6

NTC's
Thematic
Dictionary
of
American
Slang

NTC's Thematic Dictionary of American Slang

Richard A. Spears, Ph.D.

NTC Publishing Group
NTC/Contemporary Publishing Company

Library of Congress Cataloging-in-Publication Data

Spears, Richard A.
    NTC's thematic dictionary of American slang / Richard A. Spears.
       p.   cm.
    Includes index.
    ISBN 0-8442-0832-9
      1. English language—United States—Slang—Dictionaries.
    2. Figures of speech—Dictionaries.   3. Americanisms—
Dictionaries.
    I. Title.
    PE2846.S66   1997
    427'.09—dc21
                                           97-24459
                                                CIP

Interior design by Terry Stone

Published by NTC Publishing Group
An imprint of NTC/Contemporary Publishing Company
4255 West Touhy Avenue, Lincolnwood (Chicago), Illinois 60646-1975 U.S.A.
Copyright © 1998 by NTC/Contemporary Publishing Company
Manufactured in the United States of America
International Standard Book Number: 0-8442-0832-9
7 8 9 0 BC 0 9 8 7 6 5 4 3 2 1

Contents

About This Dictionary

This dictionary is a collection of slang and colloquial expressions in frequent use in the United States in the twentieth century. It contains expressions that are familiar to many Americans and other expressions that are used primarily within small groups of people. The entries represent the language of the underworld, the nursery, the college campus, California beaches, urban back streets, and Wall Street. We hear from prisoners, surfers, junkies, Valley Girls, blacks, weight lifters, surfers, and just plain folks. Fad words, metaphors, wordplay, and various figures of speech make up the body of the dictionary.

The slang and colloquial expressions in this dictionary are arranged according to theme. There is a list of themes on page ix. Writers and students seeking a slang or colloquial manner of expressing something can easily find likely candidates by using the themes to locate a selection of expressions.

There is an index on page 453 that allows the user to find a particular slang or colloquial expression by showing the theme under which the expression is listed.

Terms and Symbols

☐   marks the beginning of an example.

Amerindian   related to native American cultures and people.

AND   indicates an alternative element, either an alternative entry form or an alternative pronunciation.

black   typically used by or originated by Americans of African descent.

blend   made up of sounds from two other words, such as *smoke + fog = smog*.

catchphrase   an expression that is meant to catch attention because of its cleverness or aptness.

combining form   a sense of a word used only in combination with another word, as with **bug** in *camera bug*.

deliberate spoonerism   a deliberate interchanging of initial consonants in a pair of words, such as "queer old dean" for "dear old queen."

euphemistic   relatively refined and having no negative connotations.

exclam.   exclamation.

in.   intransitive. Expressions that are intransitive verbs or intransitive verb phrases (an intransitive verb, its auxiliaries, and modifiers) are marked *in.*

interj.   interjection.

interrog.   interrogative.

initialism   an abbreviation consisting of the initial letters of the words being shortened. The letters are pronounced one by one, as with "IBM."

mod.   modifier. Expressions serving to modify, restrict, or qualify (adjectives, adjective phrases, adverbs, adverb phrases, etc.) are marked *mod.*

n.   nominal. Expressions functioning as nominals (nouns, noun phrases, etc.) are marked *n.*

phr.   phrase.

prep.   preposition.

pro.   pronoun.

see   Go to the entry indicated.

see also   Find additional information at the entry indicated.

sent.   sentence.

tr.   transitive. Expressions that are transitive verbs or transitive verb phrases (a transitive verb and its auxiliaries, object(s), and modifier(s) are marked *tr.*

List of Themes

The following is a list of the 1,100 themes used to classify the slang and colloquial expressions found in this dictionary. The themes are also used as guide words at the top of each page in the dictionary. Use this list to explore the various themes conveniently.

ABANDONMENT

ditch *tr.* to dispose of someone or something; to abandon someone or something. □ *The crooks ditched the car and continued on foot.* □ *The flyboy ditched the plane in the lake and waded ashore.*

drop someone or something like a hot potato *tr.* to disassociate oneself from someone or something instantly. □ *When we learned of the conviction, we dropped him like a hot potato.* □ *I dropped the idea like a hot potato.*

high and dry *mod.* abandoned; unsupported. (Like a ship beached or stranded ashore.) □ *He went off and left me high and dry.* □ *Here I sit high and dry—no food, no money, no nothing.*

walk *in.* to walk out on someone. □ *They had a big fight, and he walked.* □ *Much more of this and I'm going to walk.*

ABBREVIATIONS

See also COMPUTER - ABBREVIATION.

alphabet soup *n.* initialisms and acronyms in general. □ *The names of these government offices are just alphabet soup.* □ *Just look at the telephone book! You can't find anything because it's filled with alphabet soup.*

LBO *n.* "leveraged buy-out." (Initialism. Securities markets.) □ *The money used for the LBO came from the issuance of junk bonds.* □ *Ms. Boone specializes in LBOs. She's made a fortune at it.*

ABILITY

able to cut something *phr.* able to manage or execute something. (Often negative.) □ *He's not able to cut his responsibilities like we thought.* □ *We thought he could cut it.* □ *Do you think you're able to cut it?*

have what it takes *tr.* to have the skills, power, intelligence, etc., to do something. (*Have got* can replace *have*.) □ *I know I've got what it takes.* □ *I guess I don't have what it takes to be a composer.*

ABSENCE

AWOL *mod.* "absent without leave"; escaped from prison or from the military. (Acronym or initialism.) □ *The kid the cops picked up was AWOL. He's had it.* □ *If I don't get back to the base, they're going to think I'm AWOL.*

ditch *tr. & in.* to skip or evade someone or something. □ *Pete ditched class today.* □ *If you ditch too often, they'll throw you out of the organization.*

play hooky *tr.* to not go to school; to not keep an appointment. □ *I played hooky today and did not go to work.* □ *Tommy is probably playing hooky from school again.*

ABSOLUTELY

for sure *phr.* "absolutely." □ *I'll be there, for sure.* □ *Am I happy? For sure!*

out-and-out *mod.* complete or total; blatant. □ *Fred was an out-and-out liar.* □ *Don't be such an out-and-out stinker!*

ABSTINENCE

take the pledge *tr.* to promise to abstain from beverage alcohol. □ *I'm not ready to take the pledge yet, but I will cut down.* □ *My aunt tried to get me to take the pledge.*

tote *n.* someone who abstains from alcohol. (From *teetotal*.) □ *I'm not a tote, but I do have a limit—rather low by your standards.* □ *Have a drink, or are you still a tote?*

ABUNDANCE

bellyful *n.* more than enough; more than one needs. □ *I've had a bellyful of your excuses.* □ *You've given us all a bellyful. Now, good night.*

chock-full *mod.* totally full. □ *The new musical is just chock-full of laughs.* □ *The trunk is chock-full. There's no more room.*

coming out of one's ears *mod.* in great abundance. □ *Mr. Wilson has money coming out of his ears.* □ *Borrow some paper from Chuck. He's got it coming out of his ears.*

crawling with someone or something *mod.* covered with someone or something; alive with someone or something. □ *The place was crawling with police and F.B.I. agents.* □ *The room was just crawling with ants.*

fat *mod.* well supplied with something; having an overabundance of something. □ *When it comes to printer paper, this place is fat.* □ *We're fat with paper, but there's not a ribbon in sight.*

go off the deep end *in.* to do or experience something in the extreme: to fall madly in love, to go crazy, to commit suicide, to fly into a rage, etc. □ *John is completely in love with Mary and wants to marry her. I was afraid he would go off the deep end, and he did.* □ *Sally was so depressed that we had to watch her day and night so she wouldn't go off the deep end.* □ *I saw what he had done, and I just went off the deep end. I was in a blind rage and didn't know what I was doing.*

go overboard *in.* to do far more than is necessary. □ *He has a tendency to go overboard at these parties.* □ *Now, don't go overboard for us. We're just folks.*

jampacked AND **jam-packed** *mod.* full. □ *This day has been jampacked with surprises.* □ *The box was jam-packed with goodies.*

knee-deep in something *mod.* having lots of something. □ *We are knee-deep in orders and loving it.* □ *Right now, we are knee-deep in trouble.*

no end of something *n.* an endless supply of something. □ *Have some candy. I have no end of chocolate drops.* □ *I've had no end of trouble ever since I bought this car.*

out the gazoo *phr.* in great plenty; everywhere. (*Gazoo* = anus. Potentially offensive. Use only with discretion.) □ *We have old magazines out the gazoo here. Can't we throw some of them away?* □ *Go away. I have problems out the gazoo. I don't need any more of them from you!*

overkill *n.* too much. □ *That is enough. Any more is just overkill.* □ *Your policy of overkill is wasteful and expensive.*

scads *n.* lots (of something). □ *I have just scads and scads of paper.* □ *Aunt Mary has scads of money.*

swimming in something *in.* having lots of something. □ *Right now we are swimming in merchandise. In a month it will be gone.* □ *The Wilmington-Thorpes are just swimming in money.*

up to one's eyeballs AND **up to one's ears** *mod.* filled up with something. □ *She's up to her ears in marriage proposals.* □ *We're up to our eyeballs in spare parts.*

up to one's knees *mod.* deep in something, such as paperwork or water. □ *We're up to our knees with orders and getting more all the time.* □ *The orders are up to our knees.*

up to one's neck *mod.* filled up with something. □ *I am up to my neck in other people's grief and anguish.* □ *We are all up to our necks in your problems.*

ABUSED

been had AND **was had** *phr.* been mistreated, cheated, or dealt with badly. □ *Look at this shirt! I was had!* □ *I've been had by that lousy gyp joint.*

black and blue *mod.* bruised, physically or emotionally. □ *I'm still black and blue from my divorce.* □ *What is that black and blue area on your leg?*

chewed *mod.* abused. □ *After that argument at the office yesterday, I really felt chewed.* □ *After an interview like that, I am too chewed to even cry.*

ACCELERATOR

hammer *n.* the accelerator of a vehicle. □ *She pressed down the hammer, and off they went.* □ *The hammer went straight to the floor.*

ACCEPTANCE

bite the bullet *tr.* to accept something difficult and try to live with it. □ *You are just going to have to bite the bullet and make the best of it.* □ *Jim bit the bullet and accepted what he knew had to be.*

eat something up *tr.* to believe something. □ *Those people really eat that stuff up about tax reduction.* □ *They'll eat up almost anything you tell them.*

face the music *tr.* to receive the rebuke that is due one. □ *You had better go in and face the music now.* □ *You have to face the music eventually.*

get in the groove *in.* to become attuned to something. □ *I was uncomfortable at first, but now I'm beginning to get in the groove.* □ *Fred began to get in the groove, and things went more smoothly.*

go down *in.* to be accepted. □ *We'll just have to wait awhile to see how all this goes down.* □ *The proposal didn't go down very well with the manager.*

go with the flow AND **go with it** *in.* to cope with adversity; to accept one's lot. □ *No, just relax and go with the flow.* □ *Go with it. Don't fight it.*

If you can't stand the heat, keep out of the kitchen. *sent.* "If you cannot accept the problems of involvement, do not get involved." □ *Yes, it's difficult to be a candidate. If you can't stand the heat, keep out of the kitchen.* □ *Relax. If you can't stand the heat, keep out of the kitchen.*

I'm there! *sent.* "I will accept your invitation and I will be there." □ *Sounds like it will be a great rally. I'm there!* □ *If you and Tom are going to get together and watch the game, I'm there!*

Like it or lump it! *exclam.* "Give up!"; "Shut up!"; "Accept it or go away!" □ *If you don't want to do it my way, like it or lump it!* □ *Too bad! Like it or lump it!*

Shit happens. *interj.* "Bad things just happen." (Potentially offensive. Use only with discretion.) □ *Tough luck, but shit happens.* □ *Shit happens. There's nothing that can be done about it.*

swallow *tr.* to believe or accept something. □ *Did they actually swallow that?* □ *Nobody's gonna swallow that nonsense.*

take one's lumps *tr.* to accept the result or punishment one deserves. □ *You've got to learn to take your lumps if you're going to be in politics.* □ *I hate taking my lumps. I'd rather pretend nothing had happened.*

take the spear (in one's chest) *tr.* to accept full blame for something; to accept the full brunt of the punishment for something. □ *The admiral got the short straw and had to take the spear in his chest.* □ *I sure didn't want to take the spear.*

That's the way the ball bounces. *sent.* "That is life."; "That is the random way things happen." □ *It's tough, I know, but that's the way the ball bounces.* □ *That's the way the ball bounces. It could be worse.*

That's the way the cookie crumbles. *sent.* "That is life."; "That is typical of the unequal share of things you are likely to get in life." □ *I lost my job. Oh, well. That's the way the cookie crumbles.* □ *Oh, gee! Too bad. That's the way the cookie crumbles.*

That's the way the mop flops. *sent.* "This is the way things happen."; "This is typical of the random patterns of events." (Contrived.) □ *Sorry to hear about that, but that's the way the mop flops.* □ *That's tough, but that's the way the mop flops.*

the way it plays *phr.* the way it is; the way things are. □ *The world is a rough place, and that's the way it plays.* □ *It's tough, but it's the way it plays.*

tough luck AND **tough cookies** *interj.* "That is too bad." □ *Tough luck, but that's the way the cookie crumbles.* □ *That's too bad, tough cookies.*

warts and all *mod.* even with the flaws. □ *It's a great performance—warts and all.*

3

□ *Yes, we admire each other very much, warts and all.*

whatever turns you on *phr.* "It's all right if it excites you or interests you." (Said originally about sexual matters.) □ *You really like pickled pigs' feet? Whatever turns you on.* □ *I can't stand that kind of music, but whatever turns you on.*

What the heck! *exclam.* "It doesn't matter!" (Often with the force of an exclamation.) □ *Oh, what the heck! Come on in. It doesn't matter.* □ *Oh, what the heck! I'll have another beer. Nobody's counting.*

ACCIDENT

accidentally-on-purpose *mod.* deliberate, but meant to look like an accident. □ *Then I accidentally-on-purpose spilled water on him.* □ *I knew it was done accidentally-on-purpose. That kind of thing doesn't just happen.*

beef *in.* to crack up and get injured as in a skateboard accident. □ *Chuck beefed and wrecked his elbow.* □ *Be careful or you'll beef!*

crack up *in.* to have a wreck. □ *The plane cracked up and killed two of the passengers.* □ *Whose car cracked up on the expressway?*

crack-up *n.* an accident; a wreck. □ *There was a terrible crack-up on the expressway.* □ *There were four cars in the crack-up.*

fender-bender *n.* a minor accident. □ *There are a couple of fender-benders on the expressway this morning, so be careful.* □ *A minor fender-bender blocked traffic for a while.*

fishtail *in.* [for the rear of a car] to whip back and forth like a fish moving its tail. □ *The Caddy fishtailed on the curb and almost spun around.* □ *It's easy to fishtail in wet weather.*

pileup *n.* a wreck; a vehicular crash where more than one vehicle is heavily damaged. □ *There is a serious pileup on the expressway.* □ *My car was ruined in a pileup on the highway.*

pratfall *n.* a fall on the buttocks; a stage fall on the buttocks. □ *I took a pratfall right on the sidewalk.* □ *If you want to*

be in musical comedy, you should learn to take a pratfall.

rear-ender AND **back-ender** *n.* an automobile wreck where one car runs into the back of another. □ *It wasn't a bad accident, just a rear-ender.* □ *My neck was hurt in a back-ender.*

wash out *in.* to have a serious wreck. □ *The little car washed out on the curve.* □ *The vehicles have a tendency to wash out when cornering.*

wipe out *in.* to crash. □ *I wiped out on the curve.* □ *The car wiped out on the curve.*

wipe out *in.* to fall off or away from something, such as a bicycle, skates, a surfboard, a skateboard, etc. □ *I wiped out and skinned my knee.* □ *If I wipe out again, my mother says I'm through.*

wipe-out 1. *n.* a wreck. □ *There was a four-car wipe-out on the expressway when I came in this morning.* □ *It was a pretty serious wipe-out, but no one was killed.* **2.** *n.* an accident on a bicycle, skates, surfboard, skateboard, etc. □ *I had a nasty wipe-out, but I only bruised my elbow.* □ *That last wipe-out wrecked my bike.*

wrap one's car around something *tr.* to drive one's car into something at fairly high speed. □ *She wrapped her car around a light pole.* □ *If he hadn't wrapped his car around a tree, he'd be here to read his own poetry tonight.*

ACCOST

buttonhole *tr.* to accost someone; to make someone listen to one. (As if grabbing someone by the coat lapel to keep him from getting away.) □ *The guy buttonholed me on my way out, and started asking me a lot of questions.* □ *See if you can buttonhole a cop and get some directions.*

ACCOUNTANT

bean-counter *n.* a statistician; an accountant. □ *When the bean-counters get finished with the numbers, you won't recognize them.* □ *The bean-counters predict a recession sometime in the next decade.*

number-cruncher *n.* someone who works with figures; an accountant. □

The number-crunchers are trying to get the annual report ready. □ *I enjoy being a number-cruncher. Math doesn't scare me.*

ACHIEVEMENT
See also **SUCCESS**.

do the trick *tr.* to do exactly what is needed. □ *This about does the trick.* □ *Does this little dudenwhacker do the trick?*

hit *tr.* to reach something; to achieve something. □ *The car hit ninety in no time at all.* □ *I hit sixty next month, and I'm going to retire.*

in the bag *mod.* achieved. □ *It's in the bag—as good as done.* □ *The election is in the bag unless the voters find out about my past.*

make it *tr.* to achieve one's goals. □ *I can see by looking around this room that you have really made it.* □ *I hope I make it someday. But if not, I tried.*

pull something off *tr.* to make something happen. □ *I didn't think he could pull it off.* □ *It takes a lot of skill to pull off something like that.*

swing *tr.* to bring something off; to execute a deal. □ *This is a very important deal. I hope I can swing it.* □ *They want to elect me president of the club. I hope they can swing it.*

ACQUIESCENCE
You're the doctor. *sent.* "I will do anything you say!"; "You are in charge!" □ *I'll do it if you say. You're the doctor!* □ *Put it over here. Okay, you're the doctor.*

ACTIVITY
bit *n.* any part of an act; any business or presentation. □ *I didn't like that bit concerning penalties.* □ *Now, in this next bit, you are to move center stage.*

get off the dime *in.* [for something or someone] to start moving. (To get off the dime that one stopped on in "stop on a dime.") □ *I wish this organization could get off the dime.* □ *If this project gets off the dime, we'll be okay.*

ACTOR
ham *n.* an actor; a bad actor. □ *What a ham! A real show-off.* □ *The cast was an assemblage of hams.*

ADDICTION
candied *mod.* addicted to cocaine. □ *Unfortunately, Paul is candied, and he lost his job so he can't buy toot.* □ *He is one of those people who gets candied at first snort.*

flaky *mod.* habituated to the use of cocaine. □ *He looks a little flaky. Look at his eyes and nose.* □ *Max is flaky. He's a walking advertisement for what he sells.*

graduate *in.* to move from casual drug use to addiction. □ *Gert graduated to smack after only a year of skin-popping.* □ *Pete graduated and went into treatment all in the same month.*

habit *n.* an addiction to a drug. □ *She has to steal to support her habit.* □ *There are many treatment programs to help with drug habits.*

have a monkey on one's back *tr.* to have a drug addiction. □ *Gert has a monkey on her back.* □ *Do you think she wants to have a monkey on her back?*

hook *tr.* to addict someone (to something). (Not necessarily drugs.) □ *The constant use of bicarb hooked him on the stuff.* □ *The pot hooked him.*

hooked (on something) *mod.* addicted to something, such as drugs. □ *Gert is hooked on horse.* □ *Everybody knows she is hooked.*

jones *n.* a drug habit; drug addiction. □ *That jones is really riding that guy.* □ *He's got a real bad jones with that dust.*

kick the habit *tr.* to voluntarily end any habit or custom, especially a drug habit. □ *She tried and tried to kick the habit.* □ *It's hard to kick the habit.*

mickey mouse habit *n.* a trivial drug habit. □ *Nothing to it. Just a little mickey mouse habit. I can stop any time I want.* □ *I don't care if it is a mickey mouse habit. It's a habit, and it's illegal.*

monkey *n.* a drug addiction. □ *That monkey of mine is getting hungry again.*

□ *Why don't you try to get rid of that monkey?*

monkey wagon *n.* drug addiction. □ *I've been riding this monkey wagon long enough.* □ *Some of these treatment centers won't get you off the monkey wagon unless you have insurance.*

nose habit *n.* an addiction to sniffed drugs, usually heroin or cocaine. □ *Max is suffering with his nose habit.* □ *One sniff of that white powder and she'll get a nose habit, for sure.*

on a tight leash *mod.* addicted to some drug. □ *Max is on a tight leash. He has to have the stuff regularly.* □ *Gert is kept on a tight leash by her habit.*

on the junk *mod.* on drugs; addicted to drugs. □ *Max has been on the junk for all of his adult life.* □ *He's not really on the junk. He's only addicted to cigarettes.*

on the mojo *mod.* addicted to morphine; using morphine. □ *How long you been on the mojo?* □ *How can you hold a steady job if you're on the mojo?*

on the needle *mod.* addicted to injectable drugs. □ *My sister's on the needle, and I want to help her.* □ *Once you're on the needle, you've had it.*

pushed *mod.* addicted to a drug. □ *He's pretty pushed, and he needs some stuff now!* □ *He used H. for years before he really got pushed.*

skag jones AND **scag jones** *n.* an addiction to heroin. (Here *jones* is a "thing.") □ *It's the scag jones that's got her down.* □ *She has a serious skag jones.*

ADDICTION - AGAIN

kick back *in.* [for an addict] to return to addiction after having been detoxified and withdrawn. □ *Gert stopped and kicked back a number of times.* □ *They may kick back a dozen times before it takes.*

off the wagon *mod.* back on drugs after a period of abstinence. □ *Max is off the wagon and shooting up again.* □ *He can't be off the wagon, because he has never stopped using, even for a day.*

ADDICTION - END

kick *tr.* to break a drug addiction voluntarily. □ *I knew I had the guts in me somewhere to kick juice.* □ *It's hard to kick that stuff.*

kick cold (turkey) *in.* to stop taking drugs without tapering off. □ *Tracy tried to kick cold turkey, but it was just too much.* □ *Kicking cold may be the only way to do it.*

on the natch *mod.* free of drugs; natural and straight. □ *Max says he wants to get on the natch, but I don't believe it.* □ *I have been on the natch for almost a year.*

twisted *mod.* suffering from drug withdrawal. □ *Frank was twisted and hurting bad.* □ *When you're twisted, your head spins, and you feel like screaming.*

ADDITIONAL

icing on the cake *n.* an extra enhancement. □ *Oh, wow! A tank full of gas in my new car. That's icing on the cake!* □ *Your coming home for a few days was the icing on the cake.*

jazzed (up) *mod.* enhanced; with something added; having been made more enticing. □ *The third act was jazzed up with a little skin.* □ *It was jazzed enough to have the police chief around asking questions.*

on the side *mod.* extra, such as with a job or a side order of food. □ *I would like an order of eggs with toast on the side, please.* □ *She is a bank teller and works as a waitress on the side.*

spare tire *n.* an unneeded person; an unproductive person. □ *Gary is a spare tire. Send him home.* □ *You spare tires over there! Get to work.*

to boot *mod.* in addition. □ *For graduation, I got a new suit and a coat to boot.* □ *She got an F on her term paper and flunked the final to boot.*

ADHESIVE

stickum *n.* glue. □ *Put some stickum on this paper and paste it up where it can be seen.* □ *There's no stickum left on this stamp.*

sticky *mod.* gooey. (Standard English.) □ *This stuff sure is sticky.* □ *What is this sticky stuff on my shoe? Oh, no!*

ADJUSTMENT

tweak *tr.* to adjust something slightly. □ *I just need to tweak this program a little bit; then I'll be with you.* □ *Tweak the tuner a little and see if you can get that station just a little bit clearer.*

ADVANTAGE

See also **BENEFIT**.

ahead of the game *mod.* being early; having an advantage in a competitive situation; having done more than necessary. (Especially with *get* or *keep*.) □ *Without a car telephone, I find it hard to get ahead of the game.* □ *If being ahead of the game is important to you and to your business, lease a mobile telephone from us.*

have a leg up on someone *tr.* to have an advantage over someone; to be ahead of someone. (*Have got* can replace *have*.) □ *Pete has a leg up on Wilbur because of his physical strength.* □ *I don't have a leg up on anyone. I'm a loser.*

ADVERTISING

See also **PROMOTION**.

flackery *n.* an advertising agency. □ *Ted works for a flackery over on Maple Street.* □ *It seems like the whole political campaign was directed by some New York flackery.*

hype 1. *n.* publicity; sales propaganda; promotion, especially if blatant and aggressive. □ *There was so much hype before the picture was released that the picture itself was a letdown.* □ *There is hype for the election all over the place.* **2.** *tr.* to publicize or promote someone or something aggressively; to overpraise someone or something. □ *Don't hype the thing to death.* □ *Let's hype it until everyone in the country has heard about it.*

hyped (up) *mod.* contrived; heavily promoted; falsely advertised. □ *I just won't pay good money to see these hyped-up movies.* □ *If it has to be hyped so much, it probably isn't very good.*

Madison Avenue *n.* in the style or image of the major U.S. center for advertising agencies. (The agencies are located on Madison Avenue in New York City.) □ *It's too much like Madison Avenue. We want a calm, sincere mood.* □ *This is plain old Madison Avenue. I want something more subtle.*

sellout *n.* the event of selling all of something. (Advertising.) □ *Come to our gigantic sellout of all name brand merchandise!* □ *This is the sellout of the century. Everything must go.*

squib *n.* a notice; a small advertisement. □ *There was a squib in the paper about your project.* □ *I read a squib about that yesterday.*

ADVICE

doctor's orders *n.* something that one is strongly advised to do. (Refers here to any advice given by anyone but a doctor.) □ *I have to spend a month in Arizona. Doctor's orders.* □ *I'm doing this on doctor's orders, but I don't like it.*

AFFAIR

one-night stand *n.* a romance or sexual relationship that lasts only one night. □ *It was not a romance, just a one-night stand.* □ *It looked like something that would last longer than a one-night stand.*

on the side *mod.* extramarital; in addition to one's spouse. □ *He is married, but also has a woman on the side.* □ *She has boyfriends on the side, but her husband knows about them.*

play around (with someone) *in.* to flirt or have an affair with someone. □ *Those two have been playing around for months.* □ *She only wants to play around with me.*

whing-ding AND **wing-ding** *n.* a love affair; a sexual affair. □ *Sam and Martha brought their little whing-ding to an end.* □ *Somebody found out about their little wing-ding.*

AGE

if one's a day *phr.* a phrase attached to an expression of someone's age. □ *She's fifty if she's a day!* □ *I'm sure he's forty-five if he's a day.*

juvie *mod.* juvenile. □ *That was sort of a juvie thing to do.* □ *Don't be so juvie.* □ *She still has a lot of juvie attitudes.*

over the hill *mod.* too old (for something). □ *You're only fifty! You're not over the hill yet.* □ *Some people seem over the hill at thirty.*

push *tr.* to approach a particular age (in years). □ *She looked like she was pushing forty-eight or fifty.* □ *He's only pushing thirty, but he looks much older.*

warhorse *n.* a tough old thing, person, or idea. □ *The conductor loves to have us play that old warhorse as an encore.* □ *What time does the old warhorse's train get in, and how long is she staying this time?*

AGENT

ten percenter *n.* an agent who collects 10 percent. □ *I've been supporting that ten percenter for years, and he was robbing me blind.* □ *The life of a ten percenter is not easy.*

AGGRESSIVENESS

bodacious *mod.* assertive; audacious. □ *That is a bodacious plan, for sure.* □ *Yes, sir! That is really bodacious.*

come on strong AND **come on like gangbusters** *in.* to seem aggressive; to impress people initially as very aggressive and assertive. □ *She has a tendency to come on strong, but she's really a softie.* □ *The new president comes on strong at first.*

fresh *mod.* a little aggressive sexually; prone to caress too eagerly. □ *Hey, buster! Don't get fresh with me!* □ *He got fresh, so I slapped him.*

mace someone's face *tr.* to do something drastic to someone, such as spraying mace in the face. (Chemical Mace™ is a brand of tear gas sold in pressurized cans for personal protection.) □ *Do you want me to mace your face? Then shut up!* □ *I look at him, and suddenly I just want to mace his face or something.*

play hardball (with someone) *tr.* to act strong and aggressive about an issue with someone. □ *Things are getting a little tough. The president has decided to play hardball on this issue.* □ *If he wants to play hardball with us, we can play that way, too.*

pull out all the stops *tr.* to use everything available; to not hold back. (Refers to pulling out all of the stops on an organ so that it will sound as loud as possible.) □ *Then the mayor decided to pull out all the stops.* □ *Don't pull out all the stops in the first round. Wait till he's tired in the third and clobber him good.*

pushy *mod.* very aggressive in dealing with other people. □ *Stop being so pushy! Who do you think you are?* □ *Who is that pushy dame?* □ *If she weren't so pushy, she would get more cooperation.*

rough-and-tumble *mod.* disorderly; aggressive. □ *That was a rough-and-tumble football game.* □ *George is too rough-and-tumble for me. He doesn't know how to act around civilized people.*

roughhouse AND **roughneck** *in.* to be boisterous. □ *Stop roughnecking in my living room.* □ *The boys broke the lamp when they were roughhousing around in the family room.*

to beat the band *mod.* very hard and very fast. □ *He's selling computers to beat the band since he started advertising.* □ *She worked to beat the band to get ready for this.*

world-beater *n.* an aggressive and ambitious person. □ *She's not a world-beater, but she's efficient.* □ *They hired an alleged world-beater to manage the office.*

AGREEMENT
See also YES.

agree to disagree *phr.* to agree to discuss something, but retain one's opinions. □ *We have accomplished nothing except that we agree to disagree.* □ *The two political parties agreed to disagree in 1971, and that was the last agreeable thing either one of them did.*

And how! *exclam.* "I agree!" □ *I am really excited you are here. And how!* □ BILL: *I am pleased you are here.* BOB: *Me too! And how!*

bury the hatchet *tr.* to make peace. (From an alleged Amerindian practice.)

□ *I'm sorry. Let's stop arguing and bury the hatchet.* □ *Tom and I buried the hatchet and we are good friends now.*

copasetic *mod.* agreeable; satisfactory. (Originally black. Probably from French.) □ *Everything is copasetic. Couldn't be better.* □ *This is one fine co-pasetic day.*

game *mod.* willing to do something. □ *Is anybody game for some pizza?* □ *I'm game, what about you?*

I've been there. *sent.* "I know from experience what you are talking about." □ *I know what you mean. I've been there.* □ *I've been there. You don't need to spell it out for me.*

jibe *in.* to agree; to be in harmony. □ *Your story just doesn't jibe with the facts.* □ *These things just don't jibe.*

meeting of the minds *n.* a consensus; an agreement. □ *At last we've reached a meeting of the minds.* □ *This meeting of the minds is nothing more than a truce.*

same here *phr.* "me too"; "I agree." □ MARY: *I think I'll have the broiled halibut.* JANE: *Same here.* □ BILL: *I feel sort of cold. What about you?* SUE: *Same here.*

see eye to eye *in.* [for two or more people] to agree on something or view something the same way. □ *We never seem to see eye to eye.* □ *Gary and Walter see eye to eye on this question.*

square *tr.* to settle or to make something right. □ *Let's talk about squaring this matter.* □ *Will twenty bucks square the matter?*

That's what I say. *sent.* "I agree with you." □ *Of course, Mary. That's what I say.* □ *That's what I say. The way to cut spending is just to do it.*

track *in.* to coincide; to agree. □ *These two things don't track. I don't know what's wrong.* □ *Your figures don't track with mine. What's wrong?*

up for something *mod.* agreeable to something. □ *I'm up for a pizza. Anybody want to chip in?* □ *Who's up for a swim?*

What someone said. *sent.* "I agree with what someone just said, although I might not have been able to say it as well or so elegantly." □ *What John said. And I agree 100 percent.* □ *What you said.*

You can say that again! *exclam.* "I agree!" □ *You can say that again! It's really hot!* □ *You can say that again! You hit the nail right on the head.*

You got it! *exclam.* "I agree to what you asked!"; "You will get what you want!" □ *You want a green one? You got it!* □ *This one? You got it!*

ALCOHOL/DRUGS

constitutional *n.* the first drink of alcohol or dose of drugs of the day. □ *He downed a constitutional and made ready to set out for the office.* □ *He never fails to drop a constitutional in the morning.*

Herb and Al *n.* marijuana and alcohol. □ *I'm afraid that Tom's best friends are Herb and Al.* □ *Wally asked us over to meet Herb and Al.*

hit *n.* a drink of liquor; a dose of a drug. □ *He had a hit of sauce and went out to finish his work.* □ *She popped a hit by the water cooler.*

(real) McCoy *n.* pure drugs or alcohol. (Always with *the.*) □ *Is this stuff the McCoy?* □ *If it's not the real McCoy, I don't want it.*

stumbles AND **stum; stumble-bumbles** *n.* barbiturates; sedatives; tranquilizers; alcohol. □ *Kelly was shocked to find a handful of stumble-bumbles in his brother's jeans.* □ *I need a strike. You got any stum?*

talk to Herb and Al *in.* to use marijuana and drink alcohol. □ *I've been out talking to Herb and Al—that's where I've been.* □ *Let's go talk to Herb and Al while we're waiting.*

ALCOHOL

alchy AND **alkie; alky** *n.* alcohol; an alcoholic beverage. □ *He showed up with a week's supply of alkie.* □ *The crooks stole most of the alchy from the bar at the club.*

ammunition *n.* liquor. □ *The cowboy walked in, downed a shot, and called for more ammunition.* □ *He's had about all the ammunition he can hold.*

antifreeze *n.* liquor; any legal or illegal alcohol. □ *With enough antifreeze, I can stand the cold.* □ *Here's some antifreeze to stop your teeth from chattering.*

beast *n.* liquor. □ *I feel a little overcome by the beast.* □ *Pour me some more of that beast.*

berps AND **burps** *n.* liquor; beer. □ *Did you bring the berps for the party?* □ *Hey, this is pretty good burps.*

booze *n.* beverage alcohol. (Slang since the 1500s.) □ *I don't care for booze. It makes me sneeze.* □ *Where's the booze?*

bottle *n.* liquor. (Always with *the* in this sense.) □ *Her only true love is the bottle.* □ *The bottle plays a big role in his life.*

breakfast of champions *n.* a first alcoholic drink of the day, taken in the morning, instead of breakfast. (Collegiate.) □ *Well, here it goes—the breakfast of champions.* □ *He calls it the breakfast of champions. I call it a bad sign of something out of hand.*

BYO(B) *mod.* "bring your own (booze or bottle)." (Initialism.) □ *A note on the invitation says that the party is BYOB.* □ *I hate BYOB parties. There's never enough to drink.*

cactus juice *n.* tequila. (A Mexican liquor.) □ *Ernie brought back a big jug of cactus juice from Mexico.* □ *This cactus juice will make your hair stand on end.*

chaser *n.* an alcoholic drink taken after a nonalcoholic one; beer, water, or some similar liquid drunk after a shot of hard liquor. □ *I could use a little chaser with this soda.* □ *I'd like a double scotch and a beer chaser.*

clear *mod.* (of liquor) undiluted; neat. □ *No soda. Clear, please.* □ *I like mine clear with just one ice cube.*

Dutch courage *n.* liquor; false courage from drinking liquor. □ *A couple of shots of Dutch courage, and he was ready to face anything.* □ *How about a little Dutch courage to help you through the first act?*

evidence *n.* liquor. (Usually with *the.* Incorporated into a suggestion that the evidence be destroyed by drinking it.) □ *There is only one thing to do with evidence like this, and that's drink it.* □ *They knocked back all the evidence very quickly.*

eyewash *n.* liquor. □ *How about some of that nice eyewash?* □ *You've been putting away a lot of that eyewash, haven't you?*

firewater *n.* whiskey. (From cowboy and Indian talk.) □ *This firewater leaves a lot to be desired.* □ *This isn't gin; it's firewater!*

gargle *n.* liquor. □ *You want some more gargle?* □ *Pour me a little of that gargle, if you please.*

gas *n.* liquor, especially inferior liquor. □ *You want some more gas?* □ *Pour me a little more of that gas, will you?*

gee *n.* a portion of liquor, a gallon or a single drink. □ *You want another gee of this booze?* □ *How about a gee for me?*

get down to some serious drinking *in.* to settle down to a long session of drinking. □ *Well, now we can get down to some serious drinking.* □ *When the kids go to bed, let's get down to some serious drinking.*

giggle goo *n.* liquor. □ *Can I pour you a little of that giggle goo?* □ *Haven't you had about enough of that giggle goo?*

grog *n.* liquor. □ *Here, have some more of this grog.* □ *That's enough grog for me.*

happy juice *n.* liquor, beer, and wine. □ *A little more happy juice, John?* □ *Too much happy juice can make you very unhappy.*

hard *mod.* fermented, as with cider. □ *This juice got hard. What shall I do with it?* □ *Where's the hard stuff?* □ *If it's hard, give it to me and I'll drink it.*

hard case *n.* a case of liquor. □ *Pete wanted a hard case delivered to his house.* □ *There's a lot of beer and a hard case in the van.*

headache *n.* liquor. □ *Pour me some more of that headache, will you?* □ *Give the man some more headache.*

holiday cheer *n.* liquor, especially liquor drunk at Christmas and New Year's. □ *I think he had a little too much holiday cheer.* □ *Would you care for a little holiday cheer?*

home-brew *n.* homemade liquor or beer. □ *Is this your own home-brew, Wally?* □ *My uncle makes his own home-brew.*

homespun *n.* homemade liquor or beer. □ *Jed offered a little of his homespun round the table.* □ *How about a swig of homespun?*

hooch AND **hootch** *n.* hard liquor; any alcoholic beverage. □ *Let's go guzzle some hooch.* □ *More hootch for you?*

idiot juice AND **idiotic** *n.* a mixture of ground nutmeg and water. (Prisons.) □ *Somehow a bunch of these guys got hold of some idiot juice.* □ *He drank about a gallon of idiotic to get the kick of one beer.*

idiot oil *n.* alcohol. □ *She drinks too much of that idiot oil.* □ *Idiot oil can wreck you as much as smack does.*

joy juice *n.* liquor; beer. □ *Joy juice makes Ted sad.* □ *Can I pour some more of this joy juice?*

jug *n.* a jug of liquor; a jar of moonshine; a can of beer. □ *Where's my jug? I need a swig.* □ *Pass her the jug, Sam.*

juice *n.* liquor; wine. □ *Let's go get some juice and get stewed.* □ *You got any juice in your room?*

jungle juice *n.* homemade liquor; any strong liquor. □ *This jungle juice will knock you for a loop.* □ *Jungle juice will do in a pinch.*

kosher *mod.* having to do with undiluted alcohol. □ *I'll take mine kosher with a little ice.* □ *Do you want this kosher or with soda?*

lace *tr.* to add alcohol to coffee or tea; to add alcohol to any food or drink. □ *Who laced the punch?* □ *I think I'll lace my coffee with a little whisky.*

light stuff *n.* low-proof liquor. □ *The light stuff is okay for parties, but not for serious drinking.* □ *Poor Sam is trying to cut down by drinking the light stuff. He drinks twice as much, though.*

loaded *mod.* spiked with liquor; containing much alcohol. □ *There's a little rum in the eggnog, but it's certainly not* what I would call loaded. □ *Wow, this punch is loaded!*

lubrication *n.* liquor. □ *A little lubrication would help this party a lot.* □ *Wally has had a little too much lubrication.*

lush *n.* liquor. □ *Who's bringing the lush to the party?* □ *Lead me to the lush.*

moonshine 1. *n.* homemade whisky; any cheap or inferior liquor. □ *This moonshine isn't the best you've made.* □ *Moonshine is supposed to be strong, not good.* **2.** *in.* to distill or traffic in illicit liquor. □ *Yeah, I moonshine a little. So what?* □ *You would be amazed at how much people moonshine back in the hills.*

mouthwash *n.* liquor; a drink of liquor. □ *I could use a shot of that mouthwash.* □ *You could use a little mouthwash after that long trip, I bet.*

muddler *n.* liquor. □ *I've had a little too much muddler, I think. Anyway, I'm muddled.* □ *Let's stop here for some muddler.*

naked *mod.* undiluted; having to do with neat liquor, especially gin. □ *No ice, please. I want mine naked.* □ *Give me a naked whisky, if you don't mind.*

Name your poison. *sent.* "State what you want to drink." (Refers to alcoholic drinks only.) □ *Okay, friend, name your poison.* □ *Step up to the bar and name your poison.*

near-beer *n.* beer with less than 1/2 percent alcohol content. (Originally from the Prohibition era.) □ *I read in the paper that near-beer is making a comeback.* □ *You can drink a lot of near-beer without getting drunk.*

nip 1. *n.* a small, quick drink of liquor. □ *Here, have a nip of this stuff.* □ *One nip is enough. That is powerful!* **2.** *in.* to take small drinks of liquor periodically. □ *Paul has been nipping since noon.* □ *After nipping all day, Fred was pretty well stewed by dinnertime.*

off the wagon *mod.* drinking liquor after a period of abstinence. □ *Poor John fell off the wagon again. Drunk as a skunk.* □ *He was off the wagon for a year the last time before he sobered up.*

old soldier *n.* an empty liquor bottle; an empty beer bottle or can. □ *Larry hid all his old soldiers under the bed.* □ *Bill hit Tom over the head with an old soldier.*

one for the road *n.* a drink; a drink before a journey. □ *Let's have one for the road.* □ *Don't have one for the road if you are going to be the driver.*

one too many *n.* one alcoholic drink too many, implying drunkenness. □ *I think I've had one too many. It's time to stop drinking.* □ *Don't drive if you've had one too many.*

on tap *mod.* having to do with beer sold from a barrel or keg. □ *Do you have any imported beers on tap here?* □ *I like beer on tap. The canned stuff tastes funny to me.*

on the juice *mod.* drinking heavily; on a drinking bout. □ *Fred spent the whole week on the juice.* □ *She won't be able to return your call. I'm afraid she's on the juice again.*

on the rocks *mod.* (of an alcoholic drink) with ice cubes. □ *I'd like mine on the rocks, please.* □ *Give me a scotch on the rocks, please.*

on the sauce *mod.* drinking regularly; alcohol intoxicated. □ *Poor old Ron is on the sauce again.* □ *He is on the sauce most of the time.*

on the squiff *mod.* on a drinking bout. □ *Bob is out on the squiff again.* □ *Max is always on the squiff, except when he's shooting dope.*

on the tank AND **on a tank** *mod.* on a drinking bout. □ *All the guys were on the tank last Saturday.* □ *Paul spent all weekend on a tank.*

painkiller *n.* liquor. □ *Pass that bottle of painkiller over here. My throat hurts.* □ *He should look happy. He's full of painkiller.*

paint remover *n.* strong or inferior whiskey or other spirits. □ *That paint remover you gave me nearly burned out my throat.* □ *What do you call that paint remover, anyway? It sure is powerful.*

plonk *n.* white wine; cheap wine; any liquor. (From French *blanc*.) □ *That plonk is really hard on the gut.* □ *How about a bottle of plonk?*

pluck AND **plug** *n.* wine; cheap wine. (Originally black.) □ *Where can I get some pluck?* □ *You spilled plug all over my car seat.*

plug *n.* a drink of beer. □ *Let me have a plug out of that bottle.* □ *I just want a plug, not the whole thing.*

poison *n.* an alcoholic drink. □ *Name your poison.* □ *How about a drink of that poison there?*

poo *n.* champagne. (From *shampoo*.) □ *How about another glass of poo?* □ *Oh, I just love poo!*

popper *n.* a can of beer (in a pop-top can). □ *Hey, toss me a popper, Fred!* □ *You ready for another popper, Tom?*

popskull *n.* fiery liquor; inferior whiskey. □ *This popskull will burn a hole in you.* □ *Where is that jug of popskull?*

pop (some) tops *tr.* to drink beer. □ *Wanna go out tonight and pop some tops?* □ *We are going to pop tops and watch the B-ball game.*

pop wine *n.* a cheap, flavorful, sparkling wine drink. □ *Even if you don't like fine wines, you'll like pop wine.* □ *They were drinking pop wine like it was water.*

pot *in.* to drink heavily. □ *He's been potting since dusk.* □ *Let's sit here and pot for a while.*

pound *tr.* to drink something quickly. □ *Dan said he could pound the cup of coffee in thirty seconds.* □ *You don't have to pound your milk. Take your time.*

pound a beer AND **pound some beers; hammer a beer; hammer some beers; slam a beer; slam some beers** *tr.* to drink a beer; to drink a beer fast. □ *On a hot day like this, I want to go home and pound a beer.* □ *Let's go down to the tavern and slam some beers.* □ *We went out and hammered some beers.*

pull 1. *n.* a drink; a drink from a flask. □ *He took another pull and kept on talking.* □ *Can I have a pull?* **2.** *tr.* to take a drink or a mouthful of liquor from a bottle or other container. □ *He pulled a* *slug from the bottle.* □ *She pulled a mouthful and then spat it out.*

pull jive *tr.* to drink liquor. □ *Let's go pull jive for a while.* □ *Don't you ever do anything but pull jive?*

Q *n.* a quart bottle of liquor. (An abbreviation.) □ *While you're there, get me a Q of whiskey.* □ *She can knock off a Q a day.*

quaff a brew *tr.* to drink a beer. □ *I went down to the bar to quaff a brew.* □ *Let's go somewhere and quaff a brew.*

queer *n.* illicit liquor, especially whiskey. (Prohibition era.) □ *Can you get me a bottle of queer?* □ *This isn't queer; it's left over from before Prohibition.*

queer-beer *n.* bad beer; beer of low alcohol content. □ *I hate this queer-beer. Get out the good stuff.* □ *Please don't serve me any of your queer-beer.*

quencher *n.* a drink of liquor or beer. □ *I could really use a quencher about now.* □ *How about a nice cold quencher?*

quick one AND **quickie** *n.* a quick drink of booze; a single beer consumed rapidly. □ *I could use a quick one about now.* □ *I only have time for a quickie.*

raw *mod.* (of alcoholic spirits) undiluted; neat. □ *No ice, please. I prefer it raw.* □ *I'll drink it raw—just the way it is now.*

sauce *n.* liquor; any alcoholic beverage. □ *Those guys have had too much sauce again.* □ *Did you bring the sauce? Can't have a good party without lots of sauce.*

shicker *n.* liquor; beer. □ *Fill it up with shicker again.* □ *How do you know when you've had enough shicker?*

shoot *tr.* to lace a drink with liquor. □ *I'm gonna shoot the punch with rum.* □ *Harry shot his date's Coke with vodka.*

silo drippings *n.* alcohol allegedly obtained at the base of a silo containing fermenting corn. □ *You actually drink this stuff? This is silo drippings.* □ *The old-timer called his moonshine "silo drippings."*

skag AND **scag** *n.* hard liquor. □ *No beer for me. Tonight it's scag.* □ *The two of them put away a quart of my finest skag.*

slosh *n.* beer; liquor. □ *How about a glass of slosh?* □ *No slosh for me. Just plain water.*

spike *tr.* to add ether or alcohol to beer, originally by injecting it through the cork with a hypodermic needle; to add alcohol to a nonalcoholic drink. (From Prohibition times.) □ *He found a man who would spike his beer for a small fee.* □ *He spiked the beer with ether, which is a dangerous thing to do.*

spiked *mod.* having to do with a drink with alcohol added; having to do with a punch with an alcoholic content. □ *Is the punch spiked? I want some without.* □ *We only have spiked punch.* □ *Max's breakfast orange juice is usually spiked.*

squeeze *n.* liquor. (Black.) □ *Let's stop on the way and get some squeeze.* □ *Freddie, where is your squeeze?*

staggers *n.* liquor. □ *He couldn't seem to get enough staggers.* □ *She poured herself a huge glass of staggers and mumbled something about cough medicine.*

straight (up) *mod.* without ice; neat. □ *I'll have a bourbon, straight up, please.* □ *I'll take mine straight.*

suck AND **suction** *n.* liquor; wine; beer; strong drink. □ *How about a little glass of suck before we leave?* □ *This is powerful suction!*

suds *n.* beer. □ *How about some suds, Bill?* □ *I can't get enough suds.*

swill *n.* liquor. □ *This swill is awful. Please give me some beer.* □ *The swill they serve here is better than you can get elsewhere.*

swizzle *n.* liquor; beer; a drink of an alcoholic beverage. □ *What a hot day. I could use some swizzle.* □ *What I need is a nice cold swizzle.*

tea *n.* liquor; alcoholic drink. □ *Would you care for more tea?* □ *Give the lady some more tea.*

throat gag *n.* liquor; strong liquor. □ *Pour me another of that throat gag, barkeep.* □ *That throat gag nearly choked me.*

tipple *n.* liquor; strong liquor. □ *This is mighty fine tipple.* □ *A little more tipple, Tom?*

tongue oil AND **tongue loosener** *n.* liquor. □ *She had a little too much tongue oil and was telling all about everybody.* □ *Barlowe poured the pigeon another shot of tongue loosener.*

tonic *n.* liquor. □ *How about some more tonic?* □ *Just a bit of tonic. I'm cutting down.*

tonsil bath *n.* liquor; a drink of liquor. □ *I could use a little tonsil bath about now.* □ *You want some more of that tonsil bath?*

tonsil paint AND **tonsil varnish** *n.* liquor; whiskey. □ *This tonsil varnish would take the paint off a barn.* □ *Give the man a cup of tonsil paint.*

tornado juice *n.* whiskey; strong whiskey. □ *You want another round of tornado juice?* □ *This tornado juice smells like antifreeze.*

turps AND **terps** *n.* liquor. (From turpentine.) □ *Don't forget to stop at the comfort station and get the turps.* □ *You got enough terps for the party?*

whiff-sniffer AND **wiff-sniffer** *n.* a prohibitionist; someone always alert for the smell of alcohol on someone's breath. (Prohibition.) □ *Martin is something of a whiff-sniffer.* □ *No wiff-sniffer is going to tell me what to do.*

woofle-water AND **wozzle-water** *n.* whiskey; liquor. □ *Haven't you had just about enough woofle-water?* □ *No more wozzle-water for me.*

ALCOHOL - BAD

meth *n.* denatured alcohol; methyl alcohol. (Streets and underworld.) □ *Oh, yeah, we drank meth. We drank anything we could get.* □ *Meth used to be pink. Now they put something in it to make you vomit.*

monkey swill *n.* inferior liquor; strong liquor. □ *This monkey swill will probably make me blind.* □ *Where did you get this monkey swill? This would kill a monkey anyway.*

rotgut 1. *n.* strong or inferior liquor, especially whisky. (Folksy.) □ *Where is that jug of rotgut you used to keep around here?* □ *The old man nearly went blind drinking all that rotgut.* **2.** *mod.* (of liquor) strong or fiery. □ *You've got to stop drinking that rotgut liquor and think of your health.* □ *I won't pay for this rotgut whisky. Give me something better.* **3.** *n.* weak or otherwise inferior beer. □ *I need a can of beer, and you give me this rotgut?* □ *She can afford something better, but she prefers rotgut.*

shoe polish *n.* liquor; whiskey; inferior whiskey. □ *Why don't you give that cruddy shoe polish to the cat?* □ *The old lush would be delighted to get some of your shoe polish.*

slop(s) *n.* bad beer; inferior liquor. □ *Why do we have to drink slops like this? Can't Tom afford to give his guests something decent?* □ *Tom's slop is better than water—dishwater, anyway.*

smoke *n.* methyl alcohol; bad liquor; any liquor. □ *The old guy was drinking smoke, and it blinded him.* □ *They call it smoke because when you mix it with water and shake it, it's cloudy.*

ALCOHOL - BEER

belch *n.* beer, especially bad beer. □ *Where did you get this belch?* □ *Pass the belch. Anything's good on a hot day.*

brew *n.* beer; a can, bottle, or glass of beer. □ *Hey, give me a cold brew, will ya?* □ *This is my favorite brew, and it's at just the right temperature.*

brew-ha *n.* a beer. □ *One brew-ha over here, innkeeper!* □ *How 'bout some brew-ha, Mike?*

brewski AND **brewsky** *n.* beer; a beer. □ *Hey, how 'bout a brewski?* □ *I'll take a nice cold brewsky.*

brewster *n.* beer; a can of beer. □ *I need another brewster over here, and another one for my buddy.* □ *Toss me a cold brewster, will you?*

bud *n.* a Budweiser™ beer; any beer. □ *How 'bout one of them buds in a green bottle?* □ *I got four kinds of bud here. Which do you want?* □ *This is real fine bud!*

chill AND **chilly** *n.* a cold can of beer. □ *Hey, toss me a chill, would ya, buddy?* □ *You ready for another chilly?*

cold blood AND **cold coffee** *n.* beer. □ *How would you like a little cold blood to start things off?* □ *A nice big cold coffee would do me fine.*

cold pop *n.* beer. □ *How about another can of that cold pop?* □ *A few cans of cold pop and John began to wobble a little.*

drafty *n.* a draft beer; beer. □ *How about a cold drafty?* □ *Another drafty, Tom?*

foam *n.* beer. □ *How about some more foam?* □ *All the guy thinks about is foam.*

frosty AND **frosty one** *n.* a beer; a cold beer. □ *Hey, toss me a frosty, will ya?* □ *I need a frosty one after all that work.*

·roth *n.* a beer. □ *Would you like some ·oth?* □ *How about another pitcher of ·th, innkeeper?*

·enie *n.* a Heineken (brand) beer. (It ·es in a green bottle.) □ *Tom ordered ·enie and had it put on his tab.* □ *Can ·e a couple of greenies over here, ·?*

·n. beer. □ *Can you stop at the fill-·ion and get some gusto?* □ *How ·other tube of gusto?*

·beer. □ *Let's stop at the happy ·get some honey.* □ *You want an-·of honey?*

·r. □ *Pretty good hop, Tom.* □ *· some hop with your ham-*

·a keg of beer. (Collegiate.) ·other kegger. It's only nine ·came here because some-·were keggers.

·of beer. □ *I could use a ·· about now.* □ *A little ·· the time when you're*

skat *n.* beer. □ *How about some skat, chum?* □ *You got any pretzels to go with the skat?*

toilet water *n.* beer; draft beer. (Alludes to the term for cologne.) □ *This toilet water has me running back and forth to the john.* □ *You want another pitcher of toilet water?*

tube *n.* a can of beer. □ *Toss me a tube, will ya?* □ *How many tubes do you think we ought to get for tonight?*

two umlauts *n.* a Löwenbräu (brand) beer. □ *I'll take a two umlauts.* □ *Calling a beer "two umlauts" is the most contrived bit of slang I have ever heard of.*

wet one *n.* a cold beer. □ *How about a wet one, Fred?* □ *I could sure use a wet one about now.*

ALCOHOL - BUBBLY

berpwater *n.* beer; ale; champagne. □ *I don't care for all that berpwater.* □ *Berpwater is for sissies.*

squirt *n.* beer or champagne. □ *I like squirt. It tickles my nose.* □ *How about a nice bubbly glass of squirt?*

ALCOHOL - CHAMPAGNE

bubble water AND **bubbles** *n.* champagne. □ *More bubble water, or do you want something stronger?* □ *I want about a gallon of bubbles, thanks.*

bubbly *n.* champagne. (Often with *the*.) □ *I'd like a big glass of bubbly, if you don't mind.* □ *The bubbly will brighten up any party.*

cham AND **chammy; sham; shammy** *n.* champagne. □ *Would you like a little more shammy?* □ *This is a stunning cham you picked for us, Tiffany. Is it famous?*

champers AND **shampers** *n.* champagne. □ *I could live on shampers.* □ *My dad sent us a bottle of French champers.*

grape(s) *n.* champagne; wine. □ *These grapes are great!* □ *No more of the grapes for me. It tickles my nose.*

laughing soup AND **laughing water** *n.* champagne. □ *Laughing soup flowed like fury at the reception.* □ *How about some more laughing water?*

Minnehaha *n.* champagne. (From Longfellow's *Song of Hiawatha. Minnehaha* means "laughing waters.") □ *Have a glass of Minnehaha.* □ *Minnehaha tickles my nose.*

shampoo *n.* champagne. □ *I just love this bubbly shampoo!* □ *There is nothing like shampoo to liven up a party!*

ALCOHOL - DRINKING

drinkies *n.* drinks; liquor. □ *Okay, kids, it's drinkies all around.* □ *What time is drinkies around here?*

drinkypoo *n.* a little drink of liquor. □ *Wouldn't you like just one more drinkypoo of Madeira?* □ *Just a little drinkypoo, my dear.*

ALCOHOL - GIN

juniper juice *n.* gin. (From the juniper berry flavoring of gin.) □ *He just lived for his daily ounce of juniper juice.* □ *Tracy used to like juniper juice before she went on the dust.*

ALCOHOL - ILLICIT

jake *n.* illegal liquor. (Prohibition.) □ *You know where I can get some jake?* □ *Why, there's no jake around here. There's a law against it, you know.*

moonlight 1. *n.* illicit liquor. □ *Where's that bottle of moonlight you used to keep under the counter?* □ *How about a sip of moonlight?* **2.** *in.* to traffic in illicit liquor. (Best done under the cover of darkness.) □ *He moonlighted during Prohibition.* □ *Jed was moonlighting around the clock.*

mountain dew *n.* illicit liquor; any liquor. □ *Mountain dew is what I want. As long as it's not store-bought.* □ *My pappy made his own mountain dew.*

swipe *n.* inferior liquor. □ *This swipe is gross. I'd rather drink water.* □ *I can't stand the swipe they serve here.*

who shot John *n.* illicit whiskey. (Prohibition.) □ *You know where I can get a little of that who shot John?* □ *He's had too much of that who shot John.*

ALCOHOL - LACKING

dry *mod.* having to do with a region where alcoholic beverages cannot be purchased. □ *Is Kansas still dry?* □ *I hate to get stuck in a dry town.* □ *Some small towns are dry, but not many.*

dry *n.* a Prohibitionist; an abstainer from alcohol. □ *The drys are in an increasing majority.* □ *Do you know even one dry?*

ALCOHOL - LOCATION

wet *mod.* having to do with an area where is it legal to sell alcohol. □ *Kansas became wet just a few years ago.* □ *Is it wet or dry in this county?*

ALCOHOL - PARAPHERNALIA

corpse *n.* an empty liquor or beer bottle. □ *Sam tossed another corpse out the window.* □ *Throw your corpses in the trash can, you jerk!*

dead soldier AND **dead man; dead marine; dead one** *n.* an empty liquor or beer bottle. □ *Toss your dead soldiers in the garbage, please.* □ *A dead marine fell off the table and woke up all the drunks.*

empties *n.* empty bottles. □ *Throw your empties in the trash.* □ *Whose empties are these, and how many are there?*

ALCOHOL - SALOON

draft board *n.* a tavern; a saloon. (Alludes to draft beer.) □ *Larry is down a the draft board, slamming some beers. □ Let's stop in the local draft board and to a couple.*

ALCOHOL - STRONG

blotto *n.* strong liquor. □ *Let's go ge little of that blotto.* □ *Let's get some bl and get blocked.*

coffin varnish *n.* strong, inferior lic □ *You want some more of this coffin nish?* □ *Do you see what that coffir nish you serve here has done to so those guys?*

conk-buster *n.* strong, inferior □ *Another shot of that conk-buste will just pass out.* □ *Jed kept a jar buster under his bed against nigh*

embalming fluid *n.* strong liq whiskey. □ *Jed seemed to fa cheap embalming fluid as his Bartender, pour out this embal and get me your best.*

greased lightning *n.* strong liquor. □ *This greased lightning of yours nearly blew my head off.* □ *No more greased lightning for me.*

hard liquor *n.* potent liquor such as whiskey, gin, rum, etc. □ *Hard liquor makes me sick.* □ *Stay off of hard liquor until your stomach feels better.*

hardware *n.* whiskey; potent liquor. □ *This hardware is enough to knock your socks off.* □ *Pour me some of that hardware, will ya?*

joy water *n.* liquor; strong liquor. □ *How about some more joy water?* □ *No more joy water for me, thanks.*

kong *n.* strong whiskey; illicit whiskey. (From the movie ape King Kong.) □ *How about a big swallow of that kong?* □ *Here, have some kong.*

scat *n.* strong, inferior whiskey. □ *That rotten scat nearly choked me.* □ *You got anything better than that scat, bartender?*

snakebite medicine *n.* inferior whiskey; strong whiskey; homemade whiskey. □ *That old-time snakebite medicine is good for what ails you.* □ *Snakebite medicine is a tremendous protection against snakebites if you can get the snake to drink the stuff before it bites you.*

tiger sweat AND **tiger juice; tiger('s) milk** *n.* bad liquor; strong liquor; any beer or liquor. □ *What is this tiger sweat, anyway?* □ *How about some more of that tiger juice?* □ *This tiger's milk would kill a tiger of any age or disposition.*

ALCOHOL - VODKA

potato soup *n.* vodka. □ *Have a bit of this potato soup, why don't you?* □ *Those Russians make fine potato soup.*

spud *n.* vodka. (Presumed to be made from potatoes.) □ *How about a glass of spud?* □ *She keeps a big jug of spud in the reefer and drinks it like water.*

ALCOHOL - WHISKEY

J.D. *n.* "Jack Daniels" whiskey. (Initialism. *Jack Daniels* is a protected trade name for a brand of whiskey.) □ *He poured a little J.D. into a glass, set it aside, and drank all of what was in the bottle.*

□ *Then he poured the glass of J.D. back into the bottle.*

(mountain) dew *n.* Scotch whiskey. □ *Mountain dew is best when it's from the old country.* □ *The real mountain dew is smoky-tasting and amber.*

ALCOHOL - WINE

berries *n.* wine. (Originally black.) □ *Lemme stop at the liquor store for some berries.* □ *No berries for me. Where's the belch?*

grape(s) *n.* champagne; wine. □ *These grapes are great!* □ *No more of the grape for me. It messes up my gut.*

grapes of wrath *n.* wine. □ *Fred had taken a little too much of the grapes of wrath.* □ *How about another dose of the grapes of wrath?*

ink *n.* cheap red wine. □ *The old wino prefers ink to anything else.* □ *All I have is some ink. Is that okay?*

jug wine *n.* cheap wine that is sold in volume, usually in gallon jugs. □ *We're having a little do tomorrow—nothing special. A little jug wine and chips.* □ *Can you stop by the juice shop and nick some jug wine?*

mickey AND **micky** *n.* a small bottle of wine. □ *See if you can get a mickey of something for a buck.* □ *The old guy just wants to get a micky to help with his wineache.*

schoolboy Scotch *n.* wine. □ *Give me a pint of that schoolboy Scotch.* □ *Man, she is stoned out of her mind on schoolboy Scotch!*

smash *n.* wine. (Black. Because it is made from smashed grapes.) □ *I got a bottle of smash in my car.* □ *This is great smash for a buck twenty-five.*

wino *n.* wine. □ *How about a little more wino?* □ *This is excellent wino.*

ALERTNESS

bright and breezy *mod.* cheery and alert. □ *You look all bright and breezy. What happened?* □ *Bright and breezy people on a day like this make me sick.*

bright-eyed and bushy-tailed *mod.* alert and ready to do something; as alert and as active as a squirrel. □ *You look all bright-eyed and bushy-tailed this morning.* □ *The child—bright-eyed and bushy-tailed—woke everyone up at dawn.* □ *Tell that bright-eyed and bushy-tailed brat to shut up!*

chipper *mod.* jolly, fresh, and alert. (Standard English.) □ *Well, you look chipper this morning.* □ *This chipper young man will show you around.*

fresh as a daisy *mod.* someone who is always alert and ready to go. □ *How can you be fresh as a daisy so early in the morning?* □ *I always feel fresh as a daisy.*

jazzed (up) *mod.* alert; having a positive state of mind. □ *I am jazzed up and ready to face life.* □ *Those guys were jazzed and ready for the game.*

Look alive! *exclam.* "Move faster!"; "Look and act alert!" □ *There's work to be done! Look alive!* □ *Look alive! It's a long, hard day ahead!*

pick up on something *in.* to become alert to something; to take notice of something; to learn or catch on to something. □ *She's real sharp. She picks up on everything.* □ *The cop picked up on the word "persuader."*

snap to (attention) *in.* to come to attention; to look alert immediately. □ *When they realized what was happening, they began to snap to.* □ *Snap to attention when the sarge comes in!*

switched on *mod.* alert and up-to-date; with it. □ *My brother is switched on and has lots of friends.* □ *I'm not switched on. In fact, I am pretty dull.*

switch on *in.* to come alive. □ *She saw her child and immediately switched on.* □ *I don't switch on until about noon.*

wired *mod.* nervous; extremely alert. □ *The guy is pretty wired because of the election.* □ *I get wired before a test.*

ALTERNATIVES

Fish or cut bait. *sent.* "Do something or get out of the way." □ *Fish or cut bait, Chuck. There's work to be done here.* □ *Decide whether you're going to watch or help. Fish or cut bait.*

hurry up and wait *phr.* to be alternately rushed and delayed in a hectic situation. (Often with the force of a modifier.) □ *I hate to hurry up and wait.* □ *It's always hurry up and wait around here.*

It cuts two ways. *sent.* "There are two sides, you know."; "There are two people involved." □ *You have to help, too. It cuts two ways.* □ *It cuts two ways, you know. It can't always all be my fault.*

scrape the bottom of the barrel *tr.* to utilize the last or only things or people available, even if unsatisfactory. □ *They were really scraping the bottom of the barrel when they picked you.* □ *You scraped the bottom of the barrel for this one. I want something better.*

shape up or ship out *phr.* "Improve or get out." □ *I'll tell you one more time. Shape up or ship out!* □ *They told me I had to shape up or ship out.*

straddle the fence *tr.* to support both sides of an issue. □ *The mayor is straddling the fence on this issue, hoping the public will forget it.* □ *The legislator wanted to straddle the fence until the last minute, and that alone cost her a lot of votes.*

ALWAYS

for keeps *mod.* forever. □ *Does that mean I'm going to have this scar for keeps?* □ *This is yours for keeps. Enjoy it.*

till hell freezes over *mod.* forever. (Use caution with *hell.*) □ *That's all right, boss; I can wait till hell freezes over for your answer.* □ *I'll be here till hell freezes over.*

till kingdom come *mod.* until the end of the world; forever. □ *Do I have to keep assembling these units till kingdom come?* □ *I'll hate her guts till kingdom come.*

AMATEUR

homegrown *mod.* local; folksy; amateur. □ *Everyone enjoyed Sally's homegrown humor.* □ *The homegrown talent at the fair was just as entertaining as anything could have been.*

AMAZEMENT

See also **SHOCK, SURPRISE**.

Don't I know it! *exclam.* "That is really true!" □ *It's bad, all right. Don't I know it!* □ *Late? Don't I know it. I'm yawning like hot cakes.*

Don't make me laugh! *exclam.* "That is a stupid suggestion!" □ *You a judge? Don't make me laugh!* □ *Don't make me laugh. Tom could never do that.*

eye-popper *n.* something astonishing. □ *The description of the theft was a real eye-popper.* □ *What an eye-popper of a story!*

For Pete's sake! AND **For pity's sake!; For the love of Mike!** *exclam.* "Good grief!" □ *For Pete's sake! How've ya been?* □ *For pity's sake! Ask the man in out of the cold!*

gaga *mod.* dazzled. □ *The family was gaga about my success.* □ *Tom was totally gaga after he got promoted.*

gee *exclam.* "Wow!" (An abbreviation of *Jesus!*, although not always recognized as such. Usually **Gee!**) □ *Gee! What a mess!* □ *Golly gee, do I have to?*

Give me a break! AND **Gimme a break** *exclam.* "I don't believe you!"; "You don't expect anyone to believe that!" □ *You say a gorilla is loose in the city? Gimme a break!* □ *Tom said he was late again because the back stairs caved in. His boss said, "Gimme a break!"*

Good call! *exclam.* "That was a good decision!" □ *Good call, Walter! You picked the right company to deal with.* □ *I guess this was Jane's choice. Good call, Jane.*

Good deal! *exclam.* "That is good!" (Old, but still heard.) □ *Everyone is here on time! Good deal!* □ *Good deal! My tax refund just arrived!*

Good golly, Miss Molly! *exclam.* "Good grief!"; "Wow!" □ *Good golly, Miss Molly! This place is a mess!* □ *Good golly, Miss Molly, that's awful!*

Good heavens! *exclam.* "My goodness!" (A mild exclamation of amazement, shock, etc.) □ *Good heavens! I didn't expect you to be here.* □ *Good heavens! There's a man at the window!*

Great Scott! *exclam.* "Good grief!" □ *Great Scott! What happened?* □ *I'm late again! Great Scott!*

hard to swallow *mod.* difficult to believe. □ *Your story is pretty hard to swallow, but I am beginning to believe it.* □ *The news was hard to swallow.*

Holy cow! *exclam.* "Wow!" □ *Holy cow! A red one!* □ *Give me a chance! Holy cow, don't rush me!*

Holy mackerel! *exclam.* "Wow!" □ *Holy mackerel! What a day!* □ *Holy mackerel! What's this?*

Holy moley! *exclam.* "Wow!" □ *Holy moley! A whole quarter!* □ *Look, here's another one! Holy moley!*

Horsefeathers! *exclam.* "Phooey!"; "Nonsense!" □ *Oh, horsefeathers! You're nuts!* □ *Horsefeathers! I did no such thing!*

Hot diggety (dog)! *exclam.* "Wow!" □ *Hot diggety dog! I won!* □ *I made it on time. Hot diggety!*

Hot dog! *exclam.* "Wow!" □ *Hot dog! It's my turn.* □ *Look at that! Hot dog! It's coming this way!*

Hot ziggety! *exclam.* "Wow!" □ *Hot ziggety! I made it!* □ *The plane's on time! Hot ziggety!*

I don't believe this! *exclam.* "What is happening right now is unbelievable!" □ *Gross! I don't believe this!* □ *I don't believe this! It can't be happening.*

(I) love it! *exclam.* "That is wonderful!" (A catch phrase.) □ *It's wonderful, Ted. I love it!* □ *Love it! More, more!* □ *You're so clever! Love it! Love it!*

Jeepers(-creepers)! *exclam.* "Wow!" □ *Jeepers-creepers! I'm sorry!* □ *Jeepers, she's wonderful!*

knockout *n.* something that is quite stunning. □ *Your new car is a knockout.* □ *Isn't her dress a knockout?*

lollapalooza *n.* something very big; something wondrous. □ *Look at that bump on your head. That's a lollapalooza!* □ *Her singing voice is a real dandy—a lollapalooza.*

Lord love a duck! *exclam.* "Wow!" □ *Lord love a duck! It's Mary!* □ *Lord love a duck, I'm tired!*

Man! *exclam.* "Wow!" □ *Man, what a bundle!* □ *Man, what an ugly mug.*

Neat! *exclam.* "Wow!" □ *Neat! I'm glad you came.* □ *Five of them! Neat!*

Neato (canito)! *exclam.* really fine. □ *Look at this! Neato canito!* □ *What a great present. Neato!*

Of all the nerve! *exclam.* "I am shocked by your domineering and high-handed behavior." □ *You want me to do your laundry? Of all the nerve!* □ *Of all the nerve! Asking me to do a thing like that.*

pie-eyed *mod.* wide-eyed with amazement. □ *He didn't cry out. He just stood there pie-eyed.* □ *Why are all those people pie-eyed? What happened?*

Puh-leez! *exclam.* "Please!"; "That is enough! You can't expect me to accept that!" (A long, drawn-out way of saying *Please!* The tone of voice shows exasperation and disgust. The spelling is highly variable.) □ *I am the one who's at fault? Puuuleeeze!* □ *Puh-leez! Don't try to make me believe that!*

Shazzam! *exclam.* "Wow!"; "Would you believe?" □ *And there was my ring—Shazzam!—right on the sidewalk!* □ *Shazzam! I passed the test!*

Shoot! *exclam.* "Darn!" (An exclamation or a very mild curse.) □ *Oh, shoot! I left my shades in the car.* □ *Shoot! I'm late!*

Son of a gun! *exclam.* "I am totally surprised!"; "I am shocked!" □ *Son of a gun! He did it!* □ *The thing just blew up! Son of a gun!*

Tah-dah! *exclam.* "Look at this!"; "Look at me!"; "Presenting. . . ." □ *Tah-dah! How do you like my new haircut?* □ *And here is—tah-dah!—our ever-late and never-punished executive secretary.*

That's the stuff! *exclam.* "That is good work!" □ *Good shot, Wally! That's the stuff!* □ *That's the stuff! Way to go!*

This is it! **1.** *exclam.* "This is exactly what I have been looking for!"; "I have found it!" □ *This is it! I got it right this time.* □ *This is it! The world's best pizza!* **2.** *exclam.* "This is the crucial moment!" □ *Okay, this is it, the last chance!* □ *Get ready, this is it! Jump now!*

Would you believe? *interrog.* "Isn't it amazing?" □ *He actually tried to get me to scratch his bare back! Would you believe?* □ *Would you believe? A three-cent per hour raise?*

Wow! *exclam.* an indication of amazement or surprise. □ *Wow! Is he ever ugly!* □ *A whole quarter! Wow! Thanks, mister.*

Ye gods! *exclam.* "Good grief!" □ *Ye gods! What is this stuff here?* □ *Ye gods! My hair is falling out.*

Zap! *exclam.* "Wow!" □ *Zap! I did it again!* □ *He said, "Zap!" indicating that he really liked the present, I guess.*

Zowie! *exclam.* "Wow!" □ *Zowie! They just pulled Mr. Big out of the river.* □ *Bruno had enough of the guy and wasted him, but good. Zowie!*

AMBITION

on the make *mod.* ambitious; attempting to be great. □ *That young lawyer is sure on the make.* □ *This university is on the make.*

AMBULANCE

meat wagon *n.* an ambulance. □ *The meat wagon showed up just as they were pulling what was left of Marty out of what was left of her car.* □ *When the meat wagon stops at all the traffic lights on the way to the hospital, you know somebody's pifted.*

AMOUNT
See also **SIZE**.

body count *n.* a count of people present. □ *The body count was about forty-five at the meeting.* □ *The body count seems to go down each month.*

cool *mod.* no less than (some amount of money). □ *He earns a cool million every year.* □ *She cleared a cool forty thousand on the Wilson deal.*

K *n.* a thousand (of anything, such as dollars, bytes, etc.). □ *This car is worth at least twenty K.* □ *I have 640 K memory in my computer.*

long dozen *n.* thirteen; a baker's dozen. □ *Don't you sell a long dozen anymore?* □ *They used to give you a long dozen in that bakery.*

neck and neck *mod.* almost even. □ *The horses were neck and neck at the finish line.* □ *They ran neck and neck for the entire race.*

nothing to sneeze at *n.* no small amount of money; something not inconsequential. □ *It's not a lot of money, but it's nothing to sneeze at.* □ *She worked hard and did not accomplish much, but it's nothing to sneeze at.*

sorry-ass *mod.* unacceptable. (Potentially offensive. Use only with discretion.) □ *This is a sorry-ass mess you've gotten us into.* □ *What a sorry-ass day this has been.*

thou *n.* one thousand. □ *I managed to get a couple of thou from the bank, but I need a little more than that.* □ *It only costs four thou. I could borrow it from my uncle.*

umpty-umpth AND **umpteenth** *mod.* thousandth, billionth, zillionth, etc. (Represents some very large, but indefinite number.) □ *This is the umpty-umpth time I've told you to keep your dog out of my yard.* □ *This is the umpteenth meeting of the joint conference committee, but still there is no budget.*

woods are full of _____ *phr.* "There are lots and lots of _____." (Always with *the.*) □ *The woods are full of cheap, compatible computer clones.* □ *The woods are full of nice-looking guys who'll mug you when it's too late.*

AMOUNT - EXCESSIVE

bit much *mod.* more than enough; more than good taste allows. (Always with *a.*) □ *That was a bit much, Paul. After all, there is such a thing as good taste.* □ *Your birthday card was a bit much, but thank you just the same.*

cap *tr.* to exceed something; to surpass something. □ *I know I can't cap that. That's just super!* □ *Who could ever cap a joke like that?*

That's all someone needs. *sent.* "That is too much."; "That is the last straw." □ *Now the sewer's backing up. That's all I need.* □ *A new mouth to feed. That's all we need!*

AMOUNT - LARGE

astronomical *mod.* extremely expensive; of any very high figure. □ *The prices here are astronomical!* □ *The market indexes have all reached astronomical heights for the second time.*

jillion *n.* an enormous, indefinite number. □ *I've got a jillion things to tell you.* □ *This car cost me about a jillion bucks.*

skillion *n.* an imaginary enormous number. □ *I have a skillion reasons why I won't marry you.* □ *About a skillion people are running in the marathon.*

AMOUNT - MANY

bokoo AND **boku** *mod.* many. (A play on French *beaucoup.*) □ *I've got bokoo things to do today.* □ *There are already boku people invited.*

gob *n.* a large amount of something. (Often in the plural.) □ *I've just got gobs of it if you need some.* □ *I need gobs of money to get through school.*

umpteen *mod.* many; innumerable. □ *I've told you umpteen times not to feed the cat right out of the can.* □ *There are umpteen ways to do this right. Can you manage to do one of them?*

AMOUNT - MAXIMUM

go the limit *in.* to do as much as possible; to get as much as possible. □ *Let's plan to do everything we can. Let's go the limit.* □ *We'll go the limit. To heck with the cost.*

max *n.* the maximum. □ *Is this the max I can have?* □ *I want the max. I'm hungry.*

to the max *mod.* maximally. □ *She is happy to the max.* □ *They worked to the max their whole shift.*

AMOUNT - MORE

more than one bargained for *n.* (getting) more than one expected. □ *This is certainly more than I bargained for!* □ *Trouble and more trouble. I'm getting more than I bargained for when I took the job.*

AMOUNT - MUCH

buttload AND **shitload** *mod.* a lot; a large amount. (Potentially offensive. Use only with discretion.) □ *I know we can sell a buttload of these recordings—if we can only get a shipment of them in time.* □ *I want to get a really good job and earn a shitload of money.*

heap AND **heaps** *n.* lots (of something). □ *I have a whole heap of papers for you.* □ *Mr. Wilson has heaps of money.*

like nobody's business *mod.* very well; very much. □ *She can sing like nobody's business. What a set of pipes!* □ *My mom can bake chocolate chip cookies like nobody's business.*

like there was no tomorrow *mod.* as if there would never be another opportunity. □ *She was drinking booze like there was no tomorrow.* □ *He lived like there was no tomorrow.*

lousy with someone or something *mod.* having lots of someone or something. (Like an infestation of lice.) □ *Old Mr. Wilson is lousy with money.* □ *Tiffany is lousy with jewels and furs, but she's got bad teeth.*

oodles *n.* lots (of something). □ *My uncle has just oodles and oodles of money.* □ *I don't have oodles, but I have enough to keep me happy.* □ *When I have spaghetti, I just love oodles of noodles.*

slew AND **slews** *n.* a lot; lots. □ *I have a whole slew of old computer programs at home in a box somewhere.* □ *She's got slews of money.*

so bad one can taste it *mod.* very much, indeed. □ *I want that car so bad I can taste it.* □ *He had to get to Philadelphia so bad he could taste it.*

stinking with something *mod.* with lots of something. □ *Mr. Wilson is just stinking with dough.* □ *Those guys are stinking with grass.*

tons of something *n.* lots of something. □ *We got tons of fried chicken, so help yourself.* □ *You are in tons of trouble.*

whole bunch(es) *mod.* a whole lot; very much. (Always with *a* in the singular.) □ *I like to spend evenings at home a whole bunch.* □ *I like pizza whole bunches.*

AMOUNT - SMALL

incy-wincy *mod.* tiny. □ *Just give me an incy-wincy bit. I'm on a diet.* □ *Well, maybe an incy-wincy bit more wouldn't hurt.*

in dribs and drabs *mod.* in small portions; bit by bit. □ *I'll have to pay you what I owe you in dribs and drabs.* □ *The whole story is being revealed in dribs and drabs.*

itty-bitty AND **itsy-bitsy** *mod.* tiny. □ *What an itty-bitty car!* □ *Give me an itsy-bitsy piece. I'm on a diet.*

not grow on trees *in.* not abundant; not expendable. (Usually said about money.) □ *I can't afford that. Money doesn't grow on trees, you know.* □ *Don't waste the glue. That stuff doesn't grow on trees, you know.*

piddling *mod.* inadequate; meager; tiny. □ *What a piddling amount of money! I can't live on that.* □ *That is a piddling steak. I want a big one.*

pinch *n.* a small amount of a powdered substance, such as salt, snuff, a spice, etc. (Not slang.) □ *He put a pinch under his lip and walked up to home plate.* □ *Do you have any oregano? I need a pinch.*

rock bottom *n.* the lowest point or level. □ *The value of the goods is at rock bottom right now.* □ *Prices have reached rock bottom.*

smidgen *n.* a tiny bit. □ *I just want a smidgen of cake. I'm on a diet.* □ *Oh, come on, more than a smidgen. Just a little?*

tad *n.* a bit; a small bit. □ *I'll take just a tad. I'm on a diet.* □ *That's a little more than a tad, but it's all right.*

AMOUNT - ZERO

goose egg *n.* a score of zero. □ *We got a goose egg in the second inning.* □ *It was double goose eggs for the final score.*

ANGER

bent *mod.* angry. □ *He was so bent there was steam coming out of his ears.* □ *Come on, don't get bent. I was only kidding.*

bent out of shape *mod.* angry; insulted. □ *Man, there is no reason to get so bent out of shape. I didn't mean any harm.* □ *I got bent out of shape because of the way I was treated.*

bitch someone off *tr.* to make someone angry. (Potentially offensive. Use only with discretion.) □ *You really bitch me off, do you know that?* □ *That foul temper of yours could bitch off anybody.*

blow *in.* to become very angry; to lose one's temper. □ *Finally I had had enough, and I blew.* □ *The brass blew, and we heard the noise all the way down here.*

blow a fuse AND **blow one's fuse; blow a gasket; blow one's cork; blow one's lid; blow one's top; blow one's stack** *tr.* to explode with anger; to lose one's temper. □ *Come on, don't blow a fuse.* □ *Go ahead, blow a gasket! What good will that do?*

blow off (some) steam AND **let off (some) steam** *tr.* to release emotional tension by talking or getting angry. □ *Don't worry. She's just blowing off steam.* □ *Let off some steam. Get it out of your system.*

blow one's cool *tr.* to become angry. □ *Now, now, don't blow your cool.* □ *I almost blew my cool when the dog wet my pants leg.*

blow up 1. *in.* to burst into anger. □ *I just knew you'd blow up.* □ *So she blew up. Why should that affect you so much?* **2.** *n.* an angry outburst; a fight. (Usually **blowup**.) □ *After the third blowup, she left him.* □ *One blowup after another. Yuck!*

boiled *mod.* angry. □ *I am so boiled at you!* □ *Now, don't get boiled. It was only a joke.*

boiling (mad) *mod.* very mad. □ *Mad, I'm not mad. I'm just boiling.* □ *She is really boiling mad.*

brassed (off) *mod.* angry; disgusted. □ *You look so brassed off at the world. Smile!* □ *I'm not brassed in the least, really.*

browned (off) *mod.* angry. □ *I am really browned off at you!* □ *The boss is browned—to say the least.*

brown someone off *tr.* to make someone angry. □ *That whole business with the cab really browned me off.* □ *I'm afraid I'm going to brown off everyone, but here goes anyway.*

burned AND **burned up** *mod.* very angry. □ *I've never been so burned up at anyone.* □ *Boy, was I burned!*

burn someone up *tr.* to make someone very angry. □ *That kind of thing just burns me up.* □ *This whole business burns all of us up.*

burn with a low blue flame *in.* to be quietly and intensely angry. □ *She just sat there with her steak in her lap, burning with a low blue flame.* □ *She was quiet, but everyone knew she would soon burn with a low blue flame.*

chap *tr.* to anger or annoy someone. □ *That whole business really chapped me.* □ *I didn't mean to chap you.*

chapped *mod.* angry; annoyed. □ *I was chapped. There was no way to get around it.* □ *Don't get so chapped. Nothing can be done now.*

cheesed off *mod.* angry; disgusted. □ *Clare was really cheesed off at the butler.* □ *The butler was cheesed off at the cook.*

conniption (fit) *n.* a burst of anger. □ *He had a conniption fit over the question of my marriage to Wally.* □ *Come on, don't have a conniption!*

dink someone off *tr.* to make someone angry. □ *Whatever you do, don't dink her off!* □ *Why did you have to start out your speech by dinking off the entire audience?*

do a slow burn *tr.* to be quietly angry. □ *I did a slow burn while I was getting my money back.* □ *I was doing a slow burn, but I didn't let it show.*

eat nails *tr.* to look and act really tough or angry. □ *Bruno looked mad enough to eat nails.* □ *They were all eating nails by the time the IRS got the mess straightened out.*

fenced *mod.* angry. (California.) □ *Boy, was that old man fenced!* □ *Too many people around here are fenced all the time.*

fireworks *n.* trouble; a display of temper. □ *After Bruno's fireworks, we calmed down a little.* □ *Cut out the fireworks, Sally. Calm down and get back to work.*

flexed out of shape *mod.* very angry; bent out of shape. □ *The boss was completely flexed out of shape.* □ *I am truly flexed out of shape.*

frost *tr.* to make someone angry. □ *That really frosts me.* □ *The little car frosted me by zooming into my parking place.*

frosted (over) *mod.* angry; annoyed. □ *The clerk was really frosted over when I asked for a better one.* □ *Why was he so frosted?*

get mad (at something) *in.* to muster great physical strength and determination in order to do something. □ *You're gonna have to get mad at it if you want to move it.* □ *Come on, you guys. Get mad.*

hacked (off) *mod.* angry; annoyed. □ *Wally was really hacked off about the accident.* □ *Oh, Wally is always hacked about something.*

have a short fuse *tr.* to be easy to anger. (*Have got* can replace *have.*) □ *He's got a short fuse, so watch out.* □ *Tracy has a short fuse and is likely to lose her temper at any time.*

have a spaz *tr.* to get angry or hysterical; to have a conniption (fit). (Teens and collegiate.) □ *If my dad hears about this, he'll have a spaz.* □ *The teacher had a spaz when I came in so late.*

have kittens *tr.* to become enraged. □ *When I heard the news, I had kittens. I was hacked!* □ *I almost had kittens, I was so mad.*

hit the ceiling AND **hit the roof** *tr.* to get very angry. □ *She really hit the ceiling when she found out what happened.* □ *My dad'll hit the roof when he finds out about this.*

hopping mad *mod.* very angry; angry and jumping up and down. □ *I was hopping mad about the broken window.* □ *The boss was hopping mad at the secretary.*

hot AND **hot under the collar** *mod.* angry. □ *Don't get so hot under the collar. Chill, man.* □ *What a hot dude!* □ *Gee, that guy is really hot. What did I do?*

hothead *n.* a person with a bad or quick temper. □ *Max is a hothead. Watch out.* □ *Don't be such a hothead, Chuck.*

huffy *mod.* angry; haughty. □ *Now, don't get huffy. I said I was sorry, didn't I?* □ *Who's the huffy old lady?* □ *She was so huffy about it.*

in a snit *mod.* in a fit of anger or irritation. □ *Don't get in a snit. It was an accident.* □ *Mary is in a snit because they didn't ask her to come to the shindig.*

kick up a storm *tr.* to create a disturbance; to put on an angry display. □ *My dad will just kick up a storm when he finds out.* □ *The demand made us all kick up a storm.*

loaded for bear *mod.* very angry. □ *By the time he finished talking, I was loaded for bear.* □ *I had been loaded for bear when I came into the room, and I left as meek as a lamb.*

lose it *tr.* to get angry; to lose one's temper. □ *It was too much for him. Ted lost it.* □ *I sat there calmly, biting my lip to keep from losing it.*

lose one's cool *tr.* to lose control; to lose one's temper. □ *Now, don't lose your cool. Relax.* □ *I'm trying not to lose my cool, but it's hard.*

on the warpath *mod.* very angry. □ *The boss is on the warpath again. Watch out!* □ *I am on the warpath about setting goals and standards again.*

pee'd off *mod.* extremely angry. □ *I certainly was pee'd off!* □ *I've never been so pee'd off in my life!*

pissed (off) *mod.* angry. (Crude. Potentially offensive, even though it is heard widely. Use only with discretion.) □ *I was so pissed off I could have screamed.* □ *He's come back, and he's sure pissed.*

piss someone off *tr.* to make someone angry. (Crude. Potentially offensive, even though it is widely used. Use only with discretion.) □ *She really pissed me off!* □ *That's enough to piss off anybody.*

pop off *in.* to lose one's temper. □ *Now, don't pop off. Keep cool.* □ *I don't know why she popped off at me. All I did was say hello.*

pop one's cork *tr.* to release one's anger; to blow one's top. □ *I'm just about to pop my cork.* □ *She tried to hold it back, but suddenly she popped her cork.*

see red *tr.* to be angry. □ *When she hung up the phone, I saw red. I've never been so angry in my life.* □ *As he continued to talk, she began to see red.*

short fuse *n.* a quick temper. □ *Fred's got a short fuse. Watch out.* □ *I knew she'd blow. She's got a short fuse.*

simmer (down) *in.* to reduce one's anger. □ *Now, now! Just simmer! Cool it!* □ *Simmer down, you guys.*

slow burn *n.* the act of becoming angry very slowly or being resentful for a long period of time. □ *His lips were pressed together and he was angry, but just having a slow burn.* □ *She wasn't angry yet, but she was doing a slow burn.*

sore *mod.* angry. □ *Come on! Don't get sore! I was only kidding.* □ *She is one sore old lady. You should give her teeth back.*

steam 1. *tr.* to anger someone. □ *She steamed him by being two hours late.* □ *The prof steamed the class with the long assignment.* **2.** *in.* to be angry. □ *She was absolutely steaming.* □ *They steamed for a while and then did as they were told.*

steamed (up) *mod.* angry. □ *Now, now, don't get so steamed up!* □ *She is really massively steamed.*

steam someone's beam *tr.* to make someone angry. □ *Being stood up really steams my beam!* □ *Come on, don't steam your beam. Remember how hard times are now.*

steam someone up *tr.* to get someone angry. □ *This whole mess steamed me up but good.* □ *The long critical statement simply steamed up the opposition.*

take it out on someone or something *tr.* to punish or harm someone or something because one is angry or disturbed about something. □ *I'm sorry about your*

difficulty, but don't take it out on me. □ *Don't take it out on the cat.*

teed off *mod.* angry. □ *I'm not teed off! I'm enraged.* □ *I was so teed off I could have spit!*

tee someone off *tr.* to make someone angry. □ *That really teed me off!* □ *Well, you sure managed to tee off everybody!*

throw a fit *tr.* to have a display of bad temper. □ *I knew you'd throw a fit when I told you.* □ *Oh, boy, did she ever throw a fit.*

ticked (off) *mod.* angry. □ *Wow, was she ticked off!* □ *Kelly was totally ticked.*

tick someone off *tr.* to make someone angry. □ *That really ticks me off!* □ *Doesn't that tick off everyone?*

torqued *mod.* angry. □ *Sure I was torqued. Who wouldn't be?* □ *Now, now! Don't get torqued!*

up in arms *mod.* angry; excited. □ *The whole town was up in arms about the planned highway.* □ *Now, don't get up in arms about it.*

vent one's spleen *tr.* to release one's anger. □ *No need to vent your spleen at me. I wasn't in on it.* □ *I just feel like I have to vent my spleen at somebody.*

work oneself (up) into a lather *tr.* to get excited or angry. □ *Now, now, don't work yourself up into a lather.* □ *He had worked himself into such a lather, I was afraid he would have a stroke.*

ANNOYANCE

backseat driver *n.* an annoying passenger who tells the driver how to drive; someone who tells others how to do things. □ *I don't need any backseat driver on this project.* □ *Stop being a backseat driver!*

Bag it! *exclam.* "Drop dead!" □ *You are not rad, and you are not awesome, so, like, bag it!* □ *Bag it yourself!*

Bag your face! *exclam.* "Go away!" □ *You outrage me. Bag your face!* □ *You are in the way. Bag your face!*

be in someone's face *mod.* irritating someone. □ *You are in my face too much,* *and I don't like it.* □ *I wish that the coach wasn't always in my face about something.*

Big deal! *exclam.* "So what!"; "What does it matter?" □ *So he snores! Big deal! Snore back!* □ *She says to me, "Your socks don't match." And I says back, "Big deal!"*

birdturd *mod.* stupid; obnoxious. (Potentially offensive. Use only with discretion. Derogatory.) □ *Of all the stupid, underhanded, birdturd tricks—this takes the cake!* □ *Get your ugly birdturd car out of my driveway!*

bite *in.* to be irritating. □ *This movie is really dumb. It bites.* □ *This party bites.*

bug *tr.* to annoy someone. □ *Stop bugging me, you twit!* □ *This kind of thing really bugs me.*

crank *n.* a crackpot; a bothersome person with a bogus message. □ *A crank called with a bomb threat.* □ *A crank came in and offered to punch me in the nose for a quarter.*

down trip *n.* any bad experience. □ *Today was a classic down trip.* □ *My vacation was a down trip.*

drag *n.* an annoying person; a burdensome person. □ *Gert could sure be a drag when she wanted.* □ *Clare was a drag whether she wanted to be or not.*

Drop dead! *exclam.* "No!"; "Beat it!"; "Go away and don't bother me!" □ *I don't care. Just drop dead!* □ *Drop dead! Beat it!*

Get away! *exclam.* "Stop being a pest!" □ *Don't bother me! Get away!* □ *Get away! Nobody is that stupid!*

get off someone's back AND **get off someone's case** *in.* to stop annoying someone. □ *I wish you'd get off my back.* □ *Get off my case! You aren't my mother.*

get on someone's case *in.* to start harassing someone about a personal problem; to annoy someone. □ *I'll get on Tom's case about being late so much.* □ *I'm sorry, I won't get on your case anymore.*

Get out of my face! *exclam.* "Stop arguing with me!"; "Stand back! Don't confront me with your arguments and chal-*

lenges!" □ *Beat it! Get out of my face!* □ *Get outa my face if you know what's good for you.*

get someone's goat *tr.* to irritate someone. □ *Don't let Mary get your goat. She's just irritable today.* □ *Everybody seems to be getting my goat today.*

get to someone *in.* [for someone or something] to annoy someone. □ *The whole business began to get to me after a while.* □ *Her remark got to me after a while.*

gig *n.* a bother; an annoyance; a job. □ *Man, this paperwork is such a gig.* □ *This day's a gig. I've had it.*

give someone a pain *tr.* to annoy or bother someone. □ *Please don't give me a pain. I've had a hard day.* □ *You give me a pain!*

give someone hell *tr.* to trouble someone. (Use caution with *hell.*) □ *My arthritis is giving me hell in this weather.* □ *This problem is giving us hell at the office.*

gripe one's soul *tr.* to annoy someone. □ *That kind of thing really gripes my soul!* □ *John, have I ever told you that you gripe my soul?*

hack *tr.* to annoy someone. □ *This really hacks me.* □ *That kind of behavior hacks her a lot.*

harsh toke *n.* anything or anyone unpleasant. □ *Sally can sure be a harsh toke when she wants.* □ *This meeting has been a real harsh toke.*

hassle *n.* a dispute; a bother. □ *The whole thing was a real hassle.* □ *It's a hassle every time I come here.*

headache *n.* an annoying person or thing. □ *Here comes that Ken Johnson. He's a real headache.* □ *Cars can be such a headache.*

hung *mod.* annoyed. □ *Susan is hung and looking for somebody to take it out on.* □ *How can you get so hung about practically nothing?*

jacked (out) *mod.* angry; annoyed. □ *Boy, was that old guy jacked out at you.* □ *Yup, he was jacked all right.*

lay off (**someone or something**) *in.* to stop bothering or harming someone or something; to stop being concerned about someone or something. □ *Lay off the booze for a while, why don't ya?* □ *Lay off me! I didn't do anything!*

Lump it! *exclam.* "Forget it!"; "Go away!" □ *Well, you can just lump it!* □ *Lump it! Drop dead!*

nag *tr.* to pester someone constantly. □ *Stop nagging me!* □ *I'll nag him until he remembers on his own.*

nark AND **narc** *tr.* to annoy someone. □ *Stop narking me!* □ *Why are you always narcing someone?*

narked *mod.* annoyed. (Usually with *at* or *with*.) □ *He's really narked at us.* □ *She is narked with you and your car.*

needle *tr.* to annoy someone. □ *Tom is always needling Frank.* □ *Stop needling me!*

Nerts! *exclam.* "Nuts!" (Partly euphemistic.) □ *Oh, nerts! I forgot my wallet.* □ *Nerts! I dropped my keys.*

nudge AND **noodge** **1.** *in.* to nag. □ *Don't noodge all the time.* □ *Stop always noodging.* **2.** *tr.* to nag someone. □ *Stop nudging me about that.* □ *I'll noodge him a little to remind him.*

Nuts! *exclam.* "No!"; "I don't believe you!"; "I don't care!" □ *Nuts! You don't know what you are talking about.* □ *Oh, nuts! I forgot my wallet.*

Nuts to you! *exclam.* "Go away!"; "Drop dead!" □ *Well, nuts to you! You are just plain rude!* □ *Nuts to you! I will NOT lend you money!*

pain *n.* a bother; an irritating thing or person. □ *That woman is such a pain.* □ *Those long meetings are a real pain.*

pesky *mod.* annoying; bothersome. □ *I am going to kill that pesky fly!* □ *I've had a pesky headache all day.*

rag on someone AND **rake on someone** *in.* to bother someone; to irritate someone; to criticize and humiliate someone. □ *I wish you would stop ragging on me. I don't know why you are so annoyed at me.* □ *Stop raking on me!*

red tape *n.* bureaucratic annoyances; bureaucratic forms and procedures. (Typically with *cut* as in the example.) □ *If you deal with the government, you will have to put up with lots of red tape.* □ *I have a friend who knows how to cut through red tape.*

someone or something from hell *n.* someone or something very intense, annoying, or challenging. (As if the person or thing were a demon from hell. Use caution with *hell*.) □ *She is the nurse from hell and just loves to give shots.* □ *I just came back from a cruise from hell and have lots of horror stories to tell about the trip.* □ *I worked for three years at that job from hell, and I'm glad to be out of it.*

stress **1.** *in.* to suffer annoyance; to experience stress. □ *I'm stressing again! Please don't annoy me!* □ *Clare finds that she is stressing more and more about little things.* **2.** *tr.* to annoy or bother someone. □ *Don't stress Wally! He's had a hard day.* □ *The whole affair about my beemer stressed me a whole lot.*

That tears it! *exclam.* "That is too much!" □ *Well, that tears it! I'm leaving!* □ *I thought yesterday's error was bad enough, but that tears it!*

Tough titty! AND **Tough titties!** *exclam.* "That's too bad!" (Crude. Potentially offensive. Use only with discretion.) □ *Tough titty! I told you it wouldn't be easy.* □ *So you missed the bus. Tough titty!*

What's eating someone? *interrog.* "What is bothering someone?" □ *Gee, Tom, what's eating you?* □ *What's eating Fred? He's in a rotten humor.*

ANTICIPATION
See also EARLY, WAITING.

jump the gun *tr.* to start too soon; to start before the starting signal. □ *Don't jump the gun again. Wait till I tell you.* □ *The secretary jumped the gun and gave out the letters too soon.*

one jump ahead of someone or something *n.* in advance of someone or something; a step ahead of someone or something. □ *I try to be one jump ahead* of the problems. □ *You have to keep one jump ahead of the boss in order to succeed.*

ANUS

asshole *n.* the anus. (Potentially offensive. Use only with discretion.) □ *He threatened to kick me in the asshole, or something like that, if I didn't leave at once.* □ *He had to tell the doctor about the pain in his asshole because he simply didn't know any other word for it.*

bazoo *n.* the anus. (Use caution with the topic.) □ *You wanna get kicked in the bazoo?* □ *Max threatened to install something in Bruno's bazoo.*

where the sun don't shine *phr.* in a dark place, namely the anus. (Often with *put it* or *shove it.* Part of the answer to the question *"Where shall I put it?"* Always with *don't;* never with *doesn't.*) □ *I don't care what you do with it. Just put it where the sun don't shine.* □ *For all I care you can shove it where the sun don't shine.*

ANXIETY

antsy *mod.* nervous; restless. □ *You look a little antsy. What's wrong?* □ *Who is that antsy guy?* □ *She gets antsy before a test.*

at loose ends *mod.* nervous and anxious; bored with nothing to do. □ *Tom usually works puzzles whenever he's at loose ends.* □ *I'm at loose ends on weekends.*

basket case *n.* a person who is a nervous wreck. □ *After that meeting, I was practically a basket case.* □ *The waiting was so intense that I was a real basket case.*

bundle of nerves *n.* a very nervous person. □ *I'm just a bundle of nerves. I wish this were over.* □ *Paul's been a bundle of nerves ever since his wreck.*

clutched *mod.* nervous. □ *I get so clutched before a test.* □ *George is clutched most of the time. He's in bad shape.*

clutch (up) *in.* to become very tense and anxious; to freeze with anxiety. □ *I have been known to clutch up before a race.* □ *Cool it, babe! Don't clutch!*

crack up *in.* to have a nervous breakdown. □ *The poor guy cracked up. It was too much for him.* □ *You would crack up,*

too, if you had been through all he went through.

creeps *n.* the jitters; a case of nerves. (Always with *the.*) □ *These movies always give me the creeps.* □ *The creeps always make me have to go to the john.*

dragged *mod.* anxious or frightened after smoking marijuana. □ *The kid was dragged. You could tell he didn't have much experience with the real world.* □ *Some of these burnouts really look dragged.*

edgy *mod.* nervous; anxious and uncertain. □ *I feel sort of edgy about the race.* □ *I'm just an edgy guy.* □ *Don't let yourself get so edgy.*

get one's bowels in an uproar *tr.* to become overly anxious or excited. □ *Cool it! Don't get your bowels in an uproar.* □ *Fred's always getting his bowels in an uproar about nothing.*

have ants in one's pants *tr.* to be nervous and anxious. □ *He seems to have ants in his pants before each game.* □ *All kids have got ants in their pants all the time at that age.*

heebie-jeebies AND **heeby-jeebies** *n.* an extreme case of anxiety or fear. □ *I have the heebie-jeebies whenever I go to the dentist.* □ *These movies give me the heeby-jeebies.*

jumpy *mod.* nervous. □ *I'm a little jumpy today, and I don't know why.* □ *Now, don't be jumpy. Everything will be all right.*

keyed (up) *mod.* nervous; anxious. □ *Sally was a little keyed up before the meet.* □ *When I get keyed, I meditate.*

nervous Nellie *n.* any nervous person, male or female. □ *Sue is such a nervous Nellie. She should calm down.* □ *Relax! Don't be such a nervous Nellie.*

nervy *mod.* nervous. □ *Mary is so nervy. Anything will set her off.* □ *Now, don't get nervy.*

psych out *in.* to have a nervous or emotional trauma; to go mad for a brief time. □ *Another day like this one and I'll psych out for sure.* □ *He looked at the bill and psyched out.*

run scared *in.* to act panicked. □ *All the politicians are running scared.* □ *Don't panic. There is no reason to run scared.*

screaming-meemies AND **screaming-meemies** *n.* a mental breakdown. □ *They sent Max away with the screaming-meemies.* □ *I need some sleep. I'm about to come down with the screaming-meemies.*

stew 1. *in.* to fret. □ *It's bad, but don't stew about it.* □ *I spent most of last night stewing about my job.* **2.** *n.* a fretful state. □ *Don't work yourself into a stew.* □ *Look at her face. That is the result of a dreadful stew. I wonder what's wrong.*

strung out AND **strung (up)** *mod.* depressed; nervous. □ *I get strung out before tests and other traumatic things.* □ *I'm a little strung out—because of the accident, I guess.*

sweat *tr. & in.* to fret (about something) while waiting for an outcome. □ *Come on, don't sweat it. It'll work out.* □ *This whole promotion business really has me sweating.*

sweat something out *tr.* to wait out something; to fret and worry until the end of something. □ *You'll just have to sweat it out. There's no way to hurry it up.* □ *We'll sweat out the wait—like everybody else.*

twit *n.* a nervous or frantic state. □ *The twit I was in made me seem sort of silly, I'm afraid.* □ *My confused state became a serious twit, and I didn't know what to do.*

up the wall *mod.* anxious; in a very bad situation. □ *He's really up the wall about Mary's illness.* □ *We were all up the wall until the matter was resolved.*

uptight *mod.* anxious. □ *Dave always seems uptight about something.* □ *He is one uptight guy.* □ *Don't get uptight before the test.*

white-knuckle 1. *mod.* having to do with an event that creates a lot of tension, especially an airplane flight. □ *I had a real white-knuckle session with the boss today.* □ *We came in during the storm on a white-knuckle flight from Chi-*

cago. **2.** *mod.* of a person who is made tense by something such as flying or sailing. □ *I'm afraid I'm a white-knuckle sailor, and you'd all be much happier if I stay on dry land.* □ *My cousin is a white-knuckle flyer and would rather take the train.*

white knuckler 1. *n.* a suspenseful event, such as an exciting movie or a rough airplane flight. □ *The movie was a real white knuckler.* □ *We sat through the white knuckler even without popcorn.* **2.** *n.* a tense and nervous person. □ *You white knucklers are just going to have to relax.* □ *I'm such a white knuckler before a test.*

willies *n.* a case of fear or anxiety. □ *That kind of movie always gives me the willies.* □ *I got the willies before the test.*

APPEALING

jazzy *mod.* stimulating; appealing. □ *That's a jazzy sweater you got.* □ *He's a real jazzy guy.*

oomph *n.* sex appeal. (Euphemistic.) □ *She had a lot of oomph, but didn't wish to become a movie star.* □ *No amount of oomph can make up for a total lack of talent.*

sexy *mod.* having great sex appeal. □ *What a sexy chick!* □ *He's not what I would call sexy, but I suppose it's a matter of taste.*

APPEARANCE

coyote-ugly *mod.* extremely ugly. (Crude, cruel, and potentially offensive.) □ *Is that your pet monkey, or is your date just coyote-ugly?* □ *Isn't that the most coyote-ugly creep you've ever seen?*

deadpan *n.* an expressionless face. □ *This guy has a super deadpan.* □ *Remember the deadpan she used to put on?*

double-bagger *n.* a very ugly person. (Cruel. With a face so ugly that it takes two paper bags to conceal it.) □ *Fred is what I would call a double-bagger. What a mug!* □ *I am no double-bagger!*

dressed to kill *mod.* dressed in fancy or stylish clothes to impress someone. □ *She is always dressed to kill.* □ *I'm never dressed to kill. I just try to be neat.*

dressed to the nines AND **dressed to the teeth** *mod.* dressed very stylishly with nothing overlooked. □ *She showed up for the picnic dressed to the nines.* □ *Clare is usually dressed to the teeth in order to impress people.*

front *n.* a respectable appearance. □ *Jan can put up a good front, but most of us know the real Jan.* □ *The front she put up collapsed as she heard the bad news.*

gussied up *mod.* dressed up in one's best clothing. (Folksy.) □ *She was all gussied up in her finest.* □ *I like to get gussied up and go out on the town.*

in fine feather *mod.* well dressed; of an excellent appearance. □ *Well, you are certainly in fine feather today.* □ *I like to be in fine feather when I have to give a speech.*

lift *n.* a device—worn under the hair at the temples—that provides some of the effects of a surgical face-lift. □ *Do you think she's wearing a lift?* □ *Lift, hell, she's got a damn pair of cranes under that hairdo.*

nuke oneself *tr.* to tan oneself at a tanning salon. □ *I nuke myself once a week in the spring so I will be ready for the summer bikini season.* □ *Leonard nuked himself in the middle of winter, and everyone thought he had been to Florida.*

scraggy *mod.* bony. □ *That dame is too scraggy for me.* □ *Who is that scraggy dame?* □ *I lost weight till I was scraggy as a hungry bear.*

snappy *mod.* sharp-looking. □ *That's a real snappy outfit you're wearing.* □ *Who's driving that snappy car over there?* □ *That car's not snappy!*

APPEARANCE - NEGATIVE

fugly *mod.* "fat and ugly." (Collegiate.) □ *Man, is that dog of yours ever fugly! What or who did it eat?* □ *This is a real fugly problem we're facing.*

scruff(y) *mod.* sloppy; unkempt. □ *Her boyfriend is a little scruffy, but he's got billies!* □ *Why don't you clean up this scruff car? It's—like—grody!*

APPLIANCE

fridge *n.* a refrigerator. □ *Put this in the fridge so it won't spoil.* □ *What's in the fridge for dinner tonight?*

nuker *n.* a microwave oven. □ *I tried to do a turkey in the nuker once and made a real mess of it.* □ *Who left the soggy bacon in the nuker?*

reefer *n.* a refrigerator. □ *Please put the milk in the reefer.* □ *A new reefer costs nearly $1,000!*

vac 1. *n.* a vacuum cleaner. □ *Where's the vac?* □ *Bring the vac and clean this place up.* **2.** *tr. & in.* to clean with a vacuum cleaner. □ *Vac while you have time!* □ *You are supposed to vac the whole house, not just your room!*

APPRECIATION

dig *tr.* to appreciate something; to like something. □ *He really digs classical music.* □ *Do you dig chocolate?*

eat something up *tr.* to appreciate something. □ *The audience really ate it up.* □ *The stuff about the federal budget went over well. They really ate up the whole story.*

swing with someone or something *in.* to appreciate someone or something. □ *Man, I can really swing with that color. Glorious!* □ *I can really swing with John. He and I are real close.*

APPROVAL

See also **SATISFACTORY, YES.**

green light *n.* the signal to go ahead with something; the okay. □ *She gave the green light to the project.* □ *When we get the green light, we'll start.*

OK AND **okay** *tr.* to approve something. □ *She refused to okay our plans.* □ *Please OK this bill so I can pay it.*

thumbs up 1. *n.* a sign of approval. □ *It was a thumbs up on the new filtration plant at Thursday's village board meeting.* □ *There was no thumbs up for the mayor as she faced certain defeat in today's balloting.* **2.** *mod.* approving; positive. □ *The new filtration plant got a thumbs up decision at the board meeting.* □ *A* *thumbs up vote assured another three years of financial assistance.*

ARGUMENT

See also **FIGHTING**.

flame *in.* to write an excited and angry note to someone in computer communication. □ *Barb is flaming again. It doesn't take much to set her off.* □ *Stop flaming a minute and try to explain your position calmly.*

flame-war *n.* an angry and excited exchange of notes in computer communication. □ *A flame-war erupted on the board last night and a lot of people said some pretty rude things.* □ *The SYSOP tried to stop the flame-war, but it kept going anyway.*

flap *n.* an argument; a minor scandal. □ *I'm sorry about that flap we had yesterday, but it was all your fault.* □ *Who started this flap, anyway?*

flip side *n.* the "other" side of something, such as an argument. □ *I want to hear the flip side of this before I make a judgment.* □ *On the flip side, he is no bargain either.*

shoot-out *n.* an argument. □ *When the shoot-out was over, the boss—confident she had won—went back into her office.* □ *A big public shoot-out like that sours morale a lot.*

step outside *in.* to leave the present area and go to another place, presumably to fight. □ *The two—who had been arguing—stepped outside to settle the matter.* □ *Do you want to step outside, smart ass?*

tangle with someone or something *in.* to quarrel or fight with someone or something. □ *I didn't want to tangle with her, so I did what she wanted.* □ *It's like tangling with a grizzly.*

ARISE

hit the deck *tr.* to get out of bed. □ *Come on, hit the deck! It's morning.* □ *Hit the deck! Time to rise and shine!*

ARMPITS

pits *n.* the armpits. (Usually crude.) □ *Man, you have a problem in your pits.* □ *Who's got the smelly pits in here?*

AROUSAL

bring someone on *tr.* to arouse sexually; to turn someone on. □ *She was trying to bring her date on, but he saw her game.* □ *This kind of music brings me on.*

get someone's motor running *tr.* to get someone sexually aroused. □ *She knows how to get his motor running.* □ *It's funny how that wild music gets her motor running.*

horny *mod.* sexually aroused. (Use caution with the topic.) □ *Tom said he was horny.* □ *Who is that horny jerk?* □ *All the guys in that fraternity are horny.*

hot *mod.* sexy; sexually aroused or arousing. □ *Man, is that chick hot!* □ *She's not my idea of hot.* □ *Wow, who was that hot hunk you were with?*

rammy *mod.* sexually excited or aroused. (Refers to the ram, a symbol of arousal.) □ *Fred was looking a little rammy, so I excused myself and left.* □ *Your rammy boyfriend is on the telephone.*

randy *mod.* sexually excited or aroused. □ *The town is full of randy sailors when the fleet's in.* □ *Wow, does he look randy!* □ *There is a randy-looking guy at the door asking for you.*

ARREST

bad rap *n.* a false criminal charge. □ *Freddy got stuck with a bad rap.* □ *All those guys get nothing but bad raps. Nobody's ever guilty.*

bag *tr.* to capture and arrest someone. (Underworld.) □ *They bagged the robber with the loot still on him.* □ *We'll be able to bag the alleged killer when we have more evidence.*

bagged *mod.* arrested. □ *"You are bagged," said the officer, clapping a hand on the suspect's shoulder.* □ *"I'm not bagged yet, copper," said the crook.*

batted AND **batted out** *mod.* arrested. (Underworld.) □ *I got batted out on my first day as a booster.* □ *This gal got batted twice last year on the same rap.*

bust 1. *n.* a raid by the police. □ *The cops staged a bust on Max's place.* □ *I knew it was a bust the minute they broke in the door.* **2.** *tr.* [for the police] to raid a place. □ *The bacon busted Bill's bar and put Bill in the slammer.* □ *We're gonna bust every bookie joint in town.*

bust 1. *tr.* to arrest someone. □ *The feds finally busted Max on a tax rap.* □ *A smokey busted Fred for not having a tail-light.* **2.** *n.* an arrest. □ *The bust was carried off without much stress.* □ *What a bust! The man was hollering and the kids were scoffing like mad.*

busted AND **bust** *mod.* arrested. □ *Max is bust again. The third time this month.* □ *I got busted for speeding.*

clipped *mod.* arrested. □ *Max got clipped as he got out of his car.* □ *He was clipped and no one read him his rights, so off he went.*

clouted *mod.* arrested. □ *Some old wino got clouted for spitting on the sidewalk.* □ *They do things like that to get clouted so they can have a warm place to stay overnight.*

collar 1. *tr.* to arrest someone. □ *The cops collared her as she was leaving the hotel.* □ *The nark tried to collar Max, but Max moved away too fast.* **2.** *n.* an arrest. □ *It was a tough collar, with all the screaming and yelling.* □ *I made the collar in broad daylight.*

collared *mod.* arrested. □ *Willard Babbit? Oh, yes. He's collared. Got him last night.* □ *Got collared during a routine traffic stop.*

cop 1. *tr.* to arrest someone. □ *The officer copped him and read him his rights.* □ *They copped Bruno with the evidence right on him.* **2.** *n.* an arrest. □ *It was a smooth cop. No muss, no fuss.* □ *The cop went off without a hitch except for a few little insults.*

copped *mod.* arrested. □ *Jed got himself copped—a speeder.* □ *I was copped for doing absolutely nothing at all.*

crashed *mod.* raided by the police. □ *Our pad got crashed, and a lot of kids were arrested.* □ *After the place was crashed, it was a mess.*

drop *in.* to get arrested. (Underworld.) □ *I'm not going to drop for you.* □ *Bruno dropped, but Mr. Big got him off.*

dropped *mod.* arrested. □ *Max was dropped only once last year.* □ *He got himself dropped on a speeding ticket.*

fall 1. *in.* to be arrested; to be charged with a crime. (Underworld.) □ *I heard that Bruno fell. Is that right?* □ *Bruno would never fall easily. Must be a frame.* **2.** *n.* one's arrest; being arrested and charged. (Underworld.) □ *Who took the fall for the bank job?* □ *Rocko will never accept a fall willingly.*

flag *tr.* to arrest someone. □ *The cop flagged Tracy for soliciting.* □ *They flagged Bob for speeding even though he was a judge.*

flagged *mod.* arrested. □ *Max almost got himself flagged for speeding.* □ *Sally was flagged, and she called her fixer to come get her out.*

gaffled *mod.* arrested. □ *Fred got himself gaffled for speeding.* □ *I can just picture Fred gaffled and acting all humble.*

glommed *mod.* arrested. (Underworld.) □ *Max got glommed on a speeding charge. I didn't even know he could drive.* □ *Glommed again! That's the story of my life.*

glued *mod.* arrested. (Underworld.) □ *Wally got glued for having over three hundred parking tickets.* □ *Max goes to great extremes to keep from getting glued.*

go down *in.* to be arrested. (Underworld.) □ *Lefty didn't want to go down for a job he didn't do.* □ *Mr. Big said that somebody had to go down for it, and he didn't care who.*

gotcha *n.* an arrest. (Underworld.) □ *The cop reached out, grasped Bruno's shoulder, and made the gotcha.* □ *It was a fair gotcha. Bruno was nabbed, and he went along quietly.*

guzzled *mod.* arrested. (Underworld.) □ *Rocko got himself guzzled on a speeding rap.* □ *Lefty is guzzled again. He's so clumsy.*

jacked up AND **jacked** *mod.* arrested. (Underworld.) □ *What time did Bruno get himself jacked up?* □ *He was jacked up at midnight.*

jammed *mod.* arrested. (Underworld.) □ *Bruno got jammed for speeding.* □ *When did he get jammed?*

knocked in *mod.* arrested. (Underworld.) □ *Would you believe that Rocko has never been knocked in?* □ *When Lefty was knocked in, they found his heater on him.*

nab *tr.* to arrest someone. □ *They nabbed Tom with a stolen watch on him.* □ *I knew they would nab him sooner or later.*

nabbed *mod.* caught by the police; arrested. □ *He got nabbed last night with a stolen watch on him.* □ *She's down at the police station. She's nabbed.*

nail *tr.* to arrest someone. □ *The cops nailed him right in his own doorway.* □ *"I'm gonna nail you," said the officer.*

nailed *mod.* arrested. □ *Okay, chum. You are nailed. Let's go.* □ *Why am I nailed? I didn't do anything.*

nick *tr.* to arrest someone. □ *The cops nicked Paul outside his house.* □ *They are going to nick Joe, too.*

nicked *mod.* arrested. □ *Paul was nicked last night.* □ *"Now I'm nicked," he said.*

pickup *n.* an arrest. (Underworld.) □ *Send Sergeant Townsend out to make the pickup.* □ *The cop made a pickup right across the street.*

pinch 1. *tr.* to arrest someone. □ *The cops pinched her in front of her house.* □ *The police captain pinched her for passing bad checks.* **2.** *n.* the arresting of someone. □ *They made the pinch in front of her house.* □ *The pinch was for forgery.*

pinched *mod.* arrested. □ *I got pinched for speeding.* □ *Sam got pinched for a parole violation.*

pinned *mod.* arrested. (Underworld.) □ *The boys in blue pinned him and took him away.* □ *He had a gun in his belt when they pinned him.*

popped *mod.* arrested. □ *Tom got popped for speeding.* □ *He was popped for hardly anything at all.*

prior *n.* a prior arrest. (Underworld.) □ *This guy has about fifteen priors.* □ *Have you ever had a prior, young man?*

put the arm on someone *tr.* to arrest someone. (Underworld.) □ *They put the arm on Max for pushing pills.* □ *They're gonna put the arm on the whole gang at once.*

roust *n.* a raid. □ *Okay, stand still. This is a roust!* □ *They pulled a big roust down on Fourth Street.*

rousted *mod.* arrested. (Underworld.) □ *Max got rousted last night.* □ *The cops rousted the dealers, but that didn't even slow down the drug trade.*

run someone in *tr.* to arrest someone; to take someone to the police station. □ *Don't argue with me, or I'll run you in.* □ *The cops ran in everybody in sight.*

scoop *n.* a general roundup and arrest of criminals. (Underworld.) □ *Max got picked up in that big drug scoop last month.* □ *There are some people who get dragged in every time there is a scoop. It cannot just be a coincidence.*

snapped (up) *mod.* arrested. □ *He got snapped up on a vag charge.* □ *The bacon busted the joint and snapped everybody in sight.*

snatched *mod.* arrested. □ *Everybody in the crack house got snatched in the bust.* □ *Bruno was snatched for the umpteenth time yesterday.*

sting 1. *n.* a well-planned scheme to entrap criminals. □ *The sting came off without a hitch.* □ *It was a well-planned sting and shouldn't have failed.* **2.** *tr.* to entrap and arrest someone. □ *The feebies stung the whole gang at once.* □ *"We've been stung!" they hollered.*

take a fall AND **take a dive** *tr.* to get arrested. (Underworld.) □ *Bruno took a fall for the bank robbery.* □ *I didn't wanna take a dive, but the cop left me no choice.*

take the fall *tr.* to get arrested for a particular crime. (Especially when others are going unpunished for the same crime.) □ *Bruno and Tony pulled the job off together, but Tony took the fall.* □ *You did it, and I won't take the fall!*

tapped *mod.* arrested. (As if one were tapped on the shoulder by a police officer.) □ *I knew I was gonna get tapped eventually, but I just couldn't stop stealing.* □ *The whole gang was tapped in a police raid.*

yanked *mod.* arrested. (Underworld.) □ *Lefty got himself yanked one too many times.* □ *Everybody in the gang got yanked at least once last week.*

ARRIVAL

blow in *in.* to arrive. □ *I just blew in last night. Where can I find a room?* □ *When I blew in, nobody was here.*

clock in *in.* to record one's arrival at a set time. □ *He clocked in three minutes late.* □ *When they clock in, give them this envelope.*

roll in *in.* to pull in; to drive up; to arrive. □ *The car rolled into the parking lot at a high speed.* □ *Four station wagons rolled in at the same time.*

ARROGANCE
See HAUGHTINESS.

ARTS

artsy-craftsy *mod.* dabbling in arts and crafts; artistic. □ *Wally is sort of artsy-craftsy.* □ *Gary's an artsy-crafty kind of guy with lots of talent.* □ *The artsy-craftsy crowd held a show in the library parking lot last Sunday.*

artsy (fartsy) *mod.* obviously or overly artistic. (Use caution with *fart*.) □ *The decorations were sort of artsy, but the overall effect was quite nice.* □ *Things are a little artsy fartsy in the south dorm, but most of the residents are really nice.*

farts *n.* "fine arts." (Use discretion with *fart*.) □ *Ted is studying over in the farts department.* □ *Fred took a course in farts and hated it.*

flick *n.* a movie. □ *That was a pretty good flick, right?* □ *Let's go see that new Woody Allen flick.*

rep *n.* repertory theater. □ *He spent a year in rep on the East Coast.* □ *Rep is the best place to get experience, but not to make connections.*

ASSISTANCE

begathon *n.* a televised appeal for contributions, especially as conducted by U.S. public television stations. □ *It seems like this station is one long begathon all year long.* □ *They made two million in the begathon last month.*

give someone five *tr.* to give someone a helping hand. □ *Hey, give me five over here for a minute, will ya?* □ *I gotta give this guy five with the crate. Be right with you.*

handout *n.* a gift of money, food, or other goods to a needy person. (Often in the negative, as in the examples.) □ *I don't want a handout, just a loan.* □ *Give him a handout and send him on his way.*

pitch in (and help) *in.* to volunteer to help; to join in completing a task. □ *Come on, you guys! Pitch in.* □ *If more people would pitch in and help, we could get this job done in no time at all.*

ASSISTANT

gopher AND **gofer** *n.* someone who goes for things and brings them back. (From *go for.*) □ *You got a gopher who can go get some coffee?* □ *Send the gofer out for cigarettes.*

ATTACK

blow *n.* a setback; an attack. □ *It was a real blow to our prestige.* □ *Acme Systems Industries suffered a blow to its plans to acquire A.B.C. Steel Widgets.*

ATTENTION

Dig up! *exclam.* "Listen up!"; "Pay attention!" □ *Dig up, man! This is important.* □ *Shut up and dig up!*

Geronimo! *exclam.* "Here I go!" (Originally said by parachutists leaving a plane. From the name of an Indian chief.) □ *There's my cue. Geronimo!* □ *Here goes nothing. Geronimo!*

ATTENTION - LACKING

asleep at the switch *mod.* inattentive to duty. (Not literal.) □ *Donald was asleep at the switch when the call came in.* □ *He sat there reading—asleep at the switch as usual.*

ATTRACTIVE

built like a brick outhouse AND **built like a brick shithouse** *mod.* well-built—either strong or attractive. (The second entry is potentially offensive. Use only with discretion.) □ *That guy's built like a brick shithouse.* □ *This garage is built like a brick outhouse. It'll last for years.*

ATTRACTIVENESS

eye-popper *n.* a very good-looking woman or girl. □ *Isn't that foxy lady an eye-popper?* □ *I may not be an eye-popper, but my virtue is exemplary.*

fat *mod.* sexy. □ *She is one fat sister!* □ *You are truly fat, Wendy.*

foxy *mod.* sexy, especially having to do with a woman. □ *Man, isn't she foxy?* □ *What a foxy dame!*

fresh *mod.* good-looking. □ *Wendy is fresh and smart too.* □ *Tom is fresh and buff.*

on fire *mod.* very attractive or sexy. □ *She is really on fire!* □ *Look at those jet-set people! Each one of them is just on fire.*

PHAT *phr.* "pretty hips and thighs." (Initialism.) □ *Now, that's what I like, PHAT.* □ *PHAT is what it's all about.*

sharp *mod.* good-looking; well-dressed. □ *You really look sharp today.* □ *That's a sharp set of wheels you got there.*

spiffed out *mod.* nicely dressed up; decked out. □ *I like to get all spiffed out every now and then.* □ *Wow, you look spiffed out! Where are you going?*

spiffed up *mod.* dressed up, brushed up, and polished up nicely. □ *See if you can get yourself a little spiffed up before we get to the front door. We wouldn't want the Wilmington-Thorpes to think you only have one suit.* □ *The house doesn't have to be too spiffed up for the Franklins. They are used to clutter.*

stacked *mod.* having to do with a person with a sexually attractive body, usually a female. □ *Wow, is she ever stacked!* □ *I like to see stacked dames like that starting to do business in this place.*

AUDIENCE

turnout *n.* an audience that has assembled for some purpose. □ *How was the turnout at the benefit?* □ *The turnout was great. We had a full house.*

AUDIO

See also **BROADCASTING**.

boom box *n.* a portable stereo radio. □ *Turn down that damn boom box, or I'll kick it in.* □ *Hey, man! You even gonna take your boom box to church, or what?*

box 1. *n.* a phonograph player. □ *My box is old, but still good.* □ *Yours is old! My box still has tubes!* **2.** *n.* a portable stereo radio. □ *Where did you get that box?* □ *Does that damn box have to be so loud?*

cans *n.* earphones. □ *The guy with the cans on his head is the radio operator.* □ *I bought a new set of cans for my stereo.*

crank something up *tr.* to increase the volume of an electronic device. □ *He cranked it up a little more and CRACK, there went both speakers!* □ *Kelly cranked up his stereo until we were nearly deafened.*

(ghetto) blaster AND **(ghetto) box** *n.* a portable stereo radio. (Often carried on the shoulder, especially by blacks.) □ *Hey, turn down that ghetto blaster in here!* □ *You can't bring that box on this bus!*

squawk box *n.* a public address system; a loudspeaker, especially if installed in a box or other housing. □ *A raspy voice came over the squawk box announcing the arrival of what we had been waiting for.* □ *The squawk box was strangely quiet through the night.*

thunderbox *n.* a portable stereo radio, often played very loudly in public. □ *Someday I'm going to smash one of these thunderboxes!* □ *Why not get a thunderbox of your own?*

AUTHORIZATION

say-so *n.* a command; an authorization. □ *I can't do it just on your say-so.* □ *We can begin as soon as we get the boss's say-so.*

AUTOMATIC

knee-jerk *mod.* automatic; quick and without thought. □ *That was only a knee-jerk response. Pay no attention.* □ *My knee-jerk response is that you should not go.*

AUTOMOBILES

See **CARS**.

AVAILABLE

off-the-shelf *mod.* readily available; purchasable without any special difficulties or delays. □ *This is just plain old off-the-shelf hand lotion. Isn't it great?* □ *Is it off-the-shelf?* □ *I don't use off-the-shelf software in my computer. I write my own.*

on tap *mod.* immediately available. □ *I have just the kind of person you're talking about on tap.* □ *The cook has any kind of food you might want on tap.*

up for grabs *mod.* available for anyone; not yet claimed. □ *It's up for grabs. Everything is still very chancy.* □ *I don't know who will get it. It's up for grabs.*

AVERAGE

See also **ORDINARY**.

middlebrow *mod.* middle-class; average or mediocre. (Between *highbrow* and *lowbrow*.) □ *She has average middlebrow tastes and drives a mid-sized Chevrolet.* □ *He's just too middlebrow.* □ *There are some who look down on middlebrow interests as trivial.*

run-of-the-mill *mod.* average; typical. (Referring to the typical quality of a product that comes out of a mill.) □ *He is just a run-of-the-mill guy.* □ *I don't want just run-of-the-mill ice cream.* □ *This stuff is just run-of-the-mill.*

so-so *mod.* average; mediocre. □ *It was just so-so. Nothing to write home about.* □ *I don't need to pay $7.50 to see a so-so movie.*

AVIATION

bird *n.* an airplane. □ *I like this bird. She's a dream to fly.* □ *The bird crashed on takeoff.*

bump *tr.* to remove someone from an airplane flight, usually involuntarily, be-cause of overbooking. □ *They bumped me, but gave me something to make up for it.* □ *Is this airline in the habit of bumping old ladies?*

chopper *n.* a helicopter. □ *The chopper that monitors the traffic goes over my house every morning at 6:00.* □ *I never want to ride in a chopper. Those things scare me.*

egg-beater *n.* a helicopter. □ *The egg-beater landed on the hospital roof.* □ *I would think that egg-beaters all over the place would disturb the patients.*

fling-wing *n.* a helicopter. □ *The fling-wing from the radio station is hovering over the traffic jam.* □ *There must be a dozen fling-wings up there making all that noise.*

flyboy *n.* a pilot. (Military.) □ *Rocko was a flyboy in Korea.* □ *Those flyboys have it easy.*

hop *tr.* to get aboard a plane or train. □ *I'll hop a plane and be there in a couple of hours.* □ *Hop a train or anything, but get here as soon as you can.*

no show AND **no-show** *n.* someone who doesn't show up for something, such as an airline flight. □ *The flight was cancelled because there were too many no-shows.* □ *I have never been a no show, but my brother does it all the time.*

on the beam *mod.* homing in on an aviation radio beam. (No longer a major navigational device.) □ *The plane was on the beam and landed safely in the fog.* □ *I couldn't get on the beam, and I flew right over the airfield.*

puddle jumper *n.* a small airplane. □ *I'm not going to fly 200 miles in that puddle jumper!* □ *My uncle has his own puddle jumper.*

rotorhead *n.* a helicopter pilot or member of a helicopter crew. (Military. Also a term of address.) □ *Radio those rotorheads and tell them to get back to the base, now!* □ *Hey, rotorhead, where's your egg-beater?*

sky *in.* to travel (to somewhere) in an airplane. □ *I decided to sky down to Or-*

lando for the weekend. □ Let's sky to New York and then go on to London.

stew *n.* a stewardess or steward on an airplane. □ The stew brought the coffee and rolls. □ My sister is a stew for a major airline.

stick *n.* the lever that controls the horizontal and vertical surfaces of the tail of an aircraft. □ The pilot pulled back on the stick, and the plane did nothing—being that he hadn't even started the engine or anything. □ You pull back on the stick, which lowers the tail and raises the nose, and up you go.

whirlybird *n.* a helicopter. □ See that whirlybird up there? It's timing your speed. Slow down. □ The whirlybird landed on the roof of the hospital.

wing *in.* to travel by airplane. □ We winged to Budapest and attended the conference. □ They winged from there to London.

zoomies *n.* members of the U.S. Air Force. (A nickname used by the Army. Persian Gulf War.) □ The zoomies attacked the airfield and damaged a lot of planes. □ The zoomies attacked the spy headquarters and caused a lot of damage.

AVOIDANCE

duck *tr.* to avoid someone or something. □ Clare is ducking her responsibility. □ You can't duck this investigation. They're on to you.

wouldn't touch someone or something with a ten-foot pole *phr.* would not get involved with someone or something. □ Forget it. I wouldn't touch it with a ten-foot pole. □ Tom said he wouldn't touch Tracy with a ten-foot pole.

AWARENESS

See also **KNOWLEDGE**.

hep *mod.* aware; informed. □ The chick is simply not hep. □ Fred is one of the most hep guys you're going to run into.

hip *mod.* informed; aware. □ The guy is just not hip. He's a nerd. □ Get hip, Tom!

onto someone or something *mod.* alerted to or aware of a deceitful plan or person. □ The cops are onto your little game here. □ Max thought he was safe, but the fuzz was onto him from the beginning.

ring a bell *tr.* to stir something in someone's memory. □ Yes, that rings a bell. I seem to remember it. □ Maybe the name Marsha will ring a bell!

tune in (to something) *in.* to become alert to something. □ She tuned in to the comments about acid rain. □ When I heard my name, I tuned in.

with (one's) eyes (wide) open *mod.* totally aware of what is going on. □ I went into this with my eyes wide open. □ We all started with our eyes open but didn't realize what could happen to us.

AWARENESS - LACKING

coo-coo AND **cuckoo** *mod.* unconscious. □ I socked him on the snoot and knocked him coo-coo. □ Rocko was cuckoo for a minute; then he was up and swinging.

gone AND **gone under** *mod.* unconscious. □ He's gone. Prop his feet up and call an ambulance. □ He's gone under. You can begin the procedure now.

half under *mod.* semi-conscious. □ I was half under and could hear what the doctor was saying. □ I was afraid they would start cutting while I was only half under.

out of it *mod.* not in with the real world. □ You never pay attention to what's going on. You're really out of it. □ Fred is out of it most of the time. He even looks dull.

B

BACKFIRE

backfire (on someone) *in.* [for a scheme meant to cause harm to someone or something] to harm the person who runs the scheme. □ *I hope this plan doesn't backfire on me.* □ *Her attempt to frame Bill for the crime backfired.*

BAD

See HORRIBLE, NASTY, UNDESIRABLE.

BADGE

button *n.* a police officer's badge or shield. □ *The guy flashed his button, so I let him in.* □ *Just because you got a button, it doesn't mean you can push innocent citizens around!*

shield *n.* a police officer's badge. □ *The fuzz flashed his shield, and I knew the game was over.* □ *If you're a cop, where's your shield?*

BALDNESS

baldy AND **baldie** *n.* a bald-headed man. □ *I'm getting to be an old baldie.* □ *I turned into a baldy in my twenties.*

chrome-dome *n.* a shiny, bald head; a man with a bald head. (Also a rude term of address.) □ *The guy with the chrome-dome suddenly grasped his chest and made a face.* □ *Hey, chrome-dome, you're blinding me!*

skin AND **skinhead** *n.* someone with a shaved or bald head. (Some such persons may also engage in political violence.) □ *Who's the skin with the earrings?* □ *That skinhead looks stoned.*

BASIC

bedrock 1. *n.* fundamentals; solid facts. □ *Let's get down to bedrock and quit wasting time.* □ *This is bedrock—the truth.* **2.** *mod.* fundamental. □ *You've been avoiding the bedrock issues all your life.* □ *Let's hear some more about these bedrock ideas.*

gut *mod.* basic; fundamental. □ *This is a gut issue, and we have to deal with it now.* □ *We are not dealing with what I would call one of the gut matters of the day.*

nuts and bolts *n.* the mundane workings of something; the basics of something. □ *I want you to learn how to write well. You have to get down to the nuts and bolts of writing.* □ *She's got a lot of good, general ideas, but when it comes to the nuts and bolts of getting something done, she's no good.*

BATHROOM

ammunition *n.* toilet tissue. □ *Could somebody help me? We're out of ammunition in here!* □ *The ammunition in Europe is better these days than it used to be.*

BEARD

See also MUSTACHE.

(face) fungus *n.* whiskers; a beard. □ *If John would shave off that face fungus, he'd look a lot better.* □ *What do you need all that fungus for anyway?*

fungus-face *n.* a bearded man. □ *Who's the fungus-face in the striped blazer?* □ *Hey, fungus-face! Who is that behind all the fuzz?*

fuzz-face *n.* a man with a beard. □ *Hey, fuzz-face, come here a minute.* □ *A couple of fuzz-faces came in and asked for mustache wax.*

BED

fart sack *n.* a sleeping bag; a bed. (Potentially offensive. Use only with discretion.) □ *Well, it's time I was getting* into the old fart sack. □ *Get out of that fart sack and get up and get going!*

rack *n.* a bed. □ *I need some more time in the rack.* □ *You don't get to see the rack very much in the army.*

sack *n.* a bed. □ *I was so tired I could hardly find my sack.* □ *Somebody put a spider in my sack.*

BEGGING

bum something (off someone) *tr.* to beg or borrow something (from someone). □ *Can I bum a cigarette off you?* □ *Can I bum a quarter for a phone call?*

mooch(er) *n.* a beggar. □ *The guy is a mooch. Get him out of here.* □ *I try to give every moocher a little change.*

schnorrer *n.* a beggar; a person who sponges off of friends and relatives. (Yiddish.) □ *Here comes that schnorrer from down the street. Look poor.* □ *Buy your own ciggies if you don't like mine. Shnorrers can't be choosers.*

thumber *n.* a beggar; a *moocher*. (As one who thumbs or begs a ride.) □ *Don't be a thumber, Frank. Go buy your own cancer sticks.* □ *There was a thumber on every corner trying to get a ride from someone.*

BEGINNINGS

back to square one *phr.* back to the beginning. (Often with *go*.) □ *Well, it looks like it's back to square one.* □ *We've got to get this done without going back to square one.*

crank something up *tr.* to start something up. □ *I'll go out and crank the car up so it can warm up.* □ *Crank up the copying machine. We've got a big job to do.*

fire away *in.* to start asking questions; to start talking. □ *Okay, I'm ready. Fire away.* □ *The cops fired away at him for an hour.*

from (the) git-go *mod.* from the very start. □ *This kind of thing has been a problem from the git-go.* □ *I warned you about this from git-go.*

get it on *tr.* to begin something. □ *Time to go back to work. Let's get it on!* □ *Get it on, you guys! Time to start your engines.*

get the show on the road *tr.* to get (something) started. □ *Let's get started! Get the show on the road!* □ *Get the show on the road. We don't have all day.*

git-go *n.* the very beginning. □ *Clear back at the git-go, I told you this wouldn't work.* □ *He's been gritching ever since git-go.*

honeymoon (period) AND **honeymoon stage** *n.* an early stage in any activity, before problems set in. □ *Of course, this is still the honeymoon stage, but everything seems to be going all right.* □ *The honeymoon is over, Carl. You have to produce now.*

jump-start someone or something *tr.* to get someone or something going or functioning. □ *I need to jump-start Bill early in the morning to get him going in time to get on the road by a decent hour.* □ *I am looking for someone to jump-start my car.*

jump (street) *n.* the beginning; the start (of something). (Prisons and streets.) □ *I knew from jump that you were going to be trouble.* □ *Way back at jump street, I spotted you as a troublemaker.*

knuckle down (to something) *in.* to get busy doing something. □ *Please knuckle down to your studies.* □ *You have to knuckle down if you want to get ahead.*

Let her rip! AND **Let it roll!** *exclam.* "Let it go!"; "Let it start!" □ *Time to start. Let her rip!* □ *There's the signal! Let it roll!*

swing into high gear *in.* to begin operating at a fast pace; to increase the rate of activity. □ *During the winter season we swing into high gear around here.* □ *The chef swings into high gear around eight o'clock in preparation for the theater crowd.*

trigger *tr.* to start something; to set something off. □ *The noise triggered an avalanche.* □ *One little thing triggered that blowup, and I want to find out what it is.*

up front *mod.* at the beginning; in advance. □ *She wanted $200 up front.* □ *The more you pay up front, the less you'll have to finance.*

BEHAVIOR

bogart AND **bogard** *in.* to act in a tough manner like Humphrey Bogart. □ *Look at him bogarting! Who needs tough guys?* □ *There's nothing funnier than a wimp trying to bogard around.*

camp it up *tr.* to overact. □ *Can you make it a little more lively without camping it up?* □ *She's so dull that she could camp it up and still look half asleep.*

get with it *in.* to modernize one's attitudes and behavior. □ *Get with it, Martin. Get real!* □ *You really have to get with it, Ernie.*

in one's something mode *phr.* behaving in a specified mode. (The *something* can be replaced by *work, sleep, hungry, angry,* etc.) □ *I'm not very alert because I'm still in my sleep mode.* □ *Todd is always in his play mode when he should be working.*

make like someone or something *in.* to act like someone or something. □ *Why don't you make like a bunny and run away? Beat it!* □ *Would you please make like a butler and hold the door open for me?*

on one's high horse *mod.* in a haughty manner or mood. □ *Larry is on his high horse again, bossing people around.* □ *The boss is on her high horse about the number of paper clips we use.*

piss-ant around *in.* to move about in a timid fashion; to behave overly cautiously. (Potentially offensive. Use only with discretion.) □ *Don't just piss-ant around here. State your business or get out.* □ *Stop piss-anting around and get busy.*

play someone for a fool *tr.* to treat someone like a fool; to act as if someone were a fool. □ *I know what you're trying to do. Don't try to play me for a fool.* □ *We played her for a fool, and she never knew it.*

redneck *mod.* in the manner of a southern bigot. □ *I don't follow that kind of redneck thinking.* □ *The candidate didn't want the redneck vote.*

Smile when you say that. *sent.* "Give some sort of a signal that you are only joking when you say something potentially offensive." □ *That's pretty rude. You'd better smile when you say that.* □ *I told him he'd better smile when he says that, or he's going to get in trouble.*

sprout wings *tr.* to be so good as to become an angel. □ *The kid is not about to sprout wings, but he probably won't get into jail again.* □ *He was so good and helpful, I thought he would sprout wings.*

stick-to-itiveness *n.* tenacity. □ *The kid has stick-to-itiveness. I like that in a kid.* □ *If I had more stick-to-itiveness, maybe I could get a job.*

straighten up and fly right *in.* to get serious and start behaving properly. □ *It's time for you to straighten up and fly right!* □ *Straighten up and fly right before you get into difficulty.*

stylin(g) *n.* looking good; showing off how good one looks. □ *Dave thinks that stylin' is his sole occupation.* □ *When you finish styling in front of the mirror, would you please dump the garbage?*

BEHAVIOR - BAD

cop a(n atti)tude *tr.* to take a negative or opposite attitude about something. □ *Look, chum, don't cop an attitude with me!* □ *I think you're copping a 'tude. Not advised, man. Not advised.*

illin' 1. *mod.* ill-behaved. □ *You are most illin' and you are bugging me, Kim. Stop it!* □ *She is the most illin' homeslice I know.* 2. *in.* behaving badly. □ *Stop illin' and pay attention.* □ *You are always illin'!*

pool-hopping *n.* sneaking into private or public swimming pools at night or during the off-hours. □ *The kids went pool-hopping, and one of them nearly drowned.* □ *Pool-hopping is illegal.*

snit *n.* a state of resentment. □ *Don't work yourself into such a snit.* □ *She threw quite a snit.*

tude *n.* a bad "attitude." □ *Hey, you really got a tude, dude.* □ *Are you pulling a tude with me?*

wenchy AND **whenchy** *mod.* bitchy; snotty. (Collegiate.) □ *I really wish you wouldn't be so wenchy with me!* □ *What's* *the matter with that wenchy chick?* □ *Then she began to get wenchy, so I left.*

BEHIND

down *mod.* behind in a score. □ *We're three points down with two minutes to play.* □ *They're twenty points down, and it looks like the Adamsville team has won.*

BELCH

belch 1. *in.* to bring up stomach gas. □ *They swallow beer by the can and see who can belch the loudest.* □ *I belched, and everybody stared.* **2.** *n.* a burp; an upward release of stomach gas. □ *That was the loudest belch I've ever heard.* □ *What I really need is a good belch.*

berp AND **burp 1.** *in.* to bring up stomach gas. □ *She burped quietly behind her hanky, so no one would notice.* □ *Try not to burp at the table.* **2.** *n.* an upward release of stomach gas. □ *The burp did not go unnoticed.* □ *What can you do when you berp in church?*

grunt *n.* a belch. □ *I heard your grunt!* □ *Does that grunt mean you like my cooking?*

BELIEF

Believe you me! *exclam.* "You should believe me!" □ *Believe you me, that was some cake!* □ *This is a fine picnic. Believe you me!*

buy *tr.* to believe something. □ *Nobody'll buy that story.* □ *It sounds good to me, but will your wife buy it?*

Go on! *exclam.* "I don't believe you!"; "I deny it!" □ *Go on! You don't really know what you are talking about!* □ *Go on! You weren't even there.*

Like hell! *exclam.* "That is not true!"; "I do not believe you!" (Use caution with hell.) □ *You're going to a Dead concert! Like hell!* □ *Like hell, you are!*

My foot! *exclam.* "I do not believe it!"; "Like hell!" (An exclamation of contradiction.) □ *You're the best in town, my foot!* □ *She's going to marry you? My foot!*

No kidding! *exclam.* "I am not kidding."; "You are not kidding (are you?)" □ *No kidding! I never thought she would*

do that. □ *No kidding, he's really going to join the Air Force.*

No lie! *exclam.* "Honest!"; "No kidding!" □ *I really did it! No lie!* □ *I was there on time. No lie! Ask my sister.*

No Shinola! *exclam.* "You are kidding!"; "No shit!" (A play on the expression indicating that a stupid person doesn't know shit from Shinola. Shinola is a brand of shoe polish. Use with caution.) □ *So taxes are too high? No Shinola!* □ *He's late again? No Shinola!*

piffle *exclam.* a mild exclamation or expression of distress. (Usually **Piffle!**) □ *You a stockbroker? Piffle!* □ *She finished her story, and I looked her straight in the eye and said, "Piffle!"*

Tell me another (one)! *exclam.* "Tell me another fairy tale!"; "That was a lie. Tell me another just as good!" □ *You a stockbroker? Tell me another one!* □ *There's no improvement in this problem! Tell me another!*

That'll be the day! *exclam.* "That will never happen!" □ *You win a medal? That'll be the day!* □ *When he gets his own car—that'll be the day!*

will not·wash *in.* will not be believed. (As if untruth were a stain that will not come out in the wash.) □ *It sounds phony. It won't wash.* □ *That'll never wash! It's totally unbelievable.*

You (had) better believe it! *exclam.* "It is true without question!" □ *It's true. You better believe it.* □ *Yes, this is the best, and you had better believe it!*

BELLY

See also STOMACH.

bay window *n.* a belly; an abdomen. □ *You are going to have to do something about that bay window.* □ *Your bay window is getting out of hand.*

bazoo *n.* the stomach or belly. □ *Look at the bazoo on that guy!* □ *You can tell that his bazoo came from too much beer.*

beer belly AND **beer gut** *n.* a large belly. □ *You're going to end up with a real beer belly hanging over your belt if you don't* *let up on that stuff.* □ *Look at the beer belly on that guy.*

labonza *n.* the belly. □ *I feel the effects of last night's celebration in my wallet and in my labonza.* □ *Look at the labonza on that creep! He's gonna deliver triplets.*

Milwaukee goiter AND **German goiter** *n.* a beer belly. (Refers to Milwaukee, Wisconsin, a major beer-brewing city, and to Germany.) □ *By the time he was twenty-six, he was balding and had a Milwaukee goiter that would tip him over if he turned too fast.* □ *He was proud of his German goiter.*

potbelly *n.* a big belly. □ *He got a potbelly from eating fried chicken.* □ *Everyone in her family has a potbelly.*

BENEFIT

See also **ADVANTAGE**.

brownie points *n.* imaginary credit for doing something well. (Originally *demerits* in railroading.) □ *How many brownie points do I get for not frowning when you take my picture?* □ *No brownie points for you, twit!*

onto a good thing *mod.* having found something that is to one's advantage, such as something easy, profitable, inexpensive, etc. □ *I think that Bill got onto a good thing when he opened his own store.* □ *I won't quit now. I'm onto a good thing, and I know it.*

perk *n.* an extra financial benefit; a monetary inducement or reward. (From *perquisite.*) □ *I don't get paid much, but the perks are good.* □ *I don't get paid much, and I don't get any perks!*

upside *n.* the good side. □ *On the upside, things might get better.* □ *There's not much to look forward to on the upside.*

What's in it for me? *interrog.* "How do I benefit from it?" □ *I might help out. What's in it for me?* □ *I might be able to contribute a little. What's in it for me?*

BEST

(el) primo *mod.* having to do with something that is top quality. (From Spanish for "the first.") □ *This stuff is*

primo. □ *I want some more of that el primo C.*

number one *mod.* top rated; best; closest. □ *We heard the number one high school band in the whole state last night.* □ *This is my number one buddy, Tom.*

numero uno *n.* "number one"; the best. (Spanish.) □ *This coffee is numero uno in my book.* □ *Mary is numero uno in our office. You'll have to ask her.*

ten *n.* the highest rank on a scale of one to ten. (Always with *a*.) □ *She's definitely a ten.* □ *On a scale of one to ten, this pizza's a ten.*

BETRAYAL

double-cross 1. *tr.* to betray someone. (Originally a more complicated switching of sides in a conspiracy wherein the *double-crosser* sides with the victim of the conspiracy—against the original conspirator.) □ *Don't even think about double-crossing me!* □ *Max double-crossed Mr. Big a few years back.* **2.** *n.* a betrayal. □ *He always remembered that double-cross.* □ *It's one double-cross Max is sorry about.*

double-crosser *n.* a person who betrays someone. (Often with *dirty.* See comments at *double-cross.*) □ *You dirty, low-down double-crosser, you!* □ *Max is the classic double-crosser.*

sellout *n.* a betrayal. □ *Any one of you could have stood up for me. What a sellout!* □ *How can you pull such a sellout?*

sell someone out *tr.* to betray someone. □ *How could you sell me out like that?* □ *She would sell out her mother.*

step out on someone *in.* to betray one's lover by going out with someone else. □ *Hank has been stepping out on Bess, and she doesn't know it yet.* □ *She would never step out on him.*

turn *in.* to go over to the other side, as with a spy or a criminal turning into an informer. (Underworld.) □ *Is there a chance that Max would turn?* □ *Max turn? Ha!*

BICYCLE

bike *n.* a motorcycle; a bicycle. □ *How much did that bike set you back?* □ *You have to wear a helmet with a bike that size, don't you?*

BIRTH

visit from the stork *n.* the birth of a baby. □ *The last visit from the stork was in March.* □ *We are expecting a visit from the stork next June.*

BISEXUAL

AC-DC AND **AC/DC** *mod.* bisexual. (Initialism.) □ *I didn't realize at first that we were in an AC-DC bar!* □ *Clare said Tom is AC/DC, but I don't believe it.*

combo *n.* a bisexual person. □ *Nobody would have thought that Fred's a combo.* □ *He's not a combo, he's just confused.*

BOASTING

big talk *n.* boasting; exaggerated claims. □ *No more big talk. I want action!* □ *I heard nothing but big talk since you got here.*

blowhard *n.* a braggart; a big talker. □ *You're just a big blowhard.* □ *When and if this blowhard finishes, let's go.*

blow one's own horn AND **toot one's own horn** *tr.* to brag. □ *Gary sure likes to toot his own horn.* □ *"I hate to blow my own horn," said Bill, lying through his teeth.*

bullshit artist AND **bullshitter** *n.* someone who excels at boasting or lying. (Potentially offensive. Use only with discretion.) □ *Jim is such a bullshit artist!* □ *He can't talk straight—nothing but a bullshitter.*

crapper *n.* a braggart. (Crude.) □ *The guy is a crapper and can't be trusted at all.* □ *Don't listen to the crapper.*

gas *in.* to talk nonsense; to brag. □ *Pay no attention. She's just gassing.* □ *Stop gassing for a minute and listen.*

gasbag *n.* a braggart. □ *What's the old gasbag going on about now?* □ *Harry is such a gasbag when he gets going about himself.*

loose cannon *n.* a loudmouth; a braggart. □ *As it turned out, he's not just a* loose cannon. *He makes sense.* □ *Some loose cannon in the State Department has been feeding the press all sorts of crap as a diversion.*

sell a wolf ticket AND **sell wolf tickets** *tr.* to boast, bluff, or lie. (Originally black.) □ *Freddie is out selling wolf tickets again.* □ *Are you trying to sell me a wolf ticket?*

talk big *in.* to brag; to make grandiose statements. □ *She talks big, but can't produce anything.* □ *He has some deep need to talk big. He can't do anything.*

throw the bull AND **throw the crap** *tr.* to chat; to boast. (Use caution with crap.) □ *Tom could really throw the bull and sound right as rain.* □ *You're just throwing the crap. Can it!*

windbag AND **bag of wind** *n.* a talkative person; a braggart. □ *Quiet, you windbag!* □ *She's nothing but a big bag of wind.*

woof *in.* to boast; to chatter. (Black.) □ *They're just woofing. Ignore them.* □ *Stop woofing, Fred. You sound silly.*

BOAT

stinkpot *n.* a motorboat. (Because the engine smells bad, especially when compared to a sailboat.) □ *Those guys in their stinkpots sure make a lot of noise.* □ *Those stinkpots just have to be polluting the lake.*

BODY

bod *n.* a body, especially a nice body. □ *You got a nice bod, Tom.* □ *If you got a good bod and enough money, why are you depressed?*

carcass *n.* one's body; a large or heavy body. □ *He hauled his carcass out of the car and lumbered into the bank.* □ *Put your carcass on a chair, and let's chew the fat.*

classis-chassis AND **classy-chassy** *n.* an attractive female figure. □ *Who's the classis-chassis in the mink?* □ *Now there is a classy-chassy if I ever saw one.*

odd-bod *n.* a peculiar body. □ *I have such an odd-bod that it's hard to find* clothes. □ *With an odd-bod like that, he'll never make good in the movies.*

vital statistics *n.* the measurements of a person's body. □ *Her vital statistics must require higher math to work out!* □ *Here are his vital statistics for those who are interested.*

BODY - DEAD

dog meat *n.* a dead person. (Typically in a threat.) □ *Make one move, and you're dog meat.* □ *They pulled another hunk of gangland dog meat out of the river.*

landowner *n.* a corpse; a dead person. □ *Now old Mr. Carlson was a landowner for real.* □ *"How would you like to become a landowner?" snarled the mugger.*

road pizza *n.* a dead animal on the road. □ *Every morning the highway is littered with road pizza.* □ *A bunch of crows were feasting on road pizza when we drove by.*

stiff *n.* a corpse. (Underworld.) □ *They pulled another stiff out of the river last night. Looks like another mob killing.* □ *They took me into a room full of stiffs to identify Rocko's bod.*

worm-food *n.* a corpse. □ *You wanna end up worm-food? Just keep smarting off.* □ *In the end, we're all worm-food.*

BOREDOM

See DULL.

BRAGGING

See BOASTING.

BRAIN

fuse box *n.* the head; the brain. □ *I'm afraid she's missing a little something in the fuse box.* □ *Jed acts like his fuse box is completely blown.*

top story AND **upper story** *n.* the brain. □ *A little weak in the upper story, but other than that, a great guy.* □ *He has nothing for a top story.*

wetware *n.* the human brain. (Compared to computer *hardware* and *software*.) □ *This isn't a hardware problem; it's a wetware problem.* □ *You need to update your wetware.*

BRAVERY

See COURAGE.

BREASTS

See also BUXOM.

B and B *mod.* "breast and buttock," having to do with entertainment featuring female nudity. □ *There were some picketers in front of the store protesting the sale of B and B mags over the counter.* □ *Many movies contain a little B and B just to get an R-rating.*

bazoom(s) *n.* the breasts. (Potentially offensive. Use only with discretion. Jocular or euphemistic.) □ *This doll has real bazooms.* □ *She has quite a—ah—bazoom.*

boob(y) *n.* a breast. (Usually plural. Potentially offensive. Use only with discretion.) □ *My boobs aren't what I might have wished for.* □ *With boobies like that, she can go anywhere she likes.*

boosiasm(s) *n.* a woman's breasts. (A blend of *bosom* and *enthusiasm*. Occurs both as a count and a noncount noun. Old but recurrent. Potentially offensive. Use only with discretion.) □ *Did you see the boosiasms on that dame?* □ *What a remarkable boosiasm!*

can *n.* a breast. (Use caution with the topic. Usually plural.) □ *Man, look at the cans on that dame!* □ *Those cans can't be real!*

knockers *n.* the breasts. (Potentially offensive. Use only with discretion.) □ *Nice knockers, huh?* □ *All you think about is knockers.*

murphy *n.* a breast. (Crude. Usually plural. Use caution with the topic.) □ *Look at the murphies on that dame!* □ *She stood about six feet tall and was turned in the light so her murphies stood out in silhouette.*

T and A AND **tits and ass** *n.* a display of "tits and ass," breasts and buttocks. □ *The magazines featuring tits and ass flourish in their under-the-counter trade.* □ *These silly T and A movies have no plot to interfere with the leers.*

tits *n.* the breasts. (Crude. Potentially offensive. Use only with discretion.) □ *Wow, nice tits, huh, Fred?* □ *All you think about is tits!*

BRIBERY

drugola *n.* a bribe paid by drug dealers to the police for protection. □ *Max pays a little drugola, but mostly the cops never come into this area anyway.* □ *A lot of drugola is simply paid in drugs.*

fix 1. *n.* a bribe. □ *Rocko never took a fix in his life.* □ *The agent paid a fix to the cops.* **2.** *n.* a scheme to influence the outcome of a contest or an election. □ *Something is wrong with this game. I smell a fix.* □ *Bruno planned a great fix, but the cops got wise.*

fixed *mod.* bribed. □ *Don't worry, the night watchman is fixed.* □ *The cop is fixed and won't give you guys any trouble.*

fixed *mod.* having the outcome prearranged. (Said of a contest, race, or election.) □ *The election was fixed, and we are going to protest.* □ *It was not fixed!* □ *The race was fixed, but we won anyway.*

grease *n.* protection money; bribery money. □ *Rocko was in charge of making sure that enough grease was spread around city hall.* □ *See that the commissioner of the park district gets a little grease to help us get the contract.*

grease someone's palm *tr.* to pay someone a bribe. □ *I had to grease the clerk's palm in order to get the job done.* □ *Are you trying to grease my palm?*

kickback *n.* money received in return for a favor. □ *The kickback the cop got wasn't enough, as it turned out.* □ *You really don't believe that the cops take kickbacks!*

on the take *mod.* taking bribes. (Underworld.) □ *I heard that the mayor is on the take.* □ *Everyone in city hall is on the take.*

palm-oil *n.* a bribe; a tip. □ *How much palm-oil does it take to get this deed recorded in reasonable time?* □ *The messenger seemed to move his legs faster after an application of palm-oil.*

payola *n.* any bribe or payoff. (Originally a bribe paid to a *disk jockey* by record producers to get extra attention for their records.) □ *The announcer was fired for taking payola.* □ *There was a big scandal of payola in the 1950s.*

plugola *n.* a bribe paid to get a free advertising *plug* (worth far more than the amount of the bribe). □ *How much plugola did you have to pay for that mention?* □ *The announcer was charged with accepting plugola.*

BROADCASTING

See also **AUDIO, TELEVISION**.

disk jockey AND **deejay; disc jockey; D.J.** *n.* a radio announcer who introduces recorded music, originally from phonograph records. □ *The disk jockey couldn't pronounce the name of the singing group.* □ *I was a D.J. for a while, but I didn't like it.*

ham *n.* an amateur radio operator. □ *My brother is a ham, and he helped a lot during the emergency.* □ *The hams helped by providing communication to the outside world.*

idiot card *n.* a large card that shows people on television what to say. □ *The floor director held up an idiot card so I could read out the telephone number.* □ *I couldn't read the number off the idiot card.*

radioland *n.* an imaginary place where radio listeners dwell. □ *Hello out there in radioland. This is Martin Jones speaking.* □ *All you folks in radioland who enjoy country music will like this next one.*

veejay AND **V.J.; video jock** *n.* a "video jockey"; a host on a television program that features music videos. (The abbreviation is an initialism. Patterned on *deejay*.) □ *Sally tried out for the veejay job, but she looked too old and stuffy for that kind of work.* □ *Most of the V.J.s on cable television are untrained amateurs.* □ *Wally tried out to be a video jock, but he's too uptown.*

BROKE

See **MONEY - LACKING**.

BROTHEL

call house *n.* a brothel. □ *The cops busted a call house on Fourth Street last week.* □ *The madame of the call house certainly looked like a lady to me.*

hook shop *n.* a brothel. □ *Guess who I saw coming out of a hook shop?* □ *There is a secret hook shop over on Maple Street.*

madam *n.* the female keeper of a brothel. □ *The madam was caught in a sting operation.* □ *The cops led the madam away, followed by a parade of you-know-whats.*

BURDEN
See also DIFFICULTIES, PROBLEM.

be a drag (on someone) *phr.* to be a burden (to someone). □ *I wish you wouldn't be such a drag on your friends.* □ *I don't want to be a drag on the department.*

freeload *in.* to sponge off someone else; to eat and drink at someone else's expense; to live off someone else. □ *Don't come around here and expect to freeload.* □ *My brother-in-law has been freeloading at our house for months.*

saddled with someone or something *mod.* burdened with someone or something. □ *I've been saddled with the children all day. Let's go out tonight.* □ *I don't want to be saddled with your work.*

stick someone with something *tr.* to burden someone with something. □ *Please don't stick me with the stick shift again.* □ *He left town and stuck me with the bill.*

strap someone with someone or something *tr.* to burden someone with someone or something. (Often passive.) □ *Don't you try to strap me with your baby brother!* □ *She was strapped with too many bills to pay each month.*

stuck with someone or something *mod.* burdened with someone or something; left with the burden of someone or something. □ *It's your problem, and you're stuck with it.* □ *Am I stuck with this kid forever?*

BUREAUCRAT
paper-pusher *n.* a bureaucrat; a clerk in the military services; any office worker. □ *If those paper-pushers can't get their work done on time, make them stay late.* □ *I don't want to talk to some paper-pusher, I want to talk to the boss.*

pencil-pusher *n.* a bureaucrat; a clerk; an office worker. □ *Look here, you lousy pencil-pusher, I want to talk to your boss!* □ *City hall is filled with a bunch of overpaid pencil-pushers.*

wonk *n.* a bureaucrat; a flunky. □ *The State Department policy wonks were up all night putting together the report.* □ *Our office was knee-deep in wonks before the reorganization.*

BUS
double-decker *n.* a two-level bus. □ *I like to ride in double-deckers.* □ *Some double-deckers don't have tops.*

BUSINESS
See also COMMERCE, COST, FINANCIAL.

biz *n.* a business; business. □ *What biz you in?* □ *I'm in the plumbing biz.*

B.O. *n.* "box office," where tickets to some event are sold. □ *The show was a big hit at the B.O.* □ *If you want your money back, you'll have to go to the B.O.*

body count *n.* the total number of unemployed people after a reorganization. □ *The pink slips are coming out every day. The body count on Monday was twenty-three.* □ *The body count will be high after the merger.*

brass tacks *n.* essential business. (Usually in "get down to brass tacks.") □ *Now that we are talking brass tacks, how much do you really want for this watch?* □ *Since we haven't gotten down to brass tacks, would it be unethical for me to buy you lunch?*

captain of industry *n.* a corporation officer; a capitalist. □ *The captains of industry manage to hang on to their money no matter what.* □ *It's fun to see those captains of industry drive up in their benzes.*

company man *n.* a man who always sides with his employers. □ *Ken's a company man—he'll always take management's side.* □ *You can depend on a company man to do as he is told.*

exec *n.* an executive. □ *The execs are well-treated around here.* □ *They are even firing the execs now.*

front man *n.* a respectable and well-known man who represents a less respectable person or organization. □ *The former adviser now serves as a front man for a large foundation.* □ *The front man came out and made an announcement.*

hands-on *mod.* having to do with an executive or manager who participates directly in operations. □ *We expect that he will be the kind of hands-on president we have been looking for.* □ *John is a hands-on manager. I wish he would stay in his office.*

head hunt *tr. & in.* to recruit someone (for a job). □ *He went to the conference to head hunt a new employee.* □ *All the managers were there to head hunt.*

headhunter *n.* someone who recruits executives for employment. (*Head* means "boss" here.) □ *The board of directors hired a headhunter to get a new manager.* □ *The headhunter brought in a few candidates, but nobody promising.*

hole in the wall *n.* a tiny shop, not much wider than its doorway. □ *I went into this little hole in the wall where they had the nicest little gifts.* □ *His office is just a hole in the wall.*

hot *mod.* selling well. □ *These things are really hot this season.* □ *Now, here's a hot item.*

land office business *n.* a large amount of business done in a short period of time. □ *We always do a land office business at this time of year.* □ *We keep going. Never do land office business—just enough to make out.*

org *n.* an organization. □ *She's a member of the org and can't be expected to use independent judgment.* □ *Come on, join the org.*

outfit *n.* a group of people; a company. □ *That outfit cheated me out of my money.* □ *I will never deal with that outfit again.*

pinstriper *n.* a businessman or businesswoman wearing a pinstriped suit. □ *Who's the pinstriper driving the beemer?* □ *Wall Street is nothing but wall-to-wall pinstripers.*

rep *n.* a representative, usually a sales representative. □ *Please ask your rep to stop by my office.* □ *Our rep will be in your area tomorrow.*

repo *tr.* to repossess a car. □ *Some guy came around and tried to repo my car.* □ *She's good at repoing family cars.*

show biz *n.* show business. □ *Well, that's show biz for you.* □ *Anybody who can make a living in show biz has to be clever and talented.*

slave market *n.* a job market where many candidates for jobs come face-to-face with potential employers. □ *I gotta go to the annual slave market this year. We're hiring for a change.* □ *There was little hope at the annual slave market. There were six jobs and 432 applicants.*

suit *n.* a businessman or businesswoman; someone who is in charge. □ *This suit comes up and asks to go to the airport.* □ *A couple of suits checked into a working-class hotel and caused some eyebrows to raise.*

sweetheart deal *n.* a deal made between friends so that both may profit well. (Such deals usually involve illegal or unethical practices.) □ *They found that the mayor was involved in a number of sweetheart deals.* □ *Most of the general contractors in town would be out of business if they didn't offer sweetheart deals to the politicians.*

swindle sheet *n.* an expense account record sheet or book. □ *I turned in my swindle sheet yesterday, and no one challenged the $400 for new shoes.* □ *The government makes it hard to put just anything on your swindle sheet these days.*

TCB *phr.* "taking care of business"; doing things that have to be done. (Black. Initialism.) □ *He's TCB; that's where he is.* □ *If I am just TCB and keeping my nose clean, I know I'm gonna be all right.*

vest *n.* an important businessman or businesswoman. □ *One of the vests complained to the management about the way I cleaned his office.* □ *Some vest jumped out the window this afternoon.*

wheeler-dealer *n.* someone who bargains aggressively. □ *She has turned into a real wheeler-dealer.* □ *Who's the wheeler-dealer who set up this deal?*

BUSY

crunch *n.* a crisis; a time of pressure or tightness, especially of a budget. □ *We seem to be in a crunch of one kind or another all the time.* □ *The budget crunch meant that we couldn't take trips to Europe anymore.*

dime store *n.* an establishment that is chaotic because of its small scale. □ *I can't stand this dime store anymore. This is no way to run a law firm.* □ *Things move so fast around here that we have become a dime store rather than an accounting office.*

Grand Central Station *n.* any busy and hectic place. (From Grand Central Station in New York City—a very busy place.) □ *This place is Grand Central Station on a Friday night.* □ *At just about closing time, this place becomes Grand Central Station.*

swamped *mod.* very, very busy. □ *I can't handle it now. I'm swamped.* □ *We're always swamped at this time of the year.*

tap dance like mad *in.* to be busy continuously; to have to move fast to distract someone. □ *When things get tough, the whole Congress tap dances like mad.* □ *Any public official knows how to tap dance like mad without getting out of breath or sweating.*

tied up *mod.* busy. □ *I was tied up and couldn't get to the phone.* □ *The phone was tied up for more than an hour.*

tight *mod.* busy; with little margin for error. □ *In a tight situation Martin can be sort of a wet rag.* □ *When the schedule is tight and we are busy as all get out, the telephone won't stop ringing.*

wrapped up (with someone or something) *mod.* busy with someone or something. □ *He's wrapped up with a client right now.* □ *I'll talk to you when I'm not wrapped up.*

zoo *n.* a confusing and chaotic place. □ *This place is a zoo on Monday mornings.*

□ *Where is the person in charge of this zoo?*

BUTTOCKS

BA *n.* "bare ass"; the naked buttocks. □ *Cover up your BA and see who's at the door.* □ *The guy was running around with his BA showing.*

backside *n.* the buttocks; one's rear. □ *She fell right on her backside.* □ *There is some mustard or something on your backside.*

B and B *mod.* "breast and buttock," having to do with entertainment featuring female nudity. □ *There were some picketers in front of the store protesting the sale of B and B mags over the counter.* □ *Many movies contain a little B and B just to get an R-rating.*

bazoo *n.* the buttocks. □ *She fell down right on her bazoo.* □ *Put your bazoo on this chair and let's have a little talk.*

behind *n.* the posterior; the buttocks. □ *I've got a boil on the behind that's driving me crazy.* □ *She needs some jeans that will flatter her behind.*

boody AND **boodie; bootie; booty** *n.* the buttocks. □ *Look at the nice little boody on that guy.* □ *Get your boodie out on that dance floor and shake it.*

bottom *n.* the buttocks. □ *Ted fell on his bottom and just sat there.* □ *My bottom is sore from sitting too long.*

bucket *n.* the buttocks. □ *Sam's getting a real fat bucket, isn't he?* □ *Haul your bucket over here and have a seat.*

buns *n.* the buttocks, especially shapely buttocks, particularly male buttocks. □ *What cute little buns!* □ *His face looks like a mule kicked him, but have you seen his buns?*

butt *n.* the buttocks. (Potentially offensive, although heard almost everywhere. Colloquial.) □ *She fell right on her butt.* □ *The doctor gave her a shot in the butt.*

caboose *n.* the buttocks. (From the name of the car at the end of a railroad train.) □ *You just plunk your caboose over there on the settee and listen up to what I have to tell you.* □ *My caboose is bigger* *than I want it, but life is too short to fret about stuff like that.*

can *n.* the buttocks. □ *The guy slipped on the ice and fell on his can.* □ *Look at the can on that guy!*

differential *n.* the buttocks; the *rear (end).* □ *I got a little ache in the differential.* □ *You're walking like there's something wrong with your differential.*

duff *n.* the buttocks. □ *Get off your duff and get busy.* □ *Don't you get tired of sitting around on your duff?*

duster *n.* the buttocks. □ *She fell down right on her duster.* □ *My duster is sore from all that riding.*

fanny *n.* the buttocks. (Euphemistic in the U.S. The term has taboo implications in the U.K.) □ *He fell down right on his fanny.* □ *There's dust or something on your fanny.*

gazoo *n.* the buttocks; the anus. □ *He fell down flat, smack on his gazoo.* □ *Look at the monstrous gazoo on that guy.*

keester AND **keyster; kiester** *n.* the buttocks; the anus. □ *Get your keester over here!* □ *He fell flat on his keyster.*

labonza *n.* the buttocks. □ *Good grief, what a gross labonza!* □ *She fell flat on her labonza.*

moon *n.* the buttocks. □ *He rubbed a plump moon where he had been kicked, but said no more.* □ *She fell square on her moon and slowly broke into a smile.*

prat(t) *n.* the buttocks. □ *Get out before I kick you in the pratt.* □ *Your father will spank your prat.*

rear (end) *n.* the tail end; the buttocks. (Euphemistic.) □ *She fell right on her rear.* □ *The dog bit her in the rear end.*

rooster *n.* the posterior; one's butt end. (Old. Because one "roosts" on it.) □ *Don't just sit there on your rooster. Get to work.* □ *I fell down smack on my rooster.*

rump *n.* the hindquarters; the buttocks; the posterior. □ *He fell on his rump.* □ *A dog doesn't have much rump.*

rusty-dusty *n.* the posterior; the buttocks.* □ *I fell down right on my rusty-dusty.* □ *I almost kicked him in the rusty-dusty.*

seat *n.* the buttocks. □ *Bob fell down on his seat.* □ *I was so angry. I wanted to kick him in the seat as he left.*

stern *n.* the posterior. □ *The little airplane crashed right into the stern of an enormous lady who didn't even notice.* □ *Haul your stern over here and sit down.*

T and A AND **tits and ass** *n.* a display of "tits and ass," breasts and buttocks. □ *The magazines featuring tits and ass flourish in their under-the-counter trade.* □ *These silly T and A movies have no plot to interfere with the leers.*

tokus AND **tukkis; tuchus** *n.* the buttocks; the *rump.* (Yiddish.) □ *She fell right on her tokus!* □ *Look at the tukkis on that fat guy.*

BUXOM

See also **BREASTS**.

brickhouse *n.* a large-breasted woman. (A confused or euphemistic reference to *built like a brick shithouse.* Potentially offensive. Use only with discretion.) □ *Clara's a real brickhouse. I don't see how she stands up.* □ *Look at the boosiasms on that brickhouse!*

top-heavy *mod.* heavy-breasted; buxom. □ *Tracy gets a little top-heavy when she is gaining weight.* □ *Who's the top-heavy number in the red tent?*

CALCULATION

notch *tr.* to count up something; to add up or score something. □ *Well, it looks like we notched another victory.* □ *The crooks notched one more theft before they were caught.*

number crunching *n.* using a computer to solve enormously complicated or complex mathematical problems. □ *I don't do a lot of number crunching, so I don't need a terribly fast machine.* □ *I use the big mainframe computer for number crunching.*

CALM

See also **RELAX**.

blissed (out) AND **blissed-out** *mod.* in a state of emotional bliss. □ *After the second movement, I was totally blissed out.* □ *What a blissed-out dame!* □ *I know a gal who can get blissed from a sunset.*

Blow on it! *exclam.* "Cool it!"; "Take it easy!" □ *It's all right, Tom. Blow on it!* □ *Hey, man. Relax. Blow on it!*

chill (out) *in.* to calm down; to be *cool;* to get *cool.* □ *All right now, people, chill . . . chill.* □ *Before we can debate this matter, you're all gonna have to chill out.*

cool *mod.* unabashed; unruffled; relaxed. □ *This chick is so cool—no matter what happens.* □ *She is totally cool and easygoing.*

cool, calm, and collected *mod.* cool; unabashed. □ *Albert is almost always cool, calm, and collected.* □ *Before a race I am anything but cool, calm, and collected.*

cool down *in.* to calm down. □ *Now, just cool down. Chill, chill. Everything's gonna be real cool.* □ *When things cool down around here, life will be much more liveable.*

cooled out *mod.* calm; unabashed. □ *Ted is a really cooled out kind of guy.* □ *When she's cooled out, she's great.*

Cool it! *exclam.* "Calm down!" □ *Take it easy! Cool it!* □ *Come on, cool it, man!*

cool off *in.* to calm down. □ *Now, it's all right. Cool off!* □ *I knew things would cool off eventually.*

cool out *in.* to calm down; to relax. □ *Now, just cool out, man. This will pass.* □ *Everybody cooled out after the emergency, and everything was fine.*

cool someone out *tr.* to calm someone; to appease someone. □ *Cool yourselves out, you people. We gotta be sensible.* □ *The manager appeared and tried to cool out everybody, but that was a waste of time.*

defrosted *mod.* cooled down; "even" with someone who has insulted, embarrassed, or angered one. □ *He yelled at her till he was defrosted, and then things settled down.* □ *Bob was finally defrosted when he insulted Heidi.*

Don't have a cow! *exclam.* "Calm down!"; "Don't get so excited!" (Made famous in the television show *The Simpsons.*) □ *Chill out, man! Don't have a cow!* □ *Aw, don't have a cow, dad!*

downbeat *mod.* cool; easygoing. □ *He is sort of a downbeat character—no stress.* □ *I wish I was downbeat like he is.* □ *I had sort of a downbeat day. Not your typical Monday.*

Drop it! *exclam.* "Forget it!"; "Never mind!" □ *Never mind! Just drop it!* □ *Drop it! I should never have brought it up.*

Easy does it. *phr.* "Calm down."; "Relax." □ *Chill, man, easy does it.* □ *Easy does it! Relax and go slow!*

evened out *mod.* back to normal; restored to sanity. □ *When things are evened out after the holidays, we can settle down.* □ *Finally, at about age thirty, you could say that Sam was evened out.*

Forget it! 1. *exclam.* "Never mind, it wasn't important!" □ *Forget it! It wasn't important.* □ *I had an objection, but just forget it.* **2.** *exclam.* "Never mind, it was no trouble at all!" □ *No trouble at all. Forget it!* □ *Forget it! It was my pleasure.*

Get a life! *exclam.* "Change your life radically!" □ *You are such a twit! Get a life!* □ *Get a life, you clown!*

keep cool *in.* to keep calm. □ *Now, keep cool. It's going to be all right.* □ *Just keep cool, man. Chill.*

keep one's cool *tr.* to remain calm and in control. □ *Relax, man! Just keep your cool.* □ *It's hard to keep your cool when you've been cheated.*

laid back *mod.* calm and relaxed. □ *Bruno is not what I would call laid back.* □ *You are really one laid back guy!*

mellow out *in.* to calm down; to get less angry. □ *When you mellow out, maybe we can talk.* □ *Come on, man, mellow out!*

play it cool 1. *tr.* to do something while not revealing insecurities or incompetence. □ *Play it cool, man. Look like you belong there.* □ *If the boss walks in, just play it cool.* **2.** *tr.* to hold one's temper. □ *Come on now. Let it pass. Play it cool.* □ *Don't let them get you mad. Play it cool.*

settle someone's hash *tr.* to calm someone down, perhaps by threats or by violence. □ *If he comes in here, I'll settle his hash.* □ *Now, that ought to settle your hash.*

take a chill pill *tr.* to calm down; to relax. □ *Take a chill pill, man! You are too excited.* □ *The police officer told Jim to take a chill pill and answer the questions.*

Take it down a thou(sand)! *in.* "Cool down!"; "Calm down!"; "Quiet down!" □ *Okay. Take it down a thousand, and let's talk this out.* □ *You are wild! Take it down a thou and let's try again to talk this out.*

take it slow *tr.* to go slowly and carefully. □ *Just relax and take it slow. You've got a good chance.* □ *You'll make it. Take it slow and keep your spirits up.*

CANCEL
See **STOPPING**.

CANDIDACY
dark horse *n.* an unknown entrant into a contest; a surprise candidate for political office. □ *The party is hoping that a dark horse will appear before the election.* □ *You'd be surprised at how eagerly people will vote for a dark horse.*

throw one's hat in the ring *tr.* to indicate that one is to be a contestant or a candidate. □ *The con claimed he needed parole so he could throw his hat in the ring for the mayoral election.* □ *I won't throw my hat into the ring until the last minute.*

CARDS
bitch *n.* the queen at cards and at chess. (Mostly jocular.) □ *You dealt me the bitch.* □ *And I take your bitch.*

deuce *n.* the two in playing cards. □ *If I could only get a deuce.* □ *Ah, here's the deuce I need.*

girl *n.* the queen of playing cards. □ *What I needed in that last hand was the girl.* □ *Come on, dealer, I need that girl!*

CARELESSNESS
butterfingers *n.* someone who cannot hold on to things. (Also a term of address.) □ *I'm such a butterfingers. I dropped my papers.* □ *Hang on to this tight, butterfingers!*

jerry-built *mod.* carelessly and awkwardly built. □ *This is an old, jerry-built house, but we love it.* □ *The lawyer's case was jerry-built, but the jury bought it anyway.*

lick and a promise *n.* a very casual treatment. (Always with *a*.) □ *A lick and a promise isn't enough. Take some time and do it right.* □ *She gave it a lick and a promise and said she was done.*

once over lightly *mod.* quickly and superficially; carelessly; cursorily. (This is hyphenated before a nominal.) □ *He looked at it once over lightly and agreed to do it.* □ *It needs more than a once-over-lightly look.*

play fast and loose (with someone or something) *in.* to treat someone or something carelessly or unfairly. □ *The broker played fast and loose with our money. Now we are nearly broke.* □ *He was playing fast and loose with his girl, so she left him.*

quick-and-dirty *mod.* rapidly and carelessly done. □ *I'm selling this car, so all I want is a quick-and-dirty repair job.* □ *They only do quick-and-dirty work at that shop.*

slap-dash *mod.* fast and careless. □ *I wish you hadn't done it in such a slap-dash fashion.* □ *This is a very slap-dash way to do something.*

toss something off *tr.* to do something quickly without much time or effort. □ *It was no big deal. I tossed it off in thirty minutes.* □ *We can toss off the entire order in—let's say—three hours.*

CARING

TLC *n.* "tender loving care." (Initialism.) □ *All he needs is a little TLC.* □ *This old car will keep running as long as I give it lots of T.L.C.*

CARING - LACKING

not give a hoot *tr.* not to care at all. □ *Go ahead. Do it if you want. I don't give a hoot.* □ *She doesn't give a hoot if you go into town without her.*

CARPENTER

wood butcher *n.* a carpenter. □ *See if you can get a wood butcher to fix this broken panel.* □ *The wood butcher tracked sawdust up the stairs.*

CARS

See also **DRIVING**.

ark *n.* an old car. □ *Why don't you get rid of that old ark and get something that's easier to park?* □ *This ark is the most comfortable car I've ever had. I'll drive it till it falls apart.*

banger *n.* the front bumper of a vehicle. □ *Other than a dent or two in the banger, this buggy's okay.* □ *How much for a used banger for this old heap?*

beater *n.* a junky old car. □ *I like my old beater even if it has no bumpers.* □ *I want an old beater that doesn't cost more than 800 bucks.*

beemer *n.* a B.M.W. automobile. □ *I had to sell my beemer when the stock market crashed.* □ *Tiffany's beemer was leased, but no one was supposed to know.*

beetle *n.* a Volkswagen automobile. □ *We wanted to buy a beetle, but decided on a domestic model.* □ *I remember when people used to put big windup keys on their beetles to make them look like windup toys.*

benz AND **Benz** *n.* a Mercedes Benz automobile. □ *I traded in my Benz for a beemer.* □ *My uncle had a Benz that he took back to Germany every two years for service.*

boat *n.* a big car; a full-size car. □ *I don't want to drive a big boat like that.* □ *How do you stop that boat? Throw out an anchor?*

buggy *n.* an automobile. □ *Other than a dent in the front bumper, this buggy is in A-1 condition.* □ *It's time to buy a new buggy.*

Caddy *n.* a Cadillac automobile. □ *What I really want is a Caddy. Keep your yuppie beemer.* □ *Who's the chick in the Caddy?*

can *n.* a car. □ *That's a good-looking can he's driving.* □ *Please don't park your old can in front of my house.*

clunker *n.* an old car. □ *He drives an old clunker and doesn't have any insurance.* □ *I gotta get rid of this clunker pretty soon.*

crate *n.* a dilapidated vehicle. □ *Where'd you get that old crate?* □ *This crate gets me to work and back. That's good enough.*

cream puff *n.* a used car that is in very good condition. □ *This one is a real cream puff. Only driven to church by a little old lady.* □ *This cream puff is loaded, air and everything.*

cruiser *n.* a car; a fast car. □ *This old hog is a real cruiser.* □ *I don't want a yuppie cruiser, just an old family wagon.*

flivver *n.* an old car. (Once a nickname for the Model-T Ford.) □ *Whose flivver is that parked out in the street?* □ *I got an old flivver to get to school and back.*

four wheels *n.* a car; transportation. □ *I need four wheels to get me around town.* □ *Without four wheels at my disposal, I feel trapped.*

fox trap *n.* an automobile customized and fixed up in a way that will attract women. □ *I put every cent I earned into my fox trap, but I still repelled women.* □ *To you it's a fox trap; to me it's a pimpmobile.*

gas-guzzler *n.* a large automobile that uses much gasoline. □ *I got rid of my gas-guzzler and got a smaller car.* □ *The old gas-guzzlers were certainly comfortable.*

goat *n.* a fast and powerful car; a Pontiac GTO. □ *Hey, man, where'd you get that goat?* □ *His goat conked out on him.*

heap *n.* an old car. □ *I've got to get my heap fixed up.* □ *Is this old heap yours?*

hog AND **hog cadillac** *n.* a large car; a souped-up car. □ *How do you like my new hog?* □ *That hog cadillac needs new shocks.*

hopped up *mod.* (having to do with a car that is) customized and speeded up. □ *As soon as I get this hog hopped up, you'll see some real speed.* □ *Sam drives a hopped up old Ford.*

(hot) rod *n.* a car that has been customized for power and speed by the owner. □ *My rod'll outrun yours any day.* □ *Is that a hot rod or a junk heap?*

Jag *n.* a Jaguar automobile. □ *What I really want is a Jag.* □ *How much will a Jag set me back?*

jump-start 1. *n.* the act of starting a car by getting power—through jumper cables—from another car. □ *I got a jump-start from a friend.* □ *Who can give me a jump-start?* **2.** *tr.* to start a car by getting power from another car. □ *I jump-started her car for her.* □ *I can't jump-start your car. My battery is low.*

junk heap *n.* a dilapidated old car; a dilapidated house or other structure. □ *They lived in that junk heap for thirty years and never painted it.* □ *Why don't you fix up that junk heap?*

lay (some) rubber *tr.* to spin one's car tires when accelerating, leaving black marks on the street. □ *At that age all they want to do is get in the car and lay some rubber.* □ *You wanna know how well I can lay some rubber in this thing?*

load *n.* an automobile. □ *Whose junky old load is that parked in front of the house?* □ *I'm saving money so I can replace this load with a new car.*

loaded *mod.* having all available accessories. (Said of a car.) □ *Did you want to see a car that's loaded, or is this to be a budget car?* □ *Now, this little gem is loaded with everything.*

nerd mobile *n.* a full-sized, uninteresting car; a family car. □ *My father always buys some kind of stupid nerd mobile.* □ *There is nothing but nerd mobiles on our block.*

pimpmobile *n.* a gaudy automobile, as might be driven by a pimp. (Use caution with *pimp*.) □ *You call that pimpmobile a car? Why all the chrome?* □ *He drove up in a pimpmobile and shocked all the neighbors.*

putt-putt *n.* a small motorized vehicle, especially a small car. □ *I hear him coming in his putt-putt now.* □ *That's not a motorcycle; it's just a little putt-putt.*

ragtop *n.* a convertible car. □ *The ragtop is making a comeback.* □ *I wanted a ragtop, but they cost nearly $3,000 more.*

rattle-trap *n.* a rattly (old) car; any rattly vehicle. □ *I hear Ted's rattle-trap in the driveway.* □ *I bought a rattle-trap for $400.*

repo *n.* a repossessed car. □ *It's a repo, and I got it cheap.* □ *I'd rather have a plain used car than a repo.*

ride *n.* a car. □ *What time are you coming by in your ride?* □ *Do you care if I leave my ride parked in your driveway?*

set of wheels *n.* a car. □ *I need a new set of wheels.* □ *Man, look at that set of wheels that chick has!*

sheen *n.* a car. (From *machine.*) □ *You have one fine sheen there.* □ *I have to get my sheen's oil changed today.*

shocks *n.* shock absorbers in an automobile. □ *That hog Cadillac needs new shocks.* □ *How much is a set of shocks for a buggy like this?*

short *n.* a car. (Streets.) □ *Man, that's some short you got!* □ *Max gets his money cracking shorts.*

stick *n.* a gearshift lever in a car. □ *I keep reaching for the stick in a car with automatic.* □ *Put the stick in reverse and move back slowly.*

stick shift 1. *mod.* having to do with a nonautomatic transmission or a car that has one. □ *I prefer a stick shift car—I don't know why.* □ *The stick shift models are cheaper—that's why.* □ *This one's stick shift.* **2.** *n.* a nonautomatic transmission. □ *I can't drive a stick shift!* □ *My husband took the other car and stuck me with the stick shift.*

tool *in.* to speed along (in a car). □ *We were tooling along at about seventy-five when the cop spotted us.* □ *I was tooling, and nobody could catch me.*

tranny *n.* an automobile transmission. □ *It looks like you get a new tranny, and I get 900 bucks.* □ *What kind of tranny does that baby have?*

trans *n.* an automobile. (From *transportation.*) □ *I don't have any trans—I can't get myself anywhere.* □ *What are you using for trans these days?*

Vette *n.* a Corvette automobile. □ *I'd rather have a Vette than a Caddy.* □ *Vettes aren't as popular as they once were.*

wheels *n.* a car; transportation by automobile. □ *I gotta get some wheels pretty soon.* □ *I'll need a ride. I don't have any wheels.*

CATALOG

wish book *n.* a large mail-order catalog. □ *The new wish book just came in the* mail. □ *Where's the wish book? I have to order something.*

CAUTION

go slow *phr.* "Be gentle."; "Handle with care." □ *Easy does it. Go slow, and you won't dent anything.* □ *Easy does it. Two people can handle this heavy old thing if they go slow.*

Heads up! *exclam.* "Look out!" □ *Heads up! Watch out for the swinging bucket!* □ *Here's a rough spot on the trail. Heads up!*

pussyfoot (around) *in.* to behave in a very cautious manner; to (metaphorically) tread softly; to hedge or equivocate. □ *Come on and say what you mean! Stop pussyfooting.* □ *You can depend on the mayor to pussyfoot around while the crisis is on.*

walk on eggs AND **walk on thin ice** *in.* to walk very cautiously; to be in a very precarious position. □ *I have to remember that I'm walking on eggs when I give this speech.* □ *Careful with ideas like that. You're walking on thin ice.*

Watch it! *exclam.* "Be careful!"; "Watch your step!"; "Careful of what you say!" □ *Watch it, buster!* □ *You're walking on thin ice. Watch it!*

CELEBRATION

See **PARTY**.

CELEBRITY

celeb *n.* a celebrity. □ *They hired a few celebs to shill for their new computer.* □ *There were celebs all over the place, but nobody I recognized.*

CEMETERY

bone factory *n.* a cemetery. □ *We must have passed by forty bone factories going across Missouri.* □ *I know I'll end up in the bone factory just like everyone else.*

bone orchard *n.* a cemetery. □ *That is a very pleasant bone orchard.* □ *Does it really matter how comfortable a bone orchard looks?*

boneyard *n.* a cemetery. □ *I'd like to be planted in a boneyard like that.* □ *I'll take a boneyard with a view of the lake.*

cement city *n.* a cemetery. □ *I'm too young to end up in cement city.* □ *There's* *a cement city outside town, and our house is just a half mile east of it.*

God's acre *n.* a cemetery. □ *When I end up in God's acre, I want everything to go on without me.* □ *They're planting somebody new in God's acre.*

Headstone City *n.* a cemetery. □ *Unless you want to move into a furnished flat in Headstone City, you had better fasten your seatbelt when you drive or ride in a car.* □ *Our house is just one block after the large Headstone City on the left.*

marble orchard AND **Marble City** *n.* a cemetery. □ *I already bought a little plot in a marble orchard.* □ *When I take a trip to Marble City, I want truckloads of flowers.*

CERTAINTY

all right *mod.* for sure; for certain. □ *He's the one who said it, all right.* □ *I was there, all right.*

bet one's bottom dollar *tr.* to be very certain of something; to bet in complete certainty of winning. (Need not refer to an actual bet.) □ *I bet my bottom dollar you never ever went to Alaska!* □ *He bet his bottom dollar on that horse, and it died at the gate.*

def *mod.* definitely. □ *I will be there. Def.* □ *This is def the best there is.*

have something cinched *tr.* to have something settled; to have the results of some act assured. □ *Don't worry. I've got it cinched.* □ *You just think you've got it cinched.*

jolly-well *mod.* certainly. □ *You jolly-well better be there on time.* □ *I jolly-well will.*

sure as hell *mod.* absolutely certain. □ *I'm sure as hell he's the one.* □ *You sure as hell better get yourself over here.*

surefire *mod.* certain; effective; fail-safe. □ *I've got a surefire method for fixing cracks in drywall.* □ *Good, yes; surefire, no.* □ *This stuff is a surefire cure.*

sure thing *n.* something that is absolutely certain. □ *It's a sure thing! You can't lose!* □ *Well, it looks like the sure*

thing didn't turn out to be so sure, after all.

CHALLENGE

ball-busting *mod.* difficult or challenging. □ *I am tired of this ball-busting job and I want out.* □ *I was given a ball-busting assignment, and it has kept me very busy.*

buy someone's wolf ticket *tr.* to challenge someone's boast or taunt. (Black.) □ *He wants me to buy his wolf ticket bad.* □ *He's such a fighter. He'll buy anybody's wolf ticket.*

call *tr.* to challenge someone. □ *I called him, but he ignored me.* □ *Are you the guy who called me? Who do you think you are?*

call someone out *tr.* to challenge someone to a fight. □ *Max wanted to call him out, but thought better of it.* □ *Did you call me out? What are you going to do about it?*

front *tr.* to challenge someone; to confront someone, perhaps in anger. □ *Don't front me unless you are ready for a fight.* □ *You better not front any of your teachers.*

Oh, yeah? *exclam.* "Is that what you think?"; "Are you trying to start a fight?" □ *Oh, yeah? What makes you think so?* □ *Oh, yeah? You want to start something?* □ *Tom said, "Bill, you are a numskull." Bill whirled around, saying, "Oh, yeah?"*

Put your money where your mouth is! *exclam.* "Stop talking big and make a bet!" (From gambling. Can also be said to someone giving investment advice.) □ *You want me to bet on that horse? Did you? Why don't you put your money where your mouth is?* □ *If this is such a good stock, you buy it. Put your money where your mouth is!*

Says who? AND **Sez who?** *interrog.* a formulaic challenge indicating disagreement with someone who has said something. □ *TOM: Says who? FRED: Says me, that's who!* □ *She drew herself up to her full height, looked him straight in the eye, and said, "Says who?"*

Says you! *exclam.* "That's just what you say!"; "You don't know what you are* talking about!" □ FRED: *You are fat and ugly.* TOM: *Says you!* □ MARY: *People who go around correcting other people were found to be very annoying in a recent survey.* BILL: *Says you!*

screamer *n.* anything challenging. □ *What a horrible assignment I got. A classic screamer.* □ *Bring on the screamers. I can handle anything.*

spoiling for a fight *phr.* argumentative; asking for a fight. □ *They were just spoiling for a fight, and they went outside to settle the matter.* □ *She was grouchy, and you could tell she had been spoiling for a fight all day.*

Want to make something of it? AND **Wanna make sumpin' of it?** *interrog.* "Do you want to fight about it?" □ *So, I'm a little ugly. Wanna make sumpin' of it?* □ *I'm warped and smelly. Want to make something of it?*

What's it to you? *interrog.* "What does it matter to you?"; "Is it any of your business?" □ *What's it to you if I don't do it?* □ *So I broke my glasses. What's it to you?*

You and who else? AND **You and what army?** *interrog.* "Who besides you is threatening me?" □ *You're gonna whup me? You and who else?* □ *You and what army are gonna yank my chain?*

You want to step outside? *interrog.* "Do you intend to start a fight?"; "Shall we go outside and fight?" □ *So, you don't like the way I talk! You want to step outside?* □ *You want to step outside? We can settle this once and for all.*

CHANCE

avs *n.* chance; the law of averages. (Streets. Always with *the*.) □ *The avs say that I ought to be dead by now.* □ *It looks like the avs finally caught up with him.*

crapshoot *n.* a gamble; a matter of chance. (Like a crap [dice] game.) □ *Basically, life is a crapshoot.* □ *The stock market isn't concerned with value anymore. It's just a crapshoot.*

sticky *mod.* chancy; awkward. □ *Things began to get a little sticky, and Barlowe*

began to move toward the door. □ *When the going got sticky, Freddy disappeared.*

take a flyer (on something) *tr.* to take a chance on something. □ *Kim was very reckless when she took a flyer on that airline stock.* □ *Fred is too wise an investor to take a flyer on some story stock like that.*

toss-up *n.* a matter of chance. (As predictable as the outcome of the toss of a coin.) □ *Nobody knew what to do. It was a toss-up.* □ *Who knows what will happen? It's a toss-up.*

CHARITY

can-shaker *n.* a fund-raiser. (As if a person were holding a can for the solicitation of coins from passersby.) □ *John was the mayor's can-shaker in the last election.* □ *Fred was a professional can-shaker for a museum. Maybe he has some ideas as to how we can raise some money.*

pot *n.* a vessel, hat, basket, etc., used to collect or receive contributions. □ *Please pass the pot.* □ *How much is left in the pot?*

CHARM

silky *mod.* smooth; unctuous. □ *Beware of anybody that silky.* □ *What a silky character. He could talk his way into the heart of some unsuspecting chick.*

suave *n.* personal polish and smoothness. □ *Man, does that guy ever have suave!* □ *You need some suave to carry off this sham.*

CHATTER

See also GOSSIP, TALKING.

blab *n.* talk; chatter; meaningless talk. □ *I never pay any attention to blab like that.* □ *Cut the blab and get to work.*

gabfest *n.* an event where much chattering or gossip takes place. □ *There's a gabfest going on in Clare's room.* □ *Say, your gabfest is a little loud.*

jabber 1. *n.* mindless chatter. □ *Stop all this jabber and get to work.* □ *I've heard enough of your jabber.* 2. *in.* to chatter. □ *Come over and we'll jabber about things over coffee.* □ *What are those kids jabbering about?*

jaw 1. *n.* a chat. □ *Come over for a jaw this weekend.* □ *I could use a good jaw with my old friend.* **2.** *in.* to chat. □ *Stop jawing and get to work.* □ *Come over, and we can jaw for a while.*

magpie *n.* a person who chatters; a person who annoys others by chattering. □ *Sally is such a magpie!* □ *Why do those horrendous magpies all go to the same movies I go to?*

rap 1. *in.* to talk or chat about something. □ *Something wrong? Let's rap about it.* □ *The kids sat down and rapped for an hour or so.* **2.** *n.* a conversation; a chat. □ *How about a rap?* □ *Let's have a rap sometime.*

run off at the mouth *in.* to talk too much; to have diarrhea of the mouth. □ *I wish you would stop running off at the mouth.* □ *Tom runs off at the mouth too much. I wish he would temper his remarks.*

shoot the breeze *tr.* to chat casually and without purpose. □ *We spent the entire afternoon just shooting the breeze.* □ *It was good to shoot the breeze with you, Mary.*

talk a blue streak *tr.* to talk fast or a lot. □ *This crazy bird suddenly began talking a blue streak.* □ *Some parrots never talk. Others talk a blue streak whenever it's light.*

talk someone ragged *tr.* to talk to someone too much; to bore someone. □ *That was not an interview. She talked me ragged.* □ *He always talks me ragged, but I always listen.*

talk someone's ear off *tr.* to talk to someone endlessly; to bore someone with too much talk. □ *My aunt always talks my ear off when she comes to visit.* □ *Stay away from Mr. Jones. He will talk your ear off if he gets a chance.*

talk to hear one's own voice *in.* to talk far more than is necessary; to talk much, in an egotistical manner. □ *Oh, he's just talking to hear his own voice.* □ *Am I just talking to hear my own voice, or are you listening to me?*

talk until one is blue in the face *in.* to talk until one is exhausted. □ *You can talk till you're blue in the face, but it won't do any good.* □ *She talked until she was blue in the face, but could not change their minds.*

wag one's chin *tr.* to talk or jabber; to chatter aimlessly. □ *The two old buzzards sat on the park bench wagging their chins all afternoon.* □ *Stop wagging your chin for a minute and listen up!*

well-oiled *mod.* talkative. □ *She was sure well-oiled. I thought she'd never stop talking.* □ *Get him well-oiled, and you'll find out about everything.*

windy *mod.* talkative. □ *She's so windy! Won't she ever let up?* □ *Here comes old windy Charlie. Once he gets started, he never stops.*

yack *n.* idle chatter. □ *I've heard enough yack to last me a lifetime.* □ *Too much yack. Where's the beef?*

yak it up *tr.* to talk incessantly or a lot. □ *Why don't you all just yak it up while I get ready to give the talk?* □ *Stop yakking it up and listen.*

yatata-yatata *n.* the sound of chatter or yak. □ *All I ever hear around here is yatata-yatata.* □ *He gets on the phone, and it's yatata-yatata for hours.*

yodeling in a canyon *in.* talking aimlessly. □ *You are just yodeling in a canyon if you think I really care about it.* □ *Stop yodeling in a canyon and start making sense.*

CHEAPNESS

cheesy *mod.* cheap; tacky. □ *I wouldn't live in a cheesy place like this if I could afford better.* □ *That was a cheesy trick to pull on somebody.*

chintzy *mod.* cheap; shoddy. □ *Nobody's gonna buy this chintzy stuff. Throw it out.* □ *What a chintzy car! The door fell off!*

cut corners *tr.* to do something more easily; to take shortcuts; to save money by finding cheaper ways to do something. □ *They're always finding ways to cut corners.* □ *I won't cut corners just to save money. I put quality first.*

cut-rate *mod.* cheap; low-priced. □ *I don't want any cut-rate stuff.* □ *Where are your cut-rate sweaters?*

dirt cheap *mod.* very cheap. □ *I picked this thing up dirt cheap.* □ *Get one of these while they're dirt cheap.*

el cheapo 1. *n.* the cheap one; the cheapest one. (Mock Spanish.) □ *I don't want one of those el cheapos.* □ *I can only afford el cheapo.* **2.** *mod.* cheap. □ *The el cheapo brand won't last.* □ *This is el cheapo. I don't want it.* □ *Is this the el cheapo model?*

on a shoestring *mod.* on practically no money; on a very tight budget. □ *I run my business on a shoestring. I never know from day to day whether I will survive.* □ *We live on a shoestring—hardly any money at all.*

penny-ante *mod.* trivial; cheap. □ *I'm sick of this penny-ante stuff. Let's get serious.* □ *Max moved from penny-ante crimes into drugs.*

rinky-dink *mod.* cheap; inferior; broken down. □ *I sold my rinky-dink old car yesterday.* □ *What a rinky-dink job! I quit!*

schlock AND **schlocky** *mod.* cheap; junky; inferior. □ *Schlocky stuff like this I can get from a no-overhead mail order.* □ *That place is nothing but a schlock shop.* □ *This thing is really schlock.*

shoestring *mod.* low-cost; cheap. □ *This is just a shoestring operation. There is no capital involved.* □ *We have nothing but a shoestring budget this year.*

sleaze AND **sleez** *n.* any junk. □ *I won't sell sleez like that! I won't even have it in my store.* □ *Look at this sleaze—and look at the price! Outrageous!*

stiff *tr.* to fail to tip someone who expects it. □ *Ya know, you can tell right away when a guy's gonna stiff you—ya just know.* □ *I guess I get stiffed two or three times a day.*

tacky *mod.* cheap; crude. □ *That was a tacky thing to do to her.* □ *That was so tacky!* □ *This is sort of a tacky gift for a wedding.*

ticky-tacky *n.* cheap and shabby material. □ *Those houses are just made of*

ticky-tacky, and they won't even be here in twenty years. □ *That stuff is just ticky-tacky. No one will buy it.*

two-bit *mod.* cheap; small-time. □ *Max is just a two-bit pusher. I want Mr. Big.* □ *I'm tired of your two-bit efforts to run this office.*

CHEATING

See **DECEPTION**.

CHECKS

bad paper *n.* bad checks; a bad check. □ *She got six months for passing bad paper.* □ *There is more bad paper passed in this town in one month than in all of Sweden for a whole year!*

bounce 1. *in.* [for a check] to be returned from the bank because of insufficient funds. □ *The check bounced, and I had to pay a penalty fee.* □ *If your check bounces, you'll have to bring us cash.* **2.** *tr.* [for a bank] to refuse to honor a check. □ *They bounced another of my checks today.* □ *The bank won't bounce any more checks because I closed the account.*

bum check *n.* a bad check; a forged check. □ *I never wrote a bum check in my life.* □ *We took in four bum checks today.*

chit *n.* a check. □ *She wrote out a chit for the balance due.* □ *I have your chit for the full amount.*

cut a check *tr.* to write a check. □ *We'll cut the check tonight and send it out in tomorrow's mail.* □ *Please cut a check for Mr. Babbit. Here's the amount.*

fly kites *tr.* to distribute or pass bad checks. (Underworld.) □ *Marty was picked up for flying kites in three different cities.* □ *She got caught flying kites in Philadelphia.*

hot check *n.* a bad check. □ *The crook got picked up after passing a hot check.* □ *The clerk got in trouble for taking a hot check.*

hot paper *n.* bad checks; a bad check. (Underworld.) □ *Tracy got caught passing hot paper.* □ *That teller can spot hot paper a mile away.*

kite 1. *n.* a worthless check. (Underworld.) □ *He finally wrote one kite too* *many, and they nabbed him.* □ *She passed kites from one end of town to the other, then dyed her hair, took off her glasses, and did it all over again.* **2.** *tr.* to write worthless checks; to raise the amount on a check. (Underworld.) □ *Chuck made a fortune kiting checks.* □ *He kited a check for $50,000.*

paper *n.* a forged check. □ *She was arrested for passing paper.* □ *The police actually lost the paper and ended up with no evidence.*

paperhanging *n.* writing and spending bad checks. (Underworld.) □ *She was accused of paperhanging and didn't even know what the cops were talking about, so they let her go.* □ *She is good at both paperhanging and acting.*

paper-pusher *n.* someone who passes bad checks. □ *The bank teller spotted a well-known paper-pusher and called the cops.* □ *The old lady was charged as a paper-pusher and sent to jail.*

rubber (check) *n.* a check that bounces; a forged check. □ *The bank says I wrote a rubber check, but I'm sure there was enough money on deposit.* □ *One rubber check after another! Can't you add?*

tinseled *mod.* forged or "decorated," as with a bad check. (Underworld.) □ *Gert got caught passing tinseled checks.* □ *He almost got caught kiting tinseled checks.*

wallpaper *n.* worthless checks. (Underworld.) □ *This flimflam artist has spread a lot of wallpaper in her day.* □ *The feds followed a trail of wallpaper from St. Louis to San Francisco and made the pinch.*

CHILDREN

army brat *n.* a child born to a parent in the army. (Such a child will live in many different places.) □ *I was an army brat and went to seven different schools before I got out of high school.* □ *We army brats tend to stick together.*

bundle of joy AND **bundle from heaven** *n.* a baby. □ *We are expecting a bundle of joy next September.* □ *When your little bundle from heaven arrives, things will be a little hectic for a while.*

dead-end kid *n.* a youth with no future, usually a male. □ *Kelly wasn't your typical dead-end kid.* □ *Max was a dead-end kid from the day he was born.*

dickens *n.* a devilish or impish child. (Also a term of address.) □ *Come here, you little dickens.* □ *You are such a cute little dickens!*

droopy-drawers *n.* someone—usually a child—whose pants are falling down. (Also a term of address.) □ *Hey, droopy-drawers, pull up your pants.* □ *Jimmy is a regular droopy-drawers. Maybe he needs suspenders.*

FLK *n.* "funny-looking kid." (Initialism. A strange-looking child, especially one being treated for social or physical problems.) □ *The therapist had two FLKs in a row.* □ *When the mother came in with an FLK in tow, Jane knew her afternoon would be busy.*

juvie *n.* a youth; a teenager under age eighteen. (Underworld.) □ *I work with juvies a lot. I try to get them back on the track.* □ *They brought in a juvie and charged him with shoplifting.*

monkey *n.* a playful child. (Also a term of address.) □ *Come here, you little monkey!* □ *Hey, monkey, where are you going?*

patter of tiny feet *n.* the sound of young children; having children in the household. □ *I really liked having the patter of tiny feet in the house.* □ *Darling, I think we're going to be hearing the patter of tiny feet soon.*

preemie *n.* a premature baby. (Medical.) □ *There were two preemies born today.* □ *I was a preemie.*

rug rat *n.* a child. (Also a term of address.) □ *You got any rug rats at your house?* □ *Hey, you cute little rug rat, come over here.*

scamp *n.* a small child. □ *Come here, you little scamp!* □ *There are three little scamps at the door saying, "Trick or treat!"*

snotnose(d) (kid) *n.* a young child; a relatively young person. (Derogatory. Potentially offensive. Use only with discretion.) □ *Some little snotnose swiped* my wallet. □ *A little snotnosed kid came in and asked for money.*

sprout *n.* a child. □ *Where are the sprouts?* □ *A little sprout came up and tried to sell me a ticket to a game.*

squirt *n.* a small person; a young child, especially a young boy. (Also a term of address.) □ *Hey, squirt, come over here.* □ *He sure is a cute little squirt.*

stinkpot *n.* a baby with a dirty diaper. (Also a term of address.) □ *Jimmy's a stinkpot. Better change him.* □ *Come here, you little stinkpot. I'll fix you.*

type *n.* a combining form indicating a specified type of person. □ *He's a caveman type. You know, sort of hairy and smelly.* □ *Ted's the brainy type, but has no guts.*

CHOCOLATE

chocoholic *n.* a person who craves chocolate. (Patterned on *alcoholic.*) □ *Cake, ice cream, pie—make it chocolate. I'm a chocoholic and I'm glad.* □ *I have a real treat for you chocoholics—triple chocolate cheesecake.*

CHOICE

See also **PREFERENCE**.

boxed in *mod.* in a bind; having few alternatives. □ *I really feel boxed in around here.* □ *I got him boxed in. He'll have to do it our way.*

channel surfer *n.* a person who practices *channel hopping.* □ *My husband is a confirmed channel surfer. I can't understand why he does it.* □ *Channel surfers try to keep up with many programs at one time.*

give someone the nod *tr.* to choose someone. □ *The committee gave Frank the nod for the job.* □ *They gave her the nod.*

make one's bed *tr.* to be the cause of one's own misery. □ *Well, I guess I made my own bed. Now I have to lie in it.* □ *"We all make our own beds," said the minister.*

only way to go *n.* the best way to do something; the best choice to make. □ *Get a four-wheel drive car. It's the only*

way to go. □ *That's it! A new house. It's the only way to go.*

picky *mod.* choosy. □ *Don't be so picky. They're all the same.* □ *Red, blue, green! What's the difference? You are too picky.*

tap someone (for something) *tr.* to select someone for some purpose or position. □ *The committee tapped John to run for Congress.* □ *I had thought they were going to tap Sally.*

CITIES

asphalt jungle *n.* the paved landscape of the city; the city viewed as a savage place. □ *I don't look forward to spending the rest of my days in an asphalt jungle.* □ *I want to go back to Kansas. I hate the asphalt jungle.*

Bean Town *n.* Boston, Massachusetts. (From *Boston baked beans.*) □ *I plan to hit Bean Town about noon.* □ *I've got a lot of buddies in Bean Town.*

Big Apple *n.* New York City. (Always with *the.*) □ *The Big Apple is filled with young kids trying to get into show biz.* □ *Max and his gang went to the Big Apple to lie low for a while.*

Big D *n.* Dallas, Texas. □ *Kelly is from Big D.* □ *What is Big D famous for?*

Chi(town) *n.* Chicago, Illinois. □ *I can't wait to get back to old Chitown.* □ *I was born in Chi.*

Frisco *n.* San Francisco, California. (Said to be objectionable to its residents.) □ *Have you ever been in Frisco?* □ *My cousin lives in Frisco.*

Motown *n.* "motor town," Detroit, Michigan. □ *Have you ever been to Motown?* □ *We went to Motown to buy a car once.*

Philly *n.* Philadelphia, Pennsylvania. □ *We stopped off in Philly for a day.* □ *We left Philly for the Big Apple at noon.*

Podunk *n.* an imaginary rural town where everything and everyone is backward, old-fashioned, and inferior. □ *I don't want a job in Podunk.* □ *This is the big city, not Podunk.*

tinseltown *n.* Hollywood, California. ☐ *Tinseltown is a very glitzy place.* ☐ *She's talented and has her eye on tinseltown.*

CLARITY

clear as vodka *mod.* very clear. ☐ *The weather is as clear as vodka.* ☐ *The river wasn't exactly as clear as vodka because it had just rained.*

CLEANLINESS

squeaky clean *mod.* very clean. (Like a clean glass that squeaks when one rubs a finger on it.) ☐ *I got this floor squeaky clean. Don't spill anything on it.* ☐ *Somebody tracked mud on my squeaky clean floor!*

CLEVERNESS

cagey *mod.* sneaky; shrewd. ☐ *Bruno is pretty cagey. You have to keep an eye on him.* ☐ *He's too cagey for me. I don't trust him at all.*

sharpie *n.* a clever operator; a clever person. ☐ *She's a real sharpie. She'll take you for everything you've got.* ☐ *A young sharpie in the first row got the answer right away.*

skunk *tr.* to outwit someone. ☐ *I skunked them. They'll never find me.* ☐ *That fish skunked me. I thought I caught him for sure this time.*

skunked *mod.* outwitted; outscored; defeated. ☐ *The home team skunked the visitors for the third year in a row.* ☐ *I was skunked on this year's fishing trip. Not even a bite.*

slick *mod.* clever; glib. ☐ *He is a slick operator.* ☐ *His talk is slick, but his action is zotz.*

smart cookie *n.* a clever person. ☐ *She's really a smart cookie if you give her a chance.* ☐ *Fred is a smart cookie and really ought to go far.*

smooth operator AND **smoothie** *n.* a clever and quiet person, especially in reference to romantic involvement. ☐ *Clare is an old smoothie till she thinks she's got everything the way she wants. Then you see the real Clare.* ☐ *Hank is a smooth operator. The girls just love him.*

swift *mod.* smart and clever. ☐ *Excuse my brother. He's not too swift.* ☐ *Dave is doing well in school. He's swift, and he likes his classes.*

CLOCK

tick-tock *n.* a watch or clock. (Juvenile.) ☐ *Wind your tick-tock before you forget.* ☐ *The tick-tock in the kitchen has broken.*

CLOTHING

See also **SHOES**.

air hose *n.* invisible socks; no socks. ☐ *All these kids run around campus in air hose. You'd think they'd get blisters.* ☐ *How do you like my new air hose? One size fits all.*

BVDs AND **beeveedees** *n.* underwear; men's underwear. (The first entry is an initialism. From *Bradley, Voorhies, and Day,* the manufacturers. Always plural.) ☐ *He stood there in his BVDs, freezing.* ☐ *If you don't wear a belt, your beeveedees will show.*

cazh *mod.* casual. (From *casual.*) ☐ *I tend to dress cazh in warm weather no matter what the occasion.* ☐ *Tom showed up dressed cazh and all the other guys were in tuxes.*

civvies *n.* civilian clothes rather than a uniform. (Originally military.) ☐ *I feel sort of funny in civvies.* ☐ *I re-upped because I couldn't stand the thought of civvies and stuff like that.*

clean *mod.* well-dressed. ☐ *Now, there's a clean dude!* ☐ *New threads, huh? Clean, baby, clean!*

clotheshorse *n.* someone who is obsessed with clothing and looking good in it. ☐ *Her brother is the real clotheshorse.* ☐ *Mary is such a clotheshorse! Look at her now.*

dap *mod.* well-dressed. (From *dapper.*) ☐ *Who is that dap-looking dude?* ☐ *Man, you look dap!*

double-barreled slingshot *n.* a brassiere. ☐ *Why does she wear a red double-barreled slingshot?* ☐ *Who dropped a double-barreled slingshot on the floor?*

dude up *in.* to dress up. □ *Let's get all duded up and go out.* □ *I got to dude up a little before we go.*

duds *n.* clothes. (Folksy. Always plural.) □ *Are those new duds?* □ *I need some new duds, too.*

fattygews *n.* fatigues. (Originally military.) □ *I'll slip into some fattygews and be right with you.* □ *Whose fattygews are piled here in the corner?*

flopper-stopper *n.* a brassiere. □ *Hey, Jimmy, does your sister wear a flopper-stopper yet?* □ *She's very shy. She won't even hang her flopper-stoppers out on the line to dry.*

fronts *n.* clothing; a sports jacket. □ *You got some good-looking fronts there.* □ *I need some new fronts.*

glad rags *n.* fancy clothes; best clothing. □ *You look pretty good in your glad rags.* □ *I'll get on my glad rags, and we'll go out tonight.*

grubbies AND **grubbers; grubs** *n.* worn-out clothing; clothing one wears for the occasional dirty job. □ *I have to go home, put some grubbies on, and paint the house.* □ *There I was, running around in my grubs when the senator stops by to say hello!*

in drag *mod.* wearing the clothing of the opposite sex. (Usually refers to women's clothing.) □ *Two actors in drag did a skit about life on the farm.* □ *Gary looks better in drag than he does in a suit.*

jock *n.* an athletic supporter (garment). □ *Somebody dropped a jock in the hall.* □ *Whose jock is that out there on Tracy's clothesline?*

laid out *mod.* well-dressed. □ *Look at those silks! Man are you laid out!* □ *She is all laid out in her Sunday best.*

melvin *n.* a situation where one's underpants ride up high between the buttocks. (Named for a person so stupid and unaware that he is comfortable with this arrangement.) □ *Look at that twit with the melvin.* □ *How could anybody go around all day with a melvin like that?*

midi **1.** *n.* a mid-length woman's garment. □ *Shall I wear my midi, or is it too hot?* □ *The midi is okay.* **2.** *mod.* having to do with a mid-length woman's garment. □ *This midi style is out, and the mini is back in.* □ *The midi length was just transitional. Who decides on these things, anyway?*

mini *n.* a miniskirt. □ *I look pretty good in a mini.* □ *I'll try a mini this time. I was too plump the last time they were in style.*

outfit *n.* a set of clothing. □ *You look lovely in that outfit.* □ *Should I wear my gray wool outfit?*

peel *in.* to strip off one's clothing. □ *I had to peel for my physical examination.* □ *She stood up on the stage and peeled right down to nothing!*

PJs *n.* pajamas. (Initialism. Usually juvenile.) □ *Get your PJs on and get into bed right now.* □ *I can't find my PJs. Where are they?*

rag *n.* any clothing, even the best. (Always plural.) □ *Man, I got some new rags that will knock your eyes out!* □ *You got soda pop all over my new rags!*

rag *n.* ugly or badly styled clothing; an ugly garment. □ *I can't wear that rag!* □ *I need some new clothes. I can't go around wearing rags like these.* □ *I wouldn't be seen in last season's rags.*

rag out *in.* to dress up. □ *I like to rag out and go to parties.* □ *I hate to rag out. I like comfortable clothes.*

shuck AND **shuck down** *tr. & in.* to undress oneself; to remove one's clothing. □ *He shucked himself quickly and jumped into bed.* □ *He shucked down and showered and was at work in twenty minutes.*

silks *n.* clothing. □ *Look at the silks on that dude!* □ *I gotta get some new silks before spring.*

skivvies *n.* underpants; underwear. □ *He stood there chattering in his skivvies waiting for additional indignities.* □ *I don't have any clean skivvies!*

Sunday best *n.* one's best clothing, which one would wear to church. □ *We are in our Sunday best, ready to go.* □ *I got mud on my Sunday best.*

tabbed *mod.* well-dressed. (Black.) □ *That dude is tabbed.* □ *She's really tabbed in some nice threads.*

tails *n.* a tuxedo with long tails. □ *Shall I wear my tails?* □ *Ralph had to rent tails for the evening.*

threads *n.* clothing. □ *When'd you get new threads, man?* □ *Good-looking threads on Wally, huh?*

tin hat *n.* a soldier's helmet. □ *Where's my tin hat?* □ *You use your tin hat for everything—washing, hauling water—you name it.*

tux *n.* a tuxedo. □ *Do I have to wear a tux?* □ *Rent your tux well in advance.*

undies *n.* underclothing; underpants, especially women's. □ *I like red undies.* □ *Where are my clean undies?*

vines *n.* clothing. (Black.) □ *I like those smokin' vines you're in.* □ *Good-looking vines on that guy, right?*

viz *n.* Levis; blue jeans. □ *How do you like my new viz?* □ *Those viz are too tight for her.*

wedgy *n.* a situation where one's underpants are drawn up tightly between the buttocks. □ *Wally skipped up behind Greg and gave him a wedgy.* □ *I think he LIKES walking around with a wedgy all day!*

weeds *n.* clothing. □ *Good-looking weeds you're wearing.* □ *These weeds came right out of the wish book. Would you believe?*

woolies *n.* long underwear. □ *It's the time of the year for woolies!* □ *I wish I'd worn my woolies today.*

CLUMSINESS

clunky *mod.* ponderous and inefficient. □ *The whole plan is too clunky. Try to prune it down.* □ *I got rid of all the clunky stuff. Now it's lean and mean.*

ham-handed *mod.* lacking dexterity; clumsy. □ *If I wasn't so ham-handed, I could probably fix the thing myself.* □ *He is the most ham-handed guy I've ever seen.*

stumbles *n.* the inability to stand up and walk straight. □ *I guess I have the stum-*bles today. Not enough sleep, I guess. □ *Whoops! I have a case of the stumbles.*

COFFEE

black *mod.* without cream or milk. (Said of coffee.) □ *I'd like mine black, please.* □ *Black coffee, good and hot, please.*

brew *n.* coffee; occasionally, tea. □ *I could use a nice cup of brew.* □ *This is my kind of brew, hot, black, and aromatic.*

java *n.* coffee. □ *How about a cup of java?* □ *Some black java would be real good.*

joe *n.* coffee. □ *How about a cup of joe?* □ *Yeah, a cup of black joe would be great.*

COINCIDENCE

speak of the devil *phr.* said when someone whose name has just been mentioned appears or is heard from. (A catchphrase.) □ *And speak of the devil, here's Ted now.* □ *Speak of the devil, that was Mary on the phone.*

COLD

freezing cold *mod.* very cold. □ *It's freezing cold out there.* □ *I won't go out in freezing cold weather.* □ *Why does it have to be so freezing cold?*

Siberian express *n.* an enormous mass of very cold air moving from Siberia across the North Pole and down onto North America. □ *The country braced itself for a return Friday of the Siberian express, with temperatures dropping to twenty below in many areas.* □ *The Siberian express seems to be aimed right at our state.*

COLLEGE

ivory tower *n.* an imaginary location where aloof academics are said to reside and work. □ *Why don't you come out of your ivory tower and see what the world is really like?* □ *Better yet, stay in your ivory tower.*

COMEDIAN

card *n.* a funny person. □ *Tracy is such a card. She cracks me up.* □ *Gee, Fred. You're a card. Somebody's gonna have to deal with you.*

top banana *n.* the lead comedian in a burlesque or vaudeville act. □ *The top* *banana didn't show up for the gig.* □ *Let me be top banana tonight.*

COMFORT

comfy *mod.* comfortable. □ *This is a very comfy chair.* □ *I find myself in a not too comfy position with regard to your further employment here.*

down with something 1. *mod.* comfortable with something; comfortable. (Usually with *get.*) □ *Let's get down with some good music.* □ *Pete wanted to get down with some grapes.* **2.** *mod.* ill with something; sick in bed with something. □ *I was down with the flu for two weeks.* □ *Fred and his wife were down with colds for weeks at a time.*

easy street *n.* a place or position in life where living is easy. □ *Easy street is no place for an active guy like Sam.* □ *Easy street is exactly what I want out of life.*

freeze someone out *tr.* to make it too cold for someone, usually by opening windows or through the use of air conditioning. □ *Turn up the heat unless you're trying to freeze us out.* □ *Are you trying to freeze out everybody? Close the door.*

COMMAND

big talk *tr.* to boss other people around. □ *Don't big talk me. I know who you are.* □ *She came in and big talked everybody, and we just naturally thought she was the owner.*

tell someone what to do with something *tr.* to tell someone to do something rude with something. (With the unspoken notion that one should stick it up one's ass.) □ *I'll tell you what you can do with it.* □ *If that's the way he wants to be, you can just tell him what to do with it.*

COMMERCE

See also BUSINESS, COST, FINANCIAL.

astronomical *mod.* extremely expensive; of any very high figure. □ *The prices here are astronomical!* □ *The market indexes have all reached astronomical heights for the second time.*

block *n.* the auction block. □ *The painting went on the block and sold for nearly*

$53 million. □ *The house had just gone on the block, and the first bid was already opened.*

bottom fishing *n.* seeking something at its lowest price; seeking something at a low cost and willing to accept inferior quality. □ *I don't think bottom fishing for stocks is always wise. There is always a good reason why the price is low.* □ *Bottom fishing probably won't get you anything of value.*

buy *n.* a purchase. □ *Man, this is a great buy.* □ *What a buy, two for the price of one.*

cats and dogs *n.* slow-selling or undesirable merchandise. □ *During the Christmas season, the merchants try to get rid of all their cats and dogs.* □ *When people are buying up even the cats and dogs, you know business is good.*

chit *n.* a bill or tabulation of charges that one signs rather than paying. □ *I don't have any cash. Can I sign a chit for it?* □ *Fred came in to pay for his chits about once a week.*

cold call *tr.* to call a sales prospect from a list of persons one has never met. □ *The broker cold called a number of people each evening for two months.* □ *Things have to be pretty bad when the senior brokers at a major house have to cold call people to get business.*

crack *n.* a unit of something (for a particular price); a use (of something). □ *You would think twice, too, if you remembered that it's $7 a crack.* □ *At $2 a crack, this is the best game on the midway.*

cuff *tr.* to put a charge on one's bill. □ *Would you cuff this for me, please?* □ *Sorry, I can't cuff anymore for you.*

cut a deal *tr.* to arrange a deal; to seal a bargain. □ *Maybe we can cut a deal. Let's talk.* □ *The two lawyers cut a deal that left me with the furniture, although she got the house.*

hard sell *n.* a high-pressure attempt to sell something. □ *I didn't want to listen to any hard sell, so I bought it from a mail-order place.* □ *I'm afraid I'm very susceptible to the hard sell.*

hit the bricks AND **hit the pavement** *tr.* to go out on strike. □ *The workers hit the pavement on Friday and haven't been back on the job since.* □ *Agree to our demands, or we hit the bricks.*

hock 1. *tr.* to pawn something. □ *I tried to hock my watch to get some money.* □ *I've got nothing left to hock.* **2.** *n.* the state of having been pawned. (Usually with *in*.) □ *My watch is already in hock.* □ *Get it out of hock or go buy a new one.*

on the street *mod.* at discount prices; as available from discounters. (As if some item were being sold on the street by a peddler.) □ *It lists at $2,200 and can be got for about $1,650 on the street.* □ *On the street it goes for about $400.*

package *n.* a combination of a variety of related things; a unified set of things. □ *You can't buy just one part. It comes as a package.* □ *The first college I applied to offered me a good aid package, so I went.*

package deal *n.* a variety of goods or services sold as a unit. □ *I got all these tools in a package deal for only $39.95.* □ *What about giving me all three shirts as a package deal?*

plastic 1. *n.* a plastic credit card. □ *Our economy depends on plastic.* □ *I don't carry any cash, just plastic.* **2.** *mod.* having to do with credit cards and their use. □ *This plastic economy is dangerous.* □ *There is too much plastic debt in most households.*

push money *n.* extra money paid to a salesperson to sell certain merchandise aggressively. □ *The manufacturer supplied a little push money that even the store manager didn't know about.* □ *I got about $300 last month in push money for selling some low-grade sweaters.*

repo man *n.* a man who repossesses cars for a living. □ *What kind of guy is lower than a repo man?* □ *I'd rather beg than get a job as a repo man.*

snap something up *tr.* to buy up something. □ *People were snapping these things up like hotcakes.* □ *The customers snapped up all the humidifiers on the second day of the cold spell.*

soft sell *n.* a polite attempt to sell something; a very gentle sales pitch. □ *Some people won't bother listening to a soft sell. You gotta let them know you believe in what you are selling.* □ *I tried the soft sell, but that didn't work.*

spiff *n.* extra money paid to a salesperson to sell certain merchandise aggressively. □ *The manufacturer supplied a little spiff that even the store manager didn't know about.* □ *I got about $300 last month in spiff for selling some low-grade shoes.*

steal *n.* a bargain. (Always with *a*.) □ *At this price, it's a steal.* □ *This car wasn't exactly a steal at this price, but it's still a good value.*

taker *n.* one who accepts an offer; a buyer. □ *Are there any takers for this fine, almost new caddy?* □ *Here's a taker. You'll not be sorry.*

to go *mod.* packaged to be taken out; packaged to be carried home to eat. □ *Do you want it to go, or will you eat it here?* □ *This stuff is to go.*

twofer *n.* an item that is selling two for the price of one. □ *Here's a good deal— a twofer—only $7.98.* □ *Everything in this store is a twofer. I only want one of these. Do I have to bring a friend who wants one, too?*

walk-in 1. *mod.* having to do with a customer who just comes in off the street. □ *Two walk-in customers wanted morning papers but nothing more.* □ *We were hoping for more walk-in trade.* **2.** *n.* a customer who walks in off the street. □ *We had a couple of walk-ins this morning, but none of the hotel residents came.* □ *We have a new sign outside to attract walk-ins.*

What you see is what you get. *sent.* "The product you are looking at is exactly what you get if you buy it." □ *It comes just like this. What you see is what you get.* □ *What you see is what you get. The ones in the box are just like this one.*

wheel and deal *in.* to negotiate, cajole, and connive—aggressively. □ *If you can't wheel and deal, you can't run for* *elective office.* □ *Any crook can wheel and deal!*

COMMOTION

ruckus *n.* a commotion; an uproar. □ *Quiet, please. Don't raise such a ruckus.* □ *The boss kicked up quite a ruckus when I came in late.*

rumpus *n.* a commotion. □ *Please don't make such a rumpus.* □ *There was quite a rumpus in Jim's room.*

COMMUNICATION

bitch box *n.* a loudspeaker, especially one that announces orders in the armed services. (From World War II and still heard.) □ *The bitch box was blaring out messages and I couldn't sleep.* □ *I hate to hear the sarge's voice over the bitch box.*

buzzword *n.* a specialist word; a technical word; a jargon word. □ *Your constant use of buzzwords makes your work sound quite trivial.* □ *What's the latest buzzword?*

Dear John letter *n.* a letter a woman writes to her boyfriend in the military service telling him that she does not love him anymore. □ *Wally got a Dear John letter today.* □ *Sally sends a Dear John letter about once a month.*

grapevine *n.* a mouth-to-mouth communications network. □ *I heard on the grapevine that Sam is moving to the East.* □ *The grapevine was right. He's already left.*

junk fax *n.* an unwanted and irritating fax message. □ *We got nothing but a whole pile of junk faxes today.* □ *I wish they would outlaw junk faxes.*

land a blow *tr.* to make a point. □ *I think I really landed a blow with that remark about extortion.* □ *The point about justice landed a blow.*

scrip(t) *n.* a note; any piece of paper with a written message. (Underworld.) □ *Hey, Mike, here's a script for you from the boss.* □ *Make him sign this script before you let him in on the deal.*

Stay tuned. 1. *sent.* "Stay tuned to this radio or television station." (A formula uttered before a commercial.) □ *I'll be*

right back after these announcements. Stay tuned.* □ *Stay tuned. Back in a minute.* **2.** *sent.* "Continue to pay attention to this matter."; "Watch for further developments." □ *Things are developing rapidly in this area. Stay tuned.* □ *Stay tuned. Pending legislation could change all this.*

take it to the street *tr.* to tell everyone about your problems. □ *If there's something bothering her, she's gonna take it to the street, first thing.* □ *Come on, don't take it to the street.*

COMMUNIST

commie *n.* a communist. □ *What are the commies up to now?* □ *The commies are selling gold today, and the price went down a lot.*

pinko 1. *mod.* having communist tendencies; in the manner of a communist. □ *Get that pinko jerk out of here!* □ *Take your old pinko laws and go to hell.* **2.** *n.* a communist. (Popular during the 1950s.) □ *Get out of here, you pinko!* □ *He called me a pinko, so I left.*

COMPETITION

big league *n.* a situation where competition is keen and a high level of performance is expected. (Usually plural. Referred originally to major league sports.) □ *In the big leagues you've got to know what you're worth.* □ *You're in the big leagues now—no more penny-ante stuff.*

dog-eat-dog *mod.* cruel; highly competitive. □ *This is a dog-eat-dog world.* □ *It's dog-eat-dog out there.*

COMPLAINT

another peep (out of you) *n.* another complaint, word, or sound from someone. (Usually in the negative.) □ *I don't want to hear another peep out of you!* □ *I've heard enough! Not another peep!*

beef *in.* to complain. □ *Stop your beefing!* □ *What's he beefing about now?*

bellyache *in.* to complain. □ *You are always bellyaching!* □ *Don't bellyache to me about it!*

bitch *in.* to complain. □ *You are always bitching!* □ *If I couldn't bitch, I would blow my top.*

bitch session *n.* an informal gathering where people gripe and air their grievances. (Potentially offensive. Use only with discretion.) □ *The bitch session went on for forty minutes.* □ *I learned never to open my mouth in those office bitch sessions.*

flak AND **flack** *n.* complaints; criticism; negative feedback. □ *Why do I have to get all the flak for what you did?* □ *We're getting a lot of flack for that news broadcast.*

gritch *in.* to complain. (A blend of *gripe* and *bitch*.) □ *Stop gritching all the time.* □ *Are you still gritching about that?*

gritchy *mod.* complaining; irritable. □ *I don't feel as gritchy today as I did yesterday.* □ *You seem quite gritchy to me.*

grouse *in.* to complain. □ *Paul is always grousing about something.* □ *Stop grousing and look on the good side of things.*

kick 1. *n.* a complaint. □ *What's the kick, man?* □ *You got another kick, troublemaker?* **2.** *in.* to complain. □ *Why are you always kicking?* □ *Ernie kicks about everything.*

kvetch AND **quetch** *in.* to complain. (From German *quetschen*, "to squeeze," via Yiddish.) □ *Quit your kvetching!* □ *He quetches from dawn to dusk.*

pet peeve *n.* a major or principal annoyance or complaint. □ *Dirty dishes in restaurants are my pet peeve.* □ *He has no pet peeve. He hates everything.*

picky *mod.* overly critical. □ *Complain, complain! What a picky old lady.* □ *I have to do it exactly right. My boss is very picky.*

pitch a bitch *tr.* to make a complaint. (Crude.) □ *You really love to pitch a bitch, don't you? What makes you happy?* □ *Complain, complain! You could pitch a bitch all day long.*

poor-mouth *in.* to speak repeatedly of how little money one has; to plead poverty. □ *She's got money, but she's always poor-mouthing anyway.* □ *Spend more time looking for a job and less time poor-mouthing.*

raise a stink (about someone or something) AND **make a stink (about someone or something)** *tr.* to make a big issue about someone or something. □ *You can depend on Fred to raise a stink.* □ *I hope you don't plan to make a stink about the problem.*

scream bloody murder *tr.* to scream very loudly; to complain or protest loudly. □ *She screams bloody murder every time I get near her.* □ *Those guys scream bloody murder long before they're hurt.*

sound off (about something) *in.* to complain about something; to gripe about something. □ *You are always sounding off about something that gripes your soul.* □ *Just sound off if you've got a beef.*

squawk 1. *in.* to complain. □ *Come on, don't squawk all the time!* □ *Some people squawk because they don't have anything else to do.* **2.** *n.* a complaint. □ *Here's another squawk from the lady on the third floor.* □ *I have a list of squawks from the mayor's office.*

static *n.* complaints. □ *I don't expect any static because of the noise. I warned the neighbors about the party.* □ *Is this guy giving you any static?*

yell one's guts out AND **yell one's head off** *tr.* to complain bitterly and loudly. □ *Some lady is yelling her head off about shoddy workmanship out in the lobby.* □ *I yell my guts out about tripe when I see tripe!*

COMPLETENESS

all the way *mod.* with everything on it, as with a hamburger. □ *I'd like one double cheeseburger—all the way.* □ *Make mine all the way, too.*

cold *mod.* (stopping something) suddenly and totally. □ *I stopped cold—afraid to move further.* □ *That remark stopped her cold.*

done deal *n.* a completed deal; something that is settled. □ *It's too late. It's a done deal.* □ *The sale of the property is a done deal. There is nothing that can be done now.*

down *mod.* finished; completed; behind one. □ *Well, I've got the test down. Now what?* □ *One down and three to go.*

full sesh *mod.* totally; completely. (California.) □ *He was really out of it full sesh.* □ *It was a great game. They went at it full sesh the whole time.*

hook, line, and sinker *mod.* totally. □ *She fell for it hook, line, and sinker.* □ *They believed every word hook, line, and sinker.*

iced *mod.* settled once and for all; done easily. □ *I've got it iced. Nothing to it.* □ *The whole business is iced. Don't fret.*

pass go *tr.* to complete a difficult or dangerous task successfully. (From "pass go and collect $200" in the game Monopoly™.) □ *Man, I tried to get there on time, but I just couldn't pass go.* □ *You had better pass go with this job, or you've had it.*

sewed up *mod.* completed. □ *I've just about got this contract sewed up.* □ *When we get it sewed up, we'll go out for a drink.*

stone *mod.* completely; totally. □ *This lecture is stone dull.* □ *I am stone mad at you.*

taped *mod.* finalized; sealed (up); cinched. (As if one were taping a package.) □ *I'll have this deal taped by Thursday. Then we can take it easy.* □ *Until this thing is taped, we can't do anything.*

through and through *mod.* thoroughly; throughout. □ *She's a born fighter, through and through.* □ *He is totally dishonest. A crook through and through.*

totally *mod.* absolutely; completely. (Standard. Achieves slang status through overuse.) □ *How totally gross!* □ *This place is totally beige.*

wall-to-wall *mod.* expansive and comprehensive. (From "wall-to-wall carpeting.") □ *The guy doesn't exactly have wall-to-wall generosity.* □ *Old Tom is wall-to-wall hostility these days. What's wrong?*

way *mod.* extremely; totally. □ *Oh, this is way gross!* □ *I feel way tired today.*

COMPLICATION

You don't know the half of it. *sent.* "Things are far more complicated than you think." □ *You think that's bad? You don't know the half of it.* □ *You don't know the half of it, and I'm too much a lady to tell.*

COMPUTER

app *n.* an application; a computer software application. □ *Ted bought a new app for word processing and he says it's a killer.* □ *Ted's killer app can run circles around your old WordSun program.*

beamer *n.* a user of IBM computers; one who is knowledgeable about IBM computers. □ *I'm no beamer! I'm a Mac fan.* □ *Fred is a confirmed beamer, especially now that computers are cheaper.*

big iron *n.* a large, mainframe computer. □ *We'll have to run this job on the big iron over at the university.* □ *What kind of big iron do they have over there?*

bit-bucket *n.* the imaginary place where lost computer data goes. □ *I guess my data went into the bit-bucket.* □ *I bet the bit-bucket is filled with some of the best stuff in the world.*

boot *tr. & in.* to start the operating system of a computer. □ *I booted the thing, but it just sat there.* □ *When I booted, all I got was a feep.*

feep 1. *n.* the beep made by a computer. □ *This thing only makes a feep when I try to run my program.* □ *What does the feep mean?* **2.** *in.* [for a computer] to make a little beep. □ *It feeps when it's angry, I think.* □ *Naw! It just feeps to get your attention.*

fix *n.* a repair made to a computer program. □ *This little fix should make the whole program run faster.* □ *I wrote a fix to make the program more efficient.*

flamer *n.* a person who writes excited and angry notes on a computer bulletin board or in a computer newsgroup. □ *There are too many flamers on this board to make it interesting and entertaining.* □ *The flamers turn everything into a screaming battle.*

garbage *n.* jumbled computer code. □ *All I get is garbage on the screen.* □ *If you put garbage into the computer, you'll get garbage out.*

hack *tr. & in.* to write clumsy or inefficient computer programs. □ *I can hack a program for you, but it won't be what you want.* □ *Well, I can hack myself.*

hacker *n.* a sloppy or inefficient computer programmer; a programmer who breaks into private computers via modem. □ *This program was written by a real hacker. It's a mess, but it works.* □ *Some hacker crashed my system!*

hardware *n.* computer parts, as opposed to computer programs. □ *What kind of hardware are you running this program on?* □ *The software is okay, so it must be the hardware that's off.*

hotkey *n.* one or more keys on a computer keyboard that will bring forth a special computer applications program. □ *The hotkeys for my thesaurus are "control" and "F2."* □ *Press the hotkey to bring up a calendar.*

iron *n.* computer hardware. □ *What kind of iron are you people running over there?* □ *This is good old compatible iron.*

kludge AND **kluge 1.** *n.* a patch or a fix in a computer program or circuit. □ *This is a messy kludge, but it will do the job.* □ *Kluges that are invisible don't bother anybody.* **2.** *tr.* to patch or fix a computer program circuit. □ *I only have time to kludge this problem.* □ *The kid kluged a program for us in an hour.*

kludgy *mod.* having to do with an inefficient or sloppily written computer program. □ *This program is too kludgy to be acceptable.* □ *Who wrote this kludgy mess?* □ *I don't care if it's kludgy. Does it work?*

liveware *n.* the human component of computer use. (Patterned on *software* and *hardware*.) □ *The hardware is okay. It's the liveware that's bad.* □ *If I don't get some sleep, you're going to see a liveware crash.*

moby *n.* a "megabyte," a measurement of computer memory size. (A megabyte is whale-sized compared to a kilobyte.) □ *My fixed disks give me a capacity of over seventy-five mobies.* □ *My new computer has one moby of random access memory.*

number-cruncher *n.* a large and powerful computer. □ *They traded in the old computer for a number-cruncher.* □ *The small one is reserved for minor projects. The really big and important jobs are run on the number-cruncher.*

nybble *n.* four bits of computer memory. (Literally, one half of a "bite," i.e., a byte.) □ *My program wouldn't work just because I had one silly little nybble wrong!* □ *You don't program a nybble! It's just half a bite.*

software rot *n.* an imaginary disease that causes computer programs to go bad over a long period of time. □ *I guess software rot finally got to my program!* □ *What you have here is not a bug, but just plain old software rot.*

SYSOP *n.* "system operator," the person who manages a computer system or bulletin board. □ *The SYSOP tried to bring order to the bulletin board discussion but failed.* □ *I sent a message to the SYSOP complaining about the number of personal messages on the board.*

up time *n.* the time when a computer is running. □ *You'll get the maximum up time with this machine.* □ *On some systems the down time is longer than the up time.*

COMPUTER - ABBREVIATIONS

BG *interj.* "big grin." (An initialism used in computer communications to show that the writer is joking or happy. Not pronounced. Often enclosed, <BG>.) □ *I haven't seen you on the board. I thought you had run away from home.* <BG> □ *Your last message was filled with misspelled words, but I think I could understand what you meant.* <BG>

BRB *interj.* "Be right back." (Used in electronic mail and computer communications. Not pronounced aloud. Often enclosed, <BRB>.) □ *I have to get off the computer for a minute.* <BRB> □ *I* *have to get off the computer to use the phone. BRB*

BTW *interj.* "By the way." (Used in computer communications. Not pronounced aloud.) □ *BTW, have you heard about the new communications software upgrade?* □ *I am, BTW, very interested in what you said about the high cost of software.*

DIDO *phr.* "dreck in, dreck out"; garbage in, garbage out. (Acronym.) □ *Look at this stuff that the printer put out. What is it? Oh, well. DIDO.* □ *As a programmer, I specialize in DIDO.*

FWIW *interj.* "for what it's worth." (Used in computer communications. Not pronounced aloud.) □ *FWIW, I understand exactly what you are saying.* □ *I think you are just too sensitive, FWIW.*

G *interj.* grin. (An initialism used in computer communications to show that the writer is grinning or happy. Usually, <G>. Not pronounced.) □ *I guess you are not interested in what I was saying to you. <G>* □ *When are you going to learn to spell? <G>*

GBG *interj.* a "great big grin." (An initialism used in computer communications to show that the writer is grinning, joking, or happy. Not pronounced. Often enclosed, <GBG>.) □ *I think you are just talking nonsense. <GBG>* □ *You are such a kook! <GBG>*

GIGO *phr.* "garbage in, garbage out." (Acronym. If you get garbage out of a computer, it's because you put garbage in.) □ *The program failed, and I know it's my fault. You know, GIGO.* □ *GIGO is my theme song. I get out just what I deserve.*

gooey AND **GUI** *n.* a "graphical user interface." (A type of computer control system that uses an orderly layout on the screen with icons and menus that are controlled by a computer mouse. *Gooey* is slang; *GUI* is a technical acronym.) □ *Some of the older programs that lack a gooey require a lot less memory to run.* □ *Many new computer users find it much easier to use a gooey than to type in commands.*

GR&D *interj.* "Grinning, running, and ducking." (Describes what one might be doing after having written a mischievous message on an electronic bulletin board. Used in computer communications. Sometimes enclosed, <GR&D>. Not pronounced aloud.) □ *I'm GR&D, but I'm glad I said it.* □ *I guess that you got just the kind of answer that you deserve. <GR&D>*

IAE AND **IAC** *interj.* "in any event"; "in any case." (Initialisms. Used in computer communications. Not pronounced aloud.) □ *IAE I will give you the answer tomorrow.* □ *I will be there IAC.*

IM(H)O *interj.* "in my (humble) opinion." (Initialism. Used in computer communications. Not pronounced aloud.) □ *IMHO, you are dead wrong.* □ *She is the person to choose, IMO.*

IOW *interj.* "in other words." (Initialism. Used in computer communications. Not pronounced aloud.) □ *IOW, you are angry at me.* □ *I have heard enough on this point. IOW, shut up.*

IYHO *interj.* "in your humble opinion." (Initialism. Used in computer communications. Not pronounced aloud.) □ *Things are in bad shape IYHO, but I think they are great.* □ *IYHO, everyone else is wrong!*

LIFO *phr.* "last in, first out." (Acronym. Refers to the order of data put in and returned from the processor.) □ *I can't remember whether the stack is LIFO or FIFO.* □ *This one is LIFO.*

LOL *interj.* "laughing out loud." (Indicates that one is laughing in response to a previous remark. Used in computer communications. Not pronounced aloud.) □ *I'm LOL about the last remark you made.* □ *LOL at your last message.*

OIC *phr.* "Oh, I see." (Initialism.) □ *OIC. That's very interesting.* □ *OIC. So that's how it's done.*

OTOH *phr.* "on the other hand." (An initialism. A computer communication abbreviation, not pronounced.) □ *That's one good idea. OTOH, there must be many other satisfactory procedures.* □

OTOH, everyone is a little forgetful now and then.

PITA *n.* "pain in the ass." (Initialism. A computer abbreviation, not pronounced.) □ *The SYSOP here is a real PITA. I wish he would leave us alone.* □ *Who is the PITA who keeps asking the same question over and over?*

PMJI *interj.* "Pardon me for jumping in." (This indicates that someone is responding to a message directed to someone else. Used in electronic mail and computer communications. Not pronounced aloud.) □ *PMJI, but I have some information that would help you with your problem.* □ *PMJI. As long as we are talking about vacations, does anyone know the price of admission to EPCOT Center in Orlando, Florida?*

RO(T)F(L) *interj.* "rolling on the floor laughing." (Used in electronic mail and computer communications. Not pronounced aloud.) □ *I was ROTFL when I read your note. That was too much.* □ *Your comment had me ROTF.*

RSN *interj.* "real soon now." (Used in electronic mail and computer communications. Not pronounced aloud.) □ *I will post the rest of my trip report RSN.* □ *I will be finished RSN. I'll let you know.*

SCSI AND **scuzzy** *n.* "small computer system interface." (Acronym.) □ *Come over and see my new SCSI. It lets me run a hard disc.* □ *Why do they call it a scuzzy? Why not just say what it is?*

WBMTTP *interj.* "Which brings me to the point." (Initialism. Used in electronic mail and computer communications. Not pronounced aloud.) □ *Of course, you may not like that approach. WBMTTP. You need someone to help you choose the proper method.* □ *I agree with what Tom said. WBMTTP. I think we spend too much time worrying about these matters.*

WIMP *mod.* "windows, icons, mouse pointer." (Acronym. Refers to a computer system, such as Macintosh or Microsoft Windows, with an elaborate user interface including resizable windows, clever icons, and a movable mouse. The term implies that such systems are for "computer weaklings.") □ *I am happier with a computer system that doesn't have all that WIMP stuff.* □ *I want all the WIMP gadgets I can get!*

WYSIWYG *phr.* "What you see is what you get."; *What you see on the screen is what will print on the printer.* (Acronym.) □ *This program gives you that WYSIWYG feature that everyone wants.* □ *I need something that's WYSIWYG. I have no imagination.*

COMPUTER - ERROR

bug *n.* a flaw in a computer program. □ *As soon as I get the bugs out, I can run my program.* □ *There is a little bug still, but it hardly causes any problems.*

glitch *n.* a defect; a bug. □ *There is a glitch in the computer program somewhere.* □ *I'm afraid there's a glitch in our plans.*

CONCEAL

blow smoke *tr.* to state something in a way that conceals the truth. □ *She is a master at blowing smoke. She belongs in government.* □ *When they began to figure him out, he began to blow smoke.*

paper over something *tr.* to try to conceal something unpleasant; to try to cover up a misdeed. □ *You can't paper this over. It has to be dealt with now!* □ *This is a severe social problem. Don't try to paper over it.*

plant something on someone 1. *tr.* to hide incriminating evidence on a person for later discovery and use in prosecution. (Allegedly a police practice used to entrap drug offenders.) □ *The cops planted snow on Max and then arrested him for carrying it.* □ *Don't touch me! You'll plant something on me!* **2.** *tr.* to conceal narcotics or other contraband on an unsuspecting person for the purpose of smuggling. (This person will bear the risk of discovery and arrest.) □ *The crooks planted the stuff on a passenger, but couldn't find him when the plane landed.* □ *Someone had planted coke on me, and the airport security officer found it.*

wash *n.* a *whitewash* or covering up (of a problem). □ *What the administration presented was not an explanation but a wash.* □ *We don't want a wash. We want the truth.*

whitewash 1. *tr.* to make something look better than it really is; to conceal something bad. □ *Now, don't try to whitewash this incident. Open up about it.* □ *The mayor's office tried to whitewash the whole affair.* **2.** *n.* an act or campaign of covering up something bad. □ *They tried to give the scandal the old whitewash, but it didn't work.* □ *It was a good whitewash, but nobody believed it for a minute.*

CONCENTRATION

get down *in.* to concentrate; to do something well. □ *I'm flunking two subjects, man. I gotta get down.* □ *Come on, Sam, pay attention. Get down and learn this stuff.*

CONCERN

beeswax *n.* business; concern. □ *Is this any of your beeswax?* □ *Tend to your own beeswax.*

I could(n't) care less. *sent.* "I don't care!" (The affirmative version does not make sense, but is widely used, nonetheless.) □ *So you're late. I couldn't care less.* □ *I could care less if you fell off a cliff.*

CONCLUSION

See also **ENDINGS, QUIT, STOPPING**.

button *n.* the termination of a recitation; the punch line of a joke. (The equivalent of a button punched to signal a response.) □ *When I got to the button, I realized that I had told the whole joke wrong.* □ *When I came to the button, I knew I was really going to insult the guy.*

capper *n.* the climax or clincher of something. □ *The capper of the evening was when the hostess got lathered before midnight and couldn't celebrate the New Year.* □ *When the butler tripped and served Mr. Wilson the entire dessert in his lap, that was the capper to an exciting evening.*

clinch *tr.* to settle something; to make something final. □ *I was able to clinch the deal, and I got a raise for it.* □ *I want to clinch this contract before the weekend.*

clincher *n.* the final element; the straw that broke the camel's back. □ *The clincher was when the clerk turned up the volume.* □ *Eating garlic by the bushel was the clincher. I had to get a new roommate.*

end *n.* the final insult; too much; the last straw. □ *This is just the end. I'm leaving.* □ *When she poured her drink down my back, that was the end.*

end of the ball game *n.* the end of everything. □ *Well, the car broke down. I guess that's the end of the ball game.* □ *It looked like the end of the ball game as we sped too fast around the curve.*

jig is up *phr.* the game is ended; the scheme has been found out. (Always with *the*.) □ *Okay, you kids. The jig's up!* □ *Who says the jig is up?*

parting shot *n.* the last word; a final comment before departing. □ *For a parting shot, she called me a miser.* □ *His parting shot concerned some comments about my ability to do simple math.*

pour cold water on something *tr.* to put an end to something; to dampen something. □ *I hate to pour cold water on your plan, but it won't work.* □ *I wanted to go to the party, but my brother poured cold water on that by taking the car.*

pull the plug (on someone or something) *tr.* to put an end to someone or something as a problem; to defuse a problem caused by someone or something. (As if one were disconnecting an electrical appliance.) □ *It's time to pull the plug on this problem.* □ *I've heard enough from Mr. Jones. It's time to pull the plug on him.*

sew something up *tr.* to finalize something; to conclude something. □ *Let's sew this up and get out of here.* □ *I'm about ready to sew up this matter.*

shape up *in.* to assume a final form or structure. □ *The game plan for the election was beginning to shape up.* □ *Her objectives began to shape up in her senior year.*

So much for that. *sent.* "That is all for that." (Also in other variants, as in the examples.) □ *It's gone, ruined, broken—so much for that.* □ *He's finished as a friend of mine. So much for him!* □ *So much for you! Good-bye!*

That's about the size of it. *sent.* "That is the way things are."; "That's all there is to tell." □ *Well, that's about the size of it. See you tomorrow.* □ *That's about the size of it. You've understood it perfectly.*

That's all she wrote. AND **That's what she wrote.** *sent.* "That is all of it." □ *Here's the last one we have to fix. There, that's all she wrote.* □ *That's what she wrote. There ain't no more.*

That's that! *exclam.* "That is final!"; "That is the end of it!" □ *I said no, and that's that!* □ *I won't go, and that's that!*

wrap something up *tr.* to finish something; to bring something to a conclusion. □ *Let's wrap this up and go home.* □ *Well, that about wraps up our little session together.*

CONCURRENTLY

on the fly *mod.* while something or someone is operating or moving. □ *I'll try to capture the data on the fly.* □ *Please try to buy some aspirin somewhere on the fly today.*

CONDITIONAL

eat one's hat *tr.* to do something extraordinary. □ *If she wins, I'll eat my hat.* □ *I'll eat my hat if our advertisement actually brings us a president.*

CONFESSION

come clean (with someone) (about something) *in.* to admit (something) to someone. □ *I wish you'd come clean with me about this problem.* □ *You're gonna have to come clean eventually.*

CONFIDENCE

walk tall *in.* to be brave and self-assured. □ *I know I can walk tall because I'm innocent.* □ *You go out on that stage and walk tall. There is no reason to be afraid.*

CONFRONTATION

get in someone's face *tr.* to provoke someone. □ *Ted's a real pain. He likes to get in your face. He'll argue about anything.* □ *I know you are angry, but don't get in my face. I had nothing to do with it.*

in-your-face *mod.* confrontational. □ *I'm really tired of this in-your-face attitude of yours.* □ *Fred is just an in-your-face kind of guy. He means no harm.*

stick it to someone *tr.* to give someone a problem; to confront someone. □ *They stuck it to me about the stopped-up drain.* □ *He was late, and the boss really stuck it to him.*

CONFUSION

balled up *mod.* confused; mixed up. (This is hyphenated before a nominal.) □ *That dame is so balled up she doesn't know anything.* □ *This is really a balled-up mess you've made.*

bamboozled *mod.* confused. □ *This stuff sure has me bamboozled.* □ *I don't know who's more bamboozled, you or me.*

buffaloed *mod.* confused; stumped. □ *These tax forms really have me buffaloed.* □ *He was so buffaloed by the problem that he didn't get any work done.*

clear as mud *mod.* not clear at all. (Often with *as.*) □ *All of this is clear as mud to me.* □ *I did all the reading, but it's still as clear as mud.*

discombobulate *tr.* to confuse or perplex someone. □ *That kind of discussion discombobulates me something awful.* □ *Don't let the heat of the argument discombobulate you.*

discombobulated AND **discomboobulated** *mod.* confused. □ *I get completely discombobulated when I think of figures that big.* □ *I'm so discomboobulated these days!* □ *She is one discombobulated gal.*

dither *n.* a state of confusion. □ *A dither like that is hard to break out of. Maybe a good night's sleep would help.* □ *I'm too far gone with this dither to sleep.*

far out *mod.* very hard to understand; arcane; highly theoretical. □ *This stuff is* too far out for me. □ I can't follow your far out line of reasoning.

freaked (out) *mod.* shocked; disoriented. (Perhaps from drugs or alcohol.) □ *I was too freaked out to reply.* □ *Man, was I freaked.*

freak someone out *tr.* to shock or disorient someone. □ *The whole business freaked me out.* □ *I didn't mean to freak out everybody with the bad news.*

fuzzword *n.* a confusing term usually meant to obscure meaning. □ *The current crop of fuzzwords contains a few that have come back from the twenties.* □ *Don't sling those fuzzwords at me!*

goofed (up) *mod.* confused; distraught. □ *I'm sort of goofed up today. I think I'm coming down with something.* □ *I was up too late last night, and now I'm all goofed up.*

haywire *mod.* disoriented. (Often from marijuana.) □ *Wally is sort of haywire from the grass.* □ *Max has been haywire for years.*

hustle *n.* hurried movement; confusion. □ *All the hustle and confusion made it hard to concentrate.* □ *I can't work when there is all this hustle around me.*

in a dither *mod.* confused; undecided. □ *Mary is sort of in a dither lately.* □ *Don't get yourself in a dither.*

in a tizzy *mod.* in a state of mental disorder. □ *Fred is all in a tizzy.* □ *The whole office is in a tizzy today.*

lay a (heavy) trip on someone *tr.* to confuse or astonish someone. □ *After he laid a heavy trip on me about how the company is almost broke, I cleaned out my desk and left.* □ *After Mary laid a trip on John about her other self, he sat down and stared at his feet.*

messed up *mod.* confused. □ *I'm sort of messed up since my divorce.* □ *Most kids are sort of messed up at this age.*

mess someone or something up *tr.* to put someone or something into disorder. □ *You messed me up a little bit, but I know you didn't mean to bump into me.* □ *Who messed up this place?*

mish-mash AND **mish-mosh** *n.* a mixture; a disorderly conglomeration. □ *What a mish-mash of colors and designs!* □ *There's no theme or focus. It's just a mish-mash.*

mixed (up) *mod.* confused; mentally troubled. (This is hyphenated before a nominal.) □ *I was a little mixed up after the accident.* □ *This kid's just a little mixed. She'll straighten out.* □ *She's a crazy, mixed-up kid.*

over one's head *mod.* confusing; too difficult to understand. □ *This stuff is too hard. It's over my head.* □ *Calculus is all over my head.*

pixilated AND **pixolated** *mod.* bewildered. □ *That little old lady is pixilated.* □ *She seems a bit young to be so pixolated.*

rattled *mod.* confused; bewildered. □ *He tends to get a little rattled at minor things.* □ *Try not to get her rattled.*

rummy *mod.* habitually confused and inept. □ *I get more rummy as I grow older.* □ *That rummy old man is here again.*

run amok *in.* to go awry. (From a Malay word meaning to run wild in a violent frenzy.) □ *Our plan ran amok.* □ *The whole company ran amok after the market crashed.*

runaround *n.* a wild-goose chase. (Especially with *give*, as in the examples.) □ *The IRS gave us the runaround when we asked for a review.* □ *The customer will never get a runaround at my store!*

scooters *mod.* crazy; confused. □ *It's days like this that make me think I'm scooters.* □ *You are driving me totally scooters with your constant beefing.*

screwup *n.* a mess; a blunder; utter confusion. (Usually **screw-up**.) □ *This is the chef's screwup, not mine.* □ *One more screwup like that and you're fired.*

stump *tr.* to confuse or puzzle someone. □ *That one really stumped me.* □ *I like to stump people with hard questions.*

throw *tr.* to confuse someone. □ *The question really threw me.* □ *When the light fixture fell, it threw us a little.*

throw someone for a loop *tr.* to confuse or surprise someone. □ *The whole business threw me for a loop.* □ *Don't let this question throw you for a loop.*

tizzy *n.* a state of confusion. □ *The kind of tizzy that this place gets into drives me up the wall.* □ *The office was in a tizzy when I left.*

topsy-turvy *mod.* upside down; in disarray. □ *The whole office is topsy-turvy.* □ *He came in and turned everything topsy-turvy.*

turn someone or something upside down *tr.* to upset someone or something; to confuse someone or something. □ *We turned his place upside down, but never found the gun.* □ *The whole business turned me upside down. It'll take days to recover.*

up a tree *mod.* confused; without an answer to a problem; in difficulty. □ *This whole business has me up a tree.* □ *I'm up a tree, and I need some help.*

up for grabs *mod.* in total chaos. □ *This is a madhouse. The whole place is up for grabs.* □ *When the market crashed, the whole office was up for grabs.*

zooie AND **zooey** *mod.* confusing and chaotic. □ *I can't get anything done in this zooie place.* □ *It's never zooey in my office, except for a little rowdiness at closing time.*

CONNECTION

tie-in *n.* a connection; a liaison. □ *And who is your tie-in with the Acme Systems Company?* □ *I got a call from Mary—my tie-in with the mayor's office—who says it's all set.*

CONSEQUENCES

It will be your ass! *sent.* "It will cost you your ass!"; "You will pay dearly!" (Potentially offensive. Use only with discretion.) □ *If you do that again, it will be your ass!* □ *It will be your ass if it isn't done right this time.*

CONSUMPTION

eat something up *tr.* to consume something rapidly, such as food or money. □ *Running this household eats my income up.* □ *The car really eats up gas.*

kill *tr.* to eat all of something; to drink all (of a bottle) of something. □ *Kill this bottle so we can get another.* □ *We finally killed the last of the turkey.*

throw something back *tr.* to eat or drink something. □ *Did you throw that whole beer back?* □ *Jed threw back a quick snort and went on with his complaining.*

wolf something down *tr.* to gobble something up; to bolt down food or drink. □ *Enjoy your food. Don't just wolf it down.* □ *But I enjoy wolfing down food more than anything.*

CONTACT

touch base (with someone) *tr.* to make contact with someone. □ *I wanted to touch base with you just in case something had gone wrong.* □ *Let's touch base on Wednesday and check on things.*

CONTENTMENT

easy *mod.* easy to please; flexible. □ *Don't worry about me. I'm easy.* □ *Fred's easy. He'll eat anything.*

CONTRACEPTION

pill *n.* a birth control pill. (Always with *the*.) □ *Is Sally on the pill?* □ *The pill has really changed my life.*

Vatican roulette *n.* the rhythm method of birth control. □ *My parents lost at Vatican roulette, and I am the booby prize.* □ *Father John tried to get us to refer to it as something other than Vatican roulette.*

CONTRACTION

gimme *phr.* "give me." (Eye-dialect. Typical spoken English. Used in writing only for effect. Used in the examples of this dictionary.) □ *Do you wanna gimme the thingy and lemme go ahead with my work?* □ *Gimme another one.*

gonna *phr.* "going to." (Eye-dialect. Used in writing only for effect. Used in the examples of this dictionary.) □ *What time you gonna be home?* □ *I'm gonna get you, you little dickens!*

gotcha *phr.* "I got you!"; "I've caught you!" (Usually **Gotcha!**) □ *I gotcha, and you can't get away.* □ *Ha, ha! Gotcha! Come here, you little dickens!*

lemme *phr.* "let me." (Eye-dialect. Typical spoken English. Used in writing only for effect. Used in the examples of this dictionary.) □ *Do you wanna gimme the thingy and lemme go ahead with my work?* □ *If you won't give me one of my own, make him lemme use his.*

outta *phr.* "out of." (Eye-dialect. Used in writing only for effect. Used in the examples of this dictionary.) □ *Get outta here!* □ *In two minutes I'm outta here!*

CONTROL

See also **DOMINANCE, MANAGE.**

Big Brother *n.* a personification of the totalitarian state. (From George Orwell's *1984.*) □ *Big Brother has changed the tax laws again.* □ *Now Big Brother has fixed it so you can't even baby-sit without paying taxes.*

bird-dog *tr.* to supervise someone; to follow someone. □ *I wish you would stop bird-dogging me!* □ *Barlowe knew somebody was bird-dogging him, but he was too smart to show it.*

call (all) the shots *tr.* to decide on the course of action; to be in charge. □ *Why do you have to call all the shots?* □ *Do what you're told. I'll call the shots.*

fed AND **the feds** *n.* a federal agent concerned with narcotics, tax collection, customs, etc. □ *Some fed was prowling around asking questions about you.* □ *The feds are onto Rocko and his gang.*

flip (out) *in.* to lose control of oneself. □ *Wow, I almost flipped out when I heard about it.* □ *He got so mad that he flipped.*

get one's hooks into someone or something *tr.* to get ahold of someone or something; to gain control of someone or something. □ *I want to get my hooks into the operation of this organization.* □ *If I could get my hooks into the control of the company, I would change things for the better.*

handle *n.* a way of dealing with something; a grasp of a problem. □ *As soon as I get a handle on this Wilson matter, I'll give you a buzz.* □ *I can't seem to get a handle on what's wrong.*

hold all the aces *tr.* to be in control of everything. □ *The boss holds all the aces on this deal.* □ *I'll come out okay. I hold all the aces.*

keep one's head right *tr.* to maintain control of oneself. □ *Chill, man, chill. You've got to keep your head right.* □ *I can keep my head right. I'm mellow.*

on a tight leash *mod.* under very careful control. □ *My father keeps my brother on a tight leash.* □ *We can't do much around here. The boss has us all on a tight leash.*

zeek out *in.* to lose control of oneself. □ *I was in a pretty bad state. I almost zeeked out.* □ *Fred zeeked out and had to be calmed down.*

CONTROL - LACKING

lose one's grip AND **lose one's hold** *tr.* to lose one's control over something. □ *When I begin to lose my grip, I will just quit.* □ *I'm losing my hold. It must be time to chuck it.*

schiz(z) out *in.* to freak out; to lose mental control. □ *What a day! I nearly schizzed out.* □ *I schizzed out during the test. Got an F.*

spastic *mod.* overly responsive; out of control. □ *She can get so spastic when I come in late.* □ *Tell the spastic jerk to shut up.* □ *My dad's spastic when it comes to drugs.*

spaz *n.* a fit or an attack; a strong reaction to a bad or funny situation. □ *My father had a spaz when he heard.* □ *Take it easy! Don't have a spaz.*

zoom out *in.* to lose control. □ *I nearly zoomed out when I got the news.* □ *Fred zoomed out and started screaming at Ernie.*

CONVERSATION

See also **TALKING.**

bull session *n.* a session of casual conversation. □ *The gals were sitting around enjoying a bull session.* □ *The bull session ran on late into the night.*

chew something over *tr.* to talk something over. □ *Why don't we do lunch* *sometime and chew this over?* □ *We can chew it over at lunch.*

chew the fat AND **chew the rag** *tr.* to chat or gossip. □ *Put your carcass over on the chair, and let's chew the fat for a while.* □ *We were just chewing the rag. Nothing important.*

chin music *n.* talk; idle chatter. □ *That's enough chin music back there.* □ *Okay, chum, make with the chin music. Let's have the whole story.*

chitchat 1. *n.* talk; idle talk. □ *That's enough chitchat. Please get to work.* □ *Please stop the chitchat there in the back row.* **2.** *n.* a short, friendly conversation. □ *I'd like to have a little chitchat with you when you have time.* □ *We had a chitchat about the problem, and I think things will work out.*

fan the breeze *tr.* to chat or gossip. □ *We're just fanning the breeze, so you didn't interrupt anything.* □ *Stop fanning the breeze and get to work.*

yack *n.* a chat. □ *We had a nice little yack and then left for work.* □ *Drop by for a yack sometime.*

COOKING

burn *tr.* to cook food. □ *Why don't you burn some chow for me?* □ *Burn your own stuff, you lazy good-for-nothing man!*

done to a turn *mod.* well-cooked; nicely cooked. □ *The entire meal was done to a turn.* □ *The turkey was done to a turn.*

nuke *tr.* to microwave something. □ *I have to nuke my dinner and then I will be right over.* □ *Let's nuke a bag of popcorn before we watch the movie you rented.*

over easy *mod.* turned carefully, said of cooking eggs. □ *I want mine cooked over easy.* □ *Over easy eggs are better than scrambled.*

straight up *mod.* sunny-side up; having to do with eggs cooked with yellow yolks facing straight up. □ *Two eggs, straight up, and a cup of coffee.* □ *I like my eggs straight up, but the white part has to be cooked solid.*

sunny-side up *mod.* (of eggs) with yolks facing up and still yellow and hot, but not cooked through. □ *I'll have my eggs sunny-side up, with toast and coffee.* □ *People who like sunny-side up eggs wouldn't dream of eating a whole raw egg.*

COOPERATION

play ball (with someone) *tr.* to cooperate with someone. □ *Are you going to play ball, or do I have to report you to the boss?* □ *You will be better off if you will play ball with me.*

takes two to tango *phr.* "requires two people to do certain things." □ *No, he didn't do it all by himself. Takes two to tango, you know.* □ *There's no such thing as a one-sided argument. It takes two to tango.*

COOPERATION - LACKING

fink out (on someone or something) *in.* to decide not to cooperate with someone or something (after all). □ *Come on, don't fink out on us now.* □ *Bob finked out on the plan.*

COPULATION

action *n.* sex; copulation. □ *Paul is over at Martha's house looking for some action.* □ *All those guys play around with girls just trying for a little action.*

ball *tr. & in.* to copulate (with someone). (Potentially offensive. Use only with discretion.) □ *Isn't there anything more to you than balling?* □ *I hear she balled him but good.*

biggie *n.* copulation. (Usually with *the.*) □ *But I don't think I'm ready for the biggie.* □ *He wanted to do the biggie!*

diddle *tr. & in.* to copulate (with someone). (Use caution with the topic. Old slang.) □ *I didn't think they'd diddle right there in the film.* □ *I'm tired of hearing who has diddled whom in Hollywood.*

fuck *tr. & in.* to copulate (with someone or some creature). (Taboo. Potentially offensive. Use only with discretion. A highly offensive word to many people. There are many additional meanings and constructions with the word. Colloquial.) □ *Two dogs were fucking out on* *the lawn.* □ *He actually said in public that he had—you know—fucked her.*

gang-bang 1. *n.* an act of group rape. □ *The fuzz was around investigating that gang-bang on the next block.* □ *There were reports of a gang-bang in the prison.* **2.** *tr. & in.* to rape in a group. □ *The pack of thugs set out to gang-bang some innocent victim.* □ *Why can't they stop gang-banging people?*

george *tr. & in.* to copulate (with someone, usually a woman). (Use caution with the topic.) □ *They say he georges her a lot.* □ *They were off somewhere georging.*

get down *in.* to copulate. □ *Hey, let's get down!* □ *All Steve wants to do is get down all the time.*

get it off *tr.* to ejaculate; to achieve sexual release; to copulate. (Potentially offensive. Use only with discretion.) □ *Harry kept saying he had to get it off or die. What's wrong with Harry?* □ *The entire crew of the yacht came ashore to get it off.*

get it on *tr.* [for people] to copulate. (Potentially offensive. Use only with discretion.) □ *Come on, baby, let's get it on.* □ *I don't want to get it on with you or any other creep.*

GIB *mod.* "good in bed"; good as a sexual partner. (Use caution with the topic. Initialism.) □ *Pete lets on that he's GIB.* □ *How does he know he's GIB?*

go all the way *in.* to copulate; to carry necking all the way to copulation. (Euphemistic. Use caution with the topic.) □ *Did they go all the way?* □ *He keeps wanting me to go all the way.*

group-grope *n.* a group of people engaged in sexual activities. □ *That party turned into a hopeless group-grope.* □ *The group-grope was busted up by you-know-who.*

jig *tr. & in.* to copulate (with someone). (Use caution with the topic.) □ *He's telling everybody that he didn't jig her.* □ *She's claiming they jigged twice.*

laid AND **layed** *mod.* copulated with. (Crude. Potentially offensive. Use only with discretion.) □ *Well, you look laid, all right.* □ *If you come home laid, don't say I didn't warn you.*

lay 1. *tr.* to copulate (with someone). (Crude. Use caution with the topic.) □ *She laid him on the spot.* □ *He said he was going to lay her. I thought he was just talking tough.* **2.** *n.* a sexual act. (Crude. Use caution with the topic.) □ *I could use a good lay about now.* □ *All the shipwrecked sailor could think about was a lay.*

make it *tr.* to copulate (with someone). □ *There was no doubt in his mind that those bedroom eyes were telling him their owner wanted to make it.* □ *She wanted to make it, but he convinced her they should wait.*

mifky-pifky (in the bushes) *n.* illicit sex; *hanky-panky.* □ *Jeff got caught again. Mifky-pifky in the bushes seems to be his style.* □ *Mifky-pifky is the way of the world in Hollywood.*

poke *tr.* [for a male] to copulate (with a female). (Crude. Use caution with the topic.) □ *They say he poked her.* □ *Your dog poked my dog, then ran away.*

pork *tr. & in.* to copulate (with someone). (Potentially offensive. Use only with discretion.) □ *He's telling everybody that he porked her.* □ *They pork all the time, just like bunnies.*

scam *in.* to copulate. □ *All you ever want to do is scam.* □ *I think those people over there are scamming.*

score *in.* to copulate. (Use caution with the topic.) □ *Fred can't think about anything but scoring with Martha.* □ *He will spend his vacation trying to score.*

screw *tr. & in.* to copulate (with someone). (Use caution with *screw* and the topic.) □ *He's telling everybody that he screwed her.* □ *They screw all the time, just like bunnies.*

scrog *tr. & in.* to have sex; to copulate (with someone). (Use caution with the topic.) □ *You know what? I think those people over in the corner are scrogging!* □ *The movie showed scene after scene of this woman scrogging some guy.*

scrump *tr. & in.* to copulate (with someone). (Use caution with the topic.) □ *You know what? I think those people over by the garage are scrumping!* □ *The movie showed a scene of some woman scrumping her lover.*

shack up (with someone) *in.* to have a one-night stand with someone; to copulate (with someone). □ *Those two just wanted to shack up for a while.* □ *He only wanted to shack up with me.*

COPY

bite *tr.* to copy something without permission; to steal something. □ *Sue bit a copy of my term paper, and I almost got in trouble.* □ *Somebody bit my jacket!*

bite on something *in.* to copy something that someone else has done; to dress the same way someone else does. □ *Nobody will bite on Sally. She has terrible taste.* □ *Jennifer is always biting on Anne, who is a careful dresser.*

dub 1. *tr. & in.* to duplicate something; to copy something. □ *Dub this and keep a copy yourself.* □ *He's busy dubbing right now.* **2.** *n.* a duplicate; a copy. □ *The dub was so poor we couldn't understand the dialog.* □ *This is an almost perfect dub of the original.*

dupe 1. *n.* a duplicate; a copy. □ *Make a dupe of this before you send it off.* □ *I've got a dupe in the files.* **2.** *tr.* to duplicate something; to copy something. □ *Dupe this and send the original back.* □ *Just a minute, I have to dupe a contract for the boss.*

take a page from someone's book *tr.* to copy or emulate. □ *I took a page from Edison's book and began inventing useful little things.* □ *Mind if I take a page from your book and apply for a job here?*

take-off *n.* an imitation of something; a copy of something. □ *This robot is capable of producing 200 circuit board take-offs per hour.* □ *My machine is a take-off of the real thing.*

CORPSE

See **BODY - DEAD**.

CORRECT

cooking with gas *in.* doing exactly right. (Always with -*ing*.) □ *That's great! Now you're cooking with gas!* □ *I knew she was finally cooking with gas when she answered all the questions correctly.*

dead on *mod.* exactly right; on target. □ *That's a good observation, Tiffany. You are dead on.* □ *Your criticism is dead on!*

on the beam *mod.* on the right course or track. □ *That is exactly right. You are right on the beam.* □ *You're on the beam. You will finish this with no problems.*

right as rain *mod.* completely correct. (Folksy. Often with *as*.) □ *Yes, indeed! You are right as rain!* □ *She was right as rain about the score.*

You got it! *exclam.* "You are right!" □ *That's it! You got it!* □ *That's the answer. You got it!*

CORRUPT

turn *tr.* to corrupt someone. □ *It was the booze that turned him.* □ *Max was trying to turn a young kid.*

turn someone out *tr.* to introduce someone to drugs, prostitution, homosexuality, etc. (Underworld.) □ *Max tried to turn the kid out.* □ *There are laws against turning out people the way Max was doing.*

COST

See also **BUSINESS, COMMERCE, FINANCIAL**.

bad news *n.* the bill for something. □ *Here comes the bad news.* □ *Okay, let's see what the bad news is.*

big-ticket *mod.* having to do with something expensive. □ *Will the government cut back on the big-ticket programs?* □ *In a survey taken last month, heads of families said they were unwilling to put big-ticket items at the bottom of their shopping lists.*

damage *n.* the cost; the amount of the bill (for something). □ *Okay, waiter. What's the damage?* □ *As soon as I pay the damage, we can go.*

eat *tr.* to absorb the cost or expense of something. □ *It was our mistake, and* *we'll have to eat it.* □ *We'll eat the costs on this one. It's the least we can do.*

for free *mod.* free from monetary charge; gratis. □ *And I get all this for free?* □ *Is all this really mine for free?*

for peanuts AND **for chicken feed** *mod.* for practically no money at all. □ *I won't work for peanuts.* □ *You surely don't expect me to do this for chicken feed, do you?*

freebie AND **freebee; freeby** *n.* something given away free. □ *They gave me a freebie with my purchase.* □ *I expect a freebee when I spend a lot of money like that.*

free lunch *n.* something free. (Often negative.) □ *There is no such thing as a free lunch.* □ *There's always somebody who'll do anything to get a free lunch.*

highway robbery *n.* a charge that is unbelievably high, but nonetheless unavoidable. (As if one had been accosted and robbed on the open road.) □ *But this is highway robbery. I demand to see the manager.* □ *Four thousand dollars! That's highway robbery!*

jack something up *tr.* to raise the price of something. □ *They kept jacking the price up with various charges, so I walked.* □ *How can they jack up the published price?*

knock something off *tr.* to lower the price of something; to knock off some dollars or cents from the price of something. □ *The store manager knocked 30 percent off the price of the coat.* □ *Can't you knock something off on this damaged item?*

nickel and dime someone (to death) *tr.* to make numerous small monetary charges that add up to a substantial sum. □ *Those waiters nickel and dimed me to death.* □ *Just give me the whole bill at one time. Don't nickel and dime me for days on end.*

out of sight *mod.* very expensive; high in price. □ *Prices at that restaurant are out of sight.* □ *The cost of medical care is out of sight.*

pric(e)y *mod.* expensive. □ *This stuff is too pricey.* □ *That's a pretty pricy car.* □ *Do you have anything less pricy?*

rock bottom *mod.* absolute lowest, especially in reference to price. □ *Prices are rock bottom this month.* □ *I am offering you the rock bottom price.* □ *You can't beat these rock bottom deals.*

set someone back *tr.* to cost someone. □ *That must have set you back a mint!* □ *This bracelet set me back plenty.*

steep *mod.* [of a price] high; expensive. □ *Isn't that price sort of steep?* □ *I don't have steep prices here.* □ *Their prices are pretty steep, but their goods are of high quality.*

tab *n.* a bill (for something). (From tabulation.) □ *What's the tab for this?* □ *Barlowe paid the tab and left quietly.*

too rich for someone's blood *mod.* too expensive for one's budget. □ *This hotel is too rich for my blood.* □ *Europe is getting too rich for our blood.*

to the tune of something *phr.* for the sum of a specific amount of money. □ *The whole thing set me back to the tune of $400.* □ *You will end up paying to the tune of twenty dollars a month.*

COUNTRY

banana republic *n.* a stereotypic small Central American country having continual political turmoil. (Formerly of interest to the U.S. only because it supplied bananas.) □ *This is no banana republic! Things like this aren't supposed to happen here!* □ *If you want to change governments like underwear, maybe you should emigrate to some banana republic.*

down under *n.* the area of Australia; Australia. □ *I've always wanted to visit down under.* □ *We spent Christmas down under.*

Nam *n.* Vietnam. □ *How long were you in Nam?* □ *Things were pretty bad in Nam.*

COUPLE

DINK AND **dink** *n.* "double income, no kids"; a (young) married couple with two incomes and no children. (Acronym.) □ *The whole neighborhood is populated by dinks. Not a single child on the block.* □ *Most dinks are young. Older couples whose children are grown up are just called old.*

COURAGE

backbone *n.* courage; integrity. □ *If you had any backbone, you would be able to deal with this.* □ *She lacks backbone, that's all.*

grit *n.* courage; nerve. □ *It takes a lot of grit to do something like that.* □ *Well, Pete has lots of grit. He can do it.*

guts *n.* courage; bravado. □ *Man, she's got guts!* □ *It takes guts to do something like that.*

gutsy *mod.* courageous; feisty. □ *She sure is a gutsy young thing.* □ *She is not gutsy.* □ *Ernie's acting sort of gutsy today. What happened?*

nervy *mod.* daring; courageous. □ *What a nervy guy!* □ *Don't get nervy with me!*

spunk *n.* courage. □ *Show some spunk. Get in there and stand up for your rights.* □ *I have the spunk, but I don't have the brains.*

spunky *mod.* gutsy; courageous. □ *I like a spunky girl—one who can really dance.* □ *The guy's a shrimp, but he's spunky.*

stand tall *in.* to be brave and proud. □ *I can still stand tall. I'm innocent.* □ *Our athletes stand tall in the knowledge that they did their best.*

take a lot of nerve *tr.* to require courage. □ *He climbed the mountain with a bruised foot. That took a lot of nerve.* □ *It took a lot of nerve to go into business for himself.*

COWARDICE

candy-ass 1. *n.* a coward. (Potentially offensive. Use only with discretion.) □ *You are such a candy-ass! Stand up for your rights.* □ *Ralph seems tough, but he's just a candy-ass.* **2.** *mod.* cowardly. □ *The candy-ass approach just isn't going to work.* □ *Stop the candy-ass stuff. Handle this issue directly.*

chicken *n.* a coward. □ *Come on, let's go. Don't be a chicken.* □ *He's no fun. He's a chicken.*

chicken-hearted *mod.* cowardly. □ *Yes, I'm a chicken-hearted softie. I hope you don't want to make something of it.* □ *He's chicken-hearted, but I still love him.*

chicken out (of something) *in.* to manage to get out of something, usually because of fear or cowardice. □ *Come on! Don't chicken out now!* □ *Freddy chickened out of the plan at the last minute.*

crap out *in.* to evade something; to chicken out (of something). □ *Now, don't crap out on me at the last minute.* □ *Fred crapped out, so there are only three of us.*

funk *n.* cowardice; terror. □ *She suffers this terrible funk whenever she has to give a talk.* □ *The dog was in such a funk that it was whimpering.*

have a yellow streak down one's back *tr.* to be cowardly. (Have got can replace have.) □ *I think that Wally has a yellow streak down his back. That's what's wrong.* □ *If you have a yellow streak down your back, you don't take many risks.*

lily-livered *mod.* cowardly. □ *Don't be so lily-livered. Give it a try.* □ *That lily-livered guy is up hiding under his bed till this blows over.*

punk out *in.* to chicken out. □ *He was supposed to ask her out, but he punked out at the last minute.* □ *Come on! Stick with it! Don't punk out!*

wimp out (of something) *in.* to chicken out (of something); to get out of something, leaving others to carry the burden. □ *Come on! Don't wimp out now that there's all this work to be done.* □ *Ted wimped out on us.*

wimpy *mod.* weak; inept; square. □ *You are just a wimpy nerd!* □ *Come on, don't be so wimpy.*

yellow *mod.* cowardly. □ *Who says I'm yellow?* □ *Bruno says you're yellow. Wanna make something of it?*

yellow-bellied *mod.* cowardly. □ *You are a yellow-bellied coward!* □ *I'm not yellow-*

bellied! □ *What yellow-bellied skunk ran off with my horse?*

CRANKSHAFT

wrinkle-rod *n.* the crankshaft of an engine. □ *You need a new wrinkle-rod, lady.* □ *A wrinkle-rod'll set you back about $199, plus installation charges, of course.*

CRAZINESS

See also **SILLINESS**.

(a)round the bend *mod.* crazy; beyond sanity. □ *I think I'm going around the bend.* □ *She sounds like she's round the bend already.*

balmy *mod.* crazy; giddy. □ *You are totally balmy if you think I will put up with that stuff.* □ *What a balmy idea!*

bats AND **batty** *mod.* crazy. □ *You're bats!* □ *You are driving me batty!*

birdy AND **birdie** *mod.* crazy; strange. □ *She acts a little birdy from time to time.* □ *Would you kindly take your birdie friends and go?*

bonkers AND **crackers** *mod.* insane; crazy. □ *Get this bonkers brother of yours out of here!* □ *I think I am going crackers.*

bonzo *mod.* crazy. □ *You are completely bonzo!* □ *I want out of this bonzo place!*

climb the wall(s) *tr.* to do something desperate when one is anxious, bored, or excited. □ *He was home for only three days; then he began to climb the wall.* □ *I was climbing the walls to get back to work.*

cockeyed *mod.* crazy. □ *Who came up with this cockeyed idea, anyway?* □ *If you didn't act so cockeyed all the time, you'd have more friends.*

coo-coo AND **cuckoo** *mod.* insane. □ *The chick is just coo-coo, that's all.* □ *How did I ever get involved in this cuckoo scheme, anyway?*

cracked *mod.* crazy. □ *You're cracked if you think I'll agree to that.* □ *You gotta be cracked if you think I'm going back in there.*

crackpot *mod.* having to do with crazy things, mainly ideas. □ *We need a crackpot idea around here just so we'll have*

something to compare your ideas to. □ *Why not start a crackpot idea contest?*

dingy *mod.* loony; giddy. □ *That friend of yours sure does act dingy sometimes.* □ *Tell the dingy drip to forget it.* □ *I'm not dingy, I'm just in love.*

dippy *mod.* crazy; loony. □ *Who is that dippy chick with the lamp shade on her head?* □ *Tom is dippy, but fun.*

drive someone around the bend *tr.* to drive someone crazy. □ *This tax stuff is about to drive me around the bend.* □ *Gert tried to drive us all around the bend.*

drive someone bonkers AND **drive someone nuts** *tr.* to drive someone crazy. □ *This cold is driving me bonkers.* □ *These tax forms are driving me nuts.*

far gone *mod.* in an extreme state. □ *Wow, that chick is far gone. Listen to her rave.* □ *He was too far gone to make any sense.*

flip *in.* to go crazy. □ *Wow, I've got so much to do, I may just flip.* □ *The guy flipped. He was the nervous type.*

flip one's wig *tr.* to go crazy; to lose control. □ *Tom nearly flipped his wig.* □ *I flipped my wig when I got the news.*

funny-farm *n.* an insane asylum; a mental hospital. □ *I think they ought to send you to the funny-farm.* □ *He's too far gone for the funny-farm.*

gaga *mod.* crazy; eccentric. □ *Sometimes you are so gaga!* □ *Sally is just naturally gaga.*

go bananas *in.* to go mildly crazy. □ *Sorry, I just went bananas for a minute.* □ *I thought he was going to go bananas.*

go haywire *in.* [for a person] to go berserk. □ *I thought for a minute that Pete was going to go haywire.* □ *Sorry, I guess I just went haywire for a minute.*

go mental *in.* go crazy; to act stupid. □ *Don't go mental, Jane. Just calm down and think about it.* □ *Another day in that history class and I know I will go mental.*

gonzo *mod.* crazy. □ *The guy is totally gonzo!* □ *Who drew this gonzo picture of me?*

go zonkers *in.* to go slightly crazy. □ *What a day! I almost went zonkers.* □ *I went a little zonkers there for a minute.*

half a bubble off plumb *phr.* giddy; crazy. □ *She is acting about half a bubble off plumb. What is wrong with her?* □ *Tom is just half a bubble off plumb, but he is all heart.*

have a screw loose AND **have a loose screw** *tr.* to be silly or eccentric. (*Have got* can replace *have.*) □ *He's sort of strange. I think he's got a loose screw.* □ *Yes, he has a screw loose somewhere.*

have bats in one's belfry *tr.* to be crazy. □ *You must really have bats in your belfry if you think I'll put up with that kind of stuff.* □ *Pay no attention to her. She has bats in her belfry.*

have rocks in one's head *tr.* to be silly or crazy. (*Have got* can replace *have.*) □ *You have rocks in your head!* □ *She's got rocks in her head if she thinks that.*

loco *mod.* crazy. (From Spanish.) □ *Who is that loco kid jumping up and down in the front seat?* □ *This zit is gonna drive me loco.*

loony AND **loonie** *mod.* crazy. □ *That is a loony idea. Forget it.* □ *I'm not really as loony as I seem.*

lose (all) one's marbles *tr.* to become crazy. □ *Have you lost all your marbles?* □ *She acts like she lost her marbles.*

meshuga AND **meshugah** *mod.* crazy. (From Hebrew *meshuggah* via Yiddish.) □ *What a meshuga day!* □ *This guy is meshugah!*

non compos *mod.* out of one's mind; *non compos mentis.* (Latin.) □ *She is strictly non compos!* □ *Don't pay any attention to her. She's non compos.*

not all there *mod.* crazy; stupid acting. □ *Tom's not all there. Really dense.* □ *You can't depend on Paul for much help. He's really not all there.*

not play with a full deck *in.* to operate as if one were not mentally sound. □ *That guy's not playing with a full deck.* □ *Look sharp, you dummies! Pretend you are playing with a full deck.*

nuts *mod.* crazy. □ *You're nuts if you think I care.* □ *That whole idea is just nuts!*

nutty as a fruitcake *mod.* very silly or stupid. □ *The whole idea is as nutty as a fruitcake.* □ *Tom is as nutty as a fruitcake. They will put him in a nuttery someday.*

nut up *in.* to go crazy; to go nuts. □ *I've got to have a vacation soon, or I'm going to nut up.* □ *Poor Sue nutted up and had to take it easy for a few months.*

off one's chump *mod.* crazy; nuts. □ *You silly clown. You're off your chump.* □ *Am I off my chump, or did that car suddenly disappear?*

off one's nut *mod.* crazy; out of one's head. □ *Shut up! You're off your nut!* □ *Don't pay any attention to her. She's off her nut.*

off one's rocker *mod.* silly; giddy; crazy. □ *That silly dame is off her rocker.* □ *You're off your rocker if you think I believe that!*

off one's trolley *mod.* silly; eccentric. □ *Don't mind Uncle Charles. He's a bit off his trolley.* □ *That silly old man is just off his trolley.*

plumb loco *mod.* completely crazy. (Folksy. *Loco* is from a Spanish word meaning "mad.") □ *You're plumb loco if you think I'll go along with that.* □ *All those people were running around like they were plumb loco.*

potty *mod.* crazy. □ *She is acting a little potty.* □ *Who is that potty old man?* □ *He got more potty as he grew older.*

schizo *mod.* schizophrenic. □ *That gal is sort of schizo, isn't she?* □ *I have never dealt with such a schizo type before.*

screwy *mod.* crazy. □ *I've never heard such a screwy idea.* □ *It's really screwy.* □ *That's the screwiest-looking hat I've ever seen.*

slip one's trolley *tr.* to become a little crazy; to lose one's composure. □ *I was afraid I would slip my trolley.* □ *He slipped his trolley and went totally bonkers.*

snap *in.* to go crazy. □ *Suddenly Rocko snapped and began beating her savagely.* □ *His mind snapped, and he's never been right since.*

squirrely *mod.* loony. □ *Who wrote this squirrely play?* □ *Good old squirrely Tom! Isn't he a wonder?* □ *No, he's just squirrely.*

weirded out *mod.* disturbed or unnerved by drugs or events. □ *I was totally weirded out and couldn't control myself.* □ *After the blowup, Fred was really weirded out.*

weird out *in.* to become emotionally disturbed or unnerved. □ *The day was just gross. I thought I would weird out at noon.* □ *I weirded out at the news of Frankie's death.*

whacked *mod.* crazy; silly. □ *Greg acts whacked all the time.* □ *Garth seems whacked, but he's just putting on.*

wigged (out) AND **wiggy** *mod.* having lost control of oneself. □ *The kid is just too wigged to do anything these days.* □ *After the bad news, she was totally wigged out.*

wig out *in.* to lose control of oneself. □ *I was afraid I would wig out if I stayed any longer.* □ *Take it easy, man. Don't wig out.*

CRIME

action *n.* illegal activity; commerce in drugs; acts of crime. (Underworld.) □ *You want a fast buck, you get in on that action over on Fourth Street.* □ *Things have been a little slow here, but there's some action on the East Coast.*

big-time *mod.* felonious. (Underworld.) □ *Max is into big-time stuff now.* □ *The gang pulled a real big-time job and got away with it.*

buttlegging *n.* the transportation of untaxed or undertaxed cigarettes across a state line. (Patterned on "bootlegging.") □ *There's another news story about buttlegging in northern Indiana tonight.* □ *Most of the guys at the plant do buttlegging on the way home from work.*

caper *n.* a criminal job: theft, kidnapping, blackmail, etc. (Underworld.) □ *Who did you work with on that bank ca-*

per? □ *The black and whites pulled up right in the middle of the caper.*

case the joint *tr.* to look over someplace to figure out how to break in, what to steal, etc. (Underworld.) □ *First of all you gotta case the joint to see where things are.* □ *You could see he was casing the joint the way he looked around.*

chop-shop *n.* a place where stolen cars are cut or broken up into car parts for resale. □ *The state is cracking down on these chop-shops.* □ *Once a stolen car gets to a chop-shop, there's no hope of identifying it.*

crib *n.* a location where thieves gather to plot; a dwelling for thieves, prostitutes, etc. (Underworld.) □ *The police busted a crib over on Fourth Street.* □ *They use a basement over there for a crib.*

dirty *mod.* illegal; on the wrong side of the law. □ *The cops knew that Max was dirty and they searched his car until they found something they could use against him.* □ *You just look at Bruno and you know he is dirty. The question is, what's he done now?*

greenwash *tr.* to launder money; to obliterate the illegal sources of money by moving it through a variety of financial institutions. (Underworld.) □ *It was shown in court that the mayor had been involved in greenwashing some of the bribe money.* □ *The treasurer hired someone to greenwash the cash.*

hit *n.* a robbery; an assassination. (Underworld.) □ *There was a hit at the bank on Maple Street last night.* □ *Somebody died in the hit last night, but they don't know who yet.*

hot *mod.* carrying contraband and subject to arrest if caught. □ *Max was hot and on the run.* □ *Lefty was hot and needed a place to stay.*

hot-wire *tr.* to start a car without a key. □ *Lefty hot-wired the car and used it for an hour or two.* □ *Isn't it illegal to hot-wire a car?*

inside job *n.* a crime perpetrated against an establishment by someone associated with the victimized establishment. (Underworld.) □ *The cops figured that it was an inside job.* □ *It was an inside job all right. The butler did it.*

jazzed (up) *mod.* forged or altered. □ *This check is jazzed. Deep-six it!* □ *Better not try to cash a jazzed check at this bank.*

juice racket *n.* a racket where exorbitant interest is charged on loans. (Underworld.) □ *The cops got one of the leaders of the juice racket.* □ *The juice racket is no picnic, I guess.*

launder *tr.* to conceal the source and nature of stolen or illicitly gotten money by moving it in and out of different financial institutions. (Underworld.) □ *The woman's sole function was to launder the money from drug deals.* □ *When you finish laundering the last job, we want you to do another.*

make a score *tr.* to do a criminal act: to buy or sell drugs, to rob someone. (Underworld.) □ *We made a score with that bank job in Adamsville, didn't we?* □ *They made quite a score off that junky.*

merchandise *n.* any contraband. (Underworld.) □ *The merchandise is still at the boss's place.* □ *How much of the merchandise can you deliver by midnight?*

mob *n.* the crime syndicate. (Underworld and journalistic.) □ *The mob has held this city in abject terror for years.* □ *One of the biggest fish in the mob was pulled from the river yesterday.*

on the run *mod.* running from the police. □ *Max is on the run from the cops.* □ *The gang of crooks is on the run. Probably somewhere in Florida.*

palm something off *tr.* to succeed in spending counterfeit money; to succeed in cashing a bad check. (Underworld.) □ *Max palmed four phony twenties off in less than an hour.* □ *Somebody palmed off a rubber check on me yesterday.*

pass *tr.* to succeed in spending counterfeit money; to succeed in cashing a bad check. □ *Beavis passed one bad check after another.* □ *He was arrested for passing bad checks.*

reach for the sky *in.* (a command) to put one's hands up, as in a robbery. □ *Okay, you guys, reach for the sky!* □ *The bank teller reached for the sky without having to be told.*

rip someone off *tr.* to assault, kill, beat, rob, rape, or cheat someone. (Note the *for* in the example.) □ *They ripped me off, but they didn't hurt me.* □ *Man, they ripped me off for $300.*

run 1. *tr.* to transport contraband, alcohol, or drugs. □ *Max used to run booze during Prohibition.* □ *The soldiers were caught running guns.* **2.** *n.* an act of transporting contraband. □ *Four soldiers were killed during a run.* □ *In their final run the cocaine smugglers made over $4 million.*

shakedown *n.* an act of extortion. (Underworld.) □ *Mary was giving Bruno the shakedown, so he tried to put her out of the way.* □ *Those bums are masters at the shakedown.*

shake someone down *tr.* to blackmail someone. (Underworld.) □ *Fred was trying to shake Tracy down, but she got the cops in on it.* □ *The police chief was trying to shake down just about everybody in town.*

shove *tr.* to pass counterfeit money. (Underworld.) □ *She got sent up for three years for shoving funny-money.* □ *He got away with shoving the stuff for months before they got onto him.*

smurf *tr. & in.* to shift illicit money from place to place to conceal its origin. (Underworld.) □ *I smurf for a living. It doesn't pay much, but you meet some very interesting people.* □ *I smurfed a fortune for a famous drug kingpin and got fourteen years up the river—with some very interesting people.*

smurfed *mod.* having to do with a bank that has been used to launder money. □ *The teller came slowly into the office. "I think we were smurfed," she said.* □ *See that this dough is smurfed by Friday.*

snatch 1. *tr.* to kidnap someone. (Underworld.) □ *We're gonna snatch the kid when the baby-sitter comes out to see what* happened. □ *The mob snatched Mrs. Davis and held her for ransom.* **2.** *n.* a kidnaping. (Underworld.) □ *The Bradley snatch had the detectives up all night for weeks.* □ *The snatch went off without a hitch.*

wide open *mod.* vice-ridden. □ *This town is wide open!* □ *Because the prison is understaffed, it is wide open.*

CRIMINAL

bagman *n.* any racketeer. □ *Some bagman from the mob was pulled out of the river yesterday.* □ *So you think you and your bagmen can just walk in here and take over!*

bookie *n.* a bookmaker for betting. □ *Max was a bookie till he got into drugs.* □ *My bookie wants his money on the spot.*

champ *n.* a dependable member of the underworld. (Underworld.) □ *Bruno would never sing. He's a champ.* □ *Lefty is a champ. He stood by me the whole time.*

gangbanger *n.* a member of a street gang. □ *The gangbangers threatened the old lady too often, and finally she pulled out a can of mace and gave them a little lesson in good manners.* □ *Unless you want to grow up to be a gangbanger, you'd better go to school every day.*

goon *n.* a hooligan; a thug; bodyguard. (Underworld.) □ *Bruno is one of Mr. Big's goons.* □ *Call off your goons!*

goon squad *n.* an organized group of thugs; a gang of toughs. (Underworld.) □ *Bruno and his goon squad are lurking about.* □ *The goon squad Mr. Big sent around scared the devil out of Max.*

gun *n.* a hired gunman; a bodyguard or a member of a gang of criminals. (Underworld and Western.) □ *Bruno and his guns came by to remind Gary of what he owed Mr. Big.* □ *Tell your guns to lay off.*

hired gun *n.* a paid assassin. (Underworld.) □ *Bruno is Mr. Big's hired gun.* □ *The cops are holding a well-known hired gun until they can prepare charges.*

hit man *n.* a hired killer. (Underworld.) □ *Bruno was the perfect hit man. Hardly any brains or conscience.* □ *To look at*

Rocko, you'd never believe he was a hit man.

hood *n.* a hoodlum. □ *A couple of hoods hassled us on the street.* □ *That hood should be behind bars.*

hustler *n.* a swindler; a *con artist.* □ *The chick is a real hustler. I wouldn't trust her at all.* □ *The hustler conned me out of a month's pay.*

iceman *n.* a killer. (Underworld.) □ *It's hard to believe that Rocko is a professional iceman.* □ *The mob employs a number of icemen.*

kingpin *n.* a major figure in organized crime. (Underworld.) □ *Mr. Big is not your typical kingpin. He likes to play the stock market, too.* □ *The drug kingpins are well protected.*

paper-hanger *n.* someone who tries to pass bad checks. (Underworld.) □ *The cops caught the paper-hanger red-handed.* □ *He's wanted as a paper-hanger in four states.*

perp *n.* a perpetrator; someone who does something, such as committing a crime. □ *The cops were almost sure that Max was the perp in this job.* □ *The perp left a good set of prints on the doorknob.*

punk *n.* a petty (male) hoodlum; a (male) juvenile delinquent. □ *We know how to deal with punks like you.* □ *The jails are packed with crooks who were just punks a few years ago.*

shark *n.* a swindler; a confidence operator. (Underworld.) □ *The sharks were lined up ten deep to get at the blue-eyed new owner of the bowling alley.* □ *The guy's a shark, and he's after your hard-earned money!*

smurf *n.* someone who "cleans" ill-gotten money by buying cashier's checks at banks and shifting funds from place to place. (Underworld. From the name of a type of cartoon character.) □ *I think the guy at the first window is a smurf. He's in here twice a week with $9,500 in cash each time.* □ *Did you get a good look at this alleged smurf?*

thoroughbred *n.* an underworld person who is trustworthy and loyal to the underworld. (Underworld.) □ *Max is an A-1 thoroughbred.* □ *The thoroughbred clammed up during the third degree.*

trigger *n.* a hired gunman. (Underworld.) □ *Rocko was a mob trigger for a while.* □ *Get your triggers outa here—then we can talk.*

vic *n.* a convict. □ *Max is a vic, but nobody cares much.* □ *We try to give the vics a chance at employment where they won't be treated badly.*

CRISIS

up against it *mod.* having a personal crisis; having a financial crisis. □ *This is my bad season. I'm really up against it.* □ *Can I bum a few bucks? I'm up against it this week.*

CRITICISM

bad-mouth *tr.* to speak ill of someone or something. □ *I wish you would stop bad-mouthing my car.* □ *Harry bad-mouths everything he doesn't understand.*

bad rap *n.* unjustified criticism. □ *This car has gotten a bad rap, and I don't know why.* □ *Butter has been getting sort of a bad rap lately.*

bag on someone *in.* to criticize someone. □ *Stop bagging on me! I'm tired of all your complaining.* □ *If you are going to bag on everyone all the time, I don't want to hear about it.*

bashing *n.* criticizing; defaming. (A combining form that follows the name of the person or thing being criticized.) □ *I am sick of your college-bashing!* □ *I hope you'll excuse the broker-bashing, but some of these guys don't play fair.* □ *On T.V. they had a long session of candidate-bashing, and then they read the sports news.*

blast 1. *tr.* to attack or criticize someone or something verbally. □ *She really blasted the plan in front of the board.* □ *He blasted his brother until we all left in embarrassment.* **2.** *n.* a verbal attack. □ *The senator leveled a blast at the administration.* □ *The administration delivered an enormous blast at the Senate hearing.*

bum rap AND **bum-rap** *tr.* to talk ill about someone; to accuse someone of something falsely. □ *You're always bum-rapping your car!* □ *Don't bum rap me! I'll sue!*

ding *tr.* to negate; to criticize. □ *Please stop dinging my little brother. He's a good kid.* □ *The reviewer dinged the book, but it sold well anyway.*

dish *tr.* to criticize someone or something. □ *The critics all dished the opening of the play mercilessly.* □ *I wish you would stop dishing me all the time.*

do a dump on someone or something AND **dump all over someone or something; dump on someone or something** *tr.* to criticize someone or something; to destroy someone or something. □ *There is no need to do a dump on me. I didn't wreck your car.* □ *The boss—mad as a wet hen—dumped all over me.* □ *That rotten jerk really did a dump on my car. Look at that fender!*

dumped on *mod.* maligned; abused. □ *I really feel dumped on.* □ *The jerk who designed this stupid congested stairway hasn't been dumped on enough.*

get down on someone *in.* to be critical of someone. □ *Don't get down on me. I didn't do it!* □ *I'm gonna get down on him for that.*

knock *tr.* to criticize someone or something. □ *Don't knock it if you haven't tried it.* □ *The papers are knocking my favorite candidate again.*

knock something into a cocked hat *tr.* to demolish a plan, a story, etc. □ *I knocked his plans into a cocked hat.* □ *You've knocked everything into a cocked hat.*

lay a (heavy) trip on someone *tr.* to criticize someone. □ *There's no need to lay a trip on me. I agree with you.* □ *When he finally does get there, I'm going to lay a heavy trip on him like he'll never forget.*

nit-picker *n.* a person who is hypercritical. □ *Mary is such a nit-picker.* □ *Nit-pickers drive me crazy.*

nit-picking *n.* too much minor criticism; overly particular criticism; nagging. □ *I am tired of all your nit-pick-*

ing. □ *Enough nit-picking! What are the major problems?*

on someone's case AND **on someone's tail** *mod.* nagging someone; annoying someone with criticism or supervision. □ *You have been on my case long enough. Mind your own business!* □ *The boss has been on my tail about the large number of telephone calls I make.*

poor-mouth *tr.* to speak ill of someone. □ *Please don't poor-mouth my brother.* □ *There's no need to poor-mouth your clothing.*

potshot *n.* a sharp criticism; a wild shot of criticism. (Usually with *take*.) □ *Please stop taking potshots at me!* □ *He took a potshot at my old car.*

pull one's punches *tr.* to hold back in one's criticism; to attenuate the intensity of one's remarks. (Also with *any* in the negative.) □ *I won't pull my punches with you. This is lousy.* □ *He never pulls any punches. He always talks straight.*

sidewalk superintendent *n.* any critic. □ *If another sidewalk superintendent comes in here and tries to tell me how to manage this office, heads will roll.* □ *I hate to be a sidewalk superintendent, but this plan is all wrong.*

slam 1. *tr.* to criticize someone or something. □ *Please don't slam my car. It's the best I can do.* □ *The secretary was slamming the boss in one room, and the boss was slamming the secretary in another.* **2.** *n.* a criticism. □ *Harry took another slam at the sales record the sales force had produced for the meeting.* □ *I don't want to hear another nasty and hateful slam at my sister. Is that clear?*

spike *tr.* to puncture an idea. □ *I explained the plan, but the boss spiked it immediately.* □ *I hate to see my ideas spiked like that.*

take someone or something apart *tr.* to criticize or defame someone or something. □ *They really took me apart, but what the hell?* □ *The editorial took the whole board apart.*

take the heat AND **take some heat** *tr.* to receive criticism (for something). □ *The*

cops have been taking some heat about the Quincy killing. □ *If you can't take the heat, stay out of the kitchen.*

tear someone or something apart *tr.* to criticize someone or something severely. □ *I was late, and the boss tore me apart.* □ *I thought my paper was good, but the prof tore it apart.*

thin-skinned *mod.* sensitive to criticism. □ *Don't be so thin-skinned. You can't expect everyone to like you.* □ *He's a thin-skinned guy.* □ *I'm too thin-skinned to be a bill collector.*

CULTURE

culture-vulture 1. *n.* an avid supporter of the arts. □ *A gaggle of culture-vultures gawked its way into the gallery.* □ *Many culture-vultures seem to be long on enthusiasm and short on taste.* **2.** *n.* someone who exploits the arts for monetary gain. □ *Mr. Babbit, a well-known culture-vulture in art circles, never could pass up a chance to grab up all the works of an up-and-coming young artist.* □ *Some culture-vultures are throwing a wine and cheese party on behalf of some of the young dolts they have grubstaked.*

highbrow 1. *mod.* having to do with an intellectual or a person with refined tastes. □ *I just don't care for highbrow music.* □ *Pete is sort of highbrow, but he's an okay guy.* **2.** *n.* an intellectual person; a person with refined tastes. □ *Sam used to be a highbrow, but he gave up his fancy ways.* □ *The highbrows usually congregate in there.*

longhair *n.* a *highbrow* with long hair; especially a musician. □ *There were a few longhairs at the bar, but none of the regulars.* □ *I am sort of a longhair, but I still watch T.V.*

CULTURE - LACKING

lowbrow *n.* a nonintellectual person; an anti-intellectual person. □ *Some lowbrow came in and made a stink about not being able to find any Gene Autry records.* □ *Not that Gene Autry is lowbrow. The guy who came in was.*

CURSING

Barfola! *interj.* "Dammit!"; "Good grief!" □ *Oh, they're late. Barfola!* □ *Barfola! You're out of your mind!*

barnyard language *n.* dirty language. □ *We don't allow any barnyard language in the house!* □ *I don't care to hear so much barnyard language.*

blankety-blank AND **blankity-blank** *mod.* damned. (From the past practice of printing blank spaces in place of banned words.) □ *I'm tired of your blankety-blank bad humor.* □ *Get this blankity-blank cat out of here!*

blasted *mod.* damned. □ *I asked her to get her blasted stockings off the shower curtain.* □ *Shut your blasted mouth!*

Dash it all! *exclam.* "Oh, phooey!"; "To hell with it all!" □ *Oh, dash it all! I'm late.* □ *I broke it! Dash it all!*

doggone(d) *mod.* darn(ed); damn(ed). □ *I sort of wish my hooter wasn't so doggone big.* □ *Who made this doggoned mess?*

Drat! *exclam.* "Damn!" □ *Drat! I'm late!* □ *Oh, drat! Another broken nail!*

flipping *mod.* damnable. (Euphemistic for *fucking*.) □ *Get this flipping dog out of here!* □ *What's the flipping idea?*

Forget you! *exclam.* "Drop dead!"; "Beat it!" □ *Oh, yeah! Forget you!* □ *Forget you! Get a life!*

freaking *mod.* damned. (Euphemistic for *fucking*.) □ *Get your freaking socks off my bed.* □ *What is this freaking mess on my plate?*

frigging 1. *mod.* damnable. (Euphemistic for *fucking*.) □ *Who made this frigging mess?* □ *I smashed up my frigging car!* **2.** *mod.* damnably. □ *What a frigging stupid thing to do!* □ *That is a dumb frigging thing to do!*

fucking *mod.* damnable. (Taboo. Potentially offensive. Use only with discretion. Colloquial.) □ *Get this fucking idiot outa here!* □ *What the fucking hell do you think you are doing?*

funking *mod.* damnable. (Euphemistic for *fucking*. Use only with caution.) □ *Who put this funking milk crate in the hall?* □ *Get the funking hell out of here.*

Go to! *exclam.* "Go to hell!" □ *Oh, you're terrible. Just go to!* □ *Go to, you creep!*

Go to blazes! AND **Go to the devil!** *exclam.* "Go to hell!" □ *Go to blazes! Stop pestering me!* □ *I'm sick of your complaining. Go to the devil!*

Hang it all! *exclam.* "Damn it all!" □ *Oh, hang it all! I'm late.* □ *He's late again! Hang it all!*

Hell! *exclam.* "Damn!" (Use caution with *hell*.) □ *Oh, hell. I'm late.* □ *Hell, I'm too early.*

Hell's bells (and buckets of blood)! *exclam.* "Dammit!" (Use caution with *hell*.) □ *Oh, hell's bells and buckets of blood! I forgot my keys.* □ *Hell's bells! I'm late.*

jiggered *mod.* damned. □ *Get that jiggered cat out of here!* □ *Well, I'll be jiggered!*

son of a bitch *exclam.* Dammit! (Use only with discretion. Usually **Son of a bitch!**) □ *Son of a bitch! Look at that drip!* □ *Look at that place burn. Son of a bitch!* □ *Son of a bitch! I didn't even see that car pull out.*

swear like a trooper *in.* to curse and swear with great facility. □ *Mrs. Wilson was known to swear like a trooper on occasion.* □ *The clerk started swearing like a trooper, and the customer started crying.*

DANCING

boogie 1. *n.* a kind of rock dance. □ *I didn't like the boogie until I learned how to do it right.* □ *The boogie will tire you out, but good!* **2.** *in.* to dance rock-style. □ *I don't like to boogie.* □ *I'm too old to boogie.*

breaker *n.* a break dancer. (Break dancing is a rhythmic and energetic impromptu performance usually done by untrained urban youths.) □ *He is one of the best breakers in the city.* □ *I'm too fat to be a breaker.*

get it on *tr.* to begin dancing. □ *Let's go out there and get it on!* □ *He wanted to get it on, but my feet hurt.*

go-go *mod.* having to do with fast-dancing young women on display in a night-club. □ *I worked as a go-go girl for a while.* □ *Those go-go places have mostly changed their style.*

hoofer *n.* a (professional) dancer. □ *Clare was a hoofer when she was younger and lighter.* □ *She was a hoofer on Broadway.*

shake a leg *tr.* to dance. □ *Let's shake a leg. The music's great.* □ *Hey, Tracy! You wanna shake a leg with me?*

shank *in.* to dance. □ *They were busy shankin' and didn't hear the gunshots.* □ *We were all shankin' to a great reggae band.*

DANGER

business end (of something) *n.* the dangerous end of something; the part of something that does something as opposed to the part one holds on to. □ *Harry burned himself on the business end of a soldering iron.* □ *The robber pointed the business end of the gun right at Kelly.*

close shave AND **close call** *n.* a narrow escape. □ *Wow, that was a close shave.* □ *The car passed this close to us—a real close call.*

hairy *mod.* hazardous; difficult. □ *That was a hairy experience!* □ *Wow, that's hairy!* □ *What a hairy ride!*

have a tiger by the tail *tr.* to have become associated with something powerful and potentially dangerous. (*Have got* can replace *have*.) □ *You have a tiger by the tail. You bit off more than you could chew.* □ *You've had a tiger by the tail ever since you took office.*

in the tube *mod.* at risk. □ *He's in the tube now, but things should straighten out soon.* □ *If you find yourself in the tube in this matter, just give me a ring.*

play with fire *in.* to do something dangerous or risky. □ *When you talk to me like that, you're playing with fire.* □ *Going out at night in a neighborhood like that is playing with fire.*

war zone *n.* an area where things get rough; a tough neighborhood. □ *Unfortunately our offices are in a war zone, and we have to be on the way home before dark.* □ *The drug dealers and the gangs have turned many of our neighborhoods into war zones.*

widow-maker *n.* a dangerous horse; anything dangerous: a gun, strong alcohol, etc. □ *I call this stuff widow-maker. It's really strong.* □ *That horse is a widow-maker. I won't ride it.*

DATING

See also **AFFAIR, FLIRTATION, LOVER, ROMANCE.**

drag *n.* a (female) date. □ *You got a drag for the dance yet?* □ *My drag finked out on me.*

fixed up *mod.* provided with a date. □ *Sam got fixed up with Martha.* □ *Okay, Sam is fixed up with a date for Saturday.*

grayhound *in.* [for a black] to date a white. □ *Somebody said you were grayhounding. Is that so?* □ *I am not grayhounding.*

heavy date *n.* an important date with someone; a date with someone important. □ *Mary has a heavy date with Sam tonight.* □ *Pete and Sally were out on a heavy date together.*

little black book *n.* a book containing the names and addresses of acquaintances who are potential dates, usually put together by men. □ *I've got a nice collection in my little black book.* □ *Am I in your little black book, or can you already tell that I wouldn't go out with you?*

PFD *n.* a "potential formal date"; someone who looks good enough to be a date to a formal affair. (Initialism. Collegiate.) □ *That gal is a real PFD.* □ *Mike is no PFD, but he is a great friend anyway.*

rush *tr.* to court or date someone, usually a woman. □ *Tom's trying to rush Betty, but she's not interested.* □ *He spent some time trying to rush her, but had to give up.*

stand someone up *tr.* to break a date by not showing up. □ *She stood him up, and he was really angry.* □ *He stood up his date while he played basketball with the guys.*

take someone out *tr.* to date someone. □ *I hope he'll take me out soon.* □ *She wanted to take him out for an evening.*

DAY

bad hair day *n.* a bad day in general. (Also used literally when one's inability to do anything with one's hair seems to color the events of the day.) □ *I'm sorry I am so glum. This has been a real bad hair day.* □ *It's just one bad hair day after another.*

day person *n.* a person who prefers to be active during the daytime. □ *I am strictly a day person. Have to be in bed early.* □ *The Count insisted that he was not a day person, and he had to remain on his home ground until nightfall.*

red-letter day *n.* an important or memorable day that might well be marked in red on the calendar. □ *Today was a red-letter day in our history.* □ *It was a red-letter day for our club.*

DEAD

belly up *mod.* dead. □ *That's the end. This company is belly up.* □ *After the fire the firm went belly up.*

blown away *mod.* dead; killed. (Underworld.) □ *Four of the mob were blown away when the cops got there.* □ *That guy was blown away weeks ago.*

boxed *mod.* dead; died. □ *My old dog is boxed. A car hit her.* □ *He's boxed. There's nothing that can be done.*

cold *mod.* dead. □ *This parrot is cold—pifted!* □ *When I'm cold and buried, I hope people will think of me fondly.*

crumped (out) *mod.* dead. □ *Our old dog crumped out at age fourteen.* □ *Uncle Dave is crumped and now there's nobody left to drive that 1952 Cadillac.* □ *I am so tired. I feel half-crumped.*

dead and gone *mod.* [of a person] long dead. □ *Old Gert's been dead and gone for quite a spell.* □ *When I'm dead and gone, I hope folks remember me at my best.*

DOA 1. *mod.* "dead on arrival." (Hospitals. Initialism.) □ *The kid was DOA, and there was nothing anybody could do.* □ *Do you want to end up DOA?* **2.** *n.* a person who is dead on arrival at a hospital. □ *They brought in two DOAs Saturday night.* □ *Drugs increase the number of DOAs considerably.*

eliminated *mod.* killed. □ *Mr. Big wanted Max eliminated.* □ *When Max is eliminated, there will be no competition.*

feeling no pain *mod.* feeling nothing; dead. □ *Now, poor Jed is feeling no pain.* □ *Your aunt is feeling no pain now. She slipped away before dawn.*

laid out *mod.* dead; having to do with a corpse arranged for a wake. (Not slang.) □ *When the remains were laid out, the children were allowed to come in.* □ *When I'm laid out and ready to be planted, make sure this little book is in my hand.*

outed AND **offed** *mod.* dead; killed. □ *The witness was outed before a subpoena could be issued.* □ *The guy was offed when we found him.*

out of the way *mod.* dead; killed. □ *The crooks put the witness out of the way before the trial.* □ *Now that her husband was out of the way, she began to get out and about more.*

phfft *mod.* finished; done for. □ *There is my cat, and zoom comes a car. My cat is phfft.* □ *Yup. Deader than a doornail. Phfft!*

piffed 1. AND **pifted** *tr.* killed. (Past tense only.) □ *He piffed his goldfish by mistake.* □ *The speeding car pifted the cat yesterday.* **2.** AND **pifted** *mod.* dead. □ *What will I do with a pifted cat?* □ *He's as piffed as they come.*

pushing up daisies *mod.* dead and buried. (Folksy. Usually in the future tense.) □ *I'll be pushing up daisies before this problem is solved.* □ *If you talk to me like that again, you'll be pushing up daisies.*

put to bed with a shovel *mod.* dead and buried. □ *You wanna be put to bed with a shovel? Just keep talking that way.* □ *Poor old Jake. He was put to bed with a shovel last March.*

six feet under *mod.* dead and buried. □ *Fred died and is six feet under.* □ *They put him six feet under two days after he died.*

stiff *mod.* dead. (Originally underworld.) □ *He's stiff. There's nothing that can be done.* □ *Yeah, he's stiff. Don't hit him no more.*

stone dead *mod.* dead; unquestionably dead; long dead. □ *The cat was stone dead and stiff as a board by the time we got to him.* □ *Old Tom is stone dead and in the ground.*

stonkered *mod.* killed. □ *The car crashed into him and he was stonkered for*

sure. □ *He was stonkered before the plane hit the ground.*

taken AND **had; took** *mod.* dead. □ *I'm sorry, your cat is taken—pifted.* □ *Your cat's took, lady, tough luck.*

wasted *mod.* dead; killed. □ *Max didn't want to end up wasted.* □ *That's silly. We all end up wasted one way or another.*

X'd out *mod.* killed. (Underworld.) □ *Mr. Big wanted Max X'd out.* □ *He wanted Bruno to see that all these small-time punks were X'd out.*

DEATH

See also MURDER.

bag *in.* to die. □ *The guy was coughing so hard that I thought he was going to bag right there.* □ *The old man bagged on the way to the hospital.*

beam up *in.* to die. (From the television program *Star Trek.*) □ *Pete Dead? I didn't think he was old enough to beam up.* □ *I was so exhausted after climbing four flights that I was afraid I would beam up.*

bite the big one *tr.* to die. □ *I was so tired that I thought I was going to bite the big one.* □ *I hope I am old and gray when I bite the big one.*

bite the dust *tr.* to die. □ *A shot rang out, and another cowboy bit the dust.* □ *I'm too young to bite the dust.*

body count *n.* the total of dead bodies after a battle. □ *The body count at Hill 49 was three.* □ *The body count seems to go down during the rainy season.*

box 1. *in.* to die. □ *I laughed so hard I thought I would box.* □ *The old man looks like he's going to box at any minute.* **2.** *n.* a coffin. □ *I want the cheapest box they sell.* □ *Put him in a box and put the box in a hole. Then the matter is closed.*

boxed on the table *mod.* died on the (operating) table. (Medical.) □ *The surgeon did the best job possible, but the patient boxed on the table.* □ *Another patient boxed on the table. That's three today.*

buy it *tr.* to die. □ *For a minute, I thought I was going to buy it.* □ *He lay* there coughing for a few minutes, and then he bought it.

buy the big one *tr.* to die. □ *I don't plan to buy the big one for at least another thirty years.* □ *She conked out for good—you know, bought the big one.*

buy the farm *tr.* to die; to get killed. □ *He bought the farm on San Juan Hill.* □ *I'm too young to buy the farm.*

cash in one's chips AND **cash in one's checks** *tr.* to die; to finish the game (of life). □ *He opened his eyes, said good-bye, and cashed in his chips.* □ *I'm too young to cash in my checks.*

cool *in.* to die; to become cold after death. □ *The patient cooled during surgery.* □ *We were afraid that he would cool.*

croak *in.* to die; to expire; to succumb. □ *I was afraid I'd croak.* □ *The parrot croaked before I got it home.*

curl up and die *in.* to retreat and die. (Often figurative.) □ *I was so embarrassed, I thought I would just curl up and die.* □ *The old cat, finishing up the last of its nine lives, just curled up and died.*

curtains *n.* death. (Underworld.) □ *It's curtains for you if you don't come across.* □ *Okay, Barlowe, this time it's curtains.*

deep six 1. *n.* a grave. (Always with *the*. Graves are usually six feet deep.) □ *When you know the deep six is at the end of the line no matter who you are, it makes you take life less seriously.* □ *The deep six can't be made attractive to many people.* **2.** *n.* burial at sea. (Always with *the*.) □ *They gave her the deep six with full honors.* □ *I think I'd want the deep six, but I'll probably kick off on dry land.*

die on someone *in.* [for a patient] to die under the care of someone. □ *Get that medicine over here fast, or this guy's gonna die on me.* □ *Come on, mister, don't die on me!*

Dutch act AND **Dutch cure** *n.* suicide. (Always with *the*.) □ *Well, Ken took the Dutch cure last week. So sad.* □ *She had tried the Dutch act many times in the past.*

eternal checkout *n.* death. (Usually with the.) □ *When the time comes for the eternal checkout, I hope I am ready to go.* □ *Hank knew the eternal checkout was just around the corner, and he suddenly got religion.*

eternity-box *n.* a coffin. □ *When I'm in my eternity-box, then you can have my stereo.* □ *I have my eternity-box all picked out.*

flatline *in.* to die. (From the flatness of the line on an EEG monitor.) □ *It appeared that the patient flatlined during the night.* □ *She just grabbed at her chest and flatlined.*

get one's ticket punched *tr.* to die; to be killed. (Literally, to be cancelled.) □ *Poor Chuck got his ticket punched while he was waiting for a bus.* □ *Watch out there, or you'll get your ticket punched.*

go home in a box *in.* to be shipped home dead. □ *Hey, I'm too young to go home in a box.* □ *You had better be careful on this camping trip, or you'll go home in a box.*

go West *in.* to die. □ *Ever since Uncle Ben went West, things have been peaceful around here.* □ *When I go West, I want flowers, hired mourners, and an enormous performance of Mozart's "Requiem."*

have one foot in the grave *tr.* to be near death. (*Have got* can replace *have*.) □ *I feel like I've got one foot in the grave.* □ *Uncle Ben has one foot in the grave, but he's still cheery.*

in cold storage *mod.* in a state of death. □ *Rocko gets paid for putting his subjects in cold storage.* □ *Poor old Jed is in cold storage.*

kick off *in.* to die. □ *We've been waiting for years for that cat to kick off.* □ *The old girl finally kicked off.*

kick the bucket *tr.* to die. □ *I'm too young to kick the bucket.* □ *The cat kicked the bucket last night.*

kiss off 1. *n.* death. (Usually **kiss-off**.) □ *When the time comes for the kiss-off, I hope I'm asleep.* □ *The kiss-off came wrapped in lead, and it was instant.* **2.** *in.* to die. □ *The cat is going to have to kiss* off one of these days soon. □ *The cat kissed off after eighteen years of joy and devotion.*

last roundup *n.* death. (Western.) □ *To everyone's surprise, he clutched the wound and faced the last roundup with a smile.* □ *When I know I'm headed for the last roundup, I'll write a will.*

lay someone out *tr.* to prepare someone for burial. (Not slang.) □ *The undertaker did not lay Aunt Fanny out to my satisfaction.* □ *The women of the town helped the young widow lay out her husband.*

lead poisoning *n.* death caused by being shot with a lead bullet. (Underworld.) □ *He pifted because of a case of lead poisoning.* □ *The fourth mobster to die of lead poisoning this month was buried today in a private service.*

lights out *n.* death; time to die. (Underworld.) □ *It's lights out for you, chum.* □ *When it's lights out, I want it to be fast.*

Nebraska sign *n.* a flat EEG indicating the death of the patient being monitored. □ *The lady in 203 is giving the Nebraska sign. I think she's boxed.* □ *I saw the Nebraska sign on my monitor, and knew it must not be hooked up right.*

OD *in.* to die from an overdose of drugs. □ *Two kids at my school ODed last weekend.* □ *I think Max may OD in a week or two.*

off *in.* to die. □ *The guy just falls down and offs, right there on Main Street.* □ *I don't want to off before my time.*

pop off *in.* to die. □ *My uncle popped off last week.* □ *I hope I'm asleep when I pop off.*

send someone to glory *tr.* to officiate at the burial services for someone. □ *The preacher sent him to glory amidst the sobs of six or seven former fans.* □ *The preacher probably gets fifty bucks for every stiff he sends to glory.*

snuff *mod.* having to do with death or killing. □ *Those snuff acts ought to be outlawed.* □ *All this snuff stuff is for sickies.*

snuff it *tr.* to die. □ *The cat leapt straight up in the air and snuffed it.* □ *I was so sick they thought I was going to snuff it.*

sprout wings *tr.* to die and become an angel. □ *I'm not ready to sprout wings yet. I've got a few more years.* □ *You wanna sprout wings, you just keep talking like that.*

step off the curb *in.* to die. □ *Ralph almost stepped off the curb during his operation.* □ *I'm too young to step off the curb.*

take a dirt nap *tr.* to die and be buried. □ *I don't want to end up taking a dirt nap during this operation.* □ *Isn't Tom a little young to take a dirt nap?*

take the (gas) pipe *tr.* to commit suicide. (Originally by inhaling gas.) □ *The kid was dropping everything in sight and finally took the pipe.* □ *Some poor old guy took the gas pipe and nearly blew the place up.*

take the (long) count *tr.* to die. □ *The poor cat took the long count at last.* □ *I'm too young to take the count.*

tap out *in.* to die; to expire. □ *My dog tapped out after being hit by a car.* □ *Mary was so tired that she thought she was going to tap out.*

turn belly up AND **go belly up** *in.* to die. (As a fish does when it dies.) □ *The cat was friendly for a moment before she turned belly up.* □ *Every fish in Greg's tank went belly up last night.*

turn one's toes up *tr.* to die. □ *I'm too young to turn my toes up.* □ *The cat turned up its toes right after church. Ah, the power of prayer.*

DEBT

deadbeat *n.* someone who doesn't pay debts or bills. □ *Some deadbeat with the same name as mine is ruining my credit rating.* □ *Pay up! Don't be a deadbeat.*

marker *n.* a personal promissory note; an IOU. □ *Max signed a marker for $3,000 and handed it to Bruno.* □ *Bruno said that he held Max's marker for three grand.*

reader *n.* a piece of paper with writing on it; a note; a prescription; an I.O.U. (Underworld.) □ *Max has my reader for $500.*

red ink *n.* debt; indebtedness as shown in red ink on a financial statement. □ *There is too much red ink in my financial statement.* □ *Too much red ink and the company will collapse.*

welcher *n.* someone who does not pay gambling debts. □ *It was Bruno's job to let the welchers know that Mr. Big was angry.* □ *Bruno set out to teach the welcher a lesson. He didn't mean to hurt him very much.*

DECEPTION
See also **CONCEAL**.

bamboozle *tr.* to deceive someone; to confuse someone. □ *Don't try to bamboozle me! I know what I want!* □ *The crooks bamboozled the old man out of his life savings.*

bite *in.* to accept a deception; to fall for something; to respond to a come-on. □ *I knew somebody would bite.* □ *We put up a sign advertising free pop, but nobody bit.*

blow someone off *tr.* to cheat someone; to deceive someone. □ *Don't try to blow me off! I know what's what.* □ *They blew off a young couple and conned a hundred bucks out of them.*

buckpasser *n.* someone who cannot accept the responsibility for something. □ *You are the most irresponsible buckpasser I have ever had to deal with!* □ *When something really goes wrong, everybody suddenly becomes a buckpasser.*

bull *tr. & in.* to lie to or deceive someone. □ *Stop bulling me!* □ *Is she bulling again?*

bullshit *tr.* to deceive someone; to lie to someone. (Use with caution.) □ *Stop bullshitting me!* □ *You wouldn't bullshit us, would you?*

bunco 1. *n.* a scheme to swindle people. (From *banca,* the name of a card game in Spanish.) □ *He's been fiddling with bunco on the West Coast.* □ *All the stuff relating to bunco comes across this desk.* 2. *tr.* to swindle someone. □ *They bun-*coed an old lady and left her penniless. □ *Fred tried to bunco a chick in Frisco, but felt sorry for her at the last minute.*

burn *n.* a deception; an instance of being cheated. □ *Man, that was a burn. That guy was really mad.* □ *We pulled off the burn without a hitch. It was a gas.*

burn artist *n.* someone who cheats or harms someone else. (Underworld.) □ *Never trust a known burn artist.* □ *The fuzz rounded up all the burn artists in the district and pumped them for info.*

burned *mod.* cheated; betrayed. □ *Man, did I get burned in that place!* □ *We sure got burned on that deal.*

caper *n.* any stunt or event; a trick or a scam. □ *That little caper the kids did with the statue from the town square was a dandy.* □ *Another caper like that and I call your parents.*

clip *tr.* to cheat someone. □ *That guy in there clipped me for a fiver.* □ *I didn't clip you or anybody else!*

clipped *mod.* cheated. □ *When Marty counted his change, he found he'd been clipped.* □ *You weren't clipped by me. I just made a mistake.*

con 1. *n.* a confidence scheme. □ *They pulled a real con on the old lady.* □ *This is an okay con you got going.* 2. *tr.* to swindle or deceive someone. □ *Don't try to con me. I know the score.* □ *Bruno conned him out of his money.*

con job *n.* an act of deception. □ *What a con job he tried to pull on us!* □ *This is not an annual report! It's a con job!*

diddle *tr.* to cheat someone; to deceive someone. □ *The clerk diddled me so I reported her.* □ *That's a good place to get diddled. You gotta watch them in there.*

dirty *mod.* low and sneaky. □ *What a dirty trick!* □ *That was really dirty!* □ *What a dirty thing to do!*

dirty pool *n.* activities conducted using unfair or sneaky tactics. □ *They're playing dirty pool now. This calls for a new plan.* □ *When they start playing dirty pool, it's time to get mean.*

dirty work *n.* sneaky activities. □ *I hear that Sam is up to his old dirty work again.* □ *He is a master at dirty work.*

do a number on someone AND **do a job on someone** *tr.* to harm or deceive someone. □ *The IRS really did a number on me.* □ *My local friendly plumber did a job on me cleaning out my drain.*

do a snow job on someone *tr.* to deceive or confuse someone. □ *Don't try to do a snow job on me. I know all the tricks.* □ *She thought she did a snow job on the teacher, but it backfired.*

dodge *n.* a swindle; a deception. □ *What sort of dodge did you get flimflammed with?* □ *Gary has a new dodge to make money, but he hasn't made any yet.*

done by mirrors AND **done with mirrors** *mod.* illusory; purposefully deceptive. □ *The whole budgetary process is done with mirrors.* □ *The self-review was done by mirrors and didn't come off too bad.*

double-dipper *n.* a person who collects two salaries; a federal employee who collects a federal pension and Social Security. □ *The voters of the state were shocked to learn that there were no laws against double-dippers.* □ *The double-dippers say they weren't doing anything wrong.*

euchre *tr.* to cheat or deceive someone. □ *Those guys'll try to euchre you, so watch out.* □ *I think the clerk euchred me.*

fake it *tr.* to pretend (to do something). □ *If you don't know the right notes, just fake it.* □ *I can't fake it anymore. I've got to be honest with you.*

fake someone out *tr.* to deceive someone, as with a football pass. □ *They faked me out, and then I stumbled over my own feet. The coach was fuming.* □ *We faked out the teacher, who thought we had gone out in the hall.*

fast one *n.* a clever and devious trick. □ *That was a fast one. I didn't know you were so devious.* □ *This was the last fast one like that you'll ever pull on me.*

flimflam 1. *n.* a confidence trick or deception. □ *The whole business sounds like a bit of flimflam to me.* □ *The crooks pulled a nasty flimflam on Betsy.* **2.** *tr. & in.* to cheat or deceive (someone). □ *Don't try to flimflam me. I wasn't born yesterday, you know.* □ *She is flimflamming over at the Adamsville fair this week.*

flimflam artist *n.* someone who practices confidence tricks or deceptions on someone else. □ *I don't trust that flimflam artist at all.* □ *Pretty soon, you'll learn how to spot a flimflam artist.*

four-flusher *n.* a cheater. □ *Bruno is a lousy four-flusher, among other unpleasant things.* □ *You dirty four-flusher!*

frame 1. *tr.* to cause an innocent person to be blamed for a crime; to contrive evidence so that someone appears to be guilty. (Originally underworld.) □ *Jimmy tried to frame his sister for painting the cat yellow.* □ *You won't frame me and get away with it!* **2.** AND **frame-up; frameup** *n.* a scheme in which an innocent person is made to take the blame for something; incrimination caused by contrived evidence. (Underworld.) □ *Bruno would never fall easy. Must be a frame.* □ *The frame-up would have worked if it weren't for one little thing.*

front *in.* to pretend. □ *Wendy, you are not real. You're just fronting all the time.* □ *Stop fronting and be yourself.*

fudge *in.* to cheat; to deceive (someone). □ *Bill, you're fudging. Wait till the starting gun fires.* □ *No fair fudging!*

give someone the shaft *tr.* to cheat or deceive someone; to mistreat someone. □ *The boss really gave Wally the shaft.* □ *Somebody always gives me the shaft.*

hanky-panky *n.* funny business; deceitfulness. □ *There's some hanky-panky going on in the treasurer's office.* □ *I am going to get this hanky-panky straightened out.*

hocus *tr.* to falsify something; to adulterate something. □ *Who hocused the check?* □ *Somebody has hocused the booze.*

hook *tr.* to cheat someone. □ *Watch the clerk in that store. He might try to hook you.* □ *They hooked me on the car deal.*

hooked (on something) *mod.* cheated. □ *I was really hooked on this travel deal.* □ *You were hooked, all right.*

hoser *n.* a cheater or deceiver. □ *Stop acting like a hoser and tell me the truth!* □ *You dirty lying hoser!*

hustle 1. *n.* a scheme to make money; a special technique for making money. (Underworld. This includes drug dealing, prostitution, and other vice activities.) □ *Each of these punks has a hustle—a specialty in crime.* □ *We all know what Max's hustle is.* **2.** *in.* to use one's special technique for making money. □ *He's out there on the streets hustling all the time.* □ *I gotta go hustle. I need some bread.* **3.** *tr.* to use a scheme on a person to try to make money. □ *Don't try to hustle me, sister. I know which end is up.* □ *Sam is always trying to hustle people.*

jeff *tr.* to persuade or deceive someone. □ *The guy tried to jeff me!* □ *You're just jeffing us!*

jive *n.* lies; deception; nonsense. □ *No more of your jive. Talk straight or don't talk.* □ *I've listened to your jive for years. You'll never change.*

lip gloss *n.* lies; deception; exaggeration. (From the name of a lipstick-like cosmetic.) □ *Everything he says is just lip gloss. He is a liar at heart.* □ *She doesn't mean it. Her words are just lip gloss.*

on the sly *mod.* secretly and deceptively. □ *She was stealing little bits of money on the sly.* □ *Martin was having an affair with the maid on the sly.*

pack of lies *n.* a whole collection or series of lies. □ *I've heard you talk about this before, and it's all a pack of lies.* □ *Her story is nothing but a pack of lies.*

palm *tr.* to conceal something in the hand as in a theft or the performance of a magic trick; to receive and conceal a tip or a bribe. □ *The kid palmed the candy bar and walked right out of the store.* □ *The waiter palmed the twenty-dollar bill and led us to a table.*

perpetrate *in.* to pose; to pretend. □ *Terry is always walking around perpe-*trating. *He sure wants people to think he's somebody.* □ *Look at her clothes. Have you ever seen anyone perpetrate like that?*

phutz AND **futz** *tr.* to swindle or cheat someone. □ *Don't futz me! Tell the truth!* □ *The muggers phutzed his wallet and watch.*

play around (with someone) *in.* to tease, deceive, or try to trick someone. □ *You're playing around with me. Leave me alone.* □ *Don't pay any attention to them. They're just playing around.*

put a con on someone *tr.* to attempt to deceive someone; to attempt to swindle someone. (Underworld.) □ *Don't try to put a con on me, Buster! I've been around too long.* □ *I wouldn't try to put a con on you. I'm not that dumb.*

put someone on *tr.* to tease or deceive someone innocently and in fun. □ *Come on! You're just putting me on!* □ *He got real mad even though they were only putting him on.*

put-up job *n.* a deception; a deceptive event. □ *That's really phony. A put-up job if I ever saw one.* □ *No put-up job is clever enough to fool me.*

racket *n.* a deception. □ *He operated a racket that robbed old ladies of their savings.* □ *This is not a service station; it's a real racket!*

rig *tr.* to arrange or tamper with the results of something. □ *The crooks rigged the election.* □ *Somebody rigged the contest so no one got first prize.*

rook *tr.* to cheat someone. □ *She tried to rook me when I paid my bill.* □ *Don't go into that store. They'll rook you.*

sandbag *tr.* to deceive someone; to fool someone about one's capabilities. □ *Don't let them sandbag you into expecting too little.* □ *The guy sandbagged me, and I wasn't expecting him to shoot the ball.*

scabbed *mod.* cheated in a drug deal; having been sold bogus or inferior drugs. □ *Max got scabbed by a dealer who got arrested the next day.* □ *This junk is junk. I've been scabbed.*

scam 1. *n.* a swindle. □ *I lost a fortune in that railroad scam.* □ *What a scam!*

I'm calling the cops. **2.** *tr.* to swindle someone; to deceive someone. □ *They were scammed by a sweet-talking southern lady who took all their money.* □ *She scammed them for every cent they had.*

screw *tr.* to cheat someone. □ *That salesman tried to screw me, but I just walked out on him.* □ *They didn't screw me. I got good value for my money.*

screwed *mod.* bested; defeated; cheated. □ *I really got screwed at the garage.* □ *If you don't want to get screwed by somebody, you have to do it yourself.*

screw someone out of something *tr.* to cheat someone of something. □ *You are trying to screw me out of what is rightfully mine!* □ *I'm not trying to screw anybody out of anything!*

shill *n.* someone planted in the crowd to urge others to buy something, participate in something, etc. □ *The guy's a shill! Don't fall for this setup!* □ *There were more shills than suckers on the midway that day.*

shit *tr.* to deceive someone; to lie to someone. (Use with caution.) □ *Stop shittin' me, you bastard!* □ *You wouldn't shit me, would you?*

short *tr.* to give someone less of something than was agreed upon. □ *You shorted me!* □ *They shorted us on the last order, so we switched suppliers.*

shuck *tr.* to swindle someone; to deceive someone. □ *The con man shucked a number of people in the town before moving on.* □ *He was going to shuck the mayor, but people were beginning to talk, so he blew town.*

skin *tr.* to cheat or overcharge someone. □ *The guy who sold me this car really skinned me.* □ *We skinned him on that stock deal.*

skin game *n.* any swindle. (Underworld.) □ *Bruno was mixed up in a skin game for a while.* □ *The con running the skin game got out of town.*

skullduggery *n.* deceitful doings; dirty work. □ *It took a lot of skullduggery to bring it off, but that was no problem for*

Janice. □ *Without skullduggery, politics wouldn't be interesting.*

smoke *n.* exaggeration; deception. □ *That's not a report. That's just smoke.* □ *If the smoke is too obvious, they'll just get suspicious.*

smoke and mirrors *n.* a strategy of deception and cover-up. □ *Her entire report was nothing but smoke and mirrors. Who could believe any of it?* □ *There is no plan. It's all just smoke and mirrors.*

sneaky *mod.* unfair and sly. □ *That was a sneaky thing to do!* □ *Jerry is sneaky. Don't trust him.*

snookered *mod.* cheated; deceived. □ *I was snookered skillfully and quickly. It was almost a pleasure.* □ *I got snookered at the service station.*

snow 1. *n.* deceitful talk; deception. □ *No snow, okay? I want straight talk.* □ *All I heard for an hour was snow. Now, what's the truth?* **2.** *tr.* to attempt to deceive someone. □ *Don't try to snow me!* □ *You can try to snow me if you want, but I'm onto your tricks.*

snowed *mod.* deceived. □ *He was one snowed coach. He still doesn't know what really happened.* □ *We really had him snowed!*

snow job *n.* a systematic deception. □ *You can generally tell when a student is trying to do a snow job.* □ *This snow job you call an explanation just won't do.*

spin doctor *n.* someone who provides an interpretation of news or an event in a way that makes the news or event work to the advantage of the entity employing the *spin doctor.* (Usually in political contexts in reference to manipulating the news.) □ *Things were going bad for the president, so he got himself a new spin doctor.* □ *A good spin doctor could have made the incident far less damaging.*

stack the deck *tr.* to arrange things secretly for a desired outcome. (From card playing, where a cheater may arrange the order of the cards that are to be dealt to the players.) □ *The president stacked the deck so I would be appointed head of* the finance committee. □ It's not fair when somebody stacks the deck.

stiff *tr.* to cheat someone. □ *The clown selling hot dogs stiffed me for about forty cents.* □ *I really got stiffed on that deal. Look at this cheap junk.*

sting *tr.* to cheat or swindle someone; to overcharge someone. □ *That street merchant stung me, but good.* □ *They are likely to sting you in any of those hock-shops.*

sucker *tr.* to trick or victimize someone. □ *That crook suckered me. I should have known better.* □ *They suckered him into selling half interest in his land.*

take *tr.* to cheat or deceive someone. □ *That clerk tried to take me.* □ *When they think you're going to count your change, they won't try to take you.*

taken AND **had; took** *mod.* cheated; deceived. □ *I counted my change, and I knew I was taken.* □ *You were really took, all right.*

take someone in AND **rope someone in** *tr.* to cheat or deceive someone. □ *He might try to take you in. Keep an eye on him and count your change.* □ *The con artists tried to rope in the old lady, but she was too clever.*

trick on someone *in.* to deceive someone. □ *What are you doing? Are you tricking on me?* □ *Mary is always tricking on people and now nobody trusts her.*

two-time *tr.* to deceive one's lover. □ *Sam wouldn't two-time Martha. He just wouldn't!* □ *Sam would and did two-time Martha!*

vicked *mod.* cheated; victimized. □ *I feel so vicked when I see where my taxes are spent.* □ *I got vicked at the stereo repair shop.*

wall job *n.* a car—in the shop for repairs—which is parked against the wall with no repairs done. (The customer is charged anyway.) □ *Places like those we surveyed may charge hundreds of dollars for what they call "wall jobs."* □ *Okay, Lefty, the Caddy looks like another wall job. Throw some plastic over it, and we'll call the old girl and tell her it needs parts.*

yench *tr.* to swindle someone or something; to victimize someone or something. (Underworld.) □ *The flimflam artist yenched a couple of banks and then moved on.* □ *Somebody tried to yench the wrong guy at the circus.*

DECLINE
See also **REDUCTION**.

fade *in.* to lose power; to lose influence. □ *Ralph is fading, and someone else will have to take over.* □ *The positive effect of the weekend faded fast.*

fall out of bed *in.* to fall far down, as with the drop in some measurement. □ *The temperature really fell out of bed last night! It was twenty-three below!* □ *The stock market fell out of bed last year at this time.*

go downhill *in.* to decline. □ *This company is going downhill at a great rate.* □ *Things began to go downhill when the county cut the maintenance budget.*

hit the skids *tr.* to decline; to decrease in value or status. □ *Jed hit the skids when he started drinking.* □ *The firm hit the skids when the dollar collapsed.*

nosedive *n.* a great drop; a great decline. (As with a bird or an airplane diving—nose first—toward the ground.) □ *This year our profits have taken a nosedive.* □ *Confidence in the government took a sudden nosedive.*

on the skids *mod.* on the decline. □ *My newly started business is on the skids.* □ *Her health is really on the skids, but she stays cheery anyway.*

run out of gas *in.* to lose momentum or interest. □ *His program is running out of gas.* □ *I hope I don't run out of gas before I finish what I set out to do.*

soft-pedal something *tr.* to play something down; to de-emphasize something. (Refers to the soft pedal on the piano.) □ *Try to soft-pedal the problems we have with the cooling system.* □ *I won't soft-pedal anything. Everyone must know the truth.*

DEFEAT
See also **OVERWHELM**.

aced *mod.* outmaneuvered; outscored. □ *Rebecca really got aced in the track meet.* □ *"You are aced, sucker!" shouted Rebecca as she passed Martha in the 100-yard sprint.*

can't win (th)em all *phr.* (one should) expect to lose every now and then. □ *It doesn't really matter. You can't win them all.* □ *Well, I can't win 'em all.*

Close, but no cigar. *phr.* "Close, but not close enough to win a prize!" □ *You almost did it. Close, but no cigar.* □ *Close, but no cigar! Give it another try.*

creamed *mod.* badly beaten; outscored. □ *We were really creamed in that last game, and the coach is steamed.* □ *Midwest U. got creamed again today by the Podunk Badgers.*

done over *mod.* beaten; outscored. □ *The other team was done over, and they knew it.* □ *Bruno felt that Max would get the idea if he was done over a little.*

done to a turn *mod.* beaten. □ *When Wilbur's opponent was done to a turn, Wilbur was declared the winner.* □ *Max was done to a turn, and Bruno walked away.*

pasted *mod.* badly beaten; outscored. □ *Our team really got pasted.* □ *He sure looked pasted the last time I saw him.*

pasting *n.* a beating; a defeat in a game. □ *Our team took quite a pasting last weekend.* □ *I gave him a pasting.*

shafted *mod.* beaten; bested; cheated. □ *I really got shafted in that deal.* □ *I've been shafted!*

shellacked *mod.* badly beaten; outscored. □ *They were shellacked, and they knew it.* □ *The team got shellacked in last week's game.*

tanked *mod.* defeated; outscored. □ *The team was tanked again—20–17.* □ *I just knew we'd get tanked today.*

Win a few, lose a few. *phr.* "Sometimes one wins; other times one loses." □ *Too bad. Sorry about that. Win a few, lose a few.* □ *"Win a few, lose a few" doesn't mean you never win at all.*

zap *tr.* to defeat someone or a team. □ *They zapped us 10–8.* □ *Tracy zapped Fred in the spelling bee.*

DEFECATION
See also **EXCREMENT**.

caca AND **kaka** *in.* to defecate. (Juvenile. Use caution with the topic.) □ *Jimmy kakad in his diaper!* □ *It's time you learned to caca in the potty.*

cack *in.* to defecate. (Use caution with the topic.) □ *The dog cacked right there on Fifth Avenue.* □ *"Dogs can't cack here," hollered the police officer.*

crap *in.* to defecate. (Crude. Potentially offensive. Use only with discretion.) □ *Your dog crapped on my lawn!* □ *I have to crap; then I'll be right with you.*

doo-doo *in.* to defecate. (Juvenile.) □ *Jimmy was reminded that he had to remember to doo-doo in the potty.* □ *He has to doo-doo before he goes to bed, too.*

dump 1. *in.* to defecate. (Crude. Potentially offensive. Use only with discretion.) □ *He dumped and then came back.* □ *He said he had to dump.* **2.** *n.* an act of defecation. (Potentially offensive. Use only with discretion.) □ *He said he needed a dump.* □ *He had a dump and then came back.*

dump one's load *in.* to defecate. (Crude. Potentially offensive. Use only with discretion. Also with *a*.) □ *He had to go dump a load.* □ *He dumped his load and settled back down to work.*

george *n.* a bowel movement. (Euphemistic. Use caution with the topic.) □ *I gotta go take a george. Back in a minute.* □ *I'm okay. Nothing a good george wouldn't cure.*

jobber AND **jobby** *n.* a bowel movement. (Juvenile.) □ *Don't forget to jobber, Jimmy.* □ *Mommy, I gotta jobby.*

poo *in.* to defecate. (Use caution with the topic.) □ *That old dog pooed on our lawn.* □ *Don't let your dog poo here!*

poop *in.* to defecate. □ *Your dog pooped on my lawn.* □ *I tried to chase the cat away while it was pooping.*

DEFLATE

take the wind out of someone's sails *tr.* to put a barrier in someone's path; to reduce the effectiveness of someone. □ *When the cops showed Max the evidence, it took the wind out of his sails.* □ *It really took the wind out of his sails when he didn't get promoted.*

DELAY

bogart AND **bogard** *in.* to stall. □ *Stop bogarting. Let's get this done!* □ *The lawyer for the other side is bogarding, and it will take weeks to get it settled.*

buy time *tr.* to use a tactic to postpone something. □ *You are just doing this to buy time.* □ *Maybe I can buy some time by asking for a continuance.*

on the shelf *mod.* postponed. □ *We'll have to put this matter on the shelf for a while.* □ *I have a plan on the shelf just waiting for an opportunity like this.*

DELICIOUS

scrumptious *mod.* excellent; tasty. □ *That cake is just scrumptious, Mary. What's in it?* □ *Who makes the most scrumptious chocolate chip cookies in the world—besides me, that is?*

yummy *mod.* delicious. □ *This stuff is really yummy.* □ *Who made this yummy cake?*

DELIRIUM TREMENS

barrel fever *n.* the delirium tremens. □ *The old man is down with barrel fever again.* □ *The barrel fever hit him in the middle of the night.*

bats *n.* the delirium tremens. (Always with *the.*) □ *My buddy is shaking because of a slight case of the bats.* □ *The bats getting you down again, Jed?*

blue devils *n.* the delirium tremens. □ *You wouldn't think that a society dame like that would have the blue devils, would you?* □ *The shakes, or the blue devils, are a sure sign of a serious drinking problem.*

clanks *n.* the delirium tremens. □ *He's suffering with the clanks again.* □ *Who's the old buzzard shaking with the clanks?*

horrors *n.* the delirium tremens. □ *The old wino had the horrors all the time.* □ *He has a bad case of the horrors.*

jerks *n.* the delirium tremens. □ *The old guy has the jerks.* □ *What can they do for the jerks—other than hospitalize the victims?*

jitters *n.* the nervous shakes. (Always with *the.*) □ *I get the jitters when I have to talk in public.* □ *Too much booze gives me the jitters.*

ork-orks *n.* the delirium tremens. □ *He has the ork-orks. He's a real drunk.* □ *Whenever he gets the ork-orks, he gets himself arrested and put in jail where he can sober up.*

pink elephants AND **pink spiders 1.** *n.* the delirium tremens. □ *He's screaming with pink elephants again.* □ *He was shaking something awful from the pink spiders.* **2.** *n.* hallucinatory creatures seen during the delirium tremens. □ *He said pink elephants were trying to kill him. He's really drunk.* □ *If you ever find yourself surrounded with pink elephants, you've got the D.T.s.*

rats *n.* the delirium tremens. (Always with *the.*) □ *The way he was shaking, I knew he had the rats.* □ *Most of those old guys down on Fourth Street have the rats.*

shakes *n.* the delirium tremens. □ *I got the shakes again. That's what I get for putting soda water in my whisky.* □ *In the last stages, they have the shakes all the time.*

snozzle-wobbles *n.* the delirium tremens. □ *Freddy had the snozzle-wobbles this morning. He has no idea what caused it.* □ *They say that a big glass of milk is good for the snozzle-wobbles.*

staggers *n.* drunkenness; the delirium tremens. (Always with *the.*) □ *He seems to have a little touch of the staggers.* □ *Larry's laid up with the staggers again.*

zings *n.* the delirium tremens. □ *The old guy was suffering from the zings.* □ *What can they do for the zings?*

DEMONSTRATION

demo 1. *n.* a demonstration (of something). □ *Can I have a demo of this* model? □ *Hey, Chuck, give this man a demo.* **2.** *tr.* to demonstrate something (to someone). □ *Let me demo this for you so you can see how it works.* □ *Will someone please demo this computer?* **3.** *tr.* to demonstrate (something) to someone. □ *I've got to go demo these people on this software.* □ *Can you demo me before you go?*

dog and pony show *n.* a demonstration; a speech, skit, or other presentation that is presented often. □ *Wally was there with his dog and pony show about water safety.* □ *I've seen that dog and pony show so many times, it's like I know all the words.*

DEPART

ankle *in.* to walk away from one's employment; to leave. □ *One more day like this, and I'm gonna ankle.* □ *I didn't fire her. I told her she could ankle if she wanted.*

bail (out) *in.* to resign or leave; to get free of someone or something. □ *I can't take any more. I'm going to bail out.* □ *Albert bailed just before he got fired.*

Beam me up, Scotty! *sent.* "Get me out of here!"; "Take me away from this mess!" (From the television program *Star Trek*.) □ *This place is really crazy! Beam me up, Scotty!* □ *I've heard enough! Beam me up, Scotty!*

Beat it! *exclam.* "Get out!"; "Go away!" □ *You bother me. Beat it!* □ *Beat it! I've had it with you.*

be casper *n.* to be leaving; to be disappearing. (In the manner of Casper, the friendly ghost—a cartoon character.) □ *We'll be casper in just a minute.* □ *I'm casper. See you later.*

Bite the ice! *exclam.* "Go to hell!" □ *If that's what you think, you can just bite the ice!* □ *Get a life! Bite the ice!*

blow *tr. & in.* to leave (someplace) in a hurry. □ *It's late. I gotta blow.* □ *They blew this place before you got here.*

Blow it out your ear! *exclam.* "Go away!"; "I don't believe it!" □ *Oh, blow it out your ear, you cornball!* □ *You are*

not way rad, you're just way out, twit! *Blow it out your ear!*

blow town *tr.* to get out of town, probably in a hurry. (Underworld.) □ *He blew town yesterday.* □ *I gotta pack and blow town. The cops are on to me.*

bolt *in.* to leave; to go away. (Not necessarily fast.) □ *Time to go, man. Let's bolt.* □ *Time to bolt. Got to get home.*

bone out *in.* to leave. □ *It's time we boned out and got home.* □ *Ted and Bill boned out after midnight.*

boogie *in.* to leave. □ *Come on, man. Let's boogie.* □ *Time to boogie. It's late.*

book *in.* to leave. □ *Time's up. Gotta book.* □ *Let's book. I'm late.*

break out *in.* to leave. □ *It's late, man. Time to break out.* □ *We broke out a little after midnight.*

Bug off! *exclam.* "Get out!"; "Go away!" □ *Bug off! Get out of here!* □ *Bug off and leave me alone!*

bug out 1. *in.* to pack up and retreat. (Military.) □ *Orders are to bug out by oh-nine-hundred.* □ *Okay, everybody, move it! We're bugging out.* **2.** *in.* to get out of somewhere fast. □ *I gotta find a way to bug out of here without getting caught.* □ *Okay, it's clear. Let's bug out.*

bust a move *tr.* to leave (a place). □ *Let's go. Time to bust a move.* □ *Let's bust a move. Lots to do tomorrow.*

bust ass out of someplace *in.* to get out of someplace in a hurry. (Use with caution.) □ *I had to bust ass out of the house and run all the way to school.* □ *Wayne busted ass out of the classroom and headed for home.*

Butt out! *exclam.* "Get out of my affairs!"; "Mind your own business!" □ *Go away! Butt out!* □ *Butt out! I'm busy.*

buzz along *in.* to depart. □ *Well, I must buzz along.* □ *It's time to buzz along to work now.*

clear out *in.* to leave; to depart. □ *Time for you people to clear out. It's past midnight.* □ *The boss gave me till next week to clear out. I'm fired—canned.*

cruise *in.* to move on; to leave. □ *Listen, I gotta cruise.* □ *Time to cruise. Monty Python's on in ten minutes.*

cut out *in.* to leave; to run away. □ *It's late. I think I'll cut out.* □ *Don't cut out now. The night is young.*

do a fade *tr.* to leave; to sneak away. □ *Max did a fade when he saw the pigmobile.* □ *It's time for me to do a fade.*

dust *in.* to leave; to depart. □ *Well, it's late. I gotta dust.* □ *They dusted out of there at about midnight.*

fade *in.* to leave. □ *I think that the time has come for me to fade. See ya.* □ *Hey, man, let's fade.*

fall out *in.* to depart. (Probably from the military command meaning "disperse.") □ *It's late, G. I have to fall out.* □ *Let's fall out. I have to get up early in the morning.*

Get lost! *exclam.* "Go away!"; "Beat it!" □ *Get lost, you're bothering me!* □ *Quit following me. Get lost!*

get out of Dodge *in.* to leave a place. (Refers to Dodge City, Kansas, and a catchphrase from Western adventures about this town.) □ *Come on, G. Let's get out of Dodge.* □ *Things are looking bad here. It's time to get out of Dodge.*

Get out of town! *exclam.* "Beat it!"; "Get out of here!" □ *Go away, you bother me! Get out of town!* □ *You'd better get out of town, my friend. You are a pest.*

get (out) while the gettin(g)'s good AND **get (out) while the goin's good** *phr.* to leave while it is still safe or possible to do so. □ *I could tell that it was time for me to get while the gettin's good.* □ *I told her she should get out while the goin's good.*

Go chase yourself! AND **Go chase your tail!; Go climb a tree!; Go fly a kite!; Go fry an egg!; Go jump in the lake!; Go soak your head!; Go soak yourself!** *exclam.* "Beat it!"; "Go away!" □ *Oh, go chase yourself! Get out of my face!* □ *Go soak your head! You're a pain in the neck.*

hit the road *tr.* to leave; to begin to travel on a road. □ *We plan to hit the road about dawn.* □ *Let's hit the road. We have a long way to go.*

hit the trail *tr.* to leave. (As if one were riding a horse.) □ *I have to hit the trail before sunset.* □ *Let's hit the trail. It's late.*

I've got to fly. AND **I('ve) gotta fly.** *sent.* "I have to leave right now." □ *Time's up. I've got to fly.* □ *I've gotta fly. See you later.*

I've got to split. *sent.* "I have to leave now." □ *See you later. I've got to split.* □ *I've got to split. Call my service.*

jam *in.* to depart. □ *It's time to jam. Let's go.* □ *I gotta jam, Tom. See ya.*

jet *in.* to leave a place rapidly; to go somewhere fast. □ *I will jet to Tom's house and show him these pictures.* □ *Let's jet. It's late.*

Let's bump this place! *tr.* "Let's get out of this place!"; "Let's leave!" □ *Time to go. Let's bump this place!* □ *Let's bump this place! It's dead here.*

Let's dump. *interj.* "Let's go." □ *It's late. Let's dump.* □ *Let's dump. I've still got a lot to do at home tonight.*

make like a tree and leave *phr.* to leave; to depart. (A pun on the leaf of a tree.) □ *I have to leave now. It's time to make like a tree and leave.* □ *Hey, Jane. Don't you have an appointment somewhere? Why don't you make like a tree and leave?*

make oneself scarce *tr.* to leave; to be in a place less frequently. □ *Here come the boys in blue. I'd better make myself scarce.* □ *I suggest that you make yourself scarce before she returns.*

make tracks *tr.* to move out of a place fast. □ *I gotta make tracks home now.* □ *Let's make tracks. We gotta hit Adamsville before noon.*

motor *in.* to depart. □ *Well, let's motor, you guys. It's getting late.* □ *I've got to motor. It's a long walk home.*

On your bike! AND **Go to your room!** *imperative.* "Get out of here!"; "Get on your motorcycle and get out!" □ *What a bad joke! No puns allowed here! On your bike!* □ *That was a ridiculous remark. Go to your room!*

pop off *in.* to leave; to depart in haste. □ *Bye, I must pop off.* □ *Got to pop off. I'm late.*

push off AND **shove off** *in.* to leave. (As if one were pushing away from a dock.) □ *Well, it looks like it's time to push off.* □ *It's time to go. Let's shove off.*

roll *in.* to leave, perhaps in a car. □ *I can't wait around any longer. Let's roll.* □ *We have to roll now. It's late.*

scat *in.* to leave. □ *It's midnight. I gotta scat.* □ *You guys scat now. I have to go to work.*

shag (off) *in.* to depart. □ *I gotta shag. It's late.* □ *Go on! Shag off!* □ *I gotta shag. Somebody's calling my name.*

skedaddle *in.* to get out; to leave in a hurry. (Folksy.) □ *Go on, skedaddle! Out!* □ *Well, I'd better skedaddle on home.*

skip (out) *in.* to leave; to run away without doing something, such as paying a bill. □ *The guy skipped when I wasn't looking.* □ *Fred skipped out, leaving me with the bill.*

sko AND **sgo** *phr.* "Let's go." (Now considered current slang even though it has been informal colloquial for decades.) □ *Sko. We're going to be late.* □ *It's time to hit the road. Sgo.*

smack the road *tr.* to leave; to depart. □ *Time to smack the road! Sgo!* □ *Let's smack the road. I have to get up early.*

split *in.* to leave. □ *Look at the clock. Time to split.* □ *Let's split. We're late.*

take a hike AND **take a walk** *tr.* to leave; to beat it. □ *Okay, I've had it with you. Take a hike! Beat it!* □ *I had enough of the boss and the whole place, so I cleaned out my desk and took a walk.*

take a powder *tr.* to leave; to leave town. (Underworld.) □ *Why don't you take a powder? Go on! Beat it!* □ *Bruno took a powder and will lie low for a while.*

Take a running jump (in the lake)! *exclam.* "Go away!"; "Get away from me!" □ *You know what you can do? You can take a running jump. Beat it!* □ *You can just take a running jump in the lake, you creep!*

take it on the lam *tr.* to get out of town; to run away. (Underworld.) □ *Both took it on the lam when things got hot.* □ *Bruno knew that the time had come to take it on the lam.*

take off *in.* [for someone] to leave in a hurry. □ *She really took off outa there.* □ *I've got to take off—I'm late.*

tear off *in.* to break away; to run away. □ *I hate to tear off, but I'm late.* □ *Don't tear off without having some of my pie.*

time to cruise *n.* "Time to leave." □ *See ya. It's time to cruise.* □ *Time to cruise. We're gone.*

toddle off *in.* to depart; to walk away. □ *She said good-bye and toddled off.* □ *The old man toddled off somewhere and got lost.*

tootle along *in.* to depart. □ *I think I'd better tootle along now.* □ *Nice talking to you. Must tootle along.*

trip *in.* to leave. □ *I gotta trip, man.* □ *Time to trip. See ya.*

turn tail (and run) *tr.* to flee; to run away in fright. □ *I couldn't just turn tail and run, but I wasn't going to fight that monster either.* □ *Sometimes turning tail is the only sensible thing to do.*

up stakes *tr.* to prepare for leaving and then leave. (*Up* has the force of a verb here. The phrase suggests pulling up tent stakes in preparation for departure.) □ *They just upped stakes and left without saying good-bye.* □ *It's that time of the year when I feel like upping stakes and moving to the country.*

Vamoose! *exclam.* "Beat it!"; "Go away!" (From Spanish.) □ *Go on, beat it! Vamoose!* □ *Vamoose! Go home!*

zoom AND **zoom off** *in.* to depart; to leave in a hurry. □ *Time's up. I've gotta zoom.* □ *Oh, you don't have to zoom off, do you?*

DEPRESSION

blah *mod.* depressed; worn-out. □ *When I get into a blah mood like this, I just want to cry.* □ *I'm really blah. Would you mind awfully if I just went home?*

blahs *n.* a state of mental depression. (Always with *the.*) □ *I've had the blahs about as long as I can stand.* □ *You look like you've got the blahs.*

blue *mod.* depressed; melancholy. □ *That music always makes me blue.* □ *I'm feeling sort of blue.* □ *I'm in a blue mood.*

blue devils *n.* melancholia; depression. □ *Hank is down with the blue devils again.* □ *How do you get rid of the blue devils?*

blue funk *n.* a state of depression. □ *I'm glad I'm out of my blue funk.* □ *You've got to get out of your blue funk and get back to work.*

bring-down *n.* something that depresses someone. □ *The news was a terrible bring-down.* □ *Just to see your face was a bring-down.*

bring someone down *tr.* to depress someone. □ *The news really brought me down.* □ *The failure of the business brought down the staff.*

bumming *mod.* down; depressed; suffering from something disagreeable. (Collegiate.) □ *I'm really bumming. I think I need somebody to talk to.* □ *Everybody's bumming. It must be the weather.*

crying towel *n.* someone or something used to comfort someone. □ *I guess I really need a crying towel today.* □ *I'm the kind of person who has to carry a crying towel at all times.*

cry in one's beer *in.* to feel sorry for oneself. □ *She calls up, crying in her beer, and talks on and on about her problems.* □ *Don't cry in your beer. Get yourself straightened out.*

down *mod.* depressed; melancholy. □ *I feel sort of down today.* □ *We're all a little down.*

downer *n.* a depressing event; a bad situation. □ *These cloudy days are always downers.* □ *My birthday party was a downer.*

funk *n.* a depressed state. □ *I've been in such a funk that I can't get my work done.* □ *As soon as I get out of my winter funk, I'll be more helpful.*

in a blue funk *mod.* sad; depressed. □ *I've been in a blue funk all week.* □ *Don't be in a blue funk. Things'll get better.*

pits *n.* the depths of despair. (Always with *the.* Often with *in* as in the example.) □ *It's always the pits with him.* □ *She's depressed and in the pits.*

way down *mod.* very depressed. □ *Poor Clare is way down. I think she has something wrong with her.* □ *Pete sure looks way down.*

DESCRIPTION

thumbnail sketch *n.* a quick and concise description. (One that could be written on someone's thumbnail.) □ *Let me give you a thumbnail sketch of what happened.* □ *The story—in a thumbnail sketch—deals with a family of storks and what happens to them during each of the four seasons.*

DESIRE

(Don't) you wish! *exclam.* "I'm sure you wish it were true." □ *You think you'll win? Don't you wish!* □ *There's no school tomorrow? You wish!*

drool (all) over someone or something *tr.* to show enormous desire for someone or something. □ *He was just drooling all over that new car.* □ *Sam was drooling over Martha like a lovesick calf.*

forbidden fruit *n.* something that is attractive because it is denied to one. (From the Garden of Eden in the Bible.) □ *A new car became Ralph's forbidden fruit.* □ *Liquor was forbidden fruit for Jed.*

have an itch for something *tr.* to have a desire for something. (*Have got* can replace *have.*) □ *I have an itch for some ice cream.* □ *We had an itch for a good movie, so we went.*

hurt for someone or something *in.* to long after someone or something; to need someone or something. □ *Sam really hurts for Mary.* □ *I sure am hurting for a nice big steak.*

money from home *n.* something as welcome as long-awaited money from home. □ *This cool drink is money from home right now.* □ *Having you visit like* *this is like getting money from home, Tracy.*

queer for something *mod.* in the mood for something; desiring something. □ *I'm queer for a beer right now.* □ *She's queer for him because of his money.*

sucker for someone or something *n.* someone who is prejudiced in favor of someone or something. □ *I'm a sucker for a pretty face.* □ *Ted is a sucker for any dessert with whipped cream on it.*

to die for *mod.* important or desirable enough to die for; worth dying for. □ *This chocolate cake is to die for!* □ *We had a beautiful room at the hotel and the service was to die for.*

wanabe AND **wanna be** *n.* someone who wants to be something or someone. □ *All these teenyboppers are wanabes, and that's why we can sell this stuff to them at any price.* □ *A wanna be came by selling chances on a raffle.*

want list *n.* a list of things that someone wants. □ *Some of the things on her want list we can take care of easily.* □ *Send me your want list, and I'll see what we can do.*

DESTRUCTION

death on something *n.* causing the death or destruction of something. □ *This kind of road is just death on tires.* □ *This candy is death on my teeth.*

DETAILS

chapter and verse *mod.* in the finest detail. (From the "chapter and verse" organization of the Bible.) □ *He could recite the law concerning state-funded libraries, chapter and verse.* □ *She knew her rights, chapter and verse.*

ins and outs *n.* the fine points (of something); the details; the intricacies. □ *I'm learning the ins and outs of this business.* □ *My father taught me the ins and outs of hog calling.*

DETECTIVE

company bull *n.* a detective or guard who works for a private firm. □ *Pete is a company bull for Acme Systems. He works nights.* □ *The company bull asked what we were doing there.*

crapper dick *n.* a police officer or detective who patrols public toilets. □ *When he flubbed up the Wilson case, they made him a crapper dick in the central business district.* □ *What's a crapper dick get paid?*

dick *n.* a detective. (Underworld. From *detective.*) □ *Some dicks were around looking for you.* □ *Barlowe is a private dick who has to keep one step ahead of the cops.*

gumshoe *n.* a policeman or a detective. (Underworld. Also a term of address. So-named for wearing silent, gum-rubber soles.) □ *Has that gumshoe been around asking questions again?* □ *Look, gumshoe, what do you want with me?*

private eye *n.* a detective who is licensed to work privately rather than for a police department. □ *I worked for a while as a private eye.* □ *The cops don't like private eyes much.*

DIARRHEA

Aztec two-step *n.* diarrhea, specifically that contracted in Mexico or South America by tourists; *Montezuma's revenge.* □ *I was there for only two days before I was struck down with the Aztec two-step.* □ *I spent a week in Cancun and never even heard of anybody with Aztec two-step.*

back-door trot(s) *n.* a case of diarrhea. (From the time when people had to go out the back door to the outhouse.) □ *I can't go out tonight. I got a case of the back-door trots.* □ *She gets the back-door trot when she drinks wine.*

Basra belly *n.* diarrhea; a case of diarrhea. □ *The Basra belly hit me while I was on the bus.* □ *How do you tell Basra belly from Montezuma's revenge?*

Delhi belly *n.* diarrhea, as suffered by tourists in India. □ *I've got a touch of the Delhi belly and will have to miss the Taj Mahal.* □ *I've got something you can take for Delhi belly.*

Hong Kong dog *n.* diarrhea; a case of diarrhea. □ *Andy has a touch of the Hong Kong dog and needs some medicine.* □ *I* *got rid of the Hong Kong dog by meditating.*

Montezuma's revenge *n.* diarrhea; tourist diarrhea. (Refers to tourists in Mexico.) □ *I had a little touch of Montezuma's revenge the second day, but other than that we had a wonderful time.* □ *Most people blame Montezuma's revenge on the water.*

movies *n.* a case of diarrhea. □ *A case of the movies kept me going all night.* □ *I can't go too far from the little boys' room. I got the movies.*

run off *in.* to have diarrhea. □ *Jimmy has been running off since midnight.* □ *At least I'm not running off anymore.*

runs *n.* diarrhea. (Always with *the*.) □ *That stuff we ate gave me the runs.* □ *I can't believe those cute little hamburgers could give anybody the runs.*

scoots *n.* diarrhea. (Always with *the*.) □ *Our vacation was ruined by a case of the scoots.* □ *I've got just the thing for the scoots. Stay at home.*

squirts *n.* a case of diarrhea. (Always with *the*.) □ *He's got the squirts and can't go out.* □ *What do you take for the squirts?*

summer complaint *n.* diarrhea, especially that experienced in the summer. □ *I've got a touch of the summer complaint.* □ *Does summer heat cause the summer complaint?*

trots *n.* diarrhea; a case of diarrhea. (Always with *the*.) □ *I got the trots and can't go out tonight.* □ *There's a lot of the trots going around.*

turistas *n.* diarrhea; a case of diarrhea. (From Spanish.) □ *Nobody ever died of the turistas—right away, anyway.* □ *Turistas can be very unpleasant.*

DIETING

battle of the bulge *n.* the attempt to keep one's waistline normal. (Named for a World War II battle.) □ *She appears to have lost the battle of the bulge.* □ *I've been fighting the battle of the bulge ever since I had the baby.*

DIFFERENCE

diff *n.* difference. □ *Aw, come on! What's the diff?* □ *The diff is about twenty dollars' worth of repairs, that's what.*

different strokes for different folks *phr.* "different things please different people." (Catchphrase.) □ *Do whatever you like. Different strokes for different folks.* □ *Different strokes for different folks. That's what I always say.*

whole new ball game *n.* a completely different situation; something completely different. (Always with *a*.) □ *Now that you're here, it's a whole new ball game.* □ *With a faster computer, it's a whole new ball game.*

DIFFICULTIES

See also **BURDEN, PROBLEM.**

ball-breaker AND **ball-buster** *n.* a difficult task demanding hard work or effort. □ *This job is a real ball-breaker.* □ *The task I got assigned was a ball-buster, for sure.*

ball-busting *mod.* obnoxious and threatening. (Originally for males, now for either sex.) □ *Tell that ball-busting bitch to mind her own business.* □ *Wally is a ball-busting guy who is probably just very insecure.*

bear *n.* a difficult task. □ *This problem is a real bear.* □ *This is a bear of a job. I'll be glad when it's over.*

between a rock and a hard place *mod.* in a very difficult position; facing a hard decision. □ *You got him caught between a rock and a hard place, for sure.* □ *I'm between a rock and a hard place. I don't know what to do.*

bind *n.* a problem. □ *I've got a little bind here I didn't anticipate.* □ *Unfortunately, a new bind has slowed down the project.*

bitch *n.* a difficult thing or person. (Use with caution.) □ *Life's a bitch.* □ *This algebra problem is a real bitch.*

bitch of a thing *n.* a really difficult thing. (Potentially offensive. Use only with discretion.) □ *What a bitch of a day!* □ *This is a bitch of a job.*

can of worms *n.* an intertwined set of problems; an array of difficulties. (Often with *open*.) □ *This whole business is a real can of worms.* □ *When you brought that up, you opened a whole new can of worms.*

devil of a time *n.* a very difficult time. (Always with *a*.) □ *I had a devil of a time with my taxes.* □ *This cold has been giving me a devil of a time.*

devil's own time *n.* a very difficult time; a hellish time. (Always with *the*.) □ *I had the devil's own time with these tax forms.* □ *My gout is giving me the devil's own time.*

facts of life *n.* the truth about life's difficulties. □ *You had better face up to the facts of life and get a job.* □ *They taught me everything in college except the facts of life.*

handful *n.* a difficult thing or person. □ *Little Jimmy is a handful.* □ *His dad can be a handful, too.*

hard time *n.* a difficult experience. □ *I had a hard time at the doctor's office.* □ *She's having a hard time with her child.*

have one's ass in a crack *tr.* to be stranded in a very difficult or uncomfortable state of affairs. (Potentially offensive. Use only with discretion. *Have got* can replace *have*.) □ *He's got his ass in a crack and needs all the help he can get.* □ *Now he's really got his ass in a crack and doesn't know what to do.*

headache department *n.* a central source of unnecessary problems; a person who habitually causes problems. □ *Here's another memo from the headache department.* □ *Mrs. Wilson is my least favorite headache department.*

hell of a mess *n.* a terrible mess. □ *This is really a hell of a mess you've gotten us into.* □ *I never dreamed I'd come back to such a hell of a mess.*

hot potato *n.* a difficult problem. □ *I sure don't want to have to deal with that hot potato.* □ *This one is a hot potato. Ignore it for a while.*

in a jam *mod.* in a difficult situation. □ *I think I'm sort of in a jam.* □ *Sam is in a jam.*

make it hot for someone *tr.* to make things difficult for someone; to put someone under pressure. (Note the variation in the examples.) □ *The cops were making it hot for him, so he blew town.* □ *The boss is making it a little hot for me, so I had better get to work on time.*

make waves *tr.* to cause difficulty. (Often in the negative.) □ *Just relax. Don't make waves.* □ *If you make waves too much around here, you won't last long.*

play hell with someone or something AND **play the devil with someone or something** *tr.* to cause difficulty for someone or something. □ *You know that this cake is going to play hell with my diet.* □ *Your decision plays hell with all my friends.*

put to it *mod.* in trouble or difficulty; hard up (for something such as money). (As if one's back were put to the wall.) □ *Sorry, I can't lend you anything. I'm a bit put to it this month.* □ *What a day. I'm really put to it.*

rough time *n.* a hard time; a bad time. □ *I didn't mean to give you such a rough time. I'm sorry.* □ *What a rough time we had getting the car started!*

shoot oneself in the foot *tr.* to cause oneself difficulty; to be the author of one's own doom. □ *I am a master at shooting myself in the foot.* □ *Again, he shot himself in the foot with his open and honest dealings with the press.*

snag *n.* a difficulty. □ *There's a little snag in our plan.* □ *We ran into a little snag, I'm sorry to say.*

stinker *n.* a serious problem. □ *This whole business is a real stinker.* □ *What a stinker of a problem.*

tale of woe *n.* a sad story; a list of personal problems; an excuse for failing to do something. □ *I listened to her tale of woe without saying anything.* □ *This tale of woe that we have all been getting from Kelly is just too much.*

tight spot *n.* a difficulty. □ *I'm in sort of a tight spot and wonder if you can help me out.* □ *Sure, I like helping people out of tight spots as long as it doesn't cost me any money.*

tough row to hoe *n.* a difficult task to carry out; a heavy set of burdens. □ *It's a tough row to hoe, but hoe it you will.* □ *This is not an easy task. This is a tough row to hoe.*

up the creek (without a paddle) AND **up a creek** *mod.* in an awkward position with no easy way out. (This creek is called "shit creek.") □ *I'm sort of up the creek and don't know what to do.* □ *You are up a creek! You got yourself into it, so get yourself out.*

wart *n.* a problem or an obstruction in a plan. □ *Okay, now we come to the wart. We don't have the money to carry out this plan.* □ *It's okay except for a little wart.*

wrinkle *n.* a minor problem. □ *A wrinkle has developed in the Wilson proposal.* □ *What are we going to do about this wrinkle in the computer system?*

DIGRESSION

riff *n.* a digression while speaking. □ *Excuse the little riff, but I had to mention it.* □ *If she didn't make so many riffs while she spoke, we could understand her better.*

DIRECTION

hang a huey *tr.* to make a U-turn. □ *Hang a huey at the next corner.* □ *Right here! Hang a huey!*

hang a left *tr.* to turn left. □ *He hung a left at the wrong corner.* □ *Hey, here! Hang a left here!*

hang a louie *tr.* to turn left. □ *You have to hang a louie at the stop sign.* □ *Go another block and hang a louie.*

hang a ralph *tr.* to turn right. □ *He skied down the easy slope and hung a ralph near a fir tree.* □ *Don't hang a ralph until you get past the traffic light.*

hang a right *tr.* to turn right. □ *Hang a right about here.* □ *I told him to hang a right at the next corner, but he went on.*

DISABLED

gimp *n.* a disabled person. (Originally underworld. Otherwise derogatory.) □ *Lefty tried to mug an old gimp with a cane.* □ *The gimp came hobbling along, muttering something under his breath.*

gimpy *mod.* crippled; lame. □ *I got a gimpy leg. I'll catch up in a minute.* □ *He's sort of gimpy since the football season.*

peg-leg *n.* a rude nickname for someone with a wooden peg for a leg. (Now used primarily in reference to theatrical pirates.) □ *See that peg-leg over there? He lost his foot to a shark.* □ *Hey, peg-leg. Race you to the bar!*

DISAGREEMENT

beef *n.* a complaint; a quarrel. □ *I gotta beef against you.* □ *Okay, what's the beef?*

blow-off *n.* a dispute; an argument. □ *After a blow-off like that, we need a breather.* □ *There was a big blow-off at the plant today.*

falling-out *n.* a disagreement. □ *Tom and Bill had a little falling-out.* □ *They patched up their little falling-out.*

I don't know. *sent.* "I disagree." □ *I don't know. I like it. What's wrong with it?* □ *I don't know. It looks good to me.*

on the outs (with someone) *mod.* in a mild dispute with someone; sharing ill will with someone. □ *Tom and Bill are on the outs again.* □ *Tom has been on the outs with Bill before. They'll work it out.*

slugfest *n.* a festival of arguing. □ *The slugfest went on until both sides were willing to compromise.* □ *The president emerged from the slugfest with control of the company still hers.*

DISAPPOINTMENT

burned *mod.* disappointed; humiliated; put down. □ *Whenever we rap, you're never happy till I'm burned.* □ *Ha! You're burned!*

comedown *n.* a letdown; a disappointment. □ *The loss of the race was a real comedown for Willard.* □ *It's hard to face a comedown like that.*

kick in the guts *n.* a severe blow to one's body or spirit. □ *The news was a kick in the guts, and I haven't recovered yet.* □ *I didn't need a kick in the guts like that.*

DISAPPROVAL

hoot *in.* to boo at someone's performance. □ *The audience hooted until the performer fled the stage in disgrace.* □ *They hooted for a few minutes after she left the stage.*

thumbs down 1. *n.* a sign of disapproval. □ *The board gave our proposal a thumbs down.* □ *Not another thumbs down!* **2.** *mod.* disapproving; negative. □ *It was thumbs down, and I was disappointed.* □ *The thumbs down decision was a victory for good sense.*

DISCARD

86 *tr.* to dispose of someone or something; to *nix* someone or something. □ *Please take this out and 86 it.* □ *He wants $400? 86 that! We can't afford it.*

chuck *tr.* to throw something away. □ *Chuck this thing. It's no good.* □ *The wrinkle-rod was so twisted we had to chuck it.*

deep-six *tr.* to jettison something, including a corpse, from a ship at sea. □ *The captain had them deep-six the garbage.* □ *They deep-sixed the body of the first mate, who had died of the shakes.*

scarf *tr.* to discard something. □ *Scarf that thing. It's no good.* □ *Bill scarfed his girl. She was seeing somebody else at the same time.*

shitcan *tr.* to throw something in the garbage can. □ *Shitcan this thing, will you?* □ *Who shitcanned my dirty socks?*

toss *tr.* to throw something away. □ *Toss it. It's no good.* □ *I'll toss this one. It's all scratched.*

DISCOURAGEMENT

bummed (out) *mod.* discouraged; depressed. □ *I feel so bummed. I think I need a nice hot bath.* □ *When you're feeling bummed out, think how many problems I have.*

bummer *n.* a disagreeable thing or person. □ *My coach is a real bummer.* □ *The game was a bummer you wouldn't believe.*

bum someone out *tr.* to discourage someone. □ *That darn blow-out bummed me out.* □ *The failure of his tires bummed out the race driver.*

rain on someone's parade AND **rain on someone or something** *in.* to spoil something for someone. □ *I hate to rain on your parade, but your plans are all wrong.* □ *She really rained on our parade.*

DISCOVERY

hit on something *in.* to discover something. □ *She hit on a new scheme for removing the impurities from drinking water.* □ *I hit on it when I wasn't able to sleep one night.*

hit the jackpot *tr.* to find exactly what was sought. □ *I hit the jackpot when I found this little cafe on Fourth Street.* □ *I wanted a small house with a fireplace, and I really hit the jackpot with this one.*

DISGUSTING

Barf City *n.* someone or something disgusting or undesirable. (*Barf* = vomit.) □ *The guy is gross! Just plain Barf City!* □ *The movie was really bad; Barf City, I'd say.*

Barf out! *exclam.* "This is awful!" (California.) □ *Look at that scrungy wimp! Barf out!* □ *Barf out! Get a life!*

barf someone out *tr.* to disgust someone. (California.) □ *This whole scene like, so, like, barfs me out.* □ *The movie barfed out everybody in the theatre.*

cruddy AND **crudy; cruddie** *mod.* nasty; awful. □ *What is this cruddy stuff on my plate?* □ *It's just chocolate mousse, and it's not cruddie.*

gee *mod.* "gross"; disgusting. (The initial letter of *gross.*) □ *This is just too gee!* □ *Tiffany is acting way gee lately.*

Geesh! *exclam.* "Good grief!" (Shows shock and disgust.) □ *What a mess! Geesh!* □ *Geesh! I love my work but hate my job!*

greldge *exclam.* "Nuts!"; "Darn!" (Usually **Greldge!**) □ *Oh, greldge! I'm late!* □ *This is the last straw! Greldge!*

grody to the max *mod.* totally disgusting. (California. From *grotesque*.) □ *Oo, this is grody to the max!* □ *This pizza is, like, grody to the max!*

gross *mod.* crude; vulgar; disgusting. (Slang only when overused.) □ *This food is gross!* □ *What a gross thing to even suggest.*

gross-out 1. *n.* something disgusting. □ *This whole day has been a total gross-out.* □ *That horror movie was a real gross-out.* **2.** *mod.* disgusting. □ *What a gross-out day this has been!* □ *Well, it looks like another gross-out movie.*

gross someone out *tr.* to disgust someone. □ *Those horrible pictures just gross me out.* □ *Jim's story totally grossed out Sally.*

grungy *mod.* dirty and smelly. □ *Get your grungy feet off the table!* □ *My feet are not grungy!* □ *What is this grungy stuff on the closet floor?*

gucky *mod.* thick and sticky. □ *This is a gucky day. Look at the sky.* □ *Yes, it is gucky.* □ *There is a lot of gucky oil and grease on the garage floor.*

Hairball! *exclam.* "How awful!" (An exclamation of disgust. From the name of the undigested mass of fur vomited by a cat.) □ *Hairball! I did it wrong again!* □ *Oh, I hate that dork! Hairball!*

holy stink *n.* anything repellent. □ *You really created a holy stink with that silly remark.* □ *What is this holy stink about broken windows?*

ick *exclam.* "Nasty!" (Usually **Ick!**) □ *Oh, ick! What now?* □ *Ick! I'm late!*

icky *mod.* distasteful; nasty. □ *What is this icky old stuff?* □ *This is icky.* □ *This was an icky day.*

icky-poo *mod.* disgusting. □ *I don't like all this icky-poo talk.* □ *What is that icky-poo stuff in the soup bowl?*

mungy *mod.* gloppy; messy. □ *Get that mungy stuff off my plate!* □ *The spaghetti was cold and mungy by the time it was served.*

obno(c) AND **obnox** *mod.* obnoxious; disgusting. □ *I wish you weren't so obnoc all the time!* □ *Beavis is totally obno, and he loves being that way.*

phooey AND **fooey** *exclam.* an expression of disgust, disagreement, or resignation. (Usually **Phooey!** or **Fooey!** Used typically when something smells or tastes bad.) □ *Who died in here? Phooey!* □ *This is the worst food I ever ate. Fooey!*

pukey AND **pukoid** *mod.* disgusting; repellent. □ *Who is that pukey-looking guy?* □ *Gosh, it's pukoid!* □ *What a pukey day!*

Rats! *exclam.* "Oh, damn!" □ *Rats! I broke a nail!* □ *Oh, rats! I'm late.*

raunch someone out *tr.* to disgust someone. □ *These dirty socks absolutely raunch me out!* □ *Wayne and Beavis enjoy raunching people out.*

rotten *mod.* smelly; disgusting. (Not slang.) □ *What is that rotten smell?* □ *Something rotten is under that board.*

scrungy *mod.* filthy. □ *This place is too scrungy for me. I'm outa here.* □ *What a scrungy guy. Put him somewhere to soak for a day or two.*

scurvy *mod.* repulsive. (Collegiate.) □ *Who is that scurvy guy who just came in?* □ *That class is scurvy. You'll wish you hadn't taken it.*

scuzz someone out *tr.* to nauseate someone. □ *He had this unreal face that almost scuzzed me out!* □ *It's not nice to scuzz out people like that, especially when you hardly know them.*

scuzzy *mod.* repellent; unkempt. □ *His clothes are always so scuzzy. He probably keeps them in a pile in his room.* □ *Whose scuzzy car is that in the driveway?*

Sheesh! *exclam.* "Damn!"; "Shit!" (Euphemistic for *Shit!*) □ *Sheesh! What a mess!* □ *Sheesh! I'm getting out of here!*

shit *exclam.* a general expression of disgust. (Usually *Shit!* Potentially offensive. Use only with discretion.) □ *Oh, shit! What a mess!* □ *Shit! That's terrible.*

sick to death (of someone or something) *mod.* totally disgusted with someone or something. □ *I am sick to death of your constant bickering.* □ *This whole bribery business just has me sick to death.*

skeevy *mod.* sleazy and disgusting. □ *This is a skeevy joint. Let's get out.* □ *Your coat looks so skeevy. Is it old?*

skrungy *mod.* disgusting. □ *What is this skrungy stuff they are serving here?* □ *That movie was too skrungy for me.*

So gross! *exclam.* "How disgusting!" (California.) □ *He put chocolate syrup on his pie! So gross!* □ *He's barfing! So gross!*

stink *in.* to be repellent. □ *This whole setup stinks.* □ *Your act stinks. Try another agent.*

turn up one's nose at someone or something *tr.* to show disdain or disgust at someone or something. □ *This is good, wholesome food. Don't turn your nose up at it.* □ *She turned up her nose at Max, which was probably a good idea.*

vomity *mod.* nasty. (Crude.) □ *What is this vomity stuff on my plate?* □ *Is that what you call vomity?* □ *That is a really vomity idea!*

Yec(c)h! *exclam.* "Horrible!"; "It's yucky!" □ *Oh, yech! What's that stuff?* □ *Yecch! It's moving!*

Yuck! *exclam.* "Horrible!" □ *Oh, yuck! Get that horrible thing out of here!* □ *Yuck! It looks alive!*

DISHONESTY

bent *mod.* dishonest; crooked. □ *I'm afraid that Paul is a little bent. He cheats on his taxes.* □ *A lot of those officeholders get bent while in office—if they weren't before.*

dirty deal *n.* an unfair deal. □ *That was a dirty deal. I feel cheated.* □ *I got a dirty deal at that shop, and I won't go back.*

fly-by-night *mod.* undependable; dishonest. □ *Bruno seems like such a fly-by-night character.* □ *He's not fly-by-night at all.* □ *Don't do business with fly-by-night people.*

monkey business AND **funny business** *n.* silliness; dishonest tricks. □ *That's enough monkey business. Now, settle down.* □ *Stop the funny business. This is serious!*

DISHWASHING

bust (some) suds *tr.* to wash dishes. □ *I don't want to spend the rest of my life busting suds.* □ *You get into that kitchen and bust some suds to pay for your meal!*

DISINTEREST

blow cold *in.* [for a person] to display disinterest. □ *Lately, he's sort of blown cold when I'm around.* □ *The committee blew cold as my plan unfolded.*

DISLIKE

butt *n.* someone or something that is disliked. (Potentially offensive. Use only with discretion.) □ *The guy's a real butt. A real squid.* □ *I wish you didn't act like such a butt all the time.*

dirty look *n.* a frown meant to show displeasure with something that has been said or done. □ *I gave him a dirty look, and he took his arm off my shoulder.* □ *What is that dirty look supposed to mean?*

spam *n.* something disliked, typically, but not necessarily, food. (From the brand name of a canned meat product.) □ *I can't eat this spam. It could be spoiled.* □ *This book is spam! I refuse to read it.*

vote with one's feet *in.* to show one's displeasure by walking out. □ *A lot of people are voting with their feet. Customers clearly don't like our goods.* □ *When the audience votes with its feet, you know you don't have a hit.*

DISMISSAL

bench *tr.* to retire someone; to withdraw someone from something. □ *I worked as a bridge painter for twenty-five years until they benched me.* □ *The manager benched the entire sales staff for cheating on their expense reports.*

brushoff *n.* a dismissal; an act of ignoring someone. □ *No brushoff for her. She just keeps hanging around.* □ *I got the brushoff, but I can take it.*

can *tr.* to dismiss someone from employment. □ *The jerk canned everybody who played a part in the gag.* □ *I'll can anybody who tries a stunt like that again.*

gate *n.* sending (someone) away. (Always with *the.*) □ *I could see in his eyes that it was the gate for me.* □ *I got the gate, but I was going to leave anyway.*

get the sack AND **get the ax** *tr.* to be dismissed from one's employment. □ *Poor Tom got the sack today. He's always late.* □ *I was afraid that Sally was going to get the ax.*

give someone the ax *tr.* to dismiss someone from employment. □ *They had to give Paul the ax because he was so unproductive.* □ *I was afraid they would give me the ax.*

kiss off *n.* the dismissal of someone or something. (Usually **kiss-off.**) □ *The kiss-off was when I lost the Wilson contract.* □ *Pete got the kiss off and is now looking for a new job.*

pink slip 1. *n.* a piece of paper giving notice of dismissal from employment; any dismissal from employment. □ *I got a pink slip today. I guess I had it coming.* □ *I hope I don't get a pink slip. I need this job.* 2. *tr.* to dismiss someone from employment. □ *They pink slipped the whole office force today.* □ *If your work doesn't improve, I will be forced to pink slip you.*

pink-slipped *mod.* fired; dismissed from employment. □ *I guess I've done it. I'm pink-slipped.* □ *Now I'm a member of the young and pink-slipped crowd.*

rif 1. *tr.* to dismiss an employee. (From the euphemistic *reduction in force.*) □ *They're going to rif John tomorrow.* □ *Who'll they rif next?* 2. *n.* a firing; a dismissal. □ *Who got the rif today?* □ *There's a rif in your future.*

riffed AND **rift** *mod.* fired; released from employment. (From *RIF, reduction in force.*) □ *Poor Walter got riffed Friday.* □ *Most of the sales force was riffed last week.*

sack 1. *tr.* to dismiss someone from employment; to fire someone. □ *The boss sacked the whole office staff last week.* □ *If I do that again, they'll sack me.* 2. *n.* a dismissal. (Always with *the.*) □ *The boss gave them all the sack.* □ *The sack is what I am afraid of.*

walking papers *n.* a notice of being fired, released, divorced, etc. □ *I hope I don't get my walking papers today. I need this job.* □ *Well, I got my walking papers today.*

DISPLAY

flash *tr.* to display something briefly. □ *You'd better not flash a wad like that around here. You won't have it long.* □ *The cop flashed her badge and made the pinch.*

grandstand *in.* to make oneself conspicuous. □ *Stop grandstanding, Sally. Everyone can see you.* □ *Don't you just hate the way that Pat grandstands all the time?*

Hollywood *n.* a gaudily dressed person in sunglasses. (Also a term of address.) □ *Hey, Hollywood! What's cooking?* □ *Ask Hollywood over there to take off his shades and make himself known.*

hotdog *in.* to show off. □ *The coach said, "Stop hotdogging and play ball, you guys."* □ *It's just like Wayne to hotdog when he should be paying attention to the game.*

one-man show *n.* an exhibition of the artistic works of one person. □ *She is having a one-man show at the Northside Gallery.* □ *I'm having a one-man show next weekend. Come and see what I have done.*

(pro)file *in.* to walk about and show something off; to walk carefully in a way that gets attention. (As if showing one's profile.) □ *Look at Albert profiling along! What a nerd.* □ *All those guys are filing and styling like they were a bunch of peacocks.*

signify *in.* to try to look more important than one really is; to brag; to strut one's stuff. (Black.) □ *See that dude signify like somebody important?* □ *First you gotta learn to signify.*

strut one's stuff *tr.* to walk proudly and show off one's best features or talents. □ *Get out there on that stage and strut your* stuff! □ *I'm going to strut my stuff and become a star.*

DISPOSAL
See DISCARD.

DIVORCE

give someone the ax *tr.* to divorce someone. □ *Mary gave Fred the ax after only six months.* □ *She gave him the ax because he wouldn't stop smoking like he promised.*

great divide *n.* a divorce. □ *How did Sam survive the great divide?* □ *The great divide cost over two grand.*

DOCTOR

bolus *n.* a physician. (From the Latin name for a pill.) □ *The bolus kept trying to get me to lose weight.* □ *There is a new bolus in town.*

bones *n.* a ship's physician. (From *sawbones.* Also the nickname of the doctor on the starship *Enterprise* of *Star Trek* fame.) □ *This fat bones actually wanted me to lose weight.* □ *This is quite a cut. You'll have to go over to the bones in Adamsville.*

butch *n.* a physician. (Derogatory. From *butcher.*) □ *The butch at the infirmary was no help at all.* □ *What does it take to be a butch besides an office and a degree?*

butcher *n.* a surgeon; a physician. (Usually derogatory, possibly jocular.) □ *I won't go back to that butcher for anything at all.* □ *He's been a butcher for seven years and pays 80 percent of his income for insurance.*

castor oil artist *n.* a medical doctor. □ *This two-bit castor oil artist tried to get me to lose weight.* □ *Check with your personal castor oil artist to see if you should be taking this medication.*

couch-doctor AND **couch-turkey** *n.* a psychiatrist; a psychoanalyst. □ *Some couch-doctor told her to go out and find a lover.* □ *I finally walked out on my couch-turkey. Now I'm getting it all together.*

dome-doctor *n.* a psychologist or psychiatrist. □ *They sent me to a dome-doc-*

tor, but it didn't help. □ *The dome-doctor lets me talk while he keeps score.*

guru *n.* a psychiatrist; a psychotherapist. □ *I go to this guru who gets a lot of money just to listen.* □ *I've started using my mirror for a guru. It's cheaper.*

gynie *n.* a gynecologist. □ *My gynie says I'm fine.* □ *She went to a new gynie last week.*

horse doctor *n.* a doctor. (Derogatory. Originally referred to a veterinarian.) □ *That horse doctor says there's nothing wrong with me.* □ *My horse doctor says everything is wrong with me.*

medico *n.* a doctor. (From Spanish.) □ *The medico says I should lose some weight.* □ *It's hard to take it seriously when a fat medico tells you to shed a few pounds.*

nutpick *n.* a psychoanalyst. □ *Bill pays a nutpick about $100 an hour just to listen.* □ *What do you have to know to be a nutpick?*

pill-pusher AND **pill-roller; pill-peddler** *n.* a nickname for a physician. □ *That pill-peddler charges too much.* □ *I went to the infirmary, but the pill-pusher wasn't in.*

quack *n.* a fraudulent physician; a derogatory term for a physician. □ *I won't go back to that quack ever again!* □ *Tell that quack to heal himself!*

sawbones *n.* a doctor. (Folksy. Referring to someone who amputates limbs.) □ *Call the sawbones. This is an emergency.* □ *Is there a sawbones in this town?*

shrink *n.* a psychoanalyst or psychotherapist. □ *I dropped a bundle on a shrink, but it didn't help me.* □ *The shrink says I have to take these pills to help me get off the drug habit.*

zit doctor *n.* a dermatologist. □ *The zit doctor I went to was a crater face!* □ *My zit doctor wears rubber gloves and has for years.*

DOG

bow-wow *n.* a dog. (Juvenile.) □ *The bow-wow frightened me.* □ *We're going to get you a bow-wow!*

Heinz 57 (variety) *n.* a mongrel breed of dog. (From the trade name of a condiment company.) □ *We have one pedigreed dog and one Heinz 57 variety.* □ *My Heinz 57 is the greatest dog of all.*

pooch *n.* a dog. (Also a term of address to a friendly dog.) □ *Hello, pooch. My goodness, you're friendly.* □ *Please take your pooch out of my garden.*

pot hound AND **pot sniffer** *n.* a dog trained to sniff out cannabis. □ *The pot hound at the airport is always busy finding marijuana.* □ *How do they train pot sniffers to find cannabis?*

DOMINANCE

See also **CONTROL**.

in the catbird seat *mod.* in a dominant or controlling position. □ *Sally's in the catbird seat—telling everybody where to go.* □ *I hold all the aces. I'm in the catbird seat.*

in the driver's seat *mod.* in control. □ *She's just not comfortable unless she's in the driver's seat.* □ *I'm in the driver's seat now, and I get to decide who gets raises.*

kick some ass (around) *tr.* to take over and start giving orders; to raise hell. (Potentially offensive. Use only with discretion.) □ *Do I have to come over there and kick some ass around?* □ *Bruno is just the one to kick some ass over there.*

throw one's weight around *tr.* to show off one's importance or power; to use one's rank or station to advantage. □ *The vice president was throwing his weight around, but that had little effect on anything.* □ *Don't pay any attention to her. She's just throwing her weight around.*

under someone's thumb *mod.* under someone's control. □ *You can't keep your kids under your thumb all their lives.* □ *I don't want all this under my thumb. I have to delegate a lot of it.*

wear the pants (in the house) *tr.* to be the boss in the house; to run a household. □ *All right, if you have to wear the pants, have it your way.* □ *Well, somebody has to wear the pants.*

world is one's oyster *phr.* one rules the world; one is in charge of everything. (Always with *the*.) □ *I feel like the world is my oyster today.* □ *The world is my oyster! I'm in love!*

DRAWBACK

catch *n.* a drawback. □ *Okay, that sounds good, but what's the catch?* □ *There's no catch. It's all on the up and up.*

stinger *n.* the drawback; the catch; the hitch. □ *Now, here's the stinger.* □ *Sounds good, but what's the stinger?*

What's the catch? *interrog.* "What is the drawback?"; "It sounds good. Are there any hidden problems?" □ *Sounds too good to be true. What's the catch?* □ *This looks like a good deal. What's the catch?*

DRINKING

beer *in.* to drink beer. □ *Fred and Tom sat in there watching the game and beering and belching like two old whales.* □ *Let's just sit here and beer for a while.*

bong *tr. & in.* to drink keg beer through a hose. □ *Everybody bonged till the keg was empty.* □ *There were no cups, so people had to bong their beer.*

bottom *tr.* to drink something to the bottom. □ *He bottomed the beer and ordered another one.* □ *Come on. Bottom that beer, and let's get out of here.*

bust (some) suds *tr.* to drink some beer. □ *Let's go out and bust some suds.* □ *I'm tired of busting suds. Let's play cards.*

crack a tube *tr.* to open a can of beer. □ *Why don't you drop over this evening, and we'll crack a few tubes?* □ *Would you crack a tube for me? My hands are too cold.*

crack open a bottle *tr.* to open a bottle of liquor. (Also with *the*.) □ *Let's crack open a bottle and celebrate.* □ *He cracked the bottle open and poured a little for everyone to try.*

crack some suds *tr.* to drink some beer. □ *Let's go out tonight and crack some suds.* □ *The guys wanted to watch the game and crack some suds.*

cut the dust *tr.* to take a drink of liquor. □ *I think I'll stop in here and cut the dust.*

□ *I want to cut the dust. Can I have a snort?*

fall off the wagon *in.* to resume continuous alcoholic drinking after having stopped. □ *Poor Jed fell off the wagon again.* □ *It looks to me like he wanted nothing more than to fall off the wagon.*

gargle *in.* to drink liquor. □ *They sat and gargled for an hour or two.* □ *Let's go out and gargle for a while.*

gusto *in.* to drink beer. □ *Don't you ever do anything but gusto?* □ *Let's go out and gusto all night!*

hang a few on *tr.* to take a few drinks; to have a few beers. □ *They went out to hang a few on.* □ *Let's hang on a few and then go on to the meeting.*

happy hour *n.* cocktail time. □ *Happy hour starts at dawn for Harry.* □ *The hotel had a nice happy hour at five.*

hold one's liquor *tr.* to be able to drink alcohol in quantity without ill effects. □ *Old Jed can sure hold his liquor—and a lot of it, too.* □ *I asked him to leave because he can't hold his liquor.*

juice something back *tr.* to drink alcohol. □ *He's been juicing it back since noon.* □ *Juice back your drink, and let's go.*

Mickey (Finn) *n.* a drink containing chloral hydrate; a drink containing a fast-acting laxative. □ *He slipped her a Mickey Finn, but she switched glasses.* □ *Once you've had a Mickey, you'll never forget it.*

pot *n.* a drinking vessel. (Old but still heard.) □ *How about a pot of beer?* □ *Care for another pot?*

rocks *n.* ice cubes. □ *No rocks, please. I like my drink warm.* □ *Can I have a few rocks in my drink, please?*

scupper up *in.* to drink liquor, especially beer. □ *Tom goes home to scupper up every evening.* □ *Come on, you guys. Scupper up, and let's get outa here.*

sixer *n.* a six-pack beverage container. (Usually refers to beer.) □ *Tom showed up with three sixers and a bushel of pretzels, and we all watched the game together.*

□ *Please stop by the store and pick up a sixer.*

slam *tr.* to drink something quickly. □ *Max slammed a couple of beers and left.* □ *Don't slam your coffee. You'll burn yourself.*

slip someone a Mickey *tr.* to secretly put a *Mickey Finn* in someone's alcoholic drink. (This drug either makes the victim ill or causes immediate diarrhea.) □ *Somebody slipped Barlowe a Mickey and sent him into action.* □ *For a ten-spot, the bartender slipped Rocko a Mickey.*

suck AND **suck something up** *tr.* to drink beer or liquor. □ *Yeah, I'll suck one up with ya.* □ *Let's go out and suck up a few.*

suck (some) brew AND **suck (some) suds** *tr.* to drink beer. □ *Wanna go suck some brew?* □ *I'm tired of sucking suds. Got any staggers?*

suds *in.* to drink beer. □ *How 'bout going out and sudsing for a while?* □ *They were sudsing when they should have been studying.*

swill *tr. & in.* to drink liquor. □ *Ted is in his room swilling like a madman.* □ *He swilled a whole case of beer yesterday. Isn't he joyful yet?*

torpedo *n.* a drink containing chloral hydrate; a knockout drink. □ *Barlowe signaled the bartender to give the stoolie a torpedo.* □ *The stoolie never knew it was a torpedo that wrecked him.*

toss something off *tr.* to drink something quickly. □ *He tossed it off and ordered another.* □ *She tossed off a Scotch in one big swig.*

What'll it be? *interrog.* "What do you want?" (Typically said when offering someone drinks.) □ *Okay, Mac, what'll it be?* □ *What'll it be, chum?*

What's yours? *interrog.* "What (or which) do you want?" (Typically said on offering drinks.) □ *"What's yours?" said the bartender.* □ *The nice young man behind the counter looked to the right and left at all 140 flavors and said, "What's yours?"*

DRINKING - BOUT

See also **PARTY - DRINKING**.

bender *n.* a drinking binge. □ *Her benders usually last about ten days.* □ *Paul is off on a bender again.*

binge *n.* a drinking spree. □ *Larry is the type who likes a good binge every now and then.* □ *A champagne binge can cost a lot of cabbage.*

guzzle *n.* a drinking spree. □ *Fred's out on another of his guzzles.* □ *It's one guzzle after another, day after day.*

hellbender *n.* a drinking bout. (Use caution with *hell*.) □ *Jed is off on another of his hellbenders.* □ *One of his hellbenders can last for a week.*

honk (-up) *n.* a drinking spree. □ *Jed's last honk-up lasted nearly a week.* □ *The guys went off on the honk to end all honks.*

jag *n.* a drinking bout; a prolonged state of alcohol or drug intoxication. □ *Is he off on another jag, or is this the same one?* □ *One more jag will kill her. Try to keep her away from the stuff.*

jingle *n.* a drinking bout. □ *Jack was out on a jingle all night.* □ *The guys planned a big jingle for Friday.*

mop *n.* a drinking bout. □ *She is off somewhere on another mop.* □ *This mop lasted about a day and a half.*

paint the town (red) *tr.* to go out and celebrate; to go on a drinking bout; to get drunk. □ *I feel great. Let's go out and paint the town.* □ *They were out painting the town red last night.*

rip *n.* a drinking bout. □ *All four of them went out on a rip.* □ *Fred had another rip last night. He's rotten now.*

session *n.* a drinking bout. □ *Your father's off on another session again.* □ *He was just sobering up from a session with the bottle.*

six-pack *in.* to while away a specified period of time drinking a six-pack of beer. □ *He sat in front of the television and six-packed the entire afternoon.* □ *He's in the back—six-packing, as usual.*

skate *n.* a drinking bout. □ *He's off on another three-day skate.* □ *Jerry hopes that this will be his last skate. He wants to dry out for good.*

stale drunk *n.* a long-standing and frequently renewed drunken state. □ *The guy's on a stale drunk. He is a mess.* □ *Are you on a stale drunk again, or is this the same one?*

stew *n.* a drinking bout. □ *One more stew like that and I'll need a vacation to recover.* □ *These frequent stews must stop. You will ruin your health.*

swill-up *n.* a drinking bout. □ *There was a swill-up at the frat house last week.* □ *I never miss a swill-up.*

tear *n.* a wild drinking bout. □ *Sally is off on a tear again.* □ *What a tear it was at Paul's on Saturday night!*

tipple *n.* a drinking bout. □ *Well, Uncle Harry's off on a tipple again.* □ *No, that's the same tipple.*

toot *n.* a binge; a drinking spree. □ *Harry's on a toot again.* □ *He's not on one again. It's the same old toot.*

twister *n.* a drunken spree. □ *Harry's off on a twister again.* □ *Not again. It's the same old twister.*

whing-ding AND **whinger** *n.* a wild drinking party; drinking spree. □ *Fred had one of the best whing-dings this town has ever seen.* □ *Yes, it was some whinger.*

DRINKING - EXCESS

barrel *tr. & in.* to drink liquor to excess. □ *Those guys are barreling like beer was going out of style.* □ *Stop barreling beer and let's go home.*

beer *tr.* to get oneself drunk on beer. □ *I beered myself, but good.* □ *Let's go beer a few.*

belt the grape *tr.* to drink wine or liquor heavily and become intoxicated. □ *He has a tendency to belt the grape—twenty-four hours a day.* □ *She's been belting the grape more than she wants.*

bend one's elbow AND **bend the elbow; lift one's elbow** *tr.* to take a drink of an alcoholic beverage; to drink alcohol to excess. □ *He's down at the tavern, bending his elbow.* □ *Paul gets lots of exercise. He bends his elbow thirty times a day.*

binge *in.* to drink heavily. □ *He has been binging since June.* □ *She binges about once a month and is stone-cold sober the rest of the time.*

booze it (up) *tr.* to drink excessively; to drink to intoxication. □ *You come home every night and booze it up. How can you keep on this way?* □ *Let's go out and booze it, okay?*

booze (up) *in.* to drink alcohol to excess; to go on a bash. □ *Let's go out and booze up!* □ *Stop boozing for a minute and listen up, guys.*

bottle *in.* to drink liquor to excess. □ *I wish there was a way I could get through the day without bottling.* □ *Let's go out and bottle into oblivion.*

chug(-a-lug) *tr. & in.* to drink down a whole beer (or other drink) without stopping. □ *The two guys tried to see who could chug-a-lug the most beer.* □ *Wally chugged two cans in a row.* □ *All four of them sat there chugging.*

cut one's wolf loose *tr.* to go on a drinking bout; to get drunk. □ *I'm gonna go out and cut my wolf loose tonight.* □ *You're going to cut your wolf loose too often and really get into trouble.*

do the drink thing *tr.* to drink alcohol heavily. □ *He's been doing the drink thing quite a lot lately.* □ *He started doing the drink thing when he got out of prison.*

elbow-bending *n.* drinking liquor; drinking liquor to excess. □ *She spends quite a bit of time at elbow-bending.* □ *That's a lot of elbow-bending for one sitting.*

fuzz AND **fuzzle** *in.* to get drunk. □ *They were just sitting there fuzzling away the day.* □ *Stop fuzzing and listen.*

gas (up) *in.* to drink excessively; to get drunk. □ *Let's go out and gas up!* □ *I come home every night and find that you've been gassing all day.*

get a can on *tr.* to get drunk. □ *Let's go out tonight and get a can on.* □ *The entire office staff got a can on to celebrate the contract.*

get there *in.* to get drunk. □ *Another hour of drinking and Pete knew he was going to get there.* □ *Those guys have all got there. Now what?*

guzzle *tr. & in.* to drink alcohol in great quantities. □ *Stop guzzling for a while and pay attention.* □ *Don't guzzle all that beer, or you'll turn into a guzzle-guts.*

hang one on *tr.* to get drunk. □ *Fred was hacked and went out to hang one on.* □ *Fred hangs one on about once a month.*

hit the bottle AND **hit the booze** *tr.* to go on a drinking bout; to get drunk. □ *Jed's hitting the bottle again.* □ *He's been hitting the booze for a week now.*

jug (up) *in.* to drink heavily. □ *Let's jug up and have a good time.* □ *We jugged till about noon and then went to sleep.*

juice *in.* to drink heavily. □ *Both of them were really juicing.* □ *Stop juicing and listen to me.*

lush (up) *in.* to drink alcohol to excess. □ *Come over sometime, and we'll lush.* □ *We sat lushing up for an hour waiting for the plane.*

powder up *in.* to drink heavily; to get drunk. □ *Let's go out and powder up.* □ *He's at the tavern powdering up.*

puff *in.* to get drunk. □ *Those guys go out and puff every Friday night.* □ *I've been puffing since dinnertime, and I'm done.*

raise hell *tr.* to go on a drinking spree and get drunk. □ *Let's go out and really raise hell.* □ *The boys went out to raise hell.*

shicker *in.* to tipple; to become alcohol intoxicated. □ *I'm gonna go out and shicker till I'm silly.* □ *Fred is shickering again this weekend.*

skate *in.* to get drunk. □ *Jerry's skating again. It's his whole life.* □ *Let's go out and skate, okay?*

slew *in.* to drink to intoxication. □ *They must have been slewing for an hour before one got up and left.* □ *Let's go out and slew till we forget who we are.*

slosh *tr. & in.* to drink liquor, including beer; to drink to excess. □ *Are you going to slosh gin all night?* □ *I slosh just because I like the taste.*

slush up *in.* to drink liquor; to get drunk. □ *They slushed up for a while and went out to look for some chicks.* □ *Don't you ever get tired of going out and slushing up with those guys?*

soak 1. *in.* to drink heavily; to get drunk. □ *The two old ladies put on their coats and went out to soak.* □ *They sat quietly soaking for an hour.* **2.** *n.* a drinking bout. □ *They sat there quietly enjoying their soak.* □ *Both guys declined to go out and stayed home and enjoyed a soak in front of the T.V.*

soak one's face *tr.* to drink heavily. □ *They're down at the tavern soaking their faces.* □ *Well, I guess I'll go soak my face for a while.*

sop *tr. & in.* to guzzle (liquor). □ *Let's go out and do some serious sopping.* □ *You've sopped booze long enough. Go home.*

souse 1. *in.* to drink excessively; to go on a drinking bout; to get drunk. (From a word meaning "to soak or pickle.") □ *They sat sousing quietly in the corner.* □ *Let us retire from the table and souse in the parlor.* **2.** *n.* a drinking bout. □ *The souse lasted longer than anyone would have thought.* □ *That was one fine souse we had.*

sozzle *in.* to drink to excess. □ *The guys are sozzling over at John's place.* □ *I wish you'd stop coming home every night and sozzling to oblivion.*

sponge AND **spunge** *in.* to drink heavily. □ *She was sponging like there was no tomorrow.* □ *What can you do with a woman who sits and spunges all day long?*

steam up *in.* to drink heavily; to get drunk. □ *Fred and Mike were steaming up in the back room.* □ *Let's go down to the tavern and steam up, okay?*

swig *tr.* to drink liquor deeply. □ *He nearly swigged the whole bottle before he needed to take a breath.* □ *She swigged a big gulp and just stood there—bottle in her hand—and became paralyzed.*

swipe *tr.* to drink liquor rapidly and to excess; to bolt a drink of liquor. □ *Ted swiped a quick one and ran out the door.*

□ *Fred sat at the bar and swiped two gins and ate an egg.*

swizzle *tr. & in.* to drink (liquor), probably to excess; to *tipple.* □ *Have you been swizzling again?* □ *Fred's uncle is always swizzling a little drink.*

take on fuel *tr.* to drink alcohol to excess. □ *They stopped at the tavern to take on fuel.* □ *They went inside to take fuel on and then came back out to watch the horses.*

tank AND **tank up** *in.* to drink too much beer; to drink to excess. □ *The two brothers were tanking up and didn't hear me come in.* □ *Let's go out this Friday and tank awhile.*

tie one on AND **lay one on; tie it on** *tr.* to get drunk. □ *The boys went out to tie one on.* □ *They laid one on, but good.*

toot *tr. & in.* to drink copiously. □ *She could toot booze from dusk to dawn.* □ *They tooted and tooted till they could toot no more.*

DRINKING - PARAPHERNALIA

church key *n.* a beer can opener. □ *Where is the church key when I need it?* □ *I have a church key in my glove compartment.*

dummy *n.* an empty liquor or beer bottle. □ *Toss your dummies over here, and I'll put them in the bin.* □ *That was a sixty-dummy party. I counted.*

em(m) *n.* an empty liquor bottle. □ *Put your ems in the garbage, not on the floor.* □ *Whose emms are all these?*

marine (recruit) AND **marine officer** *n.* an empty beer or liquor bottle. □ *Every now and then the gentle muttering of the customers was accented by the breaking of a marine as it hit the floor.* □ *The guy in a uniform tossed the marine officer in the barrel and giggled.*

mickey AND **micky** *n.* a hip flask for liquor. □ *He took a little swig out of a mickey he carries in his pocket.* □ *His micky made a clunk as he sat down.*

MT *n.* an empty bottle. (Initialism.) □ *Put your MTs in the garbage.* □ *Here's another MT for your collection.*

119

setup *n.* a glass with ice for an alcoholic beverage. (Usually plural.) □ *Can we have a couple of setups brought to our room, please?* □ *Who ordered the setups?*

soldier *n.* a liquor bottle; an empty liquor bottle. □ *Toss your soldier into the garbage, please.* □ *There was a broken soldier on the floor and a cap on the table.*

DRINKING - PLACE
See also TAVERN.

nitery *n.* a nightclub. □ *We'll hit a few niteries and then come back to my place.* □ *There is a cheap nitery over on Twelfth Street where Chuck has a job.*

spot *n.* a nightclub; a night spot. □ *It was a nice little spot, with a combo and a canary.* □ *We went to a spot with a jukebox for entertainment.*

DRINKING - PORTION
beerbong 1. *n.* a can of beer prepared for drinking in one gulp. (An opening is made in the bottom of a can of beer. The can, with the opening placed in the mouth, is turned upright, and the tab opener is pulled, releasing all the beer directly into the mouth.) □ *Do you know how to make a beerbong?* □ *A beerbong is a great way to liven up a party.* **2.** *in.* to drink beer as described in sense 1. □ *Those guys who were beerbonging all barfed after it was over.* □ *I tried beerbonging once, just once.*

belt 1. *n.* a swallow of liquor. □ *He took a belt and rolled it around in his mouth before draining it down into his rumbling belly.* □ *Three more quick belts and he was ready to sit down and talk.* **2.** *tr.* to drink (something). □ *He belted his drink and asked for another.* □ *Don't belt it! Savor it! Go slowly.*

coffin nail *n.* a drink of liquor. □ *How about another coffin nail?* □ *Coffin nail sounds bad. Drink sounds good.*

double *n.* a drink consisting of two servings of liquor. □ *Make mine a double, bartender.* □ *Sam usually has two doubles on the way home.*

drop *n.* a small drink of liquor; a small serving of liquor. □ *I'll take just another drop of that dew, if you don't mind.* □ *Can I give you another drop?*

eye-opener *n.* a wake-up drink of liquor; a strong drink anytime. □ *He knocked back a quick eye-opener and finished dressing.* □ *One eye-opener led to another.*

finger *n.* an amount of liquor poured into a glass equal to the width of a finger. □ *Tracy said she only drank one finger, but the glass was five inches in diameter!* □ *No fingers for you, chum. You've had enough.*

flash *n.* a drink of liquor. □ *I'll have just a flash; then I've got to run.* □ *Here, have a flash, and let's chat a little longer.*

geezer *n.* a drink of liquor. □ *Toss down a geezer of this stuff and see how you like it.* □ *Can I have another geezer of this firewater?*

glug *n.* a gulp or shot of liquor. □ *Have another glug of this moonshine.* □ *I took one glug and spit it out.*

hit me AND **hit me again** *tr.* "Serve me (another) drink." □ *Hit me again, bartender.* □ *It's empty. Hit me.*

hoist one *tr.* to have a drink. □ *Let's go out and hoist one sometime.* □ *Hey, Sam. Let's you and me hoist one.*

hooter *n.* a drink of liquor. □ *He tossed back a big hooter of booze and stood there a minute.* □ *Have another hooter?*

jigger *n.* a drink of whiskey. (The standard term for a small container used for measuring the right amount of liquor for a drink.) □ *How about another jigger of that shine?* □ *Okay, I'll have a jigger.*

jollop *n.* a drink of liquor. □ *She poured a big jollop into each of the glasses and then drank them one by one.* □ *"Have another jollop," she said to herself.*

jolt *n.* a drink of strong liquor. □ *Can you give me a little jolt of shine?* □ *He knocked back a jolt and asked for another.*

kick in the wrist *n.* a drink of liquor. □ *You want another kick in the wrist?* □ *I'll take another kick in the wrist.*

knock back a drink *tr.* to drink a beer; to have a quick drink of liquor. □ *He knocked back three beers in a row.* □ *Let's knock back another one or two and leave.*

knock one over AND **knock one back** *tr.* to take a drink of liquor. □ *He knocked one over right away and demanded another.* □ *He knocked back one and belched grossly.*

knock something down *tr.* to drink a portion of liquor. □ *Here, knock this down and let's go.* □ *He knocked down a bottle of beer and called for another.*

load 1. *n.* as much liquor as one can hold. □ *Harry had quite a load of booze.* □ *Mary is carrying a load.* **2.** *n.* a drink of liquor. □ *Can I have a load from your bottle?* □ *Help yourself to a load.*

short 1. *n.* a small drink of hard liquor or of beer. □ *One short, bartender.* □ *I'll have a short and a pack of cigarettes.* **2.** *mod.* having to do with a single drink of undiluted liquor. □ *I'll take mine short, innkeeper.* □ *Who ordered a short one?*

short one *n.* a small or quickly drunk drink of liquor, including beer. □ *How about a short one, innkeeper?* □ *Give my friend here a short one.*

short-snort *n.* a quick drink of whisky from a bottle, flask, or jug. □ *He grabbed a short-snort and went back to his carving.* □ *Jed offered the visitor a short-snort from a jar of shine.*

shot *n.* a small or quickly drunk drink of liquor, usually whiskey. □ *Here, have a shot of this stuff.* □ *He stopped at every bar on the strip for a quick shot.*

shot in the arm *n.* a drink of liquor. □ *I could use a little shot in the arm.* □ *How about a little shot in the arm, bartender?*

shot in the neck *n.* a drink of straight whiskey. □ *Wally took a little shot in the neck before heading out into the cold.* □ *A shot in the neck was just what was needed.*

skinful *n.* an intoxicating quantity of liquor; enough liquor. □ *He's got a skinful and can't drive.* □ *She knows enough to stop drinking before she gets a skinful.*

slash *n.* a drink of liquor. □ *Just one slash, and I have to be going.* □ *How about a slash? You ready yet?*

slug *n.* a drink of liquor; a shot of whiskey. □ *Have a slug of this stuff. It will—I'm sorry to say, ma'am—put hair on your chest.* □ *A couple more slugs and he was ready to face the huge bull-necked ruffian.*

smile AND **smiler; smiley** *n.* a drink of liquor; liquor. □ *Come over and join me for a smiley.* □ *Here, have a smiler on me.*

sniff *n.* a drink of liquor. □ *I'd like just a sniff of that Scotch.* □ *Sure, have a sniff of whatever you want.*

spot *n.* a small drink of liquor. □ *I'll just have a spot, please.* □ *Just a spot for me, too.*

swig *n.* a deep drink of liquor; a swallow of liquor. □ *She took a swig of rum and leaped into the lagoon.* □ *One swig of that stuff was enough for me.*

swill *n.* a drink of liquor. □ *How about a swill out of your glass?* □ *Here, you can have a little swill of mine.*

tall one *n.* a large drink; a long drink. □ *She ordered a tall one and sat back to cool off.* □ *Give me a tall one, John.*

three fingers *n.* a measurement of liquor in a glass. □ *I'll take three fingers. It's been a hard day.* □ *Your wife told me not to give you three fingers anymore.*

tipple 1. *tr. & in.* to drink liquor; to sip at a vessel of liquor. □ *He's been tippling beer since early morning.* □ *Actually, he's been tippling since 1943.* **2.** *n.* a drink of liquor. □ *How about a little tipple?* □ *I'll take just a little tipple—for my arthritis, you know.*

toss *tr.* to drink some liquor; to take a drink of liquor. □ *He tossed some whiskey and left.* □ *Toss that drink, and let's get out of here!*

triple *n.* a large alcoholic drink containing three measures of hard liquor. □ *It was a hard day. Make it a triple, John.* □ *One triple, but no more. You're cutting down, remember?*

two fingers *n.* a measurement of liquor in a glass. □ *I'll take two fingers of that* tiger milk, John. □ Just two fingers tonight, John?

wash *n.* a drink that follows a previous drink; a chaser. □ *He ordered a beer wash with his snort.* □ *Can I have a wash with this, bartender?*

whack AND **wack** *n.* a drink of liquor. □ *Take a whack of this stuff.* □ *Hey, give me another wack of that. It helps.*

DRINKING - TOAST

Down the hatch! *exclam.* "Let's drink it!" □ *Down the hatch! Have another?* □ *Bottoms up! Down the hatch!*

Drink up! *exclam.* "Finish your drink!"; "Finish that drink, and we'll have another!" □ *Okay, drink up! It's closing time.* □ *Drink up, and let's get going.*

DRIVING

fender-bender *n.* a reckless driver (who causes minor accidents). □ *I can't get insurance on my seventeen-year-old, who is a hopeless fender-bender.* □ *Don't give up on young fender-benders.*

leadfoot *n.* a speeder in an automobile. □ *There is a leadfoot driving behind me and wanting to pass.* □ *Tom was a real leadfoot until he got a few speeding tickets.*

road hog *n.* someone who takes too much space on a road or highway; someone who seems to run other people off the road. □ *Get over! Road hog!* □ *A road hog nearly ran me off the road.*

speeder *n.* a speeding ticket. □ *The cop who gave Mary a speeder Wednesday gave her another one Friday.* □ *Actually, that's three speeders in one week counting the one she got Monday.*

Sunday driver *n.* a slow and leisurely driver who appears to be sightseeing and enjoying the view, holding up traffic in the process. (Also a term of address.) □ *I'm a Sunday driver, and I'm sorry. I just can't bear to go faster.* □ *Move over, you Sunday driver!*

swamper *n.* a truck driver's helper or assistant. □ *This guy and his swamper showed up to deliver the stuff, but neither* one of them would touch it. □ *He told the swamper to get some coffee for everybody.*

tag *n.* a car license plate or sticker. □ *The car had Kansas tags and was towing a trailer.* □ *Don't forget to get a new tag for this year.*

tailgate *tr. & in.* to follow (someone) too closely in a car. □ *That guy tailgating me is drunk, I think.* □ *Ease off a little; you're tailgating.*

ticket *n.* a driving license. □ *I finally got a ticket to drive a big truck.* □ *I showed her my ticket, and she let me off with a warning.*

turn on a dime *in.* to turn sharply; to turn in a small radius. □ *This baby will turn on a dime.* □ *A car that will turn on a dime at high speed without turning turtle is what I want.*

wheel *tr. & in.* to drive a car. □ *I'm gonna wheel over later this afternoon.* □ *Let's wheel my heap over to Marty's place.*

wheel man *n.* the (male) driver of a criminal escape car. (Underworld.) □ *Lefty was the wheel man for the bank job.* □ *We need a new wheel man while Lefty's away.*

DRUGS

candy *n.* drugs in general. □ *I gotta go get some candy from the candy man.* □ *This candy is powerful stuff.*

carry 1. *in.* to carry drugs on one's person. □ *If you get busted while you're carrying, you are in big trouble with the man.* □ *You gotta learn when you can carry and when you can't.* **2.** *n.* drugs carried on the person as an emergency supply in case of arrest. (Underworld.) □ *I lost my carry somewhere.* □ *The cops found my carry, and I spent three days in the clink climbing the walls.*

crack house *n.* a house or dwelling where crack is sold and used. □ *The police are continuing their efforts to close down crack houses in the area.* □ *In one dilapidated neighborhood, there is a crack house on every block.*

discipline *n.* drugs. □ *Max has been on a little too much of that discipline lately.*

□ *She smokes this stuff she calls discipline. Smells like pot to me.*

dope *n.* drugs in general; marijuana. □ *Lay off the dope, will ya?* □ *How much dope do you do in a week, anyway?*

drop *n.* a place at which drugs, alcohol, or other contraband is left to be claimed by the recipient. □ *The police discovered the drop and waited for the runner.* □ *They switched drops constantly just in case of discovery.*

druggie AND **druggy** *n.* a drug addict or user. □ *That druggy loves to hang out here.* □ *There are too many druggies in this neighborhood.*

Dutch courage *n.* drugs. □ *Max deals in Dutch courage, as he calls it.* □ *Too much Dutch courage and you're in permanent trouble.*

Ecstasy *n.* a hallucinogen similar to LSD. □ *Chemicals with names like "Ecstasy" are being put on the streets every day.* □ *Ecstasy is just one of a dozen drugs with similar formulas.*

freaker *n.* a *freaked (out)* person. (Collegiate.) □ *Some poor freaker sat in the corner and rocked.* □ *Who's the freaker in the corner?*

gunk *n.* glue sniffed as a drug. □ *This kid is high on gunk.* □ *I thought that it was illegal to sell gunk.*

hard *mod.* having to do with an addictive drug. □ *Gert's on hard stuff now.* □ *Hard drugs are easier to get than ever before.*

hardware *n.* hard drugs or hard liquor. □ *No wine for me. Give me the hardware.* □ *This hardware is pretty powerful.*

hash-house *n.* a place where hashish is sold and used. □ *This hash-house is due for a raid. Let's hit it.* □ *The fuzz raided a hash-house over on Maple Street.*

head drug *n.* a drug that affects the mind rather than the body; a psychoactive drug. □ *It's these head drugs that get the kids into so much trouble.* □ *Head drugs are just as addictive as other drugs, but in a different way.*

heeled *mod.* carrying drugs. □ *Max is heeled and ready to deal.* □ *Gert was heeled when they arrested her.*

hold *tr. & in.* to possess drugs. □ *Gert was holding coke when she was arrested.* □ *Max is holding and wants to deal.*

huffer *n.* a person (teenager) who inhales glue vapors or some other solvent for a *high*. □ *The age of the huffers has come to an end. Now they start out on crack.* □ *His schoolwork suffered because he was a huffer.*

in action *mod.* selling or using drugs. □ *Max is in action about twenty hours a day.* □ *In this neighborhood, somebody is in action twenty-four hours a day.*

jock(e)y *n.* an addictive drug. (Because such a drug rides one like a jockey rides a horse.) □ *That jockey rode her for years.* □ *She fought that jocky, and it finally won.*

light stuff *n.* marijuana and nonaddictive drugs. □ *Sure, it's innocent. Sure, they're just kids. Do you know what kids do when they get through with the light stuff? They do coke, they shoot H, and they do the big one somewhere in an alley!* □ *The cops just found some light stuff in his pockets. They let him go.*

(ma)hoska *n.* narcotics; any contraband. (Underworld.) □ *The tall pinstriper asked where he could get some mahoska.* □ *The hoska must be for a friend. He's a blower if I ever saw one.*

Mickey (Finn) *n.* chloral hydrate as put in drinks to knock people out. □ *There was a Mickey Finn in this drink, wasn't there?* □ *Now where would I get a Mickey?*

mojo *n.* heroin; morphine; cannabis. □ *This mojo is no good.* □ *Why don't you try to kick the mojo?*

monster 1. *n.* any powerful drug affecting the central nervous system. □ *This PCP is a monster. Why don't the cops put a stop to it?* □ *That monster just about did me in.* **2.** *mod.* having to do with a powerful or addictive drug. □ *Where the devil did you get that monster dust?* □ *That is monster C, and it will make you its slave.*

mooch *n.* narcotics. □ *Mooch is what Minnie the Moocher is famous for.* □ *He's gonna have to work hard to get off the mooch.*

moonrock *n.* a form of crystallized cocaine that contains heroin. □ *Max was caught with a supply of moonrock on him.* □ *He was trying to start the little kids out on moonrock.*

narc(o) 1. *n.* a narcotic. □ *She's been taking narcs.* □ *How long has he been on narcs?* **2.** *mod.* having to do with narcotics. □ *Does he have a narc problem?* □ *She is a narco officer.*

narky *n.* a narcotic drug. □ *They caught him with a lot of narky in his pockets.* □ *The mugger wanted money to buy some narky.*

needle candy *n.* narcotics that are taken by injection. □ *Max likes needle candy best of all.* □ *Some people prefer needle candy to food.*

nose (candy) *n.* powdered drugs that are inhaled, primarily cocaine, sometimes heroin. □ *Max has some nose candy for sale.* □ *Hey, man! Where can I get some nose?*

nose hit *n.* marijuana smoke taken through the nose from the burning end of the cigarette. □ *Max likes to take nose hits.* □ *Come on, Max. Give me a nose hit!*

OD 1. *n.* an overdose of a drug. (Initialism. Drugs.) □ *Max took an OD and was sent to the hospital.* □ *If you take an OD and no one is around, you may end up dead.* **2.** *in.* to purposely or accidentally give oneself a fatal dose of drugs. □ *Max ODed on heroin.* □ *I knew he would OD someday.*

popper AND **popsie** *n.* an ampoule of amyl nitrite, a drug that is inhaled when the ampoule is broken. (Usually plural.) □ *You got a popper I can have?* □ *He had a popsie in his pocket that broke when he sat down.*

push *in.* to recruit new drug users and sell drugs to them; to deal in drugs. □ *He was pushing for two years before the cops got him.* □ *Man, look at that guy push. He hooks two new kids every day.*

put someone on *tr.* to introduce someone to cannabis use, usually smoking. □ *Where did you get that stuff? Who put you on?* □ *My brother uses it, and he put me on.*

scene *n.* the drug-use environment; the drug scene. □ *The longer you spend in a scene like this, the harder it is to sober up and go straight.* □ *This coke scene is a bad one. It will shorten your life.*

shit *n.* drugs in general; heroin; marijuana. □ *Lay off the shit, Harry! You're gonna end up hooked.* □ *So Marty scores a bag of shit—I mean skag—you know, H.—and we get out the apps to shoot.*

short *n.* a purchase of drugs that counts or weighs out less than the amount agreed upon. □ *You gave me a short. Fix it now, or this thing goes off accidentally in your ear.* □ *Max knew that Bruno ended up with a short, and Bruno wasn't stable enough to talk about things like that. Max blew.*

smoke-in *n.* a young people's public gathering of the 1960s where marijuana was smoked in open defiance of the law. □ *My uncle was at a smoke-in. He says the reporters were getting kids to pose for shots.* □ *They say you could get a high just by being near a smoke-in.*

soft *mod.* having to do with nonaddictive drugs. □ *The soft stuff just leads to hard stuff.* □ *This acid is not exactly soft.* □ *Soft drugs just take longer to turn you into a zombie.*

stepped on *mod.* having to do with diluted drugs. □ *That smack you bought was really stepped on.* □ *This stuff is too stepped on. It's sugar, and it won't do.*

stretch *tr.* to cut or dilute a drug. □ *Max was known for stretching the stuff a little too much.* □ *Let's stretch this stuff, sell it, and then blow town.*

turn on, tune in, drop out *phr.* a slogan promoting the use of LSD among young people. □ *The key phrase in the heyday of acid was "turn on, tune in, drop out."* □ *Millions heard "turn on, tune in, drop out" and did just that.*

unk-jay *n.* dope; junk. (Underworld. Pig Latin for *junk*.) □ *The creep deals in unk-jay, you know—narcotics.* □ *Stay away from the unk-jay.*

up high *n.* a stimulating rather than a depressing drug high. □ *She was always looking for a good up high. When she couldn't find quality, she went after quantity.* □ *Many of them have to have an up high. They are too close to clinical depression to chance anything else.*

DRUGS - ADDED

dust *tr.* to add a powdered drug to the end of a (tobacco or cannabis) cigarette. □ *Pete dusted one, then lit it up.* □ *Max never dusts them before he sells them.*

lace *tr.* to add a bit of one drug to another; to add drugs to any food or drink. □ *Somebody laced the ice cubes with acid.* □ *This fag is laced with opium.*

DRUGS - AMPHETAMINE

amps *n.* amphetamines. □ *I never do any drugs except maybe a few amps now and then, and the odd downer, and maybe a little grass on weekends, but nothing really hard.* □ *Paul is on a roller coaster of amps and damps.*

benny AND **bennie** *n.* a Benzedrine™ capsule or tablet. □ *You got a benny or two you could spare a poor man?* □ *A couple of bennies will chase away the blues.*

benz *n.* Benzedrine™. □ *Benz will pep you up, but you give it all back later.* □ *Stay off the benz. Coffee is enough to perk anybody up.*

blue *n.* an amphetamine tablet or capsule, especially a blue one. □ *How are blues different from reds and yellows?* □ *I'm sort of wired. You got any blues?*

cartwheel *n.* a round, white cross-scored amphetamine tablet. □ *He took cartwheels in the morning and fender-benders at night.* □ *Cartwheels were the favorite diet pill of the 1960s.*

chicken powder *n.* powdered amphetamine. □ *Those kids seem to be satisfied with chicken powder.* □ *Nobody is satisfied with chicken powder for very long.*

go-pills *n.* amphetamines. □ *She took go-pills to start the day.* □ *After a while, these go-pills just demand to be taken.*

gorilla biscuits AND **gorilla pills** *n.* amphetamines. □ *Tracy is big on those gorilla pills.* □ *Stay away from gorilla biscuits.*

jelly babies *n.* an amphetamine tablet or capsule. □ *You got any jelly babies?* □ *Are there any jelly babies in this neighborhood?*

leapers *n.* amphetamines. □ *You can tell Bruno's on leapers. He's wired as hell.* □ *He needs some barbs to balance the leapers, or maybe he just ought to go cold turkey and go straight.*

lid proppers AND **lid poppers** *n.* amphetamine tablets or capsules. (Refers to the eyelids.) □ *Kelly has to have a couple of lid proppers each morning.* □ *Are lid poppers habit-forming?*

meth *n.* methamphetamine. □ *Usually meth is injected, having almost an immediate effect.* □ *Meth comes in little glass tubes.*

pepper-upper *n.* an amphetamine tablet or capsule. □ *I need me a little pepper-upper. Can I have a prescription?* □ *You need more sleep, not a pepper-upper.*

pep pill *n.* a stimulant pill or capsule, such as an amphetamine. □ *The doctor prescribed some kind of pep pills, but I refused to take them.* □ *Got any pep pills or anything?*

speed 1. *n.* methamphetamine; amphetamine in general. □ *Speed is a monstrous problem in some cities.* □ *Kids think that speed won't get them into trouble.* **2.** *in.* to use methamphetamine; to be high on methamphetamine or amphetamine. □ *Kids who speed think it is a harmless blow-off.* □ *If they speed rather than study—speed is a problem.*

speeder *n.* an amphetamine or methamphetamine tablet, capsule, or ampoule. □ *Somebody dropped some speeders on the floor of the car, and my father spazzed out.* □ *Fred took a speeder before the exam, but he went to sleep anyway.*

DRUGS - ANALGESIC

cets AND **sets** *n.* tablets of Darvocet™, a painkiller. □ *You got any cets I can bum off you?* □ *I don't know anything about sets or any of that stuff.*

mep(s) *n.* meperidine, Demerol™, a painkiller. □ *The nurse was sneaking a little meps now and then.* □ *For some people, mep is highly addictive.*

DRUGS - BARBITURATE

barb *n.* a barbiturate; a barbiturate capsule. □ *Old Joey is hooked on barbs.* □ *You got a barb I can bum?*

blue devils *n.* capsules of Amytal™, a barbiturate. □ *How much for a little box of blue devils?* □ *Got no red devils. Will blue devils do it to you?*

canary *n.* a capsule of Nembutal™, a barbiturate. (The capsule is yellow.) □ *You got any canaries? I need a downer.* □ *There are a couple of blues, which ought to do the same as canaries.*

downer AND **down; downie** *n.* a barbiturate or a tranquilizer. □ *She favors downers.* □ *Too much booze with those downers, and you're dead.*

downer *n.* a bad drug experience. □ *That stuff you gave me was a real downer.* □ *Dust is a downer for most people.*

idiot pills *n.* barbiturates. □ *Lay off those idiot pills, why don't you?* □ *She takes idiot pills every night.*

jack-ups *n.* capsules of a barbiturate drug. □ *Walter took a few jack-ups and went on to work.* □ *Gert took her jack-ups with whiskey. She's gonna get pifted.*

King Kong pills AND **King Kong specials** *n.* barbiturates. □ *Watch out for those King Kong pills.* □ *Don't mix these King Kong specials with booze.*

M and Ms *n.* capsules of Seconal™, a barbiturate. (From the brand name of a type of brightly colored candy pellets.) □ *Is there somewhere around here I can get some M and Ms?* □ *No M and Ms for me. I'm on blues.*

sec AND **secs** *n.* a Seconal™ barbiturate capsule. □ *Max likes amies better than secs.* □ *I started taking sec in the hospital and just couldn't stop.*

sleeper *n.* a sleeping pill. □ *I just took one little sleeper.* □ *She took a handful of sleepers with a glass of booze, and that was it.*

tooie AND **tooey; tuie** *n.* a capsule of Tuinal™, a barbiturate. □ *You got any tooies?* □ *The cops saw a few tuies on the sidewalk and made the arrest.*

DRUGS - COCAINE

big-C *n.* cocaine. □ *When she started taking big-C, she was only eight.* □ *They use kids to deliver big-C because they know they're not going to get put in prison.*

blower *n.* cocaine. □ *What's the best-quality blower around here?* □ *George says he can't live without blower.*

cane *n.* cocaine. □ *What the hell did you pay for this cane?* □ *Even the kids can afford to buy cane now. The social problems of the twenty-first century are starting right here.*

cee *n.* cocaine. □ *Where can I get a little bit of cee?* □ *Ask Max for some cee, but ask him nice.*

Charles *n.* cocaine. □ *I want to meet Charles somewhere.* □ *Is there a house where I can buy some Charles somewhere close?*

crack *n.* crystalline, smokable cocaine. □ *This crack seems to have become the drug of choice for punks of all ages.* □ *Crack became popular when it became easy and cheap to process. It's been around for years in medicinal form.*

crystal 1. *n.* crystallized cocaine. □ *I wonder how much crystal is used in this country each day.* □ *Crystal—an older name for crack—was a favorite many years ago.* 2. *n.* liquid Methedrine™ in glass ampoules. □ *I hear that Wally's shooting crystal. Is that true?* □ *Max has lots of crystal right now.*

flake *n.* a medicinal form of crystallized cocaine. □ *Where can I get some flake around here?* □ *Max specializes in flake.*

free base AND **(free)base** 1. *n.* a smokable, pure extract of cocaine. □ *Max is* real big on free base. □ *Bruno likes base, too.* **2.** *in.* to smoke a pure extract of cocaine. □ *Rocko has never freebased in his life.* □ *Rocko won't base, smoke, or anything.*

heaven dust *n.* cocaine. □ *A little heaven dust and Pat was as good as new.* □ *She left her desk to take on a little heaven dust.*

hooter *n.* cocaine. □ *Max is known for his high-quality hooter.* □ *Where can I get some hooter around here?*

hubbas *n.* crystallized cocaine. □ *A ten-year-old died yesterday from hubbas.* □ *They arrested an eight-year-old for selling hubbas.*

ice *n.* cocaine; crystalline cocaine. □ *Max deals mostly in ice, but can get you almost anything.* □ *This ice isn't good enough.*

icicles *n.* pure cocaine in a crystallized form. □ *Are icicles the same as crack?* □ *Icicles are probably more pure than crack.*

incentive *n.* cocaine. □ *Maybe a little of that incentive would make me work harder.* □ *That's pretty expensive incentive.*

initiative *n.* cocaine. □ *Maybe I need some more of that initiative to get me going.* □ *That kind of initiative is pretty expensive.*

joy flakes AND **joy dust** *n.* powdered or crystallized cocaine. □ *Is joy flakes the same as crack?* □ *Joy dust is sort of crack without the press coverage.*

Lady Snow *n.* cocaine. □ *I spent the afternoon with Lady Snow.* □ *Lady Snow is about the only friend I have left.*

leaf *n.* cocaine. (Sometimes with *the*. Cocaine is extracted from the leaves of the coca plant.) □ *Sure I like plants. I am especially fond of the leaf.* □ *The entire shipment of leaf was seized by the feds.*

line *n.* a dose of finely cut cocaine arranged in a line, ready for insufflation or *snorting*. □ *Let's you and me go do some lines, okay?* □ *See these lines here? Watch what happens to them.*

rails *n.* powdered cocaine arranged into lines. □ *Max makes the rails too messy.* □ *Max put the rails on something smooth.*

rock 1. AND **rock candy** *n.* crack, a crystallized form of cocaine. □ *Some call it rock, and some call it crack.* □ *Rock is pretty expensive.* **2.** *n.* a crystallized form of heroin used for smoking. □ *Max is hooked on rock—the kind that you smoke.* □ *Powder is everywhere, but you can hardly find rock anymore.*

sea *n.* cocaine. (A spelling-out of *C.*) □ *There is a bunch using sea over at Fred's place.* □ *I never used sea before. I hear there's nothing like it.*

toke *in.* to smoke crystallized cocaine. □ *She almost blew herself up toking.* □ *They were toking when her mother called on the phone.*

tootonium *n.* an imaginary, potent type of cocaine. (A play on titanium.) □ *He called it tootonium. She called it trouble.* □ *You want some real tootonium, babe?*

tootuncommon *n.* an imaginary, potent type of cocaine; any potent cocaine. (A play on King Tutankhamen.) □ *Max laughed when the student asked for tootuncommon.* □ *Which is better, tootonium or tootuncommon?*

DRUGS - FEELING

crank bugs *n.* a drug-induced hallucination that insects are crawling under one's skin. □ *I have crank bugs, and I'm cartooning, too.* □ *There's no such thing as crank bugs, so stop scratching them.*

DRUGS - HASHISH

clay *n.* good-quality hashish. □ *I like the feel of this clay. I'll take it.* □ *Ask Bruno where you can dig up some clay.*

hash *n.* hashish; cannabis in general. □ *The amount of hash that moves into this city in a single day would astound you.* □ *Hash is still the favorite first drug other than alcohol.*

heavy hash *n.* potent cannabis. □ *Man, you came up with some real heavy hash.* □ *This is heavy hash, and it will cost you.*

heesh *n.* hashish; cannabis. □ *Ernie started out on heesh and moved on from there.* □ *Who's dealing heesh around here?*

DRUGS - HEROIN

big-H *n.* heroin. □ *She's on big-H now. Soon she'll be hooked for good.* □ *The big-H in this town is so watered down, you can joy pop for years and never get hooked.*

China white 1. AND **Chinese white** *n.* pure or nearly pure heroin. □ *Beware of that China white.* □ *You never see Chinese white anymore. There's too many other kinds of junk for anybody to bother with it.* **2.** *n.* fentanyl, a synthetic narcotic analgesic. □ *That Chinese white can paralyze your lungs.* □ *All the hopheads I know of stay away from China white.*

Chinese red *n.* heroin. □ *Chinese red is really high quality.* □ *No, Chinese red is cheap.*

gulf *n.* heroin from the Persian Gulf region. □ *This gulf is flooding the country.* □ *Those pushers can call anything gulf. How does anybody know where it's from?*

H *n.* heroin. □ *Now he's shooting H.* □ *First it was M.; now it's H.*

hazel *n.* heroin. □ *Gert needs some hazel, but anything will help her.* □ *She wants to spend the evening with hazel.*

heavy soul *n.* heroin. (Black.) □ *Tyrone is hung up on some heavy soul.* □ *That heavy soul will be on your back forever.*

hero (of the underworld) *n.* heroin. □ *Don says he knows the hero of the underworld well.* □ *Bruno stays away from hero.*

horse *n.* heroin. □ *Now, horse is all that Gert will touch.* □ *Horse is still very popular in the big cities.*

horseradish *n.* heroin. □ *Max can get you some horseradish.* □ *Gert is hooked on horseradish.*

noise *n.* heroin. □ *Man, I need some noise now! I hurt!* □ *Max is hooked on noise.*

scat *n.* heroin. (From an old term for dung.) □ *Max is trying to sell scat in the neighborhood again.* □ *That scat's gonna get that man killed.*

skag AND **scag** *n.* heroin, especially poor-quality heroin; any powerful drug. □ *Just lay off the skag—if you can.* □ *Scag has sent a lot of my friends to the bone orchard.*

tragic-magic *n.* heroin. □ *This tragic-magic, which has swept over the land, has taken too many of our youth.* □ *This tragic-magic stuff has hurt lots of my friends.*

DRUGS - LSD

acid *n.* lysergic acid diethylamide (LSD). □ *Acid and pot! That's all you think about.* □ *Freddy got hold of some bad acid and freaked out.*

blotter *n.* the drug LSD, sold on bits of blotting paper. □ *Most of the acid in this town is blotter.* □ *Blotter can bring one to five dollars a pop.*

cid AND **sid** *n.* the hallucinogenic drug LSD. (From *acid. Sid* can be capitalized.) □ *Where can I go to drop a little cid?* □ *Bruno can tell you where Sid is these days.* □ *You know where I can rap with Sid?*

cube *n.* a sugar cube impregnated with LSD. (Often in the plural.) □ *First they took it on cubes. Then on little bits of paper.* □ *The cubes were usually bluish.*

headfucker *n.* a potent psychoactive drug; LSD. (Potentially offensive. Use only with discretion.) □ *This stuff is a real headfucker. Stay away from it.* □ *John's first experience with a headfucker was not one he's likely to forget.*

LSD *n.* lysergic acid diethylamide, a hallucinogenic drug. (Initialism. Drugs. A mainstay of the 1960s and 1970s drug culture.) □ *Is there much LSD still around?* □ *LSD isn't the problem it used to be, but it's far from gone.*

mickey mouse *n.* a bit of blotter impregnated with LSD with a picture of the Walt Disney Company's Mickey Mouse on it. □ *How much is the mickey mouse?* □ *The mickey mouse is more than you want to pay.*

mind-bender AND **mind-blower** *n.* a hallucinogenic drug, typically LSD. □

You wanna try some mind-blower? □ *That mind-bender takes a long time to wear off.*

sidney *n.* the hallucinogenic drug LSD. (Also capitalized.) □ *Is Sidney working tonight?* □ *Sidney and I have a little business trip planned.*

DRUGS - MARIJUANA

bhang (ganjah) *n.* marijuana; marijuana resin. □ *It's the bhang ganjah that gives the stuff its kick.* □ *Can you get bhang ganjah by itself?*

blow jive *tr.* to smoke marijuana. □ *Man, let's go out and blow some jive!* □ *You would rather blow jive than eat, I think.*

blow smoke *tr.* to smoke marijuana. □ *Max sits around blowing smoke when he's not selling.* □ *The whole sales force blows smoke during office hours.*

burn *tr.* to smoke cannabis. □ *Jim spent Saturday out in the field burning grass.* □ *The two of them sat there burning reefers for hours on end.*

Cambodian red AND **cam (red)** *n.* a reddish brown marijuana grown in Cambodia. □ *Where did you get cam red?* □ *Cam is hard to find in the last few years.*

cigarette with no name AND **no-brand cigarette; no-name cigarette** *n.* a marijuana cigarette. □ *You got one of them cigarettes with no name?* □ *He spends his whole life burning those no-name cigarettes.*

climb *n.* a marijuana cigarette. (The means to a high.) □ *I need a climb to set me straight.* □ *Here, have a swallow of this climb.*

coli *n.* marijuana. (From broccoli.) □ *There's a little bag of coli in the fridge.* □ *Who got into my stash and took the coli?*

Colombian (gold) AND **Columbian (gold)** *n.* a potent marijuana from Colombia. (Columbian is a misspelling.) □ *Colombian gold seems to be a favorite around here.* □ *Columbian is cheap and abundant in almost every city.*

crying weed *n.* marijuana. □ *I must have got hold of some crying weed. This*

stuff leaves me cold. □ *On a rainy day, crying weed seems just right.*

doobie AND **dooby; duby** *n.* a marijuana cigarette; a fat marijuana cigarette. □ *Max sells doobies like they were candy.* □ *Want a doobie?*

dubage AND **doobage** *n.* drugs; marijuana. □ *I detect the smell of dubage in the hallway!* □ *Bill kept his doobage in an old shoe in his closet.*

gizzy *n.* marijuana. □ *The cops found a little gizzy in the guy's pocket.* □ *Where'd you get this gizzy?*

grass *n.* marijuana. □ *These kids manage to find this grass somewhere.* □ *Almost everybody knows that grass means marijuana.*

greefo AND **griefo** *n.* marijuana or a marijuana cigarette. (Mexican Spanish for *weed.*) □ *Max had a soggy greefo in his mouth.* □ *He tossed Fred a griefo and held out his hand for some bread.*

gungeon *n.* a potent type of marijuana from Africa or Jamaica; a cigarette made of this marijuana. □ *Where can I get some of that gungeon?* □ *Is this gungeon really from Africa?*

gunny *n.* a potent marijuana from Jamaica or Africa. □ *Is this gunny really from Jamaica?* □ *This gunny is just junk, plain old junk.*

gyve *n.* marijuana; a marijuana cigarette. □ *Why are you always smoking gyve?* □ *How about a hit of that gyve?*

harsh toke *n.* an irritating puff of a marijuana cigarette. □ *Wow, that was a harsh toke. Yuck!* □ *Pat got a harsh toke and coughed a lot.*

hemp *n.* cannabis. □ *The guy sort of smells like hemp.* □ *I smell hemp in here.*

herb AND **erb** *n.* marijuana. □ *Bruno is very fond of herb.* □ *Carl has found a way to synthesize the erb.*

homegrown *n.* marijuana grown domestically or locally. □ *She'd rather use homegrown than have to deal with Max.* □ *This homegrown is from the pots in her room.*

incense *n.* marijuana. □ *I think I smell some incense somewhere in this building.* □ *Hank likes to burn a little incense every now and then.*

J AND **jay** *n.* a marijuana cigarette; marijuana. (From the initial letter of *joint*.) □ *Toss me a J, huh?* □ *A jay is two clams.*

jane *n.* marijuana. □ *You got any jane?* □ *Max has jane coming out of his ears.*

jive *n.* drugs; marijuana. □ *Stop using all that jive all the time.* □ *That jive is gonna be the end of you.*

jivestick AND **gyvestick** *n.* a marijuana cigarette. □ *Max flipped a jivestick to Bruno and smiled.* □ *He had a gyvestick stuck behind his ear.*

joint *n.* a marijuana cigarette. □ *He always has a joint with him.* □ *The joint wasn't enough to carry him very long.*

K AND **kee; key; ki** *n.* a kilogram of cannabis. □ *You want a whole K?* □ *Well, how much is a ki?*

kid stuff *n.* marijuana, a drug for "beginners." □ *That grass is kid stuff.* □ *He's still using kid stuff.*

killer *n.* a marijuana cigarette. □ *How about a killer, Max?* □ *He's always smoking a killer.*

killer weed *n.* very potent marijuana. □ *Wow, this stuff is killer weed!* □ *This killer weed is oregano, I think.*

ladyfinger *n.* a marijuana cigarette. □ *Bruno knows how to roll a ladyfinger.* □ *Hell, any old joint is a ladyfinger. Don't be so particular.*

lawn *n.* poor quality marijuana. □ *This isn't good grass; it's lawn.* □ *Put this lawn in your pipe and smoke it.*

lid *n.* one half to one ounce of marijuana. □ *How much a lid?* □ *It looks like a matchbox to me. Why do they call it a lid?*

lumbo AND **limbo** *n.* Colombian marijuana. □ *He showed up with a bag of lumbo.* □ *Hey, Max! You are just in time with the limbo, man.*

lum(s) *n.* cannabis from Colombia. (The "lum" is based on the misspelling "Columbia.") □ *Bruno preferred lums,* but he would take what he could get. □ *If it weren't for lum, our trade deficit wouldn't be so bad.*

manicure *n.* good-quality, cleaned marijuana. □ *Ah, this manicure should bring some good coin.* □ *You got any high Q manicure?*

Mary Jane AND **Mary J.; Maryjane** *n.* marijuana. □ *I can't live another day without Mary Jane!* □ *I could sure rap with Mary Jane about now.*

monster weed *n.* cannabis; powerful marijuana. □ *Where on earth does she get that monster weed she's been blowing?* □ *This is what they call monster weed. Stay away from it. It may have angel dust on it.*

mother *n.* marijuana. □ *She grows her own mother in a pot in her room.* □ *This mother is way rad!*

mother nature('s) *n.* marijuana. □ *No chemicals for me. I find that mother nature is everything I need.* □ *See if you can get some of mother nature's.*

mu *n.* marijuana. □ *This mu is stale.* □ *Are mu and bu the same thing?*

mudbud *n.* homegrown marijuana. □ *Mudbud, hell! It's garbage.* □ *If you sell your mudbud, you're a pusher!*

nose-burner AND **nose-warmer** *n.* a marijuana cigarette stub. □ *Hey, man! Can I have a hit of that little nose-burner?* □ *The cops found a nose-warmer under the chair.*

number *n.* a marijuana cigarette. □ *Max lit up a number just as the boss came in.* □ *Can I have a hit off your number?*

off-brand cigarette *n.* a marijuana cigarette. □ *Max smokes nothing but those off-brand cigarettes.* □ *I smell an off-brand cigarette in here.*

pot *n.* cannabis; marijuana. (Originally drugs, now widely known.) □ *She had pot on her when she was arrested.* □ *The cops found pot growing next to city hall.*

Prince Albert *n.* cannabis in general, especially marijuana sold or transported in a Prince Albert™ pipe tobacco can. (From the 1960s, but still heard.) □ *I've* *heard that Max smokes Prince Albert. □ Where can I get a can of Prince Albert?*

ragweed *n.* inferior marijuana. □ *This stuff is ragweed. You can have it! □ Max just sells ragweed except to his friends.*

reefer AND **reef** *n.* cannabis; a marijuana cigarette. □ *He had a reefer in his hand when he was busted. □ Don't stall the reef. Pass it on.*

roach *n.* the butt end of a marijuana cigarette. □ *The cops found a roach on the bathroom floor. □ Hey, give me that roach!*

sin *n.* synthetic marijuana. (From synthetic.) □ *Most of this stuff the kids put down good money for is not sin, but angel dust. □ Max was caught up in the quest for sin.*

sinse AND **sense (bud)** *n.* seedless marijuana. (From Spanish *sinsemilla,* "seedless.") □ *Where's the sinse I was saving? □ Sense bud is all that Tiffany will touch.*

spliff AND **shpleef; spleef; splim** *n.* marijuana; a marijuana cigarette; hashish. (Originally Jamaican.) □ *They consume an enormous amount of spliff and try to sell it to the tourists. □ It's really high-quality splim.*

straw *n.* marijuana. □ *He stood right on the corner, selling straw by the handful from a bucket at his feet—and nobody even called the cops. □ This straw is not the best quality I've seen.*

stum *n.* marijuana. □ *Where can I get some stum? □ This stum is cashed. Trash it.*

sub *n.* a large marijuana cigarette. □ *Look at the size of that sub! □ Max makes a sub when he's got low-power straw.*

supergrass *n.* high-quality marijuana. □ *Tiffany picked up some pot she called supergrass. It looks like alfalfa to me. □ The cannabis that is the richest in resin is sometimes called supergrass.*

T *n.* marijuana. □ *Can't you stay off that T? □ All she thinks about is smoking T and where she's gonna get more of it.*

tea *n.* marijuana. □ *Max has tea and canaries on him now. No dust. □ Can't you lay off that tea awhile?*

up pot *n.* stimulating marijuana, as opposed to relaxing marijuana. □ *I can only handle up pot. Everything else makes me cry. □ Tell him you really don't want up pot unless it's cheap.*

wacky-tabbacky *n.* marijuana. (Collegiate.) □ *You got any of that wacky-tabbacky? □ He gets that silly look in his eye from smoking wacky-tabbacky.*

wana *n.* marijuana. □ *Got any wana on you? □ How much is this wana, man?*

weed *n.* marijuana; a marijuana cigarette. □ *This is good weed, man. □ This weed is green but decent.*

DRUGS - MESCALINE
mesc *n.* mescaline, a hallucinatory substance. □ *Tiffany is totally hooked on mesc. I don't know where she gets it. □ Jerry refuses to take mesc or any other dope.*

DRUGS - METHADONE
meth *n.* methadone. □ *Sometimes meth means methadone, a drug used in drug treatment. □ Jerry gets meth from a clinic in the city.*

DRUGS - MUSHROOMS
magic mushrooms AND **sacred mushrooms** *n.* mushrooms of the genus *Psilocybe,* which cause visions or hallucinations when eaten. □ *Magic mushrooms are okay because they are natural, or something like that. □ This is the so-called "sacred mushroom," named for its use in Amerindian ritual.*

shroom *in.* to take or eat peyote cactus. □ *They spent all afternoon shrooming. □ You shroom too much.*

shrooms *n.* the tips of the peyote cactus that contain mescaline. (From *mushrooms.* Not really a mushroom.) □ *I got some shrooms. Ya wanna come over? □ Shrooms and me don't mix.*

DRUGS - NEED
hard up *mod.* in need of drugs or alcohol. □ *Gert was hard up and needed a fix. □ The old hobo was hard up for a drink.*

hurting *mod.* seriously in need of something, such as a dose of drugs. □ *Gert is hurting. She needs something soon.* □ *When Ernie is hurting, he takes barbs.*

DRUGS - OPIUM

big-O *n.* opium. □ *The big-O is making a comeback, I hear.* □ *Most of the users of big-O died out thirty years ago.*

chase the dragon *tr.* to inhale opium fumes through a straw. □ *Harry thinks that chasing the dragon sounds like real fun.* □ *Chasing the dragon may sound good, but it smells awful.*

DRUGS - PARAPHERNALIA

bag *n.* a container of drugs. (Not necessarily a real bag.) □ *Two bags of H. for two dimes?* □ *The man flipped a couple of bags out from a little stack he had held under his wrist by a rubber band.*

banger *n.* a hypodermic syringe. □ *Jed dropped his banger and really panicked when it broke.* □ *His banger and other stuff were upstairs under a loose board.*

biz *n.* apparatus for injecting drugs. □ *The biz is right there in the towel on top of the stack.* □ *Use your own biz. I got that disease, I think.*

blinky AND **winky** *n.* a device for smoking crystallized cocaine. □ *He broke his blinky and is desperate for a new one.* □ *Hold the winky here and wait till I tell you.*

bong AND **bhong** *n.* a marijuana smoking device that cools the smoke by passing it through water. □ *This bong is really getting sort of nasty.* □ *Fill up your bong and let's get going.*

bowl *n.* a pipe or other device for smoking cannabis. □ *Where is my bowl? I got some real Q gold.* □ *There's somebody's bowl out in the hall. Go get it before the neighbors call the fuzz.*

carburetor *n.* a device for smoking cannabis that mixes the smoke with air. □ *I have a carburetor with the rest of my stash.* □ *Max showed Walter how to use a carburetor.*

chillum *n.* a pipe or device used for the smoking of marijuana. □ *He keeps a chillum in his stash.* □ *Ernie carries a chillum with him. He's trying to sell it.*

clip *n.* a holder for a marijuana cigarette butt. □ *She's got a clip if you need it.* □ *My clip's at home in my stash.*

cokespoon AND **(flake) spoon** *n.* a small spoon used to carry powdered cocaine to a nostril. □ *Wally wears a cokespoon around his neck.* □ *The principal wrote a letter to Mrs. Simpson telling her that Jimmy had brought a flake spoon to school.*

crutch *n.* a device to hold a marijuana cigarette butt. □ *Here's a crutch so you can finish your smoke.* □ *I lost my crutch.*

glass gun *n.* a hypodermic syringe. □ *Gert broke her glass gun and had to improvise.* □ *A lot of those bangsters don't even use a glass gun.*

hash cannon *n.* a device used in the smoking of cannabis. □ *Gert kept a hash cannon in her stash.* □ *Don had a hash cannon in his office as a sample of a device for smoking pot.*

hash pipe *n.* a small pipe for smoking cannabis. □ *John kept a hash pipe on the shelf just for show.* □ *The cops found a hash pipe in her pocket.*

hype AND **hipe** *n.* a hypodermic syringe and needle. □ *She forgot to clean the hype.* □ *He got an infection from a dirty hipe.*

party bowl *n.* a marijuana pipe large enough to serve a number of smokers. □ *When they arrested Max, he had two pipes and a party bowl with him.* □ *The cops thought the party bowl was a flower vase!*

roach clip AND **roach pick** *n.* a device to hold a *roach* (= marijuana cigarette butt) and make it smokable. □ *When the cops find a roach clip on you, you've had it.* □ *They found two roach picks and a pipe.*

scoop *n.* a folded matchbook cover used to *snort* cocaine or heroin. □ *I need a scoop. It's no good without one.* □ *I burned up the scoop by accident. Sorry.*

spike *n.* a hypodermic needle; a hypodermic syringe and needle; a medicine dropper and a needle. □ *The addict caught some strange disease from a dirty spike.* □ *What'll I do? I broke my spike.*

straw *n.* papers for rolling marijuana cigarettes. □ *I need some straw.* □ *I can't manage the straw with one hand. How do these cowboys do it?*

tote *n.* a small pipe for smoking cannabis. □ *Her father found a tote in her room and really hit the ceiling.* □ *The cops found a tote in her purse and called in her father.*

DRUGS - PARTY

coke party *n.* a gathering where cocaine is consumed. □ *There's a coke party in the warehouse after closing tonight.* □ *Tom's hosting a coke party for his yuppie friends.*

free base party *n.* a gathering where *free base* (= crystallized cocaine) is used. □ *Max has a free base party about once a week.* □ *The cops broke up a free base party in Beverly Hills.*

DRUGS - PCP

angel dust AND **angel hair; dust of angels** *n.* the common name for phencyclidine (PCP). □ *Angel dust is getting to be quite a problem in this town.* □ *I thought that angel hair and stuff like that was a problem of the sixties.*

DOA *n.* phencyclidine (PCP). (Because it is deadly.) □ *Stay away from DOA. There's a good reason why it's called that.* □ *The kids use DOA no matter what.*

hog *n.* phencyclidine (PCP), an animal tranquilizer. □ *We're glad to learn that the demand for hog is tapering off.* □ *Max won't sell hog to kids these days.*

killer weed *n.* phencyclidine (PCP), an animal tranquilizer. □ *Killer weed seems to be a favorite around here just now.* □ *Killer weed, K.J.—it's all exactly the same stuff.*

DRUGS - PEYOTE

cactus (buttons) *n.* peyote cactus containing mescaline. □ *Gert came back from vacation with a bag of cactus buttons.* □ *"Who ate all my cactus?" screamed Gert.*

mystic biscuit *n.* a chunk of peyote cactus. □ *Wally thought he got a piece of mystic biscuit, but it was just a moldy raisin.* □ *Max was selling mystic biscuit to the college kids.*

DRUGS - PORTION

bang *n.* an injection of a drug; any dose of a drug. □ *I need a bang pretty fast.* □ *If Max doesn't have a bang by noon, he gets desperate.*

bang in the arm *n.* an injection of narcotics. □ *The guy looked like he needed a bang in the arm right then!* □ *One good bang in the arm leads to another, they always say.*

belt *n.* an injection of a drug. □ *I could use a belt of smack to hold off the pain.* □ *Gimme a belt in the leg, will you? My arms are finished.*

bindle *n.* a packet of drugs. □ *She had a bindle of H. in her purse.* □ *That bindle was more important than money.*

bong *n.* a puff or *hit* of marijuana taken through a smoking device. □ *I'll take two bongs, and then I gotta go.* □ *I only got one bong!*

bop *n.* a drug in pill form; a dose of a drug. □ *Give me a bop of that stuff, will ya?* □ *You gonna drop both of them bops?*

can *n.* a measurement of marijuana. □ *How much do you want for a can?* □ *A can is too much except for a party.*

cap 1. *n.* a capsule of a drug. □ *Do you want it in caps or elixir?* □ *She spilled the caps on the floor and had to find every single one of them.* **2.** *tr.* to make a capsule. □ *I must have capped 300 placebos today.* □ *Max capped some H. for a pal.*

charge *n.* a dose or portion of a drug. □ *I need a charge to tide me over.* □ *Just a little charge till I can get to my candy man.*

check *n.* a dose of a drug in a capsule or folded in a paper. □ *Max handed me a check, and I slipped him some long green.* □ *How much you want for a check?*

cop a fix *tr.* to obtain a dose of drugs. □ *She was gonna, like, die if she didn't cop* *a fix pretty soon.* □ *She carries her apps so she can cop a fix whenever.*

doll *n.* a pill. (Usually plural.) □ *She took stuff, yeah, but only dolls.* □ *Taking dolls is different from shooting up.*

fix(-up) *n.* a dose of a drug, especially for an addict who is in need of drugs. (It fixes the suffering of withdrawal.) □ *It was clear that the prisoner needed a fix, but there was nothing the cops would do for him.* □ *Max arranged to get a fix-up into the con.*

hype *n.* an injection of drugs. □ *Ernie needed a hype real bad.* □ *Max told him who could help him with a hype.*

jolt *n.* a portion or dose of a drug. □ *How about a little jolt as a taste?* □ *A jolt costs.*

jug *n.* a glass vial of liquid amphetamine intended for injection. □ *His mother found a jug and took it to a drugstore to find out what it was.* □ *Any kid can get jugs just by asking around.*

load *n.* a dose of drugs; an injection of drugs. □ *She shoots a load every day or two.* □ *He scored enough for a load only yesterday.*

pill *n.* a drug in capsule form. □ *Stop taking those pills!* □ *The doctor prescribed these pills.*

poke *n.* a puff of a marijuana cigarette or pipe. □ *Can I have a poke of that?* □ *Hey! One poke is enough!*

shoot-up *n.* an injection of heroin. □ *The way Ernie was yawning, I knew he needed a shoot-up.* □ *"Just one more shoot-up. That's all. Then, never again!" moaned Ernie, rather unconvincingly.*

shot *n.* an injection of drugs. □ *Just one shot of that stuff and you're hooked for life.* □ *A shot of skag put the poor guy straight for a while.*

shot in the arm *n.* an injection of narcotics. □ *You might say that I really needed this shot in the arm.* □ *It's nothing. Just a little shot in the arm.*

sip *n.* a puff of a marijuana cigarette. □ *How about a sip of your joint?* □ *He*

took a big sip and held it so long he almost turned blue.

snort *n.* a nasal dose of a drug, usually cocaine. □ *Here, take a snort.* □ *I don't want a snort. I'm clean, and I'm going to stay that way.*

strike *n.* a dose of drugs. □ *I need a strike. You got any stumbles?* □ *Just one strike, Max, come on, just one. I'll pay you tomorrow, Max, come on, just one little strike. Anything, Max. I really hurt, Max.*

swallow *n.* a puff of cigarette smoke. □ *He took just one swallow and started coughing.* □ *Can I have a swallow of your fag?*

toke *n.* a puff of marijuana smoke. □ *After a big toke, he settled back to drift.* □ *Harry took a big toke and sighed.*

toot *n.* a line or dose of cocaine; cocaine. □ *These tootheads get sort of frantic when they can't get a toot.* □ *What do you spend on a toot, anyway?*

tote *n.* a small portion of cannabis. □ *The cops found a tote when they tossed Max, but that was all.* □ *How much do you want for just a tote?*

DRUGS - POWDER

dust *n.* a powdered drug: heroin, phencyclidine (PCP), cocaine; fine cannabis. □ *It's the dust that can really do you damage.* □ *Wally got hold of some kind of dust and took it to the police.*

snow AND **snowball; snowflakes; snow stuff** *n.* a powdered or crystalline narcotic: morphine, heroin, or cocaine. (Now almost always the latter.) □ *Now, snow is almost old-fashioned.* □ *The price of snow has come down a lot as South America exports more of it.*

DRUGS - PURCHASE

dope up *in.* to purchase a supply of drugs. □ *Where's my old friend Max? I gotta dope up.* □ *Max is doping up, himself. He doesn't grow it himself, you know.*

fix *in.* to buy a dose of drugs; to take drugs. □ *Max had to fix before he could even talk to me.* □ *Tracy was in the other room fixing.*

get a fix AND **get a gift** *tr.* to buy drugs. □ *Gert had to get home and get a fix.* □ *What did Tracy mean when she said she had to get a gift fast?*

DRUGS - REACTION
goof *in.* to scratch, nod, and slobber after an injection of heroin. □ *She just rocks and goofs for hours.* □ *She has been goofing for an hour.*

DRUGS - REHABILITATION
take the cure *tr.* to enter into any treatment program or treatment center. (Especially those dealing with drugs and alcohol.) □ *I wanted to take the cure, but I just couldn't bring myself to do it.* □ *It's hard to get them to realize that they are the ones who have to decide to take the cure.*

turn over *in.* to get off of drugs. (Like turn over a new leaf.) □ *He wanted to turn over, but just couldn't.* □ *There is a clinic on Maple Street that'll help heads turn over.*

DRUGS - RUINED
brain-burned AND **brain-fried** *mod.* brain-damaged from drugs. □ *The kid is a little brain-burned, but still has a chance at an independent life.* □ *Man, you're gonna get brain-burned from this stuff.*

burned out *mod.* no longer affected by a particular drug. □ *It's no good. I'm just burned out. The stuff doesn't affect me at all.* □ *She was burned out on Q.*

burnout *n.* a person who is ruined by drugs. □ *The kid's a burnout. What can you do?* □ *Two burnouts sat on the school steps and stared at their feet.*

DRUGS - SELLER
bagman *n.* a drug dealer. □ *Sam was a bagman for a well-known dealer for a while.* □ *We don't just want the bagman. We want to arrest Mr. Big.*

carrier *n.* a narcotics seller or transporter. □ *The carrier has the most dangerous job of all.* □ *You'll never see an old carrier.*

drug lord *n.* a drug dealer high up in the distribution chain. □ *The drug lords like Mr. Big seem never to get arrested.* □ *Max*

had always admired the sheer power of the domestic drug lord.

man AND **the man** *n.* a drug seller or pusher. □ *The man won't give you credit, you numskull!* □ *When your man doesn't show, there's always a good reason.*

DRUGS - STRONG
Cadillac *n.* a powerful drug, especially cocaine. □ *Just a pinch of Cadillac in my junk seems to keep me a little more lively.* □ *Nothing but Cadillac for Max!*

DRUGS - SUPPLY
load *n.* a drug supply; a *stash.* □ *My load is up in the closet.* □ *If his load dwindles, he gets more easily.*

main stash *n.* the home of a drug user described in terms of where one's major store of drugs is kept. □ *His apps are in his main stash.* □ *My main stash is on Maple, but I'm usually not there.*

stash *n.* a concealed supply of drugs, especially marijuana; drugs and equipment to use them stored in a secret place. □ *Max's stash was never located by the fuzz.* □ *My stash is down to nothing.*

DRUGS - TRANQUILIZERS
blue *n.* a 10-mg tablet of Valium™. □ *A blue is enough to put most people into a stupor. Why do you want two?* □ *In treatment they kept giving me blues to calm me down. Now I can't live without them.*

happy pills *n.* tranquilizers. □ *She asked the doctor for some happy pills.* □ *She is now hooked on happy pills.*

lude *n.* a capsule of Quaalude™, a tranquilizer. □ *A couple of ludes put Max in a better mood.* □ *I don't know what he gave me. Mary said it was a lude or something.*

mickey AND **micky** *n.* a tranquilizer. □ *Whatever that mickey was you gave me, it helped.* □ *Maybe a little mickey would help me relax.*

vals *n.* Valium™ tranquilizers. □ *I'm taking vals for this, but the doctor says to get off of them as soon as possible.* □ *Vals really calm you down.*

DRUGS - USE

blow 1. *tr.* to *snort* any powdered drug; to take snuff. □ *Those guys spend all their time blowing coke.* □ *Are you blowing something good?* **2.** *in.* to smoke marijuana. □ *He sits there blowing by the hour. How can he afford it?* □ *They say that blowing that much will affect your brain.* **3.** *n.* cocaine. □ *You can get some good blow over at that crack house.* □ *What's blow cost around here?*

bogart AND **bogard** *in.* to monopolize a communal marijuana cigarette; to hold a communal marijuana cigarette so long—Bogart style—that one drools on it. (From *Humphrey Bogart,* the screen actor.) □ *Come on, man. Don't bogart on us!* □ *Stop bogarding and take a hit!*

bong AND **bhong** *tr. & in.* to smoke marijuana or other drugs with a smoking device. □ *You can't just bong for the rest of your life!* □ *Wanna go bong a bowl?*

do *tr. & in.* to use a drug or drugs in general. □ *Is Tracy doing dust again?* □ *Tracy never stopped doing. She just switched from dust to splash.*

do a line *tr.* to *snort* a dose of a powdered drug, usually cocaine. □ *Max slipped into a doorway to do a line.* □ *Ernie has to do a line about every four hours—night and day.*

do drugs AND **do dope** *tr.* to take drugs; to use drugs habitually. □ *Rocko doesn't do drugs, and he doesn't drink.* □ *Max started doing dope when he was very young.*

dope up *in.* to inject drugs; to take a dose of a narcotic. □ *I'm hurting, man, I gotta dope up, now!* □ *She slipped into the back room to dope up.*

do some bongs *tr.* to smoke some marijuana, usually with a water pipe. □ *All the kids think that doing bongs is the greatest thing on earth.* □ *Hey, dude, wanna do some bongs?*

do the drug thing *tr.* to be involved with drugs; to take drugs. □ *Man, you gotta stop doing the drug thing.* □ *All she thinks about is doing the drug thing.*

drop *tr.* to take a drug, specifically *acid.* □ *Ted dropped some stuff and went on a trip.* □ *Now he doesn't drop even once a month.*

drop a bop *tr.* to take a drug in pill form. □ *Tyrone dropped a bop and went on his way.* □ *Wanna come over and drop a bop or two?*

drug *in.* to use drugs. □ *There is no way that she will stop drugging by herself.* □ *Why does she drug so heavily?*

fire a line *tr.* to *snort* a *line* of cocaine. □ *Max left to fire a line.* □ *Rocko has never fired a line in his life.*

fire up *in.* to light a marijuana cigarette. □ *Max fires up at every chance.* □ *Rocko says he never fired up in his life.*

free-basing AND **baseballing; basing** *n.* using crystallized cocaine as a recreational drug. □ *Rocko refuses to try free-basing.* □ *He saw what basing did to his brother.*

get narkied *in.* to inject drugs; to become addicted. □ *Rocko only got narkied once in his life.* □ *Gert couldn't wait to get narkied.*

get one's nose cold *tr.* to *snort* cocaine. □ *Max is always ready to get his nose cold.* □ *Rocko has never gotten his nose cold in his life.*

get one's wings *tr.* to use heavy drugs for the first time; to succeed in becoming a drug addict. □ *Gert got her wings after fiddling around with stuff for a long time.* □ *Max got his wings at about age twelve.*

get straight AND **get right** *in.* to take a dose of a drug to end drug craving. □ *Gert needed a fix to get straight.* □ *I need to get right before anything else.*

go down the line *in.* to *snort* a *line* of cocaine. □ *Gert had to leave the office to go down the line.* □ *They found her in the john, going down the line.*

goof *in.* to use heroin or some other addictive drugs without intending to become addicted; to play around (with heroin). □ *Gert spent the first few years just goofing.* □ *She was goofing, and you know what that leads to.*

horn *tr.* to sniff or *snort* a narcotic. □ *Ernie horned a line and paused for a minute.* □ *He'd rather horn it than shoot it.*

jab pop *in.* to inject (drugs). □ *Gert was jab popping when she died.* □ *Jab popping is a ticket to cement city.*

one and one *mod.* having to do with the use of both nostrils in snorting a drug, usually cocaine. □ *Max always takes it one and one. It's the only way he can get enough.* □ *He does it one and one because it hits him faster that way.*

on the street *mod.* using drugs; selling drugs; looking for drugs. □ *Fred spent a year on the street before he was arrested.* □ *Max will be on the street all his life.*

plugged in *mod.* excited by drugs; having to do with the drug culture. □ *Those guys are really plugged in.* □ *That punker is plugged in, for sure.*

pop *tr.* to take or swallow a pill, tablet, or capsule. □ *Here, pop a couple of these.* □ *He pops uppers from dawn to dusk.*

scoop *tr. & in.* to inhale cocaine or heroin, using a folded matchbook cover. □ *Max is scooping for the fourth time today.* □ *He scooped two lines together.*

session *n.* a marijuana-smoking session; time spent on a drug high. (Collegiate.) □ *What a fine session that was!* □ *Max was terribly hungry after the session.*

shoot (up) *tr. & in.* to inject a specific drug into the bloodstream. □ *He actually had to leave the meeting to shoot.* □ *The two of them were shooting up skag.*

shoot up (on something) *in.* to inject (a drug). □ *About that time we both began shooting up on skag.* □ *He couldn't wait to get home and shoot up.*

smell it up AND **smell the stuff** *tr.* to sniff or inhale powdered drugs, usually cocaine. □ *One of those guys shoots it; the other smells it up.* □ *You don't breathe it in; you just smell the stuff.*

snork *in.* to smoke marijuana or hashish. □ *Let's get down to some serious snorking.* □ *They snorked until they could snork no more.*

snort *tr. & in.* to sniff (insufflate) a powdered drug, now usually cocaine. □ *Here, snort this.* □ *You're snorting every time I see you.*

switch on *in.* to get high on drugs; to begin taking LSD or some other hallucinogens. □ *One by one, each of my friends switched on.* □ *There was some old man who seemed to get pleasure from getting kids to switch on. Maybe he was a dealer.*

take it through the nose *tr.* to inhale cocaine. □ *Max liked taking it through the nose better than anything, except maybe a shot in the arm.* □ *He went into the john, and most of us knew he had to take it through the nose right then.*

toke *tr. & in.* to puff a marijuana cigarette. □ *He sat on a stone to toke one before bean time.* □ *He tokes for a good bit of every day.*

toot *tr. & in.* to inhale a portion of cocaine. □ *She had to leave the office to toot.* □ *She tooted a couple of lines and came back.*

turn on *in.* to take a drug. □ *Pete just can't wait to light up and turn on.* □ *He will turn on with anybody at the drop of a hat.*

up *in.* to take a stimulant drug. □ *She has to up every morning.* □ *Ted upped before going in to take the test.*

use *tr. & in.* to use (drugs); to take drugs habitually. □ *I tried to stop using, but I couldn't.* □ *I couldn't face myself if I started using the stuff again.*

DRUGS - USER

baseman AND **basehead** *n.* someone who is using *free base*, a form of cocaine; someone who is "on base." □ *They say that all those rich guys are basemen.* □ *The baseheads in the dorm finally got caught.* □ *The stuff is so powerful that one whiff and you're a basehead.*

beanhead *n.* a drug user who uses pills habitually. □ *You beanheads are just as much junkies as the jerks who shoot.* □ *There's no harm in being a beanhead.*

blower *n.* a cocaine user. □ *I can spot a blower any day.* □ *Max is a blower, among other things.*

candy man *n.* a drug dealer. □ *Lefty said he had to go meet with the candy man.* □ *Max is sort of a candy man.*

C-head 1. *n.* a cocaine user. □ *I don't want any C-head operating on me!* □ *How much money does a C-head need to get through the day?* **2.** *n.* an LSD user who takes LSD on sugar cubes. □ *Frank was a C-head in the sixties.* □ *Why don't you C-heads grow up?*

chippy AND **chippie; chippy (user)** *n.* an occasional user of an addictive drug. □ *The chippy users rarely end up in the hospital.* □ *Who can stay a chippie very long?*

cokeaholic *n.* a cocaine addict. □ *It's hard to get a cokeaholic to get treatment.* □ *When I realized I was a cokeaholic, I decided to stop, but I couldn't.*

cokehead *n.* a heavy cocaine user; a co-caine addict. □ *We got a few depressed cokeheads in the emergency room who have tried suicide.* □ *As a banker, I see two or three cokeheads file for bankruptcy each year.*

connection *n.* a seller of drugs; some-one who is a source for drugs. □ *Max's connection got rousted.* □ *This connection you keep taking about—is he dependable?*

courier *n.* a small-time drug seller; a drug runner; a carrier of contraband. □ *The cops can catch the couriers whenever they want. It's the big guys they're after.* □ *The couriers are expendable.*

crackhead *n.* a user of *crack*. □ *They brought an eight-year-old crackhead in for treatment.* □ *Crackheads are a very seri-ous problem in the nation's workforce.*

drughead *n.* a heavy drug user; an ad-dict. □ *They find a drughead in the river about once a month.* □ *The drugheads are taking over this neighborhood.*

freakout *freaked (out)* person. □ *Some poor freakout sat in the corner and rocked.* □ *Who's the freakout in the corner?*

free-baser *n.* a user of *free base*. □ *Of course Max is a free-baser! What doesn't*

he do? □ *Some of these free-basers have heart attacks.*

garbage freak AND **garbagehead** *n.* an addict who will take any drug. □ *We don't know what she took. She was such a garbage freak.* □ *The garbageheads will take beans or anything else.*

gluey AND **gluer** *n.* a person, usually a teenager, who sniffs glue. □ *Teddy is a gluey. That's why he's failing in school.* □ *The gluers stand a chance of having brain damage.*

good-time man *n.* a man who sells drugs. □ *Max is the main good-time man in this neighborhood.* □ *The fuzz wants to see all the good-time men behind bars.*

grasshead AND **grasser; grasshopper** *n.* a marijuana smoker. □ *The grassheads are taking over this neighborhood.* □ *Imagine, a seven-year-old grasser!*

guru *n.* an experienced LSD user who guides someone else on a *trip*. □ *Max volunteered to serve as a guru, but he never showed up.* □ *A guru can be a big help.*

hash-head *n.* a smoker of cannabis. □ *You can't stay a hash-head all your life.* □ *Kelly was almost a hopeless hash-head.*

hay burner AND **hay head** *n.* a mari-juana smoker. □ *Some hay burner was around trying to sell raffle tickets that looked handmade.* □ *Another hay head came in and applied for the job.*

head *n.* a member of the drug culture; a hippie or a person who drops out of mainstream society because of drug use. (From the 1960s and 1970s.) □ *You still see a few heads around, even today.* □ *Some of the heads became very, very straight.*

hit man *n.* a man hired by a helpless ad-dict to inject drugs. □ *Gert needed a hit man when she was sick.* □ *Max refuses to be a hit man. He says that's not what he does best.*

hog *n.* an addict who requires very large doses to sustain the habit. □ *Gert isn't a hog. She tries to keep her habit small.* □ *Ernie is turning into a hog. He just can't get enough.*

hophead *n.* a drug user; someone under the effects of drugs. ☐ *The hopheads are taking over this part of town.* ☐ *What happens to these hopheads when they grow up?*

horner *n.* a cocaine user. ☐ *Sure, Max is a horner. He sells the stuff to support his own habit.* ☐ *I think the new employee is a horner.*

hype *n.* a drug addict who injects drugs. ☐ *Gert's been a hype for about a year.* ☐ *The hypes have a rough time in prison.*

hyper *n.* a drug user who injects drugs with a hypodermic syringe. ☐ *How long have you been a hyper, Gert?* ☐ *Max has been a hyper since he was twenty-four.*

jabber *n.* a drug addict who injects drugs. ☐ *The guy's a jabber. Look at those tracks.* ☐ *These scars show that the victim was a jabber.*

jerker *n.* a heavy user of cocaine. ☐ *The new guy is a jerker. You can see it in his eyes.* ☐ *The jerkers who need immediate treatment are sent from ER up to detox.*

junkie AND **junky** *n.* a drug dealer. ☐ *Max is a junkie.* ☐ *Junkies should be put into the jug.*

junkie AND **junky** *n.* a drug user; an addict. ☐ *The junkies can be helped, you know.* ☐ *Junkies have to steal to support their habits.*

kick freak *n.* a nonaddicted drug user. ☐ *Ernie used to be a kick freak, but all that has changed.* ☐ *Yeah, the kick freak became a junky.*

kite *n.* a drug user who is always *high*. ☐ *The guy's a kite. He won't make any sense no matter what you ask him.* ☐ *Gert is a kite, and she's getting worse.*

meth monster *n.* a habitual user of methamphetamine. ☐ *Sometimes a meth monster will do okay in school.* ☐ *These teenage meth monsters can be a real menace when they need juice.*

mojo *n.* a narcotics addict. ☐ *These mojos will rob you blind if you don't keep an eye on them.* ☐ *Bruno's no mojo, and if he was nobody'd mention it.*

moocher *n.* a drug addict. ☐ *The guy's a moocher and can't be trusted.* ☐ *These moochers will do anything to get a few bucks for a load.*

mother *n.* a drug dealer; one's own drug dealer upon whom one depends. ☐ *Bruno is my mother.* ☐ *If you can't trust your mother, who can you trust?*

mule *n.* someone who delivers or smuggles drugs for a drug dealer. ☐ *The jerks use a twelve-year-old kid for a mule!* ☐ *A car drove by, and suddenly the mule was riddled with machine gun bullets.*

OD *n.* a person who has taken an overdose of drugs. (Hospitals.) ☐ *This OD has just stopped breathing.* ☐ *How many ODs did you get in here last weekend?*

pillhead AND **pill freak** *n.* a drug user who prefers drugs in pill or capsule form. ☐ *You pill freaks should try some of this stuff.* ☐ *I don't smoke. I'm strictly a pillhead.*

pill-popper AND **popper; pill-dropper** *n.* anyone who takes pills frequently or habitually. ☐ *Poor Sue is a pill-popper.* ☐ *I knew she was always ill, but I didn't know she was a pill-dropper.* ☐ *The pill-popper thought she wouldn't get hooked.*

pusher *n.* a drug dealer who works hard to establish new addicts and customers. ☐ *That pusher over on Eighth Street was just mobbed by a group of angry parents.* ☐ *They said that pushers should be locked up forever.*

space cadet *n.* a person who is always high on drugs. ☐ *Max has been a space cadet since he was twelve.* ☐ *The space cadets can usually be found sitting on a bench outside the principal's office.*

speed demon *n.* a habitual user of methamphetamine. ☐ *A couple of speed demons mugged the old lady.* ☐ *When they are high, most speed demons don't know what they are doing.*

speeder AND **speedster** *n.* a user of amphetamines or methamphetamine; a person who is hyperactive from amphetamine use. ☐ *That kid is really hyped up—must be a speeder.* ☐ *The speedsters can seem crazy when they're on a run.*

speed freak AND **speedhead** *n.* a drug user who injects methamphetamine; an amphetamine user. □ *Hank is a speed freak, but he's not on skag.* □ *Speed freaks, not heroin addicts, account for a high proportion of drug-related crime.*

street pusher *n.* a drug dealer who works at the retail level on the streets. □ *It's the street pushers who take the risk and end up doing a few months in the pen.* □ *Max was a street pusher until he got busted.*

swingman *n.* a drug seller; a drug *connection.* □ *Max couldn't deliver till he met with his swingman.* □ *Bruno wants to be a swingman with the mob.*

user *n.* a drug user; a drug addict. □ *I want to stop being a user, but I can't do it by myself.* □ *I'm no user! Maybe a joint now and then, and an upper on a dreary morning—but I'm no user!*

weedhead AND **weed-eater** *n.* a smoker of marijuana. □ *Max is a confirmed weed-eater.* □ *The weedheads are taking over this neighborhood.*

zonker *n.* a marijuana smoker. □ *A lot of these zonkers may take six years to get through high school.* □ *You are turning into a first-class zonker.*

DRUGS - WEAK

choked *mod.* having to do with overly diluted drugs. □ *This stuff is choked. Don't score with that guy again.* □ *Why is this stuff so stepped on—you know, choked?*

DRUNK

See INTOXICATED - ALCOHOL.

DRUNKARD

alchy AND **alkie; alky** *n.* a drunkard. □ *You see alchy after alchy all up and down Maxwell Street.* □ *Some alkie came in and asked for a quarter.*

barfly *n.* a drunkard. □ *You're nothing but an old barfly!* □ *Some barfly staggered out of the tavern straight into the side of a car.*

barrel *n.* a drunkard. □ *The barrel was full up and through for the evening.* □ *A tired and weepy barrel staggered in and fell into a booth in the corner.*

bat *n.* a drunkard; a person on a drinking spree. □ *Somebody give that bat a hand before he falls down.* □ *A tired old bat—still waving a bottle—met me on the stairs.*

belcher 1. *n.* a beer drinker. □ *Look at the belly on that belcher!* □ *Harry is a confirmed belcher.* **2.** *n.* a hard drinker; a drunkard. □ *A couple of belchers wandered in about midnight. Other than that, the night is dead.* □ *I'm a belcher, and I know it.*

bender *n.* a heavy drinker; a drunkard. □ *This bender comes up to me and nearly kills me with his breath, asking for a match.* □ *In the dim light I could make out a few of the regular benders, but Harold wasn't there.*

blotter *n.* a drunkard. □ *The guy's a blotter. He'll drink anything and lots of it.* □ *They say that Mr. Franklin is a blotter and needs treatment.*

booze artist *n.* a drunken person; a drunkard. □ *Pete was a booze artist for a decade before he realized what he was doing.* □ *A wobbly booze artist sat musing on the stool in the corner.*

bottle *n.* a drunkard. □ *The bar was empty save for an old bottle propped against the side of a booth.* □ *That old girl is just a bottle. There's more booze in her than outside.*

bottle baby *n.* an alcoholic. □ *The bottle babies sat there, waiting to be thrown out at closing time.* □ *There is help for bottle babies.*

brewster *n* a beer drinker; a beer drunkard. □ *Fred has become a committed brewster. He pounds one beer after another.* □ *A dedicated brewster can put away a six-pack in half an hour.*

bubblehead *n.* a heavy drinker of champagne. □ *It takes a pretty good bankroll to be a real high-class bubblehead.* □ *Part-time bubbleheads go into operation at weddings and other celebrations.*

budhead *n.* a beer drinker. □ *You're a budhead, and you're getting worse.* □

Here comes Charlie, my favorite budhead. How about a brew, Charlie?

Christmas tree *n.* a drunkard. (From being *lit* like a Christmas tree.) □ *Some old Christmas tree staggered by, muttering to herself.* □ *A well-dressed Christmas tree sat in the corner—lit up, of course.*

crock *n.* a drunkard. □ *Give the old crock some money, anything to get him outa here before he barfs or something.* □ *The crock wants booze, not money.*

dip(so) *n.* a drunkard. (From *dipsomaniac.*) □ *Buy the dip a drink. That'll shut him up for a while.* □ *She's sort of a closet dipso.*

falling-down drunk *n.* a drunken person who falls down. □ *Poor old Jed is turning into a falling-down drunk.* □ *One more falling-down drunk in this neighborhood will not be anything new.*

gargler *n.* a drinker; a drunkard. □ *You are going to turn into a gargler if you don't let up on your drinking.* □ *Some old gargler froze to death last night.*

ginhead *n.* a drunkard. □ *Gert could have ended up a ginhead, but she went another route instead.* □ *A couple of ginheads sat in the corner booth silently.*

glow worm *n.* a drunkard; an alcoholic. □ *You are turning into a regular glow worm.* □ *Gary came out of the bar and tripped over a napping glow worm near the entrance to the alley.*

groghound *n.* a drunkard. □ *I'm afraid that Ernie is getting to be a groghound.* □ *I'm an old groghound from way back.*

guzzle-guts *n.* a drunkard; a heavy drinker. □ *Old guzzle-guts here would like another drink.* □ *Don't call me guzzle-guts. I hardly ever have a drop.*

guzzler *n.* a heavy drinker. □ *Harry is getting to be quite a guzzler.* □ *A couple of guzzlers at the bar were carrying on a low conversation when Barlowe came in.*

hammerhead *n.* a drunkard. □ *These hammerheads can't even hold a simple job for the most part.* □ *A couple of hammerheads stood in the alley, looking suspicious.*

heister *n.* a drunkard. □ *Two old heisters were lifting drink after drink and tossing them down.* □ *Wally is getting to be quite a heister.*

hellbender *n.* a heavy drinker; a drunkard. (The *bender* refers to bending the elbow with a drink in hand. Use caution with *hell.*) □ *Wally is a hellbender from way back.* □ *Jed is a world-class hellbender.*

hooch hound AND **hooch head** *n.* a drunkard. □ *Jed is a classic hooch hound. He lives for the stuff.* □ *The party turned into a drinking session for hooch heads.*

hoo(t)cher *n.* a drunkard. □ *Ernie isn't a hoocher, you can say that for him.* □ *A hootcher staggered in and staggered right out again.*

hophead *n.* an alcoholic or a drunkard. □ *I'm afraid that Wally is becoming a hophead.* □ *Ernie is a well-established and incurable hophead.*

horner *n.* a heavy drinker; a drunkard. □ *Wally is a real horner. He has an enormous capacity.* □ *Jed is the king of horners around here.*

jagster *n.* someone on a drinking spree; a heavy drinker. □ *Gary is a typical jagster. Drunk for a week and sober for three.* □ *There's not a lot that a doctor can do for a jagster like that.*

jerker *n.* a drunkard; an alcoholic. □ *Some of the jerkers have the DTs.* □ *Ask the jerker to come in and have a drink.*

jingler *mod.* a drunkard; an alcoholic. □ *The jinglers have taken over the streets.* □ *Where do all these jinglers sleep?*

job *n.* a drunkard. □ *What does this old job want besides a drink?* □ *Give the job a drink and make somebody happy today.*

jugger *n.* an alcoholic; a drunkard. □ *A couple of old juggers sat in the alley, trying to figure out how to get some more.* □ *He's a jugger, and he will never change.*

jughead *n.* a drunkard. □ *Buy the jughead a drink. That'll shut him up.* □ *You don't see jugheads at parties as much as you used to.*

juice freak *n.* someone who prefers alcohol to drugs. □ *Freddy is a juice freak. He won't touch dolls.* □ *Juice freaks end up with addictions, too.*

juicehead AND **juicer** *n.* a heavy drinker; a drunkard. □ *Hank is turning into a regular juicehead.* □ *The tavern is always filled with juicers on Friday night.*

lapper *n.* a drunkard. □ *The street was empty except for an old lapper staggering home.* □ *The party was ruined by the antics of a few lappers.*

lush *n.* a drunkard. □ *I was afraid of it for some time, but now I know. Tracy is a lush.* □ *There were four confirmed lushes at the party, but they all passed out and didn't bother us much.*

mooner *n.* a drunkard. □ *This old mooner from up in the hills wandered into town last Friday and died in the town square.* □ *There must be dozens of mooners who beg in town in the day and drink in the woods at night.*

mop *n.* a heavy drinker; a drunkard. □ *The guy's a mop. There is nothing you can do till he decides he's had enough.* □ *The mops hang out here looking for handouts.*

oilhead *n.* a drunkard; an alcoholic. □ *There is an old oilhead over there on the street corner.* □ *Paul gave the oilhead a quarter, knowing it would be spent on cheap wine.*

one of the faithful *n.* a drunkard. □ *Here comes Mr. Franklin—one of the faithful—staggering down the street.* □ *I saw one of the faithful standing at the bar.*

Otis *n.* a drunkard. (From the name of a television character who is the town drunk. Also a term of address.) □ *Look at Otis over there, propped up against the wall.* □ *Have another beer, Otis?*

pickler *n.* a drunkard; an alcoholic. □ *What a pickler. He could drink all night.* □ *The cops brought in about thirty picklers last night.*

plonko *n.* a drunkard. □ *Get that smelly plonko out of here!* □ *He's a plonko if I ever saw one.*

rumdum AND **rum-dum** *n.* a drunkard; a ruined alcoholic. □ *Get that smelly rumdum out of here.* □ *I don't want to end up like a dirty rum-dum.*

rummy *n.* a drunkard; an alcoholic; an alcoholic hobo. □ *Ask that rummy to leave before he throws up.* □ *There is a rummy at the door asking for a handout.*

shuffler *n.* a drunkard; a *tippler.* □ *The tavern was full of aged shufflers hoping for a handout.* □ *Some shuffler barfed in the shrubbery.*

sipster *n.* a tippler; a drunkard. □ *The old lady is a sipster who says she drinks a little wine to help her arthritis.* □ *Most sipsters have a really fine excuse like that.*

skate *n.* a drunkard; a person on a drinking spree. □ *Jerry's a skate and he knows it.* □ *A couple of skates celebrating the new year ran into my car.*

soak *n.* a drunkard. □ *Some old soak lay moaning in the gutter.* □ *Hank is getting to be a real soak.*

soaker *n.* a drunkard; a *tippler.* □ *Uncle Charlie was a soaker, and the family never realized it.* □ *Give the old soaker a drink to shut him up.*

sop *n.* a drunkard; an alcoholic. □ *What does the old sop want, a handout?* □ *Give the old sop a buck and tell him to beat it.*

souse *n.* a drunkard. □ *The best thing you can do for a souse like John is to take away his car keys.* □ *It's hard to live with a souse.*

sozzler *n.* a drunkard. □ *The sozzler leaned against the tavern window. I thought he would break it.* □ *A sozzler staggered by—reeking of gin.*

spud *n.* a vodka drunkard. □ *That silly spud thinks we can't smell what's on her breath.* □ *The old spud on the third floor fell down a flight or two and broke his hip.*

spunge *n.* a drunkard; a *tippler.* □ *She was a spunge, and she wasn't going to do anything about it.* □ *Is there treatment for spunges like her?*

squiff *n.* a drunkard. □ *It's no fun living with a squiff.* □ *Is there anything that can be done for a confirmed squiff?*

stew *n.* a drunkard. □ *Who is that stew in the corner?* □ *There are three stews sleeping in the alley.*

stew bum *n.* a drunkard; an alcoholic. □ *You're going to end up a stew bum if you don't lay off the moonshine.* □ *Those stew bums could use a bath.*

stick *n.* a drunkard. □ *Some stick threw up on my car.* □ *Get that stick out of here before he makes a mess.*

stiff *n.* a drunkard. □ *Some stiff staggered by—belching clouds of some beery smell.* □ *The guy's a stiff, and you want to run him for mayor? Even in this town that's going too far.*

suds-swiller *n.* a beer-drinker. □ *Ted is a suds-swiller and Bill won't touch the stuff. What strange roommates.* □ *Wayne's goal in life is to be a professional suds-swiller.*

swizzle-stick *n.* a drunkard. (From the name of a short stick used to stir an alcoholic drink.) □ *That guy is a swizzle-stick. Don't give him any more.* □ *You had better slow down, or you will turn into a swizzle-stick.*

tank AND **tank up** *n.* a drunkard. (Usually **tank-up**.) □ *You're turning into a real tank, Harry.* □ *Who's the tank-up carrying the thermos of whiskey?*

tanker *n.* a drinker; a drunkard. □ *When I came into the bar, a few tankers were in the back.* □ *Who's the tanker carrying the thermos of gin?*

thirsty soul *n.* a drunkard; a person in need of a drink. □ *Yes, I'd call Bill a thirsty soul—he always seems thirsty for booze.* □ *There was a long line of thirsty souls waiting for the liquor joint to open.*

tippler *n.* a drunkard. □ *Uncle Ben was a tippler—a harmless one.* □ *He started drinking at fifteen and has been a tippler ever since.*

toast *n.* a drunkard. □ *The old toast stumbled in front of a car.* □ *A couple of toasts tried to get us to buy them drinks.*

tooter *n.* a drunkard. □ *Hank offered the tooter a drink, which was gratefully accepted, of course.* □ *I think you are turning into a tooter.*

two-fisted drinker *n.* a heavy drinker; someone who drinks with both hands. □ *Harry was a two-fisted drinker, a caveman, and a lady-killer.* □ *The world is filled with guys who aspire to be two-fisted drinkers.*

whale *n.* a drunkard; a person with an enormous capacity for liquor. □ *Arthur is getting to be a regular whale. What does he drink?* □ *A pair of whales was in the corner booth tanking up.*

wino *n.* a wine drunkard. □ *By midnight the winos had gone into their stupors, and we got that part of town to ourselves.* □ *I gave the wino some money to help him stop the shakes.*

yeaster *n.* a beer-drinker. □ *A couple of yeasters in the back of the tavern were singing a dirty song.* □ *Who's the yeaster with the bloodshot eyes?*

zonker *n.* a drunkard. □ *The zonker just can't help himself.* □ *If I had known she was a confirmed zonker, I never would have given her a drink.*

DULL

beige *mod.* boring; insipid. □ *The party is beige. Let's cruise.* □ *Let's blow this beige joint!* □ *This day is way beige! Bag it!*

big drink of water *n.* a boring person or thing. (A pun on "hard to take.") □ *She is a big drink of water, but she could be worse.* □ *The lecture was a big drink of water.*

blah *mod.* bland; dull. □ *What a blah performance!* □ *After a blah day like this I need something really exciting, like a hot bath.*

bore the pants off (of) someone *tr.* to bore someone exceedingly. □ *You bore the pants off me!* □ *The lecture bored the pants off of everybody.*

dead 1. *mod.* dull; lifeless; flat. □ *This meal is sort of dead because I am out of onions.* □ *The pop went dead because someone left it open.* □ *Who wants dead pop?* **2.** *mod.* quiet and uneventful; boring. □ *The day was totally dead.* □ *What a dead day!* □ *Things were sure dead around this town this summer.*

dead from the neck up *mod.* no longer open to new ideas. □ *My uncle is dead from the neck up. A real fossil.* □ *Everyone on the board of directors is dead from the neck up.*

deadly (dull) *mod.* very dull. □ *The lecture was deadly dull, and I went to sleep.* □ *What a deadly dull prof.* □ *Her story was really deadly. I am sorry I was awake for part of it.*

deadpan *mod.* dull and lifeless. (Usually said of a face, expression, etc.) □ *What a deadpan expression!* □ *Her face is totally deadpan.* □ *He has such a deadpan approach to everything.*

deadpan *n.* a person with an expressionless face. □ *The guy's a perfect deadpan.* □ *When you come onstage, look like a deadpan.*

drag *n.* something dull and boring. □ *This day's a drag.* □ *What a drag. Let's go someplace interesting.*

dry-as-dust *mod.* dull; lifeless. □ *I can't take another one of his dry-as-dust lectures.* □ *All her ideas are dry-as-dust.* □ *Some dry-as-dust old crock talked endlessly about old bones.*

dull as dishwater *mod.* very dull. □ *She's cute, but dull as dishwater.* □ *Life can be as dull as dishwater.*

dullsville 1. *n.* a dull place. □ *This place is just dullsville!* □ *Home is dullsville to a teenager.* **2.** *n.* something dull. □ *The lecture was downtown dullsville for sure.* □ *When each movie I see turns into dullsville, I want to give up seeing them.*

ho-hum *mod.* dull; causing yawns. □ *Clare played another ho-hum concert at the music hall last night.* □ *It was a ho-hum lecture.*

L7 *mod.* dull; square. (The L and the 7 form a square.) □ *This guy was real, like, you know, L7.* □ *Who is the most L7 person you know?*

mope *n.* a tired and ineffectual person. □ *I can't afford to pay mopes around here. Get to work or get out!* □ *I feel like such a mope today.*

sleepfest *n.* something, such as a dull lecture, that induces a long period of sleep. □ *The history lecture today was a real sleepfest.* □ *The play was a sleepfest. Half the audience left before it was over.*

snooze *n.* something that is boring enough to put someone to sleep. □ *The play was a snooze. I left before it was over.* □ *It wasn't a lecture; it was a snooze.*

turn someone off *tr.* to dull someone's interest in someone or something. □ *The prof turned me off to the subject.* □ *The preacher set out to turn off the congregation to sin.*

vanilla *mod.* plain; dull. □ *The entire production was sort of vanilla, but it was okay.* □ *No more vanilla music, please.* □ *The vacation was vanilla, but restful.*

whitebread *mod.* plain; dull. □ *Naw, the whole thing is too whitebread.* □ *If I wanted a whitebread vacation, I'd have gone to the beach.*

yawner *n.* a boring show or performance. □ *It was a yawner from the opening curtain straight through to the end.* □ *Your lecture, sir, was a total yawner.*

zhlubby *mod.* dull; boorish. □ *Who is the zhlubby type with the plaid pants?* □ *That guy is so zhlubby!* □ *I can't sit through this zhlubby thing one more minute.*

DUPE

cherry *n.* an inexperienced person; a novice. □ *He's just a cherry. He don't know from nothing.* □ *She's a cherry when it comes to computers.*

chump *n.* a stupid person; a gullible person. □ *You are such a chump.* □ *See if that chump will loan you some money.*

clay pigeon *n.* a gullible person; a pigeon. (Underworld.) □ *We need a clay pigeon to divert attention from the snatch.* □ *Who's gonna be the clay pigeon for the bank caper?*

easy mark *n.* a likely victim. □ *Martin looks like an easy mark, but he's really quite savvy.* □ *Mary is an easy mark because she is so unsuspecting.*

fall guy *n.* a victim; a dupe. (Originally underworld.) □ *Rocko wasn't going to be* *the fall guy for this caper.* □ *I didn't want to be the fall guy, so I sat out the last job.*

gopher AND **gofer** *n.* a dupe; a pawn; an underling. □ *The guy's just a gopher. He has no say in anything.* □ *I'll send a gofer over to pick up the papers.*

john *n.* a victim of a crime or deception; a *sucker*. □ *The john went straight to the cops and told the whole thing.* □ *Clobber the john a good one when he turns around.*

mark *n.* a dupe; a victim selected for a theft or a swindle. (Underworld.) □ *I bumped the mark on the shoulder, and he put his hand on his wallet just like always.* □ *We picked the marks out of the crowd in front of the two-dollar window.*

patsy *n.* a victim of a *scam*. (Underworld.) □ *That guy over there looks like a perfect patsy.* □ *We got nearly twenty-five hundred bucks off that patsy.*

pigeon *n.* a dupe; a *sucker*; someone singled out to be cheated. □ *There's our pigeon now. Don't let him see us sizing him up.* □ *Be alert for pickpockets. Don't be some crook's pigeon.*

schlemiel AND **schlemihl; shlemiel** *n.* a gullible person; a *loser*. (From Hebrew *Shelumiel* via Yiddish.) □ *See if you can get that schlemiel to buy the Brooklyn Bridge.* □ *The stupid shlemiel says he already bought it yesterday.*

schnook AND **schnuck; shnook** *n.* a naive person; a dope. (Yiddish.) □ *The guy's a schnook with a heart of gold.* □ *What's a good-looking dame like her doing with a shnook like him?*

setup *n.* a person who is set up for some swindle; a *mark*. (Underworld.) □ *Is he the setup? He's a cop!* □ *The setup got wise at the last minute.*

soft touch *n.* a gullible person; a likely victim of a scheme. □ *John is a soft touch for a few bucks.* □ *Here comes the perfect soft touch—a nerd with a gleam in his eye.*

spring chicken *n.* a young and naive person, especially a young woman. (Usually in the negative.) □ *Well, I may not be a spring chicken, but I got some spizzerinktum left.* □ *I am a spring chicken, but I lie about my age to get served in bars.*

sucker *n.* a dupe; an easy mark. □ *See if you can sell that sucker the Brooklyn Bridge.* □ *The sucker says he doesn't need a bridge, thank you.*

tool *n.* a dupe; someone who can be victimized easily. □ *They were looking for some tool to drive the getaway car.* □ *Who's the tool with the briefcase?*

touch *n.* a likely target for begging; someone who is asked for a loan. □ *He was just the kind of touch we were looking for, not too bright and not too poor.* □ *The touch looked around him and gave the stiff two bits.*

yap *n.* a naive person; a dupe. □ *The poor yap was made a fool of.* □ *See if you can get that yap to bring over a left-handed monkey wrench.*

DWELLING
See **LODGING**.

EAGERNESS

eager-beaver *n.* a person who is very eager to do something. □ *Rocko is an eager-beaver when it comes to collecting money for Mr. Big.* □ *The eager-beavers were trying to buy tickets yesterday!*

go-getter *n.* an energetic person. □ *Wally is a real go-getter. He'll go places.* □ *Sally was really cut out to be a go-getter.*

hungry 1. *mod.* ambitious. □ *He gets ahead because he's hungry.* □ *We like to hire the hungry ones.* **2** *mod.* eager to make money. □ *He doesn't sell enough because he's not hungry enough.* □ *When he gets hungry for wealth, he'll get busy.*

raring to go *mod.* anxious and eager to go. □ *Come on, I'm raring to go!* □ *The whole family is raring to go on vacation.*

rough and ready *mod.* vigorous and eager. □ *After a good night's sleep, I feel rough and ready—I could take on a bear.* □ *My friend is the rough and ready type. I'd rather sit and think about things.*

with bells on *mod.* ready to go; eager. □ *She was here on time with bells on.* □ *I promise to be there at five in the morning with bells on.*

EARLY

See also **ANTICIPATION**.

early bird *n.* a person who arrives early. □ *The early birds get the best seats.* □ *There were some early birds who arrived before the tea things were laid.*

firstest with the mostest *mod.* the earliest and in the largest numbers; the earliest with more of what's needed. (Always with *the*.) □ *Pete got the prize for being the firstest with the mostest.* □ *I always like to be there early—the firstest with the mostest.*

EARN

bring home the bacon *tr.* to earn a livelihood; to earn money to buy food. □ *When I have to bring home the bacon, I hope I have an interesting job.* □ *I have to bring home the bacon for six kids.*

clear *tr.* to earn a specific net amount of money. □ *She cleared a cool forty thousand on that Wilson deal.* □ *We just want to clear a decent profit. Nothing greedy.*

do some fine coin *tr.* to make a large sum of money. □ *When I get my big break, I'm going to do some fine coin.* □ *Max did some fine coin on that last house-painting job.*

gravy *n.* extra or easy money; easy profit. □ *Virtually every cent that came in was pure gravy—no expenses and no materials costs at all.* □ *After I pay expenses, the rest is pure gravy.*

hand over fist *mod.* repeatedly and energetically, especially as with taking in money in a great volume. □ *We were taking in fees hand over fist, and the people were lined up for blocks.* □ *The money came in hand over fist at the B.O.*

knock down something *tr.* to earn a certain amount of money. □ *I'm lucky to knock down $20,000.* □ *She must knock down about twenty thou a year.*

make a bundle AND **make a pile** *tr.* to make a lot of money. □ *I made a bundle off that last deal.* □ *I want to buy a few stocks and make a pile in a few years.*

make a killing *tr.* to make an enormous profit; to become an enormous success. □ *The company made a killing from the sale of its subsidiary.* □ *I wanted to make a killing as a banker, but it didn't work out.*

pull down an amount of money *tr.* to earn a stated amount of money. ("An amount of money" is expressed as a figure or other indication of an actual amount.) □ *She pulls down about $40,000 a year.* □ *They pull down pretty good salaries.*

quick buck AND **fast buck** *n.* a quickly or easily earned profit. □ *I'm always on the lookout to make a fast buck.* □ *I need to make a quick buck without much effort.*

rack up something *tr.* to earn something; to collect or acquire something. □ *They all racked up a lot of profits.* □ *We racked up twenty points in the game last Saturday.*

scale *n.* the regular union rate of pay; union wages. □ *Even the big stars work for scale.* □ *We pay scale and not a penny more. I don't care who you think you are!*

take *n.* the amount of money taken in at some event; the money received for the tickets that have been purchased. □ *What was the take for the concert?* □ *The take was much larger than we expected.*

EARS

dumbo *n.* someone with large ears. (Also a rude term of address. The name of a cartoon character elephant whose ears were large enough to fly with.) □ *Wow, look at that dumbo with size twenty ears!* □ *I better get new glasses, or I'm going to be a dumbo when my head starts growing.*

EARTHY

funky *mod.* basic and simple; earthy. □ *Everything she does is so funky.* □ *I like to be around funky people.*

EASY

ace in the hole *n.* something important held in reserve. □ *The twenty-dollar bill I keep in my shoe is my ace in the hole.* □ *Mary's beautiful singing voice was her ace in the hole in case everything else failed.*

bed of roses *n.* a luxurious situation; an easy life. □ *Who said life would be a bed of roses?* □ *If I had a million bucks, I would be in a bed of roses.*

beer and skittles *n.* something very easy to do; an easy time of it. □ *Did you think*

life was all beer and skittles? □ *All you want is beer and skittles. Don't you know you have to work hard for what you want?*

blow-off *n.* something that can be done easily or without much effort. □ *Oh, that is just a blow-off. Nothing to it.* □ *The test was a blow-off.*

breeze *n.* an easy task. □ *Nothing to it. It was a breeze.* □ *I went through it like a breeze.*

cakewalk *n.* something very easy. □ *Nothing to it. It's a cakewalk.* □ *The game was a cakewalk from beginning to end.*

cinch *n.* something very easy. □ *No sweat! It was a cinch!* □ *What a cinch. Anybody can do it.*

clear sailing *mod.* easy going. □ *It'll be clear sailing from now on.* □ *When this is finished, it'll be clear sailing.*

cruise *tr.* to pass a course easily. □ *I'm gonna cruise that math course.* □ *Tom really cruised English this semester.*

cushy *mod.* soft; easy. (From *cushion*.) □ *He's got sort of a cushy job.* □ *That's a cushy kind of life to lead.*

dead cinch *n.* an absolute certainty; an easy thing to do. □ *It's a dead cinch. I foresee no problems.* □ *The job was no dead cinch, but we did it on time.*

dead easy *mod.* very easy. □ *This whole job is dead easy.* □ *It was so dead easy, Frank did it with one hand.*

free ride *n.* an easy time; participation without contributing anything. □ *You've had a free ride long enough. You have to do your share of the work now.* □ *No more free rides around here. Get off your duff and get a job!*

gut *mod.* easy. (Said of a course in high school or college.) □ *That's a gut course. Nothing to it.* □ *I won't take any more gut economics courses. Even those are hard.*

hands down *mod.* easily; unquestionably. □ *She won the contest hands down.* □ *They declared her the winner hands down.*

no-brainer *n.* an easy question that takes no thinking to answer; a simple problem that requires no intellect to solve; a dilemma that requires no pondering to resolve. □ *Of course, the question is a no-brainer. The answer has to be yes.* □ *His proposal of marriage was a no-brainer. She turned him down flat on the spot.*

Nothing to it! *exclam.* "It is very easy!" □ *Look, anybody can do it! Nothing to it!* □ *Changing a light bulb is easy. Nothing to it!*

over the hump *mod.* over the hard part; past the midpoint. □ *Things should be easy from now on. We are over the hump.* □ *When you get over the hump, life is much better.*

piece of cake *n.* something easy to do. □ *No problem. When you know what you're doing, it's a piece of cake.* □ *Glad to help. It was a piece of cake.*

sail (right) through something *in.* to get through something easily. □ *I sailed right through my homework.* □ *We sailed through the examination with no difficulty.*

snap *n.* an easy thing to do. (Always with *a*.) □ *Nothing to it. It's a snap.* □ *The whole thing was a snap.*

snap course *n.* an easy course (in school). □ *I took a snap course in algebra and flunked it.* □ *I need at least one snap course a semester to pass.*

soft berth *n.* an easy situation; employment at an easy job. □ *Fred ended up with a real soft berth.* □ *I hope I can arrange a soft berth for my brother, who just applied for a job here.*

take it easy *exclam.* "Let up!"; "Not so hard!"; "Be gentle!" (Usually **Take it easy!**) □ *Take it easy! That hurts!* □ *Take it easy; he's just a kid!*

tea party *n.* something easy; a pleasant and unstressful event. □ *It was not a tea party, but it wasn't bad either.* □ *The test was a real tea party. No sweat.*

walk *n.* something easy. (Always with *a*.) □ *That game was a walk!* □ *What a walk! I've never had such an easy time of it!*

walkover *n.* an easy victory; an easy task. (From sports.) □ *The game was a*

walkover. *No problem.* □ *Learning the computer's operating system was no walkover for me.*

waltz *n.* an easy task. □ *The job was a waltz. We did it in a day.* □ *The coach promised them that the game would be a waltz.*

without a hitch *mod.* with no problem(s). □ *Everything went off without a hitch.* □ *We hoped the job would go off without a hitch.*

EATING

artillery *n.* flatware; cutlery. □ *Who put out the artillery? I didn't get a fork.* □ *Go get your own artillery. This ain't the Ritz.*

bean time *n.* dinnertime. □ *Hey, you guys! It's bean time!* □ *I'm hungry. When's bean time around here?*

(blind) munchies *n.* a craving for food or snacks. (Originally drugs.) □ *There is nothing like potato chips when you've got the munchies.* □ *By midnight I had the blind munchies.*

bottomless pit *n.* a very hungry person. □ *The guy is a bottomless pit. There isn't enough food in town to fill him up.* □ *I've got two boys, and they're both bottomless pits.*

brown-bag 1. *n.* a bag lunch. □ *Bring a brown-bag, and we'll talk and eat at the same time.* □ *I lost my brown-bag, but I'll come to talk anyway.* **2.** *in.* to carry a bag lunch. □ *He's back to brown-bagging while he saves up for his vacation.* □ *I like to brown-bag. I don't eat so much when I do.* **3.** *mod.* having to do with an event during which people eat their own bag lunches. □ *These brown-bag affairs seem so tacky.* □ *The brown-bag meeting wasn't very useful.* □ *It's brown-bag. Come if you can.*

chew *in.* to eat. □ *She's in the kitchen, chewing.* □ *Man, I'm hungry. It's time to chew!*

chow *tr. & in.* to eat (something). □ *I've been chowing canned tuna and stale bagels to save money.* □ *When do we chow?*

chow down *in.* to eat; to take a meal. □ *Over there is where we chow down.* □ *It's past my time to chow down.*

chow hound *n.* someone who loves to eat; a heavy eater. □ *Harry is a real chow hound, and he's got love handles to prove it.* □ *Okay, listen up, all you chow hounds. There's extra beans tonight!*

chow something down *tr.* to eat something, probably quickly or without good manners. □ *We can chow this pizza down in about two minutes!* □ *I found a box of cookies and chowed it down before anybody knew what I was doing.*

chuck *in.* to eat voraciously. □ *Don't just chuck, man, enjoy your food.* □ *The two guys sat guzzling and chucking till they were full.*

dish something out *tr.* to serve food to people. (Standard English.) □ *I'll dish it out, and you take it to the table.* □ *Careful how you dish out the mashed potatoes. There may not be enough.*

dog *tr.* to eat something; to eat something as a dog eats. □ *He dogged his hamburger and ran out the door to catch the bus.* □ *Here, dog a couple of crackers and cheese. That should keep you from starving.*

down *tr.* to eat or drink something quickly. □ *He downed a can of soda and burped like a thunderclap.* □ *She downed her sandwich in record time.*

DQ *n.* "Dairy Queen," a trade name for a franchise fast-food store specializing in frozen desserts. (Initialism. Teens and collegiate.) □ *Let's go to DQ, okay?* □ *The DQ is closed for the winter.*

eat up *in.* to eat in enjoyment. (Usually a command.) □ *Come on, now. Sit down and eat up!* □ *Eat up! There's plenty more where this came from.*

feed one's face *tr.* to put food in one's mouth; to eat (something). □ *You're always feeding your face. You're going to get fat.* □ *Stop feeding your face and listen to me.*

fly light *in.* to skip a meal or eating. □ *Nothing for me, thanks. I'm flying light today.* □ *I fly light until about dinnertime.*

garbage something down *tr.* to gobble something up; to bolt something down. □ *Don't garbage your food down!* □ *That guy will garbage down almost anything.*

grub *in.* to eat (a meal). □ *When do we grub?* □ *Let's grub and get going.*

hook something down *tr.* to swallow something. □ *He hooked a drink down and turned to face his brother.* □ *Hook down one of these cookies and see what you think about them.*

nosh *in.* to snack. □ *You nosh too much.* □ *Every time I see you, you're noshing.*

nosher *n.* someone who is always eating snacks. □ *I don't know of a single nosher who's not fat.* □ *Fred's a nosher. He's always eating.*

nosh on something *in.* to make a snack of something. □ *After Thanksgiving, we noshed on turkey for three days.* □ *Who's been noshing on the chocolate cake?*

put on the feedbag AND **put on the nosebag; tie on the nosebag** *tr.* to prepare to eat; to eat a meal. (Refers to a bag of feed tied under a horse's mouth.) □ *I'm starved. Must be time to put on the feedbag.* □ *Let's go tie on the nosebag. It's nearly noon.*

put something away *tr.* to eat something. □ *Are you going to put this cake away?* □ *Did you put away that whole pizza?*

scarf 1. *tr.* to eat something. □ *Andy scarfed the whole pie.* □ *Are you going to scarf the whole thing?* **2.** *in.* to eat. □ *I'll be with you as soon as I scarf.* □ *I gotta go scarf now.*

scarf something down *tr.* to eat something, perhaps in a hurry; to swallow something, perhaps in a hurry. □ *Are you going to scarf this whole thing down?* □ *Here, scarf down this sandwich.*

scoff *tr. & in.* to eat (something). □ *He's upstairs scoffing in his room.* □ *She scoffed three hamburgers and a large order of fries.*

sink *tr.* to swallow some food or drink. □ *Here, sink a bite of this stuff.* □ *Larry stopped at a tavern to sink a short one.*

slob up *in.* to eat. □ *What time do you people slob up around here?* □ *Fred stopped slobbing up long enough to change the channel on the T.V. set.*

throw down *in.* to eat; to gobble one's food. (The opposite of *throw up* = to vomit.) □ *Man, I'm starved. Let's find a hamburger joint and throw down.* □ *What time are you going to throw down tonight?*

veggy AND **veggie** *n.* a vegetarian. □ *We have a lovely salad bar for the veggies among you.* □ *She's a veggy, so make sure there's a nice selection of appropriate goodies.*

whip something off *tr.* to finish something quickly, especially food or drink. □ *Did you just whip that whole pizza off?* □ *Lemme whip off this sandwich, and I'll be right with you.* □ *She whipped off the dishes in ten minutes.*

EAVESDROPPING

walls have ears *phr.* "Someone may be listening." (Sometimes with *the.*) □ *Talk softly. Walls have ears.* □ *The walls have ears, so be careful about what you say.*

wire *tr.* to install electronic eavesdropping equipment. □ *Somebody wired the mayor's office.* □ *They say the mayor wired his own office to make himself look like a victim.*

EFFECT

get one right here *tr.* to affect one deeply in a specific way. (Usually accompanied with a hand gesture showing exactly where one is affected: the heart = lovingly, the stomach or bowels = sickeningly.) □ *That sort of thing gets me right here.* □ *Pete clasped his hand to his chest and said, "That sort of thing gets me right here."*

get to someone *in.* [for someone or something] to touch someone emotionally. □ *Lovely flowers and things like that get to me.* □ *Sad music gets to me and makes me cry.*

EFFEMINATE

sissified *mod.* effeminate; sissy-style. □ *Don't act so sissified.* □ *I'm not comfortable in a sissified place like that.*

swish 1. *mod.* overly fancy; effeminate; displaying effeminacy. □ *The lobby of the theater was a little swish, but not offensive.* □ *Who is your swish little friend?* **2.** *n.* elaborate decoration; effeminacy. □ *There's a little too much swish here. Get rid of the gold drapes.* □ *What this place needs is more swish. Hang some baubles here and there.*

EFFICIENCY

lean and mean *mod.* capable and ready for hard, efficient work. □ *Ron got himself lean and mean and is ready to play in Saturday's game.* □ *The management is lean and mean and looks to turn a profit next year.*

run on all cylinders 1. *in.* to operate sensibly and intelligently. □ *Pay attention to what you are doing. Start running on all cylinders.* □ *She doesn't run on all cylinders this early in the morning.* **2.** *in.* to run well and smoothly. □ *This department is running on all cylinders now.* □ *My plan is now running on all cylinders.*

EFFORT

bust a gut (to do something) *tr.* to make a great effort (to do something). (Potentially offensive. Use only with discretion.) □ *I busted a gut trying to get just the thing you wanted!* □ *Don't bust a gut, but try to get here on time.*

bust (one's) ass (to do something) AND **break one's balls to do something; bust one's butt to do something; bust one's nuts to do something** *tr.* to work very hard to do something. (The expressions with *balls* and *nuts* are said typically, but not necessarily, of a male. Potentially offensive. Use only with discretion.) □ *I've been busting my nuts to get this thing done on time, and now they don't want it!* □ *You are expected to bust your nuts every minute you are at work.*

do or die *mod.* having to try as hard as one can. □ *He has the obsessive do or die attitude.* □ *I was determined to get there—do or die.*

elbow grease *n.* effort. □ *Put out a little elbow grease.* □ *All this job needs is a little more elbow grease.*

get one's teeth into something AND **sink one's teeth into something** *tr.* to undertake to do something. □ *I can't wait to sink my teeth into that Wallace job.* □ *Here, sink your teeth into this and see if you can't manage this project.*

level best *n.* one's very best effort. □ *I will do my level best to find your husband.* □ *Don't go to a whole lot of trouble. Your level best is good enough.*

EJECTION

boot 1. *tr.* to dismiss or eject someone. □ *I booted him myself.* □ *Bruno, boot that guy at once!* **2.** *n.* a dismissal or ejection. □ *I got the boot even though I had worked there for a decade.* □ *Seven people got the boot.*

boot someone out *tr.* to throw someone out; to kick someone out. □ *Are you going to boot me out?* □ *I don't boot out anybody. Bruno does that. Bruno, come here.*

bounce *tr.* to throw someone out. □ *Bruno bounced me, and I ran to my car and beat it.* □ *The owner came out and bounced us.*

bum's rush *n.* the ejection of a person from a place. □ *I got the bum's rush at that bar. Do I look that bad?* □ *Give this dame the bum's rush. She can't pay for nothin'.*

give someone the gate *tr.* to get rid of someone. □ *The chick was a pest, so I gave her the gate.* □ *He threatened to give me the gate, so I left.*

old heave-ho *n.* a dismissal; a physical removal of someone from a place. □ *I thought my job was secure, but today I got the old heave-ho.* □ *You had better act right, or my friend will give you the old heave-ho.*

throw one out on one's ear *tr.* to remove someone from a place forcibly. □ *Straighten up, or I'll throw you out on your ear.* □ *The caretaker caught us and threw us out on our ear.*

unload *tr.* to get rid of someone or something. □ *We're gonna unload all the cats and dogs during the Christmas rush.* □ *Lemme unload this dame, and then we can go out and have a little fun.*

ELBOW

crazy bone *n.* the elbow. □ *Ouch! I hit my crazy bone!* □ *Ken hit his crazy bone as he went into church, and was yelling "Oh! Oh! Oh!" as if the Spirit had got into him or something.*

ELECTRICITY

brown out *in.* [for the electricity] to fade and dim down. (Something less than a blackout.) □ *The power kept browning out.* □ *The lights started to brown out, and I thought maybe I didn't pay the bill for the juice.*

brownout *n.* a period of dimming or fading of the electricity. □ *There was another brownout today.* □ *They keep building all these expensive power stations, and then we still have brownouts.*

juice *n.* electricity. □ *The juice has been off since dawn.* □ *Turn on the juice, and let's see if it runs.*

ELECTRONICS

gender-bender *n.* a device that changes electrical plugs or sockets to the opposite gender—male to female, female to male. □ *You need what's called a gender-bender to match those plugs.* □ *I tried a gender-bender, but it won't work.*

ELEGANCE

chi-chi *mod.* elegant. □ *Oh, you look so chi-chi in that lace blouse.* □ *Her living room is so chi-chi that you are afraid to go in.*

class 1. *n.* high style; elegance. □ *The dame's got class, but no brains.* □ *Class isn't worth much in this neighborhood.* **2.** *mod.* first-rate; high-class. □ *I've always regarded the firm as a class outfit.* □ *This was a class suburb just a few years ago.*

class act *n.* a high-quality act; a high-quality way of doing things. □ *I like the way you move on the field, Jerry. It's a real class act.* □ *The prof puts on a real class act, but he grades very hard.*

classy *mod.* elegant; dandy. □ *Pretty classy place you got here.* □ *How much does a classy car like this cost?*

fancy-schmancy *mod.* fancy; very fancy. □ *This one is just too fancy-schmancy for Heidi.* □ *She likes everything fancy-*

schmancy. □ *I don't care for these fancy-schmancy get-togethers.*

piss elegant *mod.* falsely elegant; pretentious. (Crude. Potentially offensive. Use only with discretion.) □ *Here comes Paul in his piss elegant car.* □ *Do we have to go to a party at that piss elegant apartment with its corny decor?*

ritzy *mod.* elegant; flamboyant. □ *That is a real ritzy car.* □ *It's really ritzy!* □ *What a ritzy coat! Is it new?*

snazzy AND **shnazzy** *mod.* elegant; classy. □ *This is a snazzy place, all right.* □ *This place is sure snazzy.* □ *Whose shnazzy new car is this?*

snitzy *mod.* classy; ritzy. □ *This is a pretty snitzy place—tablecloths and everything.* □ *Tiffany is too snitzy for me.*

swank *n.* class; visible quality. □ *He doesn't have swank. He's a cornball!* □ *This place has swank. I like it.*

swanky *mod.* classy; *ritzy.* □ *What a swanky joint!* □ *This place is too swanky. I like to eat where I can pronounce the names of the food.*

ELIMINATE

scratch *tr.* to eliminate something from a list; to cancel something. □ *Scratch Fred. He can't make the party.* □ *We decided to scratch the idea of a new car. The old one will have to do.*

X'd out *mod.* eliminated; crossed-out. □ *But the Babbits are X'd out.* □ *Put the X'd out Babbits back where they were.*

EMBARRASSMENT

have egg on one's face *tr.* to be embarrassed by something one has done. (As if one went out in public with a dirty face. *Have got* can replace *have.*) □ *I was completely wrong, and now I have egg on my face.* □ *She's really got egg on her face!*

ice *tr.* to embarrass someone; to make someone look foolish. □ *Don't ice me in front of my friends.* □ *Why does she feel like she has to ice everybody?*

EMOTION

blow a hype *tr.* to overreact. □ *I was afraid she would blow a hype about the* broken window. □ *Come on, don't blow a hype. It's only a car.*

cut up (about someone or something) *mod.* emotionally upset about someone or something. □ *She was all cut up about her divorce.* □ *You could see how cut up she was.*

hearts and flowers *n.* sentimentality. □ *The movie was so full of hearts and flowers that I was bored.* □ *I didn't care for the hearts and flowers part.*

jag *n.* a prolonged state of emotional excess. □ *I've been on a jag and can't get my work done.* □ *She's off on a jag again.*

schmaltz AND **shmaltz** *n.* extreme sentimentality; corny sweetness. (From a Yiddish word meaning fat or oil.) □ *I didn't like that movie. Too much schmaltz.* □ *You aren't playing this piece right. It needs a little shmaltz.*

schmaltzy AND **shmaltzy** *mod.* overly sweet and sentimental. □ *This movie is too schmaltzy for me.* □ *What a shmaltzy movie!*

spaz-out *n.* an emotional display. □ *There's no need for a spaz-out!* □ *She threw a hell of a spaz-out.*

sticky *mod.* sentimental. □ *Things were getting a little sticky the more Harriet drank. She tried to kiss me, and I left.* □ *There's a sticky part in the movie, but other than that it's pretty good.*

syrupy *mod.* overly sentimental. □ *I can't stand syrupy movies.* □ *That music is too syrupy.* □ *All this syrupy talk is making me tired.*

toot *n.* a session of high emotion. □ *She's on a toot about how nobody loves her anymore.* □ *Those toots wore everybody out.*

tore (up) AND **torn (up)** *mod.* distraught; emotionally upset. □ *I knew you'd be tore up.* □ *Fred's really torn up about the accident.*

turn on the waterworks *in.* to begin to cry. □ *His lower lip was quivering, and I knew he was going to turn on the waterworks.* □ *Now, now! Don't turn on the waterworks. Cheer up!*

weeper *n.* a sad movie, novel, television program, etc. □ *I can't seem to get enough of these weepers.* □ *Not another weeper!*

work oneself up *tr.* to allow oneself to become emotionally upset. □ *Todd worked himself up, and I thought he would scream.* □ *Don't work yourself up over Tracy. She's not worth it.*

EMOTION - LACKING

hard-nosed *mod.* stern and businesslike; unsympathetic. □ *She's pretty hard-nosed and tends to put people off.* □ *It takes a hard-nosed manager to run a place like this.*

leave someone cold *tr.* to leave someone unaffected. □ *He said it was dull, and it left him cold.* □ *The music's good, but the story left the producer cold.*

EMPLOYMENT

See also OCCUPATION.

back to the salt mines *phr.* back to the workplace. □ *Well, it's Monday morning. Back to the salt mines.* □ *Break's over! Back to the salt mines, everybody.*

bread and butter *n.* one's livelihood. □ *It's bread and butter to me. I have to do it.* □ *I can't give it up. It's my bread and butter.*

burnout *n.* someone no longer effective on the job. □ *As a teacher, Fred is a burnout.* □ *We try to find some other employment for the burnouts.*

daily grind *n.* the tedious pattern of daily work. □ *Well, it's Monday. Time to start another week of the daily grind.* □ *The daily grind really gets me down.*

Don't call us, we'll call you. *sent.* a formulaic expression given to job applicants who have just interviewed or auditioned for a job. □ *Thank you, Eddie Evans. Don't call us, we'll call you.* □ *Stupendous, Gloria, just stupendous. What glamour and radiance! Don't call us, we'll call you.*

gig *n.* a onetime job; an engagement. (Musicians.) □ *I had a gig out on the west side, but I couldn't get there.* □ *The gig was canceled because of the snow.*

graveyard shift *n.* the night shift of work in a factory, usually starting at about midnight. □ *I'd prefer not to work the graveyard shift.* □ *The pay is pretty good on the graveyard shift.*

land a job *tr.* to find a job and be hired. □ *As soon as I land a job and start to bring in some money, I'm going to get a stereo.* □ *I managed to land a job at a factory.*

moonlight *in.* to work at a second job. □ *Larry had to moonlight to earn enough to feed his family.* □ *A lot of people have to moonlight to make ends meet.*

nine-to-five *mod.* typical in terms of working hours; structured and scheduled, starting and ending at set times. (From the expression *from nine to five*, normal working hours.) □ *I work nine-to-five.* □ *I really wanted a nine-to-five job until I finally got one.* □ *I can't stand the nine-to-five rat race.*

racket *n.* any job or business. □ *I've been in this racket for twenty years and never made any money.* □ *I'm a stockbroker. What's your racket?*

swing shift *n.* an evening work shift in a factory, usually from mid-afternoon to midnight. □ *I don't mind the swing shift. I'm a night person anyway.* □ *My brother works the swing shift, so I never get to see him.*

visiting fireman *n.* someone paying a visit to observe one's workplace. □ *We have a couple of visiting firemen coming today.* □ *Be sure to have these plans out when the visiting firemen come by.*

when the eagle flies AND **day the eagle flies** *phr.* payday. (The *eagle* is the one found on U.S. currency.) □ *I'll pay you back when the eagle flies.* □ *I'll find you the day the eagle flies.*

ENCOUNTER

brush *n.* an encounter; a close shave. □ *My brush with the bear was so close I could smell its breath—which was vile, I might add.* □ *It seemed like a brush with death.*

face-off *n.* a confrontation. (From hockey.) □ *For a minute it looked like we* *were headed toward a nasty face-off.* □ *The face-off continued for a few moments till both of them realized that there was no point in fighting.*

ENCOURAGEMENT

Go for it! *exclam.* "Do it!"; "Try it!" □ *Go for it! Give it a try!* □ *It looked like something I wanted to do, so I decided to go for it.*

Keep the faith (baby)! *exclam.* a statement of general encouragement or solidarity. □ *You said it! Keep the faith, baby!* □ *Keep the faith! See ya later.*

kick in the (seat of the) pants AND **kick in the ass; kick in the butt; kick in the teeth** *n.* a strong message of encouragement or demand. (Use *ass* and *butt* with discretion.) □ *All he needs is a kick in the seat of the pants to get him going.* □ *A kick in the butt will get her moving.*

Now you're talking! *exclam.* "What you are saying is making sense!" □ *Now you're talking! You've got a great idea!* □ *"Now you're talking!" said the coach when I told him I was going to win.*

Party on! *exclam.* "That's right!" □ *Party on, Beavis! You are totally right!* □ *Party on, Waldo! You said it!*

pep talk *n.* an informal speech of encouragement. □ *The coach gave the team a good pep talk, but they lost anyway.* □ *The pep talk grew into a real gripe session.*

shot in the arm *n.* a boost or act of encouragement. □ *The pep talk was a real shot in the arm for all the guys.* □ *The good test grade was a shot in the arm for Gary.*

sweetener *n.* extra encouragement, usually in the form of money. □ *Money makes the best sweetener around.* □ *Let me add a little sweetener, and we'll see if he goes for it.*

That-a-boy! *exclam.* "That is the way to do it." (Said to a boy or man.) □ *Come on, Chuck. That-a-boy!* □ *That-a-boy, Chuck. You can do it!*

That's the ticket! *exclam.* "That is exactly what is needed!" □ *Good! That's the ticket! Now you're cooking with gas.* □ *That's the ticket! Perfect!*

(That's the) way to go! *exclam.* "Nicely done!" □ *Way to go, Charlie!* □ *That's the way to go! You did it!*

There you go. *sent.* "Hooray! You did it right!" (Usually **There you go!**) □ *There you go! That's the way!* □ *Good shot, Chuck! There ya go!*

up and at them AND **up an' at 'em; up an' Adam** *phr.* to get up and go at people or things; to get active and get busy. ("Adam" is a misunderstanding of "at 'em.") □ *Come on, you guys! Up and at 'em! Can't sleep all day.* □ *Up an' Adam! The sun is shining.*

ENDEARMENT

babe *n.* a term of endearment for a woman or a man. (Also a term of address.) □ *Look, babe, get in there and tackle that guy! We're losing!* □ *Say, babes, bring me a beer, would you?*

babycakes AND **honeycakes** *n.* a term of endearment; sweetie; dear. (Also a term of address.) □ *My babycakes gave me a flimsy nightie for my birthday.* □ *Look, honeycakes, I found some lipstick on your collar.*

ENDINGS
See also CONCLUSION, QUIT, STOPPING.

done for *mod.* lost; dead; doomed. □ *I'm sorry, this whole scheme is done for.* □ *I knew I was done for.*

in the (home) stretch *mod.* in the last stage of the process. (From horse racing.) □ *We're in the homestretch with this project and can't change it now.* □ *We're in the stretch. Only three more days till we graduate.*

kibosh *n.* the end; the final blow; the thing that terminates something. (Usually with *the.*) □ *The kibosh was a real corker.* □ *They thought the kibosh was overdone.*

kiss of death *n.* the direct cause of the end of someone or something. □ *The ordinance was the kiss of death for our budding jazz band.* □ *Your attitude was the kiss of death for your employment here.*

mopping-up operation *n.* a clean-up operation; the final stages in a project where the loose ends are taken care of. □ *It's all over except a small mopping-up operation.* □ *The mopping-up operation should cost just under $20 million.*

on one's (or its) last legs *mod.* about to expire or become nonfunctional. □ *This car is on its last legs. We have to get a new one.* □ *Poor old Chuck is on his last legs.*

till the fat lady sings AND **when the fat lady sings** *mod.* at the end; a long time from now. (Supposedly from a tale about a child—sitting through an opera—who asks a parent when it will be over. "Not until the fat lady sings" is the answer.) □ *Relax. It won't be over till the fat lady sings.* □ *We can leave with everybody else when the fat lady sings.*

To hell with that! *exclam.* "That's the end of that!"; "No more of that!" (Use caution with *hell*.) □ *To hell with that! That's no excuse!* □ *I've heard stories like that before, and I don't believe any of them. To hell with that.*

turn turtle *in.* to turn over, as with a ship. □ *The old dog finally turned turtle, and that was the end.* □ *The car struck a pole and turned turtle.*

ENDLESS

bottomless pit *n.* an endless source of something, usually something troublesome. □ *This house is a bottomless pit. Keeping it up is endless.* □ *Our problems come from a bottomless pit. There is just no end to them.*

ENDURE

hack it *tr.* to stand up to something; to endure something. □ *It's hard, but I'm sure I can hack it.* □ *I'm afraid you can't hack it. It just isn't working out.*

hold water *tr.* [for an idea, plan, etc.] to survive evaluation or scrutiny. □ *Nothing you've said so far holds water.* □ *Her story doesn't hold water.*

stomach *tr.* to tolerate someone or something. (Usually negative.) □ *Bruno couldn't stomach the opera, and he left after the first ten minutes.* □ *I can't stomach movies like that.*

take it *tr.* to endure something, physically or mentally. □ *I just can't take it anymore.* □ *If you can't take it, quit.*

take it on the chin AND **take it on the nose 1.** *tr.* to stand up to something adverse, such as criticism. □ *They laid some rude chops on him, but he took it on the chin.* □ *I knew he could take it on the nose.* **2.** *tr.* to receive the full brunt of something. □ *Why do I have to take it on the chin for something I didn't do?* □ *If you did it, you have to learn to take it on the chin.*

tough something out *tr.* to carry on with something despite difficulties or setbacks. □ *Sorry, you'll just have to tough it out.* □ *I think I can tough it out for another month.*

unflappable *mod.* not subject to distraction; imperturbable. □ *Isn't he great? Truly unflappable.* □ *She is totally unflappable.* □ *I wish I was that unflappable.*

up to here *mod.* having as much as one can bear. □ *I'm up to here with your excuses!* □ *We are all up to here with this mystery.*

wear *tr.* to tolerate something. (Usually negative.) □ *That's no good. I won't wear it.* □ *I don't mind, but my wife won't wear it.*

ENERGETIC

ball of fire AND **fireball, go-getter** *n.* an energetic and ambitious person. □ *That guy is a real ball of fire when it comes to sales.* □ *I don't want to hire some young fireball. I need wisdom and thoughtfulness.*

bounce *n.* pep; energy. □ *All these kids have a lot of bounce.* □ *I never have any bounce when I wake up early.*

go-go *mod.* vigorous; energetic; frantically moving. □ *He's a real go-go guy, always up to something.* □ *I bought some silly go-go stock, and it collapsed immediately.*

go to town *in.* to do something with gusto; to do something with great speed and energy. □ *The main office is really going to town on collecting overdue pay-*

ments. □ *Man, our team is really going to town.*

heller AND **hell raiser** *n.* a rowdy person; a hell-raising person. (Use caution with *hell.*) □ *Ernie was a real heller when he was younger.* □ *A bunch of hell raisers kept me up late last night.*

like crazy AND **like mad** *mod.* furiously; very much, fast, many, or actively. □ *They're buying tickets like crazy.* □ *Look at those people on the bank. They're catching fish like mad!*

like gangbusters *mod.* with great excitement and fury. (From the phrase "Come on like 'Gangbusters,' " a radio show that "came on" with lots of noise and excitement.) □ *She works like gangbusters and gets the job done.* □ *They are selling tickets like gangbusters.*

(live) wire *n.* an energetic and vivacious person. □ *Tracy is a real live wire.* □ *With a wire like Tracy in charge, things will get done, that's for sure.*

moxie *n.* energy; spunk; spirit. □ *Now, here's a gal with real moxie.* □ *Come on. Show some moxie!*

oomph *n.* energy; drive and vitality. □ *Come on, you guys. Let's get some oomph behind it. PUSH!* □ *You need more oomph if you want to work at heavy labor.*

peppy *mod.* vigorous; energetic. □ *She's such a peppy thing.* □ *I sure don't feel very peppy right now.*

perky *mod.* energetic; alert. □ *Most poodles are quite perky.* □ *A perky hostess keeps parties alive.*

pistol *n.* a person who is bright, quick, or energetic. (Implying "hot as a pistol" or "quick as a pistol.") □ *She's a bright kid. A real pistol.* □ *Ask that pistol to step over here for a minute, would you?*

ringtailed snorter *n.* someone or something energetic and powerful. □ *Old Charlie is a real ringtailed snorter.* □ *Ask that ringtailed snorter to calm down and come over here for a minute.*

spizzerinktum *n.* energy; vitality. □ *The kid's got spizzerinktum! I like that.* □ *Put more spizzerinktum into it!*

vim and vigor *n.* energy; enthusiasm. □ *Show more vim and vigor! Let us know you're alive.* □ *She's sure got a lot of vim and vigor.*

zappy *mod.* energetic. □ *How can you be so zappy at this time of the morning?* □ *That music is a little too zappy for me.*

zing *n.* energy; dynamism. □ *Put some zing into this dance number. You wanna put the audience to sleep?* □ *This whole business needs more zing.*

zip *n.* vigor; spunk. □ *Put some zip into it. It's too ho-hum.* □ *This whole thing lacks the zip it needs to survive.*

zippy *mod.* lively; active. □ *Wow, is that kid zippy! Look at him dance!* □ *This is a real zippy number.*

zowie *n.* energy; sparkle; zest. □ *This one sounds better because the drummer has more zowie.* □ *Put some zowie into it. It's not raining inside tonight.*

ENGINE

carb *n.* an engine carburetor. □ *This car needs a new carb.* □ *I learned how to clean and adjust a carb by the time I was in high school.*

egg-beater *n.* an outboard boat motor. □ *My egg-beater has been acting up, so I didn't go out on the lake today.* □ *By the time you get about twenty egg-beaters on the lake at once, it's really pretty noisy.*

give it the gun *tr.* to gun an engine; to rev an engine up. □ *Give it the gun for a minute.* □ *I gave it the gun, and it backfired.*

goose 1. *tr.* to rev up an engine; to press down hard on the accelerator of a car. □ *Why don't you goose the thing and see how fast it'll go?* □ *Don't goose it too much.* **2.** *n.* an act of suddenly pressing down the accelerator of a car. □ *Give it a good goose and see what happens.* □ *One more goose, but don't hold it down so long.*

gun *tr.* to race an engine; to rev up an engine. □ *See how loud it is when I gun it?* □ *Gun the thing again and let me hear it.*

pickup *n.* the power of a car's engine as reflected in the car's ability to reach a high speed quickly. □ *This car has more pickup than I really need.* □ *Little cars hardly ever have enough pickup.*

purr (like a cat) *in.* [for an engine] to run well and smoothly. □ *My car really purred after I got it tuned up.* □ *New spark plugs and this old heap will really purr like a cat.*

rev something up *tr.* to speed up an engine in short bursts. □ *Rev it up a few times and see if it stalls.* □ *Tom sat at the traffic light revving up his engine.*

squirrels *n.* a car engine's horsepower. □ *What kind of squirrels you got under the hood?* □ *I got 440 squirrels and a gaggle of carburetors.*

vroom AND **varoom** *interj.* the noise of a loud engine. (Onomatopoetic.) □ *Vroom, varoom went the engine as Vic gunned it over and over.* □ *Suddenly, vroom, a plane passed low overhead.*

ENJOYMENT

get one's rocks off (on something) *tr.* to enjoy something. (Other taboo meanings, also.) □ *I really get my rocks off on heavy metal.* □ *I've listened to the stuff, but I sure don't get my rocks off on it.*

good-time it *tr.* to celebrate; to spend money and have a good time. □ *You're always good-timing it. Don't you ever study?* □ *I just want to good-time it for the rest of my life.*

rare old time *n.* a fine and enjoyable time at a party or something similar. (Folksy.) □ *That was a rare old time at Tom's the other night.* □ *I haven't had a rare old time like that in years.*

ENMITY

blood-and-guts *mod.* acrimonious. □ *There are too many blood-and-guts arguments around here.* □ *Old blood-and-guts Wally is here making threats again.*

ENTHUSIASM

gung-ho *mod.* zealous; enthusiastic. □ *We're really gung-ho about the possibilities of this product.* □ *Pete always seems*

so gung-ho about everything. □ *He's a gung-ho guy.*

on fire *mod.* doing very well; very enthusiastic. □ *Jill's new book is really on fire. Everyone is buying it.* □ *Fred is on fire in his new job. He'll get promoted in no time.*

rah-rah *mod.* having to do with college and college enthusiasm. □ *That gal is so rah-rah. What energy!* □ *It was sort of a rah-rah party.*

up a storm *mod.* with an enthusiastic spirit. (Note syntax in examples. Usually with *sing, dance, talk, blow, play.*) □ *We talked up a storm until past midnight.* □ *Can't she dance up a storm?*

ENTICEMENT

come-on *n.* a lure; bait. □ *Forty people responded to the come-on published in the Sunday paper.* □ *It's just a come-on. Nobody is giving away a decent color TV just for listening to a sales pitch.*

ENTRANCE

zoom *tr.* to gain entry to someplace without paying. □ *Both of them zoomed the circus, and both of them got arrested.* □ *Let's go zoom Martha's party!*

EQUIPMENT

outfit *n.* a set of things; the items needed for some task. □ *I got a fine chemistry outfit for my birthday.* □ *My tool kit has everything I need. It's the whole outfit.*

ERROR
See also WRONG.

blooper 1. *n.* an embarrassing broadcasting error that must be bleeped or blooped out of the program. □ *I made a blooper, and they cut it out of the program.* □ *There is a record you can buy that lets you hear the famous bloopers of the past.* **2.** *n.* any error. □ *Another day, another blooper.* □ *That was a real blooper. Did you get fired?*

blow one's lines *tr.* to forget one's lines in a play; to speak one's lines incorrectly in a play. □ *There I was in my first major role, and I blow my lines!* □ *If you blow your lines, just try to cover it up.*

boner *n.* a silly error; a gaffe. □ *Well, that was a bad boner.* □ *What a boner! You must be embarrassed.*

boo-boo *n.* an error. □ *It's only a small boo-boo. Don't stress yourself.* □ *Another boo-boo like that, and you are through.*

chunk *in.* to do badly; to blunder. □ *Sorry. I really chunked on that last deal.* □ *She is so afraid of chunking that she will hardly do anything.*

clinker *n.* a mistake; (in music) a misplayed note. □ *That was a bad clinker in the middle of the soft passage.* □ *Look at the score, man! That series of clinkers just isn't there.*

flub something up *tr.* to do something incorrectly; to *mess up* a procedure. □ *Now, don't flub this up.* □ *I never flub up anything.*

flub (up) 1. AND **flub-up** *n.* an error; a blunder. □ *I tried not to make a flub, but I did.* □ *Who is responsible for this flub-up?* **2.** *in.* to mess up; to *foul up.* □ *You are flubbing up again, aren't you?* □ *I do my best to keep from flubbing.*

fluff *tr. & in.* to make an error; to do something incorrectly. □ *Todd fluffs his lines in the same place every night.* □ *Don't fluff again, please.*

foozle 1. *n.* an error; a messed-up task. □ *Who made this foozle?* □ *What a stupid foozle!* **2.** *tr.* to mess something up; to bungle something. □ *I'm afraid I'll foozle the camera if I open it up.* □ *Who foozled the copying machine?*

foozlified *mod.* bungled. □ *This job is really foozlified. Who was in charge?* □ *I've never seen such a foozlified mess in my life!*

foul up 1. *in.* to blunder; to *mess up.* □ *Please don't foul up this time.* □ *The quarterback fouled up in the first quarter, and that lost us the game.* **2.** *n.* a blunder; an error. (Usually **foul-up.**) □ *That was a fine foul-up! Is that your specialty?* □ *I can produce a serious foul-up with both hands tied behind me.*

fudge factor *n.* a margin of error. □ *I never use a fudge factor. I measure correctly, and I cut the material exactly the way I measured it.* □ *I built in a fudge factor of three inches.*

goof 1. AND **goof up** *in.* to make a blunder. □ *Whoops, I goofed!* □ *This time, you goofed.* **2.** *n.* a blunder; an error. □ *Who made this silly goof?* □ *This goof-up is yours, not mine.*

goofed (up) *mod.* messed up; out of order. □ *All my papers are goofed up.* □ *Everything on my desk is goofed. Who's been here?*

goof something up AND **goof up on something** *tr.* to mess something up. □ *Now, don't goof it up this time.* □ *I hope I don't goof up the report again.* □ *I hope I don't goof up on the report again.*

have the wrong number *tr.* to be addressing the wrong person. (This use is in addition to the same expression used for a wrong telephone number. *Have got* can replace *have.*) □ *You have the wrong number. Walter is my brother. We look alike, though.* □ *No, I'm Sally. You have the wrong number.*

howler *n.* a serious and funny mistake. □ *Who is responsible for this howler on the Wilson account?* □ *That howler cost us plenty.*

lay an egg *tr.* [for someone] to do something bad or poorly. □ *I guess I really laid an egg, huh?* □ *The cast laid an egg in both performances.*

make a boo-boo *tr.* to make an error. □ *Everybody makes a boo-boo every now and then.* □ *Whoops! I made a boo-boo.*

mess up *in.* to make an error; to do something wrong. □ *I hope I don't mess up on the quiz.* □ *You really messed up!*

miss the boat *tr.* to have made an error; to be wrong. □ *If you think you can do that, you have just missed the boat.* □ *The guy's missed the boat. He's a lunkhead.*

off the track *mod.* not on a productive course; following the wrong lead. □ *You are off the track just a little. Let me help you.* □ *I was off the track for a while, but now everything is okay.*

pull a boner *tr.* to make a silly error. □ *That was dumb. You really pulled a boner.* □ *Tom is always pulling boners.*

screw up *in.* to mess up. □ *I hope I don't screw up this time.* □ *The waiter screwed up again.*

slip (up) 1. *in.* to make an error. □ *Don't slip up and pay this bill twice, please.* □ *I slipped and gave the guy a 35 percent tip.* **2.** AND **slip(-up)** *n.* an error. □ *That was a silly slip-up. I'm sorry.* □ *That slip cost us nearly $2,000.*

snafu *n.* an error; a foul-up. (Acronym. From *situation normal, all fouled (fucked) up.* Also capitalized.) □ *Your being last is not just a snafu. It's a disaster.* □ *What a SNAFU! All the power went off when you turned on the coffeepot.*

way off (base) *mod.* on the wrong track; completely wrong. □ *I think you're way off base. Try again.* □ *Sorry. You are way off. You should just give up.*

ESCAPE

blow the joint *tr.* to get out of a place, probably in a hurry. (Underworld.) □ *Come on, let's blow the joint before there's trouble.* □ *They blew the joint about an hour ago.*

break *n.* an escape from prison; a prison breakout. □ *I hear there's a break planned for tonight.* □ *Two cons got shot in the break.*

cut and run *in.* to stop what one is doing and flee. □ *The cops were coming, so we cut and run.* □ *At the first warning, we cut and run.*

fly the coop *tr.* to escape from somewhere; to get away. □ *I was afraid he would fly the coop if I didn't tie him up.* □ *I flew the coop before my dad got home.*

getaway *n.* an escape from the law. (Originally underworld.) □ *Lefty made a quick getaway.* □ *There was no time to make a getaway, so we had to talk to Mrs. Wilson.*

give someone the slip *tr.* to escape from a pursuer. □ *We were on his tail until he gave us the slip.* □ *I can give her the slip in no time at all.*

go over the hill *in.* to escape from a prison or from the military service. □ *Jim went over the hill, and they caught him.* □ *Jed and Tom planned to go over the hill last night. What happened?*

go over the wall *in.* to escape from a prison. □ *Lefty tried to go over the wall, but the warden got wind of it.* □ *Nobody goes over the wall in this joint.*

go south AND **head south** *in.* to make an escape; to disappear. □ *Lefty went south the minute he got out of the pen.* □ *The mugger headed south just after the crime.*

hoof it *tr.* to run away. □ *I saw them coming and hoofed it home.* □ *Lefty hoofed it when he saw the uniform.*

on the lam *mod.* running from the police. (Underworld.) □ *Max has been on the lam for a week now.* □ *When the boss found out you was on the lam, he got real mad.*

over the hill *mod.* escaped from prison or the military. □ *Two privates went over the hill last night.* □ *They broke out of jail and went over the hill.*

scram *in.* to exit fast; to get out of a place in a hurry. □ *I gotta scram. I'm late.* □ *Go on, scram! Get out of here fast!*

squirrel out of something *in.* to wiggle out of something; to manage to extricate oneself from a situation one does not wish to be in. □ *He will do anything he can to squirrel out of going to the dance.* □ *Don't try to squirrel out of it. Go through with it.*

ESSENCE

guts *n.* the essence of something. □ *Let's discuss the real guts of this issue.* □ *The guts of your proposal are really easy to understand.*

nitty-gritty *n.* the essence; the essential points. (Usually in *get down to the nitty-gritty.*) □ *What's the nitty-gritty about the broken window?* □ *Once we are down to the nitty-gritty, we can begin to sort things out.*

pure and simple *mod.* basically; simply; essentially. □ *Max is a crook, pure and simple.* □ *It's a pure and simple fact. The guy is a bum.*

ESTIMATION

ballpark estimate AND **ballpark figure** *n.* a rough estimate. □ *I can only give you a ballpark estimate at this time.* □ *All I need is a ballpark figure. Exactness comes later.*

let's say *phr.* introduces an estimate or a speculation. □ *I need about—let's say—twenty pounds.* □ *Let's say I go over and talk to him. What do you think?*

EVASION

tear loose (from someone or something) *in.* to manage to break away from someone or something. □ *The quarterback tore loose and took twenty yards for a first down.* □ *Barlowe tore loose from Rocko and made for the door.*

weasel out of something *in.* to get out of doing something; to wiggle out of a responsibility. □ *I know how to weasel out of something like that. You get a headache.* □ *You can't just weasel out now when we need you!*

wiggle out of something *in.* to successfully avoid doing something. □ *We wiggled out of the appointment.* □ *Don't try to wiggle out of it. I saw you with her.*

EVEN

even-Steven 1. *mod.* evenly divided. □ *He made the two piles of diamonds even-Steven and then let me choose which one I wanted.* □ *The cake is not exactly cut even-Steven.* **2.** *mod.* even; balanced. □ *Now we're even-Steven.* □ *Now that we've given each other black eyes, are we even-Steven?*

EVENT

barnburner *n.* an attention-getting event or development. □ *The current barnburner in Washington is the Wilson investigation.* □ *This is a real barnburner! Everyone will want to see it.*

catch *tr.* to view something; to attend something. □ *We'll take the chicks to catch a film after we eat.* □ *Did you catch* Gone with the Wind *on TV?*

do *n.* a party; a social event. □ *We had a smashing time at your little do.* □ *I'm having a do for a friend this weekend. Would you like to come?*

fanny-bumper *n.* an event that draws so many people that they bump into one another. □ *The fire on Thirty-fourth Street turned into a real fanny-bumper.* □ *There was a typically dull fanny-bumper in the village last night.*

freaker *n.* an incident that causes someone to *freak (out)*. (Collegiate.) □ *Wasn't that weird? A real freaker.* □ *Did you see that near miss? What a freaker!*

gangbusters *n.* a wild, busy, and successful event. □ *Our party was truly gangbusters, for sure.* □ *The explosion and fire two streets over was really gangbusters for a while.*

goings-on *n.* happenings; events. □ *There are sure some strange goings-on around here.* □ *Some big goings-on downtown tied up the traffic.*

good trip *n.* any good time. □ *This meeting was a good trip.* □ *Compared to the last class, this one is a good trip.*

happening *n.* an event. □ *The concert was a real happening.* □ *Well, class is never a happening, but it's never dull.*

hoo-ha *n.* a commotion. □ *What is all this hoo-ha about?* □ *A deer created quite a hoo-ha by running frantically through the department store.*

howl *n.* something funny. □ *What a howl the surprise party turned out to be when the guest of honor didn't show up.* □ *The gag was a real howl.*

joy ride *n.* a drinking bout or party. □ *There's a little joy ride over at Tom's.* □ *Some joy ride! They ran out of booze.*

make the scene *tr.* to attend an event. □ *We plan to make the scene, but you know how things are.* □ *I hope everybody can make the scene.*

rally 1. *n.* get-together of some kind; a party, usually informal, possibly spontaneous. □ *There's a rally over at Tom's tonight.* □ *The rally was a flop. Everyone left early.* **2.** *in.* to hold a get-together of some kind. (Collegiate.) □ *Let's rally tonight about midnight.* □ *They rallied until dawn.*

roast 1. *tr.* to put on an entertaining program where the guest of honor is teased and insulted. □ *They roasted Dave when he retired.* □ *If they roast me at the dinner, I'll cry.* **2.** *n.* an entertaining program where the guest of honor is insulted all in fun. □ *It was a wonderful roast. The guest of honor was pleased with the quality of the insults.* □ *It was a little too polite for a real roast.*

standee *n.* someone who must stand (at some event). □ *There were about forty standees in addition to the full house.* □ *Can I get in as a standee, or do I have to wait for the next showing?*

EVERYTHING

all that jazz *n.* all that stuff; all that nonsense. □ *I need some glue, paper, string, and all that jazz to make a kite.* □ *She told me I was selfish, hateful, rude, ugly, and all that jazz.*

everything from soup to nuts *n.* everything imaginable. □ *It looks like she brought everything from soup to nuts.* □ *I have everything from soup to nuts in my briefcase.*

from A to Z *mod.* of a complete and wide variety. □ *We have just about everything from A to Z.* □ *She ordered everything on the menu from A to Z.*

kit and caboodle *n.* everything; all parts and property. (Often with *whole.*) □ *I want you out of here—kit and caboodle—by noon.* □ *She moved in to stay, kit and caboodle.* □ *She plunked her whole kit and caboodle right in my way.*

the works *n.* the entire amount; everything. □ *I'd like my hamburger with onions, pickles, catsup, mustard—the works.* □ *She's getting the works at the beauty shop—cut, wash, dye, and set.*

whole bag of tricks *n.* everything; every possibility. □ *Well, now. I've used my whole bag of tricks, and we still haven't solved this.* □ *It may take my whole bag of tricks to do it, but I'll try.*

whole ball of wax *n.* everything; the whole thing. (Always with *the.*) □ *Well, that just about ruins the whole ball of wax.* □ *Your comments threatened the whole ball of wax, that's what.*

whole enchilada *n.* the whole thing; everything. (From Spanish. Always with *the.*) □ *Nobody, but nobody, ever gets the whole enchilada.* □ *Max wants the whole enchilada.*

whole nine yards *n.* the entire amount; everything. (Always with *the.* Origin unknown.) □ *For you I'll go the whole nine yards.* □ *You're worth the whole nine yards.*

whole schmear *n.* the entire amount; the entire affair. (Yiddish. Always with *the.*) □ *You just wrecked the whole schmear, that's what.* □ *I'll take a hamburger with everything on it—the whole schmear.*

whole shebang AND **whole shooting match** *n.* the whole affair; everything and everyone. (Folksy. Always with *the.*) □ *The whole shebang is just about washed up.* □ *I'm fed up with the whole shooting match.*

EVERYWHERE

whole wide world *n.* everywhere; everywhere and everything. (Always with *the.*) □ *It's the best in the whole wide world.* □ *I've searched the whole wide world for just the right hat.*

EVIDENCE

(bang) dead to rights *mod.* in the act; (guilty) without question. □ *We caught her dead to rights with the loot still on her.* □ *There he was, bang dead to rights with the gun still smoking.*

have someone dead to rights *tr.* to have caught someone red-handed; to have irrefutable evidence about someone's misdeed. □ *We've got you dead to rights on this one.* □ *The cops had him dead to rights.*

paper *n.* a written document; written evidence supporting something. (Often with *some.*) □ *Don't tell me over the phone! I want paper!* □ *Come on, send me some paper. Let's make this official.*

tip-off *n.* a clue; an indication. □ *The tip-off was when the dog started wagging his tail. We knew you were hiding somewhere close.* □ *The broken twig was just the tip-off Barlowe needed.*

EXACTLY

just the ticket *n.* just the perfect thing. □ *This little jigger is just the ticket.* □ *A nice cup of tea will be just the ticket.*

just what the doctor ordered *n.* exactly what is needed. □ *This nice cool beer is just what the doctor ordered.* □ *A nice chat with friends is just what the doctor ordered.*

EXAGGERATION

glorified *mod.* overblown; over-hyped; phony. □ *Why, this is just a glorified potato chip!* □ *She's just a glorified dancehall girl.*

make a federal case out of something *tr.* to exaggerate the importance of an error; to overdo something. □ *Do you have to make a federal case out of everything?* □ *I only spilled my milk. Why make a federal case out of it?*

EXAMINATION

case the joint *tr.* to look a place over. □ *The dog came in and cased the joint, sniffing out friends and foes.* □ *The old lady entered slowly, casing the joint for the face of someone of her era, and finally took a seat.*

check something out *tr.* to examine something; to think about something. □ *It's something we all have to be concerned with. Check it out.* □ *Check out this Billy Biggles album.*

dope something out *tr.* to figure out something from the information available. □ *I think I can dope this thing out from the evidence available.* □ *We can dope out the truth from her testimony if we have to.*

eyeball *tr.* to look hard at someone or something. □ *I eyeballed the contract and saw the figures.* □ *The two eyeballed each other and walked on.*

going-over *n.* an examination. □ *After a thorough going-over, the doctor pronounced me alive.* □ *I gave your car a good going-over, and I fixed a lot of little things.*

loaded question *n.* a question to which an honest answer will reveal things the speaker might otherwise wish to conceal. □ *Now, that's a loaded question, and I don't think I have to answer it.* □ *I didn't mean it to be a loaded question.*

look-see *n.* a look; a visual examination. □ *Let's go and have a look-see at this monster of yours.* □ *Take a look-see at this one and see if you like it.*

once-over *n.* a visual examination, especially of a person of the opposite sex. (Always with *the.*) □ *The way she was giving him the once-over, I knew she would say something to him.* □ *Tom, you are always giving the girls the once-over.*

once-over lightly *n.* a perfunctory examination; a quick glance. □ *Please give it more than the usual once-over lightly.* □ *Once-over lightly is not enough.*

scope (on) someone *tr.* to evaluate a member of the opposite sex visually. □ *He scoped every girl who came in the door.* □ *He wouldn't like it if somebody scoped on him. Or would he?*

scope someone out *tr.* to look someone over; to check someone out. □ *Nobody was scoping Dave out, though.* □ *Dave was scoping out all the girls.*

skin-search *n.* a search of the naked body by legal authorities. □ *These clowns were actually doing skin-searches on traffic offenders!* □ *Aren't there laws against frivolous skin-searches?*

strip-search *tr.* to search someone's entire naked body. □ *The cops strip-searched the good-looking chick who ran a red light.* □ *Now it takes a court order to strip-search someone.*

work someone over *tr.* to give someone's body a thorough examination or treatment. □ *The doctors worked her over to the tune of $1,500, but couldn't find anything wrong with her.* □ *The dermatologist worked over her entire body looking for moles.*

EXCELLENCE

awesome *exclam.* "Great!"; "Excellent!" (Usually **Awesome!** Standard English, but used often in slang.) □ *You own that gorgeous hog? Awesome!* □ *Awesome! I'm impressed.*

bad *mod.* suitable; excellent; good. (Black.) □ *I got some new silks that are really bad.* □ *That is a bad man dancing there.* □ *Look at those really bad shoes on that guy.*

bang-up *mod.* really excellent. □ *We had a bang-up time at your bash.* □ *I like to throw a bang-up party once or twice a year.* □ *Another bang-up day at the factory!*

beaut *n.* someone or something excellent, not necessarily beautiful. □ *Man, this fishing rod's a beaut!* □ *This is a beaut of a day!*

beautiful *mod.* very satisfying; excellent. □ *This wine is really beautiful!* □ *Man, this place is beautiful. You got your own sink and toilet right in the room and good strong bars to keep the riffraff out.*

berries *n.* the best; the finest. (Always with *the*. A noun with the force of an adjective.) □ *Those people are really the berries.* □ *Man, this stuff is the berries!*

bitchin' AND **bitchen** (Potentially offensive. Use only with discretion.) **1.** *mod.* excellent; great; classy. □ *This is a totally bitchin' pair of jeans!* □ *This is a way bitchen rally, my man!* **2.** *exclam.* "Terrific!" (Usually **Bitchin'!**) □ *Bitchin'! Let's do it again!* □ *Four of them? Bitchen!*

bogus *mod.* great; excellent. □ *Man, this place is really bogus!* □ *Sam and Charlie had a really bogus time at the jig.*

bold *mod.* great; outstanding. □ *Bold move, Charles. You outfoxed them.* □ *The movie we saw last night was really bold.*

Bonus! *exclam.* "That's great!"; "That's good enough to earn a bonus!" □ *Bonus! That's the best news I've heard in a long time!* □ *The teacher's sick? Bonus!*

brutal *mod.* excellent; powerful. □ *Man, what a brutal tune!* □ *That last wave was brutal to the max.*

cat's meow *n.* something really fine. □ *This stuff is really the cat's meow.* □ *Hearing all the old big band music again is the cat's meow.*

chillin' *mod.* great; excellent. □ *I had one chillin' time last night.* □ *Everybody there was chillin'.*

choice *mod.* nice; cool. □ *We had a choice time at Tom's party.* □ *This new tunage is real choice.*

cold *mod.* excellent. (Very *cool.*) □ *That last pitch was cold, man.* □ *Hey, G! That's a cold ride.*

cool *mod.* good; excellent. □ *This is a really cool setup!* □ *Then this, like, cool muscleman comes over and asks Tiffany if she'd like to dance.*

Cool beans! AND **Cool bananas!** *exclam.* "Wow!" □ *Cool beans, man. That's great!* □ *You got a car? Cool bananas!*

cosmic *mod.* excellent; powerful. □ *This pizza is absolutely cosmic!* □ *Who wants to see a really cosmic movie?*

crack *mod.* (of a person) excellent; topflight. □ *The dealer's crack salesman was no help at all.* □ *With our crack staff, we can have everything worked out in no time.*

crackerjack *mod.* excellent; industrious. □ *Fred is a crackerjack stockbroker, but his personal life is a mess.* □ *Clare is a crackerjack teacher, but she is looking for something that pays a real salary.*

cranking *mod.* exciting; excellent. □ *This record is really cranking!* □ *We had a massively cranking time at your set.*

crazy *mod.* cool. □ *This stuff is really crazy, man. I love it!* □ *What a crazy dress. It makes you look like a million.*

daisy *n.* an excellent thing. □ *This little car is a real daisy.* □ *I want a daisy of a haircut. Something unusual with bangs or something.*

dank *mod.* very good. □ *We stopped for a while in this real dank little bistro on the main boulevard.* □ *This wine is so dank!*

darb *n.* an excellent person or thing. □ *Carl is a real darb. I'm glad to know him.* □ *What a swell darb of a car!*

deathly *mod.* excellent. □ *Did you see Kelly's deathly new convertible?* □ *That's a deathly idea!*

163

decent *mod.* good; very good. □ *This is some pretty decent jazz.* □ *Your threads are decent, all right.*

def *mod.* better; *cool.* (Originally Black. From *definitive.*) □ *Man, that yogurt is def!* □ *What a def set of threads!*

diesel *mod.* really good. □ *Fred had a really diesel idea, but no money to carry it out.* □ *I am set for a diesel evening and I intend to enjoy it.*

dilly *n.* something excellent. □ *This little car is a real dilly.* □ *What a dilly of an apartment!*

doosie AND **doozie; doozy** *n.* something extraordinary, good or bad. □ *The trade show was a real doozy this year.* □ *Old Gert was a real doozy.*

dope *mod.* best; most excellent. □ *My roommate is really dope. Great guy!* □ *We had a great time there. It was dope and dudical.*

drop-dead *mod.* stunning enough to make one drop dead. □ *I had my living room done in a bright drop-dead red that makes your blood run cold!* □ *She stood up and made this drop-dead announcement about getting married, and I thought I would just scream.*

ducky *mod.* okay; good. (Often used sarcastically.) □ *Now, isn't that just ducky?* □ *That's a ducky idea!*

dude *mod.* excellent. □ *The game was severely dude! We won!* □ *This whole day has been dude and fat.*

dudical *mod.* really good. □ *It is truly dudical to see you here, Dave.* □ *What a dudical crib!*

evil *mod.* excellent. □ *This wine is really evil!* □ *Man, what evil fronts!*

Excellent! *exclam.* "Fine!" (Like *awesome,* this expression is a standard word used frequently in slang contexts.) □ *A new stereo? Excellent!* □ *Excellent! Way rad!*

fab *mod.* fabulous. □ *Man, what a fab stereo!* □ *Your pad is not what I'd call fab. Just okay.*

Fantabulous! *exclam.* "Great!" (A blend of *fantastic* and *fabulous.*) □ *You're here at last. Fantabulous!* □ *Fantabulous! It's finished.*

far out *mod.* cool; great; extraordinary. □ *This jazz is really far out!* □ *You want to hear some far out heavy metal?*

fat *mod.* great; excellent. □ *The fireworks in the park were really fat this year!* □ *Mary thought the rally was fat, but left early anyway.*

fer shur *phr.* "for sure"; "absolutely." (Eye-dialect. Used in writing only for effect.) □ *This is way rad, fer shur.* □ *I'll be there. Fer shur!*

fine and dandy *mod.* nice; good; well. (Often sarcastic.) □ *Well, that's just fine and dandy. Couldn't be better.* □ *I feel fine and dandy, and I'm going to have a good time here.*

fresh *mod.* cool; okay. □ *Gee, that's not fresh. Too bad.* □ *That stuff's really fresh. It's a winner.*

froody *mod.* grand; wonderful. □ *The curtains parted to the most froody, funky set I've ever seen.* □ *Man, is this froody!* □ *Oh, you have some froody ideas, all right. But can you carry them out?*

frosty *mod.* cool; really *cool* and *mellow.* □ *That music is really frosty.* □ *We had a frosty time, didn't we?*

funky-fresh *mod.* very good. □ *This tunage is funky-fresh—to my ears, anyway.* □ *Mary is funky-fresh when she works out, but a real slow runner when she's been lazy.*

gear *mod.* excellent. □ *This jazz is really gear!* □ *Man, what a gear pizza!*

(g)narly *mod.* excellent; great. (California.) □ *This pizza is too gnarly for words!* □ *Who is that narly guy in the white sweater?*

gone *mod.* cool; out of this world. □ *This ice cream is gone, man, gone!* □ *She is one real gone chick.*

groovy *mod.* cool; pleasant. □ *Man, this music is groovy.* □ *What a groovy day!*

heavy *mod.* really fine. □ *Man, this is some heavy chocolate cake!* □ *This stuff is really heavy!* □ *This is a real heavy thing you're doing for me.*

hellacious *mod.* wild; excellent. (Use caution with *hell*.) □ *What a hellacious good time we had!* □ *Sally throws one hellacious party.*

hell of a someone or something AND **helluva someone or something** *n.* a very good person or thing. (Use caution with *hell*.) □ *He is one hell of a guy. We really like him.* □ *We had a helluva good time.*

honey of a something *n.* a very special something; an excellent example of something. □ *This is a honey of a car. Wanna drive it?* □ *Now, here's a honey of a little stereo receiver.*

hotshot AND **hot-shot** *mod.* brilliant; great. □ *Wally is becoming a real hot-shot tenor with the local opera company.* □ *So, you're the hot-shot guy who's going to straighten this place out.*

hotsy-totsy *mod.* fine; great. □ *Well, isn't that just hotsy-totsy.* □ *I don't feel so hotsy-totsy.*

humdinger AND **hummer** *n.* someone or something excellent. □ *Now, this one is a real humdinger.* □ *Yup, he's a hummer all right.*

hype *mod.* really good; excellent. □ *Now this is a truly hype pizza!* □ *This rally is really hype!*

ice *mod.* excellent; very *cool*. □ *Her answer was ice, and she really put down that guy.* □ *Man, this stuff is ice!*

in fine feather *mod.* in good form; in good spirits. □ *Mary is really in fine feather tonight.* □ *I feel in fine feather and ready to go!*

in rare form *mod.* well-tuned for a good performance; at one's best. □ *He is in rare form today.* □ *We are not exactly in rare form on Monday mornings.*

jamming *mod.* excellent. □ *This music is really jamming.* □ *What a jamming class session.*

keeper *n.* something that can be kept; something that qualifies. □ *This fish is a keeper. Throw the others out.* □ *The chipped one is not a keeper.*

kickin' AND **kicken** *mod.* wild; super; excellent. □ *Your rally was really kickin'.* □ *I don't know where you get your clothes, but that jacket's kickin'.*

killer 1. *n.* something extraordinary. □ *That jacket is a real killer!* □ *That car is a killer. I like it!* **2.** *mod.* extraordinary; great. □ *What a killer jacket you're wearing!* □ *This is a killer hamburger, all right.*

killer-diller *n.* an excellent thing or person. □ *She is just a real killer-diller.* □ *This story is a real killer-diller.*

like a million (dollars) *mod.* very good or well. (Usually with *feel*.) □ *This old buggy runs like a million dollars.* □ *Man, I feel like a million.*

live *mod.* cool; great. □ *Everything's live! No problem!* □ *It's live and ice. No problem, man.*

Love you! *exclam.* "You are great!" (Almost meaningless patter.) □ *See ya around, Martin. Let's do lunch! Love ya! Bye-bye.* □ *Nice talking to you, babe. Love you!*

major *mod.* excellent; serious; severe. (Collegiate.) □ *This rally is, like, major!* □ *Wally is one of the most major beach guys!*

massive *mod.* excellent. (California.) □ *The bash at Tiffany's was, like, massive!* □ *That was a totally massive party, Tiff.*

mean 1. *mod.* having to do with someone or something that is very good; *cool*. □ *This music is mean, man, mean. What a great sound!* □ *This is the meanest wine I ever drank.* **2.** *mod.* having to do with an excellent example of the art of doing something well habitually. (Always with *a* as in the examples.) □ *John plays the piano quite well. Fred says that John plays a mean piano.* □ *You may say that your mother bakes delicious pies, but all my friends say she bakes a mean pie.* □ *Tom says that his father plays a mean game of golf.*

mint *mod.* good-looking; superior. (As in mint condition.) □ *Look at that guy. He's really mint, right?* □ *These tunes are mint, all right!*

most *n.* something that is the best. (Always with *the*.) □ *This noodle stuff is the most, Mom!* □ *Sally is the most! Can she dance!*

neat *mod.* great; *cool*; fine. □ *What a neat idea!* □ *That was not a very neat thing to do.*

nifty *mod.* neat; smart. □ *That is a pretty nifty car you have there.* □ *Yes, it is nifty.*

not too shabby *mod.* (with emphasis on *shabby*) "nice"; "well done." □ *Is that your car? Not too shabby!* □ *That play was not too shabby.*

Oh, boy! *exclam.* "Wow!" □ *Oh, boy! What a mess!* □ *Oh, boy! That was a great play!*

on it *mod.* really good. □ *Man, Weasel is really on it! What a rad lad!* □ *Susan is on it, and getting lots of attention for her running style.*

organic *mod.* great. □ *This is one fine, organic rally! I'm glad I stopped by.* □ *Wow, this whole day was organic!*

peach *n.* someone or something excellent. (Usually a person.) □ *That guy's a real peach.* □ *This is a peach of a car!*

peachy (keen) *mod.* fine; excellent. □ *Your idea is really peachy!* □ *What a peachy keen idea!*

primo *mod.* great; first-class. □ *This pizza is really primo.* □ *Sally is primo. You can't do better than Sally.*

rad *mod.* great; wonderful; excellent; exciting. (California. From *radical*.) □ *Oh my God, that's, like, really rad!* □ *What a rad swimsuit!*

radical *mod.* great; excellent. (California.) □ *It's so, like, radical!* □ *My boyfriend, he's, like, so radical!*

rattling *mod.* excellent. (Collegiate.) □ *Her party was really rattling.* □ *What a rattling place to live!*

righteous *mod.* good; of good quality. (Originally black.) □ *She is a righteous mama.* □ *Max told me about some righteous grass he's got.* □ *This stuff is really righteous!*

rocking *mod.* excellent. (Collegiate.) □ *Man, what a rocking party!* □ *This set is really rocking.* □ *We had a rocking time!*

rosy *mod.* good; satisfactory. □ *Things are looking rosy now that the economy is improving.* □ *Doesn't look like a very rosy future.* □ *When the stock market crashed, nothing looked rosy.*

savage *mod.* excellent. (Collegiate.) □ *This is really a savage piece of music.* □ *Man, Fred is a totally savage guy.* □ *Wow, is he savage!*

scorching *mod.* really hot; about to win something big. □ *Let me roll again. I'm really scorching.* □ *Here comes a scorching runner!* □ *He says he's scorching. Get out of his way.*

serious *mod.* good; profound; excellent. □ *He plays some serious guitar.* □ *Man, these tunes are, like, serious.*

slick *mod.* excellent. □ *This is a real slick setup you got here.* □ *That is a slick idea.* □ *The idea is not so slick!*

sly *mod.* excellent; *cool*. □ *Look at Jim's sly new ride.* □ *That is really a sly jacket you got there.*

smashing *mod.* excellent; really tremendous. □ *We had a smashing time at your little do.* □ *This whole meal has been smashing.*

smokin' *mod.* really *hot*; overpowering. □ *Those threads on that dude are really smokin'.* □ *If you wanna hear some smokin' vinyl, just stay tuned.*

solid *mod.* good; great; *cool*. □ *Man, this music is solid!* □ *Listen to that solid beat.*

some pumpkins AND **some punkins** *mod.* great or special. □ *That chick is some punkins!* □ *Isn't this little gadget really some pumpkins?*

spiffy *mod.* excellent. □ *This is a real spiffy place you've got here, Sam.* □ *Come have a look at my spiffy new car.* □ *Doesn't look so spiffy to me.*

standout *n.* an extraordinary thing or person. □ *Bob is a real standout in our bowling league.* □ *This car is a real standout as a speed machine.*

stellar *mod.* excellent; grand. □ *It was a stellar performance, and the applause was thunderous.* □ *Ronald Simpson gave us a stellar characterization of Boris, but the chorus was a disappointment.* □ *The chorus was stellar!*

stokin' *mod.* excellent; wild. □ *That car is really stokin'.* □ *We had a stokin' time at Fred's house.*

stone groove *n.* something really satisfying; a fine party or concert. □ *This affair is not what I would call a stone groove. Stone beige, maybe.* □ *Ted's do was a stone groove.*

straight *mod.* excellent. □ *This news is truly straight and I am happy to hear it.* □ *You are a straight G.*

stupid fresh *mod.* very, very good. □ *Her looks were stupid fresh. Bonus!* □ *This ice cream is stupid fresh and needs to be eaten in great volumes.*

super *mod.* fine; excellent. □ *This report is just super!* □ *Who made the super pie?*

super-duper AND **super-dooper** *mod.* excellent. □ *That's just super-duper. Couldn't have asked for better.* □ *Where is this super-dooper car of yours?*

superfly *mod.* excellent; wonderful. □ *This dude is really superfly.* □ *I don't care about this superfly gent of yours. If he doesn't have a job, I don't want you seeing him anymore. Ya hear?*

surf *mod.* wonderful; with it. (California.) □ *This party is, like, surf.* □ *This is not what I would call a surf day.*

sweet *mod.* good; profitable; excellent. □ *I got involved in a sweet deal having to do with a better job.* □ *Fred offered Bill a sweet contract, but Bill turned it down.*

swell *mod.* fine; excellent. (Also sarcastic use.) □ *Where did you get that swell hat?* □ *Oh that's just swell! Yuck!*

swellelegant *mod.* really fine. (From *swell* and *elegant*.) □ *Gee, this place is sure swellelegant!* □ *It is not swellelegant.* □ *Her car is just swellelegant.*

swinging *mod.* great. □ *We had a swinging time at John's rally.* □ *The concert was swinging—nothing like it, ever.*

tall *mod.* high-quality. □ *This is one tall pizza, man.* □ *You're bringing in some tall ideas, man.*

tawny *mod.* excellent. □ *Who is throwing this tawny party anyway?* □ *This pizza is, like, tawny!*

terrific *mod.* excellent. □ *Glad to hear it. That's just terrific.* □ *What a terrific idea!*

toast *mod.* excellent. □ *This stuff is toast!* □ *Your silks are real toast.*

too much *mod.* overwhelming; excellent. □ *It's wonderful. It's just too much!* □ *You are so kind. This is too much.*

top *tr.* to surpass someone or something. □ *Can you top this one?* □ *I'll try to top your joke.*

top-drawer *mod.* top-quality. □ *Podunk U. is a really top-drawer school.* □ *I want to hire a young MBA who's top-drawer.*

top-flight *mod.* of the highest caliber. □ *This candy is top-flight in every sense.* □ *We are looking for a top-flight manager for our new division.*

tripped out *mod.* great; excellent. □ *This party is really tripped out, right?* □ *We had a tripped-out time in class today. The teacher brought his pet rabbit.*

tubular *mod.* excellent. (Surfing and later general youth slang. Having to do with a *tube* [wave] that is good to surf in.) □ *That pizza was totally tubular!* □ *This whole week is, like, tubular.*

vicious *mod.* great; excellent. □ *Man, this burger is really vicious.* □ *That guy is one vicious driver, all right.* □ *That was a really vicious concert last night.*

wail *in.* to be great. □ *Things really started to wail about midnight when the band really got going.* □ *This pizza really wails.*

wailing AND **whaling** *mod.* excellent. (Teens.) □ *Man, that's wailing!* □ *What a whaling guitar!*

way rad *mod.* quite excellent. (California.) □ *Oh, Tiff! That's way rad!* □ *You are? Way rad!*

whale on *mod.* excellent. □ *This is one whale on rally.* □ *We had a whale on time at Bob's house.*

whipped *mod.* great. □ *The band was whipped and the food was unbelievable.* □ *You look whipped, Sam. Things going well?*

wicked *mod.* excellent; impressive. □ *Now, this is what I call a wicked guitar.* □ *Man, this wine is wicked!*

winner *n.* an excellent person or thing. □ *This one is a real winner.* □ *He's no winner, but he'll do.*

world-class *mod.* absolutely top rate. □ *Now, this is a world-class computer. Lots and lots of memory.* □ *I want to see one of your world-class automobiles, whatever that might mean.* □ *This one isn't world-class.*

EXCITEMENT

action *n.* excitement; activity in general; whatever is happening. □ *This place is dull. I want some action.* □ *How do I find out where the action is in this town?*

(all) shook up *mod.* excited; disturbed; upset. □ *She stole my heart, and I'm all shook up.* □ *They were pretty shook up after the accident.*

all the way live *mod.* very exciting; excellent. (California.) □ *Man, this place is all the way live.* □ *Oh, Tiffany is just, like, all the way live!*

belt *n.* a kick or a thrill. □ *We all got quite a belt from your jokes.* □ *Kelly gets a belt from roller coasters.*

charge *n.* a thrill. □ *Seeing my kid up there on that stage was a real charge.* □ *I got a tremendous charge out of your last letter.*

charged (up) *mod.* excited. □ *The audience was charged up and ready for the star to come out.* □ *The charged-up quarterback made some wonderful plays.*

fired up *mod.* excited; enthusiastic. □ *How can you be so fired up at this time of the morning?* □ *It's impossible to get Martin fired up at all.*

fire someone or something up *tr.* to motivate someone; to make someone enthusiastic. □ *See if you can fire John up and get him to paint the house.* □ *I have*

to fire up the electorate if I want them to vote for me.

fireworks *n.* excitement. □ *When the fireworks are over, come in and we'll talk.* □ *What're all the fireworks about around here?*

get it up *tr.* to get excited about something. (Other taboo meanings, also.) □ *I just couldn't get it up about going off to college.* □ *Paul just couldn't get it up about life in general.*

get someone going *tr.* to get someone excited; to get someone talking excitedly. □ *I guess I really got him going on the subject of politics.* □ *The whole business really makes me mad. Don't get me going.*

get someone's motor running *tr.* to get someone excited. □ *What'll I have to do to get your motor running about algebra?* □ *I've got some news that'll really get your motor running.*

go ape (over someone or something) *in.* to become very excited over someone or something. □ *I just go ape over chocolate.* □ *Sam went ape over Mary.*

go into orbit *in.* to become very excited. □ *Wow, I thought the manager was going to go into orbit, she was so mad.* □ *The entire staff went into orbit when they got the news.*

hairy-ass(ed) *mod.* wild; exciting. (Potentially offensive. Use only with discretion.) □ *We had a real hairy-ass time on the roller coaster.* □ *The last part of the climb was really hairy-assed.*

have a ball *tr.* to have an exciting time. □ *I plan to have a ball while I'm there.* □ *Come on, everybody! Let's have a ball!*

have a whale of a time *tr.* to have an exciting time; to have a big time. □ *We had a whale of a time at your party.* □ *Yes, we really had a whale of a time.*

high on something *mod.* excited or enthusiastic about something. □ *Tom is really high on the idea of going to Yellowstone this summer.* □ *I'm not high on going, but I will.*

hopped up *mod.* excited. □ *Paul is certainly hopped up about something.* □ *Why are you so hopped up?*

hyped (up) *mod.* excited; stimulated. □ *They were all hyped up before the game.* □ *She said she had to get hyped before the tennis match.*

hyper 1. *mod.* excited; overreacting. □ *I'm a little hyper because of the doctor's report.* □ *Here's another hyper patient.* □ *Now, now, don't get hyper.* **2.** *n.* a person who is always overly excited or hyperactive. □ *Pat is such a hyper. Just can't seem to relax.* □ *My dad is a hyper.*

jacked up AND **jacked** *mod.* excited. □ *Don was really jacked up about the election.* □ *The gang was jacked up and ready to party.*

jazz someone or something up *tr.* to make someone or something more exciting or sexy; to make someone or something appeal more to contemporary and youthful tastes. □ *Let's jazz this up a little bit.* □ *They jazzed up the old girl till she looked like a teenager.* □ *Don't jazz up the first number too much.*

kicky *mod.* exciting and energetic. □ *Man, what a kicky idea!* □ *She is a real kicky gal.*

knockout *mod.* very exciting. □ *It was a real knockout evening.* □ *What a knockout idea!*

out of this world *mod.* wonderful and exciting. □ *This pie is out of this world.* □ *My boyfriend is just out of this world.*

panic *n.* a very funny or exciting person or thing. □ *John's party was a real panic.* □ *Paul is a panic. He tells a joke a minute.*

pizzazz *n.* punch; glitter and excitement. □ *Listen to the way she put pizzazz into that song!* □ *This script lacks pizzazz.*

psyched (out) *mod.* excited; overwhelmed; thrilled. □ *She's really psyched out.* □ *That's great. I'm really psyched!* □ *What a psyched out way to talk!*

pump (someone) up *tr.* to excite someone; to make someone enthusiastic. □ *The coach gave a pep talk to pump the* players up for the big game. □ *Tom pumped us up at the sales meeting.*

revved up *mod.* excited, perhaps by drugs. □ *Max is revved up from too much dope.* □ *The kids were all revved up, ready to party.*

rooting-tooting *mod.* exciting; renowned; famous; illustrious. (A vague adjective of praise.) □ *We really had a rooting-tooting time last weekend.* □ *She's a rooting-tooting dancer from Omaha.*

rush *n.* any excitement; any burst of good feeling. □ *I got a real rush from helping out.* □ *The wonderful ending to the movie gave me a rush.*

Schwing! *exclam.* "How exciting!"; "How stimulating!"; "Wow!" (Originally said on seeing an extremely good-looking or sexually attractive girl.) □ *Did you see her? Schwing!* □ *Nice car. Schwing!*

screamer *n.* someone or something very exciting or attention-getting. □ *This guy is a real screamer! Wait'll you meet him.* □ *Her political campaign is a real screamer.*

sexy *mod.* neat; exciting. □ *That's a sexy set of wheels.* □ *You play really sexy music.* □ *Your idea is real sexy.*

slam-bang *mod.* wild; exciting. □ *It was a slam-bang weekend, and I loved every minute of it.* □ *Wow, did we ever have a slam-bang time!*

snazz AND **shnazz** *n.* class; glitter and excitement. □ *The curtain opened on a dazzling display of snazz and bright lights.* □ *There was lots of snazz and glitz, but no real substance.*

snazz something up *tr.* to make something classy or exciting. □ *Come on, let's try to snazz this up.* □ *What can I do to snazz up my face?*

spaz out *in.* to overreact to something; to become overly excited about something. □ *I knew you would spaz out! It's not that bad!* □ *Come on, don't spaz out!*

steam someone up *tr.* to get someone excited. □ *Steam yourselves up and get in there and win this game!* □ *The coach can really steam up those guys.*

stoked (on someone or something) *mod.* excited by someone or something. □ *We were stoked on Mary. She is the greatest.* □ *Everyone is stoked on spring.* □ *Now, don't get too stoked, you are the one who has to run.*

swing *in.* [for a party or other event] to be fun or exciting. □ *This party really swings!* □ *I've never been to a gathering that swings like this one.*

switched on *mod.* excited. □ *I get switched on by that kind of music.* □ *I am never switched on by raucous music.*

thriller-diller *n.* something like a movie, book, or television program that is thrilling. □ *The film was a real thriller-diller. I remember having to force myself to exhale.* □ *I can read one of these thriller-dillers in a couple of hours.*

turned on *mod.* made alert to what is new and exciting. □ *I want to hire someone who's really turned on—a real comer.* □ *A young, turned-on MBA would be just right.*

turn-on *n.* someone or something that excites someone. □ *The concert was a real turn-on.* □ *David can be a real turn-on when he's in a good mood.*

turn someone on *tr.* to excite or interest someone. □ *Fast music with a good beat turns me on.* □ *That stuff doesn't turn on anyone.*

wig out *in.* to have a good time at a party, etc. □ *We wigged out at John's do.* □ *Come on, let's wig out!*

wild *mod.* exciting; eccentric. □ *Things are really wild here.* □ *We had a wild time.*

wild and woolly *mod.* exciting. □ *Things get a little wild and woolly on a Friday evening at Wally's place.* □ *The ride home was a little wild and woolly.*

wow *n.* something exciting. □ *The game was a real wow.* □ *For a pretty good wow, try the Empire Theater's production of Mame this weekend.*

EXCREMENT

See also DEFECATION.

alley apple *n.* a piece of horse manure. □ *The route of the parade was littered with alley apples after about twenty minutes.* □ *Harry is collecting alley apples for his garden.*

bull-pucky *n.* bull dung. □ *Why didn't you watch where you were going? Didn't you expect to find bull-pucky in a barnyard?* □ *How can you tell it's bull-pucky?*

caca AND **kaka** *n.* dung; feces. (Juvenile. From Spanish. Use caution with the topic.) □ *There's fresh caca in the front yard.* □ *Don't worry. It's dog kaka.*

cack *n.* dung; feces. (Use caution with the topic.) □ *Wipe that cack off your shoes before you come in here!* □ *The sidewalks are just covered with cack!*

cow chips *n.* dried cow dung. □ *There's a whole field of cow chips out there! Why do you want to buy a bag of the stuff at a nursery?* □ *Break up these cow chips and work them into the soil around the base of the bushes.*

cow-doots *n.* cow dung; masses of cow dung. □ *Don was walking through the pasture gathering cow-doots to use as fertilizer.* □ *Don't step in the cow-doots.*

cow flop AND **cow plop** *n.* a mass of cow dung. □ *Mrs. Wilson is out in the pasture gathering cow flops for her garden.* □ *Cow plops are not all the same, you know.*

crap *n.* dung. (Potentially offensive. Use only with discretion. Colloquial.) □ *There's dog crap on the lawn.* □ *Don't step in that crap.*

dog *n.* dog dung. □ *There's some dog on the lawn.* □ *Don't step in the dog.*

dog-doo AND **dog-dew; dog-do** *n.* dog dung. □ *Don't step in the dog-doo.* □ *When the snow melts, the sidewalks are covered with dog-doo.*

doo(-doo) *n.* dung, especially animal dung. □ *Don't step in the doo-doo.* □ *There's a lot of pigeon doo in the attic.*

duky *n.* feces. (Originally black and primarily juvenile.) □ *The doggie made duky in the backyard.* □ *Mommy, there's duky in Jimmy's diaper.*

hockey AND **hocky** *mod.* dung. □ *Watch out for that hocky there in the gutter.* □ *Don't step in the fresh hockey.*

horse *n.* horse dung. □ *I use horse on my vegetables.* □ *I got a job shoveling horse out of the stables.*

horse hockey *n.* horse dung. □ *I try to get horse hockey for my garden.* □ *You don't see horse hockey in the streets anymore.*

meadow muffin *n.* a mass of cow dung. □ *Jill stepped in a meadow muffin while she was bird-watching.* □ *Andy's mom gathered dried meadow muffins to put in her flower garden.*

mess *n.* dung. (Usually with *a*.) □ *There is a dog mess on the lawn again this morning.* □ *There's a mess in Jimmy's diapers, Mom.*

poo AND **poo-poo** *n.* fecal material. (Mostly juvenile. Use caution with the topic.) □ *Don't step in that dog poo!* □ *There's poo on your shoe, I think.*

poop *n.* fecal matter. (Use caution with the topic.) □ *Don't step in the poop.* □ *There's poop on the sidewalk.*

pooper-scooper *n.* a device used to pick up and carry away dog feces from public places. □ *I never leave home without my pooper-scooper.* □ *Tracy actually got a ticket for walking her dog without a pooper-scooper in sight!*

road apple *n.* a lump of horse excrement. □ *Don't step on the road apples.* □ *There must be horses around here. I see road apples.*

shit (Use only with discretion.) *n.* dung. □ *Don't step in that shit there.* □ *There's dog shit in my yard!*

shitsky *n.* dung. (Potentially offensive. Use only with discretion.) □ *There's some shitsky on your shoe.* □ *Some rude dog has left a little pile of grade-A shitsky on the sidewalk.*

skid marks *n.* unclean, brownish marks on one's underpants. (Use only with discretion.) □ *Just looking at him, you know he's the type who has skid marks and enjoys popping zits.* □ *There is hardly any-thing a genteel person can say about skid marks that is acceptable in public.*

turd (Potentially offensive. Use only with discretion. Colloquial.) *n.* a lump of fecal material. □ *There is a dog turd on the lawn.* □ *There are some little mouse turds in the kitchen.*

EXCUSE

copout *n.* a poor excuse to get out of something. □ *This is a silly copout.* □ *That's not a good reason. That's just a copout.*

if you'll pardon the expression *phr.* "excuse the expression I am about to say." □ *This thing is—if you'll pardon the expression—loused up.* □ *I'm really jacked, if you'll pardon the expression.*

EXERCISE

daily dozen *n.* a short set of daily exercises. □ *I need to do my daily dozen before breakfast.* □ *A daily dozen would be good for you.*

pump (some) iron *tr.* to lift weights. □ *Andy went down to the gym to pump some iron.* □ *Mary's hobbies are pumping iron and running.*

pump something up *tr.* to flex and tense a muscle until it is expanded to its fullest size, as with thighs and forearms. (Bodybuilding.) □ *He really can pump up his pecs.* □ *She pumped up her thighs and struck a pose.*

stretch one's legs *tr.* to stand up and perhaps walk about. □ *I need to get out of here and stretch my legs for a while.* □ *Most of us stood up to stretch our legs at intermission.*

EXHAUSTION

beat *mod.* exhausted; worn-out. □ *I'm just beat!* □ *The whole family was beat after the game.*

blue in the face *mod.* pale from exhaustion or exertion. □ *I laughed until I was blue in the face.* □ *She worked hard enough to be blue in the face.*

burned out AND **burnt out** *mod.* tired; bored. □ *I'm burned out after all that partying.* □ *I don't want to work with burnt-out people. I need energy.*

bushed *mod.* exhausted. □ *I am just bushed.* □ *Another hard day! I am more bushed than ever.*

cashed *mod.* exhausted. □ *I'm just cashed—really pooped.* □ *After the game, the team was cashed and couldn't even celebrate.*

clanked *mod.* exhausted; pooped. □ *At the end of the race, the chick was totally clanked.* □ *I'm really clanked, man. Gotta take a rest.*

conk out *in.* [for someone] to collapse. □ *I was so tired I just went home and conked out.* □ *I was afraid I would conk out while I was driving.*

creased *mod.* exhausted. □ *What a day. I am totally creased.* □ *Here is one creased football player. Let him hit the rack.*

dead *mod.* very tired. □ *I am just dead from all that jogging.* □ *I went home from the office, dead as usual.*

dopey *mod.* sleepy. □ *I feel sort of dopey.* □ *The soft music made him dopey.*

dragged out *mod.* exhausted; worn-out. □ *I feel so dragged out. I think I need some iron.* □ *After the game, the whole team was dragged out.*

drain *tr.* to wear someone out. □ *Arguing like that drains me something awful.* □ *Your constant bickering is meant to drain me till I submit. Is that it?*

fagged out *mod.* exhausted. □ *I'm really fagged out after all that running.* □ *John, you sure look fagged out.*

flack (out) *in.* to collapse in exhaustion; to go to sleep. □ *I just have to go home now and flack out.* □ *Betsy flacked out at nine every night.*

flaked out *mod.* unconscious; exhausted; tired out. □ *Tom? He's upstairs flaked out from work.* □ *There are too many flaked-out people working at dangerous machines.*

flake (out) *in.* to pass out from exhaustion; to fall asleep. □ *I just flaked out. I had had it.* □ *After jogging, I usually flake for a while.*

flat on one's ass *mod.* completely exhausted. (Potentially offensive. Use only with discretion.) □ *I'm just flat on my ass. I need some rest.* □ *After the day of the marathon, Pete was flat on his ass for a week.*

freaked (out) *mod.* tired out; exhausted. □ *I'm too freaked out to go on without some rest.* □ *The chick is really freaked. Let her rest.*

groggy *mod.* tired; in a stupor. □ *He was too groggy to care what happened to him.* □ *Who's that groggy guy?* □ *I'm still groggy by ten in the morning.*

hacked *mod.* worn-out; ready to quit. □ *What a day! I'm hacked.* □ *We were all hacked at the end of the climb.*

knocked out *mod.* exhausted. □ *We were all knocked out at the end of the day.* □ *I'm knocked out after just a little bit of work.*

maxed out *mod.* exhausted; tired. □ *I am just maxed out. I haven't been getting enough sleep.* □ *I had to stop work because I was too maxed.*

peter out *in.* to give out; to wear out. □ *I'm about to peter out. I need a rest.* □ *What'll we do when the money peters out?*

pooped (out) *mod.* exhausted; worn-out. (Said of a person or an animal.) □ *I'm really pooped out.* □ *The horse looked sort of pooped in the final stretch.*

poop out *in.* to quit; to wear out and stop. □ *He pooped out after about an hour.* □ *I think I'm going to poop out pretty soon.*

puggled *mod.* exhausted; bewildered. □ *I have had a long day, and I'm really puggled.* □ *Who is that puggled old man?*

shagged out *mod.* exhausted. □ *What a day! I'm shagged out!* □ *You guys look sort of shagged out.*

shot *mod.* exhausted; worn-out. □ *I really feel shot today.* □ *Here's your pen back. It's shot anyway.* □ *This thing is shot. Let's get a new one.*

stoked out *mod.* exhausted. □ *I ran all the way and got stoked out.* □ *Alex is totally stoked out.*

strung-out shape *n.* a tired and exhausted condition. □ *They were sort of* *in strung-out shape, tired and ready for the sack.* □ *I've never been in such strung-out shape, but I've never run a marathon before.*

tapped AND **tapped out** *mod.* exhausted. □ *I need a nap. I'm tapped out.* □ *I've had it. I'm tapped.*

through the mill *mod.* abused; well-worn. □ *That was some convention. I've really been through the mill.* □ *I feel like I've gone through the mill. I'm pooped.*

veggy AND **veggie** *n.* someone who is tired or exhausted. □ *I want to be a veggy this weekend. I'll just stay at home and relax.* □ *I am just a veggie after all the activity of the last week.*

washed out *mod.* exhausted; tired. □ *I feel too washed out to go to work today.* □ *Poor Ted really looks washed out.*

wash out *in.* to slow down or collapse from exhaustion. □ *The whole play began to wash out during the second act. It was a lost cause by the third.* □ *Finally, after a long day, I just washed out. They had to call the paramedics.*

wasted *mod.* exhausted. □ *I worked two shifts and I'm totally wasted.* □ *Mary was wasted and went to bed.*

wiped (out) *mod.* (of a person or thing) exhausted. □ *I'm so wiped out that I just want to go home and go to bed.* □ *Wow, am I wiped out!*

wipe someone out *tr.* to exhaust or tire someone. □ *The game wiped me out.* □ *Jogging always wipes me out.*

woozy *mod.* sleepy; disoriented. □ *Aren't you woozy at this time of day?* □ *Who is that woozy gal by the window?* □ *I'm still sort of woozy. Give me a minute or two to wake up.*

zapped *mod.* tired; exhausted. □ *I'm too zapped to go on.* □ *I'm way zapped. Good night.*

zombie *n.* a very tired person. □ *I feel like such a zombie. Maybe I'm not eating right.* □ *I'm just a zombie at this hour of the morning.*

zoned (out) *mod.* exhausted. □ *After a day like this, I'm really zoned.* □ *Gotta get to bed. I'm just zoned out.*

zonk *tr.* to tire someone out. □ *The pills zonked me, but they made my cold better.* □ *Jogging always zonks me.*

zonked (out) *mod.* exhausted; asleep. □ *She was totally zonked out by the time I got home.* □ *I'm zonked. Good night.*

zonk out *in.* to collapse from exhaustion; to go into a stupor from drugs or exhaustion. □ *I'm gonna go home and zonk out.* □ *I went home after the trip and just zonked out.*

EXIT
See **DEPART**.

EXPERIENCE
graduate *n.* a person experienced in life, especially sexually experienced. □ *Tracy is a graduate. Nothing is new to her.* □ *You need someone who is a graduate for this kind of a job.*

old hand (at something) *n.* someone experienced at doing something. □ *I'm an old hand at fixing cars.* □ *Do you need help with your painting? I'm an old hand.*

taste blood *tr.* to experience something exciting, and perhaps dangerous, for the first time. □ *She had tasted blood once, and she knew that the life of a race-car driver was for her.* □ *Once you taste blood, you're hooked.*

EXPERIENCE - LACKING
raw *mod.* inexperienced; brand-new. □ *The raw recruit did as well as could be expected.* □ *She'll get better. She's just a little raw.*

rookie AND **rooky** *mod.* new; inexperienced. □ *Fred is a rookie first baseman for the home team.* □ *A rooky cop can make arrests just like the other cops.*

EXPERT
See **SKILL**.

EXPLANATION
clue someone in *tr.* to set someone straight (about something); to inform someone of the facts. □ *What's going on? Clue me in.* □ *I think I'd better clue in Sam about the rally.*

I'm listening. *sent.* "Keep talking.";
"Make your explanation now." □ *You
did it wrong. I'm listening.* □ *I'm sure
there's an explanation. Well, I'm listening.*

lay something out *tr.* to explain a plan
of action or a sequence of events. □ *Let
me lay it out for you.* □ *Lay out the plan
very carefully, and don't skip anything.*

Let's have it! *exclam.* "Please tell (us) the
news!" □ *What's happened? Let's have it!*
□ *Don't beat around the bush. Let's have
it!*

long story short *phr.* "to make a long
story short." □ *Okay, long story short:
everything that goes up comes down, okay?*
□ *Then the guy comes over, and—long
story short—"You got a match?"*

megillah *n.* a long and complicated
story. (From Hebrew *megillah* via Yiddish.) □ *He struggled through this
megillah and nobody believed him.* □ *You
come in here with this megillah about a
flat tire and how your brother-in-law stole
your jack and how your arthritis is kicking up—what do you think I am, some
sort of shoulder to cry on?*

run it down *tr.* to tell the whole story;
to tell the truth. □ *Come on! What happened? Run it down for me!* □ *I don't care
what happened. Run it down. I can take
it.*

shoot *in.* to start to tell (something). □
We're ready. Go ahead. Shoot! □ *Okay,
shoot. I'm all ears.*

sob story *n.* a sad story that is likely to
draw tears. □ *I've heard nothing but sob
stories today. Isn't anybody happy?* □ *She
had quite a sob story, and I listened to the
whole thing.*

Sock it to me! *exclam.* "Come on, let me
have it!" (Refers to bad news.) □ *Come
on! I can take it. Sock it to me!* □ *Sock it
to me, man. I'm ready.*

Spit it out! *exclam.* "Say it!" □ *Come on,
don't be shy! Spit it out!* □ *Say what you
have to say and leave. Hurry up! Spit it
out!*

EXPLOSIVES

soup *n.* nitroglycerin, a liquid explosive.
(Underworld.) □ *Lefty was a master with*
the soup till he blew off his hand. □ *Take
care of that soup and treat it like eggs.*

EXPRESSION

like *interj.* an emphatic or meaningless
word that, when said frequently, marks
the speaker as speaking in a very casual
or slangy mode. (Use caution with *like*.)
□ *This is, like, so silly!* □ *She is like, so,
like, way rad!*

like, you know *interj.* a combining of
the expressions *like* and *you know*.
(Never used in formal writing.) □ *She
is, well, like, you know, P.G.* □ *This is,
well, like, you know, too much!*

EXTINGUISH

kill *tr.* to douse a light. □ *Kill that light!*
□ *Would you kill the light so they can't see
we're home?*

EXTORTION

bleed *tr.* to drain someone of money
through extortion or continuous demands for payment. □ *You can't bleed me
anymore. I'm tapped.* □ *I'm going to bleed
you till I get what I deserve.*

bleed someone white AND **bleed someone dry** *tr.* to take all of someone's
money; to extort money from someone.
□ *The creeps tried to bleed me white.* □
*Max got some picture of Fred and Paul to-
gether and tried to bleed both of them dry.*

chisel *tr. & in.* to extort (money). □
Lefty tried to chisel forty bucks outa me.
□ *He's always chiseling. That's his hus-
tle.*

soak *tr.* to overcharge someone; to extort money from someone. □ *They
soaked me for twenty dollars for the parts,
but at least it runs now.* □ *The cleaners
soaked me for the cleaning job.*

EXTRAVAGANCE

big-time *mod.* outstanding; extravagant.
□ *This is one of your real big-time stars.*
□ *I can't stand any more of this big-time
living.*

put on the dog AND **put on the ritz** *tr.*
to make things extra special for a special event. □ *Frank's really putting on the
dog for the big party Friday night.* □ *They
really put on the ritz for us.*

EXTREME

hard-core *mod.* extreme; entrenched. □ *She spent some time teaching hard-core illiterates in a medium-sized town.* □ *There are too many hard-core cases of poverty there.*

in spades *mod.* in the best way possible; extravagantly. □ *He flunked the test in spades.* □ *They won the championship in spades.*

way out AND **way-out** *mod.* extreme; arcane. □ *Some of your ideas are really way out.* □ *What a way-out hairdo.*

EYELIDS

lid *n.* an eyelid. □ *Her lids began to close, and the professor raised his voice to a roar.* □ *Pop your lids open! It's morning!*

shutters *n.* the eyelids. □ *Her shutters dropped slowly, and she was asleep.* □ *She blinked those yummy shutters over those bedroom eyes, and my knees turned to mush.*

EYES

blinkers *n.* the eyes. □ *As I opened my blinkers, guess who I saw?* □ *Look at those classy blinkers!*

lamps *n.* the eyes. (Crude.) □ *His lamps are closed. He's asleep or dead.* □ *Look at them blue lamps that dame's got.*

light *n.* an eye. (Crude. Usually plural.) □ *You want I should poke your lights out?* □ *Open your lights and watch for the turn-off sign.*

peepers *n.* the eyes. □ *Come on, use your peepers. Take a good look.* □ *My peepers are tired.*

FACE

map *n.* one's face. □ *There was fear and hatred all over his map.* □ *With a map like that, she could really go somewhere.*

mug *n.* the face. (Crude.) □ *Wipe that smile off your mug!* □ *What a gorgeous mug!*

mush *n.* one's face. (Crude.) □ *Put some paint on your mush, and let's get going.* □ *With a mush like that, you ought to be in pictures. Maybe another* King Kong *remake.*

pan *n.* the face. □ *Look at that guy! I've never seen such an ugly pan in my life.* □ *I stared her right in the pan and told her to shut up.*

picklepuss *n.* a person who has a puckered-up mouth; a child who is about to cry. □ *Don't be such a picklepuss. Smile!* □ *She is such a picklepuss. Nothing seems to please her.*

puss *n.* the face. □ *I ought to poke you right in the puss!* □ *Look at the puss on that guy! What an ugly face!*

smacker *n.* the face. □ *What a gorgeous smacker on that chick.* □ *She ought to give that ugly smacker back to the horse before it runs into something.*

FAILURE

barf *in.* [for a computer] to fail to function. □ *The whole system barfed about noon, and all the data was lost.* □ *My little computer barfs about once a day. Something is wrong.*

bomb 1. *n.* a bad performance or an inherently bad show. □ *They tried as hard as they could, but the thing was a bomb from act one on.* □ *The latest bomb on Broadway, like all bombs, will only go off once. This one finished to a chorus of boos* before the final curtain. **2.** *in.* to fail. □ *My first try bombed, but things got better.* □ *It bombed the minute the first curtain went up.*

bomb (out) *in.* [for a computer or computer program] to fail. □ *You expect a program to bomb a time or two.* □ *The whole thing bombed out at just the wrong time.*

brick 1. *n.* any failure. □ *Charlie is responsible for another brick in the accounting department.* □ *This whole thing is a mess. Whose brick is this anyway?* **2.** *in.* to fail. □ *The whole project bricked because we sat on the contract too long.* □ *The company almost bricked because of delays in signing contracts.*

bum out *in.* to have any bad experience; to fail. □ *We bummed out at the concert. I dropped my music, and Larry broke a string.* □ *The test was horrible. I bummed out, for sure.*

bust *n.* a failure. □ *The whole project was a bust from the beginning.* □ *My whole life is a bust.*

choke *in.* [for a computer] to fail to take in information being fed to it. (Computers.) □ *If you don't have your modem and your software set the same way as the host, your machine will choke.* □ *I did what you told me, but it choked anyway.*

cut one's losses *tr.* to do something to stop a loss of something. □ *I knew I had to do something to cut my losses, but it was almost too late.* □ *Sell some of the high-priced stuff to cut your losses.*

dead duck *n.* a person or thing doomed to failure or disaster. □ *This whole plan was a dead duck from the beginning.* □

Wally is a dead duck because he flunked astronomy.

drop the ball *tr.* to fail at something; to allow something to fail. □ *I didn't want to be the one who dropped the ball, but I knew that someone would flub up.* □ *Sam dropped the ball, and we lost the contract.*

dud *n.* a failure; something that fails to perform as intended. □ *The whole idea turned out to be a dud.* □ *The play was a dud from start to finish.*

fail *n.* a failing grade; a grade of F. □ *Sorry, this paper's a fail if I ever saw one.* □ *I pulled a fail in stat.*

fizzle 1. *n.* a failure; something that sputters away. □ *The whole project was a fizzle.* □ *Her first play was no fizzle.* **2.** *in.* to fail. □ *The whole plan fizzled, and we had to start over.* □ *The play began to fizzle in the second act.*

flag 1. *tr.* to fail a course. □ *Pat flagged English again.* □ *I'm afraid I flagged algebra.* **2.** *n.* the grade of F. □ *I'll get a flag on algebra for the semester.* □ *I got three flags and an A.*

flop *n.* a failure. □ *What do you mean your life is a flop?* □ *The play was a flop. The entire audience left during the second act.*

flub the dub *tr.* to fail to do the right thing. □ *Martin is flubbing the dub with the fund-raising campaign.* □ *Please don't flub the dub this time.*

flunk 1. *tr. & in.* to earn a failing grade in a course. □ *I'm flunking in English lit.* □ *Wilbur is flunking everything.* **2.** *tr.* to assign someone a failing grade. □ *Good grief! She flunked me!* □ *I'm sorry, but I am going to have to flunk half the class.*

flunk out (of something) *in.* to leave school or a course because of failure. □ *Fred flunked out of school and never tried to go back.* □ *That's it. All F's. I've flunked out.*

fold *in.* to fail; to close. □ *The play folded in the second week.* □ *I was afraid my business would fold because of the recession.*

go down in flames *in.* to fail spectacularly. □ *The whole team went down in flames.* □ *I'd hate for all your planning to go down in flames.*

goose egg *n.* a failure; a zero. □ *The outcome was a real goose egg. A total mess.* □ *The result of three weeks' planning is one big goose egg.*

go over like a lead balloon *in.* [for something meant to be good] to fail to be good. □ *The joke went over like a lead balloon.* □ *I'm afraid your plan went over like a lead balloon.*

hacker *n.* a generally unsuccessful person. □ *Poor Pete is just a hacker. He'll never go anyplace.* □ *Hackers keep trying, but they never succeed.*

lay an egg *tr.* [for something] to fail. □ *The community theater laid an egg last night with the opening performance of Death of a Salesman.* □ *The film was fun to make, but it laid an egg at the box office.*

loser *n.* an inept person; an undesirable or annoying person; a social failure. □ *Dave is a real loser.* □ *Only losers wear clothes like that.* □ *Those guys are all losers. They'll never amount to anything.*

losing streak *n.* a period of bad luck, especially in gambling. □ *After a prolonged losing streak, Diamond Jane retired and opened some sort of manicure parlor outside Las Vegas.* □ *I've been on a three-year losing streak in my business. I'm just about done.*

louse something up *tr.* to botch something up. □ *Please don't louse the typewriter ribbon up this time.* □ *Jack loused up my effort to win approval for my plan.*

no-win situation *n.* a situation in which there is no hope of success. □ *I find myself in a no-win situation again.* □ *The team—in a no-win situation—punted.*

put the skids under someone or something *tr.* to cause someone or something to fail. □ *The mayor put the skids under my plan.* □ *Tom tried to talk, but the boss put the skids under him.*

strike out *in.* to fail. □ *Well, we struck out again, but we'll keep trying.* □ *I hear you struck out on that Acme proposal. Better luck next time.*

take the pipe AND **take the gas pipe** *tr.* to fail to perform under pressure; to cave in. □ *He tends to take the pipe when the going gets rough.* □ *Don't take the gas pipe, man. Stick in there!*

tube *in.* to fail. □ *The whole plan tubed at the last minute.* □ *I tubed, and I'm sorry.*

tube it *tr.* to fail a test. □ *I tubed it, and I'll probably get a D in the course.* □ *I was afraid I'd tube it, so I studied my head off.*

turkey *n.* a failure; a sham. □ *This whole business is a turkey.* □ *The turkey at the town theater closed on its first night.*

turn belly up AND **go belly up** *in.* to fail. □ *I sort of felt that the whole thing would go belly up, and I was right.* □ *The computer—on its last legs anyway—turned belly up right in the middle of an important job.*

underwhelm *tr. & in.* to fail to impress (someone). □ *Your talents simply underwhelm me.* □ *As we were being underwhelmed by a buxom soprano, my thoughts drifted to more pleasant matters.* □ *We know you are trying, but you just underwhelm.*

wash out *in.* to fail and be removed from something, such as school. □ *I studied all I could, but I still washed out.* □ *I don't want to wash out. It's my whole future.*

washout *n.* a failure; a fiasco. □ *The whole project was a washout. A lost cause from beginning to end.* □ *I am beginning to think that Sally's specialty is washouts.*

FAKE

bogue *mod.* fake; bogus. □ *Keep your bogue gold watch. I don't want it!* □ *She is so, like, bogue!*

crank *mod.* bogus. □ *We had four crank calls threatening to blow up the Eiffel Tower.* □ *A crank letter promised us a million dollars if we would play "My Blue Heaven" for two hours each morning.*

trumped-up *mod.* made up; contrived. □ *They put Larry in the slammer on some trumped-up charge.* □ *It was a silly, trumped-up idea. Just forget it.*

FALL

go Rinso *in.* to fall; to collapse in price. (A play on "to go *down the drain*." *Rinso* is a laundry soap that goes down the drain after it is used. Used in the context of the securities markets or other financial setting.) □ *All my drug stocks went Rinso when the president attacked the drug industry.* □ *I knew my bank account would go Rinso after last month's bills came in.*

go south AND **head south** *in.* to fall; to go down. □ *All the stock market indexes went south today.* □ *The market headed south today at the opening bell.*

hit the deck *tr.* to fall down; to drop down. □ *Hit the deck. Don't let them see you.* □ *I hit the deck the minute I heard the shots.*

kiss the dust *tr.* to fall to the earth, because of death or because of being struck. (Western movies.) □ *I'll see that you kiss the dust before sunset, cowboy!* □ *You'll kiss the dust before I will, sheriff.*

take a nosedive *tr.* to collapse; to fall. □ *The market took a nosedive again today.* □ *She slipped on the ice and took a nosedive.*

tank *in.* for something to fall. □ *The entire stock market tanked on Friday.* □ *My investments did not tank when the market collapsed.*

FALSE

hokey *mod.* contrived; phony. □ *What a hokey way to deal with a perfectly honest request.* □ *That idea is too hokey.* □ *That's a pretty hokey idea, but it may work.*

Hollywood *mod.* having phony glitter. □ *Who is this Hollywood dame who just came in?* □ *This whole thing is just too Hollywood.*

phony *mod.* bogus; fake. □ *This money looks phony to me.* □ *I can't stand phony vanilla flavoring.*

phony as a three-dollar bill AND **queer as a three-dollar bill** *mod.* phony; bogus. □ *This guy's as phony as a three-dollar bill.* □ *The whole deal stinks. It's as queer as a three-dollar bill.*

plastic *mod.* phony; false. □ *She wears too much makeup and looks totally plastic.* □ *I'm tired of living in such a plastic society.*

plastic punk *n.* falsely stylish. □ *Most music videos are just plastic punk.* □ *Isn't all punk really plastic punk?*

pseudo *mod.* false; bogus. □ *This is a very pseudo position that you are taking.* □ *She is just too pseudo.* □ *What a pseudo hairdo!*

queer *mod.* counterfeit. □ *This bill is queer.* □ *I don't want any queer money.*

thick *mod.* unbelievable. □ *This stuff is getting thick.* □ *This story is too thick for me. I'm cruising outa here.*

FAN

addict *n.* someone showing a marked preference for something or someone. (A combining form not related to drug addiction.) □ *Sam is a real opera addict. He just loves the stuff.* □ *My uncle is a mystery addict.*

bug *n.* someone who is enthusiastic about something. (A combining form.) □ *Mary is a camera bug.* □ *Al has turned into a real compact disc bug.*

nut *n.* an enthusiast (about something). □ *Paul is a nut about chocolate cake.* □ *Mary is a party nut.*

trekkie *n.* a fan of *Star Trek*, the television series and the movies. □ *There is a convention of trekkies in Milwaukee this weekend.* □ *The trekkies seem to have their own language.*

FANTASY

airy-fairy *mod.* insubstantial; of wishful thinking. □ *Haven't you outgrown that kind of airy-fairy thinking yet?* □ *Her ideas are too airy-fairy.* □ *I don't care to hear any more of your airy-fairy ideas.*

FARMER

hayseed *n.* a farmer; a rustic character, usually a male. □ *I'm not just some hayseed fresh off the farm.* □ *It's hard for these hayseeds to adjust to city life.*

FARMING

aggie *mod.* agricultural. □ *She spent a year at some aggie college, but didn't like it.* □ *Her aggie interests faded fast.*

FASHIONABLE

boheme *n.* a (feminine) personal style consisting of no makeup, large baggy clothing, long skirts, and comfortable shoes. (Collegiate.) □ *She looks so good in boheme!* □ *Boheme is not you.*

fly *mod.* nice-looking; stylish. □ *I like your fly shoes, Sam.* □ *This guy is really fly.*

geek-chic *n.* stylish or fashionable only for social outcasts. □ *Tom is the guy who always wears the tacky geek-chic jacket.* □ *Why do you have to buy all this geek-chic stuff? Don't they give it away somewhere?*

glitz *n.* flashiness and glamour. □ *The place was a morass of eager sales geeks and phony glitz.* □ *The glitz was blinding, and the substance was invisible.*

glitzy *mod.* fashionable; glamorous. □ *It was a real glitzy place to hold a meeting.* □ *Some glitzy blonde sang a couple of songs, and then the band played again.*

happening *mod.* fashionable; trendy; positive. (Collegiate.) □ *Oh, Tiffany, your skirt is really happening!* □ *Wow, that's happening!*

in *mod.* current; fashionable. □ *This kind of thing is in now.* □ *What's in around here in the way of clothing?*

in thing to do *n.* the fashionable or orthodox thing to do. (Always with *the*.) □ *Cutting your hair short on the sides is the in thing to do.* □ *Smoking is no longer the in thing to do.*

mod *mod.* contemporary and fashionable in clothing and ideas. □ *Your clothes are mod, but you're just a plain, old-fashioned prude.* □ *Your mod friends might appreciate this article in the paper.*

on the bandwagon *mod.* with the majority; following the latest fad. (Often with *hop, get, climb,* or *jump*.) □ *Come on! Hop on the bandwagon! Everyone else is joining.* □ *Tom always has to climb on the bandwagon. He does no independent thinking.*

rage *n.* the current fad; an irresistible fad. (Always with *the;* often with *all the.* Old but recurrent.) □ *Get a haircut like mine! It's all the rage!* □ *One rage after another. Can't I find something that will stay the same for a while?*

swing *in.* [for a person] to be up to date and modern. □ *Tom really swings. Look at those blue suede shoes!* □ *I used to swing, but then age and good taste overtook me.*

switch on *in.* to become modern and participate in current fads and events. □ *I am too old to switch on.* □ *Most kids I know switched on when they went to high school.*

tuned in *mod.* aware; up-to-date. □ *Jan is tuned in and alert to what is going on around her.* □ *Hey, Jill! Get tuned in, why don't you?*

with it *mod.* up-to-date; contemporary. □ *Martin is not exactly with it.* □ *Come on, chum. Get with it.*

FAT

all (that) meat and no potatoes *phr.* said of a tremendously fat person. (A rude catchphrase.) □ *Look at that guy— all meat and no potatoes.* □ *All that meat and no potatoes. She should go on a diet.*

chunky *mod.* stout; fat. □ *Harry—the chow hound—is getting a little chunky.* □ *It's not all fat! He's always been a chunky brute.*

fat city *n.* fatness (expressed as a place). □ *I've had it with fat city. I'm going on a diet.* □ *Sally is well on her way to fat city.*

(love) handles *n.* rolls of fat around the waist that can be held on to during love-making. □ *Ted worked out daily, trying to get rid of his love handles.* □ *Not only did he grow a belly, but he's got handles on his handles.*

padded *mod.* plump or fat. □ *He didn't hurt himself when he fell down. He's well padded there.* □ *Your clothes would fit better if you weren't so—ah—padded.*

porky *mod.* fat; obese; pig-like. □ *You are beginning to look a little porky.* □ *See that porky man over there?*

spare tire *n.* a thickness in the waist; a roll of fat around one's waist. □ *I've got to get rid of this spare tire.* □ *The spare tire started when I was twenty-six.*

(well-)upholstered *mod.* chubby; plump. □ *Fortunately, he was upholstered enough that the fall didn't really hurt.* □ *My well-upholstered brother has to go on a diet.*

FEAR
See also **FRIGHT**.

cold feet *n.* a wave of timidity or fearfulness. □ *Suddenly I had cold feet and couldn't sing a note.* □ *You sort of expect a candy-ass like that to have cold feet.*

creepy *mod.* eerie; frightening. □ *I have this creepy feeling that someone is just this very moment reading something that I wrote.* □ *This is the creepiest old house I have ever been in.*

fraidy cat *n.* a coward; a person who is frightened of everything. (Used in children's taunts.) □ *Don't be a fraidy cat. Go ahead, jump!* □ *Carl is such a fraidy cat.*

I'm shaking (in fear). *sent.* "You don't really frighten me at all." (A mocking response to a threat.) □ *Oh, what you said! I'm shaking. Not!* □ *Your threats really scare me. I'm shaking in fear.*

in a cold sweat *mod.* in a state of fear. □ *He stood there in a cold sweat, waiting for something to happen.* □ *I was in a cold sweat while they counted the ballots.*

FEELINGS

vibes *n.* vibrations; atmosphere; feelings. (Usually with *good* or *bad.*) □ *I just don't get good vibes about this deal.* □ *The vibes are just plain bad.*

FEET

crunchers *n.* the feet. □ *My crunchers are sore from all this walking.* □ *New shoes can be hard on your crunchers.*

gunboats AND **battleships** *n.* big feet; big shoes. □ *Hasn't he got the biggest gunboats you ever saw?* □ *Whose battleships are these under the coffee table?*

trotters *n.* the feet. □ *My trotters are sort of aching.* □ *Sit down and give your trotters a rest.*

FEMININE

lacy *mod.* feminine; effeminate. □ *He's sort of lacy, but when he settles down to work, the sparks fly.* □ *This place is too lacy.* □ *The hotel lobby is a little lacy, but it's clean.*

FIDELITY

seven-year itch *n.* a real or imagined longing for other women in a man's seventh year of marriage. □ *Looks like Jack has the seven-year itch.* □ *The seven-year itch is just a rumor.*

FIGHTING

See also ARGUMENT.

back *n.* one's support or second in a fight. (From *backup*.) □ *Fred served as Tom's back in the scuffle.* □ *I need a back I can depend on.*

blood and guts *n.* strife; acrimony. □ *There is a lot of blood and guts around here, but we get our work done.* □ *Cut out the blood and guts and grow up.*

crowd *tr.* to gang up on someone. □ *Some guys were crowding Todd, so we chased them off.* □ *They moved in from all sides, carrying clubs, and began to crowd us.*

down *tr.* to throw someone down, as in wrestling; to knock someone down, as in a fight. □ *Wilbur downed his opponent and won the match.* □ *Paul downed the guy with one blow.*

knockdown drag-out fight *n.* a prolonged and hard fight. □ *Trying to get my proposal accepted was a knockdown drag-out fight.* □ *I don't want to get involved in a knockdown drag-out fight over this business.*

mix it up (with someone) *tr.* to fight with someone; to quarrel with someone. □ *Max and Bruno mixed it up for a while, and then things calmed down.* □ *Max came out of the shop and began to mix it up with Bruno.*

square off *in.* to prepare to fight; to prepare to argue or compete. □ *They were squaring off, so I asked them if they'd like to step outside.* □ *Let's square off and debate this thing properly.*

FINALITY

last straw *n.* the final act or insult; the act that finally calls for a response. □ *This is the last straw. I'm calling the police.* □ *Someone's leaving the eggshells in the sink was the last straw.*

Period! *exclam.* "... and that's final!" (A way of indicating that there will be no more discussion or negotiation.) □ *I don't want to hear any more about it! Period!* □ *My final offer is $30. Period!*

FINANCIAL

See also BUSINESS, COMMERCE, COST.

aggie *n.* an agricultural futures contract. (Securities markets. Usually plural.) □ *The March aggies are looking good right now.* □ *Let's take a look at the aggies and see how the bellies are doing.*

ak AND **ok** *n.* October. (Securities markets: options and futures trading.) □ *The ak futures are looking worse by the hour.* □ *When the oks expire on Friday, we'll start looking at the des index.*

angel *n.* a secret financier. □ *Who was the angel for your new play?* □ *I was hoping for an angel to see this project through, but all the fat-cats seem to have disappeared.*

arb *n.* an arbitrageur; a market speculator. (Securities markets.) □ *The arbs are at it again, buying up companies like hotcakes.* □ *I wanted to be an arb, but it takes about $40 million to get in the door.*

backer *n.* a supporter; a financier of a play, political campaign, etc. □ *I had a lot of generous backers for the play.* □ *I was hoping for a backer, but the project was too chancy.*

beans *n.* soybean futures contracts. (Securities markets. Usually with *the*.) □ *The beans are headed south.* □ *Buy the jan beans and sell puts on the bellies.*

bellies *n.* pork bellies; pork belly futures. (Securities markets. Often with *the*.) □ *What are the dec bellies doing?* □ *Buy the bellies and sell the beans.*

Big Blue *n.* the stock of International Business Machines or the company itself. (Securities markets.) □ *I have 400 shares of Big Blue that I would like to sell.*

☐ *Big Blue led the market lower again today.*

big board *n.* the New York Stock Exchange. (Securities markets.) ☐ *On the big board, stocks were down again today, bringing the loss this week on the Dow to nearly 175 points.* ☐ *Is that stock on the big board or where?*

blue chip 1. *n.* stock shares of a large company that has a high value. (Securities markets.) ☐ *The blue chips took another nosedive in today's trading.* ☐ *I buy nothing but blue chips.* **2.** *mod.* having to do with the stock of large, valuable companies. (Securities markets.) ☐ *The blue chip rally ran for a third day.* ☐ *It was another blue chip–led sell off.*

bottom line *n.* the grand total; the final figure on a balance sheet. (Securities markets. Always with *the.*) ☐ *The company's bottom line is in bad shape.* ☐ *If the bottom line is positive, everything is okay.*

budget squeeze AND **budget crunch** *n.* a situation where there is not enough money in the budget. ☐ *Facing another budget squeeze, the legislators were forced to put off their pay increase.* ☐ *The budget crunch hasn't begun to affect us yet.*

cash cow *n.* a dependable source of money; a good investment. ☐ *I put most of my money in a dependable cash cow that pays off once a month.* ☐ *Mr. Wilson turned out to be the cash cow we needed to start our repertoire company.*

Cash is king. *sent.* "It is best to keep one's investment money in cash." (Said when the prices in the securities market are too high. It is better to build up cash and wait for a break in the market.) ☐ *Things look a little pricy now. I'd say that cash is king for the moment.* ☐ *I'm holding a little cash for a little bottom fishing, but I wouldn't say that cash is king.*

Cash is trash. *sent.* "It is unwise to keep one's investment money in cash." (Said when there are good opportunities in securities and it is foolish to stay on the sidelines in cash.) ☐ *If you've got money sitting around in a money market fund while the market is steaming ahead, you*

are losing dollars. Right now cash is trash. ☐ *Cash is trash. Get into the market or you stand to lose a bundle.*

churn *tr.* [for a stockbroker] to cause a heavy turnover in the portfolio of an investor. (The broker collects commissions on each transaction.) ☐ *I reported my broker for churning my account.* ☐ *They churn accounts to earn the commissions.*

crash 1. *in.* [for a securities market] to lose a significant portion of its value in a short time. ☐ *The market crashed and scared the stuffing out of everybody.* ☐ *When the bond market crashed, the press didn't even realize it.* **2.** *n.* a collapse of a securities market. ☐ *After the crash, a lot of people swore off the market for good.* ☐ *A crash like that was too much for a lot of people.*

crater *in.* to collapse and go down as with a falling stock price. ☐ *The stock cratered and probably won't recover for a year or two.* ☐ *When my portfolio cratered, I thought it was the end of the world. Then most of the prices came back up in a month.*

cuff quote *n.* an off-the-cuff quote of a financial instrument price. (Securities markets.) ☐ *This is just a cuff quote, but I would say it's about ninety-four.* ☐ *I can give you a cuff quote of ninety-two, but don't hold me to it.*

deadcat bounce *n.* a small, knee-jerk rally in one of the financial markets. (A dead cat—or any other animal—will bounce only slightly after being dropped. Refers to a stock index or security price that bounces up only slightly after a precipitous fall. Securities market.) ☐ *The whole market gave only a deadcat bounce after the string of losses this past week.* ☐ *I was expecting more than a deadcat bounce because of the good news.*

dead-catty *mod.* with only a slight bounce. (Said of a slight rise in the stock market after a big drop.) ☐ *We expected the stock to go up a lot today, but the increase was no better than dead-catty.* ☐

It was just a dead-catty day in spite of the good economic news.

deal stock *n.* a stock that is a takeover candidate. (Securities markets.) □ *I try to spot the deal stocks early and buy them before others do.* □ *You can lose a lot of money on deal stocks, too.*

deduck 1. *n.* a tax deduction. (From *deduct.*) □ *Interest is no longer a deduck.* □ *I need a few more deducks this year.* **2.** AND **duck** *n.* a deduction from one's paycheck. □ *More of my pay goes to ducks than I get myself.* □ *What's this duck for?*

des *n.* December. (Securities markets. Futures and options trading.) □ *The bean futures for des fell out of bed yesterday.* □ *Are these figures des or March?*

fed AND **the Fed** *n.* the Federal Reserve Board. □ *The Fed is not likely to raise interest rates again very soon.* □ *There is no way to predict what the Fed is going to do.*

fill or kill AND **F.O.K.** *phr.* a broker's notation advising the stock exchange to fill a stock order or kill it. (The abbreviation is an initialism. Securities markets.) □ *Get rid of this order. It was fill or kill, and it should have been killed yesterday.* □ *Where? I don't see that it's marked F.O.K.*

gazumph 1. *tr.* to raise the price of a house after it is sold. □ *They tried to gazumph the price at the closing.* □ *I just knew that the owner was going to gazumph the final figure.* **2.** *tr.* to subject someone to the raising of the price of a house after it is sold. □ *They tried to gazumph me!* □ *If they try to gazumph you, tell them to forget the deal.*

golden handcuffs *n.* monetary inducements to stay on the job. (Usually for highly paid executives in large corporations.) □ *The company provided a variety of golden handcuffs to keep its execs happy through a takeover.* □ *The golden handcuffs included a half million in stock options for one of the vice presidents.*

golden parachute *n.* a special kind of severance pay for persons who may be forced to leave a job. (Usually for highly paid executives in large corporations. If the company is taken over and the executives are fired, they are very well provided for.) □ *My golden parachute was so attractive that I wanted to get fired.* □ *If all the golden parachutes were used at the same time, it would bankrupt the company.*

go public *in.* to sell to the public shares of a privately owned company. (Securities markets.) □ *The company decided not to go public because the economy was so bad at the time.* □ *We'll go public at a later time.*

greenmail *n.* a money-making scheme wherein a very wealthy person buys a large number of shares of a company, threatens to take control of the company, and then offers to sell the stock to the company at an exorbitant price in lieu of a takeover. (Securities markets.) □ *Mr. Smith made about $20 million in greenmail last year.* □ *One state is trying to outlaw greenmail to protect its industrial base.*

guru *n.* a stockbroker or other financial adviser. (Securities markets.) □ *My guru says to sell all my bonds.* □ *My guru just went bankrupt.*

hamburgers *n.* shares in the McDonald's corporation. (Securities markets. New York Stock Exchange jargon.) □ *I want 400 shares of hamburgers.* □ *Hamburgers just dropped a point.*

Hold some, fold some. *sent.* to hold some of your stocks and sell some. (Securities markets.) □ *My best advice right now is to hold some, fold some. There is no real trend to the market.* □ *The stock market was so lackluster that I decided to hold some, fold some.*

(I-)beam *n.* "IBM," International Business Machines stock shares. (Securities markets.) □ *I-beam fell out of bed and took the market with it.* □ *How much beam do you own?*

in play *mod.* having to do with a company (or its stock) that is a candidate for acquisition by another company. (Securities markets.) □ *The company was in play, but nobody was buying it.* □ *These* deal stocks—which are in play right now—offer excellent buying opportunities.

in the black *mod.* financially solvent; profitable; not in debt. ☐ *Now that the company is in the black, there's a good chance it will become a deal stock.* ☐ *We're in the black now and making a profit.*

in the hole *mod.* in debt; running a deficit. ☐ *Looks like we are in the hole again this month.* ☐ *We always end the month in the hole.*

jan *n.* January in the financial futures markets. (Securities markets.) ☐ *The bean futures for jan fell out of bed yesterday.* ☐ *Are these figures jan or March?*

juice *n.* orange juice futures market. (Securities markets. Usually with *the*.) ☐ *The juice opened a little high today, but fell quickly under profit taking.* ☐ *It's time to sell the juice and buy bellies.*

junk bond *n.* a low-rated corporate bond that pays higher interest because of greater risk. ☐ *Don't put all your money into junk bonds.* ☐ *Junk bonds pay a lot of interest.*

Ma Bell *n.* AT&T, the American Telephone and Telegraph Company; any telephone company. ☐ *I forgot to pay Ma Bell this month.* ☐ *Ma Bell is still one of the largest firms in the nation.*

merger-mania *n.* an apparent need for companies to merge with one another. (Securities markets and journalism.) ☐ *Merger-mania is in the news again tonight with Ford's offer to take over GMC.* ☐ *The market meltdown put an end to merger-mania.*

over-the-counter *mod.* having to do with stocks that are sold through dealers rather than through a stock exchange.* ☐ *You can make or lose a lot of money on over-the-counter stocks.* ☐ *Is this stock over-the-counter or available on the exchange?*

play *n.* an attractive investment; a way to make some money in the securities markets. ☐ *I just heard about a good play in the options market.* ☐ *Not talking it over with your friends first was a bad play.*

☐ *Buying bonds at a discount is an interesting play.*

poison pill *n.* an element introduced into the restructuring of a corporation so that it becomes undesirable for another corporation to take it over. ☐ *Acme Corporation approved a poison pill to prevent a hostile takeover.* ☐ *Mr. Boone would have bought the company if it weren't for the poison pill.*

quant AND **quan** *n.* a technician who works in securities market analysis. ☐ *He was a quant on Wall Street for two years.* ☐ *The quants have been warning us about the danger for a month.*

rocks *n.* Xerox Inc. (Securities markets, New York Stock Exchange.) ☐ *When she says, "Buy me a thousand rocks at the market," that means she wants one thousand shares of Xerox at whatever the market price is at the moment.* ☐ *Rocks is down a point and a half.*

run-up *n.* a movement upward in the value of one or more securities. (Securities markets.) ☐ *The market's had a good run-up in the last week.* ☐ *I'm afraid that if it has a run-up to 3,000, it will fall to zero.*

shark repellent *n.* something that prevents corporate takeovers. (Securities markets.) ☐ *Acme Systems tried again to get its board to approve a shark repellent to keep the Widget cartel from acquiring it.* ☐ *The shark repellent wasn't enough.*

short 1. *n.* the sale of borrowed shares of stock; a short sale. (Securities markets.) ☐ *I think that IBM is a good short in here. The high-tech companies are in for a pullback.* ☐ *There is a lot of covering of shorts this week. After that the market is in for a steady decline.* **2.** *tr.* to sell borrowed stock. (Securities markets.) ☐ *I wouldn't short IBM. It's a long-term hold.* ☐ *The way the deficit is running, I'd short the whole market.*

spot market *n.* the open market where deals are made on the spot. (Securities markets.) ☐ *Oil reached nearly twenty-five dollars a barrel on the spot market.* ☐ *Gold prices on the spot market finally* reached $600 per ounce and then promptly collapsed.

steenth *n.* "one sixteenth," used in quoting securities prices. (Securities markets.) □ *This issue was only up a few steenths for the whole week.* □ *Acme Systems was down a steenth at midday.*

story stock *n.* shares in a company that are bought because of an appealing story about the company. □ *I never buy a story stock. By the time I hear about it, it's already gone up as much as it ever will.* □ *Acme Widgets is another story stock that I advise all my clients to buy.*

street *n.* Wall Street in New York City. (Always with *the*. Usually capitalized.) □ *The Street doesn't seem to believe the policymakers in Washington.* □ *If you want excitement and stress, the Street is the place to be.*

take something public *tr.* to sell shares in a company to the general public. (Securities markets.) □ *The board decided not to take the company public.* □ *We're going to take it public whenever the market looks good.*

teenie AND **teeny** *n.* a sixteenth. (Securities markets. From six*teenth*. One sixteenth of a point in a stock price.) □ *It's going at three and two teenies at the moment.* □ *My forty thousand shares have dropped to three teenies each, and I think I am going to go down to the beach and jump.*

wash *n.* the almost simultaneous sale and purchase of the same stock, usually to make the stock appear to be trading actively. (Securities markets. The practice is illegal. Tax loss selling must be done in such a way as to avoid appearing to be a *wash*.) □ *I sold the stock and couldn't buy it back for thirty days to avoid an illegal wash.* □ *The IRS ruled that the sale was a wash and that I couldn't take the tax loss.*

whipsaw *tr.* [for the stock market] to reduce the capital of investors by frightening them into selling when stock prices are low and encouraging them to buy when prices are high. (Securities markets.) □ *A lot of people were whip-*

sawed in the recent market volatility. □ *The market will whipsaw the investor who is not cautious.*

FINGER

(little) pinkie AND **(little) pinky** *n.* the littlest finger on either hand. □ *Ouch! I smashed my pinky.* □ *My little pinkie nearly froze because there's a hole in my glove.*

FIREFIGHTER

smoke eater *n.* a firefighter. □ *A couple of off-duty smoke eaters wandered around the store doing a little shopping.* □ *The smoke eaters took a long time getting there.*

FIST

bunch of fives *n.* the fist. □ *How would you like a bunch of fives right in the kisser?* □ *He ended up with a bunch of fives in the gut.*

dukes *n.* the fists. □ *Okay, brother, put your dukes up.* □ *The guy's got dukes like hams.*

FLAMBOYANT

pimpish *mod.* flamboyant in dress and manner, as with a pimp. (Use caution with *pimp* and the topic.) □ *Where did you get that pimpish hat, Ron?* □ *Take the feathers off it, and it won't look quite so pimpish.*

with a bang *mod.* in a flamboyant or exciting manner. (Especially with *go out, quit, finish.*) □ *The party started off with a bang.* □ *The old year went out with a bang.*

with flying colors *mod.* flamboyantly; boldly. □ *Heidi won first place with flying colors.* □ *Paul came home with flying colors after the match.*

FLATTERY

apple-polisher *n.* a flatterer. □ *Doesn't that wimpy apple-polisher know how stupid he looks?* □ *Everybody at the office seems to be an apple-polisher but me.*

brown-nose 1. AND **brown-noser** *n.* a sycophant; one who flatters for self-serving motives. □ *You are just a plain old brown-nose.* □ *That brown-noser actually gave the boss a bottle of wine for her birth-*

day. **2.** *tr. & in.* to curry favor with someone; to be a sycophant. □ *Don't you brown-nose me!* □ *Don keeps brown-nosing, and the professor pretends not to notice.*

cookie pusher *n.* someone who flatters other people for self-serving motives. □ *When you've got a whole office full of cookie pushers, there's always someone to take you to lunch.* □ *Another cookie pusher came in today to tell me what a great teacher I am.*

egg-sucker *n.* a flatterer; a sycophant. □ *The guy is a chronic egg-sucker. Ignore him.* □ *Who's the egg-sucker who brought the teacher candy?*

grade-grubbing *n.* flattering a teacher in hopes of a higher grade. □ *Some teachers don't mind a lot of grade-grubbing.* □ *So you've come in to do some grade-grubbing.*

kiss someone's ass *tr.* to fawn over someone; to flatter and curry favor with someone. (Potentially offensive. Use *ass* with discretion.) □ *What does he expect me to do? Kiss his ass?* □ *I won't kiss your ass for anything.*

kiss up to someone *in.* to flatter someone; to make over someone. □ *I'm not going to kiss up to anybody to get what's rightfully mine.* □ *If I have to kiss up to her, I guess I will.*

soft soap *n.* flattering talk; sweet talk. □ *I don't mind a little soft soap. It won't affect what I do, though.* □ *Don't waste my time with soft soap. I know you don't mean it.*

stroke *tr. & in.* to flatter someone; to soothe and comfort someone. □ *She strokes everybody to keep them on her side during the bad times.* □ *She learned long ago that stroking puts people at ease.*

FLATULENCE

backfire *in.* to release intestinal gas anally, perhaps audibly. (Use caution with the topic.) □ *Whew! Somebody backfired!* □ *It was noisy when Dave backfired, and hardly anyone heard what happened.*

barking spider AND **trumpet spider** *n.* the imaginary source of the sound of an audible release of intestinal gas. □ *Hey, Chuck! Did I hear a barking spider over there?* □ *Heidi, do you know anything about the trumpet spider I keep hearing?*

beef 1. *in.* to break wind; to release intestinal gas audibly. (Use caution with the topic.) □ *Who beefed?* □ *Wally warned everybody that he was going to beef.* **2.** *n.* an act of breaking wind. (Use caution with the topic.) □ *All right! Who's beef was that?* □ *Jimmy made another beef!*

cut the cheese AND **cut the mustard** *tr.* to release intestinal gas. (Crude. Use caution with the topic.) □ *Who cut the cheese?* □ *People who cut the mustard in the car have to get out and walk.*

fart 1. *n.* a release of intestinal gas, perhaps with a noise. (Potentially offensive in both senses. Use only with discretion. Less offensive in the U.K., and it is now used more openly in the U.S.) □ *Did I hear a fart?* □ *Who is responsible for that fart?* **2.** *in.* to release intestinal gas, perhaps with a noise. □ *Who farted?* □ *Somebody farted.*

gas *n.* intestinal gas. □ *The baby has gas and will cry for a while longer.* □ *I'm not too well, but I think it's just gas.*

traf *n.* a release of intestinal gas. (This is *fart* spelled backwards. Use caution with the topic.) □ *Who let the traf?* □ *This place smells like a traf.*

windy *mod.* flatulent; having intestinal gas. □ *I feel a little windy.* □ *If you're windy, why don't you take the day off?*

FLIRTATION

come-hither look *n.* an alluring or seductive look or glance, usually done by a woman. □ *She blinked her bedroom eyes and gave him a come-hither look.* □ *She had mastered the come-hither look, but was not ready for the next part.*

come on *n.* an invitation; a sexual invitation. (Usually **come-on.**) □ *She stared at him with her bedroom eyes, giving him that age-old come-on.* □ *Who could resist a come-on like that?*

come on to someone *in.* to make advances to a person. □ *He came on to her, but she beat it outa there fast.* □ *She didn't even know he was coming on to her, till they got to his place.*

get one's hooks into someone *tr.* [for a woman] to succeed in "capturing" a specific man. □ *She just can't wait to get her hooks into Chuck.* □ *When she got her hooks into him, she decided he wasn't so great after all.*

goo-goo eyes *n.* flirtatious eyes. (Often with *make.*) □ *Mary was making goo-goo eyes at Sam.* □ *Who's the chick over there with the goo-goo eyes?*

hanky-panky *n.* sexual play; sexual misconduct. □ *Sam and Mary are up to a little hanky-panky, I've heard.* □ *There's some hanky-panky going on in the storeroom.*

hit on someone *in.* to flirt with someone; to make a pass at someone. □ *The women were all hitting on George, but he didn't complain.* □ *I just knew he was going to hit on me—but he didn't.*

pass *n.* a sexual advance or invitation. (Usually with *make.*) □ *He made a pass at me, so I slapped him.* □ *When he made a pass at me, he got a pass right back.*

paw *tr.* to feel someone or handle someone sexually. □ *If you paw me again, I'll slap you!* □ *I can't stand men who paw you to pieces.*

Your place or mine? *interrog.* "Shall we carry on an affair at your dwelling or mine?" □ *Then I said to her, "Your place or mine?" Then she clobbered me.* □ *Your place or mine? It doesn't matter.*

FOCUS

angle *n.* slant; bias; focus. □ *Let's try to get a good angle on this news story so the wire service will buy it from us.* □ *I think that by studying the Maya I will be able to develop a new angle on why they disappeared.*

cut to the chase *in.* to focus on what is important; to abandon the preliminaries and deal with the major points. □ *All right, let's stop the idle chatter and cut to the chase.* □ *After a few introductory*

comments, we cut to the chase and began negotiating.

zoom in (on someone or something) *in.* to focus or concentrate narrowly on someone or something. □ *The conversation zoomed in on Sally and her recent narrow escape from drowning.* □ *Let's zoom in on the question of salary.*

FOG

socked in *mod.* fogged in. □ *The airport was completely socked in.* □ *We couldn't take off because we were socked in.*

FOOD

blood *n.* catsup. □ *Somebody pass the blood.* □ *How 'bout some blood for my burger?*

burger *n.* a hamburger sandwich; a hamburger patty. □ *You ready for another burger?* □ *He's cooking burgers out on the grill right now.*

burnt offering *n.* burned food; a badly cooked meal. □ *Everything I try to cook turns out to be a burnt offering.* □ *All I have to look forward to after work is a burnt offering.*

carbos *n.* carbohydrates. (Bodybuilding.) □ *You need more protein and less carbos.* □ *Too many carbos will make you fat.*

cat-soup *n.* catsup; ketchup. □ *Do you want some cat-soup on your burger?* □ *No, I never use cat-soup.*

chow *n.* food. □ *I need some chow before I go out and shovel snow.* □ *What time is chow served around here?*

chuck *n.* food. □ *Man, this chuck is okay.* □ *Who cooked this chuck, man? It's garbage!*

coffee and *n.* coffee and a doughnut or a pastry. □ *I'll have coffee and.* □ *We stopped at a little shop for coffee and.*

dagwood (sandwich) *n.* a tall sandwich with many layers of food. (From the comic strip character *Dagwood* by Chick Young.) □ *I really like to make an old-fashioned dagwood sandwich every now and then.* □ *How many calories are there in a dagwood, on the average?*

double-decker *n.* a sandwich of two layers. □ *He put away a giant double-decker and a glass of milk.* □ *How can anybody eat a double-decker that is so thick?*

geedunk *n.* ice cream. □ *Let's go out and get some geedunk for dessert.* □ *Pineapple on chocolate geedunk? Yuck!*

goober-grease *n.* peanut butter. □ *Pass me some of that goober-grease, will ya?* □ *This goober-grease is stale.*

grass *n.* lettuce; salad greens. □ *I could use a little more grass in my diet.* □ *Do you want some dressing on your grass?*

grub *n.* food. □ *Hey, this grub's pretty good.* □ *What time's grub?*

hamburg *n.* a hamburger. □ *I'd like a couple of hamburgs and a shake.* □ *This hamburg is as greasy as they come.*

hen fruit *n.* hen's eggs. □ *I always have hen fruit for breakfast.* □ *There's nothing like hen fruit and bacon.*

junk food *n.* food that is typically high in fats and salt and low in nutritional value; food from a fast-food restaurant. □ *Stay away from junk food. It's bad for you.* □ *Junk food tastes good no matter how greasy it is.*

lube *n.* butter. □ *Pass the lube, will ya, huh?* □ *We're outa lube.*

mayo *n.* mayonnaise. □ *You want mayo or mustard?* □ *I'll take both mayo and mustard, thank you.*

munchies *n.* snacks, such as potato chips; any casual food. □ *What kind of munchies are we going to have?* □ *The munchies at the party were great!*

murphy *n.* a potato. □ *I spent half my tour of duty peeling murphies.* □ *Look, this murphy looks like my mother-in-law.*

mystery meat *n.* any unidentified meat. (Collegiate.) □ *What is the mystery meat tonight?* □ *There are no hints as to what this mystery meat is—except its strange pinkish color.*

nosh *n.* a snack. (From German via Yiddish.) □ *How about a little nosh?* □ *I don't want a nosh. I need a whole meal.*

OJ *n.* orange juice. (Initialism.) □ *I like to have a big glass of fresh OJ every morning.* □ *The price of OJ is going to go up again soon.*

rabbit food *n.* lettuce; salad greens. □ *I think I need a little more rabbit food in my diet.* □ *Rabbit food tends to have a lot of vitamin C.*

red hot *n.* a hot dog; a frankfurter. □ *"Get your red hots right here!" shouted the vendor.* □ *In Chicago they never eat red hots with catsup. Imagine!*

salt horse *n.* corned or salted beef. □ *We had salt horse on toast for dinner.* □ *We made spaghetti sauce with salt horse because that was the only meat we could find.*

scarf *n.* food. □ *I want some good scarf. This stuff stinks.* □ *No more fried scarf for me.*

scoff *n.* food. □ *This scoff is gross!* □ *I want some good old American scoff.*

scream *n.* ice cream. (Collegiate.) □ *How about a nice big dish of scream?* □ *It's too cold for scream. Ask me in June.*

sinker *n.* a doughnut. □ *This sinker must be four days old.* □ *All our sinkers are brought in fresh on Monday.*

slumgullion *n.* a meat stew; any food. □ *What is this slumgullion tonight? It looks like what we had last night, only thinner.* □ *This is the best slumgullion I've ever had—which puts it right up there with dishwater.*

spot of lunch *n.* a small amount of lunch. □ *How about a spot of lunch?* □ *I had a spot of lunch at my desk, thanks.*

spud *n.* a potato. □ *I'd like a few more spuds.* □ *Mashed spuds are the best of all.*

square (meal) *n.* a good and nutritious meal. (Always with a quantifier when *square* is used without *meal*.) □ *I need three squares a day—at least.* □ *The old soak looks like he could use a square meal.*

submarine AND **sub** *n.* a long sandwich containing many different foods. □ *He ordered a submarine, but he couldn't finish it.* □ *He took what was left of the sub home with him.*

three squares *n.* three balanced meals a day. □ *I was glad to get back home to* *three squares.* □ *If I could limit myself to three squares, I could lose some weight.*

too rich for someone's blood *mod.* too high in fat content for one's diet. □ *This dessert is too rich for my blood.* □ *Most ice cream is too rich for my blood.*

trotters *n.* pig's feet. □ *Trotters are okay if you can't tell what they are.* □ *Pickled trotters are good in the summer.*

tube steak *n.* a frankfurter or a wiener. □ *Are we having tube steak again for dinner?* □ *I could live on tube steak. Nothing is better!*

veg *n.* a vegetable. □ *You want a veg with this?* □ *That's not my favorite veg.*

veggy AND **veggie** *n.* a vegetable. (Usually plural.) □ *Do you want any veggies with this?* □ *No veggies for me.*

weenie *n.* a wiener (sausage), as in a hot dog (sandwich). □ *They gave us some yucky beans with weenies in them.* □ *It's weenies again for dinner.*

worms *n.* noodles; spaghetti. □ *Let's have worms tonight.* □ *Are the worms ready for the sauce yet?*

worms in blood *n.* spaghetti in tomato sauce. □ *We're having worms in blood for dinner tonight.* □ *I'm getting tired of worms in blood every Wednesday.*

za *n.* pizza. (Collegiate.) □ *I'm gonna spring for some za.* □ *Who wants some of this za?*

FOOLPROOF

goof-proof 1. *mod.* foolproof; not subject to misuse. □ *I want a goof-proof scheme.* □ *This scheme is not goof-proof, but it's pretty sound.* □ *Now, this time I've made it goof-proof.* **2.** *tr.* to make something foolproof; to take action to see that something cannot be misused. □ *I'll try to goof-proof my scheme.* □ *See if this can be goof-proofed by Monday evening.*

FOOT

dog *n.* a foot. (Usually plural.) □ *My dogs are killing me.* □ *I gotta get home and soak my dogs.*

hock *n.* a foot. □ *My hocks are sore from all that walking.* □ *Have you ever seen such humongous hocks?*

FORBIDDEN

no-no *n.* something that is not (to be) done. (Essentially juvenile.) □ *You can't smoke in here. That's a no-no.* □ *She seems to delight in doing all the no-nos.*

verboten *mod.* forbidden. (German.) □ *That is strictly verboten.* □ *You said a verboten word around here.*

FORCE

bulldoze *tr.* to apply pressure or force to get someone to do something. □ *You think you can bulldoze people into doing what you want!* □ *Don't bulldoze me! I push back.*

ram something down someone's throat *tr.* to force something upon someone. (Not literal.) □ *Don't try to ram that nonsense down my throat.* □ *They're always trying to ram something down our throats.*

sandbag *tr.* to force someone to do something. □ *I don't want to have to sandbag you. Please cooperate.* □ *Don't let them sandbag you into buying something you don't need.*

steamroller *tr.* to force something to be approved; to force something to happen. □ *He plans to steamroller this bill through Congress, but it just won't work.* □ *When you can't steamroller something, try soft soap.*

strong-arm 1. *tr.* to force someone (to do something). □ *Bruno tried to strong-arm Frank into cooperating.* □ *Don't strong-arm me, you creep!* **2.** *mod.* forceful; by physical force. □ *The strong-arm approach got him nowhere.* □ *Too much strong-arm stuff isn't good.*

strong-arm tactics *n.* tactics based on the use of force. □ *No more strong-arm tactics. You need to be more subtle.* □ *Strong-arm tactics are out. The boss says be gentle and don't break anybody.*

FRANKNESS

lay it on the line *tr.* to speak very frankly and directly. □ *I'm going to have to lay it on the line with you, I guess.* □ *Go ahead; lay it on the line. I want to know exactly what you think.*

straight from the shoulder *mod.* very direct, without attenuation or embellishment. □ *Okay, I'll give it to you straight from the shoulder.* □ *Right straight from the shoulder: clean out your desk; you're through.*

talk turkey *tr.* to talk serious business; to talk frankly. □ *We've got to sit down and talk turkey—get this thing wrapped up.* □ *It's time to talk turkey and quit messing around.*

FREEDOM

fresh and sweet *mod.* just out of jail. (Streets.) □ *Tracy is fresh and sweet and back on the street.* □ *Hey, Lefty, you look all fresh and sweet.*

off the hook *mod.* no longer in jeopardy; no longer obligated. □ *I'll let you off the hook this time, but never again.* □ *We're off the hook. We don't need to worry anymore.*

street *n.* the real, free world, as opposed to prison. (Always with *the.*) □ *The street just isn't the same as stir.* □ *It's good to be back on the street.*

street time *n.* time not spent in prison. (Underworld.) □ *I had three months' street time; then they nailed me again.* □ *I want out of this place. I need a little street time to renew some old acquaintances.*

FRIEND

amigo *n.* a friend. (Spanish. Also a term of address.) □ *Me and my amigo want to rent a couple of horses.* □ *Hey, amigo, let's go somewhere for a drink.*

BF *n.* "best friend." (Initialism. Collegiate.) □ *You would have thought you and she were BFs to hear her talk.* □ *Sharon is my BF.*

blood *n.* a buddy among blacks. (Also a term of address.) □ *Hey, blood! Where you been?* □ *The bloods aren't going to like this.*

bosom buddy *n.* a very close male or female friend. □ *We are bosom buddies, but we can still get into a big fight every now and then.* □ *Oh, yes, Sharon is my bosom buddy.*

chum *n.* a pal; a good friend. □ *This is my chum, Wally.* □ *We've been chums for years. Went to college together.*

good buddy *n.* a friend; a partner. (Citizens band radio. Also a term of address.) □ *Well, good buddy, what's new with you?* □ *John's my good buddy.*

goombah *n.* a buddy; a trusted friend. (Also a term of address. Ultimately from Italian.) □ *Hey, goombah! How goes it?* □ *He's my goombah. I can trust him.*

holmes *n.* one's pal or friend. □ *Hey, holmes, how ya living?* □ *What do you think about that, holmes?*

homeboy AND **homegirl** *n.* a buddy; a pal. (Originally between blacks. Also a term of address. *Homeboy* is for males and *homegirl* is for females.) □ *Come on, homeboy. Help out a friend.* □ *She's my homegirl, and I'd do anything for her.*

homes AND **homey; homie** *n.* a buddy; a pal. (Originally between blacks. Also a term of address.) □ *Hey, homes! How's it going?* □ *Me and my homie want to go with you.*

homeslice *n.* a homeboy; a homegirl. □ *Ask my homeslice over there if he wants to go with you.* □ *Well, homeslice, what now?*

hoser *n.* a good guy or buddy. □ *You're a real hoser, Ted.* □ *Old Fred is a good hoser. He'll help.*

man *n.* one's friend; a buddy, not necessarily male. (Also a term of address.) □ *Look, man, take it easy!* □ *Hey, man. That one's mine!*

my man *n.* my brother or buddy. (Originally black.) □ *This is my man Sam, who's gonna show you how to boogie.* □ *Come on, my man, we have to be taking care of business.*

pal *n.* a close male friend or buddy. □ *Be nice to him. He's my pal.* □ *Hey, be a pal. Give me a match.*

palsy-walsy *n.* a good friend, *pal*, or buddy. (Also a term of address.) □ *Look here, palsy-walsy, let's you and me get out of here.* □ *Meet my old palsy-walsy, John. We've known each other since we were kids.*

Sherlock *n.* one's pal or buddy. (A play on *homes, holmes,* and *Sherlock Holmes.*) □ *Come on, Sherlock, let's go!* □ *What's happening, Sherlock?*

son of a bitch *n.* old buddy. (Used between close male companions. Use with caution.) □ *Why, you old son of a bitch! How are you?* □ *Where you been keeping yourself, you son of a bitch?*

son of a gun *n.* old buddy. □ *You old son of a gun! How are you?* □ *I went to school with this son of a gun! He's my old buddy.*

sport *n.* friend; chum. (A term of address.) □ *Well, sport, looks like we have a little problem here.* □ *Hey, sport, what's new?*

FRIENDLINESS
See also **KINDNESS**.

be down (with someone) *n.* be friends with someone; to be okay or on good terms with someone. (*Down* = okay.) □ *It's okay. I'm down with Chuck.* □ *Chuck and I are down.*

break the ice *tr.* to attempt to become friends with someone. □ *He tried to break the ice, but she was a little cold.* □ *A nice smile does a lot to break the ice.*

buddy-buddy *mod.* friendly; too friendly. □ *Why is that guy so buddy-buddy with me?* □ *Don't try to get too buddy-buddy with these people. They don't like strangers.* □ *What a buddy-buddy phony!*

buddy up to someone *in.* to become very friendly toward someone. □ *Why are you buddying up to me? I don't even know you.* □ *Try to buddy up to him and pretend you are interested in what he is doing.*

chummy *mod.* friendly. □ *I'm glad to see that you are a little more chummy this morning.* □ *Don't get too chummy with me. I'm a real son of a bitch.*

come on *in.* to begin to become friendly. □ *After a few minutes, they began to come on to each other.* □ *When the nervousness of meeting a blind date passed, Sam and Mary began to come on, and we could see it would be a success.*

pal around (with someone) *in.* to be friends with someone; to move about socially with someone. □ *Tom and Heidi have palled around for years.* □ *Young people like to pal around with one another.*

pally (with someone) *mod.* friendly or overly friendly with someone. □ *I don't know why Sue acts so pally. I hardly know her.* □ *She doesn't seem pally with me.*

palsy-walsy *mod.* friendly; overly friendly. (Often with *with.*) □ *Why is Tom so palsy-walsy with everyone?* □ *That guy is a little too palsy-walsy.*

FRIGHT
See also **FEAR**.

chill *tr.* to frighten someone. (Standard English.) □ *The specter chilled everyone who saw it.* □ *The prospect of having to go in there alone chilled Wally, but good.*

scared shitless *mod.* very frightened. (Potentially offensive. Use caution with *shit.*) □ *He wasn't just frightened. He was scared shitless!* □ *He had to go to court and was scared shitless about it.*

scared stiff *mod.* frightened; unable to move from fear. □ *The poor little kid stood there—scared stiff.* □ *I was scared stiff for hours after the accident.*

scare the hell out of someone *tr.* to frighten someone badly. (Use caution with *hell.*) □ *These figures scare the hell out of me.* □ *The door blew shut and scared the hell out of me.*

scare the pants off someone *tr.* to frighten someone suddenly. □ *The piano lid fell and scared the pants off my parents.* □ *It takes a lot to scare the pants off a hardened criminal.*

spook *tr.* to frighten or startle someone or something. □ *Something I did spooked the teller, and she set off the silent alarm.* □ *Don't spook the cattle. They'll stampede.*

spooked *mod.* frightened or startled. □ *The guy looked sort of spooked. He was sweating and panting like someone had scared him to death.* □ *The horse was spooked and rolled its eyes and snorted a lot.*

FRUSTRATION

drive someone up the wall *tr.* to frustrate someone; to drive someone to distraction. □ *These days of waiting drive me up the wall.* □ *Staying in the house drove us all up the wall.*

FUEL

motion-lotion *n.* gasoline; motor fuel. (Citizens band radio.) □ *Let's stop up ahead for some motion-lotion.* □ *I'm about out of motion-lotion.*

FUN

barrel of fun *n.* a tremendous amount of fun. □ *Tracy is just a barrel of fun on dates.* □ *We had a barrel of fun at your party.*

gas *in.* to have a good time. □ *We gassed all evening.* □ *Let's go out and gas tonight, how about it?*

FUNCTIONAL

in business *mod.* operating; equipped to operate. □ *We're in business now, and things are running smoothly.* □ *Now it works. Now we're in business.*

FURNITURE

kidney-buster *n.* an uncomfortable or poorly built seat in a vehicle. □ *I have to get this kidney-buster replaced.* □ *This kidney-buster is going to ruin my back.*

rocker *n.* a rocking chair. (Not slang.) □ *I love to spend a sunny afternoon in my rocker.* □ *Children love rockers, but they can tip over in them.*

GADGET

baby *n.* a thing; a gadget; a machine, such as a car. □ *This baby is a real bear.* □ *Hand me that baby with the sharp point, will you?* □ *What kind of tranny does that baby have?*

bells and whistles *n.* extra, fancy gadgets. □ *I like machines with all the bells and whistles.* □ *All those bells and whistles add to the cost.*

dingbat *n.* a name for a gadget. □ *Isn't there supposed to be a little red dingbat that goes in this hole?* □ *Is this the dingbat you mean?*

dingus *n.* a thing or gadget. □ *I have a little dingus that helps me clean venetian blinds.* □ *Toss me one of those dinguses that holds the wire in the groove, will ya?*

doodad *n.* a name for a gadget. □ *What are these little doodads?* □ *I don't know what they're called. If they had names, they wouldn't be doodads, now would they?*

do(o)jigger AND **do(o)hickey; do(o)hickie** *n.* a name for a gadget. □ *Toss me that little red doojigger, will you?* □ *Jim has one of those doohickies that will tighten the bit in the drill.*

doowacky *n.* a thing; a nameless gadget. □ *Where is the doowacky I laid here?* □ *Is this your doowacky? I was going to throw it away.*

fakus *n.* a gadget; something with no name or a forgotten name. □ *This little fakus goes right in here.* □ *Hand me that long fakus with the hole in one end.*

gazinkus AND **gazunkus** *n.* a gadget. □ *Where is the gazinkus I use for opening paint cans?* □ *Is this the little gazunkus you were looking for?*

geegaw AND **gewgaw; googaw** *n.* a gadget; a bauble. □ *Now, that's a cute little geegaw.* □ *What do you do with these gewgaws? Hang them on a tree?*

gizmo *n.* a gadget. □ *What is this silly little gizmo on the bottom for?* □ *This gizmo turns it on.*

goofus *n.* a gadget. □ *Where is that little goofus I use to pry open these cans?* □ *Here's just the little goofus you're looking for.*

jigger *n.* a gadget. □ *Toss me one of those copper jiggers there in the box.* □ *This kind of jigger?*

jobber AND **jobby** *n.* a gadget. □ *Where is the little jobber I use to tighten this?* □ *Do you mean this little jobber?*

sucker *n.* a gadget; a thing. □ *Now, you put this little sucker right into this slot.* □ *Where is that sucker that looks like a screw?*

thingamajig AND **thingy** *n.* a gadget for which the proper name has been forgotten or is unknown. □ *Hand me that thingamajig with the copper base, will you?* □ *What're ya supposed to do with this thingy?*

unit *n.* a gadget. □ *Now, take one of the red units—put the copper strip in the slot—place the whole thing in this larger unit—and you're done.* □ *Hand me that unit on the thingy there.*

whang(y)doodle *n.* a gadget. □ *Toss me one of the little whangdoodles, would ya?* □ *This whangydoodle is a little bent.*

whatchamacallit *n.* a name for a person or thing whose real name has been forgotten or is being avoided. □ *Did you invite whatchamacallit to the party?* □ *I lost* *my—you know—my whatchamacallit— my watch!*

whatsis AND **whatsit; whatzit; whazzit** *n.* a name for a person or thing whose real name has been forgotten or is being avoided. □ *Hand me that whatsis, will you?* □ *Put this little whatzit on the top and another on the bottom.*

whing-ding AND **wing-ding** *n.* a gadget. □ *This whing-ding is broken. Where can I find another?* □ *I've never seen one of these little wing-dings so banged up.*

widget *n.* a gadget. □ *Now, try to fit this widget into this slot here.* □ *What is the real name of this widget?*

GAMBLING

See also **CHANCE**.

bet someone dollars to doughnuts *tr.* to bet something of value against something worth considerably less. □ *I bet you dollars to doughnuts that she is on time.* □ *He bet me dollars to doughnuts that it would snow today.*

bones *n.* dice. □ *Toss me the bones and get out your checkbooks.* □ *Throw them bones and hope for the best.*

cube *n.* a die, one of a pair of dice. (Usually in the plural.) □ *Toss me the cubes.* □ *She shook the cubes, saying "Baby needs shoes!"*

get down *in.* to lay one's money on the table. (Gambling.) □ *Okay, everybody get down.* □ *Get down, and let's get going!*

high roller *n.* a big gambler who risks much money; anyone who takes risks. (Refers to rolling dice.) □ *Rocko is a high roller and isn't afraid to lose some money.* □ *He's a high roller from way back.*

hit me AND **hit me again** *tr.* (in gambling) "Deal me a card." □ *Hit me again, dealer!* □ *Okay, hit me.*

hustler *n.* a gambler in a pool hall. □ *Wasn't he the guy who played the hustler in that famous movie?* □ *He made a lot of money as a hustler.*

make book on something *tr.* to make or accept bets on something. □ *Well, she might. But I wouldn't make book on it.* □

Don't make book on my success in this game.

odds-on *mod.* having to do with the thing or person favored to win. □ *My horse is an odds-on favorite to win.* □ *My plan is odds-on to be selected.*

scratch sheet *n.* a daily horse-racing newsletter at the racetrack. □ *I picked up a scratch sheet from Lucky Louie and proceeded to lay down my life's saving on a horse named Felicity Anne.* □ *Even the cost of a scratch sheet is going up, and I'm trying to economize!*

see *tr.* to equal or raise someone's bet in poker. □ *I see your five and raise you ten.* □ *Well, can you see me or not?*

snake eyes *n.* the two in dice, one spot on each die. □ *Well, it's snake eyes again. That's all for me.* □ *The baby needs shoes, and all I get is snake eyes.*

spot someone (something) *tr.* to give an advantage to someone. □ *I'll spot you twenty points.* □ *No need to spot me. I'm the greatest!*

GAS

See **FLATULENCE**.

GATHERING

be-in *n.* a gathering of hippies. □ *A meeting of happy people, yes; a be-in this is not.* □ *This is just like a sixties be-in. Lots of phony love.*

love-in 1. *n.* an event during the 1960s where one or more couples made love in a public place. □ *My uncle was at one of those love-ins, and he said if anything was going on, it was going on under blankets.* □ *I think the only people who went to love-ins were reporters.* **2.** *n.* an event in the 1960s where everyone became euphoric—with the help of marijuana—about love and respect for their fellow humans. □ *The meeting was no love-in, but we got along.* □ *Everyone at the annual company love-in was throwing love bombs around at each other.*

GAY

blade *n.* a homosexual man. (From "gay blade.") □ *This blade comes up and says, like, "Gotta match?"* □ *Some blade came over and offered to buy me a drink.*

butch *mod.* virile and masculine. (In a homosexual context.) □ *That's a real butch haircut, Claude.* □ *Really, Clare. How butch!*

camp *mod.* having to do with homosexual persons and matters. □ *What a camp way of walking!* □ *She is so camp, I could scream!*

camp it up *tr.* to overdo effeminacy; [for a homosexual male] to act too effeminate in public. □ *Can't you even walk across the room without camping it up?* □ *John just loves to burst into the most sedate hotel in town and camp it up in the lobby.*

fag AND **faggot** *n.* a homosexual. (Potentially offensive. Use only with discretion. Usually derogatory. Resented by homosexuals.) □ *Who's the fag with the fancy hat?* □ *Don't act like a faggot, Gary.*

fairy *n.* a homosexual. (Potentially offensive. Use only with discretion. Derogatory. Resented by homosexuals.) □ *I hear that you-know-who is a fairy.* □ *Who goes around calling people fairies?*

flamer *n.* a blatantly obvious homosexual male. (Primarily and originally for males.) □ *Todd is such a flamer!* □ *He tries not to be a flamer, but what can he do?*

fruit *n.* a homosexual male. (Objected to by homosexual persons.) □ *Bob thinks that you-know-who is a fruit.* □ *Who's the fruit who just came in?*

fruitcake *n.* a homosexual male. (Objected to by homosexual persons.) □ *Ken said that you-know-who is a fruitcake.* □ *Who's the fruitcake who just came in?*

gay as pink ink *mod.* having to do with an obviously homosexual person, usually a male. □ *Who said Ron's as gay as pink ink?* □ *These two guys—as gay as pink ink—came in together.*

homo 1. *mod.* homosexual. (Often derogatory. Resented by homosexual persons.) □ *Is this one of those homo bars?* □ *Where'd you get those homo shoes?* **2.** *n.* a homosexual person. (Often derogatory. Resented by homosexual per-

sons.) □ *Somebody said she is a homo.* □ *So what if he's a homo? He can still vote, can't he?*

queen *n.* a homosexual male. □ *Tom is getting to be such a queen.* □ *What kind of a queen is Tom?*

queer 1. *mod.* homosexual or bisexual. (Derogatory. Potentially offensive. Use only with discretion.) □ *Who is that queer character?* □ *Isn't he queer?* □ *She doesn't like being called queer.* **2.** *n.* a homosexual male, occasionally a female. (Derogatory. Usually offensive. Use only with discretion. Once resented by homosexuals, coming back into use.) □ *Tell that queer to get out of here.* □ *She came to the dance with a queer.*

queer as a three-dollar bill *mod.* definitely or obviously homosexual. (Usually derogatory. Potentially offensive. Use only with discretion.) □ *That guy is as queer as a three-dollar bill.* □ *He's wearing makeup. He's queer as a three-dollar bill.*

queer-beer 1. *mod.* having to do with homosexuals; homosexual. (Usually derogatory. Resented by homosexuals.) □ *I won't wear that queer-beer outfit!* □ *Don't call me a queer-beer fruitcake!* **2.** *n.* a homosexual male, possibly a female. □ *They say she's a queer-beer.* □ *That queer-beer is staring at you.*

swing both ways *in.* to be bisexual. □ *They say that Gary swings both ways, but I wouldn't know.* □ *Since he swings both ways, he may stand a better chance at finding a date.*

that way *mod.* homosexual. □ *Ken said that you-know-who was acting sort of that way. What a gossip!* □ *Somebody said that Ken talks that way because he is that way.*

GENERALITY

shotgun *mod.* broad; general. □ *It was a shotgun attempt to include everyone.* □ *A shotgun approach to a problem like this is useless. You must get specific.*

GENEROSITY

blow someone to something *tr.* to treat someone to something, such as a meal, a movie, a drink, etc. □ *Let me blow you* *to a meal.* □ *I think I'll blow myself to a fancy dessert.*

pass for something *in.* to pay for something; to treat someone by paying for something. □ *Come on. Let's go out. I'll pass for dinner.* □ *I'll pass for drinks if you want.*

pop for something *in.* to pay for a treat (for someone). □ *Let's have some ice cream. I'll pop for it.* □ *It's about time you popped for coffee.*

spring for something AND **bounce for something** *in.* to treat (someone) by buying something. □ *I'm bouncing for pizza. Any takers?* □ *Ralph sprang for drinks, and we all had a great time.*

stake someone to something *tr.* to treat someone to something. □ *Can I stake you to a drink to celebrate?* □ *Let me stake you to a big ice cream cone.*

GENETIC

in one's blood *mod.* inborn; part of one's genetic makeup. □ *It's in my blood. I can't help it.* □ *Running is in his blood. He loves it.*

GENTILE

goy *n.* a gentile. (From Hebrew. Not necessarily derogatory.) □ *But the goys can do anything they want on Sunday!* □ *Leave that kind of thing to the goys.*

GENUINE

genuine article *n.* the real thing rather than a substitute. □ *Is this the genuine article or some cheap, made-in-U.S.A. substitute?* □ *I'll take the genuine article, thanks.*

(real) McCoy *n.* something authentic. (Always with *the.*) □ *This is the real McCoy. Nothing else like it.* □ *This is no copy. It's the McCoy.*

GIFT

stocking-stuffer *n.* a small gift that is suitable for putting inside a Christmas stocking. □ *This will make the perfect stocking-stuffer.* □ *I got some little stocking-stuffers for the kids.*

GLASSES

four-eyes *n.* someone who wears glasses. (Also a rude term of address.) □ *Well,* *I've got to the age where I'm a four-eyes.* □ *Hey, four-eyes, betcha you can't see this!*

specs *n.* eyeglasses; spectacles. □ *I broke my specs.* □ *I need specs to find where I left my specs.*

GLUTTONY

blimp out *in.* to overeat. □ *I love to buy a bag of chips and just blimp out.* □ *I only blimp out on weekends.*

foodaholic *n.* a glutton. □ *Kelly is a foodaholic and has a real eating problem.* □ *What a foodaholic! She ate a whole large pizza!*

jammed up AND **jammed** *mod.* glutted; full of food or drink. □ *I'm jammed up. I can't eat another bite.* □ *After dinner, I am so jammed up that I need a nap.*

mac out *in.* to overeat, especially the type of food served at McDonald's fast-food restaurants. (From the Big Mac™ sandwich.) □ *I've been in Europe for a month, and I just want to get home and mac out.* □ *I mac out every weekend. It's like going to church.*

make a pig (out of) of oneself *tr.* to overeat; to take more of something than anyone else gets; to be selfish. □ *Please don't make a pig out of yourself.* □ *I have a tendency to make a pig of myself at affairs like this.*

munch out *in.* to eat ravenously. □ *I had to munch out after the party. I can't imagine why.* □ *I can munch out for no reason at all.*

oink out *in.* to overeat. □ *I oink out every weekend.* □ *This Thursday starts a four-day weekend, and I plan to oink out every day.*

pig out *in.* to overeat; to overindulge in food or drink. □ *I always pig out on Fridays.* □ *I can't help myself when I see ice cream. I have to pig out.*

pork out *in.* to overindulge in food and drink. □ *Whenever I see french fries, I know I'm going to pork out.* □ *We porked out on pizza.*

root *in.* to eat food like a pig. □ *Don't root. Slow down and enjoy your food.* □

Max is downstairs rooting now. It won't take that slob long to eat.

scarf out *in.* to overeat. □ *I scarf out every weekend.* □ *My brother scarfs out every day—around the clock!*

tear into something *in.* to begin eating food with gusto. □ *The family tore into the mountain of food like they hadn't eaten since breakfast—which was true, in fact.* □ *Jimmy tore into the turkey leg and cleaned it off in no time.*

GOALS

aim for the sky AND **reach for the sky; shoot for the sky** *in.* to aspire to something; to set one's goals high. □ *Shoot for the sky, son. Don't settle for second best.* □ *Set your sights high. Aim for the sky!*

where it's at *phr.* "what one is aiming for"; "what is needed." (This does not refer to a place.) □ *Keep on trying. That's where it's at!* □ *Good strong friends. That's where it's at.*

GOOD-BYE

See you. AND **See ya.** *interj.* "Good-bye." □ *Good game, Tom. See ya.* □ *See you, old chum. Give me a ring.*

See you later. *interj.* "Good-bye." (Common colloquial. Also said to people one knows one will never see again.) □ *Nice talking to you. See you later.* □ *Have a great trip, Mary. See you later.*

See you later, alligator. *interj.* "Good-bye." (From the 1930s. Answered with "After while, crocodile.") □ Tom: *Bye.* Bill: *See you later, alligator.* □ Bill: *See you later, alligator.* Tom: *After while, crocodile.*

adios muchachos *phr.* "the end"; "good-bye everyone." (Spanish.) □ *If you step out in front of a car like that again, it's adios muchachos.* □ *I've got a gun aimed at your navel. If you move so much as one muscle, you can just say adios muchachos.*

BCNU *phr.* "Be seeing you." (An initialism. Appears in informal written contexts.) □ *Bye for now. BCNU.* □ *Todd always closes his notes with "BCNU."*

Catch you later. *sent.* "I will talk to you again when I next see you." □ *Can't talk now. Catch you later.* □ *Sorry, gotta rush. Catch you later.*

ciao AND **chow** *interj.* "Good-bye"; "Hello." (Italian.) □ *See ya. Ciao.* □ *Chow, baby. Call my service.*

Have a blimp! *exclam.* "Have a good year!" (A play on Goodyear Tire and Rubber Company, which operates the Goodyear blimp.) □ *Good-bye. Have a blimp!* □ *Have a blimp! See you next summer.*

Have a nice day. *sent.* a formulaic way of saying good-bye. □ *Thank you for shopping at Wallace's. Have a nice day.* □ *See you tomorrow. Have a nice day.*

I'm history. *sent.* "Good-bye, I am leaving." □ *I'm history. See you tomorrow.* □ *Later. I'm history.*

I'm out of here. AND **I'm outa here.** *sent.* "I am leaving this minute." □ *In three minutes I'm outa here.* □ *I'm out of here. Bye.*

It's been a slice! *sent.* "It's been good." □ *Good-bye and thank you. It's been a slice!* □ *It's been a slice. I hope to see you again some day.*

Keep in touch. *sent.* "Good-bye." (Sometimes a sarcastic way of saying good-bye to someone one doesn't care about.) □ *Nice talking to you. Keep in touch.* □ *Sorry, we can't use you anymore. Keep in touch.*

Keep on trucking. *sent.* "Keep doing what you are doing."; "Keep taking care of business." □ *See ya, man. Keep on trucking.* □ *Keep on trucking. Things'll get better.*

Later. *interj.* "Good-bye." □ *It's time to cruise. Later.* □ *Later. Gotta go.*

nice meeting you *phr.* "it is nice to have met you." (Said when leaving someone whose acquaintance you have just made.) □ *I must go now, Fred. Nice meeting you.* □ *Well, nice meeting you. I must get home now.*

nice talking to you *phr.* "it's been pleasant, good-bye." (A leave-taking formula, sometimes with an air of dismissal.) □ *Do tell. Well, nice talking to you.* □ *Nice talking to you. Call my service.*

seeyabye *interj.* "bye." (California.) □ *Oh, that's, like, so, like, rad. Okay, seeyabye.* □ *Gotta go now. Seeyabye.*

So long. *interj.* "Good-bye." □ *So long, see ya later.* □ *It's been good talking to you. So long.*

Take care. *phr.* "Good-bye, be careful." □ *See you later. Take care.* □ *Take care. See you in Philly.*

Ta-ta. *interj.* "Good-bye." □ *See ya later. Ta-ta.* □ *Ta-ta. Take care.*

Toodle(-oo). *interj.* "Good-bye." □ *Take it easy. Toodle-oo.* □ *See ya! Toodle!*

GOOSE

honker *n.* a goose. (Juvenile.) □ *A whole flock of honkers settled on our pond.* □ *Can we have honker for Thanksgiving dinner?*

GOSSIP

See also **CHATTER, TALKING**.

beak *in.* to gossip; to chatter. □ *We stood around and beaked for a while.* □ *Stop beaking and get to work.*

big-mouth *tr.* to spread secrets around. □ *Why do you always have to big-mouth everything around?* □ *Don't you big-mouth this, but I'm going to have a baby.*

blabbermouth *n.* someone who talks too much and tells secrets. □ *You are such a blabbermouth!* □ *See if you can get your brother—who is a blabbermouth—to keep this still.*

cat *n.* a gossipy woman. □ *She is such a cat!* □ *Mary can be such a cat, you know.*

dirt *n.* scandal; incriminating secrets. □ *What's the dirt on Tracy?* □ *I don't want to know about anybody's dirt!*

dirty linen AND **dirty laundry** *n.* scandal; unpleasant private matters. □ *I wish you wouldn't put our dirty linen out for everyone to see.* □ *I've heard enough about her dirty laundry.*

dish *tr.* to spread gossip about someone or something. □ *The critics all dished the opening of the play mercilessly.* □ *I wish you would stop dishing me all the time.*

dish the dirt *tr.* to spread gossip; to gossip. □ *Let's sit down, have a drink, and dish the dirt.* □ *David goes down to the tavern to dish the dirt.*

ear-duster *n.* a gossipy person. □ *Sally is sort of an ear-duster, but she's all heart.* □ *I can be an ear-duster, I know, but have you heard about Sally and her you-know-what?*

earful *n.* a tremendous amount of gossip. □ *I got a big earful about Sally.* □ *I can give you an earful about the mayor.*

flapjaw *n.* chatter; gossip. □ *Too much flapjaw for me to concentrate in here.* □ *Could you all turn down the flapjaw a little?*

furphy *n.* a groundless rumor. □ *I heard a furphy about you yesterday.* □ *Who started that furphy, anyway?*

gab 1. *in.* to chatter; to gossip. □ *Can you stop gabbing just for a minute?* □ *We like to gab. Leave us alone.* **2.** *n.* mindless chatter; gossip. □ *I like to listen in on other people's gab.* □ *Enough of this gab—on with the show!*

hen party *n.* a gossipy party attended by women. □ *I have a hen party every few weeks. We love to get together.* □ *I wouldn't be caught dead at one of those hen parties.*

latrine rumor *n.* any rumor, especially one that is alleged to spread at the latrine [general toilet facilities]. (Military.) □ *Somebody started spreading a latrine rumor about the colonel's wife.* □ *That's just a latrine rumor. The colonel isn't married.*

latrine wireless *n.* the free exchange of information and gossip at the general toilet facilities. □ *It came over the latrine wireless this morning. We're all shipping out.* □ *The latrine wireless was virtually silent while you were in sick bay.*

peg someone *tr.* to gossip about someone. □ *Kim is always pegging Jill. What's her problem?* □ *Don't peg me all the time. I've never done anything to you!*

rank on someone *in.* to attack someone verbally; to gossip about someone. □ *Please stop ranking on my family!* □ *Tom keeps ranking on Jennifer, and she is really mad about it.*

scuttlebutt *n.* gossip. □ *What's the scuttlebutt on the steeple clock? Why did it stop?* □ *Don't pay any attention to the scuttlebutt around here.*

shoot the bull AND **shoot the crap; shoot the shit** *tr.* to chat and gossip. (The same as *throw the bull.* Use caution with *crap, shit.*) □ *Let's get together sometime and shoot the bull.* □ *You spend too much time shooting the crap.*

yackety-yak *n.* chatter; gossip. □ *No more yackety-yak* □ *That's enough yackety-yak. Quiet!*

yap *in.* to chatter; to gossip. □ *Who's yapping so much in here?* □ *Did you just come here to yap?*

yenta *n.* a gossip, usually a woman. (Regarded as Yiddish.) □ *She can be such a yenta when she's got news.* □ *Tracy is a yenta if ever there was one.*

GOVERNMENT

Uncle (Sam) AND **Uncle Sugar** *n.* the personification of the U.S. □ *Uncle Sugar wants a little more of your money this year.* □ *Tell Uncle to spend a little less.*

GRATITUDE

TGIF *interj.* "Thank God it's Friday." (Initialism.) □ *It was a rough week. TGIF.* □ *Everybody was muttering TGIF by Friday afternoon.*

thanks a bunch *phr.* "thanks." □ *Thanks a bunch for your help.* □ *He said "thanks a bunch" and walked out.*

thank you very much *phr.* a (sometimes sarcastic) tag added to a statement for emphasis. (Often used when there is really nothing to thank anyone for.) □ *I will manage somehow to find my own way out, thank you very much.* □ *We are probably the only people in town who might be able to help you, thank you very much.* □ *You've been quite annoying, thank you very much!*

GREED

line one's own pocket(s) *tr.* to make money for oneself in a greedy or dishonest fashion. □ *They are interested in lining their pockets first and serving the people second.* □ *You can't blame them for wanting to line their own pockets.*

suckabuck *mod.* greedy; exhibiting greed. □ *I refuse to do business with this suckabuck company anymore.* □ *She is such a suckabuck landlady that it makes me want to move.*

GREETING

ciao AND **chow** "Good-bye"; "Hello." (Italian.) □ *See ya. Ciao.* □ *Chow, baby. Call my service.*

earth to _____ *phr.* "Hello _____, are you listening?" (A means of getting the attention of someone who is ignoring you or who is daydreaming. As if one were on the earth, trying to contact someone in a spaceship.) □ *Earth to Mom! Earth to Mom! What's for dinner?* □ *Earth to Fred! Are you asleep? Say something, Fred!*

Give me (some) skin! AND **Give me five!; Slip me five!** *exclam.* "Shake my hand!" (A request for some form of hand touching in greeting.) □ *Hey, man! Give me some skin!* □ *Give me five, my man!*

give someone five *tr.* to slap hands in greeting. □ *Jerry gave John five as they passed in the corridor.* □ *Don tried to give me five in class, but missed.*

glad-hand *tr.* to greet someone effusively. □ *The senator was glad-handing everyone in sight.* □ *He glad-handed Ernie and got a real earful.*

Have a good one. AND **Have a nice one.** *sent.* "Have a good morning, afternoon, or evening," as appropriate. (A general formulaic expression used at any time of the day or night.) □ *Thank you. Have a good one.* □ *See you tomorrow, Todd. Have a nice one.*

hey *interj.* hello. (A standard greeting in much of the South, and now, among the young.) □ *Hey, Walter. How are you?* □ *Hey, Chuck! Living large.*

Hey, bum! *interj.* hello. □ *Hey, bum! What's poppin'?* □ *Hey, bum! So good to see your smiling face.*

high five 1. *n.* a greeting where the palm of the hand is raised and slapped against another person's palm similarly raised. □ *They exchanged a high five and went* *on with the show.* □ *How about a high five, man?* **2.** *tr. & in.* to greet someone as described in sense 1. □ *They high fived and went off together.* □ *Ted high-fived Sam, and they stopped to talk.*

hit me *tr.* "Give me the high five." □ *Hit me! Where you been? Hit me again!* □ *Long time no see. Hit me, man.*

Hiya! *exclam.* "Hi!" (From *Hi, you!*) □ *Hiya! Good to see ya!* □ *Hiya! Where you been keeping yourself?*

howdy *interj.* "hello." (Folksy.) □ *Howdy, friend.* □ *Well, howdy. Long time no see.*

How goes it? *interrog.* "How are you?"; "How are things going?" □ *Nice to see you. How goes it?* □ *How goes it? Everything okay?*

How ya living? *interrog.* "How are you doing?" (The response is *Living large.*) □ *How ya living, man?* □ *Yo! How ya living?*

knock someone some skin *tr.* to shake hands with someone. □ *Hey, man, knock me some skin!* □ *Pete knocked Sam some skin, and they left the building together.*

Long time no see. *phr.* "I haven't seen you in a long time." □ *Hey, John! Long time no see!* □ *Long time no see! How ya been?*

low five *n.* the slapping of hands at waist level as a greeting. □ *They turned to each other, throwing a quick low five as they passed.* □ *The two eight-year-olds tried to give each other a low five, but they both hurt their hands.*

press (the) flesh *tr.* to shake hands. □ *Hey, chum! Glad to press flesh with you!* □ *He wanted to press the flesh, but I refused even to touch him.*

Que pasa? *interrog.* "Hello, what's going on?" (Spanish.) □ *Hey, man! Que pasa?* □ *What's happening? Que pasa?*

sieg-heil someone *tr.* to show homage to someone; to salute and obey someone. □ *The guy expects all his underlings to sieg-heil him and worship the ground he walks on.* □ *I won't sieg-heil her. She'll have to earn my respect.*

Skin me! *exclam.* "Give me some skin!"; "Shake my hand!" (Originally black.) □ *Hey, man, skin me!* □ *Hey, old buddy. Don't walk on! Skin me!*

slip someone five *tr.* to shake someone's hand. □ *Billy slipped me five, and we sat down to discuss old times.* □ *Come on, man, slip me five!*

(T)sup? *interrog.* "What's up?"; "What is happening?"; "What have you been doing?" □ *Hi! Tsup?* □ TONY: *Sup?* TIFFANY: *Like, nothing.*

What can I do you for? *interrog.* "How can I help you?"; "How can I serve you?" □ *Good morning. What can I do for you?* □ *Now it's your turn. What can I do for you?*

What do you say? *interrog.* "Hello, how are you?" □ *Hi, Jim. What do you say?* □ *What do you say, man?*

What is it? *interrog.* "Hello, what is happening?" □ *What is it? (T)sup?* □ *What is it? What's happening?*

What's buzzin' (cousin)? *interrog.* "What's happening?" □ *Hey, chum! What's buzzin', cousin?* □ *What's buzzin' around here?*

What's cooking? *interrog.* "What is happening?"; "What's about to happen?" □ *What's cooking? Anything interesting?* □ *What's cooking, anyway?*

What's going down? *interrog.* "What's happening?" □ *I can't figure out what's going down around here.* □ *Hey, man, what's going down?*

What's going on? *interrog.* "What is happening here?" □ *I hear a lot of noise. What's going on?* □ *What's all this broken glass? What's going on?*

What's happ(ening)? *interrog.* "Hello, what's new?" □ *Hey, dude! What's happening?* □ *What's happ? How's it goin'?*

What's new? *interrog.* "Hello, how are you?"; "What has happened since I last saw you?" □ *Hi, Jim! What's new?* □ *What's new with you?*

What's poppin'? *interrog.* "Hello, what is happening?" □ *What's poppin'? Anything new?* □ *What's poppin', G?*

What's shakin' (bacon)? *interrog.* "How are you?"; "What is new?" □ *What's shakin' bacon? What's going down?* □ *Hi, Jim. What's shakin'?*

What's the good word? *interrog.* "Hello, how are you?" □ *Hi, Jim! What's the good word?* □ *Haven't seen you in a long time. What's the good word?*

What's up? *interrog.* "What is going on?"; "What is happening?" □ *Hi, Jim! What's up?* □ *Haven't seen you in a month of Sundays. What's up?*

What's up, G? *interrog.* "Hello, what is up, guy?" □ *What's up, G? How ya living?* □ *What's up, G? Anything new?*

What's your age? *interrog.* "Hello, how are you?" □ *What's your age? Tsup?* □ *Yo, Sam! What's your age?*

Where (have) you been keeping yourself? *interrog.* "I haven't seen you in a long time. Where have you been?" □ *Long time no see. Where've you been keeping yourself?* □ *I haven't seen you in a long time. Where you been keeping yourself?*

Word. *interj.* "Hello." □ *Word. What's new.* □ *Word. Living large?*

Yello. *interj.* "Hello." (Said with any intonation that would be appropriate with hello.) □ *Yello, Dave Jones speaking.* □ *Yello, Smith residence.*

You guys bitchin'? *interrog.* "Hello, how are you?" (Use with caution.) □ *Tsup? You guys bitchin'?* □ *You guys bitchin'? What's poppin'?*

GRIEF

tear someone up *tr.* to cause someone much grief. □ *I know this news will tear him up.* □ *The situation really tore up his father.*

GROOMING

stickum *n.* any thick and sticky substance, especially hair dressing. □ *Use some stickum on your hair!* □ *He uses too much stickum on his hair.*

GROUCHY

bitchy *mod.* spiteful; moody; rude; complaining. (Potentially offensive. Use only with discretion.) □ *Don't be so bitchy!* □ *Who needs a house full of bitchy kids?*

crank *n.* a crabby person. (Collegiate.) □ *Why are you such a crank? Is something wrong in your life?* □ *The prof is such a crank; he jokes only about once a semester.*

cranky *mod.* irritable; fretful. □ *Don't be cranky. We're almost there.* □ *Max is cranky today. The fuzz is on his tail.*

crusty *mod.* feisty; gruff. □ *Jed is a crusty old man.* □ *Unlike most crusty, avuncular old men, Jed hasn't a single redeeming quality.*

gritch *n.* a complainer; a griper. □ *You are getting to be such a gritch.* □ *Don't be such a gritch!*

meany AND **meanie** *n.* a mean or grouchy person. □ *Come on! Don't be such a meany.* □ *I don't want to be a meanie, but if you don't turn down that radio, I don't know what I'll do.*

mingy *mod.* "mean" and "stingy." □ *Why can't you borrow it? I'm just mingy, that's all.* □ *What a mingy jerk!* □ *Aw, don't be so mingy!*

on the rag *mod.* ill-tempered. □ *Bill is on the rag and making trouble for everyone.* □ *Wow, Wayne, you are on the rag. What's eating you?*

sobersides *n.* a very serious person; a grumpy old man. □ *Old sobersides can't manage to laugh at anything.* □ *Some sobersides came over and asked us to watch our language.*

sorehead *n.* a grumpy person. (Also a term of address.) □ *She's sort of a sorehead right now. Wait a day or two and then ask her.* □ *The boss is a sorehead, but she's all we have.*

sourpuss *n.* a grouchy or frowning person. □ *What a sourpuss! He makes King Kong look sweet.* □ *Don't be a sourpuss, babycakes.*

GROUP

combo *n.* a combination of people or things. □ *Those two make an interesting combo.* □ *The dish was a combo of fish, garlic, and cream.*

posse *n.* the group of teenagers or children that one plays with or hangs out with. □ *Hank and his posse are in the backyard playing.* □ *A whole posse of kids just ran through my flower garden.*

GROWTH

snowball *in.* to grow at an increasing rate. (As a snowball rolling down a hill might increase in size.) □ *The problem began to snowball, and we had to close down for a while.* □ *Offers to help with money and prayers began to snowball, and we had to get volunteers to help answer the phones.*

GUESSING

whistle in the dark *in.* to guess aimlessly; to speculate as to a fact. □ *Am I close, or am I just whistling in the dark?* □ *She was whistling in the dark. She has no idea of what's going on.*

Your guess is as good as mine. *sent.* "I don't know either." □ *I don't know. Your guess is as good as mine.* □ *Your guess is as good as mine as to when the train will get in.*

GUILT

lay a (heavy) trip on someone AND **lay a guilt trip on someone** *tr.* to attempt to make someone feel very guilty. □ *Why do you have to lay a guilt trip on me? Why don't you go to a shrink?* □ *Of course, she just had to lay a trip on him about being bossy, self-centered, and aloof.*

lay something on someone *tr.* to attempt to make someone feel guilty about something. □ *Don't lay that stuff on me. Face your own problem.* □ *Every week she calls up to lay a guilt trip on me about something or other.*

take the rap (for something) *tr.* to take the blame for something. (Originally underworld.) □ *I didn't want to take the rap for the job, but, after all, I was guilty.* □ *I threw the rock, but John took the rap.*

HAIR

do AND **doo** *n.* a hairdo. □ *Nice do. Is it new?* □ *I can't go out in this rain and get my doo wet!*

gumb(e)y *n.* a tall, squared-off and slanting haircut that looks like the Gumby character's head. □ *Wayne came to school sporting a gumby and got a lot of attention.* □ *Ted got sent to the principal's office because of his gumby.*

mop *n.* hair; a hairdo. □ *How do you like my new mop?* □ *Why don't you comb that mop?*

piece *n.* a tiny ponytail worn by males. □ *Even the little boys—six and seven years old—want to wear a piece.* □ *Tony pointed out that lots of pirates wore pieces.*

spiked *mod.* having to do with hair that stands up straight. □ *His spiked hair wouldn't look so bad if it wasn't orange.* □ *Both orange and spiked is too much.* □ *Is spiked hair a fad or the way of the future?*

zipper head *n.* a man with his hair parted in the middle. □ *Why are there so many zipper heads around here? Is this hair style on sale or something?* □ *Some zipper head behind the counter told me I couldn't come in without a shirt.*

HANDKERCHIEF

blower *n.* a handkerchief. □ *He pulled a crusty blower from his back pocket.* □ *And what does he do when he doesn't have a blower?*

hanky AND **hankie** *n.* a handkerchief, especially if lacy and feminine. □ *Do you have a hanky I can borrow?* □ *Here, use my hankie.*

snotrag *n.* a handkerchief. (Crude. Potentially offensive. Use only with dis-

cretion.) □ *I guess I should use my snotrag.* □ *Don't you carry a snotrag?*

HANDS

grabbers *n.* the hands. □ *Keep your grabbers to yourself.* □ *Wash your grubby little grabbers before coming to the table.*

hooks *n.* the hands. □ *Get your hooks off my newspaper!* □ *Don't stand there with your hooks in your pocket. Get busy!*

meathooks *n.* the hands. □ *Get your meathooks off my car!* □ *If your meathooks so much as brush by my jacket again, you are finished!*

mitt *n.* a hand. □ *Get your mitts off my glass.* □ *The kid's got mitts on him like a gorilla.*

paw *n.* someone's hand. (Jocular.) □ *Get your paws off me!* □ *That dog bit my paw.*

HANGOVER

barrel fever *n.* a hangover. □ *Man, have I ever got barrel fever.* □ *That business last night gave me a touch of barrel fever.*

bighead *n.* a headache and other ill effects from drinking. □ *I got a case of the bighead. Too much soda in my drinks, I guess.* □ *You look like you have the bighead this morning.*

bigheaded *mod.* having a hangover. □ *Tiffany is a little bigheaded this morning.* □ *I feel sort of bigheaded.*

bottleache *n.* a hangover; the delirium tremens. □ *A lot of these guys really suffer from the bottleache, but what can they do?* □ *I got a touch of the bottleache this morning.*

brown bottle flu *n.* a hangover or sickness from drinking. (Probably from beer, which is often sold in brown bottles.) □ *The jerks in the back row of my* history class show up every Monday morning with the brown bottle flu. □ Wayne had a case of the brown bottle flu and didn't make the meeting.

have a (big) head *tr.* to have a hangover. (*Have got* can replace *have.*) □ *Oh, man, do I have a head!* □ *Tom has a head this morning and won't be coming into work.*

head *n.* a hangover. (Always with *a.*) □ *Boy, do I have a head this morning.* □ *How do you get rid of a head so you can go to work?*

hung *mod.* hungover. □ *John is really hung this morning.* □ *I'm miserable when I'm hung.*

hungover *mod.* having a hangover from too much alcohol. □ *John is really hungover today.* □ *I can't eat when I'm hungover.*

morning after (the night before) *n.* a hangover. (Always with *the.*) □ *Do worries about the morning after keep you from having a good time at parties?* □ *She's suffering from the morning after the night before.*

mouth *n.* a hangover. (Always with *a.*) □ *I've got quite a mouth this morning. I guess I overdid it.* □ *What a mouth! It tastes like a bird slept in it!*

roached *mod.* hungover; exhausted. □ *I'm roached. I feel lousy.* □ *What a day! I've never been so roached.*

woefits AND **woofits** *n.* a hangover. □ *The poor guy is suffering from the woefits.* □ *That's a bad case of the woofits.*

HAPPENING

come down *in.* to happen. □ *Hey, man! What's coming down?* □ *When something like this comes down, I have to stop and think things over.*

go down *in.* to happen. □ *Hey, man! What's going down?* □ *Something strange is going down around here.*

popping *in.* happening. □ *Is anything popping around here?* □ *Things are always popping at the gym.*

HAPPINESS

bliss out *in.* to become euphoric. □ *I blissed out just because it is spring and I*

am with you. □ *I always bliss out from talk like that, but I still love Wally.*

buck up *in.* to cheer up; to perk up. □ *Come on, now, buck up. Things can't be all that bad.* □ *She began to buck up when I showed her the results of the tests.*

feel groovy *in.* to feel really good and mellow. □ *It's a beautiful day, and I really feel groovy.* □ *Everybody is feeling groovy and smiling and all.*

happy camper *n.* a happy person. (Often in the negative.) □ *Fred flunked algebra and he is not a happy camper.* □ *I am not a happy camper. I am tired, hungry, and I need a shower.*

high, wide, and handsome *mod.* happy; carefree. □ *Wally is high, wide, and handsome after his great triumph.* □ *He sure looks high, wide, and handsome. I'm glad he's happy.*

in orbit *mod.* ecstatic; euphoric. □ *She was just in orbit when she got the letter.* □ *Pete was in orbit over the promotion.*

put a smile on someone's face *tr.* to please someone; to make someone happy. □ *We are going to give Andy a pretty good raise, and I know that'll put a smile on his face.* □ *I was able to pay a few dollars down, and that put a smile on the clerk's face.*

up *mod.* happy; cheery; not depressed. □ *I'm up today. Let's celebrate.* □ *This is not an up party. Let's cruise.*

upbeat *mod.* bright and cheery; not negative. □ *I'd prefer to open the conference with an upbeat topic.* □ *That topic is not upbeat.* □ *This piece of music has an upbeat flavor to it.*

HARASSMENT

bullyrag *tr. & in.* to harass someone. □ *Don't bullyrag me just because you're upset.* □ *Pete is bullyragging again.*

give someone a melvin *tr.* to jerk up someone's pants or underwear, drawing the fabric up sharply between the buttocks. (It is assumed that some *geek* named Melvin goes about with his underwear in this uncomfortable position.) □ *If you even try to give me a melvin, I'll bust you one.* □ *Tom came up* behind Fred, and with a deft motion, gave Fred a melvin that he would never forget.

goose 1. *tr.* to (attempt to) poke something, such as a finger, in someone's anus. □ *Freddy tried to goose me!* □ *Don't goose me!* **2.** *n.* an attempt to *goose* someone as in sense 1. □ *Harry is a master of the rude goose.* □ *He tried to give me a goose.*

hassle *tr.* to harass someone; to bother someone; to give someone a hard time. □ *Listen, please don't hassle me. I've had a hard day.* □ *Please make this dame stop hassling me!*

jack someone around *tr.* to hassle someone; to harass someone. □ *The IRS is jacking my brother around.* □ *The boss was jacking Gert around, so she just walked out.*

jerk someone around AND **jerk someone over** *tr.* to hassle someone; to waste someone's time. □ *Stop jerking me around and give me my money back.* □ *They sure like to jerk people around in that music shop.*

rank *tr.* to give someone a hard time. □ *Stop ranking me!* □ *The dean was ranking the boys for pulling the prank.* □ *When he finished with the boys, he started ranking their parents.*

razz *tr.* to tease someone. □ *Please stop razzing me.* □ *I was just razzing you. I didn't mean any harm.*

rip on someone *in.* to give someone a hard time. □ *Fred was ripping on me, and I heard about it.* □ *Stop ripping on my friend!*

yank *tr.* to harass someone. □ *Stop yanking me!* □ *Yank the welcher a little and see what that does.*

yank someone around *tr.* to harass someone; to give someone a hard time. □ *Listen, I don't mean to yank you around all the time, but we have to have the drawings by Monday.* □ *Please stop yanking me around.*

yank someone's chain *tr.* to harass someone; to give someone a hard time. (As if one were a dog wearing a choke collar, on a leash.) □ *Stop yanking my*

chain! □ *Do you really think you can just yank my chain whenever you want?*

zing *tr.* to assault someone verbally. □ *She zinged him with another clever remark.* □ *He zinged her back till he decided they were even.*

HARM
See also **INJURY**.

basted *mod.* beaten; harmed. □ *The team got basted three games in a row.* □ *We were really basted in the market crash.*

bean *tr.* to hit someone on the head. □ *The lady beaned me with her umbrella.* □ *A board fell off the scaffold and beaned the worker.*

cut one's own throat *tr.* to do something that harms oneself. □ *If I do that, I'd be cutting my own throat.* □ *He's just cutting his own throat, and he knows it.*

do someone dirt *tr.* to do ill to someone; to harm someone's reputation. □ *You really did me dirt.* □ *It seemed that the lawyer was determined to do me dirt right there in the courtroom.*

screwed, blued, and tattooed *mod.* badly mistreated; badly *screwed*. □ *I got a bad deal. I got screwed, blued, and tattooed.* □ *When John bought his wreck of a car, he got screwed, blued, and tattooed.*

shaft *tr.* to do wrong to someone. □ *The jerk shafted me, but good.* □ *We are going to shaft this guy in a way that he will remember.*

touch a sore point *tr.* to mention something that upsets someone. □ *I touched a sore point with Larry when I mentioned taxes.* □ *That touched a real sore point with me.*

HAT
brim *n.* a hat. □ *Man, that is one fine brim you got.* □ *New silks call for a new brim.*

hard hat *n.* a protective helmet worn around construction sites. (Standard English.) □ *You'll need a hard hat to come into this area.* □ *John swiped a hard hat from the construction site.*

HAUGHTINESS

biggity *mod.* haughty; aloof. □ *Kelly is too biggity for my taste.* □ *Who is that biggity guy with the mustache?*

bigheaded *mod.* conceited. □ *Now, don't get bigheaded, but you are a top drummer in my book.* □ *Look at him swagger. He is so bigheaded.* □ *What a bigheaded jerk!*

dicty *mod.* snobbish. (Black.) □ *Those people can be so dicty!* □ *That dicty lady told me I could come to the back to get a tip if I wanted.*

ego tripper *n.* a person who habitually goes on an *ego trip.* □ *Not another ego tripper running for public office!* □ *You have to be an ego tripper to be a palm-presser.*

hincty *mod.* snobbish; fussy; aloof. (Black.) □ *Some of those people are so hincty.* □ *That hincty lady told me to turn my radio down.*

holier-than-thou *mod.* superior in piety; condescending. □ *She has such a holier-than-thou attitude.* □ *Tracy can act so holier-than-thou sometimes.*

hot stuff *n.* a person who acts superior (to others). (Also a term of address.) □ *What makes you think you're such hot stuff?* □ *Hey, hot stuff, come down here and say that.*

pull an attitude *tr.* to be haughty; to put on airs. □ *Don't pull an attitude with me, chum!* □ *Mary pulled an attitude and sat around pouting all evening.*

snooty *mod.* haughty; conceited. □ *Don't be so snooty!* □ *Tiffany can be snooty if she wants to, and she usually wants to.* □ *What a snooty waiter!*

standoffish *mod.* aloof. □ *Bob is sort of standoffish until he gets to know you.* □ *Don't be so standoffish! Join in the fun.* □ *I am a standoffish guy.*

stuck-up *mod.* conceited. □ *Tom is really stuck-up.* □ *What a stuck-up jerk.* □ *Don't be so stuck-up. Unbend a little.*

uppity *mod.* haughty. (Folksy.) □ *Why is she so uppity?* □ *Don't be uppity. Remember who you are!*

HAUNT

dog *tr.* to stay with one and haunt one. □ *Will this memory dog me all the days of my life?* □ *The thought of all that cake and ice cream dogged me all during my diet.*

HEAD

attic *n.* the head, thought of as the location of one's intellect. □ *She's just got nothing in the attic. That's what's wrong with her.* □ *Ken has an attic full of fear and resentment he needs to clean out before he will feel comfortable again.*

bean *n.* the head. □ *I got a bump right here on my bean.* □ *Put your brim on your bean and cruise.*

biscuit *n.* the head. □ *She got a nasty little bump on the biscuit.* □ *He wears a tin can on his biscuit in case he tumbles.*

block *n.* the head. □ *That block of yours is pretty dense.* □ *Try to get this stuff through your block before the test.*

can *n.* the head. □ *What do you have in your can, anyway? Lard?* □ *Jerry landed one on Frank's can. Frank crumpled.*

conk AND **konk** *n.* the head. □ *Put your brim on your conk, and let's cruise.* □ *Where'd you get that nasty bump on your konk?*

gourd *n.* the head. □ *I raised up and got a nasty blow on the gourd.* □ *My gourd aches something awful.*

knowledge-box *n.* the head. □ *Now, I want to get this into your knowledge-box once and for all.* □ *My knowledge-box is just spinning with all this information.*

noodle *n.* (one's) head. □ *That's using your noodle.* □ *Put your hat on your noodle, and let's go.*

nut *n.* (one's) head. □ *A brick fell and hit him on the nut.* □ *The baseball came in fast. Clonk! Right on the nut!*

potato *n.* the head. □ *I got a nasty bump on my potato.* □ *Put your hat on your potato, and let's get out of here.*

think-box *n.* the skull; the head. □ *A little weak in the think-box, but other than that, okay.* □ *Use your think-box for* *something other than to hold your ears apart.*

HEALTHY

in action *mod.* healthy and getting around. □ *After I got well, I was in action again immediately.* □ *When will she be in action again?*

in the pink *mod.* feeling quite well; feeling on top of the world. □ *I'm in the pink today. Feeling great.* □ *When she's in the pink again, she'll give you a ring.*

HEART

pump *n.* the heart. □ *He has the pump of a forty-year-old.* □ *My pump's getting sort of weak.*

ticker *n.* a heart. □ *I've got a good strong ticker.* □ *His ticker finally gave out.*

tick-tock *n.* a heart. □ *My tick-tock is as strong as an ox's.* □ *How long does an ox's tick-tock last, anyway?*

HEAT

scorcher *n.* a very hot day. □ *This is really a scorcher, isn't it?* □ *Wow! What a scorcher!*

sizzler *n.* a very hot day. □ *Today will be another sizzler. A low-pressure center over Alabama is pumping hot and humid air into the area.* □ *What a sizzler! I'm sweating like a horse.*

sticky *mod.* having to do with hot and humid weather. □ *It's so sticky today!* □ *I can't take another sticky day like this.*

HEIGHT

lift *n.* a tall heel on shoes that makes someone seem taller. (Usually plural.) □ *I feel better in my lifts.* □ *Some people wear lifts just to make them a little more confident.*

sawed-off *mod.* short of stature. □ *Mike is sawed-off.* □ *Tom called Mike a sawed-off little runt.* □ *Well, Mike is a sawed-off runt, isn't he?*

HELL

773H *n.* "hell." (This is the printed word *hell* rotated 180 degrees. Jocular.) □ *What the 773H is going on around here?* □ *This place is one 773H of a mess!*

(blue) blazes *n.* hell. □ *You can go straight to blue blazes as far as I care.* □ *It's as hot as blazes here.*

H-E-double-toothpicks *n.* "hell." (It is not usually written and can be spelled a number of different ways.) □ *Oh, H-E-double-toothpicks! I did it wrong again!* □ *Here she comes again. H-E-double-toothpicks!*

HELP

See **ASSISTANCE**.

HETEROSEXUAL

breeder *n.* a heterosexual. (In a homosexual context.) □ *Don't invite Wally. He's a breeder.* □ *Why not? The breeders invited us to their party.*

straight *n.* a nonhomosexual; a heterosexual. (Often from the homosexual point of view.) □ *Walter invited a few straights to the affair, just to keep things calm.* □ *The straights really get upset if you camp it up too much.*

HIDING

hole up *in.* to hide (somewhere). □ *Lefty wanted to hole up somewhere till things cooled down.* □ *I just want to hole up until the whole matter is settled.*

HINDER

chill someone's action *tr.* to squelch someone; to prevent someone from accomplishing something. □ *Freddie is trying to chill my action, and I'm a little steamed about that.* □ *Just wait! I'll chill his action—just you wait.*

HOBO

bagman *n.* a tramp. □ *Two old bagmen wandered slowly down the lane.* □ *The bagman asked politely for some work that he would be paid for in food.*

bindle *n.* a packet or bundle; a hobo's pack. □ *The guy had a bindle tied to a stick, just like an old-time tramp.* □ *Throw your bindle over yonder, and plunk your butt on that empty crate.*

carry the stick *tr.* to live as a hobo, on the streets. (Streets. From the stick that supports the hobo's bundle.) □ *I even carried the stick for a while in the sixties.*

□ *I was afraid I'd be carrying the stick if I got laid off.*

gook *n.* a tramp. □ *Some old gook was asking for a handout.* □ *Give the gook some food and wish him well.*

skid row bum *n.* a down-and-out person; a low alcoholic beggar. □ *Do you want to end up a skid row bum?* □ *Even a skid row bum has some pride.*

stiff *n.* a fellow worker; a fellow tramp. (Originally hobos.) □ *He's just another working stiff like me.* □ *This stiff wants some help finding a flop for the night.*

stumblebum *n.* a tramp or bum, especially drunk and stumbling. □ *The poor old stumblebum got to the other side of the street the best he could.* □ *You are headed toward being a stumblebum if you don't lay off the sauce.*

vag *n.* a vagrant person; a person who does not work and who wanders from place to place. □ *A couple of vags on the curb were trying to hitch a ride.* □ *You vags, move on. Go on, move it!*

HOMELESSNESS
See also **HOBO**.

streeter *n.* an urban "street person." □ *These streeters have to be bright and clever just to survive.* □ *A couple of streeters taught me how to get a meal for nothing.*

street people *n.* people who live in the streets; homeless people. □ *There are a lot of cold street people at this time of the year.* □ *Some of the street people prefer that kind of life.*

HOMOSEXUAL
See **GAY**.

HONESTY
See also **TRUTH**.

honest injun *interj.* "It is true." □ *You actually did that? Honest injun?* □ *Sure I did, honest injun.*

keep one's nose clean *tr.* to keep out of trouble, especially trouble with the law. □ *Okay, chum. Keep your nose clean.* □ *I can keep my nose clean. Don't worry.*

legit *mod.* honest; legal. □ *If she's not legit, I won't work with her.* □ *Is this deal legit?*

on the level *mod.* honest; straightforward. □ *Come on now. Be on the level with me.* □ *Is the ad on the level?*

on the up-and-up *mod.* legitimate; open and aboveboard. □ *Is this deal on the up-and-up? What's the catch?* □ *Everything I do is on the up-and-up. I am totally honest.*

square shooter *n.* an honest person. □ *I trust Sam. He's a square shooter.* □ *He wouldn't do anything shabby. He's a square shooter.*

square with someone *in.* to become honest with someone. □ *I want you to square with me. Tell the truth this time.* □ *Okay, I'll square with you. Terry did it.*

straight *mod.* honest; unembellished. □ *This is the straight truth.* □ *Have I ever been anything but straight with you?*

straight arrow *n.* an honest person; a law-abiding citizen. □ *Wally is really a straight arrow at heart—as long as he's not around Max.* □ *Max is not a straight arrow. Slime is more like it.*

straight shooter *n.* an honest person. □ *I trust Mike; he's a straight shooter.* □ *We need a straight shooter in office who will work for the people rather than some political party.*

straight talk *n.* direct and honest talk. □ *It's about time for a little straight talk around here.* □ *If they want straight talk and can handle straight talk, give 'em straight talk.*

straight up *mod.* upright. □ *A fine guy— really straight up.* □ *She is one of the most straight-up brokers in town.*

swear on a stack of Bibles *in.* to make a very solemn pledge of one's honesty. (Folksy. Official oaths are sometimes taken with one hand on a Bible. This phrase implies that more Bibles make an even stronger oath.) □ *I swear on a stack of Bibles that I was in Atlanta on the night of January sixteenth.* □ *It's true! I swear on a stack of Bibles it's true!*

up front *mod.* open; honest; forthcoming. □ *She is a very up-front gal—trust her.* □ *I wish the salesman had been more up front about it.*

HOPE

pie in the sky 1. *n.* a reward; a special "heavenly reward." □ *Don't hold out for pie in the sky. Get realistic.* □ *If he didn't hope for some heavenly pie in the sky, he would probably be a real crook.* **2.** *mod.* having to do with a hope for a special reward. (This is hyphenated before a nominal.) □ *Get rid of your pie-in-the-sky ideas!* □ *What these pie-in-the-sky people really want is money.*

HORRIBLE

See also UNDESIRABLE.

hellacious *mod.* terrible. □ *The food was just hellacious. Yuck!* □ *The heat was hellacious, and the mosquitoes wouldn't leave us alone.*

like death warmed over *mod.* horrible; deathlike. □ *Oh, my God! You look like death warmed over!* □ *A tall, black-garbed gentleman lay there, looking like death warmed over.*

unearthly *mod.* weird; terrible. □ *What was that unearthly noise?* □ *There was an unearthly smell coming out of the kitchen.* □ *That's not unearthly!*

ungodly *mod.* horrendous; inconceivable. □ *What is that ungodly noise?* □ *What do you want at this ungodly hour?*

HORSE

hay burner *n.* a worthless racehorse; any old and worn-out horse. □ *Send that old hay burner to the glue factory.* □ *I went to a dude ranch, and they gave me an old hay burner to ride.*

nag *n.* a worn-out horse. □ *I bet a week's pay on that nag. Look what happened!* □ *The cowboy came riding into town on an old gray nag.*

stud *n.* a male horse used for breeding purposes. (Not slang.) □ *Last spring, we rented out all our studs and made some money.* □ *The mare kicked the stud and put us all out of business for a while.*

HOSPITAL

bone factory *n.* a hospital. □ *Lemme outa this bone factory!* □ *After about two months in the bone factory, I was back on the job.*

HOUSING

See LODGING.

HUMILIATION

burn someone down *tr.* to humiliate someone. □ *Man, don't you ever burn me down like that again!* □ *You just want to burn down everybody to make yourself seem better.*

turn someone's water off *tr.* to deflate someone; to silence someone. □ *He said you were stupid, huh? Well, I guess that turns your water off!* □ *That really turned off her water.*

HUMILITY

eat crow *tr.* to display total humility, especially when shown to be wrong. □ *Well, it looks like I was wrong, and I'm going to have to eat crow.* □ *I'll be eating crow if I'm not shown to be right.*

walk soft *in.* to take it easy; to be gentle and humble. □ *I try to walk soft and not rock the boat.* □ *The guy's a tyrant. He walks soft just to mislead people.*

HUNGER

Big Mac attack *n.* a sudden and desperate need for a Big Mac sandwich, a product of the McDonald's restaurant chain. (*Big Mac* is a protected trade name of McDonald's.) □ *I feel a Big Mac attack coming on!* □ *I just can't fight off a Big Mac attack.*

chuckers AND **chucks** *n.* a great hunger; an enormous appetite. (Usually with *the.*) □ *Oh, man, I really got the chucks. What time is chow?* □ *The chuckers got my stomach asking if my throat is cut.*

hungries *n.* hunger. (Always with *the.*) □ *Jimmy's crying because he's got the hungries.* □ *I get the hungries about this time every day.*

peckish *mod.* hungry. □ *I'm just a little peckish right now. I need a bite to eat.* □ *Wow, you look peckish!*

HURRY

boogie down (to somewhere) *in.* to hurry (to somewhere); to go (somewhere). □ *So, why don't you boogie down to the store and load up with bud and berries for the weekend?* □ *I'm gonna boogie down and see what's going on.*

Get a wiggle on! *exclam.* to hurry up. □ *Get a wiggle on! We don't have all day!* □ *Hey, you guys! Get a wiggle on! We gotta finish before nightfall.*

Get the lead out! *exclam.* "Get moving!"; "Hurry up!" (Crude. It is assumed that one has bowels full of lead. Use with caution.) □ *Come on, you turkeys. Get the lead out!* □ *Shake the lead out! I want it done today, not next week.*

Giddy up! *exclam.* "Move faster!" (Said to a horse to start it moving. Also said to people or things as a joke.) □ *Giddy up, Charlie! It's time to start moving.* □ *Let's get going, chum. Giddy up!*

Hop to it! *exclam.* "Get moving!"; "Hurry up!" □ *Hop to it! I don't pay you to stand around.* □ *I need it now! Hop to it!*

hustle *in.* to move rapidly; to hurry. □ *Come on, hustle, you guys.* □ *It's late. I've got to hustle.*

Make it snappy! *exclam.* "Hurry up!"; "Make it fast!" □ *We're late, Tracy. Make it snappy!* □ *Make it snappy, Fred. The cops are headed up the walk now.*

Rise and shine! *exclam.* "Get up and get going!" □ *Get up! Rise and shine! It's late.* □ *Okay, you guys, rise and shine!*

scoot *in.* to run or scurry quickly from one place to another. □ *I scooted from the bank to the cleaners and then on to the dentist's.* □ *The shoppers scooted from store to store spending money like it was going out of style.*

shake a leg *tr.* to hurry; to move faster. (Often as a command.) □ *Let's shake a leg, you guys. We gotta be there in twenty minutes.* □ *She told me to shake a leg, so I hurried the best I could.*

Shake it (up)! *exclam.* "Hurry!"; "Move faster!" □ *Get going, chum! Shake it up!* □ *We're late. Shake it!*

Snap it up! *exclam.* "Hurry up!" □ *We're late. Snap it up!* □ *Come on, snap it up! I don't have all day.*

Snap to it! *exclam.* "Get busy!" □ *Come on, snap to it!* □ *Snap to it, we've got lots to do.*

Where's the fire? *interrog.* "Why are you going so fast?"; "What's the hurry?" □ *Going a little fast there, weren't you? Where's the fire?* □ *Where's the fire? We have an hour to get there.*

zap *in.* to move to somewhere very fast. □ *I'll zap over and see if the duplicating is ready yet.* □ *He's zapping to the drugstore for some aspirin.*

zip *in.* to move to a place fast. □ *I'll zip to the office and get a new form.* □ *He's just zipped out to get pizza.*

zip along *in.* to move along rapidly. □ *Things are really zipping along here.* □ *Days are zipping along, and we're all getting lots done.*

HYGIENE

B.O. *n.* (bad) "body odor." (Initialism.) □ *Man, do you have B.O.!* □ *Now, here is a product that will end your worries about B.O.*

B.O. juice *n.* a deodorant; an underarm deodorant. □ *Who took my B.O. juice? I've got to go to class.* □ *Help this man find his B.O. juice, fast! He really needs it.*

foo-foo water *n.* aftershave lotion; cologne. □ *Don't use so much of that foo-foo water.* □ *I got three bottles of foo-foo water for my birthday.*

foxy *mod.* smelly with perspiration odor. □ *Somebody in this taxi is a little foxy.* □ *Who's got the foxy pits?* □ *Subway cars can sure get foxy in the summer.*

funky *mod.* unkempt. □ *Your hair is sort of funky. Comb it.* □ *John's room is funky and disorganized.*

GAPO *n.* "giant armpit odor"; a bad underarm odor. □ *Who's got the GAPO?* □ *That cab driver really has the GAPO.*

grubby *mod.* unclean; untidy; unshaven. □ *Pete looks sort of grubby today. What's* *wrong?* □ *Who's that grubby guy?* □ *I feel grubby, and I want a shower.*

jungle mouth *n.* a case of very bad breath; breath like the rotting jungle floor. □ *My husband woke up with jungle mouth, and I could hardly stand to be around him.* □ *Wow, Wayne really has a bad case of jungle mouth.*

pit stop *n.* an underarm deodorant. (Because it *stops* arm*pit* odor.) □ *Man, do you need some pit stop!* □ *Can I borrow your pit stop? I need it bad.*

slickum *n.* hair dressing, especially if thick and heavy. □ *What kind of slickum do you have on your hair—bear grease?* □ *His hair was plastered down with slickum, and he looked like something in an old movie.*

IDEA

wrinkle *n.* a new idea; a new aspect of something. □ *Fred came up with a new wrinkle for the ad campaign.* □ *Here's a wrinkle for you. Nobody has ever tried this one.*

IDENTIFICATION

card *tr.* to check people's ID cards for age or other eligibility. □ *They card everybody at the football games, even the parents.* □ *The bartender was carding people, so we left quietly.*

carded AND **proofed** *mod.* [for an ID card to be] examined to determine whether one has reached the legal drinking age. □ *Dave got carded at the party even though he is thirty and looks it.* □ *All the students were proofed at the door.*

finger *tr.* to point someone out; to identify someone (as having done something, been somewhere, etc.). □ *Pete fingered Marty as being the one who arrived first.* □ *Nobody would dare finger Rocko as the one who did it.*

ID 1. *n.* some kind of identification card. (Initialism.) □ *Can you show me an I.D.?* □ *I don't have any ID on me.* **2.** *tr.* to determine the identity of someone; to check someone for a valid identification card. □ *They IDed us at the door.* □ *I hate being I.D.ed.* □ *The cops IDed the driver in less than thirty minutes.*

lost-and-found badge *n.* a military identification tag; a military dog tag. (From the Persian Gulf War.) □ *Ted's lost-and-found badge was stolen while he was on leave.* □ *My father still keeps his lost-and-found badge from the Korean War.*

make 1. *tr.* to identify someone. (Underworld.) □ *We tried to make him down at the station but came up with nothing.* □ *Given another second or two I could have made the guy—but he covered his face.* **2.** *n.* an identification. (Underworld.) □ *We ran a make on her. She's got two priors.* □ *The make didn't come through until after she was released.*

make someone *tr.* to identify someone. □ *The cop stared at Max and tried to make him, but failed to identify him and let him go.* □ *The cops took Bruno downtown, where the police chief made him for the third time in a month.*

nail *tr.* to identify someone. □ *They nailed him from his picture.* □ *The officer nailed Freddy, thanks to the description the victim provided.*

nailed *mod.* correctly identified. □ *The thugs sure got nailed fast.* □ *The killer was nailed with the help of the F.B.I.*

put the finger on someone *tr.* to identify someone (for someone else, such as the police). (Underworld.) □ *The old lady put the finger on the punk who mugged her.* □ *Tyrone put the finger on the killer, then got out of town fast.*

run a make on someone *tr.* to perform an identity check on someone. (Underworld.) □ *The cops ran a make on Lefty and learned about his prison record.* □ *We tried to run a make on him and came up with nothing.*

tab *tr.* to identify someone. □ *I couldn't quite tab her, but when she started talking I knew right away who she was.* □ *I tabbed him right away.*

IGNORE

Bag that! *tr.* "Forget that!" □ *Bag that! The number I gave you was wrong.* □ *There are four—no, bag that!—six of the red ones and three blue ones.*

blow someone or something off *tr.* to neglect or ignore someone or something. □ *Get it done now. Don't blow it off!* □ *Don't blow me off. Listen! I want it done now!*

Bump that! *tr.* "Forget that!" □ *Bump that! I was wrong.* □ *I gave you the wrong number. Bump that!*

check that *tr.* cancel that; ignore that (last remark). □ *Check that. I was wrong.* □ *At four, no, check that, at three o'clock this afternoon, a bomb exploded at the riverside.*

fan *tr.* to ignore someone or something; to cut a class. □ *You have to meet with your teacher? Oh, fan that. It doesn't matter.* □ *Mary fanned her history class and missed an important test.*

freeze 1. *n.* the act of ignoring someone. □ *Everybody seems to be giving me the freeze.* □ *I got the freeze from Julie. What did I do wrong?* **2.** *tr.* to ignore someone. □ *Don't freeze me, gang! I use a mouthwash!* □ *They froze him because he didn't send thank-you notes for his birthday presents.*

freeze someone out *tr.* to lock someone out socially. □ *We didn't want to freeze you out. You failed to pay your dues, however.* □ *They froze out the newcomers.*

give someone the brushoff *tr.* to repel someone; to ignore someone. □ *Sam was afraid that Mary was going to give him the brushoff.* □ *The manager gave her the brushoff when she asked for a raise.*

give someone the go-by *tr.* to bypass someone; to ignore someone. □ *Gert gave us all the go-by when she was so sick.* □ *I didn't mean to give you the go-by. I'm preoccupied, that's all.*

go-by *n.* an instance of ignoring or passing by (someone). □ *I got the go-by from her every time I saw her.* □ *I find the go-by very insulting.*

ice *tr.* to ignore someone. (Underworld.) □ *Max iced Bruno for obvious reasons.* □ *The members of the gang iced Bruno, and that really made him worry.*

kiss something off *tr.* to forget about something; to ignore something. □ *Just kiss it off. You've lost your chance.* □ *Just kiss off any idea you might have had about running for office.*

let something ride *tr.* to let something remain as is; to ignore something (for a while). □ *Don't bother with it now. Let it ride for a day or two.* □ *Let it ride. It's not that important.*

put the chill on someone AND **put the freeze on someone** *tr.* to ignore someone. □ *She was pretty snooty till we all put the chill on her.* □ *Let's put the freeze on Ted until he starts acting better.*

switch off *in.* to become oblivious to everything. □ *I want to go home and switch off—just forget this whole day.* □ *I have to switch off when I go home.*

toss something off *tr.* to ignore criticism; to ignore defeat or a setback. □ *She just tossed it off like nothing had happened.* □ *How could she just toss off such a horrible thing?*

tune out *in.* to begin to ignore everything. □ *I got bored and tuned out.* □ *The entire class had tuned out, so no one heard the teacher ask the question.*

tune someone or something out *tr.* to ignore or disregard someone or something. □ *I heard enough and tuned her out.* □ *I managed to tune out the constant clamor in the streets.*

IMMEDIATELY

in a flash *mod.* right away; immediately. □ *Get over here in a flash, or else.* □ *I'll be there in a flash.*

in a jiff(y) *mod.* right away; immediately. □ *I'll be there in a jiffy.* □ *The clerk'll be with you in a jiff.*

in nothing flat *mod.* immediately. □ *I'll be there in nothing flat.* □ *She changed the tire in nothing flat.*

pronto *mod.* fast; immediately. (From Spanish. Common in Western movies.)

□ *You get over here, pronto.* □ *I want to see you in my office, pronto.*

today *mod.* now; immediately. (Sarcastic.) □ *I want it done, now—today.* □ *Come on. Sam. Move it. Today!*

IMPACT

bonk *tr.* to strike one's head. □ *He bonked his head on the shelf.* □ *I bonked my bean.*

bop *tr.* to strike someone or something. □ *I bopped the car on the hood and made a dent.* □ *You wanna get bopped in the beezer?*

brain *tr.* to hit someone (in the head). □ *I ought to brain you for that!* □ *She almost brained me with her umbrella.*

clunk 1. *tr.* to strike someone or something. □ *A small truck clunked me from behind.* □ *The branch clunked the roof as it fell.* **2.** *n.* a hit; the sound of a hit. □ *I heard a clunk on the roof. Must be reindeer.* □ *The clunk on the roof was a falling branch.*

ding *tr.* to shoot, dent, or knock something. □ *The rock dinged my left fender.* □ *The bullet dinged Rocko's right arm.*

right in the kisser *mod.* right in the mouth or face. □ *Max poked the cop right in the kisser.* □ *He caught one right in the kisser.*

scrunch *tr.* to crush or crunch. □ *I sat on my cookies and scrunched them.* □ *I hate crowds. I am afraid people will scrunch me.*

whump AND **whomp; womp** *n.* the sound made when two flat surfaces fall together. □ *I heard the whump when the shed collapsed.* □ *The whomp woke everyone up.*

zing *tr.* to make something penetrate; to shoot or fire something. □ *The crook zinged a couple of slugs into the floor and scared everyone to death.* □ *The kid zinged a paper clip into the wall.*

IMPETUOUS

go off half-cocked *in.* to proceed without knowing all the facts. □ *I waited because I didn't want to go off half-cocked.*

□ *The boss went off half-cocked and exploded into a rage about the mess.*

IMPORTANCE

big deal *n.* something really important. □ *Don't make such a big deal out of it!* □ *This isn't a big deal as I see it.*

biggie *n.* something or someone important. □ *This one's a biggie. Treat him well.* □ *As problems go, this one's a biggie.*

big league AND **big-league** *mod.* professional; *big-time.* (From baseball.) □ *He works for one of the big-league accounting firms.* □ *When I'm a big-league star, I'll send you free tickets.*

big-name *mod.* famous; important. □ *Some big-name star I've never heard of was there pretending to serve dinner.* □ *The big-name ballplayers make millions.*

play in the big leagues *in.* to become involved in something of large or important proportions. □ *You had better shape up if you want to play in the big leagues.* □ *The conductor shouted at the oboist, "You're playing in the big leagues now. Tune up or ship out."*

red-hot *mod.* important; in great demand. □ *This is a red-hot item. Everybody wants one.* □ *The stock market is a red-hot issue right now.*

walk heavy *in.* to be important. (Black.) □ *Harry's been walking heavy since he graduated.* □ *Why have you been walking heavy, man?*

IMPORTANCE - LACKING

NBD *interj.* "no big deal." (Initialism.) □ *Don't worry. NBD.* □ *So you're a little late. NBD.*

IMPRESS

blown away *mod.* overwhelmed; greatly impressed. (Often with *with* or *by*.) □ *We were just blown away by your good words.* □ *Like it? I was blown away.*

blow someone's mind *tr.* to impress someone; to overwhelm someone. □ *This whole business just blows my mind.* □ *Your credentials really blow my mind!*

wow *tr.* to delight or impress someone. □ *She wowed them with her cleverness.* □

That ought to wow them right out of their seats.

zap *tr.* to impress someone. □ *My big idea really zapped the boss. I may get a raise.* □ *I like to have something to zap the board with at every meeting.*

zoom someone out *tr.* to impress someone.* □ *You can't zoom me out, you twit!* □ *Freddie is trying to zoom out Tiffany again.*

IMPRESSIVE

awesome *mod.* impressive. □ *Let me have a look at this awesome new box of yours.* □ *That thing is really awesome.*

grandstand play *n.* something done exceedingly well to impress an audience or a group of spectators. □ *The grandstand play caught the attention of the crowd just as they were leaving.* □ *He tried one final grandstand play, but the audience continued to give him the raspberry.*

IMPROVEMENT

beef something up *tr.* to add strength or substance to something. □ *Let's beef this up with a little more on the drums.* □ *They beefed up the offer with another thousand dollars.*

clean up one's act *tr.* to reform one's conduct; to improve one's performance. □ *We were told to clean up our act or move out.* □ *I cleaned up my act, but not in time. I got kicked out.*

Get real! *exclam.* "Start acting realistically!" □ *Hey, chum! You are way off base! Get real!* □ *Get real! Wake up to reality!*

lift *n.* a brief spiritual or ego-lifting occurrence. □ *Your kind words have given me quite a lift.* □ *I could use a lift today. I am glummer than usual.*

out of the woods *mod.* freed from a previous state of uncertainty or danger; no longer critical. □ *As soon as her temperature is down, she'll be out of the woods.* □ *We're out of the woods now, and things aren't so chancy.*

shakeout *n.* an event that eliminates the weak or unproductive elements from a system. □ *After a shakeout that lasted a month, we went into full production.* □ *There was a big shakeout at the plant, and a whole lot of people got pink-slipped.*

shape up *in.* to improve; to reform. □ *I want to get things shaped up around here.* □ *I guess I'd better shape up if I want to stay in school.*

soup something up *tr.* to increase the power of something. □ *He souped his car up so it will do nearly 120.* □ *If only I could soup up this computer to run just a little faster.*

sweeten *tr.* to make a bargain or agreement better or more attractive. □ *Okay, I'll sweeten the deal. I'll throw in a lighted mirror on the visor.* □ *Sweeten the deal with air, and I'll buy the car.*

IMPUDENCE

crust *n.* nerve; gall. □ *She's got a lot of crust—coming in here like that.* □ *It takes crust to sell this stuff to somebody. You really gotta push.*

fresh *mod.* cheeky; impudent. □ *Ken sure is fresh sometimes.* □ *Kids get some pretty fresh ideas.*

get smart (with someone) *in.* to become fresh with someone; to talk back to someone. □ *Don't you get smart with me!* □ *If you get smart again, I'll bop you.*

guff *n.* back talk; complaining. □ *I don't want to hear any more of your guff.* □ *That's enough of your guff!*

jive *n.* back talk. □ *Cut the jive, man!* □ *Don't you give me any of that jive!*

lip *n.* back talk; impudent talk. □ *Don't give me any more of your lip!* □ *I've had enough of her lip.*

mouth off *in.* to give (someone) back talk. □ *If you mouth off, I will ground you for three weeks.* □ *Don't mouth off at me, buster!*

snotty AND **snottie** *mod.* rude. □ *What makes her so snotty?* □ *What a snotty waiter!* □ *Now, there's no reason to get snottie with me.*

take a lot of nerve *tr.* to be very rude; to require a lot of rudeness (to behave so badly). □ *He walked out on her, and that* *took a lot of nerve! □ That took a lot of nerve! You took my parking place!*

INCREASE

hike 1. *n.* a monetary increase. □ *I need a pay hike.* □ *Another hike in the electric rates takes place this spring.* **2.** *tr.* to increase an amount of money. □ *I wanted them to hike my salary, but they refused.* □ *The utilities all hike their rates at least once a year.*

pickup *n.* a sudden increase in something, such as speed or tempo in music. □ *We need a bit of a pickup at measure forty-three.* □ *There will be a pickup in sales during the Christmas season.*

up *tr.* to increase something. □ *She tried to up the price on me, thinking I wouldn't notice.* □ *The bank upped its rates again.*

INDECISION

fence hanger *n.* someone who cannot decide which side to be on. □ *We need to find a way to persuade the fence hangers to come over to our side.* □ *The senator stated he would be a fence hanger until the very minute of the vote.*

up in the air *mod.* (of an issue) undecided. □ *The whole matter is still up in the air.* □ *The question of who will attend is still up in the air.*

up in the air (about someone or something) *mod.* undecided about someone or something. □ *I'm sort of up in the air about whether to marry Mary or not.* □ *Mary's up in the air, too.*

waffle (around) *in.* to be indecisive. □ *Don't waffle around so long. Make up your mind.* □ *She spent three days waffling over the color of the car and finally decided on red.*

wishy-washy *mod.* indecisive; insipid; weak. □ *Don't be such a wishy-washy wimp.* □ *She is so wishy-washy!*

yo-yo *in.* to vacillate; to be *wishy-washy*. □ *Stop yo-yoing and make up your mind.* □ *He's always got to yo-yo a little before deciding.*

INDEPENDENCE

cut loose *in.* to let go; to become independent. □ *It was hard to cut loose from home.* □ *I guess it's time I cut loose.*

on one's own hook *mod.* all by oneself. □ *I don't need any help. I can do it on my own hook.* □ *She did it on her own hook without having to call on anyone.*

INDULGENCE

binge *n.* any spree of self-indulgence: emotional, gluttonous, etc. □ *About Thanksgiving time I start a month-long eating binge.* □ *The crying binge started when Marty got off the train.*

splurge *in.* to indulge oneself with much spending or eating. □ *I have to splurge every now and then. I deserve it.* □ *I splurge every weekend.*

spoiled rotten *mod.* indulged; greatly spoiled. □ *This kid is spoiled rotten!* □ *I was spoiled rotten when I was a child, so I'm used to this kind of wasteful luxury.*

INEFFICIENT

poky *mod.* slow; lagging and inefficient. □ *Hurry up! Don't be so poky.* □ *What a poky old horse.*

INFERIORITY

bottom of the barrel AND **bottom of the heap** *n.* the location of persons or things of the very lowest quality. (Usually with *from.*) □ *That last secretary you sent me was really from the bottom of the barrel.* □ *I don't need any candidates from the bottom of the heap.*

bottom out *in.* to reach the lowest or worst point of something. □ *All my problems seem to be bottoming out. They can't get much worse.* □ *Interest rates bottomed out last February.*

INFLUENCE

clout *n.* influence; power. □ *You have clout with the mayor. You try it.* □ *I don't have any clout at all.*

cozy up (to someone) *in.* to become overly friendly with someone in hope of gaining special favors. □ *Tracy cozied up to the prof, hoping for a good grade at least.* □ *She failed to read the syllabus,* *which advised students not to cozy up to the professor or call him at home.*

fix *tr.* to influence the outcome of a contest or an election. □ *Who fixed this race?* □ *Bruno knows what it takes to fix an election—cash.*

money talks *phr.* "money can buy cooperation"; "having money makes one influential." □ *I know that money talks, but I don't have the scratch to say anything with.* □ *Like they say, money talks, but don't try making it talk to a cop.*

suck AND **suction** *n.* influence. □ *He thinks he has suck, but he's just a pain in the neck.* □ *Who has some suction with the boss?*

suck up to someone *in.* to attempt to gain influence with or favor from someone. □ *In school, Max was always sucking up to the teacher.* □ *Don't suck up to me. It won't do any good.*

wallop *n.* influence. □ *The gal has a lot of wallop in city hall.* □ *I don't have enough wallop to make that kind of demand.*

INFLUENCE - LACKING

cut no ice (with someone) *tr.* to have no influence on someone; to fail to convince someone. □ *I don't care who you are. It cuts no ice with me.* □ *So you're the mayor's daughter. It still cuts no ice.*

INFORM

See TATTLING.

INFORMATION

411 *n.* information; the details about something or someone. (In the U.S., the telephone number of directory assistance or "information" is 411.) □ *What's the 411 on the new guy in the front office?* □ *I heard some interesting 411 on the guy down the street.*

ammo *n.* information or evidence that can be used to support an argument or a charge. □ *I want to get some ammo on the mayor. I think he's a crook.* □ *Try to keep my traffic tickets a secret. The opposition will use them as ammo in the next election.*

big noise *n.* the important current news; the current scandal. □ *What's the big noise around town now?* □ *There's a big noise up on Capitol Hill. Something about budget cuts.*

bum steer *n.* a false lead; false information. □ *You sure gave me a bum steer when you told me who he was.* □ *We spent all day checking out what turned out to be a bum steer.*

dish something out *tr.* to distribute information, news, etc. □ *The press secretaries were dishing reports out as fast as they could write them.* □ *The company dishes out propaganda on a regular basis.*

dope *n.* news. □ *What's the dope on the new mayor?* □ *I got some dope on the tavern fire if you want to hear it.*

get down to the nitty-gritty *in.* to get down to the basic facts. □ *Stop messing around and get down to the nitty-gritty.* □ *If we could only get down to the nitty-gritty and stop wasting time.*

handout *n.* an informational sheet of paper "handed out" to people. □ *As you can see on your handout, 40 percent of those who started never finished.* □ *I didn't get a handout.*

hip *tr.* to tell someone; to inform someone. □ *Hey, man, hip me to what's going on!* □ *What's happening? Take a minute and hip me!*

hit pay dirt AND **strike pay dirt** *tr.* to get to the basic facts of something. □ *Now we're beginning to hit pay dirt.* □ *When we figured out the code, we really struck pay dirt.*

(hot) skinny *n.* inside information. □ *What's the skinny on the tower clock?* □ *I've got the hot skinny on Mary and her boyfriend.*

hot tip *n.* a special bit of information that ought to be reliable. □ *Ted got a hot tip on a horse.* □ *I phoned in a hot tip about a news story to the papers.*

inside dope *n.* the inside story; special or privileged information. □ *Can you give me the inside dope on Marty?* □ *What's the inside dope on the candidate's drug addiction?*

lowdown *n.* the facts on something. □ *What's the lowdown on that funny statue in the park?* □ *Give me the lowdown on the project we just started.*

on the street *mod.* widely known. □ *Sue put it on the street, and now everyone knows.* □ *It's on the street. There isn't anyone who hasn't heard it.*

poop *n.* information; the detailed knowledge of something. □ *What's the poop on the broken glass in the hall?* □ *Tell me all the poop.*

poop sheet *n.* a sheet containing information. □ *Where is the poop sheet on to-day's meeting?* □ *You can't tell one from the other without a poop sheet.*

roundup *n.* a collection or summary of news items, such as a weather roundup, news roundup, etc. □ *Tune in at eleven for a roundup of the day's news.* □ *Now for a weather roundup.*

rundown *n.* a summary bringing some-one up to date. □ *Can you give me a run-down on what's happened since noon?* □ *I need a rundown on the current situation in Alaska.*

scoop 1. *n.* a news story gathered by a reporter before any other reporter hears of it. □ *I got a great scoop! I was right there when it happened.* □ *That was no scoop at all. It was on live television. Didn't you see the cameras?* **2.** *tr.* to beat someone—such as another reporter—in the race to get a news story first. □ *They scooped the other paper on both stories.* □ *Larry scooped me twice last month.*

straight dope *n.* the true information. □ *He gave us the straight dope.* □ *I want the straight dope. I can take it.*

straight from the horse's mouth *mod.* directly from the source. (As if a race-horse were giving racing tips.) □ *Of course it's true. I got it straight from the horse's mouth.* □ *This came straight from the horse's mouth. It's Zeerocks Copy in the sixth race.*

straight low *n.* the absolute truth. (Prisons.) □ *Can you give me the straight low on this mess?* □ *Nobody ain't gonna tell*

no warden the straight low; you can be sure of that.

swap notes (on someone or something) *tr.* to share information on someone or something. □ *The two chicks sat around swapping notes on guys they knew.* □ *The mechanics were swapping notes on rude customers they had dealt with in the last month.*

throw-away *n.* a flyer or handbill. □ *The throw-away announced a big, city-wide TGIF.* □ *I passed out the throw-aways, but not many people would take them.*

INJURY
See also **HARM**.

gimp *in.* to limp about. □ *I've been gimping a little bit since my accident.* □ *I'll gimp over there as soon as I can. It'll take awhile on these crutches.*

goose egg *n.* a bump on the head. □ *You've got quite a goose egg there.* □ *I walked into a door and got a big goose egg on my forehead.*

in bad shape AND **in a bad way** *mod.* in-jured or debilitated in any manner. □ *Fred had a little accident, and he's in bad shape.* □ *Tom needs exercise. He's in bad shape.*

rip *n.* a tear in the flesh of the hand, as in an athletic event where the flesh comes in contact with solid material, such as in gymnastics and weightlifting. □ *I keep getting rips from the bar.* □ *Sally has a rip on her palm.*

shiner *n.* a black eye. □ *Wow, look at Marty's shiner!* □ *I got this shiner by walking into a door.*

shot up *mod.* severely injured by gun-shots. □ *Tom got himself shot up in a hunting accident.* □ *He was pretty badly shot up in the police action.*

INNOCENCE
smell like a rose *in.* to seem innocent. □ *I came out of the whole mess smelling like a rose, even though I caused all the trouble.* □ *Tiffany pretended that she was the only one who should smell like a rose, but I knew different.*

INOFFENSIVE

sugarcoated *mod.* palatable; inoffensive; easy to take. □ *Math is so sugarcoated these days. Even I could learn it.* □ *Stop giving them sugarcoated knowledge.*

INSECT

skeeter *n.* a mosquito. (Folksy.) □ *A skeeter bit me on the arm.* □ *There are a lot of skeeters out tonight.*

INSINCERITY

fair-weather *mod.* temporary; insincere. (From *fair-weather sailor.*) □ *I need something more than a fair-weather friend to help me through all this.* □ *Well, I see you are just a fair-weather golfer like me.*

jive *mod.* deceptive; insincere. □ *Don't give me all those jive excuses.* □ *I listened to her little jive speech and then fired her.*

smarmy *mod.* insincere and obsequious. □ *He's obnoxious but brazen rather than smarmy.* □ *He's a smarmy creep.* □ *The guy is so smarmy, I can't stand him.*

INSULT

bird *n.* a rude gesture made with the middle finger. (Usually with *the.*) □ *The kid gave me the bird, so I bopped him.* □ *A lot of little kids give people the bird all the time because they see it on television.*

blow off *n.* the final insult; an event that causes a dispute. (Usually **blow-off.**) □ *The blow-off was a call from some dame named Monica who asked for Snookums.* □ *When the blow-off happened, nobody was expecting anything.*

cheap shot *n.* a remark that takes advantage of someone else's vulnerability. □ *It's easy to get a laugh with a cheap shot at cats.* □ *People who wouldn't dare utter anything negative about blacks, Poles, or women just love to take a cheap shot at yuppies.*

chop *n.* a rude remark; a cutting remark. □ *Jerry made some chop about the way I dress.* □ *That was a rotten chop! Take it back!*

dirty crack *n.* a rude remark. □ *Who made that dirty crack?* □ *Another dirty crack like that and I'll leave.*

(dirty) dozens *n.* a game of trading insulting remarks about relatives. (Originally Black. Always with *the.*) □ *Man, what's with you? Always the dirty dozens. You just gotta start something all the time.* □ *Freddy is out giving the dozens to Marty.*

dis(s) (on someone) *tr.* to belittle someone; to show disrespect for someone. (From either a nonstandard transitive verb *disrespect* or from *dismiss [as insignificant].*) □ *Gary is such a complainer. All he does is diss on people.* □ *Please stop dissing my little sister. She didn't do any of those things.* □ *Don't dis my ride! It's only temporary.*

finger wave *n.* the act of giving someone the finger; displaying the middle finger upright as a sign of derision. (The gesture is taboo.) □ *Two little kids gave the cop the finger wave.* □ *The salute turned into a finger wave when the major turned away.*

flip someone off AND **flip someone out** *tr.* to give someone the finger. (Collegiate.) □ *Did you flip me off?* □ *Ernie flipped Tom out, and Tom flattened Ernie. Ah, life in the big city.*

flip someone the bird *tr.* to give someone the finger; to display the *digitus impudicus* to someone. □ *Max flipped the cop the bird—and that was just the wrong thing to do.* □ *The little kid flipped the cop the bird and didn't even know what it meant.*

give someone the finger 1. *tr.* to display the middle finger upright as a sign of derision. (The gesture is taboo.) □ *Did one of you guys give Ted the finger?* □ *Somebody gave the cop the finger.* **2.** *tr.* to mistreat someone; to insult someone. □ *You've been giving me the finger ever since I started working here. What's wrong?* □ *I'm tired of everybody giving me the finger around here just because I'm new.*

kicker *n.* a clever but stinging remark; a sharp criticism. □ *I waited for the kicker, and finally it came.* □ *The kicker really made me mad.*

lah-di-dah *interj.* a jeer; a mocking response. □ *So you have a new car! Well, lah-di-dah.* □ *Lah-di-dah! Excuse me!*

play the dozens AND **shoot the dozens** *tr.* to trade insulting remarks concerning relatives with another person. (Chiefly black.) □ *They're out playing the dozens.* □ *Stop shooting the dozens and go do your homework.*

put-down *n.* an insult; an intentionally cruel and deflating insult. □ *Another put-down like that and I'm going home.* □ *Don't cry. It was just a little friendly put-down.*

put someone's nose out of joint *tr.* to cause someone to feel slighted; to cause someone to take offense. □ *I'm sorry we didn't invite you. We didn't mean to put your nose out of joint.* □ *Now, now, that shouldn't put your nose out of joint. We're sorry.*

scorcher *n.* a caustic remark. □ *Bob made a real scorcher about Tom's shoes.* □ *He is a master at the rude scorcher.*

scorching *mod.* caustic. □ *That remark was really scorching.* □ *What a scorching glare you got from her!*

shine someone *tr.* to insult someone; to deceive someone. □ *Stop shining me. I'm cool, man, ice.* □ *Bill is always shining Carla.*

slap in the face *n.* an insult; a rejection. □ *That remark was a real slap in the face.* □ *Her departure was a slap in the face to the manager who had refused to give her a raise.*

snide remark *n.* a caustic, haughty, or insulting remark. □ *You're really quick with the snide remark. Ever say anything nice to anybody?* □ *I did not appreciate that snide remark.*

take a dig at someone AND **take a jab at someone** *tr.* to insult or needle someone. □ *Why did you take a jab at Sam?* □ *You're always taking digs at people who think they're your friends.*

trash *tr.* to libel someone. □ *He seemed content to trash the mayor.* □ *Who is the chick who was trashing Max in the newspapers?*

Were you born in a barn? *interrog.* "Weren't you trained to close the door by yourself?" □ *Close the door! Were you born in a barn?* □ *You sure are careless with that door. Were you born in a barn?*

zinger *n.* a stinging remark. □ *She got off another zinger at her brother.* □ *I did not appreciate that zinger.*

INTELLIGENCE

brain *n.* a good student; a very intelligent person. □ *I'm no brain, but I get good grades.* □ *Who was the brain who figured this out?*

brains *n.* the person(s) in charge of thinking something through. □ *Who's the brains around this joint?* □ *Bruno is not what I would call the brains of the gang.*

conehead *n.* an intellectual; a *pointy-head.* □ *The coneheads have decided that we are all making too much money.* □ *They build fences around universities to keep the coneheads in.*

double-dome 1. *mod.* intellectual. □ *No more of your double-dome ideas.* □ *Most kids need to be exposed to double-dome profs at college for a while.* **2.** *n.* an intellectual. □ *It's not that what the double-domes say is wrong, it's that they are so sure that they are right that scares me.* □ *I'd rather be just folks than a double-dome.*

egghead *n.* an intellectual person. □ *The eggheads aren't exactly taking over the world.* □ *My uncle was an egghead, but nobody in our family thought he knew very much.*

mental giant *n.* a genius. □ *I'm no mental giant, but I do know trouble when I see it.* □ *Don was a mental giant but didn't ever take advantage of it.*

one smart apple *n.* a smart or clever person. □ *That Sue is one smart apple.* □ *My brother is one smart apple.*

on the beam *mod.* smart; clever. □ *That was well done, Tom. You're on the beam.* □ *She is really on the beam. Glad she came along.*

pointy-head *n.* a studious thinker; an intellectual. □ *The pointy-heads seem to* be living in a world of their own. □ Why do pointy-heads spend so much time arguing about nothing?

sharp mod. clever; intelligent. □ She's a real sharp chick! Got lots of savvy. □ She's sharp enough to see right through everything you say.

smarts n. intelligence. □ She's got plenty of smarts but no spunk. □ I got the smarts to do the job. All I need is someone to trust me.

INTEREST

groove on someone or something in. to show interest in someone or something; to relate to someone or something. □ Fred was beginning to groove on new age music when he met Phil. □ Sam is really grooving on Mary.

heavy into someone or something mod. much concerned with someone or something; obsessed with someone or something. □ Freddie was heavy into auto racing and always went to the races. □ Sam is heavy into Mary.

thing n. one's interest. □ This isn't exactly my thing, but I'll give it a try. □ This is just your thing! Enjoy it!

turn on in. to become interested or excited. □ She turned on when she heard her name called. □ He really turned on when he saw the cake.

turn onto someone or something in. to become interested in someone or something. □ Jeff turned onto electronics at the age of fourteen. □ I tried to get her to turn onto me, but she could only think of John.

INTERJECTION

Yo! interj. "Hello!"; "Attention, please!"; "Wait a minute!" □ Yo, Michael! What's new? □ Yo! Come over here.

yo mama interj. "so you say." (Black.) □ Not enough bread! Yo mama. □ Yo mama! The hell you say!

INTERROGATION

third degree n. a session of questioning, usually by the police. □ Max got the third degree, but—being the thoroughbred he is—he was a clam. □ They gave Bruno the third degree, but he refused to say anything.

INTERRUPTION

buttinsky AND **buttinski** n. someone who interrupts; someone who gets involved in other people's business. □ Frank is such a buttinsky. □ I hate to be a buttinski, but what are you talking about?

pop off in. to make an unnecessary remark; to interrupt with a remark; to sound off. □ Please don't pop off all the time. □ Bob keeps popping off when he should be listening.

INTESTINES

guts n. the belly; the intestines. □ Ted poked Frank right in the guts. □ I've got some kind of pain in the guts.

INTOXICATED - ALCOHOL/DRUGS

(a)round the bend mod. alcohol or drug intoxicated. □ One more of those, and you'll be around the bend. □ From the look in her eye, I'd say she is completely round the bend now.

baked mod. alcohol or drug intoxicated. □ All four of them went out and got baked. □ I've never seen anybody so baked.

belted mod. alcohol or drug intoxicated. □ How many belts does it take to get belted? □ We were belted out of our minds.

bent mod. alcohol or drug intoxicated. □ I've never seen two guys so bent. □ I can get bent on a glass of wine.

bent out of shape n. alcohol or drug intoxicated. □ I was so bent out of shape I thought I'd never recover. □ I've been polluted, but never as bent out of shape as this.

blasted mod. alcohol or drug intoxicated. □ I got myself blasted. I'm really sorry. □ I got so blasted I swore never to blow another joint.

blind(ed) mod. alcohol or drug intoxicated. □ I guess she was blinded. She couldn't stand up. □ They were both blind as they come.

221

blissed (out) AND **blissed-out** *mod.* alcohol or drug intoxicated. □ *She is more than blissed. She is stoned.* □ *My friend is a little blissed out. Can she sit here?*

blitzed (out) *mod.* alcohol or drug intoxicated. □ *To say she is blitzed out is putting it mildly!* □ *I want to go out and get totally blitzed. I'll show her who's in charge!*

blocked *mod.* alcohol or drug intoxicated. □ *Man, he is really blocked.* □ *How can anybody get so blocked on four beers?*

blowed (away) *mod.* alcohol or drug intoxicated. □ *I was so blowed away I couldn't see straight.* □ *I'm afraid I am way blowed.*

blown away AND **blown** *mod.* alcohol or drug intoxicated. □ *I drank till I was blown, and then I drank some more.* □ *Whatever that pill was, Cecilia is totally blown away.*

blown (out) *mod.* alcohol or drug intoxicated. □ *Fred is totally blown out and will have a huge hangover tomorrow.* □ *Fred stood at the door and told us he was blown—something that was totally obvious anyway.*

bombed (out) *mod.* alcohol or drug intoxicated. (Possibly from *embalmed.*) □ *They were bombed and looked nearly dead.* □ *How can I drive when I'm bombed out?*

boxed (up) *mod.* alcohol or drug intoxicated. □ *I am way boxed, and I feel sick.* □ *She got boxed up on gin.*

cooked *mod.* alcohol or drug intoxicated. □ *Pete is cooked, fried, boiled, baked—drunk.* □ *Gary is calling a cab. He's too cooked to drive.*

cop a head *tr.* to become alcohol or drug intoxicated. □ *He was mad and depressed and went home, having decided to cop a head.* □ *The two old codgers sat there copping a head, or trying to anyway.*

edged *mod.* alcohol or drug intoxicated. □ *They set out to be edged by midnight.* □ *We were edged and full of rich food. We needed only to sleep.*

far out *mod.* alcohol or drug intoxicated. □ *How'd you get so far out?* □ *Three beers and Wally was really far out.*

feel groovy *in.* to be alcohol or drug intoxicated. □ *Looks like Kelly is feeling groovy on gin again.* □ *Bruno feels groovy because of what he is smoking.*

foxy *mod.* alcohol or drug intoxicated. □ *Gary is a little foxy. Let him rest awhile.* □ *He's worse than foxy—he's stinking drunk.*

fried *mod.* alcohol or drug intoxicated. □ *How the hell did you get so fried?* □ *The chick got totally fried on three beers.*

funked out *mod.* alcohol or drug intoxicated. □ *Do you think you can go through life funked out all the time?* □ *Are you funked out again?*

gassed (up) *mod.* alcohol or drug intoxicated. □ *Fred is gassed up and very wobbly.* □ *He was too gassed up to drive home.*

glass(y)-eyed *mod.* alcohol or drug intoxicated. □ *Mary is looking sort of glassy-eyed, and it's only midnight.* □ *Ernie is usually glass-eyed, but tonight it's much worse.*

glow *n.* a mild state of drug or alcohol intoxication. □ *She had a nice glow, but was by no means stewed.* □ *What was supposed to be a nice glow turned out to be a terrifying hallucination.*

gone AND **gone under** *mod.* alcohol or drug intoxicated. □ *Those chicks are gone—too much to drink.* □ *Ted is really gone under.*

high *mod.* alcohol or drug intoxicated. □ *Wally is a little high for so early in the evening.* □ *They went out for the evening to get high, and for no other reason.*

in orbit *mod.* alcohol or drug intoxicated. □ *Gary is in orbit and can't see a hole in a ladder.* □ *After having a six-pack all to herself, Julie was in orbit.*

in the ozone *mod.* alcohol or drug intoxicated. □ *Four beers and Tom is in the ozone.* □ *We were in the ozone, but we still made a lot of sense.*

jazzed (up) *mod.* alcohol or drug intoxicated. □ *Dave was a bit jazzed up, but not terribly.* □ *Gert was jazzed out of her mind.*

keyed (up) AND **keyed up to the roof** *mod.* alcohol or drug intoxicated. □ *He was a mite keyed, but still technically sober.* □ *She was so keyed up she could hardly stand up.*

killed (off) *mod.* alcohol or drug intoxicated. □ *The team went out drinking and came home killed off.* □ *Man, were those guys killed.*

knocked out *mod.* alcohol or drug intoxicated. □ *They were all knocked out by midnight.* □ *Gary was knocked out when we dropped by, so we tried to sober him up.*

KOed *mod.* alcohol or drug intoxicated. (Initialism.) □ *Both guys were KOed and spent the night.* □ *How could anybody get so KOed on a six-pack?*

laid back *mod.* alcohol or drug intoxicated. □ *He's a little laid back and can't come to the phone.* □ *How can those guys work when they are laid back by noon?*

laid out *mod.* alcohol or drug intoxicated. □ *Man, you got yourself laid out!* □ *I'm too laid out to go to work today.*

loaded *mod.* alcohol or drug intoxicated. □ *If you're loaded, don't drive.* □ *I'm not loaded. I'm just a little tipsy.*

mellow *mod.* slightly alcohol or drug intoxicated. □ *I got mellow and stopped drinking right there.* □ *I'm only mellow, but you drive anyway.*

messed up *mod.* alcohol or drug intoxicated. □ *Somehow I must have got messed up. What caused it, do you think?* □ *Everybody at the party was too messed up to drive home.*

off *mod.* alcohol or drug intoxicated. □ *She is truly off.* □ *Tom is so off he can't stand up.*

oiled *mod.* alcohol or drug intoxicated. □ *Will this stuff make me really oiled?* □ *She's not just drunk; she's totally oiled.*

ossified *mod.* alcohol or drug intoxicated. □ *How can anybody be so ossified* on four beers? □ *I've never seen anybody so ossified.*

out *mod.* alcohol or drug intoxicated. □ *All four of them were totally out.* □ *Those guys are really out!*

out of it *mod.* alcohol or drug intoxicated. □ *Two drinks and she was totally out of it.* □ *When they are out of it, they are quite dangerous.*

out of sight *mod.* heavily alcohol or drug intoxicated. □ *They've been drinking since noon, and they're out of sight.* □ *Man, is she ever out of sight!*

pasted *mod.* alcohol or drug intoxicated. □ *Poor Tom is totally pasted.* □ *Max got pasted on beer.*

plowed (under) *mod.* alcohol or drug intoxicated. □ *She was plowed under for a week.* □ *They went out and got plowed.*

polluted *mod.* alcohol or drug intoxicated. □ *Those guys are really polluted.* □ *Madam, you are polluted!*

popped *mod.* alcohol or drug intoxicated. □ *She looks glassy-eyed because she's popped.* □ *They went out last night and got good and popped.*

primed *mod.* alcohol or drug intoxicated. □ *The entire fraternity got primed.* □ *The whole college was primed by midnight.*

psyched (out) *mod.* alcohol or drug intoxicated. □ *She's just lying there psyched out.* □ *Two beers and a red devil and he was psyched out.*

racked (up) *mod.* alcohol or drug intoxicated. □ *They drank till they were good and racked.* □ *Man, are you racked. What did you drink? A gallon?* □ *They all got racked up last weekend.*

riffed *mod.* alcohol or drug intoxicated. □ *That guy is really riffed!* □ *I can't keep getting riffed every night like this.*

ripped (up) AND **ripped (off)** *mod.* alcohol or drug intoxicated; under the effects of marijuana. □ *Why do you have to get ripped up like that?* □ *Max was ripped out of his mind on uppers.*

schnockered AND **schnoggered; shnockered; snoggered** *mod.* alcohol or drug intoxicated. □ *How can anybody be so schnockered on four beers?* □ *I've never seen anybody so schnockered.*

scorched *mod.* alcohol or drug intoxicated. □ *Who wants to go out and get scorched?* □ *How can anybody get so scorched on four beers?*

sent *mod.* alcohol or drug intoxicated. □ *Two glasses and she's sent.* □ *He's not just sent; he's stoned.*

shot-up AND **shot-away** *mod.* alcohol or drug intoxicated. □ *Well, you see, he's shot-up and can't come to the phone.* □ *How can anybody get so shot-away in so little time?*

skulled *mod.* alcohol or drug intoxicated. □ *He's too skulled to drive.* □ *He had got himself skulled in less than twenty minutes.*

smashed *mod.* alcohol or drug intoxicated. □ *He was so smashed he couldn't stand up.* □ *Tracy can drink a lot without ever getting smashed.*

smeared *mod.* alcohol or drug intoxicated. □ *I feel sort of smeared. Maybe I should have drunk less.* □ *Bob and Jim found themselves smeared at the end of the day.*

spiked *mod.* alcohol or drug intoxicated. □ *I knew that Mrs. Wilmington-Thorpe was spiked when she belched like a real country thunder-boomer.* □ *Her old man was just as spiked, and he made worse noises.*

stoned (out) *mod.* alcohol or drug intoxicated. □ *Fred is really stoned out.* □ *I have never seen anybody so stoned who could still talk.*

stoned out of one's squash *mod.* alcohol or drug intoxicated. □ *Tracy will drink a little now and then, but she never gets stoned out of her squash.* □ *Well, she was stoned out of her squash last night!*

stoned silly *mod.* alcohol or drug intoxicated. □ *I hate to get stoned silly in public. At home—ah, that's a different matter.* □ *He got stoned silly at the rally, and for all I know is still there on the floor in the corner.*

teed (up) *mod.* alcohol or drug intoxicated. □ *She was totally teed up by midnight.* □ *Tom was too teed to drive.*

tore (up) AND **torn (up)** *mod.* alcohol or drug intoxicated. □ *He wasn't just drunk—he was massively tore up.* □ *Boy, was she torn.*

trashed *mod.* alcohol or drug intoxicated. (Collegiate.) □ *They were trashed beyond help.* □ *Let's all get trashed and raid the girls' dorm.*

wasted *mod.* alcohol or drug intoxicated. □ *I really feel wasted. What did I drink?* □ *I've never seen a bartender get wasted before.*

way out AND **way-out** *mod.* heavily alcohol or drug intoxicated. □ *That guy is way out—can't even walk.* □ *She was so way-out, she was almost unconscious.*

whacked (out) *mod.* alcohol or drug intoxicated. □ *Gee, is he ever whacked!* □ *Dave was so whacked out he couldn't stand up.*

wigged (out) AND **wiggy** *mod.* alcohol or drug intoxicated. □ *How did you get so wigged out?* □ *The kid got a little wigged and slipped under the table.*

wiped (out) AND **wiped over** *mod.* alcohol or drug intoxicated. □ *Harry was too wiped out to drive.* □ *Oh, man! I'm really wiped.*

wired AND **wired up** *mod.* alcohol or drug intoxicated. □ *Ken was so wired up he couldn't remember his name.* □ *Tiff is, like, totally wired up.*

wrecked *mod.* alcohol or drug intoxicated. □ *Four beers and I was wrecked.* □ *Larry was far too wrecked to drive.*

zonked (out) AND **zounked (out)** *mod.* alcohol or drug intoxicated. □ *She's too zonked to drive.* □ *Jed was almost zounked out to unconsciousness.*

zootied *mod.* intoxicated with drugs or alcohol. □ *Hank seems to be zootied. What's he on?* □ *Garth acts like a yutz whether he's zootied or not.*

zunked *mod.* alcohol or drug intoxicated. □ *That poor guy is so zunked he can't see.* □ *The party went on and on.*

When the preacher got himself zunked on the punch, I knew it had reached the end.

INTOXICATED - ALCOHOL

aced *mod.* alcohol intoxicated. □ *How can anybody be so aced on three beers?* □ *I've never seen anybody that aced in my life.*

activated *mod.* tipsy; alcohol intoxicated. □ *All four of them went out and got a little activated.* □ *Will this stuff get me seriously activated?*

alkied (up) *mod.* alcohol intoxicated. □ *That old bum looks completely alkied up.* □ *She spends a lot of time alkied.*

annihilated *mod.* very drunk; intoxicated with a drug. □ *The boys came in annihilated and their father had plenty to say to them.* □ *Pete and Gary went out and got annihilated.*

antifreezed *mod.* alcohol intoxicated. □ *Man, I feel totally antifreezed.* □ *He appears to be frozen even though he's antifreezed.*

aped *mod.* alcohol intoxicated. □ *I've never seen my brother so totally aped before.* □ *He comes home aped about once a month.*

bagged AND **in the bag** *mod.* alcohol intoxicated. □ *How can anybody be so bagged on four beers?* □ *She just sat there and got bagged.*

balmed *mod.* alcohol intoxicated. □ *Tom was totally balmed and went to bed.* □ *Fred and Wilma went out and got totally balmed.*

balmy *mod.* alcohol intoxicated. □ *She's not just drunk, she's a little balmy.* □ *How can anybody be so balmy on four beers?*

bamboozled *mod.* alcohol intoxicated. (Collegiate.) □ *She's not just drunk, she's totally bamboozled.* □ *She just sat there and got bamboozled as the dickens.*

banjaxed *mod.* alcohol intoxicated. □ *She just sat there and got banjaxed.* □ *All four of them went out and got banjaxed.*

barreled (up) *mod.* alcohol intoxicated. □ *Those guys are really barreled up!* □ *She spends a lot of time barreled.*

bashed *mod.* alcohol intoxicated. □ *All four of them went out and got bashed.* □ *I've never seen anybody so bashed.*

basted *mod.* alcohol intoxicated. □ *I got totally basted.* □ *I got so basted I vowed never to touch another drop.*

bats AND **batty** *mod.* alcohol intoxicated; confused and drunk. □ *The guy was bats—stewed to his ears.* □ *She was sort of batty from the wine.*

batted *mod.* alcohol intoxicated. □ *She spends a lot of time batted.* □ *Will this stuff get me batted?*

battered *mod.* alcohol intoxicated. □ *Man, was I battered. I will never drink another drop.* □ *Those guys really got battered at the party.*

belly up *mod.* alcohol intoxicated. □ *Sylvia was boiled—belly up—glassy-eyed.* □ *After four beers, I was belly up, for sure.*

bewottled *mod.* alcohol intoxicated. □ *Sam was so bewottled that he could hardly walk.* □ *Garth and Wayne were severely bewottled.*

binged *mod.* alcohol intoxicated. □ *She sat there, binged out of her mind.* □ *I'm gonna go out and get myself binged, but good.*

blah *mod.* alcohol intoxicated; very drunk. □ *I got myself blah in about twenty minutes.* □ *We are going to get totally blah tonight.*

blimped *mod.* alcohol intoxicated; swollen with drinking. □ *I am still a little blimped from our party last night.* □ *I'm bigheaded and still blimped this morning.*

blind drunk *mod.* heavily alcohol intoxicated. □ *You came in blind drunk last night. What's going on?* □ *They drank till they were blind drunk.*

blooey *mod.* alcohol intoxicated. □ *Bruno is totally blooey. He can't even open his eyes.* □ *Man, I'm blooey. I'm stoned to the bones.*

blotto *mod.* alcohol intoxicated; dead drunk. □ *Let's get some smash and get blotto.* □ *She just lay there—blotto.*

blown (up) *mod.* alcohol intoxicated. □ *I guess I'm a little too blown up to drive.* □ *You are blown as blazes, you twit!*

blue *mod.* alcohol intoxicated. □ *What have you been drinking? You're getting a little blue.* □ *You might say I'm blue. Others might note that I am stoned.*

blue around the gills AND **green around the gills** *mod.* alcohol intoxicated. □ *In the middle of the drink, I knew I was getting blue around the gills.* □ *Marty—now thoroughly green around the gills—slid neatly under the table, and everyone pretended not to notice.*

boiled *mod.* alcohol intoxicated. □ *How can you get so boiled on wine?* □ *The two were boiled and not much use to us.*

bonkers AND **crackers** *mod.* slightly intoxicated. □ *I'm just a little bonkers, nothing really serious.* □ *She's too bonkers to drive.*

boozed *mod.* alcohol intoxicated. □ *Wow, is he ever boozed!* □ *I think I am a little boozed.*

boozy-woozy *mod.* alcohol intoxicated. □ *The boozy-woozy man clung to the railing and sang at the top of his voice.* □ *I think I am just an itty-bitty boozy-woozy.*

both sheets in the wind *mod.* alcohol intoxicated. □ *She's both sheets in the wind at the moment.* □ *She's not just both sheets in the wind—they're all in the wind.*

brewed *mod.* alcohol intoxicated. □ *Fred is brewed every evening by 9:00. I think he has a problem.* □ *He tries to get brewed as soon as he can after work.*

bruised *mod.* alcohol intoxicated. □ *I am bruised. My head hurts, and my gut feels yucky.* □ *How can anybody get so bruised on so little booze?*

burn with a low blue flame *in.* to be heavily alcohol intoxicated. □ *Yeah, he's burning with a low blue flame.* □ *He's not just drunk, he's burning with a low blue flame.*

busted *mod.* alcohol intoxicated. □ *I went to a beer bust and got busted.* □ *Jim is busted again—really boiled.*

buzzing *mod.* drunk. □ *Sally was buzzing after only a few drinks.* □ *She was really buzzing and Molly had to take her home.*

canned *mod.* alcohol intoxicated. □ *I'll drive. I'm too canned to walk.* □ *Man, am I canned!*

carrying a (heavy) load *mod.* alcohol intoxicated. □ *Marty is carrying a heavy load.* □ *Your father's carrying a load again. What are we going to do?*

chipper *mod.* alcohol intoxicated. □ *Larry here is chipper already!* □ *A glass of wine will make her chipper almost immediately.*

chucked *mod.* alcohol intoxicated. □ *I'm too chucked to drive.* □ *How did you get so chucked?*

clear *mod.* alcohol intoxicated. □ *Man, is she ever clear!* □ *He was clear, you know, polluted.*

clobbered *mod.* alcohol intoxicated. □ *He's the kind of guy who goes home and gets clobbered after work.* □ *The whole fraternity celebrated by getting themselves clobbered.*

comboozelated *mod.* alcohol intoxicated. (Collegiate.) □ *I believe I am just a little comboozelated.* □ *How did you get so comboozelated?*

commode-hugging drunk *mod.* heavily alcohol intoxicated; drunk and vomiting. □ *Bruno got commode-hugging drunk in the space of two hours.* □ *I could tell by the sounds coming from the bathroom that Ernie had come home commode-hugging drunk again.*

corked (up) AND **corky** *mod.* alcohol intoxicated. □ *You seem to be a little corked.* □ *You'd be corked up, too, if you'd drunk as much as I have.*

corkscrewed (up) *mod.* courageous because of alcohol; with one's courage screwed by alcohol. □ *After getting himself corkscrewed up, he went into the boss's office for a word.* □ *He used a bit of vodka to get corkscrewed enough to demand a raise.*

corned *mod.* alcohol intoxicated. □ *The old-timer is corned on moonshine.* □ *Let's go out and get corned.*

country drunk *mod.* alcohol intoxicated; drunk and disorganized. (Folksy.) □ *Them good old boys know how to get country drunk.* □ *The cowboy, really country drunk this time, got to town somehow and started a fight.*

crash *in.* to pass out from drinking alcohol to excess. □ *About midnight I crashed, and I woke up here.* □ *Let's get Wilbur home before he crashes for good.*

crashed *mod.* alcohol intoxicated. □ *Fred is crashed. Leave him alone.* □ *There were two crashed freshmen asleep on the lawn.*

creamed *mod.* alcohol intoxicated. □ *Man, Tony is totally creamed!* □ *I got myself creamed last night, didn't I?*

crocked *mod.* alcohol intoxicated. □ *What do you get out of getting crocked every night?* □ *Oh, my God! You're crocked again!*

cross-eyed (drunk) *mod.* alcohol intoxicated. □ *What's the point of getting cross-eyed drunk?* □ *He sat on the bar stool, cross-eyed and crying.*

crumped (out) *mod.* alcohol intoxicated. □ *She was too crumped out to drive herself home.* □ *Are you crumped out again?*

crying drunk *mod.* alcohol intoxicated and weeping. □ *She was crying drunk and feeling sorry for herself.* □ *I really hate it when they come in here crying drunk.*

cut *mod.* alcohol intoxicated. □ *She's too cut to drive.* □ *He got cut on beer, which is unusual for him.*

dead drunk *mod.* alcohol intoxicated; totally inebriated. □ *They were both dead drunk. They could only lie there and snore.* □ *Marty is dead drunk again.*

dead to the world *mod.* alcohol intoxicated. □ *Six beers and he was dead to the world.* □ *By midnight almost everybody was dead to the world.*

dinged out *mod.* alcohol intoxicated. □ *Gary is dinged out and can't drive.* □ *He got dinged out on a couple of quarts of foam.*

dipsy *mod.* tipsy; alcohol intoxicated. □ *I think that Jed is permanently dipsy.* □ *The cop pulled the dipsy dame over and arrested her.* □ *He was too dipsy to drive.*

discombobulated AND **discomboobulated** *mod.* alcohol intoxicated. □ *From the way she is walking, I'd say she is discombobulated.* □ *You'd be discomboobulated, too, if you'd drunk as much as she has.*

down *mod.* alcohol intoxicated. □ *Five beers and he was down.* □ *They were all down by midnight.*

drunk back *mod.* alcohol intoxicated; very drunk. □ *The whole bunch was drunk back by midnight.* □ *Larry was drunk back and couldn't drive us home.*

electrified *mod.* alcohol intoxicated. □ *Her eyes were staring straight ahead, and I knew she was electrified.* □ *By midnight we were all electrified.*

elevated *mod.* alcohol intoxicated; tipsy. □ *Jerry was too elevated to drive home.* □ *Sam was elevated from the drinking he did.*

eliminated *mod.* alcohol intoxicated. □ *By midnight, Wally was eliminated.* □ *How can anybody get eliminated on four beers?*

embalmed *mod.* alcohol intoxicated. □ *By morning they were all embalmed.* □ *Bob was too embalmed to stand up.*

faced *mod.* alcohol intoxicated. □ *Lord, is he faced!* □ *Who is that guy on the corner who looks so faced?*

falling-down drunk *mod.* alcohol intoxicated; very drunk. □ *Poor Fred is falling-down drunk and has no way to get home.* □ *She's not just tipsy; she's falling-down drunk.*

far gone *mod.* alcohol intoxicated. □ *Larry's far gone and looking sick.* □ *Wow, is she ever far gone!*

feeling no pain *mod.* numbed by alcohol and feeling nothing; alcohol intoxicated. □ *She fell off the wagon and is feeling no pain.* □ *He drank the whole thing, and he's feeling no pain.*

feshnushkied *mod.* alcohol intoxicated. □ *Wow, is that guy ever feshnushkied!* □ *Gert is too feshnushkied to drive home.*

flabbergasted *mod.* alcohol intoxicated. □ *I thought you were cutting down, and here you are totally flabbergasted again.* □ *After about six beers, Harry became flabbergasted and slid under the table.*

flaked out *mod.* alcohol intoxicated. □ *You are too flaked out to drive home. Give me your keys.* □ *Man, is she flaked out!*

flaky AND **flako** *mod.* alcohol intoxicated. □ *Man, is she flako!* □ *Paul was flaky and couldn't drive.*

flooey *mod.* alcohol intoxicated. □ *You're flooey again. That's every night this week.* □ *Wow, is she flooey!*

floored *mod.* alcohol intoxicated. □ *He's totally floored. Can't see a hole in a ladder.* □ *You'd be floored, too, if you'd drunk a dozen beers.*

fold *in.* to collapse from drinking. □ *Dave had just one more drink, and then he folded.* □ *She folded neatly and slid beneath the table.*

folded *mod.* alcohol intoxicated. □ *Pete is folded. That's the third time this week.* □ *Man, is he folded!*

foozlified *mod.* alcohol intoxicated. □ *Why do you always come home foozlified?* □ *Fred is foozlified and can't see his hand in front of him.*

four sheets in the wind AND **four sheets (to the wind)** *mod.* alcohol intoxicated. □ *She's not just tipsy. She's four sheets!* □ *After only three beers, Gary was four sheets to the wind.*

fractured *mod.* alcohol intoxicated. □ *This is the third night this week that Pete has rolled in fractured.* □ *He was so fractured he couldn't see.*

funky-drunk *mod.* alcohol intoxicated; stinking drunk. □ *The guy is funky-drunk, and I think he's going to be sick.* □ *Wow, is she ever funky-drunk!*

fuzzed AND **fuzzled; fuzzy** *mod.* alcohol intoxicated. □ *You are too fuzzed all the time to hold the job. Pack!* □ *Why do you come home every night fuzzled?*

giffed *mod.* alcohol intoxicated. (From TGIF "Thank God it's Friday." Said of people who celebrate the end of the workweek with liquor.) □ *He left the tavern pretty giffed.* □ *She was pretty giffed for just a few beers.*

glad *mod.* alcohol intoxicated. □ *After a few beers she was a mite glad.* □ *In fact, she was too glad to stand up.*

glazed (drunk) AND **glazed (over)** *mod.* alcohol intoxicated. □ *She has had too much. She's glazed drunk.* □ *Fred looks a little glazed. I think he's done for.*

glued *mod.* alcohol intoxicated. □ *Fred is glued and can't stand up.* □ *About three more beers and I'll be glued.*

goggle-eyed AND **googly-eyed** *mod.* alcohol intoxicated and staring. □ *Wally was goggle-eyed and couldn't stand up.* □ *He's too googly-eyed to drive home.*

goofy *mod.* alcohol intoxicated. □ *Wow, is she goofy!* □ *They went out and got themselves good and goofy.*

gooned *mod.* drunk. □ *Wayne came home gooned, and his dad went loco and grounded him.* □ *His date was gooned by ten, and he had to take her home.*

grape shot *mod.* alcohol intoxicated; drunk on wine. □ *After the reception, Hank found himself a little grape shot.* □ *Man, is that guy ever grape shot! How can he hold enough to get that way?*

greased *mod.* alcohol intoxicated. □ *He went out and got himself greased, even though he knew it would probably kill him.* □ *She is way too greased to drive.*

groggy AND **groggified** *mod.* alcohol intoxicated. □ *John was a little groggy—from the grog, of course.* □ *He was too groggified to drive.*

guzzled *mod.* alcohol intoxicated. □ *Sam was plenty guzzled when he got home.* □ *Todd was too guzzled to drive home.*

half-baked *mod.* alcohol intoxicated. □ *We're getting half-baked, come hell or high water.* □ *Fred got himself sort of half-baked every Saturday night.*

half-blind *mod.* alcohol intoxicated. □ *Fred got himself half-blind in no time at all.* □ *Get that half-blind jerk out of here!* □ *Four cans of beer and she was half-blind.*

half-canned *mod.* alcohol intoxicated; tipsy. □ *He's half-canned and will be no help at all.* □ *Old Don is half-canned and can't drive home.*

half-cocked *mod.* alcohol intoxicated. □ *He just sat there, half-cocked and singing.* □ *Old Jed got himself half-cocked at the reception.*

half-crocked *mod.* alcohol intoxicated. □ *Sam and John set out to get half-crocked.* □ *They came home half-crocked at midnight.*

half in the bag *mod.* alcohol intoxicated. □ *Jerry was half in the bag when we found him.* □ *They were all half in the bag by midnight.*

half-lit *mod.* alcohol intoxicated. □ *John was half-lit in no time at all.* □ *Harry was half-lit by noon.*

half-sprung *mod.* tipsy; alcohol intoxicated. □ *Ted was half-sprung and could hardly stand up.* □ *They were half-sprung by noon.*

half-stewed *mod.* tipsy; alcohol intoxicated. □ *Poor Fred was half-stewed and still had to give a speech.* □ *We were half-stewed and had a lot of drinking yet to do.*

half under *mod.* alcohol intoxicated; tipsy. □ *He was half under and could barely stand up.* □ *Only four beers and she was half under.*

half up the pole *mod.* alcohol intoxicated; tipsy. □ *She drank till she was half up the pole.* □ *Don was half up the pole when we picked him up to come here.*

hammered *mod.* alcohol intoxicated. □ *Man, old Fred was really hammered.* □ *She got so hammered she couldn't see.*

happy *mod.* alcohol intoxicated; tipsy. □ *She seems a little happy. Must have had*

a few already. □ *She's not happy. She's stewed.*

hard up *mod.* alcohol intoxicated. □ *After a couple of six packs, Wally found himself a little hard up.* □ *The whole gang was hard up by midnight.*

have a buzz on *tr.* to be tipsy or alcohol intoxicated. (*Have got* can replace *have.*) □ *Pete has a buzz on and is giggling a lot.* □ *Both of them had a buzz on by the end of the celebration.*

have a glow on *tr.* to be alcohol intoxicated; to be tipsy. (*Have got* can replace *have.*) □ *Since you already have a glow on, I guess you won't want another drink.* □ *Jed had a glow on and was just becoming civil.*

have a load on *tr.* to be alcohol intoxicated. (*Have got* can replace *have.*) □ *Fred has a load on and is finished for the evening.* □ *You have a load on every time I see you.*

have an edge on *tr.* to be alcohol intoxicated. □ *I've got an edge on and shouldn't drive home.* □ *Bob has an edge on even though he hardly drank anything.*

have a skinful *tr.* [for someone] to contain too much alcohol; to be alcohol intoxicated. □ *Pete had a skinful and just sat there quietly.* □ *What is wrong with her is that she has a skinful, that's what.*

have one's brain on a leash *in.* to be drunk. □ *Wayne had his brain on a leash before he even got to the party.* □ *Some guy who had his brain on a leash ran his car off the road.*

heeled *mod.* alcohol intoxicated. □ *Sally was too heeled to drive home.* □ *Man, were those guys heeled!*

hepped (up) *n. mod.* alcohol intoxicated. □ *Wally is a little too hepped up to drive home.* □ *Harry's too hepped to stand up.*

hiddy AND **hidi** *mod.* hideously drunk; very drunk. □ *Fred was totally hidi. He fell asleep under the table.* □ *Susan was not just drunk, she was hiddy—you know, bombed.*

hit under the wing *mod.* alcohol intoxicated. □ *Jed got hit under the wing.* □

Sally was a little hit under the wing, but she wasn't bad off at all.

honked AND **honkers** *mod.* alcohol intoxicated. □ *Wally was too honked to stand up.* □ *Man, is that guy honkers!*

hooched (up) *mod.* alcohol intoxicated. □ *Sally is too hooched to drive.* □ *She got herself hooched up and couldn't give her talk.*

hooted *mod.* alcohol intoxicated. □ *Jed got himself good and hooted.* □ *Ted is too hooted to drive.*

horizontal *mod.* alcohol intoxicated. □ *The boss was horizontal at the Christmas party.* □ *Stewed? No, he's totally horizontal!*

hot *mod.* alcohol intoxicated. □ *You could see that Wally was pretty hot from all the whisky.* □ *He was too hot to stand up.*

howling (drunk) *mod.* alcohol intoxicated; loudly drunk. □ *Wally got howling drunk and ran in the streets with his coat off.* □ *He was just howling!*

illuminated *mod.* alcohol intoxicated. □ *Paul is a bit illuminated.* □ *He's too illuminated to drive home.*

impaired *mod.* alcohol intoxicated. (Borrowed from the euphemistic *impaired physician*.) □ *Don is a bit impaired because he drinks like a fish.* □ *He was so impaired he couldn't see his hand in front of his face.* □ *The impaired driver was arrested.*

in a heap *mod.* alcohol intoxicated. □ *Poor Jed's in a heap again.* □ *The guys were all in a heap after the blast.*

in bad shape AND **in a bad way** *mod.* alcohol intoxicated. □ *Two glasses of that stuff and I'm in really bad shape.* □ *Fred is in bad shape. I think he's going to toss his cookies.*

in rare form *mod.* alcohol intoxicated. □ *Gert is in rare form, but she'll have time to sleep it off.* □ *When Harry was finally in rare form, he slid beneath the table.*

inside out *mod.* drunk. □ *Wayne spends every weekend inside out.* □ *Beavis looked forward to the day he could go out and get inside out.*

in the bag *mod.* alcohol intoxicated. □ *Kelly looks like he is in the bag.* □ *John is in the bag and mean as hell.*

in the grip of the grape *mod.* drunk on wine; drunk. □ *Wayne was in the grip of the grape and couldn't talk straight.* □ *Sue was in the grip of the grape after only three glasses of wine.*

in the gun *mod.* alcohol intoxicated. □ *Ted is in the gun again.* □ *When Fred is in the gun, he's mean.*

in the pink *mod.* alcohol intoxicated. □ *Pete is in the pink and singing at the top of his lungs.* □ *When he's in the pink, he's a handful.*

in the suds *mod.* alcohol intoxicated. □ *Fred is in the suds and can't see.* □ *When Bob is in the suds, he's mean.*

jagged *mod.* alcohol intoxicated. □ *Man, is that chick jagged!* □ *Let's go out and get jagged.*

jambled *mod.* alcohol intoxicated. □ *Jerry was too jambled to stand up.* □ *Let's go out and get good and jambled.*

jammed *mod.* alcohol intoxicated. □ *I'm a little jammed, but I think I can still drive.* □ *They were jammed by midnight.*

jiggered *mod.* alcohol intoxicated. □ *Todd was more than just a little jiggered.* □ *Bill was too jiggered to stand up.*

jingle *n.* a buzz or tingle from alcohol. □ *He had a little jingle, but he wasn't even tipsy.* □ *This stuff gives me a little jingle, but that's all.*

jingled *mod.* alcohol intoxicated. □ *She was a little jingled, but not worse than that.* □ *Let's go out and get good and jingled.*

jolly *mod.* alcohol intoxicated; tipsy. □ *Everybody was jolly and singing by the time the food arrived.* □ *Kelly was a little too jolly, and her sister told her to slow down.*

jugged (up) *mod.* alcohol intoxicated. □ *I'm not jugged up. I'm not even tipsy.* □ *Fred was too jugged to drive home.*

juicy *mod.* alcohol intoxicated. □ *Mary is just a little bit juicy, I'm afraid.* □ *She's so juicy she can't stand up!*

jungled *mod.* alcohol intoxicated. □ *Pete is a little jungled.* □ *He was jungled before he came here.*

Kentucky fried *mod.* alcohol intoxicated. (Based on the trade name "Kentucky Fried Chicken.") □ *Man, is that guy really Kentucky fried!* □ *I've never seen anybody so downright Kentucky fried on six beers.*

kited *mod.* alcohol intoxicated. (From high as a kite.) □ *Tracy was too kited to see her hand in front of her.* □ *Both guys were kited by midnight.*

knocked up *mod.* alcohol intoxicated. □ *Bill was knocked up and didn't want to drive.* □ *Wow, was that guy knocked up!*

laid to the bone *mod.* alcohol intoxicated. □ *He got himself laid to the bone.* □ *We were all laid to the bone by midnight.*

lathered *mod.* alcohol intoxicated. □ *The two brothers sat there and got lathered.* □ *She is too lathered to drive.*

light *mod.* alcohol intoxicated. □ *I began to feel a little light along about the fourth beer.* □ *I feel a little light. You'd better drive.*

liquefied *mod.* alcohol intoxicated. □ *Ten beers and I am absolutely liquefied!* □ *She is too liquefied to walk, let alone drive.*

lit AND **lit up** *mod.* drunk. □ *She was always lit by bedtime.* □ *Todd was lit up like a Christmas tree at our office party.*

loaded for bear *mod.* alcohol intoxicated. □ *He is loaded for bear and anything else.* □ *He's been drinking mule since dawn, and he's loaded for bear.*

loaded to the gills AND **loaded to the barrel** *mod.* alcohol intoxicated. □ *He's loaded to the gills. Couldn't see a hole in a ladder.* □ *Man, he's loaded to the barrel and fighting mad.*

loony AND **loonie** *mod.* alcohol intoxicated. □ *She's acting a little loonie. Let's get her home before she's sick.* □ *A couple of drinks and she's as loonie as hotcakes.*

looped AND **loopy** *mod.* alcohol intoxicated. □ *Sam is too looped to drive.* □ *She got loopy very quickly and had to be helped to a chair.*

loop-legged *mod.* alcohol intoxicated. □ *He's too loop-legged to drive.* □ *She has this strange tendency to get a little loop-legged when she has four or five drinks.*

loose *mod.* very drunk. □ *Mary was a little loose and had to be driven home.* □ *Don is too loose to stand up.*

lost in the sauce *mod.* alcohol intoxicated and bewildered. □ *Bill spends many days lost in the sauce.* □ *Sally got lost in the sauce at the party and made quite a spectacle of herself.*

lubricated *mod.* alcohol intoxicated. □ *They are sufficiently lubricated for the night.* □ *He's not fit to talk to until he's lubricated a bit.*

maggot(t)y *mod.* alcohol intoxicated; very drunk. (A play on *rotten*.) □ *Rotten, hell. They were absolutely maggotty!* □ *How can anybody reach the state of being maggoty on three beers?*

mashed *mod.* alcohol intoxicated. □ *Both guys were totally mashed. I called my brother, who came and rescued me.* □ *Bruno was mashed, but he wouldn't let anyone else drive.*

maxed out *mod.* alcohol intoxicated. □ *Sam was maxed out and seemed happy enough to sit under the table and whimper.* □ *I hadn't seen Barlowe so maxed out in years. He was nearly paralyzed.*

Mickey finished *mod.* alcohol intoxicated; totally drunk. (A play on *Mickey Finn*.) □ *I guess the old guy is about Mickey finished. He's plootered!* □ *What gets into guys that makes them want to get Mickey finished before they stop?*

milled *mod.* alcohol intoxicated. □ *She was cut up with all that booze—milled, I guess.* □ *She was too milled to drive and couldn't walk, either.*

mixed (up) *mod.* alcohol intoxicated. (This is hyphenated before a nominal.) □ *I'm just a little mixed up, nothing serious. No reason you should be swaying* around like that. □ Jerry's too mixed to drive home.

moist around the edges mod. alcohol intoxicated. □ Charlie is more than moist around the edges. He is soused. □ Didn't that guy seem a little moist around the edges?

moonlit mod. alcohol intoxicated, with moonshine. □ He's on the jug again. See, he's all moonlit. □ He's too moonlit to drive.

mopped AND **moppy** mod. alcohol intoxicated. □ Jack was a little moppy to be driving. □ He's not mopped; he's sloshed.

muddled (up) mod. alcohol intoxicated. □ I've had a little too much muddler, I think. Anyway, I'm muddled. □ Larry is too muddled up to drive.

muggy mod. alcohol intoxicated. □ George is just a little muggy. It doesn't take much anymore. □ I'm too muggy to drive.

nipped mod. alcohol intoxicated. □ All four of them went out and got nipped. □ How can anybody be so nipped on four beers?

non compos AND **non compos poopoo** mod. alcohol intoxicated. □ That gal isn't just drunk. She's non compos poopoo. □ Two glasses and he was non compos.

obliterated mod. drunk. □ Fred was obliterated and couldn't walk to his car, let alone drive it. □ Three beers and Sally became obliterated.

off one's nut mod. alcohol intoxicated. □ Those guys are really off their nuts! □ She just sat there and got more and more off her nut.

on the blink mod. alcohol intoxicated; on a drinking spree. □ They all went out and got on the blink. □ My brother is a little bit on the blink this morning.

on the fritz mod. alcohol intoxicated. □ Sue is a bit on the fritz. □ She drank till she was totally on the fritz.

Otis mod. drunk. □ Gary was completely Otis and couldn't walk straight. □ Fred was Otis by midnight and began looking like he was going to barf.

out cold mod. alcohol intoxicated. □ Four beers and he was out cold. □ He sat in his chair at the table, out cold.

out like a light mod. heavily alcohol intoxicated. □ Those guys are really out like a light! □ All four of them drank till they were out like a light.

out of one's skull mod. alcohol intoxicated. □ Oh, man, I drank till I was out of my skull. □ Two beers and he was out of his skull.

out of the way mod. alcohol intoxicated. □ She spends a lot of time out of the way. □ After a few more drinks, Bill will be out of the way.

overserved mod. having to do with a drunken person in a bar; alcohol intoxicated. (Euphemistic.) □ Four customers were overserved and had to leave. □ The overserved guy there in the corner is going to be sick.

packaged mod. alcohol intoxicated. □ Man, Max was really packaged last night! □ By midnight she was totally packaged.

pafisticated mod. alcohol intoxicated. (A corruption of "sophisticated.") □ Whenever I drink champagne, I get totally pafisticated. □ Look at her drive. She is a real pafisticated lady.

paid mod. alcohol intoxicated. □ I think I'll go out and get paid tonight. □ Tom went to the tavern and spent all his money on getting paid.

parboiled mod. alcohol intoxicated. □ Sally stayed at the bar just long enough to get parboiled. □ She's not really stewed, just parboiled.

pee'd mod. alcohol intoxicated. □ This old boy is really pee'd. □ His old lady gets pee'd after a few beers.

peonied mod. alcohol intoxicated. □ Man, was she peonied! Really stoned. □ Let's go get peonied, just for the hell of it.

pepped (up) AND **peppy** mod. alcohol intoxicated. □ That guy looks a little pepped up. Don't give him any more booze. □ I feel sort of pepped up. Time to stop drinking.

perked (up) *mod.* alcohol intoxicated. □ *Three beers and he's perked.* □ *No more. She's done. She's perked up for good.*

petrified *mod.* alcohol intoxicated. (Literally, turned into stone. Another way of saying *stoned*.) □ *She's not drunk; she's petrified.* □ *He drank moonshine till he was petrified.*

phfft *mod.* alcohol intoxicated. □ *You won't wake him up for hours yet. He's phfft.* □ *Three beers and she's phfft, for sure.*

pickled *mod.* alcohol intoxicated. (Very common.) □ *She's usually pickled by noon.* □ *It only takes a few drinks to get him pickled.*

pie-eyed *mod.* alcohol intoxicated. □ *That guy is really pie-eyed. Send him home.* □ *We've got a pie-eyed bus driver. I want to get off!*

piffed AND **pifted** *mod.* alcohol intoxicated. □ *That guy is really piffed.* □ *How can anybody get that piffed on four beers?*

piffled *mod.* alcohol intoxicated. □ *Three glasses of booze and she was totally piffled.* □ *He was so piffled he couldn't talk!*

piff(l)icated *mod.* alcohol intoxicated. □ *How can anybody drink so much and not get totally pifflicated?* □ *Get that pifficated stuffed shirt out of here!*

pigeon-eyed *mod.* alcohol intoxicated. □ *How can anyone get so pigeon-eyed on so little booze?* □ *Who is that pigeon-eyed guy over there who is having such a hard time standing up?*

pilfered *mod.* alcohol intoxicated. □ *I've had too much. I'm beginning to feel pilfered.* □ *That old boy is really pilfered.*

pinked *mod.* alcohol intoxicated; tipsy. □ *She's sitting there looking a bit pinked.* □ *I want to get pinked. Fill it up, bartender.*

pipped (up) *mod.* alcohol intoxicated. □ *I'm not drunk. Just a little pipped up.* □ *She's pipped and ready to get sick.*

pissed *mod.* alcohol intoxicated. (Potentially offensive. Use only with discretion.) □ *He was really pissed.* □ *He was so pissed he could hardly stand up.*

pixilated AND **pixolated** *mod.* alcohol intoxicated; tipsy. □ *She seems a bit pixilated. She's probably been drinking.* □ *Martha, you mustn't drive. I think you are pixilated.*

plastered *mod.* alcohol intoxicated. □ *She's really plastered.* □ *She's so plastered she can't see.*

plastered to the wall *mod.* heavily alcohol intoxicated. □ *He's not just drunk; he's plastered to the wall!* □ *How can anybody get plastered to the wall on just four beers?*

pleasantly plastered *mod.* mildly alcohol intoxicated; mellow with drink. □ *He wasn't really stoned. Just pleasantly plastered.* □ *I get to the point that I am pleasantly plastered, and then I stop.*

plonked (up) *mod.* alcohol intoxicated. □ *He sure is plonked up.* □ *She is totally plonked.*

plootered *mod.* alcohol intoxicated. □ *We went out and got totally plootered.* □ *How can anyone get so plootered on a bottle of wine?*

plotzed *mod.* alcohol intoxicated; really drunk. □ *They all came home plotzed.* □ *Two bottles and she was plotzed.*

polished (up) *mod.* alcohol intoxicated. □ *One glass of that stuff and I was polished up.* □ *How much of that do I have to drink to get good and polished?*

pooped (out) *mod.* alcohol intoxicated. □ *How much of that stuff does it take to get pooped?* □ *He's been drinking all night and is totally pooped out.*

poopied *mod.* alcohol intoxicated. □ *She was so poopied that she giggled all the way home.* □ *They got real poopied last night.*

pop-eyed *mod.* alcohol intoxicated, with bulging eyes. □ *What's he been drinking? He's pop-eyed as hell.* □ *She drank until she was totally pop-eyed.*

powdered (up) *mod.* alcohol intoxicated. □ *Those guys are powdered up.* □

Most of the bums in the gutter are really powdered.

preserved *mod.* alcohol intoxicated. ☐ *He's really preserved.* ☐ *He drank a quart of vodka and is totally preserved.*

puggled *mod.* alcohol intoxicated. ☐ *When he started pouring his drink down his collar, I knew he was puggled.* ☐ *The whole gang got puggled last night.*

pummelled *mod.* alcohol intoxicated. (Collegiate.) ☐ *Can you imagine getting pummelled on peppermint schnapps?* ☐ *They get pummelled every Friday night.*

pushed *mod.* alcohol intoxicated. ☐ *Tom is a little pushed and can't walk very straight.* ☐ *How can you be so pushed on so little booze?*

putrid *mod.* alcohol intoxicated. ☐ *That guy is stinking drunk. Putrid, in fact.* ☐ *They went out last night and got putrid.*

put to bed with a shovel *mod.* alcohol intoxicated. ☐ *He wasn't just tipsy. He was put to bed with a shovel!* ☐ *Dead drunk? Yes, put to bed with a shovel.*

quartzed *mod.* alcohol intoxicated. ☐ *She is really quartzed!* ☐ *How can anybody get so quartzed on a bottle of wine?*

queer *mod.* alcohol intoxicated. ☐ *After a glass or two, he got a little queer.* ☐ *She was so queer she could hardly stagger home.*

queered *mod.* alcohol intoxicated. (In the sense "made bogus.") ☐ *I feel sort of queered.* ☐ *How can anybody get so queered on two beers?*

rack up *in.* to become alcohol intoxicated. ☐ *Let's go down to the tavern and rack up.* ☐ *I think I'll rack up.*

rattled *mod.* tipsy; alcohol intoxicated. ☐ *After an hour of drinking, Bill was more than a little rattled.* ☐ *Being rattled from beer, I stopped drinking beer and began on the rum.*

raunchy AND **raunchie; ronchie** *mod.* alcohol intoxicated. ☐ *Those guys were raunchy as hell.* ☐ *Let's go out and get good and ronchie.*

ripe *mod.* alcohol intoxicated. ☐ *Yes, they were ripe all right. Stinking drunk.* ☐ *Bill was so ripe that they took him home.*

roasted *mod.* alcohol intoxicated. ☐ *He was stewed, roasted, and boiled.* ☐ *He's out getting roasted with the boys.*

rotten *mod.* alcohol intoxicated. ☐ *It takes a case of beer to get Wilbur rotten.* ☐ *When he gets rotten, he's sort of dangerous.*

rumdum AND **rum-dum** *mod.* alcohol intoxicated. ☐ *The old lady got rumdum on gin.* ☐ *Two glasses and she was rumdum and asleep.*

rummed (up) *mod.* alcohol intoxicated. ☐ *Sailors like to go into town and get rummed up.* ☐ *Those boys are really rummed.*

rummy *mod.* alcohol intoxicated. ☐ *She's rummy, and she's going to be sick.* ☐ *Who's the rummy old girl?* ☐ *How long does it take a heavy drinker like Bob to get rummy?*

sauced *mod.* alcohol intoxicated. ☐ *She went out and got herself sauced.* ☐ *Man, do you look sauced.*

sawed *mod.* alcohol intoxicated. ☐ *I got sawed last weekend, and I still have a headache.* ☐ *She drank a lot, but never got sawed.*

scammered *mod.* alcohol intoxicated. ☐ *She is scammered out of her mind.* ☐ *Two bottles of that stuff and she was scammered.*

screeching (drunk) *mod.* alcohol intoxicated; very drunk. ☐ *How can anybody be so screeching drunk on four beers?* ☐ *She's not just drunk; she's screeching.*

screwed AND **screwed tight** *mod.* alcohol intoxicated. ☐ *She spends a lot of time screwed.* ☐ *She's not just drunk; she's screwed tight.*

screwed, blued, and tattooed *mod.* alcohol intoxicated. ☐ *Who wants to go out and get screwed, blued, and tattooed?* ☐ *All four of them went out and got screwed, blued, and tattooed.*

screwy *mod.* alcohol intoxicated. □ *How can anybody be so screwy on five beers?* □ *I've never seen anybody so screwy.*

scronched *mod.* alcohol intoxicated. □ *She just sat there and got scronched.* □ *He spends a lot of time totally scronched.*

seeing pink elephants AND **seeing pink spiders; seeing snakes** *tr.* alcohol intoxicated; recovering from a drinking bout; having the delirium tremens. □ *When I got to the point of seeing pink elephants, I knew that something had to be done.* □ *The old one who's shaking—he's probably seeing snakes.*

sewed up *mod.* alcohol intoxicated. □ *She's not just drunk; she's sewed up.* □ *Will this stuff get me sewed up?*

SF *mod.* alcohol intoxicated. (Initialism. From *shit-faced.*) □ *Fred was really SF last night.* □ *How can that guy get so SF?*

shagged *mod.* alcohol intoxicated. □ *She is mucho shagged!* □ *Nobody is not too shagged to drive—or something like that.*

shaved *mod.* alcohol intoxicated. □ *I feel a tad shaved.* □ *So what if I'm a bit shaved? I shtill have all my shenses.*

shellacked *mod.* alcohol intoxicated; overcome by booze. □ *Ernie was so shellacked he couldn't see.* □ *How did he get so shellacked? I didn't see him drink anything.*

shicker AND **schicker; schickered** *mod.* alcohol intoxicated. (From Hebrew *shiqor* via Yiddish.) □ *It took her about ten minutes to get schicker and three days to get sober.* □ *He's schickered, and he's not going anywhere tonight.*

shined *mod.* alcohol intoxicated, especially by *moonshine.* □ *Tipsy? He's shined from dawn to dusk.* □ *The old farmer seemed a bit shined.*

shit-faced AND **shitty** *mod.* alcohol intoxicated. (Potentially offensive. Use only with discretion.) □ *I'm shit-faced, and I know it.* □ *Move over. You're too shitty to drive.*

shot *mod.* alcohol intoxicated. □ *They are a little noisy, I guess, but after all they are shot, you know, plastered.* □ *I am half shot now. I'll quit before I'm shot.*

shot in the neck *mod.* alcohol intoxicated. □ *He's shot in the neck, but he's not bleeding.* □ *What's wrong with Harry is that he's shot in the neck every day by supper.*

shredded *mod.* alcohol intoxicated. (Collegiate.) □ *We are all too shredded to drive home. What shall we do?* □ *I believe that each of us is shredded enough to fly home. Let's vote on that.*

sizzled *mod.* alcohol intoxicated. □ *I'd like to go out tonight and get sizzled—maybe that would help me forget Tiffany.* □ *Harold got himself sizzled and couldn't drive to the dance.*

skunk-drunk *mod.* alcohol intoxicated. □ *He was skunk-drunk and didn't want to be bothered.* □ *Some skunk-drunk character came in and started talking big.*

skunked *mod.* alcohol intoxicated. □ *Kelly got skunked on suds—very unusual for him.* □ *He was so skunked he couldn't find his house.*

slaughtered *mod.* drunk. □ *Ted and Bill came home slaughtered and caught hell for it.* □ *Garth went out and got himself slaughtered again last night.*

slewed AND **slewy; slued; sloughed (up)** *mod.* alcohol intoxicated. □ *Wallace is too slewed to drive.* □ *She knows how to stop drinking before she gets slewy.*

slightly rattled *mod.* tipsy; alcohol intoxicated. □ *He's only slightly rattled. He'll recover by morning.* □ *She can be stone blind and still seem only slightly rattled.*

slopped *mod.* alcohol intoxicated. □ *I've never seen a senior citizen so inelegantly slopped as was Walter.* □ *He was so slopped, he could walk without his cane.*

sloshed (to the ears) *mod.* alcohol intoxicated. □ *Man, is he sloshed to the ears!* □ *He is as sloshed as they come.*

slugged *mod.* alcohol intoxicated. □ *I'm slugged—skunked, you know, corned. And I think I am going to sick up.* □ *Ted realized that he was slugged out of his mind, but tried to get the bartender to serve him another drink.*

slushed (up) *mod.* alcohol intoxicated. □ *I hate to come home slushed and wake up everybody. I have to sing, you see.* □ *This chick is so slushed that she doesn't know her name.*

snapped (up) *mod.* alcohol intoxicated. □ *Let's go out and get ourselves good and snapped.* □ *Pete was snapped up by eight-thirty.*

snooted *mod.* alcohol intoxicated. □ *He got himself thoroughly snooted.* □ *She's snooted and will never get home by herself.*

snoozamorooed *mod.* alcohol intoxicated. □ *Man, was she snoozamorooed!* □ *He went and got himself snoozamorooed before the wedding.*

snotted *mod.* alcohol intoxicated. (Potentially offensive. Use only with discretion.) □ *He got himself totally snotted in two hours.* □ *He was too snotted to stand up.*

snozzled *mod.* alcohol intoxicated. □ *How can anybody be so snozzled on four beers?* □ *Those guys are really snozzled!*

snuffy *mod.* alcohol intoxicated. □ *She was a little snuffy, but nothing debilitating.* □ *Who's the snuffy little guy in the corner booth?*

soaked *mod.* alcohol intoxicated. □ *All the guys came home soaked.* □ *Frank was too soaked to drive home.*

socked *mod.* alcohol intoxicated. □ *I don't know what was in that punch, but I was socked.* □ *She got socked out of her mind.*

soft *mod.* alcohol intoxicated. □ *After a few hours at the party, it appeared that most people were getting soft.* □ *Hard liquor makes people soft.*

soggy *mod.* alcohol intoxicated. □ *The two old ladies got a little soggy, but nothing uncouth.* □ *They weren't sopping wet, just soggy.*

sopping (wet) AND **soppy** *mod.* alcohol intoxicated. □ *After about six beers, Ralph found himself a little soppy.* □ *He's soused—you know, sopping wet.*

so-so *mod.* tipsy; alcohol intoxicated. □ *They were so-so after a while—in front of the television with all that beer and stuff.* □ *He's so-so, but he can still stand up.*

soupy *mod.* alcohol intoxicated; drunk and vomiting. □ *Then he got sort of soupy and broke up the party.* □ *These young kids tend to get soupy rather than pass out.*

soused *mod.* alcohol intoxicated. □ *We were really soused.* □ *All we need right now is a soused bus driver.*

southern-fried *mod.* alcohol intoxicated. (An elaboration of *fried*, referring to *fried chicken*.) □ *Ted and Bill went out and got themselves southern-fried.* □ *When Bob came home southern-fried, his wife nearly killed him.*

sozzled AND **sossled**; **sozzly** *mod.* alcohol intoxicated. □ *Man, was she sozzled.* □ *She was so sozzly she didn't even know her name, or my name, or anybody's name.*

spifflicated AND **spificated** *mod.* alcohol intoxicated. □ *Mrs. Wilmington-Thorpe drank champagne until she was nearly spifflicated.* □ *Being spificated on champagne is not as bad as it sounds.*

squiffed AND **squiffy** *mod.* alcohol intoxicated. □ *She was a little squiffed, but still entertaining.* □ *The hostess was so squiffed she could hardly stand.*

squiff out *in.* to collapse from drink. □ *Hank squiffed out at midnight, right on the dot.* □ *She kept from squiffing out because she didn't trust her date.*

starched AND **starchy** *mod.* alcohol intoxicated. □ *Man, was he starched!* □ *No, he wasn't quite stiff, but he was starched.*

steamed (up) *mod.* alcohol intoxicated and fighting. □ *He was really steamed—and could hardly stand up.* □ *By midnight, Larry was too steamed to drive home, and he had to spend the night.*

stewed to the gills AND **stewed to the ears** *mod.* alcohol intoxicated. □ *Why does a grown man have to get stewed to the gills every night of his life if there isn't something a little wrong with him?* □

Here's old Charlie—stewed to the ears, as always.

stewed (up) AND **stew** *mod.* alcohol intoxicated. □ *Gary was too stewed to remember his name.* □ *The kid was stewed up and scared to death of what his parents were going to do to him.*

stiff AND **stiffed** *mod.* alcohol intoxicated; dead drunk. □ *Kelly was too stiff to find his keys.* □ *She knows how to stop drinking before she gets stiffed.*

stinking (drunk) *mod.* alcohol intoxicated. □ *He was really stinking.* □ *She came within an inch of getting stinking drunk.*

stone blind *mod.* heavily alcohol intoxicated. □ *Jerry drank the sauce till he was stone blind.* □ *When he was stone blind, he drank some more.*

stonkered *mod.* alcohol intoxicated. □ *My buddy here is stonkered and needs a ride, and can I have one, too?* □ *Wally was stonkered beyond any help.*

stozzled *mod.* alcohol intoxicated. □ *My buddy is too stozzled to drive home. Can you give him a lift?* □ *Marty can drink and drink and never get stozzled or even tipsy.*

stuccoed *mod.* alcohol intoxicated. (A play on *plastered.*) □ *The guy was too stuccoed to drive and couldn't stand up to walk.* □ *I can drink without getting stuccoed, mainly because I drink soda.*

stung *mod.* alcohol intoxicated. □ *I'm a little stung by the mule, but I can find my way home if you'll just remind me how to open this door.* □ *She can drink that stuff all evening and never get stung.*

stunned *mod.* alcohol intoxicated. □ *I was simply stunned with the stuff.* □ *Kelly was stunned and had to be carried home to recover.*

stupid *mod.* drunk. □ *These kids are so stupid they can't see straight. They're all going to be sick.* □ *Wayne was too stupid to walk, let alone drive.*

swacked *mod.* alcohol intoxicated. □ *Tracy is too swacked to drive home. Can somebody give her a lift?* □ *He walked straight out of the office and went straight into the bar with the intention of getting swacked.*

swamped *mod.* alcohol intoxicated. □ *Look at him! He's swamped—stoned out of his mind.* □ *Those old boys used to go out and get swamped every Saturday night.*

swigged AND **swiggled** *mod.* alcohol intoxicated; tipsy. □ *Man, is she ever swigged!* □ *He is too swiggled to drive.*

swizzled *mod.* alcohol intoxicated. □ *Fred went out and got himself swizzled.* □ *Man, he is really swizzled!*

swoozled *mod.* alcohol intoxicated. □ *How can anybody be so swoozled on three beers?* □ *Those guys are really swoozled!*

tacky *mod.* alcohol intoxicated. □ *Tom was a little tacky, so he gave me his car keys.* □ *Bruno seems tacky, but that's just the way he is.*

tanked AND **tanked up** *mod.* alcohol intoxicated. □ *She was too tanked to drive.* □ *That old codger is really tanked.*

tanky *mod.* alcohol intoxicated. □ *The guy was just a little tanky.* □ *He found a way to slow down and keep from getting tanky at parties.*

tanned *mod.* alcohol intoxicated. (Preserved like a tanned hide of an animal.) □ *She was completely tanned.* □ *Tom is too tanned to drive. Get him out of that car.*

that way *mod.* alcohol intoxicated. □ *Daddy's that way again.* □ *I'm sorry, but Fred's that way again and can't drive to work.*

thawed *mod.* alcohol intoxicated. □ *Tad is sort of soppy, you might say, thawed.* □ *Do you think he's too thawed to drive us home?*

three sheets in the wind AND **three sheets (to the wind); two sheets to the wind** *mod.* alcohol intoxicated and unsteady. (Sheets are the ropes used to manage a ship's sails. It is assumed that if these ropes were blowing in the wind, the ship would be unmanageable.) □ *He was three sheets to the wind and didn't pay attention to my warning.* □ *By midnight, he was three sheets.*

tiddled *mod.* alcohol intoxicated. □ *He had a tendency to get a little tiddled.* □ *Jack's too tiddled to drive.*

tiffled *mod.* alcohol intoxicated. □ *Harry was too tiffled to drive.* □ *Mary got a little tiffled, but nothing really gross.*

tight *mod.* alcohol intoxicated. □ *Frank was tight and didn't want to drive.* □ *The host got tight and had to go to bed.*

tight as a tick *mod.* alcohol intoxicated. □ *The old man was tight as a tick, but still lucid.* □ *The host got tight as a tick and fell in the pool.*

tipply *mod.* alcohol intoxicated. □ *Ben is too tipply to drive home.* □ *I feel a little tipply.*

toasted *mod.* alcohol intoxicated. □ *The chick got toasted on two glasses of cheap white wine.* □ *I'm not toasted, just a little breathless.*

tongue-tied *mod.* alcohol intoxicated. □ *He was tongue-tied and couldn't stand up.* □ *She's not just tipsy; she's tongue-tied.*

topsy-boozy AND **topsy-boosy** *mod.* alcohol intoxicated. □ *Gary drank until he was topsy-boozy.* □ *She was so topsy-boosy she couldn't stand up.*

topsy-turvy *mod.* alcohol intoxicated. □ *Four glasses of gin and the jerk was totally topsy-turvy.* □ *She was too topsy-turvy to stand up.*

torqued *mod.* alcohol intoxicated. □ *Fred was really torqued and trying to pick fights with everyone.* □ *Mary gets torqued on just a few drinks.*

totaled *mod.* alcohol intoxicated. □ *Tom was too totaled to talk.* □ *Jed was totaled and couldn't see to pay the bill.*

touched *mod.* alcohol intoxicated. □ *She was acting a little touched, but we didn't smell anything on her breath.* □ *Jed is a mite touched, wouldn't you say? Can't talk, walk, or see.*

toxicated AND **toxy** *mod.* alcohol intoxicated. □ *He was just a tad toxy, but no one in the audience could tell.* □ *The boss showed up toxicated after lunch and shocked the secretaries.*

trammeled *mod.* alcohol intoxicated. (Collegiate.) □ *Jim came home trammeled and was sick on the carpet.* □ *Wow, is she trammeled!*

tubed *mod.* alcohol intoxicated. □ *They were both tubed and giggling.* □ *You really look tubed, man!*

tuned *mod.* tipsy; drunk. □ *Wally was a little tuned so Sally swiped his car keys.* □ *Tom was too tuned to stand up, let alone drive.*

tweased *mod.* alcohol intoxicated. □ *Jim came in a little tweased last night.* □ *How tweased can anybody get on two beers?*

tweeked *mod.* alcohol intoxicated. (Collegiate.) □ *They're not really bombed—just tweeked a little.* □ *Fred was too tweeked to stand up.*

twisted *mod.* alcohol intoxicated. □ *She was so twisted she couldn't see.* □ *That chick is really twisted bad.*

under the affluence of incohol *mod.* alcohol intoxicated. (A deliberate spoonerism on *under the influence of alcohol*.) □ *Perhaps I am under the affluence of incohol just a little bit.* □ *You are very, very much under the affluence of incohol, as you have so aptly put it.*

under the table *mod.* alcohol intoxicated. □ *Jed was under the table by midnight.* □ *By 3:00 in the morning, everyone was under the table.*

under the weather *mod.* alcohol intoxicated. □ *Daddy's under the weather again.* □ *Wally's just a tad under the weather.*

up a tree *mod.* alcohol intoxicated. □ *Only two glasses of booze and he was up a tree for sure.* □ *My buddy here is up a tree and needs a crash for the night.*

upholstered *mod.* alcohol intoxicated. □ *She was a little upholstered, but not seriously impaired.* □ *He drank till he was comfortably upholstered.*

up the pole *mod.* alcohol intoxicated. □ *You sound a little up the pole. Why don't you call back when you're sober?* □ *She's up the pole and shouldn't drive.*

varnished *mod.* alcohol intoxicated. □ *Really varnished, he was. Couldn't see a hole in a ladder.* □ *That lady is too varnished to drive. If you see her getting into a car, call the cops.*

vegetable *mod.* alcohol intoxicated. □ *He's a tad vegetable but not in a stupor.* □ *Helen drank till she was totally vegetable.*

vomatose *mod.* drunk, vomiting, and nearly comatose. (From *vomit* and *comatose*.) □ *Claude is completely vomatose. What a party!* □ *Beavis got himself vomatose and messed up the driveway.*

walking on rocky socks *mod.* alcohol intoxicated. □ *She's sort of walking on rocky socks.* □ *He looks like he's walking on rocky socks.*

wall-eyed *mod.* alcohol intoxicated. □ *Wow, is he ever wall-eyed!* □ *Who's the wall-eyed guy carrying the ham sandwich?*

warped *mod.* drug intoxicated. □ *Too many yellows made Jerry warped as the dickens.* □ *I think Max is permanently warped.*

waxed *mod.* alcohol intoxicated. □ *Tom is too waxed to talk.* □ *Sam got waxed and had to be taken home.*

well-fixed AND **well-heeled** *mod.* alcohol intoxicated. □ *By midnight, he was pretty well-fixed.* □ *You might say he is well-fixed. You might say he's dead drunk, too.*

well-oiled *mod.* alcohol intoxicated. □ *He was well-oiled and couldn't stand up.* □ *Get him well-oiled and break the news to him.*

wet *mod.* alcohol intoxicated. □ *The jerk is wet and can't drive home.* □ *He's been drinking since noon and is pretty wet.*

whazood AND **waa-zooed** *mod.* alcohol intoxicated. □ *Man, is she whazood!* □ *Pete was too waa-zooed to stand up.*

whiffled *mod.* alcohol intoxicated. □ *Jed found himself a mite whiffled, but nobody else knew.* □ *That guy really looks whiffled.*

whipped *mod.* alcohol intoxicated. □ *He slid under the table—whipped, for sure.* □ *She was too whipped to find money to pay her bill.*

whittled *mod.* alcohol intoxicated; filled with liquor. □ *Fred's whittled and can't hardly see.* □ *Why does he keep getting so whittled?*

whooshed *mod.* alcohol intoxicated. □ *Jerry was totally whooshed by midnight.* □ *Hank was whooshed but thought he could drive home.*

wing heavy *mod.* alcohol intoxicated. □ *Ken's a little wing heavy and can't fly straight.* □ *From the way he's staggering, I'd say he's more than a little wing heavy.*

woofled *mod.* alcohol intoxicated. □ *Good grief, was he woofled!* □ *Did I get woofled last night? I just don't remember.*

woozy *mod.* alcohol intoxicated. □ *I felt a little woozy, but that didn't stop me from having more.* □ *Woozy as I am, I can still drive. Now, give me back my keys.*

zagged *mod.* alcohol intoxicated. □ *How can anybody get so zagged on three beers?* □ *Wow, is she zagged!*

zapped *mod.* alcohol intoxicated. □ *We all got zapped and then went home.* □ *Marty is too zapped to stand up.*

zissified *mod.* alcohol intoxicated. □ *Two of them were zissified on rum. The rest just got a little wrecked.* □ *Man, is she zissified!*

zoned (out) *mod.* alcohol intoxicated. □ *What's the matter with your eyes? Get a little zoned last night?* □ *Yeah, I'm sort of zoned out.*

zoobang *mod.* alcohol intoxicated. □ *Boy howdy! Are you ever zoobang!* □ *So, you think I'm zoobang? You want to step outside?*

zooed *mod.* drunk. □ *Sam likes to go out and get zooed every weekend.* □ *Garth is so silly when he's zooed.*

zooted *mod.* alcohol intoxicated. □ *Both of them were zooted to the max.* □ *She was too zooted to even see straight.*

zorked *mod.* alcohol intoxicated. □ *She was zorked beyond help.* □ *Everybody was essentially zorked by midnight.*

zozzled *mod.* drunk. □ *Dave was too zozzled to drive.* □ *John had a few, but he didn't get zozzled or anything like that.*

INTOXICATED - DRUGS

backed up *mod.* drug intoxicated. □ *Oh my God, I am really backed up!* □ *Old Benny's really backed up.*

beaned up *mod.* high on amphetamines. □ *Ernie is beaned up again.* □ *Two students were beaned up and were sent home.*

blixed *mod.* mildly drug intoxicated. □ *He was a little blixed when I last saw him.* □ *He has been blixed for hours.*

bonged (out) *mod.* exhausted from too much marijuana. □ *I was bonged all through the holidays.* □ *She was still bonged out after the first week of classes.*

charged (up) 1. *mod.* slightly overdosed with drugs. □ *He was talking fast and nodding his head back and forth. I think he was charged.* □ *The kid is usually charged up by class time.* **2.** *mod.* drug intoxicated. □ *The way she sat there nodding, you knew she was completely charged up.* □ *Paul was one charged up guy after the session.*

crisp *mod.* drug intoxicated. □ *The crisp guy waving the bra is the one we are after.* □ *Man, is he crisp!*

destroyed *mod.* drug intoxicated. □ *Wow, what happened to Tracy? She looks destroyed.* □ *The kid who took angel dust is destroyed most of the time.*

dopey *mod.* drug intoxicated. □ *He looks sort of dopey.* □ *The chick is too dopey to drive. See that she gets home, Ralphy, huh?*

drug (out) AND **drug out** *mod.* down; depressed. □ *Man, am I drug!* □ *We are all drug out after that meeting.*

enhanced *mod.* high on marijuana. □ *Max is sort of enhanced, as usual.* □ *Fred is enhanced by dinnertime each day.*

fixed *mod.* doped; intoxicated. □ *Max is comfortable now that he's fixed.* □ *He was fixed and broke—in a real mess, I'd say.*

GBed *mod.* "goofballed"; drug intoxicated. □ *Pete is GBed again.* □ *Gert got GBed fairly often before the accident.*

gonged *mod.* drug intoxicated. (Originally intoxicated on opium.) □ *Bruno found himself in the alley, gonged.* □ *Ernie was too gonged to stand up.*

gouch off *in.* to pass out under the influence of drugs. □ *After taking the stuff, Gary gouched off.* □ *After the fix, Gert waited patiently to gouch off.*

groovy *mod.* drug intoxicated. □ *Three beers and he was a little groovy.* □ *She's groovy, but she can still stand up.*

hopped up *mod.* stimulated by drugs. □ *The two of them were hopped up most of the time.* □ *Two hopped-up kids were hunkered down in the alley.*

horsed AND **on the horse** *mod.* under the effects of heroin; addicted to heroin. □ *Gert was totally horsed.* □ *How long have you been on the horse?*

hurt *mod.* drug intoxicated. (Black.) □ *Gert was really hurt and nodding and drooling.* □ *One hit of that horse trank and he was really hurt.*

hyped (up) *mod.* drug intoxicated. □ *Gert is happiest when she's hyped.* □ *Here comes another hyped-up musician.*

jacked up AND **jacked** *mod.* high on drugs. □ *He's jacked up, and he may have ODed.* □ *The poor kid is jacked up most of the time now.*

laid AND **layed** *mod.* drug intoxicated. □ *Man, did I get myself laid.* □ *Are you too layed to drive home?*

monolithic *mod.* heavily drug intoxicated. (A play on *stoned.*) □ *She's not just stoned, she's monolithic!* □ *I was monolithic—dead drunk.*

nodded out *mod.* in heroin euphoria; under the influence of heroin. □ *Max nodded out after his fix.* □ *He is upstairs nodded out.*

numbed out *mod.* nearly paralyzed by phencyclidine (PCP). □ *The teenager was nearly numbed out when they brought her in.* □ *Max was totally numbed out on angel dust.*

on the beam AND **beaming** *mod.* under the effects of marijuana. □ *Walter is on the beam again. How can he hold a job?*

□ *The only time that Max is happy is when he is beaming.*

out of this world *mod.* drug intoxicated. □ *Man, is she ever out of this world! What did she drink?* □ *He drank until he was out of this world.*

overamped *mod.* high on amphetamines; overdosed with amphetamines. □ *Max is overamped again.* □ *Two students were overamped and got sent to the counselor.*

over the hump *mod.* drug intoxicated. □ *Max is over the hump now. He is stoned.* □ *This stuff makes you sick at first. Then suddenly you are over the hump and floating.*

phazed AND **phased** *mod.* intoxicated with marijuana. □ *Man, I was phazed out of my mind!* □ *How much booze does it take you to get really phased?*

phumfed *mod.* drug intoxicated. □ *You can't get your work done when you are totally phumfed.* □ *She gets phumfed on pot every afternoon.*

scattered *mod.* drug intoxicated; confused by drug use. □ *Those poor kids are so scattered, they can't even get themselves to class.* □ *Fred must spend half his life scattered and sleeping.*

skagged out *mod.* drug intoxicated; very high. □ *Max was rocking back and forth on the top step—skagged out, as usual.* □ *He got to the point where being skagged out was more important than eating.*

skating *mod.* drug intoxicated. □ *He's high, all right—I'd say he's skating.* □ *He took some wicked silo and is totally skating.*

snaved in *mod.* drug intoxicated. □ *The poor guy was as snaved in as they come. Really fried.* □ *By midnight they were so snaved in they couldn't walk.*

stoned out of one's head AND **stoned out of one's gourd** *mod.* under the effects of marijuana. □ *Tiffany was stoned out of her head and started giggling.* □ *The guy was stoned out of his gourd and should never have been driving.*

strung out 1. AND **strung (up)** *mod.* drug intoxicated and bewildered. □

Bruno is really strung out lately. What's he shooting now? □ *Tim is sort of strung out and doesn't even remember what he took.* **2.** *mod.* badly addicted to heroin; dissipated by heroin. □ *Harry's strung out for good, I guess.* □ *Clare is strung out and can't deny her problem any longer.*

taken AND **had; took** *mod.* drug intoxicated; unconscious from drugs. □ *The guy in the corner booth was taken and crying in his beer.* □ *His eyes were bloodshot, his hands were shaking—he was had.*

tall *mod.* high on drugs; intoxicated with marijuana. □ *When Jerry gets a little tall, he gets overwhelmed with a sense of guilt.* □ *She seems a little tall. What's she on?*

turned on *mod.* drug intoxicated. □ *Jerry's turned on by noon—every day.* □ *The kid over there looks sort of turned on. Let's go talk to him a bit.*

wide *mod.* drug intoxicated. □ *Who is that wide dude?* □ *How'd you get so wide, man?*

zapped *mod.* drug intoxicated. □ *We all got zapped and then went home.* □ *Marty is too zapped to stand up.*

zerked (out) *mod.* drug intoxicated; heavily drug intoxicated. □ *Gary looked really zerked out, and I thought he was really stoned.* □ *Max gets zerked out every weekend.*

zipped *mod.* drug intoxicated. □ *That tootsie left them zipped.* □ *The kid is too zipped to talk.*

zoned (out) *mod.* drug intoxicated. □ *What's the matter with your eyes? Get a little zoned last night?* □ *Yeah, I'm sort of zoned out.*

INTOXICATION

going high *n.* a long-lasting type of drug high. □ *Freddie had a going high and was in trouble.* □ *Gert was always after a real going high.*

high *n.* a state of euphoria caused by drugs or alcohol. □ *His life is nothing but one high after another.* □ *Her only goal is a high.*

hold one's high *tr.* to behave reasonably well under the influence of drugs. □

Gert is having a harder and harder time holding her high. □ *Ernie can't hold his high. What a creep!*

joy ride *n.* a state of euphoria from drug use. □ *This stuff is a real joy ride.* □ *Ernie's on a little joy ride right now and can't come to the phone.*

rolling buzz *n.* a long-lasting drug high. □ *What I want is a nice rolling buzz.* □ *That stuff will give you a rolling buzz without putting you to sleep.*

INTOXICATION - BAD

bummer AND **bum trip** *n.* a bad drug experience. □ *She almost didn't get back from a bum trip.* □ *This bummer comes from mixing pills.*

bum out *in.* to have a bad experience with drugs. □ *I bummed out on angel dust.* □ *She bummed out once too often and gave up the stuff altogether.*

freak (out) *n.* a bad drug experience; a psychotic reaction to the drug LSD. (Usually **freak-out** or **freakout**.) □ *The poor kid had a freak-out and never really recovered.* □ *Some of them get turned off to drugs by a really good freakout.*

horrors *n.* frightening hallucinations from drugs. □ *Once he had gone through the horrors, he swore off for good.* □ *Pete had the horrors and had to be hospitalized.*

vegged out *mod.* debilitated by drugs or alcohol. □ *Ernie is vegged out and has quit his job and everything.* □ *Won't be long till Larry is vegged out altogether.*

INTOXICATION - DRUGS

bad trip *n.* a bad experience with a drug. □ *My first trip was a bad trip, and I never took another.* □ *The guide is supposed to talk you down from a bad trip.*

blow someone's mind *tr.* [for a drug] to intoxicate someone. □ *This stuff will blow your mind.* □ *That blue acid blew my mind.*

free trip *n.* an echo or a *flashback* of an L.S.D. experience. □ *The kid got a free trip, and it scared her to death.* □ *If these free trips continue, we may have to run some tests.*

good trip *n.* a good session with LSD or some other drug. □ *Paul said he had a good trip, but he looks like the devil.* □ *One good trip deserves another. At least that's what my guru says.*

trip *n.* a *high* from a drug. □ *Me and Sid went on a little trip.* □ *The trip was great, but once was enough.*

INTOXICATION - END

bring someone down *tr.* to terminate one's own or someone else's drug experience. □ *It took a lot to bring her down.* □ *We brought down the two of them carefully.*

come down hard *in.* to come out of a drug use session badly. □ *Mike came down hard, and it took them a long time to calm him down.* □ *Some kids who come down hard will need treatment, but none of them get it unless they look like they are bad off.*

INTOXICATION - ONSET

belt *n.* the *rush* or jolt from an injection of a drug. □ *This stuff has one hell of a belt.* □ *The belt nearly knocked her over.*

blast *n.* the kick from taking or injecting a drug. □ *That stuff really gives me a blast.* □ *With a blast like that, somebody's gonna get hooked fast.*

burn *n.* the charge or *rush* after the injection of a drug into a vein. □ *Man, wait'll you taste the burn from this stuff.* □ *I don't want a big burn; just drag it out for about an hour.*

buzz *n.* the initial effects of drinking alcohol or taking certain drugs. □ *Sam got a little buzz from the wine, but he still needed something stronger.* □ *She took a hit and leaned back, waiting for the buzz.*

call *n.* the early effects of a drug. □ *You may not get the call on this stuff for twenty minutes or more.* □ *A guy like this is only happy when he senses the call.*

charge *n.* a drug's initial onset. □ *This stuff has no charge at all.* □ *What kind of charge do you expect out of half-cashed weed?*

come on *in.* to feel the effects of a drug; for a drug to take effect. □ *After what* seemed a long time, I began to come on to the stuff. □ When I came on, I decided I didn't like it, but then it was too late.

edge *n.* drunkenness; the early stage of intoxication from alcohol or drugs. □ *She was beginning to show a little edge, but she obviously still could drive.* □ *The edge was starting, so Kelly slowed down her drinking.*

get off (on something) *in.* to take a drug and experience a *rush.* □ *Max likes to get off, but he's got his business to run.* □ *Tracy likes getting off better than anything else.*

go up *in.* to start to feel the effects of a drug. □ *Gert started to go up and suddenly fell asleep.* □ *The guy couldn't wait to get home and go up.*

jag *n.* a drug rush. □ *This stuff has no jag at all.* □ *How big a jag do you want?*

jolt *n.* the *rush* from an injection of drugs. □ *This stuff doesn't have much jolt.* □ *What kind of jolt do you want?*

kick *n.* the jolt from a drug or a drink of strong liquor. □ *This stuff really has a kick.* □ *The kick nearly knocked Harry over.*

lift AND **lift-up** *n.* drug euphoria. □ *This stuff'll give you quite a lift.* □ *The lift-up from the shot jarred her bones.*

org *n.* the *rush* caused by potent drugs. (From *orgasm.*) □ *Max hated the vomiting when he first took it, but he loved the org.* □ *Does this stuff give you a real org?*

rush *n.* a burst of energy or good feeling from a drug; the explosive euphoria of some kinds of drugs. □ *Man, this stuff really gives me a rush.* □ *What kind of rush does this have?*

tag *n.* euphoria from drug use; a drug rush. □ *This tag from this mojo is something to behold.* □ *This trash has no tag at all.*

trip *in.* to experience a *high* from a drug, especially LSD. □ *Don't bother Max. He's tripping.* □ *He trips about every other day.*

zoom AND **zoom off** *in.* to have a drug rush. □ *Sam zoomed off and thought he*

had gone to heaven. □ *Max knows how to keep zooming for about twenty minutes.*

INTOXICATION - RECOVERY

come down *in.* to begin to recover from the effects of alcohol or drug intoxication. □ *She came down slow, which was good.* □ *It was hard to get her to come down.*

sleep it off *tr.* to sleep while the effects of drugs or alcohol wear off. □ *I'm polluted, I guesh. Have to get home and shleep it off.* □ *She'll be okay when she sleeps it off.*

INTOXICATION - SEVERE

overjolt AND **OJ** 1. *n.* an overdose of drugs, especially of heroin. (The abbreviation is an initialism. Drugs.) □ *Ted is suffering from a serious OJ.* □ *That overjolt nearly killed her.* 2. *in.* to take an overdose of drugs, especially of heroin. □ *She overjolted once too often.* □ *If you OJ again, you will probably die.*

INTOXICATION - SLEEP

flake (out) *in.* to fall asleep after drug use. □ *An hour after she took the stuff, she just flaked.* □ *Pete popped a few pills and flaked out.*

INTRUSION

crash *tr. & in.* to attend a party or other event uninvited. □ *Some clown tried to crash the rally, but my dad called the cops.* □ *The boys who tried to crash also broke a window.*

crasher *n.* a person who attends a party uninvited. □ *The crashers ruined the party, and my dad called the cops.* □ *The crashers were no more rude than the guests.*

fifth wheel *n.* an extra and unneeded person. □ *I feel like such a fifth wheel around here.* □ *Hank is just a fifth wheel. Send him home.*

get a toehold *tr.* to work one's way into some association or relationship. □ *As soon as I get a toehold in the company, I'll be more relaxed.* □ *Once he gets a toehold, you'll never get rid of him.*

sound off (about something) *in.* to speak out of turn about something. □

Who asked you to sound off about this? □ *Don't just sound off without raising your hand.*

third wheel *n.* an extra person; a person who gets in the way. (Such a person is as useful as a third wheel on a bicycle.) □ *I feel like such a third wheel around here.* □ *Well, let's face it. We don't need you. You are a third wheel.*

IRRELEVANCE

dead *mod.* (of an issue) no longer germane; no longer of any importance. □ *Forget it! It's a dead issue.* □ *The project is dead. Don't waste any more time on it.*

dead horse *n.* a *dead issue*, especially one that is referred to continually. (Often with *beat, whip.*) □ *Forget it! Don't waste time whipping a dead horse.* □ *The whole business is a dead horse. Forget it.*

dead issue *n.* an issue that doesn't matter anymore. □ *It's a dead issue. Forget it.* □ *The question of my late arrival is a dead issue.*

dead letter *n.* an issue that does not matter anymore. □ *This contract is a dead letter. Forget it!* □ *The mayor's plan for our raises is a dead letter.*

out of the picture *mod.* no longer relevant to a situation; departed; dead. □ *Now that Tom is out of the picture, we needn't concern ourselves about his objections.* □ *With her husband out of the picture, she can begin living.*

JAIL

away *mod.* in prison. (Underworld.) □ *My cousin is away for a year.* □ *The judge wanted to put him away for two years, but decided on one instead.*

big house *n.* a state or federal penitentiary. (Always with *the*.) □ *It's either go straight now or spend the rest of your life in the big house.* □ *Two years in the big house is like two years in a custom-made hell.*

brig *n.* jail. (From the term for a naval prison or a shipboard jail.) □ *Throw this jerk in the brig.* □ *The brig in that one-horse town is a mess.*

calaboose *n.* jail. (From a Spanish word.) □ *One night in the calaboose is enough.* □ *Are we going to tell what happened, or are we going to spend the night in the calaboose?*

can *n.* jail. (Usually with *the*.) □ *I had to spend the night in the can, but it wasn't too bad.* □ *You've seen one can, you've seen 'em all.*

clink *n.* jail. □ *We'll throw you in the clink if you don't talk.* □ *One night in the clink was enough.*

con *n.* a convict. □ *One of the cons keeps a snake in his cell for a pet.* □ *Is that guy in the gray pajamas one of the escaped cons?*

cooler *n.* jail. (Usually with *the*.) □ *Do you want to talk, or do you want to spend a little time in the cooler?* □ *Let me outa this cooler!*

drunk tank *n.* a jail cell where drunks are kept. □ *A couple of hours in the drunk tank really made me think about alcohol.* □ *They hose down the drunk tank every hour on Friday and Saturday nights.*

Graybar Hotel AND **Graystone College** *n.* a jail; a prison. □ *The two cops had to spend two years in Graybar Hotel with some of the inmates they had caught over the past few years.* □ *Max has graduated from Graystone College three times in the last ten years.*

hoosegow *n.* a jail. □ *Learning to read can shorten one's time in the hoosegow.* □ *The judge threw the punk in the hoosegow for a few days.*

house of many doors *n.* a prison. □ *Max faced a sentence of a few years in the house of many doors.* □ *Bruno just got out of the house with many doors and is looking for somebody to pull a job with.*

joint *n.* a jail; a prison. (Underworld.) □ *Lefty just got out of the joint.* □ *He learned a lot in the joint that he was anxious to try out.*

jug *n.* jail. (Usually with *the*.) □ *Take it easy. I don't want to end up in the jug.* □ *A couple of days in the jug would do you fine.*

junk tank *n.* a jail cell where addicts are kept. □ *That junk tank is a very dangerous place.* □ *Nobody sleeps in the junk tank.*

pen *n.* a penitentiary; prison. (Underworld.) □ *Max got sent to the pen for fifteen years.* □ *After a few years in the pen, he began to appreciate freedom.*

poky *n.* jail; a jail cell. □ *She spent a day in the poky.* □ *Have you ever been in the poky?*

screw *n.* a jailer. (Underworld.) □ *See if you can get the screw's attention.* □ *I'm sick, screw! Let me out!*

slammer *n.* a jail. □ *I got out of the slammer on Monday and was back in by Wednesday.* □ *The slammer in this town is like a hotel.*

stir *n.* prison. (Underworld.) □ *I can't stand being in stir!* □ *Stir is very dull— and dangerous.*

stir crazy *mod.* anxious and mentally disturbed from being confined, as in prison. □ *I was going stir crazy in my little room, so I moved to a bigger place.* □ *I get sort of stir crazy in the winter.*

tank *n.* a jail cell for holding drunks. □ *Maybe a night in the tank would give you a chance to think about being a full-time drunk.* □ *One night in the tank was enough to make John take the pledge.*

yardbird *n.* a convict. □ *Who's the yardbird with the headphones on his noodle?* □ *So, Charlie was a yardbird. So what?*

JEER

bazoo *n.* a jeer. □ *They gave Ted the old bazoo when he fumbled the ball.* □ *A chorus of bazoos and hoots rebuked the coach when he threw the chair on the court.*

bird *n.* a derisive noise made with the lips; a raspberry. □ *The third time he fumbled, he was greeted by two thousand mouths making the bird.* □ *You guys making the bird aren't perfect either.*

Bronx cheer *n.* a rude noise made with the lips; a *raspberry.* □ *The little air compressor in the corner of the parking lot made a noise like a Bronx cheer.* □ *He got only a Bronx cheer for his efforts.*

give someone the raspberry *tr.* to make a rude noise with the lips at someone. □ *The audience gave him the raspberry, which gave him some second thoughts about his choice of career.* □ *Even after his grandstand play, they gave him the raspberry.*

JEWELRY

ice *n.* diamonds; jewels. (Underworld.) □ *That old dame has tons of ice in her hotel room.* □ *Look at the ice on her!*

rock *n.* a diamond or other gemstone. □ *Look at the size of that rock in her ring.*

□ *How many rocks are there decorating the edges of your watch?*

sparkler *n.* a diamond; gemstones. □ *Look at the sparklers on that old dame.* □ *Janice has a new sparkler on her finger.*

JOINING

ace in (to something) *in.* to happen onto something good; to manage to get into something. □ *I hope I can ace into the afternoon physics class.* □ *I don't know how I aced in. I guess I was just lucky.*

get in on the act *in.* to become involved in something with someone else. (The involvement is not necessarily welcome.) □ *Everybody wants to get in on the act.* □ *Why are you trying to get in on the act?*

get into something *in.* to become deeply involved with something. □ *I got into computers when I was in junior high school.* □ *When did you get into foreign films?*

in deep *mod.* deeply involved (with someone or something). □ *Mary and Sam are in deep.* □ *Max is in deep with the mob.*

rope someone in *tr.* to cause someone to get involved in some project. □ *She's always trying to rope me into her club.* □ *Let's rope in someone to help with cleaning up.*

thick *mod.* involved (with someone). □ *Sam and Mary are really thick.* □ *They're thick as can be.*

wired into someone or something *mod.* concerned with someone or something; really involved with someone or something. □ *Mary is really wired into classical music.* □ *Sam and Martha are totally wired into each other.*

JOKING
See also **LAUGHTER**.

corker *n.* someone or something good, funny, or entertaining. □ *That was a real corker. I thought I'd die laughing.* □ *Tracy is quite a corker. I bet she's fun at parties.*

crack *n.* a joke; a smart-aleck remark. □ *Another crack like that and your nose will* be a little flatter than it is. □ Who made that crack?

dirty joke *n.* an obscene joke. □ Fred told a dirty joke that shocked almost everyone. □ No dirty jokes around here. We get enough of that on television.

gag *n.* a joke; a trick. □ She tells the best gags. □ What a great gag! Everybody will love it.

gas *n.* a joke; a prank; a wild time. □ The party was a gas. □ What a gas! I had a great time.

get a buzz out of someone or something *tr.* to get some humor from someone or something. □ I thought you'd get a buzz out of that gag. □ I hope you get a buzz out of Ted. He's a funny guy.

hoot *n.* a joke; something laughable. □ The whole business was a terrific hoot. □ The skit was a hoot, and everyone enjoyed it.

joke *tr.* to tease someone; to make fun of someone. □ Everybody was joking my roommate because of her accent. □ Don't joke me, man. I do the best I can.

josh *tr. & in.* to tease someone; to kid someone. □ Stop joshing. Be serious. □ You're just joshing me!

killer *n.* a very funny joke. □ That last one was a killer! □ She told a killer about a red-nosed juicer.

rib-tickler *n.* a joke; something very funny. □ That was a real rib-tickler. I'll remember that joke. □ She told a rib-tickler, and everybody laughed.

riot *n.* someone or something entertaining or funny. □ Tom was a riot last night. □ Her joke was a real riot.

rip snorter *n.* a remarkable person or thing; a hilarious joke. (Folksy.) □ Old Fred is a real rip snorter. □ Her new car is a rip snorter, I tell you. □ Let me tell

you a rip snorter about a farmer and his cow. □ Judy can tell some rip snorters.

scream *n.* someone or something very funny. (Always with a.) □ The joke Tom told was really a scream. □ Tom is always a scream at parties.

stitch *n.* a very funny person. (Always with a.) □ Harry is a stitch. What a sense of humor! □ Clare is a stitch, too. Her jokes can slay you.

straight man *n.* someone who sets up jokes or gags so that someone else can say the punch line. □ I need a straight man to pick up on all my jokes. □ I'm tired of being a straight man for a has-been comic.

yak *n.* a joke. □ That was a lousy yak. □ Don't tell that yak again. It's not a winner.

yuck *n.* a joke. □ Come on! Chill out! It was just a yuck. □ Not a very good yuck if you ask me.

JUNKYARD

boneyard *n.* a junkyard. □ I got a used right-hand door from a boneyard. □ This old car's ready for the boneyard.

JUSTICE

comeuppance *n.* a well-deserved rebuke. □ He finally got the comeuppance that he's needed for so long. □ I gave her a comeuppance she'll never forget.

kangaroo court *n.* a bogus or extra-legal court. □ Is this a newspaper office or a kangaroo court? □ You have turned this interview into a kangaroo court.

serve someone right *tr.* to be just what someone deserves. □ It would serve you right if you lost your money. □ He fell down. It serves him right.

That'll teach someone. *sent.* "That is what someone deserves." □ That'll teach you to pull out in front of me. □ I hit him on the head. That'll teach him.

KEY

twister *n.* a key. (Underworld.) □ *You got the twister for this joint?* □ *Bruno snatched the jailer's twisters and waited until midnight to try something.*

KINDNESS

See also **FRIENDLINESS**.

Be my guest. *sent.* "Please go in front of me."; "Please make yourself comfortable in my home." □ *John stood aside at the open door and said to Walter, "Be my guest."* □ *Help yourself to whatever you need. Be my guest.*

big of someone *mod.* nice of someone. (Often sarcastic.) □ *A whole pound. Wow, that is really big of you!* □ *Three daisies he gave me! "Oh, that's big of you!" I said, batting my eyes.*

cut someone a break *tr.* to give someone a break. □ *Come on, cut me a break! I'm a good guy!* □ *I was only a few minutes late! Cut me a break! Don't dock my pay!*

Give me a break! AND **Gimme a break** *exclam.* "Don't be so harsh!"; "Give me a chance!" □ *I'm sorry! I'll do better! Give me a break!* □ *I was only late once! Gimme a break!*

Have a heart! *exclam.* "Be compassionate!"; "Be kind!" □ *Have a heart! Give me another chance.* □ *Come on! Have a heart!*

softhearted *mod.* tender-hearted; sympathetic. □ *She is too softhearted to handle this job.* □ *He is a softhearted guy who can help our cause a lot.*

soft touch *n.* a gentle way of handling someone or something. □ *Bess has a soft touch and can bring both sides together.* □ *Kelly lacks the kind of soft touch needed for this kind of negotiation.*

KINSHIP

cuz *n.* cousin. (Old colloquial.) □ *I've got to go to Denver to visit my cuz.* □ *My cuz came to visit for the weekend.*

dad *n.* one's father; any father; any old man. (Also a term of address. Capitalized when referring to one's own father.) □ *Hey, Dad, can I use the car tonight?* □ *Well, dad, how's it going?*

empty-nesters *n.* parents whose children have grown and moved out. □ *There are a few adjustments that empty-nesters have to make.* □ *I don't mind being an empty-nester. There's more room.*

ex *n.* a former spouse or lover. □ *My ex is in town, but we don't talk much anymore.* □ *Her ex remarried.*

folks *n.* one's parents. (Always with the possessive.) □ *I'll have to ask my folks if I can go.* □ *Her folks are sort of mad at her.*

fossil *n.* a parent. □ *My fossils would never agree to anything like that.* □ *Would your fossils permit that?*

hubby *n.* a husband. □ *My hubby will be late tonight.* □ *Where is your hubby tonight?*

mom *n.* a mother. (Also a term of address. Capitalized when used as the name of one's own mother.) □ *My mom is the greatest!* □ *Mom, can I have a bigger allowance?*

old lady AND **old woman** *n.* (one's) mother. □ *I'll ask my old lady if I can go.* □ *What time does your old lady get home?*

old lady AND **old woman** *n.* (one's) wife. □ *I wonder what my old lady is cooking* for dinner tonight. □ *My old lady doesn't like for me to go out without her.*

old man *n.* (one's) father. □ *I'll ask my old man if I can go.* □ *What time does your old man get home?*

old man *n.* (one's) husband. □ *My old man is downstairs fixing the furnace.* □ *My old man is sick and can't come with me.*

(parental) units *n.* parents. (Teens. Also a term of address.) □ *I don't think my parental units will let me stay out that late.* □ *Hey, units! I need to talk to you about something really important.*

pops *n.* one's father; any older man. (Also a term of address.) □ *Hey, pops! How you doing?* □ *Well, pops, what do you think?*

rent(al)s *n.* one's parents. (Teens. Also a term of address.) □ *I'll have to ask my rents.* □ *Hey, rentals, let's go out for dinner.*

sis *n.* sister. (Also a term of address and a common pet name for one's sister.) □ *Come on, sis. We're going to be late.* □ *Well, sis, good luck.*

wallet *n.* a college student's father and financial source. □ *My wallet won't send me another penny this semester.* □ *Why don't you tell your wallet you are starving?*

whole fam damily *n.* the entire family. (Always with *the*. A deliberate spoonerism for "whole damn family.") □ *The whole fam damily has had this virus. Yuck!* □ *There's enough here for the whole fam damily.*

KISS

bill and coo *in.* to kiss and cuddle. (In the manner of lovebirds.) □ *Keep an eye on those kids. They aren't going to be satisfied with billing and cooing forever, you know.* □ *If they bill and coo enough now, maybe they will remember how when they're older.*

chew face *tr.* to kiss. (More jocular than crude.) □ *A couple of kids were in a doorway chewin' face.* □ *Hey Tracy! Wanna go chew face?*

eat face *tr.* to kiss deeply. □ *There were some kids eating face over in the corner.* □ *Tim and Karen were in the back seat eating face.*

fish-kiss 1. *tr. & in.* to kiss (someone) with puckered up lips. (Collegiate.) □ *He can fish-kiss like an expert, which is like being an expert at nothing.* □ *He fish-kissed me, then ran back to his car.* **2.** *n.* a kiss made with puckered up lips. (Collegiate.) □ *One more fish-kiss tonight, and I am going to scream.* □ *The actor planted a big fish-kiss right on her lips and frightened her.*

French kiss 1. *n.* kissing using the tongue; open-mouth kissing. □ *What's French about a French kiss?* □ *I didn't know whether I was going to get a French kiss or a fish-kiss.* **2.** *tr.* to kiss someone using the tongue. □ *Kids like to try to French kiss each other at an early age. It's part of growing up.* □ *He tried to French kiss me, but I stopped him.*

get lip *tr.* to get some kissing; to *neck.* (Teens.) □ *Jim's been out getting lip again. Look at the lipstick.* □ *These kids talk about getting lip. Ye gods, how crude!*

grouse *in.* to *neck;* to pet and kiss. □ *They stopped grousing in order to come up for air.* □ *They were grousing in the back seat the whole trip.*

grovel *in.* to fondle or pet. □ *They spent the whole time in the back seat groveling.* □ *He always wants to go out and grovel.*

heavy necking *n.* hugging and kissing, plus intimate caresses. □ *Mary and Sam are past heavy necking.* □ *The teacher caught them at some heavy necking in the closet.*

hickey AND **hicky** *n.* a love bite; a mark on the skin caused by biting or sucking. □ *He's mad at her because she gave him a hicky.* □ *She wore a high collar to cover up a hickey.*

kissyface 1. *n.* kissing. □ *There was a lot of kissyface going on in the back seat.* □ *They're mostly involved with kissyface at this age.* **2.** *mod.* feeling the need to kiss and be kissed. □ *I feel all kissyface.* □

They were both sort of kissyface, so they left.

lip *tr. & in.* to kiss someone intimately. □ *The two of them were in the corner, lipping intently.* □ *Hey, honeycakes, I really want to lip you.*

make out *in.* to neck and pet. □ *I still like to make out, but it's hard with dentures.* □ *He started making out when he was twelve.*

mash *in.* to neck and pet. (Collegiate.) □ *Who are those two mashing in the corner?* □ *I can't spend every evening mashing with you!*

maw *tr. & in.* to kiss and pet; to smooch. (Probably from *maul.*) □ *Come on, don't maw me. You've been watching too many movies—or too few.* □ *Let's go out somewhere and maw.*

monkey bite *n.* a kiss that leaves a blotch or mark. □ *Who gave you that monkey bite?* □ *Do you have some makeup that'll cover this monkey bite?*

mush *n.* romance; lovemaking; kissing. □ *I can't stand movies with lots of mush in them.* □ *When an actor looks at an actress like that, you just know that there's gonna be some mush.*

neck *in.* to cuddle and kiss. (Always in reference to lovers or boy-girl relationships.) □ *There are some teenagers in the back room, necking.* □ *Let's go somewhere quiet and neck.*

park *in.* to *neck* or to make love, especially in a parked car. □ *Do kids still park, or do they just watch television?* □ *They still park, but they don't have a name for it anymore.*

pitch (the) woo *tr.* to kiss and caress; to woo (someone). (Old but still heard.) □ *They were out by the barn pitching woo.* □ *Old Ted can hardly see anymore, but he can still pitch the woo.*

play tonsil hockey *tr.* to kiss deeply, using the tongue. □ *Kids sit around in cars, playing tonsil hockey all evening.* □ *Sally's mother caught her playing tonsil hockey with George and grounded her.*

smacker *n.* a kiss. □ *He planted a smacker square on her lips. She kicked him*

in the shins for his trouble. □ *Barlowe was greeted at the door by a lovely, cuddly chick in a nightie—eyes closed and lips parted for a better than average smacker. He really wished—just for a moment— that he hadn't rung the wrong doorbell.*

smooch 1. *in.* to kiss and *neck.* □ *Too much smooching in a movie ruins it for me.* □ *I like to smooch myself, but I don't enjoy watching somebody else.* **2.** *n.* a kiss. □ *I like a good smooch from my hubby.* □ *Hey, sweetie, how about a smooch?*

soul kiss 1. *n.* a kiss where the kissers' tongues interact. □ *He tried to give me a soul kiss, but I pulled away.* □ *Yes, a soul kiss sounds silly—till you try it with somebody you really like.* **2.** *in.* [for two people] to kiss with interacting tongues. □ *They were soul kissing and making noises.* □ *The creep had bad breath and wanted to soul kiss!*

spoon *in.* to neck and pet. □ *They like to go out and spoon under the stars.* □ *Do you remember spooning with me years ago?*

suck face *tr.* to kiss. □ *The kid said he was going out to suck face. It sounds awful.* □ *Sally said she didn't want to suck face.*

swap spits *tr.* to kiss with someone. □ *A couple of kids were in the car swapping spits.* □ *Tiffany and Wilbur were off somewhere swapping spits, I guess.*

KNEES

dukes *n.* the knees. □ *He went down on his dukes and prayed for all sorts of good stuff.* □ *He cracked one of his dukes on the railing.*

prayerbones *n.* the knees. □ *Okay, down on your prayerbones.* □ *He pushed one of his prayerbones into my gut.*

KNOWLEDGE

See also **AWARENESS**.

down (pat) *mod.* learned; memorized. □ *I got all the dates down pat.* □ *I've got the dates down, but not the names.*

hit the fan *tr.* to become publicly known; to become a scandal. (From the phrase "when the shit hit the fan.") □ *I* *wasn't even in the country when it hit the fan.* □ *It hit the fan, and within ten minutes the press had spread it all over the world.*

know from something *in.* to know about something. □ *Do you know from timers—I mean, how timers work?* □ *I don't know from babies! Don't ask me about feeding them!*

street smarts *n.* the knowledge and ability to survive on the urban street. □ *If you don't have street smarts, you won't last long out there.* □ *You either pick up street smarts, or you don't.*

think-tank *n.* a place where great minds are assembled to try to think up solutions to problems or to envision the future. □ *She spent a few months in a California think-tank, then came back to teach.* □ *What sort of solutions are coming out of the think-tanks of the nation?*

KNOWLEDGEABLE

down *mod.* prepared; knowledgeable. □ *Are you down for the test tomorrow?* □ *Everything's down for the party.*

fly *mod.* knowledgeable; alert and in the know. □ *This dude is fly; there's no question about it.* □ *We don't need any more fly birds around here.*

in the know *mod.* knowledgeable (about something); having inside knowledge (about something). □ *Ask Harry. He's usually in the know.* □ *Sure, I'm in the know. But I'm not telling.*

know which end is up *tr.* to be alert and knowledgeable. □ *Don't try to hustle me, sister. I know which end is up.* □ *Poor Jed doesn't even know which end is up.*

on the ball *mod.* knowledgeable; competent; attentive. □ *This guy is really on the ball.* □ *If you were on the ball, this wouldn't have happened.*

savvy 1. *n.* knowledge; know-how. □ *She really has savvy when it comes to clocks.* □ *I don't have the savvy necessary to do the job.* **2.** *mod.* knowledgeable. □ *What a savvy gal!* □ *She is truly savvy!* □ *He is one of the most savvy directors in New York.*

wise to someone or something *mod.* having found out about someone or something. (Underworld.) □ *The cops are wise to the plan.* □ *I'm wise to Lefty. He's a wire.*

KNOWLEDGE - LACKING

beats me *phr.* "(the answer is) not known to me." (The emphasis is on *me*.) □ *I don't know the answer. Beats me!* □ *Beats me how those things stay in the air.*

Don't ask me. *sent.* "I don't know either." (With the emphasis on *me*.) □ *I don't know. Don't ask me.* □ *Don't ask me. I wasn't there.*

for all I know *phr.* "as far as I know"; "I really don't know." □ *For all I know, they just did it for a lark.* □ *She came in late because she had an accident, for all I know.*

not know beans (about something) *tr.* to know nothing about something. □ *Don't pay any attention to her. She doesn't know beans.* □ *I don't know beans about fixing cars.*

Search me. *sent.* "I don't know." (There is a heavy stress on both words.) □ TOM: *How do crickets make that chirping noise?* BILL: *Search me.* □ *You can search me. How should I know?*

LABOR

sewer hog *n.* a ditchdigger; a sewer worker. □ *A sewer hog doesn't get a lot of chances to pal around with the gentry, but the pay's plenty good.* □ *Fred worked as a sewer hog and made a fortune.*

LAUGHTER

See also **JOKING**.

belly laugh AND **belly laff** *n.* a loud, deep, uninhibited laugh. □ *I don't want to hear giggles when I tell a joke. I want long belly laughs.* □ *I let out a loud belly laff at the preacher's joke. A no-no, for sure.*

buzz *n.* a chuckle. □ *She gets a buzz out of reading the comics.* □ *Here's a little joke that'll give you a buzz.*

canned *mod.* having to do with prerecorded laughter or applause that is added to the sound track of a television program. □ *Canned laughter really sounds phony.* □ *The dialogue was funny enough that they didn't need to have the laughter canned.*

crack someone up *tr.* to make someone laugh. □ *She giggled, and that cracked us all up.* □ *The lecturer would talk along sort of boring like, and then all of a sudden he would crack up everybody with a joke.*

crack up *in.* to break out in laughter. □ *The whole audience cracked up.* □ *I knew I would crack up during the love scene.*

die *in.* to die (figuratively) from laughter or some other emotionally intense response. □ *The whole audience died laughing.* □ *He laughed till he died.*

double up (with laughter) *in.* to laugh so hard that one bends over. □ *We all just doubled up with laughter.* □ *I doubled up when I heard the punch line.*

fracture *tr.* to cause someone to laugh very hard. □ *Now, this joke'll fracture you.* □ *I like to tell a few that fracture everybody.*

fractured *mod.* demolished by laughter. □ *The class was fractured, and the laughter didn't stop until the teacher managed to get up off the floor.* □ *The whole audience was fractured by the time my ten minutes were up.*

gig *n.* a giggle; a bit of laughter. □ *Her little story gave us all a good gig.* □ *I had a nice little gig over what happened to Tom.*

have kittens *tr.* to laugh very hard; to enjoy something enormously. □ *It was so funny, I had kittens laughing.* □ *She had kittens laughing about it.*

hoot *in.* to laugh loudly. □ *The audience screamed and hooted with appreciation.* □ *They howled and hooted. I know they just loved it.*

horse laugh *n.* a mocking and sarcastic laugh. □ *He came out with a horse laugh that caused some eyebrows to raise.* □ *The horse laugh from the back of the room did not go unnoticed.*

howl *in.* to laugh very hard. □ *Everybody howled at my mistake.* □ *John howled when the joke was told.*

lay an egg *tr.* to laugh very hard; to cackle long and loudly. (As if one were a chicken.) □ *Half the audience laid an egg when I told this one.* □ *I didn't know whether to cry or lay an egg.*

split a gut *tr.* to laugh very hard. □ *He laughed until he nearly split a gut.* □ *The audience split a gut laughing.*

yack *n.* a laugh from a joke. □ *We had a good yack over it.* □ *The audience produced a feeble yak that was mostly from embarrassment.*

yock **1.** *n.* a loud laugh. □ *Sue let out an enormous yock and quickly covered her mouth.* □ *Who came out with that uncivil yock?* **2.** *in.* to laugh loudly. □ *Everybody yocked at the joke, and when things calmed down, I announced the mass firings.* □ *Stop yocking and listen to this.*

LAW-ABIDING

clean *mod.* not breaking any law. (Police and underworld.) □ *I'm clean, officer. You can't charge me with anything.* □ *This guy is clean. Let him go.*

go straight *in.* to stop breaking the law. □ *Lefty thought about going straight once, but pulled himself out of it.* □ *I think I'll give all this up and go straight—someday.*

jump smooth *in.* to give up illegal activities; to become *straight*. (Underworld.) □ *Freddy jumped smooth just in time.* □ *After a night in the junk tank, I knew I had to jump smooth.*

LAWYER

(ambulance) chaser *n.* a lawyer or entrepreneur who hurries to the scene of an accident to try to get the business of any injured persons. □ *The insurance companies are cracking down on ambulance chasers.* □ *Two minutes after the spectacular wreck, seven chasers with police radios showed up and began harassing the victims.*

fixer *n.* a lawyer. □ *I'll get my fixer on it first thing in the morning.* □ *Bruno's fixer didn't show up in court.*

legal-beagle AND **legal-eagle** *n.* a lawyer. □ *I've got a legal-beagle who can get me out of this scrape.* □ *She keeps a whole bunch of legal-eagles to handle that sort of thing.*

lip *n.* a lawyer. (Underworld.) □ *So I brought in my lip, and he got me off the rap.* □ *How much do you pay your lip?*

mouth(piece) *n.* a lawyer specializing in criminal cases. (Underworld.) □ *The guy hired a mouthpiece and beat the rap.* □ *I won't answer anything without my mouth right here by me.*

shark *n.* a lawyer. (Derogatory.) □ *Some shark is trying to squeeze a few grand out of me.* □ *Hire another shark to go after him.*

shyster *n.* an unethical or unscrupulous lawyer. (Also a rude term of address.) □ *Look, you cheap shyster, I paid you to help me, not ruin me!* □ *My ex-wife's shyster called again today to say she wants more money.*

LAZY

bone idle *mod.* very lazy; completely idle or unproductive. □ *Your problem is that you are bone idle.* □ *Take your bone-idle brother and move out!*

couch potato AND **cookie pusher** *n.* a lazy, do-nothing television watcher. □ *Is Martin a couch potato or a cookie pusher? That is the question!* □ *I'm just looking for a cookie pusher to fire today.*

hangout *n.* a place to loaf or *hang (around).* □ *I dropped by one of his favorite hangouts, but he wasn't there.* □ *We went over to the hangout and sat around talking.*

piker *n.* a lazy person; a shirker. □ *All right, you pikers. Pick up your shovels and get back to work.* □ *Come on, you lazy piker. There's plenty left for you to do.*

sofa spud *n.* someone who spends a great deal of time sitting and watching television. □ *Sofa spuds have been getting a lot of attention in the newspapers.* □ *These sofa spuds usually watch sports on television.*

LEGAL

beat the rap *tr.* to get free from a specific criminal charge. □ *I tried, but I couldn't beat the rap.* □ *I beat it twice, but there is no third time.*

beef *n.* a criminal charge or complaint. □ *Well, officer, what's the beef?* □ *The beef is that you appear to have left the bank Monday with about seventy-five grand that isn't yours. That's the beef!*

bend the law *tr.* to cheat a little bit without breaking the law. (Jocular.) □ *I didn't break the law. I just bent the law a little.* □ *Nobody ever got arrested for bending the law.*

bum rap *n.* a false criminal charge. (Underworld. The same as *bad rap.*) □ *This is a bum rap, and you know it.* □ *If a crook didn't scream that he got a bum rap, I might think he was really innocent.*

cop a plea *tr.* to plead guilty to a lesser charge. □ *Rocko copped a plea and got off with a week in the slammer.* □ *I wanted to cop a plea, but didn't have the chance.*

cop out *in.* to plead guilty (to a lesser charge). (Underworld.) □ *Frank copped out and got off with a night in the cooler.* □ *I decided not to cop out and got a mouthpiece instead.*

jump bail *tr.* to fail to show up in court and forfeit bail. □ *Lefty jumped bail, and now he's a fugitive.* □ *Once you've jumped bail, everybody is after you.*

palimony *n.* alimony—living expenses—paid to a common-law wife or to a former girlfriend. □ *He left her, and she took him to court to try to get him to pay palimony.* □ *With a good lawyer, she got more palimony than she could ever have gotten as alimony if they had been married.*

sue the pants off (of) someone *tr.* to sue someone for a lot of money. □ *If they do it, I'll sue the pants off of them.* □ *He sued the pants off his landlord.*

take the fifth AND **five it** *tr.* to refuse to testify to a U.S. legislative committee by invoking the protection of the Fifth Amendment to the U.S. Constitution. □ *His lawyer told him to take the fifth.* □ *After every question, the lawyer just sat there and said, "Five it."*

LEGS

gams *n.* a woman's legs, especially if attractive. □ *Is she the one with the gorgeous gams?* □ *Look at the gams on that chick!*

hams *n.* legs; hips. □ *Her great hams extended over the sides of the chair.* □ *I got* to do something to get the size of these hams down.

pin *n.* someone's leg. (Usually plural.) □ *My pins are a little wobbly.* □ *Stand up on your pins and speak your mind.*

rainbow *n.* a bowlegged person. (Also a rude term of address.) □ *Hey, rainbow! Are you a cowboy?* □ *Ask that rainbow if he has to have special trousers made.*

stems *n.* legs. □ *Look at the stems on that dame!* □ *My feet are sore, and my stems ache all the time.*

sticks *n.* a person's legs. (Always plural.) □ *Get those sticks moving! Get over here now!* □ *He's got good sticks under him, but he won't use them.*

stumps *n.* a person's legs. □ *My stumps are sore from all that walking.* □ *You need good strong stumps to do that kind of climbing.*

underpinnings *n.* the legs. □ *He has good underpinnings—ought to be able to run faster.* □ *With underpinnings like that, he ought to be able to win the marathon.*

understanding *n.* the feet. (A pun. Always singular.) □ *The boy has a good understanding. Really big gunboats, in fact.* □ *I always had a good understanding—even when I was a kid.*

LEISURE

catch some rays AND **bag some rays** *tr.* to get some sunshine; to tan in the sun. □ *We wanted to catch some rays, but the sun never came out the whole time we were there.* □ *I went to Hawaii to bag some rays.*

cruise *in.* to drive around looking for friends or social activity. □ *We went out cruising, but didn't see anybody.* □ *Let's go cruise for a while.*

friz *n.* a Frisbee™. □ *If I could find my friz, we could go out and whirl a few.* □ *Whose friz is that in the tree?*

rumpus room *n.* a family recreation room. (Old but still heard.) □ *Our rumpus room has a pool table.* □ *If you kids are going to play rough, you'll have to go down to the rumpus room.*

UVs *n.* "ultraviolet" rays from the sun; sunshine. (Initialism.) □ *I wanna get some UVs before we go home.* □ *Watch out for those UVs.*

LEND

spot someone (something) *tr.* to lend someone something. □ *Can you spot me a few bucks?* □ *I can spot you a whole hundred!*

stake someone to something *tr.* to lend or give someone money to buy something. □ *Can you stake me to a decent meal?* □ *Stake the man to a meal and a flop, and he'll tell us what we want to know.*

LESBIAN

dike *n.* a lesbian; a homosexual woman, especially one with masculine traits. (Derogatory. Potentially offensive. Use only with discretion. Resented by lesbians.) □ *Why does she work so hard to look like a dike?* □ *Who's the dike in the cowboy boots?*

LICE

bosom chums AND **bosom friends** *n.* lice. □ *The old guy sat there scratching at his bosom chums.* □ *"Nobody seems to like my bosom friends," he muttered.*

cooties *n.* real or imagined lice. □ *Randy pulled back from me like I had cooties or something. What's wrong with me?* □ *You have cooties, crotch-pheasants, and bad breath. What do you expect?*

crab *n.* a louse. (Usually plural.) □ *He's scratching like he's got crabs.* □ *The old wino and his crabs wandered into the flophouse for a little peace and quiet.*

crotch-pheasant *n.* a louse. (Usually in the plural.) □ *He appears to be afflicted with what you might call crotch-pheasants.* □ *There is a special medicine that will get rid of crotch-pheasants.*

pants rabbits *n.* lice. □ *Max is sure scratching a lot. Do you think he's got pants rabbits?* □ *I don't want to be around people who have pants rabbits and stuff like that.*

seam-squirrels *n.* lice. □ *I got an itch. Must be seam-squirrels.* □ *Where would you get seam-squirrels?*

walking dandruff AND **galloping dandruff** *n.* lice. □ *He's hopping around like he's got walking dandruff.* □ *I don't know anybody with galloping dandruff—I hope.*

LIFESTYLE

cruise *in.* to move through life at a comfortable pace. □ *I just want to get a good job and cruise for a while.* □ *I'm cruising just the way I want now.*

drop out *in.* to withdraw from a conventional lifestyle. □ *Sometimes I just want to drop out and raise pigs or something.* □ *Ted dropped out and bought a farm.*

fat city *n.* a state of wealth and comfort; easy street. □ *She's living in fat city ever since she inherited her fortune.* □ *I could settle down in fat city without any trouble.*

go through the changes *in.* to experience life's changes. □ *A good day, a bad day—it's all part of going through the changes.* □ *Nothing new with me, just going through the changes.*

LT *in.* "living together." □ *Guess who're LT?* □ *They have been LT for some time.*

on easy street *mod.* in a state of financial independence and comfort. □ *I want to live on easy street when I grow up.* □ *When I get this contract signed, I'll be on easy street.*

taking care of business *tr.* doing what one is meant to do; coping with life as it is. (Black.) □ *If the dude is taking care of business, what else do you want out of him?* □ *Walter is taking care of business. Back in a minute.*

LIMITATION

max out *in.* to reach one's maximum in something, such as weight in weight lifting or credit on a credit card. □ *Andy finally maxed out at 300 pounds.* □ *Randy just knew when he had maxed out. Something in his body told him to stop.*

LIMITATION - LACKING

no holds barred *mod.* without restriction. (There is no affirmative version of this.) □ *I want you to get that contract. Do anything—no holds barred.* □ *Try anything that will work, no holds barred.*

rat hole *n.* a bottomless pit. (Typically with *throw* and *down* as in the examples.) □ *Why do they keep throwing money down that rat hole?* □ *That rat hole will absorb as much money as they can supply.* □ *The transportation system is beyond help. Giving it more subsidies is just throwing money down a rat hole.*

sky's the limit *phr.* "there is no upper limit." (Always with *the.*) □ *I can afford it. The sky's the limit.* □ *You can do anything you set your mind to, Billy. The sky's the limit.*

LINT

ghost turd *n.* a wad of lint, as found under a bed. (Use caution with *turd.*) □ *There's a lot of ghost turds under the bed.* □ *Sweep out those ghost turds and get rid of them.*

house moss *n.* little blobs of lint. □ *There is some house moss under the sofa.* □ *Sweep up this house moss, please.*

LIST

blacklist *n.* a list of the names of banned people; a list of people undesirable to some group. □ *Am I on your blacklist?* □ *I hear they keep a blacklist on all the people they disagree with.*

drop-dead list *n.* an imaginary list of annoying people whom one could live happily without. □ *You are right at the top of my drop-dead list.* □ *I put Max on my drop-dead list.*

hit list *n.* a list of people to whom something is going to happen. □ *Ralph is on my hit list for contributing money for the orphans.* □ *She's on our hit list for volunteers.*

laundry list *n.* any long list of things. □ *He came to the interview with a laundry list of things.* □ *Now I have a laundry list of items we need to discuss.*

shopping list *n.* a list of things, especially questions or things one wants. □ *I have a shopping list of absolute musts.* □ *He showed up for the interview with a shopping list so long that it took two pages.*

sucker list *n.* a list of potential dupes; a list of people who might be taken in by deception. □ *I'm sure on their sucker list. They are trying to get me to go to a lecture and receive a free clock or something.* □ *Here's the sucker list. Call them all and try to get them interested.*

take names *tr.* to make a list of wrongdoers. (Often figuratively, as with a schoolteacher, whose major weapon is to take names and send them to the principal.) □ *The boss is madder than hell, and he's taking names.* □ *Gary is coming by to talk about the little riot last night, and I think he's taking names.*

wish list *n.* a list of things one wishes to have. □ *I put a new car at the top of my wish list.* □ *I have a CD player on my wish list.*

LISTENING

listen up *in.* to listen carefully. (Usually a command.) □ *Now, listen up! This is important.* □ *Listen up, you guys!*

LOCATION

burg *n.* a small town. (Disdainful.) □ *I can't stand another day in this burg.* □ *This burg is getting on my nerves.*

glue factory *n.* the place where old horses are sent so their bones can be made into glue; a similar, imaginary place for people. □ *I'm not as young as I used to be, but I'm not ready for the glue factory yet.* □ *If you can't keep up, we'll send you to the glue factory.*

hotbed of something *n.* a nest of something; a gathering place of a kind of people. □ *This office is a hotbed of lazy people.* □ *My class is a hotbed of nerds.*

main drag *n.* the main street. □ *I have a shop over on the main drag.* □ *The main drag is solid with traffic on Saturday nights.*

one-horse town *n.* a very small town; a small and backward town. □ *I refuse to spend a whole week in that one-horse town!* □ *I grew up in a one-horse town, and I liked it very much.*

passion-pit *n.* a drive-in movie theatre; any place where young people go to neck, such as an area where teenagers park. (Dated but still heard.) □ *She wanted me to drive down to the passion-pit, but I said I had a headache.* □ *My* mother used to tell me about her trips to the passion-pit.

rust belt *n.* the industrial north of the U.S. □ *The economy in the rust belt is slowing down.* □ *The salt they put on the roads in the winter made my car all rusty. I guess that's why they call this area the rust belt.*

scene *n.* a place; a setting. □ *This scene is no good. Let's split.* □ *I need a different scene. Life is too hectic here.*

skid row *n.* the name for a place populated with ruined alcoholics and other down-and-out people. □ *I don't want to end up on skid row. How can I get rid of this monkey?* □ *Just because they're on skid row, it doesn't mean they're beyond help.*

stamping ground *n.* one's favorite or customary location. □ *Adamsville is my old stamping ground. I was born there, you know.* □ *I like to go back and look at my old stamping ground every now and then.*

sticks *n.* a rural or backwoods area. (Always with *the* and always plural.) □ *I hated living in the sticks.* □ *You hear a lot about how things are in the sticks. They're worse.*

sun belt *n.* the southern U.S. states, where it is generally warm and sunny. □ *I want to retire to the sun belt.* □ *The population of the sun belt is exploding.*

tall timbers *n.* some remote, well-forested place; the *boondocks.* □ *Oh, Chuck lives out in the tall timbers somewhere. He only has a post office box number.* □ *You're not going to move me out into the tall timbers somewhere!*

turf *n.* (one's) ground or territory. □ *When you're on my turf, you do what I say—savvy?* □ *This is my turf, and what I say goes.*

up front *mod.* in the forefront; under fire (at the front). □ *You guys who are up front are gonna get the most fire.* □ *You two go up front and see if you can help.*

where the action is *phr.* where important things are happening. □ *I want to*

be where the action is. □ *Right there in city hall. That's where the action is.*

wide place in the road *n.* a very small town. □ *The town is little more than a wide place in the road.* □ *We stopped at a wide place in the road called Adamsville.*

wrong side of the tracks *n.* the poor side of town. □ *Fred's ashamed that he's from the wrong side of the tracks, so to speak.* □ *I'm glad I'm from the wrong side of the tracks. I know what life is really like.*

X marks the spot. *sent.* "This is the exact place!" (A catchphrase.) □ *This is where it happened. X marks the spot.* □ *X marks the spot where we first met.*

You can't get there from here. *sent.* "Where you want to go is in a very remote location." (A catchphrase.) □ *Well, you can't get there from here.* □ *Adamsville? Sorry, you can't get there from here.*

LOCATION - UNDESIRABLE

armpit *n.* any undesirable place. (A nickname for an undesirable town or city.) □ *Who wants to spend a weekend in an armpit?* □ *The town should be called the armpit of the nation.*

clip joint *n.* a business establishment that cheats customers. □ *That place is a clip joint. Stay away.* □ *The clip joint on Fourth Street was busted last night.*

creep joint AND **creep dive** *n.* an unpleasant place populated by creeps. □ *You shouldn't go into a creep joint like that alone.* □ *Why would anyone want to work in a creep dive like that?*

dump *n.* a low or cheap establishment. □ *I want out of this dump.* □ *My mama didn't raise me to spend the rest of my days in a run-down dump like this.*

hellhole *n.* a hot and crowded place; any unpleasant place. (Use caution with *hell.*) □ *I want out of this hellhole.* □ *The theater was an overcrowded hellhole. Luckily there was no fire.*

joint *n.* a low-class establishment. □ *Let's get out of this crummy joint.* □ *This joint bores me.*

rat hole *n.* a run-down place; a *dump* or a *joint.* □ *I refuse to live in this rat hole* *any longer.* □ *Why don't you clean up this rat hole?*

taco stand *n.* a lousy place; a *tacky* place. □ *It's time to get out of this taco stand and go somewhere decent.* □ *Why doesn't somebody clean up this taco stand?*

trap *n.* a low place; a *dive.* □ *I want out of this trap!* □ *This trap is a mess. Clean it up!*

LODGING

ba(t)ch (it) *tr. & in.* to live alone like a bachelor. □ *I tried to bach it for a while, but I got too lonely.* □ *I didn't want to batch, but I had to.*

buddy up (with someone) *in.* to share living space with someone; to share something with someone. □ *Let's buddy up, okay?* □ *There weren't enough to go around, so we had to buddy up.*

cliff-dweller *n.* someone who lives in a tall apartment building. □ *I could never survive as a cliff-dweller in a big city.* □ *The majority of cliff-dwellers wouldn't choose to live in any other way.*

crash 1. *in.* to spend the night. □ *I crashed at a friend's place in the city.* □ *You have a place I can crash?* **2.** *n.* a place to sleep. □ *I think I know of a crash for tonight.* □ *Molly's on the phone, looking for a crash.*

crash pad *n.* a place to stay the night on short notice. □ *I've got a crash pad in the city for emergencies like this.* □ *I gotta find a crash pad for tonight.*

crib *n.* a dwelling. (Underworld.) □ *Where's your crib, man?* □ *My good threads are all back at my crib.*

digs *n.* a dwelling; a dwelling and its furnishings. □ *You got some pretty swell digs here.* □ *Nice digs. You like it here?*

fleabag *n.* a cheap hotel; a *flophouse.* □ *I won't stay in this fleabag for one minute.* □ *Rocko never stays in fleabags. He's too proud. Bruno doesn't care.*

flop *n.* a place to sleep for the night; a bed in a *flophouse.* (Streets.) □ *The old man was looking for a flop for the night.* □ *Do you know where I can find a flop?*

flophouse *n.* a very cheap hotel offering only rows of beds. □ *This place is a flophouse! I won't stay here for a moment.* □ *All some of those guys need in life is a flop in a flophouse.*

hut *n.* a house. □ *I've got to go to my hut and pick up some bills.* □ *Where's your hut? I'll come and visit you.*

layout *n.* a place; a place to live. □ *How much does a layout like this set you back a month?* □ *This is a nice layout you got here.*

pad *n.* a place to live; one's room or dwelling. □ *Why don't you come over to my pad for a while?* □ *This is a nice pad you've got here.*

put someone up *tr.* to provide someone with temporary shelter; to let someone stay the night. □ *Can you put me up for a few days?* □ *I could put up a football team, there's so much room here.*

setup *n.* a place to live. □ *She's got a little setup over on Maple.* □ *This is a pretty nice setup. What's the rent?*

shack up (with someone) *in.* to move in with someone temporarily, presumably for sexual purposes. □ *They shacked up for over a year until her parents found out and stopped sending her money.* □ *They decided to shack up.*

take someone in *tr.* to give shelter to someone. □ *We took her in and gave her some soup and a place to stay.* □ *Mrs. Wilson takes in almost every young person who needs her help.*

LONELY

hard up *mod.* desperate for companionship. □ *Freddie said he was hard up and needed a date.* □ *Mary must be hard up to date a jerk like that.*

LOOT

boodle *n.* loot; the proceeds from a crime. (Underworld.) □ *All of the boodle was recovered in a suitcase.* □ *They divvied up the boodle and got out of town.*

cut *n.* a share of the loot or the profits. (Originally underworld.) □ *I want my cut now.* □ *You'll get your cut when everybody else does.*

haul *n.* the proceeds from a theft; loot. (Underworld.) □ *They divvied up the haul from the bank job.* □ *The cops thought they must have got a pretty good haul.*

rip *n.* the loot from a *rip-off.* □ *I want my share of the rip, now!* □ *Give him some of the rip and tell him to beat it.*

LOSE
See **DEFEAT, LOSS.**

LOSS

kiss something good-bye *tr.* to face and accept the loss of something. □ *Well, you can kiss that 100 bucks good-bye.* □ *I kissed my chance for success good-bye.*

lose a bundle *tr.* to lose a lot of money. □ *Don lost a bundle on that land purchase.* □ *I know I would lose a bundle if I got on a riverboat and gambled.*

lose one's shirt *tr.* to go broke; to lose everything of value, even one's shirt. □ *I lost my shirt on that bank deal.* □ *Try not to lose your shirt in the market again.*

take a bath (on something) *tr.* to have large financial losses on an investment. □ *Fred took a bath on that gold-mining stock.* □ *The broker warned me that I might take a bath if I bought this stuff.*

take someone to the cleaners *tr.* to take all of someone's money. □ *The lawyers took the insurance company to the cleaners, but I still didn't get enough to pay for my losses.* □ *The con artists took the old man to the cleaners.*

tank *tr. & in.* to lose a game deliberately. □ *Wilbur would never tank.* □ *The manager got wind of a plan to tank Friday's game.*

tap out *in.* to lose one's money in gambling or in the securities markets. □ *I'm gonna tap out in about three more rolls—just watch.* □ *I really tapped out on that gold-mining stock.*

throw a game *tr.* to lose a game on purpose. □ *I know Wilbur. He could never throw a game.* □ *There's a couple of those guys who would throw a game if they got enough money to do it.*

wash out *in.* to lose a large amount of money. □ *Fred washed out on that stock deal.* □ *Lefty and Bruno washed out at the track.*

Win a few, lose a few. *phr.* "Sometimes one wins; other times one loses." □ *Too bad. Sorry about that. Win a few, lose a few.* □ *"Win a few, lose a few," doesn't mean you never win at all.*

LOUDNESS

full blast *mod.* as strongly as possible. □ *He honked the horn full blast for a long time.* □ *The whistle blew full blast and woke everyone up.*

LOVE

heart *tr.* to love someone or something. (Teens.) □ *Oh, I just, like, heart your letter.* □ *She's hearting him more every day.*

steamy *mod.* lewd; sensuous; passionate. □ *They cut a couple of steamy scenes out of the movie because of complaints.* □ *Hank and Bess were having a steamy session on the couch.* □ *The session was really steamy.*

LOVER

baby *n.* a lover; one's sweetheart. (Also a term of address.) □ *Come over here and kiss me, baby.* □ *Look, baby, I think we can work this out.*

cuddle bunny *n.* a female lover. □ *All you want is a cuddle bunny with big tits! Grow up, Maxwell Wilson!* □ *Who is that cuddle bunny driving the Caddy?*

dreamboat *n.* just the kind of lover one has always dreamed of. (Also a term of address.) □ *Oh, Pete is my dreamboat.* □ *A face man makes a great dreamboat, as long as you never get to know him.*

honeybunch *n.* a sweetheart. (Also a term of address.) □ *Look, honeybunch, let's hurry up. We're late.* □ *I can't wait to get back and see my honeybunch.*

HTH *n.* "hometown honey," a sweetheart from home or still at home. (Initialism. Collegiate.) □ *Wally is my HTH, but I think I've outgrown him.* □ *I heard that Mary is Sam's HTH.*

old flame *n.* a former sweetheart or lover. □ *Mary's old flame, Tom, will be at* *the party.* □ *It is best to forget an old flame.*

one and only *n.* one's lover or sweetheart. □ *I bought a gift for my one and only.* □ *She's my one and only, and I love her.*

squeeze *n.* one's lover. □ *I'll see if my squeeze wants to go.* □ *Get your squeeze, and let's go sink a few.*

steady *n.* a boyfriend or girlfriend. □ *She showed up with Tom, her steady for the last few months.* □ *My steady is laid up with a cold. I'll come alone.*

two-timer *n.* one who deceives one's lover. □ *Sam just isn't my idea of the typical two-timer.* □ *Of course not. Two-timers rarely look like two-timers.*

LUCK

ace out *in.* to be fortunate or lucky. □ *I really aced out on that test in English.* □ *Freddy aced out at the dentist's office with only one cavity.*

Better luck next time. *sent.* "I wish you luck when you try again." □ *So you goofed up. Better luck next time.* □ *You blew it, you stupid twit. Better luck next time.*

Break a leg! *exclam.* "Good luck!" (A special theatrical way of wishing a performer good luck. Saying "good luck" is a jinx.) □ *"Break a leg!" shouted the stage manager to the heroine.* □ *Let's all go and do our best. Break a leg!*

Lots of luck! **1.** *exclam.* "Good luck!" □ *I'm glad you're giving it a try. Lots of luck!* □ *Lots of luck in your new job!* **2.** *exclam.* "You don't have a chance!"; "Good luck, you'll need it!" (Sarcastic.) □ *Think you stand a chance? Lots of luck!* □ *You, a senator? Lots of luck!*

luck of the draw *n.* the results of chance; the lack of any choice. □ *Why do I always end up with the luck of the draw?* □ *The team was assembled by chance. It was just the luck of the draw that we could work so well together.*

luck out *in.* to be fortunate; to strike it lucky. □ *I really lucked out when I ordered the duck. It's excellent.* □ *I didn't*

luck out at all. I rarely make the right choice.

lucky dog *n.* a lucky person, perhaps undeserving. (Also a term of address.) □ *You lucky dog!* □ *Max was a lucky dog because he won the football pool.*

narrow squeak *n.* a success almost not achieved; a lucky or marginal success; a problem almost not surmounted. □ *That was a narrow squeak. I don't know how I survived.* □ *Another narrow squeak like that and I'll give up.*

Rots of ruck! *exclam.* "Lots of luck!" (Mocking a Japanese pronunciation.) □ *Have a good trip, and rots of ruck!* □ *Good-bye, and rots of ruck!*

LUCKY

get hot *in.* to begin to get lucky, as in gambling. □ *I knew I was getting hot when I got all the right cards.* □ *If I could only get hot, I might win back everything I lost.*

hot *mod.* having a run of good luck in gambling. □ *I'm hot tonight! Here I go again.* □ *I was hot when I started. I'm broke now.*

LUCK - LACKING

out of luck *mod.* unfortunate; in a hopeless position. □ *If you think you are going to get any sympathy from me, you're just out of luck.* □ *I was out of luck. There were no eggs left in the store.*

rotten luck *n.* bad luck. □ *Of all the rotten luck!* □ *I've had nothing but rotten luck all day.*

tough break *n.* a bit of bad luck. □ *Tough break. Sorry about that.* □ *You've had a lot of tough breaks lately.*

LUGGAGE

keester AND **keyster; kiester** *n.* a chest; a suitcase. □ *The old lady was hauling the most enormous keester.* □ *The keester was full of cash.*

LUNGS

air-bags *n.* the lungs. □ *Fill those air-bags with good Colorado air!* □ *I've had a cold or something in my air-bags for about three days now.*

LUXURY

lap of luxury *n.* a luxurious situation. □ *I rather enjoy living in the lap of luxury.* □ *You call this pigpen the lap of luxury?*

LYING

cooked up *mod.* contrived. (This is hyphenated before a nominal.) □ *The whole thing seems so cooked up.* □ *What a cooked-up story! Of course, you don't believe it.*

fairy tale AND **bedtime story** *n.* a simplistic and condescending explanation for something; a lie. □ *I don't want to hear a fairy tale, just the facts, ma'am.* □ *What you're telling me sounds like a bedtime story. Come back when you can be more straightforward.*

fib 1. *n.* a small lie. □ *It was just a little fib. I'm sorry.* □ *Is this another one of your fibs?* **2.** *in.* to tell a small lie. □ *Stop fibbing and tell me the truth.* □ *Did you fib to the teacher?*

fibber *n.* a liar. □ *Harry can be a fibber sometimes. You got to watch him.* □ *Jimmy is turning into a little fibber.*

fish story AND **fish tale** *n.* a great big lie. (Like the fisherman who exaggerates the size of the fish that got away.) □ *That's just a fish story. Tell me another!* □ *He's a master at the fish tale. Maybe he should be a politician.*

lollapalooza *n.* a big lie. □ *She just told a lollapalooza.* □ *What a lollapalooza! You expect me to believe that?*

talk through one's hat *in.* to say baseless things; to speak carelessly and tell lies. □ *Pay no attention to my friend here. He's just talking through his hat.* □ *You don't know what you are talking about. You're just talking through your hat.*

whopper *n.* a very big lie. □ *That one's a whopper. I don't believe a word of it.* □ *She sure told a whopper, didn't she?*

MACHINERY

fire something up *tr.* to start something, such as an engine; to light something. □ *Fire this thing up, and let's get going.* □ *Andy fired up the snow blower and started to clear a path.*

guts *n.* the inner workings of anything. □ *There's something wrong in the guts of this clock.* □ *My tape recorder needs all new guts.*

MAIL

dead letter *n.* a letter that cannot move through the post office because the addressee does not exist or because the address is wrong or illegible. (Standard English.) □ *Every now and then they open the dead letters to see if they can figure out who they were meant for.* □ *Sometimes dead letters have return addresses in them.*

junk mail *n.* unwanted or annoying advertising mail. □ *All we got was junk mail today.* □ *I read everything that comes in the mail, even the junk mail.*

snail-mail *n.* post office mail; regular mail as opposed to electronic mail. (Refers to the slowness of regular mail in comparison to electronic mail or faxes.) □ *I'll send you the full text by snail-mail.* □ *There are lots of color pictures in the article, so I will send you the original by snail-mail.*

MAKEUP

war paint *n.* a woman's makeup. □ *She'll be ready when she gets on her war paint.* □ *She doesn't look half bad without war paint.*

MALFUNCTION

bite the dust *tr.* to break; to fail; to give out. □ *My car finally bit the dust.* □ *This pen has bitten the dust.*

conk out *in.* [for something] to break down; to quit running. □ *My car conked out finally.* □ *I hope my computer doesn't conk out.*

crash 1. *in.* [for a computer] to stop working. □ *This thing crashes every time I hit a certain key.* □ *My machine hasn't crashed since I got it.* **2.** *n.* a total failure of a computer. □ *Most of my data was lost in the crash.* □ *Crashes are to teach you to back up your data.* **3.** *in.* [for any electronic device] to fail. □ *My stereo crashed, so I've been watching TV.* □ *My TV crashed, and I had to go out to watch at somebody else's house.*

crum something up *tr.* to mess something up; to make something crummy. □ *Who crummed the bird feeder up?* □ *Now, don't crum up this deal.*

die on someone *in.* [for something] to quit running for someone. □ *My car died on me, and I couldn't get it started.* □ *My stereo died on me, and I had to listen to the radio.*

down time *n.* the time when a computer is not operating. □ *I can't afford a lot of down time in the system I buy.* □ *We had too much down time with the other machine.*

go blooey AND **go flooey** *in.* to fall apart; to go out of order. □ *Suddenly, all my plans went blooey.* □ *I just hope everything doesn't go flooey at the last minute.*

go haywire *in.* [for something] to go out of order; to break down. □ *My stereo's* *gone haywire.* □ *I'm afraid my car's gone haywire. It won't start.*

gronk (out) *in.* to *conk out*; to crash, as with a car or a computer. □ *My car gronked out on the way to work this morning.* □ *The program gronks every time I start to run it.*

MAN

beach bum *n.* a young man who frequents beaches. □ *A bronzed beach bum helped me find my lotion.* □ *Some of those beach bums are getting to look sort of old.*

blade *n.* a young man, witty and worldly. □ *One of those blades kept winking at me.* □ *A couple of blades from the international jet set ordered vintage wine for everyone.*

brews brothers *n.* (male) beer-drinking college students. (A play on *The Blues Brothers,* a popular movie released in 1980.) □ *The brews brothers were making a lot of noise last night. Don't those guys do anything but drink?* □ *You guys look like the devil and you smell like the brews brothers.*

cat *n.* a fellow; a *guy;* a *dude.* □ *Now, this cat wants to borrow some money from me. What should I do?* □ *Ask the cat what he's got for security.*

cool cat *n.* someone who is *cool,* usually a male. □ *Monty is a cool cat. I really like him.* □ *There is a shortage of cool cats on this turf.*

drugstore cowboy *n.* a male who hangs around drugstores and other public places trying to impress women. □ *You don't see the old drugstore cowboys around this part of town anymore.* □ *The drugstore cowboys of years ago are all hidden away shooting up something.*

fair-haired boy *n.* a promising young man; a young man who receives favoritism. □ *Ted is the boss's fair-haired boy now, but he'll just like the rest of us in a month.* □ *He'd have been fired if he wasn't the fair-haired boy.*

frat-rat *n.* a member of a fraternity. (Collegiate.) □ *The frat-rats are having a rally tonight.* □ *Is Frank a frat-rat, or is he independent?*

G *n.* "guy." □ *What's up, G?* □ *Tom's a real chilled out G.*

greaser *n.* a rough and aggressive male, usually with long, greased-down hair. □ *Who's the greaser who just swaggered in?* □ *Donna has been going out with a real greaser.*

hombre *n.* a man. (From Spanish.) □ *Who's that hombre who just came in?* □ *Now, he's a strange sort of hombre.*

john *n.* a man. □ *Some john was around asking for you.* □ *This john came up and asked if I had seen the girl in a picture he had.*

joker *n.* a man; a guy. □ *Who was that joker I saw you with last night?* □ *Some joker was at the door selling something.*

MCP AND **male chauvinist pig** *n.* a male who acts superior to and aggressively toward women. (From the woman's liberation movements of the 1970s.) □ *The guy is just a male chauvinist pig, and he'll never change.* □ *Don't you just hate walking through a room filled with MCPs and just knowing what they are thinking about you?*

Mr. Right *n.* the one man who is right for a woman. □ *Someday Mr. Right will come along and sweep you off your feet.* □ *I'm tired of waiting for Mr. Right. Where is Mr. Maybe?*

pal *n.* a term of address for a stranger, usually a male. □ *Hey, pal. Got a match?* □ *Look, pal, I was in line in front of you!*

pimp *n.* a man who solicits business for a prostitute. (Use caution with *pimp* and the topic.) □ *The guy with the diamond rings looks like a pimp.* □ *The cops took in three hookers and their pimp.*

tackhead *n.* an overdressed male. □ *Gary is sort of a tackhead when it comes to clothing.* □ *Don't be such a tackhead, Tom. Loosen up.*

MANAGE

See also **CONTROL**.

box someone in *tr.* to put someone into a bind; to reduce the number of someone's alternatives. □ *I don't want to box you in, but you are running out of options.*

☐ *I want to box in the whole staff, so they'll have to do it my way.*

head cook and bottle washer AND **chief cook and bottle washer** *n.* someone who is in charge of something trivial. ☐ *I'm the head cook and bottle washer around here.* ☐ *I want to see the chief cook and bottle washer.*

hold the fort *tr.* to remain behind and take care of things. ☐ *Hold the fort. I'll be there in a while.* ☐ *I left John there to hold the fort.*

honcho *tr.* to manage or boss something. ☐ *Who's supposed to honcho this affair?* ☐ *I'll honcho it until Larry gets here.*

movers and shakers *n.* people who get things done; organizers and managers. ☐ *The movers and shakers in this firm haven't exactly been working overtime.* ☐ *Who are the movers and shakers around here?*

point man *n.* anyone whose job it is to score successes against the opposition. ☐ *The president expects the secretary of defense to be point man for this new legislation.* ☐ *I am a diplomat, not a point man. Ask someone else to play your little games.*

quarterback *tr.* to manage, lead, or direct someone or something. ☐ *Who is going to quarterback this organization after you go?* ☐ *I quarterbacked the whole company for more years than I care to remember.*

ramrod *tr.* to lead something; to act as the driving force behind something. ☐ *Who is going to ramrod this project?* ☐ *Don't ramrod us into something we don't really want.*

Simon Legree *n.* a very hard taskmaster; a hard boss. (From the name of the slave driver in *Uncle Tom's Cabin*.) ☐ *She's a regular Simon Legree.* ☐ *Ask Simon Legree if I will be able to stop work and go home for breakfast now.*

super *n.* superintendent. ☐ *The super comes by every now and then to check on things.* ☐ *Call the super and ask for some help.*

MAN - ATTRACTIVE

beauhunk *n.* a good-looking male. (Based on *bohunk*. A play on *beau* = boyfriend, and *hunk*.) ☐ *Who is that gorgeous beauhunk over there?* ☐ *Jennifer went out with a real beauhunk who turned out to be a dipwad.*

face man *n.* a good-looking young man with no personality. (Collegiate.) ☐ *Harry is just a face man and as dull as dishwater.* ☐ *Norm is the perfect face man—all looks and no brains.*

freak daddy *n.* a good-looking male. ☐ *Tony is a real freak daddy, and I intend to get him to take me out.* ☐ *Jane wants to get her hands on the freak daddy in her history class.*

hunk *n.* a strong and sexually attractive male. ☐ *Larry is a real hunk.* ☐ *Who was that hot hunk I saw you with?*

stud-muffin *n.* a really good-looking guy; a stud. ☐ *Who's the stud-muffin with Sally?* ☐ *Did you see that stud-muffin come in?*

MAN - FRIEND

dude *n.* a male friend; a guy. (Also a term of address.) ☐ *Who's the dude with the cowboy boots?* ☐ *Hey, dude, what's happ?*

old man *n.* (one's) boyfriend. ☐ *Ask your old man to come to the party, too.* ☐ *I got my old man to take me to see that movie I told you about.*

MAN - GOOD

quality Joe *n.* an innocent or straight (male) person. (Underworld.) ☐ *Lefty is not what I would call your average quality Joe.* ☐ *These quality Joes just don't understand how it is on the street.*

right guy *n.* a good man; a straight guy. ☐ *Tom is a right guy. No trouble with him.* ☐ *I'm glad you're a right guy. I can trust you.*

MAN - IMPORTANT

big man on campus *n.* an important male college student. ☐ *Hank acts like such a big man on campus.* ☐ *Let some big man on campus do the dirty work for a change.*

big-time operator *n.* a man who chases women. □ *This big-time operator comes up and asks me to go home with him.* □ *That twit thinks he's a big-time operator. A stud he's not.*

BMOC *n.* "big man on campus," an important or self-important male college student. (Initialism. Collegiate.) □ *Who's the BMOC who keeps trying to get elected class president?* □ *When this BMOC asked me to leave, I ignored him.*

boss man *n.* the man in charge. □ *The boss man's coming. Watch out!* □ *I guess the boss man is about ready to retire.*

MAN - MEEK

Caspar Milquetoast *n.* a very timid man. (From the name of a character in a cartoon.) □ *I'm a little sensitive—not a Caspar Milquetoast, but I have feelings.* □ *He's no Caspar Milquetoast. He's quite a tennis player, in fact.*

milquetoast *n.* a shy coward; an effeminate male. □ *This little milquetoast goes up to the biker, looks at him sort of sad like, and then karate chops him into a quivering pulp.* □ *Some guy who looked like a milquetoast came in and asked for a set of brass knuckles.*

pipsqueak *n.* a small or timid man or boy. (Also a term of address.) □ *Shut up, you little pipsqueak, or I'll hit you.* □ *I may be a pipsqueak, but I am a gentleman.*

pussycat *n.* a timid male; a mild-mannered and passive male. □ *That guy is a wimp, a real pussycat.* □ *He seems mean, but underneath he's a pussycat.*

weak sister *n.* a timid male. □ *It looks like Dave is the weak sister on the team.* □ *Another weak sister and we'll have to quit. We've got to pull together.*

MAN - MUSCULAR

beef *n.* a large and muscular male. □ *Let's get one of those beefs in here to help.* □ *The two beefs pushed and pushed, but couldn't budge the crate.*

beefcake **1.** *n.* a display of the male physique. □ *There was some beefcake at the party just to liven things up.* □ *There was one calendar showing beefcake rather* than the usual cheesecake. **2.** *n.* a muscularly handsome male. □ *She's been going out with a real beefcake.* □ *I prefer skinny guys to a beefcake.*

muscleman *n.* a man who builds muscles through bodybuilding exercises. □ *That muscleman doesn't have a single ounce of fat on him.* □ *Being a muscleman requires most of your time.*

superjock *n.* a very well-built man regardless of athletic ability. □ *My boyfriend is a superjock, and does he look good!* □ *No nerd has ever been a superjock.*

MAN - NEGATIVE

badass *n.* a tough guy; a belligerent and arrogant person, usually a male. □ *Don't be such a badass all the time.* □ *Tom is the classic badass. A real bum.*

beast *n.* a crude, violent, or sexually aggressive male. □ *That beast scares the hell out of me.* □ *Oh, Martin, you're such a beast!*

but-boy *n.* someone, usually a male, who raises objections frequently. (The opposite of a *yes-man*.) □ *I wish you wouldn't be such a but-boy, Higgins. Can't you ever agree with anyone?* □ *Hank is such a but-boy. He doesn't know when to just let something go by.*

fag *n.* a repellent male. □ *You creepy fag. Stop it!* □ *Bruno is such a fag!*

heavy *n.* a (male) villain. (Especially in movies, etc.) □ *He is well-known for playing heavies in the movies.* □ *Do I always have to be the heavy?*

heel *n.* a low and despicable man. □ *You are the most impossible heel!* □ *The guy is a heel, and he seems to work at it, too.*

King Grod *n.* a very repellent male. (California.) □ *You are just King Grod! So gross!* □ *Ralph is almost King Grod!*

lone wolf *n.* a man who stays to himself. □ *Fred is sort of a lone wolf until he has a few drinks.* □ *It's the lone wolves you read about in the paper when they pull a drowning person from the river.*

louse *n.* a thoroughly repellent person, usually a male. □ *You can be such a louse!*

□ *Max turned out to be a louse, and his wife of two weeks left him.*

punk AND **punk kid** *n.* an inexperienced boy or youth. (Derogatory. Also a term of address.) □ *Ask that punk to come over here.* □ *Look here, punk, I need some help.*

SOB *n.* a "son of a bitch"; a despised person, usually a male. (Initialism only. Crude. Also a rude and provocative term of address.) □ *Tell that SOB to mind his own business.* □ *Look here, you SOB, get out!*

tough guy *n.* a tough man; a man who might be part of the underworld. □ *He was your typical tough guy—jutting chin, gruff voice—but he was just our decorator checking up on the drapes.* □ *So, you want to be a tough guy, huh?*

worm *n.* a repellent person, usually a male. □ *Gad, you are a worm, Tom.* □ *I'd like Fred better if he wasn't such a worm.*

yegg *n.* an obnoxious male. □ *Don't act like such a yegg, Bill.* □ *A couple of drunken yeggs were talking a little too loud, so Bruno showed them the door.*

MAN - OLD

buzzard *n.* an old man; a mean old man. (Especially with *old.*) □ *Who's the buzzard in the wing-tip shoes?* □ *Some old buzzard is at the door asking for Mary Wilson.*

dirty old man *n.* a lecherous old man. (Usually jocular.) □ *Jimmy, you are getting to be a dirty old man!* □ *What a terrible joke. You are a dirty old man!*

gaffer *n.* an old man; a rustic old man. (From *grandfather.*) □ *Nobody out there but some old gaffer with a cane.* □ *The old gaffer smiled and moved on.*

geezer *n.* a strange old man; a *buzzard.* □ *Who's the old geezer with the straw hat on?* □ *He is a nice geezer, but a little talkative.*

sugar daddy *n.* an older man who takes care of a younger person, especially a young athlete or a young woman. □ *Mr. Wilson is sort of a sugar daddy to the whole team.* □ *I thought sugar daddies were illegal.*

MAN - RECKLESS

cowboy *n.* a reckless and independent man; a reckless driver. (Also a term of address.) □ *Come on, cowboy, finish your coffee and get moving.* □ *Some cowboy in a new Caddy cut in front of me.*

MAN - SEX

birdwatcher *n.* a *girl* watcher; someone, usually a man, who enjoys watching women go by. □ *Harry is a dedicated birdwatcher.* □ *You birdwatchers should just mind your own business.*

charmer *n.* a seducer; a *make-out artist.* □ *You always have to act like some half-ass charmer, scamming like it really mattered! Grow up!* □ *Willard is such a charmer! Too bad he's married.*

chippy-chaser *n.* a man who chases sexually loose women. □ *He tried to be such a charmer—you know, a chippy-chaser, but he is so inept.* □ *Max used to be a chippy-chaser, but the scag has him sort of debilitated these days.*

hustler *n.* a man who is notoriously good with women. □ *That guy's a hustler. Watch out.* □ *He thinks he's a hustler. The chicks think he's a wimp.*

lady-killer *n.* a man who is very successful with women. □ *Bruno is anything but a lady-killer.* □ *We saw an old-time lady-killer with a close-cut black mustache and everything.*

make-out artist *n.* a seducer; a lecher, usually a male. □ *The guy thinks he's a make-out artist, but the women all think he's a nerd.* □ *He might have been a make-out artist in his youth, but I doubt it.*

scammer *n.* a lecher; a fast worker with the opposite sex. □ *Bob thinks he's a great scammer, but he's just a wimp.* □ *Do scammers have a great future? What's for an encore?*

stud *n.* a human male viewed as very successful with women. □ *Fred thinks he is a real stud.* □ *Man, look at that stud over there. Think he's going steady with anyone?*

studhammer *n.* a male who is successful sexually with women. □ *Alex is a real* studhammer. □ *The guy thinks he is a studhammer, but he is just a jerk.*

tomcat *n.* a sexually active male; a *stud.* □ *Old Fred's getting to be quite a tomcat.* □ *His goal in life is to die a tomcat at age ninety.*

wolf *n.* a bold and aggressive male. □ *He sees himself as a lady-killer. The chicks see him as an old-fashioned wolf.* □ *And this wolf comes up to me and starts holding my hand.*

MAN - STRANGE

gunzel-butt *n.* a strange-looking male. (Underworld.) □ *Bruno told the gunzel-butt where to get off.* □ *Rocko is no gunzel-butt. He's a thinker.*

MAN - STRONG

bruiser *n.* a big, rough male. □ *That big bruiser must weigh a ton.* □ *They call that 320-pound bruiser "The Fridge."*

cave man *n.* a strong, virile man. □ *He's sort of a cave man, big and hairy.* □ *I don't care for cave men.*

gazoony *n.* a bully or strong-arm man. (Underworld.) □ *Bruno didn't like being called a gazoony, although that is what he is.* □ *A couple of gazoonies stood outside looking menacing.*

husky *n.* a strong man; a thug. □ *Tell your husky to lay off, Bruno.* □ *A couple of huskies helped me get my car unstuck.*

knuckle-dragger *n.* a strong, ape-like man. □ *Bruno is Mr. Big's favorite knuckle-dragger.* □ *Call off your knuckle-draggers. I'll pay you whatever you want.*

macho *n.* a masculine or virile male. □ *He's such a macho. He even chews tobacco.* □ *Watch out for that macho over there. He's cruising for a bruising.*

muscleman *n.* a strong bully; a goon. (Underworld.) □ *Bruno is a muscleman for the kingpin of a local drug ring.* □ *Tell your muscleman to lay off.*

powerhouse *n.* a very big, strong person, usually a male. □ *Ted is a real powerhouse. I'd hate to have him mad at me.* □ *Each member of the football team is a powerhouse.*

strong-arm man *n.* a bully; a man who is employed to use physical power to force someone to do something. □ *Bruno is Mr. Big's strong-arm man.* □ *The mob employs hundreds of strong-arm men.*

tiger *n.* a strong and virile man. □ *The guy's a tiger. Watch out for him.* □ *Isn't Bruno a tiger?*

MAN - STUPID

Clyde *n.* an oaf; a *square* male. □ *Well, Clyde, I think you're way off base.* □ *A dull Clyde, that's my old Bill, but I still love him.*

dick *n.* a stupid male. (Potentially offensive. Use only with discretion.) □ *You stupid dick!* □ *What stupid dick put this thing here in the way?*

dildo *n.* a stupid person, usually a male. (Potentially offensive. Use only with discretion. The term refers to an artificial penis.) □ *Hank can be such a dildo sometimes.* □ *You silly dildo!*

duffer *n.* a foolish oaf; a (male) bumbler. □ *Some old duffer is weeding our garden for us. He's lost, I think.* □ *Pete's just a duffer—he's not really serious at it.*

dumb ox *n.* a large and stupid person, usually a man. □ *What does that dumb ox want?* □ *Do you think I'm going to argue with that big dumb ox?*

honyock *n.* someone, usually a male, who acts like a peasant; a crude or unsophisticated person; a rustic oaf. (Old. Also a rude or playful term of address.) □ *Steve seems like such a honyock until you get to know him.* □ *Come here, you silly honyock.*

jake *n.* a stupid person, usually a male. □ *Some loony jake told me we are going the wrong way.* □ *Who's the jake in the plaid pants?*

lug *n.* a stupid male. □ *Is this lug bothering you, lady?* □ *Some lug on a tractor was holding up traffic.*

MAN - UGLY

cromagnon *n.* an ugly male. (Collegiate.) □ *Who is that cromagnon you were with last night?* □ *That was no cro-*

magnon. That was your blind date for next weekend.

melvin *n.* a studious or unattractive male. (Teens and collegiate.) □ *Gary is such a melvin!* □ *Do you think I would go out with that melvin?*

neanderthal *n.* a large and ugly male. □ *Tell that neanderthal to get out of here.* □ *Tom, don't act like such a neanderthal.*

MAN - VULGAR

animal *n.* a male who acts like a beast in terms of manners, cleanliness, or sexual aggressiveness. (Also a term of address.) □ *You are an animal!* □ *Stop picking your nose, animal.*

ape *n.* a hoodlum or strong-arm man, especially if big and strong. (Underworld.) □ *Tell your ape to let me go!* □ *You take your apes and get out of here!*

MARBLES

aggie *n.* an agate marble or a glass imitation of one. □ *I found the old aggies I played with when I was a kid.* □ *Somebody stole my prize aggie!*

MARINE

bullet-stopper *n.* a U.S. Marine. (From the Persian Gulf War.) □ *The bullet-stoppers shipped out before we even got to the desert.* □ *About a dozen bullet-stoppers came into the bar and the army guys tried to start a fight.*

jarhead *n.* a U.S. Marine. □ *The jarheads got there first and let them know what was what.* □ *Do you want to spend a few years as a gravel-pounder or a jarhead? You get free clothes with both jobs.*

self-propelled sandbag *n.* a U.S. Marine. (Persian Gulf War.) □ *Once those self-propelled sandbags hit the bars, you army guys had better just go home.* □ *Those guys are just self-propelled sandbags. They are fearless.*

MASCULINE

macho *mod.* masculine; virile. (From Spanish. Used as a derogation by feminists.) □ *Does the world really need one more macho man?* □ *He's hardly macho.* □ *You know—that bright-eyed macho type.*

MEAN

badass *mod.* tough; bad; belligerent. (Use with caution.) □ *Tom is one badass cop!* □ *Stop acting like such a badass punk!*

hard *mod.* tough. (Akin to *hardhearted*; *hard as nails*.) □ *Sally is really hard. She can stand anything.* □ *Only the hard guys get through basic training.*

hardboiled *mod.* tough; heartless. □ *She is a hardboiled old gal.* □ *Do you have to act so hardboiled?*

in cold blood *mod.* without feeling; with cruel intent. □ *Rocko kills in cold blood and never gives it a thought.* □ *The prof flunked me in cold blood.*

low-life *mod.* mean; belligerent. □ *Don't be so low-life, man!* □ *We don't need any low-life characters around here.*

MECHANIC

grease monkey *n.* a mechanic. □ *I took my car to my favorite grease monkey, who says I need a new something or other.* □ *How much money does a grease monkey make?*

MEDDLE

diddle with something *in.* to play with something; to toy with something. □ *Here, don't diddle with that watch.* □ *Stop diddling with your nose, Jimmy!*

mess around (with something) AND **mess about (with something); monkey around (with something)** *in.* to play with or fiddle with something. □ *Don't mess around with the ashtray.* □ *You'll break it if you don't stop messing about with it.*

mess with someone or something AND **monkey with someone or something** *in.* to bother or interfere with someone or something. □ *Come on, don't monkey with it.* □ *Don't mess with me unless you want trouble.*

nosy parker *n.* a nosy person. (Also a term of address.) □ *Mary can be such a nosy parker.* □ *Look, you nosy parker, mind your own business.*

put one's nose in (where it's not wanted) AND **stick one's nose in (where**

it's not wanted) *tr.* to interfere in someone else's business. □ *Why do you always have to stick your nose in?* □ *Please don't put your nose in where it's not wanted!*

screw around with someone or something *in.* to fiddle with or *mess around (with someone or something).* □ *Andy screwed around with his clock until he broke it.* □ *Look, chum! Don't screw around with me!*

screw someone or something up *tr.* to interfere with someone or something; to mess up someone or something. □ *Try again and don't screw it up this time.* □ *You really screwed up my brother by not being on time.*

MEDICAL

bury the hatchet *tr.* to leave surgical instruments in the patient. (Medical.) □ *Did Dr. Smith bury the hatchet again?* □ *The idea that a doctor would bury the hatchet is a very old joke.*

doc(s)-in-a-box *n.* a walk-in emergency healthcare center, as found in shopping centers. □ *I was cut and went immediately to the docs-in-a-box in the mall.* □ *The doc-in-a-box finally closed because of lack of customers.*

gas-passer *n.* a jocular nickname for an anesthetist. (Hospitals.) □ *My gosh! The gas-passer charged almost as much as the surgeon.* □ *The gas-passer put a needle in my arm.*

gork 1. *tr.* to give a patient sedation. (Hospitals.) □ *Dr. Wilson says to gork the patient in 226.* □ *He'll quiet down after we gork him.* **2.** AND **GORK** *phr.* an alleged hospital chart notation of the diagnosis "God only really knows." (Hospitals.) □ *I see old Mr. Kelly is in again with a hundred complaints. His chart says GORK.* □ *He's down with gork again.*

gorked (out) *mod.* heavily sedated; knocked out. (Hospitals.) □ *Once the patient was gorked, he was more cooperative.* □ *The guy in 226 is totally gorked out now.*

lift *n.* a surgical face-lift. □ *He had a lift on his vacation, but his face still looked* two sizes too big. □ *We've got three lifts and a nose job in O.R. this morning.*

McDoctor(s) AND **McDoc(s)** *n.* a jocular term for a walk-in emergency medical clinic as found in shopping malls. □ *They took the kid to McDoctors, or whatever it is, over in the mall.* □ *McDocs is not cheap, but it's handy.*

nose job *n.* a plastic surgery operation to change the appearance of one's nose. □ *How much does a nose job cost?* □ *I don't want a nose job. What I got is good enough.*

T and A *n.* an operation to remove one's tonsils and adenoids. (Hospitals.) □ *She was scheduled for a T and A this morning at six sharp.* □ *The T and A went off without a hitch.*

veggie *n.* a comatose patient in a hospital. (Medical.) □ *Mary's aunt has been a veggie in the hospital for more than a year.* □ *I don't want to lie there and rot as a veggie. I want someone to pull the plug.*

MEDICAL - PARAPHERNALIA

silver goose *n.* a proctoscope. □ *The patient seems to have a real phobia about the silver goose.* □ *When the nurse brought in the silver goose, the patient nearly fainted.*

MEDICINE

bicarb *n.* bicarbonate of soda, used for an upset stomach. □ *I sure could use a little bicarb after that chili she served.* □ *I can't stand that sweet-tasting stuff. I want bicarb.*

liquid cork *n.* a medicine that stops diarrhea. □ *This nasty-tasting stuff is a good liquid cork for what you have.* □ *This liquid cork isn't so bad if you get it good and cold before you take it.*

on the pill *mod.* taking birth control pills. □ *Is it true that Mary is on the pill?* □ *She was on the pill, but she isn't now.*

over-the-counter *mod.* having to do with medication sold without a prescription. □ *Over-the-counter drugs can be helpful in some diseases.* □ *Is this medication over-the-counter or by prescription only?*

tab *n.* a tablet (of medicine). □ *Take a couple of aspirin tabs and call me in the morning.* □ *These tabs must have got wet. They're ruined.*

MEEKNESS

kiss-ass 1. *mod.* subservient. (Potentially offensive. Use *ass* with discretion.) □ *Don't be such a kiss-ass jerk. Tell off your boss.* □ *He is a little kiss-ass bastard who'll do anything to get ahead.* **2.** *in.* to act subservient (to someone). (Potentially offensive. Use only with discretion.) □ *Stop kiss-assing around and stand up to your employer.* □ *That guy will kiss-ass his way to the top.*

softie AND **softy** *n.* a gentle person; a very agreeable person. □ *He shouldn't give you much trouble. He's such a softie.* □ *The judge who tried the case was anything but a softie.*

MEETING

connect with someone *in.* to meet someone; to talk to someone on the telephone. □ *Let's try to connect on this matter tomorrow.* □ *We connected over a drink and discussed the matter fully.*

Let's do lunch (sometime). *sent.* "Let us have lunch together sometime." □ *Great seeing you, Martin, absolutely great. Let's do lunch.* □ *Let's do lunch sometime so we can catch up.*

meet *n.* a meeting or an appointment. (Mostly underworld.) □ *If this meet works out, we could score a cool million.* □ *What time is the meet?*

pow-wow 1. *n.* a meeting; a conference. (From an Amerindian word.) □ *There's a big pow-wow about money at the home office.* □ *Let's have a pow-wow on that issue.* **2.** *in.* to hold a meeting or a conference. □ *Let's pow-wow on that tomorrow.* □ *The senators were pow-wowing on how to get the law passed.*

MENSES

Aunt Flo *n.* a woman's menstrual period. (Used especially in expressions. Refers to the menstrual flow.) □ *I am sorry to announce that Aunt Flo has come for a visit.* □ *It's Aunt Flo again. She is such a pest.*

curse *n.* the menses. (Always with *the.*) □ *The curse struck this morning.* □ *Oh, the woes of the curse!*

have a little visitor *tr.* to have received the menses. (*Have got* can replace *have.*) □ *Mary said she has a little visitor.* □ *She has a little visitor and will call you later.*

monthlies *n.* the period of menstruation. □ *It's her monthlies. You know how she feels then.* □ *The monthlies have struck again!*

on the rag *mod.* menstruating. (Potentially offensive. Use with caution.) □ *Kim's on the rag and in a bad mood.* □ *Sue doesn't go swimming when she's on the rag.*

visit from Flo *n.* a menstrual period. □ *I am expecting a visit from Flo, but she seems late.* □ *I just had a visit from Flo. I hate the old hag!*

MENTAL

booby hatch *n.* a mental hospital. □ *I was afraid they would send me to the booby hatch.* □ *Don't you mean send you back to the booby hatch?*

laughing academy *n.* a mental hospital; an insane asylum. □ *About four years in the laughing academy would get you straightened out.* □ *I'm not ready for the laughing academy. A little while longer around here and I will be, though.*

loony bin *n.* an insane asylum; a mental hospital. □ *I feel like I'm about ready for the loony bin.* □ *Today's loony bins are far different from those of just a few decades ago.*

mental 1. *mod.* mentally retarded. (Use caution with the topic. Derogatory.) □ *The girl's mental. Leave her alone.* □ *Everybody in this ward is mental.* **2.** *n.* a mentally retarded person. (Use caution with the topic. Derogatory.) □ *He's a mental. He'll need some help.* □ *Who doesn't need help? Mentals are normal on that point.*

noid *n.* a "paranoid" person. □ *Some of those noids write hilarious letters to the editor.* □ *Who's the noid screaming about Big Brother?*

nuthouse AND **nut factory; nut-foundry; nuthatch** *n.* an insane asylum. □ *The judge spent three years in the nuthouse.* □ *They're going to send you to the nut-foundry some day.*

nuttery *n.* an insane asylum; the place where nuts are kept. □ *If you keep acting so odd, we'll have to put you in a nuttery.* □ *This place is a nuttery! I've never seen so many silly people.*

retard *n.* a rude nickname for a retarded person. (Derogatory and unkind.) □ *That retard is having a rough time.* □ *Don't call my brother a retard!*

scatterbrain *n.* a forgetful person; someone who is mentally disorganized. □ *I'm getting to be such a scatterbrain, I think.* □ *Aunt Martha is a real scatterbrain. She always forgets where her glasses are.*

where someone's head is at *phr.* the state of one's mental well-being. □ *As soon as I figure where my head is at, I'll be okay.* □ *He doesn't know where his head is at.*

MENTION

bring something up *tr.* to mention something. (Standard English.) □ *Why did you have to bring that up?* □ *Then they brought up the question of money.*

MIDDLE

smack(-dab) in the middle *mod.* exactly in the middle. □ *I came in smack-dab in the middle of the play.* □ *Not too big and not too small. Just smack in the middle.*

MILITARY

See also **SOLDIER.**

bust *tr.* to reduce someone's rank. (Originally military, now also in civilian use as with the police.) □ *I'm going to bust you to private!* □ *The brass busted her on the spot.*

goon-platoon *n.* a platoon of misfits; a platoon that is noted for its errors. (Military.) □ *Well, the goon-platoon's done it again!* □ *Which side is the goon-platoon on?*

rotsee *n.* "ROTC," the Reserve Officers Training Corps. □ *I joined rotsee to help pay my way through school.* □ *How long have you been in the rotsee program?*

scrambled eggs *n.* decorations on a military officer's uniform. □ *I know his rank is high because of the scrambled eggs, but I don't know how high.* □ *I'll be glad when I get some scrambled eggs on me.*

MILK

moo juice AND **cow juice** *n.* milk. □ *How about another glass of moo juice?* □ *While you're at the store, get some more cow juice.*

shake *n.* a milkshake. □ *I'd like a chocolate shake, please.* □ *A shake only costs sixty cents.*

tin cow *n.* canned milk. □ *This tin cow is okay in coffee or something, but you can't drink it.* □ *Tin cow was all we could get.*

MIMIC

copycat *n.* someone who mimics or copies the actions of others. □ *Don't be such a copycat. Find a style that suits you.* □ *Jim is a real copycat. He can say anything you say, just the way you say it.*

MISCHIEF

for the devil of it AND **for the heck of it; for the hell of it** *mod.* because it is slightly evil; for no good reason. (Use caution with *hell.*) □ *The kids broke the window just for the devil of it.* □ *We just drove over for the heck of it.*

full of the devil AND **full of Old Nick** *mod.* always making mischief. □ *Little Chuckie is sure full of the devil.* □ *In this weather, the kids are always full of Old Nick.*

highjinks AND **hijinks** *n.* tricks; capers. □ *Enough of your hijinks! Get busy.* □ *I like to hear about the kids and their latest hijinks.*

monkeyshines *n.* tricks; small acts of mischief. □ *You and your silly monkeyshines!* □ *These kids are a lot of fun despite their monkeyshines.*

MODERN

now generation *n.* the (once current) generation of young people who seemed to want only instant gratification. □ *All* *those people in the now generation want to start out with fancy cars and nice houses. □ What will happen to the now generation when times are hard?*

MONEY

ace *n.* one dollar. □ *Give me an ace. I have to get some telephone change.* □ *It only costs an ace. Buy two.*

adobe dollar *n.* a Mexican peso. □ *How many of these adobe dollars does it take to buy a can of pop here?* □ *One greenback will get you about 2,400 adobe dollars these days.*

almighty dollar *n.* the dollar viewed as a symbol of power or greed. □ *You don't care about anything but the almighty dollar.* □ *The world's economy seems to depend on an adequate supply of the almighty dollar.*

and change *phr.* plus a few cents; plus a few hundredths. (Used in citing a price or other decimal figure to indicate an additional fraction of a full unit.) □ *This one only costs $10 and change.* □ *The New York Stock Exchange was up seven points and change for the third broken record this week.*

ante *n.* an amount of money that must be contributed before playing certain card games, such as poker. □ *What's the ante to join this game?* □ *That's a pretty high ante. Forget it!*

bank *n.* money; ready cash. □ *I can't go out with you. No bank.* □ *I'm a little low on bank at the moment.*

bankroll *n.* a roll or wad of currency; one's cash assets. □ *My bankroll is getting a little low.* □ *Don't show that bankroll around here!*

beat *mod.* broke. □ *Man, I'm beat. I got no copper, no bread.* □ *All we need is another beat mouth to feed.*

behind the eight ball *mod.* broke. □ *Sorry, I'm really behind the eight ball this month. I can't make a contribution.* □ *I was behind the eight ball again and couldn't make my car payment.*

big bucks *n.* a lot of money. □ *To me, $400 is big bucks.* □ *She gets paid big bucks to worry about stuff like that.*

billie AND **bill(y)** *n.* paper money; a bill. (California.) □ *Do you have any billies on you?* □ *Nope, no billies on me.*

birdseed *n.* a small amount of money. □ *That's just birdseed compared to what I spend.* □ *Forty billion is birdseed to a government with a $600 billion budget.*

blow *tr.* to waste money; to spend money. □ *Mary blew $40 on a second-hand radio.* □ *We blew it all at a fancy restaurant.*

bones *n.* dollars; money; cash. □ *You got any bones on you I can borrow?* □ *The tickets only cost a few bones, but the play was lousy and I want my money back.*

bottom dollar *n.* one's last dollar. □ *I lost my bottom dollar on that deal.* □ *I'm down to my bottom dollar. How about a little loan?*

bread *n.* money. □ *I need to get some bread to live on.* □ *You got any bread you can spare?*

buck *n.* a dollar. □ *Gimme a buck for a bottle of wine, will you, mister?* □ *Here's a buck; get me some cigarettes.*

buckage *n.* money. □ *I am a little low on buckage at the moment.* □ *Can you spare a little buckage until payday?*

bundle *n.* a large amount of money. □ *He still has a bundle from the sale of his house.* □ *You must think I have a real bundle.*

C *n.* the sum of $100, as in *C-note*. (Underworld. The "C" is the Roman numeral 100.) □ *Four Cs for an old junker like that? You're crazy!* □ *This suit cost me two Cs.*

cabbage *n.* money. □ *How much cabbage you want for this heater?* □ *I don't make enough cabbage to go on a trip like that!*

cake *n.* money. □ *I can't scrape together enough cake to do the job.* □ *I don't have cake in my pocket, in the bank, or under my mattress. What am I going to do?*

capital *n.* cash; money. □ *I'm a little short of capital right now.* □ *Do you think I could borrow a little capital until payday?*

cash flow *n.* cash; ready money. □ *When I get a little cash flow at the end of the week, I'll treat you to a hamburger.* □ *There wasn't enough cash flow to pay the rent.*

cent *n.* one dollar. (Underworld.) □ *One cent for one joint? Not bad.* □ *A cent for this thing?*

century note *n.* a one-hundred-dollar bill. (Underworld. The "C" is the Roman numeral for "100.") □ *I got a couple of century notes for driving these guys home from the bank.* □ *Here's a century note for your trouble, young man.*

change *n.* money. □ *It takes a lot of change to buy a car like that.* □ *I don't have the change to get one of those videotape machines.*

chicken feed *n.* a small amount of money. □ *Sure, I can afford it. It's just chicken feed.* □ *It may be chicken feed to you, but that's a month's rent to me.*

chips *n.* money. □ *I managed to put away a few chips when I worked for Acme Systems.* □ *She saved some chips over the years and bought herself a little place on the beach.*

chump change *n.* a small amount of money; the kind of salary or amount of money a *chump* would work for. □ *I refuse to work for chump change! I want a real job.* □ *It may be chump change, but it's better than nothing.*

clam *n.* a dollar. (Underworld.) □ *Forty clams for a sweater that doesn't even have arms!* □ *You got a couple of clams I can bum for a little bottle?*

C-note AND **C-spot** *n.* a one-hundred-dollar bill. (The "C" is the Roman numeral for "100.") □ *How much ammo will a C-note buy these days?* □ *That guy wanted a C-spot to fix my muffler.*

coin *n.* money. □ *I'm sort of short of coin right now. Can it wait?* □ *He made a lot of coin on the last picture.*

color of someone's money *n.* the amount of money someone has in hand. □ *Well, I can tell if we can make a deal if I could see the color of your money.* □ *Lemme see the color of your money. Then we'll talk.*

copper *n.* money. (From *copper penny.*) □ *How much copper you got on you?* □ *That car takes too much copper to run.*

deuce *n.* two dollars. □ *Can you loan me a deuce till payday?* □ *Sure, here's a deuce. Don't spend it all in one place.*

dinero *n.* money. (Spanish.) □ *I don't have as much dinero as I need, but other than that, I'm doing okay.* □ *You got some dinero I can borrow?*

doowacky *n.* money. □ *You got some doowacky I can borrow?* □ *I'm out of doowacky myself.*

do-re-mi AND **do-re-me** *n.* money. (From *dough.*) □ *It takes too much do-re-mi to live in this part of town.* □ *Do you have a little do-re-me you could loan me?*

double saw(buck) *n.* a twenty-dollar bill. □ *This whole thing only cost a double sawbuck.* □ *Can you loan me a double sawbuck till payday?*

dough *n.* money. □ *I got a lot of dough for that ring I found.* □ *I need some dough to buy groceries.*

ducats AND **duc-ducs** *n.* money. □ *Who's got enough ducats to pay for the tickets?* □ *I've got duc-ducs galore!*

easy money *n.* money earned or gained with little or no difficulty. □ *You know where I can get some easy money?* □ *All you guys want easy money. Don't you want to work for it?*

ends *n.* money. (Streets.) □ *You got enough ends to get you through the week?* □ *We don't have enough ends to pay the gas bill.*

federal diploma *n.* a U.S. bank note. □ *I could use a few extra of those federal diplomas.* □ *How many federal diplomas you got with you?*

filthy lucre *n.* money. □ *I sure could use a little of that filthy lucre.* □ *I don't want to touch any of your filthy lucre.*

fin AND **finn** *n.* a five-dollar bill. (Germanic via Yiddish.) □ *Who says I owe* *you a fin?* □ *I gave the old guy a finn, and he nearly passed out.*

fiver *n.* a five-dollar bill. □ *This thing only cost me a fiver.* □ *Give him a fiver, and let's get outa here.*

folding money AND **folding stuff** *n.* U.S. paper bank notes, as opposed to coins. □ *Sorry, I don't have any folding money with me. Can you pick up the bill?* □ *I sure could use some more of that folding stuff.*

four bits *n.* fifty cents. (A *bit* is equal to twelve and one-half cents.) □ *You got four bits I can borrow?* □ *Here's four bits. Keep the change.*

front *in.* to pay out money in advance of receiving goods; to pay up front. □ *I fronted about $550 for the new computer.* □ *How much do you want her to front for this?*

front money *n.* money paid in advance; earnest money. □ *How much front money do you need?* □ *I put up a lot of front money and have nothing to show for it.*

geetis AND **geedus; geetus** *n.* money. □ *That kind of car takes a lot of geetis, doesn't it?* □ *I don't have the geetis to throw around on something like that.*

gold *n.* money. □ *Do you have enough gold to pay the bill?* □ *There's no gold in my pockets.*

grand AND **G** *n.* one thousand dollars. □ *That car probably cost about twenty grand.* □ *Four Gs for that thing?*

green AND **green folding; green paper; green stuff** *n.* money; paper money. □ *How much green you got on you?* □ *I have so much green stuff, I don't know what to do with it.*

greenback *n.* a dollar bill. □ *She came out of the bank and dropped this pack of greenbacks right there on the street.* □ *It's only ten greenbacks. Anybody can afford that.*

hard coin *n.* lots of money. □ *A car like that takes hard coin.* □ *Old Freddie is earning some hard coin these days.*

heavy bread AND **heavy money** *n.* a great deal of money. □ *Man, that car cost some heavy bread.* □ *It takes heavy money to run a household like this.*

hush money *n.* money paid to buy someone's silence. □ *They paid enough hush money to silence an army.* □ *There was some hush money paid to someone in city hall.*

ice *n.* money given as a bribe, especially to the police. (Underworld.) □ *Did you give Ervine the ice?* □ *A lot of those cops take ice.*

in the chips *mod.* wealthy; with lots of money. □ *I'm in the chips this month. Let's go squander it.* □ *If I was in the chips, I'd buy a Jag.*

jack *n.* money. □ *I don't have the jack for a deal like that.* □ *How much jack will it take?*

kilobucks *n.* a tremendous sum of money. □ *These boondoggles waste kilobucks!* □ *How many kilobucks does a set of wheels like that cost?*

lace *n.* money. (Underworld.) □ *You got any lace in those pockets?* □ *My lace won't reach that far. I can't afford it.*

lettuce *n.* money. □ *Put your lettuce on the table; then we'll talk.* □ *How much lettuce do you have left?*

long bread AND **long green** *n.* money. □ *Man, that must have cost you some long bread!* □ *Look at the long green you get for doing the job!*

loot *n.* money in general. □ *I left home without any loot.* □ *It takes too much loot to eat at that restaurant.*

mad money *n.* money to be spent in a frivolous fashion. □ *This is my mad money, and I'll do with it as I please.* □ *I got $100 in mad money for my birthday.*

mazuma AND **mazulla** *n.* money. (From Hebrew *mezu* via Yiddish.) □ *How much mazuma do you want for this?* □ *She's got more mazuma than she knows what to do with.*

megabucks *n.* a lot of money; *big bucks.* □ *A stereo that size must cost megabucks.*

□ *Mr. Wilson has megabucks in pharmaceutical stocks.*

mint *n.* a lot of money. □ *He makes a mint. He can afford a little generosity.* □ *That kind of car costs a mint!*

money from home *n.* easily gotten money. (Underworld.) □ *There is nothing to a simple con job like this. It's money from home.* □ *This job is like taking candy from a kid. It's money from home.*

moolah *n.* money. (Originally underworld.) □ *That is a whole lot of moolah!* □ *There was no moolah in that safe!*

necessary *n.* money; an income. (Always with *the*.) □ *I can always use more of the necessary.* □ *I gotta have more of the necessary, man.*

nest egg *n.* money saved for some important purpose, such as retirement. □ *I lost most of my nest egg in the market crash.* □ *It takes years to build up a nest egg.*

package *n.* a lot of money; a *bundle.* □ *She made quite a package on that bank deal.* □ *I came away from the dog track with a nice little package.*

peanuts *n.* practically no money at all. □ *They want me to do everything, but they only pay peanuts.* □ *The cost is just peanuts compared to what you get for the money.*

pile *n.* a large amount of money. □ *She really made a pile in the stock market.* □ *That old lady has a pile of money stashed in the bank.*

pot *n.* a sum of money collected; a pool of money. □ *Clare won the whole pot.* □ *How large is the pot this month?*

pounds *n.* dollars; money. □ *How many pounds does this thing cost?* □ *I don't have any pounds on me.*

pretty penny *n.* a sizable amount of money. □ *I imagine that your jacket cost you a pretty penny.* □ *This watch cost me a pretty penny, and I intend to take care of it.*

rivets *n.* dollars; money. □ *You got enough rivets on you for a snack?* □ *Who can come up with that many rivets?*

rocks *n.* money; dollars. (Underworld.) □ *How many rocks do you want for that?* □ *Twenty rocks for that?*

roll *n.* a bankroll; lots of money. □ *I earned a roll off that last deal.* □ *He's got a roll right there in his pocket.*

sawbuck *n.* a ten-dollar bill. (From the time when the "10" was indicated by the Roman numeral "X," which looks like the crosspiece that supports wood that is being sawed.) □ *It cost me a sawbuck to have my car pulled out of the mud.* □ *Can I borrow a sawbuck till payday?*

scratch *n.* money. □ *I just don't have the scratch.* □ *How much scratch does it take to buy a car like this one?*

shekels *n.* dollars; money. □ *You got a few shekels you can spare?* □ *These things cost plenty of shekels.*

silver *n.* money. □ *What kind of silver is that going to take?* □ *I have some silver stashed at home if you need it.*

simoleon *n.* a dollar. (Underworld.) □ *How many simoleons is this going to cost me?* □ *For only one simoleon, you get a ticket to the greatest show on earth.*

single *n.* one dollar; a dollar bill. □ *I don't have enough singles in the register to get me through the morning.* □ *I got a couple of singles I can lend you.*

six bits *n.* seventy-five cents. (A *bit* is equal to twelve and one-half U.S. cents.) □ *You got six bits I can borrow?* □ *Just try one of these things. It's only six bits.*

skin *n.* a dollar bill. □ *This ticket cost me a couple of skins—and it's not worth it.* □ *You got a skin for the tollbooth?*

slush fund *n.* a fund of money that can be used for various unofficial and discretionary purposes. □ *How much is left in the slush fund?* □ *The slush fund is bankrupt.*

smacker *n.* a dollar. (Underworld.) □ *You got a couple of smackers for the toll booth?* □ *Don't waste your hard-earned smackers like that. Run on through.*

small fortune *n.* a rather sizable amount of money. □ *This set of wheels cost me a* small fortune. □ I've got a small fortune tied up in test equipment.

smart money *n.* money belonging to smart or clever people. □ *Most of the smart money is going into utility stocks right now.* □ *Watch and see what the smart money is doing.*

soft money *n.* easy money; money obtained without much effort. □ *Don't become dependent on soft money.* □ *There's not even very much soft money around now.*

spending money *n.* cash, as opposed to money in the bank. □ *I'm a little short of spending money at the present. Could I borrow ten dollars?* □ *I don't have any spending money either.*

spinach *n.* money. (Because it is green.) □ *How much spinach you got on you?* □ *Look at this! One hundred dollars in good old American spinach!*

spondulicks AND **spondulics; spondulix** *n.* money. □ *How much spondulicks will this set me back?* □ *I don't have enough spondulix to swing the deal.*

Suzy *n.* a U.S. one-dollar coin bearing a likeness of Susan B. Anthony. □ *I've got two Suzys I want to get rid of.* □ *Someday I'm going to buy a car or something with a barrel of Suzys.*

tenner *n.* a ten-dollar bill. □ *For a tenner, the bum led Barlowe to the place where the crate still lay in the alley.* □ *Barlowe slipped him a tenner and faded into the fog.*

ten-spot *n.* a ten-dollar bill. □ *I slipped him a ten-spot, and suddenly there was a table available.* □ *It will cost you a ten-spot to get the book—in paperback, that is.*

thin dime *n.* a dime, thought of as a very small amount of money. (A concept eroded by inflation.) □ *For only one thin dime you will receive our exciting catalog of novelties and tricks.* □ *This whole mess isn't worth one thin dime.*

tight money *n.* money that is hard to get. □ *This is tight money. Go easy on it. It's hard to get.* □ *In these days of tight money, no new expenditures will be approved.*

two bits *n.* twenty-five cents; a quarter coin. □ *Can I bum two bits for the phone?* □ *Here's two bits for your piggy bank.*

wad *n.* a bundle of money; a bankroll. (Originally underworld.) □ *I lost my wad on a rotten horse in the seventh race.* □ *You'd better not flash a wad like that around here. You won't have it long.*

wampum *n.* money. (From an Amerindian word.) □ *I don't have enough wampum to swing the deal.* □ *How much wampum do you want for this thing?*

war chest *n.* a political campaign fund. □ *They say the vice president has over $1 million in his war chest.* □ *When the war chest gave out, the candidate dropped out of the race.*

wherewithal *n.* money. □ *I don't have the wherewithal to invest in anything like that.* □ *I've got the interest but not the wherewithal.*

yard *n.* a one-hundred-dollar bill. (Underworld.) □ *The guy wanted a yard just to fix a little dent in the fender.* □ *Pay him a yard to shut up about what he saw.*

MONEY - LACKING

cleaned out *mod.* broke; with no money. □ *I'm cleaned out. Not a cent left.* □ *Tom's cleaned out. He's broke. He'll have to go home.*

clean someone out *tr.* to get all of someone's money. □ *The bill for supper cleaned me out, and we couldn't go to the flick.* □ *The robbers cleaned out everybody on the train.*

dead broke *mod.* completely broke; without any money. □ *I'm dead broke—not a nickel to my name.* □ *I've been dead broke for a month now.*

financially embarrassed *mod.* broke. □ *I'm a bit financially embarrassed at the moment.* □ *Gary found himself financially embarrassed when the time came to pay the bill.*

flat broke *mod.* having no money at all. □ *Sorry, I'm flat broke. Not a cent on me.* □ *You may be flat broke, but you will find a way to pay your electricity bill or you will live in the dark.*

flat on one's ass *mod.* broke; financially destroyed. (Potentially offensive. Use only with discretion. An elaboration of *flat broke.*) □ *Sorry, I can't help you. I'm broke—flat on my ass.* □ *The guy's flat on his ass. Can you help him out with a loan?*

in deep *mod.* deeply in debt. (Often with *with* or *to.*) □ *Bruno is in deep with his bookie.* □ *I'm in deep to the department store.*

shorts AND **case of the shorts** *n.* the lack of money. (Always with *the.*) □ *Here I am with a case of the shorts again.* □ *The shorts always come around at the end of the month.*

stone broke *mod.* completely broke. □ *I'm sorry, I'm stone broke. Can I send you a check?* □ *What could I do? She was stone broke.*

strapped *mod.* broke; short of money. □ *I'm sorry, I can't pay you right now. I'm strapped.* □ *They're really strapped for money at the present time.*

tapped AND **tapped out** *mod.* broke. □ *The consumer is just about tapped. Don't expect much buying in that sector.* □ *I'm tapped out. Nothing left for you or anybody else this month.*

wiped (out) *mod.* broke. □ *I'm totally wiped out. Not enough bread for grub.* □ *Medical bills left us totally wiped out.*

MONEY - NEGATIVE

funny-money *n.* any substitute money: counterfeit money, military scrip, etc. □ *I don't want any funny-money. Real U.S. greenbacks or forget the deal.* □ *Who'll change my funny-money back to bucks?*

MONEY - SOURCE

deep pockets *n.* a good source of money. □ *We need to find some deep pockets to finance this venture.* □ *Deep pockets are hard to find since the stock market crashed.*

MOTIVATION

jack someone up *tr.* to motivate someone; to stimulate someone to do something. □ *I'll jack him up and try to get some action out of him.* □ *What does it take to jack up that lazy guy?*

wherewithal *n.* motivation; gumption. □ *I just don't have the wherewithal to do the job.* □ *As soon as I get some wherewithal, I'll get a new computer.*

MOTIVES

angle *n.* a selfish motive; an ulterior motive. □ *Okay, Ted, I know you better than to think that you are doing this out of the kindness of your heart. What's your angle?* □ *I don't have any angle. I have reformed.*

MOTORCYCLES

ape hangers *n.* long steering handles on a motorcycle. □ *Who is that guy riding the bike with ape hangers?* □ *Aren't ape hangers sort of dangerous?*

bike *n.* a motorcycle; a bicycle. □ *How much did that bike set you back?* □ *You have to wear a helmet with a bike that size, don't you?*

biker *n.* a motorcycle rider. □ *Four bikers roared by and woke up the baby.* □ *That biker is wearing about a dozen earrings.*

skid-lid *n.* a motorcycle helmet. □ *The law has no business telling me I gotta wear a skid-lid.* □ *Don't you use a skid-lid?*

MOUTH

bazoo *n.* the mouth. □ *You would have to open your big bazoo and tell everything.* □ *Don't talk with a full bazoo.*

fly trap *n.* the mouth. □ *Close your fly trap. You talk too much.* □ *Don't talk with your fly trap full.*

hatch *n.* the mouth. □ *Shut your hatch!* □ *Pop this in your hatch.*

kisser *n.* the face; the mouth. □ *I poked him right in the kisser.* □ *There he stood with a bloody kisser.*

puke hole *n.* a mouth. (Rude.) □ *Shut your puke hole and listen to what I am telling you!* □ *Do you want me to punch you in the puke hole?*

Q-sign *n.* the rounded, open mouth of a dead person with the tongue hanging out like the tail of a capital Q. (A semi-jocular usage. Hospitals.) □ *The old lady in the corner room is giving the Q-sign.* □ *I can't handle another Q-sign today.*

trap *n.* the mouth. (Crude.) □ *Shut your trap!* □ *Put this in your trap and chew it up.*

yap *n.* the mouth. □ *Shut your yap!* □ *You have a big yap, you know?*

MOVEMENT

belly up (to something) *in.* to move up to something, often a bar. □ *The man swaggered in and bellied up to the counter and demanded my immediate attention.* □ *As he bellied up, he said, "Do you know who I am?"*

full steam ahead *mod.* with determination. □ *We started moving full steam ahead on the project.* □ *Full steam ahead! Let's see how fast this will go!*

mope AND **mope around** *in.* to move around slowly and sadly. □ *I feel like moping and nothing else.* □ *He just mopes around all day and won't eat anything.*

on the run *mod.* while one is moving from place to place. □ *I will try to get some aspirin today on the run.* □ *I will think about it on the run.*

scooch 1. *in.* to move (oneself), while seated, forward, backward, or sideways by sliding. □ *Scooch over here by me.* □ *Why don't you scooch over here?* **2.** *tr.* to push or move something. □ *Scooch your chair over where the light is better.* □ *Scooch the potted palm to the edge of the deck and push it overboard.*

sleepwalk *n.* a movement toward something without effort. (A movement that could be done "in one's sleep.") □ *Getting the degree was a sleepwalk. Getting a job was hell.* □ *It was no sleepwalk, but it didn't make me slave away either.*

step right up *phr.* "come forward and do not be bashful." □ *There are still a few of these left. Step right up and get yours.* □ *Step right up and buy a ticket to the greatest show on earth!*

streak *in.* to move rapidly from one place to another. □ *The train streaked into the station and came to a stop just inches from the end of the track.* □ *I've got to streak over to the library in a big hurry.*

vroom AND **varoom** *in.* to move rapidly from place to place; to travel at high speed, making the noise of a loud engine. □ *Let's vroom over to Larry's and see what's happening.* □ *The little boy varoomed down the sidewalk on his tricycle.*

zoom up *in.* to drive or pull up to a place. □ *A car zoomed up, and seven kids got out.* □ *Let's zoom up to the door and see if she's home.*

MOVEMENT - LACKING

dead in the water *mod.* stalled; immobile. (Originally nautical.) □ *This whole company is dead in the water.* □ *The project is dead in the water for the time being.*

down for the count *mod.* inactive for the duration (of something). (From boxing.) □ *I've got a terrible cold, and I think I'm down for the count.* □ *Fred is down for the count. He's in jail.*

freeze *in.* to hold perfectly still. (Also a command given by a police officer that implies there is a gun pointed at a suspect.) □ *I froze, and the bull didn't see me.* □ *The fuzz shouted, "Freeze, or you're dead meat!"*

get nowhere fast *in.* to make very poor progress. □ *We are getting nowhere fast around here.* □ *I'm getting nowhere fast in this job. I quit.*

MOVEMENT - STYLE

style *in.* to show off; to strut around. (Black.) □ *Look at that brother style!* □ *Why don't you style over here and meet my man?*

MOVIES

clip *n.* a music video; a short film. □ *This next clip is something you'll all recognize.* □ *Stay tuned for more great clips.*

horse opera *n.* a Western movie. □ *They're showing a series of old horse operas at the theater tonight.* □ *Haven't I seen this horse opera before? About a hundred times maybe?*

nabe *n.* a neighborhood theater. □ *Do I have to go downtown to see that movie, or is it playing at the nabes yet?* □ *Why drive all the way out there when you can see it at the nabe for half the cost?*

oater *n.* a Western movie. (From the oats that the horses eat.) □ *I don't want to see an oater. Isn't anything else showing?* □ *Let's go out and see a good old-fashioned oater.*

rush *n.* a quick print of a day's shooting of a film. (Filmmaking. Usually plural.) □ *After today's shooting, we'll watch yesterday's rushes.* □ *Rush these rushes right over to Mr. Hitchcock's office.*

shoot 'em up 1. *n.* a Western action movie. □ *I like a good shoot 'em up every now and then.* □ *Most films are more sophisticated nowadays than the old shoot 'em ups.* **2.** *mod.* having to do with a Western action film. □ *He was a shoot 'em up star in the thirties.* □ *I like the good old shoot 'em up movies.*

sneak *n.* a sneak preview of a movie. □ *There was a good sneak at the Granada last night.* □ *The sneak was better than the flick they had advertised.*

snuff film *n.* a film that vividly portrays actual death or killing. □ *Who would watch a snuff film, anyway?* □ *Some of these snuff films have a loyal following of real sickies.*

take *n.* a section of a film that is pronounced acceptable just after it is shot. □ *It's a take. Get it over to the lab.* □ *After seven straight takes the crew demanded a break.*

tearjerker *n.* a very sad story or film. □ *The film was a real tearjerker.* □ *I don't care to read a steady diet of tearjerkers.*

MUCUS

boogie AND **booger** *n.* a piece of nasal mucus. (Crude. Use only with discretion.) □ *That's no way to take care of a booger!* □ *Is that a boogie on your lip, or what?*

hock a luggie *tr.* to cough up and spit out phlegm. □ *Wayne hocked a luggie right outside the classroom door and the teacher sent him to the principal's office.* □ *Tom suppressed the urge to hock a luggie over the bridge railing.*

lunger *n.* a large and nasty mass of phlegm coughed up from the lungs and spat out. □ *Wayne loved to pretend that he was going to plant a lunger on somebody's shoe.* □ *Sharon walked around a lunger on the sidewalk, but Beavis stepped right in it.*

nose-lunger *n.* a mass of nasal mucus. □ *Wayne blew a nose-lunger onto the wall and giggled.* □ *Beavis thought the funniest thing in the world was having a nose-lunger dangling from his chin.*

skeet *n.* a blob of nasal mucus. (Collegiate.) □ *God, Fred, there's a gross skeet hanging outta your nose!* □ *That wasn't stew; that was skeets!*

skeet shooting *n.* the act of blowing one's nose by pinching one nostril and using no tissue or handkerchief. □ *There is nothing more disgusting than a bunch of college boys belching and skeet shooting.* □ *Bill's mother caught him skeet shooting and really gave him a lot of trouble.*

snot *n.* nasal mucus. (Potentially offensive. Use only with discretion.) □ *Oh, God, there's snot on your cheek.* □ *He sneezed and got snot all over the newspaper.*

snotty AND **snottie** *mod.* nasty with nasal mucus. (Potentially offensive. Use only with discretion.) □ *Keep your snotty old handkerchief to yourself.* □ *Don't leave your snottie tissues all over the house!*

MURDER
See also DEATH.

blot someone out *tr.* to kill someone. (Underworld.) □ *Sorry, chum, we got orders to blot you out.* □ *They blotted out the witness before the trial.*

blow someone away *tr.* to kill someone; to shoot someone. (Underworld.) □ *The boss said we was to blow you away if you gives us any trouble.* □ *We blow away guys like you every day.*

bump someone off *tr.* to kill someone. (Originally underworld.) □ *What am I supposed to do, bump her off?* □ *The mob bumped off the witness before the trial.*

cack AND **kack; kak** *tr.* to kill someone. □ *Max threatened to cack Veronica if she* *didn't straighten up.* □ *The witness got kacked before she could testify.*

cancel someone's Christmas *tr.* to kill someone; to destroy someone. (Underworld. The dead person will miss Christmas.) □ *If he keeps bugging me, I'm gonna cancel his Christmas.* □ *Bruno threatened to cancel Max's Christmas if Max didn't pay up.*

chill *tr.* to kill someone. (Underworld.) □ *Rocko had orders to chill Barlowe or not to show his face again.* □ *I'll chill you with one blast from my cannon, you creep.*

clip *tr.* to kill someone. □ *Rocko had orders to clip both Max and Bruno.* □ *Max and Bruno had set out to clip Rocko first.*

croak *tr.* to kill someone or some creature. □ *The car croaked the cat just like that.* □ *Somebody croaked my parrot.*

deep-six *tr.* to kill or dispose of someone. (Underworld.) □ *Mr. Big ordered Bruno to deep-six Max.* □ *The thugs tried to deep-six the witness, but failed.*

drop *tr.* to kill someone or something. □ *He dropped the deer with one shot.* □ *Lefty tried to drop the leader of the gang.*

dust *tr.* to kill someone. (Underworld.) □ *The gang set out to dust the witnesses, but only got one of them.* □ *Max knew that Bruno was out to dust him.*

erase *tr.* to kill someone. □ *Bruno had orders to erase Max.* □ *Mr. Big decided who was gonna erase who.*

frag *tr.* to assassinate an unpopular military officer in Vietnam. (Military.) □ *The guy was so certain that nobody was going to frag him that he got careless and Charlie got him.* □ *I saw some creeps frag a guy once.*

give someone the business *tr.* to kill someone. (Underworld.) □ *Lefty wanted to give Rocko the business for being so damn perfect.* □ *Mr. Big told Bruno to give Max the business.*

hit *tr.* to kill someone; to assassinate someone. (Underworld.) □ *Bruno was told to hit Max.* □ *The thug set out to hit the mayor, but got nabbed first.*

hose someone down *tr.* to kill someone. (Underworld. From the image of spraying someone with bullets.) □ *Mr. Big told Bruno to hose Max down.* □ *The thugs tried to hose down the witness.*

hush someone up *tr.* to kill someone. □ *Nobody knew how to get to Mr. Big to hush him up.* □ *Mr. Big told Bruno to hush up Max.*

ice *tr.* to kill someone; to kill an informer. (Underworld.) □ *Mr. Big ordered Bruno to ice you-know-who.* □ *Somebody set out to ice Tracy—the dirty squealer.*

joy ride *n.* a ride where the passenger does not return alive. (Underworld.) □ *Mr. Big wanted Bruno to take Max on a joy ride.* □ *You're going on a little joy ride with me. Now, get moving.*

kiss someone off *tr.* to kill someone. □ *Bruno had instructions to kiss Max off.* □ *Max wanted to kiss off Bruno, too.*

knock someone off *tr.* to kill someone. (Underworld.) □ *The mob knocked the witnesses off.* □ *The cops would be happy if someone wanted to knock off Mr. Big.*

liquidate *tr.* to kill someone. (Underworld.) □ *The boss wants me to liquidate Mr. Bruno.* □ *They used a machine gun to liquidate a few troublesome characters.*

off *tr.* to dispose of someone or something; to kill someone. □ *The crooks offed the witness before the trial.* □ *Forget the whole idea! Just off it once and for all.*

put someone out of the way *tr.* to kill someone. □ *The crooks tried to put the witness out of the way.* □ *Sorry, my friend, we no longer need you. Bruno is going to have to put you out of the way.*

put someone to bed with a shovel *tr.* to bury someone; to kill and bury someone. □ *Shut up! You want me to put you to bed with a shovel?* □ *The leader of the gang was getting sort of tired and old, so one of the younger thugs put him to bed with a shovel.*

rub someone out *tr.* to kill someone. (Underworld.) □ *The gunman was eager to rub somebody out.* □ *The crooks tried to rub out the witness.*

scrag *tr.* to kill someone or something. (Originally underworld to "strangle.") □ *The gang decided that somebody was going to have to scrag the witness.* □ *A truck almost scragged Max.*

send someone to glory *tr.* to kill someone. □ *One shot sent him to glory.* □ *You want me to send you to glory or something?*

skrag *tr.* to murder someone. (Underworld.) □ *These thugs tried to skrag me, I swear.* □ *Barlowe wanted to skrag him right then and there.*

smoke *tr.* to annihilate someone; to shoot someone. (Underworld.) □ *Rocko tried time and time again to smoke Barlowe, always without success.* □ *You want me to smoke you on the spot, or are you gonna cooperate?*

snuff *tr.* to kill someone or some creature. (Underworld.) □ *The mob tried to snuff Max, but he moved too fast for them.* □ *Somebody snuffed my cat!*

spoil *tr.* to kill someone or something. □ *It was Bruno's job to make sure that nobody got close enough to Mr. Big to spoil him.* □ *Rocko was determined to spoil Barlowe.*

take care of someone *tr.* to kill someone. (Underworld.) □ *The boss told Bruno to take care of Max.* □ *I'm gonna take care of you once and for all.*

take someone off *tr.* to kill someone. (Underworld.) □ *The mob took the witness off a week before the trial.* □ *Barlowe didn't want to have to take off Lefty—like hell, he didn't.*

take someone out *tr.* to kill someone. (Underworld.) □ *The boss told Rocko to take out Barlowe.* □ *Barlowe was sure he could keep Rocko from taking him out.*

top *tr.* to kill someone. □ *Max was out to top Bruno.* □ *Bruno was gonna top Max first.*

wash someone away *tr.* to kill someone. (Underworld.) □ *Bruno was charged with trying to wash Max away.* □ *The mob triggers came by and tried to wash away a druggy type.*

waste *tr.* to kill someone. (Underworld.) □ *Bruno had orders to waste Max.* □ *The mob's triggers sped by in a car and wasted four pushers.*

whack someone (out) *tr.* to kill somebody. (Underworld.) □ *Bruno made another try at whacking Max out last evening.* □ *He really wants to whack out Mr. Big.* □ *He really wants to whack Mr. Big.*

wipe *n.* a murder; a killing. (Underworld.) □ *Who's responsible for that wipe downtown last night?* □ *The victim of the latest mob wipe was hauled out of the river this morning.*

wipe someone out *tr.* to eliminate someone; to kill someone. (Underworld.) □ *Max almost wiped Bruno out.* □ *Who wiped out Lefty?*

zap *tr.* to kill someone. □ *The stress from it all nearly zapped him.* □ *I was afraid that one of those thugs would zap me.*

zotz *tr.* to kill someone. □ *Max threatened to zotz Bruno, but it was just a threat.* □ *The gunman stepped up to the wall and zotzed two of the guards.*

MUSCLE

pump *n.* a pumped-up muscle. (Bodybuilding.) □ *Look at the size of that pump.* □ *He's tired and can't quite make a pump.*

MUSCLES

abs *n.* the abdominal muscles. (Bodybuilding.) □ *Look at the abs on that guy. Like a crossword puzzle.* □ *I do situps to harden my abs.*

buff(ed) *mod.* strong; muscular. □ *Bill is buffed and short-tempered. Stay away from him.* □ *He has such buff legs! Does he have a job or does he just work out?*

cut (up) *mod.* having well-defined abdominal muscles. □ *Greg is really cut up. He works out every day.* □ *Andy works hard to try to get a gut that's cut.*

delts *n.* the deltoid muscles. (Bodybuilding.) □ *Look at the delts on that dame!* □ *How do you get delts like that?*

lats *n.* the latissimus dorsi; the muscles of the back. (Bodybuilding.) □ *Your lats* *are coming along fine. Now let's start working on your delts.* □ *Nice lats on that guy.*

pecks AND **pecs; pects** *n.* the pectoral muscles. (From weightlifting and body-building.) □ *Look at the pecks on that guy!* □ *With pects like that he needs a bra.*

six-pack *n.* a well-muscled abdomen. □ *Tom's gut is a real six-pack. He must work out every day.* □ *What do you do with a six-pack like that? Walk around with your shirt open?*

yoked *mod.* having well-marked abdominal muscles. □ *That guy is really yoked. I wonder how much he works out.* □ *I'm too fat to ever get yoked.*

MUSIC

air guitar *n.* an imaginary guitar, played along with real music. □ *Dave stood near the window while his roommate played air guitar in front of the mirror.* □ *Jed, who sees himself as some sort of rock star, plays air guitar when he's happy or sad.*

bari AND **bary** *n.* a baritone saxophone, the saxophone with a pitch range approximating that of the human baritone voice. (Musicians.) □ *Wally played the bari when he was in college.* □ *A fine bary will cost thousands of dollars.*

beat *n.* (in music) the rhythm, especially the bass. □ *Man, that is just the kind of beat I like.* □ *The notes are nice, but it has no beat!*

beat box *n.* the person who provides the (verbal) rhythmic beat in a rap song. □ *What makes him sound so good is his beat box.* □ *Let me be the beat box this time.*

beat something out *tr.* to play something on the piano. □ *It'll just take me a few minutes to beat this out.* □ *He beat out a cheery song on the old ivories.*

blow *in.* to play a musical instrument, not necessarily a wind instrument. □ *Man, listen to her blow.* □ *She blows, and everybody listens.*

bone *n.* a trombone. □ *Herman is just a wonder on the bone.* □ *She plays the bone like nobody's business.*

boom *in.* to listen to music, as with a boom box. □ *You don't do anything but hang around and boom all day!* □ *If you're going to boom all the time, why don't you get some headphones?*

boom sticks *n.* drumsticks. (Musicians.) □ *He always carries his boom sticks in his back pocket, and he beats on walls, radiators, desks—you name it.* □ *I need new boom sticks. They keep breaking.*

bop *n.* a style of jazz popular in the 1940s. □ *We heard some bop in an old movie.* □ *Bop is not popular, but it is by no means dead.*

box *n.* a piano. □ *Man, he plays a mean box.* □ *She sure can pound the devil out of that box!*

break *n.* a solo played when the rest of the band stops. □ *This is your break, Andy. Let's hear it, man.* □ *It wasn't much of a break, but I gave it everything.*

chart *n.* a musical score. (Musicians.) □ *Come on, man! Look at the chart! You're making clinkers like hotcakes.* □ *Lemme borrow your chart for a while, okay?*

combo *n.* a small group of musicians; a small band. (From *combination*.) □ *Andy started his own combo and made money from day one.* □ *You can make a good living with a combo.*

cool *mod.* [of music] mellow; smooth. □ *This stuff is so cool, I'm just floating.* □ *Doesn't he blow a cool trumpet?*

cut *n.* a single song or section of music on a record. □ *This next cut is one everybody likes.* □ *Let's listen to another cut of the same album.*

deadhead *n.* a follower of the rock group "The Grateful Dead." □ *What do these deadheads see in that group?* □ *My son was a deadhead and used to travel all over listening to those guys.*

ear candy *n.* soft and pleasant popular music; music that is sweet to the ear. □ *I find that kind of ear candy more annoying than heavy metal.* □ *People joke about it, but ear candy is restful.*

elevator music *n.* dull, uninteresting music of the type that can be heard in elevators or shops. (As compared to exciting jazz or rock.) □ *I don't want to have to hear elevator music all day.* □ *Elevator music is better than listening to someone chewing food.*

fake book *n.* a book with basic melody and chord changes for hundreds of popular songs. □ *Somebody lifted my fake book.* □ *I thought fake books were illegal.*

flip side *n.* the "other" side of a phonograph record. □ *On the flip side, we have another version of "Love Me Tender" sung by Beverly Mills.* □ *Give a listen to the flip side sometime.*

funk *n.* a kind of blues rock; jazz based on gospel music. □ *Man, groove on that funk, would ya?* □ *Now, this is the kind of funk I've been looking for.*

groan box *n.* an accordion. □ *Clare is pretty good at the groan box.* □ *I used to play the groan box when I was a kid.*

groupie *n.* a young person who follows a band seeking the attention of the band members. □ *Would you believe that Sally was a groupie when she was 19?* □ *You mean all those young girls are groupies?*

gutbucket *n.* an earthy style of music. □ *I'd like to hear some good old-fashioned gutbucket.* □ *You don't hear much gutbucket in public places these days.*

hides *n.* drums. □ *Andy can really bang those hides.* □ *They say his hides are worth about 4,000 clams.*

hot number *n.* an exciting piece of music. □ *Now, here's a hot number by the Wanderers.* □ *Another hot number after this message.*

ivories *n.* piano keys. (From when piano keys were made from real elephant ivory.) □ *She can really bang those ivories.* □ *I'd say she has mastered the ivories.*

jam *in.* [for musicians] to play together, improvising. □ *They jammed until the neighbors complained.* □ *Come over and let's jam, okay?*

joybox *n.* a piano. □ *Can you play this joybox at all?* □ *Your joybox needs some tuning.*

label mate *n.* someone who records on the same label (as the speaker). (Record industry.) □ *Frank Duke is my label mate, and we like to get together and gossip about the record industry.* □ *I feel like a real success because my label mates are so good.*

leerics *n.* sexually suggestive song lyrics. □ *For those of you out there who go in for leerics, listen carefully to this tune.* □ *A group of parents has banded together in the eastern suburbs to fight the naughty leerics of some of the current hot rock tunes.*

licorice stick *n.* a clarinet. (Jazz musicians.) □ *Man, can he play the licorice stick.* □ *Frank makes the old licorice stick talk.*

longhair *mod.* highbrow; [of music] classical. □ *I don't care for longhair music.* □ *It's too longhair.* □ *Longhair stuff like symphonies and art galleries bores me to tears.*

map *n.* sheet music. (Jazz musicians.) □ *Check my map and see where you come in.* □ *I left the map at home. Can I look at yours?*

platter *n.* a phonograph record. (Old but still heard.) □ *Now, here's an interesting platter.* □ *They call it a platter because it looks like a serving platter.*

pop *n.* popular music. □ *I like most pop, but not if it's too loud.* □ *Pop is the only music I like.*

pound something out *tr.* to play something loudly on the piano, perhaps with difficulty. □ *Here, pound this one out. A little softer, please.* □ *She was pounding out a nice little tune.*

punk *mod.* having to do with punkers or their music. □ *I am tired of your red punk hair. Try it brown for a change.* □ *This music sounds too punk for me.*

riff *n.* a short, repeated line of music played by a particular performer. □ *Jim just sat there and forgot his riff.* □ *Listen to this riff, Tom.*

roadie AND **roady** 1. *in.* to help rock groups set up. □ *Let's go downtown and roadie tonight. The Red Drips are in town.*

□ *I hate to roady. It's, like, work!* **2.** AND **roadster** *n.* someone who helps rock groups set up for performances. □ *I want to be a roadie when I grow up.* □ *I was a roadster for a while, but I didn't like it.*

rocker *n.* a rock and roll singer, song, or fan. □ *Do all rockers have red hair?* □ *Let's listen to a good rocker.*

scat *n.* nonsense syllables sung to music. (Refers to a [primarily black] jazz practice in the jazz era.) □ *She used to do scat but moved on to blues.* □ *He could sing scat like nobody's business.*

sent *mod.* carried away by mellow music. □ *She's really sent. Look at her as she listens.* □ *All the musicians were sent. Maybe they were on something.*

set *n.* a period of time that a band plays without a break; a thirty-minute jam session. □ *I'll talk to you after this set.* □ *We do two sets and then take a twenty-minute break.*

side *n.* a side of a record. □ *Let's cruise over to Sam's pad and hear some sides.* □ *Now, here's a side you may remember.*

skins *n.* drums. (Musicians.) □ *Andy can really make the skins talk.* □ *Buddy could beat those skins like nobody's business.*

sounds *n.* music; records. □ *I got some new sounds. Ya wanna come over and listen?* □ *Man, these sounds are massive!*

(squeeze-)box *n.* an accordion. □ *My brother plays the squeeze-box—not very well, but who can tell?* □ *The band consisted of drums, clarinet, and a box. A real winner.*

tag *n.* the coda or ending section of a piece of music. □ *Now, I want everybody to slow down and watch me on the tag.* □ *Give everything you've got on the tag.*

tickle the ivories *tr.* to play the piano. □ *I used to be able to tickle the ivories real nice.* □ *She sat down to tickle the ivories for a while.*

tinklebox *n.* a piano. □ *She's okay on the tinklebox.* □ *The tinklebox in the bar seemed to be a bit loud.*

track *in.* [for a laser beam, a phonograph stylus, a tape head, etc.] to successfully transfer information to or from a recording medium. □ *Something here won't track. Must be the stylus.* □ *This thing won't track. What's wrong?*

tunage *n.* music; tunes. □ *Why don't you come over and we'll do some tunage?* □ *My stereo is down and I'm running a tunage deficit.*

tunes *n.* a record; a record album; music in general. □ *I got some new tunes. Wanna come over and listen?* □ *The old tunes are good enough for me.*

vinyl *n.* phonograph records. □ *This is one of the best tunes on vinyl.* □ *I got some new vinyl. Come over and listen.*

wax *n.* a phonograph recording; a substance onto which a recording is put. □ *This is one of the finest pieces of music ever put on wax.* □ *Now here's some wax I'll bet you've never heard before.*

MUSTACHE
See also **BEARD**.

soup-strainer *n.* a mustache. □ *Jerry had a big, bushy soup-strainer that he was very proud of.* □ *It's not a soup-strainer— just a neat little black line.*

stash *n.* a mustache. □ *Jerry has this enormous stash that he keeps waxed and trimmed.* □ *I cut my stash off because it was too much trouble to remember not to cut it off.*

N

NAIVETE

blue-eyed *mod.* innocent. □ *Look, you little blue-eyed sweetie, I know your game!* □ *He's sure his blue-eyed wonder couldn't have hit my child.* □ *Don't try to look so blue-eyed.*

FOB *mod.* "Fresh off the boat"; as gullible and trusting as a new immigrant. (Initialism. A play on the initials of "Free on Board.") □ *That new guy is really FOB. What a wimp!* □ *Where did you get those FOB shoes? Blue suede is back?*

just off the boat *mod.* to be freshly immigrated and perhaps gullible and naive. □ *I'm not just off the boat. I know what's going on.* □ *He may act like he's just off the boat, but he's all right.*

NAKEDNESS

air one's pores *tr.* to undress oneself; to become naked. □ *I'm fixing to air my pores and take a shower.* □ *Me and Wilbur, that's my brother, both fell in the creek and had to air our pores awhile so our pants could dry out.*

bare-assed *mod.* naked. (Potentially offensive. Use only with discretion.) □ *Man, that little store has the biggest display of bare-assed girlie magazines I have ever seen.* □ *And she stood there at the window, drunk and bare-assed for all the world to see.*

buck naked *mod.* entirely naked. (Folksy. From the color of buckskin leather.) □ *He stood there buck naked, scratching his belly.* □ *They all slipped off their trousers and went swimming buck naked.* □ *Who's that buck naked dancer?*

butt naked *mod.* totally nude. (Collegiate. Potentially offensive. Use only with discretion.) □ *She just stood there butt naked, looking at us.* □ *My roommate sleeps butt naked.*

gaucho *tr. & in.* to expose the buttocks (at someone), usually through a car window. □ *Victor gauchoed the cops as they went by.* □ *Victor would gaucho at the drop of a hat—so to speak.*

girlie magazine *n.* a magazine featuring pictures of nude women. □ *The girlie magazines were hidden under the counter.* □ *Some creepy character asked Sally if she would pose for a girlie magazine.*

girlie show *n.* a performance featuring nude women. □ *Bob and Pete went to the city and tried to get into a girlie show.* □ *This movie has turned out to be nothing but a girlie show.*

hang a BA (at someone) *tr.* to display one's buttocks to someone in derision. (A BA is a "bare ass.") □ *Victor was angry and hung a BA at the cop.* □ *He went to the window and hung a BA—just for the hell of it.*

in the buff *mod.* naked. □ *You-know-who sleeps in the buff.* □ *You can save hundreds of dollars in a lifetime by not buying pajamas and sleeping in the buff instead.*

moon *tr. & in.* to show (someone) one's nude posterior through a window (usually of an automobile). □ *When the plane flew over Cuba, this guy named Victor actually mooned a Russian M.I.G. that flew by.* □ *The kids were mooning, and they got arrested for indecent exposure.*

nudie *n.* a movie featuring nudes. □ *There is a nudie playing over at the Roxie Theater.* □ *I didn't know this movie was a nudie!*

skinny-dip 1. *in.* to swim in the nude. □ *We used to go skinny-dipping when I was a kid.* □ *There was an old creek on the farm where we used to skinny-dip.* **2.** *n.* a swim in the nude. □ *A nice skinny-dip in a quiet glade takes you back to nature.* □ *Randy, who fears fish, didn't take a skinny-dip with the others.*

streak 1. *in.* to run about in a public place naked. □ *This kid was streaking back and forth until the cops caught him.* □ *He streaked on a dare.* **2.** *tr.* to grace or ornament a public place or event with a naked run. □ *Charles streaked the baseball game, but nobody noticed him.* □ *I wanted to streak her party but decided against it.* **3.** *n.* a naked run in a public place. □ *There was a streak at the end of the game, but people were leaving then and didn't see it.* □ *That was no streak; that was the coach in his long underwear being chased by the owner of the team.*

streaker *n.* someone who runs naked in public places. □ *The streaker ran through a glass door and was severely injured.* □ *Streakers seemed to take over the whole country in 1973.*

stripper *n.* a striptease artist. □ *Tracy worked for a while as a stripper.* □ *Strippers from all over assembled here for their fourth annual convention and immediately took off on a sight-seeing tour.*

topless *mod.* having to do with someone wearing no clothing above the waist, usually a woman. □ *The topless places are beginning to dress up a little.* □ *The cops closed down the topless joint on Maple Street.*

NASTY

See also **HORRIBLE, UNDESIRABLE.**

creeping-crud *n.* any nasty, slimy substance. □ *You got creeping-crud all over my pants leg.* □ *That's not creeping-crud! That's my pecan pie!*

crud *n.* nastiness; junk; worthless matter. □ *This is just crud. Get rid of it.* □ *Get all that old crud out of the attic so we can have room for newer stuff.*

glop *n.* unappetizing food; *gunk;* anything undesirable. □ *Do we have the same old glop again tonight?* □ *No, this is different glop.*

gobbledygook *n.* any mess, especially of food. □ *Dinner was just gobbledygook again.* □ *Do we have the same old gobbledygook tonight?*

goo *n.* some sticky substance; *gunk.* □ *What is this goo on my shoe?* □ *There is some sort of goo on my plate. Is that meant to be my dinner?*

gook *n.* a slimy substance; a sediment or residue. □ *There was a lot of gook in my crankcase.* □ *Too much of that gook will ruin your engine.*

goop AND **goup** *n.* slop; *gunk;* bad food. □ *I refuse to eat this goop.* □ *You get used to this goup after a while.*

goozlum *n.* any gummy, sticky substance: syrup, gravy, soup, etc. □ *Do you want some of this wonderful goozlum on your ice cream?* □ *Just keep putting that goozlum on my spuds.*

greldge *n.* something nasty or *yucky.* □ *What is this greldge on my shoe?* □ *That's not greldge, that's just plain mud.*

gronk *n.* a nasty substance, such as dirt that collects between the toes. □ *I don't want to hear any more at all about your gronk.* □ *What is this gronk here?*

grunge AND **grunch** *n.* any nasty substance; dirt; *gunk.* □ *There's some gritty grunge on the kitchen floor.* □ *What's that grunch on your tie?*

guck *n.* a thick, sticky substance; *yuck.* □ *What is this guck on the bottom of my shoe?* □ *The doctor painted some nasty guck on my throat and told me not to swallow for a while.*

gunk *n.* any nasty, messy stuff. □ *What is this gunk on the counter?* □ *Get this gunk up off the floor before it dries.*

ick *n.* any nasty substance. □ *What is this ick on my shoe?* □ *That's not ick; it's good clean mud.*

mung AND **MUNG** *n.* something that is "mashed until no good"; anything nasty or gloppy. (An acronym, but possibly a coinage before it became an acronym.) □ *Get this mung off my plate.* □ *This* *mung is cruel and unusual punishment. I demand to see the warden.*

scrunge *n.* nastiness; gunk. □ *What is this scrunge on my shoe?* □ *When you find some scrunge on your shoe or something, never try to find out what it is. Just wipe it off.*

scuz(z) *n.* filth. □ *What is this scuzz all over the floor?* □ *There is some scuzz on your shoe.*

swill *n.* any nasty food or drink. □ *Let's go over to the ptomaine-domain and get our evening swill.* □ *Man does not live by swill alone. Let's go to McDuck's instead.*

NAVEL

belly button *n.* the navel. □ *Is your belly button an insy or an outsy?* □ *Do dogs have belly buttons?*

insy *n.* a navel that recedes and does not protrude. □ *Is yours an insy or an outsy?* □ *It's an outsy. So what?*

outsy *n.* a navel that protrudes. □ *Is yours an insy or an outsy?* □ *I have an outsy. Why on earth do you ask?*

NECK

scrag *n.* the neck. (Underworld.) □ *The cop grabbed him by the scrag and pushed him along to the squad car.* □ *It's gonna be your scrag in the noose when this thing's over.*

NEGOTIATION

(bargaining) chip *n.* something to be used in negotiations. □ *I want to use this incident as a bargaining chip in future negotiations.* □ *I need a few chips to use when we get down to drawing up the contract.*

NEIGHBORHOOD

nabe *n.* a neighborhood; one's own neighborhood. □ *I can't wait to get back to my own nabe.* □ *Hey, man, welcome back to the old nabe!*

NEW

(brand) spanking new *mod.* completely new. □ *My car is spanking new.* □ *Look at that brand spanking new car!*

Johnnie-come-lately AND **JCL** *n.* someone new to a situation or status. □ *This Johnnie-come-lately doesn't know what it was like in the old days.* □ *I'm just a Johnnie-come-lately, but I'm eager.*

NEWS

break *in.* [for a news story] to unfold rapidly. (Journalism.) □ *As the story continues to break, we will bring you the latest.* □ *Something is breaking on the Wilson murder. Get over to the D.A.'s office, quick.*

NEWSPAPER

rag *n.* a newspaper. □ *I'm tired of reading this rag day after day. Can't we get a different paper?* □ *What a rag! It's only good for putting in the bottom of birdcages!*

scandal sheet *n.* a tabloid newspaper featuring lurid news. □ *I like to read a scandal sheet every now and then.* □ *I'm tired of this scandal sheet. Let's get a classy newspaper today.*

screamer *n.* a newspaper headline. □ *Did you see the screamer in the paper today? "The King Died."* □ *I never read screamers.*

NICKNAME

ace *n.* a nickname for a foolish and ineffectual person. (Sarcastic. Usually a term of address.) □ *Hey, ace, hand me that monkey wrench—if you know what one is.* □ *Look, ace, you can't expect to fix an engine without getting dirty.*

angel *n.* a sweetheart. (Also a term of address.) □ *See my angel standing over there? Isn't he gorgeous?* □ *Okay, angel, let's get in the car.*

handle *n.* a person's name or nickname. (Western jargon and then citizens band radio.) □ *Well, what's your handle so I'll know what to call you?* □ *My handle is Goober. You can call me Goob.*

Mac(k) *n.* a generic name for a man. (Also a term of address.) □ *Look, Mac, you want to make some big money?* □ *Hey, Mack! Come here a minute.*

moniker AND **monniker** *n.* a nickname. □ *What's your moniker, chum?* □ *With a monniker like that, you must get in a lot of fights.*

snookums *n.* a nickname for a child or a lover. (Also a term of address.) □ *Now, now, snookums, it's all right.* □ *Does my little snookums want to play?*

so-and-so *n.* a euphemistic way of addressing someone with an insulting term of address. (This is usually euphemistic for "son of a bitch." However, it is also used for good friends, especially male to male, to show affection.) □ *This lousy so-and-so tried to take me for 400 bucks.* □ *Terry, you old so-and-so, how ya been?*

Stretch *n.* a nickname for a tall person, usually male. □ *Well, Stretch, think you'll go out for basketball this season?* □ *Come on, Stretch, let's get it in the basket!*

tag *n.* a name. □ *I know the face, but I forgot the tag.* □ *Everybody knows that tag well.*

whoozis AND **whoozit** *n.* a name for a person whose real name is forgotten or being avoided. □ *I met whoozis—you know, with the big whatsis—today.* □ *Is whoozit coming to my birthday party?*

NIGHT

night person *n.* a person who prefers to be active in the nighttime. (The plural is with *people.*) □ *I can't function in the morning. I'm strictly a night person.* □ *Night people prefer to sleep in the daytime.*

NO

See also **REFUSAL**.

hang up *in.* to say no; to cancel out of something. □ *I hung up. That's not for me anyway.* □ *If you don't want to do it, just hang up. I'll understand.*

naw *interj.* "no." □ *Naw, I didn't do that.* □ *Naw, I won't go.*

NBT *n.* "no big thing." (Initialism.) □ *Hey, man! Don't make a fuss! It's NBT.* □ *Listen up, Fred. This is NBT, but listen anyway.*

nix **1.** *interj.* "no." (Both senses from German *nichts.*) □ *The man said nix, and he means nix.* □ *Nix, I won't do it.* **2.** *exclam.* "No!"; "Stop it!"; "I disagree!" (Usually **Nix!**) □ *Nix! I won't do it.* □ *"Nix," said Paul. "I can't permit that."*

no can do *phr.* "It can't be done."; "I can't do it." □ *Sorry. No can do.* □ *Lend you $200? No can do.*

no dice *interj.* "no"; not possible. □ *When I asked about a loan, he said, "No dice."* □ *No. It can't be done; no dice.*

nope *interj.* "no." □ *I won't do it! Nope. I won't!* □ *She asked him to do it, but he said, "Nope."*

no sale *interj.* "no." □ *I wanted to go to Florida for the holidays, but my father said, "No sale."* □ *No sale. You can't do it.*

no soap *interj.* "no." □ *I can't do it. No soap.* □ *No soap, I don't lend anyone money.*

Not! *interj.* "Not really so!" (A tag phrase added to the end of a statement, changing it from affirmative to negative. There is usually a pause before *Not!,* which is said on a level pitch somewhat higher than the sentence that comes before.) □ *Of course I'm going to pay $100 a ticket to see a rock concert. Not!* □ *I am deeply in love with Kim. Not!*

not a chance *interj.* "no." □ *Me lend you money? Not a chance!* □ *I won't go, not a chance. Don't ask.*

Nothing doing! *exclam.* "No!" □ *Me, go to the opera? Nothing doing!* □ *Nothing doing! I refuse to do it.*

No way! *exclam.* "No!" □ *Me join the Army? No way!* □ *She can't do that. No way!*

NOISE

dull roar *n.* a relatively quiet degree of noisiness. □ *Hey, simmer down to a dull roar!* □ *Try to keep it at a dull roar if you can.*

peep *n.* a noise; an utterance. □ *Don't you make another peep!* □ *I don't want to hear another peep out of you.*

plop *n.* the sound of dropping something soft and bulky, such as a hunk of meat. □ *When the roast fell on the floor, it made a nasty plop.* □ *When I heard the plop, I looked up and saw our dinner on the floor.*

racket *n.* noise. □ *Cut out that racket! Shut up!* □ *Who's making all that racket?*

NONFUNCTIONING

bum *mod.* bad; faulty. □ *This is a bum fuse. No wonder it won't run.* □ *The screw has a bum head and won't turn.*

dead *mod.* no longer effective; no longer of any consequence. □ *You're dead, Fred. You can't help us anymore.* □ *That guy is dead—out of power.*

down *mod.* (of a machine) inoperative. (Originally said of a computer.) □ *The system is down. Come back later.* □ *How long has it been down?*

gone goose *n.* someone or something finished or done for. □ *I'm afraid that your old car is a gone goose.* □ *This old thing is a gone goose.*

goner *n.* someone or something finished or nearly finished. □ *This one's a goner. Toss it.* □ *The horse was a goner, so it had to be destroyed.*

haywire *mod.* out of order. (Folksy.) □ *This telephone has gone haywire.* □ *My stereo is haywire, so I've been listening to the radio.*

on the blink *mod.* out of order; ill. □ *I was a little on the blink yesterday and decided to stay at home.* □ *My refrigerator is on the blink again.*

on the fritz *mod.* not functioning properly. □ *This TV is on the fritz again.* □ *My watch is on the fritz.*

out of kilter *mod.* not functioning properly; on the fritz; out of w(h)ack. □ *My car's engine is out of kilter and needs some repair work.* □ *My coffeepot is out of kilter, so I have to make coffee in a pan.*

out of w(h)ack *mod.* out of adjustment; inoperative. □ *My watch is out of whack.* □ *I think my left eye is out of wack a little. Maybe I need glasses.*

NONINTELLECTUAL

lowbrow *mod.* nonintellectual; anti-intellectual. □ *I like my lowbrow music and my lowbrow friends!* □ *What's lowbrow about soft rock?*

NONSENSE

applesauce *n.* nonsense. □ *Don't give me that applesauce. I know better.* □ *That's just applesauce!*

bafflegab *n.* confusing jargon. □ *Don't throw that bafflegab at me. Use English.* □ *Watch out for the bafflegab they use to try to sell that stuff.*

baloney AND **bologna** *n.* nonsense. (Also as an exclamation.) □ *Don't give me all that baloney!* □ *That's just a lot of bologna. Don't believe it for a minute.* □ *Baloney! You're nuts!*

banana oil *n.* nonsense. □ *That is the silliest banana oil I have ever heard!* □ *I refuse to listen to any more of your childish banana oil.*

beans *n.* nonsense. (Refers to beans that produce *gas*, which is *hot air* or nonsense.) □ *Come on, talk straight. No more beans!* □ *Stop feeding me beans.*

birdseed *n.* nonsense. □ *Cut the birdseed. I'm not stupid, you know.* □ *I've heard enough birdseed here to last for a lifetime.*

blah-blah *phr.* a phrase echoic of gibberish or incessant chattering. (It can be repeated many times.) □ *Why all this blah-blah-blah?* □ *She's going blah-blah on the phone all the time.*

bosh *n.* nonsense; idle talk. (Also an exclamation, **Bosh!**) □ *That is enough of your bosh!* □ *Oh, bosh! You don't know what you're talking about.*

BS *n.* nonsense. (Initialism for *bullshit*.) □ *I've heard enough of your BS.* □ *Less BS and more facts, please.*

bull *n.* nonsense. □ *That's just a lot of bull.* □ *Don't give me that bull! I won't buy it.*

bull-pucky *n.* nonsense. □ *Don't give me that bull-pucky!* □ *That's all just bull-pucky. Don't believe a word of it.*

bullshit *n.* nonsense; lies; deception. (Potentially offensive. Use only with discretion.) □ *Don't give me all that bullshit!* □ *That's just bullshit.*

bunkum AND **buncombe** *n.* nonsense. □ *That's just plain bunkum.* □ *Another can-*

didate for governor means just that much more buncombe.

claptrap n. nonsense; something worthless. □ This is enough claptrap. I'm leaving. □ I know claptrap when I see it, and your play was claptrap.

cockamamie mod. ridiculous; inconceivable. □ What a cockamamie idea! □ That is the most cockamamie thing I ever heard of.

corral dust n. nonsense, lies, and exaggeration. (Euphemistic for bullshit.) □ The way Judy handles the corral dust, she must be running for political office. □ That stuff is all corral dust. Don't believe a word of it.

crap n. nonsense; lies. □ I've had enough of your crap. Now talk straight, or out you go. □ Cut the crap!

crock n. nonsense. □ What a crock! You don't know what you are talking about! □ This whole business is a crock. Hell, life's a crock!

crock of shit n. something really awful; a great mass of nonsense. (Potentially offensive. Use only with discretion.) □ That whole place is just a crock of shit. Nobody knows what's what. □ You went on vacation and left this office with a real crock of shit.

eyewash n. nonsense; deception. □ Aw, that's just a lot of eyewash! □ It's not eyewash! It's true!

fadoodle n. something ridiculous; nonsense. □ Oh, stop your silly fadoodle! □ That's nothing but fadoodle!

falderal AND **folderol** n. wasted effort; nonsense. □ I had about enough of your falderal. □ Stop the folderol and get to work.

flapdoodle AND **flamdoodle** n. nonsense. □ I've heard enough of this flapdoodle. □ Cut out the flamdoodle and speak the truth.

flimflam n. nonsense. □ Beware of the flimflam they will try to pull on you. □ I can spot flimflam a mile away.

fluff n. nonsense; irrelevant stuff. □ This is just a lot of fluff. Nothing substantial at all. □ Cut out the fluff and talk straight.

fudge n. nonsense; deception. □ Cut out the fudge and talk straight. □ I've heard enough of your fudge. Let's get honest, okay?

full of beans mod. full of nonsense. □ Oh, be quiet. You're just full of beans. □ Pay no attention to John. He's full of beans.

full of hops mod. full of nonsense. (As if one were full of beer, which contains hops.) □ Aw, you're just full of hops! □ The guy was full of hops. Nothing he said made any sense.

full of hot air AND **full of bull; full of it** mod. full of nonsense. □ You're full of hot air. I don't believe you. □ Aw, you're just full of it! Be quiet!

full of prunes mod. full of nonsense. □ You're just silly. Completely full of prunes. □ Oh, you're full of prunes. Get a life!

fun and games n. nonsense; a waste of time. □ I've had enough fun and games. Let's get on with the business. □ You spend too much time with fun and games!

garbage n. nonsense; gibberish. □ He's just talking garbage. □ I've heard too much garbage here today.

gas n. nonsense. □ All we got in class today was gas. □ Hey, that's about enough of your gas.

gibber-gabber n. nonsense; gossip and chatter. □ There sure is a lot of gibber-gabber coming from your room, Jimmy. □ What's all this gibber-gabber about?

gobbledygook n. nonsense; officialese or government gibberish. □ I can't understand all this gobbledygook. □ They must have a full-time staff to dream up all this gobbledygook.

gubbish n. nonsense; useless information. (Computers. A combination of garbage and rubbish.) □ There's nothing but gubbish on my printout. □ I can't make any sense out of this gubbish.

guff n. nonsense; bunkum. □ Wow, that vice president guy can sure dish out the guff! □ No more guff outa you, okay?

hand someone something *tr.* to tell someone something; to tell someone nonsense. □ *Don't hand me that stuff! That's silly!* □ *She handed me a line about being a famous author.*

hogwash *n.* nonsense. □ *Now that's just hogwash, and you know it.* □ *Hogwash! That's about enough of your lies!*

hokum *n.* nonsense. □ *All that is just hokum.* □ *No more hokum. I want the truth.*

hooey *n.* nonsense. □ *The whole newspaper is nothing but hooey today.* □ *What's all this hooey about getting a new car?*

hoo-ha *n.* nonsense. □ *What is all this hoo-ha about your leaving the company?* □ *Stop talking hoo-ha and tell the truth.*

horse hockey *n.* nonsense. □ *I've heard enough of your horse hockey.* □ *The guy specializes in producing horse hockey for the gossip columns.*

hot air *n.* boasting; lying; nonsense. □ *I've heard enough of your hot air.* □ *That's just a lot of hot air. Ignore it.*

kafooster *n.* nonsense. □ *We've heard enough of your kafooster.* □ *This kafooster about me being a cheater is too much.*

malark(e)y *n.* nonsense; flattery. □ *Don't give me that malarky.* □ *What ridiculous malarkey!*

mickey mouse *n.* nonsense; something trivial. (From the world-famous mouse character by the same name, owned by The Walt Disney Company.) □ *This is just a lot of mickey mouse.* □ *This mickey mouse is wasting my time.*

monkey talk *n.* distorted speech, as uttered while drug intoxicated. □ *Max slapped the poor junky to get him to stop the monkey talk.* □ *Their pupils are pinpoint-sized, and they talk monkey talk. That's how you can tell they're on H.*

moonshine *n.* nonsense; humbug. □ *That's just moonshine! I don't believe a word.* □ *He's a master at moonshine.*

mush *n.* nonsense. □ *What mush! Come on, talk straight!* □ *That's just mush. Don't believe it.*

noise *n.* empty talk; nonsense. □ *I've had enough of your noise. Shut up!* □ *That's nothing but noise. I want the truth.*

nurts AND **nerts** *n.* nonsense. □ *Don't talk that kind of nurts to me!* □ *Oh, that's just nerts. I don't believe a word of it.*

phedinkus *n.* nonsense. □ *Stop your silly phedinkus!* □ *That's just phedinkus. No one will believe you.*

phooey AND **fooey** *n.* nonsense. □ *Your story is just a lot of phooey.* □ *I've heard enough fooey. Let's get out of here.*

piffle *n.* nonsense. □ *What utter piffle!* □ *The entire report was piffle from beginning to end.*

poo AND **poo-poo** *n.* nonsense. □ *Don't give me that poo!* □ *I've heard enough of your poo-poo.*

poppycock *n.* nonsense. (From Dutch.) □ *I've heard enough of your poppycock.* □ *That's nothing but poppycock.*

razzmatazz AND **razzamatazz** *n.* nonsense. □ *Cut out the razzmatazz. How dumb do you think I am?* □ *Don't give me all that razzamatazz!*

rot *n.* nonsense. □ *Don't give me any more of your rot. Speak straight with me.* □ *That's just rot. Don't believe any of it!*

rubbish *n.* nonsense. (Also an exclamation.) □ *I'm tired of listening to your rubbish.* □ *Rubbish! That's the stupidest thing I've ever heard.*

schmegegge AND **schmegeggy** *n.* nonsense. □ *I've heard enough of your schmegegge. Out!* □ *I don't hear anything but schmegeggy coming out of Washington.*

shit *n.* nonsense. (Potentially offensive. Use only with discretion.) □ *Don't give me that shit! I know you're lying.* □ *I'm tired of your shit!*

slobber *n.* nonsense. (From the term for saliva running out of the mouth.) □ *I've heard enough of your slobber. Can it!* □ *Another hour of professorial slobber!*

tripe *n.* nonsense. □ *I don't want to hear any more of that tripe.* □ *That's just tripe. Pay no attention.*

291

whang(y)doodle *n.* nonsense. □ *Now, that's enough of your whangdoodle.* □ *All I ever hear out of you is whangydoodle.*

yap *n.* nonsense; gibberish. □ *That's just yap. Forget it. They mean no harm.* □ *That windbag can produce an enormous amount of yap.*

NONSENSE - LACKING

not just whistling Dixie *tr.* "not talking nonsense." (Folksy. Refers to a song titled "Dixie.") □ *Man, you are right! You're not just whistling Dixie.* □ *When you say she is wrong, you're not just whistling Dixie.*

NOSE

beak *n.* a nose. □ *What a beak on that guy!* □ *I want some glasses that sit in just the right place on my wonderful beak.*

beezer *n.* the nose. □ *I've got a zit on my beezer.* □ *I was afraid he would bop me on the beezer.*

hooter *n.* a nose; a big nose. □ *I sort of wish my hooter wasn't so doggone big.* □ *He blew his hooter and went back to his reading.*

horn *n.* the nose. □ *He scratched his horn with his pencil and opened his mouth to speak.* □ *He had the most humongous horn I have ever seen on man or beast.*

schnozz AND **schnozzle; schnozzola; shnozz** *n.* the nose. (From German *Schnauze* via Yiddish.) □ *Look at the schnozz on that guy!* □ *With a schnozzola like that he should be in the circus.*

smeller *n.* (one's) nose. □ *I think my smeller's gone bad because of my cold.* □ *He's got a fine strawberry on the end of his smeller.*

snoot *n.* the nose. □ *You wanna get bopped on the snoot?* □ *That's one fine zit you got on your snoot.*

NOTHING

beans *n.* nothing. □ *You act like you don't know beans about it.* □ *I have nothing I can give you. Nothing, zotz, beans!*

dick *n.* nothing. (Potentially offensive. Use only with discretion.) □ *The whole idea isn't worth dick.* □ *I was supposed to get a lot of money out of this deal, but all I got was dick!*

diddly-squat AND **(doodly-)squat** *n.* nothing. (Folksy. Originally black or southern.) □ *This contract isn't worth diddly-squat.* □ *I get paid almost doodly-squat for a full day's work.*

jack *n.* nothing. □ *This new television program isn't worth jack!* □ *Your last idea wasn't worth jack. Do I pay you to come up with stuff that bad?*

jackshit *n.* nothing. (Potentially offensive. Use only with discretion.) □ *This car isn't worth jackshit.* □ *Your comments aren't worth jackshit. Keep them to yourself.*

nada *n.* nothing; none. (Spanish.) □ *I asked him, but he didn't say nada.* □ *The score was nada to nada.*

nix *n.* nothing. □ *What did I get for all my trouble? Nix!* □ *I got nix for a tip. And after I was so helpful!*

squat *n.* nothing. □ *I worked all day on this, and she didn't pay me squat.* □ *I earn just a little more than squat, but I am very pleased with my life.*

zilch *n.* nothing. □ *And what do I get? Zilch, that's what!* □ *"Even zilch is too much," said the clerk.*

zip 1. *n.* a score or grade of zero. □ *Well, you got zip on the last test. Sorry about that.* □ *The prof said that zip is better than nothing, but I don't see how it could be.* **2.** *n.* nothing. □ *There was no mail today. Nothing. Zip.* □ *I got zip from the booking agency all week.*

zotz *n.* zero; nothing. □ *I went out to get the mail, but there was zotz.* □ *All I got for a raise was little more than zotz.*

NUMBER

bazillion *n.* an indefinite, enormous number. □ *Ernie gave me a bazillion good reasons why he shouldn't do it.* □ *Next year's bazillion-dollar budget should make things even worse.*

double-deuces *n.* the number 22. □ *The National Weather Service says it's going down to the double-deuces tonight.* □

He's double-deuces today—that's right, twenty-two years old!

double nickels AND **double buffalo** *n.* the number 55; the 55-mile-per-hour speed limit. (Originally citizens band radio. The buffalo is on one side of the nickel and accounts for the 5.) □ *You'd better travel right on those double nickels in through here. The bears are hungry.* □ *The double buffalo is enforced on this road.*

NUPTIALS

hitched *mod.* married. (Folksy.) □ *Sam and Mary decided to get hitched.* □ *They went out of state to get hitched.*

pop the question *tr.* [for a man] to ask a woman to marry him. (Could also be used by a woman asking a man.) □ *She waited for years for him to pop the question.* □ *Finally she popped the question.*

shotgun wedding *n.* a forced wedding, presumably because the bride is pregnant. □ *It was a shotgun wedding, but they sure are in love.* □ *I thought shotgun weddings went out with feuds and things like that.*

take the plunge *tr.* to marry someone. □ *I'm not ready to take the plunge yet.* □ *Sam and Mary took the plunge.*

tie the knot 1. *tr.* to marry a mate. □ *We tied the knot in a little chapel on the Arkansas border.* □ *They finally tied the knot.* **2.** *tr.* [for a cleric] to unite a couple in marriage. □ *It was hard to find somebody to tie the knot at that hour.* □ *It only took a few minutes for the ship's captain to tie the knot.*

OATHS

(Aw) shucks! *exclam.* a mild oath. (Folksy.) □ *Shucks, ma'am. It wasn't anything at all.* □ *Aw shucks, I ain't never been this close to a woman before.*

OBEDIENCE

suck someone's hind tit *tr.* to do someone's bidding no matter how unpleasant or impossible; to *kiss someone's ass.* (Potentially offensive. Use only with discretion.) □ *What am I supposed to do—suck his hind tit?* □ *She acts like everybody has to suck her hind tit to keep their jobs.*

OBLIGATION

if one knows what's good for one *phr.* "one had better do what is expected of one." □ *You'd better be on time if you know what's good for you.* □ *If you know what's good for you, you'll call and apologize.*

(must) do AND **must** *n.* something that someone ought to do. (Always with *a.*) □ *Seeing the Eiffel Tower is a must do in Paris.* □ *This is a do when you're in town.*

OBSCENE

See also **RUDE, VULGAR.**

barnyard *mod.* smutty; obscene. (Refers to the dung found in barnyards.) □ *Those barnyard movies belong in the barnyard.* □ *You are thinking barnyard thoughts again. I see it in your eyes.*

blue *mod.* obscene; vulgar; dirty. □ *Those blue jokes don't go over very well around here.* □ *Enough of your blue interests. Get out and take all these magazines with you.* □ *That one was really blue.*

dirty *mod.* obscene. □ *You have a dirty mind.* □ *The movie was too dirty for me.* □ *How would you know what's dirty and what's not?*

dirty-minded *mod.* having a tendency to see the lewd or obscene aspects of anything; having a tendency to place an obscene interpretation on the words and actions of others. □ *Bruno is sort of dirty-minded, but he wouldn't do anything really vile.* □ *He's a vile, dirty-minded jerk.* □ *Most of those guys are dirty-minded.*

dirty word *n.* a curse word; an informal word concerned with sex or excrement. □ *No dirty words are allowed on this computer bulletin board.* □ *Some kid got the microphone and yelled a dirty word into it.*

(Do) you eat with that mouth? AND **(Do) you kiss your momma with that mouth?** *interrog.* "Do you actually eat with the mouth you use to talk that filth?"; "Do you actually use that filthy mouth to kiss your mother?" (A catchphrase said to someone who talks dirty all the time.) □ *That's a lot of foul talk. Do you eat with that mouth?* □ *You talk dirt a lot. You eat with that mouth?*

have one's mind in the gutter *tr.* to think or suggest something obscene. (*Have got* can replace *have.*) □ *Tiffany has her mind in the gutter. That's why she laughs at all that dirty stuff.* □ *You always have your mind in the gutter.*

trashy *mod.* crude; obscene. □ *What a trashy movie!* □ *Cut out the trashy talk, you guys.*

OBSERVATION

catch something *tr.* to see or listen to something. (More specific than the colloquial sense, to *manage to hear something*.) □ *I will try to catch that new movie this weekend.* □ *Did you catch that radio program about cancer last night?*

eagle-eye *n.* a busybody; a person who watches or monitors other people's actions: a floorwalker, a detective, a hall monitor. □ *Some old eagle-eye across the street saw me standing in the cold and called my wife, who came down and let me in.* □ *The store detective is an eagle-eye and caught the kleptomaniac.*

get a load of something or someone *tr.* to look at someone or something. □ *Wow, get a load of Fred!* □ *Get a load of the chrome on that set of wheels!*

glom *tr.* to take a look at someone or something. (Underworld.) □ *Glom this layout for a minute.* □ *Come over here and glom the view of the bank from this window.*

lamp *tr.* to look at someone or something. (The *lamps* are the eyes.) □ *I lamped the paper and then threw it away.* □ *Here, lamp this tire for a minute. It's low, isn't it?*

people-watching *n.* observing different kinds of people as a pastime. □ *Let's eat at the greasy spoon over on Maple. The food is gross, but the people-watching is good.* □ *I enjoy people-watching, especially at airports.*

sidewalk superintendent *n.* someone who—out of curiosity—watches excavations being dug and buildings being built. □ *All day, the lines of sidewalk superintendents oozed by.* □ *I don't want any advice from a sidewalk superintendent.*

stakeout 1. *n.* a (police) assignment where someone is positioned to observe someone or something. □ *The two top cops were out on a stakeout.* □ *The stakeout at the warehouse backfired. They only found cats.* **2.** *n.* a person who is positioned to observe someone or something. □ *The stakeout stuck out like a sore thumb, standing there under the street-* *light reading a paper.* □ *The stakeout was one of Barlowe's best operatives.*

stake someone or something out 1. *tr.* to position a person so that someone or something can be observed or followed. □ *The cops staked the car out and made the arrest.* □ *Barlowe staked out the apartment building and watched patiently for an hour.* **2.** *tr.* to position a person to observe someone or something. □ *He staked his best operative out in front of the building.* □ *We staked out two men to keep watch.*

take a gander (at someone or something) *tr.* to look at someone or something. □ *Wow, take a gander at this chick!* □ *I wanted to take a gander at the new computer before they started using it.*

Watch my lips! AND **Read my lips!** *exclam.* "I am going to say something rude to you that I will not say out loud!" □ *You jerk! Watch my lips!* □ *Hey, chum! Read my lips!*

OBSESSION

bug *n.* an obsession or urge. □ *I've got this bug about making money.* □ *I have a bug that causes me to eat tons of pasta.*

hang-up *n.* a problem or concern; an obsession. □ *She's got some serious hang-ups about cats.* □ *I don't have any hang-ups at all. Well, almost none.*

happy *mod.* obsessed with something. (A combining form showing a strong interest in the thing that is named before *happy*.) □ *All those guys are girl-happy at this age.* □ *Pete's car-happy right now. That's all he thinks about.*

have something on the brain *tr.* to be obsessed with something. (*Have got* can replace *have*.) □ *You've just got girls on the brain, you silly twit.* □ *I have money on the brain, I guess.*

one-track mind *n.* a (person's) mind obsessed with only one thing. □ *When it comes to food, Tom has a one-track mind.* □ *Mary has a one-track mind. All she thinks about is Tom.*

stuck on someone or something *mod.* enamored with someone or something; obsessed with someone or something. □

Tom is stuck on himself—as conceited as can be. □ *I'm really stuck on this stuff. It's just yummy.*

wrapped up (in someone or something) *mod.* concerned or obsessed with someone or something. □ *Sally is pretty wrapped up in herself.* □ *I'm too wrapped up in my charity work to get a job.*

OBSTRUCTION

stonewall 1. *tr.* to obstruct something or someone. □ *And again, the mayor tried to stonewall the investigation.* □ *If you continue to stonewall, we'll call in the FBI.* **2.** *n.* an obstructionist act. □ *His answer to the committee was another stonewall that caught them all by surprise.* □ *The stonewall they were faced with was almost too much.*

OBTAIN

bag *tr.* to obtain something. □ *I'll try to bag a couple of tickets for you.* □ *See if you can bag one of the red ones.*

clock *tr.* to earn, score, or total up someone or something. (As if the person or thing gained were being metered or clocked.) □ *Sam clocked a date with Sally, and is he ever proud!* □ *Amy clocked nearly $12 an hour in overtime last weekend.*

latch onto something *tr.* to obtain something. □ *I have to latch onto a hundred bucks by Friday night.* □ *I latched onto a good book about repairing plumbing.*

nick *tr.* to get or take something. □ *Would you please nick me a slice of bread?* □ *Tom nicked a copy of the test for Sam, who also needed one.*

score *tr. & in.* to obtain something; to obtain drugs or sex. □ *Max spent an hour trying to score some pot.* □ *Fred is always trying to score with women.*

OBVIOUS

ob *mod.* obvious. □ *Of course I understand it. It's completely ob.* □ *It's pretty ob that you are just trying to start something.*

stick out like a sore thumb *in.* to be very obvious. □ *That zit really sticks out like a sore thumb.* □ *Do you think I would*

stick out like a sore thumb at the party if I wore this coat?

OCCUPATION
See also EMPLOYMENT.

chips *n.* a carpenter. (Also a term of address.) □ *Tell our chips to come up here and put in a new floorboard.* □ *Tell me, chips, how fast can you build a coffin?*

civil serpent *n.* a civil servant. □ *You have no idea the kinds of things civil serpents have to put up with.* □ *I'm a civil serpent with the state.*

desk jockey *n.* someone who works at a desk in an office. (Patterned on *disc jockey*.) □ *I couldn't stand being a cooped-up desk jockey.* □ *The desk jockeys at our place don't get paid very well.*

gabmeister *n.* a talk show host or hostess. □ *Todd Remington, a late-night gabmeister, startled his audience by suddenly walking offstage.* □ *There are so many of these gabmeisters that I can hardly keep them straight.*

goober-grabber *n.* someone who picks peanuts. (Typically someone native to Georgia, where peanuts are grown.) □ *My nephew moved from Chicago to Atlanta, where he became a goober-grabber in no time at all.* □ *One of the local goober-grabbers took us to a peanut boil.*

hardhat *n.* construction worker. (Usually derogatory.) □ *The hardhats didn't care much for the actress's politics.* □ *Some hardhat was waving a flag and shouting something I couldn't understand.*

moonshiner *n.* a maker of illicit whisky. □ *Moonshiners in the Georgia hills are using sophisticated electronic warning systems to keep one step ahead of the feds.* □ *I have an uncle who was a moonshiner for a while.*

powder monkey *n.* a specialist in the use of dynamite. □ *I won't stay around while the powder monkey is working.* □ *How long do powder monkeys usually live?*

OCEAN

big drink *n.* the Atlantic Ocean; an ocean. □ *We flew over the big drink in* an hour or two. □ *When you're over the big drink, you really get to feel how tiny we humans are.*

ODOR

funk *n.* a bad odor; a stench. □ *What is that ghastly funk in here?* □ *Open the windows and clear out this funk.*

funky *mod.* smelly and obnoxious. □ *Get your funky old socks outa here.* □ *This place is really funky. Open some windows.*

ripe *mod.* foul; smelly. □ *Whooey! This place is ripe. What died?* □ *Get your ripe old socks out of here!* □ *The fish seems quite ripe.*

smell to (high) heaven *in.* to smell very bad. □ *This kitchen smells to high heaven. What besides garlic are you cooking?* □ *Where has this dog been? It smells to heaven.*

stinkpot *n.* anything smelly. □ *What are you barbecuing in this old stinkpot?* □ *Why don't you drive this stinkpot into a service station and get it tuned?*

OFFENDED

get one's nose out of joint *tr.* to feel slighted by something someone has done; to take offense at something. □ *You get your nose out of joint too easily about stuff like that.* □ *Now, don't get your nose out of joint. She didn't mean it.*

OFFICER

big gun *n.* an important and powerful person, such as an officer of a company. (Often with *bring in*, as in the example.) □ *It went up to the big guns, who said no immediately.* □ *I knew they would bring in the big guns at the last minute.*

brass *n.* high-ranking military or civilian officers. □ *We'll see what the brass has to say first.* □ *The brass said no to your promotion.*

brass hat *n.* a member of the *brass*. □ *When are the brass hats going to start paying attention to the important things?* □ *A brass hat came up to me and asked me where I was going.*

chief *n.* the person in charge. (Also a term of address.) □ *Okay, chief, where*

to? □ *You got a couple of clams to pay the toll with, chief?*

in *n.* someone in a special position; someone who is serving in an elective office. □ *Well, now that I am an in, there's going to be some changes.* □ *When Ralph is one of the ins, he'll throw the crooks out.*

lame duck *mod.* having to do with someone in the last period of a term in an elective office. □ *You don't expect much from a lame duck president.* □ *Lame duck congresses tend to do things they wouldn't dare do otherwise.*

prexy *n.* a president. □ *The prexy broke the tied vote.* □ *This year's prexy will retire in March.*

veep *n.* a vice president. □ *The veep is going to preside today.* □ *Now we have to elect a veep. Any nominations?*

OLD

oldie but goodie *n.* something (or even someone) that is old but still likeable. □ *I love that piece of music. It's an oldie but goodie.* □ *Mary is an oldie but goodie. I'm glad she's still around.*

OLD-FASHIONED

back number *n.* an old-fashioned person. (Like an out-of-print issue of a magazine.) □ *Some old back number wearing gaiters wants to have a word with you.* □ *Oh, Dad! You're getting to be such a back number!*

buzzard meat *n.* someone or something that is dead or outdated. □ *If you don't watch out, you're going to become buzzard meat!* □ *That old car is buzzard meat. It will hardly run.*

cube *n.* a very *square* person. □ *This nerd was the most unbelievable cube you have ever seen.* □ *Not just an L7, a real cube.*

fossil *n.* an old-fashioned person. □ *Some old fossil called the police about the noise.* □ *Oh, Tad, you are such a fossil.*

fuddy-duddy AND **fud** *n.* a stuffy person; an old-fashioned person, especially a male. □ *Pay no attention to him. He's just an old fud.* □ *There seems to be a con-*

vention of fuddy-duddies in the park today.

granddad *n.* someone who is old-fashioned or out-of-date. □ *Tom is just a silly granddad. He is dull and old-fashioned.* □ *Don't be such a granddad. Live a little.*

groovy *mod.* out-of-date; passé. (California.) □ *Your clothes are so groovy. It barfs me out.* □ *Oh, how groovy!*

moldy fig *n.* an old-fashioned person; a square. □ *Don't be a moldy fig! Lighten up!* □ *Some moldy fig objected to our music.*

mossback *n.* an old *square;* a *stick in the mud.* □ *Walter, you are such an old mossback.* □ *I enjoy appearing to be a mossback. People expect so little from you.*

old fogey *n.* an old-fashioned person; an old man. □ *My uncle is an old fogey. He must be the most old-fashioned man in the world.* □ *Don't be such an old fogey.*

old-hat *mod.* old-fashioned or outmoded. □ *That's just old-hat. This is the modern world!* □ *Her latest work is nothing but old-hat. She's through.*

out *mod.* out of fashion. (The opposite of *in*.) □ *That kind of clothing is strictly out.* □ *You need to tell me which of my dresses is out this season.*

square *mod.* law-abiding; stodgy. □ *Man, you are really square.* □ *I come from a very square family.*

stick-in-the-mud *n.* a dull and old-fashioned person. □ *Don't be such an old stick-in-the-mud.* □ *Some stick-in-the-mud objected to the kind of music we wanted to play in church.*

trad *mod.* "traditional"; old-fashioned. □ *The approach is sort of trad, but so what?* □ *A more trad style might make the grownups more comfortable.*

uncool *mod. square;* dull and orthodox. □ *Oh, what an uncool weirdo!* □ *This place is uncool. Let's cruise.*

OPINION

bounce something off (of) someone *tr.* to try out an idea on someone; to get someone's opinion of an idea. □ *Let me bounce this off of you.* □ *I bounced the idea off Gary, but he wasn't at all impressed.*

get a load off one's mind *tr.* to say what one is thinking; to speak one's mind; to talk something out. □ *I'm sorry, but I just had to get a load off my mind.* □ *I think you'll feel better after you get a load off your mind.*

hard-liner *n.* a person who takes a strict position (on something). □ *Tom is sort of a hard-liner when it comes to spending public money.* □ *The mayor is a hard-liner on the question of care for the elderly.*

How does that grab you? *interrog.* "What do you think of that?" □ *Looks good, okay? How does that grab you?* □ *How does that grab you? Enough salt?*

slant *n.* a biased view; a unique perception. □ *You can probably give us yet another slant on this problem.* □ *You provided us with a fresh slant on this question.*

stand pat (on something) *in.* to stick firmly to one's position or opinions. □ *I am going to stand pat on this issue.* □ *I thought you would stand pat in the absence of new information.*

OPPORTUNITY

break *n.* a chance; an opportunity. □ *Come on, give me a break!* □ *I got my first break in show biz when I was only twelve.*

fair shake *n.* a fair chance. (From shaking dice.) □ *I want to give you both a fair shake.* □ *All I want from you is a fair shake.*

fat chance *n.* a very poor chance. (Sarcastic.) □ *Fat chance I'll ever get a new car.* □ *Me, get an A? Fat chance.*

golden opportunity *n.* a very good opportunity. □ *This is my golden opportunity, and I can't pass it up.* □ *You get a golden opportunity like this very rarely.*

OPPOSITION

anti 1. *mod.* against someone or something. (Sometimes with the force of a preposition.) □ *I'm not anti the proposal, I just have some questions.* □ *Four are in favor, and two are anti.* **2.** *n.* someone who is against someone or something. □ *She's an anti. Don't even ask her.* □ *All the antis are going to vote for it this time.*

blackball *tr.* to vote against someone in a secret ballot. □ *Someone blackballed the prospective member.* □ *I chose to blackball her, and I'm not sorry.*

cross someone (up) AND **cross up someone** *tr.* to go against someone; to thwart someone. □ *Don't cross me up if you know what's good for you.* □ *I told you not to cross me again!*

ORDINARY
See also **AVERAGE**.

everyday joe *n.* an ordinary man. □ *What does the everyday joe make of all this nonsense?* □ *Do you know even one everyday joe?*

grassroots *n.* the common people, especially rural people. □ *We really haven't heard anything from the grassroots yet.* □ *The grassroots isn't organized on most issues.*

great unwashed *n.* most of the common people; the hoi polloi. (Always with *the.*) □ *The great unwashed could probably tell us a lot about life in the big city.* □ *I usually find myself more in agreement with the great unwashed than with the elite.*

Jane Doe *n.* a general term for a woman. (The mate of *John Doe.*) □ *A Jane Doe was pulled out of the river this morning.* □ *There was an accident involving a Jane Doe.*

Jane Q. Public *n.* a general term for a female representative of the public. (The mate of *John Q. Public.*) □ *And what does Jane Q. Public think about all this?* □ *Jane Q. Public doesn't care at all.*

Joe Blow AND **Joe Doakes** *n.* a typical or average male American citizen. □ *What do you think Joe Blow really thinks about all this?* □ *According to surveys, Joe Doakes can hardly read.*

Joe Citizen *n.* a general term for a male representative of the public. □ *Joe Citizen hasn't spoken yet.* □ *Joe Citizen is watching T.V.*

Joe Six-pack *n.* the average guy who sits around drinking beer by the six-pack. □ *Joe Six-pack likes that kind of television program.* □ *All Joe Six-pack wants is a good game on T.V.*

John Doe *n.* a general term for a man. (The mate of *Jane Doe.*) □ *John Doe was the name at the bottom of the check.* □ *Oh, you mean John Doe isn't his real name?*

John Q. Public *n.* a general term for a male representative of the public. (The mate of *Jane Q. Public.*) □ *John Q. Public doesn't seem to like the new tax forms.* □ *John Q. Public tends not to like regimentation.*

man on the street 1. *mod.* common; everyday. (This is hyphenated before a nominal.) □ *These man-on-the-street interviews all seem sort of phony.* □ *The man-on-the-street opinion spots are fun to make, but we can't show half of them.* **2.** *n.* the common man; just anyone selected at random. □ *But what does the man on the street think about all this?* □ *The man on the street really doesn't care about most of what you think is important.*

rank and file *n.* the common members of something. □ *What will the rank and file think of the proposal?* □ *The rank and file will vote on it tomorrow.*

ORGANIZATION

get it (all) together *tr.* to get oneself organized; to get mentally adjusted. □ *When I get it together, I'll try to go back to school.* □ *Try to get it all together and come back to work next week, okay?*

get one's act together AND **get one's shit together; get one's stuff together 1.** *tr.* to organize oneself; to get one's possessions organized. (Use caution with *shit.*) □ *Let me get my act together, and I'll be right with you.* □ *I'll get my stuff together and be right with you.* **2.** AND **get one's head together** *tr.* to calm down and get mentally organized. (Use caution with *shit.*) □ *As soon as I get my head together, I can be of more help.* □ *Get your act together and start living again.*

get on the stick *in.* to get organized and get busy. □ *Get on the stick and get this job done!* □ *Come on, you guys. Let's get on the stick!*

have it all together *tr.* to be mentally and physically organized; to be of sound mind. (*Have got* can replace *have.*) □ *I don't have it all together today.* □ *Try me again later when I have it all together.*

shake-up *n.* a reorganization. □ *After a shake-up like the one we've just been through, everybody's a little upset.* □ *Fred and Clare both survived the shake-up.*

together *mod.* organized. □ *I'm not together yet. Lemme call you back.* □ *That chick's really got it together.*

OVERWHELM

ace *tr.* to surpass someone or something; to beat someone or something; to ace someone out. □ *The Japanese firm aced the Americans by getting the device onto the shelves first.* □ *Fred aced Tom in the contest for the best beard.*

ace someone out *tr.* to maneuver someone out; to win out over someone. □ *I plan to ace you out in the first lap.* □ *Martha aced out Rebecca to win the first-place trophy.*

beat someone out *tr.* to outdistance someone; to perform better than someone. □ *We have to beat the other company out, and then we'll have the contract.* □ *I beat out Walter in the footrace.*

blow someone away *tr.* to overwhelm someone; to amaze someone. □ *The music about blew me away.* □ *The whole idea just blew her away.*

blow someone's doors off *tr.* to defeat someone; to surpass someone. (As if someone were going by another vehicle on the highway at such a high speed that the doors would be blown off in passing.) □ *We're gonna really blow your doors off in the next game.* □ *They blew our doors off in sales last year.*

break someone's balls *tr.* to wreck or ruin someone; to overwork someone; to overwhelm someone. (Usually used with males, but not necessarily. Potentially offensive. Use only with discretion.) □

The boss acts like he's trying to break everybody's balls all the time. □ *No need to break my balls. I'll do it!*

cream *tr.* to beat someone; to outscore someone. □ *The other team creamed us, but we had better team spirit.* □ *We'll cream 'em next week.*

dust *tr.* to defeat someone; to win out over someone. □ *We dusted the other team, 87–54.* □ *In the second game, they dusted us.*

get the drop on someone *tr.* to succeed in getting an advantage over someone. □ *I guess I got the drop on you because I was early.* □ *I got the drop on almost everybody by sending in my registration by mail.*

knocked out *mod.* overwhelmed. □ *We were just knocked out when we heard your news.* □ *Were we surprised? We were knocked out—elated!*

murder AND **slaughter** *tr.* to overwhelm; to beat someone in a sports contest. □ *The other team murdered us.* □ *We went out on the field prepared to slaughter them.*

paste *tr.* to defeat a person or a team, usually in a game of some type. □ *The Warriors pasted the Rockets, 70–49.* □ *They really pasted our team in last week's game.*

shellack *tr.* to beat someone; to outscore someone. □ *We're gonna shellack those bums Friday night.* □ *We'll be shellacking every team in the league this year.*

shoo-in *n.* an easy winner. □ *She's a shoo-in. Nobody can touch her.* □ *My horse was a shoo-in. It won by a mile.*

slay *tr.* to overwhelm someone with one's performance or other excellence. □ *These jokes always slay the audience.* □ *Oh, you slay me with your silly remarks.*

smear *tr.* to defeat someone; to outscore someone. □ *We smeared them 50–20.* □ *They said they would smear us, but we smeared them.*

smoke *tr.* to beat someone in a contest; to outrun, outdistance, or outplay someone. □ *Jill smoked Dave in the bicycle race.* □ *I will smoke you in the race!*

stomp (on) someone *tr. & in.* to beat someone; to misuse someone. □ *We are gonna stomp you guys next game.* □ *One team stomped on the other so hard and fast, the scoreboard couldn't keep up.*

take *tr.* to defeat someone, as in a fight. □ *Max thought he could take the guy, but he wasn't sure.* □ *I know I can take you. Make my day!*

take someone to the cleaners *tr.* to defeat or best someone. □ *We took the other team to the cleaners.* □ *Look at the height they've got! They'll take us to the cleaners!*

trash *tr.* to beat, as in a ball game. □ *You trashed us this game, but watch out next season!* □ *The Jets trashed the Wall-bangers, 48–13.*

trounce *tr.* to beat or outscore someone. □ *They really trounced us.* □ *Western trounced Eastern for the tenth year in a row.*

whump AND **whomp; womp** *tr.* to beat or outscore someone. □ *They set out to whump us, and they sure did.* □ *The Red-skins womped the Walleyes.*

Win a few, lose a few. *phr.* "Sometimes one wins; other times one loses." □ *Too bad. Sorry about that. Win a few, lose a few.* □ *"Win a few, lose a few," doesn't mean you never win at all.*

You can't win them all. AND **You can't win 'em all.** *sent.* "No one succeeds all the time." (Said when someone fails.) □ *Don't fret about it, Tom. You can't win them all.* □ *You can't win 'em all, but you can't lose 'em all, either.*

zonk *tr.* to overpower someone or something. □ *We zonked the dog with a kick.* □ *It took two cops to zonk the creep.*

PACIFIER

passy *n.* a baby's pacifier. (Baby talk.) □ *Does little Johnnie want his passy?* □ *Mommy, Mary threw her passy on the floor.*

PAIN

oof *exclam.* the sound one makes when one is struck in the abdomen. (Usually **Oof!**) □ *So then Bob hit him in the belly. Oof!* □ *"Oof!" cried Tom. He couldn't talk any more after that.*

stitch *n.* a sharp pain, usually in the side. □ *I got a stitch and had to drop out of the marathon.* □ *A stitch in the side can be very painful.*

PANIC

freak (out) *in.* to panic; to lose control. □ *I was so frightened, I thought I would freak.* □ *Come on, relax. Don't freak out.*

hit the panic button AND **press the panic button; push the panic button** *tr.* to panic. □ *She hit the panic button and just went to pieces.* □ *Don't press the panic button. Relax and keep your eyes open.*

PARADOX

catch-22 *n.* a directive that is impossible to obey without violating some other, equally important, directive. □ *There was nothing I could do. It was a classic catch-22.* □ *I had my choice between catch-22s. What do you call that kind of a dilemma?*

PARODY

send someone or something up *tr.* to perform a parody of someone or something. □ *Last week, he sent the president up.* □ *In his act, he sends up famous people.*

send-up *n.* a parody. □ *It was his delightful send-up of the current administration that catapulted Roger Rogers to national fame.* □ *I enjoy a good send-up, even if it is about me.*

take-off *n.* a parody of someone or something. (Usually with *on.*) □ *The comedian did a take-off on the wealthy senator.* □ *The take-off on the dean didn't go over well.*

PARTY

ball *n.* a wild time at a party; a good time. □ *We really had a ball. See ya!* □ *Your birthday party was a ball!*

bash *n.* a wild party; a night on the town. □ *What a bash! I'm exhausted!*

blast *n.* an exciting party. □ *Fred knows how to put on a real blast!* □ *What a blast we had!*

boogie 1. *n.* a party where the *boogie* is danced. □ *There's a boogie over at Steve's tonight.* □ *One more boogie and I'm through for the year.* **2.** *in.* to party. □ *We're going to boogie at Steve's tonight.* □ *I have boogied every night for a week. I'm dead tired.*

hop *n.* a dancing party for young people. □ *The kids are out at some school-sponsored hop.* □ *The hop was a lot of fun.*

party animal *n.* someone who loves parties. □ *My boyfriend and I are real party animals. Let's party!* □ *If you weren't such a party animal, you'd have more time for studying.*

party-hearty *in.* to have a great time; to celebrate. (Originally teenage. The past tense is variable.) □ *Let's get some stuff and party-hearty.* □ *The whole class decided to celebrate and party-hearty.*

party-pooper *n.* the first person to leave a party; someone who ruins a party because of dullness or by leaving early. □ *Don't leave! Don't be a party-pooper!* □ *Don't invite Martha. She's such a party-pooper.*

petting-party *n.* a session of kissing and caressing. □ *I just want to watch the movie. I didn't come here for some teenage petting-party!* □ *We went to the passion-pit for a petting-party.*

rage *in.* to *party*; to celebrate. (Collegiate.) □ *Man, are we going to rage tonight!* □ *Fred and Mary were raging over at the frat house last weekend.*

rave *n.* a party; a wild celebration. □ *What a rave! A real fine party.* □ *Let's have a little rave next Friday.*

set *n.* a party. □ *Your set was a totally major bash!* □ *Let's throw a set tonight and invite some chicks.*

shindig *n.* a party; a dance. (Folksy.) □ *What a fancy shindig! They even have glass glasses!* □ *What time do we have to be at that shindig Saturday night?*

sock hop *n.* a dance party where everyone dances in stocking feet. (From the 1950s.) □ *My mother told us about a sock hop she went to. It doesn't sound like fun at all.* □ *Sock hops were popular in schools that had new and expensive floors in their gymnasiums.*

stag *mod.* having to do with a gathering for men only. □ *The party is stag, so Tom and I are going together.* □ *Stag parties cease to be fun after a while.*

stag-party *n.* a party for men only. □ *Sally was hired to dance at a stag-party.* □ *They hired a stripper for the stag-party—you know, the kind that jumps out of a cake.*

streak *n.* an exciting time; a wild party. □ *That rally was a streak!* □ *We had a streak at Tom's.*

tailgate *in.* to have a *tailgate party.* □ *We planned to tailgate before the game, but it was massively cold.* □ *The people who were tailgating next to us asked to borrow our salt.*

tailgate party *n.* a small party held on the folded down tailgate of a station wagon in a parking lot. (Something that is done before a ball game, concert, etc.) □ *They had a tailgate party before the Bears game.* □ *The tailgate party was a success, except for the cold.*

PARTY - DRINKING
See also DRINKING - BOUT.

beer blast AND **beer bust** *n.* a beer-drinking party; a beer binge. □ *Kelly's having a beer blast at his place, starting tonight.* □ *There is a beer bust somewhere around here almost every night.*

blow AND **blow-out** *n.* a drinking party. □ *What a blow over at Joe's. I'll never get sober.* □ *Man, come to my blow-out. It's the best place to go.*

brew-out *n.* a beer blast; a beer *blow-out.* □ *Were you at Tom's brew-out? I was too bombed to see who was there.* □ *Was that Tom's brew-out I was at?*

bust *n.* a riotous drinking party. □ *There was a big bust in the park until two in the morning.* □ *There was no beer at the bust. Only wine.*

hoo(t)chfest *n.* a drinking bout; a drinking party. □ *We stopped by Sally's to join in the hoochfest for a while.* □ *Let's throw a big hootchfest next month.*

hopfest *n.* a beer-drinking party. □ *We went to a big hopfest over at Wally's, but it broke up early.* □ *That was some hopfest! No potato chips!*

kegger *n.* a party where beer is served from a keg. (Teens and collegiate.) □ *Tiffany is having a kegger, and a few of her intimates are invited.* □ *Isn't there a kegger somewhere tonight?*

keg party *n.* a party where liquor, especially beer, is served. □ *There is a free keg party at Freddy's.* □ *The keg party ended early owing to the arrival of uninvited nabs.*

tea party *n.* a wild drinking party. (Like the Mad Hatter's party in Lewis Carroll's *Alice in Wonderland.*) □ *There was a loud tea party going on in the corner booth when Barlowe came in.* □ *I'm having a little tea party Friday. Wanna come?*

PARTY - DRUGS

grass party *n.* a marijuana-smoking party. □ *The goon squad raided Pete's grass party without any warning.* □ *Sally tried to have a grass party, but didn't have any grass.*

kick party *n.* a party where some drug is used. □ *The kick party broke up early with the help of Johnny-be-good.* □ *There was a kick party at one of the crack houses, and even little children went in.*

pot party *n.* a communal marijuana smoking session; a party where marijuana is smoked. □ *I didn't know you were taking me to a pot party!* □ *There was a bust at Max's pot party.*

PASS

ace *tr.* to pass a test easily, with an A grade. □ *Man, I really aced that test.* □ *I knew I wouldn't ace it, but I never thought I'd flunk it!*

PASSENGER

straphanger *n.* a subway passenger. □ *I didn't think I could get used to being a straphanger.* □ *Straphangers learn to blot out their surroundings.*

PAST

ancient history *n.* someone or something completely forgotten, especially past romances. □ *Bob? I never think about Bob anymore. He's ancient history.* □ *That business about joining the army is ancient history.*

dead and gone *mod.* (of a thing) gone long ago. □ *That kind of thinking is dead and gone.* □ *The horse and buggy days are dead and gone.*

flashback *n.* a memory of the past; a portrayal of the past in a story. □ *Suddenly, Fred had a wonderful flashback to his childhood.* □ *The next scene in the film was a flashback to the time of Ivan the Terrible.*

has-been 1. *mod.* former; burnt-out. □ *Some has-been singer croaked through "The Star-Spangled Banner."* □ *Now I'm a has-been football player, and nobody even knows my name.* **2.** *n.* someone who used to be important; a person whose career has ended. □ *Marty is just a has-*

been. *There's no future for him.* □ *An old has-been was hired to host the midnight show.*

history *n.* someone or something in the past. □ *Dave? Oh, he's just history. I never go out with him anymore.* □ *Susan is just history. We're through.* □ *Don't make a move! If this gun goes off, you're history.*

PATIENCE

Keep your shirt on! AND **Keep your pants on!** *exclam.* "Just wait a minute!" □ *I'll be right with you. Keep your shirt on!* □ *Keep your pants on! You're next.*

PAUSE

breather *n.* a rest period; a lull. □ *I really need a breather.* □ *As soon as we've had a breather, it's back to work.*

come up for air *in.* to pause for a break. □ *The kissers—being only human—had to come up for air eventually.* □ *They were taking in money so fast at the box office that there wasn't a minute to come up for air.*

PAWNSHOP

hockshop *n.* a pawnshop. □ *We took the watch to a hockshop, but couldn't get enough money for it.* □ *The cops checked all the hockshops in town for the murder weapon.*

PEACE

dove *n.* someone who supports a peace-seeking U.S. defense policy. □ *The doves want to sell the tanks and distribute the money to the poor.* □ *The hawks want to ignore the poor and the doves and buy tanks with the money.*

Vietnik *n.* someone—looking like a beatnik—who opposed the Vietnam War. □ *The Vietniks' message was sort of distorted by the press.* □ *I knew a Vietnik who moved to Canada.*

PENIS

cock *n.* the penis. (Taboo. Potentially offensive. Use only with discretion.) □ *He made some joke about a cock, but nobody laughed.* □ *The streaker covered his cock and ran across the field.*

dick *n.* the penis. (Widely heard, but potentially offensive. Use only with discretion.) □ *She told some dirty joke about a dick, but everybody just sat there and looked straight ahead.* □ *He covered his dick and stooped down, then reached up to pull down the shade.*

dork *n.* the penis. (Potentially offensive. Use only with discretion.) □ *Paul told a joke about a dork, but everybody just sat there and looked straight ahead.* □ *He covered his dork and squatted down; then he reached up and pulled down the shade.*

johnson *n.* a penis. (Again, a "thing." Use caution with the topic.) □ *Zip up, or your johnson'll get out.* □ *He covered his johnson and ran for the dressing room.*

joint *n.* a penis. (Use caution with the topic.) □ *He told some joke about a joint, but people just turned away.* □ *He covered his joint and ran for the dressing room.*

jones *n.* a penis. (Use caution with the topic.) □ *Zip up, man. You want your jones getting out?* □ *Cut out all this talk about joneses!*

putz *n.* a penis. (Yiddish. Use caution with *putz* and topic.) □ *Tell him to cover his putz and run and grab a towel.* □ *He told some joke about a putz, but nobody laughed.*

schmuck *n.* a penis. (Yiddish. Use caution with the topic.) □ *If I hear that joke about a camel's schmuck one more time, I'm going to scream.* □ *There are probably better names than schmuck for what you are talking about.*

weenie *n.* the penis. (Essentially juvenile and jocular. Use caution with the topic.) □ *Tell him to cover his weenie and run and grab a towel.* □ *He told some joke about a weenie, but nobody got it.*

PEOPLE

See also **MAN, WOMAN**.

buzhie *n.* a middle-class person. (From *bourgeoisie*.) □ *My mother was a buzhie, but my father was a Bohemian type.* □ *I live in a neighborhood of buzhies.*

guy *n.* a person. (Usually a male when used in the singular.) □ *Hey you guys, let's go!* □ *When you guys finish getting your makeup on, we can go back to the guys.*

PIP *n.* "postindustrial person." (Acronym. Refers to a person as a member of a group that has become useless because of technological change.) □ *The world really doesn't really need more PIPs, except as consumers, of course.* □ *Not so! The world needs plenty of PIPs to pay taxes.*

single *n.* an unmarried person. (Usually plural.) □ *I'm holding a little party for singles.* □ *Todd's a single—just recently.*

warm body *n.* just anyone who can be counted on to stay alive. □ *See if you can get a couple of warm bodies to stand at the door and hand out programs.* □ *You mean among all these warm bodies nobody knows calculus?*

PEOPLE - AMERINDIAN

apple *n.* an Amerindian who behaves more like a European than an Amerindian. (Like the apple, the person is red on the outside and white on the inside. Patterned on *Oreo*. Potentially offensive. Use only with discretion.) □ *Stop acting like an apple all the time!* □ *Sam is your typical apple. Can't decide who he really is.*

PEOPLE - ATTRACTIVE

ankle *n.* an attractive woman or *girl*. (Typically with *some*.) □ *Now, there's some ankle I've never seen around here before.* □ *Do you get ankle like that around here all the time?*

cutie *n.* a cute thing or person. (Also a term of address.) □ *Your baby is a real cutie.* □ *Come here, cutie, let me fix your collar.*

cutie pie *n.* a cute person, typically a woman or a baby. (Also a term of address.) □ *She is such a cutie pie.* □ *What's your name, cutie pie?*

glamour puss *n.* a person with a beautiful face. □ *I'm no glamour puss, but I'm no dog either.* □ *Now, Sally is what I would call a glamour puss.*

(good) looker *n.* a good-looking person. □ *Fred is not exactly a good looker, but he is pleasant enough.* □ *Mary is really a looker. I sure would like to go out with her.*

knockout *n.* a good-looking man or woman. □ *Your date is a real knockout.* □ *Who is that knockout I saw you with last weekend?*

package *n.* someone who is cute or sexually attractive. (Primarily refers to females as bundles of sexual charms.) □ *How do you like that little package who just came in?* □ *She's quite a package, if you like the giggly type.*

stunner *n.* a stunningly good-looking woman. □ *Did you see that stunner who just came in?* □ *I think that she is a stunner, and I go to all her movies—over and over.*

PEOPLE - BLACK

oreo *n.* an American of African descent who behaves more white than black. (Like the Oreo brand cookie, the person is black on the outside and white on the inside. Potentially offensive. Use only with discretion. Also a derogatory term of address.) □ *They called Sam an oreo because he wears a suit and works downtown.* □ *I'm not an oreo, I'm just doing my best with what God gave me.*

(soul) brother *n.* a black person's male, black friend. □ *Another brother took a fall last night.* □ *Terry's a soul brother, and I'll do anything for him.*

PEOPLE - COLD

cold fish *n.* a dull and unresponsive person. □ *I hate to shake hands with a cold fish like that. He didn't even smile.* □ *I hate going out with a cold fish.*

iceberg *n.* a cold and unemotional person. □ *Sally can be such an iceberg!* □ *What an insensitive iceberg!*

PEOPLE - CRAZY

crackpot *n.* a fake; a person with strange or crazy plans. □ *Some crackpot called to tell us that the sky is falling in.* □ *I'm no crackpot! I saw some of the sky floating in the lake. If it had fallen on land, someone might have been killed.*

crazy *n.* a crazy person. □ *The guy's a crazy, and he keeps coming in here asking for money.* □ *I think the crazies are taking over the world.*

loony AND **loonie** *n.* a crazy person. (From *lunatic.*) □ *I'm beginning to feel like a loonie the longer I stay around here.* □ *Don't be a loony. Use common sense.*

nut *n.* an odd or strange person; a crazy person. □ *Who is that nut over there in the corner?* □ *Some nut is going to try to fly from the top of one building to another.*

nutter *n.* a nutty person. □ *Sally is such a nutter. She would forget her head if it wasn't screwed on.* □ *That guy is a real nutter. Thinks he can get a cab at this hour.*

psycho *n.* a psychopathic person; a crazy person. □ *Get that psycho out of here!* □ *Pat is turning into a real psycho.*

schizo *n.* a schizophrenic person. □ *That guy is an absolute schizo!* □ *Keep that schizo away from me.*

sicky *n.* someone who seems mentally deranged. □ *The dame's a sicky. Watch out for yourself.* □ *Some sicky drew these obscene pictures on the wall.*

squirrel-food *n.* a nut; a loony person. □ *The driver of the car—squirrel-food, for sure—just sat there smiling.* □ *Some squirrel-food came over and asked for a sky hook.*

weirdo *n.* a strange person. □ *She is sure a weirdo lately.* □ *Don't be such a weirdo!*

PEOPLE - DULL

jeff *n.* a boring or *square* person. □ *That jeff bugs me.* □ *Don't be a jeff, man!*

L7 *n.* a *square*; a dull person. □ *That guy is an L7.* □ *Who is that L7 in the wingtip shoes?*

lame AND **laine; lane** *n.* a *square* person. (Streets. Underworld.) □ *Let's see if that lame over there has anything we want in his pockets.* □ *He won't drink anything at all. He is such a laine!*

neb(bish) *n.* a dull person; a *jerk.* (From Yiddish.) □ *Tracy is such a nebbish. Why doesn't she just give up?* □ *You are such a neb!*

nerd AND **nurd** *n.* a dull and bookish person, usually a male. □ *Fred can be such a nerd!* □ *That whole gang of boys is just a bunch of nurds.*

newt *n.* a stupid person; a dull and uninteresting person. □ *Look, you silly newt, you are wrong!* □ *Don't act like such a newt.*

poindexter *n.* a bookish person; a well-mannered good student, usually male. □ *Charles is a poindexter, but he's a good guy.* □ *I'm no poindexter. In fact, my grades are pretty low.*

stuffed shirt *n.* a dull and stuffy person, usually a male. □ *Mr. Wilson is a stuffed shirt, and people would tell him so if he didn't have so much money.* □ *I don't want to listen to that stuffed shirt anymore.*

PEOPLE - EARLY

early bird *n.* a person who gets up early. □ *I never miss sunrise. I'm an early bird.* □ *The early birds saw the corpse on the street and called the cops.*

PEOPLE - EAST ASIAN

banana *n.* an American of East Asian descent who acts "too much" like a Caucasian. (The person is yellow on the outside and white on the inside. Patterned on *Oreo*. Use discretion with racial and ethnic terms.) □ *Stop acting like such a banana!* □ *Dave is the classic banana. Can't quite figure out who he really is.*

gook *n.* a derogatory nickname for various East Asians. (Crude.) □ *Nobody wanted to go to war against the gooks.* □ *Let the gooks fight it out amongst themselves.*

gooner *n.* a term for an East Asian. (Derogatory. Military.) □ *These gooners sure can cook.* □ *See if one of the gooners will show you how to do it.*

PEOPLE - FAT

blimp *n.* a nickname for an obese person. (Cruel.) □ *Look at that blimp who just came in.* □ *This enormous blimp managed to get on the plane, but couldn't get into a seat.*

blob *n.* a very fat person. □ *What a blob!* □ *You'd think being a blob like that would get old after a while.*

blubber gut(s) *n.* a fat person. (Also a rude term of address.) □ *Hey, blubber guts! Get a girdle.* □ *Why doesn't that blubber gut do something about all that weight?*

bowser *n.* a person with a dog face or ugly face. (Typically applied to females.) □ *What a bowser! She belongs in a stable!* □ *Fred went out with a real bowser, but said he had a good time anyway.*

chubbo *n.* a fat person. (From *chubby*.) □ *Mary is a happy little chubbo. She'll probably outgrow all her baby fat.* □ *Look at those chubbos gobbling all those French fries.*

crisco *n.* a fat person. (Cruel. Also a rude term of address. The brand name of a baking shortening.) □ *Some crisco came in and ordered ten large fries.* □ *Hey, crisco! Go on a diet!*

fatso *n.* a fat person. (Cruel. Also a rude term of address.) □ *Hey, fatso! Go on a diet!* □ *Some fatso tried to get on the plane and couldn't even get through the door!*

fatty *n.* a derogatory nickname for a fat person. (Cruel. Also a rude term of address.) □ *OK, fatty, you get the biggest piece of cake because you deserve it.* □ *That fatty over there is going to eat up all the snacks.*

gutbucket *n.* a fat person, usually a man. □ *Harry is getting to be a real gutbucket.* □ *Look at the gutbucket waddling down the street.*

lard ass *n.* a fat person. (Crude. Derogatory. Also a rude term of address. Potentially offensive. Use only with discretion.) □ *Who's the lard ass with the sixty-inch waist?* □ *Hey, lard ass, get moving!*

oinker *n.* a very fat person. (Refers to the fatness of a pig.) □ *Sally is getting to be quite an oinker, don't you think?* □ *Who is that oinker who just came into the cafeteria? There won't be any food left for the rest of us.*

pig *n.* someone who eats too much; a glutton. □ *Stop being a pig! Save some for other people.* □ *I try to cut down on calories, but whenever I see red meat I make a pig of myself.*

porker *n.* a fat person. □ *Sally is not exactly a porker, but she is not skinny either.* □ *I was a porker until I started exercising.*

tub of lard AND **tub of guts** *n.* a fat person. (Cruel. Also a rude term of address.) □ *Who's that tub of guts who just came in?* □ *That tub of lard can hardly get through the door.*

whale *n.* a very fat person. (Cruel.) □ *Tracy is getting to be such a whale.* □ *Well, Gert's the whale if you ask me.*

PEOPLE - FOOLISH

goof *n.* a foolish oaf; a goofy person. □ *Sometimes I'm such a goof. I really messed up.* □ *Don't be a goof. Get with it.*

PEOPLE - FRIEND

backslapper *n.* someone who is overly friendly and outgoing. □ *At election time, city hall is filled with backslappers and baby-kissers.* □ *In the used car dealership, this backslapper comes up to me and tells me he's got something that will last me a lifetime.*

blood (brother) *n.* a fellow black male. □ *One of the bloods came up to say hello.* □ *This blood brother keeps asking me for money.*

bucko *n.* friend; pal. (Also a term of address. Can also be used with a sneer to convey contempt.) □ *Hey, bucko, come here a minute.* □ *Ask your bucko there if he wants to join us.*

bunkie *n.* a roommate. □ *My bunkie is from Iowa.* □ *I wish I had a bunkie. Things get lonely in a single room.*

glad-hander *n.* someone who displays effusive friendship. □ *What a morass of eager glad-handers and glitz!* □ *The glad-handers were out in full force at the Independence Day parade.*

pard *n.* partner. (From *pardner.* Also a term of address.) □ *Come on, pard, let's go find some action.* □ *This is my old pard, Clarence.*

PEOPLE - GOOD

clean-cut *mod.* having to do with a person who is neat and tidy. □ *He's a very clean-cut guy, and polite, too.* □ *He's sort of clean-cut looking, but with bushy hair.*

comer *n.* someone with a bright future. □ *Fred is a real comer. You'll be hearing a lot about him.* □ *A comer like that can command a high salary.*

diamond in the rough *n.* a person who is wonderful despite a rough exterior; a person with great potential. □ *Sam looks a little tacky, but he's a diamond in the rough.* □ *He's a diamond in the rough— a little hard to take at times, but okay mostly.*

do-gooder *n.* a person who is always trying to help others. (Often derogatory.) □ *The do-gooders are demanding a bigger cut of the pie.* □ *I don't consider myself a do-gooder, but I try to help people.*

Dutch uncle *n.* someone who gives avuncular advice; a man who gives advice with the directness of one's own relatives. □ *If I can be a Dutch uncle for a minute, I could give you some good advice.* □ *Dutch uncles can be as big of a pain as parents.*

good Joe *n.* a good fellow. □ *Fred's a little slow on the uptake, but he's a good Joe.* □ *Frank's a good Joe. He'll help us.*

good old boy AND **good ole boy** *n.* a good guy; a dependable companion. (Folksy.) □ *Tom is a good old boy. He'll help.* □ *One of these good ole boys will give you a hand.*

good-time Charlie *n.* a man who is always trying to have a good experience; an optimist. □ *Wally is such a good-time Charley. Who would believe the trouble he's had?* □ *Some good-time Charley is making a lot of noise.*

mensch *n.* a mature and responsible person. (From German via Yiddish.) □ *Now there goes a real mensch!* □ *I am honored to invite such a mensch into my home.*

Mr. Nice Guy *n.* a friendly, forgiving fellow. □ *You'll find that I am Mr. Nice Guy as long as you play fair with me.* □ *Oh, my boss is a Mr. Nice Guy. He'll let me off, I'm sure.*

square *n.* a person who behaves properly. □ *You are a square if I ever saw one.*

☐ *Ask that square what her favorite kind of music is.*

square john AND **square apple** *n.* someone who obeys the rules; a *square.* ☐ *Fred is a square john. There's no point in worrying about him.* ☐ *All those square apples can take care of themselves.*

straight *n.* a square person (who does not use drugs, etc.). ☐ *The guy's a straight. He's gonna turn us over to the cops!* ☐ *The straights are putting pressure on city hall to clean up this neighborhood.*

sweetheart AND **sweetie(-pie)** *n.* (one's) dear child, husband, wife, lover, etc. (Often a term of address.) ☐ *Look, sweetheart, can't we afford a new car?* ☐ *Pick up your toys, sweetie. Aunt Matilda is coming over for a visit.*

white hat *n.* a good guy; a hero. (From Western movies where you could tell the good guys from the bad guys by the color of their hats: white for good, black for bad.) ☐ *He seems like a white hat, but he's a worm.* ☐ *The white hats don't always win, you know.*

PEOPLE - IMPORTANT

Big Brother *n.* someone who personifies the totalitarian state: the police, parents, teachers. ☐ *Old Big Brother grounded me for a week.* ☐ *Big Brother says the paper is due tomorrow, or else.*

big cheese *n.* the boss; the key figure; the leader. ☐ *Here's a note from the big cheese telling me to come in for a chat.* ☐ *The big cheese is giving everyone a bonus at the end of the year.*

big enchilada *n.* the boss; the leader. ☐ *I wanna see the big enchilada!* ☐ *The big enchilada has sent word that it's safe to return.*

big fish *n.* the boss; the leader. (Underworld.) ☐ *We took in the little guys, but the big fish got away.* ☐ *The big fish ordered the killing.*

big name *n.* a famous and important person. ☐ *Lots of big names were there lending their support to the cause.* ☐ *One of the big names invited for the event canceled out at the last minute.*

big noise *n.* an important person. ☐ *If you're such a big noise, why don't you get this line moving?* ☐ *She's the big noise in Washington right now.*

bigshot 1. *n.* a very important person. ☐ *So, you really think you're a big shot.* ☐ *I'm no big shot, but I do have a little power around here.* **2.** *mod.* mighty; overbearing; overly important. ☐ *If you think that a bigshot title impresses me, you're wrong.* ☐ *Your bigshot ideas are getting us nowhere.*

big-time operator AND **BTO** *n.* someone who does business in a big way. (The abbreviation is an initialism.) ☐ *If you're such a BTO, why are we standing here in the rain?* ☐ *He's no big-time operator!*

big wheel *n.* a very important person. ☐ *Some big wheel wrote the order. Don't blame me.* ☐ *Kelly was a big wheel with the gas company for a while.*

bigwig *n.* an important person; a self-important person. ☐ *The bigwig in charge of that sort of thing will be in tomorrow.* ☐ *Some bigwig in a pinstripe suit waltzed through and asked me to leave.*

boss *mod.* excellent; powerful; superior. ☐ *That is a boss tune.* ☐ *This rally is really boss.*

face card *n.* an important person; a self-important person. (As with the royal characters in playing cards.) ☐ *Who's the face card getting out of the benz?* ☐ *Mr. Big is the face card in the local mob.*

gun *n.* a leader; the key member of a group. ☐ *Who's the gun around here?* ☐ *Bruno is the gun, and what he says goes.*

heavyweight *n.* an important person; a successful person; a leader. ☐ *Mr. Wilson is a heavyweight in local government.* ☐ *They'll bring out the heavyweights next time. Just wait and see.*

hell-on-wheels *n.* a very impressive person or thing; an extreme type of person or thing. (Use caution with *hell.*) ☐ *Fred is really hell-on-wheels when it comes to getting those little jobs done on time.* ☐ *This little machine is hell-on-wheels for general woodworking purposes.*

high mucky-muck *n.* an important person; the person in charge. □ *When the high mucky-mucks meet, they will decide what to do about the problem.* □ *Ted's father is a high mucky-muck at the gas company.*

high ups AND **higher ups** *n.* the people in charge. □ *I have to speak to the high ups about the refund.* □ *One of the higher ups is coming down to talk to you.*

honcho *n.* the head man; the boss. (Useable for either sex.) □ *The marketing honcho couldn't say when the product would be on the shelves.* □ *The top honcho at the water department was no help at all.*

hotshot *n.* an important and energetic person. (Often used sarcastically. Also a term of address.) □ *If you're such a hotshot, why not straighten out the whole thing?* □ *Look, hotshot, get busy, will you?*

key figure *n.* an important person in an event; a person central to an event. □ *Wally is a key figure in the investigation.* □ *Bruno is not exactly a key figure, but he can lead us to Mr. Big.*

main squeeze *n.* one's boss; the person in charge. □ *The main squeeze has a lot of responsibility.* □ *The main squeeze is out of town for a week.*

Mr. Big *n.* an important man; the boss man. □ *So you're Mr. Big. I thought you'd be taller.* □ *The office suite of Acme's Mr. Big was cold and ostentatious, as was its occupant.*

old man *n.* the boss; a high-ranking officer. (Always with *the*.) □ *The old man says do it, so you had better do it.* □ *Quiet! Here comes the old man.*

pin *n.* an important criminal leader. □ *The pin sent me. He says you're to come with me.* □ *The mob's getting careless. The cops think they caught the pin this time.*

somebody *n.* an important person. (Often with *a*.) □ *Aren't you a somebody?* □ *If she was somebody, you wouldn't have to ask.*

straw boss *n.* a foreman; anyone who is second in command. □ *The straw boss gave the order, and off we went.* □ *I don't mind being a straw boss as long as they pay me.*

top banana *n.* the boss; the leader or head of something. □ *You'll have to ask the top banana. He's out right now.* □ *Who's top banana around here?*

top brass *n.* the highest leader(s); the boss(es). (Originally military.) □ *The top brass turned thumbs down on the proposal.* □ *You'll have to check it out with the top brass. She'll be home around five.*

top dog *n.* the person in charge or in power; a company officer. □ *The reporter tried to get hold of one of the top dogs, but couldn't get past the secretary.* □ *A top dog from the executive suite read a prepared statement.*

VIP 1. *n.* a "very important person." (Initialism.) □ *Who's the VIP in the Mercedes?* □ *That's no VIP; that's the boss.* **2.** *mod.* something reserved for a *VIP*. (Initialism.) □ *My smile and casual manner didn't get me into the VIP lounge.* □ *They gave us the VIP treatment.*

PEOPLE - MALE

fella *n.* a fellow; a guy. (Also a term of address.) □ *Who's the fella with the dark glasses?* □ *Hey, fella. Got a match?*

PEOPLE - MEEK

Barney *n.* a nerd; a wimp. (From the Flintstones character or the children's dinosaur character.) □ *Sam's an old Barney—a real loser.* □ *If you weren't such a Barney, you'd stick up for your own rights.*

blob *n.* a useless dishrag of a person; a wimp. □ *You blob! Show some spunk!* □ *I'm amazed that blob can tie his own shoes.*

cream puff *n.* a weakling; a wimp. □ *Don't be a cream puff all your life! Join a health club!* □ *We're having a cream puff special this week for you clowns who can't climb stairs without panting.*

doormat *n.* a weak-willed person who is abused by others. □ *I always feel like a doormat.* □ *Why do people treat me like a doormat?*

gutless wonder *n.* a totally spineless person. □ *George, don't be such a gutless wonder! Stand up for your rights!* □ *Here comes that gutless wonder, Martin.*

(limp) dishrag *n.* a totally helpless person; a cowardly and spineless person. □ *He's sweet, but he's a dishrag.* □ *A limp dishrag is no help at all in a crisis.*

namby-pamby *mod.* overly nice; effeminate and weak, when said of a male. □ *Fred is too namby-pamby when it comes to making up his mind.* □ *What a namby-pamby guy!*

puppy *n.* a *wimp*; a softie. □ *That silly puppy is still waiting outside your door.* □ *Oh, Paul, you're such a puppy!*

rubber sock *n.* a timid person; a passive and compliant person. □ *What a rubber sock. She's afraid of her own shadow.* □ *Come on! Stand up for your rights. Don't be such a rubber sock!*

softie AND **softy** *n.* a weakling; a coward. □ *He's too much of a softie to fight back.* □ *Don't worry—he's a softie.*

wallflower *n.* a shy person. □ *Clare was sort of a wallflower until she graduated.* □ *Don't be a wallflower. Come to the reception.*

wet noodle *n.* a dupe; a *wimp*. □ *Don't be such a wet noodle. Don't let them push you around.* □ *Martin is such a wet noodle.*

wet sock AND **wet rag** *n.* a *wimp*; a useless *jerk*. □ *Don't be such a wet sock! Stand up for your rights!* □ *Well, in a tight situation, Martin is sort of a wet rag.*

wimp *n.* a weak and retiring person; a square. □ *Don't be a wimp. Stand up for your rights.* □ *What a wimp. People walk all over her.*

wuss(y) *n.* a *wimp*; a weak person. □ *Don't be such a wuss. Stand up for your rights.* □ *Wussies like you will never get ahead.*

yellow-belly *n.* a coward. □ *He's not a yellow-belly. He's cautious.* □ *Tell the yellow-belly to come outside and say that.*

PEOPLE - MIXED

salt and pepper *mod.* interracial, including black and white. □ *It was sort of a salt and pepper meeting, with representatives from all neighborhoods.* □ *We achieved a salt and pepper agreement that made everyone happy.*

PEOPLE - MODERN

swinger *n.* a youthful, socially active, and knowledgeable person. □ *Those kids are real swingers.* □ *Tom is a swinger. Look at those mod shoes.*

PEOPLE - NEGATIVE

AH *n.* a really wretched person, male or female; an abbreviation of *asshole*. (Initialism. Both written and pronounced.) □ *Stop being such an AH.* □ *Bill is a total AH, and he is getting on everyone's nerves.*

asshole *n.* an obnoxious person. (Crude and provocative. Also a rude term of address.) □ *Shut up and get out, you asshole!* □ *Some days it seems like only the assholes got up, and everyone else stayed in bed.*

bad egg *n.* a repellent person. □ *You're not such a bad egg after all.* □ *She's a real bad egg.*

bad trip *n.* any bad experience or person. □ *This class is a bad trip.* □ *Harry can be such a bad trip.*

ball-breaker AND **ball-buster** *n.* a hard or cruel boss. (Originally for males, now for either sex.) □ *The boss is a real ball-breaker, and I don't know how long I can go on with this job.* □ *They have special management schools to train ball-breakers.*

barf-out *n.* an unpleasant person or thing. □ *What a barf-out! I want my money back.* □ *That guy is a real barf-out.*

bathtub scum *n.* a totally despised person. □ *Look out, bathtub scum, outa my way!* □ *John is bathtub scum at its worst.*

birdturd *n.* an obnoxious person. (Potentially offensive. Use only with discretion. Derogatory. Also a term of address.) □ *You silly birdturd. Wake up!* □ *Clare can be such a birdturd when she wants.*

bitch of a someone *n.* a really difficult person. (Potentially offensive. Use only with discretion.) □ *What a bitch of a salesclerk.* □ *He is really a bitch of a boss.*

BM *n.* a disgusting and annoying person. (Use with caution. From *bowel movement.* A way of calling a person a *shit.* Derogatory.) □ *The guy's a real BM. A total pain.* □ *The new guy has to be the world's worst BM.*

boody AND **boodie; bootie; booty** *n.* someone or something disliked. □ *Why don't you clean up all this boody? This place is a mess.* □ *Who are those boodies blocking the doorway?*

boogieman *n.* an imaginary man who is said to frighten people; a false threat of any kind. □ *Don't turn me into a boogieman. Spank the child yourself.* □ *The press has made the secretary into some sort of boogieman.*

creeping-crud *n.* a repellent person. □ *Wally has become such a creeping-crud since he inherited all that money.* □ *Don't be a creeping-crud. Just go back to being a plain crud.*

crud *n.* a repellent person. □ *Don't be such a crud!* □ *That crud kept trying to paw me!*

crumb *n.* a repellent person. □ *The old man was a crumb and tried to cheat us.* □ *Micky is a crumb, and he treats me like dirt.*

crumbum *n.* a repellent person; a bum. □ *A skid row crumbum asked us for a buck.* □ *I gave the crumbum a buck and hoped he would leave.*

cull *n.* a socially unacceptable person. □ *Who's the cull driving the Edsel?* □ *This place is filled with culls. Let's split.*

dingbat *n.* any undesirable person. (Also a rude term of address.) □ *Look, dingbat, stop laughing!* □ *I'm tired of reading about that dingbat in the paper every day.*

dirty dog *n.* a low and sneaky person. □ *What a low, dirty dog.* □ *That dirty dog tried to get fresh with me!*

dirty joke *n.* a very ugly or very stupid person. □ *Look at that face. That's a dirty joke.* □ *Beavis is sort of a dirty joke that nobody can laugh at.*

dog's mother *n.* a bitch; a bitchy person. (Euphemistic.) □ *If Sally insists on being a dog's mother on this matter, I'll tell her what I think of her.* □ *Stop being a dog's mother and chill out!*

douche bag *n.* a repellent person; a disliked person. (Crude.) □ *Oh, shut up, you old douche bag!* □ *Don't be a douche bag!*

duck-squeezer *n.* someone with strong concerns about the environment and conservation, especially rescuing oil-covered ducks. □ *Some duck-squeezers were complaining about what the new dam might do.* □ *The duck-squeezers were picketing the dam site.*

eagle freak *n.* someone with strong concerns about the environment and conservation, especially the preservation of the eagle. □ *The eagle freaks oppose building the dam.* □ *They call me an eagle freak, which doesn't bother me at all.*

eco freak AND **eco nut** *n.* someone with strong concerns about the environment and conservation. (Mildly derogatory. From *ecology.*) □ *They call me an eco freak, which is okay by me.* □ *It's we eco nuts who think about the future of our planet.*

fart *n.* an obnoxious or a stupid person. (Also a provocative term of address.) □ *Who's the old fart with the enormous mustache?* □ *Who called me an old fart?*

freeloader *n.* someone who eats and drinks at someone else's expense; a parasitic person. □ *Ken is sort of a freeloader, but he's a lot of fun anyway.* □ *There are a lot of freeloaders here. We are going to have to ask to see tickets.*

fussbudget *n.* someone who fusses all the time, especially a baby. □ *Oh, Gary, don't be such a fussbudget.* □ *He is such a fussbudget. Get him a passy.*

geek AND **geke** *n.* a disgusting and repellent person; a creep. □ *The convention was a seething morass of pushy sales geeks and glad-handers.* □ *Who's the geke who just came in?*

gomer AND **goomer** *n.* a person unwelcome in a hospital. (Supposedly an acronym for "Get out of my emergency room.") □ *That gomer with the allergy is back in ER.* □ *I don't want that goomer back in the emergency room.*

goody two-shoes *n.* someone who tries to behave better than anyone else. (Also a term of address.) □ *Well, goody two-shoes, so you decided to come sit with us.* □ *I'm no goody two-shoes. I just like to keep my nose clean.*

grave-dancer *n.* someone who profits over someone else's misfortune. (From *dance on someone's grave.*) □ *I don't want to seem like a grave-dancer, but his defeat places me in line for a promotion.* □ *The guy's a grave-dancer. Anything to get ahead.*

grod AND **groddess** *n.* an especially sloppy man or woman. (Patterned on *god* and *goddess.*) □ *Hello, grods and groddesses, what's new?* □ *She is the groddess of scraggly ends.*

grub *n.* a sloppy person. □ *Don is such a grub all the time.* □ *Sorry I look like a grub. I've been doing some plumbing.*

grunge *n.* an ugly or nasty person; a repellent person. □ *Heidi thinks that Max is a grunge.* □ *Some grunch came by and dropped off this strange package for you.*

grunt *n.* a low-ranking or subservient person. (Someone who is likely to utter a grunt because of the discomforts of menial labor.) □ *Get one of the grunts over here to clean this up.* □ *Let's hire a grunt to do this kind of work.*

gug *n.* a repellent person. □ *Oo, he's such a gug!* □ *Rocko is not a gug!*

gym shoe *n.* a disliked person. □ *Who is the gym shoe who comes to class in a sport coat?* □ *Fred is such a gym shoe. Will he ever get with it?*

hack *n.* anyone who does poor or undesirable work. □ *Oh, he's just a hack. What can you expect?* □ *There's always plenty of work for a hack.*

hairball AND **furball** *n.* an obnoxious person. □ *I wish that the guys I date*

didn't always turn out to be hairballs. □ *Stop being such a furball, Wally.*

hippy AND **hippie** *n.* a long-haired, drug-using youth of the 1960s and 1970s. □ *That guy looks like a hippy left over from the sixties.* □ *Who's that has-been hippie who just came in?*

hip-shooter *n.* someone who talks without thinking; someone who speaks very frankly. □ *He's just a loudmouthed hip-shooter. Pay no attention.* □ *The press secretary was a hyper and a hip-shooter. She won't last long.*

hipster *n.* a youth of the 1950s, characterized by an interest in jazz and cool things. □ *Can you imagine your father as a hipster?* □ *Were the hipsters the ones with the big shoulder pads?*

hodad AND **hodaddy** *n.* an obnoxious person; a repellent person. (California.) □ *Ted is a total hodad.* □ *Who's the hodaddy in the plaid pants?*

hole *n.* a despised person; an *asshole.* (Use caution with the topic. Also a term of address.) □ *Sam is such a hole. He needs human being lessons.* □ *You stupid hole! Watch what you're doing!*

holy terror *n.* a devilish person; a badly behaving child. □ *Jimmy has become a holy terror lately.* □ *Why is the boss such a holy terror today?*

ick *n.* a disliked person. □ *Tell that ick to leave. He's polluting the place.* □ *Oh, Todd, don't be an ick.*

jackal *n.* a low and devious person. □ *You are nothing but a slimy jackal!* □ *What does that jackal want here?*

killjoy *n.* a person who takes the fun out of things for other people; a *party-pooper.* □ *Don't be such a killjoy!* □ *Larry is such a killjoy when he gets nervous.*

know-it-all *n.* someone who gives the impression of knowing everything. □ *Pete is such a know-it-all!* □ *That know-it-all isn't of much use to our committee.*

kvetch AND **quetch** *n.* a complainer. □ *What a kvetch you are!* □ *We don't need another quetch around here.*

lightweight *n.* an inconsequential person; someone who accomplishes very little. □ *Don't worry about her. She's just a lightweight.* □ *Those lightweights don't know how to run things right.*

long knife *n.* a destroyer; a hatchet man. □ *The secretary was acting as a long knife for the President.* □ *One of his long knives came over to pressure us into cooperating.*

loudmouth *n.* a person who talks too much or too loudly. □ *I try not to be a loudmouth, but I sometimes get carried away.* □ *There are a number of loudmouths in here who are competing with one another.*

low-life *n.* a low person; a repellent person. □ *This low-life smells like bacon.* □ *Hey, low-life, keep out of my way.*

low rent *n.* a low person; someone without grace or spirit. (Also a rude term of address.) □ *Look, low rent, where is what you owe me?* □ *This low rent here thinks he can push Bruno around, huh?*

maggot *n.* a low and wretched person; a vile person. □ *You maggot! Take your hands off me!* □ *Only a maggot would do something like that.*

megabitch *n.* a truly obnoxious *bitch.* □ *Bob, you are such a megabitch!* □ *Anne called herself a megabitch and said she didn't care what people thought of her.*

nark AND **narc** *n.* any unpleasant person. □ *Tell that narc to get lost.* □ *Stop being such a narc. Beat it!*

nudge AND **noodge** *n.* someone who nags. □ *Sally can be such a nudge!* □ *I really can't stand a noodge.*

nudnik *n.* a bore; a pest; a crank. (From Russian via Yiddish. Also a term of address.) □ *Tell that nudnik to stay away from here. He is such a pest.* □ *Heidi can be such a nudnik!*

pain in the ass AND **pain in the butt; pain in the rear** *n.* a very annoying thing or person. (Crude. Potentially offensive. Use only with discretion. An elaboration of *pain.* Use caution with *ass. Butt* is less offensive. *Rear* is euphemistic.) □ *That guy is a real pain in the ass.* □ *Things like that give me a pain in the butt.* □ *You are nothing but a pain in the rear.*

pain in the neck *n.* a difficult or annoying thing or person. □ *This tax form is a pain in the neck.* □ *My boss is a pain in the neck.*

pig *n.* a dirty or slovenly person. □ *Max is a pig. I don't think he bathes enough.* □ *Jimmy, change your clothes. Look at that mud, you little pig!*

polecat *n.* a mean and deceitful person, usually male. (Folksy. *Polecat* is another U.S. word for skunk.) □ *You dirty polecat!* □ *Tell that polecat I want to talk to him.*

pond scum *n.* a mean and wretched person; a worthless male. (Collegiate. An elaboration of *scum,* less crude than *scumbag.* Also a rude term of address.) □ *Tell that pond scum to beat it.* □ *Get your hands off me, you pond scum!*

poohead *n.* an obnoxious person. □ *Wally, don't be such a poohead!* □ *What poohead left the window open?*

puke *n.* a disgusting person. □ *I can't stand that puke!* □ *Make that puke get out of here, or I will scream!*

rat *n.* a wretched acting person. (Also a term of address.) □ *You dirty rat, you!* □ *Stop acting like a dirty rat!*

real bitch *n.* a very difficult or annoying thing or person. (Can refer to male or female. Use with caution.) □ *This math problem is a real bitch.* □ *Fred is a true problem. A real bitch.*

redneck *n.* a stereotypic southern bigot. (Derogatory. Also a term of address.) □ *Those rednecks can hardly read.* □ *Look, you stupid redneck, try to understand.*

retread *n.* a burned-out person; a made-over person. □ *Chuck is just a retread. He's through.* □ *I need somebody fresh and alive, not some tired retread.*

rotten apple *n.* a single bad person or thing. □ *There always is a rotten apple to spoil it for the rest of us.* □ *Tom sure has turned out to be the rotten apple.*

rotten egg *n.* a bad or despised person; a *stinker.* □ *That guy is a real rotten egg.*

□ *She sure has turned out to be a rotten egg.*

roughhouse AND **roughneck** *n.* a mean kid; a boisterous child, usually male. □ *Jimmy! Stop acting like such a roughhouse.* □ *Tell that young roughneck to straighten up and behave.*

royal pain *n.* someone or something irritating; a severe annoyance. □ *You are a royal pain!* □ *Her questions were a royal pain, but I had to answer them as part of my job.*

schlepper AND **shlepper** *n.* an annoying person who always wants a bargain or a favor. □ *Why am I surrounded by people who want something from me? Is this a schlepper colony or what?* □ *Tell the shleppers that they'll get their money after I close the sale on my wife and kids.*

schmuck *n.* a *jerk;* a repellent male. (Also a rude term of address. Yiddish.) □ *Who is that stupid schmuck over there?* □ *Ask that schmuck how long he will be on the phone.*

schtoonk AND **shtoonk** *n.* a detestable person. (Yiddish.) □ *The schtoonk from downstairs was here to talk to you. I told him you died.* □ *Who needs a shtoonk like that?*

screaming-meemie AND **screamie-meemie** *n.* a screaming child or adult. □ *Oh, don't be such a screaming-meemie!* □ *Jennifer has been a terrible screamie-meemie all day long!*

scum *n.* a wretched person. (Also a rude and provocative term of address.) □ *Who is that scum? Who does she think she is?* □ *Look, you scum, I'm gonna fix you once and for all!*

scumbag *n.* a mean and wretched person, usually a male. (Also a rude term of address.) □ *That scumbag is going to get caught someday.* □ *All those guys are scumbags. I don't want to have anything to do with any of them.*

scut *n.* a despicable person. (Teens and collegiate.) □ *How can you be, like, such a scut?* □ *It's scuts like that who give all us really rad kids a bad name.*

scuz(z) *n.* a nasty person; an undesirable person; a scraggly person. □ *And this scuzz comes up to me and asks me to dance, and I'm, like, "What?"* □ *I told the scuz, like, I was feeling sick, so I couldn't dance with anybody.*

scuzzbag *n.* a despicable person. (Also a rude term of address.) □ *Who is that scuzzbag who just came in?* □ *Look, scuzzbag, we don't want your kind around here.*

scuzzo *n.* a repellent person. □ *There's the scuzzo who thinks I like him.* □ *How do you get rid of a scuzzo like that?*

second fiddle *n.* a person in a secondary role; the second best. (Frequently with *play.*) □ *I won't stay around here playing second fiddle for someone half my age and ability!* □ *There are worse things than being second fiddle.*

shit *n.* a despicable person. (Crude. Also a rude and provocative term of address.) □ *Tell that stupid shit to get out of here, or I'll bust him one.* □ *What a shit you are!*

shithead *n.* a despicable person. (Crude. Also a rude and provocative term of address. Potentially offensive. Use only with discretion.) □ *You stupid shithead!* □ *The guy is somewhere between an asshole and a shithead.*

shitsky *n.* a despicable person. (Provocative. Potentially offensive. Use only with discretion.) □ *The stupid shitsky is back on skag again.* □ *With a shitsky like that on your side, who needs enemies?*

shower scum *n.* a despised person; despised people. □ *Who is the shower scum who put a cigarette butt in my houseplant?* □ *I wish the shower scum of the neighborhood wouldn't throw trash in my yard.*

shuck *n.* an insincere person. □ *The guy's a shuck. Don't believe a thing he says!* □ *Who needs a shuck for a legislator?*

sidewinder *n.* a sneaky and despicable man. (Western jargon. From the name of the sidewinder rattlesnake.) □ *You dirty, lowdown sidewinder! That's too* much! □ *What sidewinder spilled my drink?*

skag AND **scag** *n.* a rotten thing or person. □ *Don't be such a skag. Who do you think you are?* □ *Gary has become more of a scag than I can stand.*

skunk *n.* a mean and hateful person. □ *What a skunk!* □ *Must you be such a skunk in front of my friends?*

sleaze AND **sleez** *n.* a low and despicable person. □ *God, what a sleaze! How can anybody be so skanky?* □ *You'd expect to find a sleez like that in a sleazoid joint like this.*

sleazebag *n.* a repellent person or place. □ *I won't go into a sleazebag like that.* □ *Who is the sleazebag leaning against the wall?*

sleazeball *n.* a repellent person. □ *He's okay if you're into sleazeballs.* □ *Who is that sleazeball with the earring?*

sleaze-bucket *n.* a repellent person, thing, or place. □ *Gad, what a sleaze-bucket! Let me out of here!* □ *Gee, Sue, your date's a real sleaze-bucket!*

sleazo 1. AND **sleazoid** *mod.* low; disreputable; sleazy. □ *Let's get out of this sleazo joint.* □ *Who wants a sleazoid car with no back seat?* **2.** *n.* a sleazy person. □ *Who is this sleazoid?* □ *Who was that sleazoid I saw you with last night?*

slime bag AND **slime bucket; slimebag; slimeball** *n.* a despicable person, usually a male. □ *Gee, a slime bag like that in the same room with me! Yuck!* □ *Who's the slime bucket in the 1962 Bonneville?*

slob *n.* a rude, fat, and unpleasant person. □ *What a slob! Comb your hair, if you can get a comb through it!* □ *Why doesn't that slob go on a diet or something? Anything!*

sludgeball *n.* a despicable and repellent person. □ *Mike is such a sludgeball! Why do you keep seeing him?* □ *He's no sludgeball; he's eccentric.*

smart aleck *n.* someone who is saucy and acts cocky. □ *A smart aleck like you ought to have no trouble at all getting his face mashed in.* □ *Don't be such a smart aleck.*

smart ass *n.* someone who makes wisecracks and acts cocky. (Potentially offensive. Use only with discretion.) □ *Some smart ass came in here and asked for a sky hook.* □ *Don't be such a smart ass!*

smart guy *n.* a man who acts cocky; a wise guy. □ *All right, smart guy, see if you like this one.* □ *Some smart guy put fresh paint on this bench.*

smart mouth *n.* someone who makes wisecracks; a cocky person who speaks out of turn. □ *Don't be a smart mouth with me!* □ *Mr. Atkins is going to get a reputation as a smart mouth.*

smarty *n.* a cocky person. (Also a term of address.) □ *Well, if you're such a smarty, why aren't you rich?* □ *Okay, smarty, do it yourself.*

smarty-pants *n.* a cocky person; a *smart aleck*. □ *Look, smarty-pants, let's cut the clowning around.* □ *That smarty-pants is going to get herself into big trouble.*

snake in the grass *n.* a sneaky and despised person. □ *How could I ever have trusted that snake in the grass?* □ *John is such a snake in the grass.*

snoop *n.* someone who prowls around looking for something. □ *Don't be a snoop.* □ *Fred is just a snoop. He went through my desk!*

snot *n.* a nasty person; an obnoxious person. □ *You needn't be such a snot about it.* □ *What a snot!*

son of a bitch *n.* a despicable person, usually a male. (Crude and provocative. Also a very insulting term of address. Abbreviated *SOB*.) □ *Tell that son of a bitch to get out of here, but fast.* □ *Look, you son of a bitch. I'm going to paste you one.*

son of a gun *n.* a despicable person, usually a male. (Euphemistic for *son of a bitch*.) □ *If that son of a gun thinks he can boss me around like that, he's got another think coming.* □ *Some son of a gun tried to sell me a used car with no engine.*

sorehead *n.* a poor loser. □ *Don't be a sorehead. You knew what you're getting into.* □ *Some sorehead at the track tried to punch a cashier.*

spaz *n.* a total jerk; someone who over-reacts to something. (Not used for a congenitally spastic condition.) □ *Some spaz is in the other room screaming about a stolen car.* □ *Relax! You don't need to be a spaz.*

sponge *n.* a parasitic person. □ *Don't be a sponge. Get your own!* □ *Here comes that sponge, Wally. Hide your wallet, pencils, glasses, and any clothes in his size.*

square peg (in a round hole) *n.* someone who does not fit in. □ *I'm a square peg in a round hole. Maybe I am meant to be eccentric.* □ *Kelly seems to be a square peg. What'll we do with him?*

stinker *n.* an unpleasant or wicked person. □ *Jerry is a real stinker. Look what he did!* □ *What stinker messed up my desk?*

stooge *n.* someone's pawn; someone controlled or maneuvered by someone else. □ *I'm not going to be your stooge!* □ *The guy's a stooge for the mob's Mr. Big. Ignore him.*

sucker *n.* an annoying person. (Also a rude term of address.) □ *Look, sucker, get out of my way!* □ *I am really sick of that sucker hanging around here.*

swellhead *n.* a conceited person. □ *Tom is getting to be such a swellhead.* □ *I wish that swellhead would spend more time elsewhere!*

trip *n.* an annoying person or thing. □ *Class was a trip today.* □ *She is such a trip.*

turd *n.* a wretched person. (Also a provocative term of address.) □ *You stupid turd!* □ *The guy acts like a real turd most of the time.*

two-time loser *n.* a confirmed *loser.* □ *Poor Max is a two-time loser.* □ *Martin is a two-time loser, or at least he looks like one.*

vegetable *n.* someone who is brain-dead; someone who acts brain-dead; a person almost totally destroyed by drugs. □ *You are such a vegetable!* □ *You want to end up a vegetable? Just keep shooting that stuff.* □ *Cable T.V. is turning me into a vegetable.*

wart *n.* an annoying person. (Also a rude term of address.) □ *Who is that wart with the inch-thick glasses?* □ *Tell the wart to leave, or we will be forced to call Bruno, who doesn't care for such persons.*

weasel *n.* a sneaky person. □ *You slimy weasel! How could you!* □ *If Fred weren't such a weasel, we could get along better.*

weisenheimer AND **wiseacre** *n.* a presumptuous *smart aleck.* (Also a term of address.) □ *Who's the wiseacre who put sugar in the salt shaker?* □ *Look, weisenheimer, watch your tongue!*

wet blanket *n.* someone who ruins a good time. (In the way that a wet blanket is used to put out a fire.) □ *Oh, Martin! Why do you have to be such a wet blanket?* □ *Don't be a wet blanket! Have some fun!*

wipeout *n.* a loser; someone who is likely to *wipe out.* □ *The guy's a wipeout, for sure.* □ *Please don't call my friend a wipeout.*

wise guy *n.* a foolish person; a *smart aleck.* □ *Look, wise guy, mind your own business!* □ *Some wise guy messed up my work.*

wrongo *n.* an undesirable thing or person; a member of the underworld. □ *The guy's a total wrongo. He's got to be guilty.* □ *This whole business is a complete wrongo. Something's fishy.*

yard dog *n.* a repellent person; an uncouth person. □ *Is that lousy yard dog hanging around the neighborhood again?* □ *Yup. It's that yard dog, Max.*

yazzihamper *n.* an obnoxious person. □ *You are the most annoying yazzihamper I know!* □ *Who's the yazzihamper in the double knit?*

young Turk *n.* a contentious young person who goes against the system. □ *The young Turks are acting up again.* □ *Not another young Turk!*

yoyo AND **yo-yo** *n.* a fool; an obnoxious person. □ *Who's the yo-yo in the plaid pants?* □ *Some yoyo wants to talk to you on the phone.*

yuck AND **yuk** *n.* someone or something disgusting. (Also a term of address.) □ *I don't want any of that yuck on my plate!* □ *Who is that yuk in the red bandana?*

zarf *n.* an ugly and repellent male. □ *Ooo, who is that zarf who just came in?* □ *That zarf is Martin, and he makes all A's, and he helps me with my homework, so just shut up!*

zod *n.* any repellent thing or person. (California.) □ *Wally is such a total zod.* □ *Is this grody zod yours or mine?*

PEOPLE - NEW

rookie AND **rooky** *n.* a person new at something; a neophyte, especially a police officer or a ballplayer. □ *Tom is a rookie on the police force.* □ *The rookie tackled the veteran player and earned a lot of cheering and applause.*

young blood *n.* a newcomer. □ *The young blood gets a desk by the window.* □ *We keep young bloods so busy they never have a chance to look out the window.*

PEOPLE - OLD

GERK AND **gerk** *n.* an elderly simpleton; an old *nerd*. (Acronym. From *geriatric* and *jerk*.) □ *Old man Johnson is a real GERK—ill-tempered and rude.* □ *A couple of gerks sat on the park bench, snoozing.*

golden-ager *n.* an old person; a senior citizen. □ *The golden-agers sat on the benches and chatted.* □ *When I'm a golden-ager, I'm going to have a part-time job.*

old-timer *n.* an old person; an old man. (Also a term of address.) □ *Hey, old-timer, how's it going?* □ *Ask that old-timer over there if it has always been this bad around here.*

PEOPLE - SAD

gloomy Gus *n.* a sad or dismal person; a pessimist. □ *Don't be such a gloomy Gus, Wally.* □ *Well, gloomy Gus just came in again.*

sad sack *n.* a sad person; a listless or depressed person. □ *Tom always looks like such a sad sack.* □ *Who is that sad sack moping in the corner?*

PEOPLE - SEX

herpie *n.* a person infected with the *herpes simplex* virus. □ *Oo, somebody said he's a herpie!* □ *Stay away from that chick. She's a herpie.*

kink *n.* a sexually deviant person. □ *He was a kink, and I broke up with him.* □ *The kinks congregate two streets over.*

lay *n.* a person considered as a potential sex partner. (Crude. Use caution with the topic.) □ *He actually said that she was a good lay.* □ *If anybody said I was a good lay, I'd sue—probably.*

pickup *n.* someone whose acquaintance is made solely for sexual purposes. □ *She's no date. She's just a pickup.* □ *She had the gall to show up at the dance with a pickup in street clothes.*

score *n.* the client of a male or female prostitute. □ *She conked the score over the head and robbed him.* □ *Three scores was a full day's work for Tracy.*

sex-machine *n.* a person obsessed with sex. □ *Heidi looks like such a sex-machine, but she is a real wallflower.* □ *John thinks of himself as a sex-machine, but no one else does.*

swinger *n.* a person who participates in innovative sexual activities. □ *Is Gary a swinger? I've heard talk about him.* □ *We watched a movie about a swinger, but everything interesting happened in dim blue light.*

PEOPLE - SHORT

duck butt AND **dusty butt** *n.* a short person, especially someone with large buttocks. (Also a rude term of address. Potentially offensive.) □ *The duck butt who just came in reminds me of somebody I once knew.* □ *Hey, dusty butt, where you been keeping yourself?*

PEOPLE - SILLY

bimbo *n.* a clown-like person. □ *What a silly bimbo!* □ *If that bimbo doesn't keep quiet, I'll bop him.*

bubblehead *n.* a fool; a giddy person. □ *You silly bubblehead. Watch where you are going!* □ *If you can't say anything without coming off like a bubblehead, keep your mouth shut.*

ditz AND **ditzo** *n.* a giddy, absent-minded person. □ *You silly ditz!* □ *I'm getting to be such a ditz!* □ *Who is the ditzo on the phone? Another wrong number?*

flake *n.* a person who acts silly or giddy. □ *Sally is such a flake!* □ *Who's the flake in the plaid pants?*

fruitcake AND **fruit loop** *n.* a foolish oaf. (Someone who is as *nutty as a fruitcake.*) □ *What a fruitcake! Doesn't even know where his head is at.* □ *Carl acts like such a loony fruit loop.*

gonzo *n.* a silly or foolish person. □ *Some gonzo is on the phone asking for the president of the universe.* □ *Tell the gonzo I'm out.*

space cadet *n.* a person who is always silly or giddy. □ *Mom, you are such a space cadet.* □ *Here comes a space cadet who looks like he has more money than he needs.*

space out *n.* a giddy person. (Usually **space-out.**) □ *Terry is becoming such a space-out!* □ *What a space out you are!*

PEOPLE - SMALL

runt *n.* a small person; someone whose growth has been stunted. (Also a rude term of address.) □ *He can't play basketball. He's just a runt.* □ *Hey, runt. Come here!*

shrimp *n.* a small person. □ *Who's the little shrimp over by the door?* □ *I'm such a shrimp. I just have short genes.*

spud *n.* a short person. (Also a term of address.) □ *He can jump pretty high for a spud.* □ *Hey, spud! I almost didn't see you!*

PEOPLE - STRANGE

bird *n.* an odd person. □ *Some old bird came up to me and tried to sell me a cookbook.* □ *This bird is too much for me. I'm leaving.*

creep *n.* a weird person; an eerie person. □ *Charlie is such a creep when he's stoned.* □ *I thought Charlie was a creep no matter what.*

dingleberry *n.* a weird person. (From a term for unclean matter clinging to anal hairs. Many users of this term do not know its source. Potentially offensive. Use only with discretion.) □ *Stop acting like such a dingleberry!* □ *Frank is such a dingleberry!*

fink *n.* any strange or undesirable person. □ *You are being such a fink. Stop it!* □ *Martin is a strange kind of fink.*

fruit *n.* a strange person. □ *Ted is such a fruit.* □ *Sam comes on like a fruit, but it's just his sense of humor.*

geekazoid *n.* a social outcast; a nerd. □ *Don't be such a geekazoid!* □ *If you weren't such a geekazoid, I'd be surprised at the dumb things you do!*

glick a strange person; a *nerd.* □ *Don't be a glick, Bill.* □ *Fred seems to be a classic glick, but he is really an all-right guy.*

goob *n.* a nerd; a simpleton. □ *Don't be a goob. Come to the party with me.* □ *Gary is such a goob. Why can't he do anything right?*

guff *n.* a strange person; a *nerd.* □ *Wally acts like a guff when we go out. I am going to break up with him.* □ *Some old guff driving an Edsel yelled at us when we crossed the street.*

gweebo *mod.* feeble; despicable; in the manner of a *gweeb.* □ *I'm not a gweebo. I'm just eccentric.* □ *Don't act so gweebo all the time.*

honker *n.* a strange or eccentric person. □ *Clare is a real honker these days. Is she all right?* □ *Martin is a classic honker.*

jack *n.* a strange person; an annoying person. □ *Wally, stop acting like such a jack!* □ *Ted is a total jack. He doesn't know his head from a hole in the ground.*

kink *n.* a strange person; a *kinky* person. □ *The guy's a kink. Watch out for him.* □ *There are kinks all over this place.*

kook *n.* a strange person. □ *She seems like a kook, but she is just grand, really.* □ *Todd's a kook, but I love him.*

oddball *n.* an eccentric person. □ *Tom is sure an oddball. He ordered a pineapple and strawberry milkshake.* □ *We oddballs love concoctions like that.*

odd bird AND **strange bird** *n.* a strange or eccentric person. □ *Mr. Wilson certainly is an odd bird.* □ *What a strange bird you are.*

odd-bod 1. *n.* a strange person. □ *Who is that odd-bod over in the corner?* □ *Ralph can be sort of an odd-bod now and then.* **2.** *n.* a person with a strange body. □ *I am such an odd-bod that it's hard to find clothes that fit.* □ *I've never seen anyone so tall. What an odd-bod!*

peanut head *n.* an oaf; a *nerd.* □ *You are so silly, Kim. You're a real peanut head!* □ *What peanut head left the door open? It's freezing in here!*

punker *n.* a *punk* rocker; a young person who dresses in the style of *punk* rockers. □ *It's not safe to walk on the street with all those weird punkers out there.* □ *The punkers don't even have a sense of rhythm.*

queer-beer *n.* any strange person. (Also a term of address.) □ *Look, queer-beer, stop that right now!* □ *What does that queer-beer think he's doing?*

queer fish *n.* a strange person; an aloof person. □ *She's a bit odd. Sort of a queer fish.* □ *He's a queer fish. Don't you agree?*

quimp *n.* a total *jerk*; a social outcast. (Also a term of address.) □ *I don't want to live in a dorm full of quimps.* □ *Who is the quimp who packed this thing wrong?*

rad *n.* a radical person. (California.) □ *He's such a rad! For sure!* □ *My brother is a rad, but he's a good guy.*

rare bird *n.* an unusual person; a person with rare talents or abilities. □ *An interesting kind of rare bird is the man who can take long vacations and still make money.* □ *She is a rare bird who enjoys opera and can understand most of it, too.*

schlub AND **zhlub** *n.* a dull, unpolished person, usually a male. (Yiddish.) □ *I spent the whole evening listening to that schlub from New Hampshire.* □ *Hank's no zhlub. He's just eccentric.*

screwball *n.* an eccentric person; a clown or a dunce. (Also a rude term of address.) □ *Tom is such a screwball!* □ *Look, you screwball, get out!*

skeezer *n.* a weird person; a *geek.* (Also a term of address.) □ *Dave is a nice guy, but sort of a skeezer.* □ *Hey, skeezer, get out of the way!*

snapper *n.* a strange person. □ *Wally is sort of a snapper, but a nice guy.* □ *Who is the snapper with the gumby haircut?*

squirrel *n.* a strange or eccentric person. □ *Martin can be such a squirrel.* □ *Freddie is a squirrel, but I love him.*

wombat *n.* a strange person; a *geek.* (Collegiate.) □ *Why does everybody think Martin is such a wombat?* □ *Who's the wombat in the 1957 Chevy?*

zombie *n.* a weird and frightening person. □ *Martin is practically a zombie. Doesn't he ever go out—in the daylight, I mean?* □ *Tracy's getting to look like a zombie. Is she well?*

PEOPLE - STUBBORN

hardhead *n.* a stubborn person. □ *You are a classic hardhead. Lighten up!* □ *I'm not really a hardhead. You bring out the worst in me.*

rockhead *n.* someone who seems to have rocks in the head; a hardheaded or stubborn person. □ *What a rockhead! That's a stupid thing to do.* □ *Why do you always have to be such a rockhead?*

PEOPLE - STUPID

airhead AND **airbrain** *n.* a stupid person. (Someone with air where there should be brains.) □ *What is that loony airhead doing there on the roof?* □ *Some airbrain put mustard in the ketchup squeezer.*

baboon *n.* a jerk; a stupid person. (Also a rude term of address.) □ *Stop acting like a baboon! Grow up!* □ *Tell that ugly baboon to get out of here.* □ *Hey, baboon, get off my lawn!*

banana-head *n.* a stupid person. □ *Kelly can be such a banana-head!* □ *Ask that banana-head why she is wearing a coat like that in July.*

BB brain *n.* a stupid person; a person with a brain the size of shot. (Also a rude term of address.) □ *What BB brain left the door open? □ Look here, BB brain, straighten up and fly right!*

bean head *n.* an oaf. (Also **beanhead**.) □ *You are such a bean head! □ Why I keep running around with a beanhead like you is beyond me.*

beef-head *n.* an oaf; a *meathead*. □ *Look you beef-head, lay off! □ This beef-head here thinks he knows how to do my job.*

beetlebrain *n.* a stupid person. □ *Some beetlebrain left a can of paint in the hall, and guess who knocked it over? □ Why are you such a beetlebrain when it comes to math?*

birdbrain *n.* a stupid-acting person. □ *You silly birdbrain. Stop it! □ I'm such a birdbrain. I forgot my driver's license, officer.*

bliss ninny *n.* a giddy and disoriented person. □ *You silly bliss ninny. Who watches over you, anyway? □ Tiffany is such a bliss ninny—all heart though.*

blithering idiot *n.* a crazy person; a totally disoriented person. □ *How can you be such a blithering idiot? □ You blithering idiot! You've buttered the tablecloth!*

blob *n.* a fool; an oaf. □ *Don't be a blob. Get up and get going. □ This blob just sits there and lets me do all the work.*

block *n.* a stupid person. (Possibly a back formation on *blockhead*.) □ *You silly block! Get out of the way. □ Wally acts like such a block!*

blockhead *n.* a stupid person. □ *Without a blockhead like you to remind me of the perils of stupidity, I might be less efficient than I am. □ Why did he call me a blockhead? I didn't do anything.*

bohunk *n.* an oaf; a simpleton. (From *Bohemian* and the source of *hunky*, probably *Hungarian*. Derogatory or teasing.) □ *Some bohunk put the wrong label on this box. □ Come here, you silly bohunk.*

bonehead 1. *n.* a stupid or stubborn person. □ *You are such a bonehead when it comes to buying cars. □ Don't be a bonehead. Cooperate!* **2.** AND **boneheaded** *mod.* stupid; stubborn. □ *Of all*

the boneheaded things to do! □ *Why am I married to the world's greatest all-time boneheaded klutz? □ Don't be so boneheaded.*

boob *n.* a stupid person; a rural oaf. □ *You boob! What have you done? □ Why did I marry a boob like you?*

bozo *n.* a clown; a *jerk;* a fool. (Also a term of address.) □ *Look, you bozo, I've had enough of your jabber. □ Those bozos are at it again. Spend, spend, spend.*

brack-brain *n.* a fool. □ *The brack-brains in Washington have done it again! □ One brack-brain around here is enough. Do you want me to leave?*

cabbagehead *n.* a fool; a stupid person. □ *What cabbagehead put this thing on upside down? □ I'm such a cabbagehead. I mailed my paycheck back to the office by mistake.*

cheesehead *n.* a stupid-acting person. □ *Is this cheesehead bothering you? □ Why do all the cheeseheads in town ride in my cab in the same day?*

chowderhead *n.* a stupid person. □ *Look, chowderhead, do what I told you. □ Don't be such a chowderhead.*

chumphead *n.* a stupid person. □ *John is not my favorite chumphead, but he's close. □ What a chumphead. You painted over the windows.*

clodhopper *n.* a stupid person; a rural oaf. □ *Some clodhopper came into town and fell in with the wrong crowd. □ You don't know it, but that clodhopper is worth about $2 million.*

clown *n.* a fool. □ *Some clown threw our paper in a puddle this morning. □ Tell that clown in the front row to can it.*

cluck AND **kluck** *n.* a stupid person; a person as stupid as a chicken. □ *Why did they send me a dumb cluck to do this work? □ Some kluck came in and asked for a left-handed monkey wrench.*

cluckhead *n.* a stupid oaf. □ *What cluckhead put sugar in the salt shaker? □ I'm getting to be such a cluckhead!*

clunkhead *n.* an oaf; a stupid dolt. □ *What clunkhead put sugar in the salt* shaker? □ *My brother can be such a clunkhead.*

conehead *n.* a fool; an oaf. □ *Some conehead put sugar in the salt shaker.* □ *You can be pretty much of a conehead yourself sometimes, you know.*

cornball *n.* a stupid or corny person. □ *He's a cornball, but he's fun.* □ *Who invited this cornball to my party?*

crackbrain *n.* a fool; a stupid oaf. □ *Did you hear about the crackbrain who found part of the sky floating in the lake?* □ *Sometimes you are quite a crackbrain yourself.*

deadhead *n.* a stupid person. □ *Who's the deadhead in the plaid pants?* □ *Wow, are you a deadhead!*

deadneck *n.* a stupid person. □ *What deadneck put sugar in the salt shaker?* □ *Who's the deadneck who painted the fence purple?*

dim bulb *n.* a dull person; a stupid person. □ *George seems to be a dim bulb, but he's a straight-A student.* □ *I feel like such a dim bulb when I do things like that.*

dimwit *n.* an oaf; a dullard. (Also a rude term of address.) □ *Oh, Dave, you can be such a dimwit!* □ *Come on, now, you're not really a dimwit.*

ding-a-ling *n.* a stupid person; a giddy person who hears bells. □ *This ding-a-ling comes up and asks me for a dollar for the orphans. I tell her I got all the orphans I can use at any price.* □ *Who's the ding-a-ling who painted the windows stuck?*

dingbat *n.* a stupid person. □ *Who is the dingbat with Bob?* □ *That's no dingbat; that's his sister.*

dinghead *n.* a stupid person. □ *Shut up, you stupid dinghead.* □ *Frank was a real dinghead when he cheated on the exam.*

dip(shit) AND **dip(head); dipstick** *n.* an oaf; a *jerk.* (The first entry is potentially offensive. Use only with discretion.) □ *Why are you acting like such a diphead?* □ *Is there a convention of dipsticks or something here today?*

dipwad *n.* a jerk. □ *Fred is such a dipwad. Why doesn't he wise up?* □ *If you weren't a big dipwad, you would give me a hand with this.*

dode *n.* a nerd; a simpleton. □ *Wally is such a dode.* □ *My roommate is a loser. I was afraid I'd end up with a dode.*

doofus *n.* a *jerk;* a *nerd.* □ *Hank, you are acting like a doofus. Stop standing on your head.* □ *My roommate is a doofus and I'm tired of putting up with her.*

dope *n.* a stupid person. □ *I'm not such a dope.* □ *That dope has done it again!*

dorf *n.* a stupid person; a weird person. □ *You are a prize-winning dorf.* □ *Is there a convention of dorfs here today or something?*

dork *n.* a *jerk;* a strange person. □ *Ye gods, Sally! You are a dork!* □ *Here comes the king of dorks again.*

dorkmeier AND **dorkmeister; dorkmunder** *n.* a total *jerk;* a simpleton. □ *Ellen, stop acting like such a dorkmeier!* □ *Fred is my idea of the perfect dorkmunder.*

dorkus maximus *n.* a simpleton or fool; a great fool. □ *Tim is now the dorkus maximus of our dorm since he broke the dorm's television set.* □ *Sally is a dorkus maximus and spaced out to boot.*

dough head *n.* a *nerd;* a simpleton. □ *Tom, don't be such a dough head. Read the instructions and do it right.* □ *Fred, you are a real dough head! Why did you do that?*

drip *n.* an oaf; a *nerd.* □ *Oh, yuck. He's such a drip.* □ *Bob is a drip, I guess, but he's harmless.*

droid *n.* a robot-like person; a *nerd.* (From *android.*) □ *Beavis is as close to a droid as we'll ever see.* □ *The droids are taking over this campus.*

droob AND **drube** *n.* a dullard; an oaf. □ *Who's the droob standing by the punch bowl?* □ *That drube is my brother!*

dumb-ass AND **stupid-ass** *mod.* stupid. (Potentially offensive. Use only with discretion.) □ *That was a dumb-ass thing to do!* □ *You can be such a stupid-ass jerk!*

dumbbell *n.* a stupid oaf. (Also a rude term of address.) □ *Look, dumbbell, pay* *attention!* □ *I'm afraid I come on like a dumbbell sometimes.*

dumb bunny *n.* a stupid person; an oaf. □ *Who's the dumb bunny in the double-knits?* □ *Don't be a dumb bunny. Pay attention to what's going on.*

dumb cluck *n.* a stupid oaf; a person as stupid as a chicken. □ *Sally is not a dumb cluck, but she is sort of slow.* □ *What a dumb cluck!*

dumb-dodo *n.* a very stupid person. □ *What a dumb-dodo you are!* □ *I'm no dumb-dodo!*

dumb-dumb AND **dum-dum** *n.* a stupid oaf; a dullard. □ *You can be such a dumb-dumb without even trying.* □ *Marvin is no dum-dum. He just looks that way.*

dumbhead *n.* a stupid person. □ *Bob is no dumbhead, but he sure is strange.* □ *I'm no dumbhead, just a little slow.*

dumbo *n.* a stupid oaf. (Also a rude term of address.) □ *Say, dumbo, could you move out of the way?* □ *Who's the dumbo in the plaid pants?*

dumbski *n.* a stupid person. □ *He's not the dumbski he seems to be.* □ *They used to think Gert was a dumbski.*

dummy *n.* a stupid person. □ *Don't be such a dummy.* □ *I'm no dummy!*

dweeb 1. *n.* an earnest student. (Collegiate.) □ *Don't call Bob a dweeb! Even if he is one.* □ *The dweebs get all the A's, so why work?* **2.** *n.* a strange or eccentric person; a nerd. □ *This place is filled with dweebs of all sizes.* □ *Here comes a dweeb. Ask him for some money.*

feather brain *n.* a stupid person. (Also a rude term of address.) □ *Gary is such a feather brain.* □ *Hey, feather brain. Wake up and get busy!*

feeb *n.* an oaf; a stupid person. (From feebleminded.) □ *Don't be a feeb. Wake up!* □ *You are such a feeb!*

fish *n.* a stupid and inept person. (Derogatory.) □ *The guy's a fish. He can't do anything right.* □ *Don't be such a fish, Martin. Anyone can work a can opener.*

flathead *n.* a stupid person. □ *Carl, don't act like such a flathead.* □ *He may seem slow, but Carl is no flathead.*

frog face *n.* a nerd; a geek. (Especially as a rude term of address.) □ *Look here, frog face, what makes you think you can talk to me that way?* □ *Wally is such a frog face. Does he take nerd classes or what?*

gazizzey AND **gazob** *n.* a fool. □ *What gazizzey put the sugar in the salt shaker?* □ *Don't call me a gazob!*

gleep *n.* a fool; an oaf. □ *What a gleep! Does he know what's what?* □ *Don't act like such a gleep!*

gomer *n.* a stupid oaf; a social reject. (From the television character Gomer Pyle.) □ *Who's that gomer in the overalls?* □ *That gomer is my Uncle Ben.*

goobrain *n.* a fool; a stupid person. (Also a rude term of address.) □ *What silly goobrain put sugar in the salt shaker?* □ *Look, goobrain, think about it for a while. You'll catch on.*

goofball AND **goofer** *n.* a stupid person; a fool. □ *You are such a silly goofball.* □ *Chuck acts like a goofer, but he's really with it.*

goofus AND **goopus** *n.* a foolish oaf. (Also a term of address.) □ *You're just acting like a goofus. Be serious!* □ *Hey, goopus! Come here!*

goon *n.* a stupid person; a fool. □ *Oh, Wally, you're such a goon sometimes.* □ *Todd is a silly goon, but he's a lot of fun at parties.*

goose *n.* a silly oaf; an oaf. □ *Oh, I'm such a silly goose!* □ *What a goose you are!*

gork *n.* a fool; a dupe. □ *Martin acts like such a gork sometimes.* □ *The gorks are taking over the world!*

gumbyhead *n.* someone who does stupid things like the character Gumby. □ *Fred is a total gumbyhead. He does all the wrong things.* □ *Don't be a gumbyhead. Don't drink and drive.*

gump *n.* a fool; an oaf. □ *Who's the gump in the yellow slacks?* □ *Don't act like such a gump!*

hamburger *n.* a stupid and worthless person—meat. □ *The guy is just hamburger. You can't teach him anything.* □ *There is a lot of hamburger around here. Who hired them?*

hammerhead *n.* a stupid person; a person whose head seems to be as solid as a hammer. □ *You can be such a hammerhead!* □ *What a hammerhead! Totally dense!*

helium head *n.* a fool; an *airhead.* □ *Well, what's that helium head done now?* □ *You can be such a helium head without even trying.*

horse's ass *n.* a fool. (Crude. Potentially offensive. Use only with discretion.) □ *My ex-husband was a real horse's ass.* □ *Stop being such a horse's ass and listen to some sense.*

jel *n.* a stupid person. (Someone who has gelatin where brains ought to be.) □ *The guy's a jel. Forget him.* □ *Oh, Wallace, don't act like such a jel.*

jive turkey *n.* a stupid person. □ *What jive turkey made this mess?* □ *Get that jive turkey out of here!*

Joe Schmo *n.* a jerk. □ *Joe Schmo doesn't really care.* □ *Let's say Joe Schmo wants a new car. What does he do?*

jughead *n.* a stupid person. □ *You can be such a jughead!* □ *I guess I'm sort of a jughead lately.*

klutz AND **klotz** *n.* a stupid and clumsy person. □ *Don't be a klutz!* □ *Some klotz put mustard in the stew.*

knothead *n.* a stupid person. □ *Don't be such a knothead!* □ *You're no knothead. You're just great!*

knucklehead *n.* a stupid person. □ *Oh, I feel like such a knucklehead!* □ *Don't worry, you're not a knucklehead.*

lame AND **laine; lane** *n.* an inept person. □ *The guy turned out to be a lame, and we had to fire him.* □ *Maybe the lane can work in the front office answering phones or something.*

lamebrain AND **lame-brain** *n.* a fool. □ *Please don't call me a lamebrain. I do my best.* □ *What a lame-brain! She put scallops in scalloped potatoes!*

lardhead *n.* a stupid person. □ *What a lardhead! Where are your brains?* □ *I'm not a lardhead. I dwell in a different dimension.*

lorg *n.* a stupid person. □ *Why is Frank such a lorg? Can't he get with it?* □ *Tell that lorg to find his own chair.*

lughead *n.* a stupid person. (Also a term of address.) □ *What a lughead! How can you be so dumb?* □ *Hey, lughead! Watch where you are going.*

lummox AND **lommix; lummux** *n.* a heavy, awkward, stupid person. □ *He looks like a big lummox, but he can really dance.* □ *Bruno is what you would call a lommix—but not to his face, of course.*

lump *n.* a stupid clod of a man. □ *I am not a lump! I am just sedate and pensive.* □ *Who is that lump leaning over the bar?*

lumpus *n.* a stupid oaf. □ *You are a silly lumpus!* □ *Is this lumpus giving you any trouble, ma'am?*

marble dome *n.* a stupid person. (Someone who has marble where brains should be.) □ *The guy's a marble dome. He has no knowledge of what's going on around him.* □ *Is this marble dome giving you any trouble?*

McFly *n.* a stupid person; a simpleton. (Also a term of address.) □ *Oh, Donna, you are such a McFly!* □ *Hey, McFly! What do you think you are doing?*

meathead *n.* a stupid oaf. □ *Don't call him a meathead. He does his best.* □ *Is this meathead bothering you, miss?*

megadork *n.* a very stupid person. □ *What a wimpy megadork!* □ *Tiffany, you are, like, such a megadork!*

mental *n.* a stupid person. □ *You're such a mental lately.* □ *Don't be a mental.*

mental midget *n.* a stupid person. □ *I hate to seem like a mental midget, but what's so great about that?* □ *This mental midget here thinks he can solve it for us.*

mess *n.* a hopeless, stupid person. □ *Harry has turned into a mess.* □ *The guy's a mess!*

mouth-breather *n.* a stupid-acting person. □ *I always end up with a mouth-breather on a blind date.* □ *Who's the mouth-breather with Fred?*

musclehead *n.* a stupid man; a man who has muscle where there should be brains. (Also a rude term of address.) □ *Look, musclehead, do exactly what I tell you!* □ *An overstuffed musclehead waddled over and offered to bend me in half if I didn't beat it.*

mushhead *n.* a stupid person. □ *Oh, good grief, I'm such a mushhead!* □ *Who is the mushhead in the cowboy boots?*

mutant *n.* a total *jerk;* a social outcast. (Also a term of address.) □ *Sam, you act like such a mutant!* □ *Hey, mutant! Get out of my way!*

nimrod *n.* a simpleton; a *nerd.* □ *Susan is a total nimrod. She does such dumb things!* □ *What stupid nimrod left the lid off the cottage cheese?*

nitwit *n.* someone who behaves stupidly. (Also a term of address.) □ *You are such a nitwit!* □ *Please stop acting like a nitwit all the time.*

no-brow *n.* a stupid person. (Patterned on *lowbrow.*) □ *Sam is a complete no-brow. No culture, no sense of style, and no money.* □ *Max is a total drip. No-brow and a phony.*

nutcake *n.* a stupid person. □ *Stop acting like such a nutcake all the time.* □ *My sister can be a real nutcake if she tries.*

palooka AND **paluka** *n.* a stupid person; an unskilled prizefighter; any mediocre person. (Also a term of address. From the name of the comic-strip prizefighter "Joe Palooka.") □ *Tell that stupid palooka to sit down and shut up.* □ *Get out of here, you paluka. You're just in the way.*

pighead *n.* someone who is both stupid and stubborn. □ *Stop acting like such a pighead!* □ *She'll never change her mind. She's a real pighead.*

poophead *n.* a person who acts very stupidly. (Also a term of address.) □ *Some-times you act like such a poophead.* □ *Look here, poophead, you're making a fool of yourself.*

potatohead *n.* a stupid person. □ *Stop acting like a potatohead.* □ *Look, potatohead, go home!*

puddinghead *n.* someone, usually a male, who acts very stupid. □ *Please stop being such a puddinghead.* □ *That puddinghead sold my antique table for junk!*

puttyhead *n.* a stupid person. (As if the person's head were soft as putty. Also a term of address.) □ *Look, you silly puttyhead, shut up!* □ *Stop acting like a puttyhead.*

putz *n.* a stupid person, typically a male; a *schmuck.* (Yiddish. Also a rude term of address.) □ *And this stupid putz just stood there smiling.* □ *Tell that putz to leave his card with the secretary.*

rattlebrain *n.* a stupid person. □ *Is that rattlebrain here again?* □ *Please try not to be such a rattlebrain! Pay attention to what you are doing.*

retard *n.* a stupid person. (Also a term of address.) □ *Don't be a retard! Get with it!* □ *Look, you retard, get busy.*

room for rent *n.* a person who acts very stupid. (Also a term of address. This implies that one's head is so empty of brains that the space could be rented out.) □ *Hey, room for rent, wake up and pay attention.* □ *My brother is a room for rent if I ever saw one. What a dope!*

rumdum AND **rum-dum** *n.* a stupid person. □ *Hey, rumdum, wise up and do what you are told.* □ *Don't be such a rum-dum.*

sap *n.* a stupid person. □ *That poor sap thinks he can convince them.* □ *Who is that miserable looking sap in the corner?*

schlemazel AND **schlemozzle; shlimazl** *n.* an awkward, bumbling person; a loser. (Yiddish.) □ *And this poor schlemazel tries to get me to help him paint his fence!* □ *That schlemozzle is afraid of his own shadow.*

schlep AND **shlep** *n.* a stupid person; a bothersome person. (Literally, a *drag.*) □ *What a schlep! The guy's a real pain.*

□ *Ask that shlep to wait in the hall until I am free. I'll sneak out the back way.*

schloomp AND **schlump; shlump** *n.* a stupid and lazy person. (From German via Yiddish.) □ *Tell that schloomp to get busy or get out.* □ *Do you work hard? I don't hire any schlumps.*

schmegegge AND **schmegeggy** *n.* a stupid person. (Yiddish.) □ *Who is that schmegegge in the plaid pants?* □ *Ask the schmegeggy standing over by the work-bench if he's seen my sky hook.*

schmendrick AND **shmendrick** *n.* a stupid and ineffectual nobody. (Yiddish.) □ *Some schmendrick from downstairs asked if you could turn down your stereo.* □ *Tell the shmendrick to drop dead.*

schmo AND **shmo; schmoe; shmoe** *n.* a foolish and naive person, usually a male. (Yiddish.) □ *What a schmo! He thinks I caused the problem.* □ *Tell the silly schmoe to beat it.*

simp *n.* a simpleton. □ *You are such a simp!* □ *Why did some simp feel it necessary to do this?*

smurfbrain *n.* a simple-minded person. (A *smurf* is an innocent little cartoon character.) □ *You can be such a smurf-brain!* □ *You're not a smurfbrain, I suppose?*

stupe AND **stoop** *n.* a stupid person. (Also a term of address.) □ *Look, stoop, just do what you are told.* □ *Don't be a stupe! Use your head!*

stupehead *n.* a stupid person; a block-head. (Also a term of address.) □ *What a stupehead!* □ *This stupehead keeps trying to sell me something.*

turkey *n.* a stupid person. □ *Who's the turkey who put the scallops in the scal-loped potatoes?* □ *You are such a turkey!*

twit *n.* a stupid person. (Also a term of address.) □ *What a yuppie twit!* □ *Hey, you twit, get off my lawn!*

veg *n.* a stupid person. □ *Where is your brain, you veg?* □ *Some veg put scallops in the scalloped potatoes.*

weenie *n.* a stupid person. □ *Gee, you can be such a weenie!* □ *Who's the wee-nie driving the old car?*

wiener nose *n.* a simpleton. (Also a de-rogatory term of address.) □ *Look, wiener nose, mind your own business.* □ *Todd, you are such a wiener nose!*

yack AND **yock; yuck; yuk** *n.* a foolish person. □ *Who's the yock wearing the red bandana?* □ *Get some yuk to do it. I'm busy.*

yahoo *n.* a rustic oaf; an uncouth *jerk.* □ *Ask that yahoo to close the door after him.* □ *What yahoo brought this dog in here?*

yutz *n.* a fool; a simpleton. □ *Don't act like such a yutz!* □ *Who is the yutz block-ing the doorway?*

zerk *n.* a stupid person; a *jerk.* □ *Who's the zerk in the plaid pants?* □ *Don't be a zerk! Do what you're told.*

zip *n.* a worthless person; a person who amounts to zero. □ *Who is that silly zip carrying all the books?* □ *Garth is such a zip. No brains in his head at all.*

zombie *n.* a very stupid person. □ *Is this some kind of gathering of zombies and mouth-breathers or something?* □ *Please ask one of those zombies to stand by the door.*

PEOPLE - TALL

big drink of water *n.* a very tall person. (Folksy.) □ *Tim is sure a big drink of wa-ter.* □ *Kelly grew into a big drink of wa-ter.*

PEOPLE - THIN

bag of bones *n.* an extremely skinny person or animal. □ *I'm just turning into a bag of bones.* □ *Get that old bag of bones off the racetrack!*

beanpole *n.* a skinny person. □ *I'm get-ting to be such a beanpole.* □ *I used to be a beanpole. Look at me now—both of me!*

bones *n.* a nickname for a skinny per-son. (Also a term of address.) □ *Well, bones, how about a nice big meal?* □ *Ask bones there what he wants to drink.*

rattlebones *n.* a nickname for a very skinny person. (Also a term of address.)

□ *Hey, rattlebones, come over here a minute.* □ *Ask rattlebones over there to have a seat.*

stringbean *n.* a thin person. (Also a term of address.) □ *Wow, is he a stringbean!* □ *Who's the stringbean standing by the punch bowl? Somebody ought to feed him.*

PEOPLE - UGLY

beast *n.* an ugly person. □ *Who is that beast with the big hat?* □ *That beast should give the monkey back its face before it bumps into something.*

pug-ugly *n.* a very ugly person. (Also a rude term of address.) □ *Ask that pug-ugly to leave. He will frighten the children.* □ *Hey, pug-ugly, try plastic surgery!*

triple-bagger *n.* a person whose ugly face is so frightful that three bags are required to conceal it. (Crude.) □ *That guy is just a triple-bagger.* □ *He's worse than a triple-bagger—if that's possible.*

PEOPLE - UNIMPORTANT

1. stooge *in.* to work as someone's underling; to serve as someone's pawn. □ *I'm not gonna stooge for you, no sirree!* □ *You will do what I tell you, and if it's stooging you will do it, and you will smile and say thank you.* **2.** *n.* an underling; a pawn. □ *Don't expect me to be your stooge!* □ *Lefty is just Tom's stooge. He'll do anything Tom tells him.*

abbreviated piece of nothing *n.* an insignificant person or thing. □ *Tell that abbreviated piece of nothing to get his tail over here, but fast.* □ *Why don't you drive your abbreviated piece of nothing over to the service station and have a muffler put on?*

blivit *n.* someone annoying and unnecessary. □ *The dame's a blivit. She adds up to one too many.* □ *Don't be a blivit. Just calm down.*

munchkin *n.* a small or insignificant person. □ *You're not going to let that munchkin push you around, are you?* □ *Who is the munchkin holding the clipboard?*

nobody *n.* an insignificant person. (Always with *a.*) □ *Don't pay any attention* to him. *He's just a nobody.* □ *That silly girl is a nobody and a pest.*

piss-ant *n.* an insignificant person. (Also a rude term of address. Regarded as impolite. A misunderstanding of French *pis-ant,* a "step ant." Use caution with *piss,* nonetheless.) □ *Get out of here, you little piss-ant.* □ *Tell that little piss-ant to come and see me.*

small beer *n.* nothing or next to nothing; an insignificant person. □ *The guy is just a small beer. Pay him no mind.* □ *Small beer or not, he's my customer, and I will see that he is taken care of.*

small change *n.* an insignificant person. (Also a rude term of address.) □ *Look, small change, why don't you just move along?* □ *The guy you think is small change happens to own this building you seem to be guarding so well.*

small fry *n.* anything or anyone small or unimportant. (*Fry* are juvenile fish.) □ *Forget the small fry. I'm going after Mr. Big.* □ *Don't worry about the small fry. You have to please the important people.*

twirp AND **twerp** *n.* an annoying runt of a person. (Also a term of address.) □ *Look, you twirp, get out!* □ *Some little twerp threatened to kick me in the shin.*

zero *n.* an insignificant person; a nobody. □ *Pay her no mind. She is a zero around here.* □ *I want to be more in life than just another zero.*

PEOPLE - VULGAR

boo-bird *n.* a person who boos frequently at games or other public events. □ *It was a big day for the boo-birds at Wrigley Field.* □ *The catcher turned and stared right at the loudmouthed boo-bird. Everybody knew what he was thinking.*

dirty mouth *n.* a person who talks dirty. □ *You are getting to be quite a dirty mouth, Gary.* □ *Some dirty mouth yelled out the most obscene things during the meeting.*

foul mouth *n.* a person who uses obscene language habitually. □ *Terry, don't be such a foul mouth.* □ *Sally is turning into a real foul mouth.*

garbage mouth *n.* someone who uses obscene language. □ *Quiet, garbage mouth! Watch your language.* □ *Who's the garbage mouth making all the noise?*

latrine lips *n.* a person who uses dirty language. □ *Hey, latrine lips! Cool it!* □ *When old latrine lips finishes shocking everyone, I have something to say.*

potty mouth AND **toilet mouth** *n.* someone who uses obscene or profane language in most social settings. (Also a term of address.) □ *That potty mouth is offending people again.* □ *Hey, toilet mouth! Cool it!*

sewermouth *n.* someone who uses vile language constantly. (Also a rude term of address.) □ *If you're going to be a sewermouth, I wish you would leave.* □ *Who's the sewermouth in the plaid jacket?*

trash mouth *n.* someone who uses obscene language. □ *Shut up, trash mouth.* □ *Some trash mouth is making everybody mad over in the park.*

PEOPLE - WHITE

blanco *n.* a white person; a Caucasian. (From Spanish. Potentially derogatory.) □ *Adios, blanco.* □ *The blancos arrived in droves.*

Charles *n.* a Caucasian. (Black. Not necessarily derogatory.) □ *And what is Charles gonna say about what you did to his car?* □ *That brother's so backward, he's still afraid to go to Charles' front door.*

honk *n.* a white male. (Black. Not necessarily derogatory.) □ *Who's the honk who keeps driving by?* □ *There are mainly honks where I work.*

honky AND **honkey; honkie; hunky 1.** *mod.* in the manner of a Caucasian; white-like. □ *Where'd you get that honky car?* □ *That's honkey music. I want to hear soul.* **2.** *n.* a Caucasian. (Black. Not necessarily derogatory. Probably a pronunciation variant of *hunky*.) □ *The honkies are taking over this neighborhood.* □ *Some honky was around asking for you.*

jeff 1. *in.* [for a black] to take on the ways of whites. □ *Cool it man; stop your jeffing.* □ *I'm not jeffing.* **2.** *n.* a Caucasian. (From *Jefferson Davis*. Potentially derogatory.) □ *The jeffs are coming around more often. What's up?* □ *Those jeffs like you, man.*

pig *n.* a Caucasian. (Black.) □ *Why do those pigs think they can walk in here like that?* □ *Who do those pigs think they are, tourists?*

silk *n.* a Caucasian. (Black.) □ *Some silk was over here, looking around sort of suspicious.* □ *He told his mama that if she doesn't treat him better, he's gonna bring some silk home for dinner and let her see what the neighbors think.*

vanilla *n.* a Caucasian. □ *Some vanilla's on the phone—selling something, I guess.* □ *That vanilla is looking at you sort of coplike.*

WASP 1. *mod.* having to do with white Anglo-Saxon protestants; *waspish.* □ *They preferred to live in a WASP neighborhood.* □ *What a silly old WASP idea.* **2.** *n.* a "white Anglo-Saxon protestant." (Usually derogatory. Acronym.) □ *Would you call Pete a WASP?* □ *The west side is where the WASPs live.*

waspish *mod.* in the manner of a *WASP.* □ *She looks sort of waspish, but she's not.* □ *Sally is a waspish kind of yuppie.*

PEOPLE - WORTHLESS

bum *n.* a vagrant; a good-for-nothing. □ *You had better get your finances in order unless you want to become a bum.* □ *There is a bunch of bums on the corner, just doing nothing.*

crock of shit *n.* a worthless person. □ *Who is that crock of shit who brought in the dead cat?* □ *Some crock of shit put my coat on the floor!*

dirt *n.* a low, worthless person. □ *He is just dirt.* □ *I am not dirt. I'm just temporarily financially embarrassed.*

jerk *n.* a stupid or worthless person. (Now both males and females.) □ *What a loony jerk!* □ *You are such a classic jerk!*

no-account *n.* a worthless person. (Also a rude term of address.) □ *Ask that no-account to come over here and explain himself.* □ *Look, you no-account! Take your problems and go away!*

no-good *n.* a worthless person. □ *Tell that no-good to leave.* □ *The no-good is back again.*

no-goodnik *n.* someone who is no good. (The *nik* is from Russian via Yiddish.) □ *That no-goodnik is pestering me again.* □ *Tell the no-goodnik to leave quietly, or I will call the police.*

slime *n.* a worthless person; a low and wretched person. □ *What a slime that guy is!* □ *Who is the slime over there with the greasy hair?*

trash *n.* a low, worthless person; worthless people. □ *The guy is trash! Stay away from him.* □ *Running around with that trash—no wonder he's in trouble.*

zob *n.* a worthless person; a nobody. □ *Another zob came in to try out for the part.* □ *Who's the zob in the plaid pants?*

PEOPLE - YOUNG

(baby) boomer *n.* someone born during the baby boom—from the last years of World War II until the early 1960s. □ *When the baby boomers get around to saving up for retirement, you're going to see a lot of investment scams.* □ *At about age forty-five, the boomers will start putting money away.*

longhair *n.* a *hippie*; a long-haired youth of the 1960s. (Usually derogatory.) □ *Tell that longhair to get out of here.* □ *There are fewer longhairs around here than there were in the sixties.*

yuppie *n.* a "young urban professional." □ *The yuppies are getting a lot of flack these days.* □ *Why pick on yuppies?*

PERCEPTION - LACKING

see no further than the end of one's nose AND **cannot see (any) further than the end of one's nose** *in.* to be narrow-minded; to lack understanding and perception. □ *She is so selfish she can see no further than the end of her nose.* □ *You don't care about anyone but yourself. You can't see any further than the end of your nose.*

PERFORMANCE

barnstorm 1. *in.* to perform stunts in a biplane in small towns. (Presumably swooping around barns.) □ *When we* used to barnstorm, everybody thought we were kooks. □ *The old biplane we used to barnstorm with is the safest plane ever built.* **2.** *tr. & in.* [for an entertainer] to perform in small towns for short engagements. □ *My great-uncle used to barnstorm Kansas and Oklahoma with his medicine show.* □ *He barnstormed for three years before his death.*

bit *n.* a small theatrical part. (From *bit part.*) □ *I worked in bits for a year and then started selling used cars.* □ *It was just a bit, but I needed the money.*

come on *in.* to begin to perform well. □ *In the second scene, the entire cast came on, and the audience loved it.* □ *The singer came on immediately. We knew we had a star.*

gig *in.* to play or perform. (Musicians.) □ *I didn't gig at all last week. I'm getting hungry for a job.* □ *I'm happiest when I'm gigging.*

kill *tr.* to be very successful with an audience; to perform very well for an audience. □ *She really killed them with that last joke.* □ *She killed them, and they died with laughter.*

knock someone dead *tr.* to put on a stunning performance or display for someone. □ *She knocked us dead with her stunning performance.* □ *Go out on that stage and knock 'em dead, Sally.*

milk 1. *tr.* to attempt to persuade an audience to laugh or applaud. □ *Mitzy tried to milk the audience for applause.* □ *She went on milking the crowd for adulation long after they had demonstrated their appreciation.* **2.** *tr.* to attempt to get recognition from an audience. □ *His performance was marred by an amateurish attempt to milk applause.* □ *If you're good, they'll let you know it. If not, don't milk cheers, applause, or laughter.*

number *n.* an act or performance; a performance specialty. □ *Ann did her number and left the stage.* □ *I'll talk to you after my number.*

one-man show *n.* a performance put on by one person. □ *It was a one-man show,* *but it was very entertaining.* □ *For a one-man show, it was very long.*

one-night stand *n.* a performance lasting only one night. □ *The band did a series of one-night stands down the East Coast.* □ *You can't make a living doing one-night stands.*

schtick AND **shtik** *n.* a routine or act that is the trademark of an entertainer, especially in vaudeville. (Yiddish.) □ *His schtick was a trained dog and cat act.* □ *Their shtik is so old! Maybe nobody will remember whose it was.*

spoof 1. *n.* a parody. □ *The first act was a spoof of a Congressional investigation.* □ *The second act was a spoof of the first act.* **2.** *tr.* to make a parody of someone or something. □ *The comedian spoofed the executive branch by sitting in a big chair and going to sleep.* □ *I like to spoof myself. It helps break the ice at parties.*

street-casting *n.* selecting amateurs to be performers or models. □ *I do a lot of street-casting. Almost everybody can act a little.* □ *Street-casting is fun, and it's cheap.*

throw-away *n.* a comedian's quickly uttered one-line joke. □ *He tossed off his best throw-away of the evening just as the curtain fell.* □ *She was an expert at the one-line throw-away.*

PERHAPS

whatever *interj.* So what.; maybe; I guess; Why not? □ *BILL: "Would you like some pizza?" TOM: "Whatever."* □ *BILL: "I bought a new car today." TOM: "Whatever."*

PERMANENCE

carved in stone *mod.* permanent or not subject to change. (Often in the negative.) □ *Now, this isn't carved in stone yet, but this looks like the way it's going to be.* □ *Is this policy carved in stone?*

once and for all *mod.* permanently. □ *I'm gonna take care of you once and for all!* □ *I would like to get this ridiculous problem settled once and for all.*

play for keeps *in.* to take serious and permanent actions. (Refers to playing a game where the money won is not re-

turned at the end of the game.) □ *Wake up and face the fact that she's playing for keeps. She wants to get married.* □ *I always play for keeps.*

PERMISSION

go-ahead *n.* permission to proceed; the signal to go ahead. □ *We're ready to go as soon as we get the go-ahead.* □ *I gave him the go-ahead, and the tanks started moving in.*

PERSISTENCE

hang tough (on something) *in.* to stick to one's position (on something). □ *I decided I'd hang tough on it. I tend to give in too easy.* □ *Yes, just hang tough.*

PERSONAL

where someone lives *phr.* "at one's core"; "in one's own personal situation." □ *That really hits you where you live, doesn't it?* □ *Yes, that gets me where I live.*

PERSUASION

arm-twister *n.* someone who uses strong persuasion. □ *I hate to seem like an arm-twister, but I really need your help on this project.* □ *My aunt works as an arm-twister, collecting overdue bills for the telephone company.*

arm-twisting *n.* powerful persuasion. □ *The boss is very good at arm-twisting.* □ *If nice talk won't work, try a little arm-twisting.*

jaw(bone) *tr.* to try to persuade someone verbally; to apply verbal pressure to someone. □ *They tried to jawbone me into doing it.* □ *Don't jaw me. I won't do it.*

pump *tr.* to press someone for an answer or information. □ *Pump him until he talks.* □ *Don't pump me! I will tell you nothing!*

shake someone down *tr.* to put pressure on someone to lend one money. □ *We tried to shake them down for a few hundred, but no deal.* □ *If you're trying to shake me down, forget it. I got a case of the shorts.*

soft soap *tr.* to attempt to convince someone (of something) by gentle persuasion. □ *We couldn't soft soap her into* it. □ *Don't try to soft soap her. She's an old battle-ax.*

sold on someone or something *mod.* convinced of the value of someone or something. □ *I'm not yet sold on your idea.* □ *The crowd was sold on Gary. Nothing he had done or could do would cool their enthusiasm.*

squeeze *tr.* to put pressure on someone. □ *The mob began to squeeze Max for money.* □ *The tight schedule squeezed us all.*

talk one's head off *tr.* to talk endlessly; to argue persuasively or vigorously. □ *I talked my head off trying to convince them.* □ *Don't waste time talking your head off to them.*

twist someone's arm *tr.* to pressure someone. □ *I had to twist her arm a little, but she agreed.* □ *Do I have to twist your arm, or will you cooperate?*

PHOTOGRAPHY

blow-up *n.* an enlarged version of a photograph, map, chart, etc. (Usually **blowup**.) □ *Here's a blow-up of the scene of the crime.* □ *Kelly sent a blowup of their wedding picture to all her relatives.*

cheesecake *n.* a display of the female form, probably wearing little clothing, often in photographs. □ *Women don't like to see all that cheesecake on the walls when they bring their cars in here to be fixed.* □ *Now they're even putting the magazines with cheesecake under the counter.*

pix *n.* pictures; photographs. □ *I got my pix back from the drugstore.* □ *Hold still and let me get your pix taken. Then you can jump around.*

Say cheese! *exclam.* "Please smile!" (A phrase said by a photographer who is trying to get someone to smile for a photograph.) □ *Come on, now. Say cheese!* □ *Say cheese for the camera, please.*

snap *n.* a snapshot. □ *I got some good snaps of the fish you caught.* □ *Here's a snap of my brother.*

PIECES

smithereens *n.* many tiny pieces or splinters. □ *The mirror was broken to smithereens.* □ *I broke my crystal bell to smithereens.*

PIG

squealer *n.* a pig; a piglet. □ *They sent their squealers to market at just the right time.* □ *I was horrified to learn that bacon comes from squealers.*

PIMPLES

crater *n.* an acne scar. □ *Ted has a nasty crater on his cheek.* □ *Walter was always sort of embarrassed about his craters.*

crater-face AND **pizza-face; pizza-puss** *n.* someone with an acne-scarred face. (Cruel. Collegiate. Also a term of address.) □ *Who's the crater-face putting the moves on Sally?* □ *Pizza-puss over there is talking sort of loud.*

goob *n.* a pimple. □ *The goobs are taking over my whole face.* □ *I have the world's greatest goob right on the end of my nose.*

goophead *n.* an inflamed pimple. (Patterned on *blackhead*.) □ *Ye gods! I'm covered with goopheads.* □ *You ought to see the goophead on your nose.*

guber AND **goober** *n.* a facial pimple. □ *Wow, look at that giant guber on my nose.* □ *How does anybody get rid of goobers?*

hickey AND **hicky** *n.* a pimple, especially if infected. □ *There is a hickey on my nose!* □ *Wouldn't you know I'd get a hickey like this right when I have to have my picture taken!*

pip *n.* a pimple; a zit. □ *Good grief, I've got ear-to-ear pips!* □ *Do you ever outgrow pips?*

strawberry *n.* a pimple from drinking excessively. □ *His disability made itself manifest by the occasional strawberry.* □ *That's a fine strawberry on your snoot.*

toddy blossom *n.* a large pimple from too much drinking. □ *He was sporting a toddy blossom that would be the envy of any bum on skid row.* □ *There was nothing she could do to hide her toddy blossom.*

zit *n.* a pimple. □ *Don't squeeze your zits on my mirror!* □ *That is one prize-winning zit on your nose.*

PLACE
See **LOCATION**.

PLACEMENT
plop *tr.* to put or place something (somewhere). □ *I don't mind cooking a turkey. You only have to plop it in the oven and forget about it.* □ *I plopped my books on the table and went straight to my room.*

PLANNING
layout *n.* a floor plan. □ *Let's see if the layout is what we want.* □ *The layout looks awkward and wasteful of space.*

set someone up (for something) *tr.* to set the scene for something to happen to someone. □ *His buddies set him up for the gag—which ended up injuring two of them severely.* □ *Who set me up for this anyway?*

take some doing *tr.* to require added effort and planning. □ *It'll take some doing, but it'll get done.* □ *It's not impossible. It'll just take some doing.*

PLAY
ball is in someone's court *phr.* to be someone else's move, play, or turn. (Always with *the.*) □ *The ball's in your court now. You do something.* □ *I can't do anything as long as the ball is in John's court.*

PLEASANT
real gone *mod.* really *cool;* mellow and pleasant. □ *Man, this music is real gone.* □ *That's a real gone drummer.* □ *You are something—real gone.*

PLEASURE
ball *in.* to enjoy oneself. □ *The whole crowd was balling and having a fine time.* □ *We balled the whole evening.*

do one's (own) thing *tr.* to do what one wants; to do what pleases oneself no matter what others think. □ *She's going to start doing her own thing for a change.* □ *I've always done my thing, and I don't see a great amount of benefit from it.*

for kicks *mod.* for fun; for a thrill. □ *We just did it for kicks. We didn't mean to* hurt anyone. □ *Let's drive over to Wally's place, just for kicks.*

fun *mod.* pleasant; entertaining. □ *We had a real fun time.* □ *His party was fun.* □ *What a fun evening!*

get behind something *in.* to enjoy something, such as a drug or music. (Originally drugs.) □ *I'm really getting behind heavy metal.* □ *Sam got behind some acid and got stuck there.*

get it on *tr.* to enjoy oneself. □ *I can really get it on with that slow jazz.* □ *Let's go listen to some new age and get it on.*

get off (on something) *in.* to get pleasure from something. □ *I don't get off on music anymore.* □ *I listen, but I just don't get off.*

get one's kicks (from someone or something) *tr.* to get pleasure from someone or something. □ *Do you get your kicks from this sort of thing?* □ *I get my kicks from Billy Simpson. What a great entertainer!*

give someone a buzz *tr.* to give someone a chuckle or a bit of enjoyment. □ *It always gives me a buzz to watch Sally do her act.* □ *Your little joke gave me a buzz.*

groove *n.* something pleasant or *cool.* □ *This day has been a real groove.* □ *Man, what a groove!*

grooved *mod.* pleased. □ *I am so grooved. I'll just kick back and meditate.* □ *You sure look grooved. What's been happening in your life?*

in the groove *mod. cool; groovy;* pleasant and delightful. □ *Man, is that combo in the groove tonight!* □ *Get in the groove!*

kick *n.* a charge or good feeling (from something); pleasure or enjoyment from something. □ *That song really gives me a kick. I love it!* □ *What a kick that gives me!*

picnic *n.* a good time; an easy time. □ *What a great class! Every day was a real picnic.* □ *Nothing to it. A real picnic.* □ *It wasn't a terrible day, but it was no picnic.*

rude *mod.* cool; pleasant. □ *Man, that's a rude bike!* □ *Sally is a rude-looking girl!*

tickled (pink) *mod.* amused; utterly delighted; pleased. □ *I am tickled pink you could come this evening.* □ *We were tickled that you thought of us.*

yummy *mod.* delightful; beautiful. □ *Who is that yummy blonde?* □ *This evening was just yummy.*

POLICE

arm *n.* a police officer. (Underworld.) □ *What'll you do if the arms come in while you're sawing the bars of your cell?* □ *So this arm says to me, "Going to a fire?"*

baby bear *n.* a beginning highway patrol officer; a *rookie* cop. (Citizens band radio.) □ *Some baby bear tried to arrest me for speeding, but I conned him out of it.* □ *He may be just a baby bear, but he can still bite hard.*

bacon *n.* the police; a police officer. □ *Keep an eye out for the bacon.* □ *That bacon is hassling me!*

bear *n.* a highway patrol officer. □ *There's a bear hiding under that bridge.* □ *A bear is overhead, watching your speed from a helicopter.*

bear cage *n.* a police station. (Citizens band radio.) □ *Have you ever been in a country bear cage?* □ *I sat for two hours in that stinking bear cage.*

bear in the air *n.* a police officer in an airplane or a helicopter. (Citizens band radio.) □ *They've got a bear in the air on duty in northern Indiana.* □ *There's a bear in the air and another regular one keeping watch over your speed.*

bear trap *n.* a hidden speed trap, one set by a *bear.* (Citizens band radio.) □ *That whole town is a glorified bear trap.* □ *I got caught in a bear trap.*

big John *n.* the police; a police officer. □ *Big John is going to have to deal with you.* □ *Big John took her in and hit her with a vice rap.*

black and white *n.* a black and white police patrol car; any police car. □ *A black and white pulled up to the curb.* □ *Call the black and whites. We got trouble here.*

blotter *n.* a police station log of arrests; a police blotter. □ *We went downtown to have a look at the blotter. There was no Matthew Wilson on it anywhere.* □ *The blotter is full of the names of petty criminals and drunks.*

blue *n.* a police officer; the police. □ *The blues will be here in a minute.* □ *One blue isn't enough to handle the job.*

blue and white *n.* a police car. □ *A blue and white suddenly appeared, and I knew we were finished.* □ *I can usually spot a blue and white before anyone else.*

blue boys AND **blue coats** *n.* the police. □ *Four blue boys held me while a fifth slipped the cuffs on me. I ain't no pushover.* □ *The blue coats climbed out of the black and white and just stood there.*

blue flu *n.* an imaginary disease afflicting police officers who call in sick during a work stoppage or slowdown. (Journalistic. Done where strikes are illegal.) □ *Another epidemic of the blue flu struck the city's police officers early today.* □ *It seems that the city's criminals and lawbreakers are immune to the blue flu. Their work goes on totally unaffected.*

blue suit *n.* a police officer. (Usually plural.) □ *The blue suits showed up about twenty minutes after I called them!* □ *Watch out for the blue suits if you are going to drive this fast!*

body shake *n.* a shakedown of the body; a skin-search. (Underworld.) □ *You can't give me a body shake. I want my lawyer!* □ *They give everybody who passes through these doors a body shake.*

book *tr.* to charge someone with a crime. □ *The cop booked him for vagrancy.* □ *She looked sort of scroungy, and they wanted to book her for something, but didn't know what.*

bull *n.* a police officer; a private detective or guard. □ *Here come the bulls. Get out.* □ *And this bull comes up and says, "Where's the fire?"*

bust *n.* the police. □ *The bust is gonna find you no matter where you hole up.* □ *Here comes the bust. Beat it!*

Charlie Irvine *n.* a police officer. (Black.) □ *Charlie Irvine was around asking after you.* □ *Look smart, dude, here comes Charlie Irvine.*

Cheese it (the cops)! *exclam.* "Run away, the cops are coming!" □ *Look out! Cheese it, the cops!* □ *If you see the fuzz coming, you're supposed to yell, "Cheese it, the cops!" But I don't know why. Then they know we're doing something wrong.*

cop *n.* a police officer. □ *The cop wasn't in any mood to put up with any monkey business.* □ *You call the cops. I've got enough trouble.*

copper *n.* a police officer. (Originally underworld. Because the *copper* "cops" or "takes.") □ *See that copper over there? He busted me once.* □ *The coppers will catch up with you some day.*

cop-shop *n.* a police station. □ *They hauled off everybody to the cop-shop.* □ *The pigs down at the cop-shop tried to act like they didn't know who Max was.*

county-mounty *n.* a highway patrol officer. (Citizens band radio.) □ *There's a county-mounty waiting under that bridge ahead of you.* □ *The county-mounty wrote me seven tickets in that one roust.*

cuffs *n.* handcuffs. □ *I felt the cuffs tighten and snap shut on my wrists.* □ *The cuffs carried the cold of the night to my bare skin.*

feeby AND **feebee** *n.* the FBI, the Federal Bureau of Investigation. □ *The locals were going to call in the feebies, but the D.A. said to wait.* □ *The feebee is in on this already.*

flatfoot AND **flatty** *n.* a police officer, especially a foot patrol officer. □ *Think about how the flatfoot on the beat is affected by this cold.* □ *The flatty stopped at the door, tried the lock, and moved on.*

fur *n.* the police. □ *I think the fur is onto you, Rocko.* □ *The fur ain't never gonna get Rocko.*

fuzz AND **fuzz man; fuzzy (tail)** *n.* the police; a jail keeper; a detective. □ *The fuzz is onto you.* □ *See if you can distract the fuzz man while I lift his keys.*

fuzz station *n.* a police station. □ *He had to spend about an hour at the fuzz station, but nothing happened to him.* □ *Drop by the fuzz station and pick up a copy of the driving rules.*

gimpy *n.* a police officer. (Also a rude term of address. A pun on *lame*, an inept person.) □ *Here comes gimpy, swinging his stick.* □ *Gimpy has been around asking about you.*

G-man *n.* a government investigative agent; an FBI agent. □ *The G-men busted in and started shooting.* □ *When I was a kid, I wanted to be a G-man.*

goldie locks *n.* a policewoman. (Citizens band radio.) □ *Goldie locks pulled me over and gave me a citation.* □ *There was a goldie locks waiting under the bridge to spring on poor unsuspecting people like me.*

goon squad *n.* the police. □ *Here comes the goon squad. Watch out!* □ *My old buddy on the goon squad tells me there'll be some action over on Maple Street tonight.*

gumshoe *n.* a policeman or a detective. (Underworld. Also a term of address. So-named for wearing silent, gum-rubber soles.) □ *Has that gumshoe been around asking questions again?* □ *Look, gumshoe, what do you want with me?*

headache man *n.* a male law enforcement agent. □ *The headache man was here to see you, Ernie.* □ *Who gave that hot tip to the headache man?*

heat *n.* the police. (Underworld. Always with *the.*) □ *The heat is gonna catch up with you, Ernie.* □ *Who tipped the heat off about me?*

hog *n.* a police officer; a *pig.* □ *The hogs are on to you.* □ *Who called the hogs?*

hot *mod.* wanted by the police. (Underworld.) □ *Lefty is hot because of his part in the bank job.* □ *Bruno was hot and wanted somebody to hide him.*

Irv AND **Ervine; Irvine** *n.* a police officer. (Black.) □ *Irv is after you, did you* *know?* □ *Tell Ervine to go catch a speeder or something.*

J. Edgar (Hoover) *n.* the police; federal officers. (Underworld.) □ *Max got out of town when he heard that the J. Edgars were on his tail.* □ *Well, J. Edgar Hoover, looks like you got me!*

Johnny-be-good *n.* a police officer. □ *Here comes Johnny-be-good, so be good.* □ *Johnny-be-good went through my pockets.*

John(ny) Law *n.* a law officer. □ *Johnny Law is supposed to be your friend.* □ *John Law showed up with a piece of paper that says you are in trouble.*

junk squad *n.* police who enforce the narcotics laws. (Underworld.) □ *The junk squad has more than it can handle trying to keep up with the hard stuff.* □ *We need a bigger junk squad in this part of town.*

juvie *n.* a police officer concerned with juveniles. (Underworld.) □ *I'm a juvie in the Shakespeare district.* □ *The juvies have to know juvenile law cold.*

Kojak *n.* a police officer. (From the television character of the same name.) □ *Ask Kojak in for a cup of coffee.* □ *Here comes Kojak. Beat it!*

lady bear *n.* a female officer of the law. □ *This lady bear asks me if I'm going to a fire.* □ *These two lady bears walked in and took a booth by the door.*

lard *n.* the police. (Streets. Derogatory.) □ *Here comes the lard!* □ *If the lard catches you violating your parole, you're through.*

law *n.* the police. (Always with *the*.) □ *She is in a little trouble with the law.* □ *Mrs. Wilson finally called the law in on her old man.*

light *n.* a police car. □ *A couple of lights turned the corner just as the robbers were pulling away.* □ *We could see the lights coming down the expressway behind us, so we pulled over to the right and let them pass.*

lineup *n.* a row of suspects arranged at a police station so that a witness can identify one of them. (Underworld.) □

I had to stand in the lineup with this bunch of yahoos. □ *When they round up all the likely suspects and put them in the lineup, they always stick in a desk sergeant to spy on the rest.*

little boy blue *n.* a (male) police officer. □ *I hear that little boy blue is looking for you.* □ *Little boy blue is coming this way, and he's mad.*

long arm of the law *n.* the police; the law. □ *The long arm of the law is going to tap you on the shoulder some day, Lefty.* □ *The long arm of the law finally caught up with Gert.*

mallet *n.* a police officer. □ *Sam was struck by a mallet this noon.* □ *Some mallet is going around asking questions about you.*

mama bear *n.* a policewoman. □ *As we came under the bridge, we saw a mama bear sitting in a pigmobile.* □ *A mama bear pulled the trucker over.*

man AND **the man** *n.* the police; the establishment. □ *You better check with the man before you get seen with me.* □ *We are about to rap a little with my man.*

men in blue AND **boys in blue** *n.* the police; policemen. □ *The men in blue are looking for you.* □ *You can depend on the boys in blue to clean things up in this town.*

metros *n.* the police; the metropolitan police. (Not used in all metropolitan areas.) □ *The metros took ten minutes to get to the scene of the crime, and the entire city is enraged.* □ *The metros showed up and managed traffic for the fire company.*

mickey mouse *n.* a police officer. (Streets.) □ *Mickey mouse is hanging around asking about you.* □ *Tell mickey mouse he knows where to find me.*

mickey mouse ears *n.* the two lights found on top of a police car. □ *There were no mickey mouse ears, but the jerk inside looked like your average ossifer.* □ *I could see the outline of the mickey mouse ears on the blue and white behind me.*

Mr. Whiskers AND **Uncle Whiskers; whiskers (man)** *n.* a federal agent. (Underworld. From the whiskers of Uncle

Sam.) □ *Mr. Whiskers is trying to get me to pay tax on those few bucks.* □ *Uncle Whiskers is on our tail. Let's blow town.*

mug shot *n.* a photograph of one's face taken for police records. (Underworld.) □ *I'm going to have to ask you to come down to the station and go through some mug shots.* □ *How can a professional photographer take a portrait that looks like a mug shot?*

nab AND **nabber** *n.* a police officer; a cop. □ *The nabs got him, and he had the evidence on his person.* □ *There's a nabber at the door who wants to talk to you.*

nail-em-and-jail-em AND **nailer** *n.* the police in general; a police officer. □ *The nailers caught Freddy last night.* □ *Old nail-em-and-jail-em is going to be knocking at your door any day now.*

narc(o) *n.* a federal narcotics agent; any narcotics enforcement officer. □ *The narcs caught him.* □ *There is a narco at our school.*

New York's finest *n.* a New York City police officer. □ *One of New York's finest gave me a parking ticket.* □ *Three of New York's finest were standing there at my door with my lost dog.*

oink *n.* a police officer. □ *There is an oink following us on a motorcycle.* □ *Here come the oinks!*

ossifer AND **occifer** *n.* a police officer. (Also an ill-advised term of address.) □ *Look here, ossifer, I was just having a little fun.* □ *Ask the occifer there if he wants to step outside and discuss it.*

paddy *n.* a police officer, especially an Irish police officer. (Usually derogatory. Also an ill-advised term of address.) □ *Tell that paddy to go catch a crook or something.* □ *Look here, paddy, I wasn't doing anything.*

paddy wagon *n.* a police van used to take suspected criminals to the police station. □ *It took two paddy wagons to carry away the people they arrested.* □ *The cop put the woman in handcuffs and then called the paddy wagon.*

penny *n.* a police officer. (A play on *copper*.) □ *The penny over on the corner told*

the boys to get moving. □ *We better get going before the pennies get here.*

Peter Jay *n.* a nickname for a police officer. □ *You walk straight, or Peter Jay is going to bust you.* □ *Here comes Peter Jay in his pigmobile.*

pig *n.* an officer; a police officer or a military officer. (Used mostly for a police officer. Widely known since the 1960s.) □ *The pigs are coming to bust up the fight.* □ *The pigs who aren't in pig heaven are driving around in pigmobiles busting innocent people like me.*

pig heaven *n.* a police station. (Chiefly black.) □ *The man came and took my brother to pig heaven.* □ *All the bacon eventually goes home to pig heaven.*

pigmobile *n.* a police car. □ *Look out, here comes the pigmobile.* □ *Hey, man! Have you ever ridden in a pigmobile?*

pork *n.* the police in general; a *pig*. (Underworld.) □ *Keep an eye out for the pork.* □ *The pork hauled all of them to the station.*

pounder *n.* a police officer; a cop on the beat. □ *The pounder gave me a parking ticket.* □ *Most pounders get sore feet.*

rap *n.* a criminal charge; the blame for something. (Underworld.) □ *I won't take the rap for something you did.* □ *The cops tried to make the rap stick, but they didn't have enough evidence.*

(rap) sheet *n.* a criminal record listing all recorded criminal charges. □ *This guy has a rap sheet a mile long.* □ *The sergeant asked if there was a sheet on the prisoner.*

roach *n.* a police officer. (Derogatory. From *cockroach*.) □ *Watch out! The roaches are coming.* □ *A roach caught him while he was at work.*

roller *n.* a police car. □ *There are rollers in the next block, driving slow, looking for someone.* □ *The roller pulled up in front of the boys, and two officers got out.*

roust *tr.* [for a police officer] to bother or interfere with someone; to arrest someone. (Underworld.) □ *The cops rousted the gang without warning.* □ *I* *was walking along doing nothing, and this cop rousts me.*

salt and pepper *n.* a black and white police car. □ *There is a salt and pepper around the corner waiting for speeders.* □ *There is a salt and pepper behind you, and it's too late to slow down.*

Sam *n.* federal agents; federal narcotics agents. (Also a term of address. From *Uncle Sam.*) □ *Sam is on the trail of the dope smugglers.* □ *Sam is working hard to put an end to all this drug trouble.*

Sam and Dave *n.* the police; police officers. (Black.) □ *Mike got hit by Sam and Dave last night.* □ *And there at the door were my old buddies Sam and Dave with a warrant.*

sham(m)us *n.* a police officer or a detective. (Probably from Yiddish.) □ *One thing that a shamus always knows is when another shamus is following him.* □ *This is it, shammus, say your prayers.*

shield *n.* a police officer's badge. □ *The fuzz flashed his shield, and I knew the game was over.* □ *If you're a cop, where's your shield?*

skull-buster *n.* a police officer. □ *Two skull-busters came up and started asking questions.* □ *Watch out for the skull-buster over there.*

Smokey (the Bear) *n.* a highway patrol officer; a police officer. (Citizens band radio.) □ *A Smokey was hiding behind a billboard!* □ *Smokey the Bear is after you!*

snatcher *n.* a police officer; a detective. (Underworld.) □ *One of the local snatchers came around to see if the door was locked.* □ *A snatcher hauled her away to the station.*

stick man *n.* a police patrol officer (who carries a stick). □ *The stick man is due here in about three minutes. Hurry.* □ *I was a stick man for a few years till my feet went bad.*

tag *tr.* to charge someone with a crime. □ *The cop tagged him with the bank caper immediately.* □ *The cop tagged me with a ticket before I knew what hit me.*

take pictures *tr.* for a highway patrol officer to use radar. (Citizens band radio.)

□ *There's a smokey under the bridge taking pictures.* □ *I didn't see the creep was taking pictures. I got nabbed.*

Tijuana taxi *n.* a police car. (Citizens band radio.) □ *There's a Tijuana taxi back a few cars watching you awful close.* □ *It's not a Tijuana taxi; it's a park ranger!*

T-man *n.* a federal narcotics agent; a treasury agent. (The "T" is from *treasury.*) □ *The T-men were at the front while Bruno crept out the back.* □ *It's curtains for you, T-man!*

Uncle nab *n.* a policeman. □ *Uncle nab is coming. Look sharp!* □ *Watch out for Uncle nab. He's been asking about you.*

Uncle (Sam) *n.* a federal agent; federal agents. □ *The cops called in Uncle Sam to help in the investigation.* □ *Uncle has some pretty strong ideas about who's in charge of this investigation.*

vag *mod.* having to do with a charge of vagrancy. □ *They booked him on a vag charge and gave him a nice warm place to sleep that night.* □ *The vag scam didn't work like it was planned.*

wagon *n.* the police wagon. □ *I called the wagon. It'll come and get these two thugs in about fifteen minutes.* □ *Look out, you guys, the wagon's coming. Don't let 'em see you!*

POLICE - PARAPHERNALIA

nippers *n.* handcuffs; leg fetters. □ *The cops put the nippers on the crooks.* □ *No, not the nippers. They hurt my arms.*

POLITENESS

welk *phr.* "You are welcome." □ Tom: *Thanks.* Bob: *Welk.* □ *"Welk," said Fred, accepting my thanks.*

POLITICIANS

baby-kisser *n.* a politician. □ *Once those baby-kissers get in office, they spend, spend, spend.* □ *There were lots of promises at the town square today when four local baby-kissers tried to rally interest in the upcoming election.*

boys in the backroom AND **backroom boys** *n.* any private male group making decisions, usually politicians. □ *The boys* *in the backroom picked the last presidential candidate.* □ *The backroom boys have decided too many things in the past. Their day is over.*

demo AND **dem** *n.* a member of the Democratic Party. □ *A couple of dems are running for the caucus, but no other party is represented.* □ *Which demos are they?*

flesh-presser AND **palm-presser** *n.* a politician. □ *It's that time of the year when the flesh-pressers really go to work.* □ *A palm-presser came to our door to ask us what we thought about his issues.*

front runner *n.* the leader; the person or thing most likely to win. □ *The press found out some juicy secrets about the front runner and made them all public.* □ *Who is the front runner in the race for senator?*

lame duck *n.* someone who is in the last period of a term in an elective office. □ *You can't expect much from a lame duck.* □ *As a lame duck, there's not a lot I can do.*

pol *n.* a politician. □ *The pols are spending my taxes like mad again.* □ *How many pols does a democracy require anyway?*

POLITICS

grassroots *mod.* having to do with or originating with the common people. □ *A grassroots movement pushed Senator Del Monte toward the nomination.* □ *Politicians love to create grassroots movements.*

Hill *n.* the U.S. Congress; the U.S. capitol building located on Capitol Hill in Washington, D.C. (Always with *the.*) □ *I really can't tell what's happening up on the Hill.* □ *The Hill moves at its own speed.*

smoke-filled room *n.* a room where a small group of people make important decisions. (Usually used in reference to political parties.) □ *The smoke-filled rooms are still producing the candidates for most offices, even as we approach the year 2000.* □ *The deal was cut in a smoke-filled room.*

PONDEROUS

like a ton of bricks *mod.* like something very ponderous and heavy. □ *The whole thing hit me like a ton of bricks.* □ *Hitting the back end of that truck was like hitting a ton of bricks.*

POPULAR

click (with someone) *in.* to catch on with someone; to intrigue someone; to become popular with someone. □ *The pink hair and multiple earrings never really seemed to click with many kids.* □ *Sam and Mary are getting along fine. I knew they'd click.*

hot *mod.* of great renown; doing quite well for the time being. □ *The opera tenor was hot, and even the lowbrows would pay to hear him.* □ *The dancer was hot and was offered movie roles and all sorts of things.*

kitsch *n.* any form of entertainment— movies, books, plays—with enormous popular appeal. □ *This kitsch sells like mad in the big city.* □ *Most people prefer kitsch to art.*

pop *mod.* popular. □ *This style is very pop.* □ *I don't care for pop stuff.*

PORNOGRAPHY

hard-core *mod.* sexually explicit; pornographic. □ *You can't sell that hard-core stuff in a store like this!* □ *You think that's hard-core?*

skin flick *n.* a movie featuring nudity. □ *We took in a skin flick when we were in the city.* □ *Max likes skin flicks better than real girls.*

soft core 1. *mod.* referring to a mild type of pornography. □ *There are more and more soft core movies on cable television.* □ *This stuff I saw was just soft core.* □ *Now, even the soft core stuff is getting harder to find at newsstands.* **2.** *n.* mild pornography. □ *They keep some soft core under the counter.* □ *The movie was a bit of soft core, but people still walked out.*

PORTION

See also **DRUGS - PORTION**.

divvy *n.* a share of something. □ *How much is my divvy?* □ *Give me my divvy so I can go home.*

gob *n.* a blob or mass of something. □ *I'd like a big gob of mashed potatoes, please.* □ *Take that horrid gob of gum out of your mouth!*

lion's share *n.* the largest portion. □ *I earn a lot, but the lion's share goes for taxes.* □ *The lion's share of the surplus cheese goes to school cafeterias.*

touch *n.* a small portion of something to eat or drink. (Folksy.) □ *I'll have just a touch. I'm on a diet, you know.* □ *Can I have another touch of that pie, please?*

POSITION

out of kilter *mod.* out of square. □ *That picture is out of kilter. Please straighten it.* □ *That corner is not square, and the wall even looks out of kilter.*

tits up *mod.* upside down; on its or someone's back. (Potentially offensive. Use only with discretion.) □ *He landed tits up in a cornfield.* □ *Her lousy pie fell tits up onto the kitchen floor.*

POSTERIOR

tail-end *n.* the back end of something or someone. □ *He was at the tail-end of the long line.* □ *Tracy fell down on her tail-end.*

POVERTY

have-nots *n.* the poor; those who have little or nothing. (Always with *the*.) □ *The have-nots seem never to be able to get ahead.* □ *What's in it for the have-nots?*

POWER

bad *mod.* powerful; intense. (Black.) □ *Man, that is really bad music!* □ *This grass is bad!*

bang for the buck *n.* value for the money spent; excitement for the money spent; the cost-to-benefit ratio. □ *I didn't get anywhere near the bang for the buck I expected.* □ *How much bang for the buck did you really think you would get from a twelve-year-old car—at any price?*

Cadillac *n.* the name of something powerful or superior. (From the name of the automobile.) □ *This product is the Cadillac of plastic kitchenware.* □ *Acme is the Cadillac of monochrome closed-circuit retail surveillance equipment.*

carry weight *tr.* to have influence. □ *I don't carry much weight around here, but Walter does.* □ *Tom carries weight with the mayor. Ask him.*

dynamite 1. *mod.* excellent; powerful. □ *I want some more of your dynamite enchiladas, please.* □ *These tacos are dynamite, too.* **2.** *n.* anything potentially powerful: a drug, news, a person. □ *This chick is really dynamite!* □ *The story about the scandal was dynamite and kept selling papers for a month.*

greased lighting *n.* something fast or powerful. □ *That little car is just greased lightning.* □ *That kid can run like greased lightning.*

heavy artillery *n.* powerful or persuasive persons or things. □ *Finally, the mayor brought out the heavy artillery and quieted things down.* □ *The heavy artillery seemed to know how to handle matters.*

horses *n.* horse power, as in an engine. □ *How many horses does this thing have?* □ *Isn't 400 horses a lot for just one car?*

juice *n.* energy; power; political influence. □ *The boss has the juice with the board to make the necessary changes.* □ *Dave left the president's staff because he just didn't have the juice anymore to be useful.*

(ma)hoska *n.* energy; strength; *moxie.* □ *The guy's got mahoska and guts!* □ *She's quick and has lots of mahoska.*

put balls on something *tr.* to make something more masculine or powerful; to give something authority and strength. (Potentially offensive. Use only with discretion.) □ *Come on, sing louder. Put some balls on it.* □ *This story is too namby-pamby. Put some balls on it.*

souped up *mod.* made more powerful. □ *That souped up car of John's sure makes a lot of noise.* □ *Why do all cars driven by males under the age of twenty have to be souped up?*

triple whammy *n.* a powerful treatment; a powerful shock. □ *The market crash, the trade figures, and the death of the secretary of defense was a powerful triple whammy in Washington politics this week.* □ *The tax bill served as a triple whammy to the family purse.*

POWER - ALCOHOL

bang *n.* the degree of potency of the alcohol in liquor. □ *This stuff has quite a bang!* □ *The bang is gone from this wine.*

jolt *n.* the degree of potency of the alcohol in liquor. □ *It doesn't have much of a jolt.* □ *Watch out. This stuff has quite a jolt.*

lift *n.* the potency of alcohol in liquor. □ *This stuff doesn't have much lift!* □ *Now, this imported stuff has enough lift to raise the dead.*

oof *n.* the potency of the alcohol in liquor; the effect of potent alcohol. □ *This stuff really has oof. How old is it?* □ *Beer doesn't have enough oof for her anymore.*

three-two AND **three point two** *n.* a weak beer containing 3.2 percent alcohol. □ *Three-two is just no good for serious sousing.* □ *James likes three point two because he can drink more of it without getting stoned.*

PRAISE

do oneself proud *tr.* to have done a very fine job. □ *That's super! You've done yourself proud!* □ *I feel like I've done myself proud.*

hand it to someone *tr.* to acknowledge someone's excellence (at something). □ *Well, I have to hand it to you. That was great!* □ *He had to hand it to her for her excellent performance.*

PRANK

See TRICK.

PRECISION

comma-counter *n.* a pedantic person. □ *Comma-counters can be such a pain.* □ *When you need a proofreader, you need a comma-counter.*

hit the spot AND **hit the bull's-eye** *tr.* to be exactly right. □ *You really hit the spot with that prediction.* □ *Pete's prediction hit the bull's-eye.*

on-target *mod.* timely; exact; incisive. □ *Your criticism is exactly on-target.* □ *We are on-target for a December completion date.*

on the button AND **on the bean** *mod.* exactly the right time or place. □ *He was there on time, right on the button.* □ *I want to see you here at noon—on the bean.*

on the money *mod.* exactly as desired; at the right amount of money. □ *Your new idea is right on the money.* □ *The bid for the new hospital came in on the money.*

on the nose *mod.* exactly on time; exactly as planned. □ *I want you there at noon on the nose.* □ *All three of them were at the appointed place, right on the nose.*

ring the bell *tr.* to be just what is needed; to *hit the spot.* □ *This cold water really rings the bell.* □ *A good hot bowl of soup would ring the bell about now.*

slap-dab *mod.* directly. □ *We put it slap-dab on his head.* □ *I found this pop bottle slap-dab on top of the car! How'd it get there?*

spit and polish *n.* orderliness; ceremonial precision and orderliness. □ *I like spit and polish. It comes from being in the military.* □ *There is no such thing as too much spit and polish.*

ticket *n.* the exact thing; the needed thing. □ *Her smile was her ticket to a new career.* □ *This degree will be your ticket to a bright and shining future.*

PREDICTION

have good vibes *tr.* to have good feelings (about someone or something). (*Have got* can replace *have.*) □ *I've got good vibes about Heidi.* □ *I know everything will go all right. I have good vibes.*

PREDICTION - LACKING

twenty-twenty hindsight AND **20/20 hindsight** *n.* an ability to figure out what one should have done after it is too late to do it. □ *Everybody has twenty-twenty hindsight!* □ *Your 20/20 hindsight is just great.*

PREFERENCE
See also CHOICE.

bag *n.* one's preference; something suited to one's preference. □ *My bag is things with whipped cream.* □ *That kind of stuff is just not my bag.*

big with someone *mod.* preferred by someone. □ *Soup is big with everybody in cold weather.* □ *This kind of ice cream is really big with my family.*

call *n.* a decision; a prediction. □ *That was a good call, Mike.* □ *The market behaved just as you said it would. Good call.*

cup of tea *n.* something preferred or desired. (Often negative.) □ *This drug scene stuff is just not my cup of tea.* □ *Driving children around all afternoon is not my cup of tea.*

get the nod *tr.* to be chosen. □ *Fred got the nod for class treasurer.* □ *I hope I get the nod for the job.*

hooked (on someone or something) *mod.* preferring someone or something; enamored of someone or something. □ *I'm really hooked on chocolate anything.* □ *Sam is hooked on Mary for good.*

(right) up one's alley *mod.* exactly one's kind of thing; exactly what one is best equipped to do. □ *That job is right up her alley.* □ *It's not exactly up my alley, but I'll try it.*

scene *n.* one's preference. □ *This nine-to-five stuff just isn't my scene. I quit.* □ *Your scene doesn't seem to involve much in the way of hard work.*

PREGNANCY
been had AND **was had** *phr.* been copulated with; been made pregnant. □ *I've been had, and I'm going to have the baby.* □ *When she said she was had, I didn't know it was on her honeymoon.*

in a familiar way *mod.* pregnant. (Euphemistic for *in a family way*.) □ *Tracy is in a familiar way, have you heard?* □ *In a familiar way again?*

in a family way AND **in the family way** *mod.* pregnant. □ *I hear that Tracy is in a family way.* □ *Is she in the family way again?*

in bad shape AND **in a bad way** *mod.* pregnant. □ *Tracy's in bad shape again, I hear.* □ *Yup, she's in bad shape all right—about three months in bad shape.*

knocked up *mod.* pregnant. □ *Tracy got knocked up again.* □ *Isn't she knocked up most of the time?*

knock someone up *tr.* to make a woman pregnant. (Crude.) □ *They say it was Bruno who knocked her up.* □ *He did not knock up Tracy. I did.*

light bulb *n.* a pregnant woman. (Jocular. Refers to the shape of a pregnant woman.) □ *Who's the light bulb on the sofa?* □ *I can't possibly fit that light bulb out there. She'll have to wait a few months before buying expensive clothing.*

PG *mod.* "pregnant." (Initialism.) □ *Do you think Sally's PG?* □ *I think I'm PG. You know, pregnant.*

pillowed *mod.* pregnant. (Refers to the swelling in a pregnant woman's abdomen.) □ *She does look a bit pillowed, doesn't she?* □ *I think I'm more than a bit pillowed.*

preg *mod.* pregnant. □ *Doesn't Sally look a little preg?* □ *Nobody is ever just a little preg.*

pumped *mod.* pregnant; impregnated. (Crude.) □ *She was so pumped, she was out to here.* □ *Look at her! She's pumped and looks due any minute.*

sprain one's ankle *tr.* to become pregnant. □ *She has, ah, sprained her ankle.* □ *From the looks of her, she must have sprained her ankle some months ago.*

storked *mod.* pregnant. □ *She got herself good and storked. Now what?* □ *I hear that Tracy is storked again.*

PREPARATION
game plan *n.* a plan of action; a scheme. (From sports.) □ *The game plan for the election was beginning to shape up.* □ *Our game plan had to be scrapped.*

grease the skids *tr.* to help prepare for the success or failure of someone or something. □ *Ray set out to grease the skids for the right things to happen.* □ *We* need someone to grease the skids for the Wilson contract.

knock something together AND **throw something together** *tr.* to assemble something—such as a meal—at the last moment. □ *I'll see if I can throw something together.* □ *I knocked together a vegetable dish at the last minute.*

lick something into shape AND **whip something into shape** *tr.* to put something into good condition, possibly with considerable effort. □ *I've got about two days more to lick this place into shape so I can sell it.* □ *I want to whip this house into shape for Saturday night.*

loaded for bear *mod.* ready for the hardest problems. □ *Bring on the hard cases. I'm loaded for bear.* □ *I'm loaded for bear, and that's good because this is going to be a rough day.*

psyched (up) *mod.* completely mentally ready (for something). □ *I'm really psyched for this test.* □ *The team isn't psyched up enough to do a good job.*

psych someone up *tr.* to get someone excited or mentally prepared for something. □ *I psyched myself up to sing in front of all those people.* □ *The coach psyched up the team for the game.*

reinvent the wheel *tr.* to make unnecessary or redundant preparations. □ *You don't need to reinvent the wheel. Read up on what others have done.* □ *I don't have time to reinvent the wheel.*

take one's belt in (a notch) AND **pull one's belt in (a notch)** *tr.* to prepare for lean times. □ *It was clear that we would have to bite the bullet and take our belt in a notch.* □ *We were able to take our belt in a notch, unlike other people who were already strained to the maximum.*

tighten one's belt *tr.* to prepare for economies. (As if one would not be able to afford enough food to make one's stomach press against one's belt.) □ *Get ready to tighten your belt. I lost my job.* □ *The entire country will have to tighten its belt.*

warm someone up *tr.* to prepare an audience for another—more famous—performer. □ *A famous singer came out to warm us up for Jack Benny.* □ *This man Bennett is a superb choice to warm up the audience.*

work oneself up to something *tr.* to get oneself mentally ready to do something. □ *I spent all morning working myself up to taking the driver's test.* □ *I had to work myself up to it little by little.*

PREPARATION - LACKING

half-baked *mod.* badly thought out. □ *That was a half-baked scheme. Was that the best you could do?* □ *It would have been approved if it weren't so half-baked.*

half-cocked *mod.* unprepared. □ *So he's half-cocked. So what?* □ *You're half-cocked for everything you do.*

PRESENTATION

give someone an earful *tr.* to tell someone surprising secrets. □ *Sally gave Wally an earful about Pete and the things he said about Mary.* □ *Wally gave Sally an earful about Todd's tax problems.*

hit someone with something *tr.* to present someone with an idea, plan, or proposal. □ *Pete hit me with a great idea just before we left.* □ *Fred hit his boss with a plan to save a bundle in the front office.*

lay something on someone *tr.* to present a plan or an idea to someone. □ *Here is this century's greatest idea. Let me lay it on you.* □ *I'm going to lay a great idea on you.*

show and tell *n.* a session where objects are presented and described. (Essentially a kindergarten or grade school activity.) □ *It was a short lecture with lots of show and tell.* □ *I can't take another show and tell session.*

PRESSURE

crowd *tr.* to pressure or threaten someone. □ *Don't crowd me!* □ *Max began to crowd Bruno, which was the wrong thing to do.*

heat *n.* pressure. □ *There's a lot of heat on Fred right now.* □ *The boss put some heat on Wally, and things are moving faster now.*

put the arm on someone *tr.* to demand something of someone, especially money. ☐ *I know Tom wants some money. He put the arm on me, but I said no.* ☐ *She put the arm on her roommate for a loan.*

put the screws on someone AND **put the heat on someone; put the squeeze on someone** *tr.* to pressure someone; to threaten someone to achieve something. ☐ *He told everything about the plan when they put the screws on him.* ☐ *The cops put the squeeze on Harry, and he spilled the beans.*

under the gun *mod.* under pressure; under scrutiny. ☐ *I've been under the gun on this one long enough.* ☐ *They've got the boss under the gun to get this thing wound up by Saturday.*

Wipe it off! *exclam.* "Wipe that smile off your face!" ☐ *It's not funny. Wipe it off!* ☐ *Wipe it off! Nothing funny here, soldier.*

PRESSURE - REDUCE

lighten up (on someone or something) *in.* to reduce the pressure (on someone or something); to calm down (about someone or something). ☐ *Cool it, man. Lighten up! We all gotta get along here.* ☐ *Lighten up on the guy. He only stepped on your toe.*

PREVIEW

teaser *n.* a brief sample of something, such as a performance. ☐ *The teaser didn't look very promising, but the reviews were great.* ☐ *The teasers they showed before the film were the best part of the evening.*

PRICE

See COST.

PRIDE

tall in the saddle *mod.* proud. (Often with *sit.*) ☐ *I'll still be tall in the saddle when you are experiencing the results of your folly.* ☐ *Despite her difficulties, she still sat tall in the saddle.*

PRISON

See JAIL.

PRIVACY

between you, me, and the lamppost AND **between you, me, and the bedpost** *phr.* "just between you and me." ☐ *Between you, me, and the lamppost, things are going to get worse before they get better.* ☐ *They're worse than you think now, just between you, me, and the bedpost.*

Keep out of this! *exclam.* "Mind your own business!" ☐ *This is not your affair. Keep out of this!* ☐ *Keep out of this! I'll settle it.*

mind your own beeswax *tr.* to "mind one's own business." (Juvenile.) ☐ *You just mind your own beeswax!* ☐ *Lay off! Mind your own beeswax!*

none of someone's beeswax *n.* none of someone's business. ☐ *It's none of your beeswax. I'm not telling.* ☐ *You'll never know. The answer is none of your beeswax.*

PRIVATE

in *mod.* private. ☐ *Is this in information?* ☐ *If it's in or something, I'm sure they won't spread it around.*

PROBLEM

See also BURDEN, DIFFICULTIES.

get it out *tr.* to tell (someone) about a problem; to pour out one's grief. ☐ *Come on, get it out. You'll feel better.* ☐ *He would feel better if he could get it out.*

hard case *n.* a person who is a real problem. ☐ *Jed has turned into a hard case. He's fighting us at every turn.* ☐ *The hard case we dealt with last week is back again.*

tough cookie *n.* a tough person. ☐ *He's a tough cookie, but I can handle him.* ☐ *There was a tough cookie in here this morning who demanded to see the manager.*

tough customer *n.* someone who is difficult to deal with. ☐ *Some of those bikers are really tough customers.* ☐ *Bruno is a tough customer. Just keep away from him.*

tough egg to crack AND **tough nut to crack** *n.* a person or thing that is hard to figure out or hard to deal with. ☐ *This* *problem is a tough egg to crack.* □ *I wish Jill wasn't such a tough nut to crack.*

What's with someone or something? *interrog.* "What is wrong with someone or something?" □ *Hey, chum! What's with you?* □ *What's with this can opener? It won't turn.*

PRODUCING

cough something up *tr.* to produce something (which someone has requested), usually money. □ *Come on, buster, cough it up, now!* □ *You owe me seven stereo amplifiers. Now, cough them up!* □ *Cough up what you owe me!*

crank something out *tr.* to produce something; to make a lot of something. □ *She can crank mystery novels out like fury. They're all good, too.* □ *That man does nothing but crank out trouble.*

knock something off *tr.* to manufacture or make something, especially in haste. □ *I'll see if I can knock another one off before lunch.* □ *They knocked off four window frames in an hour.*

PRODUCT

brainchild *n.* someone's good idea, viewed as an offspring of the brain. □ *Is this your brainchild? It won't work.* □ *Listen to this. It's my best brainchild.*

cheapie *n.* a cheaply made article. □ *I don't want a cheapie. I can afford better.* □ *It broke. I guess it was a cheapie.*

copy *n.* a piece, as in an item produced. □ *We sell the toy at $14 a copy.* □ *These cars cost over $20,000 a copy.*

hot item *n.* an item that sells well. □ *This little thing is a hot item this season.* □ *Now here's a hot item that everybody is looking for.*

schlock *n.* inferior merchandise. (From German *schlacke,* "dregs" via Yiddish.) □ *That store has nothing but schlock.* □ *For this schlock I should pay good money?*

widget *n.* a hypothetical product made by a hypothetical company. □ *Someone said that your company is manufacturing widgets.* □ *No, we stopped making widgets last year. Too much foreign competition.*

PROFESSOR

prof *n.* a professor. (Collegiate.) □ *The prof was dull and the room was hot, and I kept closing my eyes.* □ *Who's the prof for that course?*

PROJECT

baby *n.* a project thought of as an offspring. (Always with a possessor.) □ *Whose baby is the Johnson account?* □ *You give the report. This project is your baby.*

PROMOTION

See also **ADVERTISING**.

ballyhoo 1. *n.* publicity. □ *I have never heard so much ballyhoo for such a lousy movie.* □ *After the ballyhoo died down, we realized that nothing at all had really changed.* **2.** *tr.* to promote or publicize someone or something. □ *They ballyhooed this movie on television for a month before it came out.* □ *We promise to ballyhoo John at election time.*

beat the drum for someone or something *tr.* to promote or support someone or something. □ *I spent a lot of time beating the drum for our plans for the future.* □ *The senator is only beating the drum for his special interests.*

boost *tr.* to praise someone or something; to support someone or something. □ *She is always boosting some cause.* □ *If she would boost me as well, I wouldn't object to the time she spends hyping other people.*

booster *n.* a supporter (of someone or some cause). □ *We don't have enough boosters to have any effect.* □ *I'm a booster of lots of good causes.*

flak AND **flack 1.** *n.* publicity; *hype.* □ *Who is going to believe this flack about being first-rate?* □ *It's all flak and no substance.* **2.** *n.* a public relations agent or officer. □ *The flak made an announcement and then disappeared.* □ *There were flacks all over the place telling lies and making false promises.*

flog *tr.* to promote something; to try to sell something aggressively. □ *Fred was flogging this car so hard, I figured he was trying to get rid of it.* □ *Don't flog it so hard. It makes people suspicious.*

get behind someone or something *in.* to support someone or something. □ *Let's all get behind the party in the next election.* □ *Everybody got behind Todd and cheered him on.*

hype artist *n.* someone who produces aggressive promotional material for a living. □ *She is a hype artist for a public relations firm.* □ *How much does a hype artist get paid for all that junk?*

hyper *n.* a person who praises or promotes someone or something. □ *She's a hyper, and she doesn't always tell things the way they are.* □ *As a hyper, she is a whiz.*

hype something up *tr.* to overpraise something; to propagandize something. □ *They hyped it up too much.* □ *Why do they hype up an election?*

ink *n.* publicity; print media coverage of someone or something. □ *The movie star's divorce got a lot of ink for a few days.* □ *The new president managed to get some ink every day, but it wasn't always good.*

package *tr.* to position or display someone or something, as in marketing, to good advantage. □ *The agent packaged the actress so that everyone thought she only did dramatic roles.* □ *If you package your plan correctly, the committee will accept it.*

plug 1. *n.* a free advertisement or a commercial boost from someone for a product. □ *I managed to get a plug on the Mike Michael Show.* □ *How about a free plug during your introduction?* **2.** *tr.* to give an advertisement or commercial boost for something without having to pay for it. □ *I want to get on that TV program and plug my new book.* □ *I can't plug your product until I have a sample I can test.*

push *tr.* to *hype* something or someone; to pressure something or someone. □ *She's always pushing her own interests.* □ *The clerk was pushing one brand so hard that I finally bought it.*

put something on the street *tr.* to make something known publicly; to tell everyone one's troubles. □ *Man, can't you keep a secret? Don't put everything on the street.* □ *She gets a little problem, and she puts it on the street right away!*

razzle-dazzle *n.* flamboyant publicity; hype. □ *After all the razzle-dazzle dies down, we'll see what things are really like.* □ *Hollywood is filled with razzle-dazzle and excitement.*

shill *in.* to advertise for something; to give a sales pitch for something. □ *Four stars of an old television show were there shilling for a major computer firm.* □ *They pay them a mint to shill like that.*

trumped up *mod.* heavily promoted; overly praised. □ *I don't care for trumped up stuff like that movie.* □ *That movie was so trumped up. I expected to see something much better than it turned out to be.*

trump something up *tr.* to promote or boost something. □ *They think they have to trump something up to get people to see it.* □ *They trumped up the movie so much that many people were disappointed when it finally came out.*

PROSTITUTION

call girl *n.* a prostitute; a prostitute who is always on call. □ *The snatcher hauled her in because she looked like a call girl.* □ *Most of the really sharp call girls look like MBAs and drive beemers.*

chippy AND **chippie** *n.* a part-time prostitute. □ *Yeah, so I'm a chippie. So what's that make you?* □ *Some little chippie stopped us to ask for a match. How amateurish.*

gook *n.* a prostitute. □ *Some old gook was standing around with too much leg on view.* □ *There are a lot of gooks around here in the center of town.*

hooker *n.* a prostitute. □ *There were some hookers standing right on that corner.* □ *Clare dresses like a hooker.*

hustler *n.* a prostitute. □ *Gert almost became a hustler to pay for a habit.* □ *A lot of hustlers are hooked on horse.*

john *n.* a prostitute's customer. □ *She led the john into an alley where Lefty* *robbed him.* □ *The john looked a little embarrassed.*

on the street *mod.* engaged in prostitution. □ *Mary said, "What am I supposed to do—go on the street?"* □ *All three of them went on the street to earn enough money to live.*

pro *n.* a prostitute. □ *Do you think she's a pro or just overly friendly?* □ *This pro comes up to me and acts like she's met me before.*

prosty AND **prostie** *n.* a prostitute. □ *The cops haul in about forty prosties a night from that one neighborhood alone.* □ *This one prosty was high on something and started screaming.*

turn a trick *tr.* to perform an act of prostitution. (Use caution with the topic.) □ *She can turn a trick and be on the streets again in six minutes flat.* □ *She's upstairs, turning a trick.*

PROXIMITY

eyeball to eyeball *mod.* face to face. □ *They approached each other eyeball to eyeball and frowned.* □ *Let's talk more when we are eyeball to eyeball.*

joined at the hip *mod.* closely connected; as thick as thieves. (As Siamese twins are joined.) □ *Those two are joined at the hip. They are always together.* □ *Sam and Martha are joined at the hip.*

nip and tuck *mod.* so close as to be almost the same; *neck and neck.* □ *They ran nip and tuck all the way to the finish line, but Tom won the race.* □ *It was too close to call—nip and tuck all the way.*

put some distance between someone and someone or something *tr.* to lengthen the distance or time between oneself and someone or something (including a place). □ *I gotta put some distance between me and that cop—fast.* □ *You need to put some distance between you and your brother's death.* □ *She needed enough money to put some distance between herself and her hometown.*

within an ace of (doing) something *mod.* very close to doing something. □ *I came within an ace of getting stoned.* □ *We were within an ace of beating the all-time record.*

PUBLICATION

charts *n.* the trade magazine rankings of current pop music. □ *The big one is back on the charts this week. Give it a listen.* □ *Number five on the charts again this week—it's "My Blue Heaven" with the Andrews Sisters.*

mag *n.* magazine. □ *I gotta stop and get a computer mag.* □ *I've seen your face in the mags, haven't I?*

pot boiler *n.* a book or other literary work of no value except for the money it earns. □ *I can write one pot boiler every six months or so.* □ *Can you produce anything but pot boilers?*

slick *n.* a high-quality magazine printed on slick [coated] paper. □ *The slicks are all carrying ads for products and services that couldn't even be mentioned a few years ago.* □ *Most of the price increase for the slicks has been because of postage increases.*

sub *n.* a subscription, as to a magazine. □ *I got a sub to a computer magazine for my birthday.* □ *Would you like to buy a sub to the local newspaper?*

think-piece *n.* a thoughtful piece of writing in a newspaper or magazine. □ *Mr. Wilson's think-piece about the need for more concern for the middle class was not well-received.* □ *This is plain propaganda disguised as a think-piece.*

PUBLICITY
See PROMOTION.

PUNISHMENT

behind bars *mod.* in jail; in prison. □ *You belong behind bars, you creep!* □ *I've got something here that will keep you behind bars for years.*

bit *n.* a jail sentence. (Underworld.) □ *I did a two-year bit in Sing Sing.* □ *He got only a four-year bit. He was afraid of getting worse.*

boxed (up) *mod.* in jail. □ *I did it, and I was boxed for a long time for it. Now lay off!* □ *Pat was boxed up for two days till we got bond money.*

burn 1. *tr.* to execute someone in the electric chair. (Underworld.) □ *I'll see that they burn you for this!* □ *The DA tried to burn me, but I got off with six months.* **2.** *in.* to die by electrocution in the electric chair. (Underworld.) □ *I ain't afraid I'll burn, copper!* □ *I'll see that you burn for this.*

campus *tr.* to restrict someone to the grounds of a college campus. (Collegiate.) □ *The dean threatened to campus the entire fraternity for a month.* □ *"We will campus you for a year, if necessary," shouted the dean, who really didn't understand young people.*

campused *mod.* restricted to the campus. (Collegiate.) □ *I can't go to town. I'm campused.* □ *She's campused and can only go to the library.*

chair *n.* the electric chair, as used in the execution of the death penalty. (Underworld. Always with *the*.) □ *You'll fry in the chair for this, Lefty!* □ *I don't wanna go to the chair!*

clip someone's wings *tr.* to restrain someone; to reduce or put an end to a teenager's privileges. □ *One more stunt like that and I'm going to clip your wings for a couple of weeks.* □ *Her father clipped her wings for getting into trouble with the cops.*

deuce *n.* a two-year prison sentence. (Underworld.) □ *Lefty served a deuce up the river.* □ *The DA made sure that Bruno got more than a deuce.*

do time *tr.* to serve a sentence in prison; to serve a specific amount of time in prison. (Underworld.) □ *Lefty had done time on a number of occasions.* □ *You'd better talk and talk fast if you don't want to do time.*

federal jug *n.* a federal prison. (Underworld.) □ *Rocko was set to spend the next twenty years in the federal jug.* □ *Lefty is fresh and sweet—just out of the federal jug.*

fry 1. *in.* to die in the electric chair. (Underworld.) □ *The DA is determined that you will fry.* □ *I don't want to fry!* **2.** *tr.* to execute someone in the electric chair.

(Underworld.) □ *They're gonna fry you for this.* □ *Nobody's gonna fry Rocko!*

get it *tr.* to get punished. □ *I just know I'm going to get it when I get home.* □ *You're going to get it all right!*

get it in the neck *tr.* to receive something bad, such as punishment or criticism. □ *You are going to get it in the neck for that remark.* □ *Jimmy was afraid he'd get it in the neck for being late.*

get one's lumps *tr.* to get the result or punishment one deserves. □ *If she keeps acting that way, she'll get her lumps.* □ *We will see that Dave gets his lumps.*

grounded *mod.* confined to one's home. (The standard punishment for a teenager.) □ *Tracy is grounded for a week because she came in late.* □ *You are grounded, and I don't want to hear aother word about it!*

hard time *n.* a prison sentence. (Underworld.) □ *Lefty did hard time for his part in the robbery.* □ *How much hard time does he have behind him?*

heads will roll *phr.* "someone will be punished." □ *When I find out who did this, heads will roll.* □ *Heads will roll when I get back to the office.*

hot seat *n.* the electric chair. (Underworld.) □ *Lefty, you're headed for the hot seat.* □ *The hot seat is just waiting for you, Lefty.*

pay one's dues (to society) *tr.* to serve a prison or jail sentence. □ *I served ten years in prison. I've paid my dues to society. The matter is settled.* □ *I took my medicine and paid my dues. Stop trying to punish me more.*

put someone away *tr.* to put someone in prison for a long time. (Underworld.) □ *They put Max away for fifteen years.* □ *The judge put away the whole gang.*

rub someone's nose in something *tr.* to remind someone of something constantly; to make a big issue about someone's mistake. (From the practice of training a puppy by rubbing its nose in the messes it makes.) □ *So I made a mistake! I wish you'd stop rubbing my nose* *in it.* □ *Rubbing my nose in it is not going to correct the mistake.*

send someone up the river *tr.* to send someone to prison. (Underworld. As done by a judge or indirectly by the police.) □ *They tried to send me up the river, but my lip got me off.* □ *I'm gonna send you up the river if it's the last thing I do.*

slap someone's wrist AND **slap someone on the wrist** *tr.* to administer a minor reprimand. □ *The judge only slapped her wrist.* □ *The courts only slap them on the wrist and send them back out on the streets.*

stretch 1. *in.* to hang (as with a death sentence). □ *You will stretch for this, Lefty!* □ *I'll live to see you stretch, you rat!* **2.** *n.* a prison term. □ *I was away for a stretch of about seven years.* □ *That's quite a stretch for tax evasion.*

throw the book at someone *tr.* [for the police] to charge someone with everything possible; [for a judge] to find someone guilty of everything possible. (As if one were being charged with violating all the laws in a law book.) □ *The judge wanted to throw the book at Bruno, but the prosecutor convinced him to go easy in hope that Bruno would lead them to Mr. Big.* □ *They threw the book at Rocko—he got 180 years.*

trip *n.* a prison sentence; a trip *up the river.* (Underworld.) □ *Yeah, me and Lefty both was on a little trip for a few years.* □ *I had a short trip, so what?*

up the river *mod.* in prison. (Underworld.) □ *Gary was up the river for a couple of years, but that doesn't make him a criminal, does it?* □ *The judge who sent him up the river was indicted for accepting bribery. If Gary had only known sooner!*

vacation *n.* a prison sentence. (Underworld.) □ *I had a little vacation upstate for a while.* □ *It was a three-year vacation, with time off for good behavior.*

whale the tar out of someone *tr.* to spank or beat someone. (Sometimes said to a child.) □ *My father threatened to whale the tar out of me.* □ *I'll whale the tar out of you when we get home if you don't settle down.*

PUNISHMENT - LACKING

soft on someone *mod.* too easy on someone. □ *The judge was viewed as being too soft on pushers.* □ *The cops are soft on speeders in this town.*

PURSUIT

dog *tr.* to follow someone. □ *The cop dogged Lefty for a week.* □ *Stop dogging me, you twit!*

on someone's tail *mod.* following someone closely. □ *There is a huge truck on my tail. What should I do?* □ *Keep on her tail and don't let her out of your sight.*

PUZZLE

brain-twister AND **brain-teaser** *n.* a puzzle. □ *This Maltese falcon case is a real brain-twister.* □ *Can you help me with this brain-teaser?*

QUALITATIVE

qual *n.* qualitative analysis. (Scientific.) □ *We'll have to turn to qual for that answer.* □ *She worked in qual for a while and then went on to management.*

QUALITY

A-1 AND **A number 1** *mod.* of the highest rating. □ *This steak is really A-1!* □ *I would like to get an A number 1 secretary for a change.*

ace *mod.* (of persons) best; top-rated. □ *She is an ace reporter with the newspaper.* □ *Frank is an ace swimmer.*

A-OK *mod.* in the best of condition. □ *I really feel A-OK.* □ *Show me the most A-OK canary you have.*

QUANTITATIVE

quant AND **quan** *n.* quantitative analysis. (Scientific and collegiate.) □ *I didn't study enough for my quant test.* □ *I flunked quan twice.*

QUESTION

Are we away? *interrog.* "Shall we go?"; "Let's go." (Really a command to depart expressed as a question.) □ *Well, it's late. Are we away?* □ *The car's warmed up. Are we away?*

or what? *phr.* "or what else can it be?" (Part of a special formula that asks if something is a good example or specimen of something. The expected answer is yes. The question "Is this an X or what?" means "If this isn't a really great X, what is it then?") □ *Look at what I am wearing! Is that a great jacket or what?* □ *That's my son. Is he a superman or what?*

sixty-four-dollar question *n.* the most important question; the question that everyone wants to know the answer to. (Always with *the*.) □ *When? Now, that is the sixty-four-dollar question.* □ *Now for the sixty-four-dollar question. What's the stock market going to do this year?*

QUIT

See also **CONCLUSION, ENDINGS, STOPPING**.

chuck it in *tr.* to quit; to give up. □ *I was so depressed, I almost chucked it in.* □ *If I didn't have to keep the job to live, I'd have chucked it in long ago.*

cold turkey *mod.* [stopping something] suddenly, without tapering off. (Said especially of stopping an addictive drug intake. Originally drugs.) □ *Martha stopped cold turkey and survived.* □ *I stopped smoking cigarettes cold turkey and had to be hospitalized.* □ *I gave up rich desserts cold turkey and lived to tell about it.*

cop out *in.* to give up and quit; to chicken out (of something). □ *Why do you want to cop out just when things are going great?* □ *I couldn't cop out on you guys if I wanted to.*

drop out *in.* to drop out of school or some organization. □ *I dropped out before I got promoted.* □ *Don't drop out of school. You'll regret it.*

go home to mama *in.* to give up something—such as a marriage—and return to one's mother's home. □ *I've had it. I'm going home to mama.* □ *Mary left him and went home to mama.*

go south AND **head south** *in.* to quit; to drop out of sight. □ *Fred got discouraged and went south. I think he gave up football permanently.* □ *After pulling the bank job, Max went south for a few months.*

hang it up *tr.* to quit something. □ *I finally had enough and decided to hang it up.* □ *Oh, hang it up! It's hopeless.*

knock off (work) *tr. & in.* to quit work, for the day or for a break. □ *What time do you knock off work?* □ *I knock off about five-thirty.*

knock the habit AND **kick the habit** *tr.* to stop using drugs; to break a drug addiction. □ *I just can't knock the habit.* □ *He tried to kick the habit by drinking lots of booze.*

lay down *in.* to give up. □ *Do you expect me to just lay down?* □ *You really think I should just lay down and let them walk all over me?*

quit while one is ahead *in.* to stop doing something while one is successful. □ *When will I learn to quit while I'm ahead?*

□ *Get into the market. Make some money and get out. Quit while you're ahead.*

rat out *in.* to quit; to fink out (on someone or something). □ *It's too late to rat out.* □ *He tried to rat out at the last minute.*

say uncle *tr.* to admit defeat; to give up. □ *He held me down until I said uncle.* □ *I never say uncle. I just keep right on going.*

throw in the towel AND **throw in the sponge; toss in the sponge** *tr.* to quit; to give up. (From boxing where a towel or sponge thrown into the ring indicates that a boxer has given up.) □ *I can tell when it's time to throw in the towel, and this is that time.* □ *The candidate who was exposed by the press as a former pickpocket tossed in the sponge at a tearful press conference.*

RACING

drag *tr.* to race a car against someone; to race someone in a car. □ *I'm planning to drag you at the fairgrounds next Saturday. Better be there.* □ *I don't drag anybody anymore. I lost my license.*

draggin'-wagon *n.* a fast car; a car customized for racing. □ *Your draggin'-wagon can't be driven in town, can it?* □ *My draggin'-wagon is in the shop.*

slick *n.* a racing tire. (Auto racing.) □ *That set of wheels has slicks. I wonder why.* □ *I have some slicks at home in the garage.*

RADAR

blip *n.* an intermittently appearing light on a radar screen. □ *A blip caught the controller's eye for an instant.* □ *Did you see that blip, Freddy?*

RADIO

See **AUDIO, BROADCASTING**.

RAIN

rain pitchforks *tr.* to rain very hard and heavy. □ *It rained pitchforks all day long.* □ *Every time I go out to rake leaves, it rains pitchforks.*

RARELY

once in a blue moon *mod.* rarely. □ *I do this only once in a blue moon.* □ *Once in a blue moon I have a little wine with dinner.*

READY

in the hopper *mod.* in process; in line to be processed. (A hopper is an "in basket" for incoming work.) □ *It's in the hopper. I'll get to it.* □ *Your job is in the hopper, and your turn is next.*

pumped (up) *mod.* excited; physically and mentally ready. □ *The team is really pumped up for Friday's game.* □ *She really plays well when she's pumped!*

REALITY

bring-down *n.* something that brings someone back to reality. □ *The bill for the week's stay was a real bring-down.* □ *I have had one bring-down after another today.*

for real *mod.* genuine; not imaginary. □ *Ken is really strange. Is he for real?* □ *This whole day just isn't for real.*

jungle *n.* a vicious area of confusion; the real world. □ *The place is a jungle out there. You'll grow up fast out there.* □ *Once you're out in that jungle, you'll appreciate home more.*

name of the game *n.* the way things are; the way things can be expected to be. (Always with *the*.) □ *The name of the game is money, money, money.* □ *I can't help it. That's the name of the game.*

That's show business (for you). *sent.* "That is the way that life really is." (Also with *biz* and *show biz*.) □ *And now the car won't start. That's show business for you.* □ *Too bad about the bad investment. That's show biz.*

There you go. *sent.* "That is the way things are, just like I told you."; "Isn't this just what you would expect?" □ *There you go. Isn't that just like a man!* □ *There you go, acting rude and ugly!*

REALITY - LACKING

unreal *mod.* unbelievable. □ *Your hairdo is so yummy—almost unreal.* □ *Who started this unreal argument?*

REASON - LACKING

no earthly reason *n.* no conceivable reason. □ *There is no earthly reason for your* behavior. □ *I can think of no earthly reason why the repairs should cost so much.*

track *in.* [for a person] to make sense. (Usually in the negative.) □ *She wasn't tracking. There was no sense in trying to talk to her before she came out of it.* □ *I gave up on the lecturer. He wasn't tracking.*

RECIPROCITY

Look who's talking! *exclam.* "You are just as guilty!"; "You are just as much at fault!" □ *Me a tax cheat? Look who's talking!* □ *Look who's talking. You were there before I was.*

So's your old man! *exclam.* "The same to you!"; "Drop dead!" (A catch phrase indicating basic disagreement or hostility.) □ *BILL: You're acting like an idiot! TOM: So's your old man!* □ *I don't know what you said, but so's your old man!*

two-way street *n.* a reciprocal situation. □ *This is a two-way street, you know. You will have to help me someday in return.* □ *Friendship is a two-way street.*

RECOVERY

snap out of something *in.* to recover from something. □ *I'll snap out of it in a while.* □ *It was an emotional blow, but he'll snap out of it in a while.*

REDHEAD

carrot top *n.* a person with red hair. (Also a term of address.) □ *Sam is a carrot top with the most beautiful hair I've ever seen.* □ *Hey, carrot top, where are you going?*

REDUCTION

See also DECLINE.

cut *tr.* to dilute something. □ *She always cuts her eggnog with cola. Yuck!* □ *You can cut the saltiness with a little sugar.*

put a damper on something *tr.* to reduce the intensity of something, such as a problem. □ *The death of the chief put a damper on the ceremony.* □ *I hate to put a damper on your party, but you are too loud!*

shave *tr.* to reduce or lessen something. □ *They shaved the waiting time to six months.* □ *The coach thought that the*

other team was shaving points, so he complained the next day.

REFRESHING

hit the spot AND **hit the bull's-eye** *tr.* to be refreshing. □ *This cold water really hits the spot.* □ *I want something hot—some coffee would really hit the bull's-eye.*

REFUSAL

See also NO.

back up *in.* to refuse to go through with something; to back out (of something). □ *Fred backed up at the last minute, leaving me with twenty pounds of hot dogs.* □ *Don't back up now, man. It's too late.*

nix *tr.* to put a stop to something; to say no to something; to ban something; to turn something down. □ *The boss nixed my plan.* □ *I wanted to say a certain word in my speech, but the management nixed it.*

pass 1. *in.* to decline something; to decline to participate in something. □ *No, thanks. I pass.* □ *I'll have to pass. I am not prepared.* **2.** *n.* an act of declining something. □ *I'll have to take a pass.* □ *Can I have a pass on that one? There is nothing I can do.*

take the fifth AND **five it** *tr.* to decline to answer any questions. □ *I'll take the fifth on that one. Ask Fred.* □ *Don't ask me. I am going to five it.*

would not be seen dead *phr.* would not do something under any circumstances. □ *I wouldn't be seen dead going out with Bruno!* □ *Martha would not be seen dead going into a place like that.*

REJECTION

blacklist *tr.* to put someone's name on a list of undesirables. □ *They blacklisted me for not belonging to the right organizations.* □ *Nobody else I know was blacklisted.*

chill *tr.* to reject someone. □ *The whole gang chilled him, and this really made him come home.* □ *She chilled me once too often. I won't take that from a dame.*

cold shoulder 1. *n.* a cool reception; the brushoff. □ *I didn't expect to be greeted by such a cold shoulder.* □ *I got the cold* *shoulder at the office today.* **2.** *tr.* to ignore someone; to give someone a cool reception. □ *The hostess cold-shouldered me, so I spilled my appetizers in the swimming pool.* □ *Tiffany cold-shouldered the guy who was putting the moves on Roberta.*

faced *mod.* rejected by a member of the opposite sex. (Collegiate.) □ *I've been faced again, and I hate it!* □ *Sally was faced by Todd, and she won't speak to him or anybody else.*

feel a draft *tr.* to sense that one is being rejected; to sense that someone is cool toward one, possibly for racial reasons.* □ *Oh, man, I feel a draft in here. Let's leave.* □ *What a reception! I sure feel a draft.*

shot down *mod.* rejected. □ *Tiffany is a cruel chick. I was shot down from day one.* □ *Fred's shot down, thanks to his best girl. He'll get over it.*

turn thumbs down (on someone or something) *tr.* to reject someone or something. □ *The board turned thumbs down on Rocko's application for parole.* □ *The committee examined the proposal and turned thumbs down.*

RELATIONSHIP

get with someone *in.* to find out about someone; to get to know someone. □ *I'd really like to get with her, but she's so distant.* □ *I was just beginning to get with Heidi when she left.*

RELAX

See also **CALM.**

chill *tr. & in.* to relax; to cause someone to relax. □ *Go out there and chill those people. They are getting wild!* □ *They are chilling now. For a while they were real rowdy.*

chiz *in.* to relax. (Collegiate.) □ *I gotta get back to my room and chiz a while.* □ *Chiz, guys, things are getting a little rough.*

Don't sweat it! *exclam.* "Don't worry about it!" □ *No problem. Don't sweat it!* □ *Don't sweat it! We'll take care of it.*

gel *in.* to relax and let one's hair down. □ *I've got to go home and gel for a while. Things are too stressful just now.* □ *If I don't get to gel a little every day, I tend to fall apart.*

get a load off one's feet AND **take a load off one's feet** *tr.* to sit down and relax. □ *Sit down and get a load off your feet.* □ *Take a load off your feet and have a drink.*

get naked *in.* to enjoy oneself thoroughly; to relax and enjoy oneself. □ *Let's all go out and get naked tonight.* □ *Man, I feel like getting naked tonight.*

grooving *mod.* enjoying; being *cool* and laid back. □ *Look at those guys grooving in front of the television set.* □ *They were just sitting there grooving.*

hang loose AND **stay loose** *in.* to relax and stay *cool.* □ *Just hang loose, man. Everything'll be all right.* □ *Stay loose, chum. See ya later.*

hold one's horses *tr.* to wait up; to relax and slow down; to be patient. (Usually a command.) □ *Hold your horses! Don't get in a hurry.* □ *Now, just hold your horses and let me explain.*

kick back *in.* to relax (and enjoy something). □ *Now you just kick back and enjoy this.* □ *I like to kick back and listen to a few tunes.*

lah-di-dah *mod.* casual; relaxed and uncaring. □ *He is so lah-di-dah with financial matters.* □ *She's not all that calm about her possessions, but she is very lah-di-dah with men.*

let it all hang out *tr.* to be yourself, assuming that you generally are not. □ *Come on. Relax! Let it all hang out.* □ *I let it all hang out, but I still feel rotten.*

maxin' *in.* relaxing. □ *I spent Saturday just maxin' around the house and doing some tunage.* □ *I spent all day maxin' and drinking beer.*

mellow *mod.* relaxed; untroubled; *laid back.* □ *Being mellow is my only goal in life.* □ *She is the mellowest fox I know.*

mellow out *in.* to become generally more relaxed; to grow less contentious. □ *Gary was nearly forty before he started to mellow out a little and take life less se-*

riously. □ *After his illness, he mellowed out and seemed more glad to be alive.*

R & R *n.* "rest and recuperation"; "rest and relaxation." (Originally military.) □ *I could use about three years of R & R after that battle.* □ *I'll need a lot of R & R to recover from that stuff they fed us.*

Skip it! *exclam.* "Forget it!"; "Never mind!" □ *I won't bother you with my question again. Skip it!* □ *Oh, skip it! It doesn't matter.*

spaz down *in.* to relax. □ *Spaz down, man! Chill out!* □ *We tried to get the crowd to spaz down, but they were very excited.*

take a break *tr.* to stop working for a rest period. □ *Let's take a break here. Be back in five minutes.* □ *I've got to take a break before I drop.*

take five *tr.* to take a five-minute break. □ *Okay, gang, take five. Be back here in five minutes, or else.* □ *She told them to take five, but they turned the five into fifty.*

take it easy *phr.* "relax and take care." □ *See you later. Take it easy.* □ *They told me to take it easy for a few days.*

take things easy *tr.* to relax temporarily and recuperate. □ *The doctor says I'm supposed to take things easy for a while.* □ *I want you to take it easy until the stitches heal.*

unlax *in.* to unwind and relax. □ *I just can't wait to get home and unlax.* □ *Unlax, man. Take it easy.*

veg (out) *in.* to cease working and take it easy; to vegetate. □ *Someday, I just want to veg out and enjoy life.* □ *I think I'll just veg this weekend.*

RELEASE

spring someone *tr.* to get someone out of jail on bond or permanently. □ *My wife came down and sprung me; otherwise, I'd still be in the slammer.* □ *The guy's mouthpiece tried to spring him, but the DA nixed it.*

walk *in.* to get out of prison; to get off from a criminal charge. (Underworld.) □ *They thought they had Bruno on a vice*

rap, but he walked. □ *I showed them my license; then I walked.*

RELIGION

holy Joe 1. *n.* a chaplain; a cleric; a clergyman. □ *I went to see the holy Joe, and he was a lot of help.* □ *Old holy Joe wants to see all of us at services.* **2.** *n.* a very pious person. □ *Martin looks stuffy, but he's no holy Joe.* □ *Don't let that holy Joe hear about what you've done.*

padre *n.* any male religious cleric: priest, monk, or chaplin. (From Spanish. Typically military. Also a term of address.) □ *I went to see the padre for some advice.* □ *Hey, padre, anything new on the religion front?*

sky-pilot *n.* a chaplain. □ *The sky-pilot says we can park in the church's lot, if we don't mess anything up or make too much noise.* □ *The sky-pilot's a good guy.*

REMAIN

stick around *in.* to remain nearby. □ *Stick around. Things are bound to get better.* □ *I think if you'll stick around, you'll get a seat sooner or later.*

REMIND

prod 1. *n.* a reminder. □ *She gave me a little prod about the report that is due Monday.* □ *Call me up and give me a little prod so I won't forget.* **2.** *tr.* to remind someone (about something). □ *Call me up and prod me just before the due date.* □ *Stop prodding me about these minor matters.*

REMOVAL

lift *tr.* to take something away. □ *It was his third offense, so they lifted his license.* □ *They lifted the rule about not having two different jobs.*

take the heat off someone *tr.* to relieve the pressure on someone; to free someone from suspicion, responsibility, a deadline, etc. □ *The confession by Rocko took the heat off the cop-shop for a while.* □ *They took the heat off us by moving the deadline.*

REPELLENT

turn-off *n.* something that repels someone. □ *The movie was a turn-off. I couldn't stand it.* □ *What a turn-off!*

REPETITION

if I've told you once, I've told you a thousand times *phr.* "I know I have told you many, many times." □ *If I've told you once, I've told you a thousand times, don't lean back in that chair.* □ *If I've told you once, I've told you a thousand times, wipe your feet!*

Run that by (me) again. AND **Run that by (me) one more time.** *sent.* "Please tell it to me again." □ *I can't believe my own ears. Can you run that by again, please?* □ *It's noisy in here. Please run that by me one more time.*

REPORTER

hack *n.* a reporter. □ *She was a hack for the newspaper for a while.* □ *Newspaper hacks have to know a little of everything.*

ink slinger *n.* a professional writer; a newspaper reporter. □ *The ink slingers have been at the candidates again.* □ *The problem is that there are too many ink slingers around.*

newshound *n.* a newspaper reporter who pursues a story with the same diligence used by a bloodhound. □ *If the newshounds get hold of this story, we'll never have any peace.* □ *Tell that newshound that I'll sue her if she prints that!*

talking head *n.* a television news reader or announcer whose head and neck appear on the screen. □ *I've had it with talking heads. I can read the paper and learn as much in twenty minutes.* □ *Some of those talking heads make millions a year.*

REPUTATION

black eye *n.* a moral blemish; an injury to the prestige of someone or something. □ *The library has gotten a black eye from this incident.* □ *That kind of behavior can give us all a black eye.*

cracked up to be *mod.* supposed to be. □ *This pizza isn't what it's cracked up to be.* □ *I wanted to find out whether this stuff was what it is cracked up to be.*

rep *n.* someone's reputation. □ *I hope this doesn't ruin my rep.* □ *I've got my own rep to think about.*

REQUEST

Don't ask. *sent.* "The answer is so depressing, you don't even want to hear it." □ *How am I? Don't ask.* □ *This has been a horrible day. How horrible, you say? Don't ask.*

hit someone (up) for something *tr.* to ask someone for something. □ *I hit Fred up for some help with the committee.* □ *He hit me up for a loan, but I said no.*

mooch *tr. & in.* to beg for money, liquor, or drugs in public places. □ *No mooching around here! Move along!* □ *Jed mooched drinks all evening.*

put the bite on someone *tr.* to try to get money out of someone. □ *You're always putting the bite on me for a few bucks. Go away.* □ *Don't put the bite on me. I'm broker than you are.*

tall order *n.* a request that is difficult to fulfill. □ *That's a tall order. Do you think anyone can do it?* □ *Well, it's a tall order, but I'll do it.*

touch 1. *n.* a request for money (from a beggar); a request for a loan. □ *I ignored the touch and walked on by.* □ *Here comes Fred, and he looks like he wants to make a touch.* **2.** *tr.* to ask someone for a loan. □ *He touched me for $100.* □ *The wino touched Martin for a fiver.*

RESCUE

saved by the bell *mod.* saved by the timely intervention of someone or something. □ *I was going to have to do my part, but someone knocked on the door and I didn't have to do it. I was saved by the bell.* □ *I wish I had been saved by the bell.*

RESENTMENT

front off about something *in.* to be brash and resentful about something. □ *Todd was fronting off about his assignment and got a detention for it.* □ *You will wish you hadn't fronted off about your supervisor.*

RESERVE

dibs on something *phr.* a claim on something. □ *I've got dibs on the yellow one!* □ *Dibs on the front seat!*

on ice *mod.* in reserve. □ *That's a great idea, but we'll have to put it on ice until we can afford to put it into action.* □ *I have two boyfriends. One I see every weekend, and the other I keep on ice for a rainy day.*

RESIDENT

coaster *n.* someone who lives near the ocean. (California.) □ *Tiffany is a coaster now, but she was born, like, somewhere else.* □ *The coasters just don't want to be beige, that's all.*

townie *n.* a permanent (nonstudent) resident of a college town. □ *The townies get upset when we make a lot of noise on Sundays.* □ *A couple of townies won the bicycle race.*

RESISTANCE

buck *tr.* to resist something. □ *Don't buck it. Do what you are told.* □ *He enjoys bucking the system.*

RESPECT

get face *tr.* to gain respect; to increase one's status. (The opposite of *lose face.*) □ *He's doing his best in life to get face.* □ *Let's do something to help her get face.*

RESPONSE

comeback *n.* a retort; back talk. □ *Hank is pretty fast with the comeback.* □ *One more snotty comeback like that and you're finished.*

Do tell. *sent.* "Is that so?" (A disinterested way of holding up one end of a conversation.) □ *So, you're a dentist. Do tell.* □ *Do tell. I've never heard that before. Nice talking to you.*

gut reaction (to something) *n.* a basic and immediate response to something. □ *Well, my gut reaction is quite negative.* □ *Her gut reaction to the plan is basically a good one.*

I'll bite. *sent.* "You want me to ask what or why, so, what or why?" □ *Okay, I'll bite. What's the answer?* □ *I'll bite. Why did the chicken cross the road?*

loaded remark *n.* a remark containing important implications. □ *Your loaded remark did not go over well with the host.* □ *In spite of your numerous loaded remarks, I do hope you will return sometime when it is convenient.*

nibble 1. *n.* a cautious or preliminary response to something. □ *My advertisement got three nibbles this morning.* □ *We will see if anyone else gives it a nibble.* **2.** *in.* to reply cautiously or tentatively to something. □ *Someone nibbled at your want ad.* □ *I hope someone who wants to buy my car nibbles at the description I posted on the bulletin board.*

Says me! AND **Sez me!** *exclam.* a formulaic answer to *Says who?* □ Tom: *Says who?* Fred: *Says me, that's who!* □ Tom: *You?* Fred: *You got it, buster. Sez me!*

RESPONSIBILITY

pass the buck *tr.* to shift the responsibility for something to someone else; to evade responsibility. □ *When things get a little tough, do what I do. Pass the buck.* □ *Don't pass the buck. Stand up and admit you were wrong.*

short end of the stick *n.* the burden, responsibility, blame, etc., for something. (Always with *the.*) □ *Here I am stuck with the short end of the stick again.* □ *I am the one who plans all this stuff, and when you jerks drop the ball, I'm left holding the short end of the stick.*

take someone or something on *tr.* to accept the task of handling a difficult person or thing. □ *I'll take it on if nobody else will do it.* □ *Nobody wanted to take on Mrs. Franklin, but it had to be done.*

RESPONSIBILITY - LACKING

flaky *mod.* unreliable. □ *She's too flaky to hold the job.* □ *He's a flaky dude.* □ *I'm getting so flaky. Must be old age.*

RESPONSIBLE

on someone's watch *mod.* while someone is on duty. □ *I am not responsible since it didn't happen on my watch.* □ *I guess I have to bear the blame since it happened on my watch.*

RESTAURANT

beanery *n.* a cheap eating establishment. (Where baked beans are served.) □ *I stopped in for a cup of brew at a little all-night beanery on Thirty-fourth.* □ *I'm tired of eating in beaneries.*

deuce *n.* a table for two. □ *Give the next couple the deuce over in the corner.* □ *You can't put three people at a deuce!*

doggy bag *n.* a bag—supplied by a restaurant—in which uneaten food can be carried home. □ *Do you have a doggy bag for my mousse?* □ *We do not have doggy bags, but we do supply foil.*

greasy spoon *n.* an untidy and unappetizing diner or restaurant. □ *Let's eat at the greasy spoon over on Maple. The food is gross, but the people-watching is good.* □ *I wouldn't be caught dead in a greasy spoon like that.*

hash-house *n.* a cheap diner. □ *Tom worked for two days as a hash-slinger in a hash-house.* □ *You see a lot of interesting people go in and out of a hash-house like this one.*

hash-slinger *n.* a cook, waiter, or waitress in a *hash-house.* □ *I worked as a hash-slinger in an all-night diner.* □ *The life of a hash-slinger is pretty tough.*

ho-jo('s) *n.* a Howard Johnson's restaurant or hotel. (Collegiate. Often with *the.*) □ *Let's hit ho-jo's for some grub.* □ *We're going to meet the others at the ho-jo.*

McD's AND **McDuck's** *n.* McDonald's, the franchised fast-food restaurant. (Teens and collegiate. The *duck* is a play on the Walt Disney character "Donald Duck.") □ *Can you take McD's tonight, or do you want some slow food?* □ *I can always handle McDuck's.*

Mickey D's *n.* McDonald's fast-food restaurant. (Teens and collegiate.) □ *Let's hit Mickey D's for chow this noon.* □ *We're going to Mickey D's for dinner, too.*

ptomaine-domain AND **ptomaine-palace** *n.* any institutional dining facility; a mess hall; a cafeteria. □ *I can't stand the food at the ptomaine-domain.*

□ *Time to go over to the ptomaine-palace and eat—if you can call it that.*

RESULTS

backlash *n.* the negative response to something. □ *Was there any backlash aimed at your suggestion?* □ *We weren't prepared for the backlash we got.*

bottom line *n.* the result; the *nitty-gritty;* the *score.* □ *The bottom line is that you really don't care.* □ *Well, when you get down to the bottom line, it's only money that matters.*

fallout *n.* the results of something; the *flack* from something. □ *The fallout from this afternoon's meeting was not as serious as some expected.* □ *It's not the crisis itself, but the fallout from the crisis that concerns us all.*

haul *n.* the proceeds from any activity: a performance, a fishing trip, a collection of goods or money for charity, etc. □ *They got a good haul from the benefit.* □ *They surveyed the haul of cans and packages and decided they had done a pretty fair job.*

hit *n.* a successful result; something that is exactly as intended. □ *It was a hit—a real winner.* □ *Your idea was right on target—a hit for sure.*

net result *n.* the final result after all the assets and liabilities have balanced out. □ *The net result was that I was fired.* □ *I don't care about the little things. What is the net result?*

score *n.* a summary; a conclusion; the sum total. □ *The score is that you are in trouble with the Internal Revenue Service.* □ *Okay, waiter, what's the score?*

score *n.* the result of a scoring: drugs, loot, winnings, etc. □ *Where's the score? How much did you get?* □ *The crooks dropped the score as they made their getaway.*

There will be hell to pay. *sent.* "Things will be so bad that one will have to bribe the devil to straighten them out." (Use caution with *hell.*) □ *If I don't get this done on time, there will be hell to pay.* □ *There'll be hell to pay if we miss the plane.*

There you are. *sent.* "This is the result."; "This is the way things turned out." □ *There you are. Didn't I warn you?* □ *Well, there you are. Another first-class mess.*

upshot (of something) *n.* the result of something; the outcome of something. (Always with *the.*) □ *The upshot of it all was that we don't get the new coffeepot.* □ *And the upshot was a new manager and raises for everyone.*

when push comes to shove AND **if push comes to shove** *phr.* "when things get a little pressed"; "when the situation gets more active or intense." □ *When push comes to shove, you know I'll be on your side.* □ *If push comes to shove, the front office can help with some statistics.*

worst-case scenario *n.* the worse possible future outcome. □ *Now, let's look at the worst-case scenario.* □ *In the worst-case scenario, we're all dead.*

You asked for it! *exclam.* "Here it comes, and you deserve it!" □ *So you want the full treatment? You asked for it!* □ *So, you wanted to hear both sides of the record? You asked for it!*

REVEAL

blab *tr.* to tell a secret; to reveal something private in public. □ *I'll tell you if you promise not to blab it.* □ *Tiffany blabbed the whole thing.*

blabbermouth *tr.* to tell secrets in public. □ *Don't blabbermouth this to everybody.* □ *Somebody blabbermouthed the story all over town.*

blow someone's cover *tr.* to reveal someone's true identity; to ruin someone's scheme for concealment. □ *The dog recognized me and blew my cover.* □ *I didn't mean to blow your cover.*

blow something wide open AND **bust something wide open** *tr.* to expose corrupt practices or a scheme; to put an end to corruption. □ *The press is trying to blow the town wide open, and the feebies are trying to hush them up so they can move about in secret.* □ *I'm going to bust this racket wide open.*

blow the lid off something *tr.* to expose a scandal or corrupt practice; to expose

political dishonesty. □ *I'm going to blow the lid off another phony candidate.* □ *The reporter blew the lid off the latest city hall scandal.*

come out in the wash *in.* to be dealt with in the normal chain of events. (As if someone were counselling someone who had caused a clothing stain.) □ *All of these things will come out in the wash.* □ *Whatever it is, it'll come out in the wash. Don't worry.*

get the goods on someone *tr.* to uncover incriminating evidence against someone. □ *The fuzz has gotten the goods on Mr. Big.* □ *The IRS tried to get the goods on Rocko, but Rocko knows all the angles.*

giveaway *n.* something that reveals a fact that was meant to be concealed. (Often with *dead.*) □ *The way he was walking was a giveaway to the fact that he was the one who was injured.* □ *The look on her face was a dead giveaway.*

go public *in.* to reveal something to the public. (Especially with *with,* as in the examples.) □ *It's too early to go public with the story.* □ *Just let me know when we can go public with this.*

have a big mouth *tr.* to speak loudly; to tell secrets. (*Have got* can replace *have.*) □ *Boy, do you have a big mouth!* □ *He has a big mouth. Don't tell him anything you don't want everybody else to know.*

open (up) one's kimono *phr.* to reveal what one is planning. (From the computer industry, referring especially to the involvement of the Japanese in this field.) □ *Sam isn't one to open his kimono much when it comes to new products.* □ *Even if Tom appears to open up his kimono on this deal, don't put much stock in what he says.*

shoot one's mouth off *tr.* to brag; to tell secrets. □ *Stop shooting your mouth off. Nobody believes you anymore.* □ *So you had to go and shoot off your mouth about the bankruptcy proceedings!*

sound off (about something) *in.* to announce something. □ *Why did you have to go and sound off about the surprise* *party?* □ *Keep it a secret. Don't sound off about it.*

spill *in.* to confess. (Underworld.) □ *The cops tried to get her to spill, but she just sat there.* □ *The gang was afraid she would spill, but she's a tough old thing.*

spill one's guts *tr.* to tell all; to confess. □ *I had to spill my guts about the broken window. I didn't want you to take the blame.* □ *Mary spilled her guts about the window. She confessed that she was trying to shield Bob.*

spill the beans AND **spill the works** *tr.* to give away a secret or a surprise. □ *There is a surprise party for Heidi on Wednesday. Please don't spill the beans.* □ *Paul spilled the beans about Heidi's party.*

take something public *tr.* to make something known to the public. □ *You gotta take it public—put it on the street—even when it's none of your business.* □ *Don't take it public. You'll just get talked about.*

tell the (whole) world *tr.* to spread around private business. □ *Well, you don't have to tell the whole world.* □ *Go ahead, tell the world!*

tip one's hand *tr.* to reveal what one is going to do; to reveal one's secrets. (From card playing.) □ *I didn't tip my hand at all. I left them guessing.* □ *They tried to get me to tip my hand.*

REVERSAL

comeback *n.* a return to a former state. □ *The aging singer tried to sober up and make a comeback.* □ *Her comeback was not a financial success, but it improved her spirits.*

flip-flop *n.* a reversal. □ *The President denied making a flip-flop. He said he simply forgot his earlier position.* □ *The manager did a flip-flop on the personnel policy.*

switcheroo *n.* a reversal; a switching around. □ *He pulled a switcheroo on us and showed up at the other door, so we missed getting his autograph.* □ *She is a master at the old switcheroo.*

turn around AND **turn over** *in.* [for something] to undergo a major, dynamic change. □ *Things turned around*

for Willard and went okay for a while. □ *When life turned over and things went more smoothly, Frank was happier.*

REWARD

for (all) one's trouble *phr.* in spite of one's efforts; in very poor payment for one's efforts. □ *He got a punch in the jaw for all his trouble.* □ *For her trouble, she got only honorable mention.*

plum *n.* a prize or reward; something that can be considered the spoils of a political office. □ *That appointment was quite a plum.* □ *My plum for getting elected was a big new office.*

RIDDANCE

palm someone or something off (on someone) *tr.* to transfer some unwanted person or thing to another person. □ *Don't palm her off on me. I don't want her.* □ *My uncle palmed off his old clothes on me.*

RIDICULE

poo(h)-poo(h) *tr.* to belittle someone or something. □ *He tends to pooh-pooh things he doesn't understand.* □ *Don't always poo-poo me when I express my opinions!*

RISK

See **DANGER**.

ROCKETS

shot *n.* a rocket launching. □ *The shot was canceled because of the weather.* □ *This shot, like the last, was a total failure.*

ROMANCE

See also **AFFAIR, DATING, FLIRTATION, LOVER, SEDUCTION**.

bird-dog *tr.* to take away another man's girlfriend. □ *Why'd you have to go and bird-dog me, your best buddy?* □ *I didn't bird-dog you. I'm just more loveable, that's all.*

bush patrol 1. *n.* a session of necking and petting. (Here *patrol* has the military meaning of assignment.) □ *Tom is out on bush patrol tonight. I don't know who with.* □ *Martha and Paul spent the evening on bush patrol.* **2.** *n.* an imaginary search through campus shrubbery to flush out the necking couples. □ *The* *dean of women put on her housecoat and went out on bush patrol.* □ *Bush patrol starts at midnight, so be in by then.*

crash and burn *in.* [for a young man] to fail brilliantly with a romance. (Collegiate.) □ *I knew I would crash and burn with her.* □ *It stands to reason that if Ken hadn't shot me down, I wouldn't have crashed and burned.*

cruise *tr.* to pursue a member of the opposite sex. □ *Tom was cruising Tiffany, but she got rid of him.* □ *Are you cruising me, Tom? You know you just barf me, like, out!*

dialog *tr.* to attempt to seduce someone. □ *Just let me dialog her for a while; then you'll see some action.* □ *Ron was dialoging this dame when her brother came in.*

get something going (with someone) *tr.* to start a romance with someone. □ *Heidi wants to get something going with Pete.* □ *Mary and Sam got something going.*

hot item *n.* a romantically serious couple. □ *Sam and Mary are quite a hot item lately.* □ *A hot item like Bill and Clare isn't likely to show up for the party.*

lay some sweet lines on someone AND **put some sweet lines on someone** *tr.* to speak kindly to someone; to *soft soap* someone. □ *I just laid some sweet lines on her, and she let me use her car.* □ *If you put some sweet lines on him, maybe he won't ground you.*

love bombs *n.* affirmations of affection. □ *These two were dropping love bombs on each other, even though they hate each other's guts.* □ *What a phony bunch of kooks. They were throwing love bombs all over the place!*

main squeeze *n.* one's steady girlfriend or boyfriend. □ *My main squeeze is coming over to talk tonight.* □ *She plans to marry her main squeeze.*

puppy love *n.* mild infatuation; infatuation as in a crush. □ *Is it really love or just puppy love?* □ *Look at them together. It may be puppy love, but it looks wonderful.*

sealed with a kiss AND **SWAK** *mod.* written and sent with love and care. (The initialism is sometimes written on love letters. Also an acronym.) □ *All her letters come SWAK.* □ *I know they are sealed with a kiss, because she says so.*

serious about someone *mod.* in love, or almost in love, with someone. □ *I'm afraid I'm getting serious about Bill.* □ *Bill, unfortunately, is pretty serious about Mary.*

soft on someone *mod.* romantically attracted to someone. □ *Fred is soft on Martha, I've heard.* □ *He looked like he was getting a little soft on Sally.*

strung out AND **strung (up)** *mod.* in love and disoriented. □ *Mary is strung out, and all because of Sam.* □ *Sam is strung out over Mary.*

sweet nothings *n.* loving comments; pleasant remarks between lovers. □ *They are out on the porch swing whispering sweet nothings in each other's ears.* □ *Thank heavens most married people never remember the sweet nothings they were once told.*

that way *mod.* in love. □ *Sam and Martha are that way. They look so happy.* □ *Well, Martha's that way, but Sam's just out for a good time.*

ROUTE

beat *n.* the area that a worker, a police officer, reporter, etc., is assigned to cover. □ *That's not on my beat. You'll have to talk to someone else.* □ *Your store is on my beat, and I want to make sure everything is okay.*

RUDE

See also **OBSCENE, VULGAR.**

base *mod.* rude; *gross.* (California.) □ *You are so, like, base!* □ *What a base creep!*

RUDENESS

catty *mod.* spiteful; snotty. □ *You know how catty Mary is—almost as catty as Gloria—well, she told me something about you that really shocked me.* □ *How can anybody be so catty?*

drop-dead *mod.* rude, as if telling someone to drop dead. □ *I couldn't stand the boss's drop-dead attitude, so I quit.* □ *She looked at me with that kind of drop-dead look that really made me mad.*

mouth off *in.* to speak out of turn. □ *Don't just mouth off. Wait your turn.* □ *Hold up your hand. I won't deal with people who mouth off.*

raunchy AND **raunchie; ronchie** *mod.* untidy; unclean; crude; tasteless. □ *Get your ronchie socks out of the living room.* □ *We decided to leave the raunchy movie about halfway through.*

RUINATION

banjaxed *mod.* demolished; ruined. □ *My car is totally banjaxed. What a mess!* □ *Everything I worked for is now banjaxed.*

beat *mod.* down and out; ruined. □ *This thing is beat. I don't want it.* □ *Who wants a beat hat?*

bitch *tr.* to ruin something. □ *You really bitched this coil of wire.* □ *Here's a clean one. Don't bitch it.*

bitch something up *tr.* to ruin something; to mess something up. (Potentially offensive. Use only with discretion.) □ *You really bitched my day up!* □ *How can one person bitch up something this easy?*

blooey *mod.* gone; destroyed. □ *Everything is finished, blooey!* □ *All my plans are blooey!*

blow *tr.* to ruin something; to ruin an opportunity. □ *You really blew it!* □ *It was my last chance, and I blew it.*

blow someone or something out of the water *tr.* to utterly destroy someone or something. (As a ship is blown up by a torpedo.) □ *This is too much. I'm gonna blow that guy out of the water.* □ *I plan to blow their plans out of the water.*

blow-up *n.* the ruination of something; the collapse of something. (Usually **blowup**.) □ *The blow-up in the financial world has ruined my chances for early retirement.* □ *After the blowup, they called one another to compare notes.*

bust something up *tr.* to ruin something; to break something up. □ *She tried to bust my marriage up!* □ *I hate to bust up the party, but we gotta go.*

chain(saw) *tr.* to destroy something; to cut something up severely. □ *The senatorial committee tried to chainsaw the nominee, but the full senate voted for confirmation.* □ *We didn't think they'd come in and chain all our plans.*

do a job on someone or something *tr.* to ruin someone or something; to give someone or something a thorough working over. □ *The cops did a job on Rocko, but he still wouldn't talk.* □ *There's no need to do a job on me, man, I'll tell you everything I know—which is zip.* □ *That punch sure did a job on my nose.*

fouled up *mod.* messed up; ruined; tangled up. □ *This is sure a fouled up mess.* □ *You sure are fouled up, you know.*

fragged *mod.* destroyed; ruined. □ *Why does your room look so fragged?* □ *My clothes are fragged, and I need a haircut.*

go down the tube(s) AND **go down the chute** *in.* to fail totally; to be ruined. □ *The whole project is likely to go down the tubes.* □ *All my plans just went down the chute.*

go sour *in.* to turn bad or unpleasant. □ *It looks like all my plans are going sour.* □ *My whole life is going sour right now.*

meltdown *n.* a total collapse of anything. (From the term used to describe the self-destruction of a nuclear reactor.) □ *There seems to have been a meltdown in the computer center, and all our records were lost.* □ *The meltdown in the securities markets was caused by a combination of things.*

muck something up *tr.* to mess something up; to ruin something. □ *Try not to muck it up this time.* □ *You seem to have mucked up this one, too.*

mung *tr.* to ruin something. □ *You munged my car!* □ *Look at it! You munged it!*

mung something up *tr.* to mess something up. □ *Don't mung it up this time.*

□ *The team munged up the play, and the coach blasted them but good.*

nuke *tr.* to destroy someone or something. (As with a nuclear weapon.) □ *Your cat ran through my garden and totally nuked my flowers!* □ *I'm going to nuke that cat the next time I see it.*

old one-two *n.* any destructive assault on an idea, thing, or person. □ *By the time the committee had given the plan the old one-two, there was nothing left I could do.* □ *I gave his proposal the old one-two. Next time he will be better prepared.*

on the rocks *mod.* in a state of ruin or bankruptcy. (Like a ship that has gone aground on the rocks and cannot be moved.) □ *That bank is on the rocks. Don't put your money in it.* □ *My finances are on the rocks just now.*

queer *tr.* to spoil something. □ *Please don't queer the deal.* □ *I was afraid his dirty look would queer his chances.*

rack up something *tr.* to wreck something. □ *Fred racked up his new car.* □ *He racked up his arm in the football game.*

rambo(ize) *tr.* to (figuratively) annihilate someone or something; to harm someone or something. (Collegiate. From the powerful film character "Rambo.") □ *The students ramboed the cafeteria, and the cops were called.* □ *Please don't rambo the other team. Just win the game.*

screwed up *mod.* ruined; messed up. □ *This is a really screwed up schedule. Let's start over again.* □ *Your schedule is completely screwed up.*

shoot someone or something down *tr.* to ruin someone or something; to debunk someone or something. □ *Just as I was making the final point, she shot me down with a simple fact I should have remembered.* □ *The boss shot down my plan immediately.*

shot down *mod.* demolished; destroyed. □ *Her idea was shot down after all her work.* □ *I felt shot down, even though I was sure of what I was getting into.*

shot to hell *mod.* ruined; decimated. □ *This thing is shot to hell. Let's get a new one.* □ *My car is shot to hell.*

take something out *tr.* to bomb or destroy something. □ *The enemy took out one of the tanks, but not the one carrying the medicine.* □ *The last flight took out two enemy bunkers and a radar installation.*

tapped AND **tapped out** *mod.* ruined. □ *We are tapped. That really did it to us.* □ *The project is completely tapped out.*

to hell and gone *mod.* gone; ruined. (Use caution with *hell*.) □ *Fred was to hell and gone before anybody figured out what he had done.* □ *The whole plan is to hell and gone. Nothing can be salvaged.*

totaled *mod.* wrecked; damaged beyond repair. (From *totally wrecked*.) □ *The car was totaled. There was nothing that could be saved.* □ *There's a place in the city that will buy totaled cars.*

wipe someone out *tr.* to ruin someone financially. □ *The loss of my job wiped us out.* □ *The storm ruined the corn crop and wiped out everyone in the county.*

RULES

do's and don'ts *n.* the rules; the things that should be done and those that should not be done. □ *I must admit that a lot of the do's and don'ts don't make much sense to me either.* □ *Better learn the do's and don'ts immediately.*

get with the program *in.* to follow the rules; to do what you are supposed to do. □ *Come on, Mark. Get with the program. Do what you are told.* □ *Jane just can't seem to get with the program. She has to do everything her way, right or wrong.*

regs *n.* regulations. □ *Follow the regs or pay the penalty.* □ *There is a list of regs posted on the back of your door.*

RURAL

boondocks AND **boonies** *n.* an isolated area; an area of wild terrain; suburbs distant from a city. (From the word for mountain in the Tagalog language. Since World War II.) □ *The weather out in the* *boonies looks cold and dry.* □ *I don't want to be stuck out in the boondocks!*

cornfed *mod.* rural; backwards; unsophisticated. □ *I enjoy her honest, cornfed humor.* □ *Jed is a homey, cornfed kind of guy. Don't know anybody who bears him any ill will.*

corny *mod.* having to do with simpleminded, overdrawn humor. □ *This corny dialog has to be revised before I'll act in this play.* □ *Don't be corny. This is serious.*

jerkwater *mod.* backwoodsy; insignificant. □ *I'm from a little jerkwater town in the Midwest.* □ *He's sort of the jerkwater type.*

local yokel *n.* a local resident of a rural place. (Mildly derogatory.) □ *One of the local yokels helped me change the tire.* □ *The local yokels all listen to the same radio station.*

Podunk *mod.* rural and backward. (Usually **podunk**.) □ *I want out of this Podunk town.* □ *This podunk place is driving me crazy.*

SADNESS
See **DEPRESSION**.

SAFETY
on the safe side *mod.* taking the risk-free path. □ *Let's be on the safe side and call first.* □ *I think you should stay on the safe side and call the doctor about this fever.*

SAILOR
anchor-clanker *n.* a sailor. (Army.) □ *The bar was suddenly filled with anchor-clankers, and the army guys began looking for a way out.* □ *How can you anchor-clankers stand being cooped up on those cans?*

salt *n.* a sailor. (Especially with *old*.) □ *A couple of salts came ashore and asked if they could buy some beer.* □ *I've sailed a little, but you could hardly call me an old salt.*

SALARY
See **EARN**.

SAMENESS
(dead) ringer (for someone) *n.* someone who is an exact duplicate of someone else. □ *You are sure a dead ringer for my brother.* □ *Isn't he a ringer for Chuck?*

same difference *n.* the same; no difference at all. □ *Pink, fuchsia, what does it matter? Same difference.* □ *Whether you go or I go, it's the same difference.*

same old story *n.* an often repeated story or situation. □ *It's the same old story. Boy meets girl, girl gets consumption, girl dies.* □ *One after one they came in. It's the same old story with each of them, "Not enough time to do my homework."*

same o(l)' same o(l)' *n.* the same old thing. □ *I'm getting tired of the same ol' same ol'.* □ *Why not something different? Do you like the same o' same o'?*

This is where I came in. *sent.* "This all seems very familiar." □ *Okay, that's enough. This is where I came in.* □ *This is where I came in. It's the same thing all over again.*

SAMPLE
demo *n.* an automobile or other machine or device that has been used by a dealer for demonstration purposes. □ *I can give you a demo for half price.* □ *Do you have any demos?*

SANITY
have all one's marbles *tr.* to have all one's mental faculties; to be mentally sound. □ *I don't think he has all his marbles.* □ *Do you think Bob has all his marbles?*

SARCASM
What else is new? *interrog.* "But isn't that what you expect?"; "What you said isn't new, so what is new?" □ *Yes, there is trouble around the world. What else is new?* □ *So, there's not enough money this week. What else is new?*

SATAN
deuce *n.* the devil. (Always with *the*.) □ *I'll knock the deuce out of you if you come around here again.* □ *Get the deuce out of here!*

dickens *n.* the devil. (Always with *the*.) □ *She was going to kick the dickens out of me.* □ *I felt as bad as the dickens, but what could I do?*

SATISFACTORY
See also **APPROVAL, YES**.

all right *mod.* okay. (This is hyphenated before a nominal. Slang when used before a nominal.) □ *Wally is an all-right guy.* □ *I'm all right.* □ *We had an all-right time at your party.*

cas *mod.* okay; fine. (Pronounced "KAZH." From *casual.*) □ *That's cas, man. Good to hear it.* □ *I agree. Cas. Totally cool.*

cricket *mod.* acceptable. □ *Is it really cricket to play under two different names?* □ *Who cares if it's cricket!*

down *mod.* okay; satisfactory; *cool;* in agreement. (The grammar error in the second example is part of the typical context.) □ *We had a fight, but we're down now.* □ *Me and him is down and always will be.* □ *This guy is really down.*

high-res AND **hi-res** *mod.* good; satisfying. (From *high-resolution,* referring to the picture quality of a computer monitor.) □ *This is a real high-res day for me.* □ *I sure feel hi-res today.*

hunky-dory *mod.* fine; okay. □ *As a matter of fact, everything is just hunky-dory.* □ *That is a hunky-dory idea all right.*

jake *mod.* okay; satisfactory. □ *All right? Then everything is jake.* □ *If you get here by nine o'clock, it'll be just jake.*

kosher 1. AND **koshe** *mod.* acceptable; orthodox. (From Hebrew *kasher,* "proper," via Yiddish.) □ *Is it kosher to do this?* □ *It's a kosher thing, okay.* □ *Her party was koshe. Everyone loved it.* □ *Of course, it's kosher. Everybody does it.* **2.** *tr.* to make something acceptable. □ *Do you want me to kosher it with the boss for you?* □ *Look, if you can kosher this stuff with my parents, I agree.*

Living large. *phr.* "Doing okay." (The response to *How ya living?*) □ *I'm living large. How you doing?* □ *Living large. So, how's it with you?*

no big deal AND **no biggie** *n.* (something) not difficult or troublesome. □ *Don't worry. It's no big deal.* □ *No problem. It's no biggie.*

no stress *interj.* "no problem"; "no bother." □ *Don't worry, man, no stress.*

□ *Relax. No stress. It doesn't bother me at all.*

no sweat *interj.* "no problem"; "Don't worry; it is no problem." □ *It's no big deal. No sweat.* □ *No sweat, don't fret about it.*

Not to worry. *phr.* "Don't worry." □ *You lost your ticket? Not to worry. I'll give you mine.* □ *Not to worry. Everything will be all right.*

oak(s) *mod.* "OK"; satisfactory; worthy. (Prisons.) □ *That guy's oaks.* □ *This stuff is oak.*

OK AND **okay 1.** *mod.* acceptable. □ *Fred is an OK guy.* □ *This cake is okay, but not what I would call first rate.* **2.** *mod.* acceptably. □ *She ran okay—nothing spectacular.* □ *They usually do it okay.* **3.** *n.* (someone's) acceptance. □ *I won't give the final okay until I see the plans.* □ *We got her OK and went on with the job.*

up to scratch AND **up to snuff** *mod.* satisfactory; up to what is expected. □ *This just isn't up to scratch. You'll have to do it again.* □ *The food was up to snuff, but the hotel staff was not at its usually efficient best.*

SAVINGS

squirrel something away *tr.* to hide something in reserve. □ *Here is some food. I squirreled it away in my suitcase.* □ *She had squirreled away quite a fortune.*

stash *tr.* to hide something (somewhere). □ *Stash this under the chair until I can think of a place to put it.* □ *Fred stashed his coat in a heap in the corner.*

SCANDAL

big stink *n.* a major issue; a scandal; a big argument. □ *There was a big stink made about my absence.* □ *Don't make such a big stink about it.*

SCARS

railroad tracks *n.* rows of needle scars on the veins of the arms. □ *Look at those railroad tracks on his arm. That means he shoots drugs.* □ *Max has railroad tracks on both arms.*

SCHEDULE
See **LIST**.

SCHEME

finagle AND **fanigle 1.** *in.* to plot and plan; to conspire; to arrange (something). □ *He's pretty good at finagling.* □ *She'd rather fanigle than ask outright.* **2.** *tr.* to acquire something through conniving. □ *She spent a lot of time trying to finagle a ride to work.* □ *Can I fanigle a buck from you?*

layout *n.* a scheme. (Underworld.) □ *Now here's the layout. Lefty goes in this side, and Ratface comes in the other way.* □ *The layout's no good. The cops are wise to your style, boss.*

play *n.* a strategy; a plan of action. □ *That was a bad play, Bill. We lost the account.* □ *Here's a play that worked for us last year at this time.*

setup *n.* a scheme; a plot. (Underworld.) □ *Okay, what's the setup for the bank job?* □ *I got a good little setup for earning some money.*

snake *in.* to scheme; to plot and plan. (Prisons.) □ *Lefty is always snaking.* □ *He spent a lot of time snaking about that job.*

SCHOOL

campi *n.* campuses. (The Latin plural of *campus* = field.) □ *I'll see you about the campi. Ciao!* □ *When will you return to the campi after vacation?*

crack a book *tr.* to open a book to study. (Usually in the negative.) □ *I never cracked a book and still passed the course.* □ *Sally didn't crack a book all semester.*

cram *in.* to study hard at the last minute for a test. □ *She spent the night cramming for the test.* □ *If you would study all the time, you wouldn't need to cram.*

crib course *n.* an easy course in college. □ *Tom signed up for three crib courses and gym. What a twit!* □ *Andy thought he was getting into a crib course, but it turned out to be really hard.*

cume AND **cum** *n.* a cumulative average, such as a grade-point average. (Pronounced "KYUM.") □ *My cume is not high enough to get into law school.* □ *My cum is a straight A.*

frog slicing *n.* biology class; a biology course. (A dysphemism.) □ *Mary found frog slicing to be interesting. She especially liked the study of conservation and ecology.* □ *Dave dreaded going to frog slicing. The smell got to him.*

geekdom *n.* the realm of the hard-studying students or *geeks.* □ *This dorm is not exactly geekdom. Almost all the guys here are on academic probation.* □ *I spent all last semester in the hallowed halls of geekdom, studying my buns off.*

grade-grubbing *mod.* having to do with students who are only concerned with getting high grades. □ *Grade-grubbing college kids are driving me crazy.* □ *Two grade-grubbing seniors came in and begged me to change their grades.*

gut *n.* an easy course in school. □ *That course is a gut.* □ *If it's a gut, it's for me.*

hook 1. *n.* the grade of C. □ *I didn't study at all and I still got a hook!* □ *I got three hooks and a D this semester.* **2.** *tr.* to earn or "pull" the grade of C on something in school. □ *History? I hooked it without any trouble.* □ *If I can just hook algebra, I'll stay off probation.*

lit *n.* literature, as a school subject. □ *I'm flunking English lit again.* □ *I hate lit. Give me numbers any day.*

nuts and bolts *n.* the subject of psychology in college. □ *I took a class in nuts and bolts and didn't learn anything at all about what makes me tick.* □ *Tom is flunking nuts and bolts because he won't participate in the required "experiments."*

pipe *n.* an easy course in school. □ *Take this course. It's a pipe.* □ *I don't want a full load of pipes. I want to learn something.*

prelims *n.* preliminary examinations. (Collegiate.) □ *I hope I pass my prelims.* □ *What do you have to do to get the degree after you pass your prelims?*

sheepskin *n.* a high school or college diploma. □ *When you get that sheepskin on the wall, you'll feel like it was all worth* *something.* □ *Where is your sheepskin from?*

skull-buster AND **skull-popper** *n.* a difficult course in school or college. □ *The course was a skull-buster, and I had to drop it.* □ *All the courses in that department are skull-poppers.*

underwater basket weaving *n.* an imaginary, very easy high school or college course. □ *If I can just find a course in underwater basket weaving, I'll have an easy semester.* □ *Mary majored in underwater basket weaving.*

SCOLDING

an earful *n.* a scolding. □ *Her mother gave her an earful when she finally got home.* □ *Tom got an earful for his part in the prank.*

catch hell (for something) *tr.* to get severely reprimanded for (doing) something. □ *I knew I'd catch hell for it.* □ *Somebody is going to catch hell for this!*

chew someone out *tr.* to scold someone. □ *I knew my dad was going to chew me out.* □ *The dean chewed out the whole fraternity.*

climb *tr.* to scold someone. □ *The boss climbed Harry for being late.* □ *Don't climb me! The train broke down!*

dish something out *tr.* to give out trouble, scoldings, criticism, etc. □ *The boss was dishing criticism out this morning, and I really got it.* □ *The teacher dished out a scolding to each one who was involved in the prank.*

dust someone's pants *tr.* to spank someone, usually a child. □ *My dad will dust my pants if he hears about this.* □ *I'm too old for somebody to dust my pants.*

give someone a (good) talking to *tr.* to scold someone; to lecture someone sternly. □ *I think I'll have to give Pete a good talking to.* □ *The teacher gave Jimmy a talking to.*

give someone a (good) working over *tr.* to scold or beat someone. □ *The boss gave me a good working over before firing me.* □ *Fred really gave her a working over about her performance on the project.*

give someone an earful *tr.* to scold someone. □ *I'm going to give Ralph an earful for doing that.* □ *Sally gave Sam an earful for the way he treated Mary.*

give someone hell *tr.* to bawl someone out; to scold someone severely. (Use caution with *hell*.) □ *The boss just gave me hell about it.* □ *I'm really going to give Tom hell when he gets home.*

give someone the business *tr.* to harass someone; to scold someone. □ *The guys have been giving me the business about my haircut.* □ *Sam was giving Tom the business about being late all the time.*

knock some heads together *tr.* to scold some people; to get some people to do what they are supposed to be doing. □ *Do I have to come in there and knock some heads together, or will you kids settle down?* □ *I knocked some heads together and got the proposal out on time.*

lay someone out *tr.* to scold someone severely. □ *Don't lay me out! I didn't do it!* □ *She really laid out the guy but good. What did he do, rob a bank?*

lay someone out in lavender *tr.* to scold or rebuke someone severely. □ *She really laid him out in lavender for that.* □ *No need to lay me out in lavender. I wasn't there.*

mouthful *n.* a tirade. □ *Paul really gave me a mouthful. I didn't know I hurt his feelings.* □ *She sure had a mouthful to say to you!*

nail someone to a cross AND **nail someone('s hide) to the wall** *tr.* to punish or scold someone severely. (Literally, to crucify someone or to nail someone's skin to the wall like that of a captured animal.) □ *That guy was really mad. He really nailed you to a cross.* □ *She must hate your guts. She sure nailed your hide to the wall.*

pin someone's ears back *tr.* to scold someone severely. □ *She really pinned his ears back.* □ *The teacher pinned the kids' ears back for chewing gum.*

raise the devil (with someone) AND **raise hell (with someone)** *tr.* to confront someone and complain or scold. □

I really raised the devil with my brother for being late. □ *It won't do any good to raise hell with me.*

rank someone (out) *tr.* to annoy or chastise someone. □ *He really ranks me out. What a pest!* □ *I ranked out the whole gang, but good!*

ream someone out *tr.* to scold someone severely. □ *The teacher really reamed him out.* □ *The coach reamed out the whole team.*

sail into someone AND **light into someone** *in.* to beat or scold someone. □ *Jimmy's mother really sailed into him for breaking the window.* □ *Jimmy lit into the cat for getting in the way.*

screw someone over *tr.* to give someone a very bad time; to scold someone severely. □ *Those guys really screwed you over. What started it?* □ *Let's get those kids in here and screw over every one of them. This stuff can't continue.*

take the starch out of someone *tr.* to reduce someone's self-assurance; to reduce someone's conceit. □ *I took the starch out of Kelly by telling him where he was headed if he didn't change his ways.* □ *That remark really took the starch out of him.*

tear into someone *in.* to scold someone severely; to attack someone. □ *I was late, and the super tore into me like a mad dog.* □ *I don't know why she tore into me. I was at work when the window was broken.*

tell someone where to get off *tr.* to tell someone when enough is enough; to tell someone off. □ *I was fed up with her bossiness. I finally told her where to get off.* □ *He told me where to get off, so I walked out on him.*

There you go. *sent.* "You are doing it again." □ *There you go! You said it again.* □ *I just told you not to put that junk on the table, and there you go.*

SCRUTINY

hot seat *n.* the position of being scrutinized. □ *I was in the hot seat for about an hour, but they didn't learn anything from me.* □ *This new information puts Tom in the hot seat, doesn't it?*

SEARCH

fishing expedition *n.* an exploratory search for facts. (This involves asking questions with no preconceived notion of what the answers might reveal.) □ *The lawyer was on a fishing expedition. There was no real wrong committed to justify a lawsuit.* □ *Your honor, counsel is just on a clumsy fishing expedition. I move for dismissal.*

gun for someone *in.* to be looking for someone, not necessarily with a gun. □ *Bruno is gunning for Max.* □ *The French prof is gunning for you.*

on the prowl *mod.* looking for someone for sexual purposes, in the manner of a prowling cat. □ *Tom looks like he is on the prowl again tonight.* □ *That whole gang of boys is on the prowl. Watch out.*

scrounge (around [for someone or something]) *in.* to look around for someone or something; to seek someone or something in every likely place. □ *Try to scrounge around for somebody to go to the party with, why don't you?* □ *I don't think there is anybody who will go with me, but I'll scrounge around.* □ *Ask John to scrounge around for a wrench.*

scrounge someone or something up *tr.* to get someone or something somehow. □ *I scrounged a doctor up in the middle of the night.* □ *See if you can scrounge up a new carburetor by noon.*

snoop *in.* to prowl around looking for something. □ *What are you snooping around here for?* □ *Somebody was around here snooping and asking questions.*

toss *tr.* to search someone. (Underworld.) □ *The cops tossed him and found nothing.* □ *The feds have a special way of tossing somebody for drugs.*

SECRECY

backroom *mod.* secret; concealed. □ *I am going to watch for backroom deals.* □ *All the candidates were selected in backroom meetings.*

closet *mod.* secret; concealed. □ *Marty is a closet chocolate fiend.* □ *I'm a closet hard rock fan.*

cover-up *n.* an act of concealing something. □ *The cover-up drew more attention than whatever it was that was covered up.* □ *The candidate accused her opponent of a cover-up.*

go underground *in.* to go into hiding; to begin to operate in secret. □ *The entire operation went underground, and we heard no more about it.* □ *We'll go underground if we have to. Nothing will stop the movement.*

hush-hush 1. *adj.* secret; undercover. □ *The matter is so hush-hush I can't talk about it over the phone.* □ *What is all this hush-hush stuff?* **2.** *adv.* secretly. □ *They did it so hush-hush that no one knew for a long time.* □ *What are all these plans you have made so hush-hush?*

under the table *mod.* secret; clandestine. (This is hyphenated before a nominal.) □ *It was strictly an under-the-table deal.* □ *The mayor made a few bucks under the table, too.*

under wraps *mod.* (held) in secret. □ *We kept it under wraps until after the election.* □ *The plan we had under wraps had to be scrapped anyway.*

SECURE

cinch *tr.* to have something settled and secured. □ *He cinched it with a simple signature and date.* □ *It only took a handshake to cinch the deal.*

cinched *mod.* settled; secured; *sealed (up).* (As one tightens the saddle girth on a horse.) □ *I've got it cinched! No sweat!* □ *This is a cinched deal—a done deal. No one can stop it from going through.*

sealed (up) *mod.* settled; secured; *cinched.* □ *The matter was sealed by Monday morning.* □ *The contract was sealed up just in time.*

sitting pretty *mod.* doing very nicely; in a very pleasant and secure position. □ *If I get the job, I'll be sitting pretty for a long time.* □ *She married a millionaire, and now she's sitting pretty.*

SEDUCTION

See also ROMANCE.

bedroom eyes *n.* seductive eyes. □ *Beware of bedroom eyes. They mean trouble.* □ *She batted those bedroom eyes at me, and I knew I was a goner.*

casting-couch *n.* a legendary couch found in the offices of casting directors for use in seducing young people by offering them roles. □ *They say she got the job on the casting-couch.* □ *They say the director got his job on the casting-couch, too.*

hustle *tr.* to attempt to seduce someone. □ *Max is hustling Tracy.* □ *I think that Tracy's hustling Max.*

line *n.* a story or argument; a story intended to seduce someone. □ *I've heard that line before.* □ *Don't feed me that line. Do you think I was born yesterday?*

move on someone *in.* to attempt to pick up someone; to attempt to seduce someone. (Collegiate.) □ *Don't try to move on my date, old chum.* □ *Harry is trying to move on Tiffany. They deserve each other.*

put the moves on someone *tr.* to attempt to seduce someone. (With *any* in the negative.) □ *At least he didn't try to put any moves on me.* □ *If somebody doesn't try to put the moves on her, she thinks she's a failure.*

rap *n.* sweet talk; seductive talk; *line.* □ *I like your rap, but that's all I like about you.* □ *Don't lay that rap on me! You're not my type.*

run down some lines *in.* to try to seduce someone; to go through a talk leading to seduction. □ *Go run down some lines with someone else.* □ *I was just standing there running down some lines with Mary when those guys broke in.*

SELF

look after number one *in.* to take care of oneself first. □ *You gotta look after number one, right?* □ *It's a good idea to look after number one. Who else will?*

number one *n.* oneself. □ *I don't know who will pay for the broken window, but old number one isn't!* □ *Everything always comes back to number one. I have to solve everybody's problems.*

numero uno *n.* oneself; *number one.* (Spanish.) □ *I always look out for numero uno.* □ *What's in it for numero uno?*

take care of number one AND **take care of numero uno** *tr.* to take care of oneself. □ *Arthur, like everybody else, is most concerned with taking care of number one.* □ *If you don't take care of numero uno, who will?*

SEPARATION

split up 1. *in.* to separate. □ *The two split up and went their separate ways.* □ *They couldn't get along, so they split up.* **2.** *n.* an act of separating or breaking up. (Usually **split-up**.) □ *Everyone was mentally prepared for the company's split-up.* □ *The split-up caused neither surprise nor grief.*

SEQUENCE

in the pipeline *mod.* backed up somewhere in a process; in process; in a queue. □ *There's a lot of goods still in the pipeline. That means no more orders for a while.* □ *Your papers are in the pipeline somewhere. You'll just have to wait.*

solid *mod.* consecutive; consecutively. □ *Larry ate for four solid days.* □ *Then he "had the flu" for three days solid.*

vicious circle *n.* a set of actions that lead to ever more unsatisfactory consequences; a set of bad actions that are repeated in a cycle. □ *It's a vicious circle, and I want out of it.* □ *Life has become one vicious circle after another.*

SERIOUSNESS

boogie *in.* to get down to work; to get down to business. □ *All right, it's time to boogie. Cool it!* □ *The whistle blew. Time to boogie.*

heart-to-heart (talk) *n.* a serious and intimate discussion. □ *We sat down and had a nice heart-to-heart for about an hour.* □ *A little heart-to-heart talk is just what you need.*

heavy *mod.* important; profound; serious. □ *This is a very heavy matter.* □ *This matter is too heavy.* □ *I have some heavy things to talk over with you, Sam.*

heavy scene *n.* a serious state of affairs; an emotionally charged situation. □ *Man, that meeting was really a heavy scene.* □ *Another heavy scene like that and I quit.*

I kid you not. *sent.* "I am not kidding." (Attributed to entertainer Jack Paar.) □ *She is a great singer. I kid you not.* □ *I kid you not. This is the best.*

I'm not kidding. *sent.* "I am telling the truth." □ *Get over here now! I'm not kidding.* □ *I'm not kidding. It was this big!*

intense *mod.* serious; *heavy.* □ *That man is so intense!* □ *This is an intense matter.* □ *Oh, wow! Now that's what I call intense!*

mean business *tr.* to be very, very serious. □ *Stop laughing! I mean business.* □ *I could tell from the look on her face that she meant business.*

straight-faced *mod.* with a serious, unsmiling face. □ *Mary couldn't stay straight-faced very long. It was just too funny.* □ *He was a very straight-faced prof, but he has a tremendous sense of humor.*

SEX

chippie *in.* to play around sexually. □ *She won't even chippie.* □ *So me and my boyfriend was chippying a little in the hall. Why was ya watching?*

chippy around *in.* to be sexually promiscuous. □ *She has been known to chippy around, but not with just anyone and never for money.* □ *She figures it's her right to chippy around.*

facts of life *n.* an explanation of human reproduction, especially as presented to a child. □ *No one ever explained the facts of life to me. I read books about it.* □ *She is so naive. She doesn't even know the facts of life.*

fomp *in.* to play around sexually. (Collegiate.) □ *Who are those two over there fomping?* □ *Jerry wanted to fomp, and I wanted to get him out of my sight.*

gender-bender *mod.* having to do with something that obscures male/female distinctions. □ *Those gender-bender hairstyles can be confusing.* □ *He always wears gender-bender clothes.*

kinky *mod.* having to do with unconventional sexual acts or people who perform them. □ *She seems to have a morbid interest in kinky stuff.* □ *He showed her a picture of some kind of kinky sex thing.*

mess around (with someone) AND **mess about (with someone); monkey around (with someone)** *in.* to play with someone sexually. □ *Those two have been messing around.* □ *Pete was messing around with Maria, and now she's storked.*

musical beds *n.* acts of sexual promiscuity; sleeping with many people. (From the name of the game "musical chairs.") □ *Mary has been playing musical beds for about a year.* □ *She thinks that playing musical beds is the way to get ahead.*

sleaze AND **sleez** *in.* to act low; to be sexually promiscuous. □ *She looks like the type who will sleaze and lie to get her own way.* □ *She earned quite a reputation sleezing around with just anybody.*

swift *mod.* sexually fast or easy, usually said of a woman. □ *Tracy is swift they say, but I find her to be a perfect lady.* □ *Clare is not only swift, she has a reputation.*

swing *in.* to be involved in sexual fads, group sex, or the swapping of sexual partners. □ *Carol says that Tom, Ted, and Heidi swing. How does she know?* □ *There is a lot less swinging going on since these strange diseases have spread.*

tomcat *in.* [for a man] to prowl around searching for sex. □ *Harry was out tomcatting again last night.* □ *He's gonna tomcat around till he catches something.*

SEX - DISPLAY

flash *in.* to display one's private parts briefly. (Use caution with the topic.) □ *The guy flashed and moved on down the street.* □ *She flashed briefly, providing the show that people came to see, and left the stage.*

flasher *n.* a man who exhibits his genitals. □ *The cops caught the flasher and took him away.* □ *Sarah said she thought she saw a flasher in the library.*

free show *n.* a peek at a private part of someone's body, usually a woman's. □ *Martin looked like the type who was always waiting for a free show that was never to be.* □ *A true gentleman takes no notice of a "free show."*

SHARING

action *n.* a share of something; a share of the winnings or of the booty. □ *I did my share of the work, and I want my share of the action.* □ *Just what did you do to earn any of the action?*

cut someone in (on something) *tr.* to permit someone to share something. □ *You promised you would cut me in on this caper.* □ *We can't cut you in. There's not enough.*

divvy something up *tr.* to divide something up. □ *We had to divvy my aunt's things up after her death.* □ *They divvied up the fish and drove back to the city.*

Dutch treat *n.* an outing for two or more where the cost is split among the participants, either evenly or in proportion to what is consumed. □ *I propose a Dutch treat to celebrate the day.* □ *We had a Dutch treat, which gave us a chance to get to know one another better.*

go Dutch *in.* [for two people] to split the cost of something, such as a meal. □ *How about dinner tonight? We'll go Dutch, okay?* □ *Yes, let's go Dutch.*

halvsies *mod.* with each (of two) paying half. □ *Let's do it halvsies.* □ *Let's make it halvsies, and I pay for the parking, too.*

piece (of the action) AND **bit of the action; slice of the action** *n.* a share in the activity or the profits. (Especially gambling activity.) □ *If you get in on that real estate deal, I want a piece, too.* □ *Deal Tom in. He wants a bit of the action.* □ *Don't be selfish. Give me a slice of the action.*

taste *n.* a share; a *piece (of the action)*. □ *I want a taste, too.* □ *Whatever the deal is, I want a taste.*

SHIP

rust bucket *n.* a naval destroyer; any ship. (Military.) □ *I'm anxious to get off this old rust bucket.* □ *Why don't I ever* *get assigned to a new ship? It's always some crummy rust bucket!*

SHOCK

See also **AMAZEMENT, SURPRISE**.

shocker *n.* something shocking. □ *Now, here's a shocker for you.* □ *Her news was quite a shocker.*

sticker shock *n.* the shock at seeing just how much a new automobile costs as determined by looking at the price tag or sticker. □ *I went to a car dealer today, and I am still suffering from sticker shock.* □ *If sticker shock is getting you down, think about getting a used car.*

What (a) nerve! *exclam.* "What insolence!"; "How rude and presumptuous!" □ *Did you hear what she said? What nerve!* □ *What a nerve! Have you ever seen such gall?*

zap *tr.* to shock someone. □ *That fake snake zapped me for a minute.* □ *The incident zapped me, but good.*

SHOES

boats *n.* big shoes. □ *Whose boats are under the coffee table?* □ *Those boats are special made, in fact.*

bucks *n.* buckskin (leather) shoes. □ *Look at my new bucks!* □ *You don't see many red bucks. Are you sure you got the right thing?*

clodhoppers *n.* big shoes. □ *Wipe the mud off those clodhoppers before you come in here.* □ *Look at the clodhoppers she's wearing!*

ends *n.* shoes. □ *You even got holes in your ends.* □ *Could you use some new ends?*

gunboats AND **battleships** *n.* big feet; big shoes. □ *Hasn't he got the biggest gunboats you ever saw?* □ *Whose battleships are these under the coffee table?*

jelly shoes AND **jellies; jelly sandals** *n.* colorful shoes made from soft, flexible plastic. (From *jelly bean*.) □ *It's too cold to wear jelly shoes.* □ *Jellies will crack in this weather.*

Jesus boots *n.* sandals. □ *Jesus boots are okay in the summer.* □ *Who is the kook in Jesus boots?*

kicks *n.* cleats or shoes; gym shoes. (Collegiate.) □ *Don't you dare wear those kicks in here!* □ *Take your kicks off before coming in.*

sneaks *n.* sneakers. □ *Are those sneaks new?* □ *She wore red sneaks and a mini.*

stumpers *n.* shoes. (Black.) □ *Make those stumpers shine!* □ *You like my new stumpers?*

tennies *n.* tennis shoes; sneakers. □ *Let me get my tennies on, and I'll be right with you.* □ *What is that stuff on your tennies?*

SICKNESS

bellyache *n.* a stomachache. □ *Oh, mama, do I have a bellyache!* □ *That stuff will give you one fine bellyache.*

big-C. *n.* cancer. (Usually with *the*.) □ *She was struck with the big-C.* □ *The big-C. will finish off quite a few of us.*

blue around the gills AND **green around the gills** *mod.* ill; nauseated. □ *You are looking a little blue around the gills.* □ *How about a little air? I feel a little green around the gills.*

boogie *n.* a tumor. (Medical slang.) □ *Looks like a little boogie down in the lung.* □ *I've got to take out three boogies before lunch and look at X rays all afternoon.*

bug *n.* an illness; the flu. □ *There's a bug going around.* □ *I picked up a bug at the office last week.*

clap *n.* gonorrhea. (Use caution with the topic.) □ *Max has had the clap a dozen times.* □ *A case of the clap can change your life for a while.*

creeping-crud *n.* any unidentified disease. □ *There is some kind of creeping-crud between my toes.* □ *I got the creeping-crud growing in my armpit.*

crotch-rot *n.* a skin irritation or disease characterized by itching in the genital area, usually said of males. □ *What will get rid of crotch-rot?* □ *Here's some medicine for crotch-rot.*

guber AND **goober** *n.* a tumor. (Jocular medical slang. Possibly because it grows beneath the surface like the goober—the peanut.) □ *Dr. Jones took a huge goober* *out of a lady this morning.* □ *The patient with the abdominal goober is going into surgery now.*

gunge *n.* a skin irritation in the groin. □ *I got the gunge. What'll I do?* □ *The sawbones'll give you something for the gunge.*

hack *n.* a cough. □ *That's a nasty hack you've got there.* □ *A hack like that can lead to pneumonia.*

hawk *in.* to cough mightily; to cough something up. □ *The cold has had me hawking for a week.* □ *He's been hawking all night.*

head *n.* a headache. □ *Man, do I have a head. You got any aspirin?* □ *Music that loud gives me a head.*

herped up *mod.* infected with the *herpes simplex* virus. □ *Why do all the boys treat me like I was herped up or something?* □ *They say all those frat guys are herped up.*

illin' *mod.* being ill; being sick. □ *She was illin' big time and could not come to class.* □ *I was illin' so I called in sick.*

nause someone out *tr.* to nauseate someone. □ *That horrible smell really nauses me out.* □ *Things like that nause me out, too.*

pukes *n.* the feeling of nausea; the feeling of impending vomiting. (Especially with *have, get.* Always with *the.*) □ *Oh my God, I've got the pukes.* □ *I hate having the pukes.*

pukish *mod.* nauseated. (Folksy.) □ *Oh, I feel so pukish.* □ *That old pukish feeling came over me, and I just let go.*

raunchy AND **raunchie; ronchie** *mod.* sick; ill. □ *I feel sort of raunchy.* □ *After I ate dinner, my stomach felt a little raunchie, so I went home.*

scrud *n.* a serious disease; a venereal disease. (Military.) □ *Oh, hell! I think I got the scrud!* □ *Poor dumb Charlie can't tell scrud from crotch rot.*

social disease *n.* a venereal disease. □ *Many people find things like—ah—social diseases difficult to discuss in public.* □

Others talk about private matters like social diseases till you're sick to death of it.

splitting headache *n.* a severe headache, as if one's head were splitting open. □ *I'm sorry, I can't. I have a splitting headache. Maybe Fred will play bridge with you.* □ *This splitting headache has been going on for hours.*

toss something off *tr.* to resist or fight off a disease. □ *I caught a little cold, but tossed it off right away.* □ *I can't toss off these viruses like I used to.*

turn someone's stomach *tr.* to nauseate someone. □ *That stuff turns my stomach. Do I have to eat it?* □ *Whatever that smell is, it's turning my stomach.*

under the weather *mod.* ill. □ *I feel sort of under the weather today.* □ *Whatever I ate for lunch is making me feel a bit under the weather.*

SIGNAL

buzz *tr.* to signal someone with a buzzer. □ *I'll buzz my secretary.* □ *Did you buzz, Gloria?*

give someone the nod *tr.* to signal someone by nodding. (Not slang.) □ *I gave Pete the nod, and he started the procedure.* □ *Just give me the nod when you are ready.*

high sign *n.* a hand signal meaning "okay." (The tip of the index or middle finger touches the tip of the thumb, and the hand is raised into the air.) □ *Tom got the high sign and began to open the door.* □ *Give me the high sign when you want me to start.*

idiot light *n.* a light (instead of a meter) on a car's dashboard that indicates the state of various things concerning the operation of the car. □ *I don't want idiot lights. I want meters!* □ *The idiot light went on, and I knew I was in some sort of trouble.*

telegraph one's punches *tr.* to signal, unintentionally, one's intentions. □ *When you go in there to negotiate, don't telegraph your punches. Don't let them see that we're broke.* □ *The mediator telegraphed his punches, and we were prepared with a strong counterargument.*

SIGNATURE

John Hancock *n.* one's signature. (Refers to the signature of John Hancock, one of the signers of the Declaration of Independence.) □ *Put your John Hancock right here, if you don't mind.* □ *Mr. Wilson's John Hancock is worth about $30 million.*

SILENCE

Bag it! *exclam.* "Shut up!" □ *Bag it! I'm reading.* □ *Oh, bag it! I've heard enough.*

Bite your tongue! *exclam.* "Be sorry you said that!"; "Take back what you said!" □ *Me a thief? Oh, bite your tongue!* □ *Why do you say that this will fail? Bite your tongue!*

Can it! *exclam.* "Shut up!" □ *I've heard enough. Can it!* □ *That's enough out of you! Can it!*

clam *n.* a tight-lipped person. □ *Suddenly, she became a clam and wouldn't talk anymore.* □ *Rocko's a clam. He won't say a word.*

clam up *in.* to get quiet. □ *The minute they got him inside the cop-shop, he clammed up.* □ *You'll clam up if you know what's good for you.*

Dry up! *exclam.* "Shut up!"; "Go away and don't bother me!" □ *Aw, dry up! I've heard enough.* □ *Dry up and beat it!*

dummy up *in.* to refuse to talk. (Underworld.) □ *Tracy dummied up when they got her into the station.* □ *Rocko dummied up right away. He's a real thoroughbred.*

Give it a rest! *exclam.* "Shut up!" (The "it" is a mouth.) □ *I've heard enough. Give it a rest!* □ *Give it a rest! You talk too much.*

Give me a break! AND **Gimme a break!** *exclam.* "That is enough!"; "Stop it!" □ *Do you have to go on and on? Give me a break!* □ *Gimme a break, you guys! That's enough!*

hush something up *tr.* to keep something a secret; to try to stop a rumor from spreading. □ *We just couldn't hush it up.* □ *We wanted to hush up the story, but there was no way to do it.*

Knock it off! *exclam.* "Be quiet!"; "Shut up!" □ *Hey, you guys! Knock it off!* □ *I'm trying to sleep! Knock it off!*

pipe down *in.* to become quiet; to cease making noise; to shut up. (Especially as a rude command.) □ *Pipe down! I'm trying to sleep.* □ *Come on! Pipe down and get back to work!*

Put up or shut up! *exclam.* "Speak now or remain silent for good!" □ *I'm tired of your whining. What's your problem? Put up or shut up!* □ *Now is your chance. Put up or shut up!*

Save it! *exclam.* "Be quiet!" □ *Save it! Keep quiet until this is over.* □ *I don't care what you think you have to say. Save it!*

shush (up) *in.* to be quiet. □ *Shush! I want to hear the weather.* □ *Shush up and listen to the lecture.*

shut up *in.* to be quiet. □ *Shut up and listen!* □ *Shut up yourself.*

Shut your face! *exclam.* "Shut up!"; "Be quiet!" □ *Oh, shut your face. I've heard enough.* □ *Can't you shut your face, you motor-mouth?*

simmer (down) *in.* to get quiet. □ *I waited till things began to simmer down, and then I started.* □ *Hey, simmer down to a dull roar!*

Stow it! *exclam.* "Shut up!" □ *Okay, stow it! I've heard enough.* □ *Stow it! That is enough of your applesauce.*

Stuff a sock in it! AND **Put a sock in it!** *exclam.* "Shut up!" □ *I've heard enough. Stuff a sock in it!* □ *Put a sock in it! You are a pain.*

Time (out)! *exclam.* "Stop talking for a minute!" (A way of interrupting someone.) □ *Time! I have something to say.* □ *Just a minute! Time out! I want to speak!*

Zip (up) your lip! AND **Zip it up!** *exclam.* "Be quiet!"; "Zip up your mouth!" □ *Shhhh! Zip up your lip!* □ *Zip your lip!* □ *Zip it up and listen!*

SILENT

doggo *mod.* hidden away; quiet and waiting. □ *This error was there, doggo, for nearly thirty years.* □ *Here is another one of your doggo deadbeats on this list.*

SILLINESS

See also CRAZINESS.

clown around *in.* to act silly; to mess around. □ *Please stop clowning around and get to sleep.* □ *We were just clowning around. We didn't mean to break anything.*

corny *mod.* having to do with overdone sentiment. □ *Harry always laughs at corny mush in a movie.* □ *The love scenes were your corny, hands-off-the-naughty-parts events, but nobody laughed.*

daffy *mod.* silly; crazy. □ *Kelly was acting daffy because she was so happy.* □ *Oh, don't be daffy!*

ditzy AND **ditsy** *mod.* giddy; unaware; flighty. □ *You are such a ditzy geek!* □ *Betty has been acting a little ditsy lately. What's wrong?*

dizzy *mod.* stupid; scatterbrained. □ *The prof is a little dizzy, but entertaining.* □ *Who is that dizzy dame?*

goofy *mod.* silly. □ *Stop acting so goofy! What will the neighbors say?* □ *You are really a goofy chick.*

in a twitter *mod.* in a giddy state; silly. □ *Don't get yourself in a twitter.* □ *We were all in a twitter over the upcoming event.*

jive-ass *mod.* foolish. (Potentially offensive. Use only with discretion.) □ *You can tell that jive-ass jerk to forget it.* □ *Don't pay any attention to that jive-ass jeff.*

OTL *phr.* "out to lunch"; spacy; giddy. (Initialism.) □ *Wally is the most OTL guy I have ever seen.* □ *Sue is OTL. She seems witless all the time.*

slap happy *mod.* silly; giddy. □ *I get slap happy when I have to stay up this late.* □ *She's a little slap happy, but a tremendous dear.*

spaced (out) AND **spacy** *mod.* silly; giddy. □ *I have such spaced out parents!* □ *He's so spaced!* □ *I love my spacy old dad.*

space out AND **space** *in.* to become giddy; to become disoriented. □ *She is spacing again. She doesn't even know where she is.* □ *I spaced out after the long climb.*

space someone out *tr.* to cause someone to become giddy. □ *The whole business just spaced me out.* □ *The spectacle spaced out the entire audience.*

tomfoolery *n.* foolishness. □ *That's enough of this tomfoolery!* □ *The entire evening was devoted to tomfoolery.*

wacky *mod.* loony; silly and giddy. □ *You are about the wackiest guy I ever met.* □ *I got a real kick out of that wacky movie we saw last night.*

zany *mod.* silly. □ *What a zany chick!* □ *Clare is so zany.* □ *That is a zany idea, but I like it.*

SINCERITY

in there *mod.* sincere; likeable. □ *Martha is really in there. Everybody likes her.* □ *I like a guy who's in there—who thinks about other people.*

Make no mistake (about it)! *sent.* an expression signifying the sincerity of the speaker's previous statements. □ *Make no mistake! This is the real thing.* □ *This is a very serious matter. Make no mistake about it.*

SINGER

canary *n.* a female singer. □ *The band had a cute canary who could really sing.* □ *The drummer and the canary just don't seem to be able to get along.*

whiskey tenor *n.* a strained tenor. □ *He's a whiskey tenor, but a good one.* □ *Four whiskey tenors do not a barbershop quartet make.*

SIREN

yelper *n.* the whooping (electronic) siren on emergency vehicles. □ *The black and white rounded the corner, yelper blasting.* □ *Turn off the yelper, Chuck, we hear you.*

SITTING

cop a squat *tr.* to sit down. □ *Hey, man! Come in and cop a squat.* □ *Cop a squat and crack a tube.*

Make a lap! *exclam.* to sit down. □ *Hey, make a lap and get out of the way!* □ *Pull up a chair and make a lap!*

park it (somewhere) *tr.* sit down somewhere; sit down and get out of the way. □ *Hey, park it! You're in the way.* □ *Max, park it over there in the corner. Stop pacing around. You make me nervous.*

plop *tr.* to sit oneself down somewhere; to place one's buttocks somewhere. (The *it* in the examples is the buttocks.) □ *Come in, Fred. Just plop it anywhere you see a chair. This place is a mess.* □ *Just plop it down right there, and we'll have our little talk.*

squat *in.* to sit (down). □ *Come on in and squat for a while.* □ *Squat over here by the fire.*

SIZE

See also **AMOUNT**.

dinky *mod.* small; undersized. □ *Isn't this a little dinky for a $14 steak?* □ *I'll take the dinky one. I'm on a diet.*

(grand)daddy (of them all) *n.* the biggest or oldest of all; the patriarch. □ *This old fish is the granddaddy of them all.* □ *This one is the daddy. Been here since the place was built.*

humongous *mod.* huge. □ *She lives in a humongous house on the hill.* □ *Wally has a humongous nose.* □ *That nose is not humongous.*

knee-high to a grasshopper *mod.* of very short stature. (Folksy.) □ *I knew you when you were knee-high to a grasshopper.* □ *I was knee-high to a grasshopper when I first heard that joke.*

man-size(d) *mod.* large-size, especially in reference to the size of servings of food. □ *This is a man-sized steak! That's what I want.* □ *For a man-size meal, open a can of Wallace's Chili tonight!*

mega *mod.* large. □ *Some mega beast boogied down to the front of the auditorium and started screaming.* □ *You see I have this, like, mega problem, ya know.*

mini *mod.* small; miniature. □ *I have a mini problem you can maybe help me with.* □ *This is just a mini office. I'll get a bigger one later.*

moby *mod.* enormous; unwieldy. (Like Herman Melville's great white whale, Moby Dick.) □ *This is a very moby old car.* □ *Why does he let himself get so moby?*

pint-sized *mod.* small; miniature. □ *I won't fit into one of those pint-sized cars.* □ *My car is not pint-sized.* □ *Tell that little pint-sized guy to beat it.*

teeny-weeny AND **teenie-weenie; teensy-weensy** *mod.* tiny. □ *It was just a teeny-weeny sin.* □ *This one is too teenie-weenie.* □ *Could you move just a teensy-weensy bit to the left?*

two-by-four *mod.* small. □ *A two-by-four office with a chair and a desk was where Barlowe hung out.* □ *I can't stand living in this two-by-four room!*

whopper *n.* something that is of relatively great size. □ *That thing's really a whopper!* □ *It was a whopper of an argument.*

whopping (great) *mod.* enormous. □ *Somebody showed up with a whopping great basin of chunks of pickled fish. Yummy!* □ *What a whopping fool he is!*

yea big *mod.* about so big. (Accompanied by a hand gesture.) □ *Oh, it was about yea big.* □ *Do you have a panel that is about yea big?*

SKATEBOARD

boogie-board *n.* a skateboard. (Teens.) □ *He fell off his boogie-board and broke his tailbone.* □ *Can you imagine a boogie-board costing $600?*

sidewalk surfing *n.* skateboarding. □ *Bill spent a lot of time sidewalk surfing until the town passed an ordinance against it.* □ *The little kids started the summer sidewalk surfing, but gave it up after a few weeks.*

skurf *in.* to skateboard. (From the words *skate* and *surf*.) □ *He skurfed from city hall to the post office.* □ *My mom won't let me skurf anymore.*

SKILL

cut the mustard *tr.* to be able to do something requiring youth or vigor. (Usually in the expression **too old to cut the mustard**.) □ *Do you really think he* *can cut the mustard?* □ *She's not too old to cut the mustard.*

fancy footwork AND **fast footwork** *n.* artful maneuvering; fast and clever thinking. □ *Ken did a lot of fancy footwork to get out of that one.* □ *Fast footwork is the key to success in politics.*

green thumb *n.* a wonderful ability to garden and grow houseplants. □ *Heidi has a green thumb and can work wonders with plants.* □ *If I had a green thumb, I could grow my own bananas.*

maven AND **mavin** *n.* an expert; a self-proclaimed expert. (From Hebrew *mevin* via Yiddish.) □ *A maven in the stock market you are not.* □ *Harriet—a well-known clothing maven in Rochester —keeps giving pointers on fabrics, but I don't listen.*

natural *n.* someone with obvious natural talent. □ *That guy is a natural!* □ *Can she ever dance! What a natural!*

natural-born *mod.* born with talent or skill. □ *She is really a natural-born dancer.* □ *Mary is a natural-born artist.*

one's bag *n.* one's preferences; one's talents. □ *Working crossword puzzles is my bag.* □ *Hey, Tom, what's your bag? What do you like to do?*

pro 1. *n.* a "professional" (at anything); someone as good as a professional. □ *I'm a pro at photography.* □ *When it comes to typing, he's a pro.* **2.** *mod.* professional. □ *I hope to play pro ball next year.* □ *This is not what I'd call a pro hammer.*

techie *n.* a person with technical skills or knowledge. □ *We'll have to take this problem to a techie.* □ *The techies say it should work, theoretically, that is.*

tricks of the trade *n.* special skills and knowledge associated with any trade or profession. □ *I know a few tricks of the trade that make things easier.* □ *I learned the tricks of the trade from my uncle.*

whiz *n.* a talented or skilled person. □ *She's a real whiz with stats.* □ *I'm no math whiz, but I can find your errors.*

whiz kid *n.* a bright young person. □ *The boss's new whiz kid doesn't seem to be* doing the job very well. □ *We need a whiz kid to get things brought up to date around here.*

SKILL - LACKING

can't hit the (broad) side of a barn *phr.* "cannot aim something accurately." □ *You're way off. You couldn't hit the broad side of a barn.* □ *Carry the paper to the wastebasket. You can't hit the side of a barn.*

SKIN

hide *n.* the skin. □ *I need to get some rays on my hide.* □ *Your hide looks pretty pale, all right.*

SKULL

headbone *n.* the skull. □ *I got a nasty bump on my headbone.* □ *Do you want I should conk your headbone, or will you be coming along politely?*

SKUNK

wood-pussy *n.* a skunk. □ *Do I smell the faint perfume of a wood-pussy?* □ *The dog had a nasty run-in with a wood-pussy.*

SKY

blue *n.* the sky; the heavens. □ *I just look up at the blue and hope for the best.* □ *The idea came to me right out of the blue.*

SLANG

jive talk *n.* slang; contemporary fad words. □ *I like to hear jive talk. It's like trying to work a puzzle.* □ *He stands by the window with a pad of paper and takes down the jive talk he hears.*

SLEEP

beauty sleep *n.* sleep; the sleep one requires. (Usually mentioned by non-beautiful men as a joke.) □ *I gotta get home and get my beauty sleep.* □ *You really need some beauty sleep. Why don't you try a week of it and see if that works?*

big Z's *n.* sleep. □ *I need me some of them big Z's.* □ *The big Z's must have set in before I could finish the movie.*

blanket drill *n.* a night's sleep; sleep. (Military.) □ *Fred is still on blanket drill. He's in for it.* □ *Blanket drill is the only thing I like in the army.*

blow Z's *tr.* to sleep. □ *I got to blow Z's for a while; then we'll talk.* □ *Him? Oh, he's in the back blowing Z's.*

catch some Z's AND **cop some Z's; cut some Z's** *tr.* to get some sleep. □ *I gotta catch some Z's before I drop.* □ *Why don't you stop a little bit and try to cop some Z's?*

dead to the world *mod.* sound asleep. □ *After all that exercise, he's dead to the world.* □ *He's dead to the world, and I can't rouse him.*

flake down *in.* to go to bed; to go to sleep. □ *Look at the time. I gotta go home and flake down.* □ *After I flake down for about three days, I'll tell you about my trip.*

forty winks *n.* a nap; sleep. (Usually with a quantifier. Either *forty* or *some, a few, a bunch of,* etc.) □ *I could use forty winks before I have to get to work.* □ *I need forty winks before I get started again.*

get some shut-eye *tr.* to get some sleep. □ *I need to get home and get some shut-eye before I do anything else.* □ *We all could use some shut-eye.*

hit the hay AND **hit the sack** *tr.* to go to bed. □ *I have to go home and hit the hay pretty soon.* □ *Let's hit the sack. We have to get an early start in the morning.*

kip *in.* to sleep. □ *He's upstairs kipping. Can he call you back?* □ *He'll kip for about another hour.*

pad out *in.* to go to bed or to sleep. □ *Man, if I don't pad out by midnight, I'm a zombie.* □ *Why don't you people go home so I can pad out?*

pound one's ear *tr.* to sleep. □ *I've got to spend more time pounding my ear.* □ *She went home to pound her ear an hour or two before work.*

rack (out) *in.* to go to sleep or to bed. □ *What time do you rack out?* □ *I've got to rack out or drop from exhaustion.* □ *If I don't rack by midnight, I'm dead the next day.*

rack time AND **rack duty** *n.* time spent in bed. (Military.) □ *I need more rack time than I'm getting.* □ *I was on rack duty for my entire leave.*

sacked out *mod.* asleep. □ *Mary is sacked out in her room.* □ *Here it is ten o'clock, and you are still sacked out!*

sack out *in.* to go to bed or go to sleep. □ *It's time for me to sack out.* □ *Let's sack out early tonight.*

sack rat *n.* someone who spends a lot of time in bed; someone who does not ever seem to get enough sleep. □ *Tom is such a sack rat. He can't seem to get enough sleep.* □ *Mary is such a sack rat that she misses classes.*

sack time 1. *n.* a period of time spent in bed. □ *I need more sack time than most people.* □ *How much sack time do you get?* **2.** *n.* time to go to bed. □ *Okay, gang, it's sack time. Go home so I can get some sleep!* □ *When is sack time around here?*

shut-eye *n.* sleep. □ *It's about time to get some shut-eye.* □ *I could use about another hour of shut-eye.*

snooze 1. *in.* to sleep; to take a little nap. □ *You can't snooze every afternoon!* □ *I snoozed a little bit before the party.* **2.** *n.* a little nap. □ *I need a little snooze.* □ *Why not go up and take a little snooze?*

turn in AND **roll in** *in.* to go to bed. □ *Well, it's about time to turn in.* □ *I can't wait to roll in tonight.*

winks *n.* some sleep. □ *I gotta have some winks. I'm pooped.* □ *A few winks would do you good.*

SMELL
See ODOR.

SMILE
Say cheese! *exclam.* "Please smile!" (A phrase said by a photographer who is trying to get someone to smile for a photograph.) □ *Come on, now. Say cheese!* □ *Say cheese for the camera, please.*

SNOBBISH
See HAUGHTINESS.

SNOW
dumped on *mod.* snowed on. □ *The entire Midwest was dumped on with about ten inches of snow.* □ *Our town really got dumped on last night.*

dump on someone or something *in.* to snow on someone or something. □ *Well, it dumped on us again last night.* □ *The cold front dumped on the northeast again today.*

fluff-stuff *n.* snow. □ *There is supposed to be an inch of fluff-stuff tonight.* □ *Fluff-stuff looks pretty, but it's no fun to shovel it.*

SOBRIETY

catch up *in.* to break the drug habit; to withdraw from drugs. □ *Bruno never tried to catch up. He's just too far gone.* □ *I just know I can catch up, if I can just get through the first week.*

clean *mod.* not using drugs; not involved with drugs. □ *There's a success story. Kelly is one clean guy if I ever saw one.* □ *I've been clean for more than a month now.*

cold sober *mod.* sober; completely sober. □ *Of course, I'm cold sober!* □ *He had a fine head on and wanted more than anything to be cold sober and alert.*

dry *mod.* sober; no longer alcohol intoxicated. □ *Tracy's dry, I hear.* □ *How long will Ernie stay dry?*

go straight *in.* to get off drugs. □ *Ernie wanted to go straight more than anything else in the world.* □ *I'll go straight one of these days.*

jober as a sudge *mod.* sober. (A deliberate spoonerism on *sober as a judge*.) □ *Me? I'm as jober as a sudge.* □ *What I mean to shay is that I am shertainly as jober as a sudge!*

on the wagon *mod.* not now drinking alcoholic liquor. □ *How long has John been on the wagon this time?* □ *He's on the wagon again.*

sober as a judge *mod.* as sober (free from alcohol) as it is possible to be. □ *Kelly—who was starched as could be—claimed to be sober as a judge.* □ *The judge was not always sober as a judge, but he could get through his court call.*

sold cober *mod.* sober. (A deliberate spoonerism on *cold sober*.) □ *What do you mean drunk? Why, I'm sold cober.* □ *Ted is always as sold cober as the next guy.*

squared up *mod.* no longer taking drugs. □ *Walter is squared up now and spends a lot of time trying to help others.* □ *Max'll never get himself squared up.*

stone(-cold) sober *mod.* absolutely sober. □ *I am stone-cold sober, or I will be by morning anyway.* □ *I found the secret to being stone sober. Don't drink.*

straight *mod.* off drugs; no longer addicted to drugs. □ *I'm straight now, and I'm gonna stay that way.* □ *I'm a straight guy.* □ *See how long you can stay straight, how 'bout it?*

SOCIAL

break the ice *tr.* to be the first one to do something. □ *No one wants to break the ice. I guess I will be first.* □ *Well, I guess we should break the ice and start dancing.*

buzhie *mod.* middle-class. □ *I can't stand this buzhie neighborhood.* □ *I live in a buzhie house and drive a buzhie car.* □ *She is so buzhie!*

frat 1. *n.* a fraternity. (Collegiate.) □ *Are you going to join a frat?* □ *My brother is in a frat.* **2.** *mod.* having to do with fraternities and their members. (Collegiate.) □ *Is there a frat party tonight?* □ *Frat life is not for me.*

on the shelf *mod.* not active socially; left to oneself in social matters. □ *I've been on the shelf long enough. I'm going to make some friends.* □ *She likes being on the shelf.*

rush 1. *n.* a period of time when fraternities and sororities are permitted to pursue new members. (Collegiate.) □ *When does rush start this year?* □ *I've got to be at school in time for rush.* **2.** *tr.* [for a fraternity or sorority member] to try to persuade someone to join. □ *The frat tried to rush me, but I'm too busy.* □ *They can't rush anyone except during rush week.*

stag *mod.* having to do with someone going to a party without a date. (Originally said of a male.) □ *He decided to ignore her and go stag.* □ *A bunch of the guys got together and went stag to the dance.*

stag line *n.* a line of dateless men at a dance. □ *She looked over the stag line and saw nobody she knew.* □ *The guys in the stag line looked so forlorn. She suddenly wanted to do something to make them all happy.*

table-hop *in.* to move from table to table in a restaurant, nightclub, bar, etc. □ *We used to table-hop, but nobody knows us anymore.* □ *They would table-hop—to the great dismay of the waiters.*

SOCIETY

how the other half lives *n.* how poorer people live; how richer people live. □ *Now I am beginning to understand how the other half lives.* □ *Most people don't care how the other half lives.*

SOFT

squooshy *mod.* soft; squishy. □ *I can't stand squooshy food!* □ *Mush is supposed to be squooshy.* □ *I like to walk barefooted in squooshy mud.*

SOLDIER

See also **MILITARY**.

crunchie *n.* a soldier; a marching infantry soldier. (Military.) □ *A couple of crunchies were complaining about the army.* □ *Crunchies have a pretty hard life.*

desert cherry *n.* a new soldier in a desert war; a soldier new to the desert in wartime. (From the Persian Gulf War.) □ *About 5,000 desert cherries arrived last week. Something is going to happen soon.* □ *The desert cherries are complaining about the scorpions again.*

dogface *n.* infantry soldier. (World War II. Also a term of address.) □ *Get those dogfaces over here on the double.* □ *Did I see a salute, dogface?*

gravel-pounder *n.* an infantry soldier. (Military.) □ *Do you really want to join the Army and be a gravel-pounder?* □ *The life of a gravel-pounder is not for me.*

ground-pounder *n.* an infantry soldier. (Military.) □ *If you join the Army, it means a lot of your life spent as a ground-pounder.* □ *You won't find me among the ground-pounders. I have flat feet.*

grunt *n.* an infantry soldier. (Military. From the gutteral sound made by a pig, and anyone doing very heavy labor.) □ *Hey, you grunts! Get in line!* □ *Get those grunts out on the field at sunrise!*

shavetail *n.* a second lieutenant; a non-commissioned officer in the army; any inexperienced person. (Military. From a nickname for an untrained mule that is marked by a shaved tail.) □ *This shavetail here is trying to tell me my job.* □ *Who's the shavetail dancing with the Colonel's daughter?*

vet *n.* a (war) veteran. □ *The vets in the hospitals across the land appreciate your kindness.* □ *The Vietnam vets had a very bad time of it.*

walking wounded *n.* soldiers who are injured but still able to walk. □ *There were enough walking wounded to start another division.* □ *Many of the walking wounded helped with the more seriously injured cases.*

weekend warrior *n.* a member of the military reserves. □ *I wanted to be a weekend warrior and get some of the educational benefits.* □ *The weekend warriors were called into active duty.*

yardbird *n.* an inept soldier. (Military.) □ *You yardbirds are going to learn discipline one way or another.* □ *How many of you yardbirds would like to go home in one piece?*

SOLUTION

put someone or something out of the way *tr.* to remove someone or something as a barrier. □ *I will put the whole problem out of the way.* □ *Yes, she is a problem, but you'll just have to put her out of the way and concentrate on this issue.*

quick fix *n.* a quick and probably none too permanent or satisfactory solution to a problem. □ *The quick fix isn't good enough in this case.* □ *He's a master of the quick fix.*

silver bullet AND **magic bullet** *n.* a specific, failsafe solution to a problem. (From the notion that a bullet made of silver is required to shoot a werewolf.) □ *I'm not suggesting that the committee* *has provided us with a silver bullet, only that their advice was timely and useful.* □ *Okay, I've got the silver bullet you need for this. Your vote on the pork storage units for my district would be greatly appreciated, of course.*

throw money at something *tr.* to try to solve a problem by spending money on it. (Often said of the U.S. federal government.) □ *This agency has thrown billions at the housing problem, but it has been nothing but a long-term disaster.* □ *Don't just throw money at it.*

SOMEONE

bod *n.* a person. □ *How many bods are coming over tonight?* □ *Who's the bod with the tight slacks?*

certain party *n.* "someone whom I do not wish to name; you can guess whom." (Always with *a*.) □ *I spoke to a certain party about the matter you mentioned.* □ *If a certain party finds out about you-know-what, what on earth will you do?*

what's his face AND **what's his name** *n.* someone whose name has been forgotten; someone whose name is being avoided. □ *Was what's his name there? I never can remember his name.* □ *I can't remember what's his face's name either.*

SORRY

sorry about that AND **sorry 'bout that** *interj.* "sorry"; "whoops." (A gross understatement, said more as a self-deprecating joke than as an apology.) □ *You spill hot cocoa on my coat, and all you can say is "Sorry 'bout that"?* □ *When the passenger stepped on my toe, she said, "Sorry about that."*

SPEECH

See also **TALKING**.

lines *n.* words; conversation. □ *I like your lines, but I don't have the time.* □ *We tossed some lines back and forth for a while and then split.*

lingo *n.* language; special vocabulary. □ *When you catch on to the lingo, everything becomes clear.* □ *If you don't like the lingo, don't listen.*

mouth full of South *n.* a southern accent. □ *You sure do have a mouth full of South.* □ *I just love to hear a man with a mouth full of South.*

yakky *mod.* talkative. □ *He's a yakky old man, but I like him.* □ *Isn't she yakky today?*

SPEECH - LACKING

tongue-tied *mod.* unable to speak from fear or confusion. (Standard English.) □ *I was tongue-tied and useless.* □ *Why do you get tongue-tied in front of a crowd?*

SPEECH - LOUD

yell one's head off AND **yell one's guts out** *tr.* to yell loud and long. □ *I was yelling my head off at the game.* □ *Stop yelling your guts out and listen to me.*

SPEED

barrel *in.* to go fast; to speed while driving. □ *He was barreling along at about ninety.* □ *She barreled out of here like a bat out of hell.*

barrel ass *in.* to move or drive carelessly and rapidly. (Potentially offensive. Use only with discretion.) □ *He was barrel assing along at nearly ninety.* □ *I'm gonna barrel ass outa here in just one minute.*

burn rubber *tr.* to run a car engine so fast that one spins the tires so that rubber is left on the street. □ *Man, this hog can really burn rubber.* □ *When George was at the age when the greatest thrill was burning rubber, he began to shave once a week.*

buzz along *in.* to drive or move along rapidly. □ *We were buzzing along at about seventy when we heard a siren.* □ *"You were buzzing along at eighty-two miles per hour," said the cop.*

clip *n.* a fast rate of speed. □ *By traveling at a good clip, we managed to get there before the wedding started.* □ *You were moving at a pretty good clip when you ran into the truck.*

cruise *in.* to travel at top speed. □ *This old caddy can really cruise.* □ *We cruised all the way to Philly.*

death on something *n.* moving very fast or skillfully on something, such as wheels. □ *He is way fast—just death on wheels.* □ *Pete is death on skis. You ought to see him go.*

flat out *mod.* at top speed. □ *They drove the thing flat out for an hour.* □ *If we run flat out, we can get there before dusk.*

go through someone like a dose of (the) salts *in.* to move through someone's digestive tract like a strong laxative. □ *That stuff they served last night went through me like a dose of salts.* □ *Careful of the coffee. It'll go through you like a dose of the salts.*

hump (along) *in.* to move along in a hurry. □ *I guess I'd better hump along over there.* □ *Come on, move it! Hump to the main office and be fast about it!*

hump it (to somewhere) *tr.* to move rapidly (to somewhere). □ *I have to hump it over to Kate's place right now.* □ *You'll have to hump it to get there in time.*

knock something out AND **knock something off** *tr.* to write something quickly. □ *Would you please knock a speech out for the senator?* □ *I'll knock off a letter explaining the whole thing.*

lickety-split *mod.* very fast. □ *They ran across the field lickety-split.* □ *We were there lickety-split in my new car.*

like a bat out of hell *mod.* very fast or sudden. (Use caution with *hell.*) □ *The cat took off like a bat out of hell.* □ *The car pulled away from the curb like a bat out of hell.*

like stink *mod.* rapidly. (As fast as a smell spreads.) □ *Those kids moved through the whole test like stink. Real eager-beavers.* □ *As long as she can run like stink, swim like stink, and smell like a flower, she gets my support.*

make *tr.* to achieve a specific speed. □ *See if this thing can make ninety.* □ *This buggy will make twice the speed of the old one.*

on the double *mod.* very fast; twice as fast. (Originally military. Refers to "double time" in marching.) □ *Get over here right now—on the double!* □ *She wants to see you in her office on the double.*

PDQ *mod.* "pretty damn quick"; very fast; very soon. (Initialism.) □ *You get those papers over here PDQ!* □ *They had better get this mess straightened out PDQ if they know what's good for them.*

put the pedal to the metal *tr.* to press a car's accelerator to the floor; to floor it. □ *Let's go, man. Put the pedal to the metal.* □ *Put the pedal to the metal, and we're out of here.*

quicker than hell *mod.* very fast. □ *You get over here quicker than hell.* □ *Be careful in the stock market. You can lose all your money quicker than hell.*

snappy *mod.* quick. □ *You can get there if you're snappy.* □ *Make it snappy. I'm in a hurry.*

speed demon *n.* a fast runner; a fast driver. □ *Tom is a speed demon. He qualified for the Olympics.* □ *Watch out, here comes another speed demon!*

speed merchant *n.* someone who does something fast: a runner, pitcher, swimmer, driver, etc. □ *Look at her go! What a speed merchant!* □ *What a pitch! That guy is a speed merchant for sure.*

tear into something *in.* to rush into a place. □ *I tore into the office and answered the phone.* □ *They tore into town and held up the bank.*

two shakes of a lamb's tail *mod.* quickly; rapidly. □ *I'll be there in two shakes of a lamb's tail.* □ *In two shakes of a lamb's tail, the entire pile of bricks had collapsed.*

wide open *mod.* as fast as possible; at full throttle. □ *I was driving along wide open when I became aware of a flashing red light.* □ *It was wide open and still wouldn't do better than eighty.*

SPEED - LACKING

at a snail's pace AND **at a snail's gallop** *mod.* very slowly. □ *Things are moving along at a snail's pace here, but we'll finish on time—have no fear.* □ *Poor old Wally is creeping at a snail's gallop because his car has a flat tire.*

SPENDING

big spender *n.* someone who spends much money. (Often sarcastic.) □ *The big spender left me a whole quarter tip!* □ *It's the big spenders who get themselves into money trouble.*

big-time spender *n.* someone who spends a lot of money. □ *Martin is the original big-time spender.* □ *A big-time spender doesn't look at the prices on the menu.*

lay something out *tr.* to spend some amount of money. □ *I can't lay that kind of money out every day!* □ *She laid out about $24,000 for that beemer.*

shell out (an amount of money) AND **shell an amount of money out** *tr. & in.* to spend a certain amount of money. □ *I'm not going to shell $400 out for that!* □ *Come on. You owe me. Shell out!*

shoot one's wad *tr.* to spend or use everything. □ *I shot my wad on junk food.* □ *I can't afford a cab. I shot my wad at the restaurant.*

shoot the works *tr.* to do everything; to use everything; to bet all one's money. □ *Okay, let's go out to dinner and shoot the works.* □ *Don't shoot the works! Save some for a cab.*

SPORTS

baller *n.* an athlete. (One who plays with footballs, basketballs, baseballs, etc.) □ *You will make a lot of money as a professional baller.* □ *Most of the high-paid ballers are out of a job by the age of forty.*

ballhead *n.* an athlete. (Perhaps a stupid one.) □ *My dorm is full of ballheads.* □ *If you want to be a ballhead, you have to have talent and stamina.*

bench *tr.* to take someone out of a ball game. □ *The coach benched Jim, who injured his arm.* □ *If you don't stop fouling, I'll bench you!*

bench jockey *n.* a player who sits on the bench and calls out advice. □ *The coach told all the bench jockeys to shut up.* □ *Do what you are told, or be a bench jockey for the rest of the season!*

bench warmer *n.* a ballplayer who spends most of the game on the bench waiting to play; a second-rate player. □ *You'll never be anything but a bench warmer.* □ *I do what I'm told so I can play every game. I don't want to be a bench warmer.*

grunt *n.* a wrestler. (Possibly in reference to a grunting pig.) □ *Two big grunts wearing outlandish costumes performed for the television cameras.* □ *One grunt threw the other grunt out of the ring.*

in play *mod.* being played; inbounds. (Said of a ball in a game.) □ *The ball's in play, so you made the wrong move.* □ *No, it wasn't in play, you twit!*

jock *n.* an athlete. □ *The jocks are all at practice now.* □ *She's dating a jock who has to be home by ten.*

jockstrap 1. *in.* to work as a professional athlete. □ *I jockstrapped for a few years and then lost my interest in it.* □ *I made a lot of money jockstrapping.* **2.** AND **jockstrapper** *n.* an athlete. (From the name of the supporting garment worn by male athletes.) □ *The jockstrappers are all at practice now.* □ *Here comes one of the best jockstrappers on the team.*

point man *n.* a ballplayer who habitually scores points. □ *Fred is supposed to be point man for our team, but tonight he is not doing so well.* □ *Paul is our favorite point man.*

ref 1. *n.* a referee. (Also a term of address.) □ *Hey, ref! Get some glasses!* □ *The ref did a fine job.* **2.** *tr.* to referee or officiate at something, such as a game. □ *Are you going to ref this one, or am I?* □ *I don't like to ref night games.*

rock-jock *n.* a mountain or rock climber. □ *The serious rock-jocks practice in North Wales.* □ *The sides of every mountain are covered with rock-jocks.*

shutout 1. *n.* a game where one team prevents the other from scoring at all. □ *He was still reveling from last week's shutout.* □ *It was another shutout at Klum Field House last night.* **2.** *mod.* having to do with a game where one team has no score. □ *Another shutout game gave the* *fans nothing to cheer about this afternoon.* □ *I was hoping for a shutout contest, and I got one.*

stanza *n.* an inning in baseball or some other division of a ball game. □ *He's doing better than he was in the last stanza.* □ *Jerry Clay is pitching again in this stanza.*

strap *n.* an athlete, not necessarily male. (From *jockstrap*.) □ *A whole gang of straps came in the bar and ordered milk.* □ *The guy's a strap all right, but he's not dumb.*

superjock *n.* an excellent athlete. □ *Mike is a real superjock. He plays four sports.* □ *All those superjocks get special meals and tutors to help them pass their classes.*

sweat sock *n.* an athlete; a *jock*. (Usually plural.) □ *I live in a dorm with a bunch of sweat socks. They feed us well, anyway.* □ *Both Bill's roommates are sweat socks and smell like it, too.*

ump *n.* an umpire. □ *The ump was gonna get killed if he didn't open his eyes.* □ *The ump has a pretty rough job.*

zebra *n.* a referee. (Because of the black and white striped shirt.) □ *The zebra blew the whistle on almost every play.* □ *There were not enough zebras to start the game.*

SPORTS - BASEBALL

apple *n.* a baseball. □ *Jim slammed the apple over the plate, but the ump called it a ball.* □ *Just when I raised my arm to throw to second, the damn apple slipped out of my hand and rolled down my arm. Now, explain that!*

away *mod.* out (in baseball). □ *Jim put the last one away, and that is three outs retiring the side.* □ *There's one away and two men left on base.*

beanball *n.* a pitched baseball that strikes the batter on the head, usually by accident. (Baseball.) □ *He got hit by a beanball and went after the pitcher with a bat.* □ *The guy is a master at throwing a beanball and living to tell about it.*

bottom *n.* the second half of a baseball inning. □ *It's the bottom of the second,*

Wilbur's up. □ *Wilbur hit a double-bagger in the bottom of the second.*

connect with something *in.* [for a batter] to hit a ball. □ *Wally connected for a double.* □ *He swung, but didn't connect with the ball.*

double-bagger *n.* a hit good for two bases in baseball. □ *Wilbur hit a nice double-bagger in the top of the fourth.* □ *The hit was good for a double-bagger.*

four-bagger *n.* a home run in baseball. □ *Wilbur hit his third four-bagger of the season.* □ *Another four-bagger for Wilbur!*

gopher ball *n.* a baseball pitch that is hit as a home run. (When it is hit, the batter will "go for" home.) □ *Wilbur hit another long gopher ball straight across center field.* □ *The center fielder did a dive over the fence trying to get the gopher ball.*

homer 1. *n.* a home run in baseball. □ *Wilbur hit one homer after another.* □ *Another homer for our team!* **2.** *tr. & in.* to hit a home run. □ *Wilbur homered another one and brought in two runs with him.* □ *Sam has never homered in six years of playing,*

pinch hitter *n.* a substitute batter in the game of baseball. □ *Sam is a pinch hitter for Ralph, who broke his wrist.* □ *Time to send in a pinch hitter.*

platter AND **plate** *n.* home base or home plate in baseball. (Usually with *the.*) □ *The batter stepped up to the platter.* □ *The ump dusted off the plate.*

power hitter *n.* a batter in the game of baseball who can hit the ball great distances. □ *Ted is a real power hitter. They'll try to walk him.* □ *I'm no power hitter, but I can run like mad.*

rock *n.* a baseball; a basketball. □ *Michael shot the rock to Scottie, who turned and dropped it in the basket.* □ *Hank hit the rock with the bat and broke the bat in half.*

round tripper *n.* a home run in baseball. □ *Ted is responsible for four round trippers in Saturday's game.* □ *He hit a round tripper in the fourth inning.*

screwball *n.* [in baseball] a (pitched) ball that does not travel in a straight line. □ *Jim threw another screwball, but somehow the batter hit it.* □ *Larry always seemed to be able to hit a screwball, no matter what.*

second sacker *n.* the second baseman in baseball. □ *The second sacker missed the throw, and the runner went on home.* □ *The shortstop and the second sacker crashed into one another trying to catch a ball.*

speedball *n.* [in baseball] a fast (pitched) ball. □ *The pitcher threw a speedball, and I didn't even see it!* □ *Tom can hit almost any speedball that Mike can throw.*

squeeze play *n.* a special play in baseball where there is a runner on third base and the batter bunts. (With an early start the runner may reach home plate.) □ *They pulled off that squeeze play like the professionals they are.* □ *The crowd roared as the squeeze play paid off.*

stick *n.* a baseball bat. (Baseball.) □ *He started to run and tripped over the stick.* □ *He holds the stick up higher than most batters.*

strike out *in.* [for a baseball batter] to be declared out after three strikes. (Baseball.) □ *And so Drew Wilson strikes out for his second time in this game!* □ *He struck out in the second inning, and manager Willy "Herky" Simpson read him out then.*

switch-hitter *n.* a ballplayer who bats either right-handed or left-handed. (Baseball.) □ *Monty is a switch-hitter, but he's batting right-handed today.* □ *I'm not a switch-hitter. In fact, I can hardly hit the ball at all.*

tag *tr.* [in baseball] to touch a runner with the baseball. □ *Wilbur tagged the runner and fell flat on his face.* □ *The catcher tagged the runner, but it was too late.*

top *n.* the first half of a baseball inning. □ *Wilbur hit a nice double-bagger in the top half of the fourth.* □ *It's the third inning at the top; Wilbur's up.*

triple-bagger AND **triple** *n.* a hit in baseball that gets the batter to third

base. □ *Wilbur connected for another triple-bagger in the fifth.* □ *It's a triple for Wilbur!*

SPORTS - BASKETBALL

air ball *n.* a basketball shot that misses everything, especially the basket. □ *Old Fred has become a master with the air ball. The net will never get worn-out.* □ *Another air ball for Fred Wilson. That's his fourth tonight.*

B-ball *n.* basketball; a basketball. □ *Let's go play some B-ball.* □ *Toss me the B-ball, huh?*

brick *n.* a missed shot in basketball. □ *Chalk up another brick for Michael.* □ *It looked close, but it was a brick.*

bucket 1. *n.* the goal (hoop and net) in basketball. □ *Freddy arced one at the bucket and missed.* □ *When he holds his arm up, his hand is as high as the top of the bucket.* **2.** *n.* a hoop or basket in basketball. □ *Four buckets in two minutes. Is that a record, or what?* □ *The last bucket put Adamsville ahead by two points.*

hoops *n.* the game of basketball. □ *You wanna go play some hoops?* □ *Welcome to another evening of college hoops, brought to you by the Nova Motor Company.*

jam 1. *tr. & in.* to force a basketball into the basket; to *slam dunk* a basketball. □ *He tried to jam it, but blew it.* □ *Andy broke the rim by trying to jam.* **2.** *n.* an act of forcing a basketball into the basket; a *slam dunk.* □ *The jam didn't work, and Fred's team rebounded the ball.* □ *One more jam for Wilbur!*

slam dunk 1. *tr. & in.* to force a basketball into the basket from above. (Usually hyphenated as a verb.) □ *Wilbur slam-dunked another one, raising the score from 108–110.* □ *Wilbur slam-dunked his way to fame and riches.* **2.** *n.* an act of making a basket as in sense 1. □ *Another slam dunk and Wilbur ties the score again!* □ *The rim will probably not withstand another slam dunk.*

slammer *n.* a *slam dunk.* □ *He really has that slammer perfected!* □ *It's another slammer for Wilbur!*

SPORTS - BOXING

KO AND **kayo 1.** *n.* a knockout. (The abbreviation is an initialism.) □ *It was a quick KO, and Wilbur was the new champ.* □ *It was a classic kayo. It was quick and effective.* **2.** *tr.* to knock someone out. □ *Wilbur planned to KO Wallace in the third round.* □ *Wilbur usually kayos his opponent.*

pull one's punches *tr.* to pull back during a boxing punch just before the full force of a blow is felt; to land lighter blows than normal upon an opponent. □ *The boxer started pulling his punches, and the ref ended the fight.* □ *He got fined for pulling his punches.*

tag 1. *n.* a blow to the body in boxing. □ *Wilbur landed another tag to the right shoulder before the gong sounded.* □ *Another tag on the head and Wilbur will be down.* **2.** *tr.* to punch someone in boxing. □ *Sam tagged his opponent on the cheek.* □ *The guy tagged him back right in the gut.*

take a fall AND **take a dive** *tr.* to fake being knocked out in a boxing match. □ *Wilbur wouldn't take a fall. He doesn't have it in him.* □ *The boxer took a dive in the second round and made everyone suspicious.*

telegraph one's punches *tr.* to signal, unintentionally, what blows one is about to strike. □ *Wilbur used to telegraph his punches until his coach beat it out of him.* □ *Don't telegraph your punches, kid! You'll be flat on your back in twenty seconds.*

throw a fight *tr.* to lose a boxing match on purpose. (Other words can replace *a.*) □ *I just know that Wilbur didn't throw that fight.* □ *The guy would never throw a fight.*

SPORTS - FOOTBALL

pill *n.* a football. □ *Hank tossed the pill to Wally, who promptly dropped it.* □ *Fred kicked the pill through the goal and won the game.*

sack 1. *tr.* to tackle someone in football. □ *I tried to sack him, but he was too fast.* □ *Sack that guy or else!* **2.** *n.* the completion of a tackle in football. □ *Andy made the sack on the ten-yard line.* □ *Who failed to make the sack?*

take someone out *tr.* to block someone, as in a football game. □ *I was supposed to take the left end out, but I was trapped under the center.* □ *Okay, Andy, you take out the center this time.*

SPORTS - GOLF

duffer *n.* an unskilled golfer. □ *Those duffers up ahead are holding up the game.* □ *Don't call me a duffer!*

stick *n.* a golf club. □ *These aren't my sticks, and you aren't my caddy. What's going on around here?* □ *I wanted a new set of sticks for Christmas, but I got a snowmobile instead.*

SPORTS - SKIING

snow bunny 1. *n.* a female skier. □ *Some cute little snow bunny came over and sat beside me.* □ *This place is swarming with snow bunnies who have never even seen a ski.* **2.** *n.* someone learning to ski. □ *This little slope is for snow bunnies.* □ *Most of the snow bunnies come here to socialize.*

SPORTS - VOLLEYBALL

V-ball *n.* volleyball. □ *You wanna play some V-ball?* □ *Playing V-ball is one of the best forms of exercise.*

SPOUSE

ball and chain *n.* a wife. (Mostly jocular.) □ *I've got to get home to my ball and chain.* □ *My ball and chain is mad at me.*

better half *n.* one's wife, and occasionally, one's husband. □ *My better half disapproved of the movie.* □ *I gotta go home to my better half.*

SPYING

bug 1. *n.* a spy device for listening to someone's conversation. □ *I found a little bug taped under my chair.* □ *The cops put bugs everywhere.* **2.** *tr.* to conceal a microphone somewhere. □ *Who bugged my office?* □ *We will have to bug the bookie joint to get the goods on those guys.*

plant *n.* a spy who secretly participates in criminal activities in order to inform on the criminals. □ *The crooks discovered the plant and fed him bogus infor-*

mation. □ *Don't tell everything you know. You don't know who's a plant and who isn't.*

spook *n.* a spy; a CIA (U.S. Central Intelligence Agency) agent. □ *I just learned that my uncle had been a spook for years.* □ *Fred is training to be a spook, but don't tell anybody.*

spook factory *n.* the CIA (U.S. Central Intelligence Agency) in Washington, D.C., where spies are said to be trained. □ *Tom got a job in the spook factory.* □ *Does the spook factory pay very well?*

wire 1. *n.* a bug; a device—usually worn by someone—for listening to someone's conversation remotely. □ *Lefty wore a wire when he chatted with Bruno.* □ *Max spotted the wire under Lefty's shirt.* **2.** *n.* a spy smuggled into a place. □ *Bruno thought Lefty was a wire.* □ *How do we know Lefty isn't a wire?*

START
See **BEGINNINGS**.

STATISTICS
stats *n.* statistics. □ *They're working out the stats now.* □ *The stats are expected to show that the trade balance is growing steadily worse.*

STEREO
See **AUDIO**.

STEROIDS
gorilla juice *n.* steroids. (Bodybuilding. Steroids build muscle tissue rapidly.) □ *Andy really wanted to get hold of some gorilla juice, but his parents said no.* □ *Do all those muscle-bound creatures take gorilla juice?*

STIMULANT
pick-me-up *n.* any food or drink that boosts energy, such as a drink of liquor, candy, or soda pop. □ *I'm pooped. I really need a pick-me-up.* □ *I can't finish the day without a little pick-me-up at lunch.*

pickup *n.* something eaten or drunk to boost energy. □ *Bartender, I need a little pickup.* □ *She stopped at a candy machine for a pickup.*

STINGY
cheapskate *n.* a miserly person; a very cheap person. □ *A 5 percent tip! What a cheapskate!* □ *I don't think of myself as a cheapskate, but I do try to watch my cash flow.*

chintzy *mod.* stingy; miserly. □ *The chintzy guy left me no tip!* □ *Don't be chintzy. Give the man a dollar for a cup of coffee.*

money grubber *n.* a stingy person. □ *Why is he such a money grubber? Is he going to take it with him?* □ *The boss is such a money grubber. He still has his first paper clip.*

penny-pincher *n.* someone who is very miserly; someone who objects to the expenditure of every penny. □ *If you weren't such a penny-pincher, you'd have some decent clothes.* □ *Let's elect some penny-pinchers to Congress.*

piker *n.* a miser; a *cheapskate*. (Also a term of address.) □ *You cheap little piker! Beat it!* □ *A 5 percent tip? You piker!*

scrooge *n.* a stingy person; a *penny-pincher*. (From the character in Charles Dickens's *A Christmas Carol*.) □ *Ask scrooge over there if you can borrow a quarter to call the cops.* □ *Don't be such a scrooge! All I want is a buck!*

tight *mod.* stingy. □ *She's really tight with her cash.* □ *You're just too tight. Gimme a fiver, Dad, come on.*

tightwad *n.* a stingy person; a miser. □ *There's no need to be such a tightwad.* □ *My dad's a tightwad.*

STINK
See **ODOR**.

STOMACH
See also **BELLY**.

basket *n.* the stomach. □ *I got a pain in the basket.* □ *You've got a lot of something in your basket. It's huge.*

breadbasket AND **dinner basket** *n.* the belly; the stomach. □ *I hit him, pow, right in the breadbasket.* □ *With a dinner basket like that, he must have a devil of a time buying clothes.*

cast-iron stomach *n.* a very strong stomach that can withstand bad food or anything nauseating. □ *If I didn't have a cast-iron stomach, I couldn't eat this stuff.* □ *Fred—known for his cast-iron stomach—ate all of his pepper soup.*

gutbucket *n.* the stomach. □ *Hey, your gutbucket's getting sort of big, isn't it?* □ *Sam poked Pete right in the gutbucket.*

labonza *n.* the pit of the stomach. □ *That kind of beautiful singing really gets you right in the labonza.* □ *She experienced the kind of gut-wrenching anger that starts in your labonza and cuts through right to the tip of your noggin.*

STOPPING

See also **CONCLUSION, ENDINGS, QUIT.**

Break it up! *exclam.* "Stop it!" (An order to two or more people to stop doing something, such as fighting.) □ *All right you two, break it up!* □ *She told the boys to break it up or get sent to the principal's office.*

Come off it! *exclam.* "Stop acting arrogantly!" □ *Oh, you're just one of us. Come off it!* □ *Come off it, Tiff. You're not the Queen of England.*

cut *tr.* to eliminate something; to stop (doing something). □ *OK, chum, cut the clowning.* □ *Cut that noise! Not another peep out of you.*

Cut it out! *exclam.* "Stop it!" □ *That's enough! Cut it out!* □ *Get your hands off me! Cut it out!*

Cut the comedy! *exclam.* "Get serious!"; "Stop acting silly!" □ *That's enough, you guys. Cut the comedy!* □ *Cut the comedy and get to work!*

Cut the crap! *exclam.* "Stop the nonsense!" □ *I've heard enough. Cut the crap!* □ *Cut the crap. Talk straight or get out.*

Give it up! *exclam.* "Quit now!"; "Enough is enough!" □ *Oh, give it up! You can't do it right.* □ *Give it up! You can't pitch!*

Give me a rest! *exclam.* "Lay off!"; "That is enough!" □ *Haven't I told you every-thing you need to know? Give me a rest.* □ *Give me a rest! I've heard enough.*

Hold everything! *exclam.* "Stop everything!" □ *Hold everything! I forgot my wallet.* □ *Hold everything! My door isn't closed.*

Hold it! *exclam.* "Stop right there!" □ *Hold it! Stop!* □ *That's enough! Hold it!*

Hold it, Buster! *exclam.* "Stop that, mister!" (Sometimes said by women in repulsing an arduous male.) □ *Hold it, Buster! Who do you think you are?* □ *Hold it, Buster! Who do you think I am?*

Keep your hands to yourself. *sent.* "Don't poke or hit other children." (Said to a child.) □ *Jimmy! Leave him alone and keep your hands to yourself.* □ *Keep your hands to yourself when you go to school.*

kibosh *tr.* to end something; to squelch something. □ *Please don't try to kibosh the scheme this time.* □ *Fred kiboshed our plan.*

kill *tr.* to stop or terminate something; to quash a story; to stop a story from being printed in a newspaper. □ *Kill that story. It's got too many errors.* □ *This issue has gone to press. Too late to kill it.*

put the kibosh on something *tr.* to squelch something. □ *The mayor put the kibosh on the whole deal.* □ *Tom was starting his presentation when Bob put the kibosh on the plan.*

scrub *tr.* to cancel something. □ *We had to scrub the whole plan because of the weather.* □ *The manager scrubbed the party because people wouldn't cooperate.*

stop on a dime *in.* to stop immediately. □ *This thing will stop on a dime.* □ *Imagine a bus that could stop on a dime.*

Stop the music! *exclam.* "Stop!"; "Stop whatever is happening!" (From an old radio game show called "Stop the Music!") □ *Stop the music! I have an announcement.* □ *"Stop the music!" hollered the conductor, making a little joke.*

Whoa! *exclam.* "Stop!" (Said to a horse or any person or thing.) □ *You've gone about far enough. Whoa!* □ *Whoa, you've gone about far enough.*

STORE

monkey wards *n.* Montgomery Ward, a department store chain. □ *I get that kind of stuff at monkey wards.* □ *They closed the monkey wards near us.*

STORE - LIQUOR

candy store *n.* a liquor store. □ *Let's stop at this candy store and get some bubbles.* □ *Somebody robbed the candy store on the corner.*

comfort station *n.* an establishment that sells liquor. □ *Let's get some belch at a comfort station along here somewhere.* □ *There's cops all around that comfort station. Somebody must have robbed it.*

filling station *n.* a liquor store. (From an old name for an automobile service station.) □ *Please stop at the filling station and get some suds on your way home.* □ *The filling station on the corner does a big business on Fridays.*

happy shop *n.* a liquor store. □ *I need something from the happy shop.* □ *Let's stop off at the happy shop.*

headache department AND **headache house** *n.* a liquor store or department. □ *I stopped in at the headache department for some supplies.* □ *The headache house is having a special on gin.*

joint *n.* a tavern; a speakeasy. (Prohibition.) □ *Lefty has his own joint over on Fourth Street.* □ *I wanted to open a joint, but I don't have the cash.*

juice house *n.* a liquor store. □ *Would you stop by the juice house for some foam?* □ *The juice house was held up last night.*

leeky store *n.* a liquor store. (Black. From *liquor*.) □ *Get me some grapes at the leeky store.* □ *The leeky store is closed till 10:00 A.M.*

LIQ *n.* a liquor store. (Initialism.) □ *Let's stop at the LIQ and get some berries.* □ *I got a headache already. I don't need anything from any LIQ to make it worse.*

oasis *n.* a place to buy liquor. □ *Let's go into this oasis here and pick up a few bottles.* □ *There is an oasis on almost every corner in this district.*

STORY

whodunit *n.* a detective story. □ *I love to read a good whodunit every now and then.* □ *I go through about three whodunits a week.*

STRANGE

dorky *mod.* strange; weird; undesirable; stupid. □ *That is a real dorky idea. Just forget it.* □ *It's just too dorky.* □ *Let me out of this dorky place!* □ *I wouldn't be caught dead wearing that dorky hat.*

double-gaited *mod.* weird; eccentric. □ *Carl is a little double-gaited at times. Tries too hard for a laugh.* □ *Wow, is he ever double-gaited!* □ *She is one of the most successful double-gaited comedians I've ever seen.*

funky *mod.* strange; far out. □ *I like your funky hat.* □ *Is he funky?* □ *He's such a funky guy.*

kinky *mod.* having to do with someone or something strange or weird. □ *The guy is so kinky that everyone avoids him.* □ *Who is that kinky dame in the net stockings?*

kookish *mod.* strange; eccentric. □ *There's a lot of kookish things going on around here.* □ *He is just too kookish.* □ *Who is the kookish one over there with the purple shades?*

oddball *mod.* strange; peculiar. □ *What an oddball combination of things!* □ *It's too oddball for me.* □ *Your oddball ideas have cost us too much money.*

offbeat *mod.* strange; unconventional. □ *That is really an offbeat idea.* □ *Tom is sort of offbeat. Well, he's weird.*

off-the-wall *mod.* strange; improbable; nonsensical. □ *What an off-the-wall guy!* □ *Your ideas are generally off-the-wall, but this one makes sense.*

(strictly) from hunger *mod.* very strange; acceptable only when nothing else is available. □ *This kind of entertainment is from hunger.* □ *The singer was strictly from hunger.*

zerking *mod.* strange; zerk-like. □ *Who is that zerking nerd over there?* □ *That zerking little guy is Martin, and I like him.*

STRAW

donkey's breakfast *n.* something made of straw: a straw hat, a straw mattress, etc. □ *I don't really want to sleep on a donkey's breakfast, but it's better than the floor.* □ *The tourist was wearing a red dress and had a donkey's breakfast on her head.*

STRENGTH

See POWER, STRONG.

STRONG

built like a brick outhouse AND **built like a brick shithouse** *mod.* well-built—either strong or attractive. (The second entry is potentially offensive. Use only with discretion.) □ *That guy's built like a brick shithouse.* □ *This garage is built like a brick outhouse. It'll last for years.*

STUBBORNNESS

bullheaded *mod.* stubborn. □ *Don't be so bullheaded.* □ *You are the most bullheaded man I've ever known.*

hardheaded *mod.* stubborn. □ *Gary is a real hardheaded guy.* □ *Anybody that hardheaded is going to have trouble with everybody.*

pigheaded *mod.* stupidly stubborn. (From the notion that pigs are immovable.) □ *You are unbelievably pigheaded!* □ *What a stupid pigheaded position to take.*

STUDENT

aggie *n.* a student of an agricultural (college) training program. (Specifically, Texas A & M.) □ *More and more aggies are going back for their MBAs.* □ *What kind of a job can an aggie get these days?*

coed *n.* a female college student. (From *coeducational.*) □ *Some of these coeds are pretty strong-minded.* □ *My daughter is a coed at Midwest University.*

dropout *n.* someone who has dropped out of school. □ *Dropouts find it very hard to get a job.* □ *Some dropouts make great successes of themselves, but not very many.*

frosh 1. *n.* a freshman. □ *Ken is just a frosh, but he looks older.* □ *Get some frosh to do it for you.* **2.** *mod.* having to do with

freshmen. □ *The frosh dorm is full again this year.* □ *This is a frosh dance. You can't come in.*

geek *n.* an earnest student; a hardworking student. □ *Martin is a geek, but he will go places with his brains.* □ *It looks like the geeks are taking over this campus. How gross!*

grade-grubber 1. *n.* a student who flatters the teacher in hopes of a higher grade. □ *Toward the end of a semester, my office is filled with grade-grubbers.* □ *A few grade-grubbers help assure old professors that the world is not really changing at all.* **2.** *n.* an earnest, hard-working student. (In the way a pig roots or grubs around for food.) □ *Martin is a grade-grubber and a real hard worker.* □ *If there are too many grade-grubbers in a class, it will really throw off the grading scale.*

grub *n.* an earnest student. (Collegiate.) □ *Martin is not exactly a grub. He gets good grades without trying.* □ *The test was so hard, even the grubs did poorly.*

grunt *n.* a hard-working student. □ *Martin isn't a grunt. Everything's easy for Martin.* □ *The grunts got B's on the test. It was that hard!*

gunner *n.* an earnest student. (Collegiate.) □ *Martin is a gunner, all right.* □ *The gunners in my algebra class always get the A's.*

gweeb *n.* a studious student. (Collegiate.) □ *I'm in a physics class full of gweebs.* □ *Martin is a gweeb, all right, but he's a good guy.*

Joe College *n.* a typical or average male college student. □ *You sure look like Joe College from the good old days.* □ *Joe College never had a computer or a laser-powered record player in the good old days.*

marksman *n.* a serious college student who works hard to get good marks (grades). □ *Sally is a marksman. She's always studying.* □ *Bill kept saying that Todd was a geek and a marksman, until Todd flunked algebra.*

power tool *n.* a student who studies most of the time. □ *Willard is a power tool if there ever was one. Studies most of* *the night.* □ *All the power tools always get the best grades.*

preppie AND **preppy 1.** *mod.* in the manner of a student at a preparatory school. □ *I just love your preppie coat.* □ *Preppy clothes are almost out of style.* **2.** *n.* a young person who dresses and acts like a student at a preparatory school. □ *Those preppies are having fun now, but how will they support themselves?* □ *Do all preppies become yuppies?*

shmen *n.* freshmen. □ *A couple of shmen wandered by—looking sort of lost.* □ *The shmen are having a party all to themselves this Friday.*

shwench *n.* a female freshman. (Collegiate.) □ *A couple of giggling shwenches showed up to cheer on the team.* □ *There's a shwench in my English class who knows more than the prof.*

soph *n.* a sophomore. □ *The sophs are holding a meeting to decide on a plan.* □ *He's just a soph, so he still might grow a little.*

squid *n.* an earnest student; a collegiate wimp. (Collegiate. Refers to sliminess.) □ *This whole campus is populated by squids and nerds.* □ *I'm no squid. I went out on a date last month.*

study animal *n.* someone who studies hard. □ *All the geeks in the dorm were study animals. Dull, dull, dull.* □ *At the end of the school year every party animal turns into a study animal.*

super-strap *n.* an earnest and hard-working student. □ *He's a melvin, a super-strap, and he doesn't do anything but study.* □ *I couldn't be a super-strap even if I had the brains. I just don't care that much.*

techie *n.* a student in a technical or engineering college. □ *Does one guy like Martin prove that all techies are nerds?* □ *Of course, one groovy guy proves that techies aren't nerds, right?*

throat *n.* an earnest student; a "cutthroat" student. (Collegiate.) □ *Martin is not a throat! He's not that smart.* □ *All the throats got A's, of course.*

tool *n.* an earnest student. □ *Of course he's a tool. See the plastic liner in his pocket?* □ *Martin is a tool, and he's proud of it.*

weasel *n.* an earnest student. (Collegiate.) □ *Who's the weasel who always gets A's?* □ *Martin is your classic weasel.*

weenie *n.* an earnest student. (Collegiate.) □ *That weenie keeps getting A's and raising the grade scale.* □ *Who's the weenie with the thick glasses?*

wonk *n.* an earnest student. (Collegiate.) □ *Who's the wonk who keeps getting the straight A's?* □ *Yes, you could call Martin a wonk. In fact, he's the classic wonk.*

zod *n.* a studious person. □ *Quiet. You don't want to disturb the zods.* □ *Dave decided to be a zod for a semester and see if he could pass his courses.*

STUDY

book *in.* to study. □ *I gotta book. Bye.* □ *I hate to book all night.*

book it *tr.* to study hard; to spend a period of time studying. (Collegiate.) □ *I am so tired of booking it every night of my life.* □ *I've got to spend the rest of the night booking it.*

geek out *in.* to study hard. □ *Big test tomorrow. I've got to get home and geek out.* □ *Bill's a geekazoid. He geeks out all the time.*

grade-grubbing *n.* working hard at one's studies in hopes of a high grade. □ *If all you're here for is grade-grubbing, you're going to miss a lot.* □ *Get a hobby. All grade-grubbing in college is no good.*

hit the books AND **pound the books** *tr.* to study hard. □ *I spent the weekend pounding the books.* □ *I gotta go home and hit the books.*

oil it *tr.* to study all night. (Literally, "burn the midnight oil.") □ *I have a test tomorrow, and I really have to oil it tonight.* □ *If you studied all semester long, you would still have to oil it before final exams.*

wonky *mod.* studious. (Collegiate.) □ *Martin is certainly the wonky type.* □ *You ought to get a little wonky yourself.*

STUN

zap *tr.* to stun someone with an imaginary ray gun. □ *Jimmy swung around the corner and zapped me.* □ *He zapped me with a water gun.*

STUNT

wheely AND **wheelie** *n.* an act of rearing up on a bike or motorcycle, balancing on the rear wheel. □ *Can you do wheelies?* □ *The kid did a wheely and scared his mother to death.*

STUPIDITY

airheaded *mod.* stupid; giddy. □ *You are the most airheaded twit I have ever met!* □ *That was an airheaded idea if I ever heard one.*

birdbrain(ed) *mod.* stupid. □ *I've never heard such a birdbrain idea in my life.* □ *Look, you birdbrained idiot, you are dead wrong!*

brain-dead *mod.* stupid. □ *I don't know why he's so dull. He's seems brain-dead half the time.* □ *I think that half my students are brain-dead.*

clucky *mod.* stupid; oafish. □ *What a clucky dame!* □ *The plan you submitted to this office was rejected by the policy committee. They noted that it was the cluckiest idea they had ever seen.*

clueless *mod.* unaware. □ *She is so dense. Totally clueless.* □ *I have never seen anyone so totally clueless. What a dunce.*

cluelessness *n.* total stupidity. □ *I just shake my head in wonder at the cluelessness of my fellow humans.* □ *This place is just infested with juvenile cluelessness!*

cornball *mod.* stupid or corny. □ *What a cornball idea!* □ *Ken is such a cornball hick!*

crackbrained *mod.* stupid; ridiculous. □ *I've heard enough of your crackbrained schemes.* □ *One more crackbrained idea and you're fired.*

dead from the neck up *mod.* stupid. (With a "dead" head.) □ *Beavis seems dead from the neck up.* □ *She acts like she is dead from the neck up.*

dopey *mod.* stupid. □ *What a dopey guy!* □ *That was a dopey thing to do.*

dumbski *mod.* stupid; dumb. □ *What a dumbski jerk!* □ *It is not a dumbski idea!*

fathead *n.* a stupid person; someone who has fat where brains ought to be. □ *You can be such a fathead!* □ *Paul, you are being a perfect fathead.*

fatheaded *mod.* stupid. □ *Now, that is really a fatheaded idea.* □ *It's not fatheaded!* □ *Let's not come up with a fatheaded plan. This one has to make sense.*

flatheaded *mod.* stupid. □ *That is really a flatheaded idea, you know?* □ *Martin seems flatheaded, but he's quite brilliant.*

klutzy *mod.* foolish; stupid. □ *That was really a klutzy thing to do.* □ *You are so klutzy!* □ *Whose klutzy idea was this?*

lamebrain AND **lamebrained** *mod.* foolish. □ *No more of your lamebrain ideas!* □ *My last scheme looked lamebrained at first, but it worked, didn't it?*

lardhead *mod.* foolish. □ *Now here's something from the lardhead department.* □ *No more of those lardhead ideas!*

McFly *mod.* stupid; simple-minded. □ *That was a McFly thing to do.* □ *Wayne is so McFly!*

meatheaded *mod.* stupid; simple-minded. □ *Of all the meatheaded ideas. This one takes the cake!* □ *How meatheaded!* □ *When someone conducts a meatheaded operation like this, we tend to lose faith in the whole system.*

nothing upstairs *phr.* no brains; stupid. □ *Tom is sort of stupid acting. You know—nothing upstairs.* □ *I know what's wrong with you. Nothing upstairs.*

not know from nothing *in.* to be stupid, innocent, and naive. (Usually with *don't*, as in the examples. Always in the negative.) □ *Tom don't know from nothing. He is really dense.* □ *Don't pay any attention to her. She don't know from nothing.*

nutty *mod.* silly; giddy; stupid. □ *What a nutty idea!* □ *That's nutty!* □ *Mary is a real nutty girl, but she is my best friend.*

one brick shy of a load *mod.* stupid; dense. □ *Joyce has done some stupid things. Sometimes I think she is one brick shy of a load.* □ *Ted is one brick shy of a* *load. He can't seem to do what he is told without messing up.*

out to lunch *mod.* absentminded; giddy; stupid acting. □ *Old Ted is so out to lunch these days. Seems to be losing his mind.* □ *Don't pay any attention to my uncle. He's out to lunch.*

punch-drunk AND **punchy** *mod.* unstable; stupid acting; bewildered. (From a term describing a boxer suffering from brain damage.) □ *I feel sort of punch-drunk after a roller-coaster ride.* □ *Who is that punchy jerk?* □ *I feel punchy when I drink too much coffee.*

soft *mod.* stupid. □ *The guy's soft in the head. He just can't think straight.* □ *She seems a little soft, but she's really bright.*

soft in the head *mod.* stupid; witless. □ *George is just soft in the head. He'll never get away with his little plan.* □ *You're soft in the head if you think I'll go along with that.*

stand there with one's bare face hanging out *phr.* to stand someplace looking helpless and stupid. □ *Say something. Don't just stand there with your bare face hanging out.* □ *She just stood there with her bare face hanging out while they took away everything she owned.*

There's nobody home. *sent.* "There are no brains in someone's head." □ *There's lots of goodwill in that head, but there's nobody home.* □ *You twit! There's nobody home—that's for sure.*

thick *mod.* stupid; *thickheaded.* □ *She's sort of thick, but she means well.* □ *Why are you so thick about money?*

thickheaded *mod.* stupid; with more bone than brain in the head. □ *He's so thickheaded he can play football without a helmet.* □ *What thickheaded dolt put scallops in the scalloped potatoes?*

three bricks shy of a load *mod.* stupid; dense; shortchanged on intelligence. □ *I would never say she was dense. Just three bricks shy of a load.* □ *Why do you act like you're three bricks shy of a load?*

totally clueless *mod.* ignorant (of something). □ *Everybody was totally clueless*

as to what to do. □ *Sorry, I'm totally clueless as to what to do.*

wet *mod.* feeble; in the manner of a nerd. □ *Tom is totally wet. What a jerk.* □ *Wayne is wet and so's his buddy.*

yo-yo *mod.* stupid. □ *Ask that yo-yo jerk to move along.* □ *That is the world's yo-yoest joke!*

SUBMARINE

sub *n.* a submarine. □ *I was aboard a sub for twenty minutes—and that was at Disney World.* □ *You have to have a special kind of personality to live on a sub.*

SUBSTITUTE

pinch hitter *n.* any substitute person. □ *In school today we had a pinch hitter. Our teacher was sick.* □ *I want my own doctor, not a pinch hitter!*

sub 1. *in.* to serve as a temporary replacement. □ *I subbed for Mary in a couple of games.* □ *Then she subbed for me to even the score.* **2.** *n.* a substitute. □ *I was a sub in the school system for a while.* □ *The coach sent in a sub for Wilbur.*

SUBTLE

low-key *mod.* not obvious. □ *Let's try to keep this low-key so as not to upset the family.* □ *It was a very low-key meeting, but we got a lot done.*

SUBURB

burb *n.* a suburb. (Usually plural.) □ *I've lived in the burbs all my life.* □ *Our burb is too far from the city for much pollution.*

burbed out *mod.* looking very middle-class and suburban; decked out like a suburban citizen. □ *She's all burbed out with new clothes and a fancy car.* □ *He looks sort of burbed out for a city guy.*

SUCCESS

See also **ACHIEVEMENT**.

big time *n.* the high level of success. □ *I've finally reached the big time!* □ *When the pressure in the big time got to be too much, the guy simply retired.*

blockbuster 1. *n.* something enormous, especially a movie or book that attracts a large audience. □ *That blockbuster should make about $20 million.* □ *I need* two blockbusters like that to pay for the last flop. **2.** *mod.* exciting and successful. □ *The new blockbuster movie made about a zillion bucks in a month.* □ *With a blockbuster novel like that in print, you should make quite a bundle.*

boffo 1. *n.* a box-office hit; a successful play, musical, movie, etc. □ *The last one was a tremendous boffo, but we only broke even.* □ *I need a boffo just once in my life.* **2.** *mod.* successful; tremendous. □ *We had a boffo time at your rally.* □ *Another boffo success for Wally!* □ *That was really boffo!*

clean up (on something) *in.* to make a lot of money on something. □ *The promoters cleaned up on the product.* □ *If we advertise, we can clean up.*

come out ahead *in.* to end up with a profit; to end up with some benefit. □ *I never seem to come out ahead at the end of the month.* □ *We'll come out ahead in the end. Just you wait.*

come out on top *in.* to end up to the better; to win. □ *Tim always has to come out on top—a classic poor loser.* □ *She made all the wrong moves and still came out on top.*

get off (on something) *in.* to do well on something. □ *Wayne is getting off on history, much to everyone's surprise.* □ *Bill got off on fixing up his car, and I may let him do mine, too.*

go great guns *in.* to do very well; to go very fast. □ *Everything is going great guns around here. We're busy and making lots of money.* □ *The project is finally going great guns, just as we planned.*

go over big *in.* to be appreciated as a success. □ *I'm sure this will go over big with the folks at home.* □ *Well, it didn't go over very big with the boss.*

go places *in.* to become very successful. □ *I knew that Sally would go places.* □ *I really want to go places in life.*

have it made (in the shade) *tr.* to have succeeded; to be set for life. (*Have got* can replace *have*.) □ *Wow, is he lucky! He has it made in the shade.* □ *Who's got it made in the shade?*

heavyweight *mod.* important; successful. □ *Vince is one of the heavyweight operators in this business.* □ *He's good, but he's no heavyweight.*

hit *n.* a success; something that meets with approval. □ *The play was a hit.* □ *The fudge with nuts in it was a great hit at the sale.*

hit pay dirt AND **strike pay dirt** *tr.* to discover something of value. □ *At last, we hit pay dirt.* □ *When we opened the last trunk, we knew we had struck pay dirt.*

hit the jackpot *tr.* to win a large amount of money. □ *I hit the jackpot in the big contest.* □ *Sally hit the jackpot in the lottery.*

in tall cotton *mod.* successful; on easy street. □ *I won some money at the track, and I'm really in tall cotton.* □ *We were in tall cotton until the IRS caught up with us.*

killing *n.* a great financial success. □ *Sally made a real killing in the stock market.* □ *Fred made a killing in real estate.*

make (it) big *tr. & in.* to become successful, especially financially. □ *I always knew that someday I would make it big.* □ *My brother made big, but it has just led to tax problems.*

make out *in.* to succeed. □ *How did you make out?* □ *I hope I make out okay tomorrow.*

on a roll *mod.* in the midst of a series of successes. □ *Don't stop me now. I'm on a roll.* □ *Things are going great for Larry. He's on a roll now.*

pan out *in.* [for something] to work out or turn out all right. □ *Don't worry. Everything will pan out okay.* □ *Nothing seems to pan out for me anymore.*

pass *n.* a passing grade or mark on a test. □ *Did you get a pass or a fail?* □ *This is my third pass this semester.*

rake something in *tr.* to take in a lot of something, usually money. □ *Our candidate will rake votes in by the thousand.* □ *They were raking in money by the bushel.*

roll *n.* a sustained period of luck or productivity. □ *I'm doing great! What a roll!* □ *The fantastic roll that this performer is on is truly exciting.*

score *in.* to succeed. □ *I knew if I kept trying I could score.* □ *It takes hard work and luck to score.*

smash hit *n.* a play, movie, musical, etc., which is a big success. □ *Her first book was a smash hit. The second was a disaster.* □ *A smash hit doesn't always make people rich.*

take off *in.* [for something] to start selling well. □ *The fluffy dog dolls began to take off, and we sold out the lot.* □ *Ticket sales really took off after the first performance.*

take things easy *tr.* to live well and comfortably. □ *I'll be glad when I can make enough money to take things easy.* □ *I make enough to take things easy.*

vivor *n.* a survivor; a street person who manages to survive. □ *Harry's a vivor, and I like him.* □ *She's no champ, but she's a vivor.*

waltz through something *in.* to get through something easily. □ *I waltzed through my comps and started on my research in my second year.* □ *I tried to waltz through my assignment, but it was too hard.*

SUDDEN

out of left field *mod.* suddenly; from an unexpected source or direction. □ *Most of your ideas are out of left field.* □ *All of his paintings are right out of left field.*

pickup *mod.* spontaneous; unplanned. (Especially with ball games where the members of the team are "picked up" from whoever is available.) □ *He stopped at the basketball court for a pickup game with the boys.* □ *A pickup game can be fun if the sides are evenly matched.*

sudden death *mod.* having to do with something short, quick, and decisive. □ *The game ended in a sudden death playoff.* □ *Okay, you've got just one more sudden death chance.*

SUFFERING

eat one's heart out 1. *tr.* to suffer from sorrow or grief. □ *She has been eating her heart out over that jerk ever since he ran away with Tracy.* □ *Don't eat your heart out. You really didn't like him that much, did you?* **2.** *tr.* to suffer from envy or jealousy. (Usually a command.) □ *Yeah, this one's all mine. Eat your heart out!* □ *Eat your heart out! I won it fair and square.*

sweat bullets *tr.* to suffer about something; to be anxious or nervous about something; to *sweat blood.* □ *They were sweating bullets, waiting for the results.* □ *The kid sat in the waiting room, sweating bullets while the surgeons worked on his brother.*

twist (slowly) in the wind *in.* to suffer the agony of some punishment, such as hanging. (Figurative only.) □ *I'll see you twist in the wind for trying to frustrate this investigation.* □ *The prosecutor was determined that Max would twist slowly in the wind for the crime.*

SUGAR

sand *n.* sugar. □ *Please pass the sand.* □ *Do you use sand in your coffee?*

SUITABLE

hand-in-glove *mod.* suiting one another naturally. □ *These two go hand-in-glove.* □ *The two parts went together like hand-in-glove.*

SUNBURN

baked *mod.* sunburned. □ *I was out in the sun until I got totally baked.* □ *If you would use some lotion, you wouldn't get so baked.*

SUNGLASSES

cheaters *n.* sunglasses. (Formerly all spectacles.) □ *Get your cheaters on. The sun's really bright.* □ *Somebody sat on my cheaters!*

shades *n.* dark glasses. □ *Where are my shades? The sun is too bright.* □ *The guy stood there—wearing shades and carrying a violin case.*

sunshades *n.* sunglasses. □ *Where are my sunshades? Did you borrow them again?* □ *I left my sunshades in the car.*

tints *n.* sunglasses. □ *Somebody sat on my tints.* □ *I have to get some prescription tints.*

SUNSHINE

rays *n.* sunshine. (Collegiate.) □ *I'm going to go out and get some rays today.* □ *I've had too many rays. I'm cooked.*

SUPERIORITY

ego trip *n.* a public expression of one's feelings of importance or superiority. □ *The guy is on another ego trip. Pay no attention.* □ *Sorry, I guess I'm on another ego trip.*

rule *in.* to dominate; to be the best. (Slang only in certain contexts. Typical in graffiti.) □ *The Rockets rule!* □ *Pizza rules around here.*

top of the heap *n.* a position superior to everyone else. □ *For some reason, Jerry has to be at the top of the heap.* □ *She fought her way to the top of the heap and means to stay there.*

SURFING

boogie-board *n.* a surfboard. (California.) □ *Get your boogie-board out there in that tube.* □ *She cracked her boogie-board apart on that big one.*

cop a tube *tr.* to catch a perfect tubular wave. □ *He was a real pro at copping a tube, and always just the right one.* □ *Mark—as drunk as all get out—said he was gonna go out and cop a tube.*

hang five AND **hang ten** *tr.* to stand toward the front of a surfboard or diving board and hang the toes of one or both feet over the edge. (Teens and collegiate.) □ *The coach told her to hang ten and not to look down.* □ *Get out there and hang five. You can swim. Nothing can go wrong.*

in the tube *mod.* in the tube of a large wave. □ *Pete is in the tube and looks great.* □ *On a day like today, I want to be out there in the tube.*

tube *n.* the inner curve of a tall wave. □ *I'm waiting for the best tube.* □ *A good tube will do, won't it?*

woody *n.* a wooden surfboard; a surfboard. □ *Who's the guy with the woody on his head?* □ *Get your woody, and let's get moving.*

SURPASS

See **OVERWHELM**.

SURPRISE

See also **AMAZEMENT, SHOCK**.

blindside *tr.* [for someone or something] to surprise someone, as if sneaking up on the blind side of a one-eyed person (or animal). □ *The new tax law blindsided about half the population.* □ *The mugger came up and blindsided her with a blow to the head before she knew what had happened.*

bomb(shell) *n.* a stunning piece of news that is "dropped" without warning. □ *I am still recovering from your bomb of last evening.* □ *After you left us with the bombshell about your marriage to the Christmas tree farmer in Montana, we began to realize that it's your life and you should do what you want.*

double take *n.* a surprised second look at something. □ *I did a double take and blushed.* □ *Fred did a double take, then recognized Tracy.*

drop a brick AND **drop a bomb(shell)** *tr.* to reveal startling information. □ *Tracy came in and dropped a brick that scared us all.* □ *You really dropped a bombshell!*

drop one's teeth *tr.* to react with great surprise. □ *I almost dropped my teeth when she told me her news.* □ *They dropped their teeth when I told them I was married.*

eye-opener *n.* a real surprise. □ *Her confession was a real eye-opener.* □ *This day has been an eye-opener for me.*

Fancy meeting you here. *sent.* "Just imagine meeting you here!"; "I am surprised to meet you here!" □ *Well, hello, Tom. Fancy meeting you here!* □ *Fancy meeting you here, Bill. How have you been?*

flabbergasted *mod.* surprised; baffled. □ *We were flabbergasted by your proposal.* □ *They all sat there flabbergasted.*

floored *mod.* surprised. □ *I was really floored by what she had to say.* □ *You looked floored when I came in. Wasn't I invited?*

have kittens *tr.* to be surprised. □ *I nearly had kittens when I heard.* □ *She had kittens when she heard about the wedding.*

hell of a note *n.* a surprising or amazing piece of news. (Use caution with *hell.*) □ *Well, that's a hell of a note!* □ *You forgot it. That's a hell of a note.*

knock someone out *tr.* to surprise someone. □ *Her stunning beauty knocked us all out.* □ *The news knocked out the entire crowd.*

knock someone's socks off *tr.* to surprise or startle someone; to overwhelm someone. □ *Wow, that explosion nearly knocked my socks off.* □ *This news'll knock your socks off.*

You could have knocked me over with a feather. *sent.* "I was completely surprised." □ *I was shocked. You could have knocked me over with a feather.* □ *You could have knocked me over with a feather, I was so zapped!*

SURRENDER

You can't fight city hall. *sent.* "You cannot fight a bureaucracy." □ *I finally gave up. You can't fight city hall.* □ *You can't fight city hall. Pay the parking ticket and forget it.*

SURVIVAL

walk *in.* to walk away from something unharmed. □ *It couldn't have been much of an accident. Both drivers walked.* □ *It was a horrible meeting, but when it was over I just walked.*

SURVIVAL - LACKING

snowball's chance in hell *n.* a very poor chance. (Usually in the negative.) □ *She doesn't have a snowball's chance in hell of getting it done on time.* □ *I know I don't have a snowball's chance in hell, but I'll try anyway.*

SUSPICION

fishy *mod.* dubious; questionable; likely to be improper or illegal. □ *Something*

here is fishy. □ *That was a pretty fishy story you told us.*

smell a rat *tr.* to suspect that something is wrong. □ *He smelled a rat the minute he came into the room.* □ *Keep everything normal. I don't want her to smell a rat. She has never had a surprise party before.*

smell fishy *in.* to seem suspicious. □ *Barlowe squinted a bit. Something smells fishy here, he thought.* □ *Something about the deal smelled fishy.*

smell to (high) heaven *in.* to give signals that cause suspicion. □ *This deal is messed up. It smells to high heaven.* □ *Something's wrong here. Somebody blabbed. This setup smells to high heaven.*

SWIMMING

belly flop 1 *n.* a failed dive where there is a loud noise when the flat of the stomach hits the water. □ *Wow, I never knew that a belly flop hurts!* □ *A belly flop gets zero points in a dive meet.* **2.** *in.* to dive into the water so that the flat of the stomach hits the water, usually making a loud noise. □ *Sam belly flopped again.* □ *I get so embarrassed when I belly flop!*

fanny-dipper *n.* a swimmer, as opposed to a surfer. (California.) □ *The fanny-dippers are not supposed to go out that far.* □ *It's too windy for fanny-dippers, let alone surfers.*

SYMBOL

gear *n.* an asterisk (*). □ *Why is there a gear after this word?* □ *The gear stands for anything you want it to stand for.*

mesh *n.* a crosshatch or octothorpe, (#). □ *Put a mesh on each end of your formula.* □ *What does the mesh stand for in this equation?*

pigpen *n.* a crosshatch or octothorpe, (#). (Computers.) □ *Put a pigpen just after the gear.* □ *There is nothing on my printout but a whole string of pigpens.*

screamer *n.* an exclamation point. (Printing.) □ *Put a screamer at the end of the line.* □ *Clean up this copy. There are too many screamers. Looks like junior high stuff.*

shout *n.* an exclamation point. □ *Put a shout at the end of the line. Make this dull story more sexy.* □ *This gal uses shouts like they were salt and pepper.*

shriek *n.* an exclamation point. (Typesetters.) □ *Where is there a shriek at the end?* □ *Take off that shriek. You use too many of those things.*

squiggle *n.* a wiggly mark. □ *What does this squiggle mean?* □ *That squiggle is my signature.*

toke *n.* a token. □ *Yeah. Just a little toke of my approval.* □ *Nothing much. Just a toke.*

wow *n.* an exclamation point. □ *Put a wow at the end of this sentence.* □ *Almost every sentence you write has a wow at the end of it.*

SYMBOL - DEATH

O-sign *n.* the rounded, open mouth of a dead person. (A semi-jocular usage. Hospitals.) □ *The guy in room 226 is giving the O-sign.* □ *That's the third O-sign we've gotten since noon.*

SYMBOL - GUILT

smoking gun *n.* the indisputable sign of guilt. □ *Mr. South was left holding the smoking gun.* □ *The chief of staff decided that the admiral should be found with the smoking gun.*

SYMPATHY

bleed for someone *in.* to sympathize with someone. □ *I really bleed for you, but there's nothing I can do.* □ *We bleed for you, we really do.*

TALKING

See also **CHATTER, CONVERSATION, GOSSIP, SPEECH.**

bad-mouth *n.* someone who speaks ill of someone or something. □ *Harry is such a bad-mouth!* □ *The world is filled with bad-mouths. We need more caring people.*

beat one's gums *tr.* to waste time talking a great deal without results. □ *I'm tired of beating my gums about this stuff.* □ *You're just beating your gums. No one is listening.*

big mouth *n.* a person who talks too much or too loudly; someone who tells secrets. (Also a term of address.) □ *Okay, big mouth! Shut up!* □ *Tell that big mouth to shut up.*

diarrhea of the mouth AND **diarrhea of the jawbone** *n.* an imaginary disease involving constant talking. □ *Wow, does he ever have diarrhea of the mouth!* □ *You're getting diarrhea of the jawbone again.*

flapjaw *n.* a talkative person. □ *Who is the flapjaw who has Sally cornered?* □ *Martin is anything but a flapjaw. I bet he doesn't say a dozen words per hour.*

foot-in-mouth disease *n.* the tendency to say the wrong thing at the wrong time. □ *I suffer a lot from foot-in-mouth disease.* □ *Well, Ralph has foot-in-mouth disease again.*

gift of gab *n.* the ability to speak well in public; the ability to persuade people verbally; the ability to speak well extemporaneously. □ *Gary has the gift of gab, but it doesn't get him anywhere.* □ *I wish I had the gift of gab. I'm just so shy.*

go *tr.* to say or utter something. (Used in writing only for effect.) □ *So I go,*

"Gross!" □ *Then she goes, "Like . . . ," and just stops talking.*

go on (and on) about someone or something *in.* to rave about someone or something endlessly. □ *He just went on and on about the trouble he was having with the post office.* □ *Why do you have to go on about your sister so?*

like *interj.* a particle meaning roughly "saying." (Always with some form of *be.* Use caution with *like.* Never used in formal writing.) □ *Tiffany was like, "Wow!"* □ *And I'm like, "Well, you should have put your hat on!"*

mushmouth *n.* a person who does not or cannot speak clearly. □ *Don't be a mushmouth. Talk plainly.* □ *How can a mushmouth like that get a job reading news on network television?*

quote, unquote *phr.* a parenthetical expression said before a word or short phrase indicating that the word or phrase would be in quotation marks if used in writing. □ *So I said to her, quote, unquote, it's time we had a little talk.* □ *I think my quote, unquote reputation is ruined.*

rap session *n.* an informal conversation session. □ *The kids settled down for a long rap session.* □ *The rap session was interrupted by a fire drill.*

ratchet-mouth AND **motor-mouth** *n.* someone who talks incessantly. (Also a term of address.) □ *Tell that ratchet-mouth to shut up!* □ *Hey, motor-mouth, quiet!*

run down some lines *in.* to converse (with someone). □ *I was running down some lines with Fred when the bell rang.* □ *Hey, man, let's run down some lines.*

run one's rhymes *tr.* to say what you have to say; to give one's speech or make one's plea. (Collegiate.) □ *Go run your rhymes with somebody else!* □ *I told him to run his rhymes elsewhere.*

schmooze AND **shmooze; schmoose 1.** *in.* to chat; to *chew the fat.* (From Hebrew *schmuos* via Yiddish.) □ *You were schmoozing when you should have been listening.* □ *We were shmoozing before quitting time, and then the boss walked by.* **2.** *n.* a session of chatting or conversing. □ *Come over, and let's have a schmooze before you go.* □ *A good schmoose is what you need.*

schmoozer *n.* someone who chats or converses well. □ *Clare can't sing a note, but what a schmoozer!* □ *Two old schmoozers sat muttering to one another all afternoon by the duck pond.*

shoot from the hip *in.* to speak quickly and without thinking. □ *She has a tendency to shoot from the hip, but that's not really a problem.* □ *I shot from the hip when I spoke. I'm sorry.*

talk like a nut *in.* to say stupid things. □ *You're talking like a nut! You don't know what you are saying.* □ *Don't talk like a nut! We can't afford a trip to Florida!*

yak AND **yack** *in.* to talk. □ *Stop yakking for a minute.* □ *I need to yack with you about something.*

TARGET

sitting duck *n.* someone who waits unsuspectingly for doom or destiny; an easy target for something bad. □ *Get out of the way! You're a sitting duck.* □ *The guy was a sitting duck for a mugging.*

TASTE

delish *mod.* delicious. □ *Oh, this cake is just delish.* □ *What a delish meal.*

goopy *mod.* gummy; syrupy. □ *I just love goopy desserts.* □ *This is not goopy enough.* □ *There is some goopy stuff coming out of the car's engine.*

nummy *mod.* tasty; yummy. (Also juvenile or baby talk.) □ *This cake is just nummy.* □ *Here, Jimmy, don't you want a spoon of this nummy food?*

TATTLING

bust *tr.* to inform on someone, leading to an arrest. □ *I busted Max to save my own skin.* □ *Tom busted Sam because there's bad blood between them.*

cheese-eater *n.* an informer; a *rat fink.* (Rats eat cheese.) □ *Some cheese-eater called the clerk and warned her we were coming.* □ *Tracy, the cheese-eater, called the police.*

crack *in.* to break down and talk under pressure. (Underworld.) □ *They kept at her till she finally cracked and talked.* □ *We knew you'd finally crack.*

dime-dropper *n.* an informer. (Underworld. Because an informer at one time could drop a dime in a public telephone and call the police or drop a dime on the sidewalk as a signal for the police to move in and make an arrest.) □ *I think that Tracy is the dime-dropper who caused the roust.* □ *The fuzz protects its dime-droppers with everything they've got.*

drop a dime *tr.* to inform the police of criminal activity. (Underworld.) □ *We were pretty sure that Tracy is the one who dropped the dime.* □ *No, almost anybody will drop a dime these days.*

fink *n.* an informer; a *stool (pigeon).* □ *Tracy has turned into a fink.* □ *Mr. Big doesn't think much of finks.*

fink (on someone) *in.* to inform on someone. □ *You won't fink on me, will ya?* □ *Rocko never finks on his friends.*

give (out) with something *in.* to give out information. □ *Come on, give out with the facts, man.* □ *Give with the info. We're in a hurry.*

nark AND **narc 1.** *in.* to inform (on someone) to the police. (Often with *on.*) □ *Don't narc on me!* □ *All right. Who narked?* **2.** *n.* a police informer. □ *Fred is a nark. He squealed.* □ *I'm going to get that narc for squealing.*

rat fink *n.* an informer. (Also a term of address.) □ *That guy is nothing but a rat fink. A dirty squealer!* □ *Fred told the teacher about the plot, and for the next two years everybody called him a rat fink.*

rat (on someone) *in.* to inform (on someone). □ *Bill said he was going to rat on that punk.* □ *If you rat on me, I'll get you!* □ *Who ratted?*

sing *in.* to inform (on someone). (Underworld.) □ *Rocko knew the stoolie would sing. He had to do something to stop her.* □ *Bruno would never sing. He's a champ.*

snitch 1. *in.* to inform (on someone). (Often with *on*.) □ *The cops were waiting for us. Who snitched?* □ *Tracy snitched on Bruno, and he nearly snuffed her.* **2.** *n.* an informer. □ *Who needs a snitch? If he can't keep his mouth shut, he can beat it.* □ *The snitch went and told the teacher.*

snitcher *n.* an informer. (Originally underworld.) □ *There's nothing worse than a snitcher.* □ *Clare is a snitcher. Watch what you say around her.*

spew one's guts (out) *tr.* to tell everything that one knows; to confess everything. (Underworld.) □ *Lefty was sitting there in the cop-shop spewing his guts out about the bank job.* □ *If he really is spewing his guts, the mob will cancel his Christmas.*

squawk *tr. & in.* to reveal or *blab* something. □ *Watch Tracy. She may decide to squawk.* □ *She squawked the whole business to the fuzz.*

squeal *in.* to inform (someone about something). □ *Who squealed to the cops?* □ *Tracy squealed on us.*

squealer *n.* an informer. (Underworld.) □ *Tracy is a terrible squealer.* □ *Some squealer let the cops know what was going to happen.*

stool (on someone) *in.* to inform (on someone). □ *Tracy would stool on anybody, even her own mother.* □ *Somebody stooled and ruined the whole layout.*

stool (pigeon) AND **stoolie** *n.* an informer. (Originally underworld.) □ *Some stool spilled the works to the boys in blue.* □ *There's nothing I hate worse than a stoolie.*

tipster *n.* someone who gives special information; an informer. □ *We got this from a tipster who has usually proven re-liable in the past.* □ *The cops got this info from their favorite tipster.*

whistle-blower *n.* someone who calls a halt to something; an informer; an enforcer; a *stool (pigeon).* □ *I don't know who the whistle-blower was, but a good time was really ruined.* □ *Some whistle-blower put Max behind bars for a few days.*

whistler *n.* someone who is a police informer; a *stoolie.* (Underworld.) □ *Tracy turned into a whistler after her last little vacation.* □ *Who's the whistler who squealed?*

TAVERN

See also DRINKING - PLACE.

bouncer *n.* a strong man hired to eject unruly people from a bar or similar place. (People supposedly bounce when thrown out.) □ *I saw the bouncer looking at me, and I got out of there fast.* □ *He was the biggest bouncer I've ever seen.*

dive *n.* a low drinking establishment; a cheap saloon. □ *I don't think I want to spend the whole evening in this dive.* □ *Hey, this dive ain't bad.*

fill-mill *n.* a tavern. □ *She stopped off at the fill-mill again this evening.* □ *She spends a lot of time at that fill-mill.*

gargle factory *n.* a saloon; a tavern. □ *Gary spends a lot of time at the gargle factory.* □ *He should open his own gargle factory.*

gin mill AND **gin dive; gin palace** *n.* a saloon; a low liquor establishment. □ *Fred hit every gin mill on the way home.* □ *You'll find Bob in some gin dive on the west side of town.*

groggery *n.* a tavern; a place to buy liquor. □ *Sam stopped at the groggery for a snort.* □ *All the groggeries are closed on Sundays.*

gutbucket *n.* a cheap saloon; a low tavern. □ *Old Jed is probably stuck in some gutbucket someplace, talking his head off.* □ *The pinstriper needed a drink so bad he stopped at one of those gutbuckets on Maple Street.*

guzzlery AND **guzzery** *n.* a bar; a liquor store. □ *Sam hit every guzzlery on Maple Street on the way home.* □ *I wouldn't be caught dead in a guzzery like that!*

juice joint *n.* a liquor establishment; a speakeasy. (Prohibition.) □ *His grandfather ran a juice joint during Prohobition.* □ *The cops raided the juice joints over and over.*

nineteenth hole *n.* a place to buy an alcoholic beverage after a golf game. (Likely to be filled with golfers who have played eighteen holes of golf.) □ *All of us gathered at the nineteenth hole to celebrate a great match.* □ *I hit a hole-in-one on the first hole and went straight to the nineteenth hole to celebrate.*

piss factory *n.* a saloon or a tavern. (Crude. Potentially offensive. Use only with discretion.) □ *What time did you leave that old piss factory?* □ *In my hometown there's a piss factory on every corner.*

puke hole *n.* a tavern. □ *Let's go in this puke hole and get a cold one.* □ *Carl spends almost every evening at the local puke hole.*

sauce parlor *n.* a tavern. □ *You spend too much time in the sauce parlor, Fred.* □ *I wouldn't be caught dead in that sauce parlor.*

speakeasy *n.* a nightclub serving liquor during Prohibition. □ *My grandfather remembers speakeasies. They were pretty crude places.* □ *You weren't supposed to talk about speakeasies so their locations would remain a secret.*

thirst-aid station *n.* a place to purchase liquor. (From *first-aid station.*) □ *Let's stop at the next thirst-aid station and get a snort.* □ *Wally stopped by the thirst-aid station for a quick snort.*

tippler *n.* a tavern keeper. □ *Another beer, faithful tippler.* □ *John is the best tippler this place has ever seen. Tip me another, John.*

watering hole *n.* a tavern. □ *Now this place is one of my favorite watering holes.* □ *I think you live down at that watering hole.*

TAXI

cabbie AND **cabby** *n.* a taxi driver. (Also a term of address.) □ *Ask the cabbie if he can change a twenty.* □ *Say, cabby, do you know the way to St. Joseph's Hospital?*

hack *n.* a taxi. □ *Go out to the street and see if you can get a hack.* □ *I drove a hack for a few months; then I quit.*

hacker *n.* a taxi driver. □ *That hacker nearly ran into the back of my car!* □ *You wonder how some of these hackers keep their licenses.*

TEASING

pull someone's leg *tr.* to kid someone; to tease someone. □ *They're just pulling your leg. Relax!* □ *Stop it! I don't believe you! You're pulling my leg.*

rib 1. *n.* a joke; an act of teasing. □ *I didn't mean any harm. It was just a little rib.* □ *That's a great rib, Sam!* **2.** *tr.* to tease someone. □ *Please don't rib me any more tonight. I've had it.* □ *Let's go rib Jennifer.*

shuck *tr. & in.* to kid someone; to tease someone. □ *Cool it! I'm just shucking.* □ *Stop shucking me!*

TECHNOLOGY

on the bleeding edge *phr.* having the most advanced technology; knowing about the most advanced technology. (Jocular. More advanced than *on the cutting edge.*) □ *This gadget is brand new. It's really on the bleeding edge.* □ *Tom is on the bleeding edge when it comes to optical storage technology.*

techie *mod.* having to do with technical people or things. □ *I don't like this techie jargon.* □ *This is the techie lounge. See how messy it is?*

tech-nerd *n.* a technically oriented, dull person, typically a male computer enthusiast. □ *My brother, who is a tech-nerd, spends more than ten hours a day on his computer.* □ *I had to consult a tech-nerd to get my VCR operating.*

TEENAGER

teenybopper *n.* a young teenager, usually a girl. □ *The teenyboppers moved around the mall in droves, not buying and not causing any trouble, just being avail-*

able for anyone who wanted to see them. □ *Somebody called Mary a, like, teeny-bopper, and she went, like, "So gross!"*

twinkie *n.* a cute, teenage *girl.* (California.) □ *The mall up from the beach is usually wall-to-wall twinkies.* □ *These twinkies ought to be a little more grown up than they seem to be.*

TEETH

biters *n.* the teeth. □ *My biters need a little work.* □ *I gotta get my biters to the dentist while there are still a few left.*

China *n.* the teeth. □ *I spent a damn fortune trying to get this China fixed up.* □ *If you would brush your China every day, you'd be okay.*

choppers *n.* the teeth. □ *I may be on my last legs, but my choppers are still my own.* □ *That horse has a nice set of choppers.*

crockery *n.* the teeth. □ *I gotta go to the dentist for some work on my crockery.* □ *Is that your own crockery?*

ivories *n.* the teeth. □ *I gotta go brush my ivories.* □ *Look at those nice white ivories!*

railroad tracks *n.* dental braces. □ *I can't smile because of these railroad tracks.* □ *My railroad tracks cost nearly $1,200.*

snappers *n.* the teeth. (Folksy.) □ *I couldn't talk to you on the phone till I got my snappers in.* □ *You got a mouthful of fine-looking snappers.*

tinsel-teeth *n.* a nickname for someone who wears dental braces. (Also a rude nickname.) □ *Tinsel-teeth is having a hard time talking.* □ *Well, tinsel-teeth, today's the day your braces come off.*

TELEPHONE

Baby Bell *n.* one of the regional telephone companies that were formerly a part of American Telephone & Telegraph Company. □ *The Baby Bells are doing better than the parent company.* □ *"If the Baby Bells get into long-distance service, say good-bye to Ma Bell," the hotshot money manager muttered in his third martini.*

beeper *n.* a portable telephone signal. □ *I have somebody call me during a meeting so my beeper will go off and get me out of it.* □ *My beeper went off, and I had to leave the meeting.*

buzz 1. *n.* a call on the telephone. □ *I'll give you a buzz tomorrow.* □ *I got a buzz from him yesterday.* **2.** *tr.* to call someone on the telephone. □ *Buzz me about noon.* □ *I'll buzz Mary and see if she can go.*

Call my service. *sent.* "Please call me through my answering service." (Not a friendly or encouraging invitation.) □ *Good to talk to ya, babe. Call my service. Love ya!* □ *I can't talk now. Call my service.*

digits *n.* numbers; phone number. □ *Tell me your digits and I'll call you and let you know the time.* □ *If I can find her digits, I'll call her.*

give someone a buzz *tr.* to give someone a telephone call. □ *Give me a buzz sometime.* □ *I'll give her buzz tonight and ask her.*

horn *n.* the telephone. □ *Get Mrs. Wilson on the horn, please.* □ *She's on the horn now. What'll I tell her?*

jingle *n.* a call on the telephone. □ *Give me a jingle when you get into town.* □ *I got a jingle from Gert today.*

ring off the hook *in.* [for a telephone] to ring endlessly or constantly. □ *The phone was ringing off the hook when I came in.* □ *We've been busy today. The phone's been ringing off the hook.*

try someone back (again) *tr.* to call someone back on the telephone (again) later. □ *I'll try her back later.* □ *When should I try back?*

TELEVISION

BO (Initialism.) *n.* "HBO," Home Box Office, the cable television channel. (Initialism and dysphemism.) □ *Is there a good movie on BO tonight?* □ *There is boxing on BO but no movie.*

boob-tube *n.* a television set. (Something for a *boob* to watch.) □ *You spend too much time in front of the boob-tube.* □ *What's on the boob-tube tonight?*

change the channel *tr.* to switch to some other topic of conversation. □ *Just a minute. I think you changed the channel. Let's go back to the part about you owing me money.* □ *Let's change the channel here before there is a fight.*

channel hopping AND **channel surfing; channel zapping** *n.* to use a remote control to move quickly from one television channel to another, pausing only a short time on each channel. □ *I wish you would stop channel hopping!* □ *Channel zapping is a way to keep up with a number of television shows at the same time.*

idiot box *n.* a television set. □ *You spend too much time watching the idiot box.* □ *What's on the idiot box tonight?*

kid-vid *n.* children's television; television programming aimed at children. □ *Kid-vid isn't good for anything other than selling cereal.* □ *I don't know. Kid-vid is fun.*

on the bird *mod.* available on the TV satellite channels. □ *There is a whole lot of good stuff on the bird, but you need a receiving dish to get it.* □ *I get a huge book every month listing what programs are on the bird.*

sitcom *n.* a situation comedy as found on television. □ *These sitcoms are made for juvenile minds.* □ *Sitcoms can be fun.*

soap *n.* a soap opera. □ *She won't schedule anything when her soap is on.* □ *Soaps are very popular on college campuses these days.*

surf *in.* to use a remote control to check a large number of TV stations. □ *Don spends almost an hour surfing before he falls asleep in front of the TV.* □ *Mary surfed until she fell asleep.*

telly *n.* a television set. (British.) □ *What's on the telly tonight?* □ *I mean, what's showing on the telly tonight?*

tube *n.* a television set. □ *What's on the tube tonight?* □ *The tube is in the shop, so I read a book.*

TEMPERATURE

play freeze-out *tr.* to open windows and doors, or turn down a thermostat, making someone cold. □ *Wow, it's cold in*

here! *Who's playing freeze-out?* □ *Is someone trying to play freeze-out?*

TEMPORARY

quick fix *mod.* having to do with a temporary or unsatisfactory solution or repair. (Usually **quick-fix.**) □ *Frank is a master of the quick-fix solution.* □ *This is no time for quick-fix efforts.*

scratch *mod.* impromptu; temporary. □ *We started a scratch game of basketball, but most of the girls had to leave at dinnertime.* □ *This is just a scratch tape. After you use it for your computer program, someone else will write something over it.*

stand-in *n.* a substitute; a temporary replacement. □ *I was a stand-in for the lead soprano, who had the sniffles.* □ *The audience booed the stand-in. They had paid to hear a star.*

TESTICLES

balls *n.* testicles. (Potentially offensive. Use only with discretion.) □ *He got hit right in the balls.* □ *The teacher preferred "testicles" to "balls," if they had to be mentioned at all.*

knockers *n.* the testicles. (Potentially offensive. Use only with discretion.) □ *Pow, right in the knockers. Ye gods, it hurt!* □ *He turned sideways to protect his knockers.*

nuts *n.* the testicles. (Potentially offensive. Use only with discretion.) □ *Chuck got kneed in the nuts in a football game.* □ *She tried to kick him in the nuts, like she'd seen on television, but he turned too quickly.*

TESTING

acid test *n.* a very thorough test. (From a test for determining true gold using acid.) □ *We put your invention through the acid test, and—I am extremely sorry to tell you—it failed miserably.* □ *I'll take this home to my kids and let them give it the acid test. If it survives them, it's a winner.*

THANKS

See GRATITUDE.

THEFT

boost *tr. & in.* to steal or shoplift something. (Underworld.) □ *He specializes in boosting meat for resale.* □ *He boosts for a living.*

burn *tr.* to cheat or rob someone. □ *Tom tried to burn me by selling me a bum watch, but I'm too clever.* □ *He will burn you if you're not careful.*

cop 1. *tr.* to take or steal something. (Originally underworld.) □ *Somebody copped the statue from the town square.* □ *Who copped the salt from this table?* **2.** *n.* a theft. (Underworld.) □ *They pulled the cop in broad daylight.* □ *It was a lousy cop. No skill. No finesse.*

crack *tr.* to break into something. (Underworld.) □ *We almost cracked the safe before the alarm went off.* □ *His specialty is cracking car trunks and stealing tires.*

five-finger discount *n.* the acquisition of something by shoplifting. □ *Bruno used his five-finger discount to get the kind of ring Tracy wanted.* □ *I got this thingy with my five-finger discount.*

fleece *tr.* to cheat someone; to steal everything from someone. (Underworld.) □ *Bruno fleeced the kids for a lot of money.* □ *Rocko never tried to fleece anybody.*

glom *tr.* to steal something. (Underworld.) □ *Lefty glommed a little car for the evening.* □ *He gloms just about everything he needs.*

Hands up! AND **Stick 'em up!** *exclam.* "Raise your hands in the air; this is a robbery!" (Underworld and Western.) □ *Hands up! Don't anybody move a muscle. This is a heist.* □ *Stick 'em up! Give me all your valuables.*

heist 1. *n.* a theft; a robbery; a *lift*. (Underworld.) □ *Lefty just had to pull one last heist.* □ *The heist went off without a hitch.* **2.** *tr.* to steal something; to rob a person or place; to *lift* something. (Underworld.) □ *The thugs heisted her and took her purse and watch.* □ *Lefty heisted a car and then drove around in it all evening.*

hook *tr.* to steal something. □ *Lefty hooked a couple of candy bars just for the hell of it.* □ *What did they hook last night?*

hot *mod.* stolen. □ *This watch is hot. Keep it.* □ *Rocko won't touch a hot watch or anything else hot.*

job *n.* a theft; a criminal act. (Police and underworld.) □ *Max and Lefty planned a bank job over in Adamsville.* □ *Who did that job at the old mansion last week?*

kipe *tr.* to steal something. □ *Where did you kipe this thing?* □ *The punk kiped a newspaper just for the heck of it.*

liberate *tr.* to steal something. (Originally military.) □ *We liberated a few reams of paper and a box of pens.* □ *The privates liberated a jeep and went into town.*

lift *tr.* to steal something. □ *She had lifted this ring. We found it on her when we arrested her.* □ *Some of these really young kids will lift something just because they like it.*

moonlight requisition *n.* a nighttime theft. (Military.) □ *It took a moonlight requisition to get the medicine we needed.* □ *They got the spare part on a moonlight requisition.*

mug *tr.* to attack and rob someone. □ *Somebody jumped out of an alley and tried to mug me.* □ *Some punk mugged Mrs. Lopez last night.*

nick *tr.* to steal something. □ *The thugs nicked a couple of apples from the fruit stand.* □ *Don't ever nick anything! Do you hear me?*

nip *tr.* to steal something. □ *The thief nipped my purse.* □ *The punk kid nipped two candy bars from the drugstore.*

pinch *tr.* to steal something. □ *The kid pinched a candy bar right off the counter.* □ *I pinched these paper clips from my office.*

pull a job *tr.* to carry out a crime, especially a robbery. (Police and underworld.) □ *Max decided that it was not a good time to pull a bank job.* □ *Bruno and Max left town after they pulled the job.*

rip *n.* a theft; a *rip-off.* □ *The crooks pulled a rip on Fourth Street last night.* □ *That was the third rip there this week.*

rip-off 1. *n.* a theft; a deception; an exploitation. □ *This sandwich is a rip-off!* □ *What a rip-off! I want my money back.* **2.** *mod.* having to do with theft and deception. □ *I consider myself to be rip-off champion of North America.* □ *All I hear is rip-off stories. Isn't anybody honest?*

rip something off *tr.* to steal something. □ *They ripped them all off.* □ *The crooks ripped off the hubcaps of my car.*

rob someone blind 1. *tr.* to overcharge someone. □ *You are trying to rob me blind. I won't pay it!* □ *Those auto repair shops can rob you blind if you don't watch out.* **2.** *tr.* to steal freely from someone. □ *Her maid was robbing her blind.* □ *I don't want them to rob me blind. Keep an eye on them.*

roll *tr.* to rob a drunkard. □ *The muggers found a drunk and rolled him.* □ *Those punks can't get much money by rolling drunks.*

scarf *tr.* to steal or *swipe* something. □ *The kid scarfed a candy bar, and the store owner called the cops.* □ *The plumber's assistant had been scarfing copper for months before they figured out what was going on.*

snag *tr.* to grab or steal something. □ *Somebody snagged the jacket I just bought.* □ *See if you can snag a couple of good seats while I get the popcorn.*

snatch 1. *tr.* to grab something; to steal something. □ *Snatch me the paper there on the table as you walk by, would you please?* □ *Somebody snatched my car.* **2.** *n.* a theft. (Underworld.) □ *The snatch went off without a hitch except that the safe was empty.* □ *Are you the guys who pulled off that First National snatch?*

snitch 1. *tr.* to steal something. □ *Who snitched my cake?* □ *Why don't you snitch the salt from one of the other tables?* **2.** *n.* a theft. (Underworld.) □ *The snitch went off without a hitch.* □ *How much loot did we get in the snitch?*

sticky fingers *n.* a tendency to steal. □ *Bruno has sticky fingers and likes wallets especially.* □ *Watch these young kids with sticky fingers who come in here "just looking."*

swipe *tr.* to steal something. □ *Max swiped a pack of cigarettes from the counter.* □ *Somebody swiped my wallet!*

take-off *n.* a robbery. (Underworld.) □ *That was some take-off Lefty pulled, huh?* □ *Yeah, Lefty sure knows take-offs.*

take someone or something off *tr.* to rob someone or something. (Underworld.) □ *Weren't you in that bunch that took the bank off in Philly?* □ *No, we never took off no bank, did we, Lefty?*

waltz off (with something) *in.* to steal something easily. □ *The thieves waltzed off with a giant screen television in broad daylight.* □ *They just picked the thing up and waltzed off. Nobody asked them any questions.*

whack something (out) *tr.* to rob a place; to swindle a business establishment. (Underworld.) □ *Did your guys whack the church collection box?* □ *Bruno's gang whacked out the bank on Maple street.*

THERMOSTAT

stat *n.* a thermostat. □ *Who turned down the stat?* □ *I'm afraid you need a new stat.*

THIEF

big juice *n.* a big-time crook. □ *Marty's big juice now that he's got himself a gang.* □ *So, you're the big juice around here.*

biter *n.* a thief. □ *Some biter made off with my algebra book.* □ *Who's the biter who took my jacket?*

booster *n.* a shoplifter. □ *The cops hauled in two boosters by noon.* □ *Gary was a part-time booster till he got into dope.*

cattle-rustler *n.* a thief who steals meat from supermarkets for resale. (Underworld.) □ *Marty is a cattle-rustler, and she's got some stuff for sale.* □ *She's a cattle-rustler to support her habit.*

chiseler *n.* a small-time crook; a cheater. (Originally underworld. Also a rude term of address.) □ *You dirty, two-bit chiseler! Give me my money back!* □ *Why did you trust a known chiseler like him?*

con man AND **con artist** *n.* someone who makes a living by swindling people. □ *Gary is a con artist, but at least he's not on the dole.* □ *He looks like a con man, but he's just a sweetie.*

dip *n.* a pickpocket. (Underworld.) □ *Watch out for dips at the racetrack.* □ *The dip tried a snatch, but the dupe turned around at the wrong time.*

kiper *n.* a thief; someone who steals. □ *The punk is a two-bit kiper and needs to be taught a lesson.* □ *You dirty little kiper. Give it back!*

klepto *n.* a kleptomaniac; one who steals small things obsessively. □ *The cops thought Gert was a klepto until she showed them her receipts.* □ *The jury awarded Gert five grand for being falsely arrested as a klepto.*

long knife *n.* an assassin. (Underworld.) □ *The boss sent one of his long knives to kill the guy.* □ *Some long knife showed up, but Marty took him out before he made his move.*

mug *n.* a thug; a goon. (Underworld.) □ *Call off your mugs. I'll come peacefully.* □ *Bruno is just another one of the mugs from the mob.*

mugger *n.* someone, usually a male, who attacks and robs people. □ *I clobbered the mugger with a tire iron I carry just for such occasions.* □ *The muggers have the downtown almost to themselves after dark.*

(rip-)off artist *n.* a con artist. □ *Fred is such an off artist.* □ *Beware of the rip-off artist who runs that shop.*

scammer *n.* a swindler; a hustler. □ *Max is a scammer if I ever saw one.* □ *There are a couple of scammers on the street corner. Watch out.*

take-off artist *n.* a thief. (Underworld.) □ *A take-off artist known as the Cat is cleaning out closets and jewelry boxes all over town.* □ *He's not a sales agent. He's a take-off artist, pure and simple.*

yegg *n.* a tramp, thief, or safecracker. (Underworld.) □ *The cops hauled in the usual yeggs, but they all had alibis.* □ *See if you can find that yegg we worked with on the bank job. He'll do.*

THIGHS

thunder-thighs *n.* big or fat thighs. (Cruel. Also a rude term of address.) □ *Here comes old thunder-thighs.* □ *Here, thunder-thighs, let me get you a chair or two.*

THING

johnson *n.* a thing. □ *What is this johnson about you snitching?* □ *He's got this smack johnson riding him.*

jones *n.* a thing. □ *There's a big turf jones down on the corner.* □ *This get-rich-quick jones will land you in the joint, Lefty.*

puppy *n.* a thing; a piece or part of something. □ *Put this little puppy right here.* □ *Where is that puppy?*

zinger *n.* something nice or fine. □ *That set of wheels is a real zinger.* □ *What a zinger of a hat!*

THINKING

brainstorm 1. *n.* a good idea; an idea that enters one's head suddenly. □ *I had a sudden brainstorm and got out of bed to write it down.* □ *This brainstorm hit me while I was in the shower.* **2.** *in.* to try to think up good ideas, especially as a group. □ *Let's brainstorm on this for a little while.* □ *They are in the meeting room now, brainstorming.*

changes *n.* an alteration in one's mental state. □ *The changes have sort of got me down.* □ *I'm forty and I'm finished with the changes, and if there's anything I don't want it's to be young again.*

chew something over *tr.* to think something over. □ *I'll have to chew it over for a while. I'm not sure now.* □ *Don't chew it over too long. The offer is only good till Friday.*

flash *n.* something suddenly remembered; something suddenly thought of. □ *I had a flash and quickly wrote it down.* □ *After we talked a while, a flash hit me. Why don't we sell the house?*

flash on something *in.* to remember something suddenly and vividly. □ *Then I flashed on a great idea.* □ *I was trying to flash on it, but I couldn't bring it to mind.*

foggiest (idea) *n.* (even) a hazy idea. (Usually in the negative. Always with *the.*) □ *I'm sorry I don't know. I haven't the foggiest.* □ *I don't have the foggiest idea of how to do this.*

Go figure. *interj.* "Try to figure it out."; "Just try to explain that!" □ *She hung up on me again. Go figure.* □ *They heat the water to make the tea hot, then they put ice in it to make it cold, then they put lemon in it to make it sour, and then they put sugar in it to make it sweet. Go figure.*

Put that in your pipe and smoke it! *exclam.* "Take that!"; "See how you like that!" □ *Everybody thinks you're a phony! Put that in your pipe and smoke it!* □ *You are the one who made the error, and we all know it. Put that in your pipe and smoke it!*

Use your head! AND **Use your noggin!; Use your noodle!** *exclam.* "Think!"; "Think it through!" □ *You know the answer. Use your head!* □ *Use your noggin! It's there for more than hanging your hat on.*

THREATENING

I don't mean maybe! *exclam.* "I am not kidding!" □ *You get over here right now, and I don't mean maybe!* □ *I will spank you if you ever do that again, and I don't mean maybe.*

on the chopping block *mod.* in serious and threatening straits. □ *Our whole future is on the chopping block.* □ *Until this is resolved, our necks are on the chopping block.*

work someone over *tr.* to threaten, intimidate, or beat someone. □ *Bruno threatened to work Sam over.* □ *Bruno had worked over Terry, and Sam knew that this was no idle threat.*

THRILL

bang *n.* a bit of excitement; a thrill; some amusement. □ *We got a bang out*

of your letter. □ *What a bang the party was!*

blast *n.* a thrill; a *kick.* □ *That gag gave me a blast.* □ *The roller coaster was a blast.*

boot *n.* a thrill; a charge. □ *I get a real boot out of my grandchildren.* □ *Their little games give me a real boot.*

buzz *n.* a thrill. □ *I got a real buzz out of that.* □ *The dancers gave the old man a buzz.*

get a bang out of someone or something AND **get a kick out of someone or something** *tr.* to get a thrill from someone or something. □ *I always get a bang out of her jokes.* □ *She gets a kick out of her grandchildren.*

jollies *n.* a charge or thrill; a sexual thrill; *kick.* □ *He got his jollies from skin flicks.* □ *This gyvestick gives Ernie all the jollies he wants.*

wham-bang *mod.* large; boisterous. □ *We had a really wham-bang time at your party.* □ *The overture was just too wham-bang for the tone of the play itself.*

THUNDERSTORM

thunder-boomer *n.* a thunderstorm. □ *There will be thunder-boomers in the boonies tonight.* □ *A few thunder-boomers may wake you up tonight.*

TICKETS

ducks *n.* tickets. □ *You got the ducks for Friday?* □ *There were no ducks left.*

in *n.* a ticket or means of getting in (someplace). □ *I lost my in. Can I still see the show?* □ *Lemme see your in or give me a buck.*

TIGHT

tight as a tick *mod.* very tight. □ *This lid is screwed on tight as a tick.* □ *The windows were closed—tight as a tick—to keep the cold out.*

TIME

calendar *n.* a month. □ *Okay, man. I'll see you in one calendar.* □ *One more calendar, then you get your jack.*

clock watcher *n.* someone—a worker or a student—who is always looking at the clock. □ *There are four clock watchers in our office.* □ *People who don't like their jobs can turn into clock watchers.*

day one *n.* the first day. □ *You haven't done anything right since day one! You're fired!* □ *She was unhappy with her new car even on day one.*

down to the wire *mod.* until the very last minute. □ *It came down to the wire before I turned the proposal in.* □ *We went right down to the wire on that one.*

game time *n.* time to go do what has to be done; time to go to work. (From sports.) □ *Okay, gang, let's get going. It's game time.* □ *Will this report be ready by game time?*

under the wire *mod.* at the very last minute. □ *I got it in just under the wire.* □ *It was in under the wire. Another ten minutes and it would not have counted.*

TIME - LONG

over the long haul *mod.* long term; over a long period of time. □ *Over the long haul, this one will prove best.* □ *This will last over the long haul.*

TIME - MAXIMUM

lifer *n.* someone who is attached to an institution for life, such as a lifetime soldier or a prisoner serving a life sentence. (Prisons and military.) □ *Me a lifer? Not in this army!* □ *The lifers begin to accept their fate after a few years.* □ *Most of the lifers are kept in this cell block.*

TIME - PERIOD

all-nighter *n.* something that lasts all night, like a party or study session. □ *After an all-nighter studying, I couldn't keep my eyes open for the test.* □ *Sam invited us to an all-nighter, but we're getting a little old for that kind of thing.*

banker's hours *n.* short work hours: 10:00 A.M. to 2:00 P.M. □ *When did you start keeping banker's hours?* □ *There aren't many bankers who keep banker's hours these days.*

donkey's years *n.* a long time. □ *I haven't seen you in donkey's years.* □ *It's been donkey's years since we talked.*

run *n.* a session or period of time spent doing something; a period of time when something happens. □ *The market had a good run today.* □ *We all have enjoyed a good run of luck.* □ *Max takes amphetamines and was on a run all week.* □ *A run like that can kill.*

stretch *n.* a period of time. (Folksy.) □ *Let's talk here for a stretch and then go up and see if dinner's ready.* □ *I sat there for a stretch and then got up and kept going.*

TIME - SHORT

flash *n.* a very short period of time; an instant. □ *I'll be there in a flash.* □ *It was just a flash between the time I said I'd be there and when I showed up.*

jiffy *n.* a very short time. □ *That was a pretty long jiffy I had to wait!* □ *Just a jiffy, I'll be there.*

sec *n.* a second. □ *I'll be with you in a sec. Keep your pants on!* □ *Just a sec. I'm on the phone.*

tick *n.* a minute; a second. □ *I'll be with you in a tick.* □ *This won't take a tick. Sit tight.*

TIME - SLEEP

lights out *n.* bedtime. □ *It's lights out, kids. Radios off, too!* □ *I was finished with it by lights out.*

TIME - THEN

then and there *mod.* right then. □ *He dropped the box right then and there and walked out on us.* □ *Right then and there, he pulled up his shirt and showed everyone the jagged scar.*

TIRES

rubber *n.* automobile tires; the rubber of automobile tires. □ *This car has some fine rubber on it.* □ *The rubber on my car is practically ruined.*

TOAST

Bottoms up. *sent.* "Let us drink up!" (A drinking toast.) □ *Well, bottoms up.* □ *They all raised their glasses, and the host said, "Bottoms up."*

Here's looking at you. *sent.* "I salute you." (A polite drinking toast.) □ *Well,* *here's looking at you.* □ *Here's looking at you. Bottoms up!*

Here's mud in your eye. *sent.* "I salute you." (A jocular drinking toast.) □ *Here's mud in your eye. Bottoms up!* □ *Well, here's mud in your eye. Care for another?*

TOBACCO

beecher *n.* a man who chews Beechnut (brand) tobacco. (Usually derogatory.) □ *Some old beecher wandered in and looked like he was going to leave a remembrance on the floor.* □ *The lobby of the county courthouse was populated by beechers and old hound dogs.*

blower *n.* a cigarette. □ *You got a blower I can bum?* □ *That's the third blower in ten minutes!*

burn 1. *n.* a cigarette. □ *Gimme a burn, huh?* □ *Fred just stood there with a burn on his lower lip and his hands in his pockets.* **2.** *tr.* to smoke a cigarette. □ *I need to burn a fag. Just a minute.* □ *This nicotine fiend needs to burn one for a fix!*

butt 1. *n.* a cigarette butt. □ *Whose butts are those in the car ashtray?* □ *Don't leave your butts in the houseplants!* **2.** *n.* a cigarette of any kind. □ *You got a butt I can bum?* □ *What kind of butt is that, anyway?*

cancer stick *n.* a tobacco cigarette. (From the notion that cigarette smoking is a major cause of lung cancer. Old but recurrent.) □ *Kelly pulled out his ninth cancer stick and lit it up.* □ *A lot of people are addicted to cancer sticks.*

chain(-smoke) *in.* to smoke cigarette after cigarette. □ *I never wanted to chain-smoke, but I got addicted.* □ *I used to chain, and my husband threatened to leave me if I didn't give it up. I quit when he left.*

chain-smoker *n.* someone who smokes cigarette after cigarette. □ *She was a chain-smoker for thirty years, and then suddenly, boom. She's gone.* □ *There are fewer chain-smokers now than there were just a few years ago.*

chas AND **chez** *n.* matches. (Collegiate. A clipping of "matches.") □ *Where are my chas?* □ *You got a couple of chez?*

choker *n.* a cigarette; a cigarette butt. □ *Put that damn choker out in my house!* □ *I can smell a choker the minute somebody lights it.*

cig *n.* a cigarette; a cigar. □ *Barlowe fumbled for a cig and thought better of it.* □ *Toss me my pack of cigs, will ya?*

ciggy AND **ciggie** *n.* a cigarette. □ *How 'bout a ciggy before we take off?* □ *Where is my pack of ciggies?*

clip a butt *tr.* to pinch out a cigarette for later smoking. (Also with *the.*) □ *Like an old soldier, Wally took a puff and then clipped the butt for later.* □ *You learn to clip a butt so you won't waste what you can't finish.*

coffin-dodger *n.* a heavy smoker. □ *I just hate these damn coffin-dodgers who light up a cigarette in a restaurant!* □ *Coffin-dodgers, chain-smokers—who cares? Let 'em commit suicide—in the privacy of their own homes, of course.*

coffin nail AND **coffin tack** *n.* a cigarette. □ *No more coffin nails for me.* □ *Every coffin tack you smoke takes a little off the end of your life.*

cop a drag *tr.* to smoke a cigarette. □ *She kept going off to the john to cop a drag.* □ *Smokers who have to leave the office to cop a drag must cost this nation billions each year.*

corpse *n.* a cigarette butt. □ *The wino picked up the corpse and put it in a little box that he carried with him.* □ *He is saving corpses to build a real smoke.*

dead soldier AND **dead man; dead marine; dead one** *n.* a cigarette butt. □ *The bum found a dead soldier on the ground and picked it up.* □ *He collected dead men to use in building a whole smoke.*

deck *n.* a pack of cigarettes. □ *Can you toss me a deck of fags, please?* □ *Why don't you stop in there and buy a deck?*

dip 1. *n.* a pinch or helping of snuff. □ *He took a dip just before he picked up the bat.* □ *After the hit, he got another dip.* **2.** *n.* a wad of chewing tobacco. □ *You* could see he had a big dip in his cheek. □ I won't tell you what he did with the dip when he was finished with it.

doofer AND **dufer** *n.* a (found or borrowed) cigarette saved for smoking at another time. (It will "do for" later.) □ Sam always has a doofer stuck behind his ear. □ He takes two fags, one to smoke and a dufer.

drag 1. *n.* a puff of a cigarette. □ He took a big drag and scratched at his tattoo. □ One more drag and he coughed for a while and stubbed out the fag. **2.** *tr.* to pull or puff on a cigarette. □ She dragged a couple and sat in the funk for a while. □ When she dragged a fag, you could see her relax and get straight.

dummy *n.* a cigarette butt. □ The tramp collected dummies until he had enough for a smoke. □ The guy tossed a dummy out the window of his car.

dust *n.* fine tobacco for rolling cigarettes. (Prisons.) □ How about a little dust for this candy bar? □ I don't want dust. I need chocolate.

fag *n.* a cigarette. □ Hey, pal, gimme a fag. □ Go buy your own fags!

funk *n.* tobacco smoke. □ The funk was so thick I couldn't see across the room. □ Most of those important decisions are made by party hacks in funk-filled back rooms.

hemp *n.* a smelly cigar. □ Get that vile hemp out of here! □ Can you imagine somebody bringing an old hemp like that in here?

jack *n.* tobacco for rolling cigarettes. □ You got some jack I can bum? □ I don't use jack at all.

jigger *n.* a cigarette. □ You got a jigger I can bum? □ Here's a pack of jiggers. Help yourself.

joint *n.* a tobacco cigarette. □ You got a filter joint on you? □ Why are beggars being choosers about their joints all of a sudden?

maggot *n.* a cigarette. □ Can I bum a maggot off of you? □ Get your own maggots.

Mexican breakfast *n.* a cigarette and a cup of coffee or a glass of water. □ After a Mexican breakfast, I went to Barlowe's hotel hoping to catch him before he went out. □ When some punk kid crosses the border into Mexico for a night of fun and games, all he can get to help him sober up and get out of the country the next day is a Mexican breakfast.

old soldier *n.* a cigarette or cigar butt; a hunk of tobacco. □ The tramp bent over to pick up an old soldier off the pavement. □ He's never had anything but an old soldier for a smoke.

OPs *n.* other people's cigarettes; begged or borrowed cigarettes. (Initialism.) □ My favorite kind of cigarettes is OPs. They're the cheapest, too. □ Ted only smokes OPs.

pill *n.* a tobacco cigarette. □ Hey, toss me a pill, huh? □ I'll trade you a pill for a match.

pimpstick *n.* a typical cigarette made by mass production. (Use caution with *pimp*. From an earlier time when *pimps* were likely to smoke machine-made cigarettes rather than the rugged roll-your-own type.) □ Hey, chum. Why do you smoke those pimpsticks? Can't you roll one yourself? □ Real cowboys never smoke pimpsticks, and they don't have tattoos, either.

plug *n.* a bite-sized, pressed mass of chewing tobacco. □ He put a plug in his cheek and walked away. □ Hey, gimme a piece of that plug!

puffer *n.* a cigar. □ Who's smoking that foul puffer? □ Can you imagine anyone smoking a puffer like that in a restaurant?

pull 1. *n.* a mouthful of smoke from a cigarette; a *drag* on a cigarette. □ A couple of pulls and she crushed out the cigarette. □ After a big pull, she blew an enormous smoke ring. **2.** *tr.* to smoke a cigarette. □ He pulled a long filter job and then went back to work. □ He stopped for a minute and pulled one.

ret *n.* a tobacco cigarette. (Collegiate.) □ You got a ret I can bum? □ Give my buddy a ret, will you?

411

root *n.* a cigarette or a cigar. □ *That root you're smoking sure stinks.* □ *You got a root I can borrow?*

seegar *n.* a cigar. (Folksy. The stress is on the first syllable.) □ *This dude came into this hamburger joint with a big seegar in his mouth, and the manager called the cops.* □ *There's nothing like a fine seegar after a nice bowl of hot chili.*

skag AND **scag 1.** *n.* a tobacco cigarette; a tobacco cigarette butt. (Military.) □ *Can I bum a scag off you?* □ *Here, have a skag on me.* **2.** *in.* to smoke a tobacco cigarette. □ *He stopped scagging for about a week.* □ *I'll skag till I die.*

slim *n.* a tobacco cigarette. □ *I'll take a slim and a little mist, thanks.* □ *You got a slim I can borrow?*

smoke 1. *n.* a tobacco cigarette; a pipe; a cigar. □ *I think I'll have a smoke now.* □ *You got a smoke I can owe you?* **2.** *n.* the act of smoking tobacco. □ *I need a smoke!* □ *I'm going to stop here for a smoke.*

smoke like a chimney *in.* to smoke a great deal of tobacco or other smokable substances. □ *My uncle smoked like a chimney when he was living.* □ *Somebody who smokes like a chimney in a restaurant ought to be thrown out.*

snipe *n.* a cigarette or cigar butt. □ *Down on skid row, a snipe won't be on the sidewalk for ten seconds.* □ *He saves a bunch of snipes until he gets enough for a real smoke.*

soldier *n.* a whole tobacco cigarette. □ *The old man almost fell over trying to pick up the soldier from the sidewalk.* □ *"Look, Jed. A soldier. My lucky day!" said the old soak to his buddy.*

square AND **square joint** *n.* a tobacco cigarette, compared to a marijuana cigarette. □ *You got a square on you?* □ *I'll take a reefer. I've heard that squares will give you cancer.*

stogie *n.* a cigar. □ *Then this guy pulls out a big stogie and starts to smoke it right there in the restaurant.* □ *Some activist type tried to get the customers to walk out*

if the manager didn't make the jerk put out his stogie.

straight *n.* a tobacco cigarette; a tobacco cigarette butt. (As opposed to a marijuana cigarette.) □ *No, I want a straight. That spliff makes me sneeze.* □ *Can I bum a straight off you?*

tailor-made *n.* a machine-made cigarette. (From an expression for something, such as an article of clothing, that is custom-made.) □ *They used to call these things tailor-made, meaning professionally made, as opposed to homemade.* □ *The cowboy in the movie refused to smoke a tailor-made.*

teaser *n.* a (found) cigarette butt. □ *The hobo picked up the teaser from the street and put it in a little bag.* □ *He saves up teasers to make a big smoke out of them.*

toke *n.* a cigarette. □ *You got a toke I can bum?* □ *I left my tokes in my jacket.*

tube *n.* a cigarette. □ *You got a tube I can bum?* □ *There's a pack of tubes in my jacket.*

weed *n.* tobacco; a cigarette or cigar. □ *I've about given up weed.* □ *This weed is gonna be the death of me.*

TOBACCO - PARAPHERNALIA

nose-warmer *n.* a short tobacco pipe. □ *Fred smokes a nose-warmer, especially in the winter.* □ *His nose-warmer almost set his mustache on fire once.*

TOILET

biffy *n.* a toilet. □ *Where's the biffy?* □ *The house we toured has a pink biffy. Can you believe it?*

can *n.* toilet. □ *Hell, I ain't tired! Where's the can?* □ *I gotta use the can before we leave.*

comfort station *n.* a restroom; toilet facilities available to the public. □ *Do you have a comfort station in this store?* □ *We need to stop and find a comfort station in the next town.*

craphouse *n.* a privy. (Potentially offensive. Use only with discretion. Colloquial.) □ *Wally's out in the craphouse reading, I guess.* □ *Where's the craphouse that used to be out there?*

crapper *n.* a toilet, privy, or restroom. (Potentially offensive. Use only with discretion.) □ *Where's the crapper around here?* □ *Old Jed never passes up a chance to use an indoor crapper.*

facilities *n.* toilet facilities. □ *Where are the facilities around here?* □ *Can I use your facilities?*

flusher *n.* a toilet. (Folksy. Compared to an outhouse.) □ *I hear they put in a flusher over at the Babbits'.* □ *That's silly. They've always had a flusher.*

gab room *n.* a women's restroom where women are said to chatter. □ *She went to the gab room to powder her nose.* □ *There was a small commotion in the gab room.*

gash bucket *n.* a refuse bucket; a bucket used as a urinal. (Underworld and military.) □ *Don't kick over the gash bucket over there!* □ *Why don't you go dump the gash bucket?*

growler *n.* a toilet. □ *Where's the growler around here?* □ *We only have one growler in this house.*

gutbucket 1. *n.* a chamber pot, especially one used in a prison cell. □ *You got something around here I can use as a gutbucket?* □ *I don't want any gutbucket around here.* **2.** *n.* a toilet. □ *Where's the gutbucket around here?* □ *The kid tried to flush his stash down the gutbucket.*

head *n.* a toilet; a restroom. (Originally nautical. Usually with *the*.) □ *Where's the head around here?* □ *Ralph is in the head. He'll be back in a minute.*

jake *n.* a toilet; a men's restroom. □ *Where's the jake?* □ *The jake is around the corner.*

jane *n.* a women's restroom; the *ruth*. □ *Where's the jane around here?* □ *The jane is upstairs.*

john *n.* a toilet; a bathroom. □ *Somebody's in the john.* □ *Is there another john around here?*

ladies' room *n.* the women's restroom. □ *Is there a ladies' room somewhere close?* □ *Sally has gone to the ladies' room.*

library *n.* a bathroom; an outhouse. □ *John is in the library at the moment.* □ *He keeps stuff like that to read in the library.*

little boys' room *n.* the boys' restroom; the men's restroom. □ *Can you tell me where the little boys' room is?* □ *Ted's in the little boys' room. He'll be right back.*

little girls' room *n.* the girls' restroom; the women's restroom. □ *Can you please tell me where the little girls' room is?* □ *Is there an attendant in the little girls' room?*

men's room *n.* a men's restroom. □ *Where's the men's room, please?* □ *I gotta use the men's room.*

Mrs. Murphy *n.* a bathroom. □ *Whose turn is it at Mrs. Murphy's?* □ *When will Mrs. Murphy be free?*

nature's call AND **call of nature** *n.* the feeling of a need to go to the toilet. □ *I think I feel nature's call coming on.* □ *A call of nature forced us to stop along the way.*

pot *n.* a toilet. (Usually with *the*.) □ *Jimmy's on the pot, Mommy.* □ *Where's the pot around here?*

potty *n.* a small toilet. (Usually juvenile.) □ *Mommy, I've got to go to the potty.* □ *I need to use the potty.*

powder room 1. *n.* a small bathroom without bathing facilities in a private home, usually located for the convenience of guests. □ *Can I use your powder room?* □ *Excuse me, where is the powder room?* **2.** *n.* the ladies' restroom in a public place, especially a restaurant; the place women go to powder their noses. (The emphasis is on comforts other than toilet facilities, such as mirrors, places to rest, and even a maid to help with emergency repairs of makeup or clothing.) □ *The ladies went to the powder room. They'll be back in a minute.* □ *She went to the powder room to clean the spill off her dress.*

privy *n.* an outdoor toilet; any toilet. □ *Uncle Paul was out in the privy.* □ *Where's the privy around here?*

puke hole *n.* a toilet. □ *Max tried to flush the dope down the puke hole, but the* cops caught him. □ Who didn't flush the puke hole?

ruth *n.* a women's restroom. □ *Where's the ruth?* □ *Point me toward the ruth!*

throne *n.* a toilet; a toilet seat. □ *And there was the cat—right on the throne, just staring at me.* □ *Somebody'd better clean the throne pretty soon.*

throne room *n.* a restroom; a bathroom. □ *Hank is in the throne room, reading, I think.* □ *Where's your throne room?*

TOILET - PARAPHERNALIA

TP AND **teepee** *n.* "toilet paper." (The abbreviation is an initialism.) □ *There's no TP in the john.* □ *Don't forget to get teepee at the store.*

TOILET - USE

check out the plumbing AND **visit the plumbing** *tr.* to go to the bathroom. □ *I think I'd better check out the plumbing before we go.* □ *I want you kids to visit the plumbing as soon as we get there.*

nature stop *n.* a stop to use the toilet, especially during road travel. (Euphemistic.) □ *I think I need a nature stop when it's convenient.* □ *I left my comb back at the last nature stop.*

pay a call *tr.* to go to the toilet; to leave to go to the toilet. □ *Excuse me. I have to pay a call.* □ *Tom left to pay a call. He should be back soon.*

pit stop *n.* a pause in a journey (usually by car) to urinate. (From the name of a service stop in automobile racing.) □ *I think we'll pull in at the next rest area. I need a pit stop.* □ *Poor Max needs a pit stop every thirty miles.*

potty *in.* to use the toilet. (Always juvenile.) □ *I've got to potty.* □ *Be sure to potty before we leave.*

powder one's nose AND **powder one's face** *tr.* to depart to the bathroom. (Usually said by women, or jocularly by men.) □ *Excuse me, I have to powder my nose.* □ *She just went out to powder her face.*

see a man about a dog *tr.* to leave a place for a mysterious reason, usually to go to the toilet. □ *I gotta see a man about a dog.* □ *Fred went to see a man about a dog. I hope he remembers to put the seat down.*

TOLERANT

thick-skinned *mod.* able to withstand much criticism. □ *You gotta be more thick-skinned if you want to be a cop.* □ *He's a real thick-skinned guy.* □ *I'm thick-skinned enough; I just don't like violence.*

TOOL

left-handed monkey wrench *n.* a nonexistent tool. (New workers are sometimes sent to fetch nonexistent tools.) □ *Hand me the left-handed monkey wrench, huh?* □ *Do you think you can dig up a left-handed monkey wrench?*

sky hook *n.* an imaginary tool. □ *I can't get this thing outa here without a sky hook.* □ *Go get me a sky hook, would ya?*

TORNADO

twister *n.* a tornado. □ *A twister touched down yesterday at an isolated farm seventy miles north of Adamsville.* □ *The twister didn't damage any homes.*

TOTALITY

clean sweep *n.* a broad movement clearing or affecting everything in the pathway. (Usually figurative.) □ *The boss and everybody in the front office got canned in a clean sweep from upstairs.* □ *Everybody got a raise. It was a clean sweep.*

TOUCH

paw *tr.* to touch someone more than is necessary or desired, without any sexual intent. □ *I don't like for people to paw me while they're shaking hands. There is no reason to shake my shoulder, too.* □ *Tom doesn't realize that he paws people and that it annoys them.*

TOUGH

See MEAN.

TOUPEE

See WIG.

TOURIST

day-tripper *n.* a tourist who makes one-day trips. □ *At about 4:00 P.M. the day-trippers start thinning out.* □ *Being a* *day-tripper is hard on your feet sometimes.*

rubberneck *n.* one who stares at something or someone; a tourist. □ *At noon the sidewalks are crowded with rubbernecks.* □ *See if that rubberneck over there has the correct time.*

TRANSFER

fork something over *tr.* to hand something over (to someone). □ *Okay, fork it over. It's mine!* □ *Okay, fork over the dough and be quick about it!*

glop *tr.* to slop or plop something (onto something). □ *She glopped something horrible onto my plate.* □ *Don't glop any of that pink stuff anywhere near me.*

schlep AND **shlep** *tr.* to drag or carry someone or something. (From German *schleppen* via Yiddish.) □ *Am I supposed to schlep this whole thing all the way back to the store?* □ *I am tired of shlepping kids from one thing to another.*

TRANSPORTATION

lift *n.* a ride; transportation. □ *Can you give me a lift?* □ *Would you like a lift over to your apartment?*

TRAP

booby trap 1. *n.* a concealed trap. (Both literal and figurative.) □ *This clause in the contract is a real booby trap. Let's rewrite it.* □ *Some kind of booby trap in the warehouse kept the robber from getting away.* **2.** *tr.* to install a concealed trap in a place. (Usually **booby-trap.**) □ *The agents booby-trapped the cellar.* □ *They booby-trapped the elevator so it turned into a cell if you didn't know the code to open the door.*

TRAVEL

bum around *in.* to wander around; to kick around. □ *I thought I'd bum around for a few years before I settled down.* □ *Those two kids bummed around Europe for two months.*

deadhead *tr. & in.* [for someone] to return an empty truck, train, airplane, etc., to where it came from. □ *I deadheaded back to Los Angeles.* □ *Who is supposed to deadhead this truck to Miami?*

flip-flop *n.* the return trip of a long journey. (Citizens band radio.) □ *Nice talking to you, Silver Streak. Catch you on the flip-flop.* □ *Didn't we chat on the flip-flop last week?*

flip side *n.* the return trip of a long journey. (Citizens band radio.) □ *See ya. Catch you on the flip side, maybe.* □ *Didn't I talk to you on the flip side last week?*

kidney-buster *n.* a rough ride; a rough road. □ *This road is a kidney-buster. I wish they'd fix it.* □ *That kidney-buster damaged my car.*

knock around AND **kick around** *in.* to wander around; to *bum around.* □ *I think I'll knock around a few months before looking for another job.* □ *We're just kicking around and keeping out of trouble.*

make *tr.* to arrive at a place; to cover a distance. □ *Can we make Boston by sunset?* □ *We made forty miles in thirty minutes.*

make for somewhere *in.* to set out for somewhere; to run or travel to somewhere. □ *Max made for Philadelphia when he heard the pigs in the Big Apple were after him.* □ *Barlowe made for the stairs, but two shots rang out, and he knew it was all over for Mary.*

on the road *mod.* traveling from place to place, not necessarily on the highways. □ *I was on the road with the circus for six months.* □ *I don't work in the main office anymore. Now I'm on the road.*

ride shotgun *tr.* to accompany and guard someone or something. (A term from the days of stage coaches and their armed guards.) □ *I have to take the beer over to the party. Why don't you come along and ride shotgun?* □ *Who's going to ride shotgun with Bill?*

roadie AND **roady** *mod.* eager to travel; eager to get on the road. □ *I get a little roady when the weather gets warm.* □ *We'd better get going. Your father looks a little roadie.*

roadtrip *n.* a sudden trip in a car. (Sometimes yelled, **Roadtrip!** to indicate an impending jaunt in an automobile.) □ *Let's make a little roadtrip to get some beer.* □ *"Roadtrip!" hollered Ken. "We're gonna go out and get some dames!"*

schlep AND **shlep** *n.* a journey; a distance to travel or carry something. □ *It takes about twenty minutes to make the schlep from here to there.* □ *That's a ten-mile shlep, and I won't go by myself.*

shotgun *exclam.* a phrase called out by someone who claims the privilege of riding in a car's passenger seat. (Usually **Shotgun!**) □ *"Shotgun!" cried Jimmy, heading for the car.* □ *Whoever yelled "shotgun" has to sit holding the cake all the way.*

stump 1. *n.* a visit or tour. □ *The old girl is off on another stump.* □ *It was a fine stump; we didn't miss anything.* **2.** *tr.* to visit or tour a place. □ *We stumped all of Europe this summer.* □ *The team stumped the countryside before even practicing for the game.*

thumb a ride *tr.* to beg a ride; to stand at the side of the street and signal to cars with one's thumb for a ride. □ *I'll thumb a ride to get there if I have to.* □ *I thumbed a ride to speed things up.*

tool around *in.* to drive or cruise around. □ *We tooled around for a while and then rented a horror movie.* □ *Let's tool around on the way home.*

TRICK

See also DECEPTION.

goof on someone *in.* to play a prank on someone; to involve someone in a deception. □ *Hey, don't goof on me. I'm your buddy!* □ *The kid goofed on Chuck, and he thought it was a pretty good joke.*

have an ace up one's sleeve *tr.* to have something useful in reserve; to have a special trick available. (*Have got* can replace *have.*) □ *I still have an ace up my sleeve that you don't know about.* □ *I don't have an ace up my sleeve. If it doesn't work, it doesn't work.*

phony *n.* a phone call where the caller hangs up the minute the telephone is answered. □ *No one was on the telephone. It was just a phony.* □ *We have had phony after phony all evening.*

pull a fast one *tr.* to outwit or outsmart someone by a clever and timely maneuver. □ *Don't try to pull a fast one on me.* □ *So you think you can pull a fast one?*

shuck *n.* a hoax. □ *What a stupid shuck!* □ *How could you fall for that old shuck?*

TP AND **teepee** *tr.* to festoon the trees and shrubbery of a residential yard with toilet paper. (A teenage prank.) □ *All the swimmers' houses get teepeed the night before a meet.* □ *Who teepeed my spruce tree?*

TRIVIAL

kitschy *mod.* trivial in spite of enormous popular appeal. □ *A lot of people like kitschy art.* □ *This stuff is too kitschy for me.*

lightweight *mod.* inconsequential. □ *This is a fairly lightweight matter.* □ *We need an executive here, not just a lightweight flunky.*

TROUBLE

be dust *n.* to be in trouble; to be worthless as dust; to be dead and turned to dust. □ *You keep acting like that and you'll be dust.* □ *Bruno said that Max was going to be dust if Mr. Big ever heard about what happened.*

behind the eight ball *mod.* in trouble; in a weak or losing position. □ *I'm behind the eight ball again.* □ *John spends a lot of time behind the eight ball.*

buy trouble *tr.* to encourage trouble; to bring on trouble. □ *I don't want to buy trouble. I have enough already.* □ *Saying something like that is just buying trouble.*

cruising for a bruising AND **cruisin' for a bruisin'** *in.* asking for trouble. □ *You are cruising for a bruising, you know that?* □ *Who's cruisin' for a bruisin'?*

double-trouble *n.* a very troublesome thing or person. □ *Oh, oh. Here comes double-trouble.* □ *That car you got is double-trouble.*

double whammy *n.* a double portion of something, especially something troublesome. (From *Li'l Abner*, a comic strip by Al Capp.) □ *We got a real double whammy of trouble down at the office.* □ *This morning was bad, but this afternoon the boss gave us a double whammy.*

get in bad (with someone) *in.* to get into trouble with someone. □ *I tried not to get in bad with Wally.* □ *We got in bad with each other from the start.*

have a run-in (with someone or something) *tr.* to have trouble with someone or something. □ *I had a run-in with Mrs. Wilson. She's a hard case.* □ *We've had a run-in before.*

hell *n.* trouble. (Use caution with *hell*.) □ *I went through all sorts of hell to get this done on time.* □ *This day was real hell.*

in deep doo-doo *mod.* in real trouble. (*Doo-doo* = dung.) □ *See what you've done. Now you are in deep doo-doo.* □ *I broke the window. Now I'm in deep doo-doo.*

in Dutch *mod.* in trouble. □ *I think I'm in Dutch with my folks.* □ *I didn't want to get in Dutch with you.*

in the soup *mod.* in trouble. □ *Now you're in the soup.* □ *I'm in the soup with the boss.*

jam *n.* a problem; trouble. □ *I hear you're in a bad jam.* □ *Well, it's not a bad jam.*

jammed up AND **jammed** *mod.* in trouble. □ *He got himself jammed up with the law.* □ *I'm sort of jammed and need some help.*

mell of a hess *n.* a "hell of a mess." (A deliberate spoonerism.) □ *What a mell of a hess you've gotten us into this time.* □ *Have you ever seen such a mell of a hess?*

raise Cain *tr.* to make a lot of trouble; to *raise hell*. □ *Fred was really raising Cain about the whole matter.* □ *Let's stop raising Cain.*

raise hell *tr.* to make a lot of trouble; to go on a rampage. □ *Stop raising hell so much of the time!* □ *Quiet! Don't raise hell around here.*

raise the devil (with something) AND **raise hell (with something)** *tr.* to cause trouble with something. □ *That idea raises hell with my plan.* □ *The onions raised the devil with my stomach.*

signify *in.* to cause trouble for fun; to stir things up. (Black.) □ *Why's that dude signifying over there?* □ *What are all these cats signifying about anyway?*

sweat *n.* trouble; bother. □ *I can handle it. It won't cause me any sweat.* □ *You really caused a lot of sweat around here.*

toast *mod.* in trouble; done for. □ *If you don't get here in twenty minutes, you're toast.* □ *I told him he was toast for not being there.*

TRUCK

eighteen-wheeler *n.* a large trailer truck. (There are a total of eighteen wheels on the cab and trailer.) □ *An eighteen-wheeler almost ran me off the road!* □ *The eighteen-wheelers rule the road at night.*

honey wagon AND **honey cart** *n.* a beer truck. □ *What time does the honey wagon bring in new supplies?* □ *I drove a honey cart in the city for a while.*

rig *n.* a large truck; an *eighteen-wheeler*. □ *Jim drives a really big rig.* □ *There were three rigs sitting in the parking lot when we got there.*

TRUCK - EXCREMENT

honey wagon AND **honey cart** *n.* any vehicle used for or designed for carrying excrement: a farm manure wagon; a tank truck used to pump out septic tanks; a tank truck used to pump out airplane toilets; a portable latrine truck used in movie making. □ *I drove a honey wagon in Hollywood for a year. How's that for glamour?* □ *The honey cart was stalled with a flat tire in front of the plane.*

TRUCK - FOOD

roach-coach *n.* a mobile snack truck. (The term was revived in the Persian Gulf War.) □ *Let's go get a sandwich at the roach-coach.* □ *Here comes the roach-coach! Let go spend some coin.* □ *The roach-coach pulled up in front of the dorm every night about eleven o'clock.*

TRUST

Trust me! *exclam.* "Believe me!"; "Honestly!" □ *It's true! Trust me!* □ *He actually said it just like Tom told you. Trust me!*

TRUTH

See also **HONESTY**.

fack *in.* to state the facts; to tell (someone) the truth. (Black.) □ *That dude is not facking with me.* □ *Now is the time to start facking. Where were you?*

gospel (truth) *n.* the honest truth. □ *You gotta believe me. It's the gospel truth!* □ *He speaks nothing but gospel. You can trust him.*

level with someone *in.* to speak truly and honestly with someone. □ *Okay, I'm gonna level with you. This thing is a steal at this price!* □ *I want you to level with me. Did you do it?*

mouthful *n.* a true statement. □ *You said a mouthful, and I agree.* □ *That is a mouthful, and I know it took courage to say it.*

naked truth *n.* the complete, unembellished truth. □ *Sorry to put it to you like this, but it's the naked truth.* □ *I can take it. Just tell me the naked truth.*

Tell it like it is. *sent.* "Speak frankly."; "Tell the truth no matter how much it hurts." □ *Come on man, tell it like it is!* □ *Well, I've got to tell it like it is.*

TRY

crack *n.* a try (that may or may not succeed). □ *Have another crack at it.* □ *One more crack and I'll have it.*

go *n.* a try (at something). □ *Let me have a go at it this time.* □ *I'd like to have another go at it, if I can.*

go for broke *in.* to choose to risk everything; to try to succeed against great odds. □ *I feel lucky today. I'll go for broke.* □ *We decided to go for broke, and that is exactly how we ended up.*

hang in there *in.* to keep trying; to persevere. □ *Hang in there. Keep trying.* □ *I'll just hang in there. Maybe things will get better.*

long shot *n.* a wild guess; an attempt at something that has little chance of succeeding. □ *Well, it was a long shot, but I had to try it.* □ *You shouldn't expect a long shot to pay off.*

one's best shot *n.* one's best attempt (at something). □ *That was his best shot, but it wasn't good enough.* □ *I always try to give something my best shot.*

pop *n.* a time; a try; a piece. (Always with *a*.) □ *Twenty dollars a pop is too much.* □ *I love records, but not at $15.98 a pop.*

punt *in.* to do something different in a pinch; to improvise. (From the act of kicking the ball in order to gain ground in football.) □ *When all else fails, punt!* □ *Everyone expected me to lose my temper, so I punted. I cried instead of getting mad.*

shot *n.* a try at something. □ *Go ahead. Give it another shot.* □ *Have a shot at this problem.*

shot in the dark *n.* a very general attempt; a wild guess. □ *It was just a shot in the dark. I had no idea I was exactly correct.* □ *Come on, try it. Even a shot in the dark may win.*

take a crack at something AND **have a crack at something** *tr.* to take a try at something. □ *She had a crack at food preparation, but that wasn't for her.* □ *Let me take a crack at it.*

take a shot (at something) *tr.* to try (to do) something. □ *I don't think I can do it, but I'll take a shot at it.* □ *Go ahead. Take a shot.*

take a whack at something *tr.* to have a try at something. □ *Let me take a whack at it.* □ *Why don't you practice a little while and take a whack at it tomorrow?*

throw *n.* a try; a time. □ *Have another throw at it, why don't you?* □ *Just one more throw, then I'll quit.*

touch *tr.* to deal with or handle someone or something. (Usually in the negative.) □ *I wouldn't touch that problem.* □ *Mr. Wilson is a real pain, and I wouldn't touch his account. Find somebody else to handle it.*

trial balloon *n.* a test of someone's reaction. □ *It was just a trial balloon, and it didn't work.* □ *The trial balloon was a great success.*

wing it *tr.* to improvise; to do something extemporaneously. □ *I lost my lecture notes, so I had to wing it.* □ *Don't worry. Just go out there and wing it.*

TWO

dynamic duo *n.* a very special pair of people or things. (From the *Batman* television program. Used mostly for humor.) □ *The dynamic duo, Beavis and Fred, showed up late and without the beer.* □ *Next time tell the dynamic duo to come earlier.*

gruesome twosome *n.* two people or things. (Jocular. Neither the things or the people have to be "gruesome.") □ *Well, it's the gruesome twosome. Come in and join the party.* □ *The gruesome twosome will both start in tonight's game.*

TYPING

pound something out *tr.* to type something on a typewriter. □ *I have finished writing it. Can I borrow your typewriter so I can pound it out?* □ *All the reporters were pounding out stories for the next edition of the paper.*

U

UGLINESS

butt-ugly *mod.* very ugly. (Potentially offensive. Use only with discretion.) □ *That is the most butt-ugly car I've ever seen.* □ *She is one butt-ugly woman.*

hurt *mod.* very ugly; damaged and ugly. (Black. Similar to *hurting.*) □ *Man, are you hurt!* □ *That poor girl is really bad hurt.*

hurting *mod.* very ugly; in pain from ugliness. □ *That dog of yours is something to behold. It's really hurting.* □ *Man, is she hurting!*

nay *mod.* ugly; unfavorable. (From *nasty.*) □ *She is really nay.* □ *What a nay thing to say.*

plug-ugly *mod.* very ugly. □ *Your dog is just plug-ugly.* □ *My plug-ugly dog happens to be pedigreed.*

pug-ugly *mod.* having to do with a very ugly person. □ *He is so pug-ugly.* □ *What a pug-ugly cat you have there!*

rasty *mod.* having to do with a harsh-looking young woman. (Collegiate.) □ *Who is that rasty dame I saw you with?* □ *That dark lipstick makes you look a little rasty.*

scary *mod.* (of women) ugly. □ *Man, is she scary!* □ *Why do I always end up with a scary woman?*

skank AND **scank** *in.* to appear ugly. □ *My face is skanking like mad. Must be the zits.* □ *Both sisters scank. Must be hereditary.*

skanky *mod.* ugly; repellent, usually said of a woman. (Collegiate.) □ *She is so skanky! That grody hairdo doesn't help either.* □ *What's wrong with being a little skanky? It's what you can do with your*

brain *that counts.* □ *She's skanky, nonetheless.*

ugly as sin *mod.* very ugly. □ *This car's as ugly as sin, but it's cheap and dependable.* □ *My old hound dog is ugly as sin but faithful as the dickens.*

UNAVAILABLE

taken AND **had; took** *mod.* already claimed as someone's mate or lover. □ *Sorry, Bill, I'm already taken. Sam and I are engaged.* □ *Forget it. She's taken.*

UNAWARE

See AWARENESS - LACKING.

UNCERTAINTY

dicey *mod.* touchy; chancy; touch and go. □ *Things are just a little dicey right now.* □ *I'm working on a dicey deal with the city right now.*

flip-flop *in.* to waiver in one's decisions. □ *I'm sorry I'm flip-flopping on this matter. I just can't seem to decide.* □ *Well, you just flip-flop all you want. I know what I want.*

iffy *mod.* marginally uncertain. □ *Things are still sort of iffy, but we'll know for sure in a few days.* □ *It's sort of an iffy matter, but things will get straightened out.*

touch and go *mod.* chancy. □ *It was touch and go for a while, but we are out of the woods now.* □ *The place was in a real tizzy. Everything was touch and go.*

UNCONSCIOUSNESS

KOed *mod.* "knocked out." (Initialism. Originally from boxing.) □ *Wilbur was KOed and got a cut over his eye.* □ *He stayed KOed for about two minutes.*

out cold *mod.* unconscious. □ *Paul was out cold when we found him.* □ *Who knocked him out cold?*

out like a light *mod.* unconscious or sleeping soundly. □ *I fell and hit my head. I was out like a light for two minutes, they tell me.* □ *I closed my eyes and was out like a light in no time at all.*

see stars *tr.* to be (knocked) unconscious. □ *If you talk to me like that again, you'll be seeing stars.* □ *I saw stars for a few seconds, and then someone threw cold water in my face.*

UNDECIDED

See **INDECISION**.

UNDERSTANDING

capish *in.* to understand. (Usually as a question. From an Italian dialect.) □ *The matter is settled. No more talk. Capish?* □ *Now, if you don't capish, let's get it clear right now.*

clear as vodka *mod.* very understandable. □ *Everything he said is as clear as vodka.* □ *I understand what John said, but everything you say is clear as vodka.*

dig *tr. & in.* to understand something. □ *I just don't dig what you are saying.* □ *Sorry. I just don't dig.*

Do I have to paint (you) a picture? AND **Do I have to draw (you) a picture?** *interrog.* "Do you understand yet?"; "How simple do I have to make it for you?" □ *This is supposed to be easy. Do I have to paint a picture?* □ *Do I have to draw you a picture, or can you visualize this?*

(Do you) get my drift? *interrog.* "Do you understand me?" □ *Get my drift? Should I explain it again?* □ *Do you get my drift, or shall I run through it again?*

get it *tr.* to understand a joke; to understand a point of information. □ *Sorry. I don't get it.* □ *Don't you get it?*

Get the message? AND **Get the picture?** *interrog.* "Do you understand?"; "Are you able to figure out what is meant?" □ *Things are tough around here, and we need everyone's cooperation. Get the picture?* □ *We don't need lazy people around here. Get the message?*

gotcha *phr.* "I understand you." □ *Gotcha! Thanks for telling me.* □ *Seven pounds, four ounces? Gotcha! I'll tell everybody.*

grok *tr.* to appreciate someone or something; to relate to someone or something. □ *I can really grok what you're saying.* □ *I don't quite grok that. Run it by again, would you?*

I hear what you are saying. 1. AND **I hear you.** *sent.* "I know just what you are trying to say." □ *Yes, yes. I hear what you are saying, and I'm with you.* □ *Yeah! I hear you!* **2.** *sent.* "I understand your position, but I am under no obligation to agree." □ *I hear you. So do what you want.* □ *I hear you, but it doesn't matter.*

I smell you. *sent.* "I understand you." □ *I smell you. No need to go on and on.* □ *That's enough. I smell you. Don't go on and on.*

know all the angles *tr.* to know all the tricks and artifices of dealing with someone or something. □ *Ask my mouthpiece about taxes. He knows all the angles.* □ *Rocko knows all the angles. That's how he keeps out of the slammer.*

know-how *n.* the knowledge of how to do something. □ *I don't have the know-how to do this job.* □ *You'll get the know-how on the job.*

know shit from Shinola AND **tell shit from Shinola** *tr.* to know what's what; to be intelligent and aware. (Always in the negative. Shinola is a brand of shoe polish. A person who doesn't *know shit from Shinola* is very stupid.) □ *Poor Tom doesn't know shit from Shinola.* □ *Fred can't tell shit from Shinola, and he's been made my boss.*

know the score *tr.* to know the way things work in the hard, cruel world. □ *Don't try to con me. I know the score.* □ *She knows the score. She wasn't born yesterday.*

know what's what *tr.* to be aware of what is going on in the world. □ *Heidi knows what's what. She can help.* □ *We don't know what's what around here yet.*

know where it's at *tr.* to know the way things really are. □ *I know where it's at. I don't need to be told.* □ *We know where it's at, and we want to change it.*

know where one is coming from *tr.* to understand someone's motivation; to understand and relate to someone's position. □ *I know where you're coming from. I've been there.* □ *We all know where he's coming from. That's why we are so worried.*

latch onto something *tr.* to begin to understand something. □ *When Fred finally latched onto the principles of algebra, he began to get better grades.* □ *Sue doesn't quite latch onto the proper stance in golf.*

make the scene *tr.* to understand a situation; to appreciate the situation. (Underworld.) □ *I can't quite make the scene, but it looks like Bruno punched the guy over here. Then he moved to the window over here, and that's when the old dame across the street saw him.* □ *I can make the scene. It's just like you said, except Bruno came in and found the guy laid out on the floor.*

on the same wavelength *mod.* thinking in the same pattern. □ *We're not on the same wavelength. Let's try again.* □ *We kept talking until we were on the same wavelength.*

psych someone out *tr.* to try to figure out what someone is likely to do. □ *Don't try to psych me out.* □ *The batter tried to psych out the pitcher, but it didn't work.*

savvy *tr. & in.* to understand (someone or something). (Adapted from Spanish *sabe*, "he knows.") □ *Do you savvy?* □ *Can you savvy at all what I am trying to tell you?* □ *I just can't savvy stuff like that.*

speak someone's language *tr.* to say something that one agrees with or understands. □ *I gotcha. Now you're speaking my language.* □ *Mary speaks Fred's language. They get along fine.*

squared away *mod.* straightened out. □ *I'm not really squared away on this stuff, but I'm beginning to see the light.* □ *We'll get everything squared away in a few days.*

suss someone out *tr.* to try to figure someone out. □ *I can't seem to suss Tom out. What a strange guy.* □ *I don't have any luck sussing out people I don't know well.*

where someone is at *phr.* "what mental condition someone is in." □ *I know where you're at. I know what you are talking about.* □ *You said it! I know just where you're at!*

wise up (to someone or something) *in.* to (finally) begin to understand someone or something; to realize and accept the facts about someone or something. (Also as a command.) □ *Sally finally wised up to Max.* □ *Come on, Sally! Wise up!*

UNDERSTANDING - LACKING

Greek to someone *n.* something incomprehensible to someone; something as mysterious as Greek writing. □ *I don't understand this. It's all Greek to me.* □ *She said it was Greek to her, and that it made no sense at all.*

UNDESIRABLE

See also **HORRIBLE, NASTY**.

baddy AND **baddie** *n.* a bad thing or person. □ *Using butter is supposed to be a real baddy.* □ *Marty has become such a baddie that no one speaks to him anymore.*

beasty *mod.* (of a person) undesirable; yucky. (California.) □ *You are like, so like, beasty!* □ *I can't stand that gross beasty jerk!*

beat *mod.* lousy; unfortunate. (Collegiate.) □ *This has been a beat day.* □ *What a beat deal you got!*

bogus *mod.* phony; false; undesirable. □ *I can't eat any more of this bogus food.* □ *This class is really bogus.*

cold *mod.* not good. □ *That new CD is real cold. The sound is bad and the performance is too.* □ *The lecture was cold and dull.*

crappy *mod.* bad; lousy; junky. □ *This is sure one crappy day!* □ *Shut your crappy mouth!*

crumbum *mod.* inferior; lousy. □ *I sent the crumbum food back to the kitchen. There was a bug in it.* □ *I want out of this crumbum place.*

crummy AND **crumby** *mod.* lousy; bad; inferior. □ *You know, this stuff is pretty crummy.* □ *It's worse than crumby.*

dank *mod.* very bad. □ *Class was so dank today. I thought I would die of terminal boredom.* □ *This is a real dank day. I hope it's over soon.*

dog *n.* something undesirable or worthless; merchandise that no one wants to buy. □ *Put the dogs out on the sale table so people will see them.* □ *They even bought all the dogs this year. Sales were great.*

dook *mod.* really bad. □ *No more of your dook ideas!* □ *This day was really dook!*

drippy *mod.* weak; ineffective; undesirable. □ *Bob can be so drippy without even trying.* □ *You are proposing some pretty drippy ideas.*

for the birds *mod.* undesirable. □ *This pizza is for the birds.* □ *I don't like this kind of life. It's for the birds.*

generic *mod.* cheap; plain; undesirable. □ *I don't want any old generic car, I want something with power and good looks.* □ *This cereal is generic. It has no taste at all.* □ *This pizza is completely generic. I can't stand it.*

grody AND **groaty** *mod.* disgusting. (From *grotesque*.) □ *What a grody view of the street from this window.* □ *These shoes are getting sort of groaty. I guess I'll throw them out.*

grotty *mod.* highly undesirable. (Originally British. From *grotesque*.) □ *Let's not see another grotty movie tonight.* □ *What is this grotty stuff they serve here?* □ *It's not grotty!*

gungy AND **grungy** *mod.* messy; nasty; worn-out. □ *Get your grungy feet off the sofa.* □ *The weather is so gungy today.*

harsh *mod.* bad. □ *She's a harsh lady and doesn't care how you feel.* □ *Man, this hamburger is harsh. What did you put in it?*

hell of a someone or something AND **helluva someone or something** *n.* a very bad person or thing. (Use caution with *hell*.) □ *That's a hell of a way to treat someone.* □ *He's a helluva driver! Watch out!*

hiddy AND **hidi** *mod.* hideous. □ *That skirt is just hiddy! Get a life!* □ *What hidi wheels! That car's owner has more money than sense.*

ill *mod.* dull; bad. □ *This is an ill pizza and I won't eat it.* □ *That broad is ill and has a face that would stop a clock.*

lame AND **laine; lane** *mod.* inept; inadequate; undesirable. □ *That guy's so lame, it's pitiful.* □ *This mark is about as laine as they come.*

lousy *mod.* rotten; poor; bad. □ *This is a lousy day.* □ *This mushy stuff is lousy. Do I have to eat it?*

lowdown *mod.* rotten; bad. □ *What a dirty, lowdown thing to do.* □ *You are a lowdown rat!*

no bargain *n.* not an especially good person or thing. □ *Fred is okay, but he's no bargain.* □ *This car gets me to work and back, but it's no bargain.*

no go *mod.* negative; inopportune. (This is hyphenated before a nominal.) □ *We're in a no-go situation.* □ *Is it go or no go?*

no great shakes *mod.* someone or something not very good. (There is no affirmative version of this.) □ *Your idea is no great shakes, but we'll try it anyway.* □ *Ted is no great shakes when it comes to brains.*

Not too shabby! *mod.* (with emphasis on *too*) very shabby; very poor indeed. (Sarcastic.) □ *Did you see that basket she missed? Not too shabby!* □ *What a way to treat someone. Not too shabby!*

nowhere *mod.* bad; no good; dull. □ *This place is really nowhere. Let's go.* □ *I want to get out of this nowhere party.*

piss-poor *mod.* very inadequate. (Crude. An elaboration of *poor*. Potentially offensive. Use only with discretion.) □ *This is a piss-poor excuse for fried chicken.*

□ *That was a piss-poor performance for a professional musician.*

pits *n.* anything really bad. (Always with the.) □ *Life is the pits.* □ *This whole day was the pits from beginning to end.*

poison *mod.* wicked; evil. □ *Stay away from her. She's poison.* □ *What a poison personality.*

punk *mod.* poor; dull; inferior. □ *The party turned punk, and we left.* □ *This is pretty punk food.*

rotten *mod.* poor or bad. □ *We have nothing but one rotten problem after another.* □ *This is the most rotten mess I've ever been in.*

rotten to the core *mod.* really bad. □ *That lousy punk is rotten to the core.* □ *The entire administration is rotten to the core.*

sad *mod.* poor; undesirable. □ *This is a sad excuse for a car!* □ *That was a sad pitch there at the end of the last inning.* □ *This steak is really sad.*

scrungy *mod.* inferior; bad. □ *I don't need scrungy merchandise like this. I'm going elsewhere.* □ *You have a very scrungy outlook on life.* □ *Life is scrungy.*

shag-nasty *mod.* nasty. □ *What a shag-nasty jerk!* □ *I want out of this shag-nasty mess.*

shit *n.* something poor in quality; junk. (Potentially offensive. Use only with discretion.) □ *This stuff is shit. Show me something better.* □ *What do you keep all this shit around here for?*

shouldn't happen to a dog *phr.* describes something that is so bad that no creature deserves it. □ *Poor guy. That shouldn't happen to a dog.* □ *This cold I got shouldn't happen to a dog.*

slummy *mod.* lousy. □ *What a slummy place!* □ *This place is not slummy!* □ *That was a slummy trick to pull on her.*

stinking *mod.* lousy; rotten. □ *What a stinking mess you've got yourself into.* □ *That was a mean, stinking thing to do. Really stinking!*

stink on ice *in.* to be really rotten. (So rotten as to reek even when frozen.) □

This show stinks on ice. □ *The whole idea stank on ice.*

stinky *mod.* bad. □ *That was a stinky thing to do.* □ *You have a very stinky attitude. Really stinky.*

suck *in.* [for someone or something] to be bad or undesirable. □ *This movie sucks!* □ *I think that the whole business sucks.*

sucky *mod.* poor; undesirable. □ *This is the suckiest movie I ever saw.* □ *This food is sucky. It really sucks!*

white elephant *n.* a useless or unwanted object. □ *How can I get rid of this white elephant?* □ *Take all those white elephants to the flea market.*

yucky *mod.* nasty. □ *What is this yucky pink stuff on my plate?* □ *This tastes yucky.*

UNEXPECTED

out of line *mod.* not in accord with what is appropriate or expected, especially in price or behavior. □ *Your behavior is quite out of line. I shall report you.* □ *Your price is out of line with the other stores.*

UNFAIR

heavy-handed *mod.* tactless; forceful; unfair. □ *Paul is a little heavy-handed at times, but mostly he's reasonable.* □ *That was a pretty heavy-handed thing to do.*

hit (someone) below the belt *tr.* to deal with someone unfairly. □ *Don't hit below the belt!* □ *You were hitting Tom below the belt when you said that.*

low-blow *n.* an unfair blow. □ *No fair! That was a low-blow.* □ *Coming in like that unannounced was a pretty low-blow.*

No fair! *exclam.* "That's not fair!" □ *No fair! I saw it first!* □ *That's no fair! We paid full price to see this movie.*

not cricket *mod.* unfair; illegitimate; unorthodox. □ *You can't do that! It's not cricket!* □ *What do you mean it's not cricket? You do it.*

raw deal *n.* an unfair deal; unfair treatment. (Always with a.) □ *You really got a raw deal.* □ *My last job was a raw deal. I hope this is better.*

shaft *n.* a bad deal; unfair treatment. □ *He really gave me the shaft.* □ *It's the shaft whenever you go into that place.*

UNFASHIONABLE

camp 1. *n.* something cute and out-of-fashion; something of such an anachronistic style as to be intriguing. □ *Camp is dull and was never interesting.* □ *My brother thinks camp is just a joke.* □ *Nobody really knows what style camp really is, and very few even care.* **2.** AND **campy** *mod.* overdone; out-of-fashion and intriguing. □ *Most camp entertainment is pretentious and overdrawn.* □ *Who needs camp movies?*

low rent *mod.* cheap; unfashionable. □ *This place is strictly low rent.* □ *Why don't you go live with some of your low rent friends?*

UNIMPORTANT

blip *n.* anything quick and insignificant; a onetime thing of little importance. □ *It was nothing, just a blip. The press blew it out of proportion.* □ *It wasn't really a fight. It was just a blip.*

never mind *phr.* "Forget it."; "It doesn't matter anymore." □ *Never mind. I forget what I was going to say.* □ *Oh, never mind. Nobody really cares anyway.*

nothing to write home about *n.* something small or inconsequential. □ *I got a little bit of a raise this year, but it was nothing to write home about.* □ *The party was nothing to write home about.*

piss-ant *mod.* insignificant; unimportant. □ *I don't have time for her little piss-ant problems.* □ *Take your piss-ant papers out of here and leave me alone.*

small potatoes *n.* something or someone insignificant. □ *This contract is small potatoes, but it keeps us in business till we get into the real money.* □ *Small potatoes are better than no potatoes at all.*

small-time *mod.* insignificant; petty. □ *I was in a lot of small-time stuff at home, but never a Broadway hit before.* □ *Broadway is not small-time.* □ *Max was involved in a lot of small-time crime when he was twelve.*

UNINTERESTED

turned off *mod.* uninterested. □ *I'm sort of turned off to stuff like that these days. Part of getting older, I guess.* □ *I can't pay attention if I'm turned off, now can I?*

UNIQUENESS

one *mod.* having to do with something unique or special. (Similar to a definite article.) □ *Tracy is one fine cook.* □ *He was left with one powerful hangover.* □ *Hank? Now there is one ugly son of a gun for you.*

That's a new one on me. *sent.* "That is truly amazing."; "I did not know that." □ *A machine that copies in four colors. That's a new one on me.* □ *A talking camera? That's a new one on me.*

UNKNOWN

dark horse *mod.* previously unknown. □ *Who would vote for a dark horse candidate?* □ *A dark horse player can win if all the others are creeps.*

UNORIGINAL

warmed over *mod.* not very original; rehashed. □ *I am not interested in reading warmed over news on a computer screen.* □ *The lecture sounded sort of warmed over, but it wasn't too dull.*

UNPLEASANT

bad news *mod.* unpleasant; unfortunate. □ *That poor guy is really bad news.* □ *It's bad news Freddy on the phone again.*

low-res AND **lo-res** *mod.* poor; unpleasant. (From *low resolution* in a computer terminal.) □ *I feel sort of low-res today.* □ *The party is lo-res. Let's cruise.*

rude *mod.* undesirable; unpleasant. □ *The prof in my history class is a rude dude, for sure.* □ *What a rude idea!*

UNSYNCHRONIZED

out of sync *mod.* uncoordinated; unsynchronized. □ *Our efforts are out of sync.* □ *My watch and your watch are out of sync.*

UNUSUAL

See **STRANGE**.

UPROAR

hoopla *n.* an outcry; a fuss or a *to-do.* □ *What's all this hoopla about?* □ *There is too much hoopla in these elections.*

stink *n.* a commotion. □ *The stink you made about money has done no good at all. You're fired.* □ *One more stink like that and out you go.*

to-do *n.* a commotion. □ *Don't make such a to-do when you come in late.* □ *They made quite a to-do about the broken window.*

UPSET

have one's ass in a sling *tr.* to be dejected or hurt; to be pouting. (Potentially offensive. Use only with discretion. *Have got* can replace *have.*) □ *She's got her ass in a sling because she got stood up.* □ *Why do you have your ass in a sling?*

illin' *mod.* upset. □ *What are you illin' about? Everything is ice.* □ *Tom was illin' and angry about the broken window.*

in a twit *mod.* upset; frantic. □ *She's all in a twit because she lost her keys.* □ *Pete was in a twit and was quite rude to us.*

jacked up AND **jacked** *mod.* upset; stressed. □ *I was really jacked up by the bad news.* □ *Don't get jacked up. It'll work out.*

slightly rattled *mod.* upset; confused. □ *Tom was slightly rattled by the trouble at the door.* □ *I'm slightly rattled. I'll get over it.*

stressed *mod.* upset; annoyed. □ *Come on, man, don't get stressed! It's only a gag.* □ *I am really stressed. I need a vacation.*

URINATION

duck *n.* a male urinal bedpan. (Hospitals.) □ *Somebody in room 212 needs a duck.* □ *Take this duck down there quick.*

go *in.* to urinate. □ *I gotta go!* □ *Jimmy's gonna go in his pants!*

piddle 1. *in.* to urinate. (Said of children and pets.) □ *Mommy! Jimmy's got to piddle!* □ *Please, Jimmy, don't piddle on the floor.* **2.** *n.* urine. □ *Where's the dog? There's piddle on the carpet.* □ *Don't step in the puppy's piddle.*

piss 1. *in.* to urinate. (All senses are potentially offensive. Use only with discretion.) □ *He went out and pissed in the woods.* □ *Don't piss on the floor.* **2.** *n.* urine. □ *There's piss on the rug. Where's that cat?* □ *Hey, stupid! There's piss on your pants leg.* **3.** *n.* an act of urination. (Especially with *take.*) □ *He went out to take a piss.* □ *Man, I gotta stop here for a piss.*

pump ship *tr.* to urinate. (Crude. From an expression meaning to pump the bilge water from a ship.) □ *He stopped and pumped ship right in the alley.* □ *I'll be with you after I pump ship.*

take a leak *tr.* to urinate. (Crude. Usually in reference to a male.) □ *I gotta go take a leak. Back in a minute.* □ *He just went out to take a leak.*

tea *n.* urine. □ *There is some tea on the floor.* □ *Is that tea on your pants leg?*

tee-tee 1. *in.* to urinate. (Juvenile.) □ *Jimmy, please go tee-tee before we leave.* □ *Jimmy, you are supposed to flush it when you tee-tee.* **2.** *n.* urine. (Juvenile.) □ *There's tee-tee on the floor.* □ *Why is tee-tee yellow?*

tinkle 1. *in.* to urinate. (Mostly juvenile use.) □ *I gotta tinkle!* □ *Jimmy, be sure and tinkle before we leave.* **2.** *n.* urine. (Essentially juvenile.) □ *There's tinkle on the bathroom floor.* □ *Mommy, why is tinkle warm?*

whiz *in.* to urinate. □ *I gotta stop here and whiz.* □ *You can't whiz in the park!*

VACATION

getaway *n.* a quick vacation. □ *We took a little getaway to the Bahamas.* □ *What you need is a weekend getaway.*

tourist trap *n.* a place set up to lure tourists in to spend money. (Can be a shop, a town, or a whole country.) □ *It looked like a tourist trap, so we didn't even stop the car.* □ *What keeps these tourists traps going?*

VALUE

worth one's salt *mod.* worth (in productivity) what it costs to keep one. □ *We decided that you are worth your salt, and you can stay on as office clerk.* □ *You're not worth your salt. Pack up!*

VAN

sin-bin *n.* a van fitted with bedding as a place for necking and lovemaking. □ *Wally said he was saving his money to buy a sin-bin so he could have more fun on dates.* □ *Some rusty old sin-bin was parked in front of the house when I got there.*

VANDALISM

trash 1. *tr.* to vandalize something. □ *Somebody trashed the statue with spray paint.* □ *Who trashed my room?* **2.** *n.* an act of vandalism. □ *Who quarterbacked the bus trash?* □ *The trash the other night was a real travesty.*

VEINS

burned out *mod.* having to do with the ruined veins of an addict. □ *These old ropes are just burned out. I don't know what to do.* □ *My veins are burnt out so I shoot in the jug.*

jug *n.* the jugular vein, used for the injection of narcotics. □ *Now Ernie has to take it in the jug.* □ *He's even got scars on his jugs.*

VERY

but *mod.* totally; very. (Note position in the sentence.) □ *Tell him to get his tail over here but fast.* □ *This thing has to be done but good.*

flat-out *mod.* totally. □ *She was flat-out mad as hell.* □ *We were all flat-out disgusted.*

good and something *mod.* thoroughly something. (Where *something* is an adjective.) □ *I am really good and mad at you for that.* □ *We are good and ready to do something about it.*

in a big way *mod.* very much; urgently. □ *I'm really interested in her in a big way.* □ *He plays to win—in a big way.*

massively *mod.* excellently; totally. □ *Max showed up for the meeting massively stoned and singing at the top of his lungs.* □ *Robert presented us with a massively gross belch that actually made the window rattle a little.*

mondo *mod.* totally; very much. (California.) □ *You are, like, mondo gross!* □ *This place is like, so like, mondo beige.*

mucho *mod.* very. (Spanish.) □ *This is a mucho happy young man.* □ *We are mucho disgusted with your performance.*

pretty *mod.* very. □ *Bob's a pretty nice guy.* □ *I'm pretty busy at the moment.*

real *mod.* very; really. □ *This is a real fine party.* □ *You did a real good thing.*

VICTIM

vic *n.* a victim. □ *We're all vics, but we all keep going.* □ *Harry is a con artist, not a vic.*

VIOLENCE

backhander *n.* a backhand slap in the face. □ *Then she gave me a powerful backhander without even looking to see who I was.* □ *Yes, officer, a perfectly strange woman came up and clobbered me with a backhander that loosened a tooth.*

beat someone's brains out *tr.* to beat someone severely. □ *She threatened to beat my brains out.* □ *Those thugs nearly beat his brains out.*

belt 1. *n.* a blow with the fist or hand. □ *Quiet or I'll give you a belt in the chops.* □ *I got a belt in the gut for my trouble.* **2.** *tr.* to strike someone. □ *Quiet or I'll belt you one!* □ *Don't belt me!*

biff 1. *tr.* to hit someone. □ *Tom biffed Fred on the snoot.* □ *Fred got biffed, and that really made him mad.* **2.** *n.* a blow. □ *The biff on the nose gave Fred a nosebleed.* □ *Tom got a biff in the gut for his trouble.*

blast *tr.* to shoot someone with a gun. □ *The speeding car drove by, and somebody tried to blast him with a machine gun.* □ *The cops blasted the crook till there was nothing left.*

blitz 1. *n.* a devastating attack. □ *After that blitz from the boss, you must feel sort of shaken.* □ *That's my second blitz this week. I feel like London.* **2.** *tr.* to attack and defeat someone or something. □ *Two of your friends came by and blitzed my refrigerator.* □ *The team from downstate blitzed our local team for the third year in a row.*

blood bath *n.* a battle; a great decimation. □ *What a blood bath! The whole town collapsed after the bank failed.* □ *There was a blood bath at the office when the manager fired twenty people.*

boff *tr.* to punch someone. □ *I was afraid she was going to boff me.* □ *Ted boffed Harry playfully.*

bonk *tr.* to strike someone on the head. □ *I bonked John on the head.* □ *He wouldn't move, so I bonked him.*

burn *tr.* to shoot someone. (Underworld.) □ *He burned the guy with a pistol, but it didn't stop him.* □ *Hold it! I've burned one guy tonight, and I ain't afraid of puttin' a hole through you.*

bust someone one *tr.* to punch someone; to give someone a punch, probably in the face. □ *You better shut up, or I'll bust you one!* □ *You want me to bust you one? I will if you do that again.*

clobber *tr.* to strike someone; to beat someone; to outscore someone. □ *I ought to clobber you, but good.* □ *She clobbered him over the head with her bouquet.*

coldcock *tr.* to knock someone out. □ *The guy who called Max out wanted to coldcock him for shorting him, but got coldcocked himself.* □ *The clerk coldcocked the would-be robber with a champagne bottle.*

crown *tr.* to hit someone on the head. □ *The clerk crowned the robber with a champagne bottle.* □ *The bride, at the end of her patience, crowned the stuttering cleric with her bouquet, shouted "I do," and began kissing the groom.*

deck *tr.* to knock someone to the ground. □ *Fred decked Bob with one blow.* □ *I was so mad I almost decked him.*

donnybrook *n.* a big argument; a brawl. □ *There was a big donnybrook at the concert, and the police were called.* □ *Who started this donnybrook?*

drop *tr.* to knock someone down. □ *Jim dropped Willard with a punch to the shoulder.* □ *The swinging board hit him and dropped him.*

drop someone *tr.* to knock someone down; to punch and knock down a person. □ *Fred dropped Bruno with one punch to the jaw.* □ *Max lost his cool and dropped Bruno.*

duke someone out *tr.* to knock someone out. □ *Wilbur tried to duke the guy out first.* □ *Bob duked out the mugger with a jab to the cheek.*

dust someone off *tr.* to give someone a good pounding or beating. □ *Bruno threatened to dust Max off.* □ *Bob dusted off Larry; then he started for Tom.*

dust-up *n.* a fight. □ *Max got in a dust-up with Bruno.* □ *There was a dust-up at* the party that ruined the evening for everyone.

enforcer *n.* a bully; a thug or body-guard. □ *Bruno is the perfect enforcer. Meaner than all get out.* □ *Rocko is too tender-hearted to be a good enforcer.*

fag-bashing *n.* doing violence to homo-sexuals. (Potentially offensive. Use only with discretion.) □ *Those bums get some kind of pleasure out of fag-bashing.* □ *What's this strange need you have for fag-bashing? What's your problem?*

fish-fight *n.* a fight between females. □ *There's a fish-fight over by the biology building.* □ *Those fish-fights can get bru-tal.*

flatten *tr.* to knock someone down with a blow. □ *Max flattened the kid with a jab to the nose.* □ *Wilbur will flatten his opponent.*

floored *mod.* knocked to the floor by a blow. □ *Wilbur was floored by his oppo-nent.* □ *The guy was floored and didn't move a muscle—ever again.*

free for all AND **free-for-all** *n.* a brawl; a general fight. □ *A free for all started on the beach over near the concession stand.* □ *The cops broke up the free-for-all.*

gang-bang *tr. & in.* to gang up on some-one or something. □ *They looked like they were going to gang-bang me.* □ *They're always gang-banging. The punks!*

going over *n.* a beating. □ *Bruno gave the guy a terrible going over.* □ *After a go-ing over like that, the guy spent two weeks in the hospital.*

hit *tr.* to attack or rob someone or some-thing. (Underworld.) □ *Lefty and his gang hit the bank for the second time.* □ *Can you believe that they tried to hit a block party on Fourth Street?*

joog *tr.* to stab someone. (Prisons.) □ *Lefty jooged the screw.* □ *Man, who'd you joog?*

knocked up *mod.* battered; beaten. □ *Sally was a little knocked up by the acci-dent.* □ *This book is a little knocked up, so I'll lower the price.*

knock someone's block off *tr.* to hit someone hard in the head. □ *Wilbur al-most knocked Tom's block off by accident.* □ *He threatened to knock my block off if I didn't do as I was told.*

knuckle sandwich *n.* a blow struck in the teeth or mouth. □ *How would you like a knuckle sandwich?* □ *He threatened to give me a knuckle sandwich.*

laid out *mod.* knocked down (by a punch). □ *He was down, laid out, and the cowboy just stood there panting.* □ *There he was, laid out on the sidewalk, and no one made a move to help him.*

land a blow *tr.* to strike someone. □ *He kept moving, and I found it almost im-possible to land a blow.* □ *The boxer landed a blow to the face of his opponent.*

lay someone out *tr.* to knock someone down with a punch. □ *I can't wait to get into that ring and lay the guy out.* □ *The boxer laid out his opponent with a blow to the head.*

make hamburger out of someone or something AND **make mincemeat out of someone or something** *tr.* to beat someone or something to a pulp; to de-stroy someone or something. □ *The puppy made mincemeat out of my paper.* □ *They threatened to make hamburger out of me.*

mess someone's face up *tr.* to beat someone around the face. (Under-world.) □ *I had to mess his face up a lit-tle, boss, but he's been real cooperative since then.* □ *You want me to mess up your face, or do you want to come along quietly?*

mess someone up *tr.* to beat someone up. (Underworld.) □ *The boss says me and the boys is supposed to mess you up a little.* □ *Is that your job—going around messing up people?*

mop the floor up with someone AND **wipe the floor up with someone** *tr.* to beat someone to a pulp. (Also with other verbs: *clean, dust,* etc.) □ *One more crack like that, and I'll have Bruno wipe the floor up with you.* □ *Bruno's job is dust-*

ing up the floor with people who don't wipe off their feet before coming in.

old one-two *n.* a series of two punches delivered quickly, one after another. (Always with *the.*) □ *Tom gave Bill the old one-two, and the argument was ended right there.* □ *Watch out for Tom. He's a master of the old one-two.*

paste *tr.* to strike someone, especially in the face. □ *I hauled off and pasted him right in the face.* □ *He tried to paste me, but I ducked.*

paste someone one *tr.* to land a blow on someone. □ *I pasted him one right on the nose.* □ *Next time you do that, I'll paste you one!*

pin someone's ears back *tr.* to beat someone, especially about the head. □ *Lefty says I'm supposed to pin your ears back.* □ *You do something like that again, and I'll pin your ears back.*

plant *tr.* to strike a blow (to a particular place on someone). □ *I planted one right on his nose.* □ *The boxer planted a good blow on his opponent's shoulder.*

pop *tr.* to hit or strike someone. □ *Please don't pop me again.* □ *She popped him lightly on the shoulder.*

pound someone's head in *tr.* to beat someone. □ *Talk nice to him, or he'll pound your head in.* □ *I was afraid that the cop was going to pound my head in.*

punch someone out *tr.* to knock someone out. □ *He threatened to punch me out.* □ *The thug punched out the cop and ran down an alley.*

punch someone's lights out *tr.* to knock someone out; to close someone's eyes with a hard blow. □ *Shut up, or I'll punch your lights out.* □ *He threatened to punch my lights out.* □ *You want me to punch out your lights?*

put someone away *tr.* to knock someone unconscious. □ *One tap on the head and I put him away.* □ *The cowboy slugged the rancher in the jaw and put him away for a while.*

rabbit punch *n.* a quick little punch. (Boxing and general slang.) □ *That couldn't have hurt you! It was just a little*

rabbit punch. □ *She battered him with about forty rabbit punches on the arm. Boy, is he ever sore!*

rhubarb *n.* a brawl, especially in a baseball game. □ *There's a noisy rhubarb down on the field.* □ *Ted got punched around a little bit in that rhubarb last week.*

rough someone up *tr.* to beat someone up; to maltreat someone. □ *Am I going to have to rough you up, or will you cooperate?* □ *The crooks roughed up the old lady before taking her purse.*

rough stuff *n.* unnecessary roughness; physical violence or threats of violence. □ *Okay, let's cut out the rough stuff!* □ *There was too much rough stuff in Friday's game.*

roundhouse punch *n.* a punch to the head made by swinging the arm in an arc rather than by a jabbing punch. □ *Jim knocked Ted down with a roundhouse punch.* □ *He let him have a roundhouse punch that would have cracked a two-by-four.*

rumble **1.** *in.* to fight. □ *The gangs are rumbling over on Fourth Street.* □ *We're going to rumble tomorrow night.* **2.** *n.* a fight; a street fight; a gang fight. □ *If there is a rumble, get out of there fast.* □ *My brother was hurt in a gang rumble.*

rump *tr.* to flog someone on the buttocks. □ *They rumped him and made him run around the frat house.* □ *I'm going to get rumped when my dad gets home.*

shellacking *n.* a beating. □ *We gave them a shellacking they'll never forget.* □ *Our team took a real shellacking.*

shiv AND **chiv** *tr.* to stab someone. (Underworld.) □ *He shivved Rocko, and Rocko deserved it.* □ *The boss told Bruno to get Rocko one way or the other—chiv him, burn him, clobber him—but get him.*

shoot-out *n.* a gunfight. □ *There was a big shoot-out at the end of the movie.* □ *In this shoot-out, there were no survivors—not even a horse!*

slugfest *n.* a fight; a festival of slugging. □ *They went out in the alley for a real* *slugfest.* □ *You wanna see a slugfest, just stick around.*

slug it out *tr.* to fight something out; to fight about something figuratively. □ *They finally went outside to slug it out.* □ *We'll just have to sit down in the conference room and slug it out.*

smell blood *tr.* to be ready for a fight; to be ready to attack; to be ready to act. (Like sharks, which are sent into a frenzy by the smell of blood.) □ *Lefty was surrounded, and you could tell that the guys from the other gang smelled blood.* □ *The lawyer heard the crash and came running—smelling blood and bucks.*

sock *tr.* to punch someone or something. □ *Wally was so mad, he tried to sock Paul.* □ *He socked the door with his fist and began to howl with pain.*

Sunday punch *n.* a very solid and destructive blow; one's best blow. □ *Barlowe sent a Sunday punch straight into Rocko's gut. Rocko's eyes bugged out; then he crumpled to the floor and wretched.* □ *Ralph aimed a Sunday punch at Frederick's nose, but missed and spun about, striking his elbow on the banister.*

swipe *n.* a blow or an act of striking someone or something. □ *Bob got a nasty swipe across the face.* □ *The cat gave the mouse a swipe with its paw.*

take a beating *tr.* to be beaten, bested, or defeated. □ *The candidate took a beating in the runoffs.* □ *The team took quite a beating.*

take a pop at someone *tr.* to punch at someone. □ *Bruno took a pop at me, but I ducked.* □ *The drunk took a pop at the cop—which was the wrong thing to do.*

take a swipe at someone or something *tr.* to poke at someone or something. □ *Max took a swipe at Bruno.* □ *The cat took a swipe at the ball.*

take a whack at someone or something *tr.* to hit at someone or something. □ *Wilbur took a whack at Martin and missed.* □ *Jerry got an ax and took a whack at the tree, but didn't do much damage.*

take someone or something apart *tr.* to beat or damage someone or something. □ *The mugger really took the old lady apart.* □ *The wreck took both cars apart.*

tear someone or something up *tr.* to rip someone or something to pieces. □ *The two drunks tore the bar up the best they could.* □ *The dog tore up the robber, and the robber sued.*

throw a punch *tr.* to jab; to punch. □ *She tried to throw a punch at me, but I blocked it.* □ *Wilbur threw a punch at the thug.*

trigger-happy *mod.* eager to fire a gun; eager to shoot someone or something. □ *Rocko is sort of trigger-happy. Watch out.* □ *Ask your trigger-happy hunters to be careful this year.*

wallop 1. *n.* a hard blow. □ *She planted a hard wallop on his right shoulder.* □ *I got quite a wallop when I walked into the door.* **2.** *tr.* to strike someone or something hard. □ *I walloped him hard on the shoulder, but he kept on laughing.* □ *The door swung open and walloped me in the back.*

wax *tr.* to beat or defeat someone; to assault someone. □ *Those guys look like they're gonna wax us but good.* □ *The muggers waxed the vest and swiped his briefcase.*

whack AND **wack 1.** *tr.* to strike someone or something. □ *Jed whacked the kid upside the head.* □ *Larry reached down and wacked the dog across the snout.* **2.** *n.* a blow or hit (at someone or something). □ *She tried to take a whack at me!* □ *She landed a nasty wack on his thigh.*

whack someone or something up *in.* to damage someone or something. □ *Bob got mad at Greg and whacked him up.* □ *Clara whacked up her car yesterday.*

whale into someone or something *tr.* to attack someone or something. □ *Jimmy's dad really whaled into him.* □ *The guy whaled into the logs and had a nice wood pile by noon.*

whipsaw *tr.* to assault a person; to gang up and beat a person. □ *The gang whipsawed the old man for about ten minutes.*

□ *What kind of creeps would whipsaw an old buzzard like that?*

VIRILITY

hairy-ass(ed) *mod.* virile. □ *This big hairy-ass guy started to push us around.* □ *He's not what I would call hairy-assed.* □ *Stop acting like a hairy-assed jerk.*

VISIBILITY - LACKING

lie doggo *in.* to remain unrecognized (for a long time). □ *This problem has lain doggo since 1967.* □ *If you don't find the typos now, they will lie doggo until the next edition.*

sleeper *n.* someone or something that achieves fame after a period of invisibility. □ *The movie* Red Willow *was undoubtedly the sleeper of the year, winning six awards.* □ *My candidate had been a sleeper, but he finally began to pull ahead in the polls.*

VISION

eagle-eye *n.* an eye or eyes with very keen vision. □ *Keep your eagle-eye trained on the entrance.* □ *My eagle-eye tells me there's trouble over there.*

eyeful *n.* the sight of something that one was not meant to see. □ *I got an eyeful of that contract. Yikes! What a giveaway!* □ *She really gave us an eyeful. Shame.*

gander *n.* a look. □ *Let me take a gander at it and see if it's done right.* □ *We should all take a gander to see what one is like.*

get an eyeball on someone or something *tr.* to manage to spot someone or something; to catch sight of someone or something. □ *When I finally got an eyeball on the speeding car, it was too far away for me to read the license plate.* □ *When Jane first got an eyeball on her blind date, she almost cringed in disappointment.*

rubberneck *in.* to stare (at something or someone), turning one's head if necessary. □ *What are all those people rubbernecking at?* □ *Traffic is stalled because of all the drivers who are rubbernecking.*

VOCABULARY

swallow the dictionary *tr.* to acquire an enormous vocabulary. (Usually in the past tense.) □ *My uncle says I've swallowed the dictionary. That's because I know so many big words.* □ *Did you just go to college to swallow the dictionary?*

VOICE

set of pipes *n.* a very loud voice; a strong singing voice. □ *She has a nice set of pipes.* □ *With a set of pipes like that, she's a winner.*

VOMIT

air one's belly *tr.* to empty one's stomach; to vomit. □ *What was in that hamburger? I think I've got to air my belly.* □ *That must have been some party. I heard you airing your belly for most of the night, after you got home.*

barf 1. *in.* to empty one's stomach; to vomit. □ *I think I'm going to barf!* □ *Don't barf here.* **2.** *n.* vomit. □ *Is that barf on your shoe?* □ *Whatever it is, it looks like barf.*

barf bag *n.* a bag available on an airplane for persons who are nauseated. □ *I hope I never even have to see anyone use a barf bag.* □ *What do they do with used barf bags?*

blow beets *tr.* to empty one's stomach; to vomit. □ *What was in that stew? I feel like I gotta blow beets.* □ *She wasted a few minutes blowing beets, just to make things worse.*

blow chunks AND **blow chow; blow grits** *tr.* to vomit. □ *She drank too much and left the room to blow chunks.* □ *The smell was so bad I thought I was going to blow chow.* □ *Where's Kim? She was blowing grits in the john the last time I saw her.*

blow (one's) cookies *tr.* to empty one's stomach; to vomit. □ *I think I'm going to blow my cookies.* □ *Okay, if any you guys gotta blow your cookies or something, do it here, not inside!*

blow one's doughnuts AND **lose one's doughnuts** *tr.* to empty one's stomach; to vomit. □ *The stuff was so vile, I thought I would blow my doughnuts.* □ *Who lost their doughnuts in the hall?*

blow one's groceries *tr.* to empty one's stomach; to vomit. □ *I gotta blow my groceries. Look out!* □ *She blew her groceries all over the front seat.*

blow (one's) lunch AND **lose (one's) lunch** *tr.* to empty one's stomach; to vomit. □ *I almost lost my lunch, I ran so hard.* □ *I wanted to blow my lunch, that's how rotten I felt.*

boff *in.* to empty one's stomach; to vomit. □ *She boffed and boffed, until she was exhausted.* □ *I think I'm gonna boff!*

boot *in.* to empty one's stomach; to vomit. □ *The kid booted and booted and will probably never smoke another cigar.* □ *I think I'm gonna boot. Gangway!*

bow to the porcelain altar *in.* to empty one's stomach; to vomit. (The *porcelain altar* is the toilet bowl.) □ *He spent the whole night bowing to the porcelain altar.* □ *I have the feeling that I will be bowing to the porcelain altar before morning.*

bring something up *tr.* to vomit something up; to cough something up. □ *See if you can get him to bring up the penny.* □ *I did, and he brought up a nickel instead!*

buick *in.* to vomit. (Onomatopoetic. Based on the automobile name.) □ *Dave buicked on the lawn and then stumbled into the house.* □ *Oh, lordy! I feel like I'm going to buick.*

cack AND **kack; kak** *in.* to empty one's stomach; to vomit. □ *I cacked all night with the flu.* □ *I've never heard anybody kack so loud in my life!*

call hughie AND **call earl** *tr.* to vomit. (Onomatopoetic from the sound of wretching.) □ *Fred spent an hour in the john calling hughie.* □ *Yuck! I have to go call earl.*

cat *in.* to empty one's stomach; to vomit. □ *I think I'm gonna cat.* □ *Looks like somebody catted in the bushes.*

cheese 1. *n.* vomit. □ *There's cheese on the sidewalk. Look out!* □ *In there, there's cheese on the bathroom floor. So gross!* **2.** *in.* to empty one's stomach; to vomit. □ *Somebody cheesed on the sidewalk.* □ *She*

popped into the bushes and cheesed soundlessly.

chew the cheese *tr.* to vomit. □ *Fred's out in the bushes, chewing the cheese.* □ *The cat's chewing the cheese on the living room carpet again.*

chuck AND **chuck up** *in.* to empty one's stomach; to vomit. □ *Look! Somebody chucked.* □ *I think I gotta chuck up!*

chuck a dummy *tr.* to empty one's stomach; to vomit. □ *He left the room—to chuck a dummy, I guess.* □ *Somebody chucked a dummy on the patio.*

chunk *in.* to empty one's stomach; to vomit. (Collegiate.) □ *I think I gotta chunk.* □ *The cat chunked all over the carpet.*

cry hughie *in.* to empty one's stomach; to vomit. □ *He is in the john crying hughie.* □ *I think I gotta go cry hughie.*

cry ruth AND **call ruth; call ralph; cry ralph** *tr.* to empty one's stomach; to vomit. □ *Someone is in the bushes crying ruth.* □ *I think I have to call ralph! Stop the car!*

drain the bilge *in.* to empty one's stomach; to vomit. □ *Fred left quickly to drain the bilge.* □ *Who drained the bilge in the bushes?*

drive the big bus AND **drive the porcelain bus; ride the porcelain bus** *tr.* to vomit into the toilet. (The *porcelain bus* is the toilet and the toilet seat is the steering wheel.) □ *Harry's in the john driving the big bus.* □ *Who do I hear driving the porcelain bus in the john?*

drop one's cookies AND **lose one's cookies** *tr.* to empty one's stomach; to vomit. □ *The runner went off to the side and dropped her cookies.* □ *If you feel like you're going to lose your cookies, don't do it on the carpet.*

duke *in.* to empty one's stomach; to vomit. (Collegiate. Rhymes with *puke.*) □ *He left to duke. I saw how green he was.* □ *She's in the john, duking like a goat.*

dump *tr. & in.* to empty one's stomach; to vomit. □ *He ran straight to the john and dumped his dinner.* □ *She turned green, and I knew she was going to dump.*

dump one's load *in.* to empty one's stomach; to vomit. □ *He's in the john dumping his load.* □ *Why can't he learn to dump his load silently?*

earl *n.* to vomit. (Onomatopoetic.) □ *I think I gotta go earl!* □ *Who's earling in the john?*

earp AND **urp** 1. *in.* to empty one's stomach; to vomit. (Onomatopoetic.) □ *Somebody earped here!* □ *I wish people could urp silently.* 2. *n.* vomit. □ *There's earp on your shoe.* □ *Throw something over the urp in the flower bed.*

fetch up *in.* to empty one's stomach; to vomit. □ *I really felt like I was going to fetch up.* □ *Somebody fetched up in here and didn't clean it up.*

flash the hash *tr.* to empty one's stomach; to vomit. □ *Dave left quickly to go out and flash the hash, I think.* □ *Who's in there flashing the hash?*

fling up *in.* to empty one's stomach; to vomit. □ *I was afraid I was going to fling up.* □ *Who flung up on the sidewalk?*

heave *in.* to empty one's stomach; to vomit. □ *He heaved and heaved and sounded like he was dying.* □ *I think I have to go heave.*

honk *in.* to vomit. (Onomatopoetic.) □ *I can hear someone in the john honking like mad.* □ *Who honked on the driveway?*

hughie *in.* to empty one's stomach; to vomit. □ *I gotta go hughie.* □ *Oo, who hughied?*

hug the porcelain god(dess) AND **hug the throne** *tr.* to vomit; to vomit while holding on to the toilet seat. □ *The girls drank a lot of beer and two of them spent the night hugging the porcelain god.* □ *I don't want to get drunk and have to hug the porcelain goddess all night.*

hurl *in.* to empty one's stomach; to vomit. (Like the *throw* in *throw up.*) □ *I think I gotta go hurl.* □ *Who's in the john hurling so loud?*

kiss the porcelain god *tr.* to empty one's stomach; to vomit. □ *He fled the room to kiss the porcelain god, I guess.* □ *Who's in there kissing the porcelain god?*

laugh at the carpet *in.* to vomit; to vomit on a carpet. □ *Tom bent over and laughed at the carpet, much to the embarrassment of the entire group.* □ *Wayne laughed at the carpet, and people moved away—not knowing what he was going to do next.*

launch (one's lunch) *tr. & in.* to empty one's stomach; to vomit. □ *When I saw that mess, I almost launched my lunch.* □ *Watch out! She's going to launch!*

liquid laugh *n.* vomit. □ *If you drink much more, you're gonna come out with a liquid laugh.* □ *There's some liquid laugh on your shoe.*

lose it *tr.* to empty one's stomach; to vomit. (Collegiate.) □ *Oh, God! I think I'm going to lose it!* □ *Go lose it in the bushes.*

pray to the porcelain god AND **pray to the enamel god** *in.* to empty one's stomach; to vomit. (Refers to being on one's knees [praying] in front of a porcelain toilet bowl.) □ *Boy, was I sick. I was praying to the porcelain god for two hours.* □ *Wayne was in the john, praying to the enamel god.* □ *I think I'd better go home and pray to the porcelain god.*

puke 1. *in.* to empty one's stomach; to vomit. □ *I think I am going to puke.* □ *Max went home and puked for an hour.* 2. *n.* vomit. □ *There's puke on the floor!* □ *Good grief, Tom. Is that puke on your shoe, or what?*

pump ship *tr.* to empty one's stomach; to vomit. (Crude.) □ *After I pumped ship, I felt better.* □ *Oh, man! I think I gotta pump ship!*

ralph AND **rolf** *in.* to empty one's stomach; to vomit. (Teens and collegiate.) □ *She went home and ralphed for an hour.* □ *I think I'm going to rolf.*

ralph something up *tr.* to vomit (something). (Teens and collegiate.) □ *The doctor gave him some stuff that made him ralph it up.* □ *He ralphed up his dinner.*

reverse gears *tr.* to wretch as a prelude to vomiting. □ *The cat is reversing gears. Throw her out the back door.* □ *Beavis is* *reversing gears and might be going to vomit. You never know with Beavis.*

ruth *in.* to empty one's stomach; to vomit. □ *I gotta go ruth!* □ *I just can't stand to ruth.*

shoot one's cookies AND **shoot one's breakfast; shoot one's supper** *tr.* to empty one's stomach; to vomit. □ *I think I'm gonna shoot my cookies.* □ *I shot my supper, and I was glad to get rid of it.*

shoot the cat *tr.* to empty one's stomach; to vomit. □ *I must have shot the cat a dozen times during the night.* □ *Shooting the cat is no fun when you're weak and dizzy.*

shoot the works *tr.* to empty one's stomach; to vomit. □ *Suddenly she turned sort of green, and I knew she was going to shoot the works.* □ *After she shot the works, she looked fine—but I was sort of pale.*

sicks *n.* nausea; vomiting. □ *Oh man, I got the sicks.* □ *He's at home with the sicks.*

sick (up) *in.* to empty one's stomach; to vomit. □ *I think I'm going to sick up. Isn't there supposed to be a barf bag in one of these seat pockets?* □ *He's got to sick, and there's no air sickness bag. Help!*

skin a goat *tr.* to empty one's stomach; to vomit. □ *Ralph went out to skin a goat.* □ *Was my cooking so bad that everybody had to skin a goat?*

sling the cat *tr.* to empty one's stomach; to vomit. □ *Suddenly Ralph left the room to sling the cat, I guess.* □ *That stuff will make you sling the cat.*

snap one's cookies *tr.* to vomit; to regurgitate. □ *I think I'm gonna snap my cookies.* □ *Some jerk snapped his cookies on the sidewalk.*

spew *in.* to empty one's stomach; to vomit. □ *After dinner, I suddenly had the urge to spew.* □ *Fred is up in the john spewing like mad.*

spew one's guts (out) *tr.* to empty one's stomach; to vomit. □ *Fred is spewing his guts out because of that lousy fish you served.* □ *He's spewing his guts because he has the flu, cabbagehead.*

talk on the big white phone *in.* to vomit into a toilet. □ *One more beer and I'm gonna have to go talk on the big white phone.* □ *She was talking on the big white phone all night.*

talk to earl *in.* to vomit. (Onomatopoetic.) □ *I think I hear Pete in the john talking to earl.* □ *Oh, my gosh! I think I have to go talk to earl!*

technicolor yawn *n.* vomit. □ *This garbage will bring on a few technicolor yawns if we serve it.* □ *Who did the technicolor yawn in the bushes?*

throw a map *tr.* to empty one's stomach; to vomit. □ *Somebody threw a map on the sidewalk.* □ *I felt like I was going to throw a map.*

throw a technicolor yawn *tr.* to vomit. □ *One look at the food, and I almost threw a technicolor yawn.* □ *John stumbled into the living room and threw a technicolor yawn on the new carpet.*

throw one's voice *tr.* to empty one's stomach; to vomit. □ *Wally's in the john throwing his voice.* □ *Another drink of that stuff and Don'll be throwing his voice all night.*

throw up one's toenails *tr.* to wretch; to vomit a lot. □ *It sounded like he was throwing up his toenails.* □ *Who's in the john throwing up her toenails?*

toss *in.* to empty one's stomach; to vomit. □ *I was afraid I was going to toss.* □ *She tossed right there on the steps and ran away.*

toss one's cookies AND **throw one's cookies; toss one's lunch; toss one's tacos** *tr.* to empty one's stomach; to vomit. □ *Right then and there, with no warning, he tossed his cookies.* □ *If you feel like tossing your cookies, please leave quietly.* □ *Fred stepped over to the bushes and raucously tossed his tacos.*

uke AND **yuke 1.** *in.* to empty one's stomach; to vomit. (Collegiate.) □ *I think somebody yuked in the back seat, Tom.* □ *My friends wouldn't uke in my car!* **2.** *n.* vomit. (Collegiate.) □ *That is uke on the floor, isn't it?* □ *Tell me that the stuff in the back seat isn't yuke!*

upchuck 1. *tr. & in.* to vomit (something). □ *Wally upchucked his whole dinner.* □ *Who upchucked over there?* **2.** *n.* vomit. □ *Is that upchuck on your shoe?* □ *There is still some upchuck on the bathroom floor.*

urge to purge *n.* the need to throw up. □ *Max felt the urge to purge and ran for the john.* □ *All this grease on the pizza gives me the urge to purge.*

woof *in.* to vomit. (Onomatopoetic.) □ *Somebody woofed on our driveway.* □ *Beavis had to woof on the way home.*

woof cookies *tr.* to vomit. □ *Bill is in the bathroom woofing cookies.* □ *Waldo had to woof cookies in the bushes.*

worship the porcelain god(dess) *tr.* to empty one's stomach; to vomit. (Collegiate. One is on one's knees before the toilet, which is the *god(dess)*.) □ *Somebody was in the john worshiping the porcelain god till all hours.* □ *I think I have to go worship the porcelain goddess. See ya.*

yak *in.* to vomit. (Onomatopoetic.) □ *Hank was in the john yakking all night.* □ *Who yakked on the carpet?*

yank *in.* to vomit. □ *Somebody or some animal yanked on the driveway.* □ *I think I gotta go yank.*

yap *in.* to empty one's stomach; to vomit. □ *Who yapped in the bushes?* □ *Ye gods, do I hear one of our guests yapping in the powder room?*

york 1. *in.* to empty one's stomach; to vomit. □ *He ate the stuff, then went* straight out and yorked. □ *Who yorked in the flowerpot?* **2.** *n.* vomit. □ *Is that york I see on the living room window?* □ *Hey, Jimmy! Come out in the snow and see the frozen york!*

zuke *in.* to vomit. □ *The cat zuked on the living room carpet.* □ *I hear someone zuking in the bathroom. What's going on?*

VULGAR

See also **OBSCENE, RUDE.**

dirty mouth *tr.* to speak ill of someone or something. □ *Please stop dirty mouthing my friends.* □ *You have dirty mouthed cats just about enough.*

off-color *mod.* dirty or smutty; *raunchy.* □ *That joke was sort of off-color.* □ *Tom told an off-color joke that embarrassed everyone.*

Pardon my French. AND **Excuse my French.** *sent.* "Excuse my use of swear words or taboo words." (Does not refer to real French.) □ *Pardon my French, but this is a hell of a day.* □ *What she needs is a kick in the butt, if you'll excuse my French.*

raunchy AND **raunchie; ronchie** *mod.* crude; tasteless; bad. □ *He told a very raunchy story at the party.* □ *Don't be so ronchie.*

raw *mod.* vulgar; crude; raucous; untamed. □ *I've had enough of your raw humor.* □ *That joke was a little raw.*

ripe *mod.* crude; *raunchy.* □ *Your jokes are a bit ripe.* □ *That was a ripe one!* □ *Stop acting so ripe.*

W

WAITING

See also **ANTICIPATION**.

mark time *tr.* to wait; to do nothing but wait. □ *I'll just mark time till things get better.* □ *Do you expect me to just stand here and mark time?*

on the back burner *mod.* out of the way; aside and out of consideration. □ *We will have to put this on the back burner for a while.* □ *She kept her boyfriend on the back burner until she decided what to do about him.*

twiddle one's thumbs *tr.* to do nothing; to wait nervously, playing with one's fingers. □ *I sat twiddling my thumbs while you were out doing I don't know what all!* □ *Don't just sit home twiddling your thumbs.*

WALKING

blisterfoot *n.* someone who walks a lot: a police patrol officer, a soldier, etc. □ *This blisterfoot puts his hand on my shoulder and says, "What's the rush, chum?"* □ *So this blisterfoot just falls down right there on the parade ground.*

foot it *tr.* to go somewhere by foot; to walk or run. □ *I have to foot it over to the drugstore for some medicine.* □ *I'm used to footing it wherever I go.*

galumph (around) *in.* to walk around. □ *I spent all day galumphing around, looking for a present for Ted.* □ *Stop galumphing long enough to eat some dinner.*

hit the bricks AND **hit the pavement** *tr.* to start walking; to go into the streets. □ *I have a long way to go. I'd better hit the bricks.* □ *Go on! Hit the pavement! Get going!*

hoofing *n.* walking; running. □ *My car's in the shop, so I'm hoofing for a few days.* □ *Two or three of the kids were hoofing around the mall, so I joined them.*

hoof it *in.* to walk instead of ride. □ *My car's broken down, so I had to hoof it to work today.* □ *Let's hoof it over to the library.*

shank it *tr.* to use one's legs to get somewhere; to walk. □ *My car needs fixing so I had to shank it to work today.* □ *I like to shank it every now and then.*

shank's mare *n.* foot travel. □ *You'll find that shank's mare is the quickest way to get across town.* □ *Is there a bus, or do I have to use shank's mare?*

WAR

hawk *n.* someone who supports a warlike U.S. defense policy. □ *The hawks want to raise taxes and buy tanks.* □ *The doves want to sell the tanks, ignore the hawks, and give the money to the poor.*

WARNING

bites *in.* [for someone or something] to be bad or threatening. □ *Watch out for Gloria. She bites!* □ *My dad bites, but don't worry, he's in a good mood.*

It's your funeral! *exclam.* "If you do it, you will suffer all the consequences!" □ *Go if you want. It's your funeral!* □ *Go ahead, swim to Cuba. It's your funeral!*

Make my day! *exclam.* "Go ahead, do what you are going to do, and I will be very happy to do what I have to do!" (A catchphrase said typically by a movie police officer who has a gun pointed at a criminal. The police officer wants the criminal to do something that will justify pulling the trigger, which the police officer will do with pleasure. Used in real life in any context, and especially in sarcasm.) □ *Move a muscle! Go for your gun! Go ahead, make my day!* □ *Make my day. Just try it.*

over my dead body *phr.* "not if I can stop you"; "you won't be able to do something if I am alive to prevent you." □ *You'll drop out of school over my dead body!* □ *Get married and move to Arizona? Over my dead body!*

Watch your mouth! AND **Watch your tongue!** *exclam.* "Pay attention to what you are saying!"; "Do not say anything rude!" □ *Hey, don't talk that way! Watch your mouth!* □ *Watch your tongue, garbage mouth!*

WASTE

boondoggle *n.* a waste of time and money; a project for spending public money, often unwisely. □ *Another Washington boondoggle came to light today as investigators revealed plans for a dam in a California canyon that doesn't have any water.* □ *This is another boondoggle—just the thing every single baby-kisser pledged to stop.*

circular file *n.* a wastebasket. □ *That letter went straight into the circular file.* □ *Most of the junk mail sits here until I can put it into the circular file.*

down the drain *mod.* gone; wasted. □ *Well, there's $400 down the drain.* □ *A lot of money went down the drain in that Wilson deal.*

dreck *n.* dirt; garbage. (From German via Yiddish.) □ *What is all this dreck in the corner?* □ *I've had enough of this dreck around here. Clean it up, or I'm leaving.*

file thirteen *n.* the wastebasket. □ *Please throw this in file thirteen. I don't need it anymore.* □ *I'm afraid that the papers you want went into file thirteen two days ago.*

out the window *mod.* gone; wasted. □ *All that work gone out the window.* □ *My $40—out the window. Why didn't I save my money?*

shitcan *n.* a trash can; a garbage can. (Potentially offensive. Use only with discretion.) □ *Just throw this in the shitcan.*

It's worthless. □ *The shitcan is full. Go dump it.*

trash *tr.* to throw something away. □ *Trash this stuff. Nobody will ever use it.* □ *I'll take it. Don't trash it.*

WASTE - TIME

blow off 1. *in.* to goof off; to waste time; to procrastinate. □ *You blow off too much.* □ *All your best time is gone— blown off.* **2.** *n.* a time-waster; a goof-off. (Usually **blow-off.**) □ *Fred is such a blow-off!* □ *Get busy. I don't pay blow-offs around here.*

dilly-dally *in.* to waste time. □ *Stop dilly-dallying around.* □ *I like to dilly-dally over a cup of coffee.*

dork off *in.* to waste time. □ *Stop dorking off and get busy.* □ *The whole class was dorking off and the teacher got furious.*

fake off *in.* to waste time; to *goof off.* □ *Hey, you guys, quit faking off!* □ *All you clowns do is fake off. Now, get busy!*

goldbrick *in.* to be lazy; to shirk one's duty. □ *Stop goldbricking and get back to work.* □ *Whoever is goldbricking when I come back gets a real talking to.*

goldbrick(er) *n.* a lazy person. □ *Pete is just a lazy goldbrick.* □ *Tell that goldbricker to get back to work.*

goof off 1. *n.* a time-waster; a *jerk.* (Usually **goof-off.**) □ *Pete is such a goof-off!* □ *I'm no goof-off, but I am no scholar either.* **2.** AND **goof around** *in.* to waste time. □ *Quit goofing off.* □ *Get busy. Stop goofing around.*

hack around *in.* to waste time. □ *You guys are always hacking around. Get busy!* □ *I wanted to hack around for a year after college, but my finances disagreed.*

hang *in.* to hang around; to spend time aimlessly. □ *Is that all you did all summer? Just hang?* □ *My mom yelled at me because I spent all day hanging with the guys.*

hang (around) *in.* to loiter; to waste away time doing nothing. □ *Don't just hang around. Get busy with something.* □

Move. Don't just hang. There's work to be done.

hang with someone *in.* to hang around with someone. □ *Dave spent the afternoon hanging with Don, and neither one got anything done.* □ *I'm going down to the corner and hang with the guys.*

horse around *in.* to work inefficiently; to *goof around.* □ *Stop horsing around and get busy.* □ *You guys are always horsing around.*

jack around *in.* to waste time; to mess around. □ *Stop jacking around and get busy.* □ *The gang was jacking around and broke your window.*

jerk around *in.* to waste time. □ *Stop jerking around and get to work.* □ *All you do is jerk around. Get a move on!*

knock around *in.* to waste time. □ *Stop knocking around and get to work!* □ *I need a couple of days a week just for knocking around.*

lazybones *n.* a lazy person. □ *I'm just a lazybones, but I don't eat much.* □ *That lazybones is out there sleeping in the shade.*

mess around (with someone) AND **mess about (with someone); monkey around (with someone)** *in.* to waste someone's time. □ *Don't mess about with me. Just answer the question, if you please.* □ *I don't have the time for this. Stop messing around.*

mickey mouse *mod.* trivial; time wasting; lousy. □ *I want out of this mickey mouse place.* □ *No more mickey mouse questions if I agree to stay?*

mooner *n.* an idler who stares at the moon. □ *If he ever outgrows being a mooner, he may be all right.* □ *I feel like a mooner tonight. There is nothing better to do.*

piddle (around) *in.* to waste time; to work aimlessly or inefficiently. □ *Stop piddling around! Get to work!* □ *Can't you get serious and stop piddling?*

piddler *n.* someone who wastes time. □ *Bob is such a piddler. He can't seem to get organized and get down to work.* □ *That piddler will never get anywhere in life.*

play around (with someone) *in.* to waste time; to waste someone's time. □ *Stop playing around and get to work.* □ *Don't play around with me!*

putz around *in.* to fiddle around; to mess around. □ *Stop putzing around and get to work.* □ *Those guys spend most of their time just putzing around.*

rat around *in.* to waste time loafing around; to *kick around.* (Collegiate.) □ *I didn't do anything but rat around all summer.* □ *If kids don't have jobs, they just rat around.*

scam *in.* to fool around and waste time. □ *Quit scamming and get busy.* □ *You'd get better grades if you didn't scam so much.*

screw around *in.* to waste time. □ *Stop screwing around and get busy.* □ *John's always screwing around and never does anything on time.*

sluff (off) *in.* to waste time; to *goof off.* □ *Watch him. He will sluff off if you don't keep after him.* □ *He won't sluff. I know I can trust him.*

spaz around *in.* to waste time; to mess around. □ *You kids are always spazzing around. Why don't you get a job?* □ *We're just spazzing around. Leave us alone.*

spin one's wheels *tr.* to waste time; to remain in a neutral position, neither advancing nor falling back. □ *I'm just spinning my wheels in this job. I need more training to get ahead.* □ *The whole project was just spinning its wheels until spring.*

WATCH

ticker *n.* a watch. □ *My ticker stopped. The battery must be dead.* □ *If your watch runs on a battery, can you really call it a ticker?*

tick-tock *n.* a watch or clock. (Juvenile.) □ *Wind your tick-tock before you forget.* □ *The tick-tock in the kitchen has broken.*

WEALTH

deep pockets *n.* a rich person. □ *The lawyer went after the doctor who was the deep pockets of the organization.* □ *I want* to find the deep pockets who arranged all this.

fat cat 1. *n.* someone with great wealth and the accompanying success. □ *I like to watch the fat cats go by in their beemers.* □ *I'm no fat cat. I'm usually financially embarrassed in fact.* **2.** *mod.* having to do with wealth or a wealthy person. (Hyphenated as a modifier.) □ *You'll never see me driving any of those fat-cat cars.* □ *I just have a bank account. No fat-cat investments.*

filthy rich 1. *mod.* very wealthy. □ *I wouldn't mind being filthy rich.* □ *There are too many filthy rich people now.* □ *Ken is filthy rich because of the money his uncle left him.* **2.** *n.* people who are very wealthy. □ *The filthy rich can afford that kind of thing, but I can't.* □ *I sort of feel sorry for the filthy rich.*

flush *mod.* wealthy; with plenty of money. □ *Today I am flush. By tomorrow, I'll be broke.* □ *I'm not exactly flush, but I can pay the bills.*

haves *n.* the wealthy; those who have money. (Always with *the*.) □ *The haves seem to be able to take care of themselves.* □ *I live in the western suburbs with the haves.*

jet-set(ters) *n.* young and wealthy people who fly by jet from resort to resort. □ *The jet-set doesn't come here anymore.* □ *Jet-setters have turned to other kinds of excitement.*

loaded *mod.* wealthy; loaded with money. □ *Mr. Wilson is loaded, but he is also generous with his money.* □ *My Uncle Fred is loaded, but he's going to take it all with him.*

moneybags *n.* a nickname for a wealthy person. □ *When old moneybags does finally buy the farm, who gets the loot?* □ *When you get to be a big moneybags, don't forget those you left behind.*

stinking rich *mod.* very rich. □ *I'd like to be stinking rich for the rest of my life.* □ *Tiffany is stinking rich, and she acts like it.*

strike it rich *tr.* to become rich suddenly. □ *I never thought I would strike it*

rich. □ *Pete is the kind of guy who wants to strike it rich and live in the lap of luxury for the rest of his life.*

well-fixed AND **well-heeled** *mod.* rich. □ *His father died and left him pretty well-fixed.* □ *Her well-fixed uncle left her a lot of money.* □ *Pete is well-fixed for life.*

WEAPONRY

ammo *n.* ammunition. □ *There they were, trapped in a foxhole with no ammo, enemy all over the place. What do you think happened?* □ *I don't know. They sent out for ammo, maybe?*

artillery *n.* guns; grenades. (Underworld.) □ *Where does Max stash the artillery?* □ *All the artillery is locked in the trunk of the getaway car.*

attitude-adjuster *n.* a police officer's nightstick; any club. □ *The officer said he would bring order to the gathering with his attitude-adjuster.* □ *Andy had a black attitude-adjuster hanging from his belt, and I wasn't going to argue with him.*

blade *n.* a knife. □ *Bring your blade over here and cut this loose.* □ *What are you carrying a blade for?*

cannon *n.* a gun; a revolver. (Underworld.) □ *Rocko pulled out his cannon and aimed it at Barlowe's throat.* □ *The cops found Rocko's cannon where Barlowe had kicked it during the struggle.*

clean *mod.* not carrying a weapon. (Police and underworld.) □ *I frisked him. He's clean.* □ *Bugsy's gang was clean except for Bugsy himself who had a small pistol.*

equalizer *n.* a gun; a pistol. (Underworld.) □ *Rocko carried an equalizer, but wouldn't dream of using it.* □ *An equalizer can be dangerous in Max's business.*

get the drop on someone *tr.* [for person A] to manage to get a gun aimed at person B before person B can aim back at person A. (The gun is then "dropped" by person B.) □ *Rocko got the drop on Max in a flash.* □ *Max was too stoned to get the drop on Rocko.*

hardware *n.* a weapon; a gun. (Underworld and Western.) □ *I think I see your* *hardware showing.* □ *Lefty keeps his hardware under his mattress.*

heat *n.* a gun; armaments. (Underworld.) □ *Lefty has his heat on him at all times.* □ *Rocko never carries heat.*

heater *n.* a pistol. (Underworld.) □ *Lefty carried his heater with him that day.* □ *Put your heaters away, boys. This is a job for reason.*

iron *n.* a gun; a revolver. (Underworld.) □ *Rocko never carries iron unless he's going to use it.* □ *What kind of iron do you carry?*

nuke *n.* a nuclear weapon. □ *Are there nukes aboard that ship?* □ *The military establishment is working on a number of new nukes.*

pack *tr.* to carry something, usually a gun. (Underworld. Any of the slang terms for gun may be used: *rod, iron, heat,* etc.) □ *I can tell that guy's packing heat from the bulge in his jacket.* □ *I never pack a rod on Sunday.*

persuader *n.* a gun or other weapon used to threaten someone. (Underworld.) □ *He pulls out this persuader, see, and aims it right at me, see.* □ *Maybe my little persuader will help you remember where the money is.*

piece *n.* a gun, especially a revolver. (Underworld.) □ *Is that guy carrying a piece?* □ *Okay, this gun is aimed at your head. Drop your piece.*

popper *n.* a handgun. (Underworld. From the sound of a gunshot.) □ *He carries a popper under his coat.* □ *It's illegal to carry a popper in this state.*

rod *n.* a gun; a revolver. (Underworld.) □ *I got a rod in my pocket. Don't move.* □ *I don't have any bullets for my rod.*

roscoe *n.* a pistol, especially a revolver. (Underworld.) □ *He's got a roscoe in his pocket.* □ *I'm going down there to talk to Max, and I'm taking my roscoe.*

sap *n.* a blackjack. (Underworld.) □ *The thug bopped him on the head with a sap.* □ *Max had a sap in his pocket when they arrested him for possession.*

Saturday night special *n.* a small, easily obtainable pistol. □ *There was another killing last night with a Saturday night special.* □ *That's the tenth shooting done with a Saturday night special this week.*

shank *n.* a knife. □ *The mugger pulled a shank on the victim.* □ *The cops found the shank in the bushes.*

shiv AND **chiv** *n.* a knife. (Underworld.) □ *Swiftly and silently his shiv found its way up under Rocko's ribs. All for a silly dame.* □ *I could tell from the way his cuff broke that there was a chiv strapped to his leg.*

shooting iron *n.* a pistol. (Cowboy and folksy.) □ *Millard "Shorty" Wilson always carried his shooting iron with him, except for one fateful day back in '92—1892, that is.* □ *He pulled out his shooting iron and got down to cleaning it.*

slug *n.* a bullet. □ *Barlowe sent a couple of slugs into Rocko's chest. Rocko crumpled soundlessly.* □ *The medico dug out the slugs like he had done it a thousand times—which he probably had.*

switch *n.* a switchblade knife. □ *They found a switch in his pocket when they searched him.* □ *Max was arrested for carrying a switch.*

zip gun *n.* a homemade handgun. (Underworld.) □ *The kid had a zip gun, so I didn't argue.* □ *Can he handle anything other than a zip gun?*

WEATHER

See **COLD, HEAT, WIND.**

WHAT

Now what? *interrog.* "What is wrong now?" □ *I ran into the room and stopped in front of Tom. "Now what?" asked Tom.* □ *I see you standing there. Now what?*

Say what? *interrog.* "What did you say?" □ *Say what? I didn't hear that.* □ *The old man held his hand to his ear and said, "Say what?"*

So what? *interrog.* "What does it matter?"; "What is the point of what you are saying?" □ *So what if I'm too old? Did that stop Rudolph Drew from trying it?* □ *I'm a crook. So what?*

What do you say? *interrog.* "What is your answer?" □ *Well, what do you say?* □ *Come on, I need an answer now. What do you say?*

What gives? *interrog.* "What is going on?"; "What is happening?" □ *Hey! What gives? Who left this here?* □ *What gives? Who's made this mess?*

What (in) the devil? *interrog.* "What has happened?"; "What?" (Often with the force of an exclamation.) □ *What in the devil? Who put sugar in the salt shaker?* □ *What the devil? Who are you? What are you doing in my room?*

What (in) the hell? **1.** *interrog.* "What has happened?"; "What?" □ *What in the hell? Who did this?* □ *What the hell happened here?* **2.** *exclam.* "What does it matter!" □ *Give her a new one. What the hell!* □ *Don't be such a cheapskate. Get the nice one. What the hell!*

What in (the) Sam Hill? *interrog.* "What has happened?"; "What?" (An elaboration of *what. Sam Hill* is *hell.* Often with the force of an exclamation.) □ *What in Sam Hill is going on around here?* □ *What in the Sam Hill do you think you are doing?*

What's the scam? AND **What's the deal?** *interrog.* "What is going on around here?" □ *There's a big rumpus down the hall. What's the scam?* □ *I gave you a $20, and you give me $5 back? What's the deal? Where's my other $5?*

What the deuce? *interrog.* "What has happened?"; "What?" (*Deuce* is an old word for devil.) □ *What the deuce! Who are you?* □ *What the deuce! Who did this?*

WHERE

middle of nowhere *n.* an isolated place. □ *I don't want to stay out here in the middle of nowhere.* □ *I was stranded in the middle of nowhere for an hour with a flat tire.*

Where in (the) Sam Hill? *interrog.* "Where?" (An intensive form of *where. Sam Hill* is *hell.*) □ *Where in Sam Hill did I put my hat?* □ *Where in the Sam Hill were you?*

Where in the world? *interrog.* "Where?" (An intensive form of *where.* See examples for variations.) □ *Where in the world have you been?* □ *Where in the world did I put my glasses?*

Where on (God's green) earth? *interrog.* "(Exactly) where?" (An intensive form of *where.* See examples for variations.) □ *Where on God's green earth did you get that ridiculous hat?* □ *Where on earth is my book?* □ *Where on God's green earth were you?*

Where's the beef? *interrog.* "Where is the substance?"; "Where is the content?" (From a television commercial where someone is looking for the meat in a fast-food hamburger.) □ *That's really clever and appealing, but where's the beef?* □ *Where's the beef? There's no substance in this proposal.*

WHO

Who (in) the hell? AND **Who (in) the devil?** *interrog.* "Who?" (An elaboration of *who.* See examples for variations.) □ *Who in the hell was that masked man?* □ *Who the devil are you?*

Who the deuce? *interrog.* "Who?" (An elaboration of *who.* The *deuce* is the devil. See examples for variations.) □ *Who the deuce do you think you are?* □ *Who the deuce is making all that noise?*

WIG

divot *n.* a toupee; a partial toupee. □ *I think that Sam is wearing a little divot.* □ *His divot slipped, but no one laughed.*

rug *n.* a wig or toupee. □ *Is that guy wearing a rug, or does his scalp really slide from side to side?* □ *I wear just a little rug to cover up a shiny spot.*

sky rug *n.* a toupee; a man's wig. □ *I think he is wearing a sky rug.* □ *He looks better in his sky rug, but that's not necessarily good.*

WILDNESS

frantic *mod.* great; wild. □ *We had a frantic time at Chez Freddy.* □ *That rally was really frantic.*

freak (out) a wild party of any type; any exciting happening. (Usually **freak-out** or **freakout**.) □ *There is a big freak-out* *at Freddy's joint tonight.* □ *What a frantic freakout!*

free-wheeling *mod.* lacking restraint; flamboyant and uncontrolled. □ *These high-spending, free-wheeling palm-pressers appear out of nowhere at election time.* □ *She's too free-wheeling.* □ *She's a free-wheeling executive type.*

hog-wild *mod.* wild; boisterous. □ *All the kids were completely hog-wild by the time I got there.* □ *Things got sort of hog-wild while you were away.*

WIN

See **DEFEAT, OVERWHELM.**

WIND

hawk *n.* the cold winter wind. □ *Man, just feel the hawk cut through you!* □ *It's the time of the year when the hawk rules!*

Mr. Hawkins *n.* the winter wind. (Originally Black.) □ *We have an appointment with Mr. Hawkins in January.* □ *Put something on your head, or Mr. Hawkins will cut you down.*

WOMAN

beach bunny *n.* a young woman who frequents beaches. □ *This little beach bunny bounced up and offered to put lotion on me.* □ *They say that most of those beach bunnies have some degree of sun blindness.*

bird *n.* a woman; a girl. □ *I like the bird you were with last night.* □ *What a bird! I want one.*

broad *n.* a woman. (Usually derogatory.) □ *This pushy broad comes up to me and asks if I have any manners!* □ *So—come on, what'd you tell the broad?*

campus queen *n.* a good-looking and popular female college student. □ *I always thought I wanted to be a campus queen, but all that has changed.* □ *I wonder what some of those campus queens look like when they get up in the morning.*

chick *n.* a girl or woman. □ *Who's the chick driving the ragtop?* □ *We're gonna take some chicks to dinner and then catch a flick.*

dudette *n.* a young woman; the feminine of *dude.* □ *Susan is one fine-looking dudette.* □ *The place was filled with good-looking dudettes, just waiting for the right guy to come along.*

girl *n.* a woman; a young woman. (Objectionable to some as demeaning to women.) □ *A bunch of us girls got together for coffee today.* □ *Would you girls care to come over to my house next week?*

mink *n.* a woman. (Black.) □ *I see your mink has some new silks, man.* □ *Take this home to your mink. She'll like it.*

moose *n.* a Japanese girlfriend; any girlfriend. (Crude. Military.) □ *She's my moose, and you'd better remember it!* □ *She's one fine moose, if you ask me.*

sister *n.* a fellow feminist. □ *We can do this thing, sisters, we can do it!* □ *The sisters will be discussing it at tonight's meeting.*

sister *n.* a fellow sorority member. □ *One of my sisters let me borrow her car.* □ *The junior sisters are putting on a skit.*

skirt *n.* a woman. □ *Some skirt comes up to me and asks where the police station is.* □ *Who's the skirt I saw you with last night?*

sosh *n.* a (young female) socialite. □ *A young sosh in a beemer kept trying to get around me.* □ *Tiffany looks like a sosh, but she's just a working girl.*

twist *n.* a girl; a woman. (Underworld. Possibly rhyming slang "twist and twirl = girl.") □ *This good-looking twist comes over to the table and asks Lefty if he'd like to dance.* □ *He says "yes," and the twist says, "Go ahead, I bet it's a scream!"*

WOMAN - ATTRACTIVE

babe *n.* a good-looking woman. □ *Who is that babe standing on the corner over there?* □ *That babe happens to be my sister.*

cheesecake *n.* a good-looking woman; good-looking women. □ *Who's the cheesecake in that low-cut job?* □ *Bring on the cheesecake!*

cupcake *n.* an attractive woman. (Also a term of address.) □ *Hey, cupcake, what ya doing?* □ *Who is that cupcake driving the beemer?*

dish *n.* a good-looking woman. □ *Wow, isn't she a dish?* □ *Now there's a dish.*

doll *n.* a pretty girl or woman. □ *Who's the doll I saw you with last night?* □ *That doll was my sister, jerk.*

fox *n.* an attractive girl or young woman. □ *Man, who was that fox I saw you with?* □ *That fox was my sister. Next question?*

foxy lady *n.* a sexually attractive woman or girl. □ *You are really a foxy lady, Tracy.* □ *A couple of foxy ladies stopped us on the street.*

freak mommy *n.* a good-looking female. □ *Wendy, you are a freak mommy, and I want to get to know you better.* □ *Sally is such a freak mommy. My eyes just water!*

number *n.* a girl; a sexually attractive girl. □ *Who is that cute little number I saw you with?* □ *She is really some number.*

piece *n.* a sexually attractive (young) woman. (Crude.) □ *She's a real piece!* □ *Who's that piece I saw you with last night?*

pigeon *n.* a cute girl or woman. □ *What a cute little pigeon.* □ *Who was the dreamy little pigeon I saw you with last night?*

slick-chick *n.* an attractive and cute girl. □ *Tiffany is a slick-chick. I wonder if she'd go out with me.* □ *Who was that slick-chick I saw you with the other night?*

stallion *n.* a tall, good-looking woman. □ *Dana is really a stallion!* □ *Who is the stallion with that dude?*

stone fox *n.* an attractive woman; a very sexy woman. □ *She is a stone fox if I ever saw one.* □ *Who is that stone fox I saw you with last night?*

tomato *n.* an attractive girl or woman. □ *There's a nice-looking tomato.* □ *A good-looking tomato brought me my change.*

WOMAN - COLD

ice queen *n.* a cold and haughty woman. □ *Tracy is not exactly an ice queen, but comes close.* □ *It's Kim who's the ice queen.*

WOMAN - FAT

Bahama-mama *n.* an obese black woman. (Derogatory.) □ *Clare has turned into a real Bahama-mama. She's gonna have to lay off eating so much.* □ *That Bahama-mama who was just in here ordered four chocolate shakes.*

cow *n.* a fat or ugly woman. (Derogatory.) □ *That cow can hardly get through the door.* □ *Wouldn't you think a cow like that would go on a diet?*

pig *n.* an ugly and fat woman. (Derogatory.) □ *Clare is a pig. Why doesn't she lose a ton or two?* □ *Every girl in that sorority is a pig.*

WOMAN - FRIEND

bitch *n.* one's girlfriend. (Crude and mostly jocular.) □ *She's my bitch, and I love her.* □ *Me and my bitch really like this kind of stuff.*

old lady AND **old woman** *n.* (one's) girlfriend. □ *My old lady and I are getting married next week.* □ *I got my old lady a bracelet for her birthday.*

pussycat *n.* a woman or young woman; one's girlfriend. (Also a term of address.) □ *Hi, pussycat. Don't I know you from somewhere?* □ *Who was that yummy pussycat I saw you with last Friday?*

sister *n.* a (female) friend. (Originally underworld. Sometimes a term of address.) □ *Hi, sister! How ya doing?* □ *Come here, sister. I gotta have a word with you.*

(soul) sister *n.* a black person's female, black friend. □ *One of the soul sisters dropped by to talk.* □ *A sister called, but didn't leave her name.*

wife *n.* a girlfriend. (Collegiate.) □ *Me and my wife are going to Fred's this Friday.* □ *Ask your wife if she wants to come along.*

WOMAN - GOOD

square john broad *n.* an honest, straightforward woman. (Underworld.) □ *Betty is okay. She's a real square john broad.* □ *We need a square john broad to give this place a look of respectability.*

WOMAN - IMPORTANT

boss lady *n.* the woman in charge. □ *You'll have to ask the boss lady.* □ *The boss lady asked again for volunteers.*

BWOC *n.* "big woman on campus," an important or self-important female college student. (Initialism. Collegiate.) □ *Some BWOC came in and asked us to leave.* □ *It's always the same BWOCs you see in the paper.*

WOMAN - MEEK

sob sister *n.* a weak woman who is prone to crying. □ *Mary is a sob sister. She wears you out fast.* □ *I had another sob sister in the office today. Went through half a box of tissues.*

WOMAN - NEGATIVE

barracuda *n.* a predatory person, especially a predatory woman. □ *She's a barracuda. Better watch out!* □ *I wouldn't get involved with those barracudas if I were you.*

battle-ax *n.* a belligerent (old) woman. (Derogatory.) □ *Tell the old battle-ax she can go straight to blazes.* □ *I can handle any battle-ax. Send her on in.*

bitch *n.* a derogatory term for a woman. (A verbal weapon. Derogatory.) □ *The stupid bitch doesn't know from nothing.* □ *You bitch! Stop it!*

bra-burner *n.* a nickname for a woman who supported the women's liberation movements of the 1960s and 1970s. (Derogatory.) □ *Didn't the bra-burners give way to whale-savers in the '70s?* □ *Mike wants to know if the bra-burners took them off first.*

doxy *n.* a gangster's woman. (Underworld. Old.) □ *Lefty's doxy dropped off this package. It's ticking.* □ *Does Max have a doxy?*

gold digger *n.* a woman who pays attention to a man solely because of his wealth. □ *Sam called Sally a gold digger, and she was devastated.* □ *"You little gold digger!" cried Sam.*

libber *n.* a woman who advocates woman's liberation movements; a feminist. (Usually derogatory.) □ *She sure sounds like a libber.* □ *This libber on the radio says men are unnecessary.*

nerd magnet *n.* a girl or woman who attracts dull males. □ *Oh, Kim, sometimes I feel like such a nerd magnet.* □ *Sally is weary of dating total drips. She is a classic nerd magnet.*

WOMAN - OLD

bluehair *n.* an old lady, especially one whose hair is tinted blue. □ *The cruise was nice but sort of dull because of all the bluehairs aboard.* □ *The bluehairs all crowded up to the door, each one trying to be first.*

old girl *n.* an old lady; a lively old lady. □ *That old girl is still going.* □ *What makes an old girl like that so feisty?*

WOMAN - SEX

floozie *n.* a promiscuous woman. □ *Tracy was enraged when Rocko called her a floozie.* □ *"I didn't call you a floozie," said Rocko. "I said you were boozy."*

glutz *n.* a slut; a woman of low morals. □ *I didn't say she is a glutz!* □ *Tracy knows some old dames she would call glutzes.*

grouse *n.* a woman; women considered sexually. □ *Who's the grouse I saw you with last night?* □ *Look at that grouse over there.*

hot number *n.* an attractive or sexy *girl* or woman. □ *She's quite a hot number.* □ *Who's that hot number I saw you with last night?*

quail *n.* any girl or woman, especially considered sexually. (Crude.) □ *Look at that cute little quail over there.* □ *Who was the quail I saw you with last night?*

red-hot mama *n.* an exciting woman; a sexually exciting or excited woman. □ *Clare is really a red-hot mama!* □ *I'm no red-hot mama, just a country girl.*

sex goddess *n.* a sexy looking female movie or television star. □ *I wonder what these sex goddesses look like when they get up in the morning.* □ *Sex goddesses get up in the afternoon.*

sex kitten *n.* a woman with enormous sexual potential. □ *He thought he was* getting a sex kitten, but she turned out to be just a plain cat. □ Clare does everything she can to look like a sex kitten.

sexpot *n.* one who flaunts one's sexuality, usually a woman. □ Tiffany is such a sexpot. □ About 20,000 young sexpots hit Hollywood every year hoping to be discovered.

WOMAN - STUPID

Barbie doll *n.* a pretty, giddy *girl* or woman. □ She's just a Barbie doll. □ Ask that little Barbie doll if she wants a drink.

bimbo *n.* a giddy woman; a sexually loose woman. □ So she's a bimbo. She still has rights. Have a heart! □ Now the bimbo is a star in the movies.

dumb Dora *n.* a stupid woman; a giddy woman. □ I'm no dumb Dora. I'm just learning. □ Who's the dumb Dora with the blonde hair and long fingernails?

Wilma *n.* a stupid woman. (From the Flintstones character. Also a term of address.) □ She is such a Wilma! What a twit! □ Well, Wilma. I see you forgot your money again.

WOMAN - TALL

long-tall-Sally *n.* a tall girl or woman. □ Isn't she a gorgeous long-tall-Sally? □ She's quite a long-tall-Sally.

WOMAN - UGLY

bag *n.* an ugly woman. (Derogatory.) □ Tell the old bag to mind her own business. □ She has turned into an absolute bag.

bear *n.* an ugly woman. (Derogatory.) □ Tell the old bear to hold her tongue. □ How can a bear like that be allowed to run around loose?

bow-wow *n.* an ugly woman; a *dog*. (Derogatory.) □ What a bow-wow! □ I would have chosen a better nose if I had been given a chance, but—all in all—I'm not such a bow-wow.

bush bitch AND **bush pig** *n.* an ugly or unpleasant female. (Derogatory.) □ Tom's been dating some bush pig from Adamsville. □ Who is that bush bitch I saw Tom with last night?

dog *n.* an ugly girl. □ I'm no dog, but I could wish for some changes. □ So she's not a movie star; she's not a dog either!

hellpig *n.* a fat and ugly girl or woman. (Derogatory.) □ Who was that hellpig you were out with last night? □ Comb your hair. You look like some hellpig!

roach *n.* an ugly girl or woman. (Derogatory. From *cockroach*.) □ Who was that roach you were with last night? □ That dame is a real roach.

skag AND **scag** *n.* a very ugly woman. (Collegiate.) □ What a skag! I wouldn't be seen with her. □ She looks like a scag without makeup.

skank AND **scank** *n.* an ugly (young) woman. (Collegiate.) □ What a skank she is! Give her a comb or something. □ Look at her! Is she a scank or what?

snag *n.* an ugly (young) woman. □ She's not a snag! She's lovely. □ Who's the snag your brother is running around with?

Zelda *n.* a dull and ugly female. □ I'm not as much of a Zelda as you think. □ Nobody's gonna call my sister a Zelda and get away with it.

WORK

beat one's brains out (to do something) *tr.* to work hard at a task. □ I'm tired of beating my brains out to do what you want. □ He beat out his brains to get here on time!

beat someone's brains out *tr.* to drive oneself hard (to accomplish something). □ I beat my brains out all day to clean this house, and you come in and track up the carpet! □ Don't beat your brains out. Just give it a good try.

benies *n.* benefits. □ The salary is good, but the benies are almost nonexistent. □ Are retirement contributions one of your benies?

buck for something *tr.* to work ambitiously for something, such as a promotion. □ I'm just bucking for recognition, and of course, a 20 percent raise. □ You can tell she's bucking for promotion.

dirty work *n.* menial work; hard work. □ Why do I always get stuck with the dirty work? □ *We should share the dirty work evenly.*

get hot *in.* to become busy or hectic. □ *Things always get hot around here toward the end of the month.* □ *When things start getting hot, we have to hire more people.*

get off one's rear *in.* to get up and get busy. □ *It's time to get off your rear and get to work.* □ *Hey, Chuck, get off your rear! There's work to be done.*

get with it *in.* to hurry up and get busy; to be more industrious with something. □ *Get with it; we've got a lot to do.* □ *Let's get with it. There's a lot of work to be done.*

gig *n.* any job of an assignment nature; a onetime job such as when a newspaper reporter is assigned to write a particular story. □ *I didn't want that election gig, but I got it anyway.* □ *Wally is tired of getting the crime gigs.*

gravy train *n.* a job that brings in a steady supply of easy money or *gravy.* □ *This kind of job is a real gravy train.* □ *The gravy train is just not for me.*

grunt work *n.* hard, menial labor; tedious work. □ *I'm tired of doing grunt work for minimum wages.* □ *Who is supposed to do the grunt work around here? Not me!*

leg work *n.* the physical work accompanying a task. □ *I don't mind making the phone calls if you do the leg work.* □ *I have a gopher to do the leg work for me.*

pay one's dues *tr.* to serve one's time in a menial role. □ *I spent some time as a bus boy, so I've paid my dues in the serving business.* □ *You have to start out at the bottom. Pay your dues, and then you'll appreciate better what you have.*

rat race *n.* a dull and repetitive situation; a dull and unrewarding job. □ *I am really tired of this rat race—day after day.* □ *She dropped out of the rat race and moved to Vermont, where she opened a barber shop.*

slave away (at something) *in.* to work very hard (doing something). □ *I'm tired of slaving away at this and getting*

nowhere. □ *I'm slaving away for $7.00 an hour and have no prospects for the future.*

split a gut *tr.* to work very hard. □ *I split a gut to get this place fixed up in a week.* □ *Don't split a gut for me. I love things that are falling apart.*

sweat blood *tr.* to work very hard at something; to endure distress in the process of accomplishing something. □ *And here I sweated blood to put you through college, and you treat me like a stranger.* □ *Everybody in the office had to sweat blood that week.*

workaholic *n.* someone who is obsessed with work. □ *Jerry is a workaholic. He can't enjoy a vacation.* □ *Are workaholics really productive?*

working stiff *n.* a working man; a man who must work to live. □ *But does the working stiff really care about all this economic stuff?* □ *All the working stiffs want is a raise.*

work oneself (up) into a lather *tr.* to work very hard and sweat very much. (In the way that a horse works up a lather.) □ *Don't work yourself up into a lather. We don't need to finish this today.* □ *I worked myself into a lather getting this stuff ready.*

work one's tail off AND **work one's buns off; work one's butt off** *tr.* to work very hard. (Use caution with *butt.*) □ *I worked my tail off to get done on time.* □ *You spend half your life working your butt off—and for what?*

WORN

beat up *mod.* visibly worn; shabby. (This is hyphenated before a nominal.) □ *Get your beat-up car painted or something!* □ *My coat is too beat up to wear to the opera.*

seen better days *tr.* showing signs of wear or exhaustion. (Always a past participle.) □ *This coat has seen better days.* □ *The pitcher has seen better days. He's about through on this team, I think.*

WORRY

eat *tr.* [for something] to bother or worry someone. □ *What's eating you,*

Bill? □ *Nothing's eating me. I'm just the nervous type.*

worry-wart *n.* someone who worries all the time. □ *Don't be such a worry-wart.* □ *I'm sorry I'm such a worry-wart.*

WORTHLESSNESS

clinker *n.* a worthless person or thing. (From the term for a cinder.) □ *This guy is such a clinker. Who needs him?* □ *Ralph has turned out to be a real clinker. We'll have to pink slip him.*

clunker *n.* someone or something worthless; a *clinker.* □ *We have to get the clunkers off the payroll.* □ *Fred? There's another clunker we don't need.*

cotton-picking AND **cotton-pickin'** *mod.* worthless; damned. (Folksy.) □ *What's the cotton-pickin' idea?* □ *Who is this cotton-picking bigwig pushing us around?*

crap *n.* junk; worthless matter. □ *Why don't you just throw this crap away?* □ *Get your crap off my bed!*

deadwood *n.* nonproductive or nonfunctional persons. □ *We'll have to cut costs by getting rid of the deadwood.* □ *Is there any way to make the deadwood productive again?*

good-for-nothing *mod.* worthless. (Usually having to do with a person.) □ *Let's get rid of this good-for-nothing car right now.* □ *Tell your good-for-nothing brother to find another place to live.*

hogwash *n.* something worthless; nonsense. □ *This stuff is hogwash. Take it away.* □ *I am tired of hearing your hogwash!*

lost cause *n.* a hopeless or worthless thing or person. □ *The whole play began to wash out during the second act. It was a lost cause by the third.* □ *Max is a lost cause. Just forget about him.*

no-account *mod.* worthless; no-good. □ *Her uncle is a no-account gambler.* □ *She is a no-account part-time dealer at the casino.*

no-good *mod.* worthless; bad. □ *Get that no-good jerk out of here!* □ *I have never heard of such a no-good car dealership before.*

not worth a damn *mod.* worthless. □ *This pen is not worth a damn.* □ *When it comes to keeping score, she's not worth a damn.*

not worth a plugged nickel *mod.* worth little or nothing. □ *This new battery is not worth a plugged nickel.* □ *Mary isn't worth a plugged nickel at baseball.*

not worth beans *mod.* worthless. □ *This paint is not worth beans. I'll have to buy another can.* □ *Sue, you're not worth beans as a painter.*

slime *n.* degrading matters; corrupt people or situations. □ *I don't want to be involved in slime like that.* □ *The press uncovered even more slime at city hall.*

tripe *n.* a bad performance; something worthless. □ *I know tripe when I see tripe, and that was tripe.* □ *The reviewer thought your play was tripe.*

WRITING

hack *n.* a professional writer who writes mediocre material to order. □ *This novel shows that even a hack can get something published these days.* □ *That hack can't even write her name!*

pad *tr.* to lengthen a piece of writing with unnecessary material. □ *This story would be better if you hadn't padded it with so much chitchat.* □ *I think I can pad the report enough to make it fill twenty pages.*

southpaw *n.* a left-handed person. □ *Micky's a southpaw and writes sort of funny.* □ *My sister is a southpaw, but I'm not.*

WRITING - PARAPHERNALIA

nerd pack *n.* a plastic sheath for holding pens in a pocket, protecting the cloth from ink. (This is the classic symbol of a bookish *nerd.*) □ *A lot of engineers have nerd packs.* □ *A real nerd wears a nerd pack in the pocket of a dirty shirt.*

WRONG

See also ERROR.

Come off it! *exclam.* "Give up your incorrect point of view!" □ *Come off it!*

You're wrong, and you know it. □ *You are arguing from a foolish position. You're dead wrong. Come off it!*

come on *exclam.* "You are wrong!" (Usually **Come on!**) □ *Come on! This is a good set of clubs!* □ *Come on! Wasteful spending occurs at all levels of all governments! Nobody is innocent!*

off base *mod.* off target; wrong; not relevant. □ *Your answer was completely off base. Try again.* □ *You are off base. I will have to deal with someone else.*

out in left field *mod.* wrong; *off base; loony.* □ *Don't pay any attention to her. She's out in left field as usual.* □ *That guy is out in left field—a real nut.*

wrongo *mod.* wrong. □ *You are totally wrongo.* □ *Wrongo, wrongo! You lose!*

You've got another think coming. *sent.* "You have made an error. Think again." □ *If you think I'm going to let you get away with that, you've got another think coming.* □ *You've got another think coming if you think I'll do it.*

YES

See also **AGREEMENT, APPROVAL, SATIS-FACTORY.**

abso-bloody-lutely *mod.* absolutely; emphatically. □ *Do I like pizza? Abso-bloody-lutely!* □ *We are abso-bloody-lutely sick to death of your wishy-washy attitude.*

absotively (posilutely) *mod.* absolutely; decidedly. □ *I will be there at ten, absotively posilutely.* □ *I am absotively exhausted!*

all right *interj.* "yes"; "okay." □ *All right. I'll do it.* □ *All right. I'm coming.*

Bingo! *exclam.* "Yes!"; "That's right!" (From the game "Bingo.") □ *Bingo! I've got the answer!* □ *And we put this little jobber here, another one here, and bingo! We're done.*

check *interj.* okay; yes; "Yes, it is on the list." □ *BILL: Four quarts of oil. TOM: Check.* □ *FRED: Are you ready? PAUL: Check.*

I am so sure! *exclam.* "I am right!" (California.) □ *You are way rad! I am so sure!* □ *This is too much. I am so sure!*

natch *interj.* "yes"; "naturally." □ *I guess it's okay. She said natch.* □ *Natch, you can borrow my car.*

okey-dokey *interj.* "yes"; OK. (Folksy.) □ *Okey-dokey, I'll be there at noon.* □ *Okey-dokey. You sure can.*

roger *interj.* "okay"; "That is correct." □ *Roger, I'll do it.* □ *Roger. Will do.*

ten-four AND **10-4** *interj.* "okay." (Citizens band radio.) □ *Ten-four, old buddy. I will do that.* □ *Please, where the answer to the question is yes or no, don't write 10-4 for yes.*

Way! *exclam.* "Yes it can!"; "Yes it does!" □ *TED: It can't be done. No way! BILL: Way! Yes, it can!* □ *Way! You will do it and you will like it!*

will do *phr.* "I will do it." □ *Will do. I'll get right on it.* □ *Fix the stuck window? Will do.*

Word. AND **Word up.** *interj.* "Correct."; "Right." □ *I hear you, man. Word.* □ *Word. I agree.* □ *Yes, it's time to go. Word up.*

yeah *interj.* "yes." □ *LEFTY: You okay? BRUNO: Yeah.* □ *LEFTY: Yeah? BRUNO: Yeah! I said yeah! Did you hear me say yeah?*

Yes! *interj.* "Absolutely yes!" (Always with a special intonation that holds the "*y*" on a higher pitch and then drops the pitch sharply. The word itself is not slang, but the word with this intonation is part of many slang contexts.) □ *That's right! Yes!* □ *Yes! Exactly right!*

you bet *interj.* "yes"; "You can bet on it." □ *Can you have two? You bet.* □ *You bet; it's all settled.*

You betcha! *interj.* "Yes!"; "You can be sure of it!" (Literally, You bet, you.) □ *Will I be there? You betcha.* □ *Can I? You betcha!*

You bet your boots! *exclam.* "You can be absolutely certain!" □ *Am I happy? You bet your boots!* □ *You bet your boots I'm mad.*

You bet your sweet life! *exclam.* "You are absolutely correct!" □ *Happy? You bet your sweet life!* □ *You bet your sweet life I am glad!*

You bet your sweet patoot(ie)! *exclam.* "You can be absolutely certain!" (Pa-

tootie is the buttocks.) □ *You bet your sweet patootie I'm serious!* □ *I'll be there! You bet your sweet patoot!*

yup AND **yep** *interj.* "yes." (Folksy.) □ *Yup, I'd say so.* □ *I think so. Yep, that's right.*

YIELD

knuckle under (to someone or something) *in.* to give in to or accept some-

one or something. □ *She always refused to knuckle under to anyone.* □ *You have to knuckle under to the system sometimes.*

YOUTH

beat *mod.* having to do with the Bohemian youths of the 1950s. □ *My brother looked sort of beat, but I was neat as a pin.* □ *Actually, I don't think I ever saw anybody who I would call beat.* □ *The beat guys are all gone now.*

ZIPPER

XYZ *tr.* "examine your zipper"; make sure your fly is zipped up. (Initialism. Said to men when necessary.) □ *I say there, Wally, XYZ.* □ *XYZ, Fred.*

Index of Slang and Colloquial Expressions

Use this index to find the theme under which a particular slang expression is listed. For instance, to find the definitions and examples for **airheaded**, look under the theme **STUPIDITY**. Some expressions have multiple entries and appear under more than one theme.

anchor-clanker SAILOR
ancient history PAST
and change MONEY
And how! AGREEMENT
angel dust DRUGS - PCP
angel FINANCIAL
angel NICKNAME
angle FOCUS
angle MOTIVES
animal MAN - VULGAR
ankle DEPART
ankle PEOPLE - ATTRACTIVE
annihilated INTOXICATED - ALCOHOL
another peep (out of you) COMPLAINT
ante MONEY
anti OPPOSITION
antifreeze ALCOHOL
antifreezed INTOXICATED - ALCOHOL
antsy ANXIETY
A-OK QUALITY
ape hangers MOTORCYCLES
ape MAN - VULGAR
aped INTOXICATED - ALCOHOL
app COMPUTER
apple PEOPLE - AMERINDIAN
apple SPORTS - BASEBALL
apple-polisher FLATTERY
applesauce NONSENSE
arb FINANCIAL
Are we away? QUESTION
ark CARS
arm POLICE
armpit LOCATION - UNDESIRABLE
arm-twister PERSUASION
arm-twisting PERSUASION
army brat CHILDREN
(a)round the bend CRAZINESS
(a)round the bend INTOXICATED -
  ALCOHOL/DRUGS
artillery EATING
artillery WEAPONRY
artsy (fartsy) ARTS
artsy-craftsy ARTS
asleep at the switch ATTENTION -
  LACKING
asphalt jungle CITIES
asshole ANUS
asshole PEOPLE - NEGATIVE
astronomical AMOUNT - LARGE
astronomical COMMERCE
at a snail's pace SPEED - LACKING
at loose ends ANXIETY
attic HEAD

attitude-adjuster WEAPONRY
Aunt Flo MENSES
avs CHANCE
(Aw) shucks! OATHS
away JAIL
away SPORTS - BASEBALL
awesome EXCELLENCE
awesome IMPRESSIVE
AWOL ABSENCE
Aztec two-step DIARRHEA
B and B BREASTS
B and B BUTTOCKS
BA BUTTOCKS
babe ENDEARMENT
babe WOMAN - ATTRACTIVE
baboon PEOPLE - STUPID
baby bear POLICE
Baby Bell TELEPHONE
(baby) boomer PEOPLE - YOUNG
baby GADGET
baby LOVER
baby PROJECT
babycakes ENDEARMENT
baby-kisser POLITICIANS
back number OLD-FASHIONED
back to square one BEGINNINGS
back to the salt mines EMPLOYMENT
back up REFUSAL
back FIGHTING
backbone COURAGE
back-door trot(s) DIARRHEA
backed up INTOXICATED - DRUGS
backer FINANCIAL
backfire (on someone) BACKFIRE
backfire FLATULENCE
backhander VIOLENCE
backlash RESULTS
backroom SECRECY
backseat driver ANNOYANCE
backside BUTTOCKS
backslapper PEOPLE - FRIEND
bacon POLICE
bad egg PEOPLE - NEGATIVE
bad hair day DAY
bad news COST
bad news UNPLEASANT
bad paper CHECKS
bad rap ARREST
bad rap CRITICISM
bad trip INTOXICATION - DRUGS
bad trip PEOPLE - NEGATIVE
bad EXCELLENCE
bad POWER

badass MAN - NEGATIVE
badass MEAN
baddy UNDESIRABLE
bad-mouth CRITICISM
bad-mouth TALKING
bafflegab NONSENSE
Bag it! ANNOYANCE
Bag it! SILENCE
bag of bones PEOPLE - THIN
bag on someone CRITICISM
Bag that! IGNORE
Bag your face! ANNOYANCE
bag ARREST
bag DEATH
bag DRUGS - PARAPHERNALIA
bag OBTAIN
bag PREFERENCE
bag WOMAN - UGLY
bagged ARREST
bagged INTOXICATED - ALCOHOL
bagman CRIMINAL
bagman DRUGS - SELLER
bagman HOBO
Bahama-mama WOMAN - FAT
bail (out) DEPART
baked INTOXICATED - ALCOHOL/DRUGS
baked SUNBURN
baldy BALDNESS
ball and chain SPOUSE
ball is in someone's court PLAY
ball of fire ENERGETIC
ball COPULATION
ball PARTY
ball PLEASURE
ball-breaker DIFFICULTIES
ball-breaker PEOPLE - NEGATIVE
ball-busting CHALLENGE
ball-busting DIFFICULTIES
balled up CONFUSION
baller SPORTS
ballhead SPORTS
ballpark estimate ESTIMATION
balls TESTICLES
ballyhoo PROMOTION
balmed INTOXICATED - ALCOHOL
balmy CRAZINESS
balmy INTOXICATED - ALCOHOL
baloney NONSENSE
bamboozle DECEPTION
bamboozled CONFUSION
bamboozled INTOXICATED - ALCOHOL
banana oil NONSENSE
banana republic COUNTRY

banana PEOPLE - EAST ASIAN
banana-head PEOPLE - STUPID
(bang) dead to rights EVIDENCE
bang for the buck POWER
bang in the arm DRUGS - PORTION
bang DRUGS - PORTION
bang POWER - ALCOHOL
bang THRILL
banger CARS
banger DRUGS - PARAPHERNALIA
bang-up EXCELLENCE
banjaxed INTOXICATED - ALCOHOL
banjaxed RUINATION
bank MONEY
banker's hours TIME - PERIOD
bankroll MONEY
barb DRUGS - BARBITURATE
Barbie doll WOMAN - STUPID
bare-assed NAKEDNESS
barf bag VOMIT
Barf City DISGUSTING
Barf out! DISGUSTING
barf someone out DISGUSTING
barf FAILURE
barf VOMIT
barfly DRUNKARD
Barfola! CURSING
barf-out PEOPLE - NEGATIVE
(bargaining) chip NEGOTIATION
bari MUSIC
barking spider FLATULENCE
barnburner EVENT
Barney PEOPLE - MEEK
barnstorm PERFORMANCE
barnyard language CURSING
barnyard OBSCENE
barracuda WOMAN - NEGATIVE
barrel ass SPEED
barrel fever DELIRIUM TREMENS
barrel fever HANGOVER
barrel of fun FUN
barrel DRINKING - EXCESS
barrel DRUNKARD
barrel SPEED
barreled (up) INTOXICATED - ALCOHOL
base RUDE
baseman DRUGS - USER
bash PARTY
bashed INTOXICATED - ALCOHOL
bashing CRITICISM
basket case ANXIETY
basket STOMACH
Basra belly DIARRHEA

basted HARM
basted INTOXICATED - ALCOHOL
bat DRUNKARD
ba(t)ch (it) LODGING
bathtub scum PEOPLE - NEGATIVE
bats CRAZINESS
bats DELIRIUM TREMENS
bats INTOXICATED - ALCOHOL
batted ARREST
batted INTOXICATED - ALCOHOL
battered INTOXICATED - ALCOHOL
battle of the bulge DIETING
battle-ax WOMAN - NEGATIVE
bay window BELLY
bazillion NUMBER
bazoo ANUS
bazoo BELLY
bazoo BUTTOCKS
bazoo JEER
bazoo MOUTH
bazoom(s) BREASTS
BB brain PEOPLE - STUPID
B-ball SPORTS - BASKETBALL
BCNU GOOD-BYE
be a drag (on someone) BURDEN
be casper DEPART
be down (with someone) FRIENDLINESS
be dust TROUBLE
be in someone's face ANNOYANCE
Be my guest. KINDNESS
beach bum MAN
beach bunny WOMAN
beak GOSSIP
beak NOSE
Beam me up, Scotty! DEPART
beam up DEATH
beamer COMPUTER
bean head PEOPLE - STUPID
bean time EATING
Bean Town CITIES
bean HARM
bean HEAD
beanball SPORTS - BASEBALL
bean-counter ACCOUNTANT
beaned up INTOXICATED - DRUGS
beanery RESTAURANT
beanhead DRUGS - USER
beanpole PEOPLE - THIN
beans FINANCIAL
beans NONSENSE
beans NOTHING
bear cage POLICE
bear in the air POLICE

bear trap POLICE
bear DIFFICULTIES
bear POLICE
bear WOMAN - UGLY
beast ALCOHOL
beast MAN - NEGATIVE
beast PEOPLE - UGLY
beasty UNDESIRABLE
beat box MUSIC
Beat it! DEPART
beat one's brains out (to do something) WORK
beat one's gums TALKING
beat someone out OVERWHELM
beat someone's brains out VIOLENCE
beat someone's brains out WORK
beat something out MUSIC
beat the drum for someone or something PROMOTION
beat the rap LEGAL
beat up WORN
beat EXHAUSTION
beat MONEY
beat MUSIC
beat ROUTE
beat RUINATION
beat UNDESIRABLE
beat YOUTH
beater CARS
beats me KNOWLEDGE - LACKING
beauhunk MAN - ATTRACTIVE
beaut EXCELLENCE
beautiful EXCELLENCE
beauty sleep SLEEP
bed of roses EASY
bedrock BASIC
bedroom eyes SEDUCTION
beecher TOBACCO
beef something up IMPROVEMENT
beef ACCIDENT
beef COMPLAINT
beef DISAGREEMENT
beef FLATULENCE
beef LEGAL
beef MAN - MUSCULAR
beefcake MAN - MUSCULAR
beef-head PEOPLE - STUPID
beemer CARS
been had ABUSED
been had PREGNANCY
beeper TELEPHONE
beer and skittles EASY
beer belly BELLY

big stink SCANDAL
big talk BOASTING
big talk COMMAND
big time SUCCESS
big wheel PEOPLE - IMPORTANT
big with someone PREFERENCE
big Z's SLEEP
big-C DRUGS - COCAINE
big-C SICKNESS
Big D CITIES
biggie COPULATION
biggie IMPORTANCE
biggity HAUGHTINESS
big-H DRUGS - HEROIN
bighead HANGOVER
bigheaded HANGOVER
bigheaded HAUGHTINESS
big-name IMPORTANCE
big-O DRUGS - OPIUM
bigshot PEOPLE - IMPORTANT
big-ticket COST
big-time operator MAN - IMPORTANT
big-time operator PEOPLE - IMPORTANT
big-time spender SPENDING
big-time CRIME
big-time EXTRAVAGANCE
bigwig PEOPLE - IMPORTANT
bike BICYCLE
bike MOTORCYCLES
biker MOTORCYCLES
bill and coo KISS
billie MONEY
bimbo PEOPLE - SILLY
bimbo WOMAN - STUPID
bind DIFFICULTIES
bindle DRUGS - PORTION
bindle HOBO
binge DRINKING - BOUT
binge DRINKING - EXCESS
binge INDULGENCE
binged INTOXICATED - ALCOHOL
Bingo! YES
bird AVIATION
bird INSULT
bird JEER
bird PEOPLE - STRANGE
bird WOMAN
birdbrain PEOPLE - STUPID
birdbrain(ed) STUPIDITY
bird-dog CONTROL
bird-dog ROMANCE
birdseed MONEY
birdseed NONSENSE

birdturd ANNOYANCE
birdturd PEOPLE - NEGATIVE
birdwatcher MAN - SEX
birdy CRAZINESS
biscuit HEAD
bit much AMOUNT - EXCESSIVE
bit ACTIVITY
bit PERFORMANCE
bit PUNISHMENT
bit-bucket COMPUTER
bitch box COMMUNICATION
bitch of a someone PEOPLE - NEGATIVE
bitch of a thing DIFFICULTIES
bitch session COMPLAINT
bitch someone off ANGER
bitch something up RUINATION
bitch CARDS
bitch COMPLAINT
bitch DIFFICULTIES
bitch RUINATION
bitch WOMAN - FRIEND
bitch WOMAN - NEGATIVE
bitchin' EXCELLENCE
bitchy GROUCHY
bite on something COPY
bite the big one DEATH
bite the bullet ACCEPTANCE
bite the dust DEATH
bite the dust MALFUNCTION
Bite the ice! DEPART
Bite your tongue! SILENCE
bite ANNOYANCE
bite COPY
bite DECEPTION
biter THIEF
biters TEETH
bites WARNING
biz BUSINESS
biz DRUGS - PARAPHERNALIA
blab CHATTER
blab REVEAL
blabbermouth GOSSIP
blabbermouth REVEAL
black and blue ABUSED
black and white POLICE
black eye REPUTATION
black COFFEE
blackball OPPOSITION
blacklist LIST
blacklist REJECTION
blade GAY
blade MAN
blade WEAPONRY

blah DEPRESSION
blah DULL
blah INTOXICATED - ALCOHOL
blah-blah NONSENSE
blahs DEPRESSION
blanco PEOPLE - WHITE
blanket drill SLEEP
blankety-blank CURSING
blast CRITICISM
blast INTOXICATION - ONSET
blast PARTY
blast THRILL
blast VIOLENCE
blasted CURSING
blasted INTOXICATED - ALCOHOL/DRUGS
bleed for someone SYMPATHY
bleed someone white EXTORTION
bleed EXTORTION
blimp out GLUTTONY
blimp PEOPLE - FAT
blimped INTOXICATED - ALCOHOL
blind drunk INTOXICATED - ALCOHOL
(blind) munchies EATING
blind(ed) INTOXICATED -
    ALCOHOL/DRUGS
blindside SURPRISE
blinkers EYES
blinky DRUGS - PARAPHERNALIA
blip RADAR
blip UNIMPORTANT
bliss ninny PEOPLE - STUPID
bliss out HAPPINESS
blissed (out) CALM
blissed (out) INTOXICATED -
    ALCOHOL/DRUGS
blisterfoot WALKING
blithering idiot PEOPLE - STUPID
blitz VIOLENCE
blitzed (out) INTOXICATED -
    ALCOHOL/DRUGS
blivit PEOPLE - UNIMPORTANT
blixed INTOXICATED - DRUGS
blob PEOPLE - FAT
blob PEOPLE - MEEK
blob PEOPLE - STUPID
block COMMERCE
block HEAD
block PEOPLE - STUPID
blockbuster SUCCESS
blocked INTOXICATED - ALCOHOL/DRUGS
blockhead PEOPLE - STUPID
blood and guts FIGHTING
blood bath VIOLENCE

blood (brother) PEOPLE - FRIEND
blood FOOD
blood FRIEND
blood-and-guts ENMITY
blooey INTOXICATED - ALCOHOL
blooey RUINATION
blooper ERROR
blot someone out MURDER
blotter DRUGS - LSD
blotter DRUNKARD
blotter POLICE
blotto ALCOHOL - STRONG
blotto INTOXICATED - ALCOHOL
blow a fuse ANGER
blow a hype EMOTION
blow beets VOMIT
blow chunks VOMIT
blow cold DISINTEREST
blow in ARRIVAL
Blow it out your ear! DEPART
blow jive DRUGS - MARIJUANA
blow off DISAGREEMENT
blow off (some) steam ANGER
blow off EASY
blow off INSULT
blow off WASTE - TIME
Blow on it! CALM
blow (one's) cookies VOMIT
blow one's cool ANGER
blow one's doughnuts VOMIT
blow one's groceries VOMIT
blow one's lines ERROR
blow (one's) lunch VOMIT
blow one's own horn BOASTING
blow smoke CONCEAL
blow smoke DRUGS - MARIJUANA
blow someone away MURDER
blow someone away OVERWHELM
blow someone off DECEPTION
blow someone or something off
    IGNORE
blow someone or something out of the
    water RUINATION
blow someone to something
    GENEROSITY
blow someone's cover REVEAL
blow someone's doors off OVERWHELM
blow someone's mind IMPRESS
blow someone's mind INTOXICATION -
    DRUGS
blow something wide open REVEAL
blow the joint ESCAPE
blow the lid off something REVEAL

blow town DEPART
blow up ANGER
blow-up PHOTOGRAPHY
blow-up RUINATION
blow Z's SLEEP
blow ANGER
blow ATTACK
blow DEPART
blow DRUGS - USE
blow MONEY
blow MUSIC
blow PARTY - DRINKING
blow RUINATION
blowed (away) INTOXICATED -
  ALCOHOL/DRUGS
blower DRUGS - COCAINE
blower DRUGS - USER
blower HANDKERCHIEF
blower TOBACCO
blowhard BOASTING
blown away DEAD
blown away IMPRESS
blown away INTOXICATED -
  ALCOHOL/DRUGS
blown (out) INTOXICATED -
  ALCOHOL/DRUGS
blown (up) INTOXICATED - ALCOHOL
blubber gut(s) PEOPLE - FAT
blue and white POLICE
blue around the gills INTOXICATED -
  ALCOHOL
blue around the gills SICKNESS
(blue) blazes HELL
blue boys POLICE
blue chip FINANCIAL
blue devils DELIRIUM TREMENS
blue devils DEPRESSION
blue devils DRUGS - BARBITURATE
blue flu POLICE
blue funk DEPRESSION
blue in the face EXHAUSTION
blue suit POLICE
blue DEPRESSION
blue DRUGS - AMPHETAMINE
blue DRUGS - TRANQUILIZERS
blue INTOXICATED - ALCOHOL
blue OBSCENE
blue POLICE
blue SKY
blue-eyed NAIVETE
bluehair WOMAN - OLD
BM PEOPLE - NEGATIVE
BMOC MAN - IMPORTANT

B.O. juice HYGIENE
B.O. BUSINESS
B.O. HYGIENE
BO TELEVISION
boat CARS
boats SHOES
bod BODY
bod SOMEONE
bodacious AGGRESSIVENESS
body count AMOUNT
body count BUSINESS
body count DEATH
body shake POLICE
boff VIOLENCE
boff VOMIT
boffo SUCCESS
bogart BEHAVIOR
bogart DELAY
bogart DRUGS - USE
bogue FAKE
bogus EXCELLENCE
bogus UNDESIRABLE
boheme FASHIONABLE
bohunk PEOPLE - STUPID
boiled ANGER
boiled INTOXICATED - ALCOHOL
boiling (mad) ANGER
bokoo AMOUNT - MANY
bold EXCELLENCE
bolt DEPART
bolus DOCTOR
bomb (out) FAILURE
bomb FAILURE
bombed (out) INTOXICATED -
  ALCOHOL/DRUGS
bomb(shell) SURPRISE
bone factory CEMETERY
bone factory HOSPITAL
bone idle LAZY
bone orchard CEMETERY
bone out DEPART
bone MUSIC
bonehead PEOPLE - STUPID
boner ERROR
bones DOCTOR
bones GAMBLING
bones MONEY
bones PEOPLE - THIN
boneyard CEMETERY
boneyard JUNKYARD
bong DRINKING
bong DRUGS - PARAPHERNALIA
bong DRUGS - PORTION

bong DRUGS - USE
bonged (out) INTOXICATED - DRUGS
bonk IMPACT
bonk VIOLENCE
bonkers CRAZINESS
bonkers INTOXICATED - ALCOHOL
Bonus! EXCELLENCE
bonzo CRAZINESS
boob PEOPLE - STUPID
boo-bird PEOPLE - VULGAR
boo-boo ERROR
boob-tube TELEVISION
booby hatch MENTAL
booby trap TRAP
boob(y) BREASTS
boodle LOOT
boody BUTTOCKS
boody PEOPLE - NEGATIVE
boogie down (to somewhere) HURRY
boogie DANCING
boogie DEPART
boogie MUCUS
boogie PARTY
boogie SERIOUSNESS
boogie SICKNESS
boogie-board SKATEBOARD
boogie-board SURFING
boogieman PEOPLE - NEGATIVE
book it STUDY
book DEPART
book POLICE
book STUDY
bookie CRIMINAL
boom box AUDIO
boom sticks MUSIC
boom MUSIC
boondocks RURAL
boondoggle WASTE
boosiasm(s) BREASTS
boost PROMOTION
boost THEFT
booster PROMOTION
booster THIEF
boot someone out EJECTION
boot COMPUTER
boot EJECTION
boot THRILL
boot VOMIT
booze artist DRUNKARD
booze it (up) DRINKING - EXCESS
booze (up) DRINKING - EXCESS
booze ALCOHOL
boozed INTOXICATED - ALCOHOL

boozy-woozy INTOXICATED - ALCOHOL
bop DRUGS - PORTION
bop IMPACT
bop MUSIC
bore the pants off (of) someone DULL
bosh NONSENSE
bosom buddy FRIEND
bosom chums LICE
boss lady WOMAN - IMPORTANT
boss man MAN - IMPORTANT
boss PEOPLE - IMPORTANT
both sheets in the wind INTOXICATED -
  ALCOHOL
bottle baby DRUNKARD
bottle ALCOHOL
bottle DRINKING - EXCESS
bottle DRUNKARD
bottleache HANGOVER
bottom dollar MONEY
bottom fishing COMMERCE
bottom line FINANCIAL
bottom line RESULTS
bottom of the barrel INFERIORITY
bottom out INFERIORITY
bottom BUTTOCKS
bottom DRINKING
bottom SPORTS - BASEBALL
bottomless pit EATING
bottomless pit ENDLESS
Bottoms up. TOAST
bounce something off (of) someone
  OPINION
bounce CHECKS
bounce EJECTION
bounce ENERGETIC
bouncer TAVERN
bow to the porcelain altar VOMIT
bowl DRUGS - PARAPHERNALIA
bowser PEOPLE - FAT
bow-wow DOG
bow-wow WOMAN - UGLY
box someone in MANAGE
box AUDIO
box DEATH
box MUSIC
boxed in CHOICE
boxed on the table DEATH
boxed (up) INTOXICATED -
  ALCOHOL/DRUGS
boxed (up) PUNISHMENT
boxed DEAD
boys in the backroom POLITICIANS
bozo PEOPLE - STUPID

bra-burner WOMAN - NEGATIVE
brack-brain PEOPLE - STUPID
brain IMPACT
brain INTELLIGENCE
brain-burned DRUGS - RUINED
brainchild PRODUCT
brain-dead STUPIDITY
brains INTELLIGENCE
brainstorm THINKING
brain-twister PUZZLE
(brand) spanking new NEW
brass hat OFFICER
brass tacks BUSINESS
brass OFFICER
brassed (off) ANGER
BRB COMPUTER - ABBREVIATION
bread and butter EMPLOYMENT
bread MONEY
breadbasket STOMACH
Break a leg! LUCK
Break it up! STOPPING
break out DEPART
break someone's balls OVERWHELM
break the ice FRIENDLINESS
break the ice SOCIAL
break ESCAPE
break MUSIC
break NEWS
break OPPORTUNITY
breaker DANCING
breakfast of champions ALCOHOL
breather PAUSE
breeder HETEROSEXUAL
breeze EASY
brew ALCOHOL - BEER
brew COFFEE
brewed INTOXICATED - ALCOHOL
brew-ha ALCOHOL - BEER
brew-out PARTY - DRINKING
brews brothers MAN
brewski ALCOHOL - BEER
brewster ALCOHOL - BEER
brewster DRUNKARD
brick FAILURE
brick SPORTS - BASKETBALL
brickhouse BUXOM
brig JAIL
bright and breezy ALERTNESS
bright-eyed and bushy-tailed
 ALERTNESS
brim HAT
bring home the bacon EARN
bring someone down DEPRESSION

bring someone down INTOXICATION -
 END
bring someone on AROUSAL
bring something up MENTION
bring something up VOMIT
bring-down DEPRESSION
bring-down REALITY
broad WOMAN
Bronx cheer JEER
brown bottle flu HANGOVER
brown out ELECTRICITY
brown someone off ANGER
brown-bag EATING
browned (off) ANGER
brownie points BENEFIT
brown-nose FLATTERY
bruised INTOXICATED - ALCOHOL
bruiser MAN - STRONG
brush ENCOUNTER
brushoff DISMISSAL
brutal EXCELLENCE
BS NONSENSE
BTW COMPUTER - ABBREVIATION
bubble water ALCOHOL - CHAMPAGNE
bubblehead DRUNKARD
bubblehead PEOPLE - SILLY
bubbly ALCOHOL - CHAMPAGNE
buck for something WORK
buck naked NAKEDNESS
buck up HAPPINESS
buck MONEY
buck RESISTANCE
buckage MONEY
bucket BUTTOCKS
bucket SPORTS - BASKETBALL
bucko PEOPLE - FRIEND
buckpasser DECEPTION
bucks SHOES
bud ALCOHOL - BEER
buddy up to someone FRIENDLINESS
buddy up (with someone) LODGING
buddy-buddy FRIENDLINESS
budget squeeze FINANCIAL
budhead DRUNKARD
buffaloed CONFUSION
buff(ed) MUSCLES
Bug off! DEPART
bug out DEPART
bug ANNOYANCE
bug COMPUTER - ERROR
bug FAN
bug OBSESSION
bug SICKNESS

butt DISLIKE
butt TOBACCO
butterfingers CARELESSNESS
buttinsky INTERRUPTION
buttlegging CRIME
buttload AMOUNT - MUCH
button BADGE
button CONCLUSION
buttonhole ACCOST
butt-ugly UGLINESS
buy it DEATH
buy someone's wolf ticket CHALLENGE
buy the big one DEATH
buy the farm DEATH
buy time DELAY
buy trouble TROUBLE
buy BELIEF
buy COMMERCE
buzhie PEOPLE
buzhie SOCIAL
buzz along DEPART
buzz along SPEED
buzz INTOXICATION - ONSET
buzz LAUGHTER
buzz SIGNAL
buzz TELEPHONE
buzz THRILL
buzzard meat OLD-FASHIONED
buzzard MAN - OLD
buzzing INTOXICATED - ALCOHOL
buzzword COMMUNICATION
BVDs CLOTHING
BWOC WOMAN - IMPORTANT
BYO(B) ALCOHOL
C MONEY
cabbage MONEY
cabbagehead PEOPLE - STUPID
cabbie TAXI
caboose BUTTOCKS
caca DEFECATION
caca EXCREMENT
cack DEFECATION
cack EXCREMENT
cack MURDER
cack VOMIT
cactus (buttons) DRUGS - PEYOTE
cactus juice ALCOHOL
Caddy CARS
Cadillac DRUGS - STRONG
Cadillac POWER
cagey CLEVERNESS
cake MONEY
cakewalk EASY

calaboose JAIL
calendar TIME
call (all) the shots CONTROL
call girl PROSTITUTION
call house BROTHEL
call hughie VOMIT
Call my service. TELEPHONE
call someone out CHALLENGE
call CHALLENGE
call INTOXICATION - ONSET
call PREFERENCE
Cambodian red DRUGS - MARIJUANA
camp it up BEHAVIOR
camp it up GAY
camp GAY
camp UNFASHIONABLE
campi SCHOOL
campus queen WOMAN
campus PUNISHMENT
campused PUNISHMENT
Can it! SILENCE
can of worms DIFFICULTIES
can BREASTS
can BUTTOCKS
can CARS
can DISMISSAL
can DRUGS - PORTION
can HEAD
can JAIL
can TOILET
canary DRUGS - BARBITURATE
canary SINGER
cancel someone's Christmas MURDER
cancer stick TOBACCO
candied ADDICTION
candy man DRUGS - USER
candy store STORE - LIQUOR
candy DRUGS
candy-ass COWARDICE
cane DRUGS - COCAINE
canned INTOXICATED - ALCOHOL
canned LAUGHTER
cannon WEAPONRY
cans AUDIO
can-shaker CHARITY
can't hit the (broad) side of a barn
    SKILL - LACKING
can't win (th)em all DEFEAT
cap AMOUNT - EXCESSIVE
cap DRUGS - PORTION
caper CRIME
caper DECEPTION
capish UNDERSTANDING

capital MONEY
capper CONCLUSION
captain of industry BUSINESS
carb ENGINE
carbos FOOD
carburetor DRUGS - PARAPHERNALIA
carcass BODY
card COMEDIAN
card IDENTIFICATION
carded IDENTIFICATION
carrier DRUGS - SELLER
carrot top REDHEAD
carry the stick HOBO
carry weight POWER
carry DRUGS
carrying a (heavy) load INTOXICATED - ALCOHOL
cartwheel DRUGS - AMPHETAMINE
carved in stone PERMANENCE
cas SATISFACTORY
case the joint CRIME
case the joint EXAMINATION
cash cow FINANCIAL
cash flow MONEY
cash in one's chips DEATH
Cash is king. FINANCIAL
Cash is trash. FINANCIAL
cashed EXHAUSTION
Casper Milquetoast MAN - MEEK
casting-couch SEDUCTION
cast-iron stomach STOMACH
castor oil artist DOCTOR
cat GOSSIP
cat MAN
cat VOMIT
catch hell (for something) SCOLDING
catch some rays LEISURE
catch some Z's SLEEP
catch something OBSERVATION
catch up SOBRIETY
Catch you later. GOOD-BYE
catch-22 PARADOX
catch DRAWBACK
catch EVENT
cats and dogs COMMERCE
cat's meow EXCELLENCE
cat-soup FOOD
cattle-rustler THIEF
catty RUDENESS
cave man MAN - STRONG
cazh CLOTHING
cee DRUGS - COCAINE
celeb CELEBRITY

cement city CEMETERY
cent MONEY
century note MONEY
certain party SOMEONE
cets DRUGS - ANALGESIC
chain(saw) RUINATION
chain(-smoke) TOBACCO
chain-smoker TOBACCO
chair PUNISHMENT
cham ALCOHOL - CHAMPAGNE
champ CRIMINAL
champers ALCOHOL - CHAMPAGNE
change the channel TELEVISION
change MONEY
changes THINKING
channel hopping TELEVISION
channel surfer CHOICE
chap ANGER
chapped ANGER
chapter and verse DETAILS
charge DRUGS - PORTION
charge EXCITEMENT
charge INTOXICATION - ONSET
charged (up) EXCITEMENT
charged (up) INTOXICATED - DRUGS
Charles DRUGS - COCAINE
Charles PEOPLE - WHITE
Charlie VIETNAM
Charlie Irvine POLICE
charmer MAN - SEX
chart MUSIC
charts PUBLICATION
chas TOBACCO
chase the dragon DRUGS - OPIUM
chaser ALCOHOL
C-head DRUGS - USER
cheap shot INSULT
cheapie PRODUCT
cheapskate STINGY
cheaters SUNGLASSES
check out the plumbing TOILET - USE
check something out EXAMINATION
check that IGNORE
check DRUGS - PORTION
check YES
Cheese it (the cops)! POLICE
cheese VOMIT
cheesecake PHOTOGRAPHY
cheesecake WOMAN - ATTRACTIVE
cheesed off ANGER
cheese-eater TATTLING
cheesehead PEOPLE - STUPID
cheesy CHEAPNESS

cherry DUPE
chew face KISS
chew someone out SCOLDING
chew something over CONVERSATION
chew something over THINKING
chew the cheese VOMIT
chew the fat CONVERSATION
chew EATING
chewed ABUSED
chi-chi ELEGANCE
chick WOMAN
chicken feed MONEY
chicken out (of something) COWARDICE
chicken powder DRUGS - AMPHETAMINE
chicken COWARDICE
chicken-hearted COWARDICE
chief OFFICER
chill (out) CALM
chill someone's action HINDER
chill ALCOHOL - BEER
chill FRIGHT
chill MURDER
chill REJECTION
chill RELAX
chillin' EXCELLENCE
chillum DRUGS - PARAPHERNALIA
chin music CONVERSATION
China white DRUGS - HEROIN
China TEETH
Chinese red DRUGS - HEROIN
chintzy CHEAPNESS
chintzy STINGY
chipper ALERTNESS
chipper INTOXICATED - ALCOHOL
chippie SEX
chippy around SEX
chippy DRUGS - USER
chippy PROSTITUTION
chippy-chaser MAN - SEX
chips MONEY
chips OCCUPATION
chisel EXTORTION
chiseler THIEF
chit CHECKS
chit COMMERCE
chitchat CONVERSATION
Chi(town) CITIES
chiz RELAX
chock-full ABUNDANCE
chocoholic CHOCOLATE
choice EXCELLENCE
choke FAILURE
choked DRUGS - WEAK

choker TOBACCO
chop INSULT
chopper AVIATION
choppers TEETH
chop-shop CRIME
chow down EATING
chow hound EATING
chow something down EATING
chow EATING
chow FOOD
chowderhead PEOPLE - STUPID
Christmas tree DRUNKARD
chrome-dome BALDNESS
chubbo PEOPLE - FAT
chuck a dummy VOMIT
chuck it in QUIT
chuck DISCARD
chuck EATING
chuck FOOD
chuck VOMIT
chucked INTOXICATED - ALCOHOL
chuckers HUNGER
chug(-a-lug) DRINKING - EXCESS
chum FRIEND
chummy FRIENDLINESS
chump change MONEY
chump DUPE
chumphead PEOPLE - STUPID
chunk ERROR
chunk VOMIT
chunky FAT
church key DRINKING - PARAPHERNALIA
churn FINANCIAL
ciao GOOD-BYE
ciao GREETING
cid DRUGS - LSD
cig TOBACCO
cigarette with no name DRUGS -
   MARIJUANA
ciggy TOBACCO
cinch EASY
cinch SECURE
cinched SECURE
circular file WASTE
civil serpent OCCUPATION
civvies CLOTHING
clam up SILENCE
clam MONEY
clam SILENCE
clanked EXHAUSTION
clanks DELIRIUM TREMENS
clap SICKNESS
claptrap NONSENSE

class act ELEGANCE
class ELEGANCE
classis-chassis BODY
classy ELEGANCE
clay pigeon DUPE
clay DRUGS - HASHISH
clean one's act up IMPROVEMENT
clean someone out MONEY - LACKING
clean sweep TOTALITY
clean up (on something) SUCCESS
clean CLOTHING
clean LAW-ABIDING
clean SOBRIETY
clean WEAPONRY
clean-cut PEOPLE - GOOD
cleaned out MONEY - LACKING
clear as mud CONFUSION
clear as vodka CLARITY
clear as vodka UNDERSTANDING
clear out DEPART
clear sailing EASY
clear ALCOHOL
clear EARN
clear INTOXICATED - ALCOHOL
click (with someone) POPULAR
cliff-dweller LODGING
climb the wall(s) CRAZINESS
climb DRUGS - MARIJUANA
climb SCOLDING
clinch CONCLUSION
clincher CONCLUSION
clink JAIL
clinker ERROR
clinker WORTHLESSNESS
clip a butt TOBACCO
clip joint LOCATION - UNDESIRABLE
clip someone's wings PUNISHMENT
clip DECEPTION
clip DRUGS - PARAPHERNALIA
clip MOVIES
clip MURDER
clip SPEED
clipped ARREST
clipped DECEPTION
clobber VIOLENCE
clobbered INTOXICATED - ALCOHOL
clock in ARRIVAL
clock watcher TIME
clock OBTAIN
clodhopper PEOPLE - STUPID
clodhoppers SHOES
Close, but no cigar. DEFEAT
close shave DANGER

closet SECRECY
clotheshorse CLOTHING
clout INFLUENCE
clouted ARREST
clown around SILLINESS
clown PEOPLE - STUPID
cluck PEOPLE - STUPID
cluckhead PEOPLE - STUPID
clucky STUPIDITY
clue someone in EXPLANATION
clueless STUPIDITY
cluelessness STUPIDITY
clunk IMPACT
clunker CARS
clunker WORTHLESSNESS
clunkhead PEOPLE - STUPID
clunky CLUMSINESS
clutch (up) ANXIETY
clutched ANXIETY
Clyde MAN - STUPID
C-note MONEY
coaster RESIDENT
cock PENIS
cockamamie NONSENSE
cockeyed CRAZINESS
coed STUDENT
coffee and FOOD
coffin nail DRINKING - PORTION
coffin nail TOBACCO
coffin varnish ALCOHOL - STRONG
coffin-dodger TOBACCO
coin MONEY
coke party DRUGS - PARTY
cokeaholic DRUGS - USER
cokehead DRUGS - USER
cokespoon DRUGS - PARAPHERNALIA
cold blood ALCOHOL - BEER
cold call COMMERCE
cold feet FEAR
cold fish PEOPLE - COLD
cold pop ALCOHOL - BEER
cold shoulder REJECTION
cold sober SOBRIETY
cold turkey QUIT
cold COMPLETENESS
cold DEAD
cold EXCELLENCE
cold UNDESIRABLE
coldcock VIOLENCE
coli DRUGS - MARIJUANA
collar ARREST
collared ARREST
Colombian (gold) DRUGS - MARIJUANA

467

color of someone's money MONEY
combo BISEXUAL
combo GROUP
combo MUSIC
comboozelated INTOXICATED - ALCOHOL
come clean (with someone) (about
  something) CONFESSION
come down hard INTOXICATION - END
come down DISAPPOINTMENT
come down HAPPENING
come down INTOXICATION - RECOVERY
Come off it! STOPPING
Come off it! WRONG
come on strong AGGRESSIVENESS
come on to someone FLIRTATION
come on FLIRTATION
come on FRIENDLINESS
come on INTOXICATION - ONSET
come on PERFORMANCE
come on WRONG
come out ahead SUCCESS
come out in the wash REVEAL
come out on top SUCCESS
come up for air PAUSE
comeback RESPONSE
comeback REVERSAL
come-hither look FLIRTATION
come-on ENTICEMENT
comer PEOPLE - GOOD
comeuppance JUSTICE
comfort station STORE - LIQUOR
comfort station TOILET
comfy COMFORT
coming out of one's ears ABUNDANCE
comma-counter PRECISION
commie COMMUNIST
commode-hugging drunk INTOXICATED
  - ALCOHOL
company bull DETECTIVE
company man BUSINESS
con job DECEPTION
con man THIEF
con DECEPTION
con JAIL
conehead INTELLIGENCE
conehead PEOPLE - STUPID
conk out EXHAUSTION
conk out MALFUNCTION
conk HEAD
conk-buster ALCOHOL - STRONG
connect with someone MEETING
connect with something SPORTS -
  BASEBALL

connection DRUGS - USER
conniption (fit) ANGER
constitutional ALCOHOL/DRUGS
coo-coo AWARENESS - LACKING
coo-coo CRAZINESS
cooked up LYING
cooked INTOXICATED - ALCOHOL/DRUGS
cookie pusher FLATTERY
cooking with gas CORRECT
Cool beans! EXCELLENCE
cool, calm, and collected CALM
cool cat MAN
cool down CALM
Cool it! CALM
cool off CALM
cool out CALM
cool someone out CALM
cool AMOUNT
cool CALM
cool DEATH
cool EXCELLENCE
cool MUSIC
cooled out CALM
cooler JAIL
cooties LICE
cop a drag TOBACCO
cop a fix DRUGS - PORTION
cop a head INTOXICATED -
  ALCOHOL/DRUGS
cop a plea LEGAL
cop a squat SITTING
cop a tube SURFING
cop a(n at)titude BEHAVIOR - BAD
cop out LEGAL
cop out QUIT
cop ARREST
cop POLICE
cop THEFT
copasetic AGREEMENT
copout EXCUSE
copped ARREST
copper MONEY
copper POLICE
cop-shop POLICE
copy PRODUCT
copycat MIMIC
corked (up) INTOXICATED - ALCOHOL
corker JOKING
corkscrewed (up) INTOXICATED -
  ALCOHOL
cornball PEOPLE - STUPID
cornball STUPIDITY
corned INTOXICATED - ALCOHOL

cornfed RURAL
corny RURAL
corny SILLINESS
corpse ALCOHOL - PARAPHERNALIA
corpse TOBACCO
corral dust NONSENSE
cosmic EXCELLENCE
cotton-picking WORTHLESSNESS
couch potato LAZY
couch-doctor DOCTOR
cough something up PRODUCING
country drunk INTOXICATED - ALCOHOL
county-mounty POLICE
courier DRUGS - USER
cover-up SECRECY
cow chips EXCREMENT
cow flop EXCREMENT
cow WOMAN - FAT
cowboy MAN - RECKLESS
cow-doots EXCREMENT
coyote-ugly APPEARANCE
cozy up (to someone) INFLUENCE
crab LICE
crack a book SCHOOL
crack a tube DRINKING
crack house DRUGS
crack open a bottle DRINKING
crack some suds DRINKING
crack someone up LAUGHTER
crack up ACCIDENT
crack up ANXIETY
crack up LAUGHTER
crack COMMERCE
crack DRUGS - COCAINE
crack EXCELLENCE
crack JOKING
crack TATTLING
crack THEFT
crack TRY
crackbrain PEOPLE - STUPID
crackbrained STUPIDITY
cracked up to be REPUTATION
cracked CRAZINESS
crackerjack EXCELLENCE
crackhead DRUGS - USER
crackpot CRAZINESS
crackpot PEOPLE - CRAZY
crack-up ACCIDENT
cram SCHOOL
crank bugs DRUGS - FEELING
crank something out PRODUCING
crank something up AUDIO
crank something up BEGINNINGS

crank ANNOYANCE
crank FAKE
crank GROUCHY
cranking EXCELLENCE
cranky GROUCHY
crap out COWARDICE
crap DEFECATION
crap EXCREMENT
crap NONSENSE
crap WORTHLESSNESS
craphouse TOILET
crapper dick DETECTIVE
crapper BOASTING
crapper TOILET
crappy UNDESIRABLE
crapshoot CHANCE
crash and burn ROMANCE
crash pad LODGING
crash FINANCIAL
crash INTOXICATED - ALCOHOL
crash INTRUSION
crash LODGING
crash MALFUNCTION
crashed ARREST
crashed INTOXICATED - ALCOHOL
crasher INTRUSION
crate CARS
crater FINANCIAL
crater PIMPLES
crater-face PIMPLES
crawling with someone or something
  ABUNDANCE
crazy bone ELBOW
crazy EXCELLENCE
crazy PEOPLE - CRAZY
cream puff CARS
cream puff PEOPLE - MEEK
cream OVERWHELM
creamed DEFEAT
creamed INTOXICATED - ALCOHOL
creased EXHAUSTION
creep joint LOCATION - UNDESIRABLE
creep PEOPLE - STRANGE
creeping-crud NASTY
creeping-crud PEOPLE - NEGATIVE
creeping-crud SICKNESS
creeps ANXIETY
creepy FEAR
crib course SCHOOL
crib CRIME
crib LODGING
cricket SATISFACTORY
crisco PEOPLE - FAT

crisp INTOXICATED - DRUGS
croak DEATH
croak MURDER
crock of shit NONSENSE
crock of shit PEOPLE - WORTHLESS
crock DRUNKARD
crock NONSENSE
crocked INTOXICATED - ALCOHOL
crockery TEETH
cromagnon MAN - UGLY
cross someone (up) OPPOSITION
cross-eyed (drunk) INTOXICATED - ALCOHOL
crotch-pheasant LICE
crotch-rot SICKNESS
crowd FIGHTING
crowd PRESSURE
crown VIOLENCE
crud NASTY
crud PEOPLE - NEGATIVE
cruddy DISGUSTING
cruise DEPART
cruise EASY
cruise LEISURE
cruise LIFESTYLE
cruise ROMANCE
cruise SPEED
cruiser CARS
cruising for a bruising TROUBLE
crum something up MALFUNCTION
crumb PEOPLE - NEGATIVE
crumbum PEOPLE - NEGATIVE
crumbum UNDESIRABLE
crummy UNDESIRABLE
crumped (out) DEAD
crumped (out) INTOXICATED - ALCOHOL
crunch BUSY
crunchers FEET
crunchie SOLDIER
crust IMPUDENCE
crusty GROUCHY
crutch DRUGS - PARAPHERNALIA
cry hughie VOMIT
cry in one's beer DEPRESSION
cry ruth VOMIT
crying drunk INTOXICATED - ALCOHOL
crying towel DEPRESSION
crying weed DRUGS - MARIJUANA
crystal DRUGS - COCAINE
cube DRUGS - LSD
cube GAMBLING
cube OLD-FASHIONED
cuddle bunny LOVER

cuff quote FINANCIAL
cuff COMMERCE
cuffs POLICE
cull PEOPLE - NEGATIVE
culture-vulture CULTURE
cume SCHOOL
cup of tea PREFERENCE
cupcake WOMAN - ATTRACTIVE
curl up and die DEATH
curse MENSES
curtains DEATH
cushy EASY
cut a check CHECKS
cut a deal COMMERCE
cut and run ESCAPE
cut corners CHEAPNESS
Cut it out! STOPPING
cut loose INDEPENDENCE
cut no ice (with someone) INFLUENCE - LACKING
cut one's losses FAILURE
cut one's own throat HARM
cut one's wolf loose DRINKING - EXCESS
cut out DEPART
cut someone a break KINDNESS
cut someone in (on something) SHARING
cut the cheese FLATULENCE
Cut the comedy! STOPPING
Cut the crap! STOPPING
cut the dust DRINKING
cut the mustard SKILL
cut to the chase FOCUS
cut up (about someone or something) EMOTION
cut (up) MUSCLES
cut INTOXICATED - ALCOHOL
cut LOOT
cut MUSIC
cut REDUCTION
cut STOPPING
cutie pie PEOPLE - ATTRACTIVE
cutie PEOPLE - ATTRACTIVE
cut-rate CHEAPNESS
cuz KINSHIP
dad KINSHIP
daffy SILLINESS
dagwood (sandwich) FOOD
daily dozen EXERCISE
daily grind EMPLOYMENT
daisy EXCELLENCE
damage COST
dank EXCELLENCE

dank UNDESIRABLE
dap CLOTHING
darb EXCELLENCE
dark horse CANDIDACY
dark horse UNKNOWN
Dash it all! CURSING
day one TIME
day person DAY
day-tripper TOURIST
dead and gone DEAD
dead and gone PAST
dead broke MONEY - LACKING
dead cinch EASY
dead drunk INTOXICATED - ALCOHOL
dead duck FAILURE
dead easy EASY
dead from the neck up DULL
dead from the neck up STUPIDITY
dead horse IRRELEVANCE
dead in the water MOVEMENT - LACKING
dead issue IRRELEVANCE
dead letter IRRELEVANCE
dead letter MAIL
dead on CORRECT
(dead) ringer (for someone) SAMENESS
dead soldier ALCOHOL - PARAPHERNALIA
dead soldier TOBACCO
dead to the world INTOXICATED -
  ALCOHOL
dead to the world SLEEP
dead DULL
dead EXHAUSTION
dead IRRELEVANCE
dead NONFUNCTIONING
deadbeat DEBT
deadcat bounce FINANCIAL
dead-catty FINANCIAL
dead-end kid CHILDREN
deadhead MUSIC
deadhead PEOPLE - STUPID
deadhead TRAVEL
deadly (dull) DULL
deadneck PEOPLE - STUPID
deadpan APPEARANCE
deadpan DULL
deadpan DULL
deadwood WORTHLESSNESS
deal stock FINANCIAL
Dear John letter COMMUNICATION
death on something DESTRUCTION
death on something SPEED
deathly EXCELLENCE
decent EXCELLENCE

deck TOBACCO
deck VIOLENCE
deduck FINANCIAL
deep pockets MONEY - SOURCE
deep pockets WEALTH
deep six DEATH
deep-six DISCARD
deep-six MURDER
def CERTAINTY
def EXCELLENCE
defrosted CALM
Delhi belly DIARRHEA
delish TASTE
delts MUSCLES
demo DEMONSTRATION
demo POLITICIANS
demo SAMPLE
des FINANCIAL
desert cherry SOLDIER
desk jockey OCCUPATION
destroyed INTOXICATED - DRUGS
deuce CARDS
deuce MONEY
deuce PUNISHMENT
deuce RESTAURANT
deuce SATAN
devil of a time DIFFICULTIES
devil's own time DIFFICULTIES
dialog ROMANCE
diamond in the rough PEOPLE - GOOD
diarrhea of the mouth TALKING
dibs on something RESERVE
dicey UNCERTAINTY
dick DETECTIVE
dick MAN - STUPID
dick NOTHING
dick PENIS
dickens CHILDREN
dickens SATAN
dicty HAUGHTINESS
diddle with something MEDDLE
diddle COPULATION
diddle DECEPTION
diddly-squat NOTHING
DIDO COMPUTER - ABBREVIATION
die on someone DEATH
die on someone MALFUNCTION
die LAUGHTER
diesel EXCELLENCE
diff DIFFERENCE
different strokes for different folks
  DIFFERENCE
differential BUTTOCKS

Dig up! ATTENTION
dig APPRECIATION
dig UNDERSTANDING
digits TELEPHONE
digs LODGING
dike LESBIAN
dildo MAN - STUPID
dilly EXCELLENCE
dilly-dally WASTE - TIME
dim bulb PEOPLE - STUPID
dime store BUSY
dime-dropper TATTLING
dimwit PEOPLE - STUPID
dinero MONEY
ding CRITICISM
ding IMPACT
ding-a-ling PEOPLE - STUPID
dingbat GADGET
dingbat PEOPLE - NEGATIVE
dingbat PEOPLE - STUPID
dinged out INTOXICATED - ALCOHOL
dinghead PEOPLE - STUPID
dingleberry PEOPLE - STRANGE
dingus GADGET
dingy CRAZINESS
dink someone off ANGER
DINK COUPLE
dinky SIZE
dip THIEF
dip TOBACCO
dippy CRAZINESS
dip(shit) PEOPLE - STUPID
dip(so) DRUNKARD
dipsy INTOXICATED - ALCOHOL
dipwad PEOPLE - STUPID
dirt cheap CHEAPNESS
dirt GOSSIP
dirt PEOPLE - WORTHLESS
dirty crack INSULT
dirty deal DISHONESTY
dirty dog PEOPLE - NEGATIVE
(dirty) dozens INSULT
dirty joke JOKING
dirty joke PEOPLE - NEGATIVE
dirty linen GOSSIP
dirty look DISLIKE
dirty mouth PEOPLE - VULGAR
dirty mouth VULGAR
dirty old man MAN - OLD
dirty pool DECEPTION
dirty word OBSCENE
dirty work DECEPTION
dirty work WORK

dirty CRIME
dirty DECEPTION
dirty OBSCENE
dirty-minded OBSCENE
discipline DRUGS
discombobulate CONFUSION
discombobulated INTOXICATED - ALCOHOL
discombobulated CONFUSION
dish something out EATING
dish something out INFORMATION
dish something out SCOLDING
dish the dirt GOSSIP
dish CRITICISM
dish GOSSIP
dish WOMAN - ATTRACTIVE
disk jockey BROADCASTING
dis(s) (on someone) INSULT
ditch ABANDONMENT
ditch ABSENCE
dither CONFUSION
ditz PEOPLE - SILLY
ditzy SILLINESS
dive TAVERN
divot WIG
divvy something up SHARING
divvy PORTION
dizzy SILLINESS
do a dump on someone or something CRITICISM
do a fade DEPART
do a job on someone or something RUINATION
do a line DRUGS - USE
do a number on someone DECEPTION
do a slow burn ANGER
do a snow job on someone DECEPTION
do drugs DRUGS - USE
Do I have to paint (you) a picture? UNDERSTANDING
do one's (own) thing PLEASURE
do oneself proud PRAISE
do or die EFFORT
do some bongs DRUGS - USE
do some fine coin EARN
do someone dirt HARM
Do tell. RESPONSE
do the drink thing DRINKING - EXCESS
do the drug thing DRUGS - USE
do the trick ACHIEVEMENT
do time PUNISHMENT
(Do) you eat with that mouth? OBSCENE

(Do you) get my drift? UNDERSTANDING
do DRUGS - USE
do EVENT
do HAIR
DOA DEAD
DOA DRUGS - PCP
doc(s)-in-a-box MEDICAL
doctor's orders ADVICE
dode PEOPLE - STUPID
dodge DECEPTION
dog and pony show DEMONSTRATION
dog meat BODY - DEAD
dog EATING
dog EXCREMENT
dog FOOT
dog HAUNT
dog PURSUIT
dog UNDESIRABLE
dog WOMAN - UGLY
dog-doo EXCREMENT
dog-eat-dog COMPETITION
dogface SOLDIER
doggo SILENT
doggone(d) CURSING
doggy bag RESTAURANT
do-gooder PEOPLE - GOOD
dog's mother PEOPLE - NEGATIVE
doll DRUGS - PORTION
doll WOMAN - ATTRACTIVE
dome-doctor DOCTOR
done by mirrors DECEPTION
done deal COMPLETENESS
done for ENDINGS
done over DEFEAT
done to a turn COOKING
done to a turn DEFEAT
donkey's breakfast STRAW
donkey's years TIME - PERIOD
donnybrook VIOLENCE
Don't ask me. KNOWLEDGE - LACKING
Don't ask. REQUEST
Don't call us, we'll call you.
    EMPLOYMENT
Don't have a cow! CALM
Don't I know it! AMAZEMENT
Don't make me laugh! AMAZEMENT
Don't sweat it! RELAX
(Don't) you wish! DESIRE
doobie DRUGS - MARIJUANA
doodad GADGET
doo(-doo) EXCREMENT
doo-doo DEFECATION
doofer TOBACCO

doofus PEOPLE - STUPID
do(o)jigger GADGET
dook UNDESIRABLE
doormat PEOPLE - MEEK
doosie EXCELLENCE
doowacky GADGET
doowacky MONEY
dope something out EXAMINATION
dope up DRUGS - PURCHASE
dope up DRUGS - USE
dope DRUGS
dope EXCELLENCE
dope INFORMATION
dope PEOPLE - STUPID
dopey EXHAUSTION
dopey INTOXICATED - DRUGS
dopey STUPIDITY
do-re-mi MONEY
dorf PEOPLE - STUPID
dork off WASTE - TIME
dork PENIS
dork PEOPLE - STUPID
dorkmeier PEOPLE - STUPID
dorkus maximus PEOPLE - STUPID
dorky STRANGE
do's and don'ts RULES
double cross BETRAYAL
double nickels NUMBER
double saw(buck) MONEY
double take SURPRISE
double up (with laughter) LAUGHTER
double whammy TROUBLE
double DRINKING - PORTION
double-bagger APPEARANCE
double-bagger SPORTS - BASEBALL
double-barreled slingshot CLOTHING
double-crosser BETRAYAL
double-decker BUS
double-decker FOOD
double-deuces NUMBER
double-dipper DECEPTION
double-dome INTELLIGENCE
double-gaited STRANGE
double-trouble TROUBLE
douche bag PEOPLE - NEGATIVE
dough head PEOPLE - STUPID
dough MONEY
dove PEACE
down for the count MOVEMENT -
    LACKING
down (pat) KNOWLEDGE
down the drain WASTE
Down the hatch! DRINKING - TOAST

down time MALFUNCTION
down to the wire TIME
down trip ANNOYANCE
down under COUNTRY
down with something COMFORT
down BEHIND
down COMPLETENESS
down DEPRESSION
down EATING
down FIGHTING
down INTOXICATED - ALCOHOL
down KNOWLEDGEABLE
down NONFUNCTIONING
down SATISFACTORY
downbeat CALM
downer DEPRESSION
downer DRUGS - BARBITURATE
downer DRUGS - BARBITURATE
doxy WOMAN - NEGATIVE
DQ EATING
draft board ALCOHOL - SALOON
drafty ALCOHOL - BEER
drag ANNOYANCE
drag DATING
drag DULL
drag RACING
drag TOBACCO
dragged out EXHAUSTION
dragged ANXIETY
draggin'-wagon RACING
drain the bilge VOMIT
drain EXHAUSTION
Drat! CURSING
dreamboat LOVER
dreck WASTE
dressed to kill APPEARANCE
dressed to the nines APPEARANCE
Drink up! DRINKING - TOAST
drinkies ALCOHOL - DRINKING
drinkypoo ALCOHOL - DRINKING
drip PEOPLE - STUPID
drippy UNDESIRABLE
drive someone around the bend
  CRAZINESS
drive someone bonkers CRAZINESS
drive someone up the wall
  FRUSTRATION
drive the big bus VOMIT
droid PEOPLE - STUPID
droob PEOPLE - STUPID
drool (all) over someone or something
  DESIRE
droopy-drawers CHILDREN

drop a bop DRUGS - USE
drop a brick SURPRISE
drop a dime TATTLING
Drop dead! ANNOYANCE
Drop it! CALM
drop one's cookies VOMIT
drop one's teeth SURPRISE
drop out LIFESTYLE
drop out QUIT
drop someone or something like a hot
  potato ABANDONMENT
drop someone VIOLENCE
drop the ball FAILURE
drop ARREST
drop DRINKING - PORTION
drop DRUGS
drop DRUGS - USE
drop MURDER
drop VIOLENCE
drop-dead list LIST
drop-dead EXCELLENCE
drop-dead RUDENESS
dropout STUDENT
dropped ARREST
drug lord DRUGS - SELLER
drug (out) INTOXICATED - DRUGS
drug DRUGS - USE
druggie DRUGS
drughead DRUGS - USER
drugola BRIBERY
drugstore cowboy MAN
drunk back INTOXICATED - ALCOHOL
drunk tank JAIL
Dry up! SILENCE
dry ALCOHOL - LACKING
dry ALCOHOL - LACKING
dry SOBRIETY
dry-as-dust DULL
dub COPY
dubage DRUGS - MARIJUANA
ducats MONEY
duck butt PEOPLE - SHORT
duck AVOIDANCE
duck URINATION
ducks TICKETS
duck-squeezer PEOPLE - NEGATIVE
ducky EXCELLENCE
dud FAILURE
dude up CLOTHING
dude EXCELLENCE
dude MAN - FRIEND
dudette WOMAN
dudical EXCELLENCE

duds CLOTHING
duff BUTTOCKS
duffer MAN - STUPID
duffer SPORTS - GOLF
duke someone out VIOLENCE
duke VOMIT
dukes FIST
dukes KNEES
duky EXCREMENT
dull as dishwater DULL
dull roar NOISE
dullsville DULL
dumb bunny PEOPLE - STUPID
dumb cluck PEOPLE - STUPID
dumb Dora WOMAN - STUPID
dumb ox MAN - STUPID
dumb-ass PEOPLE - STUPID
dumbbell PEOPLE - STUPID
dumb-dodo PEOPLE - STUPID
dumb-dumb PEOPLE - STUPID
dumbhead PEOPLE - STUPID
dumbo EARS
dumbo PEOPLE - STUPID
dumbski PEOPLE - STUPID
dumbski STUPIDITY
dummy up SILENCE
dummy DRINKING - PARAPHERNALIA
dummy PEOPLE - STUPID
dummy TOBACCO
dump on someone or something SNOW
dump one's load DEFECATION
dump one's load VOMIT
dump DEFECATION
dump LOCATION - UNDESIRABLE
dump VOMIT
dumped on CRITICISM
dumped on SNOW
dupe COPY
dust someone off VIOLENCE
dust someone's pants SCOLDING
dust DEPART
dust DRUGS - ADDED
dust DRUGS - POWDER
dust MURDER
dust OVERWHELM
dust TOBACCO
duster BUTTOCKS
dust-up VIOLENCE
Dutch act DEATH
Dutch courage ALCOHOL
Dutch courage DRUGS
Dutch treat SHARING
Dutch uncle PEOPLE - GOOD

dweeb PEOPLE - STUPID
dynamic duo TWO
dynamite POWER
eager-beaver EAGERNESS
eagle freak PEOPLE - NEGATIVE
eagle-eye OBSERVATION
eagle-eye VISION
ear candy MUSIC
ear-duster GOSSIP
earful GOSSIP
earl VOMIT
early bird EARLY
early bird PEOPLE - EARLY
earp VOMIT
earth to _____ GREETING
Easy does it. CALM
easy mark DUPE
easy money MONEY
easy street COMFORT
easy CONTENTMENT
eat crow HUMILITY
eat face KISS
eat nails ANGER
eat one's hat CONDITIONAL
eat one's heart out SUFFERING
eat something up ACCEPTANCE
eat something up APPRECIATION
eat something up CONSUMPTION
eat up EATING
eat COST
eat WORRY
eco freak PEOPLE - NEGATIVE
Ecstasy DRUGS
edge INTOXICATION - ONSET
edged INTOXICATED - ALCOHOL/DRUGS
edgy ANXIETY
egg-beater AVIATION
egg-beater ENGINE
egghead INTELLIGENCE
egg-sucker FLATTERY
ego trip SUPERIORITY
ego tripper HAUGHTINESS
eighteen-wheeler TRUCK
el cheapo CHEAPNESS
(el) primo BEST
elbow-bending DRINKING - EXCESS
elbow-grease EFFORT
electrified INTOXICATED - ALCOHOL
elevated INTOXICATED - ALCOHOL
elevator music MUSIC
eliminated DEAD
eliminated INTOXICATED - ALCOHOL
embalmed INTOXICATED - ALCOHOL

embalming fluid ALCOHOL - STRONG
em(m) DRINKING - PARAPHERNALIA
empties ALCOHOL - PARAPHERNALIA
empty-nesters KINSHIP
end of the ball game CONCLUSION
end CONCLUSION
ends MONEY
ends SHOES
enforcer VIOLENCE
enhanced INTOXICATED - DRUGS
equalizer WEAPONRY
erase MURDER
eternal checkout DEATH
eternity-box DEATH
euchre DECEPTION
evened out CALM
even-Steven EVEN
everyday joe ORDINARY
everything from soup to nuts
  EVERYTHING
evidence ALCOHOL
evil EXCELLENCE
ex KINSHIP
Excellent! EXCELLENCE
exec BUSINESS
eyeball to eyeball PROXIMITY
eyeball EXAMINATION
eyeful VISION
eye-opener DRINKING - PORTION
eye-opener SURPRISE
eye-popper AMAZEMENT
eye-popper ATTRACTIVENESS
eyewash ALCOHOL
eyewash NONSENSE
fab EXCELLENCE
face card PEOPLE - IMPORTANT
(face) fungus BEARD
face man MAN - ATTRACTIVE
face the music ACCEPTANCE
faced INTOXICATED - ALCOHOL
faced REJECTION
face-off ENCOUNTER
facilities TOILET
fack TRUTH
facts of life DIFFICULTIES
facts of life SEX
fade DECLINE
fade DEPART
fadoodle NONSENSE
fag GAY
fag MAN - NEGATIVE
fag TOBACCO
fag-bashing VIOLENCE

fagged out EXHAUSTION
fail FAILURE
fair shake OPPORTUNITY
fair-haired boy MAN
fair-weather INSINCERITY
fairy tale LYING
fairy GAY
fake book MUSIC
fake it DECEPTION
fake off WASTE - TIME
fake someone out DECEPTION
fakus GADGET
falderal NONSENSE
fall guy DUPE
fall off the wagon DRINKING
fall out of bed DECLINE
fall out DEPART
fall ARREST
falling-down drunk DRUNKARD
falling-down drunk INTOXICATED -
  ALCOHOL
falling-out DISAGREEMENT
fallout RESULTS
falpjaw GOSSIP
fan the breeze CONVERSATION
fan IGNORE
fancy footwork SKILL
Fancy meeting you here. SURPRISE
fancy-schmancy ELEGANCE
fanny BUTTOCKS
fanny-bumper EVENT
fanny-dipper SWIMMING
Fantabulous! EXCELLENCE
far gone CRAZINESS
far gone INTOXICATED - ALCOHOL
far out CONFUSION
far out EXCELLENCE
far out INTOXICATED - ALCOHOL/DRUGS
fart sack BED
fart FLATULENCE
fart PEOPLE - NEGATIVE
farts ARTS
fast one DECEPTION
fat cat WEALTH
fat chance OPPORTUNITY
fat city FAT
fat city LIFESTYLE
fat ABUNDANCE
fat ATTRACTIVENESS
fat EXCELLENCE
fathead STUPIDITY
fatheaded STUPIDITY
fatso PEOPLE - FAT

fatty PEOPLE - FAT
fattygews CLOTHING
feather brain PEOPLE - STUPID
fed CONTROL
fed FINANCIAL
federal diploma MONEY
federal jug PUNISHMENT
feeb PEOPLE - STUPID
feeby POLICE
feed one's face EATING
feel a draft REJECTION
feel groovy HAPPINESS
feel groovy INTOXICATED -
  ALCOHOL/DRUGS
feeling no pain DEAD
feeling no pain INTOXICATED - ALCOHOL
feep COMPUTER
fella PEOPLE - MALE
fence hanger INDECISION
fenced ANGER
fender-bender ACCIDENT
fender-bender DRIVING
fer shur EXCELLENCE
feshnushkied INTOXICATED - ALCOHOL
fetch up VOMIT
fib LYING
fibber LYING
fifth wheel INTRUSION
file thirteen WASTE
fill or kill FINANCIAL
filling station STORE - LIQUOR
fill-mill TAVERN
filthy lucre MONEY
filthy rich WEALTH
fin MONEY
finagle SCHEME
financially embarrassed MONEY -
  LACKING
fine and dandy EXCELLENCE
finger wave INSULT
finger DRINKING - PORTION
finger IDENTIFICATION
fink (on someone) TATTLING
fink out (on someone or something)
  COOPERATION - LACKING
fink PEOPLE - STRANGE
fink TATTLING
fire a line DRUGS - USE
fire away BEGINNINGS
fire someone or something up
  EXCITEMENT
fire something up MACHINERY
fire up DRUGS - USE

fired up EXCITEMENT
firewater ALCOHOL
fireworks ANGER
fireworks EXCITEMENT
firstest with the mostest EARLY
Fish or cut bait. ALTERNATIVES
fish story LYING
fish PEOPLE - STUPID
fish-fight VIOLENCE
fishing expedition SEARCH
fish-kiss KISS
fishtail ACCIDENT
fishy SUSPICION
five-finger discount THEFT
fiver MONEY
fix (up) DRUGS - PORTION
fix BRIBERY
fix COMPUTER
fix DRUGS - PURCHASE
fix INFLUENCE
fixed up DATING
fixed BRIBERY
fixed BRIBERY
fixed INTOXICATED - DRUGS
fixer LAWYER
fizzle FAILURE
flabbergasted INTOXICATED - ALCOHOL
flabbergasted SURPRISE
flack (out) EXHAUSTION
flackery ADVERTISING
flag ARREST
flag FAILURE
flagged ARREST
flak PROMOTION
flak COMPLAINT
flake down SLEEP
flake (out) EXHAUSTION
flake (out) INTOXICATION - SLEEP
flake DRUGS - COCAINE
flake PEOPLE - SILLY
flaked out EXHAUSTION
flaked out INTOXICATED - ALCOHOL
flaky INTOXICATED - ALCOHOL
flaky ADDICTION
flaky RESPONSIBILITY - LACKING
flame ARGUMENT
flamer COMPUTER
flamer GAY
flame-war ARGUMENT
flap ARGUMENT
flapdoodle NONSENSE
flapjaw TALKING
flash on something THINKING

flash the hash VOMIT
flash DISPLAY
flash DRINKING - PORTION
flash SEX - DISPLAY
flash THINKING
flash TIME - SHORT
flashback PAST
flasher SEX - DISPLAY
flat broke MONEY - LACKING
flat on one's ass EXHAUSTION
flat on one's ass MONEY - LACKING
flat out SPEED
flatfoot POLICE
flathead PEOPLE - STUPID
flatheaded STUPIDITY
flatline DEATH
flat-out VERY
flatten VIOLENCE
fleabag LODGING
fleece THEFT
flesh-presser POLITICIANS
flexed out of shape ANGER
flick ARTS
flimflam artist DECEPTION
flimflam DECEPTION
flimflam NONSENSE
fling up VOMIT
fling-wing AVIATION
flip one's wig CRAZINESS
flip (out) CONTROL
flip side MUSIC
flip side TRAVEL
flip someone off INSULT
flip someone the bird INSULT
flip CRAZINESS
flip-flop REVERSAL
flip-flop TRAVEL
flip-flop UNCERTAINTY
flipping CURSING
flipside ARGUMENT
flivver CARS
FLK CHILDREN
flog PROMOTION
flooey INTOXICATED - ALCOHOL
floored INTOXICATED - ALCOHOL
floored SURPRISE
floored VIOLENCE
floozie WOMAN - SEX
flop FAILURE
flop LODGING
flophouse LODGING
flopper-stopper CLOTHING
flub something up ERROR

flub the dub FAILURE
flub (up) ERROR
fluff ERROR
fluff NONSENSE
fluff-stuff SNOW
flunk out (of something) FAILURE
flunk FAILURE
flush WEALTH
flusher TOILET
fly kites CHECKS
fly light EATING
fly the coop ESCAPE
fly trap MOUTH
fly FASHIONABLE
fly KNOWLEDGEABLE
flyboy AVIATION
fly-by-night DISHONESTY
foam ALCOHOL - BEER
FOB NAIVETE
foggiest (idea) THINKING
fold FAILURE
fold INTOXICATED - ALCOHOL
folded INTOXICATED - ALCOHOL
folding money MONEY
folks KINSHIP
fomp SEX
foodaholic GLUTTONY
foo-foo water HYGIENE
foot it WALKING
foot-in-mouth disease TALKING
foozle ERROR
foozlified ERROR
foozlified INTOXICATED - ALCOHOL
for all I know KNOWLEDGE - LACKING
for (all) one's trouble REWARD
for free COST
for keeps ALWAYS
for kicks PLEASURE
for peanuts COST
For Pete's sake! AMAZEMENT
for real REALITY
for sure ABSOLUTELY
for the birds UNDESIRABLE
for the devil of it MISCHIEF
forbidden fruit DESIRE
Forget it! CALM
Forget you! CURSING
fork something over TRANSFER
forty winks SLEEP
fossil KINSHIP
fossil OLD-FASHIONED
foul mouth PEOPLE - VULGAR
foul up ERROR

fouled up RUINATION
four sheets in the wind INTOXICATED - ALCOHOL
four wheels CARS
four-bagger SPORTS - BASEBALL
four bits MONEY
four-eyes GLASSES
four-flusher DECEPTION
fox trap CARS
fox WOMAN - ATTRACTIVE
foxy lady WOMAN - ATTRACTIVE
foxy ATTRACTIVENESS
foxy HYGIENE
foxy INTOXICATED - ALCOHOL/DRUGS
fracture LAUGHTER
fractured INTOXICATED - ALCOHOL
fractured LAUGHTER
frag MURDER
fragged RUINATION
fraidy cat FEAR
frame DECEPTION
frantic WILDNESS
frat SOCIAL
frat-rat MAN
freak daddy MAN - ATTRACTIVE
freak mommy WOMAN - ATTRACTIVE
freak (out) INTOXICATION - BAD
freak (out) PANIC
freak (out) WILDNESS
freak someone out CONFUSION
freaked (out) CONFUSION
freaked (out) EXHAUSTION
freaker DRUGS
freaker EVENT
freaking CURSING
freakout DRUGS - USER
free base party DRUGS - PARTY
free base DRUGS - COCAINE
free for all VIOLENCE
free lunch COST
free ride EASY
free show SEX - DISPLAY
free trip INTOXICATION - DRUGS
free-baser DRUGS - USER
free-basing DRUGS - USE
freebie COST
freeload BURDEN
freeloader PEOPLE - NEGATIVE
free-wheeling WILDNESS
freeze someone out COMFORT
freeze someone out IGNORE
freeze IGNORE
freeze MOVEMENT - LACKING

freezing cold COLD
French kiss KISS
fresh and sweet FREEDOM
fresh as a daisy ALERTNESS
fresh AGGRESSIVENESS
fresh ATTRACTIVENESS
fresh EXCELLENCE
fresh IMPUDENCE
fridge APPLIANCE
fried INTOXICATED - ALCOHOL/DRUGS
frigging CURSING
Frisco CITIES
friz LEISURE
frog face PEOPLE - STUPID
frog slicing SCHOOL
from A to Z EVERYTHING
from (the) git-go BEGINNINGS
front man BUSINESS
front money MONEY
front off about something RESENTMENT
front runner POLITICIANS
front APPEARANCE
front CHALLENGE
front DECEPTION
front MONEY
fronts CLOTHING
froody EXCELLENCE
frosh STUDENT
frost ANGER
frosted (over) ANGER
frosty ALCOHOL - BEER
frosty EXCELLENCE
froth ALCOHOL - BEER
fruit GAY
fruit PEOPLE - STRANGE
fruitcake GAY
fruitcake PEOPLE - SILLY
fry PUNISHMENT
fuck COPULATION
fucking CURSING
fuddy-duddy OLD-FASHIONED
fudge factor ERROR
fudge DECEPTION
fudge NONSENSE
fugly APPEARANCE - NEGATIVE
full blast LOUDNESS
full of beans NONSENSE
full of hops NONSENSE
full of hot air NONSENSE
full of prunes NONSENSE
full of the devil MISCHIEF
full sesh COMPLETENESS
full steam ahead MOVEMENT

fun and games NONSENSE
fun PLEASURE
fungus-face BEARD
funk COWARDICE
funk DEPRESSION
funk MUSIC
funk ODOR
funk TOBACCO
funked out INTOXICATED -
  ALCOHOL/DRUGS
funking CURSING
funky EARTHY
funky HYGIENE
funky ODOR
funky STRANGE
funky-drunk INTOXICATED - ALCOHOL
funky-fresh EXCELLENCE
funny-farm CRAZINESS
funny-money MONEY - NEGATIVE
fur POLICE
furphy GOSSIP
fuse box BRAIN
fussbudget PEOPLE - NEGATIVE
fuzz station POLICE
fuzz DRINKING - EXCESS
fuzz POLICE
fuzzed INTOXICATED - ALCOHOL
fuzz-face BEARD
fuzzword CONFUSION
FWIW COMPUTER - ABBREVIATION
G COMPUTER - ABBREVIATION
G MAN
gab room TOILET
gab GOSSIP
gabfest CHATTER
gabmeister OCCUPATION
gaffer MAN - OLD
gaffled ARREST
gag JOKING
gaga AMAZEMENT
gaga CRAZINESS
galumph (around) WALKING
game plan PREPARATION
game time TIME
game AGREEMENT
gams LEGS
gander VISION
gang-bang COPULATION
gang-bang VIOLENCE
gangbanger CRIMINAL
gangbusters EVENT
GAPO HYGIENE
garbage freak DRUGS - USER

garbage mouth PEOPLE - VULGAR
garbage something down EATING
garbage COMPUTER
garbage NONSENSE
gargle factory TAVERN
gargle ALCOHOL
gargle DRINKING
gargler DRUNKARD
gas (up) DRINKING - EXCESS
gas ALCOHOL
gas BOASTING
gas FLATULENCE
gas FUN
gas JOKING
gas NONSENSE
gasbag BOASTING
gas-guzzler CARS
gash bucket TOILET
gas-passer MEDICAL
gassed (up) INTOXICATED -
  ALCOHOL/DRUGS
gate DISMISSAL
gaucho NAKEDNESS
gay as pink ink GAY
gazinkus GADGET
gazizzey PEOPLE - STUPID
gazoo BUTTOCKS
gazoony MAN - STRONG
gazumph FINANCIAL
GBed INTOXICATED - DRUGS
GBG COMPUTER - ABBREVIATION
gear EXCELLENCE
gear SYMBOL
gee ALCOHOL
gee AMAZEMENT
gee DISGUSTING
geedunk FOOD
geegaw GADGET
geek out STUDY
geek PEOPLE - NEGATIVE
geek STUDENT
geekazoid PEOPLE - STRANGE
geek-chic FASHIONABLE
geekdom SCHOOL
Geesh! DISGUSTING
geetis MONEY
geezer DRINKING - PORTION
geezer MAN - OLD
gel RELAX
gender-bender ELECTRONICS
gender-bender SEX
generic UNDESIRABLE
genuine article GENUINE

george COPULATION
george DEFECATION
GERK PEOPLE - OLD
Geronimo! ATTENTION
get a bang out of someone or
  something THRILL
get a buzz out of someone or
  something JOKING
get a can on DRINKING - EXCESS
get a fix DRUGS - PURCHASE
Get a life! CALM
get a load of something or someone
  OBSERVATION
get a load off one's feet RELAX
get a load off one's mind OPINION
get a toehold INTRUSION
Get a wiggle on! HURRY
get an eyeball on someone or
  something VISION
Get away! ANNOYANCE
get behind someone or something
  PROMOTION
get behind something PLEASURE
get down on someone CRITICISM
get down to some serious drinking
  ALCOHOL
get down to the nitty-gritty
  INFORMATION
get down CONCENTRATION
get down COPULATION
get down GAMBLING
get face RESPECT
get hot LUCKY
get hot WORK
get in bad (with someone) TROUBLE
get in on the act JOINING
get in someone's face CONFRONTATION
get in the groove ACCEPTANCE
get into something JOINING
get it (all) together ORGANIZATION
get it in the neck PUNISHMENT
get it off COPULATION
get it on BEGINNINGS
get it on COPULATION
get it on DANCING
get it on PLEASURE
get it out PROBLEM
get it up EXCITEMENT
get it PUNISHMENT
get it UNDERSTANDING
get lip KISS
Get lost! DEPART
get mad (at something) ANGER

get naked RELAX
get narkied DRUGS - USE
get nowhere fast MOVEMENT - LACKING
get off (on something) INTOXICATION -
  ONSET
get off (on something) PLEASURE
get off (on something) SUCCESS
get off one's rear WORK
get off someone's back ANNOYANCE
get off the dime ACTIVITY
get on someone's case ANNOYANCE
get on the stick ORGANIZATION
get one right here EFFECT
get one's act together ORGANIZATION
get one's bowels in an uproar ANXIETY
get one's hooks into someone or
  something CONTROL
get one's hooks into someone
  FLIRTATION
get one's kicks (from someone or
  something) PLEASURE
get one's lumps PUNISHMENT
get one's nose cold DRUGS - USE
get one's nose out of joint OFFENDED
get one's rocks off (on something)
  ENJOYMENT
get one's teeth into something EFFORT
get one's ticket punched DEATH
get one's wings DRUGS - USE
get out of Dodge DEPART
Get out of my face! ANNOYANCE
Get out of town! DEPART
get (out) while the gettin(g)'s good
  DEPART
Get real! IMPROVEMENT
get smart (with someone) IMPUDENCE
get some shut-eye SLEEP
get someone going EXCITEMENT
get someone's goat ANNOYANCE
get someone's motor running AROUSAL
get someone's motor running
  EXCITEMENT
get something going (with someone)
  ROMANCE
get straight DRUGS - USE
get the drop on someone OVERWHELM
get the drop on someone WEAPONRY
get the goods on someone REVEAL
Get the lead out! HURRY
Get the message? UNDERSTANDING
get the nod PREFERENCE
get the sack DISMISSAL
get the show on the road BEGINNINGS

get there DRINKING - EXCESS
get to someone ANNOYANCE
get to someone EFFECT
get with it BEHAVIOR
get with it WORK
get with someone RELATIONSHIP
get with the program RULES
getaway ESCAPE
getaway VACATION
(ghetto) blaster AUDIO
ghost turd LINT
GIB COPULATION
gibber-gabber NONSENSE
Giddy up! HURRY
giffed INTOXICATED - ALCOHOL
gift of gab TALKING
gig ANNOYANCE
gig EMPLOYMENT
gig LAUGHTER
gig PERFORMANCE
gig WORK
giggle goo ALCOHOL
GIGO COMPUTER - ABBREVIATION
gimme CONTRACTION
gimp DISABLED
gimp INJURY
gimpy DISABLED
gimpy POLICE
gin mill TAVERN
ginhead DRUNKARD
girl CARDS
girl WOMAN
girlie magazine NAKEDNESS
girlie show NAKEDNESS
git-go BEGINNINGS
Give it a rest! SILENCE
give it the gun ENGINE
Give it up! STOPPING
Give me a break! AMAZEMENT
Give me a break! KINDNESS
Give me a break! SILENCE
Give me a rest! STOPPING
Give me (some) skin! GREETING
give (out) with something TATTLING
give someone a buzz PLEASURE
give someone a buzz TELEPHONE
give someone a (good) talking to
  SCOLDING
give someone a (good) working over
  SCOLDING
give someone a melvin HARASSMENT
give someone a pain ANNOYANCE
give someone an earful PRESENTATION

give someone an earful SCOLDING
give someone five ASSISTANCE
give someone five GREETING
give someone hell ANNOYANCE
give someone hell SCOLDING
give someone the ax DISMISSAL
give someone the ax DIVORCE
give someone the brushoff IGNORE
give someone the business MURDER
give someone the business SCOLDING
give someone the finger INSULT
give someone the gate EJECTION
give someone the go-by IGNORE
give someone the nod CHOICE
give someone the nod SIGNAL
give someone the raspberry JEER
give someone the shaft DECEPTION
give someone the slip ESCAPE
giveaway REVEAL
gizmo GADGET
gizzy DRUGS - MARIJUANA
glad rags CLOTHING
glad INTOXICATED - ALCOHOL
glad-hand GREETING
glad-hander PEOPLE - FRIEND
glamour puss PEOPLE - ATTRACTIVE
glass gun DRUGS - PARAPHERNALIA
glass(y)-eyed INTOXICATED -
  ALCOHOL/DRUGS
glazed (drunk) INTOXICATED - ALCOHOL
gleep PEOPLE - STUPID
glick PEOPLE - STRANGE
glitch COMPUTER - ERROR
glitz FASHIONABLE
glitzy FASHIONABLE
glom OBSERVATION
glom THEFT
glommed ARREST
gloomy Gus PEOPLE - SAD
glop NASTY
glop TRANSFER
glorified EXAGGERATION
glow worm DRUNKARD
glow INTOXICATED - ALCOHOL/DRUGS
glue factory LOCATION
glued ARREST
glued INTOXICATED - ALCOHOL
gluey DRUGS - USER
glug DRINKING - PORTION
glutz WOMAN - SEX
G-man POLICE
(g)narly EXCELLENCE
go all the way COPULATION

go ape (over someone or something) EXCITEMENT
go bananas CRAZINESS
go blooey MALFUNCTION
Go chase yourself! DEPART
go down in flames FAILURE
go down the line DRUGS - USE
go down the tube(s) RUINATION
go down ACCEPTANCE
go down ARREST
go down HAPPENING
go downhill DECLINE
go Dutch SHARING
Go figure. THINKING
go for broke TRY
Go for it! ENCOURAGEMENT
go great guns SUCCESS
go haywire CRAZINESS
go haywire MALFUNCTION
go home in a box DEATH
go home to mama QUIT
go into orbit EXCITEMENT
go mental CRAZINESS
go off half-cocked IMPETUOUS
go off the deep end ABUNDANCE
go on (and on) about someone or something TALKING
Go on! BELIEF
go over big SUCCESS
go over like a lead balloon FAILURE
go over the hill ESCAPE
go over the wall ESCAPE
go overboard ABUNDANCE
go places SUCCESS
go public FINANCIAL
go public REVEAL
go Rinso FALL
go slow CAUTION
go sour RUINATION
go south ESCAPE
go south FALL
go south QUIT
go straight LAW-ABIDING
go straight SOBRIETY
go the limit AMOUNT - MAXIMUM
go through someone like a dose of (the) salts SPEED
go through the changes LIFESTYLE
Go to blazes! CURSING
go to town ENERGETIC
Go to! CURSING
go underground SECRECY
go up INTOXICATION - ONSET

go West DEATH
go with the flow ACCEPTANCE
go zonkers CRAZINESS
go TALKING
go TRY
go URINATION
go-ahead PERMISSION
goat CARS
gob AMOUNT - MANY
gob PORTION
gobbledygook NASTY
gobbledygook NONSENSE
go-by IGNORE
God's acre CEMETERY
go-getter EAGERNESS
goggle-eyed INTOXICATED - ALCOHOL
go-go DANCING
go-go ENERGETIC
going high INTOXICATION
going over EXAMINATION
going over VIOLENCE
goings-on EVENT
gold digger WOMAN - NEGATIVE
gold MONEY
goldbrick WASTE - TIME
goldbrick(er) WASTE - TIME
golden handcuffs FINANCIAL
golden opportunity OPPORTUNITY
golden parachute FINANCIAL
golden-ager PEOPLE - OLD
goldie locks POLICE
gomer PEOPLE - NEGATIVE
gomer PEOPLE - STUPID
gone goose NONFUNCTIONING
gone AWARENESS - LACKING
gone EXCELLENCE
gone INTOXICATED - ALCOHOL/DRUGS
goner NONFUNCTIONING
gonged INTOXICATED - DRUGS
gonna CONTRACTION
gonzo CRAZINESS
gonzo PEOPLE - SILLY
goo NASTY
goob PEOPLE - STRANGE
goob PIMPLES
goober-grabber OCCUPATION
goober-grease FOOD
goobrain PEOPLE - STUPID
good and something VERY
good buddy FRIEND
Good call! AMAZEMENT
Good deal! AMAZEMENT
Good golly, Miss Molly! AMAZEMENT

Good heavens! AMAZEMENT
good Joe PEOPLE - GOOD
(good) looker PEOPLE - ATTRACTIVE
good old boy PEOPLE - GOOD
good trip EVENT
good trip INTOXICATION - DRUGS
good-for-nothing WORTHLESSNESS
good-time Charlie PEOPLE - GOOD
good-time it ENJOYMENT
good-time man DRUGS - USER
goody two-shoes PEOPLE - NEGATIVE
gooey COMPUTER - ABBREVIATION
goof off WASTE - TIME
goof on someone TRICK
goof something up ERROR
goof DRUGS - REACTION
goof DRUGS - USE
goof ERROR
goof PEOPLE - FOOLISH
goofball PEOPLE - STUPID
goofed (up) CONFUSION
goofed (up) ERROR
goof-proof FOOLPROOF
goofus GADGET
goofus PEOPLE - STUPID
goofy INTOXICATED - ALCOHOL
goofy SILLINESS
goo-goo eyes FLIRTATION
gook HOBO
gook NASTY
gook PEOPLE - EAST ASIAN
gook PROSTITUTION
goombah FRIEND
goon squad CRIMINAL
goon squad POLICE
goon CRIMINAL
goon PEOPLE - STUPID
gooned INTOXICATED - ALCOHOL
gooner PEOPLE - EAST ASIAN
goon-platoon MILITARY
goop NASTY
goophead PIMPLES
goopy TASTE
goose egg AMOUNT - ZERO
goose egg FAILURE
goose egg INJURY
goose ENGINE
goose HARASSMENT
goose PEOPLE - STUPID
goozlum NASTY
gopher ball SPORTS - BASEBALL
gopher ASSISTANT
gopher DUPE

go-pills DRUGS - AMPHETAMINE
gorilla biscuits DRUGS - AMPHETAMINE
gorilla juice STEROIDS
gork MEDICAL
gork PEOPLE - STUPID
gorked (out) MEDICAL
gospel (truth) TRUTH
gotcha ARREST
gotcha CONTRACTION
gotcha UNDERSTANDING
gouch off INTOXICATED - DRUGS
gourd HEAD
goy GENTILE
grabbers HANDS
grade-grubber STUDENT
grade-grubbing SCHOOL
grade-grubbing STUDY
grade-grubbing FLATTERY
graduate ADDICTION
graduate EXPERIENCE
Grand Central Station BUSY
grand MONEY
granddad OLD-FASHIONED
(grand)daddy (of them all) SIZE
grandstand play IMPRESSIVE
grandstand DISPLAY
grape shot INTOXICATED - ALCOHOL
grapes of wrath ALCOHOL - WINE
grape(s) ALCOHOL - CHAMPAGNE
grape(s) ALCOHOL - WINE
grapevine COMMUNICATION
grass party PARTY - DRUGS
grass DRUGS - MARIJUANA
grass FOOD
grasshead DRUGS - USER
grassroots ORDINARY
grassroots POLITICS
grave-dancer PEOPLE - NEGATIVE
gravel-pounder SOLDIER
graveyard shift EMPLOYMENT
gravy train WORK
gravy EARN
Graybar Hotel JAIL
grayhound DATING
GR&D COMPUTER - ABBREVIATION
grease monkey MECHANIC
grease someone's palm BRIBERY
grease the skids PREPARATION
grease BRIBERY
greased lighting POWER
greased lightning ALCOHOL - STRONG
greased INTOXICATED - ALCOHOL
greaser MAN

greasy spoon RESTAURANT
great divide DIVORCE
Great Scott! AMAZEMENT
great unwashed ORDINARY
greefo DRUGS - MARIJUANA
Greek to someone UNDERSTANDING - LACKING
green light APPROVAL
green thumb SKILL
green MONEY
greenback MONEY
greenie ALCOHOL - BEER
greenmail FINANCIAL
greenwash CRIME
greldge DISGUSTING
greldge NASTY
gripe one's soul ANNOYANCE
grit COURAGE
gritch COMPLAINT
gritch GROUCHY
gritchy COMPLAINT
groan box MUSIC
grod PEOPLE - NEGATIVE
grody to the max DISGUSTING
grody UNDESIRABLE
grog ALCOHOL
groggery TAVERN
groggy EXHAUSTION
groggy INTOXICATED - ALCOHOL
groghound DRUNKARD
grok UNDERSTANDING
gronk (out) MALFUNCTION
gronk NASTY
groove on someone or something INTEREST
groove PLEASURE
grooved PLEASURE
grooving RELAX
groovy EXCELLENCE
groovy INTOXICATED - DRUGS
groovy OLD-FASHIONED
gross someone out DISGUSTING
gross DISGUSTING
gross-out DISGUSTING
grotty UNDESIRABLE
grounded PUNISHMENT
ground-pounder SOLDIER
group-grope COPULATION
groupie MUSIC
grouse COMPLAINT
grouse KISS
grouse WOMAN - SEX
grovel KISS

growler TOILET
grub EATING
grub FOOD
grub PEOPLE - NEGATIVE
grub STUDENT
grubbies CLOTHING
grubby HYGIENE
gruesome twosome TWO
grunge NASTY
grunge PEOPLE - NEGATIVE
grungy DISGUSTING
grunt work WORK
grunt BELCH
grunt PEOPLE - NEGATIVE
grunt SOLDIER
grunt SPORTS
grunt STUDENT
gubbish NONSENSE
guber PIMPLES
guber SICKNESS
guck NASTY
gucky DISGUSTING
guff IMPUDENCE
guff NONSENSE
guff PEOPLE - STRANGE
gug PEOPLE - NEGATIVE
gulf DRUGS - HEROIN
gumb(e)y HAIR
gumbyhead PEOPLE - STUPID
gump PEOPLE - STUPID
gumshoe DETECTIVE
gumshoe POLICE
gun for someone SEARCH
gun CRIMINAL
gun ENGINE
gun PEOPLE - IMPORTANT
gunboats FEET
gunboats SHOES
gunge SICKNESS
gungeon DRUGS - MARIJUANA
gung-ho ENTHUSIASM
gungy UNDESIRABLE
gunk DRUGS
gunk NASTY
gunner STUDENT
gunny DRUGS - MARIJUANA
gunzel-butt MAN - STRANGE
guru DOCTOR
guru DRUGS - USER
guru FINANCIAL
gussied up APPEARANCE
gusto ALCOHOL - BEER
gusto DRINKING

gut reaction (to something) RESPONSE
gut BASIC
gut EASY
gut SCHOOL
gutbucket MUSIC
gutbucket PEOPLE - FAT
gutbucket STOMACH
gutbucket TAVERN
gutbucket TOILET
gutless wonder PEOPLE - MEEK
guts COURAGE
guts ESSENCE
guts INTESTINES
guts MACHINERY
gutsy COURAGE
guy PEOPLE
guzzle DRINKING - BOUT
guzzle DRINKING - EXCESS
guzzled ARREST
guzzled INTOXICATED - ALCOHOL
guzzle-guts DRUNKARD
guzzler DRUNKARD
guzzlery TAVERN
gweeb STUDENT
gweebo PEOPLE - STRANGE
gym shoe PEOPLE - NEGATIVE
gynie DOCTOR
gyve DRUGS - MARIJUANA
H DRUGS - HEROIN
habit ADDICTION
hack around WASTE - TIME
hack it ENDURE
hack ANNOYANCE
hack COMPUTER
hack PEOPLE - NEGATIVE
hack REPORTER
hack SICKNESS
hack TAXI
hack WRITING
hacked (off) ANGER
hacked EXHAUSTION
hacker COMPUTER
hacker FAILURE
hacker TAXI
Hairball! DISGUSTING
hairball PEOPLE - NEGATIVE
hairy DANGER
hairy-ass(ed) EXCITEMENT
hairy-ass(ed) VIRILITY
half a bubble off plumb CRAZINESS
half in the bag INTOXICATED - ALCOHOL
half under AWARENESS - LACKING
half under INTOXICATED - ALCOHOL

half up the pole INTOXICATED - ALCOHOL
half-baked INTOXICATED - ALCOHOL
half-baked PREPARATION - LACKING
half-blind INTOXICATED - ALCOHOL
half-canned INTOXICATED - ALCOHOL
half-cocked INTOXICATED - ALCOHOL
half-cocked PREPARATION - LACKING
half-crocked INTOXICATED - ALCOHOL
half-lit INTOXICATED - ALCOHOL
half-sprung INTOXICATED - ALCOHOL
half-stewed INTOXICATED - ALCOHOL
halvsies SHARING
ham ACTOR
ham BROADCASTING
hamburg FOOD
hamburger PEOPLE - STUPID
hamburgers FINANCIAL
ham-handed CLUMSINESS
hammer ACCELERATOR
hammered INTOXICATED - ALCOHOL
hammerhead DRUNKARD
hammerhead PEOPLE - STUPID
hams LEGS
hand it to someone PRAISE
hand over fist EARN
hand someone something NONSENSE
handful DIFFICULTIES
hand-in-glove SUITABLE
handle CONTROL
handle NICKNAME
handout ASSISTANCE
handout INFORMATION
hands down EASY
Hands up! THEFT
hands-on BUSINESS
hang a BA (at someone) NAKEDNESS
hang a few on DRINKING
hang a huey DIRECTION
hang a left DIRECTION
hang a louie DIRECTION
hang a ralph DIRECTION
hang a right DIRECTION
hang (around) WASTE - TIME
hang five SURFING
hang in there TRY
Hang it all! CURSING
hang it up QUIT
hang loose RELAX
hang one on DRINKING - EXCESS
hang tough (on something)
    PERSISTENCE
hang up NO
hang-up OBSESSION

hang with someone WASTE - TIME
hang WASTE - TIME
hangout LAZY
hanky HANDKERCHIEF
hanky-panky DECEPTION
hanky-panky FLIRTATION
happening EVENT
happening FASHIONABLE
happy camper HAPPINESS
happy hour DRINKING
happy juice ALCOHOL
happy pills DRUGS - TRANQUILIZERS
happy shop STORE - LIQUOR
happy INTOXICATED - ALCOHOL
happy OBSESSION
hard case ALCOHOL
hard case PROBLEM
hard coin MONEY
hard liquor ALCOHOL - STRONG
hard sell COMMERCE
hard time DIFFICULTIES
hard time PUNISHMENT
hard to swallow AMAZEMENT
hard up DRUGS - NEED
hard up INTOXICATED - ALCOHOL
hard up LONELY
hard ALCOHOL
hard DRUGS
hard MEAN
hardboiled MEAN
hard-core EXTREME
hard-core PORNOGRAPHY
hardhat HAT
hardhat OCCUPATION
hardhead PEOPLE - STUBBORN
hardheaded STUBBORNNESS
hard-liner OPINION
hard-nosed EMOTION - LACKING
hardware ALCOHOL - STRONG
hardware COMPUTER
hardware DRUGS
hardware WEAPONRY
harsh toke ANNOYANCE
harsh toke DRUGS - MARIJUANA
harsh UNDESIRABLE
has-been PAST
hash cannon DRUGS - PARAPHERNALIA
hash pipe DRUGS - PARAPHERNALIA
hash DRUGS - HASHISH
hash-head DRUGS - USER
hash-house DRUGS
hash-house RESTAURANT
hash-slinger RESTAURANT

hassle ANNOYANCE
hassle HARASSMENT
hatch MOUTH
haul LOOT
haul RESULTS
have a ball EXCITEMENT
have a (big) head HANGOVER
have a big mouth REVEAL
Have a blimp! GOOD-BYE
have a buzz on INTOXICATED - ALCOHOL
have a glow on INTOXICATED - ALCOHOL
Have a good one. GREETING
Have a heart! KINDNESS
have a leg up on someone ADVANTAGE
have a little visitor MENSES
have a load on INTOXICATED - ALCOHOL
have a monkey on one's back
    ADDICTION
Have a nice day. GOOD-BYE
have a run-in (with someone or
    something) TROUBLE
have a screw loose CRAZINESS
have a short fuse ANGER
have a skinful INTOXICATED - ALCOHOL
have a spaz ANGER
have a tiger by the tail DANGER
have a whale of a time EXCITEMENT
have a yellow streak down one's back
    COWARDICE
have all one's marbles SANITY
have an ace up one's sleeve TRICK
have an edge on INTOXICATED - ALCOHOL
have an itch for something DESIRE
have ants in one's pants ANXIETY
have bats in one's belfry CRAZINESS
have egg on one's face EMBARRASSMENT
have good vibes PREDICTION
have it all together ORGANIZATION
have it made (in the shade) SUCCESS
have kittens ANGER
have kittens LAUGHTER
have kittens SURPRISE
have one foot in the grave DEATH
have one's ass in a crack DIFFICULTIES
have one's ass in a sling UPSET
have one's brain on a leash INTOXICATED
    - ALCOHOL
have one's mind in the gutter OBSCENE
have rocks in one's head CRAZINESS
have someone dead to rights EVIDENCE
have something cinched CERTAINTY
have something on the brain
    OBSESSION

have the wrong number ERROR
have what it takes ABILITY
have-nots POVERTY
haves WEALTH
hawk SICKNESS
hawk WAR
hawk WIND
hay burner DRUGS - USER
hay burner HORSE
hayseed FARMER
haywire CONFUSION
haywire NONFUNCTIONING
hazel DRUGS - HEROIN
head cook and bottle washer MANAGE
head drug DRUGS
head hunt BUSINESS
head DRUGS - USER
head HANGOVER
head SICKNESS
head TOILET
headache department DIFFICULTIES
headache department STORE - LIQUOR
headache man POLICE
headache ALCOHOL
headache ANNOYANCE
headbone SKULL
headfucker DRUGS - LSD
headhunter BUSINESS
Heads up! CAUTION
heads will roll PUNISHMENT
Headstone City CEMETERY
heap AMOUNT - MUCH
heap CARS
heart LOVE
hearts and flowers EMOTION
heart-to-heart (talk) SERIOUSNESS
heat POLICE
heat PRESSURE
heat WEAPONRY
heater WEAPONRY
heave VOMIT
heaven dust DRUGS - COCAINE
heavy artillery POWER
heavy bread MONEY
heavy date DATING
heavy hash DRUGS - HASHISH
heavy into someone or something
 INTEREST
heavy necking KISS
heavy scene SERIOUSNESS
heavy soul DRUGS - HEROIN
heavy EXCELLENCE
heavy MAN - NEGATIVE

heavy SERIOUSNESS
heavy-handed UNFAIR
heavyweight PEOPLE - IMPORTANT
heavyweight SUCCESS
H-E-double-toothpicks HELL
heebie-jeebies ANXIETY
heel MAN - NEGATIVE
heeled DRUGS
heeled INTOXICATED - ALCOHOL
heesh DRUGS - HASHISH
Heinz 57 (variety) DOG
heist THEFT
heister DRUNKARD
helium head PEOPLE - STUPID
hell of a mess DIFFICULTIES
hell of a note SURPRISE
hell of a someone or something
 EXCELLENCE
hell of a someone or something
 UNDESIRABLE
Hell! CURSING
hell TROUBLE
hellacious EXCELLENCE
hellacious HORRIBLE
hellbender DRINKING - BOUT
hellbender DRUNKARD
heller ENERGETIC
hellhole LOCATION - UNDESIRABLE
hell-on-wheels PEOPLE - IMPORTANT
hellpig WOMAN - UGLY
Hell's bells (and buckets of blood)!
 CURSING
hemp DRUGS - MARIJUANA
hemp TOBACCO
hen fruit FOOD
hen party GOSSIP
hep AWARENESS
hepped (up) INTOXICATED - ALCOHOL
Herb and Al ALCOHOL/DRUGS
herb DRUGS - MARIJUANA
Here's looking at you. TOAST
Here's mud in your eye. TOAST
hero (of the underworld) DRUGS -
 HEROIN
herped up SICKNESS
herpie PEOPLE - SEX
Hey, bum! GREETING
hey GREETING
hickey KISS
hickey PIMPLES
hiddy INTOXICATED - ALCOHOL
hiddy UNDESIRABLE
hide SKIN

hides MUSIC
high and dry ABANDONMENT
high five GREETING
high mucky-muck PEOPLE - IMPORTANT
high on something EXCITEMENT
high roller GAMBLING
high sign SIGNAL
high ups PEOPLE - IMPORTANT
high, wide, and handsome HAPPINESS
high INTOXICATED - ALCOHOL/DRUGS
high INTOXICATION
highbrow CULTURE
highjinks MISCHIEF
high-res SATISFACTORY
highway robbery COST
hike INCREASE
Hill POLITICS
hincty HAUGHTINESS
hip AWARENESS
hip INFORMATION
hippy PEOPLE - NEGATIVE
hip-shooter PEOPLE - NEGATIVE
hipster PEOPLE - NEGATIVE
hired gun CRIMINAL
history PAST
hit list LIST
hit man CRIMINAL
hit man DRUGS - USER
hit me DRINKING - PORTION
hit me GAMBLING
hit me GREETING
hit on someone FLIRTATION
hit on something DISCOVERY
hit pay dirt INFORMATION
hit pay dirt SUCCESS
hit (someone) below the belt UNFAIR
hit someone (up) for something
  REQUEST
hit someone with something
  PRESENTATION
hit the books STUDY
hit the bottle DRINKING - EXCESS
hit the bricks COMMERCE
hit the bricks WALKING
hit the ceiling ANGER
hit the deck ARISE
hit the deck FALL
hit the fan KNOWLEDGE
hit the hay SLEEP
hit the jackpot DISCOVERY
hit the jackpot SUCCESS
hit the panic button PANIC
hit the road DEPART

hit the skids DECLINE
hit the spot PRECISION
hit the spot REFRESHING
hit the trail DEPART
hit under the wing INTOXICATED -
  ALCOHOL
hit ACHIEVEMENT
hit ALCOHOL/DRUGS
hit CRIME
hit MURDER
hit RESULTS
hit SUCCESS
hit VIOLENCE
hitched NUPTIALS
Hiya! GREETING
hock a luggie MUCUS
hock COMMERCE
hock FOOT
hockey EXCREMENT
hockshop PAWNSHOP
hocus DECEPTION
hodad PEOPLE - NEGATIVE
hog CARS
hog DRUGS - PCP
hog DRUGS - USER
hog POLICE
hogwash NONSENSE
hogwash WORTHLESSNESS
hog-wild WILDNESS
ho-hum DULL
hoist one DRINKING - PORTION
ho-jo('s) RESTAURANT
hokey FALSE
hokum NONSENSE
hold all the aces CONTROL
Hold everything! STOPPING
Hold it, Buster! STOPPING
Hold it! STOPPING
hold one's high INTOXICATION
hold one's horses RELAX
hold one's liquor DRINKING
Hold some, fold some. FINANCIAL
hold the fort MANAGE
hold water ENDURE
hold DRUGS
hole in the wall BUSINESS
hole up HIDING
hole PEOPLE - NEGATIVE
holiday cheer ALCOHOL
holier-than-thou HAUGHTINESS
Hollywood DISPLAY
Hollywood FALSE
holmes FRIEND

Holy cow! AMAZEMENT
holy Joe RELIGION
Holy mackerel! AMAZEMENT
Holy moley! AMAZEMENT
holy stink DISGUSTING
holy terror PEOPLE - NEGATIVE
hombre MAN
homeboy FRIEND
home-brew ALCOHOL
homegrown AMATEUR
homegrown DRUGS - MARIJUANA
homer SPORTS - BASEBALL
homes FRIEND
homeslice FRIEND
homespun ALCOHOL
homo GAY
honcho MANAGE
honcho PEOPLE - IMPORTANT
honest injun HONESTY
honey of a something EXCELLENCE
honey wagon TRUCK
honey wagon TRUCK - EXCREMENT
honey ALCOHOL - BEER
honeybunch LOVER
honeymoon (period) BEGINNINGS
Hong Kong dog DIARRHEA
honk (up) DRINKING - BOUT
honk PEOPLE - WHITE
honk VOMIT
honked INTOXICATED - ALCOHOL
honker GOOSE
honker PEOPLE - STRANGE
honky PEOPLE - WHITE
honyock MAN - STUPID
hooch hound DRUNKARD
hooch ALCOHOL
hooched (up) INTOXICATED - ALCOHOL
hood CRIMINAL
hooey NONSENSE
hoof it ESCAPE
hoof it WALKING
hoofer DANCING
hoofing WALKING
hoo-ha EVENT
hoo-ha NONSENSE
hook, line, and sinker COMPLETENESS
hook shop BROTHEL
hook something down EATING
hook ADDICTION
hook DECEPTION
hook SCHOOL
hook THEFT

hooked (on someone or something)
    PREFERENCE
hooked (on something) ADDICTION
hooked (on something) DECEPTION
hooker PROSTITUTION
hooks HANDS
hoopla UPROAR
hoops SPORTS - BASKETBALL
hoosegow JAIL
hoot DISAPPROVAL
hoot JOKING
hoot LAUGHTER
hoo(t)cher DRUNKARD
hoo(t)chfest PARTY - DRINKING
hooted INTOXICATED - ALCOHOL
hooter DRINKING - PORTION
hooter DRUGS - COCAINE
hooter NOSE
Hop to it! HURRY
hop ALCOHOL - BEER
hop AVIATION
hop PARTY
hopfest PARTY - DRINKING
hophead DRUGS - USER
hophead DRUNKARD
hopped up CARS
hopped up EXCITEMENT
hopped up INTOXICATED - DRUGS
hopping mad ANGER
horizontal INTOXICATED - ALCOHOL
horn DRUGS - USE
horn NOSE
horn TELEPHONE
horner DRUGS - USER
horner DRUNKARD
horny AROUSAL
horrors DELIRIUM TREMENS
horrors INTOXICATION - BAD
horse around WASTE - TIME
horse doctor DOCTOR
horse hockey EXCREMENT
horse hockey NONSENSE
horse laugh LAUGHTER
horse opera MOVIES
horse DRUGS - HEROIN
horse EXCREMENT
horsed INTOXICATED - DRUGS
Horsefeathers! AMAZEMENT
horseradish DRUGS - HEROIN
horse's ass PEOPLE - STUPID
horses POWER
hose someone down MURDER
hoser DECEPTION

hoser FRIEND
hot AROUSAL
hot air NONSENSE
hot check CHECKS
Hot diggety (dog)! AMAZEMENT
Hot dog! AMAZEMENT
hot head ANGER
hot item PRODUCT
hot item ROMANCE
hot number MUSIC
hot number WOMAN - SEX
hot paper CHECKS
hot potato DIFFICULTIES
(hot) rod CARS
hot seat PUNISHMENT
hot seat SCRUTINY
(hot) skinny INFORMATION
hot stuff HAUGHTINESS
hot tip INFORMATION
hot wire CRIME
Hot ziggety! AMAZEMENT
hot ANGER
hot BUSINESS
hot CRIME
hot INTOXICATED - ALCOHOL
hot LUCKY
hot POLICE
hot POPULAR
hot THEFT
hotbed of something LOCATION
hotdog DISPLAY
hotkey COMPUTER
hotshot EXCELLENCE
hotshot PEOPLE - IMPORTANT
hotsy-totsy EXCELLENCE
house moss LINT
house of many doors JAIL
How does that grab you? OPINION
How goes it? GREETING
how the other half lives SOCIETY
How ya living? GREETING
howdy GREETING
howl EVENT
howl LAUGHTER
howler ERROR
howling (drunk) INTOXICATED -
   ALCOHOL
HTH LOVER
hubbas DRUGS - COCAINE
hubby KINSHIP
huffer DRUGS
huffy ANGER
hug the porcelain god(dess) VOMIT

hughie VOMIT
humdinger EXCELLENCE
humongous SIZE
hump (along) SPEED
hump it (to somewhere) SPEED
hung ANNOYANCE
hung HANGOVER
hungover HANGOVER
hungries HUNGER
hungry EAGERNESS
hunk MAN - ATTRACTIVE
hunky-dory SATISFACTORY
hurl VOMIT
hurry up and wait ALTERNATIVES
hurt for someone or something DESIRE
hurt INTOXICATED - DRUGS
hurt UGLINESS
hurting DRUGS - NEED
hurting UGLINESS
hush money MONEY
hush someone up MURDER
hush something up SILENCE
hush-hush SECRECY
husky MAN - STRONG
hustle CONFUSION
hustle DECEPTION
hustle HURRY
hustle SEDUCTION
hustler CRIMINAL
hustler GAMBLING
hustler MAN - SEX
hustler PROSTITUTION
hut LODGING
hype artist PROMOTION
hype something up PROMOTION
hype ADVERTISING
hype DRUGS - PARAPHERNALIA
hype DRUGS - PORTION
hype DRUGS - USER
hype EXCELLENCE
hyped (up) ADVERTISING
hyped (up) EXCITEMENT
hyped (up) INTOXICATED - DRUGS
hyper DRUGS - USER
hyper EXCITEMENT
hyper PROMOTION
I am so sure! YES
I could(n't) care less. CONCERN
I don't believe this! AMAZEMENT
I don't know. DISAGREEMENT
I don't mean maybe! THREATENING
I hear what you are saying.
   UNDERSTANDING

I kid you not. SERIOUSNESS
(I) love it! AMAZEMENT
I smell you. UNDERSTANDING
IAE COMPUTER - ABBREVIATION
(I-)beam FINANCIAL
ice queen WOMAN - COLD
ice DRUGS - COCAINE
ice EMBARRASSMENT
ice EXCELLENCE
ice IGNORE
ice JEWELRY
ice MONEY
ice MURDER
iceberg PEOPLE - COLD
iced COMPLETENESS
iceman CRIMINAL
icicles DRUGS - COCAINE
icing on the cake ADDITIONAL
ick DISGUSTING
ick NASTY
ick PEOPLE - NEGATIVE
icky DISGUSTING
icky-poo DISGUSTING
ID IDENTIFICATION
idiot box TELEVISION
idiot card BROADCASTING
idiot juice ALCOHOL
idiot light SIGNAL
idiot oil ALCOHOL
idiot pills DRUGS - BARBITURATE
if I've told you once, I've told you a
   thousand times REPETITION
if one knows what's good for one
   OBLIGATION
if one's a day AGE
If you can't stand the heat, keep out of
   the kitchen. ACCEPTANCE
if you'll pardon the expression EXCUSE
iffy UNCERTAINTY
I'll bite. RESPONSE
ill UNDESIRABLE
illin' BEHAVIOR - BAD
illin' SICKNESS
illin' UPSET
illuminated INTOXICATED - ALCOHOL
I'm history. GOOD-BYE
I'm listening. EXPLANATION
I'm not kidding. SERIOUSNESS
I'm out of here. GOOD-BYE
I'm shaking (in fear). FEAR
I'm there! ACCEPTANCE
IM(H)O COMPUTER - ABBREVIATION
impaired INTOXICATED - ALCOHOL

in a big way VERY
in a blue funk DEPRESSION
in a cold sweat FEAR
in a dither CONFUSION
in a familiar way PREGNANCY
in a family way PREGNANCY
in a flash IMMEDIATELY
in a heap INTOXICATED - ALCOHOL
in a jam DIFFICULTIES
in a jiff(y) IMMEDIATELY
in a snit ANGER
in a tizzy CONFUSION
in a twit UPSET
in a twitter SILLINESS
in action DRUGS
in action HEALTHY
in bad shape INJURY
in bad shape INTOXICATED - ALCOHOL
in bad shape PREGNANCY
in business FUNCTIONAL
in cold blood MEAN
in cold storage DEATH
in deep doo-doo TROUBLE
in deep JOINING
in deep MONEY - LACKING
in drag CLOTHING
in dribs and drabs AMOUNT - SMALL
in Dutch TROUBLE
in fine feather APPEARANCE
in fine feather EXCELLENCE
in nothing flat IMMEDIATELY
in one's blood GENETIC
in one's something mode BEHAVIOR
in orbit HAPPINESS
in orbit INTOXICATED - ALCOHOL/DRUGS
in play FINANCIAL
in play SPORTS
in rare form EXCELLENCE
in rare form INTOXICATED - ALCOHOL
in spades EXTREME
in tall cotton SUCCESS
in the bag ACHIEVEMENT
in the bag INTOXICATED - ALCOHOL
in the black FINANCIAL
in the buff NAKEDNESS
in the catbird seat DOMINANCE
in the chips MONEY
in the driver's seat DOMINANCE
in the grip of the grape INTOXICATED -
   ALCOHOL
in the groove PLEASURE
in the gun INTOXICATED - ALCOHOL
in the hole FINANCIAL

jazzy APPEALING
J.D. ALCOHOL - WHISKEY
Jeepers(-creepers)! AMAZEMENT
jeff DECEPTION
jeff PEOPLE - DULL
jeff PEOPLE - WHITE
jel PEOPLE - STUPID
jelly babies DRUGS - AMPHETAMINE
jelly shoes SHOES
jerk around WASTE - TIME
jerk someone around HARASSMENT
jerk PEOPLE - WORTHLESS
jerker DRUGS - USER
jerker DRUNKARD
jerks DELIRIUM TREMENS
jerkwater RURAL
jerry-built CARELESSNESS
Jesus boots SHOES
jet DEPART
jet-set(ters) WEALTH
jibe AGREEMENT
jiffy TIME - SHORT
jig is up CONCLUSION
jig COPULATION
jigger DRINKING - PORTION
jigger GADGET
jigger TOBACCO
jiggered CURSING
jiggered INTOXICATED - ALCOHOL
jillion AMOUNT - LARGE
jingle DRINKING - BOUT
jingle INTOXICATED - ALCOHOL
jingle TELEPHONE
jingled INTOXICATED - ALCOHOL
jingler DRUNKARD
jitters DELIRIUM TREMENS
jive talk SLANG
jive turkey PEOPLE - STUPID
jive DECEPTION
jive DRUGS - MARIJUANA
jive IMPUDENCE
jive INSINCERITY
jive-ass SILLINESS
jivestick DRUGS - MARIJUANA
job DRUNKARD
job THEFT
jobber DEFECATION
jobber GADGET
jober as a sudge SOBRIETY
jock CLOTHING
jock SPORTS
jock(e)y DRUGS
jockstrap SPORTS

Joe Blow ORDINARY
Joe Citizen ORDINARY
Joe College STUDENT
Joe Schmo PEOPLE - STUPID
Joe Six-pack ORDINARY
joe COFFEE
John Doe ORDINARY
John Hancock SIGNATURE
John Q. Public ORDINARY
john DUPE
john MAN
john PROSTITUTION
john TOILET
Johnnie-come-lately NEW
John(ny) Law POLICE
Johnny-be-good POLICE
johnson PENIS
johnson THING
joined at the hip PROXIMITY
joint DRUGS - MARIJUANA
joint JAIL
joint LOCATION - UNDESIRABLE
joint PENIS
joint STORE - LIQUOR
joint TOBACCO
joke JOKING
joker MAN
jollies THRILL
jollop DRINKING - PORTION
jolly INTOXICATED - ALCOHOL
jolly-well CERTAINTY
jolt DRINKING - PORTION
jolt DRUGS - PORTION
jolt INTOXICATION - ONSET
jolt POWER - ALCOHOL
jones ADDICTION
jones PENIS
jones THING
joog VIOLENCE
josh JOKING
joy flakes DRUGS - COCAINE
joy juice ALCOHOL
joy ride EVENT
joy ride INTOXICATION
joy ride MURDER
joy water ALCOHOL - STRONG
joybox MUSIC
jug (up) DRINKING - EXCESS
jug wine ALCOHOL - WINE
jug ALCOHOL
jug DRUGS - PORTION
jug JAIL
jug VEINS

killer weed DRUGS - PCP
killer DRUGS - MARIJUANA
killer EXCELLENCE
killer JOKING
killer-diller EXCELLENCE
killing SUCCESS
killjoy PEOPLE - NEGATIVE
kilobucks MONEY
King Grod MAN - NEGATIVE
King Kong pills DRUGS - BARBITURATE
kingpin CRIMINAL
kink PEOPLE - SEX
kink PEOPLE - STRANGE
kinky SEX
kinky STRANGE
kip SLEEP
kipe THEFT
kiper THIEF
kiss of death ENDINGS
kiss off DEATH
kiss off DISMISSAL
kiss someone off MURDER
kiss someone's ass FLATTERY
kiss something good-bye LOSS
kiss something off IGNORE
kiss the dust FALL
kiss the porcelain god VOMIT
kiss up to someone FLATTERY
kiss-ass MEEKNESS
kisser MOUTH
kissyface KISS
kit and caboodle EVERYTHING
kite CHECKS
kite DRUGS - USER
kited INTOXICATED - ALCOHOL
kitsch POPULAR
kitschy TRIVIAL
klepto THIEF
kludge COMPUTER
kludgy COMPUTER
klutz PEOPLE - STUPID
klutzy STUPIDITY
knee-deep in something ABUNDANCE
knee-high to a grasshopper SIZE
knee-jerk AUTOMATIC
knock around TRAVEL
knock around WASTE - TIME
knock back a drink DRINKING -
   PORTION
Knock it off! SILENCE
knock off (work) QUIT
knock one over DRINKING - PORTION
knock some heads together SCOLDING

knock someone dead PERFORMANCE
knock someone off MURDER
knock someone out SURPRISE
knock someone some skin GREETING
knock someone up PREGNANCY
knock someone's block off VIOLENCE
knock someone's socks off SURPRISE
knock something down DRINKING -
   PORTION
knock something down EARN
knock something into a cocked hat
   CRITICISM
knock something off COST
knock something off PRODUCING
knock something off SPEED
knock something together
   PREPARATION
knock the habit QUIT
knock CRITICISM
knockdown drag-out fight FIGHTING
knocked in ARREST
knocked out EXHAUSTION
knocked out INTOXICATED -
   ALCOHOL/DRUGS
knocked out OVERWHELM
knocked up INTOXICATED - ALCOHOL
knocked up PREGNANCY
knocked up VIOLENCE
knockers BREASTS
knockers TESTICLES
knockout AMAZEMENT
knockout EXCITEMENT
knockout PEOPLE - ATTRACTIVE
knothead PEOPLE - STUPID
know all the angles UNDERSTANDING
know from something KNOWLEDGE
know shit from Shinola
   UNDERSTANDING
know the score UNDERSTANDING
know what's what UNDERSTANDING
know where it's at UNDERSTANDING
know where one is coming from
   UNDERSTANDING
know which end is up KNOWLEDGEABLE
know-how UNDERSTANDING
know-it-all PEOPLE - NEGATIVE
knowledge-box HEAD
knuckle down (to something)
   BEGINNINGS
knuckle sandwich VIOLENCE
knuckle under (to someone or
   something) YIELD
knuckle-dragger MAN - STRONG

knucklehead PEOPLE - STUPID
KO SPORTS - BOXING
KOed INTOXICATED - ALCOHOL/DRUGS
KOed UNCONSCIOUSNESS
Kojak POLICE
kong ALCOHOL - STRONG
kook PEOPLE - STRANGE
kookish STRANGE
kosher ALCOHOL
kosher SATISFACTORY
kvetch COMPLAINT
kvetch PEOPLE - NEGATIVE
L7 DULL
L7 PEOPLE - DULL
label mate MUSIC
labonza BELLY
labonza BUTTOCKS
labonza STOMACH
lace ALCOHOL
lace DRUGS - ADDED
lace MONEY
lacy FEMININE
ladies' room TOILET
lady bear POLICE
Lady Snow DRUGS - COCAINE
ladyfinger DRUGS - MARIJUANA
lady-killer MAN - SEX
lah-di-dah INSULT
lah-di-dah RELAX
laid back CALM
laid back INTOXICATED - ALCOHOL/DRUGS
laid out CLOTHING
laid out DEAD
laid out INTOXICATED - ALCOHOL/DRUGS
laid out VIOLENCE
laid to the bone INTOXICATED - ALCOHOL
laid COPULATION
laid INTOXICATED - DRUGS
lame duck OFFICER
lame duck POLITICIANS
lame PEOPLE - DULL
lame PEOPLE - STUPID
lame UNDESIRABLE
lamebrain PEOPLE - STUPID
lamebrain STUPIDITY
lamp OBSERVATION
lamps EYES
land a blow COMMUNICATION
land a blow VIOLENCE
land a job EMPLOYMENT
land office business BUSINESS
landowner BODY - DEAD
lap of luxury LUXURY

lapper DRUNKARD
lard ass PEOPLE - FAT
lard POLICE
lardhead PEOPLE - STUPID
lardhead STUPIDITY
last roundup DEATH
last straw FINALITY
latch onto something OBTAIN
latch onto something UNDERSTANDING
Later. GOOD-BYE
lathered INTOXICATED - ALCOHOL
latrine lips PEOPLE - VULGAR
latrine rumor GOSSIP
latrine wireless GOSSIP
lats MUSCLES
laugh at the carpet VOMIT
laughing academy MENTAL
laughing soup ALCOHOL - CHAMPAGNE
launch (one's lunch) VOMIT
launder CRIME
laundry list LIST
law POLICE
lawn DRUGS - MARIJUANA
lay a (heavy) trip on someone
 CONFUSION
lay a (heavy) trip on someone
 CRITICISM
lay a (heavy) trip on someone GUILT
lay an egg ERROR
lay an egg FAILURE
lay an egg LAUGHTER
lay down QUIT
lay it on the line FRANKNESS
lay off (someone or something)
 ANNOYANCE
lay (some) rubber CARS
lay some sweet lines on someone
 ROMANCE
lay someone out in lavender SCOLDING
lay someone out DEATH
lay someone out SCOLDING
lay someone out VIOLENCE
lay something on someone GUILT
lay something on someone
 PRESENTATION
lay something out EXPLANATION
lay something out SPENDING
lay COPULATION
lay PEOPLE - SEX
layout LODGING
layout PLANNING
layout SCHEME
lazybones WASTE - TIME

LBO ABBREVIATIONS
lead poisoning DEATH
leadfoot DRIVING
leaf DRUGS - COCAINE
lean and mean EFFICIENCY
leapers DRUGS - AMPHETAMINE
leave someone cold EMOTION - LACKING
leeky store STORE - LIQUOR
leerics MUSIC
left-handed monkey wrench TOOL
leg work WORK
legal-beagle LAWYER
legit HONESTY
lemme CONTRACTION
Let her rip! BEGINNINGS
let it all hang out RELAX
let something ride IGNORE
Let's bump this place! DEPART
Let's do lunch (sometime). MEETING
Let's dump. DEPART
Let's have it! EXPLANATION
let's say ESTIMATION
lettuce MONEY
level best EFFORT
level with someone TRUTH
libber WOMAN - NEGATIVE
liberate THEFT
library TOILET
lick and a promise CARELESSNESS
lick something into shape PREPARATION
lickety-split SPEED
licorice stick MUSIC
lid proppers DRUGS - AMPHETAMINE
lid DRUGS - MARIJUANA
lid EYELIDS
lie doggo VISIBILITY - LACKING
lifer TIME - MAXIMUM
LIFO COMPUTER - ABBREVIATION
lift APPEARANCE
lift HEIGHT
lift IMPROVEMENT
lift INTOXICATION - ONSET
lift MEDICAL
lift POWER - ALCOHOL
lift REMOVAL
lift THEFT
lift TRANSPORTATION
light bulb PREGNANCY
light stuff ALCOHOL
light stuff DRUGS
light EYES
light INTOXICATED - ALCOHOL
light POLICE

lighten up (on someone or something)
PRESSURE - REDUCE
lights out DEATH
lights out TIME - SLEEP
lightweight PEOPLE - NEGATIVE
lightweight TRIVIAL
like a bat out of hell SPEED
like a million (dollars) EXCELLENCE
like a ton of bricks PONDEROUS
like crazy ENERGETIC
like death warmed over HORRIBLE
like gangbusters ENERGETIC
Like hell! BELIEF
Like it or lump it! ACCEPTANCE
like nobody's business AMOUNT - MUCH
like stink SPEED
like there was no tomorrow AMOUNT -
MUCH
like, you know EXPRESSION
like EXPRESSION
like TALKING
lily-livered COWARDICE
(limp) dishrag PEOPLE - MEEK
line one's own pocket(s) GREED
line DRUGS - COCAINE
line SEDUCTION
lines SPEECH
lineup POLICE
lingo SPEECH
lion's share PORTION
lip gloss DECEPTION
lip IMPUDENCE
lip KISS
lip LAWYER
LIQ STORE - LIQUOR
liquefied INTOXICATED - ALCOHOL
liquid cork MEDICINE
liquid laugh VOMIT
liquidate MURDER
listen up LISTENING
lit INTOXICATED - ALCOHOL
lit SCHOOL
little black book DATING
little boy blue POLICE
little boys' room TOILET
little girls' room TOILET
(little) pinkie FINGER
(live) wire ENERGETIC
live EXCELLENCE
liveware COMPUTER
Living large. SATISFACTORY
load CARS
load DRINKING - PORTION

load DRUGS - PORTION
load DRUGS - SUPPLY
loaded for bear ANGER
loaded for bear INTOXICATED - ALCOHOL
loaded for bear PREPARATION
loaded question EXAMINATION
loaded remark RESPONSE
loaded to the gills INTOXICATED - ALCOHOL
loaded ALCOHOL
loaded CARS
loaded INTOXICATED - ALCOHOL/DRUGS
loaded WEALTH
local yokel RURAL
loco CRAZINESS
LOL COMPUTER - ABBREVIATION
lollapalooza AMAZEMENT
lollapalooza LYING
lone wolf MAN - NEGATIVE
long arm of the law POLICE
long bread MONEY
long dozen AMOUNT
long knife PEOPLE - NEGATIVE
long knife THIEF
long shot TRY
long story short EXPLANATION
Long time no see. GREETING
longhair CULTURE
longhair MUSIC
longhair PEOPLE - YOUNG
long-tall-Sally WOMAN - TALL
look after number one SELF
Look alive! ALERTNESS
Look who's talking! RECIPROCITY
look-see EXAMINATION
loony bin MENTAL
loony CRAZINESS
loony INTOXICATED - ALCOHOL
loony PEOPLE - CRAZY
looped INTOXICATED - ALCOHOL
loop-legged INTOXICATED - ALCOHOL
loose cannon BOASTING
loose INTOXICATED - ALCOHOL
loot MONEY
Lord love a duck! AMAZEMENT
lorg PEOPLE - STUPID
lose a bundle LOSS
lose (all) one's marbles CRAZINESS
lose it ANGER
lose it VOMIT
lose one's cool ANGER
lose one's grip CONTROL - LACKING
lose one's shirt LOSS

loser FAILURE
losing streak FAILURE
lost cause WORTHLESSNESS
lost in the sauce INTOXICATED - ALCOHOL
lost-and-found badge IDENTIFICATION
Lots of luck! LUCK
loudmouth PEOPLE - NEGATIVE
louse something up FAILURE
louse MAN - NEGATIVE
lousy with someone or something
   AMOUNT - MUCH
lousy UNDESIRABLE
love bombs ROMANCE
(love) handles FAT
Love you! EXCELLENCE
love-in GATHERING
low five GREETING
low rent PEOPLE - NEGATIVE
low rent UNFASHIONABLE
low-blow UNFAIR
lowbrow CULTURE - LACKING
lowbrow NONINTELLECTUAL
lowdown INFORMATION
lowdown UNDESIRABLE
low-key SUBTLE
low-life MEAN
low-life PEOPLE - NEGATIVE
low-res UNPLEASANT
LSD DRUGS - LSD
LT LIFESTYLE
lube FOOD
lubricated INTOXICATED - ALCOHOL
lubrication ALCOHOL
luck of the draw LUCK
luck out LUCK
lucky dog LUCK
lude DRUGS - TRANQUILIZERS
lug MAN - STUPID
lughead PEOPLE - STUPID
lumbo DRUGS - MARIJUANA
lummox PEOPLE - STUPID
Lump it! ANNOYANCE
lump PEOPLE - STUPID
lumpus PEOPLE - STUPID
lum(s) DRUGS - MARIJUANA
lunger MUCUS
lush (up) DRINKING - EXCESS
lush ALCOHOL
lush DRUNKARD
M and Ms DRUGS - BARBITURATE
Ma Bell FINANCIAL
mac out GLUTTONY
mace someone's face AGGRESSIVENESS

macho MAN - STRONG
macho MASCULINE
Mac(k) NICKNAME
mad money MONEY
madam BROTHEL
Madison Avenue ADVERTISING
mag PUBLICATION
maggot PEOPLE - NEGATIVE
maggot TOBACCO
maggot(t)y INTOXICATED - ALCOHOL
magic mushrooms DRUGS -
  MUSHROOMS
magpie CHATTER
(ma)hoska DRUGS
(ma)hoska POWER
main drag LOCATION
main squeeze PEOPLE - IMPORTANT
main squeeze ROMANCE
main stash DRUGS - SUPPLY
major EXCELLENCE
make a boo-boo ERROR
make a bundle EARN
make a federal case out of something
  EXAGGERATION
make a killing EARN
Make a lap! SITTING
make a pig (out of) of oneself
  GLUTTONY
make a score CRIME
make book on something GAMBLING
make for somewhere TRAVEL
make hamburger out of someone or
  something VIOLENCE
make (it) big SUCCESS
make it hot for someone DIFFICULTIES
Make it snappy! HURRY
make it ACHIEVEMENT
make it COPULATION
make like a tree and leave DEPART
make like someone or something
  BEHAVIOR
Make my day! WARNING
Make no mistake (about it)! SINCERITY
make one's bed CHOICE
make oneself scarce DEPART
make out KISS
make out SUCCESS
make someone IDENTIFICATION
make the scene EVENT
make the scene UNDERSTANDING
make tracks DEPART
make waves DIFFICULTIES
make IDENTIFICATION

make SPEED
make TRAVEL
make-out artist MAN - SEX
malark(e)y NONSENSE
mallet POLICE
mama bear POLICE
man on the street ORDINARY
Man! AMAZEMENT
man DRUGS - SELLER
man FRIEND
man POLICE
manicure DRUGS - MARIJUANA
man-size(d) SIZE
map FACE
map MUSIC
marble dome PEOPLE - STUPID
marble orchard CEMETERY
marine (recruit) DRINKING -
  PARAPHERNALIA
mark time WAITING
mark DUPE
marker DEBT
marksman STUDENT
Mary Jane DRUGS - MARIJUANA
mash KISS
mashed INTOXICATED - ALCOHOL
massive EXCELLENCE
massively VERY
maven SKILL
maw KISS
max out LIMITATION
max AMOUNT - MAXIMUM
maxed out EXHAUSTION
maxed out INTOXICATED - ALCOHOL
maxin' RELAX
mayo FOOD
mazuma MONEY
McDoctor(s) MEDICAL
McD's RESTAURANT
McFly PEOPLE - STUPID
McFly STUPIDITY
MCP MAN
meadow muffin EXCREMENT
mean business SERIOUSNESS
mean EXCELLENCE
meany GROUCHY
meat wagon AMBULANCE
meathead PEOPLE - STUPID
meatheaded STUPIDITY
meathooks HANDS
medico DOCTOR
meet MEETING
meeting of the minds AGREEMENT

mega SIZE
megabitch PEOPLE - NEGATIVE
megabucks MONEY
megadork PEOPLE - STUPID
megillah EXPLANATION
mell of a hess TROUBLE
mellow out CALM
mellow out RELAX
mellow INTOXICATED - ALCOHOL/DRUGS
mellow RELAX
meltdown RUINATION
melvin CLOTHING
melvin MAN - UGLY
men in blue POLICE
men's room TOILET
mensch PEOPLE - GOOD
mental giant INTELLIGENCE
mental midget PEOPLE - STUPID
mental MENTAL
mental PEOPLE - STUPID
mep(s) DRUGS - ANALGESIC
merchandise CRIME
merger-mania FINANCIAL
mesc DRUGS - MESCALINE
mesh SYMBOL
meshuga CRAZINESS
mess around (with someone) SEX
mess around (with someone) WASTE -
    TIME
mess around (with something)
    MEDDLE
mess someone or something up
    CONFUSION
mess someone up VIOLENCE
mess someone's face up VIOLENCE
mess up ERROR
mess with someone or something
    MEDDLE
mess EXCREMENT
mess PEOPLE - STUPID
messed up CONFUSION
messed up INTOXICATED -
    ALCOHOL/DRUGS
meth monster DRUGS - USER
meth ALCOHOL - BAD
meth DRUGS - AMPHETAMINE
meth DRUGS - METHADONE
metros POLICE
Mexican breakfast TOBACCO
Mickey D's RESTAURANT
Mickey finished INTOXICATED - ALCOHOL
Mickey (Finn) DRINKING
Mickey (Finn) DRUGS

mickey mouse ears POLICE
mickey mouse habit ADDICTION
mickey mouse DRUGS - LSD
mickey mouse NONSENSE
mickey mouse POLICE
mickey mouse WASTE - TIME
mickey ALCOHOL - WINE
mickey DRINKING - PARAPHERNALIA
mickey DRUGS - TRANQUILIZERS
middle of nowhere WHERE
middlebrow AVERAGE
midi CLOTHING
mifky-pifky (in the bushes)
    COPULATION
milk PERFORMANCE
milled INTOXICATED - ALCOHOL
milquetoast MAN - MEEK
Milwaukee goiter BELLY
mind your own beeswax PRIVACY
mind-bender DRUGS - LSD
mingy GROUCHY
mini CLOTHING
mini SIZE
mink WOMAN
Minnehaha ALCOHOL - CHAMPAGNE
mint EXCELLENCE
mint MONEY
mish-mash CONFUSION
miss the boat ERROR
mitt HANDS
mix it up (with someone) FIGHTING
mixed (up) CONFUSION
mixed (up) INTOXICATED - ALCOHOL
mob CRIME
moby COMPUTER
moby SIZE
mod FASHIONABLE
moist around the edges INTOXICATED -
    ALCOHOL
mojo DRUGS
mojo DRUGS - USER
moldy fig OLD-FASHIONED
mom KINSHIP
mondo VERY
money from home DESIRE
money from home MONEY
money grubber STINGY
money talks INFLUENCE
moneybags WEALTH
moniker NICKNAME
monkey bite KISS
monkey business DISHONESTY
monkey swill ALCOHOL - BAD

monkey talk NONSENSE
monkey wagon ADDICTION
monkey wards STORE
monkey ADDICTION
monkey CHILDREN
monkeyshines MISCHIEF
monolithic INTOXICATED - DRUGS
monster weed DRUGS - MARIJUANA
monster DRUGS
Montezuma's revenge DIARRHEA
monthlies MENSES
moo juice MILK
mooch DRUGS
mooch REQUEST
mooch(er) BEGGING
moocher DRUGS - USER
moolah MONEY
moon BUTTOCKS
moon NAKEDNESS
mooner DRUNKARD
mooner WASTE - TIME
moonlight requisition THEFT
moonlight ALCOHOL - ILLICIT
moonlight EMPLOYMENT
moonlit INTOXICATED - ALCOHOL
moonrock DRUGS
moonshine ALCOHOL
moonshine NONSENSE
moonshiner OCCUPATION
moose WOMAN
mop the floor up with someone
  VIOLENCE
mop DRINKING - BOUT
mop DRUNKARD
mop HAIR
mope DULL
mope MOVEMENT
mopped INTOXICATED - ALCOHOL
mopping-up operation ENDINGS
more than one bargained for AMOUNT
  - MORE
morning after (the night before)
  HANGOVER
mossback OLD-FASHIONED
most EXCELLENCE
mother nature('s) DRUGS - MARIJUANA
mother DRUGS - MARIJUANA
mother DRUGS - USER
motion-lotion FUEL
motor DEPART
Motown CITIES
(mountain) dew ALCOHOL - WHISKEY
mountain dew ALCOHOL - ILLICIT

mouth full of South SPEECH
mouth off IMPUDENCE
mouth off RUDENESS
mouth HANGOVER
mouth-breather PEOPLE - STUPID
mouthful SCOLDING
mouthful TRUTH
mouth(piece) LAWYER
mouthwash ALCOHOL
move on someone SEDUCTION
movers and shakers MANAGE
movies DIARRHEA
moxie ENERGETIC
Mr. Big PEOPLE - IMPORTANT
Mr. Hawkins WIND
Mr. Nice Guy PEOPLE - GOOD
Mr. Right MAN
Mr. Whiskers POLICE
Mrs. Murphy TOILET
MT DRINKING - PARAPHERNALIA
mu DRUGS - MARIJUANA
mucho VERY
muck something up RUINATION
mudbud DRUGS - MARIJUANA
muddled (up) INTOXICATED - ALCOHOL
muddler ALCOHOL
mug shot POLICE
mug FACE
mug THEFT
mug THIEF
mugger THIEF
muggy INTOXICATED - ALCOHOL
mule DRUGS - USER
munch out GLUTTONY
munchies FOOD
munchkin PEOPLE - UNIMPORTANT
mung something up RUINATION
mung NASTY
mung RUINATION
mungy DISGUSTING
murder OVERWHELM
murphy BREASTS
murphy FOOD
musclehead PEOPLE - STUPID
muscleman MAN - MUSCULAR
muscleman MAN - STRONG
mush FACE
mush KISS
mush NONSENSE
mushhead PEOPLE - STUPID
mushmouth TALKING
musical beds SEX
(must) do OBLIGATION

mutant PEOPLE - STUPID
My foot! BELIEF
my man FRIEND
mystery meat FOOD
mystic biscuit DRUGS - PEYOTE
nab ARREST
nab POLICE
nabbed ARREST
nabe MOVIES
nabe NEIGHBORHOOD
nada NOTHING
nag ANNOYANCE
nag HORSE
nail someone to a cross SCOLDING
nail ARREST
nail IDENTIFICATION
nailed ARREST
nailed IDENTIFICATION
nail-em-and-jail-em POLICE
naked truth TRUTH
naked ALCOHOL
Nam COUNTRY
namby-pamby PEOPLE - MEEK
name of the game REALITY
Name your poison. ALCOHOL
narc(o) DRUGS
narc(o) POLICE
nark ANNOYANCE
nark PEOPLE - NEGATIVE
nark TATTLING
narked ANNOYANCE
narky DRUGS
narrow squeak LUCK
natch YES
natural SKILL
natural-born SKILL
nature stop TOILET - USE
nature's call TOILET
nause someone out SICKNESS
naw NO
nay UGLINESS
NBD IMPORTANCE - LACKING
NBT NO
neanderthal MAN - UGLY
near-beer ALCOHOL
Neat! AMAZEMENT
neat EXCELLENCE
Neato (canito)! AMAZEMENT
neb(bish) PEOPLE - DULL
Nebraska sign DEATH
necessary MONEY
neck and neck AMOUNT
neck KISS

needle candy DRUGS
needle ANNOYANCE
nerd magnet WOMAN - NEGATIVE
nerd mobile CARS
nerd pack WRITING -PARAPHERNALIA
nerd PEOPLE - DULL
Nerts! ANNOYANCE
nervous Nellie ANXIETY
nervy ANXIETY
nervy COURAGE
nest egg MONEY
net result RESULTS
never mind UNIMPORTANT
New York's finest POLICE
newshound REPORTER
newt PEOPLE - DULL
nibble RESPONSE
nice meeting you GOOD-BYE
nice talking to you GOOD-BYE
nick ARREST
nick OBTAIN
nick THEFT
nicked ARREST
nickel and dime someone (to death)
  COST
nifty EXCELLENCE
night person NIGHT
nimrod PEOPLE - STUPID
nineteenth hole TAVERN
nine-to-five EMPLOYMENT
nip and tuck PROXIMITY
nip ALCOHOL
nip THEFT
nipped INTOXICATED - ALCOHOL
nippers POLICE; PARAPHERNALIA
nitery DRINKING - PLACE
nit-picker CRITICISM
nit-picking CRITICISM
nitty-gritty ESSENCE
nitwit PEOPLE - STUPID
nix NO
nix NOTHING
nix REFUSAL
no bargain UNDESIRABLE
no big deal SATISFACTORY
no can do NO
no dice NO
no earthly reason REASON - LACKING
no end of something ABUNDANCE
No fair! UNFAIR
no go UNDESIRABLE
no great shakes UNDESIRABLE
no holds barred LIMITATION - LACKING

No kidding! BELIEF
No lie! BELIEF
no sale NO
No Shinola! BELIEF
no show AVIATION
no soap NO
no stress SATISFACTORY
no sweat SATISFACTORY
No way! NO
no-account PEOPLE - WORTHLESS
no-account WORTHLESSNESS
nobody PEOPLE - UNIMPORTANT
no-brainer EASY
no-brow PEOPLE - STUPID
nodded out INTOXICATED - DRUGS
no-good PEOPLE - WORTHLESS
no-good WORTHLESSNESS
no-goodnik PEOPLE - WORTHLESS
noid MENTAL
noise DRUGS - HEROIN
noise NONSENSE
non compos CRAZINESS
non compos INTOXICATED - ALCOHOL
none of someone's beeswax PRIVACY
no-no FORBIDDEN
noodle HEAD
nope NO
nose (candy) DRUGS
nose habit ADDICTION
nose hit DRUGS
nose job MEDICAL
nose-burner DRUGS - MARIJUANA
nosedive DECLINE
nose-lunger MUCUS
nose-warmer TOBACCO - PARAPHERNALIA
nosh on something EATING
nosh EATING
nosh FOOD
nosher EATING
nosy parker MEDDLE
not a chance NO
not all there CRAZINESS
not cricket UNFAIR
not give a hoot CARING - LACKING
not grow on trees AMOUNT - SMALL
not just whistling Dixie NONSENSE -
  LACKING
not know beans (about something)
  KNOWLEDGE - LACKING
not know from nothing STUPIDITY
not play with a full deck CRAZINESS
Not to worry. SATISFACTORY
Not too shabby! UNDESIRABLE

not too shabby EXCELLENCE
not worth a damn WORTHLESSNESS
not worth a plugged nickel
  WORTHLESSNESS
not worth beans WORTHLESSNESS
Not! NO
notch CALCULATION
Nothing doing! NO
Nothing to it! EASY
nothing to sneeze at AMOUNT
nothing to write home about
  UNIMPORTANT
nothing upstairs STUPIDITY
now generation MODERN
Now what? WHAT
Now you're talking! ENCOURAGEMENT
nowhere UNDESIRABLE
no-win situation FAILURE
nudge ANNOYANCE
nudge PEOPLE - NEGATIVE
nudie NAKEDNESS
nudnik PEOPLE - NEGATIVE
nuke oneself APPEARANCE
nuke COOKING
nuke RUINATION
nuke WEAPONRY
nuker APPLIANCE
numbed out INTOXICATED - DRUGS
number crunching CALCULATION
number one BEST
number one SELF
number DRUGS - MARIJUANA
number PERFORMANCE
number WOMAN - ATTRACTIVE
number-cruncher ACCOUNTANT
number-cruncher COMPUTER
numero uno BEST
numero uno SELF
nummy TASTE
nurts NONSENSE
nut up CRAZINESS
nut FAN
nut HEAD
nut PEOPLE - CRAZY
nutcake PEOPLE - STUPID
nuthouse MENTAL
nutpick DOCTOR
nuts and bolts BASIC
nuts and bolts SCHOOL
Nuts to you! ANNOYANCE
Nuts! ANNOYANCE
nuts CRAZINESS
nuts TESTICLES

nutter PEOPLE - CRAZY
nuttery MENTAL
nutty as a fruitcake CRAZINESS
nutty STUPIDITY
nybble COMPUTER
oak(s) SATISFACTORY
oasis STORE - LIQUOR
oater MOVIES
ob OBVIOUS
obliterated INTOXICATED - ALCOHOL
obno(c) DISGUSTING
OD DEATH
OD DRUGS
OD DRUGS - USER
odd bird PEOPLE - STRANGE
oddball PEOPLE - STRANGE
oddball STRANGE
odd-bod BODY
odd-bod PEOPLE - STRANGE
odds-on GAMBLING
Of all the nerve! AMAZEMENT
off base WRONG
off one's chump CRAZINESS
off one's nut CRAZINESS
off one's nut INTOXICATED - ALCOHOL
off one's rocker CRAZINESS
off one's trolley CRAZINESS
off the hook FREEDOM
off the track ERROR
off the wagon ADDICTION - AGAIN
off the wagon ALCOHOL
off DEATH
off INTOXICATED - ALCOHOL/DRUGS
off MURDER
offbeat STRANGE
off-brand cigarette DRUGS - MARIJUANA
off-color VULGAR
off-the-shelf AVAILABLE
off-the-wall STRANGE
Oh, boy! EXCELLENCE
Oh, yeah? CHALLENGE
OIC COMPUTER - ABBREVIATION
oil it STUDY
oiled INTOXICATED - ALCOHOL/DRUGS
oilhead DRUNKARD
oink out GLUTTONY
oink POLICE
oinker PEOPLE - FAT
OJ FOOD
OK APPROVAL
OK SATISFACTORY
okey-dokey YES
old flame LOVER

old fogey OLD-FASHIONED
old girl WOMAN - OLD
old hand (at something) EXPERIENCE
old-hat OLD-FASHIONED
old heave-ho EJECTION
old lady KINSHIP
old lady KINSHIP
old lady WOMAN - FRIEND
old man KINSHIP
old man KINSHIP
old man MAN - FRIEND
old man PEOPLE - IMPORTANT
old one-two RUINATION
old one-two VIOLENCE
old soldier ALCOHOL
old soldier TOBACCO
oldie but goodie OLD
old-timer PEOPLE - OLD
on a roll SUCCESS
on a shoestring CHEAPNESS
on a tight leash ADDICTION
on a tight leash CONTROL
on easy street LIFESTYLE
on fire ATTRACTIVENESS
on fire ENTHUSIASM
on ice RESERVE
on it EXCELLENCE
on one's high horse BEHAVIOR
on one's (or its) last legs ENDINGS
on one's own hook INDEPENDENCE
on someone's case CRITICISM
on someone's tail PURSUIT
on someone's watch RESPONSIBLE
on tap ALCOHOL
on tap AVAILABLE
on the back burner WAITING
on the ball KNOWLEDGEABLE
on the bandwagon FASHIONABLE
on the beam AVIATION
on the beam CORRECT
on the beam INTELLIGENCE
on the beam INTOXICATED - DRUGS
on the bird TELEVISION
on the bleeding edge TECHNOLOGY
on the blink INTOXICATED - ALCOHOL
on the blink NONFUNCTIONING
on the button PRECISION
on the chopping block THREATENING
on the double SPEED
on the fly CONCURRENTLY
on the fritz INTOXICATED - ALCOHOL
on the fritz NONFUNCTIONING
on the juice ALCOHOL

on the junk ADDICTION
on the lam ESCAPE
on the level HONESTY
on the make AMBITION
on the mojo ADDICTION
on the money PRECISION
on the natch ADDICTION - END
on the needle ADDICTION
on the nose PRECISION
on the outs (with someone)
  DISAGREEMENT
on the pill MEDICINE
on the prowl SEARCH
on the rag GROUCHY
on the rag MENSES
on the road TRAVEL
on the rocks ALCOHOL
on the rocks RUINATION
on the run CRIME
on the run MOVEMENT
on the safe side SAFETY
on the same wavelength
  UNDERSTANDING
on the sauce ALCOHOL
on the shelf DELAY
on the shelf SOCIAL
on the side ADDITIONAL
on the side AFFAIR
on the skids DECLINE
on the sly DECEPTION
on the squiff ALCOHOL
on the street COMMERCE
on the street DRUGS - USE
on the street INFORMATION
on the street PROSTITUTION
on the take BRIBERY
on the tank ALCOHOL
on the up-and-up HONESTY
on the wagon SOBRIETY
on the warpath ANGER
On your bike! DEPART
once and for all PERMANENCE
once in a blue moon RARELY
once over lightly CARELESSNESS
once-over lightly EXAMINATION
once-over EXAMINATION
one and one DRUGS - USE
one and only LOVER
one brick shy of a load STUPIDITY
one for the road ALCOHOL
one jump ahead of someone or
  something ANTICIPATION
one of the faithful DRUNKARD

one smart apple INTELLIGENCE
one too many ALCOHOL
one UNIQUENESS
one-horse town LOCATION
one-man show DISPLAY
one-man show PERFORMANCE
one-night stand AFFAIR
one-night stand PERFORMANCE
one's bag SKILL
one's best shot TRY
one-track mind OBSESSION
only way to go CHOICE
on-target PRECISION
onto a good thing BENEFIT
onto someone or something
  AWARENESS
oodles AMOUNT - MUCH
oof PAIN
oof POWER - ALCOHOL
oomph APPEALING
oomph ENERGETIC
open (up) one's kimono REVEAL
OPs TOBACCO
or what? QUESTION
oreo PEOPLE - BLACK
org BUSINESS
org INTOXICATION - ONSET
organic EXCELLENCE
ork-orks DELIRIUM TREMENS
O-sign SYMBOL - DEATH
ossifer POLICE
ossified INTOXICATED - ALCOHOL/DRUGS
Otis DRUNKARD
Otis INTOXICATED - ALCOHOL
OTL SILLINESS
OTOH COMPUTER - ABBREVIATION
out cold INTOXICATED - ALCOHOL
out cold UNCONSCIOUSNESS
out in left field WRONG
out like a light INTOXICATED - ALCOHOL
out like a light UNCONSCIOUSNESS
out of it AWARENESS - LACKING
out of it INTOXICATED - ALCOHOL/DRUGS
out of kilter NONFUNCTIONING
out of kilter POSITION
out of left field SUDDEN
out of line UNEXPECTED
out of luck LUCK - LACKING
out of one's skull INTOXICATED -
  ALCOHOL
out of sight COST
out of sight INTOXICATED -
  ALCOHOL/DRUGS

pasted DEFEAT
pasted INTOXICATED - ALCOHOL/DRUGS
pasting DEFEAT
patsy DUPE
patter of tiny feet CHILDREN
paw FLIRTATION
paw HANDS
paw TOUCH
pay a call TOILET - USE
pay one's dues (to society) PUNISHMENT
pay one's dues WORK
payola BRIBERY
PDQ SPEED
peach EXCELLENCE
peachy (keen) EXCELLENCE
peanut head PEOPLE - STRANGE
peanuts MONEY
peckish HUNGER
pecks MUSCLES
pee'd off ANGER
pee'd INTOXICATED - ALCOHOL
peel CLOTHING
peep NOISE
peepers EYES
peg someone GOSSIP
peg-leg DISABLED
pen JAIL
pencil-pusher BUREAUCRAT
penny POLICE
penny-ante CHEAPNESS
penny-pincher STINGY
peonied INTOXICATED - ALCOHOL
people-watching OBSERVATION
pep pill DRUGS - AMPHETAMINE
pep talk ENCOURAGEMENT
pepped (up) INTOXICATED - ALCOHOL
pepper-upper DRUGS - AMPHETAMINE
peppy ENERGETIC
Period! FINALITY
perk BENEFIT
perked (up) INTOXICATED - ALCOHOL
perky ENERGETIC
perp CRIMINAL
perpetrate DECEPTION
persuader WEAPONRY
pesky ANNOYANCE
pet peeve COMPLAINT
Peter Jay POLICE
peter out EXHAUSTION
petrified INTOXICATED - ALCOHOL
petting-party PARTY
PFD DATING
PG PREGNANCY

PHAT ATTRACTIVENESS
phazed INTOXICATED - DRUGS
phedinkus NONSENSE
phfft DEAD
phfft INTOXICATED - ALCOHOL
Philly CITIES
phony as a three-dollar bill FALSE
phony FALSE
phony TRICK
phooey DISGUSTING
phooey NONSENSE
phumfed INTOXICATED - DRUGS
phutz DECEPTION
pick up on something ALERTNESS
pickled INTOXICATED - ALCOHOL
picklepuss FACE
pickler DRUNKARD
pick-me-up STIMULANT
pickup ARREST
pickup ENGINE
pickup INCREASE
pickup PEOPLE - SEX
pickup STIMULANT
pickup SUDDEN
picky CHOICE
picky COMPLAINT
picnic PLEASURE
piddle (around) WASTE - TIME
piddle URINATION
piddler WASTE - TIME
piddling AMOUNT - SMALL
pie in the sky HOPE
piece of cake EASY
piece (of the action) SHARING
piece HAIR
piece WEAPONRY
piece WOMAN - ATTRACTIVE
pie-eyed AMAZEMENT
pie-eyed INTOXICATED - ALCOHOL
piffed DEAD
piffed INTOXICATED - ALCOHOL
piffle BELIEF
piffle NONSENSE
piffled INTOXICATED - ALCOHOL
piff(l)icated INTOXICATED - ALCOHOL
pig heaven POLICE
pig out GLUTTONY
pig PEOPLE - FAT
pig PEOPLE - NEGATIVE
pig PEOPLE - WHITE
pig POLICE
pig WOMAN - FAT
pigeon DUPE

pigeon WOMAN - ATTRACTIVE
pigeon-eyed INTOXICATED - ALCOHOL
pighead PEOPLE - STUPID
pigheaded STUBBORNNESS
pigmobile POLICE
pigpen SYMBOL
piker LAZY
piker STINGY
pile MONEY
pileup ACCIDENT
pilfered INTOXICATED - ALCOHOL
pill CONTRACEPTION
pill DRUGS - PORTION
pill SPORTS - FOOTBALL
pill TOBACCO
pillhead DRUGS - USER
pillowed PREGNANCY
pill-popper DRUGS - USER
pill-pusher DOCTOR
pimp MAN
pimpish FLAMBOYANT
pimpmobile CARS
pimpstick TOBACCO
pin someone's ears back SCOLDING
pin someone's ears back VIOLENCE
pin LEGS
pin PEOPLE - IMPORTANT
pinch hitter SPORTS - BASEBALL
pinch hitter SUBSTITUTE
pinch AMOUNT - SMALL
pinch ARREST
pinch THEFT
pinched ARREST
pink elephants DELIRIUM TREMENS
pink slip DISMISSAL
pinked INTOXICATED - ALCOHOL
pinko COMMUNIST
pink-slipped DISMISSAL
pinned ARREST
pinstriper BUSINESS
pint-sized SIZE
PIP PEOPLE
pip PIMPLES
pipe down SILENCE
pipe SCHOOL
pipped (up) INTOXICATED - ALCOHOL
pipsqueak MAN - MEEK
piss elegant ELEGANCE
piss factory TAVERN
piss someone off ANGER
piss URINATION
piss-ant around BEHAVIOR
piss-ant PEOPLE - UNIMPORTANT

piss-ant UNIMPORTANT
piss-poor UNDESIRABLE
pissed (off) ANGER
pissed INTOXICATED - ALCOHOL
pistol ENERGETIC
pit stop HYGIENE
pit stop TOILET - USE
PITA COMPUTER - ABBREVIATION
pitch a bitch COMPLAINT
pitch in (and help) ASSISTANCE
pitch (the) woo KISS
pits ARMPITS
pits DEPRESSION
pits UNDESIRABLE
pix PHOTOGRAPHY
pixilated CONFUSION
pixilated INTOXICATED - ALCOHOL
pizzazz EXCITEMENT
PJs CLOTHING
plant something on someone CONCEAL
plant SPYING
plant VIOLENCE
plastered to the wall INTOXICATED -
   ALCOHOL
plastered INTOXICATED - ALCOHOL
plastic punk FALSE
plastic COMMERCE
plastic FALSE
platter MUSIC
platter SPORTS - BASEBALL
play around (with someone) AFFAIR
play around (with someone)
   DECEPTION
play around (with someone) WASTE -
   TIME
play ball (with someone) COOPERATION
play fast and loose (with someone or
   something) CARELESSNESS
play for keeps PERMANENCE
play freeze-out TEMPERATURE
play hardball (with someone)
   AGGRESSIVENESS
play hell with someone or something
   DIFFICULTIES
play hooky ABSENCE
play in the big leagues IMPORTANCE
play it cool CALM
play someone for a fool BEHAVIOR
play the dozens INSULT
play tonsil hockey KISS
play with fire DANGER
play FINANCIAL
play SCHEME

pleasantly plastered INTOXICATED - ALCOHOL
plonk ALCOHOL
plonked (up) INTOXICATED - ALCOHOL
plonko DRUNKARD
plootered INTOXICATED - ALCOHOL
plop NOISE
plop PLACEMENT
plop SITTING
plotzed INTOXICATED - ALCOHOL
plowed (under) INTOXICATED - ALCOHOL/DRUGS
pluck ALCOHOL
plug ALCOHOL
plug PROMOTION
plug TOBACCO
plugged in DRUGS - USE
plugola BRIBERY
plug-ugly UGLINESS
plum REWARD
plumb loco CRAZINESS
PMJI COMPUTER - ABBREVIATION
Podunk CITIES
Podunk RURAL
poindexter PEOPLE - DULL
point man MANAGE
point man SPORTS
pointy-head INTELLIGENCE
poison pill FINANCIAL
poison ALCOHOL
poison UNDESIRABLE
poke COPULATION
poke DRUGS - PORTION
poky INEFFICIENT
poky JAIL
pol POLITICIANS
polecat PEOPLE - NEGATIVE
polished (up) INTOXICATED - ALCOHOL
polluted INTOXICATED - ALCOHOL/DRUGS
pond scum PEOPLE - NEGATIVE
poo ALCOHOL
poo DEFECATION
poo EXCREMENT
poo NONSENSE
pooch DOG
poohead PEOPLE - NEGATIVE
poo(h)-poo(h) RIDICULE
pool-hopping BEHAVIOR - BAD
poop out EXHAUSTION
poop sheet INFORMATION
poop DEFECATION
poop EXCREMENT
poop INFORMATION

pooped (out) EXHAUSTION
pooped (out) INTOXICATED - ALCOHOL
pooper-scooper EXCREMENT
poophead PEOPLE - STUPID
poopied INTOXICATED - ALCOHOL
poor-mouth COMPLAINT
poor-mouth CRITICISM
pop for something GENEROSITY
pop off ANGER
pop off DEATH
pop off DEPART
pop off INTERRUPTION
pop one's cork ANGER
pop (some) tops ALCOHOL
pop the question NUPTIALS
pop wine ALCOHOL
pop DRUGS - USE
pop MUSIC
pop POPULAR
pop TRY
pop VIOLENCE
pop-eyed INTOXICATED - ALCOHOL
popped ARREST
popped INTOXICATED - ALCOHOL/DRUGS
popper ALCOHOL
popper DRUGS
popper WEAPONRY
popping HAPPENING
poppycock NONSENSE
pops KINSHIP
popskull ALCOHOL
pork out GLUTTONY
pork COPULATION
pork POLICE
porker PEOPLE - FAT
porky FAT
posse GROUP
pot boiler PUBLICATION
pot hound DOG
pot party PARTY - DRUGS
pot ALCOHOL
pot CHARITY
pot DRINKING
pot DRUGS - MARIJUANA
pot MONEY
pot TOILET
potato soup ALCOHOL - VODKA
potato HEAD
potatohead PEOPLE - STUPID
potbelly BELLY
potshot CRITICISM
potty mouth PEOPLE - VULGAR
potty CRAZINESS

potty TOILET
potty TOILET - USE
pound a beer ALCOHOL
pound one's ear SLEEP
pound someone's head in VIOLENCE
pound something out MUSIC
pound something out TYPING
pound ALCOHOL
pounder POLICE
pounds MONEY
pour cold water on something
  CONCLUSION
powder monkey OCCUPATION
powder one's nose TOILET - USE
powder room TOILET
powder up DRINKING - EXCESS
powdered (up) INTOXICATED - ALCOHOL
power hitter SPORTS - BASEBALL
power tool STUDENT
powerhouse MAN - STRONG
pow-wow MEETING
pratfall ACCIDENT
prat(t) BUTTOCKS
pray to the porcelain god VOMIT
prayerbones KNEES
preemie CHILDREN
preg PREGNANCY
prelims SCHOOL
preppie STUDENT
preserved INTOXICATED - ALCOHOL
press (the) flesh GREETING
pretty penny MONEY
pretty VERY
prexy OFFICER
pric(e)y COST
primed INTOXICATED - ALCOHOL/DRUGS
primo EXCELLENCE
Prince Albert DRUGS - MARIJUANA
prior ARREST
private eye DETECTIVE
privy TOILET
pro PROSTITUTION
pro SKILL
prod REMIND
prof PROFESSOR
(pro)file DISPLAY
pronto IMMEDIATELY
prosty PROSTITUTION
pseudo FALSE
psych out ANXIETY
psych someone out UNDERSTANDING
psych someone up PREPARATION
psyched (out) EXCITEMENT

psyched (out) INTOXICATED -
  ALCOHOL/DRUGS
psyched (up) PREPARATION
psycho PEOPLE - CRAZY
ptomaine-domain RESTAURANT
puddinghead PEOPLE - STUPID
puddle jumper AVIATION
puff DRINKING - EXCESS
puffer TOBACCO
puggled EXHAUSTION
puggled INTOXICATED - ALCOHOL
pug-ugly PEOPLE - UGLY
pug-ugly UGLINESS
Puh-leez! AMAZEMENT
puke hole MOUTH
puke hole TAVERN
puke hole TOILET
puke PEOPLE - NEGATIVE
puke VOMIT
pukes SICKNESS
pukey DISGUSTING
pukish SICKNESS
pull a boner ERROR
pull a fast one TRICK
pull a job THEFT
pull an attitude HAUGHTINESS
pull down an amount of money EARN
pull jive ALCOHOL
pull one's punches CRITICISM
pull one's punches SPORTS - BOXING
pull out all the stops AGGRESSIVENESS
pull someone's leg TEASING
pull something off ACHIEVEMENT
pull the plug (on someone or
  something) CONCLUSION
pull ALCOHOL
pull TOBACCO
pummelled INTOXICATED - ALCOHOL
pump ship URINATION
pump ship VOMIT
pump (some) iron EXERCISE
pump (someone) up EXCITEMENT
pump something up EXERCISE
pump HEART
pump MUSCLE
pump PERSUASION
pumped (up) READY
pumped PREGNANCY
punch someone out VIOLENCE
punch someone's lights out VIOLENCE
punch-drunk STUPIDITY
punk out COWARDICE
punk CRIMINAL

punk MAN - NEGATIVE
punk MUSIC
punk UNDESIRABLE
punker PEOPLE - STRANGE
punt TRY
puppy love ROMANCE
puppy PEOPLE - MEEK
puppy THING
pure and simple ESSENCE
purr (like a cat) ENGINE
push money COMMERCE
push off DEPART
push AGE
push DRUGS
push PROMOTION
pushed ADDICTION
pushed INTOXICATED - ALCOHOL
pusher DRUGS - USER
pushing up daisies DEAD
pushy AGGRESSIVENESS
puss FACE
pussycat MAN - MEEK
pussycat WOMAN - FRIEND
pussyfoot (around) CAUTION
put a con on someone DECEPTION
put a damper on something REDUCTION
put a smile on someone's face
    HAPPINESS
put balls on something POWER
put on the dog EXTRAVAGANCE
put on the feedbag EATING
put one's nose in (where it's not
    wanted) MEDDLE
put some distance between someone
    and someone or something PROXIMITY
put someone away PUNISHMENT
put someone away VIOLENCE
put someone on DECEPTION
put someone on DRUGS
put someone or something out of the
    way SOLUTION
put someone out of the way MURDER
put someone to bed with a shovel
    MURDER
put someone up LODGING
put someone's nose out of joint INSULT
put something away EATING
put something on the street
    PROMOTION
Put that in your pipe and smoke it!
    THINKING
put the arm on someone ARREST
put the arm on someone PRESSURE

put the bite on someone REQUEST
put the chill on someone IGNORE
put the finger on someone
    IDENTIFICATION
put the kibosh on something STOPPING
put the moves on someone SEDUCTION
put the pedal to the metal SPEED
put the screws on someone PRESSURE
put the skids under someone or
    something FAILURE
put to bed with a shovel DEAD
put to bed with a shovel INTOXICATED -
    ALCOHOL
put to it DIFFICULTIES
Put up or shut up! SILENCE
Put your money where your mouth is!
    CHALLENGE
put-down INSULT
putrid INTOXICATED - ALCOHOL
putt-putt CARS
puttyhead PEOPLE - STUPID
put-up job DECEPTION
putz around WASTE - TIME
putz PENIS
putz PEOPLE - STUPID
Q ALCOHOL
Q-sign MOUTH
quack DOCTOR
quaff a brew ALCOHOL
quail WOMAN - SEX
qual QUALITATIVE
quality Joe MAN - GOOD
quant FINANCIAL
quant QUANTITATIVE
quarterback MANAGE
quartzed INTOXICATED - ALCOHOL
Que pasa? GREETING
queen GAY
queer as a three-dollar bill GAY
queer fish PEOPLE - STRANGE
queer for something DESIRE
queer ALCOHOL
queer FALSE
queer GAY
queer INTOXICATED - ALCOHOL
queer RUINATION
queer-beer ALCOHOL
queer-beer GAY
queer-beer PEOPLE - STRANGE
queered INTOXICATED - ALCOHOL
quencher ALCOHOL
quick buck EARN
quick fix SOLUTION

quick fix TEMPORARY
quick one ALCOHOL
quick-and-dirty CARELESSNESS
quicker than hell SPEED
quimp PEOPLE - STRANGE
quit while one is ahead QUIT
quote, unquote TALKING
R&R RELAX
rabbit food FOOD
rabbit punch VIOLENCE
rack (out) SLEEP
rack up something EARN
rack up something RUINATION
rack time SLEEP
rack up INTOXICATED - ALCOHOL
rack BED
racked (up) INTOXICATED -
ALCOHOL/DRUGS
racket DECEPTION
racket EMPLOYMENT
racket NOISE
rad EXCELLENCE
rad PEOPLE - STRANGE
radical EXCELLENCE
radioland BROADCASTING
rag on someone ANNOYANCE
rag out CLOTHING
rag CLOTHING
rag CLOTHING
rag NEWSPAPER
rage FASHIONABLE
rage PARTY
ragtop CARS
ragweed DRUGS - MARIJUANA
rah-rah ENTHUSIASM
railroad tracks SCARS
railroad tracks TEETH
rails DRUGS - COCAINE
rain on someone's parade
DISCOURAGEMENT
rain pitchforks RAIN
rainbow LEGS
raise a stink (about someone or
something) COMPLAINT
raise Cain TROUBLE
raise hell DRINKING - EXCESS
raise hell TROUBLE
raise the devil (with someone)
SCOLDING
raise the devil (with something)
TROUBLE
rake something in SUCCESS
rally EVENT

ralph something up VOMIT
ralph VOMIT
ram something down someone's throat
FORCE
rambo(ize) RUINATION
rammy AROUSAL
ramrod MANAGE
randy AROUSAL
rank and file ORDINARY
rank on someone GOSSIP
rank someone (out) SCOLDING
rank HARASSMENT
rap session TALKING
(rap) sheet POLICE
rap CHATTER
rap POLICE
rap SEDUCTION
rare bird PEOPLE - STRANGE
rare old time ENJOYMENT
raring to go EAGERNESS
rasty UGLINESS
rat around WASTE - TIME
rat fink TATTLING
rat (on someone) TATTLING
rat out QUIT
rat race WORK
rat PEOPLE - NEGATIVE
ratchet-mouth TALKING
rathole LIMITATION - LACKING
rathole LOCATION - UNDESIRABLE
Rats! DISGUSTING
rats DELIRIUM TREMENS
rattlebones PEOPLE - THIN
rattlebrain PEOPLE - STUPID
rattled CONFUSION
rattled INTOXICATED - ALCOHOL
rattle-trap CARS
rattling EXCELLENCE
raunch someone out DISGUSTING
raunchy INTOXICATED - ALCOHOL
raunchy RUDENESS
raunchy SICKNESS
raunchy VULGAR
rave PARTY
raw deal UNFAIR
raw ALCOHOL
raw EXPERIENCE - LACKING
raw VULGAR
rays SUNSHINE
razz HARASSMENT
razzle-dazzle PROMOTION
razzmatazz NONSENSE
reach for the sky CRIME

reader DEBT
real bitch PEOPLE - NEGATIVE
real gone PLEASANT
(real) McCoy ALCOHOL/DRUGS
(real) McCoy GENUINE
real VERY
ream someone out SCOLDING
rear (end) BUTTOCKS
rear-ender ACCIDENT
red hot FOOD
red hot IMPORTANCE
red ink DEBT
red tape ANNOYANCE
red-hot mama WOMAN - SEX
red-letter day DAY
redneck BEHAVIOR
redneck PEOPLE - NEGATIVE
reefer APPLIANCE
reefer DRUGS - MARIJUANA
ref SPORTS
regs RULES
reinvent the wheel PREPARATION
rent(al)s KINSHIP
rep ARTS
rep BUSINESS
rep REPUTATION
repo man COMMERCE
repo BUSINESS
repo CARS
ret TOBACCO
retard MENTAL
retard PEOPLE - STUPID
retread PEOPLE - NEGATIVE
rev something up ENGINE
reverse gears VOMIT
revved up EXCITEMENT
rhubarb VIOLENCE
rib TEASING
rib-tickler JOKING
ride shotgun TRAVEL
ride CARS
rif DISMISSAL
riff DIGRESSION
riff MUSIC
riffed DISMISSAL
riffed INTOXICATED - ALCOHOL/DRUGS
rig DECEPTION
rig TRUCK
right as rain CORRECT
right guy MAN - GOOD
right in the kisser IMPACT
(right) up one's alley PREFERENCE
righteous EXCELLENCE

ring a bell AWARENESS
ring off the hook TELEPHONE
ring the bell PRECISION
ringtailed snorter ENERGETIC
rinky-dink CHEAPNESS
riot JOKING
rip on someone HARASSMENT
rip snorter JOKING
rip someone off CRIME
rip something off THEFT
rip DRINKING - BOUT
rip INJURY
rip LOOT
rip THEFT
ripe INTOXICATED - ALCOHOL
ripe ODOR
ripe VULGAR
(rip-)off artist THIEF
rip-off THEFT
ripped (up) INTOXICATED -
  ALCOHOL/DRUGS
Rise and shine! HURRY
ritzy ELEGANCE
rivets MONEY
roach clip DRUGS - PARAPHERNALIA
roach DRUGS - MARIJUANA
roach POLICE
roach WOMAN - UGLY
roach-coach TRUCK - FOOD
roached HANGOVER
road apple EXCREMENT
road hog DRIVING
road pizza BODY - DEAD
roadie MUSIC
roadie TRAVEL
roadtrip TRAVEL
roast EVENT
roasted INTOXICATED - ALCOHOL
rob someone blind THEFT
rock bottom AMOUNT - SMALL
rock bottom COST
rock DRUGS - COCAINE
rock JEWELRY
rock SPORTS - BASEBALL
rocker FURNITURE
rocker MUSIC
rockhead PEOPLE - STUBBORN
rocking EXCELLENCE
rock-jock SPORTS
rocks DRINKING
rocks FINANCIAL
rocks MONEY
rod WEAPONRY

sack rat SLEEP
sack time SLEEP
sack BED
sack DISMISSAL
sack SPORTS - FOOTBALL
sacked out SLEEP
sad sack PEOPLE - SAD
sad UNDESIRABLE
saddled with someone or something
  BURDEN
sail into someone SCOLDING
sail (right) through something EASY
salt and pepper PEOPLE - MIXED
salt and pepper POLICE
salt horse FOOD
salt SAILOR
Sam and Dave POLICE
Sam POLICE
same difference SAMENESS
same here AGREEMENT
same o(l)' same o(l)' SAMENESS
same old story SAMENESS
sand SUGAR
sandbag DECEPTION
sandbag FORCE
sap PEOPLE - STUPID
sap WEAPONRY
Saturday night special WEAPONRY
sauce parlor TAVERN
sauce ALCOHOL
sauced INTOXICATED - ALCOHOL
savage EXCELLENCE
Save it! SILENCE
saved by the bell RESCUE
savvy KNOWLEDGEABLE
savvy UNDERSTANDING
sawbones DOCTOR
sawbuck MONEY
sawed INTOXICATED - ALCOHOL
sawed-off HEIGHT
Say cheese! PHOTOGRAPHY
Say cheese! SMILE
say uncle QUIT
Say what? WHAT
Says me! RESPONSE
Says who? CHALLENGE
Says you! CHALLENGE
say-so AUTHORIZATION
scabbed DECEPTION
scads ABUNDANCE
scale EARN
scam COPULATION
scam DECEPTION

scam WASTE - TIME
scammer MAN - SEX
scammer THIEF
scammered INTOXICATED - ALCOHOL
scamp CHILDREN
scandal sheet NEWSPAPER
scare the hell out of someone FRIGHT
scare the pants off someone FRIGHT
scared shitless FRIGHT
scared stiff FRIGHT
scarf out GLUTTONY
scarf something down EATING
scarf DISCARD
scarf EATING
scarf FOOD
scarf THEFT
scary UGLINESS
scat ALCOHOL - STRONG
scat DEPART
scat DRUGS - HEROIN
scat MUSIC
scatterbrain MENTAL
scattered INTOXICATED - DRUGS
scene DRUGS
scene LOCATION
scene PREFERENCE
schizo CRAZINESS
schizo PEOPLE - CRAZY
schiz(z) out CONTROL - LACKING
schlemazel PEOPLE - STUPID
schlemiel DUPE
schlep PEOPLE - STUPID
schlep TRANSFER
schlep TRAVEL
schlepper PEOPLE - NEGATIVE
schlock CHEAPNESS
schlock PRODUCT
schloomp PEOPLE - STUPID
schlub PEOPLE - STRANGE
schmaltz EMOTION
schmaltzy EMOTION
schmegegge NONSENSE
schmegegge PEOPLE - STUPID
schmendrick PEOPLE - STUPID
schmo PEOPLE - STUPID
schmooze TALKING
schmoozer TALKING
schmuck PENIS
schmuck PEOPLE - NEGATIVE
schnockered INTOXICATED -
  ALCOHOL/DRUGS
schnook DUPE
schnorrer BEGGING

sealed with a kiss ROMANCE
seam-squirrels LICE
Search me. KNOWLEDGE - LACKING
seat BUTTOCKS
sec DRUGS - BARBITURATE
sec TIME - SHORT
second fiddle PEOPLE - NEGATIVE
second sacker SPORTS - BASEBALL
see GAMBLING
see a man about a dog TOILET - USE
see eye to eye AGREEMENT
see no further than the end of one's
  nose PERCEPTION - LACKING
see red ANGER
see stars UNCONSCIOUSNESS
See you later, alligator. GOOD-BYE
See you later. GOOD-BYE
See you. GOOD-BYE
seegar TOBACCO
seeing pink elephants INTOXICATED -
  ALCOHOL
seen better days WORN
seeyabye GOOD-BYE
self-propelled sandbag MARINE
sell a wolf ticket BOASTING
sell someone out BETRAYAL
sellout ADVERTISING
sellout BETRAYAL
send someone or something up
  PARODY
send someone to glory DEATH
send someone to glory MURDER
send someone up the river PUNISHMENT
send-up PARODY
sent INTOXICATED - ALCOHOL/DRUGS
sent MUSIC
serious about someone ROMANCE
serious EXCELLENCE
serve someone right JUSTICE
session DRINKING - BOUT
session DRUGS - USE
set of pipes VOICE
set of wheels CARS
set someone back COST
set someone up (for something)
  PLANNING
set MUSIC
set PARTY
settle someone's hash CALM
setup DRINKING - PARAPHERNALIA
setup DUPE
setup LODGING
setup SCHEME

seven-year itch FIDELITY
sew something up CONCLUSION
sewed up COMPLETENESS
sewed up INTOXICATED - ALCOHOL
sewer hog LABOR
sewermouth PEOPLE - VULGAR
sex goddess WOMAN - SEX
sex kitten WOMAN - SEX
sex pot WOMAN - SEX
sex-machine PEOPLE - SEX
sexy APPEALING
sexy EXCITEMENT
SF INTOXICATED - ALCOHOL
shack up (with someone) COPULATION
shack up (with someone) LODGING
shades SUNGLASSES
shaft HARM
shaft UNFAIR
shafted DEFEAT
shag (off) DEPART
shagged out EXHAUSTION
shagged INTOXICATED - ALCOHOL
shag-nasty UNDESIRABLE
shake a leg DANCING
shake a leg HURRY
Shake it (up)! HURRY
shake someone down CRIME
shake someone down PERSUASION
shake MILK
shakedown CRIME
shakeout IMPROVEMENT
shakes DELIRIUM TREMENS
shake-up ORGANIZATION
sham(m)us POLICE
shampoo ALCOHOL - CHAMPAGNE
shank it WALKING
shank DANCING
shank WEAPONRY
shank's mare WALKING
shape up or ship out ALTERNATIVES
shape up CONCLUSION
shape up IMPROVEMENT
shark repellent FINANCIAL
shark CRIMINAL
shark LAWYER
sharp ATTRACTIVENESS
sharp INTELLIGENCE
sharpie CLEVERNESS
shave REDUCTION
shaved INTOXICATED - ALCOHOL
shavetail SOLDIER
Shazzam! AMAZEMENT
sheen CARS

shroom DRUGS - MUSHROOMS
shrooms DRUGS - MUSHROOMS
shuck CLOTHING
shuck DECEPTION
shuck PEOPLE - NEGATIVE
shuck TEASING
shuck TRICK
shuffler DRUNKARD
shush (up) SILENCE
shut up SILENCE
Shut your face! SILENCE
shut-eye SLEEP
shutout SPORTS
shutters EYELIDS
shwench STUDENT
shyster LAWYER
Siberian express COLD
sick to death (of someone or
  something) DISGUSTING
sick (up) VOMIT
sicks VOMIT
sicky PEOPLE - CRAZY
side MUSIC
sidewalk superintendent CRITICISM
sidewalk superintendent OBSERVATION
sidewalk surfing SKATEBOARD
sidewinder PEOPLE - NEGATIVE
sidney DRUGS - LSD
sieg-heil someone GREETING
signify DISPLAY
signify TROUBLE
silk PEOPLE - WHITE
silks CLOTHING
silky CHARM
silo drippings ALCOHOL
silver bullet SOLUTION
silver goose MEDICAL - PARAPHERNALIA
silver MONEY
simmer (down) ANGER
simmer (down) SILENCE
simoleon MONEY
Simon Legree MANAGE
simp PEOPLE - STUPID
sin DRUGS - MARIJUANA
sin-bin VAN
sing TATTLING
single MONEY
single PEOPLE
sink EATING
sinker FOOD
sinse DRUGS - MARIJUANA
sip DRUGS - PORTION
sipster DRUNKARD

sis KINSHIP
sissified EFFEMINATE
sister WOMAN
sister WOMAN
sister WOMAN - FRIEND
sitcom TELEVISION
sitting duck TARGET
sitting pretty SECURE
six bits MONEY
six feet under DEAD
sixer DRINKING
six-pack DRINKING - BOUT
six-pack MUSCLES
sixty-four-dollar question QUESTION
sizzled INTOXICATED - ALCOHOL
sizzler HEAT
skag jones ADDICTION
skag ALCOHOL
skag DRUGS - HEROIN
skag PEOPLE - NEGATIVE
skag TOBACCO
skag WOMAN - UGLY
skagged out INTOXICATED - DRUGS
skank UGLINESS
skank WOMAN - UGLY
skanky UGLINESS
skat ALCOHOL - BEER
skate DRINKING - BOUT
skate DRINKING - EXCESS
skate DRUNKARD
skating INTOXICATED - DRUGS
skedaddle DEPART
skeet shooting MUCUS
skeet MUCUS
skeeter INSECT
skeevy DISGUSTING
skeezer PEOPLE - STRANGE
skid marks EXCREMENT
skid row bum HOBO
skid row LOCATION
skid-lid MOTORCYCLES
skillion AMOUNT - LARGE
skin a goat VOMIT
skin flick PORNOGRAPHY
skin game DECEPTION
Skin me! GREETING
skin BALDNESS
skin DECEPTION
skin MONEY
skinful DRINKING - PORTION
skinny-dip NAKEDNESS
skins MUSIC
skin-search EXAMINATION

smarmy INSINCERITY
smart aleck PEOPLE - NEGATIVE
smart ass PEOPLE - NEGATIVE
smart cookie CLEVERNESS
smart guy PEOPLE - NEGATIVE
smart money MONEY
smart mouth PEOPLE - NEGATIVE
smarts INTELLIGENCE
smarty PEOPLE - NEGATIVE
smarty-pants PEOPLE - NEGATIVE
smash hit SUCCESS
smash ALCOHOL - WINE
smashed INTOXICATED - ALCOHOL/DRUGS
smashing EXCELLENCE
smear OVERWHELM
smeared INTOXICATED - ALCOHOL/DRUGS
smell a rat SUSPICION
smell blood VIOLENCE
smell fishy SUSPICION
smell it up DRUGS - USE
smell like a rose INNOCENCE
smell to (high) heaven ODOR
smell to (high) heaven SUSPICION
smeller NOSE
smidgen AMOUNT - SMALL
Smile when you say that. BEHAVIOR
smile DRINKING - PORTION
smithereens PIECES
smoke and mirrors DECEPTION
smoke eater FIRE FIGHTER
smoke like a chimney TOBACCO
smoke ALCOHOL - BAD
smoke DECEPTION
smoke MURDER
smoke OVERWHELM
smoke TOBACCO
smoke-filled room POLITICS
smoke-in DRUGS
Smokey (the Bear) POLICE
smokin' EXCELLENCE
smoking gun SYMBOL - GUILT
smooch KISS
smooth operator CLEVERNESS
smurf CRIME
smurf CRIMINAL
smurfbrain PEOPLE - STUPID
smurfed CRIME
snafu ERROR
snag DIFFICULTIES
snag THEFT
snag WOMAN - UGLY
snail-mail MAIL
snake eyes GAMBLING

snake in the grass PEOPLE - NEGATIVE
snake SCHEME
snakebite medicine ALCOHOL - STRONG
snap course EASY
Snap it up! HURRY
snap one's cookies VOMIT
snap out of something RECOVERY
snap something up COMMERCE
snap to (attention) ALERTNESS
Snap to it! HURRY
snap CRAZINESS
snap EASY
snap PHOTOGRAPHY
snapped (up) ARREST
snapped (up) INTOXICATED - ALCOHOL
snapper PEOPLE - STRANGE
snappers TEETH
snappy APPEARANCE
snappy SPEED
snatch CRIME
snatch THEFT
snatched ARREST
snatcher POLICE
snaved in INTOXICATED - DRUGS
snazz something up EXCITEMENT
snazz EXCITEMENT
snazzy ELEGANCE
sneak MOVIES
sneaks SHOES
sneaky DECEPTION
snide remark INSULT
sniff DRINKING - PORTION
snipe TOBACCO
snit BEHAVIOR - BAD
snitch TATTLING
snitch THEFT
snitcher TATTLING
snitzy ELEGANCE
snookered DECEPTION
snookums NICKNAME
snoop PEOPLE - NEGATIVE
snoop SEARCH
snoot NOSE
snooted INTOXICATED - ALCOHOL
snooty HAUGHTINESS
snoozamorooed INTOXICATED - ALCOHOL
snooze DULL
snooze SLEEP
snork DRUGS - USE
snort DRUGS - PORTION
snort DRUGS - USE
snot MUCUS
snot PEOPLE - NEGATIVE

snotnose(d) (kid) CHILDREN
snotrag HANDKERCHIEF
snotted INTOXICATED - ALCOHOL
snotty IMPUDENCE
snotty MUCUS
snow bunny SPORTS - SKIING
snow job DECEPTION
snow DECEPTION
snow DRUGS - POWDER
snowball GROWTH
snowball's chance in hell SURVIVAL -
 LACKING
snowed DECEPTION
snozzled INTOXICATED - ALCOHOL
snozzle-wobbles DELIRIUM TREMENS
snuff film MOVIES
snuff it DEATH
snuff DEATH
snuff MURDER
snuffy INTOXICATED - ALCOHOL
so bad one can taste it AMOUNT - MUCH
So gross! DISGUSTING
So long. GOOD-BYE
So much for that. CONCLUSION
So what? WHAT
soak one's face DRINKING - EXCESS
soak DRINKING - EXCESS
soak DRUNKARD
soak EXTORTION
soaked INTOXICATED - ALCOHOL
soaker DRUNKARD
so-and-so NICKNAME
soap TELEVISION
sob sister WOMAN - MEEK
sob story EXPLANATION
SOB MAN - NEGATIVE
sober as a judge SOBRIETY
sobersides GROUCHY
social disease SICKNESS
sock hop PARTY
Sock it to me! EXPLANATION
sock VIOLENCE
socked in FOG
socked INTOXICATED - ALCOHOL
sofa spud LAZY
soft berth EASY
soft core PORNOGRAPHY
soft in the head STUPIDITY
soft money MONEY
soft on someone PUNISHMENT - LACKING
soft on someone ROMANCE
soft pedal something DECLINE
soft sell COMMERCE

soft soap FLATTERY
soft soap PERSUASION
soft touch DUPE
soft touch KINDNESS
soft DRUGS
soft INTOXICATED - ALCOHOL
soft STUPIDITY
soft-hearted KINDNESS
softie MEEKNESS
softie PEOPLE - MEEK
software rot COMPUTER
soggy INTOXICATED - ALCOHOL
sold cober SOBRIETY
sold on someone or something
 PERSUASION
soldier DRINKING - PARAPHERNALIA
soldier TOBACCO
solid EXCELLENCE
solid SEQUENCE
some pumpkins EXCELLENCE
somebody PEOPLE - IMPORTANT
someone or something from hell
 ANNOYANCE
son of a bitch CURSING
son of a bitch FRIEND
son of a bitch PEOPLE - NEGATIVE
Son of a gun! AMAZEMENT
son of a gun FRIEND
son of a gun PEOPLE - NEGATIVE
sop DRINKING - EXCESS
sop DRUNKARD
soph STUDENT
sopping (wet) INTOXICATED - ALCOHOL
sore ANGER
sorehead GROUCHY
sorehead PEOPLE - NEGATIVE
sorry about that SORRY
sorry-ass AMOUNT
So's your old man! RECIPROCITY
sosh WOMAN
so-so INTOXICATED - ALCOHOL
so-so AVERAGE
(soul) brother PEOPLE - BLACK
soul kiss KISS
(soul) sister WOMAN - FRIEND
sound off (about something)
 COMPLAINT
sound off (about something)
 INTRUSION
sound off (about something) REVEAL
sounds MUSIC
soup something up IMPROVEMENT
soup EXPLOSIVES

souped up POWER
soup-strainer MUSTACHE
soupy INTOXICATED - ALCOHOL
sourpuss GROUCHY
souse DRINKING - EXCESS
souse DRUNKARD
soused INTOXICATED - ALCOHOL
southern-fried INTOXICATED - ALCOHOL
southpaw WRITING
sozzle DRINKING - EXCESS
sozzled INTOXICATED - ALCOHOL
sozzler DRUNKARD
space cadet DRUGS - USER
space cadet PEOPLE - SILLY
space out PEOPLE - SILLY
space out SILLINESS
space someone out SILLINESS
spaced (out) SILLINESS
spam DISLIKE
spare tire ADDITIONAL
spare tire FAT
sparkler JEWELRY
spastic CONTROL - LACKING
spaz around WASTE - TIME
spaz down RELAX
spaz out EXCITEMENT
spaz CONTROL - LACKING
spaz PEOPLE - NEGATIVE
spaz-out EMOTION
speak of the devil COINCIDENCE
speak someone's language
  UNDERSTANDING
speakeasy TAVERN
specs GLASSES
speed demon DRUGS - USER
speed demon SPEED
speed freak DRUGS - USER
speed merchant SPEED
speed DRUGS - AMPHETAMINE
speedball SPORTS - BASEBALL
speeder DRIVING
speeder DRUGS - AMPHETAMINE
speeder DRUGS - USER
spending money MONEY
spew one's guts (out) TATTLING
spew one's guts (out) VOMIT
spew VOMIT
spiff COMMERCE
spiffed out ATTRACTIVENESS
spiffed up ATTRACTIVENESS
spifflicated INTOXICATED - ALCOHOL
spiffy EXCELLENCE
spike ALCOHOL

spike CRITICISM
spike DRUGS - PARAPHERNALIA
spiked ALCOHOL
spiked HAIR
spiked INTOXICATED - ALCOHOL/DRUGS
spill one's guts REVEAL
spill the beans REVEAL
spill REVEAL
spin doctor DECEPTION
spin one's wheels WASTE - TIME
spinach MONEY
spit and polish PRECISION
Spit it out! EXPLANATION
spizzerinktum ENERGETIC
spliff DRUGS - MARIJUANA
split a gut LAUGHTER
split a gut WORK
split up SEPARATION
split DEPART
splitting headache SICKNESS
splurge INDULGENCE
spoil MURDER
spoiled rotten INDULGENCE
spoiling for a fight CHALLENGE
spondulicks MONEY
sponge DRINKING - EXCESS
sponge PEOPLE - NEGATIVE
spoof PERFORMANCE
spook factory SPYING
spook FRIGHT
spook SPYING
spooked FRIGHT
spoon KISS
sport FRIEND
spot market FINANCIAL
spot of lunch FOOD
spot someone (something) GAMBLING
spot someone (something) LEND
spot DRINKING - PLACE
spot DRINKING - PORTION
sprain one's ankle PREGNANCY
spring chicken DUPE
spring for something GENEROSITY
spring someone RELEASE
sprout wings BEHAVIOR
sprout wings DEATH
sprout CHILDREN
spud ALCOHOL - VODKA
spud DRUNKARD
spud FOOD
spud PEOPLE - SMALL
spunge DRUNKARD
spunk COURAGE

spunky COURAGE
square john broad WOMAN - GOOD
square john PEOPLE - GOOD
square (meal) FOOD
square off FIGHTING
square peg (in a round hole) PEOPLE - NEGATIVE
square shooter HONESTY
square with someone HONESTY
square AGREEMENT
square OLD-FASHIONED
square PEOPLE - GOOD
square TOBACCO
squared away UNDERSTANDING
squared up SOBRIETY
squat NOTHING
squat SITTING
squawk box AUDIO
squawk COMPLAINT
squawk TATTLING
squeaky clean CLEANLINESS
squeal TATTLING
squealer PIG
squealer TATTLING
squeeze play SPORTS - BASEBALL
squeeze ALCOHOL
squeeze LOVER
squeeze PERSUASION
(squeeze-)box MUSIC
squib ADVERTISING
squid STUDENT
squiff out INTOXICATED - ALCOHOL
squiff DRUNKARD
squiffed INTOXICATED - ALCOHOL
squiggle SYMBOL
squirrel out of something ESCAPE
squirrel something away SAVINGS
squirrel PEOPLE - STRANGE
squirrel-food PEOPLE - CRAZY
squirrels ENGINE
squirrely CRAZINESS
squirt ALCOHOL - BUBBLY
squirt CHILDREN
squirts DIARRHEA
squooshy SOFT
stack the deck DECEPTION
stacked ATTRACTIVENESS
stag line SOCIAL
stag PARTY
stag SOCIAL
staggers ALCOHOL
staggers DELIRIUM TREMENS
stag-party PARTY

stake someone or something out OBSERVATION
stake someone to something GENEROSITY
stake someone to something LEND
stakeout OBSERVATION
stale drunk DRINKING - BOUT
stallion WOMAN - ATTRACTIVE
stamping ground LOCATION
stand pat (on something) OPINION
stand someone up DATING
stand tall COURAGE
stand there with one's bare face hanging out STUPIDITY
standee EVENT
stand-in TEMPORARY
standoffish HAUGHTINESS
stand-out EXCELLENCE
stanza SPORTS
starched INTOXICATED - ALCOHOL
stash DRUGS - SUPPLY
stash MUSTACHE
stash SAVINGS
stat THERMOSTAT
static COMPLAINT
stats STATISTICS
Stay tuned. COMMUNICATION
steady LOVER
steal COMMERCE
steam someone up ANGER
steam someone up EXCITEMENT
steam someone's beam ANGER
steam up DRINKING - EXCESS
steam ANGER
steamed (up) ANGER
steamed (up) INTOXICATED - ALCOHOL
steamroller FORCE
steamy LOVE
steenth FINANCIAL
steep COST
stellar EXCELLENCE
stems LEGS
step off the curb DEATH
step out on someone BETRAYAL
step outside ARGUMENT
step right up MOVEMENT
stepped on DRUGS
stern BUTTOCKS
stew bum DRUNKARD
stew ANXIETY
stew AVIATION
stew DRINKING - BOUT
stew DRUNKARD

stewed to the gills INTOXICATED - ALCOHOL
stewed (up) INTOXICATED - ALCOHOL
stick around REMAIN
stick it to someone CONFRONTATION
stick man POLICE
stick out like a sore thumb OBVIOUS
stick shift CARS
stick someone with something BURDEN
stick AVIATION
stick CARS
stick DRUNKARD
stick LEGS
stick LOCATION
stick SPORTS - BASEBALL
stick SPORTS - GOLF
sticker shock SHOCK
stick-in-the-mud OLD-FASHIONED
stick-to-itiveness BEHAVIOR
stickum ADHESIVE
stickum GROOMING
sticky fingers THEFT
sticky ADHESIVE
sticky CHANCE
sticky EMOTION
sticky HEAT
stiff BODY - DEAD
stiff CHEAPNESS
stiff DEAD
stiff DECEPTION
stiff DRUNKARD
stiff HOBO
stiff INTOXICATED - ALCOHOL
sting ARREST
sting DECEPTION
stinger DRAWBACK
stink on ice UNDESIRABLE
stink DISGUSTING
stink UPROAR
stinker DIFFICULTIES
stinker PEOPLE - NEGATIVE
stinking (drunk) INTOXICATED - ALCOHOL
stinking rich WEALTH
stinking with something AMOUNT - MUCH
stinking UNDESIRABLE
stinkpot BOAT
stinkpot CHILDREN
stinkpot ODOR
stinky UNDESIRABLE
stir crazy JAIL
stir JAIL

stitch JOKING
stitch PAIN
stocking-stuffer GIFT
stogie TOBACCO
stoked (on someone or something) EXCITEMENT
stoked out EXHAUSTION
stokin' EXCELLENCE
stomach ENDURE
stomp (on) someone OVERWHELM
stone blind INTOXICATED - ALCOHOL
stone broke MONEY - LACKING
stone dead DEAD
stone fox WOMAN - ATTRACTIVE
stone groove EXCELLENCE
stone COMPLETENESS
stone(-cold) sober SOBRIETY
stoned out of one's head INTOXICATED - DRUGS
stoned out of one's squash INTOXICATED - ALCOHOL/DRUGS
stoned (out) INTOXICATED - ALCOHOL/DRUGS
stoned silly INTOXICATED - ALCOHOL/DRUGS
stonewall OBSTRUCTION
stonkered DEAD
stonkered INTOXICATED - ALCOHOL
stooge PEOPLE - NEGATIVE
stool (on someone) TATTLING
stool (pigeon) TATTLING
stop on a dime STOPPING
Stop the music! STOPPING
storked PREGNANCY
story stock FINANCIAL
Stow it! SILENCE
stozzled INTOXICATED - ALCOHOL
straddle the fence ALTERNATIVES
straight arrow HONESTY
straight dope INFORMATION
straight from the horse's mouth INFORMATION
straight from the shoulder FRANKNESS
straight low INFORMATION
straight man JOKING
straight shooter HONESTY
straight talk HONESTY
straight (up) ALCOHOL
straight up COOKING
straight up HONESTY
straight EXCELLENCE
straight HETEROSEXUAL
straight HONESTY

suds-swiller DRUNKARD
sue the pants off (of) someone LEGAL
sugar daddy MAN - OLD
sugarcoated INOFFENSIVE
suit BUSINESS
summer complaint DIARRHEA
sun belt LOCATION
Sunday best CLOTHING
Sunday driver DRIVING
Sunday punch VIOLENCE
sunny-side up COOKING
sunshades SUNGLASSES
super EXCELLENCE
super MANAGE
super-duper EXCELLENCE
superfly EXCELLENCE
supergrass DRUGS - MARIJUANA
superjock MAN - MUSCULAR
superjock SPORTS
super-strap STUDENT
sure as hell CERTAINTY
sure thing CERTAINTY
surefire CERTAINTY
surf EXCELLENCE
surf TELEVISION
suss someone out UNDERSTANDING
Suzy MONEY
swacked INTOXICATED - ALCOHOL
swallow the dictionary VOCABULARY
swallow ACCEPTANCE
swallow DRUGS - PORTION
swamped BUSY
swamped INTOXICATED - ALCOHOL
swamper DRIVING
swank ELEGANCE
swanky ELEGANCE
swap notes (on someone or
  something) INFORMATION
swap spits KISS
swear like a trooper CURSING
swear on a stack of Bibles HONESTY
sweat blood WORK
sweat bullets SUFFERING
sweat sock SPORTS
sweat something out ANXIETY
sweat ANXIETY
sweat TROUBLE
sweet nothings ROMANCE
sweet EXCELLENCE
sweeten IMPROVEMENT
sweetener ENCOURAGEMENT
sweetheart deal BUSINESS
sweetheart PEOPLE - GOOD

swell EXCELLENCE
swellelegant EXCELLENCE
swellhead PEOPLE - NEGATIVE
swift CLEVERNESS
swift SEX
swig DRINKING - EXCESS
swig DRINKING - PORTION
swigged INTOXICATED - ALCOHOL
swill ALCOHOL
swill DRINKING
swill DRINKING - PORTION
swill NASTY
swill-up DRINKING - BOUT
swimming in something ABUNDANCE
swindle sheet BUSINESS
swing both ways GAY
swing into high gear BEGINNINGS
swing shift EMPLOYMENT
swing with someone or something
  APPRECIATION
swing ACHIEVEMENT
swing EXCITEMENT
swing FASHIONABLE
swing SEX
swinger PEOPLE - MODERN
swinger PEOPLE - SEX
swinging EXCELLENCE
swingman DRUGS - USER
swipe ALCOHOL - ILLICIT
swipe DRINKING - EXCESS
swipe THEFT
swipe VIOLENCE
swish EFFEMINATE
switch off IGNORE
switch on ALERTNESS
switch on DRUGS - USE
switch on FASHIONABLE
switch WEAPONRY
switched on ALERTNESS
switched on EXCITEMENT
switcheroo REVERSAL
switch-hitter SPORTS - BASEBALL
swizzle ALCOHOL
swizzle DRINKING - EXCESS
swizzled INTOXICATED - ALCOHOL
swizzle-stick DRUNKARD
swoozled INTOXICATED - ALCOHOL
syrupy EMOTION
SYSOP COMPUTER
T and A BREASTS
T and A BUTTOCKS
T and A MEDICAL
T DRUGS - MARIJUANA

take the rap (for something) GUILT
take the spear (in one's chest)
  ACCEPTANCE
take the starch out of someone
  SCOLDING
take the wind out of someone's sails
  DEFLATE
take things easy RELAX
take things easy SUCCESS
take DECEPTION
take EARN
take MOVIES
take OVERWHELM
taken DEAD
taken DECEPTION
taken INTOXICATED - DRUGS
taken UNAVAILABLE
take-off artist THIEF
take-off COPY
take-off PARODY
take-off THEFT
taker COMMERCE
takes two to tango COOPERATION
taking care of business LIFESTYLE
tale of woe DIFFICULTIES
talk a blue streak CHATTER
talk big BOASTING
talk like a nut TALKING
talk on the big white phone VOMIT
talk one's head off PERSUASION
talk someone ragged CHATTER
talk someone's ear off CHATTER
talk through one's hat LYING
talk to earl VOMIT
talk to hear one's own voice CHATTER
talk to Herb and Al ALCOHOL/DRUGS
talk turkey FRANKNESS
talk until one is blue in the face
  CHATTER
talking head REPORTER
tall in the saddle PRIDE
tall one DRINKING - PORTION
tall order REQUEST
tall timbers LOCATION
tall EXCELLENCE
tall INTOXICATED - DRUGS
tangle with someone or something
  ARGUMENT
tank DRINKING - EXCESS
tank DRUNKARD
tank FALL
tank JAIL
tank LOSS

tanked DEFEAT
tanked INTOXICATED - ALCOHOL
tanker DRUNKARD
tanky INTOXICATED - ALCOHOL
tanned INTOXICATED - ALCOHOL
tap dance like mad BUSY
tap out DEATH
tap out LOSS
tap someone (for something) CHOICE
taped COMPLETENESS
tapped ARREST
tapped EXHAUSTION
tapped MONEY - LACKING
tapped RUINATION
taste blood EXPERIENCE
taste SHARING
Ta-ta. GOOD-BYE
tawny EXCELLENCE
TCB BUSINESS
tea party EASY
tea party PARTY - DRINKING
tea ALCOHOL
tea DRUGS - MARIJUANA
tea URINATION
tear into someone SCOLDING
tear into something GLUTTONY
tear into something SPEED
tear loose (from someone or
  something) EVASION
tear off DEPART
tear someone or something apart
  CRITICISM
tear someone or something up
  VIOLENCE
tear someone up GRIEF
tear DRINKING - BOUT
tearjerker MOVIES
teaser PREVIEW
teaser TOBACCO
techie SKILL
techie STUDENT
techie TECHNOLOGY
tech-nerd TECHNOLOGY
technicolor yawn VOMIT
tee someone off ANGER
teed off ANGER
teed (up) INTOXICATED - ALCOHOL/DRUGS
teenie FINANCIAL
teenybopper TEENAGER
teeny-weeny SIZE
tee-tee URINATION
telegraph one's punches SIGNAL

telegraph one's punches SPORTS - BOXING
Tell it like it is. TRUTH
Tell me another (one)! BELIEF
tell someone what to do with something COMMAND
tell someone where to get off SCOLDING
tell the (whole) world REVEAL
telly TELEVISION
ten percenter AGENT
ten BEST
ten-four YES
tenner MONEY
tennies SHOES
ten-spot MONEY
terrific EXCELLENCE
TGIF GRATITUDE
thank you very much GRATITUDE
thanks a bunch GRATITUDE
That tears it! ANNOYANCE
that way GAY
that way INTOXICATED - ALCOHOL
that way ROMANCE
That-a-boy! ENCOURAGEMENT
That'll be the day! BELIEF
That'll teach someone. JUSTICE
That's a new one on me. UNIQUENESS
That's about the size of it. CONCLUSION
That's all she wrote. CONCLUSION
That's all someone needs. AMOUNT - EXCESSIVE
That's show business (for you). REALITY
That's that! CONCLUSION
That's the stuff! AMAZEMENT
That's the ticket! ENCOURAGEMENT
That's the way the ball bounces. ACCEPTANCE
That's the way the cookie crumbles. ACCEPTANCE
That's the way the mop flops. ACCEPTANCE
(That's the) way to go! ENCOURAGEMENT
That's what I say. AGREEMENT
thawed INTOXICATED - ALCOHOL
the way it plays ACCEPTANCE
the works EVERYTHING
then and there TIME - THEN
There will be hell to pay. RESULTS
There you are. RESULTS
There you go. ENCOURAGEMENT
There you go. REALITY

There you go. SCOLDING
There's nobody home. STUPIDITY
thick FALSE
thick JOINING
thick STUPIDITY
thickheaded STUPIDITY
thick-skinned TOLERANT
thin dime MONEY
thing INTEREST
thingamajig GADGET
think-box HEAD
think-piece PUBLICATION
think-tank KNOWLEDGE
thin-skinned CRITICISM
third degree INTERROGATION
third wheel INTRUSION
thirst-aid station TAVERN
thirsty soul DRUNKARD
This is it! AMAZEMENT
This is where I came in. SAMENESS
thoroughbred CRIMINAL
thou AMOUNT
threads CLOTHING
three bricks shy of a load STUPIDITY
three fingers DRINKING - PORTION
three sheets in the wind INTOXICATED - ALCOHOL
three squares FOOD
three-two POWER - ALCOHOL
thriller-diller EXCITEMENT
throat gag ALCOHOL
throat STUDENT
throne room TOILET
throne TOILET
through and through COMPLETENESS
through the mill EXHAUSTION
throw a fight SPORTS - BOXING
throw a fit ANGER
throw a game LOSS
throw a map VOMIT
throw a punch VIOLENCE
throw a technicolor yawn VOMIT
throw down EATING
throw in the towel QUIT
throw money at something SOLUTION
throw one out on one's ear EJECTION
throw one's hat in the ring CANDIDACY
throw one's voice VOMIT
throw one's weight around DOMINANCE
throw someone for a loop CONFUSION
throw something back CONSUMPTION
throw the book at someone PUNISHMENT

throw the bull BOASTING
throw up one's toenails VOMIT
throw CONFUSION
throw TRY
throw-away INFORMATION
throw-away PERFORMANCE
thumb a ride TRAVEL
thumber BEGGING
thumbnail sketch DESCRIPTION
thumbs down DISAPPROVAL
thumbs up APPROVAL
thunder-boomer THUNDERSTORM
thunderbox AUDIO
thunder-thighs THIGHS
tick someone off ANGER
tick TIME - SHORT
ticked (off) ANGER
ticker HEART
ticker WATCH
ticket DRIVING
ticket PRECISION
tickle the ivories MUSIC
tickled (pink) PLEASURE
tick-tock CLOCK
tick-tock HEART
tick-tock WATCH
ticky-tacky CHEAPNESS
tiddled INTOXICATED - ALCOHOL
tie one on DRINKING - EXCESS
tie the knot NUPTIALS
tied up BUSY
tie-in CONNECTION
tiffled INTOXICATED - ALCOHOL
tiger sweat ALCOHOL - STRONG
tiger MAN - STRONG
tight as a tick INTOXICATED - ALCOHOL
tight as a tick TIGHT
tight money MONEY
tight spot DIFFICULTIES
tight BUSY
tight INTOXICATED - ALCOHOL
tight STINGY
tighten one's belt PREPARATION
tightwad STINGY
Tijuana taxi POLICE
till hell freezes over ALWAYS
till kingdom come ALWAYS
till the fat lady sings ENDINGS
Time (out)! SILENCE
time to cruise DEPART
tin cow MILK
tin hat CLOTHING
tinkle URINATION

tinklebox MUSIC
tinseled CHECKS
tinsel-teeth TEETH
tinseltown CITIES
tints SUNGLASSES
tip one's hand REVEAL
tip-off EVIDENCE
tipple ALCOHOL
tipple DRINKING - BOUT
tipple DRINKING - PORTION
tippler DRUNKARD
tippler TAVERN
tipply INTOXICATED - ALCOHOL
tipster TATTLING
tits up POSITION
tits BREASTS
tizzy CONFUSION
TLC CARING
T-man POLICE
to beat the band AGGRESSIVENESS
to boot ADDITIONAL
to die for DESIRE
to go COMMERCE
to hell and gone RUINATION
To hell with that! ENDINGS
to the max AMOUNT - MAXIMUM
to the tune of something COST
toast DRUNKARD
toast EXCELLENCE
toast TROUBLE
toasted INTOXICATED - ALCOHOL
today IMMEDIATELY
toddle off DEPART
toddy blossom PIMPLES
to-do UPROAR
together ORGANIZATION
toilet water ALCOHOL - BEER
toke DRUGS - COCAINE
toke DRUGS - PORTION
toke DRUGS - USE
toke SYMBOL
toke TOBACCO
tokus BUTTOCKS
tomato WOMAN - ATTRACTIVE
tomcat MAN - SEX
tomcat SEX
tomfoolery SILLINESS
tongue oil ALCOHOL
tongue-tied INTOXICATED - ALCOHOL
tongue-tied SPEECH - LACKING
tonic ALCOHOL
tons of something AMOUNT - MUCH
tonsil bath ALCOHOL

tonsil paint ALCOHOL
too much EXCELLENCE
too rich for someone's blood COST
too rich for someone's blood FOOD
Toodle(-oo). GOOD-BYE
tooie DRUGS - BARBITURATE
tool around TRAVEL
tool CARS
tool DUPE
tool STUDENT
toot DRINKING - BOUT
toot DRINKING - EXCESS
toot DRUGS - PORTION
toot DRUGS - USE
toot EMOTION
tooter DRUNKARD
tootle along DEPART
tootonium DRUGS - COCAINE
tootuncommon DRUGS - COCAINE
top banana COMEDIAN
top banana PEOPLE - IMPORTANT
top brass PEOPLE - IMPORTANT
top dog PEOPLE - IMPORTANT
top heavy BUXOM
top of the heap SUPERIORITY
top story BRAIN
top EXCELLENCE
top MURDER
top SPORTS - BASEBALL
top-drawer EXCELLENCE
top-flight EXCELLENCE
topless NAKEDNESS
topsy-boozy INTOXICATED - ALCOHOL
topsy-turvy CONFUSION
topsy-turvy INTOXICATED - ALCOHOL
tore (up) EMOTION
tore (up) INTOXICATED - ALCOHOL/DRUGS
tornado juice ALCOHOL
torpedo DRINKING
torqued ANGER
torqued INTOXICATED - ALCOHOL
toss one's cookies VOMIT
toss something off CARELESSNESS
toss something off DRINKING
toss something off IGNORE
toss something off SICKNESS
toss DISCARD
toss DRINKING - PORTION
toss SEARCH
toss VOMIT
toss-up CHANCE
totaled INTOXICATED - ALCOHOL
totaled RUINATION

totally clueless STUPIDITY
totally COMPLETENESS
tote ABSTINENCE
tote DRUGS - PARAPHERNALIA
tote DRUGS - PORTION
touch a sore point HARM
touch and go UNCERTAINTY
touch base (with someone)
  CONTACT
touch DUPE
touch PORTION
touch REQUEST
touch TRY
touched INTOXICATED - ALCOHOL
tough break LUCK - LACKING
tough cookie PROBLEM
tough customer PROBLEM
tough egg to crack PROBLEM
tough guy MAN - NEGATIVE
tough luck ACCEPTANCE
tough row to hoe DIFFICULTIES
tough something out ENDURE
Tough titty! ANNOYANCE
tourist trap VACATION
townie RESIDENT
toxicated INTOXICATED - ALCOHOL
TP TOILET - PARAPHERNALIA
TP TRICK
track AGREEMENT
track MUSIC
track REASON - LACKING
trad OLD-FASHIONED
traf FLATULENCE
tragic-magic DRUGS - HEROIN
trammeled INTOXICATED - ALCOHOL
tranny CARS
trans CARS
trap LOCATION - UNDESIRABLE
trap MOUTH
trash mouth PEOPLE - VULGAR
trash INSULT
trash OVERWHELM
trash PEOPLE - WORTHLESS
trash VANDALISM
trash WASTE
trashed INTOXICATED - ALCOHOL/DRUGS
trashy OBSCENE
trekkie FAN
trial balloon TRY
trick on someone DECEPTION
tricks of the trade SKILL
trigger BEGINNINGS
trigger CRIMINAL

trigger-happy VIOLENCE
trip DEPART
trip INTOXICATION - DRUGS
trip INTOXICATION - ONSET
trip PEOPLE - NEGATIVE
trip PUNISHMENT
tripe NONSENSE
tripe WORTHLESSNESS
triple whammy POWER
triple DRINKING - PORTION
triple-bagger PEOPLE - UGLY
triple-bagger SPORTS - BASEBALL
tripped out EXCELLENCE
trots DIARRHEA
trotters FEET
trotters FOOD
trounce OVERWHELM
trump something up PROMOTION
trumped up FAKE
trumped up PROMOTION
Trust me! TRUST
try someone back (again) TELEPHONE
(T)sup? GREETING
tub of lard PEOPLE - FAT
tube it FAILURE
tube steak FOOD
tube ALCOHOL - BEER
tube FAILURE
tube SURFING
tube TELEVISION
tube TOBACCO
tubed INTOXICATED - ALCOHOL
tubular EXCELLENCE
tude BEHAVIOR - BAD
tunage EXCELLENCE
tunage MUSIC
tune in (to something) AWARENESS
tune out IGNORE
tune someone or something out
  IGNORE
tuned in FASHIONABLE
tuned INTOXICATED - ALCOHOL
tunes MUSIC
turd EXCREMENT
turd PEOPLE - NEGATIVE
turf LOCATION
turistas DIARRHEA
turkey FAILURE
turkey PEOPLE - STUPID
turn a trick PROSTITUTION
turn around REVERSAL
turn belly up DEATH
turn belly up FAILURE

turn in SLEEP
turn on a dime DRIVING
turn on the waterworks EMOTION
turn on, tune in, drop out DRUGS
turn on DRUGS - USE
turn on EXCITEMENT
turn on INTEREST
turn one's toes up DEATH
turn onto someone or something
  INTEREST
turn over DRUGS - REHABILITATION
turn someone off DULL
turn someone on EXCITEMENT
turn someone or something upside
  down CONFUSION
turn someone out CORRUPT
turn someone's stomach SICKNESS
turn someone's water off HUMILIATION
turn tail (and run) DEPART
turn thumbs down (on someone or
  something) REJECTION
turn turtle ENDINGS
turn up one's nose at someone or
  something DISGUSTING
turn BETRAYAL
turn CORRUPT
turned off UNINTERESTED
turned on EXCITEMENT
turned on INTOXICATED - DRUGS
turn-off REPELLENT
turnout AUDIENCE
turps ALCOHOL
tux CLOTHING
tweak ADJUSTMENT
tweased INTOXICATED - ALCOHOL
tweeked INTOXICATED - ALCOHOL
twenty-twenty hindsight PREDICTION -
  LACKING
twiddle one's thumbs WAITING
twinkie TEENAGER
twirp PEOPLE - UNIMPORTANT
twist (slowly) in the wind SUFFERING
twist someone's arm PERSUASION
twist WOMAN
twisted ADDICTION - END
twisted INTOXICATED - ALCOHOL
twister DRINKING - BOUT
twister KEY
twister TORNADO
twit ANXIETY
twit PEOPLE - STUPID
two fingers DRINKING - PORTION
two shakes of a lamb's tail SPEED

two umlauts ALCOHOL - BEER
two-bit CHEAPNESS
two bits MONEY
two-by-four SIZE
twofer COMMERCE
two-fisted drinker DRUNKARD
two-time loser PEOPLE - NEGATIVE
two-time DECEPTION
two-timer LOVER
two-way street RECIPROCITY
type CHILDREN
ugly as sin UGLINESS
uke VOMIT
ump SPORTS
umpteen AMOUNT - MANY
umpty-umpth AMOUNT
Uncle nab POLICE
Uncle (Sam) GOVERNMENT
Uncle (Sam) POLICE
uncool OLD-FASHIONED
under someone's thumb DOMINANCE
under the affluence of incohol
  INTOXICATED - ALCOHOL
under the gun PRESSURE
under the table INTOXICATED - ALCOHOL
under the table SECRECY
under the weather INTOXICATED -
  ALCOHOL
under the weather SICKNESS
under the wire TIME
under wraps SECRECY
underpinnings LEGS
understanding LEGS
underwater basket weaving SCHOOL
underwhelm FAILURE
undies CLOTHING
unearthly HORRIBLE
unflappable ENDURE
ungodly HORRIBLE
unit GADGET
unk-jay DRUGS
unlax RELAX
unload EJECTION
unreal REALITY - LACKING
up a storm ENTHUSIASM
up a tree CONFUSION
up a tree INTOXICATED - ALCOHOL
up against it CRISIS
up and at them ENCOURAGEMENT
up for grabs AVAILABLE
up for grabs CONFUSION
up for something AGREEMENT
up front BEGINNINGS

up front HONESTY
up front LOCATION
up high DRUGS
up in arms ANGER
up in the air (about someone or
  something) INDECISION
up in the air INDECISION
up pot DRUGS - MARIJUANA
up stakes DEPART
up the creek (without a paddle)
  DIFFICULTIES
up the pole INTOXICATED - ALCOHOL
up the river PUNISHMENT
up the wall ANXIETY
up time COMPUTER
up to here ENDURE
up to one's eyeballs ABUNDANCE
up to one's knees ABUNDANCE
up to one's neck ABUNDANCE
up to scratch SATISFACTORY
up DRUGS - USE
up HAPPINESS
up INCREASE
upbeat HAPPINESS
upchuck VOMIT
upholstered INTOXICATED - ALCOHOL
uppity HAUGHTINESS
upshot (of something) RESULTS
upside BENEFIT
uptight ANXIETY
urge to purge VOMIT
Use your head! THINKING
use DRUGS - USE
user DRUGS - USER
UVs LEISURE
vac APPLIANCE
vacation PUNISHMENT
vag HOBO
vag POLICE
vals DRUGS - TRANQUILIZERS
Vamoose! DEPART
vanilla DULL
vanilla PEOPLE - WHITE
varnished INTOXICATED - ALCOHOL
Vatican roulette CONTRACEPTION
V-ball SPORTS - VOLLEYBALL
veejay BROADCASTING
veep OFFICER
veg (out) RELAX
veg FOOD
veg PEOPLE - STUPID
vegetable INTOXICATED - ALCOHOL
vegetable PEOPLE - NEGATIVE

vegged out INTOXICATION - BAD
veggie MEDICAL
veggy EATING
veggy EXHAUSTION
veggy FOOD
vent one's spleen ANGER
verboten FORBIDDEN
vest BUSINESS
vet SOLDIER
vette CARS
vibes FEELINGS
vic CRIMINAL
vic VICTIM
vicious circle SEQUENCE
vicious EXCELLENCE
vicked DECEPTION
Vietnik PEACE
vim and vigor ENERGETIC
vines CLOTHING
vinyl MUSIC
VIP PEOPLE - IMPORTANT
visit from Flo MENSES
visit from the stork BIRTH
visiting fireman EMPLOYMENT
vital statistics BODY
vivor SUCCESS
viz CLOTHING
vomatose INTOXICATED - ALCOHOL
vomity DISGUSTING
vote with one's feet DISLIKE
vroom ENGINE
vroom MOVEMENT
wacky SILLINESS
wacky-tabbacky DRUGS - MARIJUANA
wad MONEY
waffle (around) INDECISION
wag one's chin CHATTER
wagon POLICE
wail EXCELLENCE
wailing EXCELLENCE
walk heavy IMPORTANCE
walk on eggs CAUTION
walk soft HUMILITY
walk tall CONFIDENCE
walk ABANDONMENT
walk EASY
walk RELEASE
walk SURVIVAL
walk-in COMMERCE
walking dandruff LICE
walking on rocky socks INTOXICATED - ALCOHOL
walking papers DISMISSAL

walking wounded SOLDIER
walkover EASY
wall job DECEPTION
wallet KINSHIP
wall-eyed INTOXICATED - ALCOHOL
wallflower PEOPLE - MEEK
wallop INFLUENCE
wallop VIOLENCE
wallpaper CHECKS
walls have ears EAVESDROPPING
wall-to-wall COMPLETENESS
waltz off (with something) THEFT
waltz through something SUCCESS
waltz EASY
wampum MONEY
wana DRUGS - MARIJUANA
wanabe DESIRE
want list DESIRE
Want to make something of it?
   CHALLENGE
war chest MONEY
war paint MAKEUP
war zone DANGER
warhorse AGE
warm body PEOPLE
warm someone up PREPARATION
warmed over UNORIGINAL
warped INTOXICATED - ALCOHOL
wart DIFFICULTIES
wart PEOPLE - NEGATIVE
warts and all ACCEPTANCE
wash out ACCIDENT
wash out EXHAUSTION
wash out FAILURE
wash out LOSS
wash someone away MURDER
wash CONCEAL
wash DRINKING - PORTION
wash FINANCIAL
washed out EXHAUSTION
washout FAILURE
WASP PEOPLE - WHITE
waspish PEOPLE - WHITE
waste MURDER
wasted DEAD
wasted EXHAUSTION
wasted INTOXICATED - ALCOHOL/DRUGS
Watch it! CAUTION
Watch my lips! OBSERVATION
Watch your mouth! WARNING
watering hole TAVERN
wax MUSIC
wax VIOLENCE

waxed INTOXICATED - ALCOHOL
way down DEPRESSION
way off (base) ERROR
way out EXTREME
way out INTOXICATED - ALCOHOL/DRUGS
way rad EXCELLENCE
Way! YES
way COMPLETENESS
WBMTTP COMPUTER - ABBREVIATION
weak sister MAN - MEEK
wear the pants (in the house)
  DOMINANCE
wear ENDURE
weasel out of something EVASION
weasel PEOPLE - NEGATIVE
weasel STUDENT
wedgy CLOTHING
weed DRUGS - MARIJUANA
weed TOBACCO
weedhead DRUGS - USER
weeds CLOTHING
weekend warrior SOLDIER
weenie FOOD
weenie PENIS
weenie PEOPLE - STUPID
weenie STUDENT
weeper EMOTION
weird out CRAZINESS
weirded out CRAZINESS
weirdo PEOPLE - CRAZY
weisenheimer PEOPLE - NEGATIVE
welcher DEBT
welk POLITENESS
well-fixed INTOXICATED - ALCOHOL
well-fixed WEALTH
well-oiled CHATTER
well-oiled INTOXICATED - ALCOHOL
(well-)upholstered FAT
wenchy BEHAVIOR - BAD
Were you born in a barn? INSULT
wet blanket PEOPLE - NEGATIVE
wet noodle PEOPLE - MEEK
wet one ALCOHOL - BEER
wet sock PEOPLE - MEEK
wet ALCOHOL - LOCATION
wet INTOXICATED - ALCOHOL
wet STUPIDITY
wetware BRAIN
whack someone or something up
  VIOLENCE
whack someone (out) MURDER
whack something (out) THEFT
whack DRINKING - PORTION

whack VIOLENCE
whacked (out) INTOXICATED -
  ALCOHOL/DRUGS
whacked CRAZINESS
whale into someone or something
  VIOLENCE
whale on EXCELLENCE
whale the tar out of someone
  PUNISHMENT
whale DRUNKARD
whale PEOPLE - FAT
wham-bang THRILL
whang(y)doodle GADGET
whang(y)doodle NONSENSE
What (a) nerve! SHOCK
What can I do you for? GREETING
What do you say? GREETING
What do you say? WHAT
What else is new? SARCASM
What gives? WHAT
What (in) the devil? WHAT
What (in) the hell? WHAT
What in (the) Sam Hill? WHAT
What is it? GREETING
What someone said. AGREEMENT
What the deuce? WHAT
What the heck! ACCEPTANCE
What you see is what you get.
  COMMERCE
whatchamacallit GADGET
whatever turns you on ACCEPTANCE
whatever PERHAPS
What'll it be? DRINKING
What's buzzin' (cousin)? GREETING
What's cooking? GREETING
What's eating someone? ANNOYANCE
What's going down? GREETING
What's going on? GREETING
What's happ(ening)? GREETING
what's his face SOMEONE
What's in it for me? BENEFIT
What's it to you? CHALLENGE
What's new? GREETING
What's poppin'? GREETING
What's shakin' (bacon)? GREETING
What's the catch? DRAWBACK
What's the good word? GREETING
What's the scam? WHAT
What's up, G? GREETING
What's up? GREETING
What's with someone or something?
  PROBLEM
What's your age? GREETING

What's yours? DRINKING
whatsis GADGET
whazood INTOXICATED - ALCOHOL
wheel and deal COMMERCE
wheel man DRIVING
wheel DRIVING
wheeler-dealer BUSINESS
wheels CARS
wheely STUNT
when push comes to shove RESULTS
when the eagle flies EMPLOYMENT
Where (have) you been keeping
  yourself? GREETING
Where in (the) Sam Hill? WHERE
Where in the world? WHERE
where it's at GOALS
Where on (God's green) earth? WHERE
where someone is at UNDERSTANDING
where someone lives PERSONAL
where someone's head is at MENTAL
where the action is LOCATION
where the sun don't shine ANUS
Where's the beef? WHERE
Where's the fire? HURRY
wherewithal MONEY
wherewithal MOTIVATION
whiffled INTOXICATED - ALCOHOL
whiff-sniffer ALCOHOL
whing-ding AFFAIR
whing-ding DRINKING - BOUT
whing-ding GADGET
whip something off EATING
whipped EXCELLENCE
whipped INTOXICATED - ALCOHOL
whipsaw FINANCIAL
whipsaw VIOLENCE
whirlybird AVIATION
whiskey tenor SINGER
whistle in the dark GUESSING
whistle-blower TATTLING
whistler TATTLING
white elephant UNDESIRABLE
white hat PEOPLE - GOOD
white knuckler ANXIETY
whitebread DULL
white-knuckle ANXIETY
whitewash CONCEAL
whittled INTOXICATED - ALCOHOL
whiz kid SKILL
whiz SKILL
whiz URINATION
Who (in) the hell? WHO
who shot John ALCOHOL - ILLICIT

Who the deuce? WHO
Whoa! STOPPING
whodunit STORY
whole bag of tricks EVERYTHING
whole ball of wax EVERYTHING
whole bunch(es) AMOUNT - MUCH
whole enchilada EVERYTHING
whole fam damily KINSHIP
whole new ball game DIFFERENCE
whole nine yards EVERYTHING
whole schmear EVERYTHING
whole shebang EVERYTHING
whole wide world EVERYWHERE
whooshed INTOXICATED - ALCOHOL
whoozis NICKNAME
whopper LYING
whopper SIZE
whopping (great) SIZE
whump IMPACT
whump OVERWHELM
wicked EXCELLENCE
wide open CRIME
wide open SPEED
wide place in the road LOCATION
wide INTOXICATED - DRUGS
widget GADGET
widget PRODUCT
widow-maker DANGER
wiener nose PEOPLE - STUPID
wife WOMAN - FRIEND
wig out CRAZINESS
wig out EXCITEMENT
wigged (out) CRAZINESS
wigged (out) INTOXICATED -
  ALCOHOL/DRUGS
wiggle out of something EVASION
wild and wooly EXCITEMENT
wild EXCITEMENT
will do YES
will not wash BELIEF
willies ANXIETY
Wilma WOMAN - STUPID
wimp out (of something) COWARDICE
WIMP COMPUTER - ABBREVIATION
wimp PEOPLE - MEEK
wimpy COWARDICE
Win a few, lose a few. DEFEAT
Win a few, lose a few. LOSS
Win a few, lose a few. OVERWHELM
windbag BOASTING
windy CHATTER
windy FLATULENCE
wing heavy INTOXICATED - ALCOHOL

wing it TRY
wing AVIATION
winks SLEEP
winner EXCELLENCE
wino ALCOHOL - WINE
wino DRUNKARD
Wipe it off! PRESSURE
wipe out ACCIDENT
wipe out ACCIDENT
wipe out PEOPLE - NEGATIVE
wipe someone out EXHAUSTION
wipe someone out MURDER
wipe someone out RUINATION
wipe MURDER
wiped (out) EXHAUSTION
wiped (out) INTOXICATED - ALCOHOL/DRUGS
wiped (out) MONEY - LACKING
wipe-out ACCIDENT
wire EAVESDROPPING
wire SPYING
wired into someone or something JOINING
wired ALERTNESS
wired INTOXICATED - ALCOHOL/DRUGS
wise guy PEOPLE - NEGATIVE
wise to someone or something KNOWLEDGEABLE
wise up (to someone or something) UNDERSTANDING
wish book CATALOG
wish list LIST
wishy-washy INDECISION
with a bang FLAMBOYANT
with bells on EAGERNESS
with flying colors FLAMBOYANT
with it FASHIONABLE
with (one's) eyes (wide) open AWARENESS
within an ace of (doing) something PROXIMITY
without a hitch EASY
woefits HANGOVER
wolf something down CONSUMPTION
wolf MAN - SEX
wombat PEOPLE - STRANGE
wonk BUREAUCRAT
wonk STUDENT
wonky STUDY
wood butcher CARPENTER
wood-pussy SKUNK
woods are full of _____ AMOUNT
woody SURFING

woof cookies VOMIT
woof BOASTING
woof VOMIT
woofled INTOXICATED - ALCOHOL
woofle-water ALCOHOL
woolies CLOTHING
woozy EXHAUSTION
woozy INTOXICATED - ALCOHOL
Word. GREETING
Word. YES
work one's tail off WORK
work oneself (up) into a lather ANGER
work oneself (up) into a lather WORK
work oneself up to something PREPARATION
work oneself up EMOTION
work someone over EXAMINATION
work someone over THREATENING
workaholic WORK
working stiff WORK
world is one's oyster DOMINANCE
world-beater AGGRESSIVENESS
world-class EXCELLENCE
worm MAN - NEGATIVE
worm-food BODY - DEAD
worms in blood FOOD
worms FOOD
worry-wart WORRY
worship the porcelain god(dess) VOMIT
worst-case scenario RESULTS
worth one's salt VALUE
would not be seen dead REFUSAL
Would you believe? AMAZEMENT
wouldn't touch someone or something with a ten-foot pole AVOIDANCE
Wow! AMAZEMENT
wow EXCITEMENT
wow IMPRESS
wow SYMBOL
wrap one's car around something ACCIDENT
wrap something up CONCLUSION
wrapped up (in someone or something) OBSESSION
wrapped up (with someone or something) BUSY
wrecked INTOXICATED - ALCOHOL/DRUGS
wrinkle DIFFICULTIES
wrinkle IDEA
wrinkle-rod CRANKSHAFT
wrong side of the tracks LOCATION
wrongo PEOPLE - NEGATIVE
wrongo WRONG

wuss(y) PEOPLE - MEEK
WYSIWYG COMPUTER - ABBREVIATION
X marks the spot. LOCATION
X'd out DEAD
X'd out ELIMINATE
XYZ ZIPPER
yack CHATTER
yack CONVERSATION
yack LAUGHTER
yack PEOPLE - STUPID
yackety-yak GOSSIP
yahoo PEOPLE - STUPID
yak it up CHATTER
yak JOKING
yak TALKING
yak VOMIT
yakky SPEECH
yank someone around HARASSMENT
yank someone's chain HARASSMENT
yank HARASSMENT
yank VOMIT
yanked ARREST
yap DUPE
yap GOSSIP
yap MOUTH
yap NONSENSE
yap VOMIT
yard dog PEOPLE - NEGATIVE
yard MONEY
yardbird JAIL
yardbird SOLDIER
yatata-yatata CHATTER
yawner DULL
yazzihamper PEOPLE - NEGATIVE
Ye gods! AMAZEMENT
yea big SIZE
yeah YES
yeaster DRUNKARD
Yec(c)h! DISGUSTING
yegg MAN - NEGATIVE
yegg THIEF
yell one's guts out COMPLAINT
yell one's head off SPEECH - LOUD
Yello. GREETING
yellow COWARDICE
yellow-bellied COWARDICE
yellow-belly PEOPLE - MEEK
yelper SIREN
yench DECEPTION
yenta GOSSIP
Yes! YES
yo mama INTERJECTION
Yo! INTERJECTION

yock LAUGHTER
yodeling in a canyon CHATTER
yoked MUSCLES
york VOMIT
You and who else? CHALLENGE
You asked for it! RESULTS
You bet your boots! YES
You bet your sweet life! YES
You bet your sweet patoot(ie)! YES
you bet YES
You betcha! YES
You can say that again! AGREEMENT
You can't fight city hall. SURRENDER
You can't get there from here.
   LOCATION
You can't win them all. OVERWHELM
You could have knocked me over with
   a feather. SURPRISE
You don't know the half of it.
   COMPLICATION
You got it! AGREEMENT
You got it! CORRECT
You guys bitchin'? GREETING
You (had) better believe it! BELIEF
You want to step outside? CHALLENGE
young blood PEOPLE - NEW
young Turk PEOPLE - NEGATIVE
Your guess is as good as mine.
   GUESSING
Your place or mine? FLIRTATION
You're the doctor. ACQUIESCENCE
You've got another think coming.
   WRONG
yo-yo INDECISION
yo-yo STUPIDITY
yoyo PEOPLE - NEGATIVE
Yuck! DISGUSTING
yuck JOKING
yuck PEOPLE - NEGATIVE
yucky UNDESIRABLE
yummy DELICIOUS
yummy PLEASURE
yup YES
yuppie PEOPLE - YOUNG
yutz PEOPLE - STUPID
za FOOD
zagged INTOXICATED - ALCOHOL
zany SILLINESS
Zap! AMAZEMENT
zap DEFEAT
zap HURRY
zap IMPRESS
zap MURDER

zap SHOCK
zap STUN
zapped EXHAUSTION
zapped INTOXICATED - ALCOHOL
zapped INTOXICATED - DRUGS
zappy ENERGETIC
zarf PEOPLE - NEGATIVE
zebra SPORTS
zeek out CONTROL
Zelda WOMAN - UGLY
zerk PEOPLE - STUPID
zerked (out) INTOXICATED - DRUGS
zerking STRANGE
zero PEOPLE - UNIMPORTANT
zhlubby DULL
zilch NOTHING
zing ENERGETIC
zing HARASSMENT
zing IMPACT
zinger INSULT
zinger THING
zings DELIRIUM TREMENS
zip along HURRY
zip gun WEAPONRY
Zip (up) your lip! SILENCE
zip ENERGETIC
zip HURRY
zip NOTHING
zip PEOPLE - STUPID
zipped INTOXICATED - DRUGS
zipper head HAIR
zippy ENERGETIC
zissified INTOXICATED - ALCOHOL
zit doctor DOCTOR
zit PIMPLES
zob PEOPLE - WORTHLESS
zod PEOPLE - NEGATIVE

zod STUDENT
zombie EXHAUSTION
zombie PEOPLE - STRANGE
zombie PEOPLE - STUPID
zoned (out) EXHAUSTION
zoned (out) INTOXICATED - ALCOHOL
zoned (out) INTOXICATED - DRUGS
zonk out EXHAUSTION
zonk EXHAUSTION
zonk OVERWHELM
zonked (out) EXHAUSTION
zonked (out) INTOXICATED - ALCOHOL/DRUGS
zonker DRUGS - USER
zonker DRUNKARD
zoo BUSY
zoobang INTOXICATED - ALCOHOL
zooed INTOXICATED - ALCOHOL
zooie CONFUSION
zoom in (on someone or something) FOCUS
zoom out CONTROL - LACKING
zoom someone out IMPRESS
zoom up MOVEMENT
zoom DEPART
zoom ENTRANCE
zoom INTOXICATION - ONSET
zoomies AVIATION
zooted INTOXICATED - ALCOHOL
zootied INTOXICATED - ALCOHOL/DRUGS
zorked INTOXICATED - ALCOHOL
zotz MURDER
zotz NOTHING
Zowie! AMAZEMENT
zowie ENERGETIC
zozzled INTOXICATED - ALCOHOL
zuke VOMIT